Resources for Teaching

THE BEDFORD INTRODUCTION TO LITERATURE

Reading • Thinking • Writing

Resources for Teaching

Fifth Edition

THE BEDFORD INTRODUCTION TO LITERATURE

Reading • Thinking • Writing

Michael Meyer
University of Connecticut

Ellen Darion

Kathleen Morgan Drowne
University of North Carolina, Chapel Hill

Quentin Miller
Gustavus Adolphus College

Julie Nash
Gustavus Adolphus College

Anne Phillips
Kansas State University

John Repp
University of Pittsburgh

Robert Spirko
University of North Carolina, Chapel Hill

Bedford/St. Martin's   Boston New York

3 2 1 0 9 8

f e d c b a

For information, write: Bedford/St. Martin's

75 Arlington Street, Boston, MA 02116

ISBN: 0-312-17139-0

Preface

This instructor's manual is designed to be a resource of commentaries, interpretations, and suggestions for teaching the works included in *The Bedford Introduction to Literature*, Fifth Edition. The entries offer advice about how to approach individual selections and suggest possible answers to many of the questions raised in the text. No attempt has been made to generate definitive readings of the works; the text selections are rich enough to accommodate multiple approaches and interpretations. Our hope is that instructors will take what they find useful and leave the rest behind. Inevitably, instructors will disagree with some of the commentaries, but perhaps such disagreements will provide starting points for class discussion.

In addition to offering approaches to selections, many of the entries suggest topics for discussion and writing. The format of the entries varies from itemized responses to specific questions to essays that present overviews of individual works. This flexibility allows each entry to be more responsive to the nature of a particular work and the questions asked about it in the text. Nearly all of the "Connections to Other Selections" questions posed in the text are answered in the manual, and every entry includes suggestions for further connections. The appendix listing selections linked by connections questions serves as a quick reference for instructors who are looking for ideas for pairing selections, and this information also appears with the appropriate individual entries for each selection. The manual includes selected bibliographies for authors treated in depth, and critical readings are mentioned throughout the manual when they are felt to be particularly useful resources for teaching a work. For more general bibliographic guides, see the annotated list of reference sources for fiction, poetry, and drama on pages 2100–2102 of the main text.

The manual also provides instructors with additional resources for teaching selections in the Albums of World Literature and the Albums of Contemporary Stories, Poems, and Plays. There is a preface to each of the albums that includes suggestions for teaching this potentially unfamiliar material, and all connections questions posed in the text for these selections, with the exception of questions that explicitly ask students to write an essay, are answered in the manual. In addition, and new to this edition, the manual provides plenty of similar suggestions for each of the three new Cultural Case Studies in the book—detailed introductory essays as well as itemized responses to questions.

An appendix that gives instructors suggestions for teaching thematic units is also included. Each of the five units includes a table of contents organized by genre and an extensive list of questions for discussion and writing. The appendix of Film, Video, and Audiocassette Resources for teaching selections in *The Bedford Introduction to Literature* has been updated and expanded for the fifth edition of the manual. The information contained in this list is incorporated into the appropriate individual manual entries for ease of reference. Finally, at the end of the manual, you will find a description of *Literature Aloud: Classic and Contemporary Stories, Poems, and Selected Scenes from THE BEDFORD INTRO-*

DUCTION TO LITERATURE — an audio recording of works from the text (available on compact disk and audiotape), along with information on how to obtain a copy.

New to this edition are chapter introductions with suggestions for approaching *The Bedford Introduction to Literature*'s editorial discussions in class and a number of "Tips from the Field"— class-tested teaching suggestions from instructors who have taught from previous editions. If you have a teaching tip that you would like to submit for the next edition of this instructor's manual, please send it to the attention of Aron Keesbury, Editor, at Bedford/St. Martins, 75 Arlington Street, Boston, MA 02116. Your teaching suggestion should be approximately 50 words long and suggest ways of teaching a particular author or selection that have been especially effective in your classroom experience. If we use your teaching suggestion, we will be happy to acknowledge you in the manual and pay you an honorarium.

This edition also offers advice on how to incorporate the many popular titles in Bedford's Case Studies in Contemporary Criticism series into the course. These volumes provide a useful supplement for instructors who want to cover the different schools of literary theory in more depth than is provided in Chapter 37 of *The Bedford Introduction to Literature*. The section of the manual that includes specific suggestions for pairing selections in the text with specific Case Studies titles will appeal to instructors who wish to supplement *The Bedford Introduction to Literature* with a longer work.

For those instructors who wish to incorporate research into their classes, the Bedford Links to Resources in Literature (at <www.bedfordstmartins.com/litlinks/litlinks .html>) are a great resource for merging the research process with the possibilities of the World Wide Web. The links are arranged alphabetically by author, by authors treated in depth, by major literary period, and by authors of Bedford's Case Studies in Contemporary Criticism and Cultural Editions series. These links have already been screened and can take students deep into the Web and into the world of the author or literary period they are studying.

The manual is conveniently arranged by genre and follows the organization of the text. Page references corresponding to the text are included at the top of each right page of the manual and after the title of each entry.

Contents

FICTION

1

Reading Fiction

In connection with the introductory material in Chapter 1, it may be useful to engage students in a comparison of the ways in which they read. For instance, how does the text on the back of a cereal box differ from a story in a news magazine? We read differently depending on our interest in the subject, our acceptance of a writer's style and voice, and our environment. Some students may read primarily while they are on the treadmill at the recreation center; others need quiet in which to concentrate. Even students who wouldn't identify themselves as readers might discover that they actually rely on reading skills more than they realize.

After focusing on the reader, students might consider the reading material. Encourage them to consider how reading fiction may be different from reading a newspaper. What different demands are being made on the reader in these contexts? Fiction invites the reader to enter a world that may or may not be familiar to them; it also asks them to think not only about the words on the page but also about their implications. Fiction is, in a sense, not only about what the writer tells the reader, but also what the writer doesn't tell the reader. It's up to the reader to invest the spaces between the words with creative (yet reasonable) meanings.

Finally, students will profit from learning that sharing their interpretations with each other can be intensely rewarding. Because they bring different experiences and values to their readings, they may discover different significant aspects of a given text. To practice building their interpretive skills, students might bring in a letter to the editor in a local newspaper, or a comic strip, or some other reading material, and explain what they think is of interest about their "text." (This may be particularly successful for students in small groups.) Students may be surprised to discover the differences between their readings — or even their similarities. An ironic editorial or a purposely ambiguous (or especially political) cartoon may provide diverse yet reasonable readings. In discussing those readings, students begin to develop the skills that will make their experience with fiction successful and rewarding.

KATE CHOPIN, *The Story of an Hour* (p. 10)

Katherine (Kate) Chopin was born in 1851 and was educated in St. Louis. The mother of six children, she produced her first novel, *At Fault*, in 1890. *Bayou Folk* (1894) and *A Night in Acadie* (1897), both collections of short stories, were followed in 1899 by Chopin's most well-known work, *The Awakening*, a work denounced by critics and judged to be "immoral." At the time of her death in 1904, Chopin left unpublished a novel, *Young*

Dr. Gosse, and a short story collection, *A Vocation and a Voice*, from which "The Story of an Hour" is taken. Her fiction commonly depicts heroines who attempt to balance personal independence with the demands of marriage, motherhood, and society.

As you begin to consider this story, lead the class into a discussion of Mrs. Mallard's character. What do they think of her? Even for the 1990s, this is in certain ways a bold story, and there are likely to be students who will describe the protagonist as callous, selfish, unnatural — even, in Mrs. Mallard's own words, "monstrous" — because of her joyous feeling of freedom after her initial grief and shock. Go through the text with the class, looking for evidence that this radical shift in feeling is genuine. To demonstrate her grief and subsequent numbness, you might point to Mrs. Mallard's weeping with "sudden, wild abandonment" (paragraph 3), the "physical exhaustion that haunted her body . . . and soul" (4), the way she sat "motionless, except when a sob came up into her throat and shook her, as a child who has cried itself to sleep continues to sob in its dreams" (7), and her look, which "indicated a suspension of intelligent thought" (8). Especially important to the defense of Mrs. Mallard's character is her effort to fight off "this thing that was approaching to possess her": "she was striving to beat it back with her will" (9-10).

Ask students to discuss (or write about) what they imagine Mrs. Mallard's marriage to have been like. If her husband "had never looked save with love upon her" (13), what was wrong with the marriage? The answer can be found in the lines "She had loved him — sometimes. Often she had not. . . . What could love, the unsolved mystery, count for in the face of this possession of self-assertion which she suddenly recognized as the strongest impulse of her being!" (15). The surprise ending aside (some readers may find it manipulative), this story is basically about a woman awakening to the idea that all the love and stability in the world can't compensate for her lack of control over her own life.

Ask the class if they can locate any symbols in the story. "The tops of trees that were all aquiver with the new spring life," sparrows "twittering" (5), "patches of blue sky showing . . . through the clouds" (6), and "the sounds, the scents, the color that filled the air" (9) all suggest the renewal and rebirth that follow.

Students could also write about the ending of the story, specifically the last three paragraphs. What is the tone here? (Ironic. First, Mrs. Mallard suffers a heart attack when she sees her husband, rather than when she learns of his death, which is when everyone originally feared she would have an attack. Second, she does not die of joy, as the doctors claim, but of shock — the shock of having to go back to her old way of life once she has realized there is another way to live.)

Chopin's story offers an opportunity to demonstrate how a reader's own values and assumptions are relevant to literary interpretation. Responses to Mrs. Mallard are — for better or worse — often informed by readers' attitudes toward marriage. Similar issues can also be engaged in the Van Der Zee and Godwin stories that follow Chopin's. Chapter 37, "Critical Strategies for Reading," includes a variety of approaches to "The Story of an Hour." Students who are exposed to this chapter early in the course will be likely to generate more pointed and sophisticated kinds of questions about the subsequent texts they read.

For additional background material, see Per Seyersted's *Kate Chopin: A Critical Biography* (Baton Rouge: Louisiana State UP, 1969); Marlene Springer's *Edith Wharton and Kate Chopin: A Reference Guide* (Boston: G. K. Hall, 1976); and Carol P. Christ's *Diving Deep and Surfacing: Women Writers on Spiritual Quest* (Boston: Beacon, 1980).

POSSIBLE CONNECTIONS TO OTHER SELECTIONS

Dagoberto Gilb, "Love in L.A." (text p. 265)
Susan Glaspell, *Trifles* (text p. 1172)
Yukio Mishima, "Patriotism" (text p. 593)

RESOURCE FOR TEACHING

Kate Chopin's "The Story of an Hour." 24 min., color, 1982, 1/2″ open reel (EIAJ), 16-mm film. A dramatization of the story, with an examination of Chopin's life. Distributed by Ishtar.

A Composite of a Romance Tip Sheet (p. 20)

This tip sheet offers an opportunity to begin discussion of the elements of fiction. Reading a romance novel is not a prerequisite for discussion, because most of us have experienced similar formulas in magazines, popular television programs, or films; also, an excerpt from a romance novel begins on text page 25. Students are usually delighted to recognize the patterns prescribed in the tip sheet and have no trouble recalling stories that fit this description. This gets class discussion off to a good start, provided the emphasis is on why readers derive pleasure from romance formulas rather than on a denigration of such reading.

Recent criticism has focused considerable attention on the audience and appeal of romance novels. (See, for example, the excerpt from Tania Modleski's *Loving with a Vengeance: Mass-Produced Fantasies for Women* [New York: Archon, 1982] on text p. 38; Janice A. Radway's *Reading the Romance: Women, Patriarchy, and Popular Literature* [Chapel Hill: University of North Carolina Press, 1984]; and Kay Mussell's *Fantasy and Reconciliation: Contemporary Formulas of Women's Romance Fiction* [Westport, CT: Greenwood, 1984].) Romance readers are typically housewives ranging in age from their twenties to midforties. Not surprisingly, the age of the heroine usually determines the approximate age of the reader, because the protagonists of Harlequin and Silhouette romances — to name only the two most popular series — are created so that consumers will readily identify with the heroines' romantic adventures in exciting settings as a means of escaping the loneliness and tedium of domesticity. (It's worth emphasizing, of course, that male readers engage in similar fantasies; Philip Larkin's "A Study of Reading Habits" on p. 684 suggests some possibilities.) The heroine is "attractive" rather than "glamorous" because she is likely to appeal to more readers who might describe themselves that way.

Romance readers are often treated to a veritable fashion show, with detailed descriptions of the heroine's clothes. This kind of window-shopping is especially apparent in television soap operas, in which the costumes and sets resemble Bloomingdale's displays more than they do real life. In a very real sense, their audience is shopping for images of success, courtship, and marriage. The hero is a man who may initially seem to be cold and cruel but ultimately provides warmth, love, and security. He is as virtuous as the heroine (if he's divorced, his ex-wife is to blame) but stronger. His being "about ten years" older emphasizes male dominance over female submissiveness, a theme that implicitly looms large in many romances.

The use of sex varies in romances, especially recent ones, in which explicitness seems to be more popular. Nevertheless, suspense and tension are produced in all romances by the teasing complications that keep lovers apart until the end. The major requirement in love scenes between the hero and heroine is that they be culminations of romantic feelings — love — rather than merely graphic sexual descriptions.

3

The simplified writing style of romances is geared for relatively inexperienced, unsophisticated readers. Probably not very many romance readers cross over to *Pride and Prejudice* or *Jane Eyre*, although some of Austen's and Brontë's readers have certainly been known to enjoy romances. Instructors who share their own reading habits with a class might reassure students that popular and high culture aren't necessarily mutually exclusive while simultaneously whetting students' appetites for the stories to come.

KAREN VAN DER ZEE, *From* A Secret Sorrow (p. 25)

Karen Van Der Zee was born and grew up in Holland. She published a number of short stories there early in her career. Although the United States is her permanent home, she and her husband, a consultant in agriculture to developing countries, often live abroad. The couple was married in Kenya, their first child was born in Ghana, and their second child arrived in the United States. Van Der Zee has contributed more than fifteen books so far to the Harlequin line.

The excerpt from *A Secret Sorrow* subscribes to much of the plotting and characterization methods described in the composite tip sheet. Kai and Faye are not definitively brought together until the final chapter, after Faye's secret is revealed and Kai expresses his unconditional love for her. Students should have no difficulty understanding how the heroine's and hero's love for each other inevitably earns them domestic bliss in the "low white ranch house under the blue skies of Texas," where the family "flourished like the crops in the fields" (paragraph 137). Kai is the traditional dominant, protective male who takes charge of their relationship (albeit tenderly). A good many prepackaged phrases describe him: he has a "hard body," and he kisses her with a "hard, desperate passion" when he isn't speaking "huskily" or lifting her face with his "bronzed hand." In contrast, Faye is "like a terrified animal" and no match for his "hot, fuming fury" when he accuses her of jeopardizing their love.

Despite the predictable action, stereotyped characterizations, clichéd language, and flaccid descriptions of lovemaking (108), some students (perhaps many) will prefer *A Secret Sorrow* to Godwin's "A Sorrowful Woman." But that's natural enough. Van Der Zee's story is accessible and familiar material, while Godwin's is puzzling and vaguely threatening because "A Sorrowful Woman" raises questions instead of resolving them. Rather than directly challenging students' preferences and forcing them to be defensive, demonstrate how Godwin's story can be reread several times and still be interesting. *A Secret Sorrow* certainly does not stand up to that test because it was written to be consumed on a first reading so that readers will buy the next book in the series.

POSSIBLE CONNECTIONS TO OTHER SELECTIONS

Edgar Rice Burroughs, From *Tarzan of the Apes* (text p. 62)
Gail Godwin, "A Sorrowful Woman" (text p. 33)

GAIL GODWIN, *A Sorrowful Woman* (p. 33)

Gail Godwin traces her beginnings as a writer to her mother, a teacher and writer, who read stories out of a blank address book, "the special book," as Godwin has called it, "a tiny book with no writing at all in it." Although she frequently contributes essays and stories to publications such as *Harper's, Esquire, Cosmopolitan,* and *Ms.* and has written four librettos, Godwin is primarily known as a novelist; her books include *The Perfectionists* (1970), *The Odd Woman* (1974), *Violet Clay* (1978), *A Mother and Two Daughters* (1982), and *The Finishing School* (1985). Born in 1937 in Birmingham, Alabama, Godwin was educated at the University of North Carolina and the University of Iowa. She worked as a reporter for the *Miami Herald* and as a travel consultant with the U.S. Embassy in London before pursuing a career as a full-time writer and teacher of writing. She has received a National Endowment for the Arts grant, a Guggenheim fellowship, and an Award in Literature from the American Institute and Academy of Arts and Letters. She was coeditor of *Best American Short Stories* in 1985 and has had her short stories collected in *Dream Children* (1976), *Real Life* (1981), and *Mr. Bedford and the Muses* (1983).

"A Sorrowful Woman" challenges the assumptions that inform romance novels. The central point of *A Secret Sorrow* is that love conquers all and that marriage and motherhood make women "beautiful, complete, [and] whole." In contrast, Godwin's story begins with an epigraph that suggests a dark fairy tale: "Once upon a time there was a wife and mother one too many times." The story opens with a pleasant description of the woman's husband ("durable, receptive, gentle") and child ("a tender golden three"), but she is saddened and sickened by the sight of them. These unnamed characters (they are offered as types) seem to have the kind of life that allows Kai and Faye to live happily ever after, but in Godwin's world, this domestic arrangement turns out to be a deadly trap for "the woman." The opening paragraph shocks us into wanting to read the rest of the story to find out why the woman is repulsed by her seemingly perfect life.

It may be tempting to accept the husband's assessment that "Mommy is sick." Students might be eager to see her as mad or suffering from a nervous breakdown, but if we settle for one of those explanations, the meaning of the story is flattened. We simply don't know enough about the woman to diagnose her behavior in psychological terms. She is, after all, presented as a type, not as an individual. She does appear mentally ill, and she becomes progressively more unstable until she withdraws from life completely, but Godwin portrays her as desperate, not simply insane, and focuses our attention on the larger question of why the sole role of wife and mother may not be fulfilling.

The woman rejects life on the terms it is offered to her and no one — including her — knows what to make of her refusal. (For a discussion of the nature of the conflict in the story see pp. 67–68 of the text.) What is clear, however, is that she cannot live in the traditional role that her husband and son (and we) expect of her. She finds that motherhood doesn't fit her and makes her feel absurd (consider the "vertical bra" in paragraph 4). When she retreats from the family, her husband accommodates her with sympathy and an "understanding" that Godwin reveals to be a means of control rather than genuine care. He tells her he wants "to be big enough to contain whatever you must do" (21). And that's the problem. What he cannot comprehend is that she needs an identity that goes beyond being his wife and his child's mother. Instead, he gives her a nightly sleeping draught; his remedy is to anesthetize his Sleeping Beauty rather than to awaken her to some other possibilities.

Neither the husband nor the wife is capable of taking any effective action. The husband can replace his wife with the "perfect girl" to help around the house, and he can even manage quite well on his own, but he has no more sense of what to do about her refusal to go on with her life than she does. Her own understanding of her situation goes no further than her realization that her life did not have to take a defined shape any more than a poem does (22). Her story is a twentieth-century female version of Herman Melville's "Bartleby, the Scrivener" (p. 113); both characters prefer not to live their lives, but neither attempts to change anything or offer alternatives. Instead, they are messengers whose behavior makes us vaguely troubled. The two stories warrant close comparison.

In the end, when spring arrives, the woman uses herself up in a final burst of domestic energy that provides the husband and son with laundry, hand-knitted sweaters, drawings, stories, love sonnets, and a feast that resembles a Thanksgiving dinner. But neither renewal nor thanks is forthcoming. Instead, the boy, unaware of his mother's death, asks, "Can we eat the turkey for supper?" (38). The irony reveals that the woman has been totally consumed by her role.

Ask students why this story appeared in *Esquire*, a magazine for men, rather than, say, *Good Housekeeping*. The discussion can sensitize them to the idea of literary markets and create an awareness of audiences as well as texts. Surely a romance writer for *Good Housekeeping* would have ended this story differently. Students will know what to suggest for such an ending.

For a discussion of Godwin's treatment of traditional role models in the story, see Judith K. Gardiner's " 'A Sorrowful Woman': Gail Godwin's Feminist Parable," *Studies in Short Fiction* 12 (1975): 286-290.

TIP FROM THE FIELD

Because many of my community college students don't understand the distinctions of formulaic writing they are supposed to make between the excerpt from Van Der Zee's *A Secret Sorrow* and Godwin's "A Sorrowful Woman," I have them focus instead on the similarities and differences between the fairy-tale nature of these two stories. I ask students to consider how each story is a fairy tale or representative of one. Students have little difficulty identifying the fairy-tale elements of Prince Charming rescuing a damsel in distress and living happily ever after in *A Secret Sorrow*. Students have more difficulty recognizing the fairy-tale ("Once upon a time there was a wife and mother one too many times") aspects of "A Sorrowful Woman," but once this heuristic device is in place, good discussion and writing will result. I find this works particularly well with older traditional students who more readily see the invalidity of the first fairy tale and may be all too familiar with the reality of the second.

— JOSEPH ZEPPETELLO, *Ulster Community College*

POSSIBLE CONNECTIONS TO OTHER SELECTIONS

Colette, "The Hand" (text p. 220)
Emily Dickinson, "Much Madness is divinest Sense — " (text p. 942)
Henrik Ibsen, *A Doll House* (text p. 1564)
Herman Melville, "Bartleby, the Scrivener" (text p. 113)
Linda Pastan, "Marks" (text p. 791)

RESOURCE FOR TEACHING

Interview [recording]. 1 cassette (56 min.). Godwin discusses the recurring themes and concerns in her fiction. Distributed by American Audio Prose Library.

PERSPECTIVE

TANIA MODLESKI, *The Popularity of Romance Novels* (p. 38)

One use of this perspective might involve a comparison of the goals of the heroines in the excerpt from *A Secret Sorrow* and the short story "A Sorrowful Woman." Is Faye embracing "patriarchal myths and institutions" (paragraph 1) even when she tries to turn

away from Kai? How is the woman in Godwin's story responding to these myths and institutions?

Another approach involves a more general discussion of popular culture. Ask students to choose one or two highly successful recent movies and explain whether these
movies depict women who "find meaning and pleasure in activities which are not wholly
male-centered" (1). A particularly fruitful discussion might arise from consideration of a
movie such as *Thelma and Louise, The River Wild*, or even the 1980s hit *Romancing the Stone*,
in which the heroine is a writer of Harlequin romance–like novels.

THOMAS JEFFERSON, *On the Dangers of Reading Fiction* (p. 39)

Draw on any story that was popular in class to argue that reading fiction is time
spent "instructively employed" and that reason and good judgment can be improved by
reading fiction — in short, to refute Jefferson's argument. Have students tell you what
they learned from any of the stories in the anthology and state why they were worth reading. Jefferson's views could also be discussed in light of the book banning and censorship
going on in this country today.

2

Writing about Fiction

Beginning to write about literature, students should establish particular goals. First, it is important to begin to understand and use the language of literary interpretation — to incorporate references to plot, characterization, setting, and other elements into an argument based on the writer's understanding of one or more literary works. Chapter introductions throughout *The Bedford Introduction to Literature* provide and define key terms (foreshadowing, irony, static vs. dynamic characterization, and other terms); encourage your students not only to learn the terms' meanings but to begin to incorporate them into their active vocabularies. Using the correct terminology, the student establishes a sense of authority and readers of the student's work are more likely to respect the student's perspective. Second, encourage students to develop a particular analytic focus for each writing task. It isn't enough to simply describe an immediate reaction to a literary work, although first responses are useful in beginning to determine a thesis. (To facilitate analytic approaches to the literature, in *The Bedford Introduction to Literature*, students are invited to generate "First Responses" after they finish reading each literary work; they then proceed to more specific questions about the texts.) After determining their initial reactions, writers should return to the literature and determine how it provoked their responses. Students' discoveries at this stage in the writing process may well lead to significant observations about the literature. Third, students should decide if a particular writing mode will facilitate explanation of their theses. If comparing two stories, for instance, or a character's perspective at the beginning of a story with his/her perspective at the end, the student should compare *to make a specific point*. The order in which the stories or topics are discussed within a paper should be purposeful; it should also be consistent throughout. Good literary interpretation manifests a sense of purpose; the writer should write to convince readers that certain aspects of a given literary work are significant and/or more complex than those readers might have imagined.

The Questions for Responsive Reading and Writing in this chapter, although broad, can provide students with ideas that will allow them to begin critically analyzing works of fiction. This list of questions is extensive and may at first seem overwhelming to your students. It is important, therefore, for students to realize that they shouldn't expect every question to apply to every text in a meaningful way, and that certain questions will apply to certain stories better than others. To make these questions seem more manageable, you might consider asking your students to apply the questions about plot to one story that your class has studied, the questions about character to another story, and so on. Or you might choose one piece of fiction and ask your students to answer (in discussion or in a brief writing assignment) one or two questions from each set. As your students learn to apply these questions to different selections, they will become more comfortable discussing fiction and, as a result, become better able to analyze fiction in their writing. You might also remind students that they must understand the literary terms used in the questions in order to answer the questions intelligently; the Glossary of Literary Terms, included at the back of the text on page 2123, provides concise definitions and examples of these terms.

A NOTE ABOUT USING STUDENT MODELS

Student writing samples are included throughout *The Bedford Introduction to Literature*. Instructors may find it constructive to discuss these samples with their own students; in tracing the authors' writing processes and the development of their ideas, literature students may develop their own strategies for writing about literature. These sample student papers include initial responses, detailed lists, and multiple drafts; they enforce instructors' advice that writing is a labor-intensive process. The final drafts demonstrate the value inherent in struggling to develop and enhance original ideas about literature.

Particularly for students who are unfamiliar with writing about literature, these sample papers demonstrate useful techniques for developing accurate thesis statements and incorporating textual evidence. Instructors might call particular attention to the way evidence supports the thesis in these sample papers. Whether paraphrased or quoted directly, textual evidence distinguishes an unconvincing paper from an effective, thought-provoking one. Competent writers don't rely on textual evidence to make their arguments for them; instead, they subordinate the evidence to their own ideas.

Because the sample papers address materials contained within *The Bedford Introduction to Literature*, students may find themselves inspired to reread the literature discussed. Instructors might find it useful to have students write responses to the student sample papers as a way of generating discussion, both about the literature and about the writing process. Working with the sample papers, readers may understand more about how different elements within the literature combine to create meanings and achieve effects; they should also recognize and appreciate in more substantial ways the subtlety of the author's technique.

A SAMPLE STUDENT PAPER IN PROGRESS

In the student sample paper contained in Chapter 2, Maya Leigh writes about the depiction of marriage in Karen Van Der Zee's novel, *A Secret Sorrow*, and in Gail Godwin's short story, "A Sorrowful Woman." Students should have read the excerpt from Van Der Zee's novel and the complete Godwin short story (both contained in Chapter 1). In addition, before introducing students to Leigh's sample paper, you may want to assign or encourage your students to respond to the questions following each text. Having generated some initial ideas about these texts, students might appreciate or understand more of Leigh's writing process.

Second, encourage students to answer the "Questions for Responsive Reading and Writing" at the beginning of Chapter 2 in reference to Van Der Zee's and Godwin's work. (This might be a productive in-class discussion or small-group assignment.) Gaining confidence in assessing plot, character, setting, point-of-view, and other literary elements, students will be better prepared to follow Leigh's ideas. They may find the numerous questions in each section overwhelming, but they will most likely develop some ideas about each element whether they answer all or only a few of the questions.

Turning to the "First Response," students should recognize the personal quality of the work. Notice the extensive use of "I" throughout: we learn a great deal about Maya as we read her response. (She has read Harlequin romances before, and she knows what she values about them: the happy endings.) In addition, it might be useful to point out that stories that don't initially meet readers' expectations or satisfy them are often better writing topics than stories that contain no surprises and no mysteries. As Leigh notes, the Godwin story "is a much more powerful story, and it is one that I could read several times, unlike the Harlequin. The Godwin woman bothers me too, because I can't really

9

see what she has to complain about" (paragraph 2). This response leads directly to Leigh's focus on the roles of the female protagonists and their relationship to marriage. At this point, students might look back at their own — or at each other's — first responses to the Van Der Zee and Godwin stories. Are there problems or striking reactions that invite the writer to study them in more detail?

After completing her "First Response," Leigh then lists her ideas about the female characters' lives: their observations about marriage, men, children, housework, and other relevant issues. She organizes her list in such a way that comparable topics appear opposite one another. For instance, she compares the female characters' status at the end of each story: in Godwin's story, the woman is "dead in the end"; in Van Der Zee's, the woman, Faye, is "beautiful, whole, complete in the end." Each woman experiences a crisis, but for Godwin's character, the crisis is "due to fear of always having husband and kid" while for Van Der Zee's protagonist, the crisis is "due to fear of never having husband and kids." Lists such as Leigh's are a useful way of generating and organizing basic observations about literature. This technique is also useful in estimating how characters develop over the course of a story, or how two characters' dialogue with one another evolves. It can even be useful simply in comparing the first few paragraphs of a story with the final ones. It enables readers to begin to identify key aspects for further study.

Two working drafts follow Leigh's lists. After students have read all of each draft, they may find themselves overwhelmed by the material or unable to explain exactly how Leigh's ideas are evolving. Invite them to break down the drafts — to study the thesis statements separately, to focus on particular paragraphs in order to understand how Leigh's topic is evolving, to see how she begins to incorporate different and more convincing textual evidence. In particular, you may want to call students' attention to the way Leigh refines her approach, corrects details of her observations, and incorporates the terminology of literary analysis as she develops these drafts. Strong papers are accurate, thought-provoking, and convincing. Ask students to identify two or three different examples in which Leigh's second draft is an improvement on the first. Dealing with these drafts, you might also call attention to basic elements of technique, among them introducing the authors' full names and story titles in the first paragraph, developing a strong thesis within that paragraph, and properly quoting and citing textual evidence throughout the essay.

Finally, having immersed themselves in Leigh's ideas and writing process, students should turn to the final product of her labor. The introduction to the final draft summarizes Leigh's improvements, particularly involving accuracy, argumentation, and mechanics (transitions, sentence clarity, conclusions). In discussion or in small groups, students could study these aspects of the essay and, additionally, identify what they find convincing or provocative about Leigh's ideas. It might be useful to assign different sections of the essay to different groups in order for students to focus more effectively on the material. In connection with studying this final version, students might return to the Godwin and Van Der Zee texts; having read Leigh's commentary, what do they notice about the literature that they hadn't been aware of while reading these stories? If students still have objections to her ideas or arguments, you may want to encourage them to formulate these objections in writing. Students might also explain how Leigh could overcome their objections or account for their questions.

Students may even find this sample student paper useful beyond their study of Chapter 2: it can serve as a model for writing about literature throughout the fiction section.

3

Plot

The introductory section of Chapter 3 provides students with specific examples of exposition, rising action, conflict, suspense, climax, and resolution. Students should practice applying these terms not only to the fiction provided in the chapter but also to other "stories" that they encounter in popular culture, including jokes, television shows, comic strips, and other sources. Students might keep a log of their reading or television watching for a week and practice identifying plot elements. They also might experiment with considering how they might rearrange these elements in a given story to create alternate effects. Students might even work in small groups to compare their readings of the same source and to practice rearranging the elements.

This chapter also explains plot techniques such as flashbacks and foreshadowing. Again, you may wish to invite students to apply these to the "stories" they follow outside of class. It might also be useful to practice in class with texts that most students might already know. Fairy tales, fables, and nursery rhymes are especially fruitful sources for further study of plot. Having "Goldilocks and the Three Bears" begin at the end or in the middle, or investing "Little Red Riding Hood" with foreshadowing in the first paragraph might enable students to discover more meaning both in the original tale and in the retelling.

EDGAR RICE BURROUGHS, *From* Tarzan of the Apes (p. 62)

Most of the sixty books Edgar Rice Burroughs wrote recorded bedtime stories he had told his children. In addition to the enormously popular Tarzan series, Burroughs wrote a good deal of science fiction, most notably a series of books that chronicle the adventures of John Carter of Mars. Before making his fortune as a writer, Burroughs was a cowboy, gold miner, policeman, and store manager. His books include *The Princess of Mars* (1917), *Tanar of Pellucidar* (1930), and *Tarzan and the Foreign Legion* (1947). *Tarzan of the Apes* (1914), the first of the Tarzan series, has been translated into more than fifty languages.

Burroughs writes that from Tarzan's "early infancy his survival had depended upon acuteness of eyesight, hearing, smell, touch, and taste far more than upon the more slowly developed organ of reason. The least developed of all in Tarzan was the sense of taste" (paragraphs 29–30). The description in the excerpt relies heavily on physical detail, almost corresponding to this discussion of Tarzan's acute sensory development. Ask students to isolate one paragraph of the Burroughs excerpt and assess the kind of description included in it. What techniques does Burroughs rely on in successfully presenting such heavy — but not excessive — detail?

Much of the plot in this excerpt functions as a device for revealing the characterizations of Tarzan and Terkoz by providing them with occurrences to which they must react. How would the excerpt change if it were altered to reflect primarily Jane's characterization? What details would be emphasized in such a narrative? Would the plot seem in any way diminished in such a representation?

POSSIBLE CONNECTIONS TO OTHER SELECTIONS

Tim O'Brien, "How to Tell a True War Story" (text p. 555)
Karen Van Der Zee, From *A Secret Sorrow* (text p. 25)

RESOURCE FOR TEACHING

Tarzan of the Apes [recording]. 6 cassettes (90 min. each). Read by Walter Costello. Distributed by Books on Tape.

PERSPECTIVE

GORE VIDAL, *The Popularity of the Tarzan Books* (p. 68)

In light of Vidal's statement that "action" is hard to write, ask students to compare the action in the excerpt from *Tarzan of the Apes* (p. 62) with the action in any story they think might stand up well against *Tarzan*. A particularly good choice would be Mishima's "Patriotism" (p. 593).

MARK HALLIDAY, *Young Man on Sixth Avenue* (p. 70)

It is difficult to estimate how students might identify with the young man described in Halliday's story. Their reaction may be dictated by their age, their experience, and their ability to empathize with others. Traditional college students might prefer the ambitious, confident man characterized in the first three paragraphs of the story to the older, more settled figure described in the three final paragraphs of the story. However, nontraditional students might identify more closely with — or appreciate the perspective of — the older man.

Ask the students how they might characterize the time and setting of this story. In 1938, for instance, America was coming out of the Great Depression. Manhattan was then, as it is now, in many ways the center of American business and culture: as Halliday notes, it is "the biggest, the most overwhelming city" (paragraph 1). In addition, the story includes numerous references not only to the year but also to such public figures as Rita Hayworth, Theodore Dreiser, Thomas Wolfe, and John O'Hara. Students might benefit from studying standard bibliographic entries about these figures, but at the least, they should know that these references enforce the theme of the story — that a person's confidence and expectations of success in youth are too often balanced by the reality of a later life that may be, at best, mundane. Consider how the reference to Rita Hayworth informs the story: in 1938, Hayworth had recently married Edward Judson, a businessman who furthered his wife's career in significant ways, in part by renaming her and transforming her from a dancer of Hispanic origin into a red-haired, much-admired American star. However, Hayworth is also significant because although she made such a vivid impression in films such as *Gilda* (1946), her potential was never realized. She ended her career a pathetic figure unable to remember lines or manage her own assets. She was eventually diagnosed as a victim of Alzheimer's disease. The distance between her youthful success and the reality of her later life parallels the experiences of the protagonist in Halliday's story.

The literary references also reinforce the theme of unrealized potential. Perhaps the most fruitful comparison that may be made is between Halliday's protagonist and Dreiser's George Hurstwood, from *Sister Carrie* (1900). Hurstwood is portrayed at the beginning of the novel as an ambitious, reasonably successful Midwestern resort manager. After leaving his position and his family to move to New York with a young woman to whom he is not married, he experiences a dramatic decline of fortune. By the end of the novel, he has succumbed to despair.

The protagonist of "Young Man on Sixth Avenue" is supremely confident at the beginning of the story. Halliday characterizes his abundant energy: "His legs were long and his legs were strong; there was no question about his legs; they were unmistakable in their length and strength; they were as bold and dependable as any American machine..." (paragraph 1). In addition, this man is confident that he conveys evident cachet; others on the street, he is sure, will notice him. When he dines with his friend John at a "witty" late lunch, "Everything was — the whole lunch was good. It was right. And what they said was both hilarious and notably well-informed" (5). All in all, this man has intelligence, style, ambition, and potential. However, in the very next paragraph, and throughout the remainder of the story, his energy has been replaced by lethargy; readers may be shocked to discover that the up-and-coming young man has become someone who dozes off "in the blue chair, with his work on his lapboard, after a pleasant dinner of macaroni and sausage and salad" (6). Not only is the man's sedentary life-style surprising, but his prosaic dinner is in sharp contrast to the earlier reference to the man's appreciation for "the right restaurant for red roast beef, not too expensive" (3), or the Seventh Avenue lunch described in paragraph five.

The narrative structure of this story emphasizes the way in which the man is surprised by the relentless march of time. In the space of three sentences, the better part of this man's life — his business success, his marriage, and his fatherhood — passes. Just as he is shocked to discover that much of his life is over, so the reader is shocked by the sudden transition from youth to middle age. In essence, Halliday elides the climax in order to enable readers to appreciate some of the confusion and surprise the man must be feeling about the passing of his own life.

Halliday provides some foreshadowing of the man's later life in paragraph four when the man encounters "an unexpected zone of deep shade." Though his future is, he thinks, quite bright, the shadow makes him shiver and pause (4). This is in striking contrast to his energetic, almost mechanized pace one block earlier. Ask students to identify what the "deep shade" represents. In addition, invite them to envision the experience of being surrounded — and dwarfed — by the tall buildings and the enclosed space of midtown New York City. For a man who conceives of his potential through metaphors of height ("he moved visibly tall with the tall potential of the not-finite twentieth-century getting that would be his inheritance" [1]), this sudden recognition of his limitations is daunting.

Finally, you may want to call students' attention to the man's different attitudes toward women at the beginning of his life and at the end. (In fact, the final paragraph details his posthumous awareness.) In the beginning, he regards women in the same way that he regards his career: "He knew they knew he would *get* some of them" (1). He's supremely confident in his effect on them: "They felt that they or their sisters would have to take him into account, and they touched their scarves a little nervously" (1). In the end, however, he has lost his confidence (or his arrogance): "Women see past him on the street in this pseudo-present and he feels they are so stupid and walks fierce for a minute..."

13

(8). What makes this character worth a second, more sympathetic evaluation is his immediate adjustment of his attitude: "his shoulders settle closer to his skeleton with the truth about these women: not especially stupid; only young" (8). It is evident in this passage that although the man may never have accomplished his early goals (something "that would have made people say 'Yes that's why you matter so much' " [7]), he has nonetheless achieved some sense of humanity and sympathy in his life.

Ask students to interpret the final sentence of the story. What does the man's memory of himself as a young man add to the story as a whole? What is the significance of the young man stepping back onto the curb in that final line? Is this more a reflection of the older man's wistful yearning for the energy of his youth, or some form of regret about the way he once approached life?

POSSIBLE CONNECTIONS TO OTHER SELECTIONS

T. S. Eliot, "The Love Song of J. Alfred Prufrock" (text p. 1045)
Herman Melville, "Bartleby, the Scrivener" (question #1, following)

CONNECTION QUESTION IN TEXT (p. 72) WITH ANSWER

1. Discuss the significance of the Manhattan setting in "Young Man on Sixth Avenue" and in Herman Melville's "Bartleby, the Scrivener" (p. 113).

    The most fruitful discussion of the significance of the Manhattan setting in "Young Man on Sixth Avenue" and "Bartleby, the Scrivener" arises from the places alluded to in each story. In "Young Man on Sixth Avenue," for instance, the protagonist crosses Forty-ninth, Forty-eighth, and Forty-seventh Streets as well as Fifth, Sixth, and Seventh Avenues. Halliday emphasizes Sixth Avenue in the title and throughout the story: "all Sixth Avenue was in fact at two o'clock a thumping bright Rita Hayworth and the young man strode south irresistibly" (paragraph 2). Sixth Avenue — the Avenue of the Americas, as it is also known — is a center of business (hence, the man's interview occurs there); it also features such landmarks as Radio City Music Hall, a symbol of American optimism and prosperity. Thus, setting confirms the robust characterization of the protagonist in the early stage of his career.

    In "Bartleby, the Scrivener," Melville alludes to several New York landmarks, including Trinity Church, where the elite go to worship. (This reveals the lawyer's status-consciousness.) In addition, the district in which the lawyer maintains his office, Wall Street, indicates his interest in wealth and prosperity at the beginning of the story and enables Melville to establish a contrast between the lawyer's enthusiasm for materialism and Bartleby's denial of it.

    Students might consult guide books or other information about New York in order to develop their ideas about setting in Halliday and Melville's stories.

WILLIAM FAULKNER, *A Rose for Emily* (p. 72)

The ending of this mystery story is as chillingly gruesome as it is surprising. Just when we think that the discovery of Homer Barron's body ("what was left of him") is the awful revelation that the narrator has been leading up to, we realize in the final climactic paragraph (and particularly in the last three words) that the strand of "iron-gray hair" on the indented pillow belongs to Emily. The details indicate that she has slept with Homer since she murdered him, because we are told in paragraph 48 that her hair hadn't turned gray until after Homer disappeared. The closing paragraph produces a gasp of horror in most readers, but by withholding this information until the very end, Faulkner allows us to develop a sympathetic understanding of Emily before we are revolted by her necrophilia.

The conclusion is skillfully foreshadowed: Emily denies her father's death; she buys arsenic; Homer disappears; and there is a terrible smell around the house. These clues are muted, however, by the narrator's rearrangement of the order of events. We learn about the smell before we know that Emily bought arsenic and that Homer disappeared. Hence, these details seem less related to one another than they would if they had been presented chronologically. Faulkner's plotting allows him to preserve suspense in a first reading. On subsequent readings we take delight in realizing how all the pieces fit together and point to the conclusion.

The gothic elements provide an appropriate atmosphere of mystery and are directly related to the conflicts in the story. Emily's decrepit house evokes an older, defunct South that resists the change imposed by garages, gasoline pumps, new construction, paved sidewalks, and a Yankee carpetbagger such as Homer. This exposition is essential to the story's theme because it explains Emily's antagonists. Emily rejects newness and change; her house smells of "dust and disuse." Her refusal to let go of the past is indicated by her insistence that her father did not die and by her necrophilia with Homer. She attempts to stop time, and although the narrator's collective "we" suggests the town's tolerance for and sympathy with such an attitude (as a representative of the North, Homer is powerful but vulgar), the story finally makes clear that living in a dead past means living with death. As much as the narrator realizes that Emily's illusions caused her to reject the changing realities of her life, he — like his fellow citizens — admires Emily with "a sort of respectful affection" (paragraph 1). She is like a "fallen monument," a reminder of an Old South that could not survive the new order of Reconstruction. Even though she murders Homer, Emily cannot stop the changes brought by the urbanization associated with him.

This story, minus its concerns about change in the South and its tribute — a rose — to Emily's strong sensibilities (in spite of her illusions and eccentricities), fits into the gothic horror tradition, but it would be a far less intriguing work if the formula were to supersede Faulkner's complex imaginative treatment.

POSSIBLE CONNECTIONS TO OTHER SELECTIONS

Stephen Crane, "The Bride Comes to Yellow Sky" (text p. 249)
Emily Dickinson, "The Soul selects her own Society —" (text p. 941)
Ralph Ellison, "Battle Royal" (text p. 223)
William Faulkner, "Barn Burning" (text p. 481)
Yukio Mishima, "Patriotism" (questions #1, 2, and 3, following)

CONNECTIONS QUESTIONS IN TEXT (p. 79) WITH ANSWERS

1. Contrast Faulkner's ordering of events with Yukio Mishima's strategy in "Patriotism" (p. 593). How does each author's arrangement of incidents create different effects on the reader?

2. To what extent do concepts of honor and tradition influence the action in "A Rose for Emily" and "Patriotism"?

3. Compare and contrast Faulkner's and Mishima's uses of death as a means of resolving conflicts having to do with love.

Answer to Questions 1–3

A number of useful connections can be made between "A Rose for Emily" and Mishima's "Patriotism" (p. 593). Mishima's plot contains no surprises, while the incidents in Faulkner's story are arranged to lead up to the final ghastly scene. Students might be asked to write about how they respond to the plotting of each story; this will encourage them to keep track of their responses and to connect them to specific events in the stories. Additionally, although Faulkner and Mishima focus on radically different cultures, they both use concepts of honor and tradition to develop conflict and reveal character. Students should be encouraged to see how important a role dignity plays in the lives of Reiko and Emily. Moreover, it is worth pointing out that death in these stories — whether suicide or murder — is, at least from the central character's point of view, a means of preserving dignity.

RESOURCES FOR TEACHING

Barn Burning. 41 min., color, 1980. Beta, VHS, 16-mm film. With Tommy Lee Jones. Same program available in "The American Short Story Series II" on manual page 591. See local retailer.

Collected Short Stories of William Faulkner, Volumes 1 and 2 [recording]. (Volume 1, 11 90-min. cassettes; Volume 2, 11 90-min. cassettes). Read by Wolfram Kandinsky and Michael Kramer. (Volume 2 includes "A Rose for Emily"). Distributed by Books on Tape.

The Long Hot Summer. 118 min., color, 1958. Beta, VHS. A film adaptation of "Barn Burning." Directed by Martin Ritt. With Paul Newman, Orson Welles, Joanne Woodward, Lee Remick, Anthony Franciosa, Angela Lansbury, and Richard Anderson. See local retailer.

The Long Hot Summer. 172 min., color, 1986. Beta, VHS. A made-for-TV version of "Barn Burning." Directed by Stuart Cooper. With Don Johnson, Cybill Shepherd, Judith Ivey, Jason Robards, and Ava Gardner. See local retailer.

A Rose for Emily. 27 min., color, 1983. Beta, VHS, ¾" U-matic cassette, 16-mm film. Distributed by Pyramid Film and Video. Available for rental from member institutions of the Consortium of College and University Media Centers.

A Rose for Emily (William Faulkner). 27 min., color, 1983. VHS. With Anjelica Huston. Narrated by John Houseman. Distributed by Pyramid Film & Video.

William Faulkner: A Life on Paper. 120 min., color, 1980. Beta, VHS, ¾" U-matic cassette. A documentary biography. With Lauren Bacall, Howard Hawks, Anita Loos, George Plimpton, Tennessee Williams, and Jill Faulkner Summers (the author's daughter). Distributed by Films, Inc.

William Faulkner's Mississippi. 49 min., color and b/w, 1965. Beta, VHS, ¾" U-matic cassette. Deals with Faulkner's life and works. Distributed by Benchmark Films. Available for rental from member institutions of the Consortium of College and University Media Centers.

PERSPECTIVES ON FAULKNER

WILLIAM FAULKNER, *On "A Rose for Emily"* (p. 79)

Ask students to consider Faulkner's statement "I was simply trying to write about people," which was made in response to a question about symbolism in this story. Have the class look at other stories in which symbols are prevalent, or at least obvious. Are the characters always realistic and convincing? Have you come across any characters who serve a symbolic function but are not entirely credible as far as motivation or behavior goes?

ANDRE DUBUS, *Killings* (p. 81)

At the heart of "Killings" is the issue of the justice of the legal system — a system of arrest, bail, trial, and sentencing — versus the ancient concept of justice known as "an eye for an eye." When Willis and Matt are discussing the matter, Willis argues that the established American legal system will prove unsatisfactory: "Know what he'll do? Five at the most" (paragraph 16). In the flashback, when Frank returns home after Strout has assaulted him, Matt wants him to press charges, but Frank refuses (38–39). The laws are simply inadequate in many respects for the circumstances surrounding the events of the story; as Matt tells his wife when she objects to Frank's seeing Mary Ann before her divorce is final, "Massachusetts has crazy laws" (58). Later in the story, as Matt forces Strout to pack his belongings, Strout attempts to defend his actions: "I wanted to try to get together with her again. . . . I couldn't even talk to her. He was always with her. I'm going to jail for it; if I ever get out I'll be an old man. Isn't that enough?" (120). In this mock trial, Matt becomes both judge and jury: "You're not going to jail" (121). Matt knows that no system of justice will deny Strout what Strout's action has denied Frank, and the thought of Strout living in freedom at any time in the future is intolerable for Matt: "just thinking of Strout in Montana or whatever place lay at the end of the lie he had told, thinking of him walking the streets there, loving a girl there . . . would be enough to slowly rot the rest of his days" (135). In the end, Matt ensures that Strout's punishment is appropriate to his crime: as Strout shot Frank, so Matt shoots Strout. In the last paragraph, Matt seems to find justice in the knowledge that both Frank and Strout will be covered by the "red and yellow leaves falling on the earth" (169).

Neither Matt nor Strout is really a "killer" (hence the title — "Killings," not "Killers"). By means of the flashbacks and the sequence in which we see Strout's house and hear his "defense," we realize that each of the murders is committed out of love. Matt cannot live with Ruth's daily pain on encountering Strout in town. He is also motivated by the love he continues to feel for his dead son. Remembering how he would stand beneath the tree behind his house as one of his children climbed it, "poised to catch the small body before it hit the earth" (77), Matt carries an undeniable burden of guilt that he could not save his son. After Frank's death, Matt feels "that all the fears he had borne while they [the children] were growing up, and all the grief he had been afraid of, had backed up like a huge wave and struck him on the beach and swept him out to sea" (77). His response to this metaphorical assault is to punish Strout. Matt is constantly reminded of that "huge wave"; as he forces Strout into the car, he recognizes "the smacking curling white at the breakwater" (87). Later, we are told that "over the engine Matt could hear through his open window the water rushing inland under the bridge" (91). Matt uses his awareness of the wave's presence to bolster his courage during his interaction with Strout. Significantly, after he has buried Strout, he throws the gun into a nearby pond (152) and the keys to Strout's car into the Merrimack River (153). In a sense, the water — the force that can drown him in grief and fear unless he opposes it in some way — represents the senseless violence that has destroyed his peaceful existence; his actions serve as defiant gestures against what he feels has "struck him on the beach and swept him out to sea."

As we learn from the interaction between Strout and Matt, Strout has also acted out of love. He attempts to explain to Matt that he wanted Mary Ann and his children back; as the earlier flashback reveals, although his life has been violent and unsuccessful in some aspects, he has not previously demonstrated that he is a "killer." Although Dubus offers these occasional insights into Strout's character, the distance between readers and Strout remains. We have a much greater understanding of Matt's thoughts and feelings than Strout's, and while other characters are referred to throughout the story by their first names, Strout is almost always referred to by his last name only.

How important is the setting? You might ask students what time and place they associate with Frank. When Matt thinks of Frank, he thinks of Frank's job as a lifeguard, of the way he smells of the beach when he comes home, of his tan. Toward the end of the story, Matt and Strout drive past "the Dairy Queen closed until spring, and the two lobster restaurants that faced each other and were crowded all summer and were now also closed" (91). Ask students why this is a significant passage. Certainly the busy summer season, replete with tourists, is associated in Matt's mind with Frank. It is appropriate that the emptiness of the fall season follows Frank's death.

Even though Matt commits a murder in this story, readers may feel tremendous sympathy for him. He is a victim who takes action against the man who caused his grief; he is also portrayed as a man of humanity who takes pains to understand other people's perspectives and the complexities of a situation. Watching his son with Mary Ann, Matt tries to imagine what Frank feels and wants Frank to find the kind of intimacy with Mary Ann that he has established with Ruth. Later, as Matt and Strout go through Strout's house, Matt attempts to understand the situation from Strout's perspective. When he is in bed with Ruth at the end of the story, Matt sees both "Frank and Mary Ann making love in her bed" (169) and Strout's lover: "The other girl was faceless, bodiless, but he felt her sleeping now" (169). Because he is such a finely drawn character, readers may find it difficult to condemn Matt for his actions in "Killings."

POSSIBLE CONNECTIONS TO OTHER SELECTIONS

Isabel Allende, "The Judge's Wife" (text p. 581)
Alison Baker, "Better Be Ready 'Bout Half Past Eight" (text p. 617)
William Faulkner, "Barn Burning" (text p. 481)
———, "A Rose for Emily" (text p. 72)
Susan Glaspell, *Trifles* (text p. 1172)
Gish Jen, "In the American Society" (text p. 643)

RESOURCES FOR TEACHING

Andre Dubus: Reading [recording]. 1 cassette (51 min.). The writer reads his work and discusses the writing process. Distributed by American Audio Prose Library.
Andre Dubus: Interview [recording]. 1 cassette (50 min.). The writer reads his work and discusses the writing process. Distributed by American Audio Prose Library.

PERSPECTIVE

THOMAS E. KENNEDY, *On Morality and Revenge in "Killings"* (p. 94)

Kennedy writes eloquently about the spiritual isolation that Matt Fowler must face as a result of killing Richard Strout. It is true that the act of murder may haunt Matt, and that Matt and Ruth probably cannot tell their other children that Frank's murder has been avenged. However, students should question Kennedy's premise that a "profound lifelong isolation awaits Fowler as a result of his act of premeditated murder" (paragraph

4). Indeed, Matt is essentially supported in his actions by much of the small, sympathetic community in which he lives. Consider Matt's close connection to his wife, Ruth, who knows of and supports his action. Consider also Matt's deep and significant friendship with his accomplice, Willis. Matt recognizes the way Willis and the other poker players reveal "affection and courtesy" (7) when he joins them for the first time after Frank's death, and Willis aids and abets both the planning and the enactment of Strout's murder. Prior to the actual murder, both Ruth and Willis admit that they would kill Strout if the opportunity presented itself. In some ways, the town itself seems almost an accomplice: Frank's funeral is well attended, and no one in town will hire Strout. Throughout "Killings," Dubus provides a number of indications that the members of Matt's community will continue to support and sustain him after Strout's death as they have throughout the events leading up to it.

The question then is whether such mute sympathy, along with Matt's personal sense that justice has been served, will be enough to sustain him afterward. Ask your students if Kennedy overemphasizes the significance of Matt's inability to make love after his encounter with Strout. Has he "isolated himself by his act" (1) of murder, as Kennedy suggests? Do they agree with Kennedy's claim that Matt "is left morally wounded to walk the earth, and [that] his suffering will spread" (4)?

A. L. BADER, *Nothing Happens in Modern Short Stories* (p. 95)

Ask students to read through relatively recent issues of *The New Yorker*, the *Atlantic*, or *Esquire* until they find a short story they really like. Does anything "happen" in the story? Is there a character change? If not, what do they like about the story?

4

Character

In the introductory section for Chapter 4, the sample passage from *Hard Times* demonstrates the intricacies of characterization. Because many students might not be familiar with Dickens's work, it might be fruitful to study the characterization in an example or two drawn from popular culture. For instance, students might decide whether the characters in their favorite television shows are static or dynamic, flat or round. They might compare comedies (typically containing stock, static characters) with dramas (often featuring characters who are allowed to change and grow). Ask students whether the title character in *Frasier* is static or dynamic, or whether the doctors on *ER* are predictable or surprising in their choices and actions. Commonly, the comedy arises from a manipulation of plot in order to force a predictable reaction from a well-established but static character; in contrast, drama's success usually depends on the complexities of characterization. It may be fruitful to discuss why these different "genres" require different manipulations of characterization.

Encourage students to get into the habit of asking themselves a series of questions about characterization after reading a story. First, is the narrator reliable? Is there any reason provided in the text that the narrator may have a particular agenda that causes her or him to alter or slant the telling of the story? (For instance, in "Bartleby, the Scrivener" [p. 113], what is the lawyer's motivation in telling the story? Is it merely that he found Bartleby an interesting character? Or, does he have something to gain from the telling?) Also, to whom is the narrator telling the story? Occasionally, we have a clear sense of audience. (In a poem such as Robert Browning's "My Last Duchess" [p. 821], for example, we know not only the identity of the listener but also his reaction to the tale.) In addition to the narrator, what other characters are significant to the story? Do the characters change in the course of the narration? Are they static or dynamic? (Sometimes, the most effective way to determine this is through a comparison of the characters.) The character's impression on the reader may be based on what the character says, what the character does, and what other characters say about the character or how they react to her or him. Students might envision themselves as private detectives building case files on each character they encounter in a story; they might share their findings in response to a given story as they develop their skills.

CHARLES DICKENS, *From* Hard Times (p. 98)

Charles Dickens (1812–1870) was the author of numerous novels, travel books, and sketches. Many of his most memorable characters are inspired by his memories of childhood, during which time his father was imprisoned for debt. Dickens later acted in amateur theatricals and performed public readings of his work. His novels and other later writings were serialized in both English and American periodicals. Among his works are *Oliver Twist, Bleak House, Great Expectations, A Christmas Carol,* and *A Tale of Two Cities.* He is buried in Poet's Corner, Westminster Abbey.

In this excerpt from *Hard Times*, Dickens's description of "the speaker," Mr. Gradgrind, works to reveal aspects of his character. In addition, other characters' responses to Gradgrind emphasize certain aspects or traits of his character. How does the final paragraph of the excerpt reveal additional information about Gradgrind? How does the information about the other grownups in the room convey a specific impression about the children who are assembled there?

As a means of starting discussion of Dickens's characterization of Mr. Gradgrind, ask students to write a short sketch in which they experience a class taught by him. They might enjoy writing about how he would interact with their actual class.

POSSIBLE CONNECTIONS TO OTHER SELECTIONS

Toni Cade Bambara, "The Lesson" (text p. 179)
Nathaniel Hawthorne, "Young Goodman Brown" (text p. 310)

RESOURCES FOR TEACHING

Charles Dickens: An Introduction to His Life and Work. 27 min., color, 1979. Beta, VHS, 3/4″ U-matic cassette, special-order formats. An introduction to Dickens's life and work. Distributed by the International Film Bureau.

The Charles Dickens Show. 52 min., color, 1973. Beta, VHS, ¾″ U-matic cassette. Deals with the writer and his times. Includes dramatization from his life and works. Distributed by the International Film Bureau.

Hard Times. 240 min., color, 1977. Beta, VHS, ¾″ U-matic cassette. A TV adaptation of the novel. Distributed by WNET/Thirteen Non-Broadcast.

Hard Times [recording]. 16 hours, 8 cassettes. Read by Frederick Davison. Distributed by Blackstone Audio.

BHARATI MUKHERJEE, *The Tenant* (p. 102)

To fully understand the complexities of the protagonist in "The Tenant," students will probably find it helpful to study her conflicting impulses. More than once in the story, Maya describes herself as a void: "She has accomplished nothing. She has changed her citizenship but she hasn't broken through into the light, the vigor, the *hustle* of the New World. She is stuck in dead space" (paragraph 76). The question is, with what will she fill that dead space? In this story, she struggles to balance impulses that reflect not only Indian and American but also colonial and postcolonial Indian culture.

Our understanding of Maya stems primarily from her thoughts. In dealing with the other characters in this story, she is rarely able to explain how she feels. As she acknowledges, "She can't talk about the dead space she lives in" (94). She can't talk to Fran openly because, although Fran has been responsible for Maya's being hired at the university, "Fran is on the Hiring, Tenure, and Reappointment Committee" (11). In addition, Maya is "too polite" to inquire about the mysterious upstairs noise at the Chatterji's apartment, and even though she would like to put Dr. Chatterji down with one of the "nasty, ironic one-liners" (52) that she is known for, we never see her do so in the course of the story. Throughout the story, she is silenced, in part by her upbringing, and in part by her ethnicity. Thus, we need to study her thoughts and actions to determine her motivation.

Much of the story demonstrates the presence for Maya of two cultures, two sets of expectations. Though she claims to have "broken with the past" (22), her syntax suggests that the break isn't complete; she immediately qualifies her assertion by adding, "But."

21

This qualification occurs throughout the story: "She is an American citizen. But" (16). By suggesting an assertion's opposite, the frequent phrase "not necessarily" also works as a qualifier: "She's not necessarily on Dr. Chatterji's side is what she wants to get across early; she's not against America and Americans" (26). She is aware of American expectations of Indian women: for instance, they should be "inventive with food, whip up exotic delights to tickle an American's palate" (5), but she also manipulates others by acting on stereotypical assumptions of Indian women when it is useful for her to do so. During her initial telephone conversation with Dr. Chatterji, for instance: " 'I don't drive,' she lies, knowing it sounds less shameful than not owning a car. She has said this so often she can get in the right degree of apology and Asian upper-class helplessness" (20).

On the other hand, Maya's actions reveal her genuine longing to surround herself with aspects of Indian culture as well. Immediately after moving to Cedar Falls, she searches the telephone book for "common Indian names, especially Bengali" (5). When meeting the Chatterjis, she wears traditional clothing: "She has dressed herself in a peach-colored nylon georgette sari, jade drop-earrings and a necklace. The color is good on dark skin" (22). She finds herself deeply moved by Mrs. Chatterji's music (55). She goes to the periodicals room of the library to satisfy her desire for news about India: "Out here, in the heartland of the new world, the India of serious newspapers unsettles. Maya longs again to feel what she had felt in the Chatterjis' living room: virtues made physical" (68). She even steals the issue of *India Abroad* (68) in order to contact Indian men through their ads in the matrimonial columns.

Caste remains an issue for Maya even though she claims to have escaped such "Old World" concerns. We are told, "She was born in 1954, six full years after India became independent. Her India was Nehru's India: a charged, progressive place" (10), and she prides herself on being a modern woman: "Maya's taken some big risks, made a break with her parents' ways. She's done things a woman from Ballygunge Park Road doesn't do, even in fantasies" (16). However, traditional ties are difficult to break. Whenever Maya thinks of her parents, or of her family, it is a colonial India she remembers. For instance, Dr. and Mrs. Chatterji remain interested in her family's ties to the British Empire, and Maya herself acknowledges a pre-Nehru female upbringing: "Maya had been in trouble with her women's group at Duke. She was too feminine. She had tried to explain the world she came out of. Her grandmother had been married off at the age of five in a village now in Bangladesh. Her great-aunt had been burned to death over a dowry problem. She herself had been trained to speak softly, arrange flowers, sing, be pliant" (22). Maya's conflict between breaking with her parents' ways and adhering to them at the same time is evident in "The Tenant."

You may want to invite students to compare Maya's situation with that of the Chatterjis' nephew, Poltoo. Though they never meet, they have much in common. Both are fighting against family expectations, both are of the same generation, and both are trained as academics. Though his aunt and uncle are horrified that Poltoo wants to marry a woman from Ghana, Maya thinks, "A good Brahmin boy in Iowa is in love with an African Muslim. It shouldn't be a big deal. But the more she watches the physicist, the more she realizes that 'Brahmin' isn't a caste, it's a metaphor. You break one small rule, and the constellation collapses" (53). Has her own constellation collapsed in the wake of her marriage to an American and her subsequent divorce? Students might discuss whether Poltoo's example has an influence on Maya's decision at the end to go to Ashoke Mehta in Connecticut. In the library, she reads of an incident in India in which "a child drawing well water — the reporter calls the child 'a new-Buddhist, a convert from the now-outlawed untouchable caste' — has been stoned. An editorial explains that the story about stoning is not a story about caste but about failed idealism; a story about promises of green fields and clean, potable water broken, a story about bribes paid and wells not dug. But no, thinks Maya, it's about caste" (67). This news report indicates that Maya's personal struggle with colonial and postcolonial values is one that is shared by many Indians, whether at home or abroad.

Mukherjee writes of the "confused world of the immigrant — the lostness that Maya and Poltoo feel. . . ." (52); significantly, both Maya and Poltoo rely on relationships to compensate for their "lostness." Throughout "The Tenant," Maya either pursues or considers relationships with a number of men. Early in the story, she hints that her taste runs to men who would be inappropriate for her, men with whom she does not wish to develop the kind of relationship she would acknowledge to her family: "Maya has slept with married men, with nameless men, with men little more than boys, but never with an Indian man. Never" (30). (Has she not slept with an Indian because it would be too appropriate?) Students should consider Maya's attitude toward men in general. "She remembers now how full of a soft, Cheeverian light Durham had been the summer she had slept with John Hadwen; and how after that, her tidy graduate-student world became monstrous, lawless. All men became John Hadwen; John became all men" (53). In a sense, Maya's sexual activity is a rebellion against her traditional upbringing. She tells us, "Love is anarchy" (53). Ask students whether Maya's intent to pursue a relationship with Ashoke Mehta continues or contrasts with her previous sexual history. What might be her motivation for pursuing such a relationship? Is this a relationship her family will approve of? In that sense, how can the proposed relationship constitute "anarchy"? It may be useful to compare her relationship with Ashoke to her involvement with Fred. She rationalizes sleeping with her landlord: "The dead space need not suffocate" (98). But Fred's attitude toward their relationship may in fact be what most propels her toward Ashoke: "Two wounded people, he will joke during their nightly contortions. It will shock her, this assumed equivalence with a man so strikingly deficient. She knows she is strange, and lonely, but being Indian is not the same, she would have thought, as being a freak" (98). Is she willing to pursue Ashoke not only because she finds him sexually attractive but also because with him, there will be no question of her being identified as "a freak"?

The title of the story prepares us to accept Maya's departure. "Tenant" has a temporary ring to it; it contrasts with "owner" or other words that indicate permanence. Also, as "tenant," she is unknown — or defined solely by her tenancy. It is understandable, then, that Maya would describe herself as "dead space." We get the impression that she won't be staying in Cedar Falls, Iowa, for very long. Perhaps Fran's comparison of Maya to Vern, who has left the Midwest to move to San Francisco and study film, is more apt than she realizes.

POSSIBLE CONNECTIONS TO OTHER SELECTIONS

Raymond Carver, "Popular Mechanics" (question #1, following)
William Faulkner, "Barn Burning" (text p. 481)
Alice Munro, "Prue" (question #2, following)

CONNECTIONS QUESTIONS IN TEXT (p. 112) WITH ANSWERS

1. Compare the use of exposition to reveal character in "The Tenant" and Raymond Carver's "Popular Mechanics" (p. 272). How does exposition or its relative absence affect your understanding of and response to the characters in each story?

Readers are privy to the protagonist's thoughts in "The Tenant"; however, in "Popular Mechanics," they are not. As a result, there is much more evidence for determining motivation in Mukherjee's story. In Carver's story, characters are determined only by what they say and do. In addition, setting reveals characterization in Carver's story. As metaphors for the disintegration of the marriage, the house darkens, and the artifacts of the characters' life together are destroyed.

2. Mukherjee describes Maya as having "broken with the past. But" (paragraph 22). How might this observation suggest a starting point for comparing "The Tenant" with Alice Munro's "Prue" (p. 454)?

Neither Maya nor Prue have made clean breaks with the past. Maya's family and cultural heritage are as much a part of her present as her past, while Prue's relationship with Gordon continues even after he has returned to his wife, divorced his wife, and developed relationships with other women. Neither protagonist is entirely honest with herself. Maya's syntax ("But.") allows for the possibility that the break is incomplete without having to acknowledge the specific ways in which her actions are a response to her family's expectations and her upbringing. Prue would claim that taking Gordon's amber cufflink is just a silly, meaningless habit, but it seems clear that her action is in some form retaliation for Gordon's involvement with the young woman who comes to his door while Prue is having dinner with him.

RESOURCE FOR TEACHING

Bharati Mukherjee: Conquering America. 30 min., color, 1994. VHS. In this interview with Bill Moyers, Mukherjee discusses America's newest immigrants and the building resentment and tensions between our country's various cultures. Distributed by Films for the Humanities and Sciences.

HERMAN MELVILLE, *Bartleby, the Scrivener* (p. 113)

Although students are usually intrigued by Bartleby's bizarre behavior, they are likely to respond to the "inscrutable scrivener" in much the same way that Ginger Nut assesses him: "I think, sir, he's a little *luny*" (paragraph 49). But to dismiss Bartleby as, say, a catatonic schizophrenic reduces the story to merely a prescient case study and tends to ignore the narrator-lawyer, the other major character. Besides, we don't learn enough about Bartleby to make anything approaching a clinical judgment because, as the lawyer tells us in the first paragraph, "No materials exist, for a full and satisfactory biography of this man." He is as disturbingly mysterious as Godwin's protagonist in "A Sorrowful Woman" (p. 33).

What makes the story so weird — a term that nearly always comes up in discussions of Bartleby — is that the lawyer and the scrivener occupy two radically different fictional worlds. We recognize the lawyer as a character from the kind of fictions that convey at least some of the realistic textures of life, but Bartleby seems to be an allegorical or symbolic intruder in that world. Melville uses Bartleby to disrupt the lawyer's assumptions about life. It's as if a Kafka character suddenly turned up in a novel by Dickens or James. Melville makes us, as much as the lawyer, feel that Bartleby is somehow out of place.

The protagonist is the lawyer; he is a dynamic character who changes while Bartleby, the antagonist, remains static throughout. (Some critics, however, see Bartleby as the story's central character. For alternative readings see the article by Stern cited at the end of this discussion.) Melville has the lawyer characterize himself in the first few paragraphs so that we understand the point of view from which we will see Bartleby. No champion of truth and justice, the lawyer makes his living doing a "snug business among rich men's bonds, and mortgages, and title-deeds" (2). He is convinced that "the easiest way of life is best"; he is an "eminently safe man" who takes pride in his "prudence," "method," and status (signified by his reference three times in the second paragraph to John Jacob Astor). His other employees, Turkey, Nippers, and Ginger Nut, are introduced to the reader before Bartleby in order to make credible the lawyer's tolerance for eccentric behavior. So long as the lawyer gets some work out of these human copying machines, he'll put up with just about everything — provided they don't publicly embarrass him or jeopardize his reputation. It is significant that he is a lawyer rather than simply a businessman because the law is founded on precedents and assumptions; Bartleby, however, is "more a man of preferences than assumptions" (149). Because Bartleby is beyond the lawyer's experience, the lawyer does not know how to respond to the scrivener's passive refusal to "come forth" and do "his duty."

Despite the title, the story is the lawyer's, because his sense of humanity enlarges as a result of his experience with Bartleby. "The bond of a common humanity" creates "presentiments of strange discoveries [that] hover[ed] round me" (91). In a sense, the lawyer discovers what Emily Dickinson's speaker describes in "There's a certain Slant of light" (p. 2082), a poem that can help students understand the significance of the lawyer's final comment, "Ah, Bartleby! Ah, humanity!" The lawyer moves beyond his initial incredulity, confusion, anger, and frustration and begins to understand that Bartleby represents a challenge to all his assumptions about life. Finally, he invests meaning in Bartleby instead of dismissing him as eccentric or mad. Melville expects the reader to puzzle out his meaning too.

Bartleby's physical characteristics foreshadow his death. When we first meet him (17), he already seems to have withdrawn from life. He is "motionless" and "pallidly neat, pitiably respectable, incurably forlorn!" He seems scarcely alive and is described as "cadaverous." With nearly all the life gone out of him, he is capable of nothing more than "silently, palely, mechanically" (20) copying until he prefers not to — a refusal that marks the beginning of his increasing insistence on not living.

Bartleby's "I would prefer not to" confuses and enrages the lawyer and his employees. This simple declaration takes on more power and significance as the story progresses (not unlike Edgar Allan Poe's use of "nevermore" in "The Raven"). Bartleby's seemingly mild statement carries with it considerable heft, because "some paramount consideration prevailed with him to reply as he did!" (39). His declaration is both humorous and deadly serious.

The Dead Letter Office is essential to understanding what motivates Bartleby's behavior. Although Melville is not specific, he suggests enough about the nature of the thwarted hopes and desires that the scrivener daily encountered in the Dead Letter Office to account for Bartleby's rejection of life. Somehow it was all too painful for him and rendered life barren and meaningless — hence his "dead-wall reveries." The lawyer makes the connection between this experience and Bartleby. But Melville has him withhold that information so that we focus on the effect Bartleby has on the narrator rather than on the causes of Bartleby's rejection of life. By the end of the story, the lawyer has a chastened view of life that challenges his assumption that "the easiest way of life is best."

You may want to ask students to identify the different walls that comprise the various settings of this story. (In addition to those in the office, the walls of the prison at the end of the story are significant.) Melville's story is subtitled "A Story of Wall Street" because Bartleby's "dead-wall reveries" represent a rejection of the materialistic values that inform the center of American financial interests. Business and money mean nothing to Bartleby, but they essentially constitute the sum total of the lawyer's life until his encounter with him. Melville sympathizes with the characters while rejecting their responses to life. He clearly does not endorse the lawyer's smug materialism, but neither does he offer Bartleby's unrelenting vision of death as an answer to the dehumanizing, mechanical meaninglessness that walls the characters in. In this story Melville presents issues, not solutions; it is exploratory rather than definitive.

This story can be usefully regarded as a kind of sit-in protest — at least on a metaphysical level — with nonnegotiable demands. Bartleby is a stubborn reminder that the lawyer's world is driven by expediency rather than principle — that the lawyer's satisfaction with life has been based on his previous avoidance of the big issues. Surprisingly, there is some delightful humor in the story as the characters' exasperation with Bartleby's behavior develops. We know that the scrivener is going to get a rise out of them. There is also humor in Bartleby's reply to the lawyer that he is "sitting upon the banister" (195) when the lawyer asks him what he's doing in his office building on a Sunday. And consider the lawyer's suggestions that Bartleby be a bartender, a bill collector, or a traveling companion "to entertain some young gentleman with your conversation" (199–210). A student once suggested that a dramatization of the story should feature Richard Nixon as the lawyer and Woody Allen as Bartleby. Ask students for their own suggestions on who might play these roles; the question encourages them to think of what goes into a characterization.

Students might be asked to trace their reactions to Bartleby while they read, then to compare them with how they respond to him after class discussion of his character.

For an excellent survey of the many varied critical approaches to the story, see Milton R. Stern's "Towards 'Bartleby the Scrivener,'" in *The Stoic Strain in American Literature*, ed. Duane J. MacMillan (Toronto: U of Toronto P, 1979), 19–41.

POSSIBLE CONNECTIONS TO OTHER SELECTIONS

Emily Dickinson, "There's a certain Slant of light" (text p. 2082)
Robert Frost, "Mending Wall" (text p. 979)
Gail Godwin, "A Sorrowful Woman" (text p. 33)
Nathaniel Hawthorne, "Young Goodman Brown" (text p. 310)
Franz Kafka, "A Hunger Artist" (text p. 528)

RESOURCES FOR TEACHING

Herman Melville. 22 min., color, 1978. Beta, VHS, ¾" U-matic cassette, 16-mm film. Ancillary materials available. Part of the "Authors" series of biographies. Distributed by Journal Films, Inc. Available for rental from member institutions of the Consortium of College and University Media Centers.

Herman Melville: Consider the Sea. 28 min., color, 1982. Beta, VHS, ¾" U-matic cassette, 16-mm film, special-order formats. Deals with the author and his relationship with the sea. Major works discussed include *Moby-Dick, Billy Budd*, and "Bartleby, the Scrivener." Distributed by the International Film Bureau. Available for rental from member institutions of the Consortium of College and University Media Centers.

Melville: Six Short Novels [recording]. 8 cassettes (60 min. each). Read by Dan Lazar. Includes "Bartleby, the Scrivener," "The Apple Tree Table," "My Chimney," and "The Happy Failure." Distributed by Books on Tape.

Herman Melville: Damned in Paradise. 90 min., color, 1986. Beta, VHS, ¾" U-matic cassette. Documents Melville's personal and intellectual history. Distributed by Pyramid Film and Video. 8 cassettes (60 min. each). Available for rental from member institutions of the Consortium of College and University Media Centers.

Bartleby. 79 min., color, 1970. VHS. Cast: Paul Scofield, John McEnery. Directed by Anthony Friedman. Distributed by: White Star.

Bartleby. 28 min., color, 1969. VHS. Distributed by Britannica Films.

Bartleby. 29 min., b/w, 1965. VHS. Videotape from the "American Story Classics" series. Distributed by Film Video Library.

Bartleby, the Scrivener [recording]. 1 cassette (90 min.). Read by Walter Zimmerman. Distributed by Jimcin Recordings.

PERSPECTIVES ON MELVILLE

NATHANIEL HAWTHORNE, *On Herman Melville's Philosophic Stance*
(p. 138)

After reading Hawthorne's description of Melville, ask students to identify aspects of the description that recall any of the characters or instances from "Bartleby, the Scrivener." In particular, how might Melville's habit of "reason[ing] of Providence and futurity, and of everything that lies beyond human ken" (paragraph 1) have influenced his portrait of the lawyer? Is there any detail from Hawthorne's description of Melville that recalls Bartleby's characterization?

DAN MCCALL, *On the Lawyer's Character in "Bartleby, the Scrivener"*
(p. 139)

McCall's topic lies at the heart of any interpretation of Melville's story: how do we perceive both Bartleby and the lawyer? While McCall presents numerous critical opinions on the subject, he fails (in this excerpt) to apply his own argument to the text itself. Ask students to rely on specific examples from the story in explaining whether they find the lawyer sympathetic or unsympathetic.

McCall's article can also provide students with an out-of-class project. Where he focuses on the lawyer's character, encourage students to identify and explain the range of responses to Bartleby himself. How has the perception of either Bartleby or the lawyer changed over the years?

LEON ROOKE, *Sweethearts* (p. 141)

Initially, students might interpret Rooke's title literally and assume that the man and woman in this one-paragraph story are indeed "lovers through thick and thin." However, readers should ask whether the first-person narrator and the woman really are "sweethearts." This is less a story about a male-female relationship than it is about what that relationship reveals about the narrator, in particular. The narrator reveals his self-doubt and insecurity through his sudden questioning of the reader: "You believe me, don't you?" When he isn't talking to (or arguing with) the woman, he's telling the reader all about his relationship with her. Indeed, the narrator is an intense, almost manic figure who seems desperate for some kind of human connection — or, he's terrified of being alone. The line in the story that best reveals this character's complexities appears toward the beginning, when he announces, "I've got to talk to someone." Later in the story, he tells the woman, "You're a life saver, that's what you are" — after all, she enables him to avoid being alone. She provides a little humanity and warmth in his otherwise empty life. Also indicative of his loneliness is his exaggeration of the depth and extent of his relationship with her. He assures readers, "She's my sweetheart, I am hers. . . . She'll be here soon, any minute now, any second now." Nonetheless, as the repetition of "now" indicates, the person he really seems to be trying to convince is himself. Finally, he establishes a contrast between his relationship with this woman and the alternative, being alone, in the last line of the story: "What you have here, in this neighborhood, on this freezing night, are two people, two sweethearts, who utterly understand each other."

Invite students to list details about the narrator that can be supported through a close reading of the text. (Is his name really "Jack," or is that just a slangy term that he uses for himself — as in "hit the road, Jack"?) There is something unstable about the narrator. First, the woman says, "You'd better get straight with yourself before you want to start making time with a woman like me." (Perhaps the references to her life, including her children, are relevant here.) Then, the woman adds, "Why are you shouting? Stop shouting, get a grip on yourself." The narrator acknowledges that he is out of control: "I can't get a grip on myself. I can't get straight with myself."

These people clearly have some kind of a history with one another. They demonstrate a certain ritual in their conversation, whether they are bickering about when and where to meet, arguing about their past meetings, or teasing each other when they don't get the responses they're hoping for: "She says, Wait now, I could be wrong. I could be. What's your name anyhow?" "I say, Hold on. Hold on, I say, I think you've got the wrong party. Let's check that number again. Do we know each other?" The humor stems from their familiarity with each other. And they clearly have been together several times before. They debate when they last saw each other ("She says, But I was over there last week. I was over there last night. Wasn't I over there last night?"). They allude to what has happened — or not happened — when they were together: the woman asks, "What about all the nights I did spend all night and nothing ever happened?" Students should consider reasons for the significance of this, particularly since the subject is raised more than once. Later in the story, the man brings it up again: "How much time am I making if you come over and nothing happens?" Later still, the woman says, "When I say nothing happens I don't mean it the way you think I mean it." This might refer to the man's inability to perform sexually; however, it also might refer to the status of the relationship — that it has never really turned into something more significant. Getting at the meaning of this thread of conversation may well enable students to understand more about the relationship enacted in "Sweethearts" as a whole.

Though students should focus on the speaker, they might also study the female character. Though she is contained within the narrator's account, she is richly characterized. Students might generate possible interpretations of the woman's acknowledgment that she is "trouble for every man I've ever known." She also appears to be more realistic about the nature of her relationship with this man, and more capable than he is of understanding his limitations. What do students suppose she might find attractive about the narrator? Why would she continue to call him when their relationship is so evidently limited?

Less proficient readers might have a hard time determining the speaker and the tone in this story. Perhaps identifying the breaks between speakers (often indicated by "I said" or "she said") and performing it in class might make more of the meaning clear. Students might experiment with reading it aloud to one another in order to determine the way the tone changes (from, at one point, intense anger, to despair, to tenderness) and to decide for themselves the actual status of the relationship.

POSSIBLE CONNECTIONS TO OTHER SELECTIONS

Margaret Atwood, "There Was Once" (text p. 247)
A. L. Bader, "Nothing Happens in Modern Short Stories" (question #1, following)
John Updike, "A & P" (text p. 576)

CONNECTION QUESTION IN TEXT (p. 142) WITH ANSWER

1. Read A. L. Bader's "Nothing Happens in Modern Short Stories" (p. 95). To what extent are Bader's comments relevant to "Sweethearts"?

    "Sweethearts" does adhere to the characteristics of the modern short story as described by Bader. Particularly if they missed the intricacies of characterization embedded in the narrative, students may indeed argue that "Sweethearts" is lacking a plot. After discussing the characterization of the narrator, encourage them to apply the elements of plot to this story. Opinions may vary to some extent; nonetheless, students should find some aspects of exposition, rising action, conflict, climax, and resolution in Rooke's story.

    In many ways, however, this demonstration of the narrator's character is in itself a complete story. Certainly the narrative unravels by the end, forcing readers to question their initial impressions of the story. It would be a mistake to overlook the narrative complexity of "Sweethearts."

5

Setting

Several aspects of setting are described in the introduction to Chapter 5. Setting may include the time, the place, and the social environment in which a story takes place; moreover, it may contribute additional significance to the meaning of the story. In addition, setting may involve traditional associations. Students might practice identifying their associations with a given place, time of day, and time of year. For instance, what do they associate with Seattle, or Birmingham, Alabama? With midnight? With autumn? Commonly, the general connotations that readers associate with a given setting are those the author has in mind as well. When a setting is specified, students should get in the habit of considering why that setting might be significant. When a setting is not specified, students should also consider the writer's rationale. It might be useful to briefly discuss in class why a writer might or might not specify a setting for a particular story.

The stories in this chapter all contain settings that operate on a metaphorical level to contribute to their meaning. Throughout the twentieth century, Yugoslavia has been known for violence and social upheaval; appropriately enough, in Fay Weldon's "IND AFF," it serves as the backdrop for a young woman's life-changing personal decisions. The title of Ernest Hemingway's story, "Soldier's Home," might refer in general to Harold Krebs's small Oklahoma town. It might also call readers' attention to the conditions Krebs encounters in his own family's house — their inability to understand his war experiences. Moreover, the title suggests a particular time — Krebs's return after the war ("Soldier is Home"). Finally, for David Updike's protagonist, summer is as much a state of mind and a significant developmental phase as it is a particular time of year. The sample stories in this chapter all enable students to reach beyond a literal setting and think more figuratively about the meanings of these works.

ERNEST HEMINGWAY, *Soldier's Home* (p. 145)

This is a war story that includes no physical violence because Hemingway focuses on the war's psychological effects on the protagonist. A truce ended the wholesale butchery of youth fighting during World War I, but the painful memory of it has made Krebs a prisoner of war. Although the story's setting is a peaceful small town in Oklahoma, Hemingway evokes the horrors that Krebs endured and brought back home with him. In a sense the real setting of this story is Belleau Wood as well as the sites of the other bloody battles Krebs experienced. (A brief student report summarizing the nature of these battles and the casualties they produced can provide a vivid context for class discussion of the story.)

Krebs cannot talk about his experiences at home because people in town have "heard too many atrocity stories to be thrilled by actualities" (paragraph 4). He has been affected as a result of his experiences in a way they'll never be, and therein lies the story's conflict. The fraternity brother who went off to war in 1917 with romantic expectations returns knowing what the real picture is (consider the ironic deflation produced by the two photographs in paragraphs 1 and 2). Krebs knows that popular visions of the glory of war are illusions and that the reality consists more typically of sickening fear. An inadvertent hint of that comes from his sister, who calls him "Hare," a nickname that suggests fright and flight. (For a poem with a similar theme see Wilfred Owen's "Dulce et Decorum Est," p. 763.) Krebs prefers silence to lying.

Krebs refuses to engage in the familiar domestic patterns of life expected of him. He also rejects the "complicated" world of the young girls in town. (Krebs's rejection of whatever is "complicated" is related to Hemingway's style on pp. 268–269 in the text.) Nothing really matters very much to him; he appears numb and unwilling to commit himself to what he regards as meaningless, trivial games. He feels more at home remembering Germany and France than living in his parents' house. Reading a history of the battles he's been in gives him a feeling of something more real than his life at home, which strikes him as petty, repressive, and blind. His father's permission to use the family car, for example, is neither wanted nor needed. (For a discussion of the symbolic significance of home in the story see p. 216 in the text.)

Krebs's mother brings the conflict to a climax. She speaks for the family and the community, urging Krebs to get back to a normal life of work, marriage, and "being really a credit to the community" (Hemingway's use of point of view in this scene [58–70] is discussed in the text on pp. 176–177). Krebs finds his mother's values little more than sentimental presuppositions that in no way relate to the person he has become. The only solution to the suffocating unreality imposed on him by his family and town is to leave home. He can neither love nor pray; he's no longer in "his Kingdom" (63). There's no going back to that prewar identity as an innocent fraternity brother from a Methodist college. The story's title, then, is ironic, for Krebs cannot go home again, because home seems to be either a lie or a place stunningly ignorant of what he discovered in the war.

A writing assignment based on a comparison of how settings are used in "Soldier's Home" and Tim O'Brien's "How to Tell a True War Story" will encourage students to relate the characters and themes to each story's setting. The landscape of home in each story is equally important but radically different in its significance.

POSSIBLE CONNECTIONS TO OTHER SELECTIONS

Gish Jen, "In the American Society" (text p. 643)
James Joyce, "Eveline" (text p. 512)
Yukio Mishima, "Patriotism" (text p. 593)
Tim O'Brien, "How to Tell a True War Story" (text p. 555)
Flannery O'Connor, "Good Country People" (text p. 392)
John Updike, "A & P" (text p. 576)

RESOURCES FOR TEACHING

Ernest Hemingway. 53 min., color, 1983. VHS. This program explores Hemingway's life and literary psyche through the eyes of those who knew him. A BBC Production. Part of the "Great Writers of the 20th Century" series. Distributed by Films for the Humanities and Sciences.

Ernest Hemingway: A Life Story [recording]. Part 1, 11 cassettes; Part 2, 10 cassettes (1 hr., 30 min., per cassette). Read by Christopher Hunt. Draws from Hemingway's diaries, letters, and unpublished writing, as well as personal testimony from the people who played a part in the author's life. Distributed by Blackstone Audio Books.

Hemingway. 18 min., b/w, 1993. Beta, VHS, ¾″ U-matic cassette, 16-mm film. A biography using rare stills and motion-picture footage. Narrated by Chet Huntley. Distributed by Thomas Klise Company. Available for rental from member institutions of the Consortium of College and University Media Centers.

Hemingway: Up in Michigan, the Early Years. 28 min., color, 1986. Beta, VHS, ¾″ U-matic cassette. A literary biography of the writer. Distributed by Centre Communications.

Soldier's Home. See "The American Short Story Series I" on manual page 591.

PERSPECTIVES

E. E. CUMMINGS, *my sweet old etcetera* (p. 151)

Compare the responses of the family members described in Cummings's poem with the reactions of the family in "Soldier's Home." What are their conceptions of the meaning of "war"? Are there any differences between the familial reactions in these works? What do the narrator of "my sweet old etcetera" and the soldier in Hemingway's story seem to value most as a result of their respective experiences in the war?

ERNEST HEMINGWAY, *On What Every Writer Needs* (p. 152)

Ask students to discuss a character (from any story) who does not have a "shit detector." How might this character think and behave differently if he or she did have such "radar"?

FAY WELDON, *IND AFF, or Out of Love in Sarajevo* (p. 153)

In this brief cautionary tale, Weldon manages to question the nature of fate and individual will, desire, and imagination, as well as question the relationship between the apparently political and the apparently personal. It is not so much the "sad story" promised by the first line as it is a fable about taking responsibility for one's actions and understanding the essentially interconnected nature of all events.

When the twenty-five-year-old unnamed narrator fell in love with her forty-six-year-old thesis director (who was already married and the father of three children), she fell in love with her idea of him rather than with him as a man. The narrator, who tells her story from the perspective of one who has learned her lesson and is now simply imparting it, has come to understand that she had confused "mere passing academic ambition with love" (48), believing this man's assessment of the world and of herself ("He said I had a good mind but not a first-class mind and somehow I didn't take it as an insult" [4]) when she should have been coming up with her own conclusions. Weldon comments in another story concerned with a young woman's infatuation with a much older man that "it was not her desire that was stirred, it was her imagination. But how is she to know this?" What the narrator wishes to believe about her lover — that this is "not just any old professor-student romance" — and what she actually feels about him are two different things.

Peter Piper (the name itself should indicate a certain lack of respect on the part of the author for such characters), the Cambridge professor who has been married to a swimming coach for twenty-four years, likes to "luxuriate in guilt and indecision" and has taken his student/mistress with him on a holiday to see whether they are "really, truly suited," to make sure that it is "the Real Thing" before they "shack up, as he put it." The narrator is desperately drawn to her teacher because he represents much more than he actually offers. To maintain her affection for Peter, she overlooks his stinginess ("Peter felt it was less confusing if we each paid our own way" [44]), his whining ("I noticed I had become used to his complaining. I supposed that when you had been married a little you simply wouldn't hear it" [12]), the fact that often when she spoke "he wasn't listening," the fact that he might not want her to go topless at the beach ("this might be the area where the age difference showed"), and his "thinning hair" because he seems authoritative (speaking in "quasi-Serbo-Croatian") and powerful. He "liked to be asked questions" and obviously adores the adoration of his student. She loves him with "inordinate Affection," she claims. "Your Ind Aff is my wife's sorrow" (27), Peter moans, blaming a girl who was born the first year of his marriage for his wife's unhappiness, absolving himself from any blame.

The question of whether particular events happen because of the inevitable buildup of insurmountable forces or, instead, because of a series of particular moments that might have been avoided with care, caution, or consideration is brought to bear not only on the narrator's relationship with Peter but on the question of World War I. With the background material effortlessly supplied by Weldon, even readers unfamiliar with the story of Princip's assassination of the archduke will be able to see the way Princip's tale parallels that of the narrator. Was the war inevitable? Was it, as Peter Piper claims, bound to "start sooner or later," because of the "social and economic tensions" that had to find "some release"? Along the same lines of reasoning, is the twenty-four-year marriage between Peter and the woman who is known only as Mrs. Piper doomed to failure, or is it instead pressured into failure by the husband's infidelity? Is it, as the narrator's sister Clare (herself married to a much older professor) claims, a fact that "if you can unhinge a marriage, it's ripe for unhinging, it would happen sooner or later, it might as well be you" (36)? Is it, in other words, the narrator who is assassinating the Piper marriage?

The climax of the story occurs when the narrator and Peter are waiting to be served wild boar in a private restaurant. She notices a waiter whom she describes as being "about my age" (showing her keenly felt awareness of the difference in age between herself and Peter). She has felt desire for Peter in her mind, and has learned to feel "a pain in her heart" as an "erotic sensation," but in looking at the virile, handsome man her own age she feels "quite violently, an associated yet different pang which got my lower stomach." She describes this desire as the "true, the real pain of Ind Aff!" Her desire for the waiter has nothing to do with his position, his authority, or his power. It has to do with his "flashing eyes, hooked nose, luxuriant black hair, sensuous mouth" (38). She asks herself in a moment of clear vision, "What was I doing with this man with thinning hair?" (41). She thinks to herself, when she automatically tells Peter that she loves him, "How much I lied." She has freed herself from the confines of his authority and declares in opposition to him that "if Princip hadn't shot the archduke, something else, some undisclosed, unsuspected variable, might have come along and defused the whole political/military situation, and neither World War I nor II ever happened" (43). She then gets up to go "home."

"This is how I fell out of love with my professor," declares the narrator, describing their affair as "a silly, sad episode, which I regret." She sees herself as silly for having confused her career ambitions with desire and silly for trying to "outdo my sister Clare," who has married her professor (but has to live in Brussels as a sort of cosmic penance). Piper eventually proves spiteful and tries to refuse the narrator's thesis, but she wins her appeal and, delightfully, can confirm for herself that she does indeed have a "first-class mind." She feels, finally, a connection to poor Princip, who should have "hung on a bit, there in

Sarajevo" because he might have "come to his senses. People do, sometimes quite quickly" (48).

POSSIBLE CONNECTIONS TO OTHER SELECTIONS

Mark Halliday, "Graded Paper" (text p. 1156)
Nathaniel Hawthorne, "The Birthmark" (question #2, following)
D. H. Lawrence, "The Horse Dealer's Daughter" (question #3, following)
Naguib Mahfouz, "The Answer Is No" (text p. 591)
Katherine Mansfield, "Miss Brill" (text p. 258)
Joyce Carol Oates, "The Lady with the Pet Dog" (question #1, following)

CONNECTIONS QUESTIONS IN TEXT (p. 159) WITH ANSWERS

1. Compare and contrast "IND AFF" and Oates's "The Lady with the Pet Dog" (p. 200) as love stories. Do you think that the stories end happily, or the way you would want them to end? Are the endings problematic?

    Both "IND AFF" and "The Lady with the Pet Dog" end with the protagonists' rediscoveries of themselves. Weldon's heroine realizes that she doesn't love Professor Piper and that she does, in fact, have a "first-class mind"; Oates's heroine discovers that she can experience love without becoming smothered by it. Students might have to define what they mean by the term *love story*: is the depiction of love strictly limited to love between two human beings, or can it be self-love? Certainly both of these heroines make decisions that embody self-love and approval. However, neither of these stories provides us with a pair of lovers going off "into the sunset." Weldon seems to support her protagonist's decision and to suggest that we shouldn't feel sympathy for the professor. Oates's depiction of her heroine is more problematic: exactly what is Anna's final observation at the end of the story? How are we to regard her lover, with his continual, nervous gestures?

2. Explain how Weldon's concept of "Ind Aff" — "inordinate affection" — can be used to make sense of the relationship between Georgiana and Aylmer in Nathaniel Hawthorne's "The Birthmark" (p. 329).

    Aylmer, the "mad scientist" of Hawthorne's "The Birthmark," might aver that his feeling for Georgiana is what Weldon describes as the opposite of "Ind Aff": "A pure and spiritual, if passionate, concern for her soul" (paragraph 26). Yet given his obsession with Georgiana's physical characteristic — the birthmark tellingly shaped as a human handprint — he might more accurately be described as displaying "Ind Aff." The long-suffering Georgiana, on the other hand, displays a love that is more pure and spiritual. It is possible that like Weldon's professor, who refuses to acknowledge his own responsibility when he tells the protagonist that "your Ind Aff is my wife's sorrow" (27), Aylmer may never perceive or accept his own responsibility for the events leading to Georgiana's death.

3. How does passion figure in "IND AFF" and in D. H. Lawrence's "The Horse Dealer's Daughter" (p. 543)? Explain how Weldon's and Lawrence's perspectives on passion suggest differing views of love and human relationships.

    Weldon's story is primarily passionless — certainly there is little sexual energy or warmth between the narrator and the professor, for whom she feels at most a sentimental and intellectual attachment. The only real passion in this story comes when the narrator looks at the young waiter: "Instead of the pain in the heart I'd become accustomed to as an erotic sensation, [I] now felt, quite violently, an associated yet different pang which got my lower stomach" (paragraph 38). In contrast, Mabel and Fergusson, the protagonists of Lawrence's story, seem to be affecting each other even before their symbolically loaded journey into the muddy pond. However, readers may have the sense that while Mabel and Fergusson's future will continue to be sparked by their almost raw emotional response to each other, they'll never quite banish the odor of the brackish water. Ask students to compare the tone of the final paragraphs of each story: how much does each paragraph convey about the protagonists' choices, perspectives, and futures?

PERSPECTIVE

FAY WELDON, *On the Importance of Place in "IND AFF"* (p. 159)

Weldon's perspective on her story, taken from an interview almost ten years after it was published, invites readers to apply biographical strategies to "IND AFF." Students might first describe the aspects of the story that seem relevant to Weldon's commentary. Second, they might consider her assessment of setting in this story. Given the political and cultural instability of this region during the past ten years, culminating in the arrival of the United Nations peacekeeping force, what additional meaning might be drawn from "IND AFF"?

RUTH PRAWER JHABVALA, *The Englishwoman* (p. 160)

A good way to start discussion of this story is to ask students to contrast the two settings described in the final paragraph of "The Englishwoman." The first half of the paragraph depicts Sadie's Indian garden: "faint silver light," "the fountain with the stone statue, and the lime trees, and the great flowering bush of queen of the night" (paragraph 40). In addition, there is a reference to Chandralekha, the relative who eventually killed herself because her family disagreed with her choice of husband. The reference is of particular significance because Sadie had sympathized with Chandralekha, had not understood the family's objections concerning caste, and had "met the man, who struck her as intelligent and of a strong character" (34). At that time, Sadie had realized that "everything that went on in the house during those days was a mystery to her" and that "the passions that were aroused, the issues that were thought to be at stake, were beyond her comprehension" (34). The reference reminds readers that despite having lived in India for thirty years, Sadie remains an alien.

In contrast to that silver, ghostly Indian garden, Sadie imagines a green and golden English landscape. Where India has been dry, muggy, and heavy, England appears dewy, fresh, and full of life. Sadie envisions "mild soft rain coming down like a curtain," "a sun as mild and soft as that rain," and winds "as cold and fresh as the waters of a mountain torrent" (40). In her mind, England is open, empty, and strikingly free of people. Encourage students to discuss the images of England here and to contrast the description in the final paragraph with earlier descriptions of setting in the story. For instance, the cold English wind is strikingly different from the stifling Indian heat Sadie remembers in connection with the day her son was ill. Then, she longed only to escape the Indian air "thick as a swamp in which fevers breed" and to "be alone with her sick child in some cool place" (19).

Once students understand the nuances of the physical setting, encourage them to connect it with the characters. How does Sadie's demeanor remind readers of the English climate? How does Annapurna embody the characteristics of Indian climate? Throughout the story, there are numerous references to the women's bodies and personalities that ally them with England and India. Sadie is "a spare, stringent, high-bred English beauty" (16); Annapurna is "a very, very physical sort of person. She is stout, with a tight glowing skin, and shining eyes and teeth, and hair glossy with black dye. She loves clothes and jewelry and rich food" (6). During her son's illness, Sadie is scared and angry, and her psychological distress manifests itself in physical discomfort. In an attempt to sympathize with and soothe her, Annapurna holds Sadie close, but Sadie's reaction is a rejection of Annapurna and in effect of India: "It's so *hot!*" (28). "Hot" here might refer not only to the actual temperature, but to temperament as well. Sadie abhors highly emotional scenes such as her husband's demonstrations when he protests Chandralekha's lover or when he hears that Sadie is leaving. Conversely, Annapurna and the other Indian characters understand, participate in, and draw strength from such scenes. On the night before she leaves for England, Sadie visits with her husband and Annapurna during their card game. Sadie "lowers her eyes away from them: she sits there, silent, prim, showing no emotion" (37). Both her husband and Annapurna sit with tears flowing down their faces. It's not only the climate that Sadie rejects; it's also the passionate emotions that she has come to find suffocating in India.

The title of this story, "The Englishwoman," is a succinct, effective indication of Sadie's status as alien in India. Have your students discuss the significance of the title. We learn that she has lived in India for thirty years; her children are half Indian, and she doesn't have especially warm memories of her life in England. We also learn that she "knows almost no one there: a few distant relatives, one old school friend; she hasn't been there for thirty years, she has no contacts, no correspondence" (29). Yet she is referred to as "the Englishwoman" throughout the story. It is particularly striking that in the final section of the story, in which Sadie's husband and Annapurna resign themselves to her leaving, Sadie has literally become "like a guest" (37) in the house. Have students examine the story for the numerous references to Sadie as "the Englishwoman" — references that imply that characters such as Annapurna may never have seen Sadie as anything but alien.

POSSIBLE CONNECTIONS TO OTHER SELECTIONS

Gail Godwin, "A Sorrowful Woman" (text p. 33)
Ernest Hemingway, "Soldier's Home" (text p. 145)
James Joyce, "Eveline" (text p. 512)

DAVID UPDIKE, *Summer* (p. 169)

"Summer" is a celebration of both a time of year and a time of life. This story of teen protagonist Homer's subtle pursuit of Sandra, his friend Fred's sister, is vitalized by the descriptions of the lake and the characters' youthful energy. From the opening description of the way Homer and Fred pass their time (in athletics, predominantly) to the closing description of the final night at the lake, Updike lavishes description on the images of summer. His story is replete with references to images that evoke all the senses. Students might trace them throughout the story.

Even the characters' names allude to aspects of the summer. "Homer" — as if from home-run — reminds us of one of the boys' favorite activities. (Baseball players are known as "the boys of summer.") Updike's characters play some form of baseball indoors as well as outside, as detailed by the first paragraph: "a variant of baseball adapted to the local geography: two pine trees as foul poles, a broomstick as the bat, the apex of the small, secluded house the dividing line between home runs and outs. On rainy days they swatted bottle tops across the living room floor." Is "Homer" also an indication that the summer — and the adventure — will end in a satisfying way? The name for the female love interest is equally apt: "Sandra" evokes summer; it recalls the lake, the sunshine; it even recalls the female protagonist of the popular 1970s musical and film *Grease*, who sings a duet with the male lead about the romance of "Summer Nights." Finally, the other prominent name contained in Updike's story also emphasizes the theme: here, Thyme equals "time." Not only is summer ending and autumn arriving, but there is the sense that Homer and his friend Fred are at the peak of their vitality. Their sense of indestructibility (drinking for the first time, "wrestl[ing] the car" [11]) and their energy (manifested through their many athletic activities) are relevant indeed. It is during this summer that they become "unofficial [tennis] champions of the lake by trouncing the elder Dewitt boys, unbeaten in several years" (13). It is no coincidence that "glum Billy Dewitt" attributes his loss to the boys' youth. Homer thinks that although Dewitt jests, he also is "hiding some greater sense of loss" (13); indeed, Dewitt's metaphorical "summer," his career as champion, is over.

Although Homer doesn't acknowledge his longing for Sandra until the end of paragraph 9, readers are given many clues that he has a crush on her prior to that point in the story. For instance, Homer lavishes description on Sandra. Instead of saying, "Sandra never tanned," he savors her image: "When she first came in her face was faintly flushed, and there was a pinkish line around the snowy band where her bathing suit strap had been, but the back of her legs remained an endearing, pale white, the color of eggshells, and her back acquired only the softest, brownish blur" (5). The words "endearing" and "softest" indicate his affection for her. He also notes with frustration that she is "strangely indifferent to his heroics" (6).

Of course, there are several hints in the story that Sandra is less oblivious to Homer's crush than he imagines. Although he hopes to impress her by winning the tennis match, she utterly distracts him by leaving at the crucial moment: "Homer watched her as she went down the path, and, impetus suddenly lost, he double faulted, stroked a routine backhand over the back fence, and the match was over" (6). Worst of all, she doesn't even focus on him as he tells her about it afterward. All she says is, "I wish I could go sailing" (7). Coming home from the hike up the mountain, she keeps "his elbow hopelessly held in the warm crook of her arm" (10). Readers must wonder how much of Sandra's summer has been a subtle, friendly campaign to drive Homer to distraction — after all, she's described more than once as appearing in front of him from nowhere, stretching or calling attention to her body in some way, teasing him with her laughter as they cruise home after her shift at the bowling alley. His favorite words for approximating her attraction are "indifference" and "oblivious": "as silently as she arrived, she would leave, walking back through the stones with the same casual sway of indifference" (5); "her life went on its oblivious, happy course without him" (10); "Homer sat at the counter and watched her serve up sloshing cups of coffee, secretly loathing the leering gazes of whiskered truck drivers, and loving her oblivious, vacant stare in answer, hip cocked, hand on counter, gazing up into the neon air above their heads" (12). As the final paragraph of the story reveals, however, Sandra has been anything but indifferent or oblivious throughout Homer's visit to the lake. Looking back on the story after having read it all, students will appreciate the humor and irony of the passages that stress her disregard for Homer.

Homer admits that "to touch her, or kiss her, seemed suddenly incongruous, absurd, contrary to something he could not put his finger on"; "he realized he had never been able to imagine the moment he distantly longed for" (14). Ask students to discuss Homer's motivation here. Why doesn't he kiss Sandra? Why doesn't he need to demonstrate his affection for her in some tangible way? What is there in the story that indicates that longing itself is enough? Is there any connection between his distanced affection for Sandra and his interest in the girl in the canoe who waves to them at the end of the summer? He tells us, "there was something in the way that she raised her arm which, when added to the distant impression of her fullness, beauty, youth, filled him with longing as their boat moved inexorably past, slapping the waves, and she disappeared behind a crop of trees" (15). Is this in some sense a metaphor for the ending of his pursuit of Sandra as the summer comes to a close?

Midway through this story, Homer, the teenage protagonist, reads one of Sir Arthur Conan Doyle's Sherlock Holmes stories (4). In many ways, "Summer" is also a detective story in which Homer discovers that his interpretation of the events at the lake has not been accurate. For an entertaining comparison, students might look up "A Scandal in Bohemia," the one Sherlock Holmes story in which Holmes meets his match, in a woman, Irene Adler. Sandra's outmaneuvering of Homer is in many ways reminiscent of both the mystery and the romance of "A Scandal in Bohemia." One of Holmes's favorite expressions for the thrill of the mystery is "the game's afoot!" Here, the game of teen romance enacted by Sandra and Homer is most satisfyingly, indeed, by the end of the story literally "afoot."

POSSIBLE CONNECTIONS TO OTHER SELECTIONS

Dagoberto Gilb, "Love in L.A." (question #2, following)
Leon Rooke, "Sweethearts" (text p. 140)
John Updike, "A & P" (question #1, following)

CONNECTIONS QUESTIONS IN TEXT (p. 173) WITH ANSWERS

1. Compare David Updike's treatment of summer as the setting of his story with John Updike's (David's father, incidentally) use of summer as the setting in "A & P" (p. 576).

   Both stories detail the characteristics of summer, both as a time of year and as a time of life. Their endings particularly, however, differ. "Summer" is romantic while "A & P" is realistic. Although both stories focus on young male protagonists who are infatuated with the idea of the young women they encounter, Homer's experience is playful; in contrast, Sammy's encounter with Queenie and her friends leads him initially to make the gesture of quitting his job and then to realize that the consequences of his actions may be more significant than he realized. For both protagonists, the end of summer is the end of innocence, but the tone with which each author invests that realization is significantly different.

2. Discuss "Summer" and Dagoberto Gilb's "Love in L.A." (p. 265) as love stories. Explain why you might prefer one over the other.

   Both Gilb and Updike's protagonists may pursue what the women they encounter represent more than the women themselves. Gilb's protagonist, Jake, is in love with his own sense of himself as a manipulator of other people; his pursuit of Mariana is based on his desire to avoid paying for the damage he's inflicted on her Toyota. Updike's protagonist, however, is less egotistical than young: he's infatuated with the idea of infatuation. However, Homer doesn't hurt Sandra in any way. Indeed, there's a playful reciprocity to their relationship that's missing from Mariana's encounter with Jake.

6

Point of View

After reading the introduction to Chapter 6, students should be able to distinguish a first-person point of view from a third-person point of view. Is the narrator a major or minor character in the story or a witness to it? Does the narrator have access to the inner thoughts of all the characters? One of the characters? None of the characters? Students should practice identifying the point of view in the stories they study. Then, they should analyze the author's choice of point of view. For instance, why is Sylvia in Toni Cade Bambara's "The Lesson" a more productive narrator than Miss Moore? (Miss Moore would have to tell us her plan if she were the narrator; instead, Bambara chose to show Sylvia's growing awareness of social and economic inequality in America — and her reaction to that awareness.) In addition, point of view is related to characterization in significant ways. Students should be aware that a narrator may have a particular agenda — that the telling of the story is slanted in some respect. Is the narrator trying to make himself look more important? Generally, point of view is designed to showcase a dynamic (rather than a static) character. Finally, in shifting point of view, as Joyce Carol Oates does in her reenvisioning of Chekhov's "The Lady with the Pet Dog," an author can expand and enrich a story. Students should know why an author chooses a particular point of view; they should also imagine the effect of changing the point of view within a given story. What would be lost or gained in changing a particular story's point of view?

TONI CADE BAMBARA, *The Lesson* (p. 179)

"So I deal in straight-up fiction myself, 'cause I value my family and friends, and mostly 'cause I lie a lot anyway." Toni Cade Bambara's "straight-up fiction" has been collected in *Gorilla, My Love* (1972) and *The Sea Birds Are Still Alive* (1977), and in 1980 she published her first novel, *The Salt Eaters*. A number of her screenplays have been produced, including "Zora" (1971), "The Johnson Girls" (1972), "Epitaph for Willie" (1982), "Tar Baby" (1984), "The Bombing of Osage" (winner of the 1986 Best Documentary Award from the Pennsylvania Association of Broadcasters and a Documentary Award from the National Black Programming Consortium), and "Cecil B. Moore: Master Tactician of Direct Action" (1987). Born in New York City in 1939, Bambara graduated from Queens College in 1959, studied at the University of Florence and the École de Mme. Étienne Decroux in Paris and New York between 1961 and 1963, and earned her M.A. from City College, New York, in 1964. She has also studied dance, linguistics, and filmmaking. Her working life demonstrates similar variety: Bambara has been employed by the New York State Department of Welfare, directed recreation programs in the psychiatry department of Metropolitan Hospital, New York City, served as program director of Colony House Community Center, New York City, and taught at various colleges and universities, including Rutgers University and Spelman College.

The title is a good way to start discussion of this story: what is the lesson Miss Moore is trying to teach Sylvia (the narrator) and her friends? Is she successful?

Miss Moore is trying to get her charges to see that they live in a "society . . . in which some people can spend on a toy what it would cost to feed a family of six or seven" (paragraph 50) and that, in Sylvia's words, "Poor people have to wake up and demand their share of the pie" (44). But despite Sylvia's ability to paraphrase Miss Moore's lecture, it is clear she hasn't completely taken it in when she goes on to say, "Don't none of us know what kind of pie she talking about in the first damn place." Miss Moore has, however, had some success: Sugar provides her with precisely the answer she was hoping to hear: "You know, Miss Moore, I don't think all of us here put together eat in a year what that sailboat costs. . . . This is not much of a democracy if you ask me. Equal chance to pursue happiness means an equal crack at the dough, don't it?" (49 and 51).

Still, the fact that Miss Moore can sense Sylvia's anger assures her that at least some of her point has gotten across. We (the readers) can sense it too, when Sylvia thinks things such as "I sure want to punch somebody in the mouth" (41), "Who are these people that spend that much for performing clowns and $1,000 for toy sailboats? What kinda work they do and how they live and how come we ain't in on it?" (44), and finally "I'm going . . . to think this day through. . . . Ain't nobody gonna beat me at nuthin" (58).

Ask the class what they think the last line of the story means. Does Sylvia think Sugar is smarter than she is because Sugar knew the answer to Miss Moore's question and she didn't? Could the "nobody" in that line refer to anyone other than Sugar?

Sylvia is annoyed and feels betrayed partly because Sugar is suddenly playing into the student/teacher game Miss Moore creates on these occasions, which the kids all usually hate; Sylvia feels Sugar shouldn't be giving Miss Moore the time of day. But Sylvia is also unhappy because to identify the problem (the unequal distribution of wealth), as Sugar has done, is to admit that there is a problem — and this is something Sylvia hasn't come to terms with. We know this from her earlier comments about Miss Moore's lecture: "And then she gets to the part about we all poor and live in the slums, which I don't feature" (3). So the last line of the story refers not only to Sugar but to Sylvia's position (and that of black people in general) in society.

Clearly Bambara intends this story to be instructive to her readers as well as to the children in Miss Moore's charge. It is not easy to make a social comment of this nature without sounding preachy; ask the class how she manages it.

Humor is one of the hallmarks of Bambara's style, and the accuracy with which she renders her characters' speech is marvelous. Her language is charged with enough energy to snare even the most lethargic reader, and she captures the rhythm and idioms of her characters' dialect precisely, brilliantly contrasting the children's "street" talk against Miss Moore's "proper speech."

POSSIBLE CONNECTIONS TO OTHER SELECTIONS

Sandra Cisneros, "Barbie-Q" (text p. 218)

Ralph Ellison, "Battle Royal" (text p. 223)

Katherine Mansfield, "Miss Brill" (text p. 258)

Flannery O'Connor, "A Good Man Is Hard to Find" (text p. 381)

RESOURCE FOR TEACHING

Interview with Toni Cade Bambara [recording]. 1 cassette (58 min.). Discussion of Bambara's origins, work habits, publishing, and writing. Distributed by American Audio Prose Library.

ANTON CHEKHOV, *The Lady with the Pet Dog* (p. 185)

It would be useful to assign Chekhov's statement "On Morality in Fiction" (p. 199) at the same time you assign this story; the commentary makes an excellent springboard for discussion of the story. Ask the class whether they think Chekhov does "all the time speak and think" in Gurov's tone and spirit, as the author says he must, in order to show what kind of a person his character is.

The story is told from Gurov's point of view, which Chekhov refuses to comment on, morally or otherwise. His aim is simply to portray Gurov as accurately as he can; here is a man who does certain things, feels certain feelings, and so on. It is by this constant exposure to Gurov's thoughts and actions that we get to know, and eventually care about, the protagonist. Initially, he is not a sympathetic character; he speaks ill of his wife and of women in general. He considers women inferior because of "bitter experience" with them (paragraph 5), but later thoughts reveal that it is he who has treated them badly. For evidence of this, direct the class to paragraph 28: "From the past he preserved the memory of carefree, good-natured women whom love made gay and who were grateful to him for the happiness he gave them . . . and of women like his wife who loved without sincerity . . . and of very beautiful, frigid women, across whose faces would suddenly flit a rapacious expression — an obstinate desire to take more from life than it could give . . . and when Gurov grew cold to them their beauty aroused his hatred, and the lace on their lingerie seemed to him to resemble scales."

The fact is that he is afraid of women, afraid of their power over him. (See the end of paragraph 5: "Some force seemed to draw him to them [the women], too.") Gurov calls women inferior to empower himself against them, so that he can control them, instead of the other way around. Yalta's atmosphere, which is deceptively festive, is the perfect place for Gurov to play his games with women and himself. It is a resort town, a place people visit for vacations, or as in Anna's case, to escape their daily lives. Since everyone is there on a temporary basis, nothing that happens there is permanent or matters in the "real" world to which the vacationers must all eventually return.

Chekhov sticks to Gurov's consciousness so closely that while we may or may not sympathize with him, we cannot help but begin to understand him. For instance, many readers will not be kindly disposed to Gurov when he becomes annoyed by Anna's distressed reaction to committing adultery (37), but even then we can comprehend what is going on in his mind. (All the other women he has had affairs with were old hands at the game; he is not used to a woman like Anna, who is genuinely disturbed by what she has done.) But in the story's third section, we see Gurov changing; he realizes that Anna is different (63), that he is unable to forget her the way he forgot the others, and that she is "the only happiness that he now desired for himself" (84). Finally, he realizes that "only now when his head was gray he had fallen in love, really, truly — for the first time in his life" (115). If the story had been told from Anna's perspective, we would miss the crucial insights and transitions Gurov experiences in the last two sections.

Chekhov's objectivity makes it possible for us to understand Gurov and Anna; his presentation of his characters is so compassionate it is clear he sympathizes with them and their situation. This is not to say he condones their actions; he is simply able to see (and to make us see) how this relationship has come about and why these characters behave the way they do. Both married young, perhaps too young to know any better, and apparently neither of their marriages is based on love. This information helps explain the characters' motivations as well as their plight at the end of the story. Living in a society where divorce was not considered an acceptable alternative, and having recognized their love for each other as too powerful to deny, they can have no resolution to this conflict. For as long as Anna and Gurov love each other, life will remain "complicated and difficult."

POSSIBLE CONNECTION TO ANOTHER SELECTION

Joyce Carol Oates, "The Lady with the Pet Dog" (text p. 200)

RESOURCES FOR TEACHING

Anton Chekhov: A Writer's Life. 37 min., color and b/w, 1974. Beta, VHS, ¾" U-matic cassette, 16-mm film. A biographical portrait of the writer. Distributed by Films for the Humanities and Sciences.

Gielgud's Chekhov. 52 min., color, 1981. Beta, VHS. Three programs: (1) "The Fugitive," "Desire for Sleep," and "Rothschild's Violin"; (2) "Volodya" and "The Boarding House"; (3) "Revenge" and "The Wallet." Distributed by Mastervision.

The Lady with the Pet Dog. 86 min., b/w, 1960. Beta, VHS. In Russian, with English subtitles. Distributed by Facets Multimedia.

PERSPECTIVE

ANTON CHEKHOV, *On Morality in Fiction* (p. 199)

Chekhov suggests that the result of combining art with "a sermon" would be bad art (or at least bad technique). Ask students whether they agree with this statement. Have them select a story that either does or does not "combine art with a sermon," and ask them to discuss whether it succeeds — both on their terms and on Chekhov's.

JOYCE CAROL OATES, *The Lady with the Pet Dog* (p. 200)

In retelling Chekhov's story, Oates is paying homage to this classic tale of adulterous love. While Oates sets her own story in twentieth-century America, she has deliberately retained many aspects of Chekhov's version. The couple meet at a renowned vacation spot, complete with beach; the woman is alone because she wanted to get away from her husband for a while; the man has children and the woman doesn't; months after their initial parting, the man seeks out the woman at a local performance she is attending with her husband. All these details evoke certain associations for a reader who knows Chekhov's story; we expect that parallel events and emotions will unfold. But Oates's version certainly stands on its own; she has integrated all the details she borrowed into a story that makes sense even if you are not familiar with Chekhov's.

Of course there are differences between the two versions, the most obvious being the perspective from which the story is told. Oates went beyond paying her respects to Chekhov, for to change the point of view is to change the story being told. (Remind the class how different Melville's "Bartleby, the Scrivener" [p. 113] would be if it were told from Bartleby's point of view.) Oates's version is Anna's story; it is her heart and mind we see here, and it is her character we begin to understand.

When the lovers first separate, Anna tells herself (in paragraph 30) that she is glad: "She understood that she was free of him . . . she would leave him soon, safely, and within a few days he would have fallen into the past, the impersonal past. . . ." He had threatened her with love, something she had grown used to living without. For here is what passed for love, or at least for conjugal relations, in her marriage (see paragraph 126): "Sometimes he failed at loving her, sometimes he succeeded, it had nothing to do with her or her pity or her ten years of love for him, it had nothing to do with a woman at all. It was a private act accomplished by a man, a husband, or a lover, in communion with his own soul, his manhood." Experiences like this having formed her attitude toward love and sex, it is easy to see why she is not eager to embark on another relationship — why, in other words, she is relieved to be parting from her lover. But in the end she realizes that her lover is different, and she lets herself love, understanding that believing in and accepting her lover are far better than the sterile life she has with her husband and the "clumsiness" (17) of his love.

This story may initially be confusing to students because of the order in which events are told. But the order is actually quite strategic. In the first two parts, we learn the profound effect Anna's lover, and indeed the very concept of the affair, has on her. A good example is this sentence in paragraph 10: "She was still panicked. . . . It made her think of mucus, of something thick and gray and congested inside her, stuck to her, that was herself and yet not herself — a poison." In paragraph 12 we learn that Anna is not happy with her husband: "For years now they had not been comfortable together." And in paragraph 20 we learn that "she did not really trust men."

In the first two sections of the story we are also given some specific history about the lovers. Anna tells her lover she believes in him (69), and we realize the significance of this statement since Anna said earlier that she did not trust men. But her lover replies by speaking "of his wife, her ambitions, her intelligence, her use of the children against him"; in other words, he speaks of his unwillingness to get a divorce. So Anna's trust is shattered; she thinks about killing him, as she thought, earlier, about killing herself. If the story were told chronologically, starting with the couple meeting, all of this information would have to be provided in the exposition, thus interrupting the narrative and lessening the tension that precedes and pervades the beginning of the affair.

POSSIBLE CONNECTIONS TO OTHER SELECTIONS

Anton Chekhov, "The Lady with the Pet Dog" (text p. 185)

Fay Weldon, "IND AFF, or Out of Love in Sarajevo" (text p. 153)

RESOURCES FOR TEACHING

Joyce Carol Oates [recording]. 1 cassette (29 min.), 1989. The author talks about her writing habits. Distributed by Letters on the Air.

Joyce Carol Oates. 28 min., color, 1994. VHS. Oates discusses her work as both a writer and teacher, her craft and methods, and the major themes of her novels, short stories, and poems. Distributed by Films for the Humanities and Sciences.

PERSPECTIVE

MATTHEW C. BRENNAN, *Point of View and Plotting in Chekhov's and Oates's "The Lady with the Pet Dog"* (p. 213)

Because Brennan so specifically refers to the text to support his observations on the differences between Chekhov's and Oates's stories, students may find it difficult to argue with him. It may be useful to ask students to define "masculine," "feminine," "linear," and "circular" and to apply their definitions to both the stories as well as to Brennan's article. Do they agree with Brennan's use of these terms?

As a writing assignment, encourage students to model Brennan's approach by creating a second version of a particular story in which they highlight a character other than the protagonist of the original version.

7

Symbolism

The three stories in Chapter 7 invite the reader to consider the complexity of symbolism. After reading the introduction, students should be aware of the difference between symbolism and allegory; they should also begin to appreciate the nuances of symbolism. In addition to the common cultural symbols described in the introduction, students might generate a list of other familiar symbols from their daily experience. For instance, what traditional, conventional, or public meanings do students associate with water? (Possible associations range from baptism rites to the territory of the unconscious.) What possible meanings are associated with dragons? In Western cultures, dragons have commonly symbolized danger or obstacles to success. In Eastern cultures, in contrast, they are often perceived to be symbols of good luck. In order to demonstrate the sophistication and breadth of common symbols, instructors might introduce students to reference works such as J. E. Cirlot's *A Dictionary of Symbols* (Philosophical Library, 1971). However, as explained in the introduction, common sense should be a reader's guide in determining the meaning of literary symbols.

SANDRA CISNEROS, *Barbie-Q* (p. 218)

The narrator of this very short story reveals, in her consuming passion for the things of Barbie's world, the dissonance between this imagined world and her actual experience. The artificial lifestyle that Mattel has created for Barbie has little practical application to the narrator's social circumstances. Barbie's clothes are stiletto heels, jewelry, "a Jackie Kennedy pillbox hat, white gloves . . . evening elegance in black glitter strapless gown with a puffy skirt at the bottom like a mermaid tail" (paragraph 1). Her wardrobe does not include sneakers, jeans, faded T-shirts, or any other clothes appropriate to everyday use. The narrator can afford only one outfit for her Barbie, which has suffered from constant wear: "From so much dressing and undressing, the black glitter wears off where her titties stick out" (1). However, she has embraced the upper-class, Anglo lifestyle that Barbie represents, which is underscored by the "Waspy" names of the dolls in paragraph 4 — "Skipper," "Scooter," and "Tutti." Cisneros provides little detail about the narrator's circumstances, but she implies the dissonance between the narrator's "real life" and the Barbie mystique when she juxtaposes the "watersoaked and sooty Barbies" found on Maxwell Street, which the narrator and her friend can afford, with the image of "new Bendable Legs Barbie and Midge . . . in nice clean boxes" (6).

The narrator explains that she has fashioned an extra outfit for Barbie from an old sock to create a "glamorous, fancy-free, off-the-shoulder look" (1) — a nice image of the incongruity between her "real" life and her Barbie-oriented fantasies. However, she clearly sees her contribution as negligible, for when she describes her Barbie wardrobe, she enumerates only the commercially produced accessories, "not including the sock dress" (2). Significantly, the narrator remains nameless.

Barbie is defined purely by her appearance. Toy makers capitalize on this by selling the identical doll in many different outfits. What does this say about a woman's individuality? What does "Barbie-Q" imply about a culture in which women are expected to emulate a doll? (Encourage students to examine the stories, or scripts, that the girls create for their Barbies [2] and to identify the "lesson" Cisneros's narrator seems to have gleaned from her dolls.) Students might examine other forms of popular culture — songs, movies, books — to identify the images that constitute an American myth of femininity. For instance, what does Scarlett ("Tomorrow is another day") O'Hara have in common with Barbie? An interesting discussion might ensue from a comparison of female- and male-oriented toys and an assessment of the cultural stereotypes they perpetuate.

POSSIBLE CONNECTIONS TO OTHER SELECTIONS

Toni Cade Bambara, "The Lesson" (text p. 179)
Raymond Carver, "Popular Mechanics" (text p. 272)
Colette, "The Hand" (text p. 220)
Ralph Ellison, "Battle Royal" (text p. 223)
Dagoberto Gilb, "Love in L.A." (text p. 265)

COLETTE [Sidonie-Gabrielle Colette], *The Hand* (p. 220)

In "The Hand," Colette's description of one night in the life of a woman and her sleeping husband forces readers to rely for meaning on the imagery associated with the husband's hand and on the wife's limited actions. By contrasting the wife's initial observations of the husband's hand with her later perceptions of it, students can clearly see her changing awareness of her lover. The husband's hand is a microcosm of the whole man, isolated as it is among the sheets. Initially, the wife focuses on its manicure, representative of the man's breeding and elegance: "The flat nails, whose ridges the nail buffer had not smoothed out, gleamed, coated with pink varnish" (paragraph 13). The glazed nails are a symbol of his refinement. However, she is distracted by the color of the nails, a too-feminine touch, which clashes with the size and strength — the masculinity — of the hand. As she discovers this incongruity, her conception of the hand, and of the man, rapidly changes from idealization to realization. She focuses primarily on male qualities of the hand, associating them with uncivilized, inhuman imagery: "The hand suddenly took on a vile, apelike appearance" (15). Her following observations of it are filled with references to its animal qualities: "tensed up in the shape of a crab," "the hand . . . lowered its claws, and became a pliant beast," "red fur" (17, 17, 19). Her husband is no longer a handsome lover; he has become a beast.

The wife's changing awareness of the hand affects her behavior. At the beginning of the story, as she gazes around the bedroom and at her sleeping lover, the hand rests next to her right elbow, and she is content. At the end of her story, her initial response is to shrink from contact with it or with anything it touches, including the piece of toast it has buttered. Her change in attitude toward the hand and its owner is presented in two stages. As she gazes at the hand and its nails, she feels in control: she makes a mental note to convince the husband not to use pink varnish. Then the hand moves, revealing the thumb as "horribly long and spatulate" (15), and she responds with a single word: " 'Oh!' whispered the young woman, as though faced with something slightly indecent" (16). The hand's altered appearance forces her beyond blissful, romantic, honeymoon notions of it and into a more realistic inspection. The setting reinforces this intrusion of reality. As she utters the first "Oh!" she suddenly becomes aware of the world outside the bedroom: "The sound of a passing car pierced the silence with a shrillness that seemed luminous" (17). As she studies the hand, she becomes more aware not only of its appearance, but also of its potential for destruction. It is described in militaristic, warlike terms: "Ready for battle," "It regrouped its forces" (17, 19). These images are reinforced by the association of the hand's power with a criminal act: "Slowly drawing itself in again, [it] grabbed a fistful of the sheet, dug into it with its curved fingers, and squeezed, squeezed with the methodical pleasure of a strangler" (19). The wife's realization of the hand's (and therefore the husband's) absolute power causes her to utter a second "Oh!" Her first whispered response has become a cry of terror. The hand is not only capable of evil and of harming the wife, but it appears to take great pleasure in such acts of cruelty, reinforcing the ultimate representation of the husband as a beast.

At the beginning of "The Hand," the wife is like a character in a fairy tale. A whirlwind romance led to her marrying a man whom she really didn't know well. After her one-night encounter with the hand, representative of her husband in a truly unconscious, natural state, details of the husband's background that previously seemed innocent take on sinister connotations: he is "recently widowed" and her involvement with him "had been little more than a kidnapping" (3). In the end, she is Beauty married to her Beast, legally and eternally. Her expectation of living life "happily ever after" has been defeated; instead, she is preparing for "her life of duplicity, of resignation, and of a lowly, delicate diplomacy" (25). Symbolizing her helplessness, she can only kiss his hand, the "monstrous hand" of the beast to whom she has entrusted her fate.

POSSIBLE CONNECTIONS TO OTHER SELECTIONS

Sandra Cisneros, "Barbie-Q" (text p. 218)
Gail Godwin, "A Sorrowful Woman" (text p. 33)
Nathaniel Hawthorne, "The Birthmark" (text p. 329)
John Updike, "A & P" (text p. 576)

RESOURCES FOR TEACHING

Colette. 13 min., color, 1979. Beta, VHS, ¾″ U-matic cassette, 16-mm film. A literary biography. Distributed by Coronet/MTI.

Colette. 30 min., b/w, 1950. 16-mm film. Still photos and live footage provide the background for Colette's own narration. In French with English subtitles. Out of print; available through Consortium (see the appendix of Film, Video, and Audiocassette Resources).

Colette Reads Colette [recording]. 1 cassette. The author reads favorite passages, in French. Distributed by Applause Productions.

RALPH ELLISON, *Battle Royal* (p. 223)

The opening paragraph of this story is fairly abstract and may be difficult for some students to grasp on first reading. But by the story's end the narrator's comments in this paragraph should have become very clear. Throughout this story Ellison is concerned with the masks, roles, and labels people impose on one another in this society. The narrator is invisible because the town's white citizens don't see him (or anyone else black) for what he is — which is, simply, a human being. What they see is a black man, or, in their vocabulary, a "nigger," "coon," or "shine." And "niggers," to their minds, are to be treated a certain way; mainly, they are to be publicly humiliated and abused. It is bitterly ironic that these men can bestow a great honor on this boy (the college scholarship) and simultaneously treat him worse than they would treat their dogs. It is equally ironic that, despite the brutal treatment the narrator receives at the hands of these men, he still wants to give his speech and is still proud to receive their gift.

The horrifying battle royal can be seen as a metaphor for the society the narrator lives in, in which nothing makes sense. Ten black boys are viciously used by some of the most important men of the town; they are forced to provide a freak show — first in the boxing ring, later on the electrified rug. In both cases they are jerked around like puppets on a string. They are, in fact, puppets; the white men are the puppeteers. If the boys refuse to fight one another, or to grab for the money with sufficient enthusiasm, it is clear the drunken white mob will hurt them much worse than they will hurt one another. White men have the power and make the decisions in this society, so the boys do as they are told. And not once do any white men — the very source of all this angry violence and confusion — get hurt.

The boys are brought in front of the naked blonde in an attempt to make them feel as uncomfortable as possible; they are not supposed to look at white women, and, left to their own devices, they wouldn't, especially in a room full of drunken white men. The blonde, with her ironic American flag tattoo, suggests all the things the boys (who are supposed to be Americans too) can't have simply because they are black: dignity, self-respect, freedom of choice, the freedom not to beat each other up or be beaten up by the white citizens present.

The blonde also serves another, very different function: at the same time that she is supposedly superior to the boys by virtue of the color of her skin, she is being used by the men; she too is a puppet. In paragraph 9, when she is being tossed into the air, the narrator sees the same "terror and disgust in her eyes" that he and the other boys are feeling.

As a high-school graduate, the narrator is extremely naive and believes that these men really respect him as he gives his speech after the battle, barely able to talk because he is choking on his own blood. In retrospect, as an educated adult, he realizes that he could not possibly have gotten an ounce of respect from any of them, and that, if he had known better at the time, he would not have respected himself. He realizes now that he was a laughing stock and that the white men were sending him the very message he read in his dream: "Keep This Nigger-Boy Running." In retrospect, too, he is able to understand his grandfather's dying words. His grandfather meant that a black man in this society didn't stand a chance by fighting racism openly. Instead, he believed blacks should pretend to play the game; white people had so much power that it was only by working within their system (by receiving scholarships to black colleges, for example, and then leading black people "in the proper paths") that blacks could hope to accomplish anything in the fight for equality. Dignity and self-respect, meanwhile, could come from within, since you would know you were agreeing them "to death and destruction" (2).

POSSIBLE CONNECTIONS TO OTHER SELECTIONS

Toni Cade Bambara, "The Lesson" (text p. 179)
Paul Laurence Dunbar, "We Wear the Mask" (text p. 808)
William Faulkner, "A Rose for Emily" (text p. 72)
Bessie Head, "The Prisoner Who Wore Glasses" (text p. 587)
M. Carl Holman, "Mr. Z" (text p. 1098)
Flannery O'Connor, "Revelation" (text p. 407)
August Wilson, *The Piano Lesson* (text p. 1962)

PERSPECTIVE

MORDECAI MARCUS, *What Is an Initiation Story?* (p. 234)

Ask students to apply one of Marcus's three categories of initiation to a story they are familiar with. Their response should explain how the initiation in the story they have chosen fits one of Marcus's categories but not the other two.

For a more creative response, ask students to write short sketches that depict one of Marcus's types of initiation. They might follow up their fictional sketches with short explanations of how their sketches fit Marcus's definitions.

FAE MYENNE NG, *A Red Sweater* (p. 235)

Students may not fully understand the symbolism of the red sweater until they comprehend some of the complexity of characterization in Ng's story. The narrator's deep ambivalence about her family and her ethnic heritage fuel her desire to give her sister this special gift; its meaning evolves as we obtain more of an understanding of the family's history and interpersonal dynamics.

The narrator is filled with conflicting emotions about her family. It is, she tells us, a "failed family" (paragraph 3); after the suicide of her middle sister (who remains nameless), "the family just sort of fell apart" (18). In addition, her parents' relationship has caused the narrator to look for a means of escape; she explains that her pregnancy and ensuing abortion became her "opportunity" (13) to leave her family behind. But she is unable to make a complete break from them; thus, she meets her elder sister, Lisa, for dinner in an annual ritual. The sisters are ambivalent about talking to each other as well: Lisa's "voice is sullen. She doesn't look at me. Once a year, I come in, asking questions. She's got the answers, but she hates them. For me, I think she's got the peace of heart, knowing that she's done her share for Mah and Deh. She thinks I have the peace, not caring. Her life is full of questions, too, but I have no answers" (29). Listening to her sister's stories, the narrator thinks, "I tell myself not to come back next year. I tell myself to apply for another transfer, to the East Coast" (68). But she still wants to hear the stories. The narrator demonstrates bitterness toward her parents, recalling their attacks on each other and their treatment of their daughters: "The stories themselves mean little. It was how hot and furious they could become. Is there no end to it? What makes their ugliness so alive, so thick and impossible to let go of?" (86–87). She also uses irony to summarize her parents' rejection of her: "My parents always had a special way of saying things" (17).

Nonetheless, she also reveals a sense of duty, love, and compassion toward them. She acknowledges, "the folks still won't see me, but I try to keep in touch with them through Lisa" (18). Her drink, Johnny Walker, "reminds me of Deh" (33), and looking into Lisa's eyes, she sees "Mah's eyes. Eyes that make you want to talk" (37). She tells us of Mah's kindness toward Deh: "Even though it was nonstop for Mah — rushing to the sweatshop in the morning, out to shop on break, and then home to cook by evening — she did this for him" (57), and she also defends her father: "his work was hard, too" (74). She sums up her attitude by saying, "their lives weren't easy. So is their discontent without reason?" (78).

She also would like to reject her Chinese heritage, particularly the misogynistic aspects of Chinese culture. She refers to the "failure" of her parents to produce a male heir at the beginning of the story, but at the end, she writes of "the bondmaids growing up in service, or the newborn daughters whose mouths were stuffed with ashes. Courtesans with the three-inch feet, . . . the frightened child-brides" (105). When the waiter asks her whether she and her sister are Chinese, she denies it (99); instead, she offers, "we're two sisters" (100). She establishes a contrast between what is Chinese and what is American: "at the Chinatown places, you have nothing to talk about except the bare issues"; there, "the food is good and the living hard. You eat a steaming rice plate, and then you feel like rushing home to sew garments or assemble radio parts or something" (22). In contrast, "in American restaurants, the atmosphere helps you along. I want nice light and a view and handsome waiters" (22). The narrator's choice of a fork over chopsticks ("The only chopsticks I own, I wear in my hair" [24]) signifies her ambivalence about her ethnicity.

And yet, she is unable to break with her heritage in the same way that she is unable to break with her family. Significantly, the time of year when the narrator and her sister meet, "January, New Year's, and February, New Year's again, double luckiness with our birthdays in between" (19), involves both American and Chinese celebrations. In addition, she acknowledges, "sometimes I get very hungry for Chinese flavors: black beans, garlic and ginger, shrimp paste and sesame oil. These are tastes we grew up with, still dream about. Crave" (50). During dinner, she suggests that maybe they should have gone to Chinatown after all (92).

Having established the narrator's family's history and patterns, ask students to compare the narrator's description of Lisa with her description of the red sweater. In the course of the evening, Lisa announces, "I don't want to think about [the family violence] anymore" (88). Though the narrator tells us, "for a long time Lisa's wanted out" (103), she also tells us that Lisa "can stay at that point of endurance forever" (103). According to the narrator, "Lisa is reed-thin and tall. She's got a body that clothes look good on. My sister slips something on, and it wraps her like skin. Fabric has pulse on her" (37). Hence, the narrator selects as Lisa's special gift the "lucky" red angora sweater.

What is the connection between the narrator's description of the sweater as "Hand Wash Only. Worn Once" (109) and the fact that Lisa "grabs at things out of despair, out of fear. Gifts grow old for her. Emotions never ripen, they sour. Everything slips away from her. Nothing sustains her. Her beauty has made her fragile" (91)? In addition, what is the narrator wishing for Lisa in giving her this gift? The narrator acknowledges, "I want her beauty to buy her out" (106), and she adds "time is what I would like to give her" (107); she also notices the dark, attractive waiter's evident interest in Lisa. Will this particular sweater be enough to help Lisa find love? Will Lisa be able to escape the dynamics of her parents' violence if she can devote herself to a love of her own? Can Lisa ultimately benefit from the sacrifices of her parents? As the narrator emphasizes, "we're the lucky generation" (105); "the idea is that the next generation can marry for love" (71). Neither the narrator nor the middle sister achieved this goal; perhaps Lisa will achieve it. Do students believe Lisa will be able to achieve this goal? Students might list the descriptions of the sweater at the beginning and the end of the story and discuss the ways in which Ng endows each description with meaning as she tells her story. For instance, understanding more of the intensity of the parents' relationship to each other, and to their daughters, we might begin to understand the narrator's choice of "fierce" and "dark red" and "made in Hong Kong" (1) in describing her gift to her sister.

Finally, students should examine Mah's philosophy: "Bones are sweeter than you know" (48). In what way does this sum up not only Mah and Deh's relationship but the narrator's relationship to her family as well? In addition, in what way is the story about Deh waiting in line at the bank four times significant? Can it apply metaphorically to Lisa as well as Deh? Studying these aspects of the story, students may understand that the narrator's gift involves not only a change of clothing but a change of life.

49

POSSIBLE CONNECTIONS TO OTHER SELECTIONS

Toni Cade Bambara, "The Lesson" (text p. 179)
Gish Jen, "In the American Society" (question #2, following)
Bharati Mukherjee, "The Tenant" (question #1, following)

CONNECTIONS QUESTIONS IN TEXT (p. 242) WITH ANSWERS

1. Compare the narrator in "A Red Sweater" with the narrator of Bharati Mukherjee's "The Tenant" (p. 102). In what sense might each narrator be described as a "tenant"?

   The narrator of "A Red Sweater" (who is not named in the story) and Maya, the protagonist of "The Tenant," share an ambivalence about both their families and their ethnicity that prevents them from fully committing to their individual, professional lives. Ng's narrator is evidently a flight attendant; significantly, she works for American Airlines (8). She tells us, "you have to be heartless [to leave]. My sister holds that heart, too close and for too long. This is her weakness, and I like to think, used to be mine" (104). However, there's a certain transitory quality to her sense of herself as independent: she tells us that, "it will be my turn one day" (88) to return and care for her parents. Maya, an academic who teaches comparative literature, is also in a transitory mode: she will leave the life she has established in Iowa to pursue a love affair with the man she has met through an ad in an Indian newspaper.

2. Discuss the ways in which Chinese immigrant life is presented in "A Red Sweater" and Gish Jen's "In the American Society" (p. 643). What significant similarities and differences do you find?

   In both "A Red Sweater" and "In the American Society," the parents of the female narrators are immigrants. However, in Jen's story, the parents have prospered: the mother worked her way up to manager at a supermarket before she quit, while the father has made enough profit at his pancake house to imagine himself a kind of Chinese "godfather" who can take care of his workers. In contrast, the parents of the narrator of "A Red Sweater" have never prospered despite their capacity for hard work. Mah has labored for a sweatshop for thirty years; Deh has tried several businesses, but all have failed. They have never reached the level of comfort and prosperity achieved by the parents in Jen's story. The parents in Jen's story found America to be, in many ways, the land of opportunity, while the parents in Ng's story have not. Their economic success determines the tenor of their marriages, as well: Jen's characters demonstrate a solidarity and a love for one another that is more easily expressed, whereas Ng's characters are all scarred by their failures. It is particularly significant that (foreshadowing the middle daughter's suicide) the father in Ng's story has threatened for years to jump to his death off the Golden Gate Bridge (63), a symbol of American prosperity and optimism.

8

Theme

In the introduction to Chapter 8, there are seven specific suggestions to help students identify and formulate themes for the stories they read. It might be useful to assign students to apply those hints to stories the class has already discussed. Also, students might practice identifying the theme of a given story before they come to class. Working in small groups or exchanging written statements about the theme, they may realize through studying their own concrete examples that theme is a significant literary element. They also might formulate statements of theme and "morals" for the same story in order to differentiate between them and to learn more about a story's perspective on a given topic.

MARGARET ATWOOD, *There Was Once* (p. 247)

Initially, students may be confused by the lack of exposition in Atwood's story. Encourage them to work through the story, identifying the speakers and developing some sense of their characterization from the few details Atwood provides. Finally, invite the students to generate ideas about the theme of the story.

"There Was Once" is primarily a dialogue. Atwood provides considerable opportunity for different characterizations of the speakers in her story, but because the speakers clearly alternate paragraphs through most of the story and have such distinctive voices, it is easy to distinguish them. Students may come up with different identities for these speakers, but certain details seem significant. Speaker A, the person attempting to tell the story, seems more conservative and traditional, particularly in comparison to Speaker B. Throughout the story, Speaker A rather mild-manneredly accepts Speaker B's objections and attempts to revise accordingly; the one moment in the story where Speaker A becomes more assertive is in paragraph 23, where he says, after a number of Speaker B's corrections, "sounds to me like you don't want to hear this story at all." At that point, Speaker B backs down: "Oh well, go on" (24).

Speaker B is clearly interested in what students might refer to as a "politically correct" agenda, using feminist rhetoric throughout the story ("Women these days have to deal with too many intimidating physical role models as it is, what with those bimbos in the ads" [12]). Throughout the story, Speaker B challenges Speaker A to consider the ways in which A's story marginalizes or objectifies the characters involved. Speaker B, for instance, claims that A doesn't understand the meaning of "poor" (8).

In paragraph 29, an interesting shift occurs. In response to Speaker B's assessment of "middle-aged men," a voice complains, *"Hey, just a minute! I'm a middle-aged — "*; students should examine this passage in its context and decide whether the speaker is Speaker A or another person, Speaker C. Though the questions in the text following Atwood's story refer only to two speakers, textual evidence suggests that there are, at this point of the story, actually three voices. Speaker C, middle-aged, begins to object to Speaker B's representation of men (a nice touch, considering Speaker B has attempted to protect and speak for all sorts of other persons of diverse socioeconomic status and race). But clearly, Speaker C has interrupted the dialogue between Speaker A and Speaker B (which resumes following paragraph 29). It is clear, through Speaker B's reference to "the two of us" in paragraph 30, that Speaker A is not the person expressing dismay in paragraph 29, and that Speaker B is referring first in paragraph 30 to Speaker C and then returning B's attention ("Go on") to Speaker A.

In paragraph 22, Speaker B condemns Speaker A's ability to tell a story that would be relevant to others: "Everything is about you." B sneers that the color of the protagonist "would probably be [Speaker A's] color, wouldn't it?" [20], implying Speaker A's single-sightedness; later, in paragraph 24, A seemingly relents a little bit, saying, "You could make her ethnic. That might help." There is irony in Speaker B's complaints that Speaker A's story is mostly about Speaker A: Speaker B spends the whole story trying to make A's story more relevant to A's own world-view, right through to the final objection, "So, why not *here*?" (42).

Many students might feel sympathy for Speaker A, who never gets to tell the story. Speaker B also seems condescending and shrill. However, is there anything of value in Speaker B's insistence on the "politically correct" agenda for this story? What do students associate with the title? Does it refer nostalgically to a time when stories could be told before being edited? Was there ever a time when fairy tales didn't carry social, cultural meaning? Students should be aware of the relevance of Atwood's subject matter; for instance, in the 1990s, HBO has produced a series of highly regarded revisionings of traditional fairy tales that reflect issues of race, class, and gender. In addition, such satiric collections of fairy tales as James Finn Garner's *Politically Correct Bedtime Stories: Modern Tales for Our Life & Times* (Macmillan, 1994) have appeared on the best-seller lists. Students might study a few of these contemporary, popular fairy-tale revisions as they develop their interpretations of the theme and significance of Atwood's "There Was Once."

POSSIBLE CONNECTIONS TO OTHER SELECTIONS

Toni Cade Bambara, "The Lesson" (text p. 179)
T. Coraghessan Boyle, "Carnal Knowledge" (question #1, following)

CONNECTION QUESTION IN TEXT (p. 249) WITH ANSWER

1. Discuss the use of satire in "There Was Once" and in T. Coraghessan Boyle's "Carnal Knowledge" (p. 276). Though these are very different types of stories, how are the themes somewhat similar?

   Both Atwood and Boyle satirize contemporary cultural movements. "Carnal Knowledge" satirizes animal rights organizations while Atwood satirizes the politically correct, or "PC" movement. The protagonist of "Carnal Knowledge," Jim, participates in picketing a fur emporium in Beverly Hills and in "liberating turkeys" only because he's interested in Alena. (Hence the play on words in the title: "carnal" refers to his lust for Alena as well as to his affinity for meat.) In "There Was Once," Speaker B emphasizes throughout the story the need to make traditional stories more inclusive and diverse — and yet, by the end of the story, it is clear that Speaker B also wants the stories to be personally relevant to her. In addition, in both stories, the characters who are the chief proponents of these causes are depicted in less admirable ways than the characters who interact with them.

Atwood and Family. 30 min., color, 1989. Beta, VHS, ¾″ U-matic cassette, 16-mm film. Atwood talks about her life and work. Distributed by the National Film Board of Canada. Available for rental from member institutions of the Consortium of College and University Media Centers.

Interview with Margaret Atwood [recording]. 1 cassette (56 min.). Covers Atwood's feminism, nationalism, themes, and craft. Distributed by American Audio Prose Library.

STEPHEN CRANE, *The Bride Comes to Yellow Sky* (p. 250)

In this story Jack Potter is conflicted between the love and duty he feels toward his new wife and the love and duty he feels toward Yellow Sky. As town marshal, protector and defender of, and friend to, Yellow Sky, he feels he has betrayed the town not only by marrying a stranger but by marrying without the town's knowledge as well. Crane is playing with some traditional western myths here — most notably the idea of the lawman's loyalty to his territory above anything else, even personal happiness.

In fact, the title and first paragraph of this story set up our expectations for a typical western. The bride's coming to Yellow Sky supplies the element of adventure and a little bit of tension (how will she react to her new home, and how will the town react to her?). The train and the plains, with their mesquite, cactus, "little groups of frame houses," and the "sweeping" vista all provide the setting we associate with western adventures. But Crane is quick to let us know that he is playing off these traditions rather than adopting them conventionally. Notice that the bride is neither pretty nor young, and that while the newly wed couple is ostensibly very happy, they are practically tortured by embarrassment.

As far as traditional westerns go, something is definitely askew here. Marshals don't usually have brides because women only get in the way in the wild world of gunslingers and Indians. And if there is a wife, she is decidedly young and pretty. She is also in the house, where she belongs, rather than in San Antonio, dragging the marshal miles away from where he belongs, taking care of the local drunk bully. Finally, while we expect this story to end in a shoot-out (though because of the comic tone we don't really expect anyone to get killed), words are exchanged instead of bullets and Scratchy Wilson is "disarmed" by the incredible fact (and sight) of Jack Potter's bride. For all we know, if Mrs. Potter hadn't been standing there, Wilson might not have believed Potter's claim that he had just gotten married (which is also his explanation for why he doesn't have a gun). So Mrs. Potter actually serves as a weapon more powerful than a gun; Wilson takes one look at her and loses interest in shooting.

What kind of shoot-out is this, where no shots are fired? What kind of West is this, with a bride in a cashmere dress (attire we can't imagine women wearing, or even having access to, in that setting)? And we're explicitly told that Scratchy Wilson's gaudy outfit is inauthentic western garb; the shirt came from New York City and the inappropriate boots are, we learn in paragraph 63, "the kind beloved in winter by little sledding boys on the hillsides of New England." The suggestion is that the romantic West of the storybooks is dead, or at least dying fast. Edwin H. Cady, in *Stephen Crane* (New York: Twayne, 1962), notes that " 'The Bride Comes to Yellow Sky' is a hilariously funny parody of neo-romantic lamentations over 'The Passing of the West.' The last marshal is tamed by a prosaic marriage and exempted from playing The Game so absurdly romanticized. . . . His occupation gone, the last Bad Man, a part-time worker anyhow, shuffles off into the sunset dragging boot tracks through the dust like the tracks of the last dinosaur" (102). When Scratchy Wilson says, "I s'pose it's all off now" (88), the specific reference is to his rampage on the town, but the larger implication is that the whole myth of the West is over as well.

Scratchy's comic and ineffective qualities are meant to suggest those same qualities in Yellow Sky, and in any part or member of the West that still adheres to this myth. The drummer in the saloon reinforces this concept; as an outsider to Yellow Sky, he helps dramatize this episode. The fact that he has been many places but hasn't encountered such a situation before suggests how ridiculous this little scene really is; people just don't go around shooting up a town this way anymore (if they ever really did), and Yellow Sky seems to be one of the last places to find this out.

Crane creates suspense by delaying the inevitable meeting between Potter and Wilson; he alternates scenes of the bride and groom en route to Yellow Sky with scenes of what is going on in Yellow Sky at the same moment. But it is a teasing rather than a gripping suspense; Crane's tone is sufficiently mocking and ironic that we don't really believe Wilson, or anybody else, is actually going to kill anyone.

POSSIBLE CONNECTIONS TO OTHER SELECTIONS

William Faulkner, "A Rose for Emily" (text p. 72)

Katherine Mansfield, "Miss Brill" (text p. 258)

Jane Martin, *Rodeo* (text p. 1657)

RESOURCES FOR TEACHING

The Bride Comes to Yellow Sky [recording]. 1 cassette (50 min.), 1983. Read by Walter Zimmerman and Jim Killavey. Illustrates the contrasting sides of Crane's art — the humorous and the gruesome. Distributed by Jimcin Recordings.

The Red Badge of Courage and Other Stories [recording]. 6 cassettes (6 hrs., 39 min.), 1976. Includes title story, "The Mystery of Heroism," "The Open Boat," and "The Bride Comes to Yellow Sky." Distributed by Listening Library.

The Red Badge of Courage and Other Stories [recording]. 9 cassettes (1 hr. each). Read by Michael Pritchard. Includes "The Bride Comes to Yellow Sky," "The Blue Hotel," and "The Open Boat." Distributed by Books on Tape.

See also "American Story Classics" series in the appendix of Film, Video, and Audio-cassette Resources.

KATHERINE MANSFIELD, *Miss Brill* (p. 258)

Mansfield's characterization of Miss Brill is a portrait of an elderly woman alone. We never learn her first name because there is no one to address her familiarly. She carefully observes the crowds in the park because they are the only people in her life, aside from the students she tutors or the old gentleman for whom she reads the newspaper. She notices that the band conductor wears a new coat, and she looks forward to her special seat in the park, which is for "sitting in other people's lives just for a minute while they talked around her" (paragraph 3). By silent participation in other people's lives — even if they are only a husband and wife quarreling over whether one of them should wear spectacles — her life is enriched.

Miss Brill is content with her solitary life of observations. She is not merely a stock characterization of a frail old lady. She prides herself on her ability to hear and watch others. She sorts out the children, parents, lovers, and old people and vicariously participates in their lives, but she does not see herself in the same light as the other people who sit on the benches: "they were odd, silent, nearly all old, and from the way they stared they looked as though they'd just come from dark little rooms or even — even cupboards!" (5). Miss Brill believes she is more vital and alive than that.

Life in the park offers all the exciting variety of a theater production to Miss Brill. She regards herself as part of a large cast, every member of which plays an important role. She feels a sense of community with them that makes her want to sing with the band. The music seems to be a confirmation of her connection with people and a fitting expression of her abiding concern that kindnesses be observed: she wants to rebuke a complaining wife; she disapproves of the haughty woman who rejects the violets picked up for her by a little boy; and she regards the man who blows smoke in the face of the woman with the ermine toque as a brute. Her reactions to these minor characters reveal her decency and sensitivity.

At the climactic moment, when she feels elated by the band's music, she is suddenly and unexpectedly made to realize that the young "hero and heroine" (actually the story's antagonists) who sit nearby regard her as an unwelcome intrusion in their lives. She hears herself described as a "stupid old thing" and the fur that she so fondly wears is dismissed as merely "funny" (11–14). This insensitive slight produces the conflict in the story and changes Miss Brill because she is suddenly made aware of how she is like the other old people in the park. She returns home defeated, no longer able to delight in the simple pleasure of a honeycake. "Her room [is] like a cupboard," where she places her fur in a box. When "she put the lid on she thought she heard something crying" (18). Her fur — Miss Brill's sense of herself — expresses for her the painful, puzzled sense that she is less vitally a part of the world than she had assumed. Her life appears to be closed down — boxed up — at the end. Having denied herself the honeycake, it seems unlikely that she'll return to the park the following Sunday. If she does, her role in the "play" she imagined will have been significantly diminished because she no longer perceives herself as an astute observer of other characters but as one of them, "odd, silent," and "old."

As a writing assignment, you might ask students to discuss the function of the minor characters mentioned in the story. They can analyze the way Mansfield uses these characters to reveal Miss Brill's character.

There is almost no physical description of Miss Brill in the story. Another writing assignment might be to develop a detailed description that is consistent with Miss Brill's behavior.

POSSIBLE CONNECTIONS TO OTHER SELECTIONS

Stephen Crane, "The Bride Comes to Yellow Sky" (text p. 250)
James Joyce, "Eveline" (text p. 512)
Fay Weldon, "IND AFF, or Out of Love in Sarajevo" (text p. 153)

PERSPECTIVE

EUDORA WELTY, *On the Plots of "The Bride Comes to Yellow Sky" and "Miss Brill"* (p. 262)

Welty asserts that "considerably more of a story is attempted" in "Miss Brill" than in "The Bride Comes to Yellow Sky"; she describes Crane's story as "playful" and a "comedy." Ask the class first whether they agree with this assessment and second whether they think that because something is playful or funny it is necessarily "less" of a story or a less serious piece of work. Ask students whether they can cite works that are both funny and serious. (Bambara's "The Lesson" [p. 179] is a good example.)

DAGOBERTO GILB, *Love in L.A.* (p. 265)

"Love in L.A." might be interpreted as "California Dreamin'." Set in the shadow of the Hollywood Freeway, it is all about pretending to be someone different and attempting to attract an audience. Although Jake drives a '58 Buick (without insurance), he dreams of "something better": a "crushed velvet interior with electric controls for the L.A. summer, a nice warm heater and defroster for the winter drives at the beach, a cruise control for those longer trips, mellow speakers front and rear of course, windows that hum closed, snuffing out that nasty exterior noise of freeways" (paragraph 1). Given the centrality of cars and freeways in southern California, this is an apt metaphor for the kind of life of wealth and status that Jake would like to lead, the person he'd be if only the reality of his situation lived up to his imagination. Instead of sitting in "a clot of near motionless traffic" (1), he'd be cruising through life. Tellingly, the "green light" (2) of his imagination is more real than the actual traffic in front of him. Lost in his fantasy, he rear-ends the car ahead of him.

Jake is conscious of "performance" throughout his encounter with Mariana. He stalls for time while he prepares lines based on both his inability (and unwillingness) to make financial reparation and his attraction to her. He also considers at least two options for escaping the situation. Students can deduce from this significant information about his character that Jake is not the upstanding individual he appears to be at the start of his conversation with Mariana. Jake's performance is further undermined by the information that emphasizes Jake's scam in action. For instance, Jake tells Mariana, "I really am sorry about hitting you like that" (12), but the text following this ("he sounded genuine" [12]) implies that he is trying to pull some sort of scam. His deception becomes more obvious throughout the exchange. After acting sincere, Jake "exaggerated greatly" (20) about his lack of identification and his vocation as a musician; later, "he lied" about whether he had insurance (28). He might think he's been convincing ("back in his car he took a moment or two to feel both proud and sad about his performance" [38]). Ask students to consider whether or not Jake feels guilty for his deceitful actions. Exactly what might he feel sad about?

Ask students to characterize the cars featured in "Love in L.A." Jake's aging Buick is big and sturdy and mechanically reliable, and he regards its lack of nicks or dents as "one of his few clear-cut accomplishments over the years" (3). Mariana's car is a newer Toyota with Florida plates. As Jake puts it, these cars are "so soft they might replace waterbeds soon" (12). There are unmistakable parallels between the cars and their owners' personalities. Jake dresses in "less than new but not unhip clothes" (6), and while he appears to be having a conversation about the damage to Mariana's car, he's really more interested in whether he can get her into bed. It's no accident that while Jake talks, he "fondle[s] the wide dimple" (12) in Mariana's (car's) rear end.

Although he seems to think he won over Mariana because she gives him her phone number, the final paragraph reveals that she hasn't been influenced by his act. It won't do her any good to trace the license number that she copies off the plate on his car, but then, he's not going to drive off thinking that his deception worked. In fact, one could argue that each character has attempted to scam the other. Jake plays his "genuine" act to escape from responsibility, while Mariana may have relied on her beauty in order to coerce him into giving her the information she needs. Neither character will be satisfied. Love, in this story, is less about genuine affection and attraction than it is about running (and deflecting) a scam. Ultimately, Jack is yet another kind of used-car salesman, and his encounter with Mariana will be only another hit-and-run statistic.

POSSIBLE CONNECTION TO ANOTHER SELECTION

Sandra Cisneros, "Barbie-Q" (text p. 218)

9

Style, Tone, and Irony

The introduction to Chapter 9 describes the intricacies of style, tone, and irony. Students might experiment individually with style, tone, and irony first by rereading some of their own work and establishing some assessment of their own natural style and tone. Second, they might learn more about these tools by rewriting common fairy tales in different voices. For instance, how might "Goldilocks and the Three Bears" sound as told by a Sam Spade character (from Dashiell Hammett's *The Maltese Falcon*)? A Walter Mitty? A politician? Students might also practice writing excuses why a paper might be late in different modes — both sincere and ironic. You may even want to introduce students to such landmark examples of irony as Jonathan Swift's "A Modest Proposal." Though the irony in literature is rarely as exaggerated as Swift's, it provides the reader with information about the story that might dramatically affect their interpretations. Inventing and practicing their own examples of different styles, tones, and ironic works, and reading other examples embodying them, students will become more confident at recognizing and responding to these literary tools in the work of professional authors.

RAYMOND CARVER, *Popular Mechanics* (p. 272)

Born in 1938 in Clatskanie, Oregon, to working-class parents, Carver grew up in Yakima, Washington, was educated at Humboldt State College in California, and did graduate work at the University of Iowa. He married at age nineteen and during his college years worked at a series of low-paying jobs to help support his family. These difficult years eventually ended in divorce. He taught at a number of universities, among them the University of California at Berkeley, the University of Iowa, the University of Texas at El Paso, and Syracuse University. Carver's collections of stories include *Will You Please Be Quiet, Please?* (1976), *What We Talk About When We Talk About Love* (1981), from which "Popular Mechanics" is taken, *Cathedral* (1984), and *Where I'm Calling From: New and Selected Stories* (1988). Though extremely brief, "Popular Mechanics" describes a stark domestic situation with a startling conclusion.

For an interesting reading of "Popular Mechanics," see "Physical and Social Laws in Ray Carver's *Popular Mechanics*," by Norman German and Jack Bedell, *Critique* 29.4 (Summer 1988): 257–260. This entry incorporates several of their ideas.

What do students think of when they think of the term *popular mechanics*? One possibility is the contemporary "how-to" magazine *Popular Mechanics*, which contains suggestions and instructions for "home improvement" projects. In its form, Carver's story reminds us of such a "how-to." Consisting of a series of very brief paragraphs, or "steps," it contains no complicated instructions or convoluted sentences. It's only when we look beneath the surface and consider the story's implications that we discover its complexities. There is a certain "mechanical" nature to the story as well, as Carver describes the couple's physical grappling over the baby: "in the near-dark he worked on her fisted fingers with one hand and with the other hand he gripped the screaming baby up under an arm near the shoulder" (paragraph 31); "she caught the baby around the wrist and leaned back" (34). As German and Bedell point out, the baby functions as some sort of wishbone during this scuffle (258). Holding him over the stove, and pulling at him from each side, the husband and wife focus solely on their own wishes rather than the baby's safety. Ask students how they interpret the last line: "In this manner, the issue was decided" (36). German and Bedell suggest that "issue" refers both to the argument and to the baby as the parents' offspring (258). As the last line implies, in this struggle there can only be losers.

Minor details of the story contribute to its effect. In the first paragraph it is "getting dark" both inside and out; the light has faded away by the end of the story. In paragraph 10, the husband looks "around the bedroom before turning off the light"; in paragraph 31, we are told that "the kitchen window gave no light." The scuffle intensifies in proportion to the increasing darkness in the house — and, as German and Bedell note, the sound level rises proportionally to the decreasing light (259). The argument over the baby's picture foreshadows the struggle in the kitchen and reveals the parents' tendency to objectify everything in their attempts to hurt each other. The flowerpot serves as yet another example of this: the symbol of a domestic harmony that has ceased to exist for these people, the pot is knocked off the wall by the parents' mutual efforts. In this story, the baby (often referred to as "it") becomes just one more object.

In class, explain the story of Solomon (1 Kings 3) and ask students to compare its outcome with Carver's conclusion. (Neither of Carver's adult characters is willing to take any responsibility: notice that the wife says, "You're hurting the baby" [29] instead of "We're hurting the baby.") Whereas 1 Kings 3 is ultimately a story about a mother's love and selflessness, "Popular Mechanics" reveals the animosity and selfishness of both parents.

POSSIBLE CONNECTION TO ANOTHER SELECTION

Sandra Cisneros, "Barbie-Q" (text p. 218)

RESOURCES FOR TEACHING

Interview with Raymond Carver [recording]. 1 cassette (51 min.). Stimulating introduction to Carver's life and work. Distributed by American Audio Prose Library.

Raymond Carver. 50 min., color, 1996. VHS. Fellow writers, Carver's wife, and others discuss his lower-middle-class roots in the Northwest as the source of inspiration for his characters and stories. A BBC Production. From the "Great Writers of the 20th Century" Series. Distributed by Films for the Humanities and Sciences.

Readings [recording]. 1 cassette (51 min.). Distributed by American Audio Prose Library.

Short Cuts. 189 min., color, 1993. Cast: Jennifer Jason Leigh, Tim Robbins, Madeleine Stowe, Frances McDormand, Peter Gallagher, Lily Tomlin, Andie MacDowell, Jack Lemmon, Lyle Lovett, Huey Lewis, Matthew Modine, Lili Taylor, Christopher Penn, Robert Downey Jr. Directed by Robert Altman. Distributed by Columbia Tristar Home Video.

PERSPECTIVE

JOHN BARTH, *On Minimalist Fiction* (p. 274)

Is minimalism defined more by a "terse, oblique, realistic or hyperrealistic" quality (paragraph 1) or by the inclusion of numerous references to contemporary popular culture? Students should identify a selection from the fiction section that in their opinion fits Barth's definition and explain why it does so. In their responses, they should explain whether the story they have chosen to write about is minimalistic in form, style, or material.

T. CORAGHESSAN BOYLE, *Carnal Knowledge* (p. 276)

Students might begin their analysis of this story by looking up a definition for the word *carnal*. *Webster's New Collegiate Dictionary* refers to "carnal" in part as "relating to or given to crude bodily pleasures and appetites," and in the *Oxford English Dictionary*, a prominent definition is "of the flesh." The question to be asked in connection with Boyle's title is, which flesh? The opening and concluding paragraphs depict Jim's thoughts about meat — from "[b]eef, mutton, pork, venison, dripping burgers and greasy ribs" (paragraph 1) to McDonald's hamburgers. While much of Jim's odyssey throughout this story involves the kind of meat he might find in a sandwich (pastrami, Thanksgiving turkey, a Big Mac), more of it focuses on his pursuit of Alena. Beginning in the first two paragraphs of "Carnal Knowledge," when Jim says, "I could never resist the veal scallopini. And then I met Alena Jorgensen," hunger is aligned with lust.

"Carnal Knowledge" is full of similar ironic parallels and *double entendres* playing Jim's participation in the Animal Liberation Front against his love affair with Alena. The connection is signified in the text by Jim's recognition that Alena's "eyes were ever so slightly mismatched, like the dog's" (11). Stunned as he might be about the way Alf was tortured by the shoe company, Jim is "moved even more by the sight of [Alena] bending over the box in her Gore-Tex bikini" (26): " 'Tortured him?' I echoed, feeling the indignation rise in me — this beautiful girl, this innocent beast" (21). He calls in sick to work the next morning not because of a fierce personal commitment to fighting "species fascism" (18), but because he envisions himself spending "the rest of the day right there beside her, peeling grapes and dropping them one by one between her parted and expectant lips" (46). Later, considering his role as a liberator of turkeys, Jim thinks "about meat and jail and the heroic proportions to which I was about to swell in Alena's eyes and what I intended to do to her when we finally got to bed" (81). Thus the overall irony of the title. When Jim comforts himself at the end of the story — " 'Meat,' and I spoke the word aloud, talking to calm myself as if I'd awakened from a bad dream, 'it's only meat' " (117) — he's talking about Alena as much as he is about his Big Mac.

There's also plentiful humor in Boyle's word choice throughout the story — word choice that foreshadows the end of the love affair, undermines Jim's attempt to be convincing in his commitment to the cause, and satirizes the animal rights movement along the way. Discovering that Alf has urinated on him, Jim is "glad to see that the thing was hobbled — it would simplify the task of running it down and beating it to death" (5). When Alena describes her work with the Animal Liberation Front, Jim "could only nod and exclaim, smile ruefully and whistle in a low 'holy cow!' sort of way" (32). Jim does begin to think more about the plight of animals — he admits that Alena "fascinated me, fixated me, made me feel like a tomcat leaping in and out of second-story windows" (55). And his ruminations at Rolfe's cabin reveal the limits of his allegiance to turkey liberation: "I was thinking of all the turkeys I'd sent to their doom, of the plucked wishbones, the pope's noses, and the crisp browned skin I used to relish as a kid. It brought a lump to my throat, and something more: I realized I was hungry" (72). From the name for the turkey farm ("Hedda Gabler's Range-Fed Turkey Ranch" [71]) to his depiction of the liberated turkeys' fate — "the road was coated in feathers, turkey feathers, . . . [a]nd more: there was flesh there too, slick and greasy, a red pulp ground into the surface of the road, thrown up like slush from the tires of the car ahead of me" (115) — Boyle never allows his reader to take Jim's odyssey seriously.

As a means of identifying the overall irony of "Carnal Knowledge," students might identify Jim's motivation. Encourage them to discuss Jim's situation. Certainly his age (and the fact that his adventure begins on his thirtieth birthday), his vocation (as a writer of advertisements), his aspirations (an evening of listening to his mother, aunt, and grandmother engage in "a spate of reminiscences," followed by "a divorced computer programmer in her midthirties with three kids and bad breath" [14]) all contribute to his participation in Alena's cause. As he admits, "I was giddy with the adolescent joy of it" (56). Some aspects of Jim's life may be all too realistic for some readers, but his career as a "liberator of turkeys" and his turn as "a turkey expressway" (97) resonate with humor, satire, and irony.

POSSIBLE CONNECTIONS TO OTHER SELECTIONS

Alison Baker, "Better Be Ready 'Bout Half Past Eight" (text p. 617)
Nathaniel Hawthorne, "Young Goodman Brown" (text p. 310)
Edgar Allan Poe, "The Purloined Letter" (text p. 564)

SUSAN MINOT, *Lust* (p. 290)

Beginning their study of this story, students might look up the meaning of "lust" in the dictionary. Definitions of the term range from "pleasure, delight" to "intense sexual desire: lasciviousness." Ask the students whether these denotations really apply to Minot's story. (They might wonder *whose* lust is referred to here.) Though they might initially be overwhelmed by the numerous sexual encounters described by the narrator, they should examine in particular the narrator's selection of metaphors and similes to come to some conclusions about the meaning of the story. Studying the narrator's analogies, readers become aware of the irony inherent in the title.

Trace the narrator's references to her encounters throughout the story. Describing her initial sexual experience, she claims that she "flipped" (paragraph 1), implying a certain exhilaration about discovering her sexuality. Being sexually active is for her a way of asserting her independence and maturity, particularly when she compares herself to her mother: the narrator "kept the dial [of birth control pills] in my top drawer like my mother and thought of her each time I tipped out the yellow tablets in the morning before chapel" (31). However, her sexual experiences don't enhance her self-confidence; rather, they steadily diminish her. She later tells us that during and after sex, she felt like "a body waiting on the rug" (6), that she was "filled absolutely with air, or with a sadness that wouldn't stop" (28). Elsewhere, she tells us, "you wonder how long you can keep it up. You begin to feel as if you're showing through, like a bathroom window that only lets in grey light, the kind you can't see out of" (64). In many of her analogies, she compares herself to a piece of meat (recalling derogatory terms for the body): "Then you start to get tired. You begin to feel diluted, like watered-down stew" (44); "you wonder about things feeling a little off-kilter. You begin to feel like a piece of pounded veal" (72); "after sex, you curl up like a shrimp, something deep inside you ruined, slammed in a place that sickens at slamming, and slowly you fill up with an overwhelming sadness, an elusive gaping worry" (79). It's evident that the narrator's encounters with these young men increasingly make her feel more like an object than a person. It is significant that she is an unnamed narrator, that none of her partners (not lovers) ever calls her by her name. The structure of the story, fragmented by her experiences with different men, also illustrates her fragmentation of self.

In addition to revealing her personal feelings through her analogies, the narrator provides some sense of the larger, cultural assumptions about gender. She asserts that there are different "rules" of behavior for young men and young women: "The more girls a boy has, the better. He has a bright look, having reaped fruits, blooming. He stalks around, sure-shouldered, and you have the feeling he's got more in him, a fatter heart, more stories to tell. For a girl, with each boy it's as though a petal gets plucked each time" (43). You may want to ask students to compare the language of these descriptions, and examine the description in paragraph 48. Here, the narrator explains the typical roles for boys and girls:

> On weekends they play touch football while we sit on the sidelines, picking blades of grass to chew on, and watch. We're always watching them run around. We shiver in the stands, knocking our boots together to keep our toes warm, and they whizz across the ice, chopping their sticks around the puck. When they're in the rink, they refuse to look at you, only eyeing each other beneath low helmets. You cheer for them, but they don't look up, even if it's a face-off when nothing's happening, even if they're doing drills before any game has started at all.

In other words, men are those who act; women are those who observe. Men have the authority in their interaction with women. The narrator describes the way her partners take the initiative: " 'come here,' he says on the porch. . . . He kisses my palm then directs my hand to his fly" (12–15); they focus on their own needs and interests rather than on hers: ". . . trying to be reasonable, in a regular voice, 'Listen I just want to have a good time.' So I'd go because I couldn't think of something to say back that wouldn't be obvious, and if you go out with them, you sort of have to do something" (25–26). The narrator uses words such as "surrender" (28) to describe the way she feels about these encounters. She doesn't demonstrate any sense of personal authority in dealing with men: "I thought the worst thing anyone could call you was a cock-teaser. So, if you flirted, you had to be prepared to go through with it" (38). The one time she tries to achieve more of a relationship with the boy she's sleeping with, his response is " 'What the hell are you talking about?' " (60). Ask students to explain the irony in the narrator's comment, "I hate those girls who push away a boy's face as if she were made out of Ivory soap, as if she's that much greater than he is" (68).

Students might discuss the way the girls in this story interact with each other. What are their value systems? We get two glimpses of the narrator with her friends Giddy and Jill. In the first, the other girls cannot imagine that the narrator is unhappy, because she "always [has] a boyfriend" (36). (Students might explain the narrator's reaction to her friends' comments here.) In the second, all three are talking with the housemother, Mrs. Gunther, whose own life history doesn't promise anything more for these young women. Having married her first boyfriend (because she was pregnant, we wonder?), she affirms for Jill, Giddy, and the narrator the passiveness of women and the centrality of male attention. Students might discuss the circumstances of the narrator's school and family life — there are certainly very few adults who seem aware of her experiences or their ramifications. In this predominantly upper-class setting, in which the narrator and her companions attend prep schools, go on ski trips, and stay at family apartments and summer houses, there is surprisingly little positive, constructive interaction with adults. The few adults who take notice of her sexual activity — the school doctor, Mrs. Gunther, the headmaster — never offer her any constructive alternative choices.

In connection with "Lust," students might consider whether the narrator's assertions about the gender roles described in Minot's story reflect their experience. In this context, it might be useful to discuss the roles of male and female characters in popular fairy tales. Compare, for instance, the roles of Prince Charming and the Sleeping Beauty, or even those of the characters in "Little Red Riding Hood." Can students think of a fairy tale in which the female character takes an authoritative stance? Two excellent essays on the subject might be relevant to such a discussion: Marcia K. Lieberman's " 'Some Day My Prince Will Come': Female Acculturation through the Fairy Tale," and Karen E. Rowe's "Feminism and Fairy Tales," both reprinted in Jack Zipes's *Don't Bet on the Prince: Contemporary Feminist Fairy Tales in North America and England* (Methuen, 1986).

Minot's story also seems relevant to recent studies about Mary Pipher's *Reviving Ophelia* and other studies about girls' loss of confidence during their teenage years. Significantly, the narrator tells us, "I could do some things well. Some things I was good at, like math or painting or even sports, but the second a boy put his arm around me, I forgot about wanting to do anything else, which felt like a relief at first until it became like sinking into a muck" (19).

POSSIBLE CONNECTIONS TO OTHER SELECTIONS

Jamaica Kincaid, "Girl" (text p. 534)
Alice Munro, "An Ounce of Cure" (question #2, following)
David Updike, "Summer" (question #1, following)

CONNECTIONS QUESTIONS IN TEXT (p. 297) WITH ANSWERS

1. Compare the treatments of youthful sexuality in "Lust" and David Updike's "Summer" (p. 169). Do you prefer one story over the other? Why?

    The teenage characters in David Updike's "Summer" are still innocent at the end of the story; their lust has gone unconsummated. Their attraction to one another appears to be more romantic or sentimental than physical — neither character feels the need to commit to a physical gesture. Indeed, we are told in "Summer" that for Homer, the protagonist, "to touch [Sandra], or kiss her, seemed suddenly incongruous, absurd, contrary to something he could not put his finger on" (paragraph 14). In contrast, the narrator of "Lust" has had only physical experience, not psychological or emotional involvement. Her partners demonstrate no desire for any relationship other than a physical one; hence, the tone of the end of "Lust" is one of disillusionment and regret. In contrast, the tone of "Summer" is upbeat, emphasizing Homer's new awareness and his joy that Sandra has returned his interest. Theirs is a much more reciprocal relationship, albeit unconsummated, than any of the encounters the narrator describes in "Lust."

2. Compare the narrators of "Lust" and Alice Munro's "An Ounce of Cure" (p. 434). What significant similarities and differences do you see between the narrators?

    Both the narrators of "Lust" and "An Ounce of Cure" are older women looking back on their adolescent experiences. However, the narrator of "An Ounce of Cure" has salvaged her self-image with the help of a sense of humor and an understanding of the cultural pressures on her parents, her neighbors, and herself at that time. Thus she as an adult can encounter the focus of her adolescent crush, Martin (in later life an undertaker), and recognize his limitations. In contrast, the narrator of "Lust," looking back on her adolescence, reveals a much stronger sense of regret: "Teenage years. You know just what you're doing and don't see the things that start to get in the way" (29). Whereas the protagonist of "An Ounce of Cure" has developed a healthy personal perspective, the narrator of "Lust" remains focused on how the boys see her, not on how she sees them: "Then comes after. After when they don't look at you. . . . Their blank look tells you that the girl they were fucking is not there anymore. You seem to have disappeared" (83).

GEORGE BOWERING, *A Short Story* (p. 298)

Bowering's style in this story is distinctive both at the sentence level (where he has a tendency to drop some apostrophes, particularly in contractions, and to use "&" for "and" and "t" for "ed") and in the overall structure of the narrative. Isolating sections of the story under headings identified as various literary elements, he calls attention to the telling of the story as much as to its subject matter. You may want to have students study the contents of each section in relationship to the headings; they should also consider the overall effect of Bowering's approach. In part, it distances the reader from the characters described in "A Short Story." It also invites readers to focus on the way the different literary elements contribute to the overall effect of the story.

Instructors might encourage students to generate ideas about each of the elements of this story. For instance, under "Setting," they might study the description of the Jacobsen home, its surrounding orchards, and the nearby lake. Though important description is included in the opening section, references to setting occur throughout the story. Overall, they emphasize the fallen or ruined quality of the valley. The cherry blossoms are past their prime; they are "shrunken to brown lace" (paragraph 1), and the lake is "spotted with brown weeds dying underwater, where the newest poison had been dumpt by the government two weeks before" (3). Ask students to consider the implications of setting, both outdoors and within the Jacobsen house.

Art's propensity for making trophies from the bodies of the animals he has shot is equally significant: the house "was panelled with knotty cedar, animal heads looking across at one another from the walls" (4). The mounted heads have always made Donna anxious; when she was a teenager and her dog died, Donna immediately took the body out and buried it before Art could take it to the taxidermist. This brief anecdote is significant because it foreshadows Donna's decision to kill her mother. Students should discuss the reasons Donna chooses to kill her mother instead of her stepfather. (After all, in the sections identified as "Flashback" and "Foreshadowing," Donna's hostility toward older men, and toward Art, is evident.) In part, her decision may be based on the fact that her mother chose Art instead of Donna. She seeks revenge on her mother for betraying her, but her action is also related to her distaste for Art and his mounted heads. She acknowledges that she and her mother "had not once spoken to each other on the telephone since Jacobsen had mounted her [Audrey] as his casual season's trophy" (40). She cannot prevent Art from adding Audrey to his collection, but she can, in effect, ruin the trophy. Hence, it is significant that she shoots her mother in the face. Students might be confused about the last paragraph of the story as well. They might focus on the setting (the tree where Donna would go for comfort when she was a teenager), the reference to Donna's dog "waiting for her to signal something" (94), and the foreshadowing provided by the episode in which Donna thinks about hurting the man who has hired her to have sex with him. Thinking of stabbing him with scissors ("fetching a jolt as they sank into the flesh of his back" [74]), she finds that "the points of her scissors were just below the joining of her ribcage, forcing the skin a little" (74). These details, along with Donna's indecision about her future, suggest that she commits suicide in the last paragraph.

Bowering emphasizes the connections between this story and the story of Adam and Eve in the Garden of Eden. He teases the reader with references to other elements of the story from Genesis: for instance, Donna defends the beauty of the valley, saying "it *is* a garden" (52); also, when she ran away as a teenager, she took, significantly, "just two apples" (59). What is the combined effect of these allusions? Why does the notion of the garden before and after the Fall resonate in this story? Students might compare Donna's sense of the valley before and after her mother's marriage to Art. The narrator explains, "Donna could not stay in that family where her first love, her first world face, lost all hope & fell in, decided to stay with the bringer of death. What polluted language in the formerly unchallenged eden" (41). In addition, students might consider the ways in which the narrator, the Jacobsens, and Donna reenact the biblical tragedy.

In addition, the narrator refers to himself as "omniscient" (17); he tells the reader not to believe that he is "God-like" (18), but he then admits, "I would like to keep you closer than your usual 'god' will allow (except for people such as yourself Leda) (no, that's not what I'm trying to do to you, reader: dont be so suspicious)" (20). His reference to Leda invokes Greek mythology; Leda was seduced by Zeus in the guise of a swan and gave birth to Helen of Troy as well as Pollux, Castor, and Clytemnestra. Instructors might briefly outline this story for students unfamiliar with Greek mythology; they might also invite students to generate ideas about the intertextuality of "A Short Story." For instance, the narrator emphasizes Donna's beauty on several occasions: he tells us, "what a beautiful sight she was, with her long legs & summer dress, sunglasses percht on top of her short feathery blondish hair" (31). Is there any connection between the narrator's praise of Donna and his reference to the story of Leda and her children?

POSSIBLE CONNECTIONS TO OTHER SELECTIONS

Andre Dubus, "Killings" (question #1, following)
Stephen King, "Suffer the Little Children" (text p. 535)

CONNECTION QUESTION IN TEXT (p. 305) WITH ANSWER

1. Compare the motives for the killings in this story and in Andre Dubus's "Killings" (p. 81).

    Students may feel sympathetic toward the characters who wield the guns in "Killings" and "A Short Story"; however, they may argue that Matt Fowler is ultimately a more sympathetic character than Donna Michaels. Both are dealing with the loss of loved ones (Matt's son, Frank, and Donna's mother, Audrey). Both of the antagonists, Richard Strout and Art Jacobsen, are depicted to some extent as selfish, destructive individuals. However, Matt is consumed with grief for his son, who was murdered by Richard Strout because he was seeing Strout's soon-to-be ex-wife, Mary Ann. He also is motivated to take action because he fears that Strout will escape imprisonment. Matt can't bear the thought that Strout will live a long life while his own son lies in a grave. He decides that the only way to ensure justice is to kill Strout; there is some suggestion at the end of the story that his action will haunt him for the rest of his life.

    Donna's mother is still alive; Audrey has chosen to marry Art instead of living as a single mother with Donna. Donna clearly resents her mother for her lack of maternal connection. It is significant that Donna encounters a more positive image of motherhood, "a mother quail & her five little ones" (paragraph 36), as she returns to the Jacobsen house. In a sense, killing Audrey is both punitive and protective: Donna punishes Audrey for leaving her; at the same time, she prevents Art from keeping Audrey as one of his many trophies. However, it is implied that she commits suicide at the end of the story. Thus, neither Matt nor Donna finds satisfaction as a result of their actions.

10

A Study of Three Authors: Nathaniel Hawthorne, Flannery O'Connor, and Alice Munro

In Chapter 10, students have the opportunity to develop some expertise in the works of Nathaniel Hawthorne, Flannery O'Connor, and Alice Munro. In addition to studying more than one work by the same author, here they have the opportunity to engage with the critics. In the section for each author, there appear not only numerous perspectives (some general, some specific to the stories contained in this chapter), but also excerpts from multiple critiques of the same story ("Complementary Critical Readings").

Instructors may want to encourage their students to study the multiple approaches to interpretation of literature in Chapter 37 before beginning to discuss the critical commentary. After some introduction to psychological, feminist, formalist, and other strategies for interpretation, students might more readily identify individual critics' ideologies or better understand their intellectual approaches to the literature as well as their ideas about the content (their close readings) of these stories. Comparing the critical stances exemplified by the examples in Chapter 10, particularly in connection with multiple stories by the same authors, students will enhance both their reading and their critical thinking skills. They may also appreciate more deeply the diverse possibilities for interpretation of these compelling stories.

NATHANIEL HAWTHORNE

Young Goodman Brown (p. 310)

Brown's name conveys several meanings that can be determined after reading this story. This is a point worth stressing with students so they do not mistakenly assume that they should perceive the following meanings on a first reading. "Young" suggests the protagonist's innocent, simple nature at the beginning of the story, when he has an as yet untested, abstract faith in life. "Goodman," in addition to being a seventeenth-century honorific somewhat like "mister," takes on an ironic meaning when Brown meets the devil. "Brown" is a common name that perhaps serves to universalize this character's experience. If Hawthorne had chosen the name "White" or "Black," he would have cast the protagonist in too absolute a moral role. "Gray" would do, but "Brown" has the additional advantage of associating the protagonist with the forest, particularly in the fall, an appropriate season for the story's movement from innocence to experience.

The opening paragraphs provide important contrasts between the village and the forest. The village represents the safe, predictable landscape of home, associated with light, faith, goodness, and community. In paragraph 8 the forest is dreary, dark, gloomy, narrow, and threatening; it represents a moral wilderness in which skepticism and evil flourish. Brown journeys into the forest to meet the devil. No specific reason is given for the journey, but most of us can understand Eve's curiosity about biting into the apple. Brown assumes that he will be able to cling to "Faith" after his encounter with the devil (although students may never have heard of this story, most will grasp its allegorical nature very quickly). But of course Brown turns out to be wrong because when he sees that the rest of the community — from all the respectable deacons, selectmen, and religious leaders to his family and beloved Faith — share the impulses he has acted on, his faith is shattered.

We know that Brown's meeting is with a supernatural figure because the old man explains that he had been in Boston only fifteen minutes before his meeting in the forest outside Salem village. His devilish nature is conveyed by his serpentine staff; indeed, he even sits under "an old tree" (10) that suggests the tree of knowledge in Genesis. We don't have to believe, however, that Brown has a literal encounter with the devil. Hawthorne tells us that the staff's wriggling like a snake probably was only an "ocular deception" (13). This kind of calculated ambiguity is used a number of times in the story to accommodate readers who are wary of supernatural events and prefer "reality" in their fiction.

Students should be asked to locate other instances of ambiguity — such as Faith's ribbons and the question at the end concerning whether Brown simply dreamed the entire sequence of events. It seems that the answer to this question doesn't really matter because in the final paragraph Hawthorne dismisses such questions and instead emphasizes the terrible results of Brown's belief — that he has been betrayed by everyone in the community. Brown's life is ruined; he becomes as stern and dark as the moral wilderness he abhors. Because he turned away from life and lost faith, "his dying hour was gloom." There is no absolute evidence either to relieve the community of responsibility for its involvement with evil or to pronounce it innocent. (A reader can, however, draw on Hawthorne's other works to demonstrate that he viewed humankind as neither wholly corrupt nor perfect; see, for example, "The Birthmark," text p. 329.)

Even if Faith has some knowledge of evil or is tempted by it, that does not mean that "evil is the nature of mankind" (65) as the devil (not Hawthorne) falsely claims. When she joyfully meets her husband on the village street, Hawthorne paints on Faith's face no ironic smile, which would indicate hypocrisy or deception. And she has her pink ribbons. There is no actual reason for Brown to shrink "from the bosom of Faith" (72). He does so because he refuses to tolerate any kind of ambiguity. He is a moral absolutist who mistakenly accepts the devil's view of humanity. In a psychological sense his rejection of the world may be seen as a projection of his own feelings of guilt, and so he repudiates all trust, love, and especially faith, because he now sees faith as a satanic joke.

Hawthorne's built-in ambiguities in "Young Goodman Brown" have encouraged many readings of the story. For a convenient sample of twelve different readings see *Nathaniel Hawthorne: Young Goodman Brown*, edited by Thomas E. Connolly (Columbus: Merrill, 1968). If a dozen students are asked to read and summarize varying interpretations, the class will have an opportunity to debate the story in detail and develop an idea of what makes one interpretation more valid than another. It's also useful for them to realize that critics can disagree.

POSSIBLE CONNECTIONS TO OTHER SELECTIONS

T. Coraghessan Boyle, "Carnal Knowledge" (text p. 276)
Nathaniel Hawthorne "The Birthmark" (text p. 329)
———, "The Minister's Black Veil" (text p. 320)
Herman Melville, "Bartleby, the Scrivener" (text p. 113)

RESOURCE FOR TEACHING

Young Goodman Brown. 30 min., color, 1972. Beta, VHS, ¾″ U-matic cassette, 16-mm film. Distributed by Pyramid Film and Video. Available for rental from member institutions of the Consortium of College and University Media Centers.

The Minister's Black Veil (p. 320)

Nathaniel Hawthorne's "The Minister's Black Veil" presents readers with unanswerable questions: Why does the minister wear the black veil? What does the veil represent? A first-person point of view would destroy the ambiguity, and therefore the intellectual challenge, of the tale. If Mr. Hooper told his congregation and Hawthorne's readers why he made the choice to wear the veil, it is likely that neither group would be affected by his action. Because Mr. Hooper does not reveal his motivation, students are forced to propose their own theories for it.

If, as Edgar Allan Poe and other critics have suggested, Mr. Hooper wears the veil as a penance for a specific sin, possibly in connection with the young woman whose funeral he conducts, he exacts a heavy toll from his parishioners. From the first moment he appears wearing the veil, "two folds of crape, which entirely concealed his features, except the mouth and chin, but probably did not intercept his sight, farther than to give a darkened aspect to all living and inanimate things" (paragraph 6), he casts a cloud upon his parishioners' faces and spirits. They cannot return his greeting. The traditional atmosphere of the church is disrupted by the congregation's horror, and after church many of Mr. Hooper's listeners reverse their normally decorous behavior to gawk or gossip: "Some talked loudly, and profaned the Sabbath-day with ostentatious laughter" (13). Later the same day, even the corpse in the coffin shudders as Mr. Hooper bends over it, though a black veil is appropriate for the occasion. The minister then officiates at a wedding, but "the same horrible black veil which had added deeper gloom to the funeral . . . could portend nothing but evil to the wedding" (22). The groom shivers, and the bride is so pale that she is associated with the dead maiden of the earlier funeral. These are short-term effects of the minister's decision to wear the black veil; a long-term effect of it on his parishioners is the breakdown of his communication with them. The good people of his church are accustomed to guiding him in church matters as well as to being led by him: "Hitherto, whenever there appeared the slightest call for such interference, he had never lacked advisors, nor shown himself averse to be guided by their judgment" (24). Yet when they approach him to discuss his reason for wearing the veil and call his attention to its adverse effect on the church, they are unable to reach him. Not even his wife-to-be, Elizabeth, can convince him to remove his mask, even for a moment. Though she is noted for her "calm energy" (25) and has a "firmer character than his own" (36), she too is affected by the veil: "But, in an instant, as it were, a new feeling took the place of sorrow: her eyes were fixed insensibly on the black veil, when, like a sudden twilight in the air, its terrors fell around her" (36). If the minister dons the black veil as a penance for his unknown sin, the fear, distrust, and isolation it inspires are greater evils that seem to defeat his purpose.

If Mr. Hooper dons the black veil to symbolize the sins of his secretive flock, he exacts a heavier toll upon himself. On the first Sunday of its appearance, the veil isolates him not only from his parishioners but from God: "It threw its obscurity between him and the holy page, as he read the Scriptures; and while he prayed, the veil lay heavily on his uplifted countenance" (10). God cannot reach him, and his congregation chooses to avoid him. "None, as on former occasions, aspired to the honor of walking by their pastor's side. Old Squire Saunders, doubtless by an accidental lapse of memory, neglected to invite Mr. Hooper to his table, where the good clergyman had been wont to bless the food, almost every Sunday since his settlement" (13). As he continues to wear the veil, the people not only avoid him but express their opinions of him in bewilderment and scorn: "Our parson has gone mad!" (9); "it was reckoned merely an eccentric whim" (44); "but with the multitude, good Mr. Hooper was irreparably a bugbear" (44). Even though he becomes a renowned speaker, and people come from great distances to hear his church services, they come for dubious, clearly not religious, reasons: "With the mere idle purpose of gazing at his figure, because it was forbidden them to behold his face" (45). The people in his village go out of their way to avoid him in the streets, while children flee at his approach. Far from being a holy man, he has become a monster. His personal life is in no better condition after his bride-to-be leaves him. He himself is frightened at his reflection in the mirror. In the end, the black veil has cost him his link with humanity: "It had separated him from cheerful brotherhood and woman's love, and kept him in that saddest of all prisons, his own heart" (47). Mr. Hooper addresses this awful personal cost on his deathbed when he cries, "Why do you tremble at me alone? . . . Tremble also at each other" (58). This is his final intimation that the wearing of the veil is connected with his parishioners' spiritual welfare.

One other possible motive is a self-righteous and total obsession with wearing the black veil — he is unable to give it up for his lover, his congregation, or his God. On his deathbed he speaks of the supposed meaning of the veil and of man's fundamental tendency to hide sins. If he is purely self-motivated, this deathbed speech is hypocritical. He has worn the black veil at an inestimable cost.

Hawthorne suggests that at the funeral over which Mr. Hooper presides, the veil is "an appropriate emblem" (18). Does Mr. Hooper's lifelong appearance in the veil suggest an ongoing funeral for the town's spirituality? What is the meaning of the minister's constant smile? Is it genuine, ironic, or the sign of a crazed intellect? In what real-life situations do people wear veils? How does Mr. Hooper's application of the black crape conform to or contrast with these traditional uses? As students attempt to answer these questions, ask them to explain how "The Minister's Black Veil" is, as Hawthorne claims, a parable. Students' definitions of the term may lead them to their own answers to these questions and their own interpretations of the story.

POSSIBLE CONNECTIONS TO OTHER SELECTIONS

Nathaniel Hawthorne, "The Birthmark" (text p. 329)
——, "Young Goodman Brown" (text p. 310)

RESOURCES FOR TEACHING

The Minister's Black Veil [recording]. 1 cassette. Read by Walter Zimmerman and John Chatty. Includes "Young Goodman Brown." Distributed by Jimcin Recordings.
The Minister's Black Veil [recording]. 1 cassette. Distributed by Spoken Arts.

The Birthmark (p. 329)

Aylmer (a variant of Elmer, meaning "noble") in this story is neither evil nor mad. An eighteenth-century scientist, he embodies the period's devotion to science and reason. However, his studies supersede all else in his life; they are his first love — even before his wife. His choice of science over love identifies him as the kind of Hawthorne character who displays an imbalance of head and heart. His intellect usurps his common sense and feelings. He loses sight of Georgiana's humanity in his monomaniacal quest to achieve an ideal perfection in her person.

Aylmer is shocked by Georgiana's birthmark because he sees it as a "visible mark of earthly imperfection" (paragraph 5). To him the "crimson hand" (a sign perhaps that humankind's fallen nature is imprinted by the devil [original sin] on all human beings) symbolizes the "fatal flaw of humanity" and is a sign of mortality, "toil and pain" (8). This extreme perspective differs from the more normal views of the birthmark in paragraph 7.

Georgiana (whose name is appropriately associated with the earthy rather than the ideal) loves her husband so completely that she is willing to risk her life to win his approval. Her feelings serve as a foil to his obsessive efforts to perfect her; she loves him despite his willingness to dehumanize her. She is unaware of his blasphemous pride, which the reader sees clearly: "What will be my triumph when I shall have corrected what Nature left imperfect in her fairest work!" (19). Though the story is set in the 1700s, Georgiana can be seen as a prototype of many nineteenth-century female characters — passive and incapable of changing the course of events that will inevitably destroy her. She becomes a martyr to her love for Aylmer. Students are likely to see her as hopelessly weak rather than nearly perfect. When Georgiana reads Aylmer's journal and observes that "his most splendid successes were almost invariably failures, if compared with the ideal at which he aimed" (51), many readers wonder why this and other grim foreshadowings about the nature of his work (see 32–37) do not alarm her. Hawthorne, however, stresses her loyal devotion to her husband more as a virtue than as a weakness.

Aminadab is also an obvious foil to Aylmer. His name spelled backward is, interestingly enough, *bad anima* (bad soul or life principle). He represents the opposite of Aylmer's aspirations for the ideal: "He seemed to represent man's physical nature." His physical features — his grimy, shaggy, low stature and "indescribable earthiness" — are in stark contrast to Aylmer's "slender figure, and pale, intellectual face," which make him "a type of the spiritual element" (25). Aminadab's "smoky aspect" is the result of his tending Aylmer's "hot and feverish" furnace, which seems demonic and evokes the destructive nature of Aylmer's efforts to spiritualize matter (57).

Although Aylmer's motives are noble, his egotism blinds him to a central fact that his science ignores, for according to Hawthorne, there can be no such thing as mortal perfection. The story's theme argues that the nature of mortal existence necessarily means humanity's "liability to sin, sorrow, decay, and death" (8). For Hawthorne, no science can change that fact of life. As soon as the birthmark fades from Georgiana's face, her life fades because mortality and perfection do not coexist. Aylmer lacks the profound wisdom to embrace the human condition. Like Young Goodman Brown, he fails to accept the terms on which life offers itself.

Students may find provocative a discussion (or writing assignment) about this story as a modern version of our obsession with attaining physical perfection, through exercise, cosmetic surgery, or some other means. Hawthorne's theme of human imperfection is largely a philosophical issue, but it can also be addressed through psychological and sociological perspectives.

Judith Fetterley offers "A Feminist Reading of 'The Birthmark' " on text page 365.

POSSIBLE CONNECTIONS TO OTHER SELECTIONS

Colette, "The Hand" (text p. 220)
Emily Dickinson, "Success is counted sweetest" (text p. 932)

Nathaniel Hawthorne, "The Minister's Black Veil" (text p. 320)

———, "Young Goodman Brown" (text p. 310)

Yukio Mishima, "Patriotism" (text p. 593)

Flannery O'Connor, "A Good Man Is Hard to Find" (text p. 381)

Fay Weldon, "IND AFF, or Out of Love in Sarajevo" (text p. 153)

RESOURCE FOR TEACHING

The Birthmark [recording]. 1 cassette (63 min.). Read by Walter Zimmerman. Distributed by Jimcin Recordings.

Rappaccini's Daughter (p. 341)

To get them into the story, you may want to encourage students to examine the motivation of all of the principal characters in "Rappaccini's Daughter." Though they might initially regard only Rappaccini himself as evil (or responsible for Beatrice's tragic end), they may come to see Baglioni and even Giovanni in a more unfavorable light. In the end, only Beatrice is a fully sympathetic character, and the tragedy of Hawthorne's story is that she is destroyed in the battle between Baglioni, Giovanni, and Rappaccini.

Like Alymer and other "scientists" in Hawthorne's fiction, Rappaccini is evil. He aspires to be more powerful than other humans; he creates Beatrice, he says, to be "endowed with marvelous gifts, against which no power nor strength could avail an enemy . . . to be able to quell the mightiest with a breath . . . to be as terrible as thou art beautiful" (paragraph 135). He views the world beyond his garden as corrupt; therefore, he wants to prepare his daughter to survive in that world: "Wouldst thou, then, have preferred the condition of a weak woman, exposed to all evil, and capable of none?" (135). He also regards Beatrice, along with the garden, as his greatest scientific achievement. Indeed, he cannot separate his role as father from his role as scientist. We learn that the plant with purple flowers, the deadliest of deadly flora in his garden, is a "sister" to Beatrice: as she explains to Giovanni, "at the hour when I first drew breath, this plant sprang from the soil, the offspring of his science, of his intellect, while I was but his earthly child" (113). It is clear from the syntax of this line that Beatrice is subordinate to the plant; she is Rappaccini's maidservant, his assistant in the garden "laboratory," his bait to entrap Giovanni. Rappaccini's claim that his goal was to empower Beatrice should be weighed against his treatment of her.

Baglioni, whom students may regard initially as one of the heroes of the story, also should be carefully studied. Though he stresses at every encounter with Giovanni that he cares for the boy as "the son of my old friend" (53), he is not inspired to become involved in the affair solely by affection for the young man. Indeed, his involvement in the case is motivated more by rivalry and jealousy. As the narrator explains, "there was a professional warfare of long continuance between him and Doctor Rappaccini, in which the latter was generally thought to have gained the advantage" (25). (The use of "warfare" to describe what might be referred to in other situations as a friendly rivalry or a fierce competition is significant.) Meeting Giovanni on the street, learning of his passion for Beatrice, and noticing Rappaccini's interest in Giovanni, Baglioni is galvanized: "it is too insufferable an impertinence in Rappaccini, thus to snatch the bud out of my own hands, as I may say; and make use of him for his infernal experiments. This daughter of his! It shall be looked to. Perchance, most learned Rappaccini, I may foil you where you little dream of it!" (53). It is significant that both Rappaccini and Baglioni regard Giovanni as an experiment ripe for their expertise: meeting Giovanni in the street, Baglioni "scrutiniz[ed] the youth with an earnest glance" (44). Immediately following, Rappaccini appears on the street and gazes upon him "with an intentness that seemed to bring out whatever was within him worthy of notice. Nevertheless, there was a peculiar quietness in the look, as if taking merely a speculative, not a human interest, in the young man" (46).

Invite students to compare other passages from the story in which Baglioni and Rappaccini are described or behave in a similar fashion. It is ironic that both are physicians: both are intent on using human lives to further their own rivalry and reputations, but at what cost to the victims? Baglioni tells Giovanni that Rappaccini "was not restrained by natural affection from offering up his child, in this horrible manner, as the victim of his insane zeal for science. For — let us do him justice — he is as true a man of science as ever distilled his own heart in an alembic" (96). There is also double irony in Baglioni's comment to himself that Rappaccini "is a wonderful man! — a wonderful man indeed! A vile empiric, however, in his practice, and therefore not to be tolerated by those who respect the good old rules of the medical profession" (100). To himself, he practices verbal irony; readers can also observe the dramatic irony in his assumption that he is one of "those who respect the good old rules." Even at the end of the story, Hawthorne stresses that Baglioni expresses triumph over Rappaccini, as much or more than he demonstrates horror for the suffering of Beatrice: "Rappaccini! Rappaccini! And is *this* the upshot of your experiment?" (138).

Giovanni himself is a slightly more complicated character. He is wildly in love with Beatrice — a love accentuated by his Italian heritage (particularly because he is from warm, romantic, sunny southern Italy) and by the story's setting in Padua. (The name of the heroine is also significant. In Italian literature, "Beatrice" is associated with goodness, light, and love. Dante's inspiration and guide in the *Divine Comedy* is also named Beatrice.) Students might feel sympathy for Giovanni, particularly when he discovers that he has become as deadly as Beatrice. In this respect, he is, like her, a victim of the scientists' rivalry. However, students should examine Giovanni's treatment of Beatrice. He seems particularly impressed with her physical beauty; indeed, before Lisabetta shows him into the garden, he is quite the voyeur. He judges Beatrice harshly after he discovers that he has become poisonous; though both characters are equally affected by Rappaccini's evil, he assumes the high moral ground: "might there not still be a hope of his returning within the limits of ordinary nature, and leading Beatrice — the redeemed Beatrice — by the hand?" (128). (His physical condition is a metaphor for his character as well — the more selfish he becomes, the more poisonous he is.) The narrator highlights Giovanni's insensitivity in order to fully characterize his flaw: "Oh, weak, and selfish, and unworthy spirit, that could dream of an earthly union and earthly happiness as possible, after such deep love had been so bitterly wronged as was Beatrice's love by Giovanni's blighting words!" (128). In the end, she condemns Giovanni as well as her father: "Farewell, Giovanni! Thy words of hatred are like lead within my heart — but they, too, will fall away as I ascend. Oh, was there not, from the first, more poison in thy nature than in mine?" (136).

There are allusions to the biblical story of Adam and Eve in the Garden of Eden throughout "Rappaccini's Daughter." The garden is described in several instances as "that Eden of poisonous flowers" (81), and Beatrice's work in the garden is described in language evocative of Eve's life before the Fall ("though I have grown up among these flowers, I know no more of them than their hues and perfumes; and sometimes, methinks I would fain rid myself of even that small knowledge" [67]). In the references to their considerable physical beauty, Beatrice and Giovanni might be seen as Adam and Eve. Encourage students to consider the ways that these allusions enrich and emphasize the theme of the story. In part, Rappaccini's assumption of the role of God reveals his malignant character. Beatrice tells Giovanni that her father "created" the garden (111); she also acknowledges, "this garden is his world" (65). The height of Rappaccini's human arrogance is his assumption of omnipotence and omniscience, and the garden is described in terms that acknowledge this: "Several [of the plants], also, would have shocked a delicate instinct by an appearance of artificiality, indicating that there had been such commixture, and, as it were, adultery of various vegetable species, that the production was no longer of God's making, but the monstrous offspring of man's depraved fancy, glowing with only an evil mockery of beauty" (63). In part, the allusions to Eden heighten the tragedy of the conclusion. Though Giovanni aligns himself with goodness (invoking God's name, asking for blessings, and assuming his redemption at the end), it is clear in the conclusion that he belongs to the same group as the other evil characters surrounding Beatrice. Finally, this revision of the story of Eden also places the Adam figure at fault instead of Eve; here, she is a victim of his involvement with the serpent, Baglioni. Students might have other ideas about the importance of the biblical allusions, and they should have the opportunity to discuss them.

POSSIBLE CONNECTIONS TO OTHER SELECTIONS

Gail Godwin, "A Sorrowful Woman" (text p. 33)
Nathaniel Hawthorne, "The Birthmark," (question #1, following)

CONNECTION QUESTION IN TEXT (p. 360) WITH ANSWER

1. Compare Rappaccini's devotion to science with Aylmer's in "The Birthmark"(p. 329). Explain the similarities and differences in the plots.

    Like Hawthorne's "The Birthmark," "Rappaccini's Daughter" is a story about humanity sacrificed to science; moreover, in both stories, the female characters fall victim to male characters' ambitions and desires. In both stories, the scientists are characterized as heartless men who have given themselves purely to experimentation — even physically, they appear heartless. Rappaccini, according to Hawthorne, "could never, even in his more youthful days, have expressed much warmth of heart" (8); Baglioni says to Giovanni that Rappaccini's attention to Giovanni is "as deep as nature itself, but without nature's warmth of love" (49). These "scientists" care little for the victims of their experiments. Rappaccini sacrifices his daughter by making her as poisonous as his garden; she cannot live a normal life. She cannot love, be loved, bear children, go out into the world. Aylmer sacrifices his wife, Georgiana, to his zeal for knowledge. Both women are characterized as the best humanity might offer; significantly, both are associated with the mark of a tiny human hand: Beatrice's attempt to save Giovanni from the dangerous plant in the middle of the garden results in his waking up the next morning with a kind of burn in the shape of fingers and a thumb; Georgiana's fatal flaw, in Aylmer's eyes, is her birthmark, the tiny handprint on her face. At the end of both stories the scientists are finally punished for their heartlessness, but the women who love them have been destroyed.

PERSPECTIVES ON HAWTHORNE

Hawthorne on Solitude (p. 360)

Students can use this letter to get a sense of how Hawthorne worried about his self-imposed solitude and how he used "nothing but thin air to concoct my stories." Ask students if tensions in the letter are manifested in any of the Hawthorne stories included in this chapter.

Hawthorne on the Power of the Writer's Imagination (p. 362)

The light of a writer's imagination cast on familiar objects and events changes our perceptions of things. Good writing causes us to encounter not merely observable facts but also meanings supplied by the author. Hawthorne's purposes as a writer go beyond a realistic presentation of the world; he sought to invest his work with his own reading of "the truth of the human heart."

Hawthorne on His Short Stories (p. 363)

Hawthorne seems a bit nervous and uncertain about characterizing his stories because he anticipates his public's objection to their ambiguities and sometimes puzzling themes. He is aware that a weird tale such as "The Minister's Black Veil" is radically different from the popular sunny magazine sketches of robust American life contemporary with it.

HERMAN MELVILLE, *On Nathaniel Hawthorne's Tragic Vision* (p. 364)

Melville admired Hawthorne's exploration of the darker side of human potential. He dedicated *Moby-Dick* to Hawthorne because he recognized in him a kindred spirit willing to risk an outward-bound voyage, even if it meant the possibility of being lost.

TWO COMPLEMENTARY CRITICAL READINGS

JUDITH FETTERLEY, *A Feminist Reading of "The Birthmark"* (p. 365)

Do students agree with Fetterley's argument that "The Birthmark" is the story of "how to murder your wife and get away with it" (paragraph 1)? How do they account for the fact that Georgiana gives her permission to Aylmer to conduct his experiment? Does this indicate that she has more power than Fetterley might assume? Do the other Hawthorne selections demonstrate a similar emphasis on woman as commodity? Could Fetterley's observation that "to those who love Georgiana, her birthmark is evidence of her beauty; to those who envy or hate her, it is an object of disgust" (4) be only slightly altered to refer to Beatrice, or Faith, or Elizabeth's distinctive traits? Encourage students to rely on the text for specific details in agreeing or disagreeing with Fetterley.

Encourage students to read the excerpt from Fetterley's discussion of "A Rose for Emily" (p. 2072). Students might then construct a model for a feminist approach to literature based on their familiarity with both Fetterley excerpts.

JAMES QUINN AND ROSS BALDESSARINI, *A Psychological Reading of "The Birthmark"* (p. 366)

In a sense, this perspective offers a defense of Aylmer in response to the argument in the preceding perspective. Quinn and Baldessarini argue that "Aylmer is another Hawthornian victim of morbid forces, largely internal, beyond his control" (paragraph 4). Do students agree that Aylmer's behavior is beyond his control? Do they accept the argument that "the first to be destroyed is Aylmer himself, who steps out of the procession of life" (8)?

How would students expect Fetterley and other proponents of feminist readings of "The Birthmark" to respond to Quinn and Baldessarini's argument that the birthmark "is suggestive of the scarlet letter — another public sign of secret and lustful sin, of 'putting hands upon' in a sexual sense. . . . It seems to Hawthorne to symbolize the fallen and sinful nature of man" (7)?

ADDITIONAL RESOURCES FOR TEACHING HAWTHORNE

SELECTED BIBLIOGRAPHY

Baym, Nina. *The Shape of Hawthorne's Career.* Ithaca: Cornell UP, 1976.

Bertani Newman, Lea. *A Reader's Guide to the Short Stories of Nathaniel Hawthorne.* Boston: G. K. Hall, 1979.

Bloom, Harold, ed. *Nathaniel Hawthorne.* New York: Chelsea, 1986.

Bunge, Nancy L. *Nathaniel Hawthorne: A Study of the Short Fiction.* New York: Twayne, 1993.

Cameron, Kenneth W. *Hawthorne among His Contemporaries.* Hartford: Transcendental, 1968.

Cantwell, Robert. *Nathaniel Hawthorne: The American Years.* New York: Hippocrene, 1971.

Crews, Frederick C. *The Sins of the Fathers: Hawthorne's Psychological Themes.* New York: Oxford UP, 1966.

Crowley, J. Donald. *Hawthorne: The Critical Heritage.* New York: Banes, 1970.

Hall, Lawrence S. *Hawthorne: Critic of Society.* New Haven: Yale UP, 1944.

Hawthorne, Nathaniel. *The Complete Novels and Selected Tales of Nathaniel Hawthorne.* Ed. Norman Holmes Pearson. New York: Modern Library, 1965.

———. *Complete Short Stories of Nathaniel Hawthorne.* Garden City: Hanover, 1959.

———. *The Letters of Nathaniel Hawthorne, 1813–1843.* Vol. 15 of *The Centenary Edition of the Works of Nathaniel Hawthorne.* Ed. Thomas Woodson et al. 18 vols. Columbus: Ohio State UP, 1985.

———. *The Letters of Nathaniel Hawthorne, 1843–1853.* Vol. 16 of *The Centenary Edition of the Works of Nathaniel Hawthorne.* Ed. Thomas Woodson et al. 18 vols. Columbus: Ohio State UP, 1985.

———. *The Letters of Nathaniel Hawthorne, 1857–1864.* Vol. 18 of *The Centenary Edition of the Works of Nathaniel Hawthorne.* Ed. Thomas Woodson et al. 18 vols. Columbus: Ohio State UP, 1987.

———. *The Portable Hawthorne.* Ed. Malcolm Cowley. New York: Viking, 1969.

Mellow, James. *Nathaniel Hawthorne in His Times.* Boston: Houghton, 1980.

Moore, Thomas R. *A Thick and Darksome Veil: The Rhetoric of Hawthorne's Sketches, Prefaces, and Essays.* Boston: Northeastern UP, 1994.

Stern, Milton. *Contexts for Hawthorne: The Marble Faun and the Politics of Openness and Closure in American Literature.* Urbana: U of Illinois P, 1991.

Stubbs, John Caldwell. *The Pursuit of Form: A Study of Hawthorne and the Romance.* Urbana: U of Illinois P, 1970.

AUDIOVISUAL RESOURCES

Favorite Stories by Nathaniel Hawthorne, Vol. 1 [recording]. 2 cassettes (2 hours 30 min.). Read by Walter Zimmerman and John Chatty. Includes "Dr. Heidegger's Experiment" and "The Minister's Black Veil." Distributed by Jimcin Recordings.

Nathaniel Hawthorne: Light in the Shadows. 23 min., color, 1982. Beta, VHS, ¾" U-matic cassette, 16-mm film, special-order formats. A background of the author's life and works, especially *The Scarlet Letter* and *The House of the Seven Gables.* Distributed by the International Film Bureau. Available for rental from member institutions of the Consortium of College and University Media Centers.

FLANNERY O'CONNOR

The Turkey (p. 373)

Eleven-year-old Ruller is caught between childhood games and the responsibilities of adulthood. In the beginning of the story, he pretends that he is chasing rustlers; he wields guns, catches crooks, and leads a posse of men (paragraph 1). Elsewhere, he also fantasizes about being a jewel thief (25) and a preacher who opens a home for wayward boys (in the manner of a Father Flannigan) (38). Many of his fantasies seem fostered by the movies — he thinks not of the real person Father Flannigan but the actor who portrays him, Bing Crosby, in the film based on Flannigan's story *Boys Town* (1938). At home, he hears just enough of his parents' and other adults' conversations to partially comprehend their anxieties. He listens at night as his parents talk about their sons; he also hears them argue. And he's witnessed his brother Hane's evolution into a "bad" boy (who drinks, swears, and sneaks in late at night). He vaguely understands his father's concern that his boys are running wild and his mother's remonstrances that she is doing the best she can to raise them. After he tears his sleeves chasing the turkey, he worries about what will happen to him when he gets home — making readers wonder what kind of punishment is exercised at the McFarney home.

When he sees the turkey, he envisions it as an opportunity to be an "unusual boy" in the most favorable sense. In this sense, his adventure with the turkey is just another of the scenarios he envisions in which he gets to play the hero: "He saw himself going in the front door with it slung over his shoulder, and them all screaming, 'Look at Ruller with that wild turkey!' " (3). In addition, however, he is anxious to prove himself, and he wants to show his parents that he is going to be a better man than his older brother. He also wants to give his parents a good reason not to argue or fight in the middle of the night: "Hane hadn't ever got a turkey. Hane hadn't ever caught anything. He guessed they'd be knocked out when they saw him; he guessed they'd talk about it in bed" (5). His greatest fear is that he will become like Hane: "He wondered suddenly if he were going 'bad.' That's what Hane had done. Hane played pool and smoked cigarettes and sneaked in at twelve-thirty and boy he thought he was something" (21). "The Turkey" thus provides a compelling, psychologically sophisticated characterization of an eleven-year-old boy.

However, this story also functions effectively on a moral level. O'Connor often incorporates within her stories allegorical meanings; commonly, her characters' most egregious flaws are that they think they can outguess or understand or manipulate God. Ruller's adventures with the turkey may be understood in this context. When he thinks he can't catch the turkey, he begins to curse, at first "cautiously" (12) and "almost inaudibly" (17); then, he begins in earnest to curse as he has heard Hane and other relatives do: "God dammit to hell, good Lord from Jerusalem" (18). He experiences waves of enthusiasm for swearing and anxiety about it as well: "He remembered the minister had said young men were going to the devil by the dozens this day and age; forsaking gentle ways; walking in the tracks of Satan" (22). He tries on the role of "bad boy" in much the same way that he chases rustlers. God even plays a role in one of his fantasies (41). In this mode, Ruller envisions the turkey as a divine message: "Maybe finding the turkey was a sign" (38); "Maybe it was to keep him from going bad. Maybe God wanted to keep him from that" (36). (It is evident that he grew up in an environment where adults interpreted their daily experiences in this way.)

Ask students to evaluate Ruller's motivation once he gets the turkey. If the turkey is a sign from God, a means of making Ruller "good," does he live up to this Divine intervention? By choosing a route home that passes through town and by showing off his prize (probably even to the man who shot it — the hunter who refers to him as "the god-dam imp" [54]), Ruller is prideful. He focuses more on the accolades he might enjoy than on the moral or spiritual significance of the gift. He's unable to imagine himself in any role other than that of the hero. Is it, then, God who punishes him by sending what one might regard as avenging angels — the country boys — to take away the turkey? Indeed, it is while he's showing off the turkey that the first reference to the "country boys" appears in the story. As he gets more and more arrogant, the threat implied by his followers is intensified: "He felt warm all over and nice as if something very fine were going to be or had been. He looked back once and saw that the country boys were following him" (58). After walking through town, he prays to God to send him a beggar (60), again so that he can show off. If he were truly humble and grateful for God's kindness, he wouldn't consider passing through town a second time. In addition, he wouldn't need to show off the turkey at home. Finally, if his religious commitment were genuine, he might consider giving the turkey, rather than his more commonplace dime, to Hetty Gilman ("an old woman whom everybody said had more money than anybody in town because she had been begging for twenty years. She sneaked into people's houses and sat until they gave her something" [63]).

Students should be aware of the way O'Connor uses irony in her description of Ruller: "almost without thinking, he turned and asked graciously, 'You all wanta see this turkey?' " (65). In order to help students understand the irony, ask them to define *gracious*. Then encourage them to find a more appropriate word to describe Ruller's motivation. His loss of the turkey to the country boys may be seen as Divine judgment for his lack of humility. It is significant that while he has the turkey, he feels "as if the ground did not need to be under him any longer" (65); after the boys have taken the turkey and walked away, he "turned toward home, almost creeping" (70). Having lost his assurance and pride, and having nothing (not even a vestige of God's love, he thinks) to show for his torn clothing and lost afternoon, Ruller "ran faster and faster, and as he turned up the road to his house, his heart was running as fast as his legs and he was certain that Something Awful was tearing behind him with its arms rigid and its fingers ready to clutch" (70).

POSSIBLE CONNECTIONS TO OTHER SELECTIONS

Nathaniel Hawthorne, "The Minister's Black Veil" (text p. 320)

Flannery O'Connor, "Good Country People" (question #2, following)

———, "Revelation" (question #1, following)

CONNECTIONS QUESTIONS IN TEXT (p. 381) WITH ANSWERS

1. Compare the endings of "The Turkey" and "Revelation" (p. 407). What, if any, sort of revelation does Ruller experience?

   Both Ruller and Ruby Turpin experience a revelation that deconstructs their prideful self-image. Ruller becomes rather pompous as he shows off his turkey; Ruby's assessment of herself as better than almost everyone she meets is completely lacking in Christian charity. In both stories, God gives each character a better understanding of his or her limitations. Both acquire some humility. Ruller and Ruby eventually may get into heaven, but not in the way they initially imagine; they need to remember God's omnipotence and omniscience. Neither character can make deals with God. In addition, both experience revelations in thoroughly undignified circumstances. Ruller's grace is achieved through his brief possession of a turkey carcass; Ruby is assaulted in a waiting room and then achieves her apocalyptic vision while she washes the pig parlor. Both characters are consumed with the question "Who do you think you are?" At the end of each story, both are sadder and wiser; they are less likely to expect blessings or to assume that they are God's chosen people.

2. Compare Ruller's problems concerning religious faith with Hulga's in "Good Country People"(p. 392).

Both Ruller and Hulga pretend to some extent that they don't believe in God or in Christian virtues. Ruller swears, plots mayhem, and condemns God for showing him the turkey and then not enabling him to catch it. Hulga acts throughout the first three-quarters of "Good Country People" as though she has turned her back on God; she sneers at her mother, Mrs. Hopewell, and the Bible salesman, Manley Pointer, for their professed faith and goes out of her way to be rude to both of them. However, both Ruller and Hulga eventually regret their disrespect for the Lord and for common courtesy ("good country" values); both encounter individuals (the country boys, the Bible salesman) who convince them that they really do fear the Lord and believe in His ways. As a result, despite anything they may have said or done earlier, both Ruller and Hulga demonstrate more of a conventional belief by the end of these stories.

A Good Man Is Hard to Find (p. 381)

This story may initially puzzle students. It certainly defies easy interpretation. As they analyze the grandmother's and the Misfit's characters, they may understand more of the story, but even after discussion, students might have more questions than answers.

At the beginning of the story, the grandmother dwells on the past. Her manners and attire are ladylike: "The grandmother had on a navy blue straw sailor hat with a bunch of white violets on the brim and a navy blue dress with a small white dot in the print. Her collars and cuffs were white organdy trimmed with lace and at her neckline she had pinned a purple spray of cloth violets containing a sachet" (paragraph 12). She is a hard contrast to the mother, a young woman in slacks who represents the contemporary woman, and the rude granddaughter, June Star, the woman of the future. The grandmother's stories, about former beaus, lost opportunities, and secret panels in houses long gone, emphasize her preoccupation with the past. Even her humor involves the past: " 'Where's the plantation?' John Wesley asked. 'Gone With the Wind,' said the grandmother. 'Ha. Ha' " (23–24). She seems incapable of accepting the present or preparing for the future. She can only focus on her personal affairs and desires.

The Misfit is striking because he forces the grandmother beyond her obsession with herself and her past. As soon as she sees him, she focuses on identifying him. Then, trying to save herself and her family, she attempts to convince him that he is (note present tense) a good man. The Misfit and the grandmother are similar in one sense: he, too, dwells on his past. His grievances about his criminal record highlight his human past, and his observations about Jesus reflect a more universal human past. After hearing his "confession," the grandmother attempts to preserve both of their futures by "saving" the Misfit: "If you would pray . . . Jesus would help you" (118). Even though the Misfit refuses her help, they are both shaken out of their selfish memories. The grandmother becomes a more Christian woman because of her encounter with the Misfit. In truth, as the Misfit explains, "She would of been a good woman, . . . if it had been somebody there to shoot her every minute of her life" (140). Jesus taught the people by his good example and his raising of the dead; the Misfit enlightens the woman by his evil example and his execution of her.

This story obviously foreshadows its violent ending by its constant references to death in the plot, the dialogue, and the setting. The grandmother dresses up for the journey so that if she is in an accident, "anyone seeing her dead on the highway would know at once that she was a lady" (12). The last city that the family drives through is Toombsboro. The Misfit and his henchmen drive a car associated with funerals: "A big black battered hearse-like automobile" (70). Is the Misfit the Death the story foreshadows, or is O'Connor simply leading up to the deaths of the family?

Does "A Good Man Is Hard to Find" seem like a genuine story, or is the plot too coincidental? Are the characters and events believable? The power of surface appearances is constantly emphasized: the old woman is a lady because of the way she dresses; she recognizes the Misfit as one of her children only after he dons the shirt worn previously by Bailey Boy. Why does O'Connor call attention to these surface appearances and their effects? If this story is an allegory, what do the Misfit and the grandmother (for whom other, more specific names are never indicated) represent? What is the effect of the epigram at the beginning of the story? It may merely warn the reader about the journey this family is making; there may, however, be added significance to the source and the religious nature of its message. What might the dragon represent?

Students may be able to make meaningful connections between this story and Faulkner's "Barn Burning" (text p. 481). What kind of people survive and prevail at the ends of these stories? Is there a distinctly southern flavor to them? How might O'Connor have been influenced by Faulkner?

TIPS FROM THE FIELD

I always do a "talk show" after teaching the section on O'Connor. I have five or six students assume characters from each of the O'Connor stories and have the rest of the class prepare questions for the "guests" on the talk show. This exercise is always popular and is especially fun if you choose "hams" to play the characters.

— ROBERT CROFT, *Gainesville College*

From my experiences trying to teach Flannery O'Connor to a class including several Japanese and Swedish students, I came to realize that a number of American students — even southern ones — also have trouble with O'Connor's use of dialect. I found that having these students read aloud some scenes from "Good Country People" and "A Good Man Is Hard to Find" effectively broke through the dialect barrier. Their ears seem to be able to make sense of O'Connor's dialogue even when their eyes can't.

— JAMES H. CLEMMER, *Austin Peay State University*

POSSIBLE CONNECTIONS TO OTHER SELECTIONS

Isabel Allende, "The Judge's Wife" (text p. 581)
Toni Cade Bambara, "The Lesson" (text p. 179)
William Faulkner, "Barn Burning" (text p. 481)
Nathaniel Hawthorne, "The Birthmark" (text p. 329)
Gish Jen, "In the American Society" (text p. 643)
Flannery O'Connor, "Revelation" (text p. 407)

Good Country People (p. 392)

The central conflict in this story is between Hulga, who believes herself to be vastly superior to everyone around her, and the Bible salesman, Manley Pointer, whom Hulga and her mother at first take to be simple, naive, "good country people." Hulga wants to seduce Pointer to shatter his alleged innocence, both physical and spiritual. She wants him to believe in nothing, as she does. Her initial impulse is meanspirited, but even her first thoughts of seducing him include a fantasy of being with him once she has enlightened him about her version of the truth. "She imagined that she took his remorse in hand and changed it into a deeper understanding of life. She took all his shame away and turned it into something useful" (paragraph 91). Despite her facade of nastiness, which she uses as a sort of defense mechanism, Hulga really does want warmth, respect, admiration, and even love. She begins to recognize these feelings in herself, ironically, as Pointer is convincing her to show him her artificial leg. She is moved by what she perceives to be his innocence, which has enabled him (she thinks) to see the truth about her: that she "ain't like anybody else" (128).

But the joke is on Hulga. No sooner does Pointer get his hands on her leg than all his apparent innocence and tenderness disappear. It was the leg he wanted all along, for his collection; the sexual activity would have been a nice fringe benefit, but he is perfectly willing to leave without it. When Hulga asks him, in paragraph 136, "aren't you just good country people?" she is, ironically, clinging to the very values that she previously denounced and satirized. She is forced to acknowledge that civility and common decency (which Pointer has flouted by taking her leg) do matter. She has been deceiving herself by pretending that these things are dispensable, that she does not need affection, and that she does not believe in, or need to believe in, anything. It has taken someone more cynical and evil than herself to make her aware of the truth.

Hulga now realizes that, compared with Pointer, she is the innocent one. O'Connor's suggestion is that Hulga will soon get the same message we do from Pointer's last words: the result of "believing in nothing" is the kind of depravity of spirit Pointer exhibits, and if she wants to save herself from that she'd better start believing.

Hulga's two names represent her inner conflict between everything she is and everything she is repressing. The name "Joy," of course, is just another of her mother's empty clichés, so she changes it to Hulga (which suggests some combination of the words *ugly, huge,* and *hulk*). By denying the "nice" name her mother gave her, she can deny the "niceness" in herself. She can, in fact, create a new self: hostile, angry, and abusive — all to hide the pain she feels because of what she is repressing. Mrs. Hopewell's name emphasizes the shallowness of her beliefs that "nothing is perfect" (11) and that "people who looked on the bright side of things would be beautiful even if they were not" (17). And Mrs. Freeman's name suggests that she is free in a way that both Joy and her mother are not.

Mrs. Freeman sees through Hulga as her mother can't; direct the class to paragraph 16, where we learn that Mrs. Freeman calls the girl "Hulga" rather than "Joy." "Mrs. Freeman's relish for using the name only irritated [Hulga]. It was as if Mrs. Freeman's beady steel-pointed eyes had penetrated far enough behind her face to reach some secret fact." This secret fact is that, as the author says in "O'Connor on Theme and Symbol" (text p. 423), "there is a wooden part of [Hulga's] soul that corresponds to her wooden leg." Mrs. Freeman's statement at the story's end, "Some can't be that simple," suggests that she has seen through the Bible salesman as well. That Mrs. Hopewell repeatedly refers to Mrs. Freeman with condescension as "good country people" becomes increasingly ironic in light of the fact that Mrs. Freeman is much smarter and a much better judge of human nature than either her employer or her employer's daughter.

The older women are introduced before Hulga so that her character can be developed in relation to theirs. By the time Hulga appears, we are as alienated by her mother's insipid thoughts and conversation as Hulga is, so we can empathize with the girl somewhat. The last two paragraphs of the story depict an unchanged, vapidly optimistic Mrs. Hopewell, who knows nothing of what has gone on between Hulga and Pointer in the barn. Her cheerful ignorance contrasts sharply with Hulga's "churning face" and emotions in the preceding paragraph; it is Mrs. Hopewell who has the most to learn.

The limited omniscient point of view lets O'Connor alternate between Mrs. Hopewell's and Hulga's perspectives, giving us access to the actions and thoughts of both characters and allowing us to make informed judgments that we would not be able to make if we were limited to Hulga's point of view.

POSSIBLE CONNECTIONS TO OTHER SELECTIONS

Ernest Hemingway, "Soldier's Home" (text p. 145)
Flannery O'Connor, "Revelation" (text p. 407)

Revelation (p. 407)

As a member of "the home-and-land owner" class, Mrs. Turpin believes herself to be superior to "niggers," "white-trash," and mere "home-owners" (paragraph 24). She takes pride in her position in the community, and far worse in O'Connor's credo, she takes pride in what she perceives to be her privileged position in relation to God. In paragraph 74 she thinks, "He had not made her a nigger or white-trash or ugly! He had made her herself and given her a little of everything. Jesus, thank you! she said. Thank you thank you thank you!" She believes that she was singled out to have this high station, along with her other virtues. In other words, she believes that she is saved and has nothing to worry about on Judgment Day. The gospel music on the radio in the doctor's office adds an extra ironic twist. Note, in paragraph 21, that Mrs. Turpin can supply the song's "last line mentally"; this is a gesture of routine rather than one that comes from the heart. Mrs. Turpin takes God and his mercy for granted; she might as well be singing along with a toothpaste commercial.

Among the signals Mrs. Turpin misses but we comprehend is the parallel between the doctor's waiting room and Mrs. Turpin's pig parlor. A close reading of paragraphs 173-181 will reveal that Mrs. Turpin sees the hogs as interchangeable rather than individuals. She is unable, however, to make the connection to the group of people in the doctor's office, or to humanity in general — which she still, this late in the story, insists on dividing into classes. It is in this context, too, that we understand Mrs. Turpin's hired woman's comment "You just had you a little fall" (147). It suggests that she has fallen from God's grace, at least in part because she thought she could earn and control it.

In paragraphs 178-186 Mrs. Turpin is addressing God; her anger and confusion stem from the fact that she really does believe herself to be a good person; it is not until the end of the story that she realizes her prideful hypocrisy. So at this point she feels that the message that she is a warthog from hell is unwarranted, that God has tricked her somehow and is being cruel and unfair. The truth is revealed to her in the story's last two paragraphs, when "a visionary light settled in her eyes" (191). According to Frederick Asals, the "abysmal" knowledge Mrs. Turpin receives is that "those like herself, who had possessed 'good order and common sense and respectable behavior,' who had been blessed with a 'God-given wit,' discover that although these gifts are apparently their worldly responsibility, they have no final value in themselves." But the message is also "life-giving," or at least has the potential to be so:

> The visionary procession of "Revelation" clearly carried into eternity . . . the purifying action of the fire itself. Indeed . . . the imaginary fire in O'Connor's fiction . . . is most often purgatorial . . . and what it signals is the infliction of a searing grace, the onset of a saving pain. (Frederick Asals, *Flannery O'Connor: The Imagination of Extremity* [Athens: U of Georgia P, 1982], 225-226)

We see that Mrs. Turpin has at least a chance for redemption, although there will be a high price to pay.

Mary Grace attacks Mrs. Turpin partly because she is a messenger from God, partly because she is disturbed, and partly, we suspect, because she recognizes (perhaps through her God-given vision as a lunatic) Mrs. Turpin for the hypocrite she is. Mary Grace's name, of course, suggests redemption. Because she is ugly and nasty, Mrs. Turpin feels superior to her, so it is fitting that Mary Grace deliver the divine message: that Mrs. Turpin might as well be a warthog from hell for all the good her "virtues" will do her on Judgment Day. Further irony comes from the title of Mary Grace's textbook; in O'Connor's Catholic vision, human development can't be studied, or controlled, by humans; it is all in the hands of God. (If it could be controlled, why would the little boy have an ulcer? Why would Mary Grace be a lunatic?)

The humor in this story (as well as in the rest of O'Connor's work) is bitter, but it helps to cut the pain of the characters by introducing a measure of buoyancy, a light at the end of the tunnel. O'Connor's is a tragicomic vision; she recognized that while humanity's folly is great, it is also funny. But humor, in literature and in life, has always operated as a defense mechanism, to help people bear their trials and tragedies. This is one of the reasons O'Connor's work resonates even for readers with no religious faith. (See question #3 after "O'Connor on the Use of Exaggeration and Distortion" [p. 423]). Humor is universal, as are O'Connor's concerns with hypocrisy and truth.

POSSIBLE CONNECTIONS TO OTHER SELECTIONS

Emily Dickinson, "What Soft — Cherubic Creatures — " (text p. 940)
Ralph Ellison, "Battle Royal" (text p. 223)
Flannery O'Connor, "Good Country People" (text p. 392)
———, "A Good Man Is Hard to Find" (text p. 381)
John Updike, "A & P" (text p. 576)

PERSPECTIVES ON O'CONNOR

O'Connor on Faith (p. 421)

At the end of "Good Country People," Hulga appears to be a likely candidate to "cherish the world at the same time that [she struggles] to endure it." Ask the students to explain how and why this change comes about.

O'Connor on the Materials of Fiction (p. 422)

Passages that appeal through the senses, that dwell on "those concrete details of life that make actual the mystery of our position on earth" abound in O'Connor's stories.

Some examples you might cite, or direct the class to, include the descriptions of Mrs. Freeman's facial expressions in the first paragraph of "Good Country People"; Hulga's appreciation of the sound of her own name (16); Hulga's perceptions of taste and touch in paragraph 113, when she and Pointer are kissing in the loft; Mrs. Turpin's visual perceptions immediately after being struck by Mary Grace's book in "Revelation" (102); the passage describing the road supposedly leading to the house with the secret panel in "A Good Man Is Hard to Find" (60).

O'Connor on the Use of Exaggeration and Distortion (p. 423)

Both the theft of Hulga's leg and Mrs. Turpin's vision can be seen as events or actions that purify the main characters.

For a specific response as to whether O'Connor's stories have anything to offer a reader without religious faith, see the comments in the last paragraph of this manual's entry for "Revelation" (pp. 80–81).

O'Connor on Theme and Symbol (p. 423)

O'Connor argues that "the peculiar problem of the short-story writer is how to make the action he describes reveal as much of the mystery of existence as possible" (paragraph 2), and she cautions against our overlooking the literal resonance of her work in pursuit of symbolic meaning. Encourage students to identify both the literal and symbolic significance of some aspect of O'Connor's fiction. For instance, Mary Grace's response to Mrs. Turpin in "Revelation," "Go back to hell where you came from, you old warthog" (112), has literal as well as symbolic impact. What is especially apt about O'Connor's choice of language here?

JOSEPHINE HENDIN, *On O'Connor's Refusal to "Do Pretty"* (p. 425)

What are the differences between the example referred to by Hendin and the instances in O'Connor's fiction in which a character refuses to "do pretty"? What exactly is O'Connor refusing in this anecdote? What are characters such as Mary Grace in "Revelation" objecting to? Are there other significant differences between the fictional and biographical examples?

CLAIRE KAHANE, *The Function of Violence in O'Connor's Fiction* (p. 425)

Ask students to assess the types of violent acts that occur in O'Connor's fiction. Is there a pattern to this violence? Do certain characters experience more violent acts than others? How would students define "violence" within the context of O'Connor's stories?

EDWARD KESSLER, *On O'Connor's Use of History* (p. 426)

Kessler asserts that "in O'Connor's fiction, the past neither justifies nor even explains what is happening" (paragraph 1). Ask students to identify O'Connor's characters' perspectives on their histories — for instance, what does the Misfit's description of his past in "A Good Man Is Hard to Find" explain about his behavior? How often are the characters' pasts in some way a source for the prideful behavior that leads to their downfalls? Based on such examples, do students agree or disagree with Kessler's argument?

TWO COMPLEMENTARY CRITICAL READINGS

A. R. COULTHARD, *On the Visionary Ending of "Revelation"* (p. 427)

Coulthard argues that "the second part of the story does not keep pace with its rollicking opening" (paragraph 1). Do students agree with this? In what way is the opening "rollicking," and how does the ending contrast with it? Ask students to concretely compare some aspect of the early portion of the story with a portion of the ending in order to confirm or contradict Coulthard's assertion.

Coulthard also suggests that "Ruby begins to grow into a sympathetic, even lovable character" (2). Are we more sympathetic toward Mrs. Turpin than we might be toward other O'Connor characters? What elements of the text might inspire our sympathy for her?

MARSHALL BRUCE GENTRY, *On the Revised Ending of "Revelation"* (p. 429)

Ask students to define the term *revelation*, and then to apply their definitions to the ending. How does O'Connor's revision of the ending increase its connection to the fiery, apocalyptic, biblical book bearing the same title? Do students agree with Gentry that "the final version makes the vision more clearly redemptive" (paragraph 2)? Does Mrs. Turpin's revelation at the end of the story seem self-produced or imposed on her?

ADDITIONAL RESOURCES FOR TEACHING O'CONNOR

SELECTED BIBLIOGRAPHY

Bacon, Jon Lance. *Flannery O'Connor and Cold War Culture.* Cambridge: Cambridge UP, 1993.

Bloom, Harold, ed. *Flannery O'Connor.* New York: Chelsea, 1986.

Brinkmeyer, Robert H., Jr. *The Art and Vision of Flannery O'Connor.* Baton Rouge: Louisiana State UP, 1989.

Feeley, Kathleen. *Flannery O'Connor: Voice of the Peacock.* New Brunswick: Rutgers UP, 1972.

Friedman, Melvin J., and Beverly Lyon Clark, eds. *Critical Essays on Flannery O'Connor.* Boston: G. K. Hall, 1985.

Grimshaw, James A. *The Flannery O'Connor Companion.* Westport: Greenwood, 1981.

Johansen, Ruthann Knechel. *The Narrative Secret of Flannery O'Connor: The Trickster as Interpreter.* Tuscaloosa: U of Alabama P, 1994.

O'Connor, Flannery. *The Complete Stories.* New York: Farrar, 1971.

——. *Conversations with Flannery O'Connor.* Ed. Rosemary M. Magee. Jackson: UP of Mississippi, 1987.

——. *The Habit of Being: The Letters of Flannery O'Connor.* Ed. Sally Fitzgerald. New York: Farrar, 1979.

——. *Mystery and Manners.* Ed. Sally Fitzgerald and Robert Fitzgerald. New York: Farrar, 1969.

——. *The Presence of Grace and Other Book Reviews.* Comp. Leo J. Zuber. Ed. Carter W. Martin. Athens: U of Georgia P, 1983.

——. *The Violent Bear It Away.* New York: Farrar, 1960.

——. *Wise Blood.* New York: Harcourt, 1952.

ALICE MUNRO

An Ounce of Cure (p. 434)

Part of the charm of "An Ounce of Cure" is Munro's humorous characterization of many aspects of adolescent life. She recalls nearly universal teenage experiences, and her wry tendencies toward both understatement and exaggeration serve her well here. Many traditional students (who would be only a year or two beyond the kind of experiences detailed in this story) will find it easy to relate to aspects of this story.

Although the plot — the narrator's recollection of her first crush, her senior year in high school, and her first experience with alcohol — will be enough to attract readers' attention, the rich characterization should also be a source for discussion. Students should realize that the strong narrative voice benefits from perspective on the events described in "An Ounce of Cure": the narrator is looking back on this story with far more wisdom, experience, and humor than she could have mustered right after it happened. In a key passage, she alludes to this added perspective and to the striking difference time makes: "Why is it a temptation to refer to this sort of thing lightly, with irony, with amazement even, at finding oneself involved with such preposterous emotions in the unaccountable past? That is what we are apt to do, speaking of love; with adolescent love, of course, it's practically obligatory" (paragraph 5). Students might identify passages that ring with irony throughout the story. They might also consider writing passages of their own that feature the same narrator telling her story the morning after her adventure at the Berrymans', or at graduation, or even at the end of her college career. It might be interesting to discover how different amounts of time affect our perspectives on the past.

One of the strengths of "An Ounce of Cure" is its strong characterization. The narrator, her mother, and even fairly minor characters are fully developed; we understand and appreciate their predicaments. For instance, the narrator's friend Joyce is the quintessential best friend — the kind of person who calls the narrator the morning after the prom to suitably denigrate the date who attended with the narrator's former boyfriend: "yes, M.C. *had* been there with M.B., and she had on a formal that must have been made out of somebody's old lace tablecloth, it just *hung*" (7). Kay Stringer, whom the narrator meets as a result of her brush with the alcohol, turns out to have "a great female instinct to manage, comfort, and control" (20) — nurselike assets that the narrator recognizes years later in a maternity ward (24). We also find an insightful perspective on Mr. Berryman's probable state of mind as he drives the narrator home: "I suppose that besides being angry and disgusted with *me*, he was worried about taking me home in this condition to my strait-laced parents, who could always say I got the liquor in his house. Plenty of Temperance people would think that enough to hold him responsible, and the town was full of Temperance people. Good relations with the town were very important to him from a business point of view" (31). Not only do we perceive an individual character's motivation here, but we also have a broader sense of the community. In keeping with the information that the narrator took a temperance pledge in seventh grade, and that her mother had to take the bus to the next town to acquire a new bottle of scotch to replace the one the narrator filled with water, we have a clear sense of a time and a place that might be nearly unrecognizable otherwise to students in the 1990s.

Munro's use of description is strikingly original. Consider, for instance, the narrator's (academic) expectation of the effects of alcohol: "I had thought of some sweeping emotional change, an upsurge of gaiety and irresponsibility, a feeling of lawlessness and escape, accompanied by a little dizziness and perhaps a tendency to giggle out loud" (13) — in part a splendid foreshadowing of some of her behavior a few hours later. The matter-of-fact sentence "I reached up and turned on a floor lamp beside the chair, and the room jumped on me" (12) eloquently and visually depicts the way the narrator felt as the alcohol worked its way into her system. Encourage students to examine the story for other moments when the description evokes a significant reader response.

On her way to disaster at the Berrymans', the narrator acknowledges, "My approach [to the alcohol] could not have been less casual if I had been the Little Mermaid drinking the witch's crystal potion" (11). It might be fruitful for students to reread the original Hans Christian Andersen fairy tale and develop an analogy between the situations of the Little Mermaid and Munro's narrator. Each heroine drinks because of great romantic longing for an unattainable boy. Considered together, these stories might lead to an especially fruitful discussion of fantasy and reality in connection with adolescence, gender, and culture.

POSSIBLE CONNECTIONS TO OTHER SELECTIONS

George Bowering, "A Short Story" (text p. 298)
Susan Minot, "Lust" (text p. 200)
David Updike, "Summer" (text p. 169)

How I Met My Husband (p. 442)

Most students will recognize and appreciate this straightforward, realistic, first-person coming-of-age story as exactly that. The narrator is looking back on herself at age fifteen, presenting these events (which do lead up to her meeting the man who will become her husband) as she remembers them, adding occasional adult insights in retrospect.

Ask the class whether the title is in any way misleading. It suggests that we will read a story about a courtship or romantic encounter — which will involve the narrator and a man the narrator will eventually marry. And we believe this is what we're reading about, just as Edie believes Chris will write to her, until the day she suddenly realizes he won't. (Most readers, especially those older and wiser than Edie, realize Chris won't write to her a little sooner than she does.) So the title becomes gently ironic, since Edie meets her husband by waiting for the mail every day, smiling not for Carmichael the mailman but in anticipation of a letter from Chris.

Direct students' attention to the last sentence of the story, particularly the last phrase: "because I like for people to think what pleases them and makes them happy." The narrator is able to speak this line now — but did she always feel this way?

Edie can feel generous because she is a mature and happy adult. But she wasn't this giving as a naive and definitely opinionated adolescent. She didn't think highly of the Peebleses, especially Mrs. Peebles, who didn't bake, had only two children and no barn work, complained about living in the country, and generally, as Edie saw it, didn't know the meaning of good hard work. And Edie certainly didn't want Alice Kelling to be happy. But in retrospect Edie disapproves of her own behavior. "You'd think I'd be ashamed of myself, setting her on the wrong track.... Women should stick together and not do things like that. I see that now, but didn't then" (paragraph 157). It is Edie's maturity, along with her own happiness, that gives her this warmer, more accepting attitude toward other people and toward life.

Prue (p. 454)

Gordon's vacillating nature is indicated in the first paragraph when we learn of his uncertain, wavering relationships with his wife and Prue. He is a big man with little or no ability to make decisions about his emotional life. Now divorced, he says he wants to marry Prue even though he is in love with a "quite young" woman who twice appears, frustrated and angry, at his door. Gordon is a successful neurologist who, ironically, makes everyone around him nervous: "He doesn't know why people laugh or throw their overnight bags at him, but he's noticed they do" (paragraph 28).

Prue's feelings for and devotion to Gordon may not be admirable, but they are believable. Through her "anecdotes," the reader senses that Prue accepts her life, even if it consists mostly of dashed hopes, broken dreams, and thwarted expectations that leave her with hardly any understanding of why such things happen to her. She, however, "never makes any real demands or complaints" about her life. She appears to be determinedly "cheerful" and ever willing to look on the bright side of people's behavior, including her lover's encounters with another woman. The only thing she allows herself to complain about is her name.

Prue's name retains for her a kind of "schoolgirl" identity that is as unsatisfactory to her as the name "Prudence," which conjures up images of "an old virgin" (3). Prue is clearly not afraid of sex; she is not a prude. As a woman in her late forties, she finds neither name suitable, though she acknowledges that her personality — "bright and thoughtful, and a cheerful spectator" — makes it hard "to grant her maturity, maternity [or any] real troubles" (3). Her life is hardly what she thought it would be, but she attends to it, along with her customers at the plant shop, with a dutiful vivacity. Her children wish more for her, and she listens to their advice, but "like a flighty daughter, [she] neglects to answer their letters" (4).

Prue is prudent: she's careful, judicious, and considerate of others, but she is also attentive to her own interests, as is evidenced by her taking Gordon's cufflink. If the conflict of this story centers on Prue's inability to have Gordon, then she resolves the conflict by taking his cufflink, which he bought when he returned to his wife, and placing it in an old tobacco tin. This tin, once stuffed with sweets and given to Prue by her children as a substitute for smoking, now serves to keep her from ruining her mental as well as her physical health. The small pieces of Gordon's life stored in the tin give her just enough satisfaction to allow her to feel in control of their relationship. This little "piece of nonsense" (39) alerts us to one possible theme for the story: as "unintense" and "civilized" (2) as Prue is, she does have flashes of deep emotion that subtly suggest how painful and bereft her life has been.

In a sense, Gordon also steals from Prue, but he does not steal only bits and pieces. Whereas Gordon is a "doughty fortress" (20) oblivious to the pain he causes, Prue's life is hidden "in the dark of the old tobacco tin," which she "more or less forgets about" (41) as much as she can. If students are invited to speculate upon what will become of Gordon and Prue, their responses will probably focus on the degree to which they think Prue can confront Gordon directly rather than symbolically. The incidents and descriptions of Prue in the story suggest that she will not make demands on Gordon, because she "doesn't take herself too seriously" (2). It seems likely that Gordon won't take her very seriously either.

POSSIBLE CONNECTIONS TO OTHER SELECTIONS

Colette, "The Hand" (text p. 220)
Katherine Mansfield, "Miss Brill" (text p. 258)

Miles City, Montana (p. 458)

Students may find the incident involving Meg and the swimming pool the most accessible aspect of "Miles City, Montana." They should study in particular the way Munro builds suspense and foreshadows Meg's ability and self-preservation. In addition, the narrator's feelings about parents and children are a significant aspect of the story, one that draws connections between Meg's experience in the pool and Steve Gauley's drowning. Finally, the narrator's thoughts about marriage and her acknowledgment that her marriage to Roger does not endure are also of importance.

The narrator's youngest daughter, Meg, is only three and a half (paragraph 7); initially, she seems far less knowledgeable than her older sister. When Cynthia says goodbye to their house as they leave on their trip to Ontario, Meg asks, "Where will we live now?" (13). Cynthia makes fun of her, and Meg seems very much the baby sister. Later, when Cynthia goes into the dressing room to change into her bathing suit, the narrator changes Meg's clothes in the car: "her body still had the solid unself-consciousness, the sweet indifference, something of the milky smell, of a baby's body" (126). These characterizations lead us to believe that Meg is more helpless than she really is and enhance the suspense of the scene where Meg falls into the pool. However, there are also several ways that Munro foreshadows Meg's survival. First, the narrator tells us that "Meg was more solidly built, more reticent — not rebellious but stubborn sometimes, mysterious. Her silences seemed to us to show her strength of character, and her negatives were taken as signs of an imperturbable independence" (32). Second, when Meg wants to see the maps of their road trip, Cynthia confidently asserts, "You won't understand" (25). However, even though Cynthia rearranges the maps in order to challenge her, Meg can still find the right location on the right map. Third, when the parents and Cynthia are playing "Who Am I," only Meg knows Cynthia's "identity." (This game is also known as "Twenty Questions." Why is it significant that Munro chooses to refer to it as "Who Am I"? Invite students to discuss the possible connections between this title and its meaning for each of the characters riding in the car.)

Munro begins the story with the description of Steve Gauley's drowning and funeral (1–6). She returns to this subject near the end of the story (154–56). Invite students to compare the circumstances of Steve Gauley's drowning with Meg's experience in the pool. (Notice that when the narrator describes each, she incorporates both memories of and suppositions about the event.) Focus as well on the narrator's thoughts about family and parenthood in connection with both events. In the earlier incident, she is the daughter, the playmate of the drowned child (notice that there is nearly the same age difference between Steve and the narrator as there is between Cynthia and Meg — and nearly the same relationship, in which the older child semitorments the younger). She remembers her parents' involvement with Steve Gauley: her father carried the body home, while her mother organized the funeral. Most clearly, she remembers feeling "a furious and sickening disgust." Encourage students to explain what it is that disgusts the child narrator about her parents. Is it that they haven't been able to protect the children? Is it that she is newly aware of her parents' limitations and imperfections? As an adult, she acknowledges, "I thought that I was understanding something about them for the first time. It was a deadly serious thing. I was understanding that they were implicated. Their big, stiff, dressed-up bodies did not stand between me and sudden death, or any kind of death" (154). Students might compare her attitude toward her parents with her assessment of Steve Gauley's father. Why is he excused from her anger? He has been a less than capable (or traditional) parent. His wife has left him; he barely keeps his house (and his child) together. Is it because he has never pretended an omnipotence that the narrator feels "he was the only one I didn't see giving consent. He couldn't prevent anything, but he wasn't implicated in anything, either — not like the others, saying the Lord's Prayer in their unnaturally weighted voices, oozing religion and dishonor" (156)?

In the end, the question remains: what does the incident in the pool tell us about the narrator, about her attitudes toward motherhood and marriage? Prior to arriving in Miles City, the narrator divides her world into different types of mothers: "I had a dread of turning into a certain kind of mother — the kind whose body sagged, who moved in a woolly-smelling, milky-smelling fog, solemn with trivial burdens. . . . I favored another approach — the mock desperation, the inflated irony of the professional mothers who wrote for magazines. In those magazine pieces, the children were splendidly self-willed, hard-edged, perverse, indomitable. So were the mothers, through their wit, indomitable" (33). Though her children display the admirable traits of magazine-children, it is possible that the narrator's instincts, her fear, her tremendous relief, and her guilt after the incident at the pool have shaken her out of her pose as an "indomitable" mother. In addition, she now has a parent's perspective of a near-drowning to contrast with her childhood observance of Steve Gauley's drowning and funeral, which provides her with insight and compassion for her own parents: "So we went on, with the two in the back seat trusting us, because of no choice, and we ourselves trusting to be forgiven, in time, for everything that had first to be seen and condemned by those children: whatever was flippant, arbitrary, careless, callous — all our natural, and particular, mistakes" (168).

Ask students to characterize the narrator's marriage to Roger. Is there any foreshadowing that the marriage will dissolve? Certainly there are the regular, petty disputes: why didn't the narrator put lettuce on the salmon sandwiches? Why hasn't the narrator sent her family the pictures that Roger carefully labels? In fact, many of their disagreements involve Roger's dissatisfaction with what he perceives as the narrator's shortcomings. There are also indications that though they agree on many things at this point in their lives, Roger, in contrast to the narrator, will grow increasingly conservative. Roger's world and the narrator's are in many ways separate. (One wonders where and how they met.) Her parents were working-class farmers; his upbringing (through his aunt and uncle's intervention) was more upper-class, privileged (private schools, summer camp). Hence, Roger cannot relax among the turkey crew, and the narrator cannot have a conversation with Roger's uncle, who regards her as suspiciously "communist" and represents the Establishment — he "was on the board of directors of several companies" (71). Roger loves to acquire; the narrator loves to free herself from acquisition (hence the extended road trip). As she tells us, "I was happy because of the shedding. I loved taking off. . . . I wanted to hide so that I could get busy at my real work, which was a sort of wooing of distant parts of myself" (22). It is significant that she describes herself as a "watcher, not a keeper" (22): this statement applies not only to her sense of herself but her identity as a wife and a mother. Ask students to free-associate with the terms "watcher" and "keeper." In what ways do these terms relate to the narrator's thoughts about her children, her husband, her parents, and her future?

POSSIBLE CONNECTIONS TO OTHER SELECTIONS

T. S. Eliot, "The Love Song of J. Alfred Prufrock" (text p. 1045)
Alice Munro, "An Ounce of Cure" (question #1, following)
Flannery O'Connor, "The Turkey" (question #2, following)

CONNECTIONS QUESTIONS IN TEXT (p. 472) **WITH ANSWERS**

1. Compare the narrator in this story with the narrator in Munro's "An Ounce of Cure" (p. 434). Explain why you think their retrospective narrations are different from or similar to each other.

    The narrators in both "Miles City, Montana" and "An Ounce of Cure" consider the ways their childhood or adolescent experiences shaped their self-images as adults. In addition, both stories examine the relationship between parents and children. For both narrators, distance adds perspective: for the woman in "Miles City, Montana," her experiences as a parent leaven her anger at her parents for their lack of omnipotence. For the narrator of "An Ounce of Cure," her adult experiences give her the ability to perceive the way that the cultural expectations fostered in her hometown affected not only her teenage self but her parents and her neighbors as well. Understanding them, she forgives them. However, the narrator of "Miles City, Montana" reflects a more somber tone about her realizations, whereas the narrator of "An Ounce of Cure" achieves a more humorous perspective.

2. How might Steve Gauley be seen as a version of Ruller in Flannery O'Connor's "The Turkey" (p. 373)? How is childhood presented in each story?

    Both Steve and Ruller might be seen as neglected children. Steve's mother has left the family; his father can barely keep the house together (literally) and food on the table. There are problems in Ruller's family as well: his older brother has become a delinquent and his parents argue frequently. Both boys try not to call attention to themselves or to cause trouble for their parents. Neither boy spends a great deal of time at home. However, we never know a great deal about Steve's character because he is more of a device for Munro's protagonist's observations: he appears only in flashback, playing with (and harassing) the protagonist on Saturdays, or as a dead body in the protagonist's father's arms. Ruller, in contrast, is much more thoroughly characterized: his stream-of-consciousness thoughts about his family, his games, and his religion are fully characterized for readers.

RESOURCE FOR TEACHING

  Interview with Alice Munro [recording]. 1 cassette (72 min.). Munro discusses influences, feminism, and Canadian literature. Distributed by American Audio Prose Library.

PERSPECTIVES ON MUNRO

GRAEME GIBSON, *An Interview with Munro on Writing* (p. 472)

  As Munro indicates in the interview, she sees herself as a writer concerned less with "ideas" than with "the surface of life." This, of course, is not to say that her stories are devoid of ideas, but rather that their ideas — or meanings — are inseparable from the materials of the stories themselves. The characters, actions, settings, and language *are* the stories' meanings rather than mere illustrations of themes that are neatly tied up in the concluding paragraph. Munro's sense of alienation from her environment also helps to explain this point, because her "different view of the world" has taught her "to disguise everything" in order to avoid "great trouble and ridicule." Symbol, metaphor, and subtlety are therefore natural as well as strategic forms of expression for Munro.

BENJAMIN DeMOTT, *On Munro's Female Protagonists* (p. 474)

DeMott's description of Munro's heroines captures some of the fascinating qualities of her female protagonists. They are sensitive, savvy, self-reliant, and smart while simultaneously revealing their vulnerabilities and limitations. Her characters seem to be exquisitely aware of their mistakes, and that is part of their personal triumph and the reason they are appealing. If they "regret" any of their experiences, they are also committed to relishing them, because, finally, they locate authority in themselves rather than in relatives, lovers, friends, or society.

CATHERINE SHELDRICK ROSS, *On the Reader's Experience in Reading Munro's Stories* (p. 474)

"Recognition" is certainly central to Munro's fiction. In her "arrangement of materials" she is less concerned with what happens next (though she does create delectably suspenseful moments in her stories, as when we wonder what Mr. Berryman will do about the narrator's drunkenness in "An Ounce of Cure") than with what her characters understand — or don't understand — about their experiences. Ask students if the reader of the stories comprehends more about the meanings of the characters' experiences than do the characters themselves.

W. R. MARTIN, *On Prue's Suppressed Passions* (p. 475)

Martin's reading of Prue's "suppressed passions" indicates that she cannot acknowledge the anger she feels about Gordon's treatment of her. Her way of coping with that anger is to take her revenge in the mildly subversive gesture of stealing a single cufflink. As small as Prue's gesture might seem, it can be read as an expression of her frustration with Gordon and as an attempt to exercise some small measure of control over him. Her taking only one cufflink indicates a very measured and precise response, a prudent one, calculated to keep him wondering about the missing cufflink, rather than forgetting about it.

GEORGE WOODCOCK, *On Symbolism in Munro's Fiction* (p. 476)

Woodcock's discussion of "visuality" and "surfaces" in Munro's fiction nicely complements what Munro says about the "surface of life" in her interview with Graeme Gibson (p. 472). The emphasis Woodcock places upon "the power of image" in Munro's short stories implies that her work must be read very closely, despite its smooth surfaces, in order to discover the layers of textured meaning embedded in what is "There." The magic of her work — its subtle effects conveyed directly by experience — is discovered in careful readings that alert readers to meanings hovering around the surface of things. If students pay attention to the details in Munro's fiction, they don't have to worry about reading between the lines.

ROBERT HAMPSON, *On the Reader's Expectations in "How I Met My Husband"* (p. 477)

Hampson carefully traces how the title sets up expectations that the story thwarts until its final three paragraphs, when we see that it is the mailman that Edie marries. Some students may feel "cheated" by this surprising turn of events, but many will be delighted by the deception because Edie's waiting finally ends at the same time that the rest of her life begins. Hampson's assertion that "the invitation to interpret in whatever way you wish undermines any claim to value in that interpretation" seems to posit a professional critic rather than a general reader as Munro's audience, an assumption that could be worth discussing with students.

TWO COMPLEMENTARY CRITICAL READINGS

Munro on Narration in "An Ounce of Cure" (p. 478)

Munro's observation that the narrator of "An Ounce of Cure" becomes an "observer" rather than a "participant" offers an important insight into the true value of the narrator's "hopelessly messy" experience of getting drunk. By observing her own life, the narrator makes a "glorious leap" from "ineptness and self-conscious miseries to being a godlike arranger of patterns and destinies." Like Munro herself, the narrator discovers that telling a story is a way of controlling its meaning and value.

LORRAINE McMULLEN, *On Munro's Ironic Humor in "An Ounce of Cure"* (p. 479)

As McMullen suggests, irony is central to Munro's "view of humanity and events." Munro characteristically demonstrates that people and events are not always what they seem to be, especially when events are regarded from the perspective that time and distance can provide — as they are in "An Ounce of Cure." Munro's use of ironic humor is the perfect vehicle for taking us from what appears to be true to a discovery of what is real.

11

Critical Case Study:
William Faulkner's "Barn Burning"

Prior to studying the short story by Faulkner contained in Chapter 11, students might study the other short story by this author anthologized in *The Bedford Introduction to Literature*, "A Rose for Emily" (text p. 72). In part, familiarity with other Faulkner works might help students feel more comfortable with the author's unique writing style. In addition, because both stories are set in Faulkner's mythic Yoknapatawpha County, they contain similar references to characters and events. (Colonel John Sartoris, for instance, is the mayor to whom Emily refers the selectmen in the matter of her taxes; he is also the namesake of the protagonist in "Barn Burning," "Sarty" Snopes.) Students might generate ideas about other connections between these stories as well. In particular, the stories' common references to the South prior to and after the Civil War are consistent: Faulkner associates grace, gentility, and a Southern aristocracy with the antebellum South, whereas the modern South is characterized by gas stations and cotton gins ("A Rose for Emily"); Ab Snopes's characterization as a man of rusty tin ("Barn Burning") is consistent with this mechanized view of the post–Civil War South.

If students are curious about Ab Snopes's career as a "privateer" (a horse thief) during the Civil War or his decision to name his youngest son Sarty, direct them to Faulkner's novel *The Unvanquished* (1938), a relatively linear narrative (originally published as a series of short stories in the *Saturday Evening Post* and *Scribner's Magazine*) about Colonel John Sartoris, his son, Bayard, and their exploits during the Civil War and Reconstruction in Jefferson.

WILLIAM FAULKNER, *Barn Burning* (p. 481)

In William Faulkner's "Barn Burning," a boy is continually placed in situations where he must decide whether to support his family and deny his conscience or to uphold society's conventions and act according to his convictions. Within this plot, Faulkner also reveals the concerns and stylistic traits most characteristic of his fiction by emphasizing the innermost thoughts, impressions, and urges of human beings, or as he identified them in his Nobel Prize acceptance speech, "the problems of the human heart in conflict with itself."

The boy, Colonel Sartoris Snopes, is faced with three distinct moments when he must decide whether to stand with his family or with the society that Abner continually battles. The first trial occurs in a small-town general store, the courtroom where Abner is accused of setting fire to another man's property. The boy's initial response is animal: he convinces himself that he and his father face a mutual enemy in the judge. When he is called forward to testify, he realizes that he is in an impossible position, caught between his father and the judge. "He aims for me to lie, he thought, again with that frantic grief and despair. And I will have to do it" (paragraph 7). He has no practical choice; his psychological and economic security stem from his father's favor. All he knows is that he must fight for his father. Yet when the moment to speak arrives, he cannot lie. Both the judge and his father realize this, and the judge settles the trial without forcing the boy to answer. That night, after the family has left the area, Abner hits Sarty, but the real blow is caused by his words: "You were fixing to tell them. You would have told him. . . . You're getting to be a man. You got to learn. You got to learn to stick to your own blood or you ain't going to have any blood to stick to you" (28–29).

Sarty can only hope that he won't be put in such a situation in the next town, but life there is no simpler. The second trial occurs when Abner sues Major de Spain over the value of the rug that he has spitefully ruined. In that courtroom scene, Sarty is hardly considered one of the family. Although he tries to help, he is banished to the back of the room, where he can watch the proceedings with other strangers. This strengthens his own sense of justice because it releases him from the restricted perception of the family. After this incident, his father addresses him as he might a stranger. His honeyed response to Sarty's attempted reassurance is even more distancing, and dangerous, than his normally harsh treatment of the boy: "His father glanced for an instant down at him, the face absolutely calm, the grizzled eyebrows tangled above the cold eyes, the voice almost pleasant, almost gentle: 'You think so? Well, we'll wait till October anyway' " (81). The father immediately mends the wagon, indicating that the family will be making another move long before harvest. His actions completely contradict the comment he has addressed to the son he no longer trusts.

Sarty's third crisis of conscience occurs in the evening, when he knows that his father is about to burn Major de Spain's barn. Finally, he is able to break free from all of his family loyalties and alert the major. He acts according to his conscience, but he must sacrifice his family ties as a result. As he experiences each psychological ordeal during this short period of time, Sarty matures from a scared, dependent child to a young man capable of making moral distinctions and acting on them.

The conflict between this son and his father is indicative of the clash Faulkner saw between the rising, mechanistic, materialistic "New South" and the receding, chivalric "Old South." Abner Snopes is representative of the new breed of southerner. A scavenger in the Civil War, fighting only for his own gain, he is associated with machines and material gain. Faulkner consistently describes him in industrial terms: "The stiff black back, the stiff and implacable limp of the figure which was not dwarfed by the house . . . that impervious quality of something cut ruthlessly from tin, depthless, as though, sidewise to the sun, it would cast no shadow" (41). Snopes clearly displays animosity toward the wealth and gentility of the fading upper classes. His son, on the other hand, feels an inward loyalty to the upper classes and demonstrates that affinity at the end of the story when he alerts Major de Spain. Named for Colonel Sartoris, an honorable southern warrior, Sarty is of the Old South. His immediate response to seeing the de Spain house is relief that his father cannot reach these people: "They are safe from him. People whose lives are a part of this peace and dignity are beyond his touch" (41). The affluence of the house and its furnishings speaks directly to the boy's soul. "The boy, deluged as though by a warm wave by a suave turn of the carpeted stair and a pendant glitter of chandeliers and a mute gleam of gold frames, heard the swift feet and saw her too, a lady" (43). Nothing else in Sarty's "poor white trash" existence has had this effect on him. At heart, Sarty is more a descendant of Major de Spain (a link indicated as well by their names) than he is of the Snopeses' lineage.

The matter of the de Spain carpet also illustrates this conflict between the Old South and the New South. Abner ruins the valuable rug to show his defiance of de Spain wealth. The major enforces the cleansing, and the penalty for ruining the carpet, not as a genuine response to its destruction but to teach Abner some southern manners: "That won't keep Mrs. de Spain quiet but maybe it will teach you to wipe your feet before you enter her house again" (63).

Does the mechanistic southerner succeed, or does old southern gentility prevail? It may be a mixed solution: Sarty escapes and can finally begin living according to his conscience. On the other hand, a blaze has been set, and there are other Snopeses to continue these acts of arson. If students are interested in reading more about the fortunes of the Snopes family, including Abner's horsetrading career and the effect of the spotted horses on the town in which Sarty has seen them advertised, they should be directed to Faulkner's Snopes trilogy: *The Hamlet, The Town,* and *The Mansion.*

Students may find themselves sympathetic to Abner Snopes's instinctual rebellion against an economic system that builds wealth for a few individuals at the expense of black and white labor: "He stood for a moment, planted stiffly on the stiff foot, looking back at the house. 'Pretty and white, ain't it?' he said. 'That's sweat. Nigger sweat. Maybe it ain't white enough yet to suit him. Maybe he wants to mix some white sweat with it'" (46). You might raise the idea of Abner's defiance as socioeconomic protest as a topic for discussion.

POSSIBLE CONNECTIONS TO OTHER SELECTIONS

Andre Dubus, "Killings" (text p. 81)
William Faulkner, "A Rose for Emily" (text p. 72)
Bessie Head, "The Prisoner Who Wore Glasses" (text p. 587)
Flannery O'Connor, "A Good Man Is Hard to Find" (text p. 381)

RESOURCES FOR TEACHING

Barn Burning. 41 min., color, 1980. Beta, VHS, 16-mm film. With Tommy Lee Jones. Same program available in "The American Short Story II" series. See local retailer.

The Long Hot Summer. 118 min., color, 1958. Beta, VHS. A film adaptation of "Barn Burning." Directed by Martin Ritt. With Paul Newman, Orson Welles, Joanne Woodward, Lee Remick, Anthony Franciosa, Angela Lansbury, and Richard Anderson. See local retailer.

The Long Hot Summer. 172 min., color, 1986. Beta, VHS. A made-for-TV version of "Barn Burning." Directed by Stuart Cooper. With Don Johnson, Cybill Shepherd, Judith Ivey, Jason Robards, and Ava Gardner. See local retailer.

William Faulkner: A Life on Paper. 2 hrs., color, 1980. Beta, VHS, ¾″ U-matic cassette. A documentary biography. With Lauren Bacall, Howard Hawks, Anita Loos, George Plimpton, Tennessee Williams, and Jill Faulkner Summers (the author's daughter). Distributed by Films, Inc.

William Faulkner's Mississippi. 49 min., color and b/w, 1965. Beta, VHS, ¾″ U-matic cassette. Deals with Faulkner's life and works. Distributed by Benchmark Films.

PERSPECTIVES ON FAULKNER

JANE HILES, *Blood Ties in "Barn Burning"* (p. 494)

In connection with Faulkner's comments on clannishness and the South, students should focus on Sarty's definition of "family" in "Barn Burning" as well as Abner Snopes's own understanding of the concept. At the heart of the story is Sarty's attempt to define the extent of his obligations to the people who have raised him and to understand where his obligations to the community supersede familial responsibilities. In a larger, more spiritual sense, Sarty does reveal a clannishness by eventually siding with the de Spains and the community against Abner.

Students should also apply Faulkner's assertion that southerners have had to learn to support each other since the Civil War to the lecture Abner delivers on the importance of family. Faulkner seems to consider the entire South to be, in some sense, a family. Does Abner's behavior during the war, and following, reveal the contradictions between what he tells Sarty to do and what he himself has done?

BENJAMIN DeMOTT, *Abner Snopes as a Victim of Class* (p. 496)

Any discussion of this perspective will center on DeMott's defense of Abner Snopes, in which he argues for our recognition of "the terrible frustration of an undeveloped mind" (paragraph 5). Are students able to see any nobler aspects in Abner's characterization? If so, where are these aspects revealed in the text?

DeMott also argues that Abner "often behaves with fearful coldness to those who try desperately to communicate the loving respect they feel for him" (1). Are there any characters in addition to Sarty who genuinely feel such emotions? Does Sarty actually feel "loving respect" for Abner? Or is it the romantic ideal of a father — and a soldier — that commands his emotions?

GAYLE EDWARD WILSON, *Conflict in "Barn Burning"* (p. 497)

Once students have a clear understanding of the differences between the Apollonian man and the Paranoid man, ask them to apply these categories to the various characters in the story. In particular, how does Major de Spain reveal characteristics of both types? Does Abner demonstrate any of the characteristics of the Apollonian man? Edward Wilson makes a good case for the application of these types to the characters in Faulkner's story, but it might be fruitful to discuss how these types fail to characterize the complexity of behavior that is revealed in "Barn Burning."

JAMES FERGUSON, *Narrative Strategy in "Barn Burning"* (p. 500)

In this brief selection, Ferguson argues that the narrative intrusions in "Barn Burning" give "the reader insights far beyond the capabilities of the youthful protagonist" (paragraph 1). Ask students to identify other instances than those cited by Ferguson in which they see such a narrative presence in "Barn Burning" and to assess the total effect of such intrusions in a more specific way. For instance, while Ferguson focuses on the way in which the passages he cites work to explain Abner's behavior, they also serve to establish the boundaries of Sarty's character — of what he is capable of comprehending.

AN EXCERPT FROM A SAMPLE PAPER (p. 503)

In this excerpt from Sonia Metzger's essay on "The Fires of Class Conflict in 'Barn Burning,'" she summarizes the arguments posed by two of the authors of critical perspectives on Faulkner's story, Benjamin DeMott and Gayle Edward Wilson. If students are having difficulty summarizing the reading materials, it might be a useful exercise for them to trace Metzger's information by rereading and studying the critical perspectives cited in her paper. If students are more competent at summarizing their reading, they might provide a detailed summary of Metzger's own argument, or of the other two perspectives in this chapter, those by Jane Hiles and James Ferguson.

In addition, students might critique the beginning of this sample student paper as it is excerpted here. The author doesn't get to her thesis until page 3 of her essay. Students might discuss their reactions to this writing strategy. In addition, they should consider ways of constructing an introduction for Metzger's paper that prepares readers for the summaries of the critics (pp. 1–2) but also presents her thesis in a more immediate fashion. Also, they might identify aspects of the text of Faulkner's short story that might serve as useful support for her thesis. Is there any material in the story that supports a counterargument? Finally, students should have the opportunity to respond, in class discussion, small groups, or even in freewriting, to Metzger's ideas. As they grapple with the content and expression of Metzger's work, they may develop important new ideas of their own about Faulkner's story, and on writing about literature in general.

12

Cultural Case Study: James Joyce's "Eveline"

As the introduction to Chapter 12 explains, students should learn to study literary texts not only from a formalist perspective (practicing close readings) but also from other extratextual perspectives. In Chapter 12, students are provided with several resources that might help them learn more about the context in which Joyce wrote "Eveline." Though this story might seem simple and straightforward, particularly until the final paragraph, students are bound to wonder why the protagonist changes her mind at the last minute. The accompanying sources — a photograph, a temperance tract, a letter from an Irish immigrant to a family member, and a synopsis of *The Bohemian Girl* — all help students understand more about the character, time, place, and situation depicted in this story. In combination with the materials about Joyce that lead into the story, these "cultural contexts" help students interpret "Eveline."

After reading the story, and before studying the materials that follow it, invite students to discuss the ways in which the introduction to Joyce's life and work (including the chronology) is particularly helpful in understanding "Eveline." For instance, Joyce's experiences as an expatriate may inform his characterization of the protagonist. In addition, how do the references to Ireland's political and religious situation at the time Joyce was writing the stories that comprise *Dubliners* add depth to the story? Finally, ask students to discuss their ideas about why the material in Joyce's story might have been controversial or subject to censorship. Are there any details in the story that seem particularly libelous?

After reading this story, students may be eager to debate the reasons Eveline refuses to accompany Frank to Buenos Aires. Most of the story leads the reader to expect that she will leave, as it focuses on the many reasons she is unhappy. It would seem that she has nothing to look forward to in Dublin: her father continually harangues her, and the members of her family whom she has truly loved are dead. Her job is not rewarding, and her manager enjoys humiliating her. Why, then, does Eveline decide to stay with her father in Dublin? Readers must examine the text closely to discover the reason for her decision.

Eveline has witnessed the gradual displacement of much of her familiar surroundings. Physically, the place where she has grown up has become more urbanized and modern, resulting in a loss of connections between the people who live there: "One time there used to be a field there in which they used to play every evening with other people's children. Then a man from Belfast bought the field and built houses in it — not like their little brown houses but bright brick houses with shining roofs. The children of the avenue used to play together in that field" (paragraph 2). In addition, her spiritual community of family and friends has been equally fragmented. The people she has loved most — Ernest and her mother — are dead. The children she once played with are either dead or have left the country. As Eveline comes to realize, "Everything changes. Now she was going to go away like the others, to leave her home" (2). Her choice is perhaps less between Frank and her family than between leaving behind the last vestiges of her community — a particular place in Dublin and a particular state of mind — or maintaining it in some fashion.

She has seen what happens when people leave Dublin — they are forgotten by those who remain behind. A good example of this is her father's friend, the priest, whose picture hangs in Eveline's house. She knows that, according to her father, "He is in Melbourne now" (4), but "during all those years she had never found out the name of the priest" (3). What can Eveline expect to be said about her if she leaves for Buenos Aires with Frank, particularly since her father dislikes Frank and has forbidden her to see him? Such a separation from her family would augment the dissolution of the only community she has known.

Students should consider what Frank represents and what he offers to Eveline. Frank has taken her to places she wouldn't ordinarily go, like the theater, and he wants to take her out of the country. He himself is foreign to her experience: he actively enjoys life, calls her by a nickname, and sings. How does he contrast with Eveline's family? What about him attracts her to begin with? How can we reconcile her quiet appreciation of his "foreign" qualities with her ultimate decision to remain in familiar surroundings?

Eveline is reminded of certain familial obligations and attachments as she waits for the evening departure time. The music of the street organ outside reminds her of the night her mother died and of Eveline's "promise to keep the home together as long as she could" (14). At that time, Eveline agreed to uphold her mother's commitment to keeping the family together in some fashion; if she leaves, she will have failed to honor her mother and her mother's values. Since her mother's death she has "had hard work to keep the house together and to see that the two young children who had been left to her charge went to school regularly and got their meals regularly" (9). However, as she thinks about the demands that have been placed upon her, she does not find her life "wholly undesirable" (9). Despite her father's violent propensities, she has observed his tender side: "Her father was becoming old lately, she noticed; he would miss her" (13). In particular she remembers two instances in which he demonstrated a commitment to his family: "Not long before, when she had been laid up for a day, he had read her out a ghost story and made toast for her at the fire. Another day, when their mother was alive, they had all gone for a picnic to the Hill of Howth. She remembered her father putting on her mother's bonnet to make the children laugh" (13). With these familial bonds before her, she prepares to leave with Frank.

The key to Eveline's decision to stay might be found in paragraph 19. Waiting for the boat's departure, "out of a maze of distress, she prayed to God to direct her, to show her what was her duty." In the end, Eveline is motivated by duty to her father and mother, and to her familiar surroundings; she cannot deny her responsibilities. While students may not agree with her decision, a well-rounded discussion of her complex motivations can be thought-provoking and rewarding.

POSSIBLE CONNECTIONS TO OTHER SELECTIONS

Ernest Hemingway, "Soldier's Home" (text p. 145)
Naguib Mahfouz, "The Answer Is No" (text p. 591)

CULTURAL CONTEXTS, "EVELINE"

Photograph of Poole Street, Dublin (p. 516)

This picture of Poole Street, Dublin, provides students with a visual representation of the setting for "Eveline." In Joyce's story, the protagonist remembers when she and her siblings and other children played in the field; now that field has been converted into "bright brick houses with shining roofs" (paragraph 2). The photograph conveys this claustrophobic character of the setting in "Eveline." The protagonist cannot see beyond the "avenue" (literally and figuratively). Within her house, the atmosphere and furnishings are characterized as dusty and "yellowing" (2). She encounters the same people and passes the same houses every day of her life. Paradoxically, she is both exhausted by and attracted to this environment. It stifles her, and yet, it is the only life she can ultimately imagine for herself. The thought of traveling to Buenos Aires (with its connotations of space, frontier, unsettledness) is anathema to her soul. Ask students to compare the protagonist's own "little brown houses" with these new domiciles. How does the "concrete pavement" contrast with "the cinder path"?

Eveline, as the person responsible for taking care of the younger children, feeding the family, and keeping the house neat (when she is not at work), has little opportunity to escape from this environment. And yet, she remains deeply attached to it. Encourage students to imagine what it would be like to grow up in such a setting. For instance, how much privacy might a family have while living in one of these row houses? What would be the benefits and drawbacks of growing up there?

Resources of Ireland (p. 517)

Students should focus on the way the authors of this temperance tract shape their argument about the condition of Ireland. (Study the use of pronouns: "we" and "our" refer to the English.) For the English, this tract is designed to arouse indignation about the waste of resources and the lack of productivity by the Irish people. Since the English, as landlords and overseers for the Irish, resent the loss of their profits and the depreciation of their property as a result of the Irish people's excessive consumption of alcohol (note that the opening line of the tract emphasizes its writers' chief concern with "the great decay of her trade and manufacturers"), you may want to ask students to explore the possible motivations for this tract. In essence, the argument is not founded in humanitarianism. If the Irish were to stop drinking and start producing linens and other commodities mentioned in the tract, they still would reap very little of the profits of their labors. Instead, the English landlords would accumulate the wealth. Why, then, would the Irish find it worthwhile to change their habits?

In connection with this text, students should explore how an awareness of the Irish propensity for alcoholism adds meaning to "Eveline." This tract is of particular relevance to Eveline's characterization of her father and her economic circumstances. Mr. Hill is commonly drunk and abusive: "Even now, though she was over nineteen, she sometimes felt herself in danger of her father's violence. She knew it was that that had given her the palpitations. When they were growing up he had never gone for her, like he used to go for Harry and Ernest, because she was a girl; but latterly he had begun to threaten her and say what he would do to her only for her dead mother's sake" (9). Her father's alcoholism is longstanding, although Eveline convinces herself that during her childhood, he was "not so bad" (2). It is also an economic reality for her that the majority of the family's financial resources (including all of her own salary and some of her brother's, as well as whatever her father earns) are to be pocketed by her father and used for alcohol. Though he gives her some funds for family groceries, he consumes a substantial amount of the family's resources. It is ironic that he refuses to give Eveline money because "he wasn't going to give her his hard-earned money to throw about the streets" (9); he himself is going to waste the same money in the local pubs.

In addition, in the closing paragraph of the excerpt, the authors reveal an inherent rivalry with the Americans (previously in the position of the Irish, tenants of the British): "Have we nothing to learn from America, where, by the associated efforts of the sober and intelligent for the purpose of discouraging the use of ardent spirits, their consumption is already diminished one-third throughout the whole Union?" (6). Students might compare the reaction of the American colonists to English rule (revolution) with the response of the Irish (despair, submission, inebriation). Students also should decide whether the tract writers are motivated more by concern for their fellow man or by greed.

In connection with this tract, written from the English perspective, it might be useful to introduce the students to all or part of Jonathan Swift's famous and satiric essay, "A Modest Proposal." Swift, an Irishman, writes with intensity about the English people's disregard for Irish citizens. His proposal that the English begin to consider Irish children as a food source highlights his indignation at the way English landlords are running Ireland and consuming its natural resources. Students might find helpful connections among this satire, the temperance tract, and Joyce's short story.

A Letter Home from an Irish Emigrant in Australia (p. 520)

In "Eveline," the protagonist prepares two letters before she leaves to meet Frank. One is addressed to her father; the other is to her brother, Harry. This alerts the reader to Eveline's close ties to her family, even when she is thinking of eloping with Frank. Students should explore the ways in which Bridget Burke's letter to her brother John also demonstrates a deep devotion to family and home. First, Bridget repeatedly asks for news of home: "I often Have a Walk with Patt & Has a long yarn of Home" (paragraph 1); she adds, "we often Have some fun talking of the Old times at Home" (1). In the final paragraph of her letter, she begs for information about home, family, and friends: "Now John I must ask you for all my Aunts & Uncles Cousins friends & Neighbours sweet Harts & all also did Cannopy die yet." She concludes, "Lett me know all about Home." Although one paragraph of her letter does focus on Bridget's observations about Australia, the majority of her letter concerns family and home in Ireland. Reading this real immigrant's reaction to life in a foreign country, we understand more about why Eveline cannot leave her home at the end of Joyce's story.

Though Bridget is living in Australia, it is clearly not a "home" to her. She goes walking with her brother, and occasionally visits her uncle and his family. She confesses, however, that she "cannot make free with any body" (1). Though the country offers success to "a Young person that can take care of himselfe" (2), Bridget nonetheless finds it "verry strange" (1). She seems to have traveled out of Ireland for economic reasons; nonetheless, she finds Australia emotionally and psychologically unsatisfying.

A Plot Synopsis of The Bohemian Girl (p. 521)

In "Eveline," Frank takes Eveline to the opera, an uncommon experience for her: "she felt elated as she sat in an unaccustomed part of the theatre with him" (10). In this respect, the opera itself is irrelevant: the opportunity to get away from her father's abuse, the humiliation of her position at The Stores, and the unending work of raising her younger siblings is most significant. However, the choice of the particular opera is also relevant. (Joyce's decision to identify the opera specifically by name indicates its relevance to the characterization and themes of his story.) "Bohemian" has several definitions: it may refer to a specific geographic area, a group of people (wanderers, gypsies), or a lifestyle (usually an unconventional one). For instance, if Eveline were to run off with Frank to Buenos Aires, she might be seen as participating in a Bohemian rejection of family connections, church strictures about marriage. (Eloping in itself might be seen as a "Bohemian" act.)

Like Joyce's short story, Balfe's opera involves a heroine's choice of husband and connection to family. The Bohemian girl, Arline, falls in love with her rescuer, Thaddeus. Eveline, in similar fashion, regards Frank as her rescuer. Arline is taken from her home; Eveline is considering eloping with Frank to South America. Eventually, Arline is able to return home with the man she loves and receive the blessings of her father. Perhaps Eveline fantasizes about such an event. In any case, the opera offers her the possibility of a sentimental, satisfying resolution.

Incidentally, students might not understand why Thaddeus dashes his drink to the ground in the first act. He is "a Polish exile," a "fugitive from the Austrian troops" (paragraph 1). When the Count proposes a toast to "the Emperor," he is demonstrating an alliance with the forces that are pursuing Thaddeus. Thus, *The Bohemian Girl* is not only a romance; it also depicts a political division. Thaddeus and the Count are on opposing sides of the conflict; so, metaphorically Frank and Mr. Hill represent different factions between which Eveline must choose an alliance.

ADDITIONAL RESOURCES FOR TEACHING JOYCE

SELECTED BIBLIOGRAPHY

Attridge, Derek, ed. *The Cambridge Companion to James Joyce.* Cambridge: Cambridge UP, 1990.

Baker, James, and Thomas F. Staley, eds. *James Joyce's Dubliners: A Critical Handbook.* Belmont: Wadsworth, 1969.

Benstock, Bernard, ed. *Critical Essays on James Joyce.* Boston: G. K. Hall, 1985.

Bloom, Harold, ed. *James Joyce's* Dubliners. New York: Chelsea, 1988.

Bowen, Zack, and James F. Carens, eds. *A Companion to Joyce Studies.* Westport: Greenwood, 1984.

The Cambridge Companion to James Joyce. Cambridge: Cambridge UP, 1990.

Ellmann, Richard. *James Joyce.* New York: Oxford UP, 1982.

Gaiser, Gottlieb, ed. *International Perspectives on James Joyce.* Troy: Whitston, 1986.

Hart, Clive. *James Joyce's Dubliners: Critical Essays.* London: Faber, 1969.

Joyce, James. *Dubliners.* New York: Viking, 1968.

———. *Finnegan's Wake.* New York: Viking, 1947.

———. *Letters.* Ed. Stuart Gilbert. New York: Viking, 1957.

———. *The Portable James Joyce.* Introduction and notes by Harry Levin. New York: Viking, 1947.

———. *Portrait of the Artist as a Young Man.* New York: Viking, 1964.

———. *Ulysses.* Ed. Hans Walter Gabler et al. New York: Random, 1984.

Leonard, Garry Martin. *Reading* Dubliners *Again: A Lacanian Perspective.* Syracuse: Syracuse UP, 1993.

McCormack, W. J., and Alistair Stead, eds. *James Joyce and Modern Literature.* London: Routledge, 1982.

Mikhail, E. H., ed. *James Joyce: Interviews and Recollections.* New York: St. Martin's, 1990.

Peterson, Richard F., et al., eds. *Work in Progress: Joyce Centenary Essays.* Carbondale: Southern Illinois UP, 1983.

Tindall, William York. *A Reader's Guide to James Joyce.* New York: Farrar, 1959.

Torchiana, Donald T. *Backgrounds for Joyce's* Dubliners. Boston: Allen, 1986.
Wright, David G. *Characters of Joyce.* Totowa: Barnes & Noble, 1983.

AUDIOVISUAL RESOURCES

"The Dead" and Other Stories from *Dubliners* [recording]. 2 cassettes (2 hrs., 15 min.). Distributed by Audio Partners.

James Joyce. 50 min., color, 1996. VHS. Critics and those who knew Joyce trace events in his life through passages in *Ulysses* and other works, including *Dubliners*, the collection of short stories, and the semiautobiographical novel, *A Portrait of the Artist as a Young Man.* A BBC Production. Part of the "Great Writers of the 20th Century" series. Distributed by Films for the Humanities and Sciences.

James Joyce's Women. 91 min., color, 1983. Beta, VHS. Actors portray Joyce's wife plus Molly Bloom and two other of his female characters. Adapted and produced by Fionnula Flanagan. With Flanagan, Timothy E. O'Grady, Chris O'Neill. See local retailer.

Dubliners **by James Joyce** [recording]. 6 cassettes (90 min. each). Read by Jim Killavey. "The Dead" and fourteen other short stories of Irish life. Distributed by Jimcin Recordings.

Dubliners [recording]. 8 cassettes (1 hr. each). Read by David Case. Distributed by Books on Tape.

13

A Collection of Stories

In Chapter 13, "A Collection of Stories," students have the opportunity to apply what they have learned about plot, characterization, setting, irony, and other literary elements in the earlier chapters of *The Bedford Introduction to Literature*. Except for the stories in the World and Contemporary Albums at the end of the chapter, no story is accompanied by specific questions, "Connections" topics for discussion, or writing exercises. Instructors might want students to prepare their own selection of questions in connection with the readings in this chapter (after all, after responding to the questions provided in all the earlier chapters, students should have developed some knowledge about how to pose questions, as well as how to respond to them). This might make a good group project; separate groups might be responsible for presenting questions for individual stories. In addition, students might follow their readings in this chapter by generating their own "First Response" questions (either for themselves or for their classmates). As they may have learned by following the exercises provided in earlier chapters, identifying an immediate response to a story and then building an understanding of how the work provokes such a response may enable them to find additional meaning in the work or learn more about an author's technique. In effect, this collection enables the students to become the instructors — to develop a more immediate relationship with the literature — without finding themselves limited to the ancillary materials provided in earlier chapters.

CHARLES JOHNSON, *Exchange Value* (p. 523)

Like Cooter, the story's character, students initially may wonder why Loftis decides not to spend Miss Bailey's money. In addition, they may notice the way the brothers begin to change after they discover their neighbor's treasure hoard. Both of them begin to behave like Miss Bailey after they steal her money. The brothers' curious reactions to sudden prosperity may be rooted to some extent in their family history and their racial identity.

Students should characterize each of the brothers prior to their discovery of Miss Bailey's cache. Loftis, the older brother, is (at thirty) a night watchman; however, he is "the kind of brother who buys *Esquire*, sews Hart, Schaffner & Marx labels in Robert Hall suits, talks properlike, packs his hair with Murray's; and he took classes in politics and stuff at the Black People's Topographical Library in the late 1960s. At thirty, he makes his bed military-style, reads *Black Scholar* on the bus he takes to the plant, and, come hell or high water, plans to make a Big Score" (paragraph 3). Students may not recognize all the references in this description; however, they can determine an accurate, general meaning through context clues. The most accessible detail may be the reference to *Esquire*: what kind of publication is *Esquire*? (How does it differ from, for instance, *Playboy*?) How does reading *Esquire* enhance Loftis's image of himself? (Students might even free-associate with his name.) They might also determine Loftis's characterization through comparison with his brother. Cooter, the first-person narrator, "can't keep no job and sorta stay close to home, watching TV, or reading World's Finest comic books, or maybe just laying dead, listening to music, imaging I see faces or foreign places in water stains on the wallpaper, 'cause some days, when I remember Papa, then Mama, killing theyselves for chump change — a pitiful li'l bowl of porridge — I get to thinking that even if I ain't had all I wanted, maybe I've had, you know, all I'm eve gonna get" (3). Loftis masterminds the break-in; he also decides that the brothers should move all Miss Bailey's goods into their apartment. He shows no qualms about seeing Miss Bailey's dead body. Cooter, on the other hand, is a follower and a dreamer who demonstrates an acquiescence to his poverty and lower-class standing. He interprets the world in a less ambitious or practical, more imaginative manner. (Students might study the numerous literary allusions embedded in his narrative, ranging from his description of the hoard as "so like picturebook scenes of plentifulness you could seal yourself off in here and settle forever" [5] to his self-characterization after stealing the money: "barricaded in by all that hope-made material, the Kid [a reference to the comic book protagonist, The Yellow Kid?] felt like a king in his counting room [a reference to the nursery rhyme]" [37].)

How do Loftis and Cooter react differently to their new-found wealth? Though Loftis first "inventories" the cache and then ponders its possibilities, Cooter is in favor of immediate gratification. He tells the reader, "Be like Miss Bailey's stuff is raw energy, and Loftis and me, like wizards, could transform her stuff into anything else at will. All we had to do, it seemed to me, was decide exactly what to exchange it for" (21). Cooter acts on his enthusiasm; he reports that he took a stack of "fifties, grabbed me a cab downtown to grease, yum, at one of them high-hat restaurants in the Loop. . . . But then I thought better of it, you know, like I'd be out of place — just another jig putting on airs — and scarfed instead at a ribjoint till both my eyes bubbled. . . . Then I copped a boss silk necktie, cashmere socks, and a whistle-slick maxi leather jacket on State Street, took cabs *everywhere*, . . ." (22). When he returns home, Loftis reproaches him, "As soon as you buy something you *lose* the power to buy something" (25). Loftis also tells Cooter a significant story: " 'Remember the time Mama give me that ring we had in the family for fifty years? And I took it to Merchandise Mart and sold it for a few pieces of candy?' He hitched his chair forward and sat with his elbows on his knees. 'That's what you did, Cooter. You crawled into a Clark bar' " (25). Loftis exchanged family heritage and history for something transitory; by hocking the ring, he squandered both its economic and sentimental value. Hence, he approaches Miss Bailey's hoard with more understanding for her eccentric behavior. He also begins to emulate her, booby-trapping the apartment and refusing to buy anything.

Cooter begins to act like Loftis (and Miss Bailey) after Loftis explains the concept of "exchange value" to him. He carefully wraps up his new jacket and adds it to "Miss Bailey's unsunned treasures" (36), he refuses to call the landlord when the toilet begins to malfunction, he begs Pookie White for food, and in the end, he stows the penny Loftis has labeled in the jar. In part, he modifies his behavior because Loftis is his big brother. In part, thinking back on his parents' experiences, he begins to understand some of Loftis's ideas. Though at the beginning he asks Loftis, " 'But why didn't she use it, huh? Tell me that?' " (20), at the end of the story he has a much clearer understanding of Miss Bailey's perspective. Claiming that it comes to him as he watches the fireman remove Miss Bailey from the building, Cooter thinks, "when Connors will her his wealth, it put her through changes, she be spellbound, possessed by the promise of life, panicky about depletion, and locked now in the past 'cause *every* purchase, you know, has to be a poor buy: a loss of life" (36). Students should discuss the economic theory embedded in this line.

Cooter's realization is also linked to race. As a black man living in a world where the white people control the wealth, he understands that his possibilities in life are limited. He remembers his father "always wanting the things white people had out in Hyde Park, where Mama did daywork sometimes" (3). When he first acquires the money, he thinks maybe it will bring him power in some way: he fantasizes about crowing about his windfall to the cook who reminds him of his old baby-sitter (22). However, he begins to realize in the course of the story that spending money means depleting the possibility for power as well. He demonstrates this realization as he muses about Miss Bailey: "maybe she'd been poor as Job's turkey for thirty years, suffering that special Negro fear of using up what little we get in this life — Loftis, he call that entropy — believing in her belly, and for all her faith, jim, that there just ain't no more coming tomorrow from grace, or the Lord, or from her own labor, like she can't kill nothing, and won't nothing die" (36).

In order for students to connect with this story, even though its diction might confuse them, they might compare it to the fairy tale of "Aladdin." Cooter invokes the comparison when he refers to "the power of that fellah Henry Conners trapped like a bottle spirit — which we could live off, so it was the future, too, pure potential"; he adds, "we had $879,543 worth of wishes, if you can deal with that" (21). Students should characterize the moment in "Aladdin" before the protagonist begins to make his wishes. What are his possibilities at that moment? Even if he gets what he desires, isn't his potential diminished after he has used up his wishes?

POSSIBLE CONNECTIONS TO OTHER SELECTIONS

Toni Cade Bambara, "The Lesson" (text p. 179)
Flannery O'Connor, "The Turkey" (text p. 373)

RESOURCES FOR TEACHING

Charles Johnson. 29 min., color, 1993. VHS. This program shows how Charles Johnson blends black folk tales, Zen parables, eighteenth-century picaresque novels, and twentieth-century philosophy into his storytelling. Distributed by Films for the Humanities and Sciences.

In Black and White: Charles Johnson. 27 min., color, 1992. VHS. Johnson describes his literary objective: to explore classic metaphysical questions from East and West against the backdrop of American life and history. Distributed by California Newsreel.

See "In Black and White: Conversations with African American Writers" on manual page 591.

FRANZ KAFKA, *A Hunger Artist* (p. 528)

Although he died relatively early in the century (in 1924, in Vienna), many consider Franz Kafka the quintessential twentieth-century writer. Influenced by the philosophers Søren Kierkegaard and Friedrich Nietzsche, and by the Talmud, Kafka's portrayals of alienation and what came to be called existential angst prefigure the particular horrors of our time with uncanny accuracy. The conflicts and ironies of Kafka's life read like some of his fiction: he was born Jewish in Catholic Czechoslovakia (Prague, 1883). His father, a German-speaking shopkeeper who dominated family life, pushed his son toward a career in business despite knowing of his love for literature. Kafka lived with his parents for most of his life in spite of deep disappointment with them. He was a passionate man who seemed cold and strange to those around him. He took a degree in law and worked as an executive in an insurance company until tuberculosis forced him to quit in 1922. Kafka published two novellas (*The Metamorphosis*, 1915, and *In the Penal Colony*, 1919) and a collection of stories (*The Country Doctor*, 1919) during his lifetime. In addition, three novels (*The Trial*, 1925; *The Castle*, 1926; *Amerika*, 1927) and one collection of stories (*The Hunger Artist*, 1924) were published posthumously. All of these works repeatedly show individuals caught in meaningless, ironic, oppressive, unrelentingly grim circumstances. Kafka's work has been an enormous influence on later writers such as Samuel Beckett, Harold Pinter, Alain Robbe-Grillet, and Gabriel García Márquez, among many others. The facts that he wished at the end of his life to have all his work burned, that his three sisters died in concentration camps, and that he thought himself an abject failure all can be described as Kafkaesque.

Kafka's symbolism in this fantastic story can be interpreted on several levels. Instead of outlining these directly, it is probably more profitable to let the discussion of symbolism spring from answers to more concrete questions. You might begin with the hunger artist himself. Ask the class why he is fasting. Why do people usually fast? Do these reasons apply to the protagonist in any way?

The hunger artist is fasting for the same reason a painter paints or a writer writes: it is his art. It is also, of course, his profession. Fasting is what he excels at and what he gets paid for. Since the usual motives for fasting are religious or spiritual, on the surface the hunger artist is *not* fasting for the usual reasons. A person fasting with the aim of religious purification would not be concerned with being "cheated of the fame he would get for fasting longer" or being "the record hunger artist of all time" (paragraph 3). This is not to paint the artist as a completely vain creature; his "capacity for fasting" is more than a matter of pride for him. He is "too frantically devoted to fasting" to consider another profession (5). Self-denial is his art, and it does have a nonmaterial, spiritual value for him.

Discuss the protagonist's change in attitude toward his art during the course of the story. While he seems initially to be fasting for some greater glory, by the end he claims he is fasting only because he "couldn't find the food" he liked (9). Is this statement merely the reflection of a deranged mind (which the protagonist possesses by now because he has been starving himself to death), or does it suggest any deeper meaning?

One possible reading of this statement is to interpret "the food he liked" metaphorically. Perhaps he made no such claim earlier in his career because he *had* "the food he liked": public acclaim, respect, approval, even reverence. In those days the public shared and appreciated his values. By the end of the story, however, the audience's interests and values have changed; the nourishment he needs simply does not exist any longer; there is no place for someone with the hunger artist's talents and beliefs.

Many critics believe the hunger artist represents the fate of the artist in the twentieth century: what was once an honored and respected position is now considered frivolous and irrelevant. Other critics believe that the artist represents the spiritual side of human beings, while the panther represents the physical. (Regardless of the strength of the spiritual side, the physical wins. The artist dies because he denied his physical needs, and he is replaced by the pure life force of the panther.) Most critics also perceive the hunger artist as a religious figure — mystic, holy man, saint, or priest. This interpretation holds that the story is about the decline of religion in the modern world.

The story provides ample evidence to support all these theories; a symbolic analysis would be an excellent writing assignment. Another writing assignment might be to discuss the tone of the story. What is it (ironic), and how does Kafka establish it? (Through the voice of the omniscient narrator, who is sufficiently detached from the artist that we can tell he doesn't share or even understand all of the artist's feelings.)

POSSIBLE CONNECTION TO ANOTHER SELECTION

Herman Melville, "Bartleby, the Scrivener" (text p. 113)

RESOURCES FOR TEACHING

Franz Kafka. 22 min., color, 1994. VHS. A literary portrait of the author. Distributed by Klise Company.

The Trials of Franz Kafka. 15 min., b/w, 198?. Beta, VHS, ¾" U-matic cassette. Kafka's life and times, told in his own words. Narrated by Kurt Vonnegut. Distributed by Films for the Humanities and Sciences.

JAMAICA KINCAID, *Girl* (p. 534)

Jamaica Kincaid (b. 1949) was born in St. John's, Antigua, in the West Indies. She later became a naturalized U.S. citizen. Her works include a short story collection, *At the Bottom of the River* (1983), the short story cycle *Annie John* (1985) — both set in Antigua — and *A Small Place* (1988). "Girl" is taken from *At the Bottom of the River*.

In this story two voices engage in what is actually a dialogue. The majority of the lines are instructions from a mother to her daughter about proper behavior. Whether the mother is training her daughter to carry out the traditional duties of women on various days of the week, explaining cooking tips, or warning her about growing up to be a "loose" woman, her advice can be taken in two ways. In one view, she is a typically scolding mother, who must nag her daughter in order to communicate with her. In another view, the entire speech is a harangue designed to entertain the reader. This double level of interpretation applies to the daughter's italicized responses as well. In one view, she can only internalize her responses because her mother gives her no opportunity to present her own views. In the other, more humorous interpretation, the daughter acts as the "straight man," responding with lines designed to set up the punch line, the ending line, of her mother's joke. Whether genuine scolding or parody, the effect is achieved at the daughter's expense.

Encourage students to read this short piece aloud. "Girl" may prompt them to write about the differences between American teenagers' responsibilities and Kincaid's character's duties. They may also be inspired to consider their own relationships with their parents or children. No matter how the students respond to the piece, they should view the "conflict" from both points of view to fully appreciate it.

POSSIBLE CONNECTIONS TO OTHER SELECTIONS

Susan Minot, "Lust" (text p. 290)
Alice Munro, "Miles City, Montana" (text p. 458)

RESOURCES FOR TEACHING

Readings [recording]. 1 cassette (60 min.). Jamaica Kincaid reads excerpts from *Annie John*, *At the Bottom of the River* (including *Girl*), and *Lucy*. Distributed by American Audio Prose Library.

Interview with Jamaica Kincaid [recording]. 1 cassette (59 min.). Kincaid describes her move from Antigua to the United States and her British Colonial education. Distributed by American Audio Prose Library.

STEPHEN KING, *Suffer the Little Children* (p. 535)

Students may favor the straightforward narration and predictable application of horror and violence in "Suffer the Little Children," which might provide them with one critical approach to the story: What are the formulas of horror fiction? Students should identify specific conventions of horror that they find in this story; in addition, if they are fans of King's work, they might also discuss the ways in which this story is characteristically his. How is King's short story similar to other horror fiction they have read? What are readers' expectations of that genre?

King's effect derives in part from the way he establishes Miss Sidley's character early in the story and then proceeds to deconstruct it. We know that Miss Sidley, "like God, . . . seemed to know everything all at once" (paragraph 2). She is the stereotypical fierce old-maid schoolteacher. She is physically unprepossessing but psychologically powerful: "Small, constantly suffering, gimlet-eyed woman. But they feared her. Her tongue was a school-yard legend. The eyes, when focused on a giggler or a whisperer, could turn the stoutest knees to water" (3). The project of the story, then, is not to challenge her physically; it is to tear down her confidence, her authority, her belief in herself. King accomplishes this by identifying one child in particular who seems to know her secrets. He also refuses to regard her with awe. His telling "side-of-the-mouth smile" (17) is his trademark. After watching him, Miss Sidley begins to second-guess herself: "She had always been a winner. She looked down at her poached eggs. Hadn't she?" (33–35). Ask students to compare the atmosphere in her classroom prior to and following Robert's pronouncement, ostensibly as part of the vocabulary exercise, that "tomorrow a bad thing will happen" (17). (If Miss Sidley — or the narrator — had pooh-poohed this suggestion, would it be more effective foreshadowing?) Where the class was previously completely obedient ("she could turn her back on her pupils with confidence" [4]), her authority now appeared to be subverted: "It seemed the whole class now regarded her with hostile, shielded eyes. Robert smiled distantly at her from his front-row seat, and she did not have the courage to take him to task" (121). The remainder of the story is full of her horrified reactions to the children and her second-guessing of her own impressions: "*It was all in your mind, Emily. All in your mind*" (146). Her downfall culminates in her being sent to an asylum, Juniper Hill, and committing suicide at the end of the story.

The title of the story, "Suffer the Little Children," is also of significance. Ask students to identify the source for this phrase. It appears in the book of Mark 10:14, in the New Testament (in the language of the King James version): "Suffer the little children to come unto me, and forbid them not, for of such is the kingdom of God." How, then, is the title ironic? How is the phrase used differently here than it is in the Bible? Jesus blesses the children and holds them up as examples to the adults; however, Miss Sidley emphasizes their "nastiness" and ultimately kills them. (They are, in King's story, aliens: what is he suggesting about the future of the world, both here and in the final paragraph of the story?) In connection with this, students might study the way Miss Sidley characterizes the children: "children had been different in her day. Not more polite — children have never had time for that — and not exactly more respectful of their elders; it was a kind of hypocrisy that had never been there before. A smiling quietness around adults that had never been there before. A kind of quiet contempt that was upsetting and unnerving" (52). In the same way that King establishes the teacher's characterization and then dismantles it, so he presents the reader with the stereotypical image of the child and then deconstructs it. But his treatment of character is highly predictable, particularly in the passages where he describes the alien-children. There are no surprises, no real plot twists, no gray areas for readers to ponder. In comparison with a more psychologically complex and terrifying story, Joyce Carol Oates's "The Night Nurse" (text p. 653), King's story is rather mundane.

Students might briefly characterize King's writing style. He relies on the grotesque (in his description of the alien faces) and the obscene for much of his effect: for instance, prim, proper Miss Sidley describes the girls in the lavatory as "bitches" (66); later, as she attempts to kill the thirteenth child, she screams, "Dirty bitch, dirty crawling, filthy unnatural *bitch*! Change! God damn you, *change*!" (153). King also relies on the use of italics for frequent effect (in effect, sensationalizing the material through appearance, rather than substance). Would the story be as effective without the use of italics, and without the dramatic paragraph breaks? Examine specific passages such as paragraphs 53, 65, and 146. Does the story itself make the reader uneasy, or is its effect related in equal measure to its arrangement on the page?

POSSIBLE CONNECTIONS TO OTHER SELECTIONS

Charles Dickens, From *Hard Times* (text p. 98)

Flannery O'Connor, "A Good Man Is Hard to Find" (text p. 381)

D. H. LAWRENCE, *The Horse Dealer's Daughter* (p. 543)

D. H. Lawrence was born in 1885 in the Nottinghamshire village of Eastwood, in England's industrial Midlands. Although he grew up feeling closer to his book-loving mother, Lawrence would finally regard his miner father's rough vitality with deep respect, and he imbued a number of his male characters with his father's qualities of mind and behavior, qualities he came to see as essentially masculine. Further, the depictions of marriage in his mature works echo the "union of opposites" embodied in his parents' relationship. No "true marriage" — no true relationship, really — could exist, Lawrence thought, without fundamental conflict.

After finishing high school, Lawrence became a clerk, then an elementary-school teacher; he spent two years at Nottingham University College, earning a teacher's certificate in 1908. During this time he worked on his first novel (*The White Peacock*, published in 1911), wrote poetry and short fiction, and read constantly. He got a job as a schoolteacher in a suburb of London and stayed for four years, until he fell in love with Frieda von Richthofen, the German wife of a professor at Nottingham. They married in Germany in 1914, by which time Lawrence's autobiographical second novel, *Sons and Lovers*, had been published to both good reviews and good sales.

The couple returned to England early in World War I. Lawrence's vehement opposition to the war (it didn't help that Frieda was German) led to trouble with the English authorities. This was, in fact, only the first in what was to become a lifelong series of conflicts with the established order. *The Rainbow* was banned soon after its publication in 1915 because of its depictions (frank for the time) of sexuality. When the war ended, Lawrence left England with his wife, only to spend the rest of his life looking for a community where he felt welcome. Often very ill with the tuberculosis that eventually killed him, Lawrence lived and wrote in Italy, Australia, Mexico, France, and New Mexico. After his death his ashes were scattered near the ranch house where he had lived outside Taos, New Mexico.

Lawrence's works include *Women in Love* (1920), *Aaron's Rod* (1922), *Kangaroo* (1923), *The Plumed Serpent* (1926), *Lady Chatterley's Lover* (1928), and *Studies in Classical American Literature* (1923).

Some students will be confused or even disturbed by Lawrence's vision of love, life, and death as presented in this story. For this reason an attempt to answer the concrete question Why does Mabel attempt suicide? might be a good way to move toward a discussion of the themes. What about Mabel's life is so oppressive, unbearable, and meaningless? What, prior to the opening of the story, had made her life worthwhile?

Mabel's life has been grim since her widowed father remarried, an action that set Mabel "hard against him." (Presumably Mabel felt the marriage violated her father's original love for her mother, who had died thirteen years before this story takes place.) Before he remarried, Mabel had been contented enough, attending her father and living "in the memory of her mother, . . . whom she had loved." But with her father's death went the family fortune — the one thing that had made Mabel feel "established," "proud," and "confident." Her brothers had always been "brutal and coarse" and had never shown any interest in her. She had no friends or acquaintances, both her parents were dead, and her poverty made her feel completely degraded. The only place she felt secure was in the churchyard where her mother was buried; her only source of happiness was tending her mother's grave and anticipating "her own glorification, approaching her dead mother, who was glorified." The fact is, Mabel has been leading a sort of living death (paragraphs 96–98).

This analysis of Mabel's situation should give students better insight into her character and can lead to a more sophisticated discussion of, or writing assignment on, the use of symbols in the story. Students should now be able to identify many of the symbolic aspects of the setting: the large house, servantless and desolate; the empty stables; the "gray, wintry day, with saddened . . . fields and an atmosphere blackened by the smoke of foundries not far off'; and "a slow, moist, heavy coldness sinking in and deadening all the faculties" (99, 106). Yet while all of these suggest death, the story contains as many symbols of life: the horses, with their "swinging . . . great rounded haunches" and their "massive, slumbrous strength" (6); "the working people," who provide Fergusson with excitement, stimulation, and gratification (106), and Mabel herself, who is literally brought back to life by Fergusson, but who also, figuratively, brings him to life. "He could never let her go away. . . . He wanted to remain like that forever, with his heart hurting him in a pain that was also life to him" (154).

This introduction to the interrelated themes of life and death and love should enable students to discuss the story more fully. You could also ask students to write about the main characters: Do they change during the course of the story, and if so, how? What brings about these changes? Why does Mabel ask Fergusson if he loves her when she does? Why does he react to her question "amazed, bewildered, and afraid" (147)? What does the last paragraph of the story suggest about Mabel and Fergusson's future, and about Lawrence's vision of relationships between men and women?

A third writing topic might be a discussion of point of view. Ask students to identify and discuss the type of narration used. Could the story have been told exclusively from Mabel's point of view, or Fergusson's? Why or why not?

POSSIBLE CONNECTIONS TO OTHER SELECTIONS

Yukio Mishima, "Patriotism" (text p. 593)
Fay Weldon, "IND AFF, or Out of Love in Sarajevo" (text p. 153)

RESOURCES FOR TEACHING

England, My England [recording]. 8 cassettes (60 min. each). Read by Richard Brown. Includes readings of *The Horse Dealer's Daughter, The Primrose Path,* and others. Distributed by Books on Tape.

D. H. Lawrence. 30 min., color, 1984. VHS, 16-mm film. A biographical portrait of the writer. Includes his views on war and censorship. Part of the "Famous Author" series. Distributed by Britannica Films.

The Horse Dealer's Daughter. 30 min., color, 1984. VHS. Close-captioned. Distributed by Monterey Home Video.

D. H. Lawrence. 53 min., color, 1984. VHS. Lawrence biographer John Worthen and others who knew the writer discuss the author's life, his many love affairs, and his turbulent marriage to his wife, Frieda. The program contains some profanity and should be previewed before being shown to students. A BBC Production. Part of the "Great Writers of the 20th Century" series. Distributed by Films for the Humanities and Sciences.

TIM O'BRIEN, *How to Tell a True War Story* (p. 555)

Tim O'Brien's work is heavily influenced by his service in Vietnam and by the "war writing" of Ernest Hemingway and Joseph Heller. His first book, *If I Die in a Combat Zone, Box Me Up and Ship Me Home* (1973) collects anecdotes of O'Brien's tour of duty, and *Going After Cacciato*, which won the National Book Award in 1978, revolves around a vision in which one of the characters decides to leave the war and walk to Paris.

O'Brien was born in 1946 in Austin, Minnesota, graduated *summa cum laude* from Macalester College, and did graduate work at Harvard University. He has written for the *Washington Post, Esquire,* and *Playboy,* among other publications, and his books include *Northern Lights* (1974) and *The Nuclear Age* (1985). His most recent novel, *In the Lake of the Woods,* was published in 1994. "How To Tell a True War Story" appears in O'Brien's short story collection, *The Things They Carried* (1990).

In "How to Tell a True War Story," O'Brien establishes the pattern of his narrative in the first seven paragraphs. The vignette about Rat, his friend, and the sister who doesn't write back is a microcosm of the story as a whole. It establishes a sequence — introduction of characters, narration of details, topped by a punch line — that the following portions of the story closely parallel, incorporating specific terminology and black humor, as well as metanarration in which instructions about how to write and tell war stories are conveyed. In its inability to identify a single moral or a distinct meaning, this vignette, like the rest of "How to Tell a True War Story" parallels American reaction to the Vietnam War.

In the opening sequence, the narrator introduces his characters: Bob "Rat" Kiley, the friend who is killed, and the dead soldier's sister — the "dumb cooze" who "never writes back" (7). O'Brien's later amplifications of the story also rely on immediate characterization: "The dead guy's name was Curt Lemon" (11); "I heard this one, for example, from Mitchell Sanders" (21); and finally, affecting the narrator most directly, "this one wakes me up" (97). Even the commentaries about telling war stories focus most immediately on the people who listen to them and respond — "Now and then, when I tell this story, someone will come up to me afterward and say she liked it. It's always a woman. Usually it's an older woman of kindly temperament and humane politics" (106). Through his characters, O'Brien can reach his readers. More important, O'Brien reminds us that stories cannot exist without storytellers and audiences.

Within the narratives, O'Brien fills the readers' minds with graphic, brutal details and terminology appropriate to the war situation. In the opening section, Rat describes how his friend's courage caused him to "volunteer for stuff nobody else would volunteer for in a million years, dangerous stuff, like doing recon or going out on these really bad-ass night patrols" (3). In later sections, the details reveal the way Curt Lemon explodes in the sunlight, the bewilderment of the patrol on the mountain, or the gruesome horror of Rat's slow, deliberate destruction of the baby buffalo. Each of the sections builds on the trauma of previous ones: the buffalo sequence is far more tortuously laid out than the story about Rat's friend.

The final sentences of each portion of the story invariably build to punch lines. They either depend on black humor for their power or reveal the seeming meaninglessness of the war effort. The punch lines also indicate some buildup of power — some exaggeration — leading to ironic endings in which little is actually accomplished. The first section, told in a tone of incredulity and cynicism, involves silence on the part of a soldier's family. Later story lines end with the ominous silence of the mountain after the patrol has expanded its force to destroy sound, and with Rat's meaningless annihilation of a mute animal. Each narrative points to the soldiers' frustrations in a variety of different situations — frustrations that affect them not only during the war, but years later: "Often in a true war story there is not even a point, or else the point doesn't hit you until twenty years later, in your sleep, and you wake up and shake your wife and start telling the story to her, except when you get to the end you've forgotten the point again" (96). Like America's involvement in Vietnam, which its citizens are still questioning, the episodes in "How to Tell a True War Story" do not deliver any neatly packaged truisms.

Students should compare the sections of the story that contain the narratives with those that tell about the narratives. Why has O'Brien included both types of narrative in his story? Students might also trace the progression of each type of narration: to what point does each build? Finally, O'Brien's artistry should be recognized. His words are forceful, but they convey the beauty and grandeur of war as well. He writes that war "is grotesque. But in truth war is also beauty. For all its horror, you can't help but gape at the awful majesty of combat" (92). Like the war it describes, O'Brien's story combines the grotesque and the beautiful to create a powerful statement about conflict.

POSSIBLE CONNECTIONS TO OTHER SELECTIONS

Edgar Rice Burroughs, From *Tarzan of the Apes* (text p. 62)

Ernest Hemingway, "Soldier's Home" (text p. 145)

Yusef Komunyakaa, "Facing It" (text p. 1162)

Yukio Mishima, "Patriotism" (text p. 593)

William Shakespeare, *A Midsummer Night's Dream* (text p. 1327)

EDGAR ALLAN POE, *The Purloined Letter* (p. 564)

"The Purloined Letter" is the third short story written by Poe to feature the detective C. Auguste Dupin and his companion, the nameless narrator. The situation described in the story is similar to the plot of Alexandre Dumas's *The Three Musketeers* (1844), a novel published a year earlier than Poe's story. In both works, a female "personage of most exalted station" (26) is threatened by a minister who knows of her affair with a man other than her husband. The hero of the story (whether Dupin or D'Artagnan and his companions) retrieves the lady's personal property, thus preserving her reputation. Students should be aware of the ways this story participates in the development of the detective fiction genre; they should also consider the way in which the power of observation — the same skill they rely on to interpret literature — is employed by the detective to solve the mystery.

Following the tradition established in "The Murders in the Rue Morgue" (1841) and "The Mystery of Marie Roget" (1842), "The Purloined Letter" showcases the intellectual genius of the detective. It also relies for its effect on the exchanges between the detective and his companion. The narrator's questions about the case allow Dupin to show off; what the narrator cannot fathom, Dupin easily explains. This use of characterization to enhance the image of the detective and make him more human is also employed by Sir Arthur Conan Doyle, near the end of the nineteenth century, in his stories about Sherlock Holmes and Dr. Watson. In the twentieth century, Agatha Christie has also emulated Poe's work in her characterization of the Belgian detective, M. Hercule Poirot, and his companion, Hastings. Unlike some of this later detective fiction, "The Purloined Letter" does not challenge the reader to compete with the detective. Instead, our role is to attend to and admire the detective as he narrates his adventure. Hence the gap in the narrative between the Prefect's first visit and his follow-up meeting with Dupin.

Poe provides explanation about the history of and relationship between the narrator and Dupin in the beginning of "The Murders in the Rue Morgue" that might be of interest to students: Dupin comes from an illustrious Parisian family; however, his economic circumstances are extremely limited. (His financial straits prompt his interest in making the Prefect pay for information in the letter.) His companion is of wealthier means; they determine to share a residence (a "time-eaten and grotesque" mansion described in Poe's typical Gothic tradition). The two share a love of books; they also venture forth only at night. When at home, during daylight hours, they close the windows and light the candles (hence the darkened indoor setting for "The Purloined Letter"). Of Dupin, the narrator observes the following: "I could not help remarking and admiring (although from his rich ideality I had been prepared to expect it) a peculiar analytic ability in Dupin. He seemed, too, to take an eager delight in its exercise — if not exactly in its display — and did not hesitate to confess the pleasure thus derived. He boasted to me, with a low chuckling laugh, that most men, in respect to himself, wore windows in their bosoms, and was wont to follow up such assertions by direct and very startling proofs of his intimate knowledge of my own." In what way does it summarize Dupin's approach to the case? Students also might apply this description to Dupin's behavior in "The Purloined Letter." What do we see when we look into his own "window"? Students should acknowledge his ego, his prejudices, and his alliances as they study the way he solves this mystery.

Monsieur Dupin solves the mystery because he is able to read and predict the behavior of both the Prefect and Minister D——. In part, Dupin finds this case easy to solve because he has had previous encounters with both men. He also shares traits with both the Prefect and Minister D——. Students should list the common traits of Dupin and the Prefect, and, more substantially, of Dupin and Minister D——. (There are curious similarities between them, ranging from the initials of their last names to their nocturnal habits to their intellectual abilities.) However, there are also significant differences between these men. The Prefect, though thorough in his methods, is shortsighted; he does not find the letter because he underestimates the Minister. He is a foil to Dupin; though both men are experienced in dealing with crime and eager to recover the Queen's property, the Prefect fails because he does not apply logic to the Minister's character as well as to the problem of his residence. Dupin outwits the Minister because the Minister fails to realize the significance of Dupin's visit. Had the Minister applied the same methods of character analysis to Dupin, chances are that he would have acted to prevent Dupin's acquisition of the letter.

Dupin provides two analogies about his methods of deduction, in paragraphs 93–96 and 108. Students should study these analogies carefully. In the first, Dupin compares his approach to the method employed by the schoolboy in his game of marbles. In the second, he compares the Minister's method of hiding the letter to the map game. Which analogy is more applicable to this case? Which analogy is more problematic? Students should discover the flaws in the marble analogy, particularly in Dupin's explanation of the way he makes his face assume the expression of his enemy, thereby discovering what the enemy is thinking.

There are examples of foreshadowing and irony throughout the earlier conversation between Dupin, the narrator, and the Prefect. Dupin suggests, "Perhaps the mystery is a little too plain" (paragraph 12); it is "a little too self-evident" (14). After we hear how he managed to obtain the letter, we realize the truth of his earlier observations. (This demonstrates the way in which he manipulates — and out-maneuvers — the Prefect throughout the story.) Dupin also levels satire at the Prefect: when he explains the situation surrounding the theft, ending with the statement that the Queen "has committed the matter to me" (30), Dupin's response is quite entertaining: " 'Than whom,' said Dupin, amid a perfect whirlwind of smoke, 'no more sagacious agent could, I suppose, be desired, or even imagined' " (31). In essence, he is literally and figuratively blowing smoke at the Prefect.

"The Purloined Letter" also shares certain characteristics with detective fiction (and series fiction) of the modern era. Students who have read books about the detectives Nancy Drew, the Hardy Boys, and other juvenile detectives might recognize the way Poe reminds his audience of the series in the opening paragraph. The narrator muses briefly over the exploits performed by his companion in the previous two cases; readers who encountered "The Purloined Letter" and were intrigued by it would want to read the rest of the stories in the series as well.

POSSIBLE CONNECTION TO ANOTHER SELECTION

T. Coraghessan Boyle, "Carnal Knowledge" (text p. 276)

RESOURCES FOR TEACHING

Edgar Allan Poe: Terror of the Soul. 1 hr., color, 1995. Beta, VHS. A biography revealing Poe's creative genius and personal experiences through dramatic recreations of important scenes from his work and life. Includes dramatizations of Poe classics such as "The Tell-Tale Heart" performed by Treat Williams, John Heard, and Rene Auberjonois. Distributed by PBS Video.

Edgar Allan Poe Stories [recording]. 2 cassettes (2 hrs., 5 min.). Six stories performed by Basil Rathbone. Distributed by Caedmon/HarperAudio.

The Fall of the House of Usher: And Other Poems and Tales [recording]. 1 cassette (44 min.). Abridged. Performed by Basil Rathbone. Includes "The Fall of the House of Usher," "The Telltale Heart," "The Haunted Palace" and "The Bells." Distributed by Caedmon/HarperAudio.

The Purloined Letter and Poems [recording]. 1 cassette (1 hr.). Abridged. Performed by Anthony Quayle. Includes "The Purloined Letter," "The Valley of Unrest" and "A Dream within a Dream." Distributed by Books on Tape.

JOHN UPDIKE, *A & P* (p. 576)

John Updike is one of those rare writers who command both popular acclaim and critical respect. The prolific novelist, short story writer, and poet was born in Shillington, Pennsylvania, in 1932, completed a bachelor's degree at Harvard University (where he worked for a time as a cartoonist for the Harvard *Lampoon*), and spent a year at Oxford University studying at the Ruskin School of Drawing and Fine Arts. After returning from England in 1955, he worked at *The New Yorker*, where he began publishing his short fiction. He left the magazine in 1957 to write full time.

Updike's great subject is the relationship between men and women, especially in marriage. The Rabbit novels (*Rabbit, Run*, 1960; *Rabbit Redux*, 1971; *Rabbit Is Rich*, 1981; and *Rabbit at Rest*, 1990; named for their protagonist, Harry "Rabbit" Angstrom) constitute perhaps the best-known examples of this preoccupation. Updike has received numerous awards, including the National Book Award, the Pulitzer Prize, and the Creative Arts Medal for Lifetime Achievement from Brandeis University. His collections of stories include *Pigeon Feathers* (1962) and *Trust Me* (1987); his novels include *The Centaur* (1963), *The Coup* (1978), and most recently, *S.* (1988). His poetry collections include *The Carpentered Hen and Other Tame Creatures* (1958) and *Tossing and Turning* (1977); his nonfiction works include a collection of essays and criticism, *Hugging the Shore* (1983), and the memoir *Self-consciousness* (1989).

Sammy's voice is what pulls us into "A & P," thanks to his engaging first-person narration. Ask the class to describe his voice — the tone he uses, the things he thinks and says, the way he says them. What kind of a person is Sammy?

While Sammy is not exactly an all-American boy — he's too much of a smart aleck and somewhat disrespectful to his elders and to women (when he's not telling us about "sheep" or "houseslaves," he's focused on someone's belly or shoulders or "sweet broad soft-looking can") — he is funny, and we excuse most of his prejudices on the ground of youth. (He is young. It is difficult to imagine the more mature, responsible Stokesie, for example, quitting his job over this incident.) Updike's mastery of the vernacular makes Sammy all the more appealing: we enjoy hearing him talk and think, and his observations about protocol in the A & P and his small town are mercilessly accurate. At the same time Sammy is critical of this context, however, he is also a part of it: "We're [the A & P is] right in the middle of town, and the women generally put on a shirt or shorts or something before they get out of the car into the street. . . . Poor kids, I began to feel sorry for them, they couldn't help it" (paragraphs 10–11). He understands how the little world he lives in works, and he knows it is inappropriate for the girls to be wearing bathing suits in the A & P.

Ask the class to identify the climax of the story (Sammy quitting his job) and to discuss why Sammy quits.

Sammy hasn't given us any evidence that he hates his job. He has a friend there, and his wonderful description of using the cash register suggests he gets a certain amount of pleasure from his mastery of the machine. He is bored, however. (His descriptions of the store's regular clientele and the view from the front of the store demonstrate this.) And, without realizing it, he's probably looking for a cause, or at least something to react to. He does, after a while, feel bad for the girls, and quitting becomes a heroic gesture. In his mind, he isn't defending the honor and dignity of just these three embarrassed girls but of everyone, including himself, who feels humiliated or restricted by the narrow parameters of the silly, limited, limiting town or society in which they live.

Ask the class what Sammy gains from quitting. In acting on what has suddenly become principle, does he gain anything?

On the surface, he certainly loses more than he gains. The gesture is lost on the girls, who hightail it out of the store too fast even to hear him. And, of course, he loses his job. But for the moment, anyway, he retains his dignity — and the last line of the story suggests he has already gained some perspective.

Ask the class whether they think Sammy should have quit and whether they agree that "once you begin a gesture it's fatal not to go through with it" (31). How do they imagine Updike feels about this statement?

The relatively somber tone of the story's last three paragraphs, along with the narrator's dramatic last line, suggests that Updike does not agree with Sammy on this point. Sammy's going to learn from this experience, but he's learning the hard way. (This can lead to an interesting paper: exploring the roles and attitudes of the two minor characters, Stokesie and Lengel, by comparing them with Sammy.)

Another good writing assignment would be to compare this story with Bambara's "The Lesson" (p. 179), a story with a similarly humorous and personable first-person narrator. Both narrator-protagonists have many critical things to say about the people around them. Both are young, use slang, and come from a different social class than some of the people they encounter, or have to think about, during the course of their respective stories. Both learn something unpleasant about the way the world works and experience a certain initiation into maturity. In what ways are Sammy's and Sylvia's experiences different? Is one story more concerned with the issue of growing up, while the other focuses more on social and political issues? In what other ways are the stories similar or different?

POSSIBLE CONNECTIONS TO OTHER SELECTIONS

Colette, "The Hand" (text p. 220)
Ernest Hemingway, "Soldier's Home" (text p. 145)
Flannery O'Connor, "Revelation" (text p. 407)

RESOURCES FOR TEACHING

John Updike. 30 min., b/w, 1966. 16-mm film. Discusses Updike's beliefs and attitudes. The author reads selections from his works. Distributed by Indiana University Instructional Support Services.

Selected Stories by John Updike [recording]. 2 cassettes (2 hrs., 49 min.), 1985. Updike reads six unabridged stories: "A & P," "Pigeon Feathers," "The Family Meadow," "The Witnesses," "The Alligators," and "Separating." Distributed by Random Audiobooks.

What Makes Rabbit Run? 29 min., color, 1986. VHS, 16-mm film. Updike reads from his works and discusses his life. Distributed by Barr Entertainment.

Writers: John Updike. 30 min., b/w, 1966. ¾" U-matic cassette, 16-mm film, special-order formats. An interview with the writer. Distributed by Indiana University Instructional Support Services. Available for rental from member institutions of the Consortium of College and University Media Centers.

AN ALBUM OF WORLD LITERATURE

Like much of the Western literature with which students and instructors may be more familiar, the stories in this album frequently are concerned with what Faulkner once identified as "the problem of the human heart in conflict with itself." In addition, world literature frequently emphasizes power structures — the relation between oppressor and oppressed — as well as calling into question the underlying political and moral systems of a particular society. World literature may also offer readers a better understanding of the rituals, beliefs, and customs of a particular culture. It may be useful to ask students whether the authors of selections in the World Album are fostering a spirit of mutual understanding and offering to meet the reader on common ground or actively challenging the reader's experience and contrasting it with their own. Some of the stories in the World Album, such as Isabel Allende's "The Judge's Wife" and Bessie Head's "The Prisoner Who Wore Glasses," show people from different races, classes, and perspectives who find a way to connect despite their differences. In that coming together, do all differences between characters vanish, or are the individuals in these stories represented as retaining a distinct racial or class identity even as they connect?

The writers of the stories in the World Album define themselves and their cultures and share that definition with readers the world over, thus preserving aspects of their culture that may be changing. Allende measures the events of her story against the folk predictions that foretell her protagonist's doom. Yukio Mishima's "Patriotism" concerns a couple who adhere to traditional samurai custom despite the pressures of a contemporary society. Bi Shumin's "Broken Transformers" depicts a "blue-collar" Chinese family's struggle with ethics and economic realities; the catalyst for their crisis is the introduction of an American toy into their son's life. Serving as microcosms of the larger society, the protagonists in these stories demonstrate the customs and beliefs that characterize their cultures. Often, despite poverty, squalor, or oppression, they succeed in bridging a gap, in bringing together opposing forces or value systems.

As students read the stories in this album, they should consider how their Western cultural experience has prepared them, and failed to prepare them, for approaching non-Western literature. What strikes them as familiar? What seems "foreign" to them? The "Connections to Other Selections" questions will enable students to connect the stories in the World Album with the other fiction selections. At the same time, they might consider how the underlying assumptions in these stories challenge their own world-views. For instance, Head's story concerns race relations between a group of black political prisoners and their white supervisor. A common American cultural assumption is that a prisoner, having been convicted of a crime, is guilty, yet Head emphasizes that Brille and his fellow prisoners are not "criminals." Naguib Mahfouz's "The Answer Is No" focuses on the effect of marriage on a woman in a Middle Eastern culture. However, it does not reinforce Western assumptions about the role of women in Middle Eastern culture. Do students find themselves adjusting their cultural assumptions? Do they find themselves questioning their own moral, legal, political, and cultural traditions? By comparing the World Album selections with their own experiences, readers of these stories may come to understand more about themselves, and to expand their world-views.

ISABEL ALLENDE, *The Judge's Wife* (p. 581)

Although the characters and the plot of this story have their parallels in every culture, there are many details in "The Judge's Wife" that are distinct cultural markers. The widespread acceptance of and reliance on superstitions, for instance, may surprise American readers. From the beginning of the story, when we are told that "Nicolas Vidal always knew he would lose his head over a woman. So it was foretold on the day of his birth, and later confirmed by the Turkish woman in the corner shop the one time he allowed her to read his fortune in the coffee grounds" (paragraph 1), Allende incorporates many folk customs and characteristics. Folk remedies are prominent: Nicolas's mother tries to "wrench him from her womb with sprigs of parsley, candle butts, douches of ashes, and other violent purgatives" (2). Some readers might scoff at and dismiss a superstition such as the fortune-teller's prediction, yet at the end of the story, it actually comes true.

The events in "The Judge's Wife" serve to underscore the rituals through which the community is maintained. Every character seems necessary to the community. Even a seemingly shy and retiring woman such as Doña Casilda makes a distinct contribution. She has such an effect on the Judge that his judgments in court alter dramatically (1), and she is the one person in town who will stand up to him and bring water and food to Juana (13). Though there are disagreements, and some of the citizens take advantage of others, there is a commitment to the community as a whole, and the community comes to the aid of its individuals. Frequently, there is a humorous aspect to events. For instance, when Juana the Forlorn is in the cage, we are told that "the Judge couldn't prevent a steady stream of people filing through the square to show their sympathy for the old woman, and was powerless to stop the prostitutes going on a sympathy strike just as the miners' fortnight holiday was beginning" (11). There's also something amusing about the game played by the Judge and Nicolas: "Whenever there was an outcry after a crime had been committed in the region, the police set out with dogs to track [Nicolas] down, but after scouring the hills invariably returned empty-handed. In all honesty they preferred it that way" (4). Although Nicolas as an outlaw is in danger of being captured whenever he has contact with the members of the community, he clearly maintains communication with them. The Turkish shopkeeper, for instance, sends him a message when the Judge and his family have left town (17).

A highly masculine "code of honor" is overtly emphasized in "The Judge's Wife." When the Judge attempts to trap Nicolas by torturing Nicolas's mother, Allende writes that "though for many years [Nicolas] had had no contact with Juana, and retained few happy childhood memories, this was a question of honor. No man can accept such an insult, his gang reasoned as they got guns and horses ready to rush into the ambush and, if need be, lay down their lives" (7). Nicolas himself says, "We'll see who's got more balls, the Judge or me" (10). His pursuit of the Judge is as a man, not as a leader of a gang. Such behavior is not only apparent but accepted and even expected by the other characters.

Ask students to compare the Judge's treatment of Juana with Nicolas's treatment of Doña Casilda. The Judge tries to capture Nicolas by assaulting his mother. We are told that her cries are heard by all of the members of the town and that only Doña Casilda will take a stand to help her. Nicolas and the town can endure Juana's cries, but the Judge gives in when he hears his own children's wails. At the end of the story, the Judge is beyond the reach of Nicolas's wrath. Paralleling the earlier incident, Nicolas decides to take revenge by "assaulting" Doña Casilda. She begs him to escape when the troops approach, but he refuses. How does his action compare with the Judge's? Who, in Nicolas's vernacular, has "got more balls"?

POSSIBLE CONNECTIONS TO OTHER SELECTIONS

Andre Dubus, "Killings" (question #1, following)
Bessie Head, "The Prisoner Who Wore Glasses" (text p. 587)
Flannery O'Connor, "A Good Man Is Hard to Find" (text p. 381)

CONNECTION QUESTION IN TEXT (p. 586) WITH ANSWER

1. Discuss Allende's treatment of justice with that of Andre Dubus in "Killings" (p. 81).

A discussion of Allende's and Dubus's stories might center on the distinction between the legal system and abstract ideas of justice. Early in "The Judge's Wife," Allende emphasizes this distinction by contrasting the severity of the Judge's sentences prior to his marriage — "the severity and stubbornness with which he executed the law even at the expense of justice had made him feared throughout the province" (paragraph 1) — with his decisions afterward, in which, for instance, "to general amazement, he found the youngster who robbed the Turkish shopkeeper innocent, on the grounds that she had been selling him short for years" (1). In "Killings," Dubus contrasts the legal system, with its tendency toward insufficient and commuted sentences, with the justice of Matt's actions. In each story, there is a sense that justice has prevailed: Strout receives the kind of treatment he subjected Frank to, while both of Allende's primary male characters are brought down as a result of their assaults on the women in each other's families. Students might discuss where their sympathies lie at the end of each story: do they support the actions of the protagonists, regardless of their results?

RESOURCES FOR TEACHING

Giving Birth, Finding Form [recording]. 1 cassette (90 min.), 1993. Authors Isabel Allende, Alice Walker, and Jean Shinoda Bolen discuss their lives through their books and illustrate how creativity can kindle the feminine spirit. Distributed by Sounds True or Norelco.

Isabel Allende: The Woman's Voice in Latin American Literature. 56 min., color, 1991. VHS. The author discusses the emotions that inform her fiction and the events that set them in motion. Distributed by Films for the Humanities and Sciences.

BESSIE HEAD, *The Prisoner Who Wore Glasses* (p. 587)

The roles the warder and the prisoner play at the beginning of this story are fairly typical. Hannetjie has power over Brille and asserts himself through both psychological and physical means: "Look 'ere . . . I don't take orders from a kaffir. I don't know what kind of kaffir you tink you are. Why don't you say Baas? I'm your Baas. Why don't you say Baas, hey?" (paragraph 14). When Brille fails to respond in a properly subdued fashion — "I'm twenty years older than you" (16) — the warder beats him. Later in the story, however, after Brille has caught Hannetjie stealing, they are on a more equal footing, as is apparent in a second encounter, in which Hannetjie asks Brille to pick up his jacket and Brille responds by saying, "Nothing in the regulations says I'm your servant" (39). As in the first encounter, Hannetjie attempts to force Brille into a properly subordinate position by insisting on a specific name: "I've told you not to call me Hannetjie. You must say, 'Baas' " (40). Rather than bowing and scraping, Brille looks straight at him and responds, "I'll tell you something about this Baas business, Hannetjie. . . . One of these days we are going to run the country. You are going to clean my car. Now I have a fifteen-year-old son and I'd die of shame if you had to tell him that I ever called you Baas" (41). Rather than beating Brille for this, Warder Hannetjie goes red in the face and picks up his jacket himself (42). These two encounters point to a movement toward equality in the relationship between Brille and Hannetjie. Ask students how each of the men has changed in the interim between these encounters. Which character has changed more? Which character displays greater humanity? Would Hannetjie have reached the level at which he works together with the inmates if Brille hadn't caught him stealing?

Whereas many South African writers have exposed their readers to gruesome descriptions of whites torturing blacks, the violence in Head's story is subordinated to what it teaches her protagonist. Surprisingly, Brille draws on personal, familial experience in coping with the warder's brutality. We are told that within the bounds of their three-bedroom house, Brille's twelve children would "get hold of each other's heads and give them a good bashing against the wall" (21). Brille's experience of having to stop this violence has prepared him to deal with Hannetjie. Head tells us that Brille "never failed to have a sense of godhead at the way in which his presence could change savages into fairly reasonable human beings" (21). As he tells his fellow inmates, "I am a father of children and I saw today that Hannetjie is just a child and stupidly truthful. I'm going to punish him severely because we need a good warder" (37). Ask students to define what Brille means by the terms "stupidly truthful," "punish him severely," and "good warder." How does Brille "punish" Hannetjie? What exactly is the lesson that Brille teaches Hannetjie?

How are we to decide what is "good" behavior and "bad" behavior in this story? Does our knowledge that Brille and his fellow inmates are political prisoners alter our opinion of them? Do we accept their "misbehavior" — eating raw cabbages, smoking, and talking when they are supposed to be working — because the system that has enslaved them is corrupt? Do we overlook the pilfering of fertilizer and other goods by both inmates and warder because the system of justice that sponsors the prison is immoral? Late in the story, Brille tells Hannetjie that "we want you on our side. We want a good warder because without a good warder we won't be able to manage the long stretch ahead" (52). How would Brille define "good warder" here? Head's final depiction of the working relationship between Span One and Warder Hannetjie seems far more ideal than the earlier presentations. Here, Hannetjie has "a way of slipping off his revolver and picking up a spade and digging alongside Span One" (53). In return, the inmates exercise their talent for pilfering commodities for the warder's farm. In the end, they seem to be "comrades" exercising a certain kind of justice, particularly as they work together to subvert, albeit in minor ways, an unjust system.

POSSIBLE CONNECTIONS TO OTHER SELECTIONS

Isabel Allende, "The Judge's Wife" (text p. 581)
Ralph Ellison, "Battle Royal" (question #1, following)
William Faulkner, "Barn Burning" (question #2, following)

CONNECTIONS QUESTIONS IN TEXT (p. 590) WITH ANSWERS

1. Discuss how the issue of race relations is presented in "The Prisoner Who Wore Glasses" and Ralph Ellison's "Battle Royal" (p. 223). Compare Brille's strategy of dealing with racial issues with the strategy suggested by the last words from the grandfather in "Battle Royal."

   Whereas the protagonist of Ralph Ellison's "Battle Royal" is forced by the white men in the story to understand the "lesson" they would have him learn, the protagonist of Head's story is actually the tutor for the white man. Brille, the prisoner who wears glasses, may seem shortsighted initially, but he is actually the most perceptive character in the story. Whereas the whites in "Battle Royal" force the narrator to subject himself to their conditions before permitting him to give his speech, Brille refuses to alter his behavior to suit the warder. Unlike the grandfather in "Battle Royal," Brille does not advocate "yessing" the white oppressors; instead, he works through several layers of power to achieve a working relationship with the warder, Hannetjie. Ellison's narrator must swallow his own blood as he delivers the speech the white men want to hear, yet Brille remains articulate and perceptive without sacrificing his pride.

2. Compare Brille's character with Abner Snopes's in William Faulkner's "Barn Burning" (p. 481). How does each character cope with oppression?

Whereas Abner Snopes is consumed with his own sense of being oppressed and his own determination to take personal revenge, Brille considers the oppressor's condition as well as his own. In addition, he is concerned with the welfare of the other members of the Span. Abner considers anyone outside his family to be the enemy. In contrast, Brille applies his understanding of his children's behavior to his oppressor, in effect making Hannetjie a member of his family. These contrasts show that although Brille wears glasses, he has a much clearer vision of his condition than Abner is capable of constructing. Students might consider why Abner and Brille's responses are so different. What experiences have shaped their perspectives of the world? What is society's opinion of each of them? Which character do we admire more?

NAGUIB MAHFOUZ, *The Answer Is No* (p. 591)

Although the title of this story ostensibly refers to the protagonist's refusal of Badran Badawi's offer of marriage, you might begin discussion of this story by having students consider what else she is refusing. Possible responses include her refusal to marry at all and her refusal to reply to Badawi's question at the end of the story. The protagonist is clearly disturbed by the reappearance of her former tutor in her life although she tells her mother that her tutor's reappearance is "of no importance at all — it's an old and long-forgotten story" (paragraph 8). However, her other responses to him reveal the depths of her psychological distress. Ask your students to examine the text for indications of her emotional state. Mahfouz writes that "a shudder passed through her body" (1) and that she "did not look in good shape" (5). She herself acknowledges that she has "not completely" forgotten him (9). The long-forgotten story is obviously not entirely forgotten in her mind. When she was fourteen and he was twenty-five years older, he used his position as her tutor to have sex with her. You may want to ask your students whether or not she was raped. Although the story does not say for sure ("Without love or desire on her part the thing had happened" [10]), many students will undoubtedly suspect that he raped her. Other students may believe that he took advantage of his situation to seduce her. However it happened, students will most likely be in agreement that given her age and naiveté, he definitely abused his power and took advantage of her.

Although Badawi makes good on his promise to marry her and proposes to her when she is of age, the protagonist turns his proposal down. She "had attained a degree of maturity that gave her an understanding of the dimensions of her tragic position" (11). Have students identify the nature of this "tragic position." Ask them also to reflect on her position in Egyptian society, where the roles of women are more traditionally defined. Although she is rich and beautiful, well educated, and empowered by her mother and father to make her own decisions, she nevertheless doesn't feel free to seek love. Presumably, she never marries because she is no longer a virgin: "She had either to accept or to close the door forever" (12).

Although "it had meant little to her to sacrifice marriage" (14), she still strives to convince herself that "solitude accompanied by self-respect [is] not loneliness" (13) and that "happiness is not confined to love and motherhood" (20). Ask students whether or not they believe her when she assures Badawi, "I'm fine" (24). Ultimately, is her unhappiness a result of Badawi's reappearance in her life, or is it more closely tied to her own psychological turmoil and uncertainty with the choices that she has made? Ask students to examine the line, "She avoids love, fears it" (20). Despite her confident exterior, she is still haunted by the sexual incident that occurred years ago. An interesting closing discussion might be to ask students what is the significance of the fact that Mahfouz never names the protagonist.

POSSIBLE CONNECTIONS TO OTHER SELECTIONS

James Joyce, "Eveline" (text p. 512)

Fay Weldon, "IND AFF, or Out of Love in Sarajevo" (question #1, following)

CONNECTION QUESTION IN TEXT (p. 593) WITH ANSWER

1. Discuss the similarities and differences between the older men in "The Answer Is No" and Fay Weldon's "IND AFF, or Out of Love in Sarajevo" (p. 153).

    Both "The Answer Is No" and "IND AFF" depict older, well-educated men who take advantage of their students' youth and inexperience. While Badawi's seduction of the protagonist of Mahfouz's story might seem unforgivable, some students might nonetheless find him a more sympathetic character than Peter Piper. Badawi at least makes good on his promise to ask for the protagonist's hand in marriage, and when he reappears in her life as the headmaster at the school where she teaches, he does express interest in and concern for the protagonist. Peter Piper, on the other hand, is entirely self-absorbed. Instead of focusing on the needs and desires of his lover, Piper "liked to luxuriate in guilt and indecision" (paragraph 6). Piper is also far more vindictive than Badawi: after his relationship with his student ends, he attempts to reject her thesis. As Weldon's protagonist notes, however, "I went to appeal, which he never thought I'd dare, and won. I had a first-class mind after all" (47). Weldon's protagonist seems to have achieved closure and triumph at the end of "IND AFF"; Mahfouz's protagonist, however, never seems to have achieved the independence or happiness that she yearns for in "The Answer Is No."

YUKIO MISHIMA, *Patriotism* (p. 593)

On the afternoon of November 25, 1970, the day he completed what is usually considered his masterpiece (the tetralogy *The Sea of Fertility*), Yukio Mishima and several members of his private "army" captured the headquarters of Japan's Eastern Ground Self-defense Forces. The group issued a series of demands that went unmet, leading to Mishima's ritual suicide, or *seppuku*, a part of the samurai tradition. For most of his life he had felt that Japan was drifting too far from its classic traditions.

Mishima was born Kimitake Hiraoka in Tokyo in 1925 to a family with samurai antecedents. When World War II began, he became convinced that he would die for his emperor, but he failed the army physical, a dishonor that may explain his lifelong devotion to bodybuilding and the martial arts. After the war, he attended law school at Tokyo University and worked for a short time at the Finance Ministry. *Confessions of a Mask*, his first novel, was published in 1949.

In addition to being an enormously prolific writer, Mishima sang, acted, modeled, designed the uniforms for his "army," and became an expert in karate and kendo. He wrote poetry, stories, plays, novels, travel books, and articles, and translated a number of No dramas. In addition to the *Sea of Fertility* tetralogy, some of his best-known novels in

English translation include *The Sound of Waves* (1954), *The Temple of the Golden Pavilion* (1956), and *The Sailor Who Fell from Grace with the Sea* (1963).

Plot (or structure) analysis provides a good opening into "Patriotism": Why does Mishima choose to reveal the entire sequence of events in the story's first paragraph? How does knowing the outcome of the story affect the reader? Suspense is clearly not important to the author here; by summarizing the story in the first paragraph, he eliminates any possibility of suspense (or even curiosity) about what happened next or how the conflict will be resolved. Ask the class what is the most important element in this story. How does Mishima hope to snare his readers and maintain their interest?

Character and theme are the heart of this story — understanding who these people are and why they do what they do. The biggest question, of course, is motivation: Why does the protagonist commit suicide? The factual answer to this question can be found in the story's first paragraph. He was "profoundly disturbed by the knowledge that his closest colleagues had been with the mutineers from the beginning, and indignant at the imminent prospect of Imperial troops attacking Imperial troops." His colleagues had mutinied, and because he had been completely uninvolved and unaware, he was about to be put "in command of a unit with orders to attack them. . . . I can't do it. It's impossible to do a thing like that."

In other words, this is a matter of honor, pure and simple. Implicit in Takeyama's statement "I knew nothing. They hadn't asked me to join" (paragraph 23) is the suggestion that he might have joined the mutiny had he been asked. Ironically, having been denied the opportunity to take a stand, he is forced into the position of defending the status quo and opposing the mutineers. He cannot make himself attack his own colleagues, but refusing to do so would mark him as a mutineer, unfaithful to the imperial troops as well. He sees himself as doomed and chooses the only honorable death — honorable for himself and for his country. (Hence the title, "Patriotism.")

This analysis helps explain the lieutenant's motivation for killing himself. Reiko's suicide may be more difficult for some students to accept. Her decision to "accompany" her husband cannot be explained as solely romantic; it must also be seen as a reflection of Mishima's belief in "traditional" Japanese values and his attitudes toward women: her husband was the "sun about which her whole world revolved" (9), and "husband and wife should be harmonious" (10).

Ask the class to identify the various rituals in the story. (In addition to the lovemaking and *seppuku*, there are, among others, the morning worship, preparing and drinking sake, bathing, and shaving.) What do these rituals tell us about the characters of the protagonist and his wife? (If there were some way out of his predicament besides suicide, he probably wouldn't recognize it, as locked into his rituals as he is. But he is locked into them by choice [as is his wife]: if he is living in the past, he is doing so because he wants to.) Have your students also locate the contrasting images in the story. (Heat and cold, dark and light, control — spiritual and physical — and lack of control.) Discuss how these help illustrate the story's theme.

The bulk of the story consists of a lengthy scene in which the couple makes love and then a lengthy scene depicting the suicides. Why does Mishima devote so much space to these scenes, and what is the effect of juxtaposing these two intensely physical activities?

The author seems to draw a parallel between the lovemaking and the suicides. Both activities are, strictly speaking, "sensual" experiences. When the lieutenant is waiting for his wife to join him on the bedding, he wonders, "Was it death he was now waiting for?

123

Or a wild ecstasy of the senses? The two seemed to overlap, almost as if the object of this bodily desire was death itself" (62). In a review of Mishima's work, Hortense Calisher wrote that Mishima "is telling us that death is one of life's satisfactions" (*New York Times Book Review*, 12 Nov. 1972: 56–60).

This is a disturbing story, and it may be helpful to provide the class with some biographical information early in the discussion. Particularly interesting is the fact that when this story was made into a movie shortly after its publication, Mishima played the role of Lieutenant Takeyama. While it is important, in reading fiction, not to equate the narrator (or protagonist) with the author, biographical facts do help explain how Mishima came to write such a story. He apparently revered the values of austerity, loyalty, and allegiance practiced by the ancient samurai, from whom his grandmother was descended. (This accounts for the symbolic use of *seppuku* in the story.) Mishima was reportedly deeply disturbed by the corruption and materialism so prevalent in modern Japan. According to the critic Donald Richie, "a romantic such as Mishima is a man who compares things as they are with things as they have been or could be and who, in the face of public indifference and private doubt, has the strength of character to live by those standards" (*Harper's*, Sept. 1972).

POSSIBLE CONNECTIONS TO OTHER SELECTIONS

Kate Chopin, "The Story of an Hour" (question #1, following)

William Faulkner, "A Rose for Emily" (text p. 72)

Nathaniel Hawthorne, "The Birthmark" (text p. 329)

Ernest Hemingway, "Soldier's Home" (text p. 145)

David Henry Hwang, *M. Butterfly* (text p. 1675)

Gish Jen, "In the American Society" (text p. 643)

D. H. Lawrence, "The Horse Dealer's Daughter" (question #3, following)

Tim O'Brien, "How to Tell a True War Story" (question #2, following)

CONNECTIONS QUESTIONS IN TEXT (p. 609) WITH ANSWERS

1. Contrast Reiko's response to her husband's death in this story with Mrs. Mallard's in Chopin's "The Story of an Hour" (p. 10). How do the differences indicate different sensibilities in the culture of each story?

   Reiko's response to her husband's death differs from Mrs. Mallard's reaction: Reiko sees "before her only the joy of herself entering a realm her husband had already made his own" (paragraph 137), whereas Mrs. Mallard focuses on the possibility of personal freedom engendered by the news that her husband has been killed. Reiko envisions herself solely as an extension of her husband; Mrs. Mallard, for a short period of time, envisions herself as independent and facing seemingly endless possibilities. This contrast indicates both the difference between nineteenth-century American culture and traditional samurai values, and Mishima's desire to uphold those traditional values he felt were being abandoned in contemporary Japan.

2. Compare and contrast Mishima's description of the couple's suicides with Tim O'Brien's descriptions of a soldier being blown up and a water buffalo being shot in "How to Tell a True War Story" (p. 555). How do these descriptions of violent actions support the theme of each story?

Mishima and O'Brien both provide graphic, shocking detail in their stories — Mishima of the ritual suicides of his characters and O'Brien of the horrors of war. Both also glorify those experiences: Mishima describes Shinji and Reiko's deaths in loving, colorful detail. His characters are clearly, in his perception, doing the right thing, and doing it perfectly. O'Brien emphasizes the beauty of war: "for all its horror, you can't help but gape at the awful majesty of combat" (paragraph 92). However, whereas Mishima presents ritual *seppuku* as a means of upholding traditional values, O'Brien is ambivalent about the moral and political implications of the Vietnam War. You might ask students what they feel O'Brien's attitude toward his subject is.

3. How does Reiko's suicide provide meaning to her life in contrast to Mabel's suicide attempt in Lawrence's "The Horse Dealer's Daughter" (p. 543)? How is human passion a central concern in both stories?

Reiko's suicide signifies her commitment to her husband and his values. In completing the ritual *seppuku*, Reiko is triumphantly affirming her fulfillment of what she sees as her place in her society. In contrast, Mabel is responding to what she sees as a lack of place for her in her society: her attempt to kill herself, far less gloriously displayed than Reiko's, comes out of despair. The two actions do have something in common, however, as both characters are motivated in part by human passion. In Mishima's story, Reiko and Shinji's passion for each other is conveyed by the descriptions of their wedding portrait, their sexual appetites for each other, and their suicides. Mabel is also motivated by several passions: her love for her mother has kept her "alive" for many years, and that love causes her unbearable pain at the thought of not being where she can at least tend to her mother's grave. In addition, Mabel's response to Fergusson is instinctual, rather than intellectual. Although she is unable to articulate the human passions that sway her, her actions throughout the story seem to be determined by them.

BI SHUMIN, *Broken Transformers* (p. 609)

Students should focus not only on the effect of American culture on this Chinese family; they should study the way the mother and son's relationship is "transformed." By examining the dynamics of the story — how the mother changes, how the son changes, and how each character's view of the other changes in the course of the story — students should attain a clear understanding of the theme and symbolism of Shumin's story.

Ask students to characterize the mother and to explain why she buys her son the Transformer in the first place. The mother, the nameless first-person narrator, begins the story with an appreciation of her son that is grounded in his complete obedience. She is forty; he is ten. Though her husband complains that she is spoiling the child and leaving him unprepared for the life he will lead as the son of poor, "blue-collar" parents, the mother attempts to give her son every advantage. As she acknowledges, "I was loath to leave him with any regrets about his childhood" (paragraph 21). Thus, though they cannot afford to squander their money, and though she desperately needs wool for a new hat and scarf, she buys her son a toy. Her gesture is prompted in large part by what she regards as her son's heroism in denying his desire: because he resolutely turns away from the display, she is moved to grant his wish. Her satisfaction with his model behavior is signified by her wish to kiss "his smooth brow, now covered with beads of salty sweet sweat" (7) — an impulse repeated later in the story when her son treats Fatty with magnanimity, even though he has broken the son's Transformer.

What the mother values most about her son is his compliance: "He had always been so obedient" (123). His behavior is evidence for the mother of her good parenting. She also feels some power because she has been able to shelter him from the world; believing what she tells him about the way the world operates, he adheres to her rules. She also values his innocence and naiveté. While he is returning the broken Giant Transformer, the mother thinks with satisfaction of her guidance: "Moreover I congratulated myself now on not having filled his heart with my own cynical suspicions" (68). Even when he presents her with the yarn at the end of the story, her initial reaction is one of gratitude for his good behavior: "I kept my eyes closed, savoring the happy moment that only a mother can experience" (109).

However, when her son finally behaves in a way other than that which she has sanctioned by demanding reparation from Fatty, her attitude toward him changes in a drastic way. Though she earlier prevented his father from striking him, she actually slaps him herself by the end of the story. She claims, "his bold expression seemed to come from a boy I didn't know" (125); she also acknowledges the significant change in their relationship when she tells us, "I had never really hit him before, but now I felt certain that this would not be the last time" (130).

"Broken Transformers" might also be seen as a rite-of-passage story about the son. Ask students to characterize his evolution as a character. At the beginning, for instance, he demonstrates some awareness of economic realities when he claims not to want a Transformer: "The paper says Transformers are only foreign kids' cast-offs. They move them into China to get our money" (14). However, students should contrast what he says and the way he stands (his body language), particularly in paragraph 7. He cannot help but look longingly at the bright display. After he receives the toy, he maintains his good behavior, finishing his homework before he begins to play. However, after Fatty has broken his toy, the son struggles to practice the principles he has been taught. Though he forgives his friend, he himself soon breaks his classmate's Transformer. The classmate's family's reaction to his mistake changes his perspective dramatically. The mother observes, upon his return from taking the broken Giant to them, "One look at him was enough to convince me that he had undergone a profound inner trauma" (71). This is his first experience that does not conform to what his mother has taught him; he has great difficulty reconciling the different codes of behavior that he has practiced and experienced. This leads to his returning to Fatty and demanding compensation. He hasn't completely abandoned his values, generously providing his mother with the wool she needs for her hat and scarf, instead of buying a new, working Transformer; nonetheless, by the end of the story, his sense of ethics is uniquely his own, not merely a mirror of his mother's.

Students should consider the ways in which Chinese culture clashes with American culture in this story. The mother regards things American as frivolous: "I hated the monstrous cartoon family which had my son glued to the TV set every Saturday and Sunday night; not only did it prevent me watching the news, but it had so captured the imagination of thousands of children that the toy replicas now pouring into the stores were sucking money from parents like locusts devouring crops" (6). Yet she also admires American ingenuity: "One has to admire the Americans. Who else would come up with the idea of turning the belly of a fighter into a robot's head and then proceed to create a machine that executes the transition so flawlessly?" (49). Ask students to examine paragraph 19: what is significant or ironic about the following: " 'Convertible Transformer fights for justice and freedom with an iron will . . .' he sang sweetly. It was the theme song from the TV series" (19).

Students should also interpret the significance of the last two paragraphs of the story. In "Broken Transformers," the toy the mother buys for her son initially represents her bond with him: "This purchase was a token of appreciation for my son's understanding and an expression of our mutual love" (17). Their mutual disillusionment with one another is evident at the end of the story when the mother acknowledges, " Now we have two Transformers that do not transform. My son has never touched them again" (133–134). In the same way that the toys no longer "work," so the bond between mother and son has been transformed into a more difficult, less idealistic, more realistic relationship.

POSSIBLE CONNECTIONS TO OTHER SELECTIONS

Sandra Cisneros, "Barbie-Q" (question #1, following)

Charles Johnson, "Exchange Value," (question #2, following)

Alice Munro, "Miles City, Montana" (text p. 458)

CONNECTIONS QUESTIONS IN TEXT (p. 617) WITH ANSWERS

1. Compare the significance of the Transformer in this story with the Barbie doll in Sandra Cisneros's "Barbie-Q" (p. 218).

   In both stories, the toys represent the children's position in and perspective on the world. In "Barbie-Q," the way the girls dress and play with their dolls represents their world-view. Whether the dolls are stand-ins for older sisters, neighbors, or characters on the television shows the girls are exposed to, they enact restricted roles: the girls dress them in the sexiest possible outfits and make them fight over boyfriends. The way the girls talk about them and play with them reveals their own limited expectations in life. The references to setting — a Latino neighborhood in Chicago — and to the "fire sale" toys reinforce the impression that the girls' circumstances and opportunities are limited.

   In "Broken Transformers," the toys also represent social class and status: for instance, the Giant belongs to a girl from a wealthy family. Though the narrator's family cannot afford a Transformer, the mother sacrifices the money intended for wool for a hat and scarf and buys her son the smallest possible model. The mother knows that her husband will not approve: "He had always maintained that I spoiled the child and warned me that ours was just an ordinary 'blue-collar family' which shouldn't aspire to the same heights of those better-off. But was it to be the case that no 'blue-collar' worker should ever own a Transformer?" (11–12). In buying the toy, the mother attempts to defy her husband's rigid view of the world and to give her son a social position among his classmates that is higher than his economic circumstances might allow. By the end of the story, however, the husband's perspective has been validated, and the son is more aware of class and economic realities.

2. Compare the conflict in "Broken Transformers" and in Charles Johnson's "Exchange Value" (p. 523).

   To some extent, the conflict in both stories involves what the characters exchange or sacrifice in order to acquire a material object. For the family in Shumin's story, the purchase of the Transformer leads eventually to their mutual disillusionment; it also eventually drains them of their resources for surviving the winter. The acquisition of the toy leads to the dissolution of the ethics and morals the mother has tried to instill in her son. In "Exchange Value," Loftis tells Cooter a story about having pawned a ring that had been in their family for fifty years in order to buy candy. Essentially, Loftis sacrifices family heritage for immediate, transitory gratification. As a result, Loftis chooses not to spend any of the money he takes from Miss Bailey's apartment. Whatever he might receive in exchange for it wouldn't be of equal or appropriate value. Though Cooter initially buys food and clothing, he too realizes by the end of the story that nothing he might buy could equal the potential, the power, of the money. In the end, like Miss Bailey, the brothers become misers and recluses: the money has significantly altered their perspectives on the world.

AN ALBUM OF CONTEMPORARY STORIES

The stories in this album, written within the past ten years, demonstrate a concern with personal and cultural origins — with the relationship between self and society — that is shared by many contemporary writers. They also depict the way people become distanced from each other and their communities. Alison Baker's gender-bending "Better Be Ready 'Bout Half Past Eight" challenges our assumptions about friendship and about the nature of masculinity and femininity. Richard Ford's representation of the parallels between a small New Jersey town's economic slump and a family's fragmentation in "Bascombe, in Realty," also alludes to aspects of American culture from the 1970s through the 1990s. Gish Jen's "In the American Society" focuses on how our ethnic and cultural heritages can affect our participation in society and our relationships with our families. Joyce Carol Oates's horror story, "The Night Nurse," depicts two women who must come to terms with their mutual past — a past rooted in their experiences as adolescents and college students — and find some resolution to their conflict. Tobias Wolff's "Powder" demonstrates the way in which a son whose parents are separated comes to appreciate and forge a enduring bond with his father.

Students might consider the ways in which each of the stories in this album can be seen as a product of contemporary experience. They might also connect the concerns depicted in these selections with those of the literature of previous generations. What concerns remain the same? What concerns seem particularly contemporary? Do these stories suggest possible directions for the next generation of fiction writers?

ALISON BAKER, *Better Be Ready 'Bout Half Past Eight* (p. 617)

In "Better Be Ready 'Bout Half Past Eight," Byron Glass moves from being self-centered and determinedly oblivious toward an awakened sense of acceptance and a recognition of his place within his community. Along the way, he is forced to confront the limitations of his assumptions about friendship, family, and his professional identity.

The crisis that initiates Byron's new awareness is brought on by his lifelong friend Zach's announcement that he is going to become a woman. Near the beginning of the story, Byron sees a license plate — "IMAQT" — and automatically assumes that the car's owner is "a woman, of course" (paragraph 44). His assumptions about the nature of femininity are stereotypical and rigid, and his insistence on a similar interpretation of masculinity is also evident. He reflects this attitude in the scene where he changes his son's diaper: " 'You know what you are, don't you?' he said, leaning over and peering into Toby's face. 'A little man. No question about that' " (85). Yet by the end of the story, Byron has realized that his son, Toby, "could grow up to be anything!" (336). Byron reacts to Zach's announcement with disbelief and derision, followed by a number of attempts to come to terms with it. Ask students to identify the points at which Byron advances in his acceptance of Zach/Zoe. For instance, Byron's wife, Emily, clarifies the situation for him when she tells Byron, "We're talking about a human being who has suffered for forty years, and you're jealous because we're giving him some lacy underpants?" (169). Students might contrast a number of scenes in order to examine Byron's changing attitude. Possible scenes to contrast include the one near the beginning when Zach comes into the office wearing makeup and the scene where Byron first uses Emily's lipstick in the bathroom, concluding with the discussion of Byron's experience wearing makeup at the shopping mall. Or, contrast Byron's discussion in Terry Wu's office with his comments to his wife when they meet Terry at the shower. Because so much of the story consists of dialogue, the most effective way to identify characterization is through what the characters say to and about each other.

Through Zach/Zoe's transformation and Byron's resulting growth, Baker challenges readers' assumptions about gender roles. Byron is depicted throughout the story as an involved parent. He feeds Toby, changes him, sings and tells stories to him, carries him in a Snugli through stores, and cradles him as he moves through the crowd at the shower. In a number of instances, Baker's depiction of Byron carrying his son evokes images of pregnancy: "from his shoulders, like a newly discovered organ of delight, hung the little bag full of Toby Glass" (335). In contrast, Emily is often associated with stereotypically masculine qualities. She is seen putting together the Baby Bouncer for Toby; we also read that "Byron's mother used to say that Emily was built like a football player" (88). Emily sings a song to her son that implies a male voice: " 'I'll be Don Ameche in a taxi, honey,' she'd sing. 'Better be ready 'bout half-past eight' " (123). Yet Byron's and Emily's love and attraction to each other are depicted in a very traditional way. This couple's acceptance of and intimacy with each other's individuality prepares us to accept Byron's eventual understanding of Zach/Zoe's new identity. At the end of the story, we see Byron physically accept Zoe: "Byron put his arm through hers and squeezed it, and he could feel her breast against his triceps as she squeezed back, her muscles hardening briefly against his own" (334). Through Zach/Zoe's sexual development, Byron becomes more accepting and finally, at the end of the story, affirms his sense of community: "[Byron] felt a rush of pleasure. On his left Emily reached for a bacon-wrapped chicken liver; on his right his oldest friend in the world gently disengaged her arm from his to touch the hands of the dozens of people who had come to wish her well" (335). With the addition of his son, Byron's world is complete.

Ask students to draw connections between the scenes in which Byron struggles with his interests in science and poetry and the scenes that concern his relationship with Zach/Zoe. Some students might associate Byron's involvement with science with his masculine side; his poetry might seem more feminine. However, instructors might easily challenge these assumptions by pointing out that in Byron's first discussion with Emily, she sits at the kitchen table, "ostensibly editing a paper on the synthesis of mRNA at the transcriptional level in the Drosophila Per protein" (25). Byron hopes to achieve an understanding of "the meaning of life" (271) through his interest in both science and poetry. Is he ultimately successful?

POSSIBLE CONNECTIONS TO OTHER SELECTIONS

T. Coraghessan Boyle, "Carnal Knowledge" (text p. 275)
Andre Dubus, "Killings" (question #1, following)
David Henry Hwang, *M. Butterfly* (text p. 1675)

2. Discuss how the endings of Baker's story and Andre Dubus's "Killings" (p. 81) affect your understanding of and emotional response to the events in each story.

   Baker's story ends with an affirmation of community and harmony, while Dubus's story is more problematic. "Better Be Ready 'Bout Half Past Eight" offers positive resolution — Byron's acceptance of Zoe, his contentment in a circle of friends and family. The final paragraph seems especially important in this context because it depicts a number of individual musicians preparing their instruments and beginning to play together. Baker emphasizes that all of the players are female — a nod to Zoe and to Byron's acceptance of "her."

   "Killings," however, ends with a father and mother in bed, contemplating the father's killing of the man who murdered their son. Some students may find resolution in the scene through the parents' intimacy and through Matt's "just" treatment of the murderer, Richard Strout. Other students may find no closure because of the effect of the killing on Matt, who "shuddered with a sob that he kept silent in his heart" (169). For these readers, Baker's story might depict human connection while Dubus's story reveals only isolation.

RICHARD FORD, *Bascombe, in Realty* (p. 632)

Initially, students may find the first half of the story, particularly the description of real estate in Haddam, New Jersey, dense and somewhat inaccessible; however, the second half, concerning the narrator's personal life, should help them understand how the story works as a whole. Thus, it makes sense to approach "Bascombe, in Realty" first through an analysis of the second half of the story. Once students have a firm grasp on the narrator's character, his comments about real estate in Haddam will make more sense to them.

The most important question for them to consider may be this: Why does Frank buy his ex-wife's house? In order to answer this question, students should generate a list, either independently or in class discussion (or small groups), of key details about the narrator. Frank tells us that he used to be a sportswriter (paragraph 8); that he has lived in Haddam since the early 1970s, when he and his wife were newlyweds (12); that he has two children, Paul and Clarissa. He is now forty-five years old (9). How is his age a factor in his decision to make significant life changes? How does his perspective at forty-five contrast with his perspective at thirty-two? He tells us that he regards himself as being in life's homestretch: "I was getting things nicely turned around for the long, leisurely canter back to the barn" (20). It is at this stage that his ex-wife, Ann, tells him that she is getting married to Charley.

Though they are divorced, he still loves Ann, and his feelings for her motivate his life changes — buying a house and changing professions. It is clear that the divorce was not his idea: "If I'd known Ann would get remarried (knowing it as demonstrated by actually thinking it) I'd have fought like a Viking instead of giving in to divorce years ago like a queasy, uninspired saint. And I'd have fought it for a good reason: because no matter where she holds the mortgage papers, she completely supposes my existence" (70). And though he has accepted the divorce, he still spends considerable amounts of time with her. Together, they make fun of the other men she dates; together, they tend to sick children. He has, he explains, spent many nights walking the halls of her house while she and the children were asleep (92); he has even spent the night on her couch when he was feeling "the jimjams" (87). He has fantasies that they will get back together, in particular a scenario in which one of them will care for the other in some serious illness, after which they will reconcile (69). What most alarms him about Ann's decision to marry Charley is that his fantasy will no longer be at all possible: "Which is how I did feel: full of emotion that Ann was going away now to start the part of her life (she was forty-two) that would end in her death. And I would play no part in it. . . . And worse, I would be unthought-of" (53). His original fantasy, harking back to his marriage vows about "in sickness and in health," has been replaced by a vision in which he receives a terse notification of Ann's death (51) — and in which Ann, on her deathbed, barely remembers him (53). Thus, his reaction is to buy her house — in a sense, to have some piece of her forever: "so she could never get rid of me, not that you ever get rid of anybody, ever, and especially somebody you've been married to!" (47). He acquires more than her house in the process. It is ironic that his new profession is also inspired by his ex-wife: " 'I'll leave the real estate ideas to you,' Ann said, and I knew she wanted to get off the phone" (48). Frank tells us how easy it was for him to acquire her house; he is also proud of the deal he works out for himself in unloading his old home. Students should be aware of and consider the significance of Frank's nearly simultaneous change in residence and profession: "I have lived here now for three years, slightly longer than I have been in my new profession of house-selling for the Lauren-Schwindell Firm" (17).

Ford is a deft writer, and though students might miss his adept use of language in their pursuit of the story's meaning, they should be made aware of it. For instance, he incorporates a nautical motif in the give-and-take of Ann and Frank's relationship after Ann becomes involved with Charley. Charley's house and habits inspire the nautical theme. His firm is "housed predictably in a converted seaman's chapel situated on stilts at the marsh edge . . . , all of it just downwind of 'the Knoll,' his equally pretentious hand-hewn, post-and-beam Nantucket Cottage adaptation. . . . Charley, I hardly need say, attended Yale, hails from New Canaan, and sails his own twenty-five-foot Alerion, built with his own methodical, well-calloused fingers, using sails he sewed himself" (18). It's apt (and playful) that the narrator muses, "I suppose now I should've seen it coming and torpedoed him the way any sane man would" (21). Extending the theme, when Ann tells Frank she's going to marry Charley, he thinks, "I was hit amidships" (22). The language is witty and playful; it also invites students to think about the image of Connecticut versus the image of New Jersey. What do students associate with each place? What do Ann and Frank associate with each place?

With a clearer understanding of Frank's interpersonal relationships and motivations, students should be able to see more meaning in the first half of the story as well. Though many of his observations seem to be general commentary about the status of his community, they are also closely linked with his personal life. In general, he observes, "maybe the thing you see coming is not even the real thing, the thing that scares you, but its aftermath" (5). By the end of the story, we realize that he is less concerned with house prices in Haddam than he is with Ann's remarriage to Charley. What significant details about the setting are provided for us, particularly in the first half of the story? Frank tells us that Haddam is in a slump — house prices are down, people are working harder and retrenching financially. Violence is beginning to impact the community: Frank himself has been mugged, the neighbors two doors down have been robbed (twice in the same week), and, most seriously, one of the realtors has been murdered (4). Though he downplays it, the narrator reveals an anxiety about the future of the community that parallels his anxiety about a life without Ann.

In discussion, students should generate some specific ideas about the meaning of the lines of poetry that conclude the story: "Let the winged Fancy roam / Pleasure never is

131

at home" (92). (Isn't this a bit ironic, coming from a real estate agent?) How do these lines relate to Frank's relationships with Ann, Paul, and Clary, and his position with the Lauren-Schwindell Firm? Frank tells us that despite his age and experiences, "I am still able to feel 'purely pleased' " (11), and he claims, "it is when I lose that ability, if that's what it is, that I'll think about life in a different light" (11). The ending suggests that he has not yet lost that ability. He demonstrates great pleasure in his acquisition of the new house. As well, his reaction to Ann's remarriage has been to act, to change (although he couldn't act to stop the divorce earlier in his life); his ability to adapt also proves to him that forty-five is still relatively young — or at least not the beginning of death, as he envisioned it when he first heard that Ann would remarry.

Finally, students should consider the way in which the publication history of "Bascombe, in Realty" is related to its literary qualities. The story was originally published in *Esquire*. How might students characterize that particular publication and its readers? What distinguishes this story as an *Esquire* story?

POSSIBLE CONNECTIONS TO OTHER SELECTIONS

Mark Halliday, "Young Man on Sixth Avenue" (question #2, following)
Susan Minot, "Lust" (text p. 290)
Alice Munro, "An Ounce of Cure" (question #1, following)

CONNECTIONS QUESTIONS IN TEXT (p. 642) WITH ANSWERS

1. Discuss the significance of the small-town settings in "Bascombe, in Realty" and Alice Munro's "An Ounce of Cure" (p. 434).

   In both stories, setting enables the narrator to understand more about his or her motivation. Both small towns try to compensate for the unpredictable quality of the world beyond their city limits. Ford's narrator tells us, "there's a feeling of a wild world being just beyond our perimeter, a new and untallied feeling among our residents" (5). In Haddam, the residents retrench: instead of selling and moving away, they dig in where they are. As a real estate agent, he compares himself to an archaeologist, "unearthing the ongoing stelae and mysterious petroglyphs of my time, fitting pieces together, deciphering partial inscriptions, discovering how the whole site is shaped and lies upon the hilltop, and which way it faced — wondering: Where is all this heading?" (15). He then studies his reasons for buying his ex-wife's house and taking up real estate as a profession. Munro's narrator is equally concerned with the way the small town she lived in has shaped its residents' responses to life. For her, an understanding of the small-town ways that motivated the community enables her to understand more about her own adolescence (and about her adult self, as well). In particular, studying the time and place in which she was raised helps her to see why her first encounter with alcohol created such a stir in the community. It also helps her to see why her neighbors and parents reacted as they did. Thus, both Ford and Munro probe not only a character but also a place and a time in developing their stories.

2. Compare the protagonist of Ford's story with that of Mark Halliday's in "Young Man on Sixth Avenue" (p. 70). To what extent does life meet their expectations?

   For the protagonist of Halliday's story, the peak of his life seems to be when he is a young, ambitious man in New York City. The pace of the city, the opportunities for "witty" lunches, the professional challenges appeal to the protagonist. This portion of his life receives the most attention in the story — most of his midlife experiences are elided. In contrast, "Bascombe, in Realty," is about the way a man can make significant life-changes at forty-five. Frank discovers that he can adapt in rewarding ways, that he doesn't have to merely accept what life brings him, that he has talents he never imagined himself having at thirty-two. Ford's story suggests, more than Halliday's, that there is more to life than a young man's perspective. Halliday's protagonist seems to feel that he missed his chance; Ford's finds that he can take those chances and prevail. Frank's future isn't entirely the way he imagined it would be (Ann does not remarry him), but he nonetheless seems a stronger, more sympathetic character for his struggles.

RESOURCES FOR TEACHING

Richard Ford: The Sportswriter (1st chapter) and Rock Springs (short story) [recording]. 1 cassette (89 min.). Distributed by American Audio Prose Library.

Interview [recording]. 1 cassette (55 min.). Pulitzer Prize–winning Ford discusses his writing and personal life. Distributed by American Audio Prose Library.

GISH JEN, *In the American Society* (p. 643)

Mr. Chang seems divided between his desire to be "a good American" and his ties to the culture and the values of China. He takes over the pancake house because it will place him firmly in an American tradition and enable him to send his daughters to college: "Those Americans always saying it. . . . Smart guys thinking in advance" (paragraph 1). Yet the more firmly established in what he sees as the American tradition he becomes, the more he invokes his Chinese heritage: "As time went on and the business continued to thrive, my father started to talk about his grandfather and the village he had reigned over in China — things my father had never talked about when he worked for other people" (2). His habit of concerning himself with his employees' lives far beyond usual business relationships comes from his memories of his grandfather and is affirmed by what he has seen of the "Godfather" movies — movies that uphold a Sicilian immigrant's culture and beliefs. The father believes what his father has taught him, that "the province comes before the town, the town comes before the family" (90). In the first part of the story, which focuses on the family business, he carries out this belief by going to great lengths to protect his workers, despite his family's concerns. You might ask students whether, in the second section of the story, which focuses on the family's social life, the father still upholds the "province" or "town" before the family. Ask students to compare the two sections. What do we see in the father in a social setting that the business setting hasn't already revealed? Are there structural similarities between the sections? Where is he most "American" in each instance? Where is he most clearly behaving according to his Chinese training?

Ask students to compare the father's transition into an "American" with the mother's. She is also trying to find a balance between the traditional ways and the new, but even at the beginning of the story she seems to have assimilated more of the American culture: "she had opinions, now, on how downtown should be zoned; she could pump her own gas and check her own oil; and . . . she herself was now interested in espadrilles, and wallpaper, and most recently, the town country club" (5). What does she seem to value most about American society? What does she perceive as its faults? How is the mother contrasted with Mrs. Lardner? Jen depicts Mrs. Lardner as larger than life, insensitive, and somewhat gushy. Is Jen relying too heavily on stereotypical American behavior in this characterization? In the end, how do "born-and-bred" Americans such as Mrs.

Lardner and Jeremy Brothers compare with Mr. and Mrs. Chang? Where do the daughters fit into the variety of cultures and values depicted in this story?

"In the American Society" offers students an opportunity to define what they think it means to be "an American." What are the most stereotypical characteristics of an American? Encourage students to consider positive and negative aspects of the American character, both past and present. It might be useful to reread this story at least once in order to focus on the small details that constitute Jen's sense of American society. In addition, instructors might compare this story with works such as Cisneros's "Barbie-Q" (text p. 218) as a means of arriving at some recognition of how existing American culture contributes to all of our conceptions of ourselves as Americans.

POSSIBLE CONNECTIONS TO OTHER SELECTIONS

Ernest Hemingway, "Soldier's Home" (text p. 145)

Yukio Mishima, "Patriotism" (question #1, following)

Flannery O'Connor, "A Good Man Is Hard to Find" (question #2, following)

CONNECTIONS QUESTIONS IN TEXT (p. 653) WITH ANSWERS

1. Discuss the role of cultural tradition in Jen's story and Mishima's "Patriotism" (p. 593).

    Jen's story provides an assessment of the difficulties of maintaining some sense of cultural tradition while assimilating into a new society; Mishima's story concerns the upholding of cultural traditions at society's expense. In Jen's story, the father emulates his grandfather's patriarchal behavior in China: he thinks it is his duty to take care of "his people." However, when he attempts to put this theory into practice in America, he finds that his employees resent his behavior, particularly his tendency to demand complete loyalty in return for his generosity. As the head waitress complains, "It's not just the blacks don't believe in slavery" (paragraph 23). Mr. Chang attempts to exact the same loyalty from his family that he expects from his employees: "In my father's mind, a family owed its head a degree of loyalty that left no room for dissent" (21). Both of his traditional expectations are disappointed in the course of the story. However, by the story's end, Mr. Chang is again the central authority as he leads his family away from Mrs. Lardner's party. As the narrator notes, "Then his shirt started moving again, and we trooped up the hill after it, into the dark" (194). The affirmation of cultural tradition is more strongly emphasized in Mishima's "Patriotism," in which Reiko and Shinji perform ritual *seppuku* after a military coup in which Shinji's friends have participated. There is never any question that the characters will fail to adhere to strict samurai tradition — in fact, the story is a loving, detailed tribute to those traditions. The end of "Patriotism" emphasizes the power of tradition far more than the closing line of "In the American Society." Mishima writes that Reiko "gathered her strength and plunged the point of the blade deep into her throat" (138).

2. Compare the purpose of the humor in Jen's story with its purpose in O'Connor's "A Good Man Is Hard to Find" (p. 381).

    The humor in Jen's story provides readers with a means of understanding Mr. Chang without condemning him. He may be overbearing and insistent on approaching Americans with the habits of Chinese customs, but he remains a sympathetic character, particularly in connection with characters such as Jeremy Brothers. Here, the humor serves to undermine the larger-than-life Americans whose behavior is outrageous (and racist). Like Jen, O'Connor uses humor as a means of helping her audience retain interest in the grandmother, who can be excused for her selfish, prideful behavior only if she is perceived as a somewhat comic figure. O'Connor's humor provides a contrast to the startling violence that characterizes her fiction. For instance, in describing the car accident, O'Connor focuses on the comic aspects of its cause: "Pitty Sing, the cat, sprang onto Bailey's shoulder" (paragraph 63). She adds that as the car rolled, "Bailey remained in the driver's seat with the cat — gray-striped with a broad white face and an orange nose — clinging to his neck like a caterpillar" (64).

JOYCE CAROL OATES, *The Night Nurse* (p. 653)

In this story, Oates effectively creates a terrifying situation for her protagonist; she also invests the story with surprising compassion. The reader's initial expectations of both protagonist and antagonist are transformed; both women discover depth of character within themselves that is surprising. Grace Burkhardt's self-satisfied assumptions about herself are challenged and dramatically altered in the course of the story; in addition, though Harriet Zink might at first remind us of a stereotypical Stephen King character (perhaps Annie, the woman who entraps and tortures the writer in *Misery*), she, too, is a surprisingly dynamic character.

"The Night Nurse" contains all the elements of a thoroughly frightening story. A hospital would seem to be a place of safety and security, well-staffed with knowledgeable, caring people. However, even before night falls, there are several suggestions that the setting might be more ambiguous than the reader initially imagines. Grace thinks of a former lover, "an intelligent man, a reasonable man, yet, on the subject of hospitals, adamantly irrational" (paragraph 33). In addition, her potential for anxiety is intensified, albeit inadvertently, by the stories she hears: "her sister, meaning well, had told her alarming tales of negligent and even hostile nurses and attendants at big-city hospitals as a way of assuring Grace that here, by contrast, in this suburban hospital, she would receive better treatment" (46). Left alone for the night, she cannot help but imagine the worst. She is also in intense physical pain. In addition, after visiting hours are over, she feels completely alone and helpless. She is immobilized; she is shivering; she cannot seem to get any help from the staff at the hospital. The "sharp smell of urine" (36), even after the bedpan has been taken away, intensifies the unpleasant impression of this setting. In addition, the eeriness of the setting is enhanced by the consistent references to the time.

What is most alarming to Grace is her lack of control. She envisions herself as a smart, capable, kind, successful woman: "Her name was Grace Burkhardt and she was forty-four years old and she was a woman accustomed, as the chief administrator of a state arts council, to exercising authority" (6). As she deals with friends and business matters on the phone after her surgery, it is most important to her to regain some authority over her own life: "Nothing meant more to her than to take back the control she'd lost back there in the pedestrian mall, to tell her story as if it were her own" (11). In the night, without anyone there, she succumbs to panic (15). She also turns, uncharacteristically, to prayer (17), a gesture that will be increasingly significant by the end of the story. Until this point in her life, she has always regarded herself as a kind person: "Hadn't she overheard, to her embarrassment, just the other day, two young women staff members at the arts council speaking of Grace Burkhardt warmly, comparing her favorably to her male predecessor" (74). This passage is ultimately ironic: Grace will leave the hospital with a much clearer sense of her pride, selfishness, and lack of charity. After her encounter with

Harriet Zink, Grace is particularly aware of her spiritual shortcomings. (Her name is especially apt in this context.) She recognizes that she was far more unkind to Harriet than she has ever acknowledged; in addition, Grace recognizes, *"I am not that strong. I am not evil, but I am not that strong. In [Harriet's] place, I could not forgive"* (111). Thus, by the end of the story, we have a deeper, richer understanding of this flawed but sympathetic character.

When we first encounter Harriet, surprisingly early in the story, long before she and Grace have their revealing conversation, she is a nameless, ominous impression: "a face floated near, a stranger's face that was at the same time familiar as a lost sister's" (8). (Given their history together and their similarities — they are both scholarship girls, from farming families — this is especially significant.) The physical description of Harriet is also ominous: "The features were indistinct but the skin was strangely flushed and shiny, like something not quite fully hatched. There was a smile, thin-lipped and tentative. No-color eyes" (10). In the phrases "not quite fully hatched" and "no-color," Oates establishes readers' initial impression of the nurse as something inhuman — an impression enhanced later by reference to the nurse's "glass marble" eyes (62) and her skin "the color of spoiled cantaloupe" (64). When the nurse is (finally) described physically, she also seems rather grotesque: "so short as to seem almost dwarfish. Hardly five feet tall. But round-bodied, with a moon face, peculiar flushed skin that was smooth and shiny as scar tissue; small close-set damp eyes; a thin pursed mouth" (28). Complete with the references to her sweat-stained armpits, she seems a disgusting creature. There is also an implied malevolence to the way she appears in or leaves the room, seemingly from nowhere (see paragraphs 20, 23, 48, and 56). Grace's impressions of her early in their conversation also enhance this impression: *"She's mad, she's come to injure me"* (65). Much to our surprise, and Grace's as well, Harriet ultimately turns out to be something other than a monster. Just when she seems poised to attack Grace, hovering over her in anger, Harriet has her own epiphany: "her expression shifted suddenly, turned unexpectedly thoughtful. She said, with the air of one making a discovery, 'Yes, I can forgive you, Grace Burkhardt. I'm a Christian woman. In my heart I'm empowered to forgive'" (106). Students might initially interpret the tone of this passage as sanctimonious or self-righteous, but the exposition and the imagery suggest a more sincere interpretation. Harriet "spoke with such sudden pride, it was as if sunshine flooded the room" (106). In contrast with all the dark, night imagery, Harriet's forgiveness warms both characters like afternoon sun.

POSSIBLE CONNECTIONS TO OTHER SELECTIONS

Nathaniel Hawthorne, "Young Goodman Brown" (question #2, following)
Stephen King, "Suffer the Little Children" (question #1, following)
Alice Munro, "Miles City, Montana" (text p. 458)

CONNECTIONS QUESTIONS IN TEXT (p. 664) WITH ANSWERS

1. How is fear made central in "The Night Nurse" and Stephen King's "Suffer the Little Children" (p. 535)? What do you think is the purpose for evoking fear in each story?

    Miss Sidley's fear is theatrical, unrealistic: the fear of aliens invading children's bodies, the fear of being tormented beyond the brink of sanity by the children's attitudes and the way their faces and bodies dissolve into grotesques. Most readers would have a hard time believing that the events described in King's "Suffer the Little Children" could actually happen. Grace Burkhardt's fear in "The Night Nurse" is far more ominous because it is realistic: the fear that your body could fail you at any time, the fear of being immobilized and completely dependent upon someone else, the fear of discovering that you are not the good, kind person that you have always envisioned yourself to be. Part of what intensifies the effect of "The Night Nurse" is that what happens to Grace could happen to any of us at any time: the accident occurs in a commonplace setting (a shopping mall), and the nurse who confronts Grace in the middle of the night could be anyone to whom we have in the past been unkind. King uses the horror in his story to limited effect: it initially shocks the reader, but it leaves no thought-provoking impression. Oates's story, with its more sophisticated theme and characterization, gives the reader much more to consider.

2. Discuss the effects of the settings in "The Night Nurse" and Hawthorne's "Young Goodman Brown" (p. 310). Pay particular attention to how the night is treated.

Young Goodman Brown travels into the woods at night for what Hawthorne terms an "evil purpose" (8). As his journey continues, the nocturnal setting is intensified: it becomes increasingly dark and ominous. Young Goodman Brown admits his character flaws at the beginning of his adventure; he knows that he should instead be home with his wife, Faith, not consorting with the Devil and his cohorts. It becomes so dark that he cannot see anything. This physical description is symbolic of his moral condition as well: by the end of the story, he has become "a stern, a sad, a darkly meditative, a distrustful, if not a desperate man" (72). In contrast, Grace Burkhardt is less self-aware (or less honest with herself) at the beginning of "The Night Nurse." She enters the hospital with a firm sense of her goodness and innocence — her accident could happen to anyone. As night falls and the hospital becomes increasingly silent and empty, however, she is forced to examine her supposed self-truths. But there is a leavening of the darkness at the end of Oates's story: after her encounter with Harriet Zink, Grace dreams of "staring into the sun as if in penance" (108). Her bedside lamp is still on as well (109). The light is representative of her growing self-awareness and acceptance of her flaws. Like Goodman Brown, Grace Burkhardt has experienced "a dark night of the soul," but unlike Hawthorne's misanthrope, Oates's protagonist emerges with a more profound, sophisticated, and constructive understanding of humanity.

TOBIAS WOLFF, *Powder* (p. 665)

"Powder" is a story about a significant moment in a relationship between a father and his son. The first-person narrator's parents are separated at the time of the events described in this story, and the narrator, who is young enough not to have gotten a driver's license yet, tells us, "my mother was still angry with [my father] for sneaking me into a nightclub during our last visit, to see Thelonious Monk" (paragraph 1). Though he tells us that his father eventually did get him home for Christmas Eve dinner, "buying a little more time before my mother decided to make the split final" (34), there is evident tension between the father and son, particularly at the beginning of the story and leading up to when the state trooper tells the father that the road is closed. The boy seems nervous; he knows that the mother is going to be angry; and he himself seems irritated that his father has dawdled so long: "as we were checking out of the lodge that morning it began to snow, and in this snow he observed some quality that made it necessary for us to get in one last run. We got in several last runs. He was indifferent to my fretting" (2). The father's dialogue with his son at the beginning of the story signals the difficulties in their relationship. The father says "Right, doctor?" (4). The son, who is supposed to respond by saying, "Right, doctor" (5), remains silent. A little later, he reproaches his father: "We should have left before, . . . Doctor" (12); significantly, the father fails to respond according to their ritual.

The turn in the story comes when the son can relinquish his criticism of his father and admire him for who he is. This comes in part when the father insists on driving past the barricades, despite the possible penalties. In contrast with the earlier dialogue, once they have committed themselves to making the trip together (father driving, son becoming "an accomplice" [19] by moving the barricades), they both participate in their routine. When the father says, "Joke, doctor" (19), the son replies, "Funny, doctor" (20).

Students should decide whether these characters are static or dynamic. The father remains consistent throughout the story: he savors the adventure, despite the possible penalties. (Though he cannot please his son's mother, he does wheedle his way out of any trouble with the state troopers.) The son is a more dynamic character: he has to move past his inflexible opinions into an appreciation of his father's talents. He characterizes himself for the reader: "I always thought ahead. I was a boy who kept his clothes on numbered hangers to ensure proper rotation. I bothered my teachers for homework assignments far ahead of their due dates so I could make up schedules" (34). However, he finally relaxes and accepts his father for the free spirit that he is: a persuasive, appealing man, a great driver, a loving father who is committed to making sure his son experiences exhilaration and joy in his life, despite his parents' problems. Though earlier in the story, the narrator manifests anxiety about traveling over the closed road ("to keep my hands from shaking I clamped them between my knees" [21]), he now notes, as his father deftly drives through the fresh snow, "I actually trusted him" (35). He also describes his father as "rumpled, kind, bankrupt of honor, flushed with certainty" (35). Compare this statement with the son's responses to and thoughts about his father earlier in the story. In addition, direct students to reread paragraph 3. The son and father have been skiing during the snowfall, and the son acknowledges his dependence on his father's skill: "By now I couldn't see the trail. There was no point in trying. I stuck to him like white on rice and did what he did and somehow made it to the bottom without sailing off a cliff." This passage foreshadows the drive down the closed road later in the day; however, the tone is quite different. Ask students to explain the ways in which the narrator changes his attitude between this journey down the mountain and the one made later on in the "purring" Austin-Healy.

In what way is this drive down the mountain a metaphor for the future of the boy's relationship with his father? The narrator describes the setting: "Down the first long stretch I watched the road behind us, to see if the trooper was on our tail. The barricade vanished. Then there was nothing but snow: snow on the road, snow kicking up from the chains, snow on the trees, snow in the sky; and our trail in the snow. I faced around and had a shock. The lie of the road behind us had been marked by our own tracks, but there were no tracks ahead of us. My father was breaking virgin snow between a line of tall trees. He was humming 'Stars Fell on Alabama' " (21). We know that the narrator's mother will eventually decide to leave his father. We also know that the father is deeply committed to being with his son. Though there are no clear solutions or easy answers, readers may get the feeling from this passage that the father will continue to find ways of loving his son.

POSSIBLE CONNECTIONS TO OTHER SELECTIONS

Margaret Atwood, "Bored" (text p. 737)
William Faulkner, "Barn Burning" (question #1, following)
David Updike, "Summer" (question #2, following)

Connections Questions in Text (p. 667) with Answers

1. Compare the relationship between the father and son in "Powder" and in Faulkner's "Barn Burning" (p. 481). How is loyalty an issue in each story?

    Sarty sees himself entirely as his father's ally in the opening scene of "Barn Burning": "He could not see the table where the Justice sat and before which his father and his father's enemy (*our enemy* he thought in that despair; *ourn! mine and hisn both! He's my father!*) stood. . . ." (1). The father, Ab Snopes, later warns Sarty that family relationships are all he can count on in life. (Ab emphasizes this by striking Sarty.) However, in the end, Sarty betrays his father; he allies himself instead with Major de Spain, the community, and the law. Though he loves the idea of his father, he can no longer support or accept his father's lawless, violent propensities. In contrast, the son in "Powder" initially regards his father with some suspicion and resentment. (The reader wonders whether he has adopted his mother's evident disapproval of his father.) In the course of the story, however, the son comes to appreciate more of his father's qualities — particularly when he realizes that the father is serious about keeping his promise to get his son home for Christmas Eve dinner. In the end, the son demonstrates admiration and love for his father and exhilaration about their adventure together: "the best was yet to come — switchbacks and hairpins impossible to describe. Except maybe to say this: if you haven't driven fresh powder, you haven't driven" (35). Thus, in contrast to Sarty, the narrator of Wolff's story manifests an enhanced, strengthened loyalty to his father by the end of the story.

2. Consider the significance of the titles of "Powder" and of David Updike's "Summer" (p. 169). What alternative titles can you think of for these two stories that help to evoke their meaning?

    Both titles rely on connotations as well as denotations to convey meaning. "Powder" refers literally to the fresh snow that has caused the troopers to close the road. However, it also carries a sense of newness, a sense of the frontier, an opportunity for adventure. It is far superior to packed, well-traveled snow. The title's exhilaration corresponds as well, by the end of the story, to the father and son's improved relationship (and mutual exploits). "Summer" also has diverse meanings. In addition to being a particular time of year, the warmest season, it also represents metaphorically a phase of life for the protagonist, Homer. He is young and athletic; he spends his summer playing tennis, canoeing, and other sports. He also experiences first love. His pursuit of Sandra, though unconsummated, is ultimately a joyful experience.

Resource for Teaching

Interview [recording]. 1 cassette (56 min.). Discussion of stories and storytelling. Distributed by American Audio Prose Library.

POETRY

Brief biographical notes for major poets are included in the first entry for each poet. Check the index for page numbers of first entries. In addition, available resources relating to specific poets and their work are included in the first entry for each poet under the heading "Resources for Teaching." Resources for each of the three poets treated in depth in Chapter 24 appear after the final perspective entry for that poet.

14

Reading Poetry

Perhaps the most difficult part of any introductory literature course is convincing the students that they can, in fact, read poetry. Often, students are intimidated by previous experiences, either in high school or other college courses; they have often accepted that they "just don't get it." Thus, it is important to develop students' confidence in themselves as readers. One way to do this is to get the students to articulate what they see actually happening in the poem, to read what is "on the page."

This chapter has several poems that lend themselves to such an application. Robert Hayden's "Those Winter Sundays, " John Updike's "Dog's Death," Wole Soyinka's "Telephone Conversation, " and Elizabeth Bishop's "The Fish, " among others, are poems that have a clear scene or situation that grounds them: they mean what they say in a concrete way. Other meanings and issues can be raised, of course, but Bishop's poem, for instance, is first and foremost about catching a fish. Students will often "get" this level of the poem, but distrust their reading, figuring that it isn't what the poem is "really about." A good reading, however, is grounded in such particulars. You might want to have students offer a one- or two-sentence summary of the action of such poems: "The speaker in Bishop's poem catches an old fish, looks into his eyes, and lets him go." Students can then be encouraged to build on these readings once their "fear of poetry" has been deflated somewhat.

Even such poems as Robert Morgan's "Mountain Graveyard" can become more accessible; what may seem to some as mere wordplay will be more powerful if students slow down and picture the scene evoked by the title.

In some cases, you may be confronted by students who already have all the answers. Such students can easily intimidate a class. A useful exercise can be done with Robert Frost's "The Road Not Taken" (Chapter 24, text p. 976). Many students have encountered this poem in high school; most have "learned" that it is a poem about making a brave choice that leads the speaker to a life of independence, or a poem of regret at lost possibilities. As the text points out, however, close attention to the verb tenses in the final stanza reveals a more ambiguous reading. You may want to distribute a copy of this poem (with no commentary) to the class, and ask them "How old is the speaker in the poem?" Focusing attention on the last two stanzas can prove instructive even to experienced readers, and emphasize the importance of careful attention and multiple readings.

There are two strategies you may find effective in working with students' resistance to poetry and helping them understand the poems they are faced with: reading aloud and short writings. On the surface, this sounds obvious, but having to understand a poem well enough to read it or hearing it spoken can make a difference in students' appreciation of poetry. Tips on encouraging reading aloud can be found in this manual in the introduction to Chapter 20.

Similarly, you might want to assign students short, informal writing to help them think through some of the issues you want to cover in class. These writings can be based on questions in the text, questions of your own, or even student-generated questions based on issues that seem to interest them in discussion. Preparing them before class discussion can help students frame ideas to share. You may want to grade these assignments only on a pass/fail basis, to give students the chance to do experimental thinking in a low-stakes environment. Chapter 15 has a number of questions and strategies you might find useful in these assignments.

MARGE PIERCY, *The Secretary Chant* (p. 671)

This poem provides an opportunity to discuss point of view in poetry. The secretary's view of herself mirrors the way she is treated. She has become a variety of objects, a list of useful items because she is looked at as an object by people outside her. Her attitude toward herself is framed by other people's perceptions of her, although we must assume that she is aware of her ability to write satire. We get an inkling of her "real" self in the last three lines; the misspelled "wonce" mocks misperceptions of her intellect, while "woman" indicates that there is much more to be learned about the speaker.

In a writing assignment, you might ask students to discuss the metaphors in this poem. What assumptions about women and secretaries do the metaphors satirize? How do sound patterns such as "Zing. Tinkle" (line 14) affect the satire?

POSSIBLE CONNECTIONS TO OTHER SELECTIONS

E. E. Cummings, "she being Brand" (text p. 721)
Katharyn Howd Machan, "Hazel Tells LaVerne" (text p. 725)

RESOURCE FOR TEACHING

Marge Piercy: At the Core [recording]. 1 cassette (58 min.), 1977. Distributed by Watershed Tapes.

ROBERT HAYDEN, *Those Winter Sundays* (p. 672)

Useful comparisons can be made between any of the poems in this book that speak of love's transcendence or amplitude and any others, like this one and Theodore Roethke's "My Papa's Waltz" (text p. 871), that speak of its difficulty — the time it sometimes takes to recognize love. Hayden's speaker looks back at his father's unappreciated Sunday labor, at last knowing it for what it was and knowing, too, that the chance for gratitude has long since passed. The poem gives a strong sense, especially in its final two lines, that the speaker has tended to "love's austere and lonely offices" (line 14). The repetition of "What did I know?" seems to be a cry into the silence not only of the past but of the poet's present situation as well. The poem plays the music of the father's furnace work, the hard consonant sounds "splintering, breaking" (6) as the poem unfolds and disappearing entirely by the poem's end.

You might begin discussion by asking students to describe the speaker's father in as much detail as possible based on the speaker's spare description. From the poem's second word, "too," the poem reaches beyond itself to suggest something about the man without naming it. What other details contribute to our impression of him? Following that discussion, you could also ask for a description of the speaker. What does his language reveal about his character? And how does this character contrast with his father's character?

POSSIBLE CONNECTIONS TO OTHER SELECTIONS

Margaret Atwood, "Bored" (text p. 737)

Andrew Hudgins, "Elegy for My Father, Who Is Not Dead" (text p. 893)

Theodore Roethke, "My Papa's Waltz" (text p. 871)

JOHN UPDIKE, *Dog's Death* (p. 673)

This narrative poem subtly traces a family's emotional response to the illness and death of their pet dog. Ask students to find the events that lead to the dog's death. How does the speaker relate these events? He tells us the dog's age when he talks about her toilet training and immediately establishes the family's relationship to her by repeating their words: "Good dog! Good dog!" (line 4). Alliteration and assonance soften the story; after they have identified these sound patterns, ask students why the repeated sounds are appropriate to the subject matter. Direct their attention to the enjambment in lines 12–13. Why does the sentence span two stanzas? Might the speaker be reluctant to tell us the dog died?

When he relates his wife's reaction to the death, the speaker describes her voice as "imperious with tears" (14). After they have established a definition of the word *imperious*, ask students to determine why it might be used here. The ambiguous "her" and "she" in the final two lines of the stanza make us puzzle out for a moment the pronouns' referent. Is the speaker talking about his wife or the dog? Are both implied? How does this distortion of identity work in a discussion of death?

The final stanza reads as a eulogy; the consonants become harder — "drawing" (18), "dissolution" (18), "diarrhoea" (19), "dragged" (19) — perhaps because the speaker is working at closing off the experience. In a writing assignment, you might ask students to discuss the three uses of "Good dog." How does the last one differ from the first two? How does the poem prepare us for the change?

POSSIBLE CONNECTIONS TO OTHER SELECTIONS

Seamus Heaney, "Mid-term Break" (text p. 892)

Jane Kenyon, "The Blue Bowl" (text p. 768)

Ronald Wallace, "Dogs" (text p. 1164)

RESOURCES FOR TEACHING

John Updike, I and II [recording]. 2 cassettes (58 min.), 1987. Distributed by New Letters on the Air.

The Poetry of John Updike [recording]. 1 cassette (47 min.), 1967. Part of YM-YWHA Poetry Center Series. Distributed by Audio-Forum.

WILLIAM HATHAWAY, *Oh, Oh* (p. 675)

The reader's delight in the surprise ending of this poem hinges on the mood set up by the language of the first fifteen lines. Which words create this idyllic mood? What happens to the poem if you replace these words with others? For example, what words could replace "amble" (line 1)? How might one wave besides "gaily" (10)? How could the caboose pass other than with a "chuckle" (15)? How does the poem read with your revisions?

Does the poet give any clues as to what lies ahead? What about the "black window" in line 9, the exact center of the poem? A writing activity dealing with denotation and connotation could develop from a study of this poem. Have students consider a picture (one of an old house works well) and describe it first as though it might be used as a setting for *Nightmare on Elm Street,* then for an episode of the *Brady Bunch*. Discuss the word choices that set the different moods.

POSSIBLE CONNECTION TO ANOTHER SELECTION

Robert Frost, "Design" (text p. 993)

ROBERT FRANCIS, *Catch* (p. 676)

This poem casts metaphor-making as a game of catch between two boys. If you are using the poem to examine metaphor, you might ask students what is missing from the central metaphor that Francis creates: that is, when two boys are playing catch, they are tossing a ball to one another. If we interpret the two players of this game as the poet and the reader, does the game of catch seem one-sided, as though one player is firing a number of balls at the other one? Once you catch the ball in a game of catch, you throw it back. Does the relationship between reader and poet work the same way?

Encourage students to enjoy listening to this poem. Like a good pitcher, Francis finds various ways of throwing strikes. Consider, for example, line 3, with its "attitudes, latitudes, interludes, altitudes," or "prosy" and "posy" later in the poem.

POSSIBLE CONNECTIONS TO OTHER SELECTIONS

Emily Dickinson, "Portraits are to daily faces" (text p. 934)
Robert Francis, "The Pitcher" (text p. 850)
Robert Wallace, "The Double-Play" (text p. 1122)

WOLE SOYINKA, *Telephone Conversation* (p. 681)

"Telephone Conversation" is a narrative poem that takes a satiric look at the emotionally charged issue of racism. One way to approach the topic of racism (and race in general) is to begin discussion of this poem by having your students paraphrase the poem. Student paraphrases will undoubtedly focus on the racial dimensions of the conversation and the racial theme of the poem. In comparing prose paraphrases to the language of the poem, students may notice several things about the poet's style that are lost in a paraphrase: the short sentences and sentence fragments, the unusual syntax of many lines, the terse language, and the fast pace. After identifying some of these characteristics, you may wish to ask students what effects these characteristics have on the tone of the poem. It may also be interesting to talk about the effect the poet achieves by printing the words of the landlady in capital letters. What are the political implications of this shift? By the end of the poem, what do readers know about the speakers based solely on the words that have passed between them?

You may want to ask students to do a Marxist reading of this poem. In addition to race, they should consider issues of class, power, and social injustice in Soyinka's poem. Although the poet's deft handling of the account leaves little doubt as to who got in the last word, given the inevitable outcome of the exchange, who seems to have "won," and how?

POSSIBLE CONNECTIONS TO OTHER SELECTIONS

Chitra Banerjee Divakaruni, "Indian Movie, New Jersey" (text p. 819)

Langston Hughes, "Ballad of the Landlord" (text p. 1025)

Gary Soto, "Mexicans Begin Jogging" (text p. 923)

ELIZABETH BISHOP, *The Fish* (p. 682)

Born in Worcester, Massachusetts, Elizabeth Bishop knew displacement early: her father died when she was an infant, and her mother was committed to an asylum when she was five. Bishop lived with relatives during her childhood and adolescence in Nova Scotia and New England; after completing a degree at Vassar College, she lived in New York City, Key West, and for sixteen years in Brazil. Travel and exile, as well as the insistent yet alien presence of the "things of the world," figure prominently in her work.

The most arresting feature of "The Fish" is its imagery. Consider, for example, the brown skin that "hung in strips / like ancient wall-paper" (lines 10–11), the ornamentation of "fine rosettes of lime" (17), or the pause to mention and comment again on "the frightening gills" (24). Not only does Bishop have an eye for the particular, even the minute, but in this poem she exhibits an ability to dissect imaginatively flesh, bones, bladder, the interior of the fish's eyes.

After you review the appearance of the fish, it might be a good idea to glance back at the syntax of the poem. Note, for example, the syntactic simplicity and parallelism of lines 5–7, conveying with their flat factuality the fish's implacable "thereness." The syntax becomes a little more complex later on, as Bishop's vision penetrates into the interior of the fish's anatomy and, eventually, into its being. The fish is no longer a mere member of its species but a kind of military hero and a survivor that has escaped at least five attempts on its life.

Bishop's skill transforms the fish into a thing of beauty and an object of admiration, almost without our realizing it. At this point in the discussion, though, it would be a good idea to step back and see what she is looking at. The scene is simply an old fish, brown and battle-scarred, with sullen jaw, staring back at the speaker (Bishop, we assume). Not an ideal setting for the epiphanic moment.

But that is, of course, what occurs — signaled to us by the repetition of the word *rainbow*. In a sense, both fish and poet have transcended themselves — the one by surviving, the other by seeing beyond the ugliness. Victory, indeed, fills up the boat.

POSSIBLE CONNECTIONS TO OTHER SELECTIONS

Joy Harjo, "Fishing" (text p. 1094)

N. Scott Momaday, "The Bear" (text p. 1110)

David Solway, "Windsurfing" (text p. 755)

RESOURCES FOR TEACHING

Delmore Schwartz, Richard Blackmur, Stephen Spender, and Elizabeth Bishop.
1 cassette. Distributed by the Library of Congress.
See "Voices and Vision" in the appendix of Film, Video, and Audiocassette Resources.

PHILIP LARKIN, *A Study of Reading Habits* (p. 684)

This poem about a speaker's developing disillusionment with reading is a clever satire of the speaker's attitude. Note the intricate rhyme pattern in the poem. The poet's use of a complex poetic form while having the poem's speaker use slang and trite phrases provides an excellent opportunity to make students aware of the difference between the poet and the speaker of a poem. Does the slang used in Larkin's poem help to identify the speaker with a particular time period? With what current words would your students replace such words as "cool" (line 4), "lark" (8), "dude" (13)? Is any of the slang used in this poem still current?

After your students have read Larkin's poem, you might ask them to discuss their previous (and present) reading habits or have them write a short essay on this subject. What do they expect to gain from reading? Escape? Pleasure? Knowledge?

POSSIBLE CONNECTIONS TO OTHER SELECTIONS

Thomas Hardy, "The Ruined Maid" (text p. 1093)

Marianne Moore, "Poetry" (text p. 1111)

ROBERT MORGAN, *Mountain Graveyard* (p. 686)

Ask students if they agree with the assertion that "Mountain Graveyard" is "unmistakably poetry." If they think it is poetry, is it a good poem? Meyer's strong argument in the text may be intimidating, but students should be encouraged to develop their own sense of what poetry is as they work through these chapters. Further, this poem and the next afford opportunities (because of their highly unorthodox forms) to lead students into a discussion of the authority of the printed word: Is a piece of literature good because "the book says so"? Is a story "art" because it is anthologized? It might be useful to return to these questions when your class finishes its consideration of poetry.

As a writing activity, have students choose another setting (college campus, supermarket, playground) and develop a set of anagrams for the new locale. Do different arrangements of the anagrams change the overall meaning of the set? Are any of the arrangements poetry?

POSSIBLE CONNECTIONS TO OTHER SELECTIONS

Helen Chasin, "The Word *Plum*" (text p. 851)

E. E. Cummings "l(a" (text p. 687)

E. E. CUMMINGS, *l(a* (p. 687)

E. E. Cummings was born in Cambridge, Massachusetts, the son of a Congregationalist minister. He earned a degree from Harvard University and began writing his iconoclastic poems after coming upon the work of Ezra Pound. His experimentation with syntax and punctuation reflects a seriously playful attitude toward language and meaning and a skepticism about institutional authority.

At first glance, "l(a" seems to be a poem spewed out by a closemouthed computer held in solitary confinement. As with Morgan's "Mountain Graveyard," however, the poem comes into its own as the reader not only deciphers but brings meaning to the text. Implied here is a simile between a falling leaf and loneliness. The use of a natural image to suggest an emotion recalls Japanese haiku (see Chapter 22).

The vertical quality of the poem illustrates the motion of a single leaf falling. Students might also point out the repetition of the digit *one* (indistinguishable in some texts from the letter *l*), along with other "aloneness" words, such as *a* and *one*. If ever a poem's medium enhanced its message, this one surely does.

POSSIBLE CONNECTION TO ANOTHER SELECTION

Robert Morgan, "Mountain Graveyard" (text p. 686)

RESOURCES FOR TEACHING

E. E. Cummings Reading His Poetry [recording]. 1 cassette. Distributed by Caedmon/HarperAudio.

E. E. Cummings Reads [recording]. 1 cassette (60 min.), 1987. From The Poet Anniversary Series. Distributed by Caedmon/HarperAudio.

E. E. Cummings Reads His Collected Poetry, 1920–1940, & Prose [recording]. 2 cassettes (79 min.). Distributed by Caedmon/HarperAudio.

E. E. Cummings Reads His Collected Poetry, 1943–1958 [recording]. 2 cassettes. Distributed by Caedmon/HarperAudio.

E. E. Cummings: The Making of a Poet. 24 min., 1978. Beta, VHS, ¾" U-matic cassette. A profile of Cummings told in his own words. Distributed by Films for the Humanities and Sciences.

E. E. Cummings: Nonlectures [recording]. 6 cassettes. 1. "I & My Parents"; 2. "I & Their Son"; 3. "Self-discovery"; 4. "I & You & Is"; 5. "I & Now & Him"; 6. "I & Am & Santa Claus." Distributed by Caedmon/HarperAudio.

Poems of E. E. Cummings [recording]. 1 cassette (60 min.), 1981. Part of Poetic Heritage Series. Distributed by Summer Stream.

E. E. Cummings: Twentieth-Century Poetry in English: Recordings of Poets Reading Their Own Poetry, No. 5 [recording]. Distributed by the Library of Congress.

See also "Poetry for People Who Hate Poetry," "Inner Ear, Parts 5 and 6," and "Caedmon Treasury of Modern Poets Reading Their Own Poetry" in the appendix of Film, Video, and Audiocassette Resources.

ANONYMOUS, *Western Wind* (p. 688)

Students should be aware that, in England, the coming of the west wind signifies the arrival of spring. How is the longing for spring in this lyric connected to the overall sense of longing or to sexual longing? These brief four lines contain examples of several poetic devices worth noting. Ask students to consider the effects of the apostrophe and the alliteration in the first line. Many modern poets would consider these techniques artificial and overdone, but this poet seems to be interested in making a strong statement in just a few words. Does it work? Also, consider the use of the expletive "Christ" (line 3). This word makes the reader feel the intensity of emotion being conveyed and turns the poem into a kind of prayer — it is both sacred and profane.

For purposes of comparison, consider this poem in conjunction with another lyric that uses the same apostrophe, Percy Bysshe Shelley's "Ode to the West Wind" (text p. 894). Students should note that "Western Wind" is much more personal and less formal in diction than Shelley's poem.

POSSIBLE CONNECTION TO ANOTHER SELECTION

Timothy Steele, "An Aubade" (text p. 761)

REGINA BARRECA, *Nighttime Fires* (p. 688)

This narrative poem has a recurrent theme, indicated by the repetitions of the word *smoke*. Smoke is the end of the father's quest, but what, exactly, is he looking for? His daughter, the speaker, provides a clue when she tells us that her father lost his job, so he had time to pursue fires. Smoke is the father's assurance that there is justice in the world because fires destroy rich and poor people alike. Ask students to look at the images the speaker uses to describe her father: What kind of man is he? How would they characterize the daughter's relationship to him? Does the mother also think of these drives as "festival, carnival" (line 15)? In some respect, the carnival is the father's performance before his family, in which the "wolf whine of the siren" (9) is matched by his "mad" (8) expression.

In a writing assignment, you might ask students to examine the metaphors describing the father. What do these figures tell us about his life? For example, in the final image of the father, his eyes are compared to "hallways filled with smoke" (31). Why is he likened to a house? What might this image tell us about his life?

POSSIBLE CONNECTIONS TO OTHER SELECTIONS

Michael S. Harper, "Grandfather" (text p. 1095)
Robert Hayden, "Those Winter Sundays" (text p. 672)

HELEN FARRIES, *Magic of Love* (p. 692)

Note the ways in which this poem fulfills the greeting-card formula, especially with its "lilting" anapests, internal rhymes, and tried-and-true (and terribly trite) metaphors, all designed to lift the reader's spirits.

You might begin discussion by asking why this poem has withstood the test of time (as greeting-card verse). The pleasure of this specific poem comes not as much from its theme, which is nothing particularly new, as from its elements of sound, especially its internal, and full, end-stopped rhyme. Because poetry evolved, at least partly, from an oral tradition — using rhymes as mnemonic devices — you may even use this poem as a vehicle for discussing the very basic history of poetry. You may ask, for example, *why* strict rhyme and meter serve as such an effective mnemonic device. Does this poem use its devices pleasurably?

POSSIBLE CONNECTION TO ANOTHER SELECTION

Langston Hughes, "Formula" (text p. 1021)

JOHN FREDERICK NIMS, *Love Poem* (p. 693)

Greeting cards must speak to the anonymous masses. Nims's poem, while maintaining a simplicity of diction and a directness of sentiment, is far stronger than the greeting-card verse, in part because it is addressing a specific person.

The poem is obviously not a piece to be carved on the pedestal of some faceless ideal; students will probably have at least some curiosity about a poem that begins "My clumsiest dear." After they have become accustomed to this violating of poetic convention, ask them to review the poem for other refreshing and surprising uses of language. They might mention, for example, the use of "shipwreck" as a verb in line 1, the play on "bull in a china shop" (line 3), or the projective quality of "undulant" in line 8 to describe the floor as it appears to the drunk. Again, unlike conventional verse, this poem concludes with an almost paradoxical twist to the most salient feature of this woman who breaks things: her absence would cause "all the toys of the world [to] break."

In a writing assignment, you might ask students to compare this poem with Shakespeare's sonnet "My mistress' eyes . . ." (text p. 882).

POSSIBLE CONNECTION TO ANOTHER SELECTION

William Shakespeare, "My mistress' eyes are nothing like the sun" (text p. 882)

RESOURCE FOR TEACHING

John Frederick Nims [recording]. 1 cassette (29 min.), 1986. A reading by the Chicago poet. Distributed by New Letters on the Air.

BRUCE SPRINGSTEEN, *Streets of Philadelphia* (p. 694)

Many of your students may be familiar with this song, which was featured in the award-winning film *Philadelphia*. For students who are unfamiliar with the movie, you may want to explain that the movie depicts the true story of a man with AIDS and his landmark court case concerning discrimination against people with AIDS, tried in the city of Philadelphia. Ask your students to consider whether knowing that this song was written to accompany this film influences their reading of the song.

Listening to a recording of the song will undoubtedly provide students with a richer understanding of the tone. It may be helpful to ask students whether their interpretations of the lyrics change when the music is added. You might ask your students to consider how the words and notes interact in this particular song and whether one seems stronger or weaker than the other. To further class discussion comparing the recording of "Streets of Philadelphia" to the printed version, read the work aloud to your students, being careful to pause only for line breaks. Then ask students to consider whether the music contributes more to their understanding of the song. Depending on the response you get, you might ask if the lack of punctuation makes the lyrics more difficult to follow without the music.

POSSIBLE CONNECTION TO ANOTHER SELECTION

Robert Francis, *On "Hard" Poetry* (text p. 697)

RESOURCES FOR TEACHING

Springsteen's *Greatest Hits* [recording]. 1 CD. Distributed by Columbia Records.
Philadelphia. 125 min., color, 1994. VHS. Film starring Tom Hanks and Denzel Washington, featuring Bruce Springsteen's hit single "Streets of Philadelphia." See local retailer.

QUEEN LATIFAH, *The Evil That Men Do* (p. 695)

Taking its title from Shakespeare's *Julius Caesar*, this rap song tackles contemporary issues from welfare to drugs to homelessness. The speaker targets not only government but also someone who puts a quarter in a video machine while neglecting the homeless. Because the speaker's message may be hard to swallow, the poem begins with a first-person justification; as in many rap lyrics, the speaker sets herself up to be larger-than-life: "Behold the Queen," she says (line 2). Even though the poem is nothing more than "thoughts in mind," the words are important "because I knew you wanted it." Then in the second stanza she shifts the focus from herself — the Queen who is "livin' positive" (4) — to one who isn't: some "poor girl [who] can't find / A way to be crack-free" (35–36). The contrast paints the "poor girl" more starkly and offers the speaker as a possible role model. In the final stanza, she takes the focus off the government and puts it on anyone who doesn't seem to care about his fellow man. A thematic inroad into the poem may be to discuss and extrapolate the meanings of "evil" and "men" as they appear in the title, and as they change over the course of the poem.

Students are likely to be more familiar with rap lyrics than their instructors are. Ask how many of them are familiar with "the Latifah with the Queen in front of it" in particular. How does her public persona influence the way they read the poem? Since rap has been propagated, at least in part, by television, you might find it productive to discuss poetry as a performance as opposed to a private experience. Consider the role of public readings of more academically accepted poets like T. S. Eliot, for instance. You may also want to compare other features of rap with more "traditional" poetic conventions: end-rhyme, allusion, alliteration, and clever turns-of-phrase. Ask students to describe these conventions and to give examples of them from this poem; then, if you have worked with other twentieth-century poetry, contrast the types of conventions apparent in rap versus other modern poems. Such a discussion, coupled with a discussion about the Shakespearean context of the title, may lead to a cultural debate about "high" and "low" art, or about what constitutes "literature." What is the effect of studying something that students may have considered "merely" entertainment in a class about something as serious as "literature"?

POSSIBLE CONNECTION TO ANOTHER SELECTION

Bruce Springsteen, "Streets of Philadelphia" (question #1, following)

CONNECTION QUESTION IN TEXT (p. 697) WITH ANSWER

1. Compare the world described in this song with that presented in "Streets of Philadelphia" (p. 694).

    Both lyrics paint a picture of loneliness in an urban environment, but the imagery in Queen Latifah's song is more concrete than that in Springsteen's. Her emphasis is much broader, much less concerned with the problems of an individual self and more with what that self perceives. In Springsteen's world, the self is reaching out for connection to another; in Latifah's world, the self is telling the rest of us what's wrong with the world and implicating us in the perpetuation of its problems.

PERSPECTIVE

ROBERT FRANCIS, *On "Hard" Poetry* (p. 697)

Discussing hard poetry through its opposite, soft poetry, may be the best way into a discussion of this piece. Hard poetry does not use excess words, does not lapse into sentimentality, does not have an undefined or loose form. The hard poem sustains tension between poet and speaker, reader and text. You may want to put Francis's ideas to the test by asking students to find specific lines from "Streets of Philadelphia" that support their argument about whether the lyrics can be characterized as "hard" poetry. Are the speaker's tone and the images used in the song sentimental — or "soft"? Students should be able to point to a number of lines that allow for multiple interpretations — that challenge the reader and create some "resistance." For example, you might ask them to discuss Springsteen's use of the adjective *faithless* in line 21. Why is the kiss of the "brother" who *receives* the speaker described as "faithless"? You might also ask students whether they feel the lyrics are tightly organized. How effective is Springsteen's use of rhyme and repetition?

POSSIBLE CONNECTIONS TO OTHER SELECTIONS

Helen Farries, "Magic of Love" (text p. 692)

Langston Hughes, "Cross" (text p. 1020)

Bruce Springsteen, "Streets of Philadelphia" (text p. 694)

MICHAEL ONDAATJE, *To a Sad Daughter* (p. 698)

This poem is a close examination of a father's relationship with his maturing daughter. The poet examines the differences between him and his daughter, and attempts to understand and communicate with her on her own level. By scrutinizing his daughter's newfound likes and dislikes, the poet hopes to come to terms with their changing relationship and "advise" his daughter on what futures lie ahead of her.

Throughout the poem the poet lists and attempts to understand his daughter's peculiar attributes, such as her fondness for hockey and horror movies. At the same time, he understands how these things will help shape and form her so that she will become the person she is destined to become. He sees the potentialities for both joy and sadness in her life and hopes to be a source of reliability for her, yet understands that she must eventually choose her own path. "One day I'll come swimming / beside your ship or someone will / and if you hear the siren / listen to it. For if you close your ears / only nothing happens. You will never change."

There is tension in this poem between the desire to protect and the desire to let the daughter go out into "all those possible worlds!" (line 59); even the poet, sometimes, unintentionally loses his connection to his daughter in the creation of his own world, the world of his poems. Here, the "yellow suburban annunciation" (81), serves to place his daughter in the hopeful world of the fully realized potentiality of his daughter.

You may enter into a discussion of this poem by asking your students to make a list of all the "advice" that the poet gives to his daughter. What does this advice say about the poet's dreams of his daughter's future? It will also be important to discuss the meaning of the reference to death in the last stanza of the poem.

POSSIBLE CONNECTIONS TO OTHER SELECTIONS

Lucille Clifton, "come home from the movies" (text p. 791)

Sylvia Plath, "Daddy" (text p. 1113)

ALICE WALKER, *a woman is not a potted plant* (p. 700)

This speaker's definition of womanhood works by contrasting against the metaphor of a potted plant and the confines a potted plant embodies. After the first three stanzas of contrast, the speaker goes on to define woman as "wilderness unbounded" (lines 27–28); even more unbounded than a flying wild animal such as a bee. The effect of describing what womanhood is *not* is a strong rhetorical device, evident in poetry dating back at least as far as the English Renaissance (as in the opening line of Ben Jonson's "To Penshurst," "Thou art *not*, Penshurst, built to envious show . . ."). Students may be interested not only in the effect of this rhetoric but in its power — as though the speaker is arguing with someone before he or she has even asserted anything. This speaker's strong voice allows her to make her point in such a way that her opinion comes across loud and clear, so her rhetorical stance is appropriate to the topic of the poem: the need to redefine womanhood.

This is truly a polemical poem, then; but students may be interested in discussing the contrast between the message — which might be described as political, or which can be said to be historical in the sense that Walker is redefining woman *against* the more "traditional" definition — and the imagery, which is completely natural. Why does she select a natural metaphor rather than a metaphor from history or politics to communicate her message? Ask students to describe any hierarchies they see in nature as a way of unpacking the hierarchy inherent in the poem's structure: the progression from a potted plant to a bee. You may want to pause at each of the steps of the hierarchy to discuss how each represents a stereotypical view of womanhood. In addition to Marge Piercy's "The Secretary Chant" (text p. 671), the title poem from Walker's collection *Her Blue Body Everything We Know* can enhance students' understanding of Walker's use of woman as a metaphor for nature.

POSSIBLE CONNECTIONS TO OTHER SELECTIONS

Marge Piercy, "The Secretary Chant" (question #1, following)
William Shakespeare, "My mistress' eyes are nothing like the sun" (text p. 882)

CONNECTION QUESTION IN TEXT (p. 701) WITH ANSWER

1. Compare Walker's take on female identity in this poem with Marge Piercy's in "The Secretary Chant" (p. 671). How are their conceptions similar? Different?

    In both cases, women have been dehumanized, yet Walker describes women in terms of nature, whereas Piercy's speaker considers herself in mechanical terms. In one sense, Walker's poem responds to the situation presented in Piercy's, arguing that women should be considered boundless. Walker's speaker is distant from her subject, though, whereas Piercy's is immersed. Consequently, Walker's speaker is much stronger, taking a firm position on how women should be regarded.

RESOURCE FOR TEACHING

Interview with Kay Bonetti [recording]. 2 cassettes (82 min.), 1988. Distributed by American Audio Prose Library.

WYATT PRUNTY, *Elderly Lady Crossing on Green* (p. 701)

"Elderly Lady Crossing on Green" undercuts the reader's expectations; although unlike William Hathaway's "Oh, Oh" (text p. 675), this poem's surprise comes early on in the poem. The reader's expectations that an elderly woman crossing a street will be feeble, helpless, and aged, are blown away first by her rejection of all of the nice gestures young people offer, then by the vision that she was not only once young, but also vicious. The poem becomes a vision of a younger version of the woman behind the wheel, driving like a maniac, disregarding all pedestrians in her path.

That the poem begins *in medias res* adds to an invisible litany of the reader's expectations, set up by the title. Having students write a list of images that come to mind when they see or think about old women, then listing these images on the board may lead to an interesting discussion of stereotypes and expectations. Why is it relatively acceptable to harbor stereotypes about the elderly in our culture while it is taboo to harbor stereotypes about race, ethnicity, gender, etc.? The speaker begins by assuming that we all know (and perhaps share) these stereotypes, and the vision of his menacing subject as a young woman points up our prejudice. We are even denied the opportunity to romanticize her past, to dwell on the fact that she was once a "widow, wife, mother, or a bride" (line 14).

Is this poem meant to be funny, as "Oh, Oh" is? Does it play up our pity even as it confounds our expectations? Much of the interpretation hinges on the last two stanzas, and you may have to work hard to get students to transfer their attention from the relatively simple fantasy about the past to the somewhat philosophical ending. Is the poem entirely a fantasy based on a woman's anger? Is she feeling alienated, "a small tug on the tidal swell" (19)? Is her rejection of nice gestures in the first stanza motivated by fear rather than cantankerousness? While exploring these questions, you might want to ask students to examine the references to death in the poem, for example: "run you flat as paint" (6), "jaywalked to eternity" (12), "the other side" (16). Why do we sometimes treat death in such a cartoonish, ostensibly humorous way?

POSSIBLE CONNECTIONS TO OTHER SELECTIONS

William Hathaway, "Oh, Oh" (question #1, following)
Aron Keesbury, "Song to a Waitress" (text p. 872)

CONNECTION QUESTION IN TEXT (p. 702) WITH ANSWER

1. Write an essay comparing the humor in this poem with that of William Hathaway's "Oh, Oh" (p. 675).

    The humor in this poem depends on the image of an elderly woman acting against our expectations: young, uncaring, and aggressive. In Hathaway's poem, the Hell's Angels act exactly as we expect them to, so the humor hinges on the speaker's perception of them as they present an element of danger in his bucolic scene. Another significant difference is that the humor in "Oh, Oh" occurs at the end of the poem, causing us to rethink the rest of the poem from the title on. In Prunty's poem, much of the humor occurs at the beginning; by the end, we feel pity for the elderly lady rather than mirth.

ALBERTO RÍOS, *Seniors* (p. 702)

You might begin your discussion of this poem by asking students to talk about its use of slang, particularly in the first stanza. The slang establishes the speaker's environment as well as his conversational tone. As the poem progresses, it focuses on the speaker, and the tone becomes more meditative. Although they modify his relationship to other people, the images of cavities, flat walls, and water (particularly in stanza III) distance the speaker from the social realm, until he is left "on the desert" in the last stanza.

Students might write an essay on these images. How does their evocation of sexual experience prepare us for the last line of the poem? What is the speaker trying to say about sex, about life? How does the language of the final stanza compare with that of the first stanza? What might this changed diction indicate in the speaker's attitude toward himself and the world?

POSSIBLE CONNECTIONS TO OTHER SELECTIONS

T. S. Eliot, "The Love Song of J. Alfred Prufrock" (question #2, following)

Sharon Olds, "Sex without Love" (question #1, following)

CONNECTIONS QUESTIONS IN TEXT (p. 703) WITH ANSWERS

1. Compare the treatment of sex in this poem with that in Sharon Olds's "Sex without Love" (p. 740).

    Olds talks about sex as a sport, noting how lovers who have sex without love treat their bodies as separate from "truth." The images Olds uses to make her point are unlike Ríos's imagery. Ríos talks about bodies as continually fading away. His speaker calls the body of the woman he first kissed almost "nonexistent" (line 18), comparing all sexual experiences to a "flagstone wall" (22), vacationing in Bermuda, swimming ("all water," 27). For Ríos's speaker, sex provides a vehicle for capturing the past; for Olds's speaker, sex is the subject for a lesson about love.

2. Think about "Seniors" as a kind of love poem and compare the speaker's voice here with the one in T. S. Eliot's "The Love Song of J. Alfred Prufrock" (p. 1045). How are these two voices used to evoke different cultures? Of what value is love in these cultures?

    J. Alfred Prufrock's voice bespeaks an empty culture, characterized by "sawdust restaurants" and "yellow smoke" as well as by empty conversations and rituals. "Prufrock" is a love poem that never comes to be because the speaker is too fearful to act: "Do I dare / Disturb the universe?" Ríos's speaker also describes a lost culture, particularly in his use of slang and his references to materialism in the first two stanzas. In fact, many of the images in "Seniors" are complemented by similar, though starker, images in "Prufrock." In each poem, love symbolizes the speaker's individual feelings of loss and the collective emptiness of the culture.

RESOURCES FOR TEACHING

Alberto A. Ríos: Reading His Poetry [recording]. 1 cassette. Distributed by Sound Photosynthesis.

See also "Birthright: Growing Up Hispanic" in the appendix of Film, Video, and Audiocassette Resources.

MARY JO SALTER, *Welcome to Hiroshima* (p. 703)

In the second person, this poem traces the speaker's reactions upon visiting Hiroshima (the site of the first atomic bomb dropped on Japan during World War II) by projecting the speaker's emotions onto the reader, the "you" who is ostensibly the subject of the poem. At first she is turned off by the crass commercialism that has taken over the town, then meditates on the irony of the eerie optimism of the place — the "mistaken cheer" (line 19) with which "humanity" has "erased its own erasure" (20). Her desire to drink in history leads her into the memorial museum, but she is struck initially by the bad taste with which the bombing is presented. Just as she is about to dismiss the experience, she is drawn in by a striking exhibit: the wristwatch of a child, jammed at the precise moment the bomb struck.

One way into the poem is to trace in detail the speaker's emotional development, paying careful attention to the imagery. You may have to coax students a little to recognize the difficulty of moving the reader from a comparison between the mushroom cloud of the A-bomb and a television advertisement for beer, to "the blood and scum afloat / on the Ohta River" (10), to the absurdity of a maraschino cherry garnishing a pizza. Getting from the town into the museum is equally jarring, and tracing the poet's use of imagery will help students to feel what the speaker is going through: from being able to compare "strings of flesh" (24) to "gloves / a mother clips to coatsleeves" (23–24) to being struck by the image of the stopped watch. Once you have established the specifics of her emotional journey, you can take on the question of why the watch is a particularly resonant symbol for this speaker.

It may also be beneficial to speculate about the motivations of the speaker. Why would a person make such a visit? It isn't likely that your students will have been to Hiroshima, but some may have visited another memorial site that recalls a historical tragedy: concentration camps in Eastern Europe or Holocaust monuments or museums in America, any number of Vietnam memorials, the site of a Native American massacre, etc. You may want to approach their experience by first asking what they hoped to feel, contrasted with what they actually did feel; but you might also want to emphasize the difference between individual memorials: how the memorial in Hiroshima is not exactly the same as the ones they might have seen. Such a discussion might branch out into considerations of how history should best be commemorated, particularly history that necessarily disturbs us. How can historical events best be felt in the present, and why might "bad taste" such as that described in the poem make itself felt?

POSSIBLE CONNECTION TO ANOTHER SELECTION

Denise Levertov, "Gathered at the River" (question #1, following)

CONNECTION QUESTION IN TEXT (p. 705) **WITH ANSWER**

1. Write an essay comparing Salter's treatment of the commemoration of Hiroshima with Denise Levertov's in "Gathered at the River" (p. 907).

   Levertov's poem is solemn throughout. The ritual that the speaker participates in is serious, and her emotions are deeply felt from the beginning of the poem through the end. In Salter's poem, the speaker is taken aback at first by the crass presentation of the victims of the atomic bomb. She expects to be moved, and she eventually is, but her experience is one of transformation; she is almost surprised by how deeply she feels the pain of the victims once she sees the exhibit of the stopped watch. Students might find it easier to access the emotions of Salter's speaker because of this transformation. You could draw a comparison between these poems about mourning and poems about faith; George Herbert's "The Collar" (p. 1097) suggests a transformation similar to that expressed in Salter's poem whereas the speakers of Gerard Manley Hopkins's poems are generally secure in their faith from the beginning, just as Levertov's speaker is secure in her emotions regarding victims of the holocaust.

JOHN DONNE, *The Sun Rising* (p. 705)

John Donne was born Roman Catholic when England was staunchly anti-Catholic, a circumstance that made his pursuit of worldly success significantly more difficult than it might otherwise have been for one with his intelligence, energy, and wit. Donne attended

Oxford and Cambridge Universities and trained in the law for a time. After a youth and young manhood full of worldly pleasure, Donne became an Anglican preacher in 1615.

This aubade uses a typical metaphysical conceit transforming two lovers in bed into a universal microcosm. The speaker entreats the sun to leave him and his lover alone and to bother others who need to get out of bed. The dialogue is ostensibly between the speaker and the sun, but students will probably wish to discuss the relationship between the speaker and his lover. What is implied by the metaphor, "She is all states, and all princes I" (line 21)? Does the speaker seem more preoccupied with his wordplay or with his lover?

The speaker's blunt message is to leave the lovers alone and bother other people who need waking to get on with the work of their ordinary lives. The tone softens in the second stanza, as Donne thinks more of his beloved. When he is with her, the world seems to be concentered in their presence. If the sun were to shine only on their room, it would be everywhere.

In the final stanza the speaker continues to expound on how, when you are in love, your heaven, earth, and kingdom are contained in your beloved. As he writes in the opening of this stanza, "She is all states, and all princes I" (21), and later, "All honor's mimic, all wealth alchemy" (24). Some students might point out that the idea that true love is a treasure worth far more than any amount of money still persists.

POSSIBLE CONNECTIONS TO OTHER SELECTIONS

John Donne, "The Flea" (text p. 1090)
Andrew Marvell, "To His Coy Mistress" (text p. 729)
Richard Wilbur, "A Late Aubade" (question #1, following)

CONNECTION QUESTION IN TEXT (p. 706) WITH ANSWER

1. Compare this lyric poem with Richard Wilbur's "A Late Aubade" (p. 732). What similarities do you find in the ideas and emotions expressed in each?

    Both speakers have in common the desire to linger in bed with their lovers, but Donne's speaker blames the sun for trying to separate them. He is implicated in the impending parting because he, too, must rise and leave. By contrast, Wilbur's speaker blames his lover, who seems to have more tasks or obligations than he does. Another difference is the scope of the rhetoric they use. Typical of "metaphysical" conceits, Donne's speaker presents the situation in grand terms, making his lover "all states" (line 21) and their bedroom the entire universe. Wilbur's speaker does not make such grand pronouncements; he simply states that it is nicer to linger in bed and kiss than to busy oneself with routine occurrences.

RESOURCES FOR TEACHING

Essential Donne [recording]. From the Essential Poets Series. Distributed by the Listening Library.

John Donne [recording]. 40 min., VHS. Discusses the poet's life and works. Distributed by Insight Media.

John Donne: Love Poems [recording]. 1 cassette. Distributed by Recorded Books.

John Donne: Selected Poems [recording]. 2 cassettes (180 min.), 1992. Read by Frederick Davidson. Distributed by Blackstone Audio Books.

The Love Poems of John Donne [recording]. 1 cassette. Distributed by Caedmon/HarperAudio.

Treasury of John Donne [recording]. 1 cassette. Distributed by Spoken Arts.

See also "Metaphysical and Devotional Poetry" and "Palgrave's Golden Treasury of English Poetry" in the appendix of Film, Video, and Audiocassette Resources.

LI HO, *A Beautiful Girl Combs Her Hair* (p. 706)

Like his predecessor Li Po, Li Ho did not serve as a civil servant, an unusual choice for poets of the T'ang Dynasty in China. He wrote poems while riding on a donkey and revised them at the end of each day.

Juxtaposition, one of the most important techniques in Chinese poetry, is amply evident in this poem, as is one of Li Ho's characteristic touches: supernatural mystery appearing alongside unvarnished description ("singing jade"; "her mirror / two phoenixes / a pool of autumn light"). The poet deftly brings the senses into play; the girl's "spilling hair" has a precise fragrance; it is not simply black but the "color of raven feathers / shining blue-black stuff"; and it defeats her "jade comb," which in the middle of the poem falls without sound.

You might ask students to think about where the speaker is in relation to this scene and what significance his location might have for his exasperation. Reading the poem without the speaker's outburst in lines 23–26 might lead to a productive discussion of the effects of metaphor and connotation. What sort of girl is this "wild goose" with blackest hair so carefully attended? How much does the speaker know of her? How much does he wish to know?

POSSIBLE CONNECTIONS TO OTHER SELECTIONS

Langston Hughes, "The English" (text p. 1024)
Sylvia Plath, "Mirror" (text p. 786)
David Solway, "Windsurfing" (text p. 755)
Cathy Song, "The White Porch" (question #1, following)

CONNECTION QUESTION IN TEXT (p. 707) WITH ANSWER

1. Compare the description of hair in this poem with that in Cathy Song's "The White Porch" (p. 772). What significant similarities do you find?

   Song's "The White Porch" has a tone similar to that of this poem, with alluring, almost seductive images of a woman's hair. Both women's hair is thick and unmanageable. Each woman gathers vegetation from the garden, again pointing to her ripe sexuality. In both poems hair serves as a way of knowing the women, a means of access to their restlessness and self-consciousness. You might ask students to comment on differences in the poems resulting from the difference in speakers. Li Ho's speaker watches the woman dress her hair and is upset by her "slovenly beauty" (line 24). The speaker in Song's poem is the possessor of the hair and of the erotic power it symbolizes and releases.

ROBERT HASS, *Happiness* (p. 707)

The speaker of this poem builds up to a definition of "happiness" that is based on his and his lover's appreciation of a natural scene of foxes eating windfall apples. After seeing this scene, they each write. These events, coupled with other details from their cozy life, cause the speaker to reflect on his mood.

Students, of course, have access to a huge genre of "Happiness is . . ." clichés in the form of greeting cards, coffee mugs, and bathroom wall hangings. It is important to get them to see how complex and specific Hass's definition of happiness is by emphasizing what's contained within the dashes of this poem. Students might find themselves eliminating those sections to get the gist of the speaker's happiness; yet these are crucial descriptions. The speaker sees something of the beauty and mystery of nature, and he twice tries to speculate about what creatures might "symbolize." The symbolic value of foxes ("the wakefulness of living things" [line 5]), of mist ("the luminous and indefinite aspect of intention" [13]), and of swans ("mystery" [17]) give the poem a dimension that students might initially resist in an attempt to glean the bottom line about happiness. The figurative meaning of natural creatures has a nice inversion in the final line, in which the speaker and his lover are compared to bats. Encourage students to explore the relationship between the speaker's attempt to situate himself and his wife or lover in nature and the process of their writing. Happiness seems to emerge from these two acts, which together amount to interpreting nature, a prominent *poetic* motif.

POSSIBLE CONNECTIONS TO OTHER SELECTIONS

James Dickey, "Deer Among Cattle" (text p. 766)

Emily Dickinson, "I like a look of Agony" (question #1, following)

CONNECTION QUESTION IN TEXT (p. 708) WITH ANSWER

1. Write an essay that compares and contrasts "Happiness" with Emily Dickinson's "I like a look of Agony" (p. 938). Do they both succeed in capturing an emotion? What message do you take away from each?

    Students may see "Happiness" as a poem that explores emotion and Dickinson's poem as one that suppresses emotion. We have a good sense of the personality of Hass's speaker, but Dickinson's speaker seems eccentric and unfamiliar. Hass's imagery churns up a genuine feeling in the speaker and in the reader, whereas Dickinson's speaker describes death in very cold, matter-of-fact terms. Yet both poems value genuine emotion, and in both cases people have little control over genuine emotion, which originates in something outside themselves.

MILLER WILLIAMS, *Excuse Me* (p. 708)

This poem goes even further than Archibald MacLeish's "Ars Poetica" (text p. 1107) or Marianne Moore's "Poetry" (text p. 1111) to reveal the negotiation between reader and poet. It goes beyond the act of reading a poem to take on a specific contemporary academic approach to literature. The speaker takes a position against the deconstructionist notion that the author is nonexistent, thereby giving himself a voice that we cannot ignore, beginning with the title. He defines a poem and advances a theory about how to read poetry in the first stanza. In the second stanza he rejects the idea of deconstruction since it eliminates one of the "players" of the game of reading poetry. Avoiding the author amounts to "sitting on one end / of a seesaw in summer, wishing you had a friend" (line 15).

This poem gives students a chance to articulate what they do when they read a poem. Do they see it as a kind of game? If so, do they see the poet as the other player? In lines

6–10, Williams seems to construct the poem as a sort of chess match, or a battle of wits — a very different sort of game than playing on a seesaw. Which one better represents students' experiences? Can they come up with another game analogy that fits the situation even better? Is this poem, like deconstruction, an intellectual exercise, or is it emotional as well?

You might also encourage students to apply Williams's definition of poetry to this poem; in what sense is it "an act / of language meant to hold its own exceptions" (4–5)? What poetic conventions does it use or reject? The final two lines of the first stanza and the final four lines of the second stanza employ end rhyme, for instance. Would the poem have had a different effect if Williams had used end rhyme throughout? What about if he hadn't used end rhyme at all?

POSSIBLE CONNECTION TO ANOTHER SELECTION

Archibald MacLeish, "Ars Poetica" (text p. 1107)

RESOURCES FOR TEACHING

Miller Williams [recording]. 1 cassette (29 min.), 1985. Distributed by New Letters on the Air.

Poems of Miller Williams [recording]. 1 cassette. Read by the author. Distributed by Spoken Arts.

The Poetry of Miller Williams [recording]. 1 cassette (26 min.), 1969. Part of the YM-YWHA Poetry Center Series. Distributed by Audio-Forum.

Writing about Poetry

Comments often overheard in introductory literature classes suggest that many students believe that they are simply incapable of understanding poetry. Thus, their attempts to find meaning in poems are often hindered by their feelings of intimidation and ineptness. The Questions for Responsive Reading and Writing in Chapter 15 may prove to be particularly useful to these insecure students because they break down general poetry analysis into smaller components, which students may feel better able to manage. These questions, however, can also aid more confident and capable students in their analysis and interpretation of poetry by offering specific places for them to begin their literary investigations.

You might also use these questions in class to teach your students how to approach writing about poetry. Have your students work individually or in small groups, exploring possible answers to these questions using assigned poems. Brief written responses to these questions might lead to longer, more detailed interpretations at a later time. Of course, not every question will relate meaningfully to every poem. To help students learn to apply a certain type of question in their analysis, you might devise an exercise in which your students decide which questions are best suited to which particular poems in a set. You might also remind them that these questions about poetry are open-ended and often require more than a one-word or one-sentence response. Ask your students to provide evidence for their answers by quoting directly from the poems they have chosen to analyze. Also, it is important for students to feel comfortable using the terminology that describes particular elements of poetry; be sure to refer them to the Glossary of Literary Terms included in the anthology (text p. 2147) if they are having trouble understanding any of these terms.

Chapter 15 includes a brief sample student paper analyzing Elizabeth Bishop's poem "Manners" (text p. 713). Ask your students to read the poem and then discuss how they might approach the assignment that was given to this student writer. What specific aspects of the poem might they choose to explore? What would they do differently from the writer of the sample? You may consider assigning your class a writing task similar to the one described in this chapter, using any poem your students have studied. The sample paper, while not necessarily a blueprint for effective poetry analysis, may offer your students a useful model of strong student writing that they may try to emulate. At the same time, you might ask your students to treat the sample student paper as an unfinished draft of an essay and have them suggest ways to revise this paper that would make it an even more effective piece.

Word Choice, Word Order, and Tone

Since poetry depends for its effects on the concentrated use of language, word choice can play a pivotal role in determining the meaning of a poem. For instance, in Martín Espada's "Latin Night at the Pawnshop," the choice of the word *apparition* as the first noun in the poem echoes Pound's "In a Station of the Metro." One word sets up an allusion to a key imagist poem, and thus puts Espada's poem in the context of that tradition. Still, students may remain unconvinced that word choice is all that important to a poem.

As an exercise to emphasize the importance of word choice, you might have students type up a short poem or section of a poem on a word processor. Most word processors now come with a thesaurus function that allows the user to replace a word with a synonym provided from a list. Have students replace either a couple of key words in the poem or a word in each line with the synonyms offered, and then read their new poems to the class. For instance, Pound's "In a Station of the Metro" can range from "The mirage of these faces in the throng / petals on a damp black bough" to "The fantasy of these mugs in the bunch / petals on a clammy dire branch." After a few such examples, it should become clear how important word choice is to the overall effect of the poem.

You might try a similar exercise for word order with some of the selections (E. E. Cummings's "in Just–" lends itself to this application). Having students think hypothetically about other options for the poem can help them develop an appreciation for the reasons a poem is the way it is. In general, counterfactuals help sharpen critical thinking skills.

The reasons a poem conveys a certain tone are sometimes hard to pin down, and can initially prove frustrating for students. A poem like Derek Walcott's "The Virgins" relies not only on careful word choice ("dead," "die," "funeral") but also on the images of dry desolation and emptiness. You might find it helpful to encourage students to look not only at word choice but also other features of the poem in their discussions of tone.

The pairing of Hardy's and Slavitt's poems about the *Titanic* can very effectively show students the workings of diction. The popularity of the James Cameron movie *Titanic* will ensure that students know something about the event itself. A similar pairing that can prove interesting is Keats's "Ode on a Grecian Urn" and Olds's "Sex Without Love." Both poems describe a beautiful aesthetic object but differ greatly in their ultimate conclusions, a difference that has much to do with tone. It may be a challenge, but having students articulate this difference in class discussion or a short writing can prove useful to their understanding of how tone and theme are related.

RANDALL JARRELL, *The Death of the Ball Turret Gunner* (p. 720)

Randall Jarrell attended Vanderbilt University and so became influenced by the Agrarian literary movement, an anti-industrial movement that sought to reinstate the values of an agricultural society. Jarrell's poem probably reflects on personal experience, as he was an air force pilot from 1942 until the end of World War II. However, like most of his poems, it evokes universal human pain and anguish, regardless of its specific circumstances.

The textual discussion of this poem calls attention to Jarrell's intentional use of ambiguity in some of his word choices, but is the overall tone of the poem ambiguous? How would you describe the speaker's attitude toward his subject? Have students look at Alfred, Lord Tennyson's "The Charge of the Light Brigade" (text p. 870) for another depiction of death in war. What are the word choices Tennyson makes in order to create the tone he wants? How does the tone of Tennyson's poem compare to that of Jarrell's?

The scene depicted in Jarrell's poem might almost be a synopsis of one of the major story lines in Joseph Heller's novel *Catch-22*. Compare Jarrell's word choices and the mood created by them to Heller's depiction of the gunner in Chapter 5 of *Catch-22*:

> That was where he wanted to be [atop the escape hatch, ready to parachute to safety] if he had to be there at all, instead of hung out there in front like some goddam cantilevered goldfish in some goddam cantilevered goldfish bowl while the goddam foul black tiers of flak were bursting and billowing and booming all around and above and below him in a climbing, cracking, staggered, banging, phantasmagorical, cosmological wickedness that jarred and tossed and shivered, clattered and pierced, and threatened to annihilate them all in one splinter of a second in one vast flash of fire. (New York: Dell, 1974, p. 50)

POSSIBLE CONNECTIONS TO OTHER SELECTIONS

Wilfred Owen, "Dulce et Decorum Est" (text p. 763)
Alfred, Lord Tennyson, "The Charge of the Light Brigade" (text p. 870)

RESOURCES FOR TEACHING

The Poetry of Randall Jarrell [recording]. 1 cassette (67 min.), 1963. Part of YM-YWHA Poetry Center Series. Distributed by Audio-Forum.

Randall Jarrell: The Bat Poet [recording]. 1 cassette. Distributed by Caedmon/HarperAudio.

Randall Jarrell Reads and Discusses His Poems Against War [recording]. 1 cassette. Distributed by Caedmon/HarperAudio.

See also "The Poet's Voice" in the appendix of Film, Video, and Audiocassette Resources.

E. E. CUMMINGS, *she being Brand* (p. 721)

This poem is a naughtily playful allegory of a young man's attempt to initiate a sexual experience with his girlfriend. Language accommodates the situation of the poem nicely, since some men seem to respond to cars and women with equal measures of affection and caretaking and refer to both cars and women as "she." Cummings drops innuendos of his witty double entendres early on. Listen, for example, to the opening eight lines, in which the poet seems to pause over words like "stiff" (line 4), "universal" (6), and even "springs" (8), which could suggest springs of affection. Knowing the "secret" of the poem, the class should enjoy lines such as "next / minute i was back in neutral tried and / again slo-wly;bare,ly nudg. ing (my" (lines 13–15). This work also offers good opportunities to discuss the function of punctuation in poetry.

Sharon Olds, "Sex without Love" (text p. 740)
Marge Piercy, "The Secretary Chant" (text p. 671)

DEREK WALCOTT, *The Virgins* (p. 723)

The speaker of this poem despairs over the effect of American tourism on his small Caribbean island. He laments the replacement of duty-free goods for real trade, implying that the bargains made available by the duty-free shops have killed other economic opportunities in the city.

Students who have not traveled or who do not understand duty-free shopping may need a little background before they can grasp the speaker's sentiment. You might want to give a little history of Caribbean economics by explaining the legacy of the slave trade in the Caribbean and moving into a consideration of the tourism industry. What kind of an economic base does tourism provide? What are the implications for people who work in the tourism industry? Students may point out that tourism seems like a "win-win" situation: local residents have jobs and their economy is stimulated by foreign dollars and tourists have a tropical playground where they can relax.

The poem acts as a counterpoint to this point of view, and complicates discussions of the American Dream: Whose dream is it, anyway? Beyond clichés about suburban middle-class security and picket fences, is there something essential, something integral about that dream that unifies our nation and gives us a necessary sense of identity? If so, how can the speaker hold the attitude that there are good things in life that are "not lost to the American Dream" (line 4)? Does prosperity for one person necessarily mean poverty for someone else? What are we left with when we mourn the passing of soulless things like condominiums and roulette wheels? A discussion of opposing images of death and life should enhance this discussion of trade. At the same time, you might want to emphasize the interplay between natural and artificial objects in the poem. The title "The Virgins" provides a nice ironic twist by suggesting the irrevocable loss of something while eliding the word that suggests possession of the islands by the head nation of the tourism empire; ask students what the difference is between "The Virgins" and "The U.S. Virgin Islands."

POSSIBLE CONNECTIONS TO OTHER SELECTIONS

Jean Toomer, "Reapers" (text p. 844)
Thom Ward, "Vasectomy" (text p. 920)

RESOURCES FOR TEACHING

Bill Moyers's A World of Ideas: Derek Walcott [video]. Color, VHS (29 min.), 1989. Distributed by PBS Video.

Derek Walcott Reads [recording]. 1 cassette (90 min.). Distributed by Caedmon/HarperAudio.

Omeros [recording]. 1 cassette (29 min.), 1990. Distributed by New Letters on the Air.

Walcott on Poetry [recording]. 1 cassette. Distributed by the Center for National Humanities.

RUTH FAINLIGHT, *Flower Feet* (p. 724)

Born in New York City, Ruth Fainlight now lives in England, where she writes many poems about women and their relationships with their families, children, pets, and others. Her interest in non-Western cultures is clear from her travel sketches of India as well as from this poem.

The terrible price of "beauty" is one consideration of this poem. Ask students to talk about the custom of binding feet. How do the speaker's descriptions of the process reveal the mentality of those who invented and sustained the custom? Notice how the speaker talks about the shoes as artifacts in the first stanza, painting their appearance in complimentary images, then, in the second stanza, undercuts their appealing exteriors by examining what they produced.

In a writing assignment, you might ask students to consider the speaker's attitude toward women. How does she feel about "nurse and mother" (line 15)? What are the larger implications of her perspective on sex discrimination sanctioned by cultural custom?

POSSIBLE CONNECTIONS TO OTHER SELECTIONS

Robert Frost, "Mending Wall" (question #1, following)
James Merrill, "Casual Wear" (question #2, following)
Janice Mirikitani, "Recipe" (text p. 803)

CONNECTIONS QUESTIONS IN TEXT (p. 725) WITH ANSWERS

1. How is the speaker's perspective on tradition and custom in this poem similar to that in Frost's "Mending Wall" (p. 979)?

    In "Mending Wall" Frost's speaker subtly disdains the custom of keeping other people at a distance. The neighbor's statement "good fences make good neighbors" does not convince the speaker that they need a fence, but he cannot end the tradition by arguing with his neighbor. Similarly, Fainlight feels helpless when confronted with the cruelty of a cultural custom that caused pain to many women. Fainlight examines a tradition that no longer continues; Frost points out a problem many Americans consider a fact of existence. Comparing the poems, students might examine the similarities between these very different cultural customs.

2. The final line of this poem is startling. Why? How is it similar in its strategy to James Merrill's "Casual Wear" (p. 817)?

    The final line of the poem is startling because we would ordinarily blame men for these women's torture, whereas Fainlight's speaker wonders at how women could torture their own daughters out of custom. Merrill's "Casual Wear" attacks its listeners similarly, using the familiar topic of women's apparel to explore the possible causes and effects of a terrorist attack. Just as Fainlight challenges our notions of sex discrimination, Merrill asks us to consider terrorism from a less glossy position than the news presents; the implication of the rich in the act is undeniable and fascinating to discuss.

KATHARYN HOWD MACHAN, *Hazel Tells LaVerne* (p. 725)

You might begin discussing this poem by talking about names and how they too have connotative value. Would our expectations be the same if the poem were titled "Sybil Speaks with Jacqueline"? By and large this poem does a good job at getting across its meaning through denotative language. But the fact that Hazel does use language almost exclusively in denotative terms is in itself a sign of her personality. As in a dramatic monologue by Robert Browning, Hazel tells more about herself, her social class, and her impenetrably matter-of-fact outlook on life than she does about her encounter with the frog. We as readers then fill in the gaps of the speaker's perceptions as well as piece together her outlook and attitude.

You might ask students to respond to Hazel's personality. She is likable; her matter-of-factness cuts through any of the fairy tales the world might try to sell her, and she's funny. Students can probably provide examples of characters from TV shows who are like Hazel and whose humor derives from their plain-spoken concreteness. We all admire the survivor who cannot be duped.

POSSIBLE CONNECTIONS TO OTHER SELECTIONS

Robert Browning, "My Last Duchess" (question #1, following)
Thomas Hardy, "The Ruined Maid" (text p. 1093)

CONNECTION QUESTION IN TEXT (p. 726) WITH ANSWER

1. Although Robert Browning's "My Last Duchess" (p. 821) is a more complex poem than Machan's, both use dramatic monologues to reveal character. How are the strategies in each poem similar?

   The speakers of each poem reveal something about themselves as they try to narrate a story. The speaker of this poem repeats the line "me a princess," indicating that her bravado is just a front for her dreams. The speaker of Browning's poem uses more sophisticated language, and he believes that he is in control of the narrative situation, but the more he talks the more he reveals about his true desires and motives. His asides are what give him away; as he pauses to consider how he should express something, he gives us the opportunity to analyze not only the content of his speech but his expression of it as well.

MARTÍN ESPADA, *Latin Night at the Pawnshop* (p. 726)

This imagist poem describes a scene of a man looking into the window of a pawnshop. In the instruments suspended there, he sees the apparition of a salsa band. The poet compares the instruments to a dead man with a toe tag.

There is nothing apparently "difficult" about this poem, so students may be quick to dismiss it, feeling that they "get the point" instantly. The challenge for discussion then becomes to fill in the considerable space around the poem. The liveliness of a salsa band coupled with the fact that the poem takes place on Christmas, a day of celebration, contribute to the blunt emotional overtones of the poem. What does the speaker's presence at a pawnshop on Christmas suggest? The speaker is implicitly mourning the passage of something vital. Unlike the Christmas ghosts of a character students are familiar with, Dickens's Scrooge, this apparition does not seem to provide any comfort or hope for the future. The apparition is the *absence* of the band, with its instruments apparently sold cheaply. As a way of pointing out what exactly has been lost, emphasize all of the economic allusions in the poem (pawnshop, Liberty Loan, golden, silver, price tags). Does the poem seek to make a broad point about class and culture in contemporary America? Consider the title as a follow-up to this question. Students may think of other examples of the various ways in which immigrants in America must "sell out" their culture for more fundamental survival needs (i.e., money).

Thom Ward, "Vasectomy" (text p. 920)

MAXINE KUMIN, *Woodchucks* (p. 727)

Maxine Kumin has a farm in southern New Hampshire, and many of her poems describe her experiences with the land and with raising and training her horses. To anyone familiar with farming, especially in New England, woodchucks are pesky creatures that seem to do their best to make a peaceable coexistence between animals and humans difficult.

In her efforts to get rid of the woodchucks, notice how Kumin arranges language as an armor to justify her acts. Like a good attorney, she has an "airtight" legal and moral case against the woodchucks. But when you read line 5, you see that her action amounts to entrapment. Language drawn from a religious sphere is also used to bolster her resolve to kill the woodchucks. The knockout bomb is described as "merciful" (line 3), and as the speaker picks up the .22, she "righteously" thrills to its feel (13). Even in her personal estimation, she is "a lapsed pacifist fallen from grace / puffed with Darwinian pieties for killing" (15–16). Where religion hesitates, science, with its promise of salvation for the fittest, moves in. What surprises Kumin is her newfound awareness that she can kill, one-on-one, with the dispatch of a "murderer" or "hawkeye killer" (23–24). She thrills to the act and yet is haunted by it. Observe with the class how particular are her memories of each woodchuck she shoots and how, afterward, she has an unquiet dream of killing.

The final lines of the poem, "If only they'd all consented to die unseen / gassed underground the quiet Nazi way," are disquieting and filled with implications. An essay topic could be organized around an evaluation of Kumin's attitude toward her act, particularly with reference to these lines. Initially, Kumin did attempt to gas the woodchucks. Now that she has shot them, does she somehow feel implicated in the mindset that fueled the Jewish Holocaust? Aside from learning that she can kill, what has she learned from this experience?

William Stafford, "Traveling through the Dark" (text p. 813)

ROBERT HERRICK, *To the Virgins, to Make Much of Time* (p. 728)

Robert Herrick, son of a well-to-do London goldsmith, rather halfheartedly became an Anglican clergyman assigned to Dean Prior in Devonshire, in the west of England. He wrote poems secretly, making up for many of them alluring, exotic, phantom mistresses. After losing his position when the Puritans rose to power, Herrick published his only book, containing some 1,200 poems, in 1648.

This is one of the better-known poems of the *carpe diem* (seize the day) tradition. Here, Herrick is advising young women in a tone of straightforward urging to make the most of their opportunities for pleasure while they are in the prime of youth and beauty. These "virgins," Herrick implies, are like the sun at its zenith or a flower in full bloom; they will soon begin to decline and may never have the same opportunities for marriage again. The word *virgins,* rather than *women,* accommodates the advice in the last stanza to "go marry" and carries with it as well the connotation of sought-for sexual fulfillment. Some of your students might point out how a young woman's situation is much more complex today than it apparently was in Herrick's time, since "seizing the day" can and often does mean pursuing opportunities for career over those for marriage.

One possible way to enter a discussion of the poem is to consider the arrangement of the argument. The speaker has a definite intent: to communicate bits of wisdom to the "virgins" of the title. What effect does the order of his points of argument have on the way the poem reads? What would happen if we were to rearrange the first three stanzas: Would the message of the poem remain exactly the same?

POSSIBLE CONNECTIONS TO OTHER SELECTIONS

Robert Frost, "Nothing Gold Can Stay" (text p. 989)
Edmund Waller, "Go, Lovely Rose" (text p. 1123)
Richard Wilbur, "A Late Aubade" (text p. 732)

RESOURCE FOR TEACHING

See "Palgrave's Golden Treasury of English Poetry" in the appendix of Film, Video, and Audiocassette Resources.

ANDREW MARVELL, *To His Coy Mistress* (p. 729)

After graduating from Cambridge University in 1639, Andrew Marvell left England to travel in Europe. Almost nothing is known of his life from this time until he became the tutor of the daughter of a powerful Yorkshire nobleman in 1650. Most of his poems seem to have been written during the next seven years. He served for a short time as John Milton's assistant when Milton was Latin secretary for the Commonwealth, and he represented Hull, his hometown, in Parliament from 1659 until he died.

This seduction poem is structured with a flawless logic. Marvell begins with a hypothetical conjecture, "Had we but world enough, and time," which he then disproves with hyperbole, promising his "mistress" that he would devote "an age at least" to praising her every part. Time is, of course, far more limited, and the second section of the poem makes clear time's ravages on beauty. The third section expounds the *carpe diem* theme: if time is limited, then seize the day and triumph over life's difficulties with love.

From his initial tone of teasing hyperbole, the poet modulates to a much more somber tone, employing the metaphysically startling imagery of the grave to underscore human mortality. Lines 31–32 are an example of understatement, calculated to make the listener react and acknowledge this world as the time and place for embracing.

Some classes may need help in recognizing that the verbs in the first part of the poem are in the subjunctive mood, while those in the last are often in the imperative. At any rate, students should easily recognize that the last section contains verbs that all imply a physical vigor that would seize time, mold it to the lovers' uses, and thus "make [time] run" (46) according to the clock of their own desires.

The poem seems far more than a simple celebration of the flesh. It confronts human mortality and suggests a psychological stance that would seize life (and face death) so that fulfilling of one's time would be a strategy of confronting time's passing.

As a writing topic you might ask students to explain the radical and somewhat abrupt change in tone between the opening twenty lines and the rest of the poem. Marvell offers more than one reason to temper his initial levity.

Refer students to Bernard Duyfhuizen's " 'To His Coy Mistress': On How a Female Might Respond" (text p. 731) for a contemporary perspective on the poem.

TIP FROM THE FIELD

I use point-of-view writing assignments that ask students to assume a persona in a poem or story and respond to the other characters or situations in the selection accordingly. For example, I have students read Andrew Marvell's "To His Coy Mistress" and then write an essay from the point of view of the wooer or the wooee.

— SANDRA ADICKES, *Winona State University*

POSSIBLE CONNECTIONS TO OTHER SELECTIONS

Diane Ackerman, "A Fine, a Private Place" (text p. 734)

John Keats, "Ode on a Grecian Urn" (text p. 741)

Carolyn Kizer, "Food for Love" (text p. 769)

Richard Wilbur, "A Late Aubade" (text p. 732)

RESOURCES FOR TEACHING

Andrew Marvell: Ralph Richardson Reads Andrew Marvell [recording]. 1 cassette. Distributed by Audio-Forum.

See also "Metaphysical and Devotional Poetry" in the appendix of Film, Video, and Audiocassette Resources.

PERSPECTIVE

BERNARD DUYFHUIZEN, *"To His Coy Mistress": On How a Female Might Respond* (p. 731)

You might ask your students in a writing assignment to use Duyfhuizen's analysis as a model in writing their own description of a female's response to a male poet's address. They could use the poems in this section (Robert Herrick's "To the Virgins, to Make Much of Time" [text p. 728] and Richard Wilbur's "A Late Aubade" [text p. 732]), or they might choose a poem like Shakespeare's "Shall I compare thee to a summer's day?" (text p. 881). Students could also choose an address by a female poet to a male — Margaret Atwood's "you fit into me" (text p. 777), for example — or a poem by a woman about a relationship with a man — Adrienne Rich's "Living in Sin" (text p. 1115) — and analyze the male's response.

RICHARD WILBUR, *A Late Aubade* (p. 732)

A prolific poet, critic, translator, and editor, Richard Wilbur (b. 1921) studied at Amherst and Harvard and was awarded the Pulitzer Prize and the National Book Award in 1957 for *Things of This World*. Influenced by the works of the Metaphysical Poets and Wallace Stevens, Wilbur's poetry has been described by poet and critic John Ciardi as often concerned with "the central driving intention of finding that artifice which will most include the most of life."

It is difficult to translate the forms of Renaissance charm and wit into the more hurried, less mannered tones of the twentieth century. So Wilbur seems to find as he writes his "late" aubade ("late," one supposes, as in "late Corinthian," as well as late in the day), in which going means staying and seizing the day dictates staying in bed. Despite the turnabout in manners and customs, this poem achieves its own special charm. You might begin discussion, though, by asking the class to evaluate the speaker here as rhetorician or persuader. Does he keep to the rules of logic, or does he beg some questions and employ loaded language in other instances? Obviously, he has no admiration for women who spend hours in either libraries or shopping malls, and with deadpan doggerel he sets up a rhyme in stanza I between "carrel" (line 1) and "Ladies' Apparel" (4) that devalues both activities. Likewise, he colors the attitude of the person being addressed by talking of planting a "raucous" (5) bed of salvia (which yield bright blue or red flowers) or lunching through a "screed" (7) (the archaism is deliberate here) of someone's loves.

The poem is an appeal to the assumed and presumed sensuality of both the speaker and the woman he addresses. Thus the Matisselike still life of chilled white wine, blue cheese, and ruddy-skinned pears with which Wilbur concludes the poem is a fitting tricolor tribute to the senses, even though the woman here is still the one who serves and waits.

A writing assignment could be organized around a comparison of Herrick's "To the Virgins, to Make Much of Time" (text p. 728), Marvell's "To His Coy Mistress" (text p. 729), and this poem. Wilbur's poem is more conversational and relaxed, reflecting a commonality of spirit between the lovers. The speaker here dwells more on the prolonged moment than on the bleak foreknowledge of death.

POSSIBLE CONNECTIONS TO OTHER SELECTIONS

John Donne, "The Sun Rising" (text p. 705)

Deborah Garrison, "She Was Waiting to Be Told" (text p. 1152)

Robert Herrick, "To the Virgins, to Make Much of Time" (questions #1 and #2, following)

Andrew Marvell, "To His Coy Mistress" (questions #1 and #2, following)

Sharon Olds, "Sex without Love" (text p. 740)

Edmund Waller, "Go, Lovely Rose" (text p. 1123)

CONNECTIONS QUESTIONS IN TEXT (p. 733) WITH ANSWERS

1. How does the man's argument in "A Late Aubade" differ from the speakers' in Herrick's and Marvell's poems? Which of the three arguments do you find most convincing?

    Unlike the other two writers, Wilbur's speaker is not immediately concerned with the passing of his youth. Herrick's and Marvell's poems try to convince their listeners to seize the moment because they feel the pressure of old age and mortality. Consequently, their rhetoric is loftier than Wilbur's, encompassing history and popular mythology. Wilbur's speaker tries to convince his lover in relatively simple language — "Isn't this better?" (line 12) — that the morning is more pleasantly spent in bed with him than elsewhere. Students are likely to find Wilbur's speaker the most convincing; his rhetoric is influenced by the "give the people what they want" philosophy of the twentieth century, whereas the other two poets are influenced by models of classical rhetoric of the English Renaissance. If the consensus tends this way, you might want to consider how rhetoric changes over time.

2. Explain how the tone of each poem is suited to its theme.

Herrick's speaker argues from a position of wisdom, even condescension, which is fitting since the theme urges young women to live the moment of their youth. Marvell's poem seems more desperate; the speaker feels the pressure of "Time's wingéd chariot" (line 22) because he, along with his lover, senses his own passing youth. Wilbur's speaker is not as young — this is a *late* aubade — so his tone, his language, and his argument are all more leisurely, as though he is not worried about losing the moment of his youth as much as he would simply like his lover to remain in bed with him.

RESOURCES FOR TEACHING

Richard Wilbur [recording]. 1 cassette (29 min.), 1990. The author reads his poems and talks about early influences and censorship. Distributed by New Letters on the Air.

Poems of Richard Wilbur [recording]. 1 cassette. Distributed by Spoken Arts.

Poetry — Richard Wilbur and Robert Lowell. 30 min., b/w, 1966. ¾" U-matic cassette, 16-mm film, special-order formats. Interviews with the two poets. Distributed by Indiana University Instructional Support Services.

Richard Wilbur Reading His Poetry [recording]. 1 cassette. Distributed by Caedmon/HarperAudio.

See also "Caedmon Treasury of Modern Poets Reading Their Own Poetry" and "Twentieth-Century Poets Reading Their Work" in the appendix of Film, Video, and Audiocassette Resources.

DIANE ACKERMAN, *A Fine, a Private Place* (p. 734)

Ackerman's poem might serve as sequel to Marvell's "To His Coy Mistress" (text p. 729) because it focuses less on the man's pursuit of his love (the subject of the speaker's rhetorical assault in Marvell's poem) than on the actual act of intercourse. The title of this poem is an allusion to the following lines from "To His Coy Mistress": "The grave's a fine and private place, / But none, I think, do there embrace" (lines 31–32). Ackerman depicts a grave of sorts — below the surface of the ocean — where the lovers in her poem, referred to at different times as "a pirate vessel" (48) and "a Spanish Galleon" (60), do embrace. Underwater, the man can phrase his desire only in physical gestures. Beginning with the description of his erection, when the woman notices "the octopus / in his swimsuit / stretch one tentacle / and ripple its silky bag" (15–18), Ackerman constructs an elaborate extended metaphor in which the lovers' bodies and their actions are construed in the highly specific imagery of the underwater world.

While Ackerman devotes significant and elaborate description to the couple and their lovemaking, enacting Marvell's speaker's plea to "tear our pleasures with rough strife" (43), there are instances in the poem in which, like Marvell, she seems to regard the woman as a commodity, as a "sea-geisha" (24). The lovers return to the surface only after the male is satisfied, and after he gives the signal. We are told that he leads the woman to safety (80). Throughout this process, even the ocean pets the woman, "cell by cell, murmuring / along her legs and neck, / caressing her / with pale, endless arms" (85–88). How does she seem to regard this?

It is only at the end of the poem that Ackerman delves into the woman's response to her experience. Whereas Marvell focuses solely on the male's perspective, Ackerman remedies this in the final lines of her poem, in which the woman continues to envision the surface world in marine terminology. She sees the snowflakes as "minnows" (109) and savors "holding a sponge / idly under tap-gush" (110–111) as it reminds her of her underwater tryst. The final stanza would seem to suggest that the woman treasures her experience underwater. Ask students to identify the poem's tone. Are we to regard the relationship portrayed in the poem as an ideal encounter?

POSSIBLE CONNECTIONS TO OTHER SELECTIONS

Marilyn Bowering, "Wishing Africa" (text p. 743)

Emily Dickinson, " 'Heaven' — is what I cannot reach!" (text p. 936)

Andrew Marvell, "To His Coy Mistress" (question #1, following)

CONNECTION QUESTION IN TEXT (p. 736) WITH ANSWER

1. Write an essay comparing the tone of Ackerman's poem with that of Marvell's "To His Coy Mistress" (p. 729). To what extent are the central ideas in the poems similar?

    Both poems value passionate sex, but Marvell's poem anticipates the sexual encounter, whereas Ackerman's poem recalls it. As a result, Marvell's poem is more rushed, hurried on by "Time's wingéd chariot" (line 21) and Ackerman's poem is more leisurely, both in terms of its tone and its length. In a sense, their messages are opposite: Marvell's speaker argues that his youth is passing away quickly and that he is hurtling toward death, so he must enjoy passion when he is young. The subject of Ackerman's poem recalls her sexual encounter during the mundane moments of her daily routine, intimating that the moment of youth lives on in memory instead of passing away forever — the fear of Marvell's speaker.

MARGARET ATWOOD, *Bored* (p. 737)

This adult speaker reflects on her boredom as a young girl spending time with her father. She recounts their activities together, and ultimately realizes that her mature perceptions differ greatly from her childhood perceptions. She ends with the wistful realization, "Now I would know." Careful readers will notice that the relationship between the speaker and the "he" of the poem is likely that of a daughter and father; she sits in the back seat, helps him to build a garden, and learns about nature from him. It might be interesting to discuss why no one else exists in the poem. Is it primarily about him or about her? If the daughter is sitting in the back seat, it is likely that her mother is sitting in the front seat; why is her mother never mentioned?

The poem's single stanza doesn't help to identify points at which the speaker's attitude, point of view, or definition of boredom shift. It may be productive to have students identify and discuss these points: when boredom transmutes into "looking hard and up close at the small / details" (lines 13–14), or when her activity merges with "what / the animals spend most of their time at" (25). How does the meaning of the word "bored" change from the title through line 37? Students might be more likely to recognize the pun with "board" (4) — an object that almost seems an extension of the speaker in the early lines. However, the more elusive pun on boring as digging or burrowing represents a crucial turn in the speaker's perspective, as it allows the speaker to connect her activities with those of the animals her father "pointed . . . out" (27–28). "Boring" — a negative word to any child — becomes a positive word from the speaker's adult perspective since it connotes digging deeper in order to find meaning, resulting in a mature appreciation of her father.

POSSIBLE CONNECTION TO ANOTHER SELECTION

Robert Hayden, "Those Winter Sundays" (question #1, following)

1. Write an essay on the speaker's attitude toward the father in this poem and in Robert
    Hayden's "Those Winter Sundays" (p. 672).

    The two poems end with strikingly similar sentiments: the penultimate line of Hay-
    den's poem is, "What did I know, what did I know," and the final line of Atwood's is
    "Now I would know." Both speakers look back on their youthful relationship with
    their fathers from the point of view of a relatively wise and experienced adult. Yet a
    much greater gulf exists between the speaker of "Those Winter Sundays" and his fa-
    ther, who is associated with "the chronic angers of that house" (line 8). Atwood's
    speaker has a more intimate relationship with her father, who whistles, boats, and
    drives a car. Hayden's speaker's father works too hard and is alienated from his family.
    The bond of love between them is apparent, but it is an intense kind of "tough love."

RESOURCE FOR TEACHING

Margaret Atwood Reads [recording]. 1 cassette (36 min.). Distributed by Caed-
mon/HarperAudio.

THOMAS HARDY, *The Convergence of the Twain* (p. 738)

Between the ages of fifteen and twenty-one, Thomas Hardy was apprenticed to an architect in his native Dorchester, an area in southwest England that he was to transform
into the "Wessex" of his novels. He went to London in 1862 to practice as an architect
and pursue a growing interest in writing. Though he enjoyed a successful career as a novelist, Hardy stopped writing fiction after publishing *Jude the Obscure* in 1895, concentrating instead on the poetry that ranks him among the major English poets.

This poem ushers in an event that some consider to be the beginning of the modern
era: the sinking of the *Titanic*. The final two stanzas support this idea. What is the true
significance of the event, according to the speaker? What are the implications of a God
who is described as both "The Immanent Will that stirs and urges everything" (line 18)
and "the Spinner of the Years" (31)? On a superficial level, the "twain" of the title signifies the ship and the iceberg; what are some of the connotative meanings of the word?

The *Titanic* as described in this poem is "gaily great" (20) in its luxurious opulence,
but Hardy also stresses the ship's "vaingloriousness" (15), planned by the "Pride of Life"
(3). It is as though in this dramatic gesture of invention and design humanity became the
tragic overreacher. In a writing assignment, you might ask the class to compare the tones
of the speakers in this poem and in Percy Bysshe Shelley's "Ozymandias" (text p. 1118).

The "marriage" between ship and iceberg is suggested through the use of several
words and phrases, such as "sinister mate," (19), "intimate welding," as in "wedding" (27),
and "consummation" in the final line.

Hardy, the master celebrator of "Hap" (see text p. 1093), assigns the disaster to Fate,
or as he allegorizes it, the "Immanent Will" (18) that directs all things and the "Spinner of
the Years" (31), who decides when time has run out.

POSSIBLE CONNECTIONS TO OTHER SELECTIONS

Stephen Crane, "A Man Said to the Universe" (text p. 805)
David R. Slavitt, "Titanic" (text p. 739)
Wallace Stevens, "The Emperor of Ice-Cream" (text p. 1120)

The Poetry of Thomas Hardy [recording]. 1 cassette. Distributed by Caedmon/HarperAudio.

See also "Introduction to English Poetry," "Romantics and Realists," and "Victorian Poetry" (recording) in the appendix of Film, Video, and Audiocassette Resources.

DAVID R. SLAVITT, *Titanic* (p. 739)

Although Slavitt's poem acknowledges the power of fate, it focuses on human attitudes rather than cosmic forces. The first stanza, for example, calls attention to our gullibility; its weary, yet affectionate tone originating in the "this is how we are" shrug of the two *who* clauses. The speaker ponders death, deciding that since "we all go down" (line 4), it would be better to do so with some company and some notice from the rest of the world. But the speaker's gentle urging that it wouldn't be "so bad, after all" (11) to go "first-class" (14) includes some simple, unambiguous descriptions of what such a mass loss of life would actually be like: "The cold water" (11–12), which would be "anesthetic and very quick" (12); the "cries on all sides" (13). Death always wins, "we all go down, mostly / alone" (4–5), so wouldn't it be fine to die "with crowds of people, friends, servants, / well fed, with music" (4–5)?

You might ask students to compare in a short paper the attitudes toward fate in "Titanic" and Hardy's "The Convergence of the Twain" (text p. 738) and how each poem's diction and tone contribute to the communication of these attitudes.

Possible Connection to Another Selection

Thomas Hardy, "The Convergence of the Twain" (questions #1 and #3, following)

Connections Questions in Text (p. 740) with Answers

1. How does "Titanic" differ in its attitude toward opulence from "The Convergence of the Twain" (p. 738)?

   In Hardy's poem, the opulence of the passengers on board the *Titanic* is emblematic of their lack of humility, and it seems partially responsible for the crash. Slavitt's poem, at least on the surface, celebrates the style with which the same passengers exited the world, arguing that, as long as we have to die, we might as well be having fun while we do it.

3. Compare the speakers' tones in "Titanic" and "The Convergence of the Twain."

   Hardy's poem is serious, formal in its use of language, form, and rhyme. "Titanic" is much more colloquial, less brooding in its tone and its language. Both poems could be described as philosophical, but Slavitt's brand of philosophy is more home-spun and optimistic.

SHARON OLDS, *Sex without Love* (p. 740)

The word *beautiful,* which begins the second sentence of this poem, may puzzle students at first. Coupled with the ambiguity of the initial question (which may indicate either the speaker's envy or her disdain), the appeal of the lovers as performing artists may signal a positive view of them. But students will soon recognize that the beautiful images of the poem are surface images only; they are also empty and somewhat violent. The textural imagery — "ice" (line 3), "hooked" (4), and even "red as steak" (6) — suggests an undertone of danger in this act. As an artist, the poet must show the lovers as beautiful forms, but as an artist with a social consciousness, she must also explore the vacuum beneath the forms.

A discussion of the poem's imagery may begin with an exploration of all the possible meanings of its initial question. The speaker examines not only the moral implications of this self-centered experience but also the mechanics of the physical act: *how* as well as *why* they do it. Discuss the shift in tone from the portrayal of the lovers as ice skaters and dancers in the initial lines to their likeness to great runners. This last metaphor solidifies the coldness of the speaker's assessment. Like great runners, the lovers concentrate only on the movement of their bodies, surrendering their mental and emotional health to the physical act. Students will see that the energy and concentration of runners are essential to a track event but not to an act of mutual communication. It is essential for the couple to think of themselves as athletes in order to escape the negative moral and potentially painful emotional implications of their act.

The religious images of the poem contrast with its athletic metaphors. Beginning with "God" (line 9) and moving into "light / rising slowly as steam off their joined / skin" (11–13), the speaker subtly distinguishes between the false, body-bound vision of the lovers and the "true religion" that is implied through their negation. Ask students to identify the speaker's tone in these lines: is she really talking about a religious experience, or is she pointing out the lovers' self-absorption? The mathematical language with which the speaker imagines her subjects talking about themselves, "just factors" (21), is undercut by her derogatory tone. Although *they* may act as if they are God, if we are searching for truth, we know that we can never really be single bodies alone in the universe. The implied "truth" here is a communal one, just the opposite of what is described.

In a writing assignment, you might ask students to explore what is not said in the poem. What is the alternative? Why would the speaker not state her idea of truth directly?

POSSIBLE CONNECTIONS TO OTHER SELECTIONS

E. E. Cummings, "she being Brand" (question #1, following)

Peter Meinke, "The ABC of Aerobics" (text p. 922)

Alberto Ríos, "Seniors" (text p. 702)

Richard Wilbur, "A Late Aubade" (question #2, following)

CONNECTIONS QUESTIONS IN TEXT (p. 741) WITH ANSWERS

1. How does the treatment of sex and love in Olds's poem compare with that in E. E. Cummings's "she being Brand" (p. 721)?

   Cummings and Olds do not share a similar notion of sex in these poems. Cummings's speaker is flippant, implying in his language that having sex is like driving a new car. Olds also talks about sex as mechanistic, but her disdain for that attitude is obvious. Cummings's speaker is less interested in the "truth" of the sexual relationship than he is in making the experience live on the page. Olds's speaker implies with regret that "truth" and love are ignored by those who have sex without love. One of the ways to reveal the different attitudes of these speakers is to compare their poems' very different images and sounds.

2. Just as Olds describes sex without love, she implies a definition of love in this poem. Consider whether the lovers in Wilbur's "A Late Aubade" (p. 732) fall within Olds's definition.

The lovers in Wilbur's poem may well fall under Olds's definition of sex without love. The speaker in "A Late Aubade" clearly cares for their physical relationship, urging his beloved to forget worldly business and get them some wine and cheese. However, Wilbur's speaker's deliberate persuasive appeal to his lover establishes verbal communication, which is not even present in Olds's poem.

JOHN KEATS, *Ode on a Grecian Urn* (p. 741)

The speaker's attitude toward this object of beauty is a rapt expression of awe at its evocative and truth-bearing power and presence. Life portrayed on the urn is forever in suspended animation: no one gets old; the "wild ecstasy" goes undiminished; the love, never consummated, is yet never consumed and wearied of. Keats seems to admire this portrait of the sensuous ideal, which exists unmarred by mortality or the vagrancy of human passion.

The significant question about this ode (beyond the meaning of the closing two lines and whether the speaker or the urn pronounces all or a part of them) appears to rest with "Cold Pastoral!" (45) and the ambivalence these words imply. Earlier, in stanza III, Keats had admired the love "for ever warm and still to be enjoyed" (26) that was portrayed on the urn. Has the temperature of the urn changed by stanza V? Has the speaker discovered, in essence, that even though the urn portrays a sensuous ideal of courtship and pursuit, it is still merely a cold form that, because it is deathless, can never feel the warmth of human life?

Still one of the best studies on this ode is the essay (bearing the same title as the ode) by Earl R. Wasserman in *The Finer Tone: Keats's Major Poems* (Baltimore: Johns Hopkins UP, 1953, 1967, 11–63). For the record, Wasserman argues that the closing lines are spoken by the poet to the reader; as Wasserman explains, the ode is *on* a Grecian Urn, not *to* the urn. Hence, "it is Keats who must make the commentary on the drama" (59). Refer students to Brook Thomas's "A New Historical Approach to Keats's 'Ode on a Grecian Urn'" (text p. 741) for a contemporary perspective on the poem.

POSSIBLE CONNECTIONS TO OTHER SELECTIONS

Emily Dickinson, "Success is counted sweetest" (text p. 932)

John Keats, "To Autumn" (question #3, following)

Andrew Marvell, "To His Coy Mistress" (question #1, following)

Richard Wilbur, "Love Calls Us to the Things of This World" (question #2, following)

CONNECTIONS QUESTIONS IN TEXT (p. 743) WITH ANSWERS

1. Write an essay comparing the view of time in this ode with that in Marvell's "To His Coy Mistress" (p. 729). Pay particular attention to the connotative language in each poem.

   In Keats's ode, time wastes human beings but does not affect art. Art provides hope, friendliness, and beauty to human beings, making their misery more understandable in its "truth." In Marvell's poem, which dwells much more in the physicality of human experience, the speaker urges his listener to "make [the sun] run" (line 46), because time will destroy her anyway. The difference in the poems' treatments of time results from their different subjects. Whereas Keats's ode discusses art *vs.* human existence, Marvell's work claims that human existence is all we have.

2. Discuss the treatment and meaning of love in this ode and in Richard Wilbur's "Love Calls Us to the Things of This World" (p. 1124).

Keats presents the moment before the kiss as the peak of a relationship because this moment is full of anticipation and ripeness, but Wilbur makes the very earthly lovers into heavenly angels. The value of anticipation over experience in Keats's mind is ambiguous, however. After all, he describes his vision as a "Cold Pastoral" in stanza V. Perhaps he thinks that loving is more important than art, but it is hard to tell. Unlike Keats's speaker, the speaker in Wilbur's poem traces the moment after the epiphany, when souls descend from fresh laundry into the living bodies of lovers waking to ordinary day.

3. Compare the tone and attitude toward life in this ode with those in Keats's "To Autumn" (p. 771).

In "To Autumn" Keats celebrates a moment at the end of fall, asking us to appreciate the passage of time in his timeless work of art. In a sense the Grecian urn, a celebration of timeless beauty in art, competes with the ephemeral season of autumn. The poems are perfectly juxtaposed; one celebrates finitude, the other immortality. "To Autumn" appeals directly to the senses, whereas in "Ode on a Grecian Urn," the urn stands between the speaker and his audience, and between the audience and the ephemeral experience frozen forever on the urn. "Ode on a Grecian Urn" creates a sense of aesthetic distance and self-consciously questions the meaning and value of art in a way that "To Autumn" does not.

GWENDOLYN BROOKS, *We Real Cool* (p. 743)

Gwendolyn Brooks, who grew up in Chicago and who won the Pulitzer Prize in 1950, has been a deeply respected and influential poet for more than forty years.

In this poem, Brooks sets forth a tableau in a montage of street language. The poetic conventions she uses include alliteration, assonance, and internal rhyme. Students may be so taken with the sounds of the poem that they will be surprised that it has a decidedly somber focal point. How does the rest of the poem prepare us for the final line? Is there a "message" implicit in the poem? If so, how is the message affected by the spare yet stunning language of the poem?

The repeated "we" sounds the menacing note of the communal pack, its members secure perhaps only when they are together. The truncated syntax reflects both a lack of and a disdain for education, yet the poem celebrates the music of its vernacular, a quality that would be mostly lost were the pronouns to appear at the beginnings of lines.

Brooks's attitude toward this chorus that finds strength in numbers is a measured anger against its self-destructiveness. The absence of "we" in the final line is a silent prophecy of their future, moving us toward an understanding of the theme of the poem: death (burial/shovel) at an early age and the corruption of a golden opportunity to spend youth more wisely. The "Golden Shovel" also bespeaks an ironic promise that the events of the last line sadly belie.

POSSIBLE CONNECTION TO ANOTHER SELECTION

Langston Hughes, "Jazzonia" (text p. 1017)

RESOURCES FOR TEACHING

Gwendolyn Brooks. 30 min., b/w, 1966. ¾" U-matic cassette, 16-mm film, special-order formats. Brooks talks about her life and poetry. Distributed by Indiana University Instructional Support Services.

Gwendolyn Brooks I & II [recording]. 1 cassette (60 min.), 1988, 1989. Distributed by New Letters on the Air.

Gwendolyn Brooks Reading Her Poetry [recording]. 1 cassette. Distributed by Caedmon/HarperAudio.

See also "The Harlem Renaissance and Beyond" in the appendix of Film, Video, and Audiocassette Resources.

MARILYN BOWERING, *Wishing Africa* (p. 743)

This poem is fueled primarily by a deep sense of dislocation on the part of the speaker. The speaker's intense desire to find "a way / of wishing Africa" (lines 17–18) reveals feelings of loss and disappointment. The split between the fractured, dislocated self and the whole, connected self is developed partly through images of color. White is primarily associated with loss and disconnection; the first two lines ("There's never enough whiskey or rain / when the blood is thin and white") suggest a loss that is further emphasized by images of the whiteness of Queen Anne's lace, butterflies, and acacia. The desire to connect with Africa, thereby connecting with the earth and the sexuality latent in the earth, is starkly contrasted with the sterile reality the speaker feels toward the end of the poem: "I am white as a geisha, / my roots indiscriminate / since my bones gave way" (35–37).

"Wishing Africa" reveals a sense of displacement not just across space, but across time as well. The third stanza suggests the speaker's understanding of heritage and ancestry ("I was not far behind / those who first / opened the ground" [21–23]), but it is now impossible to connect meaningfully with the identity of the past. The speaker "had a soul" (40), but now feels soulless, alone, and far from enjoying the abundant life that the past seems to have held.

POSSIBLE CONNECTIONS TO OTHER SELECTIONS

Diane Ackerman, "A Fine, a Private Place" (question #1, following)

Rainer Maria Rilke, "The Panther" (question #2, following)

CONNECTIONS QUESTIONS IN TEXT (p. 745) WITH ANSWERS

1. What does the use of sensuality in this poem and in Diane Ackerman's "A Fine, a Private Place" (p. 734) reveal about the speaker in each poem?

    The speaker in each poem remembers a past time through sensual descriptions, but the speaker in Bowering's poem has lost her vitality. As the poem progresses, the descriptions lack the sensuality that typified them in the first stanza. In Ackerman's poem, the speaker retains her vitality, continuing to live the moment of her passion even as she bites into a peach and muses about her past.

2. In an essay compare the themes of "Wishing Africa" and Rainer Maria Rilke's "The Panther" (p. 767).

    This poem embodies the remorse of one who has been "greedy" (line 41) and "indiscriminate" (36). "The Panther" is a poem about being confined and growing weary; the same could be said of Bowering's poem, but it is a "small, personal pruning" (38) that preserves her speaker. The forces that confine the panther in Rilke's poem come from outside itself, as the last stanza emphasizes.

D. H. LAWRENCE, *The English Are So Nice!* (p. 745)

With a heavily ironic tone, this poem attacks what the speaker feels to be British hypocrisy in dealing with foreign people. Beginning with the assertion that the English "are the nicest people in the world" and leading the reader through sarcastic redefinitions of English niceness, the speaker shows that the English are just the opposite of nice. It may be interesting to note that the speaker speaks of the English not only in the third person, but also in the first, enhancing the ironic effect, and validating his point. (Note also the way Lawrence makes use of British diction: "as well" [line 5], "are they now?" [10], "Of course, naturally" [13], "you know" [17], etc.)

With modern cynicism, Lawrence critiques what has always been a cornerstone of the British character: their politeness and belief in good manners in all social situations. Your class's definitions or examples of the word "nice" might differ considerably from this equation with manners. The distinction between niceness and manners is an important one, for Lawrence is critiquing not the general hypocrisy of people who think they are nice but aren't, but specifically the English *appearance* of niceness to foreigners. This is a poem about a certain kind of xenophobia. It might be an interesting exercise to ask students if they are able to come up with a certain American trait that might be perceived by people from other countries as hypocrisy, too. How do Americans perceive their best qualities?

POSSIBLE CONNECTIONS TO OTHER SELECTIONS

Elizabeth Bishop, "Manners" (text p. 713)
Langston Hughes, "The English" (question #1, following)

CONNECTION QUESTION IN TEXT (p. 745) WITH ANSWER

1. Write an essay that compares and contrasts the English in this poem with the way they're presented in Langston Hughes's "The English" (p. 1024).

   The style of "The English Are So Nice!", particularly the poet's aggressive repetition of the word "nice," may be productively compared to Hughes's "The English." Both poems take on a similar topic and were published only two years apart. The tone of each poem affects the respective "messages"; Lawrence in taking the point of view of an Englishman is more sarcastic than Hughes. Hughes's poem has a different effect because of the object of English behavior (countries from or to which the British "buy, sell, or rob" oil, fruit, cocoa beans, or gold); and because the speaker is more straightforward with his disparaging diction — consider "rob" in line 9.

LOUIS SIMPSON, *In the Suburbs* (p. 746)

Students may resist this spare poem's desolate presentation of the fate of the American suburbanite. The suburban phenomenon began a dozen years before Simpson published his poem, but the poem is as relevant as ever since Americans continue to move to the suburbs. At least some of your students are likely to be from suburban households. A discussion of the American Dream may be a productive place to begin, perhaps even before students have read the poem. It might also be useful to have them define "middle class," in terms of both yearly income and lifestyle choices. Once you have established (and perhaps complicated) their sense of the middle class in America, you can work your way into the poem: where does the speaker of this poem get off equating a middle-class existence with a "waste" (line 2) of life? Does "middleclass" (3) necessarily mean suburban or vice versa? Is the situation as fatalistic as the poet suggests it is? (Half of the poem's six lines contain the phrase "were born to" (lines 2, 3, 5), and the first line is "There's no way out").

This apparently simple poem is complicated considerably by the final two lines. The poet connects a suburban lifestyle with one of religious devotion. Because of the negative diction ("no way out" in line 1, "waste" in line 2, for example) the comparison invites a discussion not only of the worst aspects of middle-class existence, but of religion, too. But what alternatives are there? Consider, too, the positive aspects of suburbia and religion. What connotations does the poem's last word, "singing," carry? At the end of the discussion, you might point out how powerful word choice can be in a simple, spare poem like this one for generating ideas.

Comparisons of this poem to John Ciardi's "Suburban" (text p. 818) are likely to yield observations of a stark difference in tone. Ciardi's poem is funny, Simpson's is quite serious. Yet do the poems share a similar attitude about what is important in life? Does the speaker of "Suburban" lead a typical middle-class life? Does the speaker in "In the Suburbs"? How do the differences in speaker and point of view affect the reader's reception of each poem?

POSSIBLE CONNECTIONS TO OTHER SELECTIONS

John Ciardi, "Suburban" (question #1, following)

Florence Cassen Mayers, "All-American Sestina" (text p. 888)

CONNECTION QUESTION IN TEXT (p. 746) WITH ANSWER

1. Write an essay on suburban life based on this poem and John Ciardi's "Suburban" (p. 818).

   Based on the speakers' attitudes in these two poems, the suburbs are, ostensibly, devoid of life, or repressed. Mrs. Friar, the neighbor in Ciardi's poem, fails, out of an overdeveloped sense of propriety, to value the "organic gold" (line 11) of the dog's "repulsive object" (5). The speaker in Simpson's poem regards suburban, middle-class life as a "waste of life" (3). Yet each poem concludes on a hopeful note, stressing the life that is beneath an otherwise sterile-seeming appearance: Simpson's poem concludes with the hopeful last word, "singing" (6); and Ciardi's hints at the "resurrection" (20) into plant life of even the foul "repulsive object."

A NOTE ON READING TRANSLATIONS

PABLO NERUDA, *Juventud*, with translations by ROBERT BLY and JACK SCHMITT (pp. 747, 748)

In this poem, Neruda uses one rolling sentence charged with intense language and studded with images both to capture the power and mystery of adolescence and to reflect elegiacally on youth from a more distant perspective. The erotic imagery in this poem is palpable in any translation, whether it is Bly's "drops of life slipping on the fingertips" (line 4), Schmitt's "sugary kisses on the teeth" (3), or the original's "la dulce pulpa erótica" (5), which even readers who know no Spanish can appreciate, if only for its sounds. As the poem progresses, the perspective seems more distant and the images more general as it is revealed that these images are memories, observed from a distance. The final image of the poem, of a guttering candle flame, yokes the poem's concern with love and youthful sensuality — the flame of passion — with the wiser-if-sadder perspective of the mature observer in whom a flame acts as beacon or guide.

While neither Bly's nor Schmitt's translation veers very far from Neruda's original, neither is exactly literal. Both translators make choices that emphasize different aspects of the Spanish poem. For instance, Bly adds the words "made" (1) and "branches" (2) to the first two lines of his poem — neither appears in the Spanish. By adding words, Bly more closely approximates the lengths and cadences of the Spanish lines, and he holds the reader's attention on the strange opening image. He achieves the same effect in the third line by converting the simpler Spanish metaphor ("los besos del azúcar") into a full-blown simile: "the kisses like sugar in the teeth" (3). Bly seems to opt for reality over mystery, preferring to let the images work by clarifying them. This approach carries him through the rest of the poem: for the Spanish "pulpa," which means pulp or flesh, Bly substitutes "fruit"; for the Spanish "mojándose" Bly chooses "sputtering" — in both instances he's choosing English idiom over absolute faithfulness to the Spanish.

If Bly angles his translation toward maintaining the overall rhythmic shape of the poem, Schmitt leans more toward maintaining a more literal link with the Spanish. Note that, whenever possible, Schmitt uses an English cognate of a Spanish word: "erotic pulp" (5) for "pulpa erótica"; "inciting" (6) for "incitantes"; and "secret" (7) for "secretos." Doing so not only keeps Schmitt's version rigidly close to the literal Spanish; it also forms a sort of linguistic bridge between the English and the Spanish, linking them to their common roots. Schmitt's choice of linguistic over rhythmic faithfulness allows him to compress his lines, making his poem move more quickly than the original. Schmitt gets some of the original's intensity in this way, opting less for an easy reading than for an energetic one.

Be sure to have at least one student who knows Spanish read Neruda's poem aloud; have it read by a few students if several know Spanish. Hearing the poem in a few voices will help students hear the music and the power of the original, which will make the choices that Bly and Schmitt have made more clear.

SAPPHO, *Hymn to Aphrodite* with four translations by HENRY T. WHARTON, T. W. HIGGINSON, RICHARD LATTIMORE, and JIM POWELL (pp. 748–751)

In this appeal to Aphrodite, Sappho asks that the lover who has spurned her be afflicted with yearning, and filled with desire for Sappho. All four of these versions of this poem, Sappho's most famous, try to conform to the original's stanzaic form — a form that has come to be known as the sapphic. A sapphic is three eleven-syllable lines followed by one five-syllable line; or two eleven-syllable lines followed by one sixteen-syllable line. The Greeks used a metrical system based on syllable length rather than stress: thus a Greek metric foot would consist of a combination of short and long syllables rather than unstressed and stressed syllables. This metric system, called quantitative, is difficult in English, where it is usually replaced — as in these versions — with a more familiar accentual-syllabic approximation.

In spite of their common formal aims and their dedication to accurately rendering the original, each of these poems is unique. Both Wharton's and Higginson's versions sound high-flown and a bit archaic — almost biblical — to our ears, and they wouldn't have sounded like ordinary speech to nineteenth-century readers, either. Compare, for instance, Higginson's elaborate image "the most lovely / Consecrated birds" (lines 9–10) with Lattimore's simple "sparrows" (9). Where Higginson's version is grandiose, full of ornate phrasing and imagery, Lattimore's is both stately and intimate. Lattimore stresses this intimacy in his closing, where Aphrodite acts as a guardian, almost maternal, where in other versions she is cast in a less consoling role: as military ally (in Wharton and Powell), as venerated deity, "Sacred protector" (28) in Higginson. Though Jim Powell's version is most faithful to the meter of the classical Greek, clearly his diction is the most up-to-date: his use of contractions and of italics to add emphasis makes his version sound almost casual at times.

Studying this poem makes clear how much of translation is interpretation, how much a translator is limited or informed by the context in which he or she is writing. You might want to discuss Higginson's editorial decision to change the pronoun for Sappho's lover from "she" to "he" in the sixth stanza, though the lover was certainly a woman in the original (21–24). The practice of editing poems in such a way was not uncommon in previous centuries — even Shakespeare was not immune. Although students may find this sort of obvious editing troubling, it is interesting to note the extent to which decisions these translators make in choosing a style or a level of diction change the poem in equally — or more — profound ways.

17

Images

Students are already very familiar with imagery through advertising. You may find it an interesting exercise to have students compare ads and poems dealing with similar subject matter: a recruitment commercial and Owen's "Dulce et Decorum Est," for instance. This may prove to be a controversial exercise — be prepared for students' resistance. You may instead (or additionally) want to have students focus on several advertisements or television shows and write a short response to the imagery they find there. This exercise can be beneficial because it will show students they already know how to read imagery, and will also help sharpen their critical thinking skills by applying analysis in an area they are unused to.

Still, students can sometimes have trouble with very imagistic poems: such poems may require more effort on the part of students than they suspect. Often, it may help to ask students to consider why it is that a poet focuses so closely on a given scene or object. Jacobson's "On Being Served Apples" can be cryptic, but students might be urged to look for a common thread: images of women. Whitman's "Cavalry Crossing a Ford" can seem like just a pretty scene unless one puts it in the context of the Civil War and realizes the possible fate in store for these men — a fate of which Whitman was all too aware from his work in a hospital. If students can be helped to see that poets often use images to emphasize significance or preserve a fleeting moment, they may appreciate the poems more.

Another important point in this chapter is that images need not be exclusively visual. Croft's "Home-Baked Bread" and Song's "The White Porch" both employ a variety of imagery to enhance the sensual themes of the poems, whereas Kizer's "Food for Love" uses similar kinds of imagery to darker thematic effect. Blake's "London" is full of auditory images, while Roethke's "The Root Cellar" and Baca's "Green Chile" use smell and taste, respectively. Baca's poem raises an interesting point about the cultural specificity of imagery, particularly when compared to a poem such as Wilbur's "A Late Aubade." Some students may, in fact, be more familiar with the taste of green chile con carne than bleu cheese and wine.

You may find that it helps to have students experiment with their own writing in this chapter: they could be asked to write a descriptive paragraph or poem concretely rendering an object, scene, or activity. This can serve to emphasize ideas raised in class about the significance of detail.

The paragraph from Hulme at the end of the chapter can also be useful in this regard, as it highlights some of these ideas. It can also provide a good starting place for discussions either now or later in the class about the distinction between poetry and prose.

WILLIAM CARLOS WILLIAMS, *Poem* (p. 753)

William Carlos Williams was born and lived most of his life in Rutherford, New Jersey, a town near Paterson, the city that provided the title and much of the subject matter of his "modern epic" poem *Paterson*. He had a thriving medical practice for fifty years, delivering more than 2,000 babies and writing his poems, novels, short stories, and essays at night and in the moments he could snatch between patient visits during the day.

This poem is an imaged motion, but the verse has a certain slant music too. Notice the *t*-sounds that align themselves in the second tercet, the consonance in "hind" (line 8) and "down" (9), the repetitions in "pit of" (10), "empty" (11), and "flowerpot" (12). Sound also helps convey the poem's sense of agility and smoothness.

Students may initially resist this poem because, being apparently simple, it may not conform to their expectations. If this situation arises, or perhaps even if it doesn't, you can use this opportunity to ask the question, "what should poetry do or be?" In all likelihood, you can convince skeptics that Williams's poem does what they don't think it does. In any case, it is an opportunity to refine a definition of poetry while exploring its power to appeal to our imagination.

POSSIBLE CONNECTIONS TO OTHER SELECTIONS

Matsuo Bashō, "Under cherry trees" (text p. 891)
Ezra Pound, "In a Station of the Metro" (text p. 772)

RESOURCES FOR TEACHING

William Carlos Williams Reads His Poetry [recording]. 1 cassette. Distributed by Caedmon/HarperAudio.
William Carlos Williams, People and the Stones: Selected Poems [recording]. 1 cassette (60 min.). Distributed by Watershed Tapes.
See also "Inner Ear, Part 1," "The Poet's Voice," "Voices and Vision," and "Caedmon Treasury of Modern Poets Reading Their Own Poetry" in the appendix of Film, Video, and Audiocassette Resources.

BONNIE JACOBSON, *On Being Served Apples* (p. 753)

An object may evoke a different response as it is placed into different environments. In "On Being Served Apples," Jacobson gives us four strikingly different images of apples, as the fruit is placed in different contexts. The colors associated with each portion of the poem provoke a variety of emotional responses, and students may be inspired to survey their assumptions about the connotations of different colors.

In addition, instructors might discuss the associations students have with the image of the apple. Do students think of bringing an apple for the teacher in connection with the first line of this poem? Students might suggest other popular associations with apple imagery, such as the role of the apple in Genesis or in the story of Snow White. Does Jacobson's poem touch on any of these familiar associations?

All four of Jacobson's images of the apple are connected with women. Note also the title: "On Being *Served* Apples." Why is it appropriate to associate apples and women in this way?

POSSIBLE CONNECTIONS TO OTHER SELECTIONS

Conrad Hilberry, "The Frying Pan" (text p. 807)
Alice Walker, "A woman is not a potted plant" (text p. 700)

WALT WHITMAN, *Cavalry Crossing a Ford* (p. 754)

Walt Whitman is, with Emily Dickinson, one of the two poetic giants of the American nineteenth century. Born in Huntington, Long Island, he grew up in Brooklyn, leaving school at age eleven for a job as an office boy in a law firm. His poetry grew out of his experiences as a reporter, teacher, laborer, and Civil War nurse. He self-published the first edition of his book — his life's work, really — *Leaves of Grass* in 1855.

Whitman's descriptive words lend a colorful, paradelike quality to this scene. The flashing arms with their musical clank along with the guidon flags fluttering gaily create an image that suggests liveliness and energy. Yet, "Behold" in lines 3 and 4, with its biblical overtones and its arresting sense of absorbing the sight ("be-hold"), is more stately than *look* or *see* and, with its long vowels, is almost ministerial. How does Whitman manage these two apparently contrasting tones?

The speaker in this poem (we can assume Whitman himself) seems to be fairly distant from the scene and possibly slightly elevated to see the entire picture. He scans the troops with a panning gaze that is, nonetheless, able to come in for some close-ups as he looks at the brown-faced men, "each group, each person, a picture" (4).

A productive discussion of this poem might take into account Whitman's lines and how their rhythm contributes to the description in the poem. Does the momentum of the lines have anything to do with the movement of the troops? To what degree is the description "arranged," and to what degree does it mirror the speaker's perception of the scene as it impresses itself upon him?

POSSIBLE CONNECTIONS TO OTHER SELECTIONS

Faiz Ahmed Faiz, "If You Look at the City from Here" (text p. 1139)
William Carlos Williams, "Poem" (text p. 753)

RESOURCES FOR TEACHING

Walt Whitman: American Poet, 1819–1892 [recording]. Color, VHS (30 min.), 1994. Distributed by Kultur.

Walt Whitman: Crossing Brooklyn Ferry & Other Poems [recording]. 1 cassette. Distributed by Caedmon/HarperAudio.

The Democratic Vistas of Walt Whitman [recording]. 1 cassette (22 min.), 1968. By Louis Untermeyer. Part of the Makers of the Modern World Series. Distributed by Audio-Forum.

Walt Whitman: Endlessly Rocking. 21 min., color, 1986. Beta, VHS, ¾″ U-matic cassette. Shows a teacher's unsuccessful attempts to interest her students in Whitman. Distributed by Centre Communications.

Walt Whitman: Frost and Whitman. 30 min., b/w, 1963. Beta, VHS, ½″ open reel (EIAJ), ¾″ U-matic cassette, 2″ quadraplex open reel. Will Geer performs excerpts from the two poets' works. Distributed by the New York State Education Department.

Walt Whitman: The Living Tradition. 20 min., color, 1983. Beta, VHS, ¾″ U-matic cassette. Allen Ginsberg reads Whitman's poetry. Distributed by Centre Communications.

Walt Whitman: Memoranda During the War: From Specimen Days [recording]. 240 min. Distributed by Recorded Books.

Walt Whitman: Orson Welles Reads "Song of Myself" [recording]. 1 cassette. Distributed by Audio-Forum.

Walt Whitman: Poet for a New Age. 29 min., color, 1972. Beta, VHS, ¾″ U-matic cassette, 16-mm film. A study of the poet. Distributed by Britannica Films.

Treasury of Walt Whitman: Leaves of Grass, I & II [recording]. 2 cassettes (92 min.). Unabridged edition. Distributed by Spoken Arts.

Walt Whitman: Twentieth Century Poetry in English, No. 13–17 [recording]. From the Leaves of Grass Centennial Series. Distributed by the Library of Congress.

Walt Whitman. 10 min., color, 1972. Beta, VHS, ¾″ U-matic cassette, 16-mm film, open captioned. Readings and a discussion of Whitman's life. Hosted by Efrem Zimbalist, Jr. Distributed by AIMS Media, Inc.

Walt Whitman. 12 min., color, 1989. Beta, VHS, ¾″ U-matic cassette. Examines Whitman's poetic language. Distributed by Films for the Humanities and Sciences.

Walt Whitman: Gary Kinnell Reads Walt Whitman [recording]. 1 cassette (59 min.). Kinnell reads excerpts from "Song of Myself," "I Sing the Body Electric," and several shorter poems. Distributed by Sound Rx.

Readings of Walt Whitman [recording]. 1 cassette, 1957. Distributed by Smithsonian/Folkways Recordings.

Walt Whitman's Civil War. 15 min., color, 1988. Beta, VHS, ¾″ U-matic cassette. Discusses Whitman's perspective on the war. Distributed by Churchill Media.

DAVID SOLWAY, *Windsurfing* (p. 755)

"Windsurfing" is a poem full of action and motion. The poem begins with "It"; the poet does not pause long enough to even explain exactly what "it" is, but instead allows the motion of the poem to mirror the motion of the windsurfer. The man who is windsurfing is referred to directly only twice; the man and the windsurfer move so forcefully together that the two share a single identity. The intensity of the motion of the windsurfer as it careens across the water is suggested through the carefully chosen verbs ("plunge" [line 20], "snapping" [37], "lashing" [38], "shearing" [39], "lunging" [27], etc.), which reveal the violence, grace, and beauty of the scene.

Because "Windsurfing" conveys one particular scene vividly, you may wish to ask students to compare the water imagery, the fluidity of motion between the man and his windsurfer, and the sensual imagery to those of other poems with similar settings (such as Matthew Arnold's "Dover Beach" [text p. 757]; and Diane Ackerman's "A Fine, a Private Place" [text p. 734]).

POSSIBLE CONNECTIONS TO OTHER SELECTIONS

Elizabeth Bishop, "The Fish" (question #2, following)
Li Ho, "A Beautiful Girl Combs Her Hair" (question #1, following)

CONNECTIONS QUESTIONS IN TEXT (p. 756) WITH ANSWERS

1. Consider the effects of the images in "Windsurfing" and Li Ho's "A Beautiful Girl Combs Her Hair" (p. 706). In an essay, explain how these images produce emotional responses in you.

   Solway's imagery moves fluidly, one metaphor leading into another with active verbs. Li Ho's imagery is somewhat more startling, juxtaposing images that seem to have less to do with one another but that create an overall impression that ultimately coheres.

2. Compare the descriptions in "Windsurfing" and Elizabeth Bishop's "The Fish" (p. 682). How does each poet appeal to your senses to describe windsurfing and fishing?

185

The fish in Bishop's poem is not in motion the way the windsurfer is. Bishop's speaker regards the fish, then looks more closely and more closely still, describing details as they impress themselves upon her and relying on simile and details to convey an impression of the fish as though she is slowly zooming in with a camera. Solway's windsurfer is moving much more quickly, and he provides us with metaphors that change at rapid-fire pace, mimicking the movement of his subject.

THEODORE ROETHKE, *Root Cellar* (p. 756)

The theme of this brief lyric with its powerful images is stated in the penultimate line: "Nothing would give up life." In the darkness of the root cellar, dank with a perpetual humidity, nothing sleeps; the atmosphere is ideal for engendering life. Normally we associate the underground with death and decay, but here decay is shown to be a source of life.

Some of the imagery in this poem is aimed at the olfactory sense, particularly when Roethke summons up the "congress of stinks" (line 6). "Congress" is an especially appropriate word choice here, for it can mean not only a political body but sexual intercourse as well. Coming together, as all these odoriferous bodies do, brings forth life out of putrefaction, mold, slime, and bulbous decay.

The sense of sight, however, also operates in the poem, and we are asked to use our imaginative powers to see shoots "lolling obscenely" (4) or hanging down "like tropical snakes" (5). Even our sense of touch is called upon to apprehend the "leaf-mold, manure, lime, piled against slippery planks" (9). Note too the consonance of *ms* and *ps* in this carefully constructed line. As ugly and odoriferous as some of these images are, the poem ends on a small cry of victory — "Even the dirt kept breathing a small breath" (11) — and this closing line recapitulates the tone of admiration, even wonder, that Roethke seems to feel as he enters the root cellar.

POSSIBLE CONNECTION TO ANOTHER SELECTION

John Keats, "To Autumn" (text p. 771)

RESOURCES FOR TEACHING

The Poetry of Theodore Roethke [recording]. 1 cassette (36 min.). Part of the YM-YWHA Poetry Center Series. Distributed by Audio-Forum.
Theodore Roethke [recording]. 48 min., 1972. A posthumous collection of Roethke reading his poetry. Distributed by Caedmon/HarperAudio.
Theodore Roethke: Twentieth-Century Poetry in English: Recordings of Poets Reading Their Own Poetry, No. 10 [recording]. Distributed by the Library of Congress.
Words for the Wind: Read by Theodore Roethke [recording]. 1 cassette, 1962. Distributed by Smithsonian/Folkways Recordings.
See also "The Poet's Voice" in the appendix of Film, Video, and Audiocassette Resources.

MATTHEW ARNOLD, *Dover Beach* (p. 757)

Matthew Arnold was born in the English village of Laleham, in the Thames valley. His father was a clergyman and a reformist educator, a powerful personality against whom the young Arnold rebelled in a number of ways, including nearly flunking out of Oxford. After several years as private secretary to a nobleman, in 1851 Arnold became an inspector of schools, a post he held for thirty-five years. For the characteristic jauntiness of his prose style, Walt Whitman once referred to him as "one of the dudes of literature."

Many of us have had the experience of looking out on a landscape and registering its beauty (and possibly its tranquillity) and its undercurrent of something lost or awry. Such is the case for the speaker of "Dover Beach" as he looks out at the shore awash in moonlight. The private moment has its wholeness, for he stands in the "sweetness" of the night air with his beloved. But all the security and peace he could expect to feel are shaken by his concerns beyond the moment and his awareness of the ravages that history brings to bear on the present. We are not fragments of our time alone, the poem seems to say; we are caught in the "turbid ebb and flow / Of human misery" (lines 17–18) that Sophocles heard so long ago.

In the third stanza, Arnold goes beyond commenting on the sadness that seems an inevitable part of the human condition, as his thoughts turn to the malaise of his own time. Faith, which once encircled humanity, is now only the overheard roar of its waters withdrawing to the rock-strewn edges of the world. In short, for whatever happens there is no solace, no consolation or reason to hope for any restoration, justice, or change. Humankind is beyond the tragic condition of Sophocles, and in this poem, Arnold seems to be tipping the balance toward a modernist existential worldview. The tone of the poem barely improves by the final stanza, for the image Arnold leaves us with is that of "ignorant armies" clashing in the night — the sound and fury once again signifying nothing.

The images of Dover Beach or some other imagined seascape work well to evoke the tone that Arnold is trying to convey. In discussion, or perhaps as a writing topic, you might ask the class to review the poem for natural details and images (in lines 9–14 or most of the third stanza, for example) that suggest the dreary, stark, and ominous portrait Arnold is painting here.

General essays on this poem appear in A. Dwight Culler's *Imaginative Reason: The Poetry of Matthew Arnold* (New Haven: Yale UP, 1966) and James Dickey's *Babel to Byzantium* (New York: Farrar, 1968).

POSSIBLE CONNECTIONS TO OTHER SELECTIONS

Anthony Hecht, "The Dover Bitch" (question #2, following)
Wilfred Owen, "Dulce et Decorum Est" (question #1, following)

CONNECTIONS QUESTIONS IN TEXT (p. 758) WITH ANSWERS

1. Explain how the images in Wilfred Owen's "Dulce et Decorum Est" (p. 763) develop further the ideas and sentiments suggested by Arnold's final line concerning "ignorant armies clash[ing] by night."

   The crippled soldiers in Owen's poem illustrate the final line of Arnold's, their decrepitude confirming what Arnold only hinted at. The gruesome images — "coughing like hags" (line 2), "blood-shod" (6), "choking, drowning" (16) — graphically demonstrate the consequences of those "ignorant armies clash[ing] by night."

2. Contrast Arnold's images with those of Anthony Hecht in his parody "The Dover Bitch" (p. 1096). How do Hecht's images create a very different mood from that of "Dover Beach"?

   In a conversational style and lighthearted tone, Hecht's speaker refers to the immediate pleasures of a more bawdy reality while defending the implied listener in Arnold's poem. Hecht's images evoke the daily life of the woman, contrasting sharply with Arnold's interest in the more philosophical issues of his day. Although we cannot assume much about the listener in Arnold's poem (is she even real?), we might presume that she would be far more respectful toward the speaker than Hecht's images imply. Indeed, Hecht intimates that the listener is a "loose woman": "I give her a good time" (26).

RESOURCES FOR TEACHING

Treasury of Matthew Arnold [recording]. 1 cassette. Distributed by Spoken Arts.
See also "Literature: The Synthesis of Poetry," "Palgrave's Golden Treasury of English Poetry," and "Victorian Poetry" (film and recording) in the appendix of Film, Video, and Audiocassette Resources.

JIMMY SANTIAGO BACA, *Green Chile* (p. 758)

You might begin a discussion of this poem by focusing on the way the differences between the red and green chiles reflect the differences between the speaker and his grandmother. Students may note that in the poem the red chiles function as decoration while the green chiles symbolize passion and tradition. For example, the speaker likes to have "red chile" (line 1) with his "eggs and potatoes for breakfast" (1, 2) and also uses them as decoration throughout his house (3, 4).

The speaker's use of red peppers could be seen as signs of the speaker's assimilation into mainstream United States culture, for the speaker eats a traditional breakfast of "eggs and potatoes" (2), whereas the grandmother prepares "green chile con carne / between soft warm leaves of corn tortillas / with beans and rice" (32–34). In contrast to the speaker, who uses red chile peppers as decoration, the grandmother views the green chile peppers as a "gentleman" (19) — more than a decoration, green chile peppers represent "passion" (31) and "ritual" (45). Considering the contrast in the function of the red and green chile peppers, ask your students to discuss what the speaker could be implying about the differences between his generation and his grandmother's generation. Is it possible that the speaker finds himself separated from the passion and intensity of the Hispanic community in which his grandmother lives? How does the image of the chile peppers work to reconcile the life-style of the speaker with the life-style of the grandmother? What could the speaker hope to convey in the sexual description of his grandmother's relationship with the green chile?

Because of the implicit and explicit connections between food and sexuality, you might ask students to further explore those links through other poems in which food and eating are framed in sexual terms — the vegetables in Roethke's "Root Cellar" (text p. 756), for example, or the food metaphors in Sally Croft's "Home-Baked Bread" (text p. 768), Carolyn Kizer's "Food for Love" (text p. 769), and Elaine Magarrell's "The Joy of Cooking" (text p. 792).

POSSIBLE CONNECTIONS TO OTHER SELECTIONS

Seamus Heaney, "The Pitchfork" (text p. 760)
Bonnie Jacobson, "On Being Served Apples" (text p. 753)

RESOURCE FOR TEACHING

Jimmy Santiago Baca [recording]. 1 cassette (29 min.), 1991. Distributed by New Letters on the Air.

SEAMUS HEANEY, *The Pitchfork* (p. 760)

This poem's agrarian worker imagines that his pitchfork approaches perfection. His flights of fancy construct him as a warrior or an athlete. He also considers the pitchfork itself and the hand that holds it.

The poem is mythical in its tone and its reverence for this "implement" (line 1). There are myths of the warrior and the athlete that pervade all cultures, including ours; slow-motion images of war scenes or athletic contests in movies testify to this fact. After discussing what is involved in these myths, you might need to coax students to recognize that myths of workers also exist, as in American folklore (John Henry, Paul Bunyan . . .). What connects these myths and what separates them?

You might follow this question with a consideration of the opposition the poem sets up between the pitchfork and the worker who handles it. Which one is the poem celebrating? It is titled "The Pitchfork," but it ends with "the opening hand" (20) of the worker. Does the pitchfork's "imagined perfection" (2) depend entirely on the worker's imagination? Or is that imagination made possible by the essence of the pitchfork, its tangible qualities discussed in the third stanza? It is, after all, the prongs of the pitchfork that seem to project the worker's imagination into "an other side / where perfection — or nearness to it — is imagined" (18–19). But this vision returns to himself, both in his "aiming" (20) and in his "opening hand" (20).

POSSIBLE CONNECTIONS TO OTHER SELECTIONS

Jimmy Santiago Baca, "Green Chile" (question #1, following)
Elizabeth Bishop, "The Fish" (text p. 682)

CONNECTION QUESTION IN TEXT (p. 760) WITH ANSWER

1. Pitchforks and green chile do not have much in common, but the images used to describe the pitchfork in this poem and the chile in Jimmy Santiago Baca's "Green Chile" (p. 758) invest these otherwise ordinary objects with significance. Write an essay that discusses how the images in these two poems give these objects qualities that are not inherent in either pitchforks or chile.

    Connecting this poem to Baca's "Green Chile" must involve a consideration of ritual, and of images that take us beyond the merely ordinary. The speaker of "Green Chile" begins, unlike Heaney, with a mundane image and moves gradually into the realm of "historical grandeur" (line 6), recasting the chile as an "oily rubbery serpent" (22) or a "tiger in mid-leap" (26), and recasting his grandmother's preparation of his lunch as a "sacrifice / to her little prince" (34–35). Like the worker in "The Pitchfork," the speaker in "Green Chile" is aware of an "old, beautiful ritual" (45).

RESOURCES FOR TEACHING

Seamus Heaney [recording]. 2 cassettes, 1990. Heaney reads his own work and a personal selection of classic poems by Shakespeare, Marvell, Hardy, Yeats, Blake, and others. Distributed by Poet's Audio Center.

Seamus Heaney: Poet in Limboland. 29 min., color, 1972. Beta, VHS, ¾" U-matic cassette, 16-mm film. Heaney discusses his poetry and political problems in Ireland. Distributed by Films for the Humanities and Sciences.

Stepping Stone [recording]. 1 cassette (72 min.), 1996. Distributed by Penguin Audiobooks.

H. D. [HILDA DOOLITTLE], *Heat* (p. 761)

Hilda Doolittle was born in Bethlehem, Pennsylvania, and educated at private schools in Philadelphia. In 1911 she moved to London, where she married English poet Richard Aldington. Although an American poet and novelist, H. D. was involved with the Bloomsbury group for a time and was an important figure in the Imagist movement as well. Ezra Pound, who encouraged her poetic aspirations and submitted her work to *Poetry* magazine under the name "H. D., Imagiste," was probably the most influential of a group of friends that included T. S. Eliot, William Carlos Williams, and D. H. Lawrence. In 1933, Freud agreed, at the request of the poet, to accept her as a subject of study, and H. D.'s later poems, such as "The Walls Do Not Fall" (1944), are markedly influenced by her own and her mentor's interests in psychoanalysis, religion, and mythology.

One way to open up discussion is to examine the nature of the heat, the wind, and the fruit as they are described in the poem. In what sense are these things abstract? What qualities are associated with each of them? Do students all have the same impression of the type of heat the speaker is describing? Heat becomes a living force in these lines, capable of occupying space and offering resistance to seemingly denser objects: "Fruit cannot drop / through this thick air —" (lines 4–5). The ripeness and fullness implied in the images of the fruit in the second stanza are somewhat threatened by the relentless heat. We can almost feel the fruit shriveling in response, deprived of oxygen, unable to participate in the natural cycle that will make them fall to the ground. A heat that is able to blunt the points of pears and round grapes (8–9) acquires the power of an elemental force.

The image of the cutting plow in lines 10 through 13 builds on the personification of the wind in the first line. The wind becomes a creative agent, a matching elemental force called up to cut through the heat and restore order in the natural world. However, the plow is also a domestic tool at the service of human beings. The poet's words conjure and direct the wind. By framing the poem as an invocation, the poet calls attention to her own ability to control this natural scene.

POSSIBLE CONNECTIONS TO OTHER SELECTIONS

Ezra Pound, "In a Station of the Metro" (text p. 772)

William Carlos Williams, "Poem" (text p. 753)

RESOURCE FOR TEACHING

H. D. [Hilda Doolittle], Helen in Egypt [recording]. 1 cassette (39 min.). Part of the Archive Series. Distributed by Watershed Tapes.

TIMOTHY STEELE, *An Aubade* (p. 761)

As the title implies, this poem partakes in the centuries-old tradition of a morning song from one lover to another. The speaker surveys the room as his lover showers, recalls her body, and spends the rest of the poem shifting between his perceptions of the bedroom and his recollections of his lover. He plans to lounge in bed doing so until she appears in the room, bringing together in the final line these two poles: his naked lover and the contents of the room.

The title tips us off to the poet's consciousness that he is partaking in a poetic tradition. Students should notice this self-awareness when they characterize the speaker. If they don't immediately describe him as a poet, have them list the poetic conventions that the poem utilizes: the alliteration of "she," "showering," and "shine" in the first two lines;

the strict scheme of end-rhyme; the poem's even pentameter, ten or tropes such as personification (the "face" of the flashlight [line 15]). The speaker emphasizes his awareness of his place in an old tradition at the end of the first stanza, comparing the folds of his sheet to "paintings from some fine old master's hand" (5).

Yet this is a contemporary poem: Does it feel like one? Do modern details such as showers and flashlights root us firmly in the twentieth century? What is the effect of mixing timeless and contemporary details as the poet does?

POSSIBLE CONNECTIONS TO OTHER SELECTIONS

Robert Herrick, "To the Virgins, to Make Much of Time" (text p. 728)

Richard Wilbur, "A Late Aubade" (question #1, following)

CONNECTION QUESTION IN TEXT (p. 762) WITH ANSWER

1. How does the tone of Steele's poem compare with Richard Wilbur's "A Late Aubade" (p. 732)? Explain why you prefer one over the other.

   Wilbur's "A Late Aubade," another aubade in which the speaker punctuates "the rosebuds-theme of centuries of verse" (line 23) also includes details from contemporary life, such as elevator cages. The tone is slightly different, though, and this difference pertains to the question of categorizing Steele's poem as a *carpe diem* poem: Wilbur's speaker is trying to lure his lover back into bed, Steele's speaker is content with the knowledge that pleasure is "brief and fugitive" (19). A close examination of this difference will challenge students to consider the ways in which both poets play with time — how they see the present as a function of both the past (memory) and the future (imagination).

WILLIAM BLAKE, *London* (p. 762)

William Blake's only formal schooling was in art, and he learned engraving as an apprentice to a prominent London engraver. After his seven years' service, Blake made his living as a printer and engraver, writing poetry on the side. The private mythology that came to dominate his poems was worked out in almost total obscurity: at the time of his death Blake had acquired some notice for his art but almost none for his writing.

This poem may seem pessimistic, but is it entirely so? If students would go so far as to call it "apocalyptic," does their knowledge of history help them to discern where the speaker's attitude comes from? The use of "chartered" (line 1) to describe streets and the River Thames makes all the boundaries in the poem seem unnatural and rigid; the cries heard are cries of pain and sadness. Like the rigidities of the chartered streets, the legislation of the "mind-forged manacles" (8) does nothing to promote civil liberty and happiness. Blake implies here that the "manacles" of religion and government that should protect individuals fail miserably to ensure good lives. Children are sold into near slavery as chimney sweeps, their own dark and stunted faces casting a pall (appall) on the benevolent state and the Christian tradition. Soldiers sent off to war die or kill other soldiers. Sexual restrictions invite prostitution and thus promote disease, which may, in turn, afflict marriages and resulting births. Social regulations ("manacles") thus induce societal ills.

The image of the soldier dying for the state, for example, (11–12), is described in a condensed and effective manner that suggests not only his lucklessness (or helplessness) but also the indifference of a government removed from the individual by class ("Palace" [12]), its insularity ("walls" [12]), and the imperturbable security of law.

Comparison of the two versions of the final stanza provides an excellent writing topic. Notice, though, how much more endemic the societal failings and wrongdoings appear in the second (revised) version. Instead of "midnight harlot's curse," the phrase becomes the "midnight streets" (13) (evil as pervasive) and "the youthful Harlot's curse" (14) (a blighting of innocence at an early age). By reversing "marriage hearse" and "infant's tear," Blake suggests not a mere (and societally sanctioned) cause-effect relation between marriage and the birth of afflicted infants but the presence of syphilis in even the youngest members of society and the conditions that would sustain its presence.

How do the urban ills of contemporary society compare with those of Blake's time? It might be an interesting exercise to ask students to write a poem about contemporary social ills, either urban or rural, in Blake's style. What has changed?

POSSIBLE CONNECTIONS TO OTHER SELECTIONS

Claribel Alegría, "I Am Mirror" (text p. 1136)
George Eliot, "In a London Drawingroom" (text p. 1092)
Faiz Ahmed Faiz, "If You Look at the City from Here" (text p. 1139)

RESOURCES FOR TEACHING

William Blake: The Book of Thel [recording]. 1 cassette. Distributed by Audio-Forum.
Essay on William Blake. 52 min., color, 1969. ¾" U-matic cassette, 16-mm film, special-order formats. A profile of the poet. Distributed by Indiana University Instructional Support Services.
William Blake: The Marriage of Heaven and Hell. 30 min., color, 1984. ¾" U-matic cassette. Dramatizes the life of Blake and his wife Catherine. With Anne Baxter and George Rose. Distributed by Modern Talking Picture Service.
Poems [recording]. 1 cassette (80 min.). Distributed by HighBridge.
The Poetry of William Blake [recording]. 1 cassette. Distributed by Caedmon/HarperAudio.
Poetry of William Blake [recording]. 1 cassette. Distributed by Spoken Arts.
William Blake. 26 min., color, 1973. 16-mm film. Hosted by Kenneth Clark. Focuses on Blake's drawings and engravings. Distributed by Pyramid Film & Video.
William Blake: Something About Poetry [recording]. 1 cassette (22 min.), 1969. Distributed by Audio-Forum.
William Blake. 30 min., VHS. A dramatization of Blake's inner world. Distributed by Insight Media.
William Blake. 57 min., color, 1976. Beta, VHS, ¾" U-matic cassette, special-order formats. A biographical portrait. Distributed by Time-Life Video.
William Blake: Selected Poems [recording]. 2 cassettes (180 min.), 1992. Includes "Tyger! Tyger!" and "A Poison Tree." Distributed by Blackstone Audio Books.
See also "Introduction to English Poetry" and "Romantic Pioneers" in the appendix of Film, Video, and Audiocassette Resources.

WILFRED OWEN, *Dulce et Decorum Est* (p. 763)

This poem is an argument against war, not against a country. So often war is an act surrounded by image-making words of glory and honor and flanked by the "nobility" of slogan sentiments. Here Owen has presented the actuality of battle and death by a particularly dehumanizing and agonizing weapon: poison gas. He wants his audience to know a little more exactly what war entails.

The famous indictment of war centers around the experiences and emotions of a disillusioned World War I soldier. It might be necessary to provide a little background about the nature of warfare during "the war to end all wars." The ground war was fought mostly in trenches, where not only did close and relentless combat last much longer than anyone initially expected, but the threat of illness from decomposing bodies and diseases that bred in the mud of the trenches was very real. You are likely to push some buttons by doing so, but you may want to try to discuss the final lines first.

Owen seems to want to collar and talk to each reader directly. After the vividness of his description, some of which is in the present tense, Owen's attitude toward the "lie" (line 27) that his "friend" (25) might tell is disdainful, and understandably so.

You may want to ask students where the notion that it is noble to fight for one's country comes from. Under what circumstances does such a notion break down? Is war still glamorized by way of songs, films, and poetry? (If students respond quickly, "No; all that ended with Vietnam," push the question a little further: what about movies that take on an abstract enemy, like the popular patriotic alien-fighting thriller *Independence Day?*)

POSSIBLE CONNECTIONS TO OTHER SELECTIONS

Matthew Arnold, "Dover Beach" (text p. 757)
Sharon Olds, "Rite of Passage" (text p. 915)

RESOURCES FOR TEACHING

Wilfred Owen: The Pity of War. 58 min., color, 1987. Beta, VHS, ¾" U-matic cassette. A documentary drawn from Owen's poems, diaries, and letters. Distributed by Films for the Humanities and Sciences.

War Requiem [video]. Color & b/w, VHS (92 min.), 1988. Written and directed by Derek Jarman, music by Benjamin Britten. Distributed by Mystic Fire Video.

War Requiem [recording]. 2 compact discs, 1993. Distributed by Deutsche Grammophone.

MARGARET HOLLEY, *Peepers* (p. 764)

This poem begins by describing the sexual frenzy of young frogs in the springtime. The imagery is of the raucous, wet, unbridled sexuality that casts spring as a kind of orgy that threatens to "last forever." The poem shifts suddenly in line 40 from a description of these young peepers to a sleeping human subject who is surprised by an overwhelming sexual feeling, culminating in a striking utterance of ecstasy in the final line/stanza: "Oh."

Students may not have spent much time contemplating the mating rituals of young amphibians, so you may have to pull back initially to consider what such a motif might represent to a poet. Is it a return to nature, a reverence for the rebirth and transformation of spring, or is it simply a new way to regard the human subject in the final 12 lines of the poem? Much depends upon the way students read the tone of the first 40 lines. There is something frightening about all of this unrestrained sexuality, especially since it comes from such small creatures who are transformed without warning from innocent seeming "berry-eyed" (line 2) things with "fetal fingers" (4) into "flying bat-fish / ready to jump /

full-tilt into anything" (10–12). The transformation is important, signalled by the allusion to Ovid in line 29. Mirroring the peepers' metamorphosis to "mature adults" in line 30, the sexual appetite of the creatures transforms into that of the human subject of the final lines. Note also the personification of the frogs beginning with line 22.

It might help at this point to list the transformations the poem suggests, then discuss how they relate to one another: infant into adult, winter into spring, animal into human, slumber into ecstasy. Once students have addressed these questions, they may be better prepared to take on some of the complexities of the final lines, such as the simile that compares the future to "a kind / but relentless scientist," or the meaning of the "immensity / that grips you." You may choose to compare this poem to others that play with the notion of spring's surprising transformations, such as Jane Kenyon's "Surprise" (text p. 806).

POSSIBLE CONNECTION TO ANOTHER SELECTION

Sylvia Plath, "Mushrooms" (text p. 842)

ELIZABETH BARRETT BROWNING, *Grief* (p. 765)

"Grief" is an ideal example of the Italian sonnet as described in Chapter 22. The first eight lines, the octave, demonstrate a rhyme scheme of *abbaabba*; the sestet's rhyme scheme is *cdccdc*. Following the traditional structure of an Italian sonnet, the octave here identifies the problem: behavior that is not true grief according to the poet's definition. Those who "through the midnight air / Beat upward to God's throne in loud access" (lines 3–4) are more flamboyant than sorrowful, according to the poet, who claims personal knowledge and understanding of the subject in the first line, with the words "I tell you." The break between the octave and the sestet occurs in the eighth line (which contains thirteen syllables, rather than the traditional ten of iambic pentameter); the beginning of the sestet provides a response and a resolution to the problem raised in the octave by describing more appropriate means of grieving: "Deep-hearted man, express / Grief for thy Dead in silence like to death —" (8–9).

As a means of clarifying Barrett Browning's distinction between grief and nongrief, encourage students to identify figures in literature or popular culture who demonstrate either artificial or genuine grief. According to this poem, for instance, Marc Antony's oration over the body of Caesar might not be seen as genuine grief.

Barrett Browning uses the following images to indicate the nature of grief: it is "passionless" (1), and "Full desertness, / In souls as countries, lieth silent-bare" (5–6). Grief is "in silence like to Death" (9), "a monumental statue set / in everlasting watch and moveless woe" (10–11). Ask students what these images have in common. Grief associated with a death might be especially well-suited to these images, but Barrett Browning more generally asserts that any true grief brings the stillness, the despair, the inability to change suggested by this poem. Indeed, the nature of grief is in part a manifestation of helplessness and recognition of the futility of action: as Barrett Browning reminds us, if grief "could weep, it could arise and go" (14).

POSSIBLE CONNECTIONS TO OTHER SELECTIONS

E. E. Cummings, "since feeling is first" (text p. 1087)
Emily Dickinson, "I like a look of Agony" (text p. 938)

Elizabeth Barrett Browning: Sonnets from the Portuguese [recording]. 1 cassette. Performed by Katherine Cornell and Anthony Quayle. Distributed by Caedmon/HarperAudio.

Elizabeth Barrett Browning: Sonnets from the Portuguese [recording]. 1 cassette. Read by Penelope Lee. Distributed by Spoken Arts.

See also "Victorian Poetry" (film and recording) in the appendix of Film, Video, and Audiocassette Resources.

JAMES DICKEY, *Deer Among Cattle* (p. 766)

The speaker of this poem, who observes a nighttime meadow scene with a flashlight, considers the contrasts between the herd of cattle grazing there and the lone deer who has joined them. He contemplates not only the differences between the "wild one" (line 5) and those "bred- / for-slaughter" (8–9), but also their subtle similarities: the deer is also "domesticated" (7) but "by darkness" (8) rather than by humankind. However, the differences far outweigh the similarities, and at the end of the poem the speaker is compelled to acknowledge the different way the "sparks from [his] hand" (19) reflect in the eyes of the deer as opposed to the cattle.

This relationship between the speaker and all of the animals together becomes more interesting than the relationship between the deer and the cattle as the poem concludes. The words "human" (4) and "inhuman" (16) set up a dichotomy in the poem that is not as easily recognizable as it might at first appear to be. The speaker's hand holds a "searing beam" (1) and "sparks" (19) — images of destruction — and he observes the scene behind a "paralyzed fence" (10) which contains "human grass" (6) and a wild animal "domesticated / by darkness" (7–8). The night becomes "the night of the hammer" in the penultimate line. Ask students to try to make sense of the speaker's attitude toward this scene by situating him within it: does he feel more part of the human realm or the animal realm? (Recall that the grass and the light in the cows' eyes are described as "human" [4] and that the grass enclosed by the fence is "a green frosted table" [12]). The speaker seems detached from the scene, but the poem begins and ends with the illumination from his flashlight, seen through his eyes.

POSSIBLE CONNECTIONS TO OTHER SELECTIONS

William Blake, "The Tyger" (text p. 868)
Rainer Maria Rilke, "The Panther" (question #1, following)

CONNECTION QUESTION IN TEXT (p. 767) WITH ANSWER

1. Discuss the idea of confinement in "Deer Among Cattle" and Rainer Maria Rilke's "The Panther" (p. 767).

   Rilke's "The Panther" involves no such speaker, no explicit "I/eye" observing the scene. Rilke's poem feels more confined than Dickey's does; there doesn't seem to be any world "behind the bars" (line 4) in "The Panther," but there is a forest beyond the field in "Deer Among Cattle." Still, it is complicated, since the deer has entered the world within the "paralyzed fence" (10), the field contained therein is described as "wide-open country" (18).

RESOURCES FOR TEACHING

James Dickey [video]. Color, VHS (30 min.), 1989. A production of the University of South Carolina and the South Carolina ETV Network. Distributed by PBS Video.

James Dickey [recording]. 1 cassette (29 min.), 1987. Distributed by New Letters on the Air.

James Dickey [recording]. 1 cassette, 1976. Distributed by Tapes for Readers.

James Dickey Reads His Poetry & Prose [recording]. 1 cassette, 1972. Distributed by Caedmon/HarperAudio.

The Poems of James Dickey [recording]. 1 cassette (52 min.), 1967. Distributed by Spoken Arts.

RAINER MARIA RILKE, *The Panther* (p. 767)

Born in Austria-Hungary (now the Czech Republic), Rainer Maria Rilke was educated in Catholic schools but later rebelled against his faith. He migrated to Munich after studying philosophy at Prague. In 1909 he went to Paris, a gathering place for many artists at the time. Rilke's images have been described as having classical plasticity: precise, chiseled, and visual. His mixture of squalor and art may have come from the time he spent in Paris.

The form and content of "The Panther" unite to indicate increasing confinement. In each of the stanzas, Rilke moves from exterior to interior and from action to inaction, leaving the reader with something more finite to consider each time — paralleling the confinement experienced by the panther. The first line of the first stanza refers to the world beyond the bars: by the end of the stanza, there are only "a thousand bars; and behind the bars, no world" (line 4). In the first line of the second stanza, the panther is moving in "cramped circles, over and over" (5); at the end of the stanza, we find "a mighty will which stands paralyzed" (8). The third stanza traces the path of an image as it penetrates "the curtain of the pupils" (9) until it "plunges into the heart and is gone" (12). This final image is so far within the panther that it remains unidentifiable. As a result, like the panther, we are forced by the form of the poem into a stillness and a recognition of our inability to control the situation. In a sense, Rilke is dropping the curtain over our own pupils.

POSSIBLE CONNECTIONS TO OTHER SELECTIONS

Marilyn Bowering, "Wishing Africa" (text p. 743)
Emily Dickinson, "A Bird came down the Walk —" (question #1, following)

CONNECTION QUESTION IN TEXT (p. 767) WITH ANSWER

1. Write an essay explaining how a sense of movement is achieved by the images and rhythms in this poem and in Dickinson's "A Bird came down the Walk —" (p. 829).

   Dickinson's bird moves with jerky movements, reflected in her brief, restless lines, until the end of the poem when the bird's movements are compared to rowing. Rilke's panther is at once more graceful and more cramped. His "ritual dance around a center / in which a mighty will stands paralyzed" (lines 7–8) is almost hypnotic so that we are especially surprised by the unexplained rushing image in the final stanza.

RESOURCES FOR TEACHING

The Poetry of Rainer Maria Rilke [recording]. 1 cassette. In German. Distributed by Caedmon/HarperAudio.

Rainer Maria Rilke: Selected Poems [recording]. 2 cassettes (118 min.), 1988. From the Spiritual Classics on Cassette Series. Distributed by Audio Literature.

JANE KENYON, *The Blue Bowl* (p. 768)

The speaker of this poem recounts how she and someone else (presumably a husband or lover) buried their dead cat the day before the poem is written. The burial is ritualistic; the speaker compares herself and her fellow undertaker to "primitives." Though they go about the burial rather methodically, the event has affected them deeply. They are "silent" (line 13) the rest of the day and seemingly empty: "we worked, / ate, stared, and slept" (13–14).

The title of this poem provides its most challenging point of interpretation. In addition to asking about the blueness of the bowl, ask students why the title focuses on the seemingly inconsequential bowl at all; why not entitle the poem "The Burial"? The bowl's blueness calls attention to other colors in the poem that may have otherwise been overlooked: the cat's "long red fur" (7) and the incongruous "white feathers / between its toes" (7–8). There is something *off*, something unsettling about the entire poem. Note how the first line, read alone, raises fundamental questions about meaning: do primitives bury cats with bowls? The speaker has difficulty communicating; she interrupts her description ("long, not to say aquiline, nose" [9]) in the same way that the robin or the neighbor of the final simile say "the wrong thing" (17).

Burial is meant to be a neat, finalizing procedure, but death is a messy business, both physically and emotionally. Nothing about it can be satisfying. In discussing the psychological implications of burial and comparing this poem to Updike's "Dog's Death" (text p. 11), students may be reluctant to leap over the next level of taboo into a comparison of human burial to pet burial. How might the nature of "The Blue Bowl" have changed if the speaker were burying a person rather than a pet? How might it have remained the same?

POSSIBLE CONNECTIONS TO OTHER SELECTIONS

Rachel Hadas, "The Red Hat" (text p. 864)
John Updike, "Dog's Death" (question #1, following)

CONNECTION QUESTION IN TEXT (p. 768) WITH ANSWER

1. Write an essay comparing the death of this cat with the dog of John Updike's "Dog's Death" (p. 673). Which poem draws a more powerful response from you? Explain why.

   One difference is that the cat of Kenyon's poem is never described as it was when it was alive. We do not see it die, whereas we witness the death of the dog in Updike's poem firsthand. Kenyon's speaker states that "There are sorrows keener than these" (line 11) as she buries the cat, but Updike's speaker shows us the grief of the family. It is likely that students will find Kenyon's poem unsettling and will find Updike's poem viscerally upsetting or pathetic.

RESOURCE FOR TEACHING

Jane Kenyon [recording]. 1 cassette, 1987. Distributed by New Letters on the Air.

SALLY CROFT, *Home-Baked Bread* (p. 768)

This poem describes a seduction by way of cooking, cleverly departing from the title of the source of the epigraph, *The Joy of Cooking*, into another popular text from the 1970s,

The Joy of Sex. The great-aunt of the second stanza is an interesting inroad. Great-aunts are generally associated more with cooking than with seduction; is this one figured into the poem as a contrast to the amorous speaker, or does she reinforce the idea that all women have their "cunning triumphs" (line 2), which are sometimes hidden or only suggested?

"Cunning triumphs," appearing amid the measured dryness of a cookbook text, certainly has the potential to arrest someone's poetic sensibilities. *Cunning* seems more appropriately applied to the feats of Odysseus than to the food in *The Joy of Cooking*. At any rate, "cunning triumphs" rises, as it were, beyond the limits of technical discourse. It shines, it sparkles, it almost titillates the kitchen soul.

"Insinuation" (3), too, is a pivotal word in the poem. It looks back on the questioning attitude of the opening lines and points toward the wily, winding seductiveness of what will follow.

At first we hear the speaker reading and questioning the cookbook. Then we hear the speaker transformed into a new identity — of Lady Who Works Cunning Triumphs. She is addressing someone she would charm and seduce.

The poem achieves a unity through the repetition of certain images, such as the room that recalls the great-aunt's bedroom as well as the other reiterated images, of honey, sweet seductiveness, warmth, and open air.

POSSIBLE CONNECTIONS TO OTHER SELECTIONS

Carolyn Kizer, "Food for Love" (text p. 769)
Elaine Magarrell, "The Joy of Cooking" (text p. 792)
Cathy Song, "The White Porch" (text p. 772)

CAROLYN KIZER, *Food for Love* (p. 769)

The speaker of "Food for Love" seems more obsessed with power and control than with any form of sentimental, romantic love. In almost every one of the first twelve lines, she assumes some sort of active stance regarding her "lover": she gleefully recounts her ability to "murder . . . with love" (line 1), "suffocate" (2), "hug" (3), "dine on" (5), and so on. While there is a highly erotic nature to her evident anticipation of dining "on your delectable marrow" (5), she uses images that suggest castration in lines 9–11: "With my female blade I'll carve my name / In your most aspiring palm." In the remainder of the poem, she exudes confidence in her ability to predict her victim's response. Here, the erotic nature has been amplified through both her perception of herself as an "Opulent mirage" (15) and her anticipation of the lover's movement toward her "in undulating dunes / Till you arrive at sudden ultramarine: / A Mediterranean to stroke your dusty shores" (19–21). Undeniably, the relationship is passionate.

Kizer constructs an elaborate extended metaphor in "Food for Love" in which the narrator's relationship to her lover is conveyed primarily through images of the desert. The lover is the narrator's "personal Sahara" (6); after the initial devastation described in the first two stanzas, the lover becomes a "total desert" (13). Mirages, oases, and succulents play a part in this scheme. Representing the replenishment that will continue this cycle, the narrator predicts that the lover will eventually be a "resurrected field in bloom" (27), yet she also promises once again to consume. As the final line indicates, the activity described in "Food for Love" is only part of an ongoing cycle in which devouring is balanced with replenishing.

Kizer's emphasis on death and resurrection invites a recognition of the similarities between the rituals of Christianity and the practices that sustain this relationship. Ask students whether they find such a connection appropriate to this poem. Which aspects of Christian tradition are most easily incorporated in a reading of this poem?

POSSIBLE CONNECTIONS TO OTHER SELECTIONS

Sally Croft, "Home-Baked Bread" (question #2, following)
Maxine Hong Kingston, "Restaurant" (text p. 849)
Elaine Magarrell, "The Joy of Cooking" (text p. 792)
Andrew Marvell, "To His Coy Mistress" (text p. 729)

CONNECTION QUESTION IN TEXT (p. 770) WITH ANSWER

2. Discuss the relationship between food and love in Kizer's poem and in "Home-Baked Bread" (p. 768).

    In Kizer's poem and in Croft's, the same senses that can taste and feel food are employed not only for the enjoyment of eating, but also to illustrate the sensuousness of sexual love. However, whereas Croft uses food to seduce her lover (the "you" in the poem), Kizer addresses the food directly — creating a metaphor of food *as* lover. Each poem uses food as a means to an end: Kizer's to devour and to create new life in the speaker; and Croft's to seduce the lover.

RESOURCES FOR TEACHING

Carolyn Kizer: An Ear to the Earth [recording]. 1 cassette (63 min.), 1977. Distributed by Watershed Tapes.
Carolyn Kizer [recording]. 1 cassette (29 min.), 1985. Distributed by New Letters on the Air.
Carolyn Kizer: Selected Poems [recording]. 1 cassette (63 min.), 1977. Distributed by Watershed Tapes.
Carolyn Kizer: Reading Her Poetry [recording]. 1 cassette. Distributed by Sound Photosynthesis.

JOHN KEATS, *To Autumn* (p. 771)

"To Autumn" was the last major lyric Keats wrote. But despite its tone and imagery, particularly in the last stanza, there is no indication that Keats had an exact foreknowledge of his impending death.

Personification is a major device in this poem. In stanza I, which suggests the early part of the day, autumn is the "bosom-friend" (line 2) of the sun and a ripener of growing things. In stanza II, which has a midday cast, autumn is a storekeeper and a harvester or gleaner. In the final stanza, which reflects "the soft-dying day" (25), the image of autumn is less directly named, but the idea of the contemplative is suggested. One sees things ripening in the opening stanza; in stanza II, autumn feels the wind and drowses in the "fume" (17) of poppies; in the final stanza, autumn and the reader both are invited to listen to the special music of the close of the day and of the year.

In his brief poetic career, Keats seems to have grown into a more serene acceptance of death, preferring the organic ebb and flow of life over the cool, unchanging fixity of the artifact.

POSSIBLE CONNECTIONS TO OTHER SELECTIONS

Robert Frost, "After Apple-Picking" (question #1, following)
John Keats, "Ode on a Grecian Urn" (text p. 741)
Theodore Roethke, "Root Cellar" (question #2, following)

CONNECTIONS QUESTIONS IN TEXT (p. 772) WITH ANSWERS

1. Compare this poem's tone and its perspective on death with those of Robert Frost's "After Apple-Picking" (p. 983).

    More metaphoric, perhaps, than literal, the apple picker's description of the recent harvest in "After Apple-Picking" could be a summary of his life. Already drowsy, he allows the time of day and the season to ease him into a reverie. The harvest he contemplates is a personal one — the apples he picked or let fall. This musing might occasion more brooding than is found in "To Autumn," in which the poet surveys more impersonally the season's reign and the year's end. "To Autumn" captures the last moments before winter, preserving them in all their ripeness and sensuality. Although both poems imply that death is near, Keats's speaker is far less willing to yield to it before appreciating the last moments of life as fully as he can.

2. Write an essay comparing the significance of the images of "mellow fruitfulness" (line 1) in "To Autumn" with that of the images of ripeness in Roethke's "Root Cellar" (text p. 756). Explain how the images in each poem lead to very different feelings about the same phenomenon.

    The images in "To Autumn" provide a sharp contrast to those in "Root Cellar." The root cellar is "a congress of stinks" (6), a place where ripeness is dank and almost obscene. Keats's images of fruitfulness are, in his word, "mellow" (1). One reason for the difference could be that Keats describes the end of a harvest, the cessation of growth, whereas Roethke traces the undying process that will begin growth all over again.

EZRA POUND, *In a Station of the Metro* (p. 772)

Ezra Pound was born in Idaho and grew up in Philadelphia, eventually attending the University of Pennsylvania. There he befriended William Carlos Williams and H. D. (Hilda Doolittle) and concentrated on his image as a poet (affecting capes, canes, and rakish hats) as well as on his studies. He later attended Hamilton College and returned to UPenn for graduate work in languages, completing a master of arts in 1906. Two years later he moved to London, beginning a lifelong voluntary exile during which he worked as secretary to William Butler Yeats; began and abandoned numerous literary movements; started his "epic including history," *The Cantos*; lived in Paris, Venice, and Rapallo (Italy); furthered the literary careers of Hemingway, Joyce, Eliot, Frost, and Marianne Moore, among others; broadcast for Mussolini and ended up under arrest for treason. Declared insane at his trial, Pound spent twelve years in a Washington, D.C., hospital. Freed through the efforts of his writer friends, Pound spent the rest of his life in Italy. Despite his glaring shortcomings, Pound is seen by many as the most technically accomplished poet and one of the most gifted critics of his generation.

Pound helped articulate the ideas of imagism, one of his early efforts to "make it new." Although the halves of this poem work as if the second half were describing the first, each of the two lines possesses its own integrity as well as a capacity to make us see those faces.

POSSIBLE CONNECTION TO ANOTHER SELECTION

Etheridge Knight, "Eastern Guard Tower" (text p. 892)

RESOURCES FOR TEACHING

Ezra Pound Reading Cantico Del Sole, Canto Ninety-Nine & Other Poems [recording]. 2 cassettes. Distributed by Caedmon/HarperAudio.

Ezra Pound: Poet's Poet. 29 min., b/w, 1970. Beta, VHS, ¾" U-matic cassette, 16-mm film. A profile of Pound and his influence on later poets. Distributed by Films for the Humanities and Sciences.

See also "Modern American Poetry," "The Poet's Voice," "Voices and Vision," and "Caedmon Treasury of Modern Poets Reading Their Own Poetry" in the appendix of Film, Video, and Audiocassette Resources.

CATHY SONG, *The White Porch* (p. 772)

The speaker in this poem establishes a conversation with her listener in the first stanza: "your" (line 10), "think" (12). She projects her listener into the future even as she captures the present moment through the description of her newly washed hair. The second stanza moves the conversation toward sexual innuendo, comparing the speaker's arousal to a flower, a flock of birds, and a sponge cake with peaches. Ask students to determine how these images give us a sense of what the speaker is like. What is her relationship to the listener? The final stanza returns us to the initial image of hair, but whereas the first stanza moves toward the future, the third plunges us back into the past. Students will enjoy comparing the images describing the mother to those describing the lover in the final lines. Like the rope ladder (an allusion to Rapunzel?), the poem is column-shaped, inviting its listener into the experience of reading it as it talks about a sexual relationship.

In a writing assignment, ask students to examine the concrete nouns and participial verbs in the poem. How do they evoke the speaker's message? How do images of domestic life summon the speaker's more "philosophical" side?

POSSIBLE CONNECTIONS TO OTHER SELECTIONS

Sally Croft, "Home-Baked Bread" (question #1, following)
Li Ho, "A Beautiful Girl Combs Her Hair" (text p. 706)

CONNECTION QUESTION IN TEXT (p. 774) WITH ANSWER

1. Compare the images used to describe the speaker's "slow arousal" in this poem with Croft's images in "Home-Baked Bread" (p. 768). What similarities do you see? What makes each description so effective?

   Croft also uses domestic images to talk about sexual intimacy and poetry writing. Both "Home-Baked Bread" and "The White Porch" invite the listener into the experience, promising food and warmth; each poem, for example, uses peaches to seduce its listener. The imagery is full of anticipation and ripeness. There is an element of danger, too, in each poem, enticing the audiences into delicious but forbidden experiences.

PERSPECTIVE

T. E. HULME, *On the Differences between Poetry and Prose* (p. 774)

As a class exercise, you might ask students to bring in examples of prose that contradict Hulme's claims. The prose poem by Carolyn Forché ("The Colonel," text p. 914) might be useful in a comparison between prose and poetry, but students might also want to bring in examples of prose they read elsewhere. In another writing assignment, you might ask students to flesh out Hulme's theory with especially vivid examples of poems that "hand over sensations bodily."

18

Figures of Speech

The material in this chapter can build on issues raised in the previous two: considerations of word choice, tone, and images both influence and reflect choices in figurative speech. You might have your students draw these connections explicitly by having them select a poem from this chapter and analyze it both in terms of its figurative language and also in terms of concepts discussed earlier. Doing so will help them understand how various elements make up the total effect of a poem.

Another possible exercise for this chapter would be to have students think about and list instances of figurative language used in their everyday speech, working either alone or in small groups. You might have them do this at the beginning of the chapter (after a brief discussion of figurative language) and again at the end: the difference in the number of instances they derive should be encouraging.

It is likely that students are already aware of the difference between simile and metaphor; the distinction will become important to them only if they can understand that it has some significance. Similes tend to call attention to the comparison itself, as in Atwood's "you fit into me" or Wordsworth's "London, 1802": the comparison becomes an important feature of the poems, foregrounding the "you and me" in Atwood's case, or Milton in Wordsworth's. Conversely, metaphors tend to focus on the *content* of the comparison, shifting the focus from the separate entities being compared to the nature of those entities, as in Dickinson's "Presentiment — is that long Shadow — on the lawn — ."

Metonymy and synecdoche can be difficult for students to grasp; for some reason, they find it more difficult to remember "metonymy" than "metaphor." You might find it useful to point out (or to have students point out) uses of metonymy in everyday language: "The White House confirms" or "University A beat University B" or "The Chancellor's office responded." This can help students get a grasp of the concepts involved and defuse their anticipation of being unable to understand these terms.

Paradox and oxymoron can be useful tools to encourage students' critical thinking skills. Puzzling out paradoxes and explaining oxymorons often require students to think in unusual ways. Poems that lend themselves to this are Donne's "Batter My Heart" and "Death Be Not Proud," as well as nearly any poem by Emily Dickinson.

WILLIAM SHAKESPEARE, *From* Macbeth *(Act V, Scene v)* (p. 776)

After asking students to identify each of the things to which Shakespeare's Macbeth compares life, and to consider how life is like each of them, have them decide which of these figures of speech is the most effective. Does one overpower the others, or does the overall effect depend on the conjunction of all of them?

Have students recall other things to which they have heard life compared. Are these common images examples of strong figurative language, or merely clichés? For example,

"Life is a bed of roses" conveys the idea that life is easy and beautiful, but it is such a well-worn phrase that it now lacks the impact it might once have had. As a writing assignment, students could come up with their own similes and metaphors and explain how life is like the image they have created.

See Robert Frost's " 'Out, Out —' " (text p. 987) for one example of how a modern poet has made use of Shakespeare's famous passage. Students familiar with William Faulkner's *The Sound and the Fury* might be able to comment on how another twentieth-century writer has used the reprinted passage from *Macbeth*.

POSSIBLE CONNECTION TO ANOTHER SELECTION

Robert Frost, " 'Out, Out —' " (text p. 987)

RESOURCES FOR TEACHING

See the first Shakespeare entry under Sonnet, Chapter 22, for resources for teaching Shakespeare's poetry (manual p. 267).

MARGARET ATWOOD, *you fit into me* (p. 777)

Students may need help with the allusions called up by the first two lines of this poem: the hook and eye that fasten a door shut; the buttonhook used to fasten women's shoes in the early twentieth century. You might ask students to compose a poem in which a figure of speech produces first pleasant associations and later unpleasant or, as in Atwood's poem, lurid ones. You might also ask the class in a brief writing assignment to determine how the simile and its expansion work. Would the poem be as successful, for example, if "eye" were not a part of the human anatomy?

POSSIBLE CONNECTION TO ANOTHER SELECTION

Emily Dickinson, "Wild Nights — Wild Nights!" (text p. 939)

RESOURCE FOR TEACHING

The Poetry and Voice of Margaret Atwood [recording]. 1 cassette (59 min.), 1977. Distributed by Caedmon/HarperAudio.

EMILY DICKINSON, *Presentiment — is that long Shadow — on the lawn —* (p. 777)

As noted in the text, Dickinson uses richly connotative words such as *shadow* and *darkness* in order to express in a few words the sense of fear and danger inherent in her "Presentiment." You might explore with your students other connotations of the word *presentiment.* Are all premonitions warnings about negative occurrences? Have any of your students had premonitions about good things? What kinds of words might one want to use in order to express — economically — the possibility of pleasant surprise? You could have students, individually or in groups, try to identify specific words and then a controlling metaphor that would be appropriate to express this alternative kind of surprise.

POSSIBLE CONNECTIONS TO OTHER SELECTIONS

Elizabeth Barrett Browning, "Grief" (text p. 765)
Emily Dickinson, "Success is counted sweetest" (text p. 932)

ANNE BRADSTREET, *The Author to Her Book* (p. 778)

This speaker regards her collection of poetry as though it were her child, considering both its penchant for brattiness and her mother's affection for it. Ask students to trace the extended metaphor in this poem, pointing out the way diction influences tone. What, for example, do the words *ill-formed* and *feeble* (line 1) tell us about the speaker's attitude toward her work? Does this attitude change at all as the poem progresses? Although her initial attitude toward the book is disdain, the speaker's reluctance to part with her creation in the final lines could be the result of both modesty and affection.

Sound patterns and meter are also good topics for discussion of this poem. The meter is iambic pentameter, but there are variations in rhythm that are linked to meaning. Line 15 presents the problem of metrical arrangement, providing an example in line 16: "Yet still thou run'st more hobbling than is meet."

In a writing assignment, you might ask students to discuss the way this poem talks about the writing process. How does Bradstreet suggest a book is written?

POSSIBLE CONNECTION TO ANOTHER SELECTION

William Shakespeare, "Not marble, nor the gilded monuments" (text p. 1116)

RESOURCE FOR TEACHING

Anne Bradstreet [recording]. 1 cassette, 1976. Distributed by Everett/Edwards, p1976.

ROSARIO CASTELLANOS, *Chess* (p. 779)

You might begin by asking students what associations they have with the game of chess. Traditionally, chess is thought of as an intellectual game — a game that relies on intricate moves and countermoves, with players anticipating one another's strategies as they plan their own. Considering the emphasis on strategy, chess could be called a "mind game" that two people agree to play. Thus, in lines 2 and 3, the reader learns that in adding chess as "one more tie to the many that already bind . . ." the players have very deliberately set up and engaged in the "mind game" of chess. Encourage students to notice the confrontational terms the poet uses to describe the competition — the board was "between" the players, they "divided" the pieces, they "swore to respect" the rules, and the "match" began (lines 5–10).

Ask students to discuss why two people might choose to add another "tie" (2) to a relationship, for although there are hints in the first stanza that what's been set up is more than a simple chess game, the final stanza leaves little doubt about the metaphoric scope of the contest. By using the hyperbolic "centuries" in line 10, the poet intensifies the sense that the players have reached a stalemate. That they are meditating "ferociously" (11) for a way to deal "the one last blow" (12) that will "annihilate the other one forever" (13) underscores the hostile nature of the contest.

While the features of the competition revealed in the second and third stanza will probably provide students with much to discuss, perhaps the most interesting feature of this poem occurs in the first stanza, where the speaker characterizes the relationship between the players with these words: "Because we were friends and sometimes loved each other" (1). There are no clues in the poem as to the gender of either player or to the nature of the "love" referred to in the opening line. Obviously, there is already some relationship between the players, since they decided to "add one more tie / to the many that already bound [them]" (2–3). Likewise, the plural word "games" implies that other interactions have taken place or exist as possibilities. While it may prove interesting for students to debate their own perceptions of the gender of the players in this poem, it may be helpful at some point to acknowledge that the real key is not the gender of the players but the nature of the relationship — are these lovers in the romantic and sexual sense, or are they friends that love? Students' understanding of the last two lines may vary depending on their understanding of the "love" relationship. Is the last blow a competitive personal rivalry, a way of ending the relationship, or something even stronger and more violent?

POSSIBLE CONNECTIONS TO OTHER SELECTIONS

Robin Becker, "Shopping" (text p. 794)
Sylvia Plath, "Daddy" (text p. 1113)

EDMUND CONTI, *Pragmatist* (p. 780)

As a writing assignment, you might ask the class to discuss whether the mixed tone of this poem is successful. Is, for example, "coming our way" (line 2) too liltingly conversational for the idea of apocalypse?

POSSIBLE CONNECTIONS TO OTHER SELECTIONS

Samuel Taylor Coleridge, "What Is an Epigram?" (text p. 889)
William Hathaway, "Oh, Oh" (text p. 675)

DYLAN THOMAS, *The Hand That Signed the Paper* (p. 781)

Dylan Thomas's *Eighteen Poems,* published in 1934, when he was twenty, began his career as a poet with a flourish: here, it seemed, was an answer to T. S. Eliot, a return to rhapsody and unembarrassed music. Thomas's poems became more craftsmanlike as he matured, but they never lost their ambition for the grand gesture, the all-embracing, bittersweet melancholy for which the Romantics strove. Thomas lived the role of the poet to the hilt: he was an alcoholic, a philanderer, a wonderful storyteller, a boor, and a justly celebrated reader of his own poems and those of others. Although he never learned to speak Welsh (he was born and grew up in Swansea, Wales), it is said that his poems carry the sounds of that language over into English. He died of alcohol poisoning during his third reading tour of the United States.

Although Thomas seems to be referring to no specific incident in this poem, the date of the poem (1936) indicates a possible concern with the political machinations leading up to the outbreak of World War II. The "five kings [who] did a king to death" (line 4) may even recall the five major powers who signed the Treaty of Versailles to end World War I but in their severe dismantling of Germany set the stage for another war. Some critics suggest that the poem, especially in the last two stanzas, refers to a wrathful God. Which words or phrases would lend credence to this reading? Students may suggest other situations in which a person in power can, by performing a seemingly simple act, adversely affect people at long range.

Discuss the title's allusion to the saying "The hand that rocks the cradle rules the world." Both phrases make observations about the power inherent in the acts of a single person. How are the acts to which they refer alike and different? How does the allusion to motherhood create irony in the poem? (Students familiar with the 1992 horror film *The*

Hand That Rocks the Cradle, which deals with a deranged babysitter, may have their own associations with this poem.)

POSSIBLE CONNECTIONS TO OTHER SELECTIONS

Alice Jones, "The Foot" (text p. 863)
Wilfred Owen, "Arms and The Boy" (text p. 1112)
Wole Soyinka, "Future Plans" (text p. 1145)

RESOURCES FOR TEACHING

The Days of Dylan Thomas. 21 min., b/w, 1965. Beta, VHS, ¾" U-matic cassette, 16-mm film. A biography of the poet. Distributed by CRM Films.

Dylan Thomas [recording]. 4 cassettes. Distributed by Caedmon/HarperAudio.

Dylan Thomas. 25 min., color, 1982. Beta, VHS, ¾" U-matic cassette. A portrait of the poet. Distributed by Films, Inc.

A Dylan Thomas Memoir. 28 min., color, 1972. Beta, VHS, ¾" U-matic cassette, 16-mm film. A character study of the poet. Distributed by Pyramid Film and Video.

Dylan Thomas Reading "And Death Shall Have No Dominion" & Other Poems [recording]. 1 cassette. Distributed by Caedmon/HarperAudio.

Dylan Thomas Reading His Poetry [recording]. 2 cassettes. Distributed by Caedmon/HarperAudio.

Dylan Thomas Reading "Quite Early One Morning" & Other Poems [recording]. 1 cassette. Distributed by Caedmon/HarperAudio.

Dylan Thomas Reading "Over Sir John's Hill" & Other Poems [recording]. 1 cassette. Distributed by Caedmon/HarperAudio.

Dylan Thomas Reads a Personal Anthology [recording]. 1 cassette. Distributed by Caedmon/HarperAudio.

An Evening with Dylan Thomas [recording]. 1 cassette. Distributed by Caedmon/HarperAudio.

Dylan Thomas: In Country Heaven — The Evolution of a Poem [recording]. 1 cassette. Distributed by Caedmon/HarperAudio.

Dylan Thomas: A Portrait. 26 min., color, 1989. Beta, VHS, ¾" U-matic cassette. A biographical film. Distributed by Films for the Humanities and Sciences.

Dylan Thomas: An Appreciation [recording]. 1 cassette. Distributed by Audio-Forum.

Dylan Thomas Soundbook [recording]. 4 cassettes. Read by the author. Distributed by Caedmon/HarperAudio.

Dylan Thomas: Under Milkwood [recording]. 2 cassettes (90 min.). Distributed by S & S Audio.

The Wales of Dylan Thomas. color, 1989. Images of Wales in Thomas's poetry, prose, and drama. Distributed by Films for the Humanities and Sciences.

JANICE TOWNLEY MOORE, *To a Wasp* (p. 782)

Discuss with students how an awareness of the intensity and seriousness of purpose that usually accompany the use of apostrophe affect their reading of this poem, which is, after all, about a common insect. In what way is the fist in the last line being waved at both the speaker and the wasp? Whose fist is it? How does the word *chortled* in the first line help us understand the speaker's view of the wasp? Discuss the paradox inherent in the notion of "delicious death" (line 11).

Figures of Speech

POSSIBLE CONNECTIONS TO OTHER SELECTIONS

John Donne, "The Flea" (text p. 1090)
David McCord, "Epitaph on a Waiter" (text p. 890)

J. PATRICK LEWIS, *The Unkindest Cut* (p. 784)

Students will enjoy this humorous quatrain that is a play on the saying "the pen is mightier than the sword." To open discussion, ask students to point out the paradox inherent in this simple poem. Discuss also the title of the poem, pointing out that the title is an allusion to Shakespeare's *Julius Caesar* (III.ii.188).

POSSIBLE CONNECTIONS TO OTHER SELECTIONS

Queen Latifah, "The Evil That Men Do" (text p. 695)
Dorothy Parker, "One Perfect Rose" (text p. 869)

MARGARET ATWOOD, *February* (p. 784)

"February," on the surface, is comprised of the ruminations of a speaker whose cat wakes her up in the morning. The feeling it evokes is familiar to everyone, particularly those who live in northern climes: "time to get this depressing season over with." The speaker initially rejects sex (suggesting that people should spay and neuter not only their animals but themselves!) and embraces the human version of hibernation ("Time to eat fat / and watch hockey"). The cat seems to be responsible for her attitude, and by the end, she entreats it to "get going / on a little optimism around here."

Though the speaker's tone is generally humorous, it might be productive to begin by encouraging students to locate all of the death imagery in the poem, obvious or otherwise. The cat's breath is "of burped-up meat and musty sofas," for instance, and "famine / crouches in the bedsheets" along with the speaker. Our efforts to propagate life seem to lead to death in the speaker's mind: "love . . . does us in," heating our bodies produces pollution, etc. How does the speaker's humorous tone interact with the apparently serious subject matter and imagery? Ask students to try to figure out why she suddenly rejects this "month of despair / with a skewered heart in the centre" in line 29, how the cat is converted into "the life principle, / more or less" (31–32). Is she shaking off the despair of the season by rejecting the cat? Is the cat somehow an emblem of winter, or is it an envoy of nature in general?

POSSIBLE CONNECTIONS TO OTHER SELECTIONS

Stephen Crane, "A Man Said to the Universe" (text p. 805)
Richard Wilbur, "A Late Aubade" (text p. 732)

SOPHIE CABOT BLACK, *August* (p. 785)

This poem, a description of an impending change from summer into autumn, is unusual for one so contemporary in that it seems so unbothered by the horrors of the modern world. It depicts both natural and human reactions to the passing of summer and anticipations of the coming of a killing season. It is a nature poem that approaches the pastoral; the human subject within it is nearly part of the landscape. Yet the theme is not typically pastoral. The world described is not idyllic; it is a world that seems to be running down toward its own destruction, brought about by the impending fall.

The language of the poem subtly reinforces this mood. The man, presumably a farmer, knows the "*tilt* and *decline* of each field, / his own *faulty* predictions" (lines 6–7). Nature seems old and sloppy, characterized by words like "tired," "loose," "unguarded," and "reckless" (10–13). It might be productive to have students draw their own associations of August or of harvest-time: what are some typical harvest rituals? As we celebrate harvest, do we seem, like the leaves at the end of this poem, "unaware" that things are about to die? This awareness contrasts nicely with the speaker of Atwood's poem "February," who is trapped by the despair of her gray month, but who knows at the end that there is hope for the coming spring.

POSSIBLE CONNECTIONS TO OTHER SELECTIONS

Margaret Atwood, "February" (question #1, following)

James Dickey, "Deer Among Cattle" (text p. 766)

Jane Kenyon, "Surprise" (text p. 806)

CONNECTION QUESTION IN TEXT (p. 786) WITH ANSWER

1. Discuss the moods created in "August" and Margaret Atwood's "February" (p. 784). To what extent do you think each poem is successful in capturing the essence of the title's subject?

   The mood of Atwood's poem is at least partially humorous, as though the speaker has resigned herself to the desperateness of the month and given up on the depression it engenders. She creates her mood obliquely, through objects such as her cat, french fries, and hockey, which would seem to have little to do with one another. Black's poem is concerned head-on with its topic; all the creatures and plants together seem attuned to the impending change of season, and it unsettles them, or makes them behave recklessly.

ERNEST SLYMAN, *Lightning Bugs* (p. 786)

This three-line poem casts lightning bugs (also called "fireflies") as spies who invade the speaker's backyard. It might be difficult to sustain a discussion about such a short poem, but you could begin by asking students to describe the speaker, the conditions under which he might make this observation, and the sights and sounds that surround him. Does his paranoia come from his sense that he is alone or from his sense that he is all too crowded?

Without the title, we would think this poem is about people. The title frames the experience by identifying the image to be captured in the lines that follow. Then, the image of the "peepholes" (line 2), coming as it does before the "snapshots" (3), makes us first imagine the bugs as human beings, who require peepholes to see who is outside. When mention of snapshots is added to this image, the bugs become like tourists, waiting for someone to come out of the house so they can take a picture. This is ironic, for it is really the bugs who are the celebrities, fascinating the speaker, who watches them.

POSSIBLE CONNECTION TO ANOTHER SELECTION

Ezra Pound, "In a Station of the Metro" (text p. 772)

SYLVIA PLATH, *Mirror* (p. 786)

Sylvia Plath grew up with an invalid father (he refused to seek treatment for what he thought was cancer but was actually diabetes) who died when she was eight. Her mother was a teacher, who by example and instruction encouraged her daughter's precocious literary ambitions (Plath published her first poem before she was nine). Plath attended Smith College on scholarship, won a Fulbright to study in England, received a number of awards for her writing, and eventually married the English poet Ted Hughes. In the last few harrowing months of her life (which she spent alone because Hughes was having an affair), she wrote most of her finest poems, sometimes at the rate of two or three a day. She killed herself on February 11, 1963.

This poem speaks from the point of view of a mirror reflecting an aging woman. The poem's brilliant use of personification may mask some other concerns in the poem; you might begin discussion by asking students to consider why the poet chooses this device. Is it possible to speak from an inhuman point of view? This speaker claims to "have no preconceptions" (line 1) and to be "unmisted by love or dislike" (3). These are decidedly inhuman characteristics, yet the speaker has a human voice and a human consciousness. Does the use of personification express some desire, in this case, to shed what can be painful human emotions? How does that desire in the poet reflect the persona of the aging woman who is the subject (or object) of the second stanza?

Without the use of personification, the poem would simply be another flat statement on a woman watching herself grow old. But that action of watching is enlivened by the mirror taking on some organic attributes. The pink wall it reflects becomes part of its heart, for example, and despite the truth it gives back to the woman, it feels important and necessary. Without the responsive quality of the mirror, it is unlikely that the last images would be quite so startling. But the personified mirror literally acquires a depth it probably would not have otherwise, and it figures in the poem as a lake, a drowning pool, and the source of the "terrible fish" (18). In the final simile, the image is no longer a mere reflection but a figure of assault coming up out of the depths of self to frighten her.

POSSIBLE CONNECTIONS TO OTHER SELECTIONS

Claribel Alegría, "I Am Mirror" (text p. 1136)

Li Ho, "A Beautiful Girl Combs Her Hair" (text p. 706)

Sylvia Plath, "Metaphors" (text p. 1115)

———, "Mushrooms" (text p. 842)

RESOURCES FOR TEACHING

Sylvia Plath: The Bell Jar. 113 min., color, 1979. Beta, VHS. Based on Plath's semi-autobiographical novel. See local retailer.

Sylvia Plath. 4 programs (30 min. each), color, 1974. VHS, ½" open reel (EIAJ), ¾" U-matic cassette, 2" quadraplex open reel. A biographical examination of the poet and her work. Distributed by New York State Education Department.

Sylvia Plath [video]. Color, VHS (1988). Distributed by Annenberg/CPB Collection and Mystic Fire.

Sylvia Plath: Letters Home. 90 min., color, 1985. Beta, VHS, ¾" U-matic cassette. Staged version of Plath's letters to her mother. Distributed by Films for the Humanities and Sciences.

Sylvia Plath, Part I: The Struggle. 30 min., color, 1974. Beta, VHS, ½" open reel (EIAJ), ¾" U-matic cassette, 2" quadraplex open reel. A dramatization of Plath's poetry by The Royal Shakespeare Company. Distributed by New York State Education Department.

Sylvia Plath, Part II: Getting There. 30 min., color, 1974. Beta, VHS, ½" open reel (EIAJ), ¾" U-matic cassette, 2" quadraplex open reel. Plath's poems are set to music by Elizabeth Swados and performed by Michele Collison. Distributed by New York State Education Department.

Sylvia Plath Reading Her Poetry [recording]. 1 cassette. Distributed by Caedmon/HarperAudio.

Sylvia Plath Reads [recording]. 1 cassette (60 min.), 1987. From The Poet Anniversary Series. Distributed by Caedmon/HarperAudio.

Sylvia Plath [recording]. 1 cassette (48 min.), 1962. A historic reading of fifteen poems recorded the month before the poet's suicide. Distributed by Poet's Audio Center.

WILLIAM WORDSWORTH, *London, 1802* (p. 787)

William Wordsworth was born in the English Lake District, in Cockermouth, West Cumberland, and grew up roaming the countryside. He completed his undergraduate degree at Cambridge University in 1791 and spent a year in revolutionary France. By the age of 27, he had settled in Somersetshire to be near Samuel Taylor Coleridge, with whom, in 1798, he published one of the most influential volumes in the history of English poetry, *Lyrical Ballads*. Wordsworth enjoyed increasing public reward as a poet (becoming poet laureate in 1843) even as his private life suffered from frequent tragedy and disappointment.

The metonymic nouns following the colon in line 3 of "London, 1802" all point to areas within British culture and civilization that Wordsworth thinks have declined since Milton's day. All things have suffered loss — from the strength of the church, the army, or the accomplishment of writers to the more immediate and individual quality of home life — in particular an "inward happiness," along with a sense of strength and security.

Milton seems to have represented for Wordsworth an epitome of the heroic, a kind of guiding star apart from other human beings, with a voice that was expansive, at one with the sublime in nature, and morally incorruptible.

POSSIBLE CONNECTIONS TO OTHER SELECTIONS

William Blake, "London" (text p. 762)
George Eliot, "In a London Drawingroom" (text p. 1092)

RESOURCES FOR TEACHING

The Poetry of Wordsworth [recording]. 1 cassette. Distributed by Caedmon/HarperAudio.

Treasury of William Wordsworth [recording]. 1 cassette. Distributed by Spoken Arts.

William Wordsworth: William and Dorothy. 52 min., color, 1989. Beta, VHS, ¾" U-matic cassette. Explores Wordsworth's poetry and his troubled relationship with his sister. Directed by Ken Russell. Distributed by Films for the Humanities and Sciences.

William Wordsworth. 28 min., color, 1989. Beta, VHS, ¾" U-matic cassette. An examination of the poet's work set against the Lake District, subject of many of the poems. Distributed by Films for the Humanities and Sciences.

William Wordsworth and the English Lakes. 15 min., color, 1989. Beta, VHS, ¾" U-matic cassette. Looks at Wordsworth's use of language. Distributed by Films for the Humanities and Sciences.

William Wordsworth: Selected Poems [recording]. 2 cassettes (180 min.). Read by Frederick Davidson. Distributed by Blackstone Audio Books.

See also "English Literature: Romantic Period," "English Romantic Poetry," "Introduction to English Poetry," "Palgrave's Golden Treasury of English Poetry," "Romantic Pioneers," and "The Young Romantics" in the appendix of Film, Video, and Audiocassette Resources.

JIM STEVENS, *Schizophrenia* (p. 788)

The ways in which personification, stanzaic form, and title combine to create meaning in this poem can be a fruitful approach to discussion. Stevens personifies the house as a victim suffering from the turmoil of its inhabitants. You might ask students to find examples of ways in which the house is physically "hurt" by their activities (see especially lines 2–5 and 17–20). The sequencing and relative lengths of the stanzas draws the reader to important statements of meaning in the poem. The poem is framed by two identical statements that "it was the house that suffered most." Moving toward the center from these identical lines, 2–5 and 17–20 deal specifically with physical things happening to the house. The next two stanzas toward the center, lines 6–9 and 13–16, depict the people doing things to the house, using it as a means of carrying out their aggressions toward one another. The very center of the poem, set off by a three-line stanza when the ones surrounding it have contained four lines, specifies what has been going on between the people themselves.

It is the title, however, that brings the poem together as a whole and allows us to relate the suffering *of* the house to the suffering *in* the house. *Schizophrenia* literally means a split mind; it is a psychosis characterized by radical changes in behavior. Have the students notice the change in behavior and its effects on the house between the beginning and end of the poem. In the first nine lines, the house is being violently abused: doors and dishes are slammed around, the carpets are intentionally scuffed, and grease, much harder to deal with than plain dirt, is ground into the tablecloth. In lines 5–9, the pattern moderates slightly: the slammed doors get locked, the dishes remain dirty instead of being slammed around, the feet stand still instead of scuffing. The third long stanza provides a transition into a mode of behavior radically opposite to what has come before. It casts the turmoil in terms of the inhabitants' violence toward one another, but also indicates that this violence is no longer occurring. Instead, what we see in lines 12–16 is the people dividing the house between them, splitting it between them to stay out of one another's way and put an end to the fighting. Note the ominous tone of line 15, an allusion to the biblical warning that "a house divided against itself cannot stand." Indeed, the effects on the house of this new kind of warfare are all seen in terms of things splitting apart — the paint coming away from the wood, the windows breaking into pieces, the front door coming loose from its hinges, and the roof tiles coming off the roof. The last word (*madhouse*) of the poem proper, before the refrain of the last line, brings the reader back to the title. You might discuss with your students whether the word refers to the house itself, which the speaker contends is suffering, or whether it means a house that contains mad people, or both. Is the idea of "home," the combination of house and people, the real victim of the madness? Would "Madhouse" have been a better title than "Schizophrenia"?

POSSIBLE CONNECTIONS TO OTHER SELECTIONS

Emily Dickinson, "One need not be a Chamber — to be Haunted —" (text p. 947)
Langston Hughes, "doorknobs" (text p. 1032)
Edgar Allan Poe, "The Haunted Palace" (text p. 800)

WALT WHITMAN, *A Noiseless Patient Spider* and *The Soul, reaching, throwing out for love* (pp. 788, 789)

In the two versions of this poem, Whitman participates in a fairly long and distinguished tradition, starting with the homely tropes of Edward Taylor or Anne Bradstreet, that explores analogies between lower forms of natural life and the human condition. In this instance, the analogy is effective since both soul and spider are isolated — and are trying to reach across vast space to forge connections between themselves and the rest of the world. The emphasis within the soul seems to be a reflective activity (musing, venturing, throwing, seeking), while the activity of the spider seems more a physical compulsion, especially with the repetition of "filament."

A valid inroad into the poem is a discussion of the term "Soul." Does "the Soul" of the title and the first line differ from the "sweet souls" of line 7 and the "latent souls of love" of the final line? In any case, what are the implications of linking the soul with some tiny earthly creature, especially one who is feared by many humans?

In the revised version, the poem is structured by the analogy, which renders the soul's casting of its "ductile anchor" as being as much a natural phenomenon as the spider's web-building. The earlier version is more a personal cry for love, and the spider analogy becomes an incidental metaphor.

POSSIBLE CONNECTIONS TO OTHER SELECTIONS ("A NOISELESS PATIENT SPIDER")

Emily Dickinson, "I heard a Fly buzz — when I died —" (text p. 959)
Walt Whitman, "The Soul, reaching, throwing out for love" (text p. 789)

CONNECTION QUESTION IN TEXT (p. 789) WITH ANSWER

1. Read the early version of "A Noiseless Patient Spider" (text p. 789). Which version is more unified by its metaphors? Which do you prefer? Why? Write an essay about the change of focus from the early version to the final one.

   The earlier version is less controlled in its use of metaphor than the revised version. There is a simpler correspondence between the action of the soul and of the spider in the revised version; in the earlier version this correspondence is complicated by the imagery of oceans associated with love, as well as of the eyes of a stranger. Students are likely to prefer the revised version for its relative simplicity, although some may favor the unbridled outpouring of the earlier version, which, with its rambling lines, exclamation points, and use of the vocative, seems stylistically closer to many of Whitman's other poems.

JOHN DONNE, *A Valediction: Forbidding Mourning* (p. 790)

The questions in the text show how richly metaphorical this metaphysical poem in fact is. Virtually every statement here is made through a comparison. The lovers should tolerate their separation with the same grace with which "virtuous men" leave this earth. They are not like the "Dull sublunary" lovers who need physical presence to sustain each other; they represent something finer. This sense of refinement is picked up and developed further in the simile in line 24, when the strength of the love between Donne and his wife is compared to gold, which does not shatter when beaten but expands to delicate, fine plate. Donne concludes his poem with the well-known compass metaphor. You might have to explain at this point what sort of compass Donne is describing, since we live in an age of computer graphics, not drafting skills. Because the compass here is used to draw circles, it is a most appropriate simile to describe unity and perfection.

POSSIBLE CONNECTIONS TO OTHER SELECTIONS

Anne Bradstreet, "To My Dear and Loving Husband" (text p. 1080)
John Donne, "The Flea" (text p. 1090)
William Shakespeare, "Shall I compare thee to a summer's day?" (text p. 881)

LINDA PASTAN, *Marks* (p. 791)

In teaching this poem, it would probably be a good idea to discuss the social expectations of motherhood and those of being a student. The latter relationship, in which the person is constantly being judged and is answerable to an authority figure, is not always ego enhancing, a point that Eugène Ionesco carried to absurd limits in *The Lesson*. The situation of the mother in Pastan's poem seems not much better; although anyone in any job or academic setting is frequently under review, is not a mother's "job" more an act of ongoing generosity than a fulfilling of job or course requirements? Class discussion could challenge the appropriateness of the metaphor here.

The speaker's increasingly bitter, ironic tone serves (as irony often does) as a weapon against the "marks" (the hurt and disillusionment) inflicted on her by her family. Can she easily leave school; leave her responsibilities?

As a writing assignment, ask students to analyze how this poem challenges and mocks its central metaphor.

POSSIBLE CONNECTIONS TO OTHER SELECTIONS

Julia Alvarez, "Woman's Work" (text p. 886)
Indira Sant, "Household Fires" (text p. 1144)

RESOURCES FOR TEACHING

Linda Pastan: Mosaic [recording]. 1 cassette (51 min.), 1988. Distributed by Watershed Tapes.
Linda Pastan [recording]. 1 cassette (29 min.). Distributed by New Letters on the Air.

LUCILLE CLIFTON, *come home from the movies* (p. 791)

The speaker in this poem contrasts activities such as spending time at the movies and dancing with planting flowers, reading newspapers, and raising children. Ask your students what kind of life each set of actions represents. The former is, in general, more glamorous but less substantial than the latter. You might wish to focus part of your discussion on lines 7–9. Although the poem has no set rhyme or metric pattern, Clifton sets these lines apart by the repeated rhythms and words she uses in them. The lines contain the most explicit statement of her urgent message to the black children. The lines fit well together because of their rhythms, but why else does Clifton choose these particular images? What specific social problems are addressed in these lines? As a writing activity, you might have students rewrite the lines as though they were addressing children in the neighborhood in which they grew up and expand upon what they have written in a short paper.

Another interesting aspect of this poem is its specificity. You could ask your students to point out words that indicate who is speaking to the "black girls and boys." Phrases like "be over" and "be cold" (lines 3–4), "our neighborhood" (4), and "our fathers" (12) indicate that the speaker is black and a member of the same poverty-stricken community as the children. Does the poem in any way address a wider audience than this? Does it have a more universal message?

POSSIBLE CONNECTIONS TO OTHER SELECTIONS

Amiri Baraka, "SOS" (text p. 1077)
Langston Hughes, "Red Silk Stockings" (text p. 1022)

RESOURCES FOR TEACHING

Lucille Clifton [recording]. 1 cassette (29 min.), 1989. Distributed by New Letters on the Air.
Lucille Clifton: The Place for Keeping [recording]. 1 cassette (45 min.). Distributed by Watershed Tapes.

ELAINE MAGARRELL, *The Joy of Cooking* (p. 792)

This grisly poem is from the point of view of a disgruntled sibling who has, on a literal level, cooked parts of her sister and brother. On a metaphorical level, she is attacking their attributes which have injured her. Ask students whether they think the poem is humorous or horrifying. They are bound to recall some news story or horror movie featuring cannibalism, even of one's family members. Is the speaker's fantasy tempered by these incidents, or does her tone and her reliance on the discourse of cookbooks make it impossible to accept the poem as anything but a metaphor with humorous intent?

The tongue and heart are extended metaphors for the siblings. The sister is described as needing spices to make her more interesting. We can imagine that hers is not an effervescent personality. The brother, characterized as a heart, seems heartless. Whereas most hearts feed six, his "barely feeds two" (line 16). He is "rather dry" (10), requiring stuffing to make him palatable. Neither sibling is complete enough when left alone to warrant the speaker's unadorning description; she must "doctor them up" to make them palatable to her audience and herself.

POSSIBLE CONNECTIONS TO OTHER SELECTIONS

Sally Croft, "Home-Baked Bread" (question #1, following)
Maxine Hong Kingston, "Restaurant" (text p. 849)
Carolyn Kizer, "Food for Love" (text p. 769)

CONNECTION QUESTION IN TEXT (p. 792) WITH ANSWER

1. Write an essay that explains how cooking becomes a way of talking about something else in this poem and in Croft's "Home-Baked Bread" (p. 768).

   Croft at first questions *The Joy of Cooking*, wondering why it should treat its subject as one would a human mystery. Carried away by the language, she moves into the role of seductress, luring her listener into the erotic sensuality of her poem. Magarrell's adaptation from the same book takes an entirely different form. Her tone is bitter. Rather than seducing her listeners, she startles and perhaps alienates them through her arresting images.

STEPHEN PERRY, *Blue Spruce* (p. 793)

Perry's poem is very visual, moving back and forth between metaphors and weaving images together on several levels. Some of the references in this poem may seem a little foreign to contemporary students — few students have had first-hand experience with a barber shop, a razor strop, horses and carriages, or even a bandstand. However, these images are central to the charm of the piece, and a good starting place may be to point out that the title, "Blue Spruce," works on many levels — it not only signifies a type of evergreen tree (and thus a connection to winter), but also was the name of a scent of aftershave lotion. Consequently, the title "Blue Spruce" points to the connection between the metaphors that help characterize the grandfather — the barber shop, the winter images of snow and ice, and the bandstand and instruments that appear beneath the evergreens. It may be helpful to ask students to trace each of these metaphors in order to see how the images are interwoven in the poem. You may also wish to discuss which aspect of the grandfather each of the images signifies (for example, the barber shop as his identity, the winter images as his age, the bandstand as his love). Students will undoubtedly have their own understandings of the symbolic value of these images, and it may be useful to have students write a short explanation of how they interpret the images in Perry's poem.

You may wish to point out that from the opening lines of the poem, the speaker establishes a connection between shaving and sexuality: "the black razor strop hung like the penis of an ox" (lines 3–4). This connection is explored throughout the poem, since it is the grandfather's sexual behavior that gets him in trouble with the town and with his family. Some students may see the grandfather's behavior as irresponsible; others may see him as irrepressible and extravagant — a man who lived life with a flourish and with a great deal of show. When asking students to determine whether the speaker wishes for readers to admire or to scorn the grandfather, you might ask them to identify where in the poem their own reaction to the grandfather begins to take shape. The speaker first mentions the possibility of hating the grandfather in lines 32–34, and many students might find it hard to admire a man who flirts with nurses at his wife's "last death" (36). An interesting related question is whether the speaker even intends to influence the reader either way. Although he pretends not to hate the grandfather (he asks, "How could you hate him?" and he does not list himself among the family members that do [31–33]) there seem to be some underlying resentments that rise to the surface with observations of his grandfather's "oompah love," his "bandstand love," his "brassy love" (25–26) and with the acknowledgment that the grandfather has acted in ways that have harmed the speaker's family (29–31; 34).

Perhaps the final analysis of the speaker's reaction to his grandfather's activities occurs in the final memory he re-creates: the moment where the grandfather, "a deep lather / of laughter" (40–41), takes the speaker from his mother and raises him into the bell of his instrument, as if he were "a note / he'd play into light —" (44–45). Have your students consider whether the speaker is saying that he feels connected to the grandfather, and that he will be the child that carries the grandfather forward into the future, or that this is simply one more example of the grandfather grandstanding his love, viewing the child as his own private hope.

POSSIBLE CONNECTIONS TO OTHER SELECTIONS

Regina Barreca, "Nighttime Fires" (text p. 688)
Theodore Roethke, "My Papa's Waltz" (text p. 871)

ROBIN BECKER, *Shopping* (p. 794)

The speaker of this poem threatens to buy a number of trinkets, articles of clothing, or objects of folk art if her lover leaves her. The tone is somewhat comic; we can assume that the speaker's lover does not want her to buy any of these things, and her seemingly inconsequential threats act as a form of revenge for something not yet done. Though comic, the threat belies the speaker's underlying fear that something may happen to elicit her revenge. What is the speaker afraid of, specifically? Why? You may want to consider the speaker's concern with loss, and the almost parenthetical reference to her sister, late in the poem (line 34). The ending of the poem is ominous as the speaker alludes to her aunt's death and her mother's behavior thereafter.

This is not the first time death is mentioned in the poem, however. One of the objects the speaker threatens to buy is an "Anasazi pot with the hole / in the bottom where the spirit / of the potter is said to escape / after her death" (20-23). This image concludes the first stanza, just as the resonant image of the speaker's dead aunt and mother concludes the second. As students are considering the nature of shopping as a metaphor, you might also ask them to decide whether the objects the speaker intends to buy have equal metaphorical value. Are they all *simply* the types of trinkets one might find at roadside shops in the American Southwest, or are there subtle differences between them which help to change the tone of the poem as it progresses? What metaphor emerges as the poem progresses and culminates with the mother's "outfit[ting] herself in an elegant suit" (35)? You may want to ask students what emotional purpose the "outfit" serves. How are the speaker and her mother similar?

POSSIBLE CONNECTIONS TO OTHER SELECTIONS

Emily Dickinson, "The Bustle in a House" (question #1, following)
Sylvia Plath, "Mirror" (text p. 786)

CONNECTION QUESTION IN TEXT (p. 795) WITH ANSWER

1. In an essay examine the relationship between love and death in "Shopping" and Emily Dickinson's "The Bustle in a House" (p. 950).

    In both poems, some comfort is taken from a routine that takes place after death, yet there is also a certain eccentricity implicit in the act. Both poems indicate that people tend to become excessively involved in themselves after death to the point that they cannot see themselves clearly.

PERSPECTIVE

JOHN R. SEARLE, *Figuring Out Metaphors* (p. 795)

In a writing assignment, ask students to find two poems in which the metaphors work and two in which they don't. The students' essays should explain their choices, that is, define the metaphors in the poems and explain why they work (or why they don't). If possible, the students should speculate about the characteristics of a successful metaphor based on the evidence of the poems they have chosen.

A class exercise or another writing assignment might involve students finding metaphors in sources other than poems — in the newspaper, for example, or in popular songs or television programs. Once found, these examples could also be analyzed as successful or unsuccessful metaphors.

19

Symbol, Allegory, and Irony

The discussion on symbol and allegory can follow naturally from the discussion of figurative language. In a sense, symbols are metaphors with one term left open, and it is up to the reader to complete them. Many of the poems in the previous chapter lend themselves well to symbolic readings — a good transition between the chapters might have students select a previously covered poem and examine its symbols.

Another exercise that can be useful is to have students brainstorm a list of symbols found in popular culture and articulate the connotations that surround them: what the American flag means, for instance. (This exercise can also illustrate how symbols can have different meanings for different groups.) This can help give students a sense of how symbols work, and how they can be simultaneously specific and general.

Students often seem to believe that every poem is immediately symbolic, which can be simultaneously encouraging and frustrating in their zeal to leap to the "real" meaning of the poem. Alternately, they may be committed to a kind of relativism, in which they believe that some poems can be symbolic of anything. While it is true that some symbols are more loosely focused than others, one of the challenges of discussion in this chapter is to encourage students to offer well-thought-out readings. It is a difficult line to walk between putting pressure on students to read critically and shutting down all discussion because the students come to believe that the teacher has "the right answer," and unless they can provide this they are better off keeping quiet. In fact, students may use silence as a tactic to bring out "the right answer" from the teacher. In this chapter, it is perhaps better to err on the side of caution and try to draw out students' own interpretations, even if these interpretations are initially somewhat off track. You may find it useful to avoid giving your own interpretations at all, relying instead on student input shaped by questions from you and from other students. Students may find this frustrating at first, particularly when they are used to being given answers by authorities, but ultimately it will sharpen their abilities as readers.

Irony can be difficult to explain directly — in this case, examples are a great help. Irony often depends on an understanding of the context, as Janice Mirikitani's "Recipe" illustrates. Without some idea of the "beauty myth," the irony in this poem will not be evident. It may be useful to compare some kinds of irony to an inside joke in that they depend on a shared bit of information before the audience can "get it." Students may in fact be quite familiar with situational irony, as in Jane Kenyon's "Surprise." They may be able to readily call incidents to mind in which all was not as it initially seemed. For an interesting take on irony, you might look at Linda Hutcheon's book *Irony's Edge: The Theory and Politics of Irony*, which is an occasionally dense but well-supported argument about the place of irony in contemporary society.

ROBERT FROST, *Acquainted with the Night* (p. 798)

This poem investigates the mind of a speaker who has seen a part of humanity and of nature that he cannot overlook. His experience has led him to see things that other people have not necessarily seen. The poem invites us to read it on more than one level, as is the case with many of Frost's poems. You might ask the students to discuss in a two-page essay the function of the clock in this poem. How does its presence modify the tone of the poem? Do we read it literally, symbolically, or as a mixture of both?

POSSIBLE CONNECTIONS TO OTHER SELECTIONS

T. S. Eliot, "The Love Song of J. Alfred Prufrock" (text p. 1045)
Robert Frost, "Stopping by Woods on a Snowy Evening" (text p. 989)
Octavio Paz, "The Street" (text p. 1143)

EDGAR ALLAN POE, *The Haunted Palace* (p. 800)

Edgar Allan Poe was born in Boston, the son of itinerant actors. He lived an often harrowing life marked by alcoholism, disease, and misfortune, managing to eke out a rather precarious existence primarily as an editor for a number of newspapers and periodicals in Philadelphia, New York, and Baltimore. Although he was renowned in his lifetime as the author of "The Raven," his most abiding ambition was to be a respected critic. He died after collapsing in a Baltimore street.

Students may have had little exposure to allegory, since it is not frequently used by modern writers. Thus it might be useful to explicate at least one stanza of the poem, discussing how a particular part of the palace corresponds to a particular part of the human body or mind. Notice the two "characters" actually personified by Poe in the poem: Thought (line 5) and Echoes (29). Does there seem to be a particular reason for singling out these two?

What is the purpose of using such archaic expressions as "Porphyrogene" (22) and "red-litten" (42)? What other words in the poem seem especially well chosen for their connotative meanings?

As a short writing assignment or subject for further class discussion, ask your students to contrast the depictions of the "windows" and the "door" of the palace when they first appear in the poem (stanzas III and IV) with their portrayal in the last stanza, after the coming of the "evil things" (33). How do they seem to change?

POSSIBLE CONNECTIONS TO OTHER SELECTIONS

Emily Dickinson, "One need not be a Chamber — to be Haunted —" (text p. 947)
Jim Stevens, "Schizophrenia" (text p. 788)

RESOURCES FOR TEACHING

Edgar Allan Poe: "The Raven," "The Bells," and Other Poems [recording]. 1 cassette. Distributed by Spoken Arts.
Edgar Allan Poe: Terror of the Soul. 1 hour, color, 1995. Beta, VHS. A biography revealing Poe's creative genius and personal experiences through dramatic re-creations of important scenes from his work and life. Distributed by PBS Video.
Poetry of Edgar Allan Poe [recording]. 2 cassettes (2 hours). Distributed by Dove Audio.
With Poe at Midnight. 60 min., color, 1979. Beta, VHS, ¾" U-matic cassette. Examines the interaction between Poe's life and work. Distributed by Media Concepts, Inc.
See also "Poetry by Americans" in the appendix of Film, Video, and Audiocassette Resources.

EDWIN ARLINGTON ROBINSON, *Richard Cory* (p. 802)

Edwin Arlington Robinson became a professional poet in the grimmest of circumstances: his father's businesses went bankrupt in 1893, one brother became a drug addict and another an alcoholic, and Robinson could afford to attend Harvard University for just two years. He eked out a livelihood from the contributions of friends and patrons, finally moving to New York City, where his work received more critical attention and public acceptance. He won three Pulitzer Prizes for his gloomy, musical verse narratives.

As a writing assignment, you might ask students to analyze how Robinson achieves the power of the final line of "Richard Cory," paying special attention to the regal language that describes Cory as well as the strong contrasts in the couplets of the final stanza.

POSSIBLE CONNECTIONS TO OTHER SELECTIONS

M. Carl Holman, "Mr. Z" (text p. 1098)
Percy Bysshe Shelley, "Ozymandias" (text p. 1118)

KENNETH FEARING, *AD* (p. 803)

How does the double meaning inherent in the title of the poem — "AD" is an abbreviation for "advertisement" as well as for "in the year of the Lord" — prepare the reader for the satire that follows? Notice how even the type used for this poem contributes to its meaning. The italicized words and phrases might occur in any high-powered advertising campaign. How is the effect of the advertising words undercut by the words in standard type? What is the effect of the reversal of type patterns in the last line?

Students should be aware that the poem alludes, in part, to the Uncle Sam "I want you" army recruiting posters. Discuss whether the purpose of the satire in "AD" is to expose a situation that exists, to correct it, or both. Is the situation to which the poem refers — the attempt to draw people into a horrifying occupation by making the work sound exciting and rewarding — confined to the pre–World War II era?

POSSIBLE CONNECTIONS TO OTHER SELECTIONS

Janice Mirikitani, "Recipe" (text p. 803)
Wole Soyinka, "Future Plans" (text p. 1145)

JANICE MIRIKITANI, *Recipe* (p. 803)

Before discussing this poem, be sure students understand the literal message of the poem — this is a recipe for "Round Eyes" (that is, caucasian eyes) written by a Japanese American poet. The poem is fairly straightforward, outlining the necessary equipment and the step-by-step process involved in making eyes that are not round into round eyes. However, a close examination shows that the poem is loaded with double meanings. For example, examine the final instruction of the recipe: "Do not cry" (line 16). Ask your students to consider the tone and stance of the speaker in light of line 16. What do the round eyes represent, and why does this speaker imply that round eyes might be desirable? Discuss what the poem implies about cultural standards of beauty and the price individuals — particularly women and women of color — are required to pay to meet these standards.

This poem also serves as an excellent example of irony. Ask students how irony functions in the poem. In order to help students appreciate the difficulty of employing a successful ironic strategy, and in order to help them examine some cultural assumptions that are often taken for granted, you might ask students to write a similar cultural critique — to choose a cultural standard of beauty or success and to write an ironic piece describing how this cultural standard may be obtained or maintained, and at what cost.

POSSIBLE CONNECTIONS TO OTHER SELECTIONS

Ruth Fainlight, "Flower Feet" (text p. 724)

Kenneth Fearing, "AD" (question #1, following)

CONNECTION QUESTION IN TEXT (p. 804) WITH ANSWER

1. Why are the formulas for an advertisement and a recipe especially suited for Fearing's and Mirikitani's respective purposes? To what extent do the ironic strategies lead to a similar tone and theme?

   Generally speaking, advertisements and recipes regard something potentially positive — either something the reader (or viewer) would *want* to buy or to make. In these two poems, the conceits of an advertisement and recipe try to convince men to die and women (Asian women in particular) to tape their eyelids up, respectively. The irony becomes apparent not only through the use of each conceit for its apparently opposite purpose, but also through the diction of each poem. Fearing's "horror" (line 4) and "dying in flames" (6) play against our ideas of an advertisement selling something; Mirikitani's "false" (line 4) and her final word — "cry" — do the same with the recipe formula.

E. E. CUMMINGS, *next to of course god america i* (p. 805)

The speaker of this poem is trapped by jingoistic clichés that render his speech almost meaningless. His intent is to manipulate his audience, convincing them that the men who have sacrificed their lives in war are "heroic" and "happy" (line 10). As a writing assignment, you might ask students to analyze how Cummings portrays character without employing direct description.

POSSIBLE CONNECTIONS TO OTHER SELECTIONS

Langston Hughes, "Un-American Investigators" (text p. 1030)

Yusef Komunyakaa, "Facing It" (text p. 1162)

Florence Cassen Mayers, "All-American Sestina" (text p. 888)

STEPHEN CRANE, *A Man Said to the Universe* (p. 805)

What sort of answer does the man in the poem expect to get from the universe? What does that say about the man? What other emotions, besides amusement, does this poem evoke? How does a reader's own perception of how the universe operates affect his or her response to the poem? Students are likely to concur that the more distance they feel between themselves and the man, the more amusing they find the poem.

POSSIBLE CONNECTIONS TO OTHER SELECTIONS

Robert Frost, " 'Out, Out' —" (text p. 987)

Langston Hughes, "Lenox Avenue: Midnight" (text p. 1022)

JANE KENYON, *Surprise* (p. 806)

From the perspective of the woman "surprised," this poem encompasses many of the conflicting emotions of a surprise party in spare, deliberate imagery. Distracted by the unnamed male, and oblivious to the gathering elsewhere, the speaker notes all of the changes around her as a result of the onset of spring. The last three lines of the poem reverse the mood, suggesting that the speaker's surprise comes at the ease with which her husband/lover has deceived her, opening up the possibility that there is something wrong with their relationship.

It might be useful to begin by asking students if they have ever been involved in a surprise party — either as the victim or as the scheming organizer. A discussion of what a surprise party intends to do leads naturally into a discussion of what it often actually does. Similarly, the poem leads us from the mundane — "pancakes at the local diner" (line 1), "casseroles" (4) — to the surprising renewal of nature in springtime, to the woman's astounding realization that the man has had such an easy time lying to her. The word "astound," with its connotations of bewilderment, direct our attention away from the surprise party and into speculation about the relationship between them. The irony centers around the renewal of the spring birthday juxtaposed against some almost funereal undertones (consider "spectral" in line 8, and "ash" in line 9, for example). The tension between images enables us to interpret their relationship in a novel, surprising way.

POSSIBLE CONNECTIONS TO OTHER SELECTIONS

William Hathaway, "Oh, Oh" (question #1, following)
Sharon Olds, "Rite of Passage" (question #2, following)

CONNECTIONS QUESTIONS IN TEXT (p. 806) WITH ANSWERS

1. Write an essay on the nature of the surprises in Kenyon's poem and in William Hathaway's "Oh, Oh" (p. 675). Include in your discussion a comparison of the tone and irony in each poem.

   "Oh, Oh" is much more humorous than this poem, but the effects are similar. In both cases, the final line tells us something that we didn't know, something that causes us to rethink the rest of the poem, especially the title. In Hathaway's poem, we know that something is coming, though, since the title clues us in. In this poem, we may at first take the "surprise" to be simply the surprise party, so we are especially surprised to learn that there is something amiss between this couple who seem to have enjoyed their breakfast and spring walk.

2. Compare and contrast in an essay the irony associated with the birthday parties in "Surprise" and Sharon Olds's "Rite of Passage" (p. 915).

   The irony in Olds's poem comes partially from the speaker's sense that her son and his friends are treating life so lightly at a birthday party. He is transformed from a frail, innocent thing to a general plotting the death of a weaker being. The young partygoers are not any more aware of this irony than the guests at the party in Kenyon's poem are. In both cases, the irony is something shared only between the poet and the reader, although any adult at Olds's party would be likely to notice something vaguely disturbing in the boys' comments.

CONRAD HILBERRY, *The Frying Pan* (p. 807)

This poem includes a visual cue, a shape meant to be both a frying pan and the symbol for womanhood minus the cross at the bottom. The former symbol represents "emptiness" (line 5) to the speaker, but the latter empowers her. The poem is about signification and the relationship between words and images.

The "mark" in the first stanza of this poem is first the mark of gender, an indelible identity afforded a woman at birth, which she can either resist or accept. The first stanza shows how this mark makes other "marks"; the woman is written into what can become imprisoning roles, such as those of housewife and mother, roles perhaps characterized by "collar and leash" (line 7). The mark may also be her written word on the page; using language, perhaps she tries to improve her position.

When the pan's handle is crossed, transforming it into the mark of the female gender, the woman speaking is herself transformed. She is "Venus / . . . the egg / and the pan it cooks in" (12–14). The symbols refer to the female reproductive system, but they generate in the female-run kitchen, intimating that this woman's freedom is perhaps not as "miraculous" as it seems. The analogy to the sun gives the woman a life-giving power. She is mother earth, to use a well-known representation of women. We must wonder, however, given the analogy to the frying egg, if the woman does not destroy herself in the process of calling attention to her heat-giving powers.

The poem's title plays with the cliché "out of the frying pan into the fire," perhaps illustrating by allusion the woman's failed gesture toward freedom. How conscious is the implication of this allusion?

POSSIBLE CONNECTION TO ANOTHER SELECTION

Julia Alvarez, "Woman's Work" (text p. 886)

WILLIAM BLAKE, *The Sick Rose* (p. 807)

This seems to be a poem that straddles the fine line between symbol and allegory. Unlike Robert Frost's "Acquainted with the Night" (text p. 129), this poem appears to demand an interpretation that will explain "rose" and "worm" so that they assume some importance within human affairs. Typically, whether "rose" is taken as an allegorical figure or a symbol (and many follow the latter course), it is connected with innocent love that succumbs to the corrupting worm. The worm signifies an illicit passion and preys on the rose's repression and vulnerability. Dark times and ill weather (an indicator of societal evil, perhaps) accompany the arrival of the worm. To be sure, this poem is more open-ended in the meanings that can be assigned to it and is therefore symbolically suggestive. The poem tends not to be didactic, as most allegories are, yet we seem to want to know, in the manner of allegory, what "rose" and "worm" mean for us.

A reading suggesting that this poem should be taken literally is in Michael Riffaterr's "The Self-sufficient Text" (*Diacritics*, Fall 1973). See also E. D. Hirsch, Jr.'s *Innocence and Experience* (Chicago: U of Chicago P, 1975), which argues that Blake is satirizing the rose's innocence: "Her ignorance *is* her spiritual disease because in accepting 'dark secret love' she has unknowingly repressed and perverted her instinctive life, her 'bed of crimson joy.' "

POSSIBLE CONNECTIONS TO OTHER SELECTIONS

William Blake, "Ah Sun-flower" (text p. 1078)
Robert Frost, "Design" (text p. 993)

PAUL LAURENCE DUNBAR, *We Wear the Mask* (p. 808)

Dunbar's racial heritage certainly provides one key to understanding "We Wear the Mask." The descriptions of the "tortured souls" (line 11) who "wear the mask that grins and lies" (1) remind us of the oppressive social conditions for African Americans in Dunbar's day, as well as the considerable and evident oppression in our own society. Dunbar allows insight into both the experience of suffering African Americans, "all our tears and sighs" (7), and the perception of the whites who enforce a particular kind of "acceptable," "civilized," or "happy" behavior. There are a number of allusions to the slave condition in Dunbar's poem. For instance, because they were prohibited from gathering together and "socializing," slaves became adept at singing — a subversive manner of communication that might contain news about the Underground Railroad or other issues of interest to slaves. Dunbar emphasizes this aspect of his heritage in lines such as "We sing, but oh the clay is vile / Beneath our feet, and long the mile" (12–13), even as he highlights the tendency of whites to perceive such singing as a sign that the slaves were happy.

For readers unaware that Dunbar was black, the poem may inspire a more general understanding of the behavior of the oppressed. This poem highlights the way individuals are expected to conform to societal expectations — a tendency students may be familiar with from their own experience. As a possible topic for discussion, ask students to consider whether such a "humanistic" interpretation of Dunbar's poem is a limited one. Is our understanding of the poem enriched by a knowledge of Dunbar's African American heritage?

POSSIBLE CONNECTIONS TO OTHER SELECTIONS

William Blake, "The Chimney Sweeper" (question #2, following)
Lucille Clifton, "come home from the movies" (text p. 791)
Langston Hughes, "Dinner Guest: Me" (question #1, following)

CONNECTIONS QUESTIONS IN TEXT (p. 808) WITH ANSWERS

1. How might the first line of this poem be used to describe the theme of Langston Hughes's "Dinner Guest: Me" (p. 1033)?

   The first line of this poem is a description of someone who is false to himself. Hughes's speaker blames himself for not standing up to the white liberal establishment, which really seeks to uphold the status quo rather than the truth about race relations.

2. Write an essay on oppression as explored in "We Wear the Mask" and William Blake's "The Chimney Sweeper" (p. 822).

   In both cases, oppression is enforced by convincing those who are oppressed that they should accept their plight happily. In both cases, the poet endorses liberation of the oppressed and believes that their cries should be heard; yet as long as people wear the mask of complacency, there will be no progress toward that end.

RESOURCES FOR TEACHING

Paul Laurence Dunbar: American Poet. 14 min., color, 1966. Beta, VHS, ¾″ U-matic cassette, 16-mm film, open-captioned. A biographical sketch of the poet. Distributed by Phoenix/BFA Films.

Paul Laurence Dunbar. 22 min., color, 1973. Beta, VHS, ¾″ U-matic cassette. A biographical tribute to the poet. Directed by Carlton Moss. Distributed by Pyramid Film and Video.

ROBERT BLY, *Snowbanks North of the House* (p. 809)

This is a series poem — a poem that presents a list of observations that may seem disconnected but that have some internal coherence. You might ask students to try to identify the link between all of the images and lines in this poem, although it may be difficult for them to put the relationship into concrete language.

This poem focuses on the idea of things that end, and the great sense of loss and loneliness that accompanies certain kinds of endings. This theme is apparent in lines that describe the high-school boy who stops reading (line 3), the son who stops calling home (4), the mother who no longer makes bread (5), the woman who ceases to love her husband (6), and the minister who falls leaving the church (7); however, it is less apparent in lines like "It will not come closer — / the one inside moves back, and the hands touch nothing, and are safe" (9) or in the final lines that describe the man in the black coat. Ask students to attempt to interpret these lines: What will not come closer? Who is the man in the black coat, and why is he portrayed the way he is? You might also ask students to explore the connections between the images in the poem that seem to defy our general expectations. Why might the poet have included lines that appear to be unrelated to the rest of the poem?

POSSIBLE CONNECTIONS TO OTHER SELECTIONS

William Blake, "London" (text p. 762)
Robert Bly, "Snowfall in the Afternoon" (text p. 1078)
Robert Frost, "Stopping by Woods on a Snowy Evening" (question #2, following)
William Butler Yeats, "The Second Coming" (text p. 1133)

CONNECTION QUESTION IN TEXT (p. 810) WITH ANSWER

2. Compare and contrast the symbolic images in "Snowbanks North of the House" and Robert Frost's "Stopping by Woods on a Snowy Evening" (p. 989).

In each poem the snow is a metaphor for a sadness underlying the speakers' ruminations. Whereas Frost's snowy setting contributes to the overall weary sadness, Bly is more direct, linking the "drift[s]" (line 1) with the "thoughts that go so far" (2).

RESOURCES FOR TEACHING

Robert Bly I & II [recording]. 1 cassette (60 min.), 1979, 1991. Distributed by New Letters on the Air.

Robert Bly: Booth and Bly, Poets. 30 min., color, 1978. ½" open reel (EIAJ), ¾" U-matic cassette. A four-part series of workshops and readings by the poets. Distributed by Nebraska Educational Television Network.

Robert Bly: An Evening of Poetry [recording]. 2 cassettes. Distributed by Sound Horizons.

Robert Bly: Fairy Tales for Men and Women [recording]. 90 min., 1987. Bly applies psychoanalytical analysis to poetry. Distributed by Ally Press.

Robert Bly: For the Stomach — Selected Poems, 1974 [recording]. 64 min. Bly reads his poetry. Distributed by Watershed Tapes.

A Home in Dark Grass: Poems & Meditations on Solitudes, Families, Disciplines [recording]. 2 cassettes (131 min.), 1991. Distributed by Ally Press Audio.

Robert Bly: The Human Shadow [recording]. 2 cassettes. Distributed by Mystic Fire.

Robert Bly: A Man Writes to Part of Himself. 57 min., color, 1978. ¾" U-matic cassette, special-order formats. Poetry and conversation with the writer. Distributed by Intermedia Arts of Minnesota.

Poems of Kabir [recording]. 2 cassettes (1 hour, 59 min.), 1977, 1995. Distributed by Audio Literature.

Poems of Kabir [recording]. 1 cassette. Ally Press.

Robert Bly: Poetry East and West [recording]. 140 min., 1983. Bly gives a poetry lecture, accompanied by the dulcimer. Distributed by Dolphin Tapes.

Robert Bly: Poetry in Motion. 30 min., color, 1981. Beta, VHS, ¾" U-matic cassette. Video biographies of three poets: Robert Bly, Frederick Marfred, and Thomas McGrath. Distributed by Intermedia Arts of Minnesota.

Robert Bly: Poetry Reading — An Ancient Tradition [recording]. 145 min., 1983. Bly talks about the oral tradition in poetry. Distributed by Dolphin Tapes.

The Poetry of Robert Bly [recording]. 1 cassette (38 min.), 1966. Part of the YM-YWHA Poetry Center Series. Distributed by Audio-Forum.

Robert Bly: Selected Poems [recording]. 2 cassettes (131 min.), 1987. Distributed by Ally Productions.

Robert Bly: The Six Powers of Poetry [recording]. 1 cassette (90 min.), 1983. A lecture from the San Jose Poetry Center. Distributed by Dolphin Tapes.

See also "Moyers: The Power of the Word" in the appendix of Film, Video, and Audiocassette Resources.

PERSPECTIVE

ROBERT BLY, *On "Snowbanks North of the House"* (p. 810)

Bly's generous perspective walks the reader through the poem line by line, explaining the emotional origin of each line as he goes. There are a couple of ways to use this perspective — both for this poem in particular, and for poetry in general. You may want to have students read the perspective after a substantial discussion of the poem. Certainly many students will view the poem differently than Bly, which will pave the way for a discussion of how author-intent and reader response can differ. Similarly, Bly's understanding of the emotional impact of the poem will, at times, coincide with that of your students. In order for students to relate to the poem, is it necessary for them to have the same specific experience that caused Bly to write each line? Consider Bly's own, more general metaphor for poetry: a "nourishing mud pond in which partly developed tadpoles can live for a while."

You may also wish to use this perspective for discussions of other poems. Bly begins by quoting William Stafford's opinion regarding assertions in a poem. This seemingly "over-analytical" approach to a poem may initially turn off some students. But it also provides an interesting inroad to the process of writing poetry and how that process, in turn, affects the reader. Perhaps a more accessible poem (because of its immediate and overt appeal to the reader) is Marianne Moore's "Poetry." How does Moore control the use of assertions to guide readers through her poem? Can your students think of other poems that use assertions similarly? Consider how Bly himself begins with a discussion of his assertions and ends by asserting that a poem is a "mud pond."

WILLIAM STAFFORD, *Traveling through the Dark* (p. 813)

This poem is a gut-wrenching narrative of a man who finds a deer by the side of the road who has been struck dead but whose unborn fawn is still alive. After hesitating a moment, he decides to pursue his original course of action and throw her over the edge of the road. Students might be taken aback by the speaker's reaction to this incident, especially the language he uses to describe the occurrence: "It is usually best to roll them into the canyon" (line 3). Do we believe that he is emotionless or simply that he must suspend his emotions in order to accomplish his task? What is the effect of the truncated final stanza?

One of the surprising qualities about this poem is just how much time Stafford takes to describe his car. Given this description, with its glowing light, its "warm exhaust," the "steady" engine that "purred," the car acquires a stronger lifelike sense than anything else in this poem, which laments the death of something beautiful in the natural world. The car, "aimed ahead," seems symbolically to foreshadow a darker, more inhuman future, in which mechanization replaces old-fashioned Fate.

Providing every physical detail of his encounter with the deer, the speaker sounds like a news reporter, calmly telling his story to his listeners. But the final stanza suggests that he is meditative and brooding, that this incident means much more to him than its details imply, that his thinking involves the fate of the deer as well as that of the human race.

The short final stanza emphasizes its contemplative tone, setting it against the previous stanzas, moving the focus away from the deer, toward the speaker and his fellow human beings. It also suggests the finality of his decision.

POSSIBLE CONNECTIONS TO OTHER SELECTIONS

Andrew Hudgins, "Seventeen" (text p. 813)
Langston Hughes, "Dream Variations" (text p. 1018)
Alden Nowlan, "The Bull Moose" (text p. 815)
John Updike, "Dog's Death" (text p. 673)

RESOURCES FOR TEACHING

William Stafford I & II [recording]. 1 cassette (60 min.), 1983, 1984. The author reads his poetry and discusses politics, poetry, and the writing process. Distributed by New Letters on the Air.

William Stafford: Troubleshooting [recording]. 1 cassette (50 min.), 1984. Distributed by Watershed Tapes.

See also "Moyers: The Power of the Word" in the appendix of Film, Video, and Audiocassette Resources.

ANDREW HUDGINS, *Seventeen* (p. 813)

This brutal poem describes the experience of a teenaged speaker who watches a dog nearly die as it spills out of a pick-up truck ahead of him. After a brief confrontation with the truck driver, it is up to the speaker to put the dog out of its misery. He does so, methodically, and indicates that some time has passed between the event and the present, during which he has been able to contemplate the meaning of it.

Seventeen is not that long ago for many college students, and it may be productive to begin by asking them to describe any defining moments or events that they experienced at or around that age. The speaker cusses at an adult for the first time in his life and expects "a beating" (line 18) in return, which is the punishment a child would have received. What he undergoes is much more painful; you might want to ask students to describe the psychological or social differences between being beaten up and having to do away with a suffering animal.

The poem relies on verbs to communicate the scene; you might want to isolate some of these verbs and discuss why the speaker chose them to paint the picture. It is interesting to note how the speaker begins to rely on adjectives — consider "blue" (33), "loose" (35), and "orange and purple" (36) — in the final six lines of the poem. Does this event somehow change the way he thinks about the world? How does the preponderance of adjectives vs. verbs reflect the speaker's emotional or mental state? Why is it significant that he didn't know the words for "butterfly weed and vetch" at the time, but now, when he writes about the scene, he both uses these words and emphasizes that he didn't know the words before?

POSSIBLE CONNECTIONS TO OTHER SELECTIONS

Jane Kenyon, "The Blue Bowl" (text p. 768)

William Stafford, "Traveling through the Dark" (question #1, following)

CONNECTION QUESTION IN TEXT (p. 814) WITH ANSWER

1. Write an essay that compares the speakers and themes of "Seventeen" and "Traveling through the Dark" (p. 813).

    In both "Seventeen" and "Traveling through the Dark" the speakers come across animals in the road. Each speaker is presented with a moral dilemma: whether and how to kill the animal. Yet William Stafford's speaker seems more detached and ruminative — less emotional; and his moral dilemma is more complex. Hudgins's speaker, though it is clear that he must kill the dog, is also undergoing a certain rite of passage that we can assume has already happened to Stafford's. "Traveling through the Dark" is, perhaps, about complicated choices; Hudgins's about growing up.

ALDEN NOWLAN, *The Bull Moose* (p. 815)

This poem describes a conflict between man and nature, one in which man, through his actions, futilely attempts to make nature (that is, the moose) look ridiculous, but is rewarded only by appearing cowardly and cruel. The speaker, observing the interactions of a lost bull moose and the townspeople, succeeds in making the townspeople and not the moose look ridiculous. The people demonstrate a complete misunderstanding of the moose; they lack respect for creatures of the wild in general and this trapped moose in particular. They condescend to the moose, treating it like a sideshow freak by feeding it beer, opening its mouth, planting "a little purple cap / of thistles on his head." Their affection for the animal is utterly skewed; they don't realize the moral problems inherent in so amiably agreeing that "it was a shame / to shoot anything so shaggy and cuddlesome." The moose's last act was one of power, strength, and dignity — it refused to die with bottles in its mouth or thistles on its head. As "the bull moose gathered his strength / like a scaffolded king, straightened and lifted its horns," it terrified the onlookers, even the wardens. But the final act of the young men, the honking of the car horns as the moose is executed, serves as both a way to mask their guilt by drowning out the sounds of the screaming moose, and as a sort of victory cry upon winning a cruel, unfair, and dishonorable battle.

POSSIBLE CONNECTION TO ANOTHER SELECTION

William Stafford, "Traveling through the Dark" (question #1, following)

CONNECTION QUESTION IN TEXT (p. 816) WITH ANSWER

1. In an essay compare and contrast how the animals portrayed in "The Bull Moose" and in Stafford's "Traveling through the Dark" (p. 813) are used as symbols.

In both poems there is a violent clash between humanity and the animal world. In Nowlan's poem, the bull moose symbolizes the reluctant power of nature, which man has abused but which continues to be fearsome. Stafford's speaker is not petty; he thinks deeply and quickly about his ability to influence nature, and though his action is painful, he is ultimately humane in letting the unborn fawn expire.

JULIO MARZÁN, *Ethnic Poetry* (p. 816)

The phrase, "The ethnic poet said" begins each of the poem's five stanzas, followed by a quotation and the response of the ethnic audience. In each case, the poet speaks in language or imagery that isn't "conventional" — it seems to disrupt conventions of typical Western poetry or thought. In each case, the audience responds by eating ethnic food or playing on ethnic instruments. In the final stanza, though, the poet quotes from Robert Frost's "Mending Wall" and the audience's response is to "deeply [understand] humanity" (line 20).

The poem invites us to consider the "proper" response to poetry as it satirizes the notion that poetry is a philosophical venture, that it is supposed to evoke in its listeners a deep understanding of human nature. The irony (and subtle humor) is made thicker by the fact that Frost's poem is about divisions between neighbors and that this poem begins with the assumption that there are differences between ethnic and other poetry. It might be interesting to apply the notion that poetry is meant to evoke a deep understanding about human nature to the poems excerpted within each stanza of "Ethnic Poetry." Is it possible to do so? Why does the "ethnic audience" choose to respond differently? What assumptions are made about the ethnicity of the poet and the audience in each stanza?

This poem may tend to touch off discussions of the "proper" response to poetry and the proper way to construct a poem. Langston Hughes's poem, "Formula" (text p. 1021), can deepen this discussion since it suggests that poetry is frequently elitist. Is it implicitly so? Has our perception of poetry made it an elitist form as much as the poet's conception that, as Hughes says, it "should treat / Of lofty things"? This is a good opportunity to get students to consider the nature of the barriers between "high" and "low" culture: where do they experience poetry in their lives besides in college courses? And what is their response to it? Do they ever *read* poetry "for fun," or do they know anyone who does? Have they ever been to a poetry reading? Is the emphasis in contemporary music on lyrics or on melody, instrumentation, etc.? Would their response to the lyrics of their favorite band be altered if those lyrics were presented in a classroom? (The general question: does our understanding of poetry depend more on the context in which we read it or on the nature of the poetry itself?)

POSSIBLE CONNECTIONS TO OTHER SELECTIONS

Robert Frost, "Mending Wall" (text p. 979)

Langston Hughes, "Formula" (question #1, following)

D. H. Lawrence, "The English Are So Nice!" (text p. 745)

CONNECTION QUESTION IN TEXT (p. 816) WITH ANSWER

1. Write an essay that discusses the speaker's ideas about what poetry should be in "Ethnic Poetry" and in Langston Hughes's "Formula" (p. 1021).

   Both poems ironically consider the notion that poetry "should treat / Of lofty things." In Hughes's poem, lofty poetry is not separated from poetry about everyday occurrences specifically by ethnicity; his concern is that poetry overlooks the pain of human existence. Marzán's concern is that listeners might tend to privilege poetry that seems deeply philosophical rather than culturally resonant.

JAMES MERRILL, *Casual Wear* (p. 817)

Merrill has been called a conversational poet. His familiarity with the lives of American aristocrats may result from his wealthy background, which especially influenced his earlier poetry.

Jeans, of course, are "casual wear," and by implication, this act of random terrorism appears to be a casual flourish of some unseen hand. That relation in sum seems to be the import of this poem. Because of the enjambment of lines between stanzas, students may not at first observe that the stanzas rhyme with an *abba* pattern — except the middle two lines of the first stanza. But then, what would rhyme with "Ferdi Plinthbower"? Rhyme, however, along with odd lengthy names, precise statistics, and descriptions of human beings as proper demographic models, detracts from our ability to feel the weight of this crime against humankind and our intuitive understanding of the moral workings of the universe. The inverse parallels between "tourist" and "terrorist" seem just too chillingly neat.

So what might Merrill actually be saying in this poem? Perhaps he is not so much speaking out against terrorist activity as talking about the media, with its formulaic scenarios, and the number-plotting social scientists, who surround such an event with their own dehumanizing mist of facts and figures. In the final irony of the poem, we know the name of the clothing designer but not that of the terrorist's victim.

Comments on Merrill's poetry include *James Merrill: Essays in Criticism,* edited by David Lehman and Charles Berger (Ithaca: Cornell UP, 1983) and Judith Moffet's *James Merrill: An Introduction to the Poetry* (New York: Columbia UP, 1984).

POSSIBLE CONNECTIONS TO OTHER SELECTIONS

W. H. Auden, "The Unknown Citizen" (text p. 1076)
Ruth Fainlight, "Flower Feet" (text p. 724)
Peter Meinke, "The ABC of Aerobics" (question #1, following)

CONNECTION QUESTION IN TEXT (p. 817) WITH ANSWER

1. Compare the satire in this poem with that in Peter Meinke's "The ABC of Aerobics" (p. 922). What is satirized in each poem? Which satire is more pointed from your perspective?

    Meinke's satire directs itself at the frantic health-conscious exercising that has become a part of our culture. Merrill's addresses a different aspect of the same culture, the materialism and media hype that eradicate the individual, leaving us with facts, figures, and wardrobe reports. Merrill's poem has a sobering life-and-death message, whereas Meinke's seems to have more hope for immediate change. Merrill's speaker is bitter; Meinke's satire is comical.

RESOURCES FOR TEACHING

James Merrill: Reflected Houses [recording]. 1 cassette (60 min.), 1988. Distributed by Watershed Tapes.
James Merrill: Voices from Sandover. 116 min., color. A dramatic adaptation of Merrill's "The Changing Light at Sandover" and a summation of the poetic thought of

this influential American poet. The cassette concludes with an interview of Merrill by Helen Vendler. Distributed by Films for the Humanities and Sciences.

See also "Poets in Person, No. 4" in the appendix of Film, Video, and Audiocassette Resources.

HENRY REED, *Naming of Parts* (p. 817)

The irony of this poem is situational. The instructor (no doubt an army sergeant addressing a group of raw recruits) is filled with self-importance as he drones on about naming the rifle parts, wholly oblivious to the silent beauty of the spring day. The season, though, arouses in the young recruit's thoughts reminders of a world far more vibrant than that of weaponry. Students should be able to distinguish between sergeant and recruit in the exchange of voices. The recruit's musings begin in the second half of the fourth line of each stanza, and the final line works to deflect the authoritative tone of the earlier part of the stanza. Discussion of rifle parts summons up with ironic aptness physical allusions, which the young recruit inevitably thinks of as he looks at the beautiful gardens in spring, assaulted by the vigorous bees.

POSSIBLE CONNECTIONS TO OTHER SELECTIONS

E. E. Cummings, "she being Brand" (text p. 721)

Linda Pastan, "Marks" (text p. 791)

JOHN CIARDI, *Suburban* (p. 818)

In "Suburban," Ciardi satirizes the artificial behavior of those who live in the suburbs. Note that Mrs. Friar seems unable to look at or refer to by name the object that incites her to phone the poet — the word *turd* does not occur until the final stanza, when the poet is returning to his own property. Ask students to compare Ciardi's perception of the turd — "organic gold" (line 11) — to Mrs. Friar's — "a large repulsive object" (5). What does the difference indicate about their contrasting worldviews?

How do the poet's tone and behavior alter when he crosses the property line? His attitude when Mrs. Friar first asks him to come over and remove the offending object — a humorous observation that his dog is in another state — is contrasted with his behavior in Mrs. Friar's yard, as he scoops and bows (16). How would Mrs. Friar have responded if Ciardi had shared his vision of what his dog, his son, and his son's girlfriend were doing in Vermont? How would she have responded if he had refused to come over? If Ciardi lacks any respect for the pseudodelicate sensibilities of his suburban neighbors, why does he humor them and conform to their accepted behavior in this instance?

Suburban neighborhoods are noted for being well-organized and highly developed; like them, the first four stanzas of the poem conform to a single pattern (note the perfect, standard indentation of the second and fourth lines in each). Yet the final line of the poem stands alone, beyond the conformity of the preceding stanzas. As Ciardi seems to be alone in his ability to accept the "turd" as an aspect of "real life," so this final line presents a different aspect of the suburbs. Ask students to assess the tonal shift and meaning of this final, isolated line, which provides a key to much of the preceding material.

POSSIBLE CONNECTIONS TO OTHER SELECTIONS

Louis Simpson, "In the Suburbs" (text p. 746)

John Updike, "Dog's Death" (question #1, following)

CONNECTION QUESTION IN TEXT (p. 819) **WITH ANSWER**

1. Compare the speakers' voices in "Suburban" and in John Updike's "Dog's Death" (p. 673).

    The speaker of Ciardi's poem is much more satirical than Updike's speaker, which is consistent with the subject matter of each. There is something raw and honest about the way Updike's speaker approaches his topic, but Ciardi's speaker has his tongue in his cheek throughout the poem, emphasizing the "I said" and "she said" of his story to comic effect. The settings of the poems are similar, but the comic presence of Mrs. Friar in this poem and the tragic death of the dog in Updike's poem alter the tones of each considerably.

RESOURCES FOR TEACHING

As If: Poems Selected and Read by John Ciardi [recording]. 1 cassette, 1955. Distributed by Smithsonian/Folkways Recordings.

John Ciardi [recording]. 1 cassette, 1991. Distributed by Audio-Forum.

John Ciardi I & II [recording]. 1 cassette (60 min.), 1983, 1984. The author reads poems about war, Italy, and aging. Distributed by New Letters on the Air.

Hans Juergensen & John Ciardi: World War II [recording]. 1 cassette (29 min.). Distributed by New Letters on the Air.

The Poetry of John Ciardi [recording]. 1 cassette (56 min.), 1964. Distributed by Audio-Forum.

John Ciardi: Twentieth-Century Poets in English: Recordings of Poets Reading Their Own Poetry, No. 27 [recording]. Distributed by the Library of Congress.

John Ciardi: You Read to Me, I'll Read to You [recording]. 1 cassette, 1992. Distributed by Spoken Arts.

CHITRA BANERJEE DIVAKARUNI, *Indian Movie, New Jersey* (p. 819)

The speaker in "Indian Movie, New Jersey" contrasts the safety and hope of the world inside the movie theater with the threats and disappointments of the world outside. The irony of the poem is that the movie theater itself underscores the thwarted possibilities and expectations that America represents — "the America that was supposed to be" (line 51).

You might begin a discussion of this poem by asking students to identify and describe a "world" they participate in, such as a university or college, that is different from the "real world" they know. One way to further the discussion is to focus on the idea of the "American Dream." Ask students to read Louis Simpson's "In the Suburbs" (text p. 746). After they read the poem, begin a discussion as to why these poets seem disillusioned by this concept. (Or do they?)

POSSIBLE CONNECTIONS TO OTHER SELECTIONS

Langston Hughes, "Theme for English B" (text p. 1027)

Tato Laviera, "AmeRícan" (text p. 918)

ROBERT BROWNING, *My Last Duchess* (p. 821)

Robert Browning lived with his parents in a London suburb until he married Elizabeth Barrett at age 34; he had previously left home only to attend boarding school and for short trips abroad. He and his wife lived in Italy for fifteen years, a period in which he produced some of his first memorable poems. *Men and Women,* published in 1855, gained Browning the initial intimations of his later fame. The poet returned to England after his wife died in 1861. His work continued to elicit increasing public (if not always critical) acclaim.

Ironically, the speaker is talking about the portrait of his last duchess (how many went before?) to the marriage broker, who is handling the current arrangement between the duke and the broker's "master," father of the bride-to-be.

The last wife's principal fault was that she was too democratic in her smiles; she did not reserve them for the duke alone. The duke holds no regard for kindness and thoughtfulness; he thinks only of money, rank, and name. He treats women as objects and possessions.

The visitor seems to want to leave early, perhaps to warn his master of the unfeeling tyrant who would marry the master's daughter at a cut rate (cf. lines 47–54).

Students may have already read this dramatic monologue in high school. The second time around they should appreciate the irony even more as the duke reveals so much of his own character while ostensibly controlling the situation.

POSSIBLE CONNECTIONS TO OTHER SELECTIONS

Mark Halliday, "Graded Paper" (text p. 1156)
Katharyn Howd Machan, "Hazel Tells LaVerne" (question #1, following)

CONNECTION QUESTION IN TEXT (p. 822) WITH ANSWER

1. Write an essay describing the ways in which the speakers of "My Last Duchess" and "Hazel Tells LaVerne" (p. 725) by Katharyn Howd Machan inadvertently reveal themselves.

   In both cases, the speaker has a story to tell, and both speakers are trying to paint a favorable picture of themselves as they do so. The speaker of Browning's poem gets himself in trouble as he continues to talk, indicating the fate of his last duchess through unsuppressed expressions of his own unfulfilled desire. As he describes the portrait, he eventually gets away from art and into the character of the duchess, wondering all the while how he should express himself. The speaker of "Hazel Tells LaVerne" reveals her unconscious desire to be taken away from her situation as she repeats the line "me a princess," focusing (without meaning to do so) on herself rather than on the frog whose story she is narrating. Students with a background in psychology might be able to flesh out the motivations behind these speakers' tales even more.

RESOURCES FOR TEACHING

Robert Browning: My Last Duchess & Other Poems [recording]. 1 cassette. Distributed by Caedmon/HarperAudio.

Robert Browning: Selected Poems [recording]. 4 cassettes (360 min.). Read by Frederick Davidson. Distributed by Blackstone Audio Books.

The Poetry of Browning [recording]. 1 cassette. Distributed by Caedmon/HarperAudio.

Robert Browning — His Life and Poetry. 21 min., color, 1972. Beta, VHS, ¾″ U-matic cassette, 16-mm film, special-order format. A dramatization of Browning's life and several of his poems, including "My Last Duchess." Distributed by International Film Bureau.

Treasury of Robert Browning [recording]. 1 cassette. Distributed by Spoken Arts.

See also "Victorian Poetry" (recording) in the appendix of Film, Video, and Audio-cassette Resources.

WILLIAM BLAKE, *The Chimney Sweeper* (p. 822)

There is an ironic distance in this poem between the speaker, who seems to be too young to make judgments, and Blake, who through his ironic perspective underscores the harm that comes from too meekly doing one's duty, not to mention the evil of a society indifferent to the plight of "thousands of sweepers" whose only pleasure is in dreams. Needless to say, sacrificing one's hair for the sake of on-the-job cleanliness is not a principle Blake would endorse.

On the surface the poem could be interpreted as a dream of desire for some beneficent angel to release the boys from their "coffins of black" (the chimneys). More likely, the dream expresses a desire for release through death from the torturous and life-threatening trials of sweeping soot from chimneys. Here again, irony operates, in that a dream of death makes it easier for the boy to face his life the next morning.

POSSIBLE CONNECTIONS TO OTHER SELECTIONS

Paul Laurence Dunbar, "We Wear the Mask" (text p. 808)
Langston Hughes, "Negro" (text p. 1016)

GARY SOTO, *Behind Grandma's House* (p. 823)

In this poem, Soto captures a moment that almost every individual experiences in growing up — the trying on of different identities to discover one that "fits." Ultimately, the grandma in the poem helps the speaker along in the process by showing him how the identity he is trying cannot work. Students may connect the episode described in this poem to times in their own lives when they've searched for an identity or tried too hard to prove something to themselves or others.

You might begin the class discussion by suggesting that the real "happening" of the poem is the arrival of the grandma, who, with total nonchalance, sets the speaker straight on what it means to be tough. Ask students why Soto limited his description of the grandma to simply "her apron flapping in a breeze, / her hair mussed" (lines 19–20). She seems a fairly "typical" grandma in appearance — clearly she's not looking for a fight — yet her simple "Let me help you" followed by a well-aimed punch teaches the speaker more about toughness than he learned through an entire alley's worth of vandalism.

POSSIBLE CONNECTION TO ANOTHER SELECTION

Sharon Olds, "Rite of Passage" (question #1, following)

CONNECTION QUESTION IN TEXT (p. 824) WITH ANSWER

1. Write an essay comparing the themes of "Behind Grandma's House" and Sharon Olds's "Rite of Passage" (p. 915).

   Both poems suggest that boys will be boys; in this poem we get the sense that some boys, like this speaker who "wanted fame" (line 1), will cross the boundaries of acceptable behavior to be accepted. In Olds's poem, it seems that all boys are capable of doing so, but for them the notion of acceptable behavior changes with context. The boy in Soto's poem is not going to achieve fame by behaving this way in front of his grandmother, or even behind her house. The boys at the birthday party in Olds's poem will only achieve fame if they conform because they are at a party. The speaker in Olds's poem is unlike the grandmother in Soto's poem because she is outnumbered; her son is bound to go through his rite of passage with his peers. Soto's speaker also grows and learns something, but it is through the discipline of an elder rather than through the coaxing of friends.

RESOURCES FOR TEACHING

Gary Soto I & II [recording]. 1 cassette (60 min.), 1982, 1992. The author reads his works and talks about the recent rise of Chicano literature. Distributed by New Letters on the Air.

See also "Poets in Person, No. 7" (recording) in the appendix of Film, Video, and Audiocassette Resources.

ROBERT BLY, *Sitting Down to Dinner* (p. 824)

This poem considers the personality of a man who, as a child, was given mixed signals as to what was truly his. The gist of the argument is that a child who is told to finish what is on *his* plate or to go to *his* room will begin to feel as though nothing is truly his. Since he has no freedom as a child, he has no imagination as an adult, and as a result, becomes "helpful and hostile at the same time" (line 11). This person both "leans toward you and leans away"; the speaker concludes by asking the reader, "Do you feel me leaning?"

Some students may relish the opportunity to complain about how they were brought up. Bly describes too much control as a "demon" in line 2. Could too much freedom also be considered a "demon"? Which is worse? Ask students to consider the symbolism of dinner, the assumption that a child's parents are commanding him to finish what's on his plate or sit on his chair. This rhetoric is no doubt familiar to students, and they might offer other examples of it from their own childhood. Be prepared, if you go this route, to monitor a debate about the proper means of child rearing: how much freedom can children handle? Where is the line between parental guidance and excessive control? Or, in connection with Heitzman's poem (see "Possible Connections," below), when does an adult's need for order interfere with or damage a child's sense of self?

A more difficult concept is the idea behind line 1: "Suppose a man can't find what is his." How do students interpret that line? What, as an adult, belongs to you? Students are likely to recognize that Bly is speaking in terms beyond material possession, but they might find it difficult to articulate exactly what he means. It might help to have them write about what they think is theirs, excluding material possessions, before discussing the poem, and to extrapolate by asking them how they think such things could be lost.

POSSIBLE CONNECTIONS TO OTHER SELECTIONS

Robert Frost, "Birches" (text p. 986)
Judy Page Heitzman, "The Schoolroom on the Second Floor of the Knitting Mill" (question #1, following)

1. In an essay consider how early childhood experiences affect adult identities in "Sitting Down to Dinner" and in Judy Page Heitzman's "The Schoolroom on the Second Floor of the Knitting Mill" (p. 1158).

   In Bly's poem, children are not allowed any volition or sense of possession; a child is told to finish "his" plate or go to "his" room even though neither one is truly his. The effect of such an upbringing is to raise an adult who has no "foundation" (line 10) and who must consequently rely on others. The situation is slightly different in Heitzman's poem, in which an adult teacher blames a child for failing to control other children. By being told that she is not a good leader, the young girl is set up for a pattern of self-blame for failure that lasts for the rest of her life. Her shame comes from the fact that her peers hear the teacher's scorn. It is not as though she is dispossessed, as is the case in Bly's poem, but rather that she is singled out and ridiculed.

PERSPECTIVE

EZRA POUND, *On Symbols* (p. 825)

Consider Pound's use of the word *natural* in the first line of the passage. Does he mean that a symbol should be drawn from an object in nature or that a symbol should have a natural, easy relationship to the idea it is meant to symbolize? Students might suggest other interpretations. Does Pound's example of the hawk at the end of the passage help to clarify his meaning? Ask students what a hawk might symbolize. Using other Pound poems in this anthology, identify the symbols the poet employs and discuss whether they are "natural" in either sense of the word. Look at Poe's "The Haunted Palace" (text p. 800), wherein the human mind and head are compared to a house, or Millay's "I will put Chaos into fourteen lines" (text p. 882), in which writing poetry is compared to rape, as examples to discuss which method of using symbols they think conveys meaning most effectively.

20

Sounds

In this chapter, encouraging students to read aloud is vital. You may find that you have to lead by example, initially. However, you will probably want to shift the focus onto student readers at some point. In some cases, you may find yourself confronting a considerable degree of resistance, particularly if there has not been much reading aloud previously. Much of this resistance stems from fear of embarrassment, and dealing with it requires either the creation of a "safe space" in which students can read without fear of others snickering, or a slightly raucous classroom environment in which students don't feel as much pressure to be "cool."

If you have a group of particularly shy students, you might find it helpful to assign students poems in advance, so that they have a chance to read the poem through a couple of times before being called on to speak out before the class. If you have a mix of extraverts and introverts, you might schedule the class so that the extraverts read "cold," and announce at the end of class the poems the introverts will read in the next session, to give them fair warning.

In most cases, the addition of student voices to the classroom will help increase involvement and raise the energy level. If the class has not featured student reading much so far, this chapter would be an appropriate time to introduce this feature of the class.

In addition to including student voices in the classroom, this chapter affords an opportunity to include the voices of the poets as well: Kinnell, Hopkins, Carroll, Brodsky, Pope, Hacker, and Kingston each have recordings available that will allow students to hear either the voice of the poet or a skilled reader reciting the poems. It is perhaps a judgment call as to whether you should introduce these readings before students have done much reading on their own, in order to provide models of reading for them, or to wait until after students have some experience, to keep from intimidating them into silence. If you have included recordings in previous chapters, this may not be an issue here. In any event, recordings can be very useful in giving students a sense of the reality of the people "behind the page," as it were. You may find it appropriate to do readings or bring in recordings of poems that have been popular with students earlier in the class, and evaluate the poets' use of sound in relation to the students' own preference of these poems.

Thematically, there are some interesting poems in this chapter. If you do not want the focus on reading to overwhelm a discussion of these poems, you could use the reading as a springboard to raise the class's interest and energy, and to give them specific features to discuss when they make connections between the sound of a poem and its "message."

ANONYMOUS, *Scarborough Fair* (p. 827)

Ballads in general and this ballad in particular are discussed more fully in the manual on page 379. Your students may or may not be acquainted with the Simon and Garfunkel version of this ballad that was used in the 1960s as an antiwar song, and the use of this traditional ballad in that context may lead to some interesting discussion about the difference between the oral and written tradition.

As a ballad, "Scarborough Fair" follows a clear pattern: four feet to a line with an *abab* rhyme scheme and repeated second and fourth lines. In addition, in all but the first stanza, the first words of the stanza are "Tell her to" followed by the introduction of an impossible task that, if performed, will reconcile the speaker of the poem to the "bonny lass" who was once his true lover. The impossible nature of these tasks is perhaps a clue as to how much hope the speaker in the poem has of reconciliation.

The effect of the refrain is soothing — readers and listeners come to expect the repeated lines, and the rhythm of these lines is peaceful. The herbs that are mentioned in the refrain are associated with female power (parsley was used to decorate tombs, sage represents wisdom, rosemary is for memory, and thyme is thought to enhance courage). In addition, both sage and rosemary had the connotation of growing in gardens where women ruled the households. Why might the poet have chosen these herbs as repeated symbols in this ballad? What message might the poet have been trying to convey?

POSSIBLE CONNECTIONS TO OTHER SELECTIONS

Anonymous, "Bonny Barbara Allan" (text p. 1074)
John Donne, "A Valediction: Forbidding Mourning" (text p. 790)

JOHN UPDIKE, *Player Piano* (p. 828)

This poem is a listening exercise in how to translate the sounds poetry can produce to musical analogues we have already heard. From light ditties through more somber 1920s chase-scene music, perhaps, to a medley of chords and light cadences, this poem explores a player piano's repertoire. In doing so, does the poem do anything *besides* impress us with its sounds? Does reading the poem allow us anything beyond the sheer joy of the sounds of words and the way they can be manipulated?

MAY SWENSON, *A Nosty Fright* (p. 828)

Since "A Nosty Fright" is much more about sound than sense, be sure to read it, or have students read it, aloud (this may be more difficult than one might anticipate, for the transposed consonants often have the effect of creating tongue-twisters). Does the fractured diction have any purpose other than humor? Remind students that people who are upset or frightened often find it difficult to speak clearly.

Notice that sometimes the poetic technique used here results in transpositions that are actual words. Do any of these seem appropriate in this poem, for instance, "Bat" in line 24, or "fright" in line 25? Do any of them seem out of place, like "mitten" (20)? Have students suggest definitions for some of the nonsense words and phrases, based on their sounds. Compare the poem to Lewis Carroll's "Jabberwocky" (text p. 841). Are the techniques for creating new words the same in both poems?

POSSIBLE CONNECTION TO ANOTHER SELECTION

Lewis Carroll [Charles Lutwidge Dodgson], "Jabberwocky" (text p. 841)

EMILY DICKINSON, *A Bird came down the Walk* — (p. 829)

Silent reading of this poem, followed by reading it aloud, will reinforce the connection between sound and sense. In particular, students should hear the difference between the irregular movement of the first three stanzas and the smoothness of the last six lines, a difference created visually by punctuation but even more obvious when the poem is heard.

One of the poetic techniques that characterizes Emily Dickinson's poetry is her use of unexpected words and images. Consider her depiction of the bird's eyes and of his flight. How can eyes be "rapid" (line 9)? How can they hurry (10)? How can feathers "unroll" (15)? How is flight like rowing (16)? What is the effect created by the use of unusual language to describe an ordinary creature?

Compare the way the sounds of poetry are used to create a sense of an animal's movement in this poem and in Rilke's "The Panther" (text p. 767). Are the panther's movements in any way like the bird's?

POSSIBLE CONNECTION TO ANOTHER SELECTION

Rainer Maria Rilke, "The Panther" (text p. 767)

GALWAY KINNELL, *Blackberry Eating* (p. 832)

Some poems are memorable for their themes, while others are enjoyed not for what they say but for how they say it. This poem seems to fall into this second category, as Kinnell tries in lieu of the blackberries themselves to offer us a blackberry language. It would probably be a good idea to read this poem aloud in class. Kinnell plays with the kinesthesia of the sound in words such as *strengths* or *squinched,* which by their compacted consonance physically suggest to him the pressure of the tongue bursting open the berry's mysterious ("black art") icy sweetness. What other words are there (you might ask) that seem to touch the inside of the body before they are spoken? Look at some of the heavily consonantal words in lines 12 and 13, marking especially words like *splurge* and *language.* Lines 4–6, besides containing good examples of consonance patterns, also express a pathetic fallacy, with Kinnell's imaginative supposition that blackberry bushes are punished with nettles for knowing the art of blackberry making. You might ask what, if anything, this image adds to the poem. Probably it underscores Kinnell's whimsical sense of the black artistry of blackberry making.

The sound then moves from the hard *b* of *blackberry* to the softer *ss* of the final lines. Many assonant *o*s occur in the first lines, *e*s and *a*s in the middle of the poem. The sounds attempt to capture the delectable berries, making the experience of reading the poem as sensuous as eating a berry.

More than providing a message of "truth" for its reader, this poem invites us into an experience of sound and image. The poem is about language in that it considers the difficulty of capturing an idea in words and communicating it effectively. Attempting to write a poem can be as much a learning experience about poetry as attempting to write about a poem. Perhaps some members of the class would like to try writing their own lyric beginning with the words *I love to.*

POSSIBLE CONNECTIONS TO OTHER SELECTIONS

Helen Chasin, "The Word *Plum*" (text p. 851)

Emily Dickinson, "I taste a liquor never brewed —" (text p. 936)

Pablo Neruda, "Sweetness, Always" (text p. 1141)

RESOURCES FOR TEACHING

Galway Kinnell I & II [recording]. 1 cassette (60 min.), 1982, 1991. Distributed by New Letters on the Air.

The Poetry of Galway Kinnell [recording]. 1 cassette (33 min.), 1965. Part of the YM-YWHA Poetry Center Series. Distributed by Audio-Forum.

The Poetry & Voice of Galway Kinnell [recording]. 1 cassette. Distributed by Caedmon/HarperAudio.

See also "Moyers: The Power of the Word" in the appendix of Film, Video, and Audiocassette Resources.

RICHARD ARMOUR, *Going to Extremes* (p. 833)

What are the "extremes" to which this poem goes? How does the poet connect the two words that describe the extremes?

Even if students are unfamiliar with scansion, they should be able to detect a difference in the way words are emphasized in lines 1 and 3 as opposed to lines 2 and 4. Ask them to describe how the sound shifts coincide with the action of the poem. In speaking lines 1 and 3 aloud, one can almost feel the sharp movements of the bottle. In lines 2 and 4, it is as though the bottle is at rest, with the person who has been shaking it now waiting to see whether or not the catsup will come. Having students actually "shake" an imaginary catsup bottle as they recite the poem might be an effective way to connect sound to sense.

POSSIBLE CONNECTION TO ANOTHER SELECTION

Margaret Atwood, "you fit into me" (text p. 777)

ROBERT SOUTHEY, From *The Cataract of Lodore* (p. 833)

Although Robert Southey is now known chiefly for his association with some of the great poets of the Romantic period, such as Wordsworth and Coleridge, he was very popular in his own time and became the poet laureate of England in 1813. He is also credited with the first published version of the children's story *The Three Bears*.

In a twenty-three-line introductory stanza that is not excerpted here, the poet reveals that his son and daughter had requested him to tell them — in verse — about the water at Lodore. He also introduces himself as the poet laureate. Does having this information in any way change your students' response to the poem that follows?

Are any lines in the poem especially memorable? Why is it appropriate that line 68, with its thirteen syllables, is metrically the longest line of the poem?

TIP FROM THE FIELD

One tip I've found helpful in teaching sound in poetry, is to have students stand in a tight circle and recite the excerpt from "The Cataract of Lodore" in round-robin fashion, one after another. Each student reads a line in the order of the poem, repeating the poem several times, faster each time. The results, in terms of student response, are remarkable.

— NANCY VEIGA, *Modesto Junior College*

POSSIBLE CONNECTION TO ANOTHER SELECTION

Greg Williamson, "Waterfall" (text p. 874)

PERSPECTIVE

DAVID LENSON, *On the Contemporary Use of Rhyme* (p. 836)

You might ask students to find contemporary poems that make subtle use of rhyme. Philip Larkin's poems are good examples of the effective use of slant rhyme and enjambment to camouflage the rhymes in a poem. Conversely, you might ask students to look for songs that don't use rhyme. Bruce Springsteen's "Streets of Philadelphia" (text p. 694) uses some rhyme, but not in every line. What is the effect of the sporadic rhyme in his song?

Students might be interested in speculating on why writers are returning to rhyme. Is more formal poetry appropriate for our time and culture? Or is it simply a question of rebelling against the norm (in our time, unrhymed poetry)?

GERARD MANLEY HOPKINS, *God's Grandeur* (p. 837)

Gerard Manley Hopkins was a deeply religious man, a Jesuit ordained in 1877. He had previously graduated from Oxford University and joined the Roman Catholic Church in 1866. He served a number of parishes before being appointed a professor of classics at University College, Dublin. Although he tried to keep his poetic vocation from interfering with his spiritual one, he wasn't successful, and he suffered greatly because of this conflict, once burning all his finished work and another time forsaking poetry for seven years.

Although this poem follows sonnet form and an exact rhyme scheme, the first eight lines still read very roughly. How does the poet achieve this effect? Note the disruptions in rhythm as well as the use of cacophonic sounds. Have students try reading line 4 aloud to better appreciate its difficulty. Is there any change in the level of disruption or the level of cacophony in the last six lines? What is the effect of the inserted "ah!" in the last line?

Compare the halting beginning and smooth ending of this poem to the similar transition that occurs in Emily Dickinson's "A Bird came down the Walk —" (text p. 829). How does Dickinson's bird compare to the bird image Hopkins evokes in the last two lines?

POSSIBLE CONNECTIONS TO OTHER SELECTIONS

Denise Levertov, "Gathered at the River" (text p. 907)
William Wordsworth, "The World Is Too Much With Us" (text p. 880)

RESOURCES FOR TEACHING

The Poetry of Gerard Manley Hopkins [recording]. 1 cassette. Distributed by Caedmon/HarperAudio.
Gerard Manley Hopkins: The Wreck of the Deutschland [recording]. 1 cassette. Distributed by Audio-Forum.
See also "Romantics and Realists" and "Victorian Poetry" [recording] in the appendix of Film, Video, and Audiocassette Resources.

EDGAR ALLAN POE, *The Bells* (p. 838)

Divided into four sections, each corresponding to a type of bell (sleigh bells, wedding bells, alarm bells, and death-knells), this poem relies heavily on onomatopoeia. As the poem's stanzas grow increasingly longer and the subject becomes increasingly heavier, the reader moves through a series of psychological adjustments, exploited by the sonorous qualities of language.

The sound of the bells also becomes increasingly heavy as the poem progresses, from tinkling to tolling. Any discussion of this poem will depend largely on the way it is read aloud in class. You might have to coax students to read the poem as it calls to be read. Take, for example, the repetition of the word *bells* at the end of each stanza. How do we know how long to pause between each utterance of this word based on the rest of the words in that stanza? You may want to ask your students to try to quantify the pauses in the poem. Is it productive to treat each pause the same in a reading? Poe's poem can be thought of as an argument for why poetry should always be read aloud; much of its effect comes from the ways its sounds fall upon the ear.

In addition to the effect of repetition and onomatopoeia, "The Bells" also serves as a model for other poetic conventions, notably alliteration and assonance, and end-stopped rhyme. Students may become so caught up in Poe's sound-play that they overlook the meaning of the words or the effect of the poem's structure. You can prompt them to elucidate the theme by having them compare parts of speech in each of the four stanzas; what does the progression of the adjectives in the four stanzas tell us (from crystalline to liquid to mad to melancholy)? The same effect can be achieved with nouns, verbs, or adverbs. Would the poem's theme change if the order of the stanzas were mixed up? Have them compare the phrases "keeping time, time, time" and "Runic rhyme" in the first and last stanzas; has the rest of the poem changed the import of these phrases? Is it ironic that the "Runic rhyme" as described in the final stanza is "happy" when the mood seems to have changed from happy to melancholy? The poem's trajectory seems to be important to its theme. A comparison to Southey's "The Cataract of Lodore" (p. 833) might highlight this difference since Southey's poem seems more driven by momentum than by a thematic focal point.

POSSIBLE CONNECTIONS TO OTHER SELECTIONS

Anonymous, "Bonny Barbara Allan" (text p. 1074)
Robert Southey, "The Cataract of Lodore" (question #1, following)

CONNECTION QUESTION IN TEXT (p. 841) WITH ANSWER

1. Compare Poe's sound effects with Robert Southey's in "The Cataract of Lodore" (p. 833). Which poem do you find more effective in its use of sound? Explain why.

   The poets use different methods to create their sound effects. Poe relies more on repetition than Southey does. "The Cataract of Lodore" strings together words that rhyme — "And rushing and flushing and brushing and gushing" (line 63) — rarely returning to a word that has already been used. Poe also combines rhyming words in quick succession — "By the twanging / And the clanging" (58–59), but the refrain always returns to bells. Southey's poem thus conveys the sense of something rushing endlessly onward, whereas Poe's poem conveys the sense of something that resounds. Each is appropriate to its subject.

LEWIS CARROLL [CHARLES LUTWIDGE DODGSON], *Jabberwocky* (p. 841)

" 'Jabberwocky' is no mere piece of sound experimentation but a serious short narrative poem describing a young man's coming of age as he seeks out and kills the tribal terror." Test that description on your students, and they will, one hopes, turn around and tell you that the fun of this poem and the justification for its being reside in its sound and word creations.

Carroll kept his own glossary for some of the words in this poem, which Alice read through her looking glass. The glossary entries and copious notes about the poem are provided by Martin Gardner in *The Annotated Alice* (New York: Bramhall House, 1960), pp. 191-197. The notes are too extensive to include here — but as a sampling, here is the first stanza "translated":

> 'Twas time for making dinner (bryllyg — to broil),
>   and the "smooth and active" (slimy + lithe) badgers
>
> Did scratch like a dog (gyre — giaour)
>   and drill holes (gimble) in the side of the hill:
>
> All unhappy were the Parrots (now extinct; they lived on veal and
>   under sundials),
>
> And the grave turtles (who lived on swallows and oysters) squeaked.

Reality bores its head through the hills and holes of "Jabberwocky," and certain words in the poem have their place in the *OED*. These include *rath,* an Irish word for a circular earthen wall; *Manx,* a Celtic name for the Isle of Man; *whiffling,* smoking, drinking, or blowing short puffs; *Caloo,* the sound and name of an arctic duck; *beamish,* old form of *beaming; chortled,* Carroll's own coinage, meaning "laughed"; and *gallumphing,* another of Carroll's creations, which according to him is a cross between *gallop* and *triumphant* and means "to march on exultantly with irregular bounding movements."

POSSIBLE CONNECTION TO ANOTHER SELECTION

May Swenson, "A Nosty Fright" (question #1, following)

CONNECTION QUESTION IN TEXT (p. 842) WITH ANSWER

1. Compare Carroll's strategies for creating sound and meaning with those used by Swenson in "A Nosty Fright" (p. 828).

    Whereas Swenson transposes letters to create amusing sound patterns and effects, Carroll combines and alters words to invent a new language for his speaker. Carroll's technique is harder to translate word for word; it requires more of his audience's imaginative effort.

RESOURCES FOR TEACHING

Treasury of Lewis Carroll [recording]. 1 cassette. Distributed by Spoken Arts.
See also "Victorian Poetry" [recording] in the appendix of Film, Video, and Audio-cassette Resources.

SYLVIA PLATH, *Mushrooms* (p. 842)

Ostensibly, the speaker of this poem is a mushroom speaking on behalf of other mushrooms pushing their way into the world and gaining strength through their ever-increasing number. Despite their unobtrusiveness and the fact that they are "meek" (line 26) and "bland-mannered" (21), the mushrooms claim that they "shall by morning / Inherit the earth" (31-32).

It may be a natural impulse to take "mushrooms" metaphorically; readers are more likely to squeeze out some truth about "human nature" than to accept the possibility that this poem might be simply an imaginative projection into the point of view of a fungus. These two readings are made possible through the noncommittal title: do students take "mushrooms" to be a metaphor for a certain type of people: "our kind" (30)? How does the poem allow us to read mushrooms as such a metaphor? Does it essentially matter whether or not we take mushrooms literally or metaphorically? Isn't the poem more about the mushrooms (whatever we take them to be) in relationship to the rest of the earth that they threaten to "inherit" (33)?

The mushrooms are personified, but they are also specifically mushrooms, growing in "loam" (5) and so forth. Students must read the poem closely, highlighting what they feel to be its key poetic conventions, in order to support their interpretation of the poem's theme and tone. Are these mushrooms threatening or sinister in any way? Do we feel pity for them, do we respect them? Are we as readers meant to side with the mushrooms or with the rest of the world? You may want to consider Plath's pervasive use of assonance and alliteration. How do the sounds — "soft fists insist on" (10), for example — contribute to our understanding of tone? How do they work with the content? Is this poem humorous?

WILLIAM HEYEN, *The Trains* (p. 843)

For students who don't know, explain that Treblinka is the name of a Nazi concentration camp located near Warsaw, Poland. To illustrate Heyen's use of sound, you may want to open discussion by reading the poem aloud to your class. By repeating the word *Treblinka*, and by relying on choppy words with sharp, hard consonant sounds, Heyen creates the sound and rhythm of the wheels of a train — a rhythm that is intensified with the repetition of *Treblinka* until it resonates within the reader. In this way the poet uses sound and rhythm to affect the reader. Ask students to provide specific examples from the poem of how sound is used to intensify the horror of Treblinka.

At first, Heyen tells the facts of the story — listing with detachment and distance the statistics of what was removed from Treblinka on freight trains. However, as the poem continues, the statistics gain strength and the reader's horror mounts with each new revelation: clothing became paper (line 7), watches were saved and kept (8), and women's hair was used for mattresses and dolls (9).

In the fourth stanza, Heyen implies that many people are indirectly linked to the atrocities of Treblinka through the legacy of the material goods culled from the Holocaust. He suggests that the words of his poem might "like to use some of that same paper" (10); "one of those watches may pulse in your own wrist" (11), much like the rhythm of breathing or a pulse; and that someone the reader *knows* may "collect dolls, or sleep on human hair" (12). Ask students to consider the effect of this stanza. Is the poet implying a collective guilt for the Holocaust? Or is he implying that the horror of Treblinka lives on through the material legacy of the dead? In the end, no one escapes Heyen's indictment, and although Commandant Stangl of Treblinka may be dead at last, his legacy lives on in word and sound within anyone who hears the story.

POSSIBLE CONNECTION TO ANOTHER SELECTION

Mary Jo Salter, "Welcome to Hiroshima" (text p. 703)

JEAN TOOMER, *Reapers* (p. 844)

"Reapers" is taken from Toomer's experimentalist novel *Cain* (1923), which combines poetry and prose and was one of the works that helped launch the Harlem Renaissance. The poem is ominous and grim in tone. Long before it was fashionable to call his people blacks, Toomer here stressed the dire nature of the scene by talking about black reapers and black horses. Scythes and mowers call to mind the image of death as a grim reaper, sometimes cutting down people in their prime. That symbolic association is enhanced by the death of the field rat, which seems to indicate also the vulnerability of the reapers to being cut down by some impersonal, indifferent force.

The sound of the rasping blade being honed to sharpness is suggested in lines 1 and 2 by the many *s*-sounds. In question 4's version of line 6, certain alliterative and assonant sounds are linked by echoing sounds, as in "fi*el*d rat," "squ*eal* ing," "b*leed*s." A cause-effect relation is underscored by Toomer's version, which places "squealing" and "bleeds" together. Finally, the caesura provides rhythmic reinforcement of the action described.

POSSIBLE CONNECTIONS TO OTHER SELECTIONS

William Blake, "The Chimney Sweeper" (text p. 822)
Countee Cullen, "Yet I Do Marvel" (text p. 1086)

JOHN DONNE, *Song* (p. 844)

This poem explores a number of supposed impossibilities, ending with "a woman true, and fair" (line 17). The poem is at once bawdy and cynical; women are promiscuous, but the speaker also feels that they cannot be otherwise. Once students have discerned the speaker's attitude and his tone, take some time to investigate the way the speaker builds his argument. What types of mysteries does he use for comparison in the first stanza?

Donne manages to mix cynicism and lightheartedness here as he verbally throws up his hands at the possibility of finding an honest mind or a woman who is both true and fair. You might spend some time in class discussion exploring how he holds at bay the darker tones of his cynicism. Can we identify with Donne's dilemma today, or have attitudes toward women changed too much? What does the humor in the poem tell us about his fundamental attitude toward women? Students will probably appreciate the hyperbole in the poem. It is as though Donne were saying, "You might as well get with child a mandrake root, as find an honest mind."

The last stanza is especially humorous. Donne claims he would not even go next door to see this reputedly loyal woman. Her reputation for loyalty might hold long enough for his friend to write a letter describing her, but by the time the speaker arrived, she would have been false to two or three other lovers.

As a writing assignment, you might ask the students to discuss the humor in this song, humor that would definitely include Donne's use of hyperbole. The students should then try to anticipate a listener's reaction to the speaker and decide whether the speaker is perfectly "straight" in his observations.

POSSIBLE CONNECTIONS TO OTHER SELECTIONS

Anonymous, "Scarborough Fair" (text p. 827)
John Donne, "The Flea" (text p. 1090)

JOSEPH BRODSKY, *Love Song* (p. 845)

The speaker of this poem creates eight hypothetical situations for his lover, following the formula, "If you were . . . I would . . ." The relationship between the speaker and the addressee is complex, based on these analogies, and the relationship between these hypotheses is just as complex. The speaker seems tender toward the addressee in the first hypothesis, for instance, but he becomes domineering and possessive in the second. Does the order of the hypotheses matter? Is there some sort of progression toward that mysterious final line?

At first, this seems like an example of light verse: a short, witty poem with a comic tone, if not necessarily a comic theme. The repetition of the formula and the easy rhyme scheme contribute to the light mood of the poem. But you may want to point out the seriousness that lies just below the surface of the poem. Each couplet has a word or image that disturbs or subverts the comic tone. The addressee is "drowning" (line 1) in the first couplet and "arrested" (3) in the second; the speaker "cuts" (4) a record and "storms" (10) the ladies' room, etc. It might be interesting to have students write a description of the speaker before you begin discussion and to compare these impressions. Do they base their description more on his actions, his imagination, or his tone? What kind of lover is he (possessive, sensitive, passionate)? The final line complicates everything that comes before, but it also renders the poem more comic. It sounds like witty doggerel, but does it tell us something about the speaker that we didn't know before?

POSSIBLE CONNECTIONS TO OTHER SELECTIONS

Aron Keesbury, "Song to a Waitress" (text p. 872)
William Shakespeare, "My mistress' eyes are nothing like the sun" (text p. 882)

RESOURCES FOR TEACHING

Joseph Brodsky: A Maddening Space [video]. Color, VHS (60 min.), 1989. Center for Visual History in association with Channel 4. Produced by Sasha Alpert, directed/written by Lawrence Pitkethly, narrated by Jason Robards. Distributed by Mystic Fire Video.

Joseph Brodsky Reads His Poetry [recording]. 1 cassette (30 min.), 1988. Distributed by Caedmon/HarperAudio.

Winter [recording]. 1 cassette (64 min.). In Russian and English. Distributed by Watershed Tapes.

THOMAS HARDY, *The Oxen* (p. 846)

So often a poem's source is childhood memory or belief, as though childhood were a period in our lives that made poetry possible. You might ask the class if they already knew of the belief about animals on which this poem rests. There is a kind of pathos about the poem, in which Hardy recalls his own readiness to believe that the oxen knelt in reverence on Christmas Eve. The feeling is of a wistful longing for a belief that probably never can be reinstated in this (even for Hardy) more mechanistic and rationalistic age. It is not so much a loss of childhood, but rather the loss of belief that is mourned. In the final stanza, the doubled *o*-sounds suggest the tones of lament and mourning.

ALEXANDER POPE, From *An Essay on Criticism* (p. 847)

Alexander Pope was born in London and, after age twelve, grew up in Windsor Forest. Because his family was Catholic, and because he had been afflicted with tuberculosis of the spine, most of his education was completed at home. Catholics couldn't attend university or hold office, chief routes to patronage in those days, so Pope became by necessity as well as by desire and talent the first writer to show that literature could be one's sole support. His work, beginning with translations of the *Iliad* and the *Odyssey,* was both critically approved and financially profitable.

You might begin discussion of this selection by reminding students that the debate over which should take precedence, sound or sense, has been of greater concern to poets than many of us realize or recall.

Pope enjoys a little self-reflective mockery in these lines, like the bumper sticker that reads "Eschew Obfuscation." What he says, he does: the iambs march with strict, tuneful regularity in line 4. The word *do* in line 10 is an expletive, or meter filler. Line 11 presents a parade of monosyllables. "Chimes" in line 12 sets up the anticipated "rhymes" in line 13, and line 21 exceeds its bounds, albeit slowly, with the long alexandrine. Line 20 ("A needless Alexandrine") is also a clever play on Pope's name and on himself.

Line 23 uses assonance and some alliteration to suggest what it means; line 24 is a fine example of "easy vigor," straightforward and brief enough; lines 32 and 33 imitate the thought through the manipulation of sounds, in particular the sibilance of the *s*-sound, the growling of the *r*s, and the forcefulness of the blocks of heavy-stressed words, as in "when loud surges lash."

In line 34 the sounds get stuck in one's throat ("rock's vast weight") and reflect this resisting struggle. Accents in line 35 on "líne tóo lábors," and on "wórds móve slów" create an almost plodding rhythm that imitates the sense of the words. These lines contrast with lines 36 and 37, which contain far more light-stressed words and employ a much more direct and smooth syntax.

Careful reading of much contemporary poetry will reveal the continuing validity of Pope's observations. In any case, the power of words fashioned into lines with close attention to sound can be amply demonstrated by observing the structure of popular songs and advertisements.

POSSIBLE CONNECTION TO ANOTHER SELECTION

Langston Hughes, "Formula" (text p. 1021)

RESOURCES FOR TEACHING

    Treasury of Alexander Pope [recording]. 1 cassette. Distributed by Spoken Arts.
    See also "English Literature: Eighteenth Century" and "Restoration and Augustan Poetry" in the appendix of Film, Video, and Audiocassette Resources.

MARILYN HACKER, *Groves of Academe* (p. 848)

From the point of view of a weary poetry professor, this poem encompasses the various responses she receives when she asks, "Tell me about the poetry you're reading." All of the responses dodge the question, focusing instead on the budding poets themselves rather than on the seemingly nonexistent poetry they are reading.

As students of poetry themselves, your students may feel uncomfortable as the subjects of this poem. They may also tend to distance themselves from the student voices in the poem. They may characterize the speaker as cynical: why doesn't she include any of the brilliant responses from students who *do* take the initiative to read poetry that isn't required in class? You might ask them if it is necessary to read poetry if you are to be a poet. If so, how does one find the time to do so in college? This may spark a lively discussion about the undergraduate experience — how valuable a commodity time is, how professors have no sense that students are taking more than one course, and so forth.

Having flushed out the attitudes of the speaker and students in the poem, you may return the discussion to the topic of "Groves of Academe" as a poem. It has an elaborate rhyme scheme, for instance, which addresses the student's question in lines 12–13. How else do Hacker's techniques play with the content of the poem? While characterizing the speaker, it is also useful to characterize the poem: is it a satire? Is the poet exaggerating the voices that she represents? (She has fit them into a rhyme scheme, so it isn't likely that she's copied them verbatim from students.) Is the humor biting — the speaker wants to foster "perversity" in herself, after all — or is it light? Point out how each of the students emphasizes themselves in their responses. Is the speaker arguing that all young poets are egotistical?

POSSIBLE CONNECTIONS TO OTHER SELECTIONS

Robert Browning, "My Last Duchess" (text p. 821)

Mark Halliday, "Graded Paper" (question #1, following)

CONNECTION QUESTION IN TEXT (p. 848) WITH ANSWER

1. Write an essay that compares the teachers in "Groves of Academe" and in Mark Halliday's "Graded Paper" (p. 1156). Which teacher would you rather have for a course? Explain why.

    Although both professors are cynical, Halliday's professor is much more pointed in his critique, which has more to do with the student's writing ability than with students' general attitude. Hacker's speaker doesn't really offer any optimism for her students, but Halliday's speaker realizes that students are not the same person that he is. They are younger, for starters, and that fact may be more valuable than he has acknowledged. Students might not be able to separate the "A-" from the rest of the comment on the paper in Halliday's poem, just as they are often blind to our own comments when a grade is attached. If it is possible, you might want to level the playing field a bit by asking students to disregard that grade and to focus on the comment only, or, if that is not possible, to imagine what kind of grader Hacker's speaker is. What students probably want is a professor who will criticize them but give them a good grade anyway. How do they feel about cynicism? Do they understand where it comes from, or do they consider it a professional flaw?

RESOURCE FOR TEACHING

The Poetry and Voice of Marilyn Hacker [recording]. 1 cassette. Distributed by Caedmon/HarperAudio.

MAXINE HONG KINGSTON, *Restaurant* (p. 849)

You may wish to begin a discussion of this poem by noting the way Kingston has structured the lines — they are rhymed couplets (though often the rhymes are slant), and they have no regular rhythm or meter. Because there is no particular meter, the rhymes are subtle and unpredictable, and the line breaks take the reader by surprise. This irregular rhythm lends a sense of breathlessness to the poem — readers rarely get to relax as they move from one line to the next, since many of the lines are heavily enjambed as they adhere to the poem's rhyme scheme. To demonstrate this breathless pacing, you might ask students to read aloud the first eight lines, where only lines five and eight are end-stopped, and where all the rest of the lines create a strong sense of tension and resolution in the reader. The breathless quality of the poem captures the breathlessness of the scene the speaker is describing — the frantic pace of a restaurant kitchen.

Have your students consider lines 15–16, when the speaker admits, "In this basement / I lose my size." Students may have different interpretations of these lines. One possible interpretation is that the speaker loses her individual identity in the basement as she slaves away. Other students might intrepret these lines to mean that the speaker had imagined herself to be "too big" for this job — above it somehow — and as a result is diminished by the reality of her situation. Although the speaker may lose size, she still demonstrates a remarkable strength, lifting "a pot as big as a tub with both hands" (18).

The final lines of the poem contain a powerful image — one that students are not likely to miss for its unavoidable irony. After the exhausting ordeal in which so many workers expend so much energy to create a meal, the "clean diners" dine in luxury — "behind glass in candlelight" (25), blissfully unaware of the effort it took to create the meal they are enjoying. This is the first moment in the poem where the speaker moves from description into something more reflective, as the frantic pace of the kitchen slows to allow the workers to observe the fruits of their labor.

Student readings of this poem may be enriched by some understanding of Marxist literary theory (text p. 2057), since Kingston presents a startling picture of difference based on privilege and wealth.

POSSIBLE CONNECTIONS TO OTHER SELECTIONS

Langston Hughes, "Dinner Guest: Me" (text p. 1033)
Carolyn Kizer, "Food for Love" (question #1, following)
Elaine Magarrell, "The Joy of Cooking" (question #1, following)

CONNECTION QUESTION IN TEXT (p. 849) WITH ANSWER

1. Write an essay analyzing how the kitchen activities described in "Restaurant," Carolyn Kizer's "Food for Love" (p. 769), and Elaine Magarrell's "The Joy of Cooking" (p. 792) are used to convey the themes of these poems.

   The kitchen in "Restaurant" is a metaphorical site in which working people must ultimately work together, and their frenetic activity stands in stark contrast to the diners who are gently illuminated in candlelight. The other two poems apply the discourse of cooking to the culinary preparation of people, which acts as a metaphor for love or revenge. In all three cases, the preparation of food represents a fundamental human interaction, whether it divides or unites people. All three poems also cast the preparation of food as a cruel yet tender activity; you might ask students how dining can be considered both a cruel and tender experience.

RESOURCES FOR TEACHING

Maxine Hong Kingston [recording]. 1 cassette, 1986. Interview. Distributed by American Prose Library.

The Stories of Maxine Hong Kingston. 54 min., color, 1990. VHS. Kingston discusses her perspective on the "Great American Melting Pot." Distributed by University of Washington Educational Media Collection.

PAUL HUMPHREY, *Blow* (p. 850)

The class may not be familiar with the term *luffed,* which is a nautical word meaning "to turn the head of the ship into the wind." The woman here is metaphorically transformed into a sailing ship — appropriately enough since both would be spoken of as "she." The marvelous final line gives a blow to the gesture of the speaker trying to quell the woman's wind-filled skirt. Here the alliteration creates a kind of humor, and the quick end-stopped monosyllables with their *t*-sounds emphasize the deftness that marks the woman's movements. Point out to the class how these short, light sounds are used, almost as a verbal photograph, to capture the moment.

POSSIBLE CONNECTION TO ANOTHER SELECTION

Robert Herrick, "Upon Julia's Clothes" (text p. 878)

ROBERT FRANCIS, *The Pitcher* (p. 850)

This poem ostensibly describes a baseball pitcher's art, but the poet seems also to be describing the art of poetry. When poems discuss poetry, it is always important to consider whether their claims are meant to be universal or whether they are meant to apply only to a specific type of poetry, usually the poetry that the poet favors. You might also consider how the poem functions on a literal level: does the metaphor ever break down? In what sense is a reader analogous to a batter?

If a pitcher is too obvious, the batter will easily figure out how to hit the balls he throws. The pitcher and batter play a cat-and-mouse game in which the pitcher must stay within the boundaries but not pitch directly to the hitter. While the other players throw directly to one another, he must seem to throw a fast ball only to throw a curve and vice versa. But he cannot throw wildly, or he has failed to do his job. In a similar way, the poet's play with language must "avoid the obvious" and "vary the avoidance." Line 4, almost (but not quite) a repetition of line 3, does what it says by avoiding the repetition.

Like the pitcher's task of avoidance within bounds, the rhymes in the poem are not quite but almost there. We have the sense of a potential never actualized. The final lines illustrate the perfect rhyme that is avoided in the previous lines, indicating the completed pitch and the finished poem.

The poet, like the pitcher, chooses his words and delivers them as he feels he must, making the reader wait patiently. Ironically, the pitcher is on the defensive side, although he appears to be on the offensive as he aims at his target. This fact may lead us to question the real relationship between poet and audience suggested in this analogy.

POSSIBLE CONNECTIONS TO OTHER SELECTIONS

Robert Francis, "Catch" (text p. 676)
Robert Wallace, "The Double-Play" (question #1, following)

CONNECTION QUESTION IN TEXT (p. 851) WITH ANSWER

1. Compare this poem with Robert Wallace's "The Double-Play" (p. 1122), another poem that explores the relation of baseball to poetry.

   Wallace's analogy discusses the importance of agility and skill in the writing of poetry, whereas Francis's concentration on the pitcher reveals his belief that poetry is more involved with moderate deception than with speed or skillful movement.

HELEN CHASIN, *The Word* Plum (p. 851)

The title of this poem suggests that it is about words. The relationship of the word *plum* to the object plum will generate an interesting discussion of the nature of language. Do words correspond to objects? Does poetry do more than point dimly to the sensuous realm?

The alliteration and assonance make our lips move the way they might when eating a plum. They also call attention to the sound of the poem, so that it is also about writing poetry.

POSSIBLE CONNECTIONS TO OTHER SELECTIONS

Galway Kinnell, "Blackberry Eating" (question #1, following)
Pablo Neruda, "Sweetness, Always" (text p. 1141)

CONNECTION QUESTION IN TEXT (p. 851) WITH ANSWER

1. How is Kinnell's "Blackberry Eating" (p. 832) similar in technique to Chasin's poem? Try writing such a poem yourself: choose a food to describe that allows you to evoke its sensuousness in sounds.

    Both poets draw a direct comparison between the sound of the words associated with eating fruit and the experience of eating the fruit itself. It is perhaps no accident that they both use such sensuous language to describe fruits, the sexual organs of plants. Both poets anthropomorphize the fruit, to a degree; Chasin emphasizes the skin and flesh of plums, and Kinnell's blackberries, who know "the black art / of blackberry-making" (lines 5–6), fairly lower themselves into his mouth. If students choose foods besides fruit to write about, do those foods share any of the sensual qualities of fruit? (If you have covered T. S. Eliot's "The Love Song of J. Alfred Prufrock" [text p. 1045], you might use these poems to make sense of Prufrock's deliberation over whether to "eat a peach.")

JOHN KEATS, *Ode to a Nightingale* (p. 851)

Earl R. Wasserman in *The Finer Tone: Keats's Major Poems* (Baltimore: Johns Hopkins UP, 1953, 1967) discusses this ode at length and places it in context with other Keats poems, including "Ode on a Grecian Urn" and "La Belle Dame sans Merci." He finds here a set of impossible contradictions, for it appears that happiness or ecstasy can be achieved only by an annihilation of self. As Wasserman writes, "By attempting to gain 'happiness,' one is brought beyond his proper bound, and yet, being mortal, he is still confined to the earthly; and thus he is left with no standards to which to refer, or rather, with two conflicting sets of standards" (183).

As a result of his complete empathic entrance into the bird's state, the poet finds himself "too happy in thine happiness." The poet has exceeded his own mortal bounds. In stanza II he longs for escape from this world — through an inebriation from the waters of poetic inspiration. Such a fading or leave-taking would be a means of fleeing from the strain of mortality (stanza III). The bird, which at first had signified beauty and oneness with nature, is now becoming identified with immortality and the ability to transcend the mortal state. The speaker admits his fascination with "easeful Death," but at the close of stanza VI, he realizes the ultimate dilemma: if he did die, the bird would go on singing but the speaker would be as responsive as "sod."

The introduction of Ruth is interesting, because she symbolizes life, family, and generational continuity. Having lost her husband, she stayed with her mother-in-law in an alien land, remarried, and bore a son.

The word *forlorn* recalls the speaker to his senses in stanza VIII, for he realizes that in this world of death, spirit, and the imagination — this ethereal world of transcendent essences — he is as nothing, and the word *forlorn*, like a bell, not only recalls him to himself but could also serve as his death summons. Note how many of the attractive sensuous details in the poem exalt physical, mortal life. At the close of stanza V, for example, Keats rescues even the flies for our poetic appreciation.

POSSIBLE CONNECTIONS TO OTHER SELECTIONS

Robert Frost, "Come In" (text p. 994)
Percy Bysshe Shelley, "Ode to the West Wind" (text p. 894)

PERSPECTIVE

DYLAN THOMAS, *On the Words in Poetry* (p. 854)

As Thomas emphasizes, the power of words often lies in their sound. Encourage students to read poetry aloud; in performance, the rhyme, rhythm, and character of a poem become more apparent. Thomas's own words on the subject of language and poetry are filled with character: "Out of them came the gusts and grunts and hiccups and heehaws of the common fun of the earth" (paragraph 2). Ask students to assess the effect of such words, identifying their denotations and connotations. Words, according to Thomas, clearly convey emotions. Thomas personifies words at the end of this excerpt, when he writes about their "forms and moods, their ups and downs, their chops and changes, their needs and demands" (2). Ask students to create a list of words that have obvious "moods" or "demands." They might also be interested in hearing some of Thomas's own poetry in connection with this perspective.

21

Patterns of Rhythm

As in Chapter 20, reading aloud can be of great benefit here. Abstract discussions of prosody will almost certainly turn students off. However, if students can understand how rhythm contributes to the overall impression a poem makes, they will be more likely to show interest in questions of meter. One way to emphasize this impression is to have students read these poems out loud.

These readings will also show that even the strictest metrical forms are not absolute — no one really reads iambic meter da-dum da-dum da-dum, and students will find attempts to do so unnatural (and perhaps humorous). There are variations in rhythm built into the language, and often into the meter of the poems themselves. Once students understand this, they can approach prosody as a descriptive rather than prescriptive activity, and can see scansion as a way of understanding effects rather than as an end in itself.

You may want to encourage this perception in the kinds of writing you have students do in this chapter. Critics almost never use exclusively prosody-based arguments about poems; students would be well advised to do the same. You might craft the writing assignments to have students talk about prosody among other features of a poem that contribute to its overall effect or meaning. This kind of assignment has the added advantage of keeping skills students have developed in previous chapters alive by continued use.

This chapter also lends itself well to the inclusion of popular culture — rap music, for instance, can be very sophisticated metrically. Students will probably immediately understand the difference in feeling between songs with a heavy beat (for instance, L.L. Cool J's "Momma Said Knock You Out") and ones where the rhythms are lighter and more trippingly phrased (the Fresh Prince's "Summertime"). Depending on the tastes of your class, the students themselves may be able to provide better and more current examples.

Another exercise you might try would be to have students look for patterns of rhythm in other kinds of language — Martin Luther King, Jr.'s "I Have a Dream" speech lends itself particularly well to this application, and can be compared in structure to the selection from Whitman's "Song of the Open Road."

From the poetry collection (Chapter 27), Philip Larkin's "This Be the Verse" is a particularly good example of the use of rhythm to help the overall impact of the poem. The rhythms Larkin employs create a cadence that emphasizes certain words and brings out a certain tone, at once flippant and cynical. In fact, in this poem the rhythms and the content work somewhat at cross purposes to produce this effect: the rhythms are light and almost singsong in places, the content dark and ultimately despairing about the human project.

WALT WHITMAN, From *Song of the Open Road* (p. 857)

Walt Whitman's poem proclaims the glorious freedom of the open road, but its form is not completely "free." The stanzas are nontraditional, rather than totally anarchic. Ask students to look for links within and between the two stanzas, for patterns that hold them together. The first stanza, after beginning with the foreign word *allons,* employs several exclamatory phrases, many of which begin with the word *let.* The second stanza also begins with a foreign word — *camerado* — and after one transitional exclamation proceeds with three phrases that repeat the word *give.* In addition, the second stanza mentions several items that are supposedly left behind in the first and replaces these old values with new ones: "my love" is offered as a replacement for money (lines 4 and 8), "myself" for preaching and law (6 and 9).

Ask students to recall other places where they have seen repetition used as a rhetorical device. They might mention speechmaking, legal documents, or the Bible. Discuss the implications of Whitman's use of a technique that characterizes the very things he wishes to abandon.

Ask students whether they find the narrator's attitude attractive or repulsive. Does he seem naive or insightful? Are they drawn to the idea of leaving books, laws, and religion behind for the "Open Road"?

POSSIBLE CONNECTIONS TO OTHER SELECTIONS

Alfred, Lord Tennyson, "The Charge of the Light Brigade" (text p. 870)

Walt Whitman, From *I Sing the Body Electric* (text p. 903)

WILLIAM WORDSWORTH, *My Heart Leaps Up* (p. 860)

The text discusses the enjambment in lines 8–9. What is the effect of the enjambment in the first two lines? Note that all the lines between are end-stopped. Is there a thematic connection between the pairs of enjambed lines? Between the end-stopped lines?

Ask students to discuss what they think Wordsworth means by "the child is father of the Man" (line 7). Do any current songs or other elements of popular culture reflect this same sentiment, or is it dismissable as a nineteenth-century Romantic impulse?

POSSIBLE CONNECTION TO ANOTHER SELECTION

William Blake, "The Lamb" (text p. 868)

TIMOTHY STEELE, *Waiting for the Storm* (p. 861)

The text thoroughly discusses the poem's metrics and how they contribute to its meaning. In addition, you may wish to discuss word choices in the poem. How can darkness be "wrinkling," as stated in line 1? Why do you suppose Steele uses such a prosaic title for a poem so full of poetic images? You might have students examine the individual images and discuss the senses to which they appeal. Is the poem mostly auditory, visual, tactile, or does it touch all of the senses? Why does Steele start and end with the images he does? Can your students suggest other prestorm sensations the poet might have included? Would their inclusion alter the mood of the poem? You might have students decide on a topic for description and brainstorm to produce images that draw on each of the senses. Are some senses harder to utilize than others?

POSSIBLE CONNECTION TO ANOTHER SELECTION

Sylvia Plath, "Mushrooms" (text p. 842)

WILLIAM BUTLER YEATS, *That the Night Come* (p. 862)

William Butler Yeats was born in Dublin and spent his youth in Dublin, London, and Sligo (his mother's family's home) in the west of Ireland. After graduating from high school, Yeats decided to attend art school (his father, J. B. Yeats, was a painter) and made poetry an avocation. He dropped out soon after and published his first poems at age twenty in the *Dublin University Review*. His poetic influences include Spenser, Shelley, Blake, and the pre-Raphaelite poets of 1890s London, but a perhaps equally important shaping force was his religious temperament. Never satisfied with Christian doctrine, he invented, piecemeal, a mythology that informs his poetry in often obscure ways. For range and power, no twentieth-century poet equals Yeats.

Discuss the central metaphor of the poem: that the woman's longing for death is like a king's longing for the consummation of his marriage. Note especially the word *desire* (line 2). How can the desire for death possibly be equated with the desire for sex? Compare this poem to one of the *carpe diem* poems students have read (text p. 728). In the *carpe diem* tradition, sexuality is opposed to death; in this poem, is sexuality equated with death? Why does the speaker call death "proud" (3)? Does the speaker see death as a proud bridegroom awaiting his bride? Is this an allusion to Donne's "Death Be Not Proud" (text p. 1090)?

POSSIBLE CONNECTION TO ANOTHER SELECTION

Emily Dickinson, "I read my sentence — steadily — " (text p. 944)

RESOURCES FOR TEACHING

Dylan Thomas Reads the Poetry of W. B. Yeats & Others [recording]. 1 cassette. Includes readings of Yeats, Louis MacNeice, George Barker, Walter de la Mare, W. H. Davies, D. H. Lawrence, and W. H. Auden. Distributed by Caedmon/HarperAudio.

The Love Poems of William Butler Yeats. 30 min., b/w, 1967. Beta, VHS, ½" open reel (EIAJ), ¾" U-matic cassette, 2" quadraplex open reel. Selections from the poet's works. Distributed by New York State Education Department.

Poems of William Butler Yeats [recording]. 1 cassette. Distributed by Spoken Arts.

The Poetry of William Butler Yeats [recording]. 1 cassette. Distributed by Caedmon/HarperAudio.

William Butler Yeats et al.: Treasury of Irish Verse, Folk Tales, & Ballads [recording]. 6 cassettes (294 min.), 1986. Distributed by Spoken Arts.

William Butler Yeats: Twentieth Century Poets Read Their Works [recording]. 6 cassettes (270 min.), 1986. Distributed by Spoken Arts.

W. B. Yeats [recording]. 1 cassette (49 min.), 1953. Read by Stephen Spender. Distributed by Audio-Forum.

Yeats Country. 19 min., color, 1965. VHS, ¾" U-matic cassette, 16-mm film. Juxtaposes Yeats's poetry with scenes of the Ireland he wrote about. Distributed by International Film Bureau.

Yeats Remembered. 30 min., VHS. Biographical film using period photographs and interviews with the poet and his family. Distributed by Insight Media.

Poems by W. B. Yeats and Poems for Several Voices [recording]. 1 cassette, 1973. Includes "Sailing to Byzantium." Also features poems by Thomas Hardy, Robert Graves, and Gerard Manley Hopkins. Read by V. C. Clinton-Beddeley, Jill Balcon, and M. Westbury. Distributed by Smithsonian/Folkways Recordings.

ALICE JONES, *The Foot* (p. 863)

The anatomical terms make "The Foot" scholarly and intellectually precise. The speaker of the poem clearly knows a great deal about the foot — the scientific terminology communicates much more than most people know about their feet. Given that poems are scanned in metrical feet, you might suggest to your students that this poem can be read as a pun; the metrical feet of a poem, such as iambs, support the poem just as human feet support people. The scholarly and foreign terms used to describe the subject of the poem obscure the function of the foot, just as overly scholarly terminology about scansion can obscure the function (and enjoyment) of a poem.

Certainly, the poem can be read not only as a pun. The first line of the poem does reveal the speaker's surprise about the human foot — that it is our "improbable" support — and the ending of the poem returns to this sense of mystery when it alludes to our connection to "an ancestor" (line 22) with a "wild / and necessary claw" (24–25). It might be interesting to have students explore one or more of the following questions in writing: What effect does the poet achieve by using language the common reader does not understand? Likewise, why would a poet write about a familiar object and make it seem foreign? Does the poet intend to humble readers by suggesting that despite all our learning we still are rooted in a past that contains ancestors with claws rather than feet?

POSSIBLE CONNECTION TO ANOTHER SELECTION

Wilfred Owen, "Arms and The Boy" (text p. 1112)

A. E. HOUSMAN, *When I was one-and-twenty* (p. 864)

The basic metrical pattern here is iambic trimeter. The first stanza is tightly rhymed, with only two rhyming sounds. The second stanza picks up on the first rhyming word of stanza I (*twenty*), but Housman in this stanza uses more rhyming words (four sounds in the eight lines), as though he were opening up to experience. Appropriately, given his unhappy romance, "rue," "two," and "true" echo one another in rhyme. Love in both stanzas is metaphorically treated with marketplace terminology. In the first stanza the wise man advises the speaker to keep his fancy free. In the second stanza the wise man observes that the heart "was never given in vain," and moreover, the cost of buying or selling this seat of affection is immeasurable. The repetition of " 'tis true" is like a shaking of the head, of one in a state of endless "rue."

You might enter a discussion of this poem by asking students about their reactions to advice from elders. They will probably have stories about how they had to learn through experience, not advice. If that is the case, what is our relationship to the speaker of the poem? Are we meant to reject his advice, too, in favor of learning on our own? Is the speaker somewhat foppish, because he believes he has aged so much in just one year?

POSSIBLE CONNECTIONS TO OTHER SELECTIONS

Margaret Atwood, "Bored" (text p. 737)

Robert Frost, "Birches" (text p. 986)

RESOURCES FOR TEACHING

A. E. Housman: "A Shropshire Lad" & Other Poetry [recording]. 1 cassette. Distributed by Caedmon/HarperAudio.

See also "Romantics and Realists" and "Victorian Poetry" [recording] in the appendix of Film, Video, and Audiocassette Resources.

RACHEL HADAS, *The Red Hat* (p. 864)

The child of the speaker of this poem has recently begun to walk to school alone. The speaker and her husband take turns secretly following the boy most of the way toward school. She finds this change toward maturity unsettling; rather than feeling joy at her child's newfound independence, she and her husband feel "empty, unanchored, perilously light" (line 21). The title of the poem, and its post-Christmas setting, emphasize the youth of the boy and the irrevocable loss of childlike innocence that is the basis for the poem's core emotion.

The poem is written in heroic couplets, but the poet prevents the rhythm from sounding singsongy with enjambment, punctuating the lines unevenly, ending a sentence midline; or often by altering the meter with a semicolon or colon. Ask students how this rhythm affects the poem's tone: Would it have been as poignant if the poet hadn't interrupted the rhythm with punctuation? If the rhymes had been end-stopped and full? Does the uneven meter have something to do with the theme of the poem? This theme is obviously related to the sometimes painful passage from childhood into adulthood, the "pull / of something more powerful than school" (lines 15–16), less commonly presented from the parent's point of view than from a child's. Who do students sympathize with? Do they better understand the child's need to be independent, or the parent's need to follow him at a distance?

POSSIBLE CONNECTIONS TO OTHER SELECTIONS

Robert Bly, "Sitting Down to Dinner" (question #1, following)
Sharon Olds, "Rite of Passage" (text p. 915)

CONNECTION QUESTION IN TEXT (p. 865) WITH ANSWER

1. In an essay discuss the themes of "The Red Hat" and Robert Bly's "Sitting Down to Dinner" (p. 824). Pay particular attention to the way parents are presented in each poem.

   In Robert Bly's "Sitting Down to Dinner," the speaker is definitely sympathetic to children rather than to their parents. Both poems will inspire discussions about the proper mix of guidance and "letting go," but also compare them as poetry. Bly seems to have an axe to grind, Hadas does not; does that observation affect how students view the form of each poem as well as the tone? Do students have different emotional responses to the two poems?

ROBERT HERRICK, *Delight in Disorder* (p. 865)

The speaker of this poem prefers in women a slightly disheveled appearance to one that presents the wearer as though she is perfect. Not coincidentally, the poem's strength is not only in its artfulness, its reliance on poetic conventions like end-rhyme and alliteration, but on the slight disorderliness of his rhythm. Vague impressions of court life in seventeenth-century England may be sufficient to initiate a discussion of the importance of dress at the time. If you are also discussing Ben Jonson's "Still to Be Neat," the next poem in this section, you might be able to get some mileage out of a discussion on the relationship between the two arts of fashion and poetry and the way they interact.

You might begin discussion of this poem by asking students what connotations the word *neat* holds for them. Then explore Herrick's use of *disorder,* as contrasted with our word *disorderly,* along with *wantonness.* Clearly, disorder and wantonness arouse in the speaker here a "fine distraction" and exercise a certain appeal that would not be present if the person addressed were prim and proper.

The speaker is bewitched but not bothered by his lady's "sweet disorder." Words are chosen to indicate a tantalizing of the passions by "erring" lace, "tempestuous" petticoats, and shoestrings tied with a "wild civility."

Herrick subtly illustrates his theme by working changes in the basic iambic tetrameter rhythm. Iambs change to trochees (cf. lines 2 and 4, for example), and in line 10 dactyls appear.

Ask students to turn back to the second question in the text and in a writing assignment analyze how patterns of rhyme and consonance work to create a subtle and pleasing artistic order.

POSSIBLE CONNECTION TO ANOTHER SELECTION

Ben Jonson, "Still to Be Neat" (text p. 866)

BEN JONSON, *Still to Be Neat* (p. 866)

Stepson of a bricklayer, Jonson was one of the first English writers to make his living by his pen. Admired for his lyrical poetry and literary criticism, Jonson is perhaps best known for his satiric comedies — including *Volpone* (1605), *The Alchemist* (1610), and *Bartholomew Fair* (1614) — and for the elaborate masques he created with designer Inigo Jones for the court of James I.

It may seem odd then that Jonson would choose to reject the elaborate fashions of the time, yet that is what Jonson is doing in this poem. The speaker dislikes the artful manners and dress of the woman. "Sweet" refers both to her smell, which is sweet, and their relationship, which presumably has some difficulties, perhaps because of her preoccupation with her own appearance. The speaker is suspicious about the reason for this preoccupation.

He asks the woman to be more sincere in her attentions to him, to pay less attention to her appearance. Neglecting herself is "sweet" to him because it is more natural, less deceptive. Words such as *adulteries* (line 11) and *face* play with the relationship between art and nature, intimating that the woman's efforts to make herself into a beautiful object only mar her natural beauty.

The disruptions in the rhythms reinforce Jonson's point until the final line. In line 6 the rhythm and the caesura in the middle of the line force the reader to slow down, emphasizing the speaker's insistence that the woman stop her artful motion and remove the mask. In the final line, the iambic tetrameter brings the speaker's point home in a succinct statement of his case.

POSSIBLE CONNECTION TO ANOTHER SELECTION

Robert Herrick, "Delight in Disorder" (questions #1 and #2, following)

CONNECTIONS QUESTIONS IN TEXT (p. 866) WITH ANSWERS

1. Write an essay comparing the themes of "Still to Be Neat" and Herrick's preceding poem, "Delight in Disorder" (p. 865). How do the speakers make similar points but from different perspectives?

Herrick's speaker asks for a similar absence of artistry and emphasis on irregularity. But the poems seem to treat the art-nature dichotomy differently. For Herrick, a "sweet disorder" may be part of the art, whereas for Jonson the relationship between art and nature is more troubled. Jonson's speaker does not want his beloved to be artful; Herrick's simply asks that the art not be "too precise in every part."

2. How does the rhythm of "Still to Be Neat" compare with that of "Delight in Disorder"? Which do you find more effective? Explain why.

With trochees interrupting the iambic rhythm throughout, Jonson's poem is more insistent than Herrick's. The speaker in "Still to Be Neat" is calling for an end to false art. Herrick's smoother rhythm and more easily flowing syllables suggest the speaker's delight in observing the disorder of his lady's dress. The differences in meter are in keeping with the different relationship between art and nature in the two poems.

RESOURCE FOR TEACHING

Poetry of the Early Seventeenth Century [recording]. 1 cassette. Distributed by Spoken Arts.

CHARLES MARTIN, *Victoria's Secret* (p. 867)

With grace and wit this poem connects the themes of our modern perception of Victorian sexuality and the aims of modern advertising, both contained in the title. The speaker begins with our "enlightened" perception that our predecessors were too proper to enjoy sex; the women were encouraged to think about shopping while the men went about their grubby, sordid business, horribly detached from the object of their lovemaking. The speaker then posits a future scenario in which our descendants will also "mock any passion / They think we were prone to, if thinking comes back into fashion" (lines 11–12). The word "fashion" precipitates the connection to the Victoria's Secret catalog, and the rest of the poem becomes a critique of the way advertisers play with our emotions and with our conceptions of ourselves.

As is the case with its title, this poem relies heavily on puns to make its point: "sheer lingerie" (17) or "complaisant negligence" (16). You may have to tease out the double meanings of some of these phrases, and you may also have to set up a discussion of the Victorian era. When considering the Victorian era, the general trend may be to feel as though "we" are more open, more liberated, than "they were back then." Martin is playing with, and satirizing exactly that notion. Once you have established this, the discussion of the various manipulative techniques that advertisers use is likely to be fruitful. It may be interesting to discuss similar techniques in poetry. Does the seemingly antiquated form of the poem mask the fact that it is a satire of contemporary society? Does this type of poem seem somehow more appropriate for satire than one with no end-rhyme or strict metrical form might?

POSSIBLE CONNECTIONS TO OTHER SELECTIONS

Robin Becker, "Shopping" (text p. 794)
Kenneth Fearing, "AD" (question #1, following)

CONNECTION QUESTION IN TEXT (p. 867) WITH ANSWER

1. Write an essay on the social criticism aimed at advertising in this poem and in Kenneth Fearing's "AD" (p. 803).

This poem analyzes advertising from the perspective of one who has studied it, someone with a sense of both history and merchandising. He concludes that advertisements appeal to our sometimes false conceptions of our own place in history, in this case, that we have arrived at a period of sexual liberation and bodily perfection that our predecessors didn't even dream of. Fearing's "AD" exploits advertising's appeal to populist sensibilities. Even something as horrifying as Nazism can be sold because it gives those who buy into it a sense of belonging. This type of advertisement appeals to our visceral emotions rather than to our sense of refinement.

WILLIAM BLAKE, *The Lamb* and *The Tyger* (pp. 868–869)

These two poems when paired make excellent examples of diction, rhythm, and sound and how these elements enhance tone. Ostensibly, each poem employs a four-stress pattern of trochaic feet, but the gliding *l*-sounds of the opening of "The Lamb" make the first stress on "Little" seem much lighter than the emphasis "Tyger" receives. The rhyme in the opening two lines of "The Lamb" is feminine, again unlike the stressed rhyme in "The Tyger." Only one question ("Who made Thee?") is asked of the lamb, and that question is repeated several times, giving the poem a sense of childlike simplicity and innocence. In this poem, moreover, there is a figural pattern of exchangeable identities between Lamb and Creator (Lamb of God), and speaker as child and Christ as God's child. Unlike the fearful symmetry of "The Tyger," this poem reflects a wholeness and innocence by the cohesiveness of these identities.

"The Tyger" poses far more questions about the creation of this powerful, regal beast, including the question in line 20: "Did he who made the Lamb make thee?" Ways of reading that question include the debate over the presence of evil in a God-created universe and the possibility of a second creator from whom darkness, evil, and fierce energy emanate. Could not the tiger stand for positive expressions of power? By and large, though, the questions in "The Tyger" go unanswered. Notice, for example, the substitution of *dare* in the final line for *could* in line 4.

As a writing assignment, you might ask students to examine several elements in each poem, including rhythm, patterns of consonance and assonance, pace, tone, even levels of ambiguity so that they are able on a fairly sophisticated level to articulate the differences between the two lyrics.

POSSIBLE CONNECTION TO ANOTHER SELECTION

William Wordsworth, "I Wandered Lonely as a Cloud" (text p. 1127)

DOROTHY PARKER, *One Perfect Rose* (p. 869)

Typical of Parker's famous wit, this poem turns a romantic trope — the tribute of a rose — into a joke. The speaker wonders why she never receives "one perfect limousine" (line 9) instead of a rose. She claims that she knows "the language of the floweret" (5): what do students suppose is the language of the limousine? That is, what sort of tribute would a limousine be?

The tone of the first two stanzas is dreamy and romantic. The speaker builds a sense of adulation for the rose as a symbol of love and beauty. The *abab* rhyme scheme and the iambic pentameter rhythm are in keeping with the poem's seemingly traditional theme.

The meaning of the rose flip-flops in the third stanza. In the first two instances, we read the rose as a beautiful symbol of love for the speaker. In line 12, it becomes a material object like any other, only far less valuable than "one perfect limousine."

The speaker is sophisticated and witty. She plays on our traditional (and somewhat sentimental) associations of love with fragile flowers and purely idealistic emotion. Then in a deft stroke she unmasks herself to reveal a materialistic strain — one that may exist in all of us.

POSSIBLE CONNECTION TO ANOTHER SELECTION

J. Patrick Lewis, "The Unkindest Cut" (text p. 784)

RESOURCES FOR TEACHING

Dorothy Parker [recording]. 2 cassettes. Read by Mary M. Lewis. Distributed by Cassette Works.

An Informal Hour with Dorothy Parker [recording]. 1 cassette. The author reads her short story "Horsie" as well as twenty-six poems. Distributed by Spoken Arts.

See also "Spoken Arts Treasury of American Jewish Poets Reading Their Poems," Vol. 1 [recording] in the appendix of Film, Video, and Audiocassette Resources.

ALFRED, LORD TENNYSON, *The Charge of the Light Brigade* (p. 870)

This poem praises and honors the light brigade, those "noble six hundred" men who charge "into the valley of Death" even though they know that they will die. The poem raises questions about the nature of bravery during wartime; the soldiers are praised for their glory, their honor, their nobility, but there is a nagging sense that their deaths could have been avoided. They knew that "someone had blundered" (line 12) but this logic is tempered by the sentiment behind the famous lines "Their's not to make reply, / Their's not to reason why, / Their's but to do and die" (13–15).

The rhyme and meter make the poem sound like a typical poem celebrating the heroes of war. The phrase "six hundred" is rhymed repeatedly, with "thundered" (21), "wondered" (31), and "sundered" (36); the word "blundered," which sounds a discordant note in the second stanza, is nearly buried by what appears to be the poem's laudatory tone. Students may debate about whether the poem focuses on praising the brigade for its courage or on criticizing the brigade for its blind obedience, which leads many of them to death. The effect would certainly be different if the sentiment of the second stanza were to come at the end of the poem. Since it doesn't, questions about the poem's tone and the speaker's attitude must take into consideration both the poem as a whole and the second stanza in particular. The "honor" that is proposed for the "noble six hundred" in the final stanza is altered not only by the second stanza but by the fact that the six hundred are less than six hundred in the stanzas IV and V.

POSSIBLE CONNECTIONS TO OTHER SELECTIONS

Wilfred Owen, "Dulce et Decorum Est" (question #1, following)
Walt Whitman, "Cavalry Crossing a Ford" (text p. 754)

CONNECTION QUESTION IN TEXT (p. 871) WITH ANSWER

1. Compare the theme of "The Charge of the Light Brigade" with Owen's "Dulce et Decorum Est" (p. 763).

261

The tone of "Dulce et Decorum Est" makes its theme much more obvious; would students go so far as to say that the speakers of the two poems share the same attitude but that they simply differ in their degrees of subtlety? Is there a certain nobility associated with the warfare Tennyson describes, with its charges on horseback and sabers, as opposed to Owen's description of World War I with its invisible enemy, its lethal gas, and the horrors of trench warfare?

RESOURCES FOR TEACHING

The Poetry of Tennyson [recording]. 1 cassette. Distributed by Caedmon/Harper-Audio.

Portrait of a Poet [recording]. 1 cassette (53 min.). Distributed by Watershed Tapes.

Treasury of Alfred, Lord Tennyson [recording]. 1 cassette. Read by Robert Speaight. Includes "Ulysses," "The Lotus Eaters," and "The Charge of the Light Brigade." Distributed by Spoken Arts.

See "England: Background of Literature," "Palgrave's Golden Treasury of English Poetry," and "Victorian Poetry" [film and recording] in the appendix of Film, Video, and Audiocassette Resources.

THEODORE ROETHKE, *My Papa's Waltz* (p. 871)

From the perspective of a man looking back at his childhood, the speaker recollects the drunken lurchings of his working-class father as he waltzed around the room. The remembrance is one of those strong early memories that, years later, one sifts through. The rhythm of the poem reflects well those moments the speaker recalls with some pain. Notice the spondees, for example, in "My right ear scraped a buckle" (line 12) or in "You beat time on my head / With a palm caked hard by dirt" (13–14). The title, with its use of *Papa*, seems to indicate a memory from early childhood — as does line 12. It also connotes a certain gentle affection for "Papa," despite all the other memories.

POSSIBLE CONNECTIONS TO OTHER SELECTIONS

Regina Barreca, "Nighttime Fires" (text p. 688)
Dylan Thomas, "Do not go gentle into that good night" (text p. 885)

ARON KEESBURY, *Song to a Waitress* (p. 872)

The speaker of this poem is a somewhat belligerent diner patron whose repeated demands for "hot" coffee in a "big fat mug" add to the depiction of a gruff man who appears to know what he wants. The scene, reminiscent of the famous Jack Nicholson routine from *Five Easy Pieces*, evokes a nearly mythical American landscape, a kind of diner frontier in which "big," "hot," "fat," and "full" are the values that matter, in which "pink, pansy / sugar packets in dainty little cups" (line 8) represent a rejected set of values.

The central irony of the poem is that it is a poem at all. Its title, "Song to a Waitress," conjures up a centuries-long tradition of a poetic form, and it is composed of three four-line stanzas completed with a rhymed couplet, reminiscent of a Shakespearean sonnet (traditionally, a love poem). Yet the poem resists these conventions, too, just as it rejects the "pink, pansy / sugar packets." The speaker's tone clashes with the very notion of poetry and with the idea that his attitude toward the waitress could be construed as a song. If you choose to have students write a response to the speaker, they will also be participating in a poetic tradition that was common during the English Renaissance, that of response to a love song, and they may reject the speaker's values from the point of view of the waitress just as the Nymph rejects those of the Shepherd. In doing so, do they choose to make use of any of the various repetitions in this poem? Do they make use of all of them?

POSSIBLE CONNECTIONS TO OTHER SELECTIONS

Jim Daniels, "Short-order Cook" (text p. 913)

Katharyn Howd Machan, "Hazel Tells LaVerne" (question #1, following)

CONNECTION QUESTION IN TEXT (p. 873) WITH ANSWER

1. Write a reply to the speaker in "Song to a Waitress" from the point of view of the waitress. You might begin by writing a prose paragraph; then try organizing it into lines of poetry. Read Katharyn Howd Machan's "Hazel Tells LaVerne" (p. 725) for a source of inspiration.

    Students should strive to get the voice of the waitress right, for which they can use Machan's poem as a source of inspiration, but they also should not ignore the metrical principles of Keesbury's poem. They should attempt to make the reply similar to the original, just as the Nymph's reply to the Shepherd undoes the Shepherd's rhetoric. In other words, you may have to remind students that they are not only creating a speaker, but that she is replying to a specific outburst by the speaker of Keesbury's poem.

EDWARD HIRSCH, *Fast Break* (p. 873)

This poem, a description of a fast break in basketball, takes the reader through the action at a frenzied pace. Like the play it describes, the poem seems chaotic or random, but the end result is a vision of perfection. The poem is one long sentence, punctuated sparingly, divided into two-line stanzas. How would the effect of the poem change if it were punctuated or divided more conventionally?

Run-ons make us feel that we are watching the basketball game as we read the poem. The one long sentence is an appropriate choice because the poem describes a few seconds of activity on a basketball court; we feel both the urgency and the rapidity of the play. In keeping with the spirit of the game, in which quick moves, sudden reversals, and surges of power are of the essence, the meter is irregular.

The tribute to the dead friend attempts to sing the praises of a short but successful life. The image of the power-forward exploding past other players in a fury (lines 25, 26) suggests someone burning through life radiant with energy and resolve. The player scores the point in the final lines. We sense both a resolution to the play and a resolution to the life.

In its attempt to capture a single moment on the court, to encircle the actions of all of the players in that moment, and to make the audience feel as if they are a part of it, this poem can be called "a momentary stay against confusion." The poem freezes a moment in time, seeming to simplify a life's journey in a single play. The poem shows us the player's life making sense.

POSSIBLE CONNECTION TO ANOTHER SELECTION

Alfred, Lord Tennyson, "The Charge of the Light Brigade" (text p. 870)

GREG WILLIAMSON, *Waterfall* (p. 874)

This poem describes both a waterfall and poetry; one serves as a metaphor for the other, but it is difficult to decide which is the metaphor and which is the object of inquiry. In the first stanza the speaker describes the waterfall by itself, in the second stanza he backs off to consider the viability of his descriptions, and in the third stanza he shifts his attention to poetry and language. His point is reinforced by the rhythm; despite a strict scheme of meter and end-rhyme, the ideas contained within the poem spill over from one line to the next, ignoring form in favor of a rhythm that can no more be controlled than the cascade of a waterfall.

A helpful starting point for discussion might be to list as a class the ways in which poetry and waterfalls are alike in order to test the poem's analogy. Where is the common ground, and how does this poem represent in verse the point the poet is trying to make? The key has something to do with flow and with the way both poems and waterfalls "obey hidden rules" (line 4). In poetry, these hidden rules include the way language does not always conform to stanzaic form in the sense that the rhythm of an idea can "spill over" from one line to the next. Do students think that poetry obeys its own "hidden rules," that at some point the poet simply loses control of language? The final stanza makes it seem as though poetry has a will of its own; what is the poet's role, in terms of the metaphor the speaker has created? This question recalls the speaker's transition from waterfall to language in the second stanza; if we consider that the poet is the "bed" and language the "water," which steers which, and to what degree?

POSSIBLE CONNECTION TO ANOTHER SELECTION

Edgar Allan Poe, "The Bells" (text p. 838)

PERSPECTIVE

LOUISE BOGAN, *On Formal Poetry* (p. 875)

You might ask students to compare Bogan's questions about form as repression with Whitman's assertion that "the rhyme and uniformity of perfect poems show the free growth of metrical laws and bud from them as unerringly and loosely as lilacs or roses on a bush, and take shapes as compact as the shapes of chestnuts and oranges and melons and pears, and shed the perfume impalpable to form" (p. 904). Students could write an essay about these perspectives on "form" in poetry, using two or three examples from the collection of poems in Chapter 27.

22

Poetic Forms

There is some degree of controversy over the role of form in poetry. The movement calling itself New Formalism advocates a widespread return to form, and criticizes what it calls the status quo of open form. (A possible introduction to this position is in Dana Gioia's "Notes on the New Formalism" in the Autumn 1987 *Hudson Review*, reprinted in *Can Poetry Matter?* Also, see Timothy Steele's *Missing Measures*.) There are also, however, several defenses of open form (perhaps the best of which is Stanley Plumly's "Chapter and Verse" in the January/February and May/June issues of *American Poetry Review*.) You might find it interesting to introduce your students to this controversy and have them find their own positions on the matter. This exercise can help students understand that there are reasons for the choice to write in or out of traditional forms, and that traditional forms are not always or necessarily conservative. In addition, it emphasizes the idea that poetry is a dynamic genre, full of conflict and contradiction.

As in previous chapters, this material will likely be most appealing to students in terms of its relation to the overall impact of a poem — form only takes on meaning when married to content and presented in context. Quizzes that ask students to give the structure of a Petrarchan sonnet tend not to work as well as those that ask students to explain how the form of a particular sonnet contributes to its overall effect. (Some historical notes might be useful in this chapter, since the importance of traditional forms has as much to do with the history of those forms as with each current instance of the form.)

The section on sonnets is particularly good at emphasizing the different uses to which the form was put; each use, however, draws on the structure of the sonnet to help create meaning and coherence in the poem. Mark Jarman's "Unholy Sonnet," in conjunction with the sonnets from Donne found in Chapter 27, make good test cases. Students can see how the sonnet form allows Jarman to engage in a cross-century and cross-faith debate with Donne; the sonnet ensures that despite the historical and religious differences, the discussion takes place on the same terrain.

Another example that can help students understand the union of form and content can be found in the section on the villanelle — the kinds of repetition this form requires can be used for emphatic statement, as both Dylan Thomas's and Julia Alvarez's poems demonstrate.

A. E. HOUSMAN, *Loveliest of trees, the cherry now* (p. 877)

The speaker in this poem greets life with a warmhearted *joie de vivre*. Although he is young, he already has a sense of life's limits. He means to enjoy the beauty of life every minute he is alive. Even then, he claims, he could not absorb all the beauties of life. The connotations of rebirth and spring are reinforced by the mention of Eastertide in line 4.

Yet behind the gaiety and cheerful resolve is an awareness of the imminence of death. You might explore, either in class discussion or as a writing assignment, the question of whether this could be considered a *carpe diem* poem.

POSSIBLE CONNECTIONS TO OTHER SELECTIONS

Robert Frost, "The Road Not Taken" (text p. 976)

Robert Herrick, "To the Virgins, to Make Much of Time" (text p. 728)

ROBERT HERRICK, *Upon Julia's Clothes* (p. 878)

Herrick uses so many of the elements of poetry — rhyme, rhythm, the sound and choice of words — so well in this brief lyric that it is worth taking some class time to analyze. The first tercet of iambic tetrameter is absolutely regular and thus suggests the sweet*ly* flow*ing* l*i*quefaction of J*u*l*ia*'s c*lo*thes. In the second tercet, trochees interrupt the established pattern to capture in rhythmic terms "that brave vibration." *Brave* is used here in the sense of "making a fine show or display," as in a banner waving.

POSSIBLE CONNECTION TO ANOTHER SELECTION

Paul Humphrey, "Blow" (question #1, following)

CONNECTION QUESTION IN TEXT (p. 878) WITH ANSWER

1. Compare the tone of this poem with that of Humphrey's "Blow" (p. 850). Are the situations and speakers similar? Is there any difference in tone between these two poems?

   The situations are dissimilar in that Herrick's subject is "my Julia" (line 1) but the speaker of Humphrey's poem has no relationship with his subject. He is more self-deprecating than Herrick's speaker is; when the woman laughs and leaves in the final lines, we sense that she is laughing at him rather than at her situation. His gallantry becomes buffoonery. Herrick's emphasis is on the speaker's reverie; he is ecstatic rather than ridiculous.

S O N N E T

JOHN KEATS, *On First Looking into Chapman's Homer* (p. 879)

The principal theme of Keats's sonnet is discovery; he uses the sudden and unexpected discovery of the Pacific Ocean by early explorers of the Americas as a metaphor for those moments in life when we feel that a previously held view has been radically shaken.

You might ask students whether they have experienced a moment of discovery similar to that which Keats describes. After they have read Keats's poem, give them a few minutes to write about a moment when they felt a sense of revelation similar to that felt by "stout Cortez" and his men, and then discuss the results.

A comparison of Keats's sonnets provides ample evidence of the poet's continual experimentation with form during his brief career. In "Chapman's Homer," Keats utilizes the characteristic division of the Italian sonnet into octave and sestet, with the opening eight lines setting up a situation or argument and the remaining six resolving it. You may wish to compare Keats's use of the sonnet form in "Chapman's Homer" with his use of the form in other poems in the chapter. In some sonnets Keats favors the Italian or Petrarchan form, but in "When I have fears" (text p. 1103) he uses the English or Shakespearean rhyme scheme (three quatrains and a couplet).

Robert Hass, "Happiness" (text p. 707)

Walt Whitman, "One Hour to Madness and Joy" (text p. 1123)

WILLIAM WORDSWORTH, *The World Is Too Much with Us* (p. 880)

Like Hopkins in "God's Grandeur" (text p. 837), Wordsworth is protesting here the preoccupation with worldliness — banking, buying, getting, spending — that makes it increasingly difficult to feel the mystery and power in the natural world. Proteus (a god of the sea) and Triton (another sea god, who stirred up storms) lie dormant, their power to kindle in the human soul a spirit of awe suppressed in the commercialized world, where people have bartered their hearts away. "Great God!" is the speaker's spontaneous and ironic response to the decline of spirituality, for it appears that the pagan world possessed a stronger sense of godliness.

POSSIBLE CONNECTIONS TO OTHER SELECTIONS

Matthew Arnold, "Dover Beach" (text p. 757)

Gerard Manley Hopkins, "God's Grandeur" (question #1, following)

CONNECTION QUESTION IN TEXT (p. 881) WITH ANSWER

1. Compare the theme of this sonnet with that of Hopkins's "God's Grandeur" (p. 837).

    Both Wordsworth's sonnet and "God's Grandeur" draw from the social and industrial worlds to discuss the greatness of creation and the human threat to that greatness. The speaker in Hopkins's sonnet places his faith in the creator, who can overcome the destructive actions of human beings. Wordsworth's sonnet returns to pagan myths for comfort, although the speaker has little hope of overcoming the bleakness of the world that is "too much with us." Hopkins dwells on bleak images of all "seared with trade," but he is convinced that nature is still available to us and that even humanity can be redeemed.

WILLIAM SHAKESPEARE, *Shall I compare thee to a summer's day?* (p. 881)

The speaker in this sonnet praises his beloved not only for her loveliness but also for her temperateness of manner. Unlike nature, which is forever changing, she shows a steady devotion. Moreover, the speaker tells us that this love will extend well into the future, even beyond the grave. Such love, like the art that celebrates it, confers a measure of immortality on the lovers and, self-reflexively, on the sonnet. Notice, for example, how the stressed words in the couplet reinforce this idea. *Long* is stressed in both lines of the couplet, along with other significant words that link continued "life" with "this," the sonnet that confers immortality, and "thee," the object the sonnet addresses.

POSSIBLE CONNECTIONS TO OTHER SELECTIONS

John Frederick Nims, "Love Poem" (text p. 693)

William Shakespeare, "My mistress' eyes are nothing like the sun" (text p. 882)

RESOURCES FOR TEACHING

William Shakespeare: Poetry and Hidden Poetry. 53 min., color, 1984. A microexamination of Shakespeare's poetry and its hidden meanings. Produced by the Royal Shakespeare Company. Distributed by Films for the Humanities and Sciences.

Selected Sonnets by Shakespeare. 40 min., color, 1984. Beta, VHS, ¾" U-matic cassette. Features readings by Ben Kingsley and Jane Lapotaire. Distributed by Films for the Humanities and Sciences.

Selected Sonnets of Shakespeare [recording]. 1 cassette. Distributed by Spoken Arts.

William Shakespeare: The Sonnets [recording]. 1 cassette. Distributed by Recorded Books.

William Shakespeare Sonnets [recording]. 2 cassettes (120 min.). Distributed by Caedmon/HarperAudio.

William Shakespeare's Sonnets. 150 min., color, 1984. Beta, VHS, ¾" U-matic cassette. An in-depth look at fifteen of Shakespeare's sonnets. With Ben Kingsley, Roger Reese, Claire Bloom, Jane Lapotaire, A. L. Rouse, and Stephen Spender. Distributed by Films for the Humanities and Sciences.

See also "Poetry for People Who Hate Poetry," "England: Background of Literature," "Introduction to English Poetry," "Medieval and Elizabethan Poetry," and "Palgrave's Golden Treasury of English Poetry" in the appendix of Film, Video, and Audiocassette Resources.

WILLIAM SHAKESPEARE, *My mistress' eyes are nothing like the sun* (p. 882)

Students may have read this sonnet in high school, and you might begin by asking them what they think the mistress looks like. Some clarification of Shakespeare's use of the term *mistress* (beloved or chosen one) may be in order. This sonnet plays with the conventions and clichés of the Petrarchan sonnet, which elaborated on the extraordinary qualities of the maiden's eyes as compared to the splendor of the sun. But Shakespeare refuses to do this and thus argues for a poetry that avoids cliché and the excess metaphor that tries to outdo reality. He is, in fact, asserting the beauty of his beloved in the last line. She is as attractive as any other woman who has been "belied" (made to seem more beautiful) by false comparison.

POSSIBLE CONNECTION TO ANOTHER SELECTION

William Shakespeare, "Shall I compare thee to a summer's day?" (text p. 881)

EDNA ST. VINCENT MILLAY, *I will put Chaos into fourteen lines* (p. 882)

In structure, Millay's list of paradoxes and resolutions adheres strictly to the verse form of the Italian, or Petrarchan, sonnet: it consists of fourteen lines of iambic pentameter with a rhyme scheme based upon an octave and a sestet. The octave is a single sentence describing the poet's efforts to force Chaos to unite with Order; the sestet recounts the happy results of such a union.

The poem accomplishes the apparently impossible feat of "containing" both Chaos "himself" and his various manifestations. The poet literally "puts Chaos into" the poem through personification, by portraying the abstract idea of Chaos as a character in a sonnet. The highly ordered verse form controls the disorderly, negative power of Chaos — "Flood, fire, and demon" (line 4) — by the physical act of shaping the words into the iambic pentameter line. One might expect that such restrictions would humble, even emasculate such a powerful figure, but according to the poet, the "sweet" sonnet form does not deprive Chaos of his energy; it concentrates the energy in a pattern of beauty and harmony — it "make[s] him good" (14).

The poet's use of figurative language reinforces the paradox inherent in the poem's structure. The image of "pious rape" in line 6 may seem irresolvably paradoxical in the 1990s, when a rape is such a highly charged negative issue. However, this is an excellent opportunity to encourage students to go beyond themselves in order to examine the poem on its own terms. The "rape" here is rape in a mythic sense; the dramatic situation in lines 3-8 recalls the creation myths of Hesiod or Genesis, with the poet herself as the agent who brings Order to Chaos and calls it "good." The poet insists that the forcible control exercised does not hurt Chaos, but actually benefits him by adding sweetness and goodness to his formidable power.

The personification of Chaos as a male entity produces another paradox in addition to the contradiction created by juxtaposing the orderly sonnet form with a disorderly central character. Because we know that the poet is female, we have a highly unusual role reversal here — the male is raped by the female in the poem. The female poet forces Chaos into the "strict confines" (5) of the sonnet until he "mingles and combines" (8) with Order.

POSSIBLE CONNECTION TO ANOTHER SELECTION

Robert Frost, "Design" (question #1, following)

CONNECTION QUESTION IN TEXT (p. 883) WITH ANSWER

1. Compare the theme of this poem with that of Robert Frost's "Design" (p. 993).

    Frost's "Design," like "I will put Chaos," is structured as an Italian sonnet, but in contrast to Millay's poem, which begins with an abstract concept and uses imagery to make it more concrete, "Design" begins with a small, concrete image and extrapolates it to a larger, more abstract one. In general, Frost tends to affirm the power of poetic form to harness the chaos of life, to create a "momentary stay against confusion," much as Millay does in "I will put Chaos." However, Frost's images of death and terror in "Design" suggest that if there is a controlling order in the universe, it is largely a force of evil. In contrast to Millay's theme, Frost suggests that Chaos can force Order to become a channel for his negative energy.

MOLLY PEACOCK, *Desire* (p. 883)

This somewhat complex treatment of desire reads almost like a riddle, and students may productively spend time trying to figure out exactly what the speaker is describing. The answer to the riddle is contained both in the title and in the final phrase: "Desire . . . the drive to feel" (line 14). But the metaphors and similes throughout the body of the poem present its chief interpretive problem: what exactly is the poet's point about desire, and why is it useful to define it the way she does?

The best way to reorganize the poem initially may be to list all of the metaphors for desire and to consider them individually; for instance, in what sense is desire "blunt" (10), "like a paw" (9)? Once you have done so, consider the metaphors together. Do they have anything in common? Students should notice that these metaphors often have to do with something animal and youthful, something wild and unsophisticated. The intimation is that socialization and civilization bring us farther away from our instinctive "drive to feel" (14), which is why desire is "what babies bring to kings" (5) as opposed to the material gifts that the three wise men brought to the infant Jesus.

Poetic Forms

POSSIBLE CONNECTIONS TO OTHER SELECTIONS

Diane Ackerman, "A Fine, a Private Place" (question #1, following)
Walt Whitman, From *I Sing the Body Electric* (text p. 903)

CONNECTION QUESTION IN TEXT (p. 884) WITH ANSWER

1. Compare the treatment of desire in this poem with that of Ackerman's "A Fine, a Private Place" (p. 734). In an essay, identify the theme of each poem and compare their conceptions of desire. How alike are these two poems?

A comparison of this poem to Ackerman's "A Fine, a Private Place" should yield some interesting results since this poem is much more abstract. If students take the themes of the two poems to be similar, they can illustrate Peacock's ideas with Ackerman's poem, demonstrating how the lovers in "A Fine, a Private Place" enact "the blind instinct for life unruled." If they consider the themes dissimilar, you might ask them how the form of each poem underscores this difference.

MARK JARMAN, *Unholy Sonnet* (p. 884)

This poem is an example of an Italian, or Petrarchan, sonnet. You may wish to begin discussion by having students read the poem aloud, since the lines are so heavily enjambed that the rhythm and rhyme occur subtly. In dealing with this piece as a sonnet, you might point out that Italian sonnets are characterized by the usual fourteen lines of iambic pentameter, but unlike other sonnet forms, this type usually contains a shift in content between the octave and the sestet — a movement from suggestion to resolution.

This shift occurs in terms of both style and content in this poem. In the opening octave, many of the lines begin with a dactylic rather than an iambic foot (lines 1–4 each begin this way), and all of the lines in the octave have feminine endings. By contrast, the sestet lines each begin with a standard iambic foot and conclude with a masculine ending. In content, the repeated use of the word "after" — which occurs five times in the octave — sets up a sense of suspense in the first part of the poem that is then resolved through the repeated "there is" in the concluding sestet. In addition, the octave uses the pronouns "us" and "our," while the answering sestet uses the pronouns "you" and "your." Ask students to consider whether this shift in pronouns affects the reading of the poem. Does it strengthen or detract from the sense of resolution contained in the poem's concluding sestet?

POSSIBLE CONNECTIONS TO OTHER SELECTIONS

John Donne, "Batter My Heart" (question #1, following)
——, "Death Be Not Proud" (question #1, following)

CONNECTION QUESTION IN TEXT (p. 884) WITH ANSWER

1. Jarman has said that his "Unholy Sonnets" (there are about twenty of them) are modeled after John Donne's *Holy Sonnets*, but that he does not share the same Christian assumptions about faith and mercy that inform Donne's sonnets. Instead, Jarman says, he "work[s] against any assumption or shared expression of faith, to write a devotional poetry against the grain." Keeping this statement in mind, write an essay comparing and contrasting the tone and theme of Jarman's sonnet with John Donne's "Batter My Heart" (p. 1089) or "Death Be Not Proud" (p. 1090).

Jarman's sonnet considers the disparity between what we are trying to do through practicing religion and what we actually do. He believes that the rituals of church-going do nothing to eradicate our basic (and base) human nature. The two sonnets by Donne describe a much more personal faith on the part of the speaker. Human activity does not interfere with his relationship with God or with his belief in eternal life through faith. The subject in Jarman's poem is collective first person and second person; in Donne's poems, the subject is first-person singular. In writing "a devotional poetry against the grain," Jarman is responding not only to Donne but to modern views of religion. Yet in terms of form, Jarman's sonnet does work as a kind of inversion of Donne's logic; all three poems end with a bold sentiment in the final couplet.

VILLANELLE

DYLAN THOMAS, *Do not go gentle into that good night* (p. 885)

This poem is a villanelle, a French verse form ordinarily treating light topics, whose five tercets and concluding quatrain employ only two end rhymes. The first and third lines of the poem must alternatively conclude the tercets and form a couplet for the quatrain. Despite these formal restrictions, Thomas's poem sounds remarkably unforced and reflects quite adequately the feeling of a man who does not want his father to die.

Just as remarkable is the poem's rich figurative language; this villanelle could be used as a summary example of almost all the points outlined in this chapter. Variety is achieved through the metonymies for death, such as "close of day" (line 2), "dark" (4), "dying of the light" (9). The overall effect is to describe death metaphorically as the end of a day and thus, in some sense, to familiarize death and lessen its threat. Even to describe death as "that good night" (1) reduces it to a gesture of good-bye. Other figures of speech include a pun on "grave" men (13) (both solemn and mortal), an oxymoron in "who see with blinding sight" (13), various similes, such as "blaze like meteors" (14), and the overall form of the apostrophe.

Thomas introduces several examples of people who might be expected to acquiesce to death gently but who, nonetheless, resist it. "Wise men" (philosophers, perhaps) want more time because so far their wisdom has not created any radical change ("forked no lightning"). Men who do good works (theologians, possibly) look back and realize that the sum total of their efforts was "frail" and if they had devoted more time to a fertile field ("green bay"), their deeds might have been more effective. "Wild men" (inspired artists, writers) know their words have caught and held time, but they know too how in various ways — with their relations with others or perhaps with alcohol and drugs — they have "grieved" the sun. Grave men at the end of their lives realize too late that joy is one means of transcending time. All these groups experience some form of knowledge that makes them wish they could prolong life and live it according to their new insights.

As a writing assignment you might ask students to analyze a character or group of people that they have read about in a short story who seem to fit into one of the categories Thomas describes. What advice would he give them? How otherwise could they lead their lives?

POSSIBLE CONNECTION TO ANOTHER SELECTION

Sylvia Plath, "Daddy" (text p. 1113)

CONNECTION QUESTION IN TEXT (p. 885) **WITH ANSWER**

1. In Thomas's poem we experience "rage against the dying of the light." Contrast this with the rage you find in Sylvia Plath's "Daddy" (p. 1113). What produces the emotion in Plath's poem?

   For Thomas, rage is an outpouring of passion, a summoning of strength that will preserve the speaker's father's vitality. In the final stanza, cursing and blessing amount to the same thing because they connote this same sense of vitality. The rage in Plath's poem is a reaction to injustice. This rage, too, gives the speaker a sense of power: the power to use language as a way of condemning her oppressor. Both poets value rage as a fundamental element of our humanity, but in each poem it springs from different sources. Plath's speaker is uncorking a pent-up emotion, whereas the father in Thomas's poem is being asked to reach into himself to squeeze out whatever emotion is left in him.

JULIA ALVAREZ, *Woman's Work* (p. 886)

This poem describes a woman whose mother tried to convince her that "woman's work" (i.e., domestic chores) is "high art." The speaker's mother is devoted to the perfection of her art, and she tries to convince the speaker to follow in her footsteps. While the mother argues that housework is an art, the speaker feels that it is a prison at the same time. The speaker rejects this life-style but still manages to become her "mother's child" (line 17) since she devotes herself wholeheartedly to her own art, writing.

The effect of the poem's departure from the villanelle form (it does not repeat line 1 exactly in lines 6, 12, and 18 but rather varies the theme in each of these lines) is to emphasize the poem's theme: redefining "woman's work" while elevating it as "high art." The speaker alters the original line each time she repeats it just as she alters her mother's definition of woman's work. The other departure from the villanelle form is that the rhymes are not always strict (tiles, outside, satisfied, pies, advised, child). How would the poem be different if the poet had kept the rhyme scheme strict, as Thomas does in "Do not go gentle . . ."? Comparisons of these poems may prove interesting, since each one may seem to exclude the other gender. Alvarez's poem is consciously a woman's poem. Is Thomas's consciously a man's poem? Would his poem change considerably if references to "men" became references to "people"? Are the traits he is lauding in others and encouraging in his father typically "masculine" traits?

POSSIBLE CONNECTIONS TO OTHER SELECTIONS

Jim Daniels, "Short-order Cook" (text p. 913)
Dylan Thomas, "Do not go gentle into that good night" (question #1, following)

CONNECTION QUESTION IN TEXT (p. 886) **WITH ANSWER**

1. Compare and contrast the themes and tone of "Woman's Work" and Dylan Thomas's "Do not go gentle into that good night" (p. 885). Will the speaker in Alvarez's poem "go gentle into that good night"? Would the speaker in Thomas's call woman's work, as described above, "high art"?

   This question highlights the differences between the two poems in terms of gender. Thomas's speaker is concerned only with the activities of men, and, in stereotypical fashion, the provinces of these men exist outside of the domestic sphere. The speaker of Alvarez's poem rejects the corollary notion — that the provinces of women exist entirely within the domestic sphere — yet she finds a compromise to her mother's wishes. It is not likely that this speaker will "go gentle into that good night"; her passion is evident from her rejection of her mother's life-style. It is equally unlikely that the speaker of Thomas's poem would call woman's work "high art," since he does not seem at all concerned about it; yet we must speculate along broad lines to back up such a statement.

SESTINA

ELIZABETH BISHOP, *Sestina* (p. 887)

This poem strikes the ear as particularly sad because it portrays unexpressed emotion in an intimate domestic setting. There seems to be no shared awareness between grandmother and child, although one suspects they are sad for similar reasons. To make matters even worse, that sadness seems as foreordained as the rain showers that the almanac predicts. Here the almanac functions for the grandmother as a soothsayer, foretelling sadness and loss. For the child, the Marvel Stove operates in the same way (line 25), its cast-iron blackness serving as a kind of mute doomsayer. Note, for example, the repetition of "tears" and "rain" in stanzas II and III and how they are connected with "grandmother," "almanac," "child," and "stove."

Bishop's father died of Bright's disease at age thirty-nine, when the poet was only eight months old. Her mother subsequently suffered several nervous breakdowns, and Bishop was sent from her home in Worcester, Massachusetts, to live with her maternal grandmother in Nova Scotia. The grandmother had lost her own father in a sailing accident when she was a child. A good summary of Bishop's childhood is offered by Robert Giroux in his introduction to *Elizabeth Bishop: The Collected Prose* (New York: Farrar, 1984). If your students enjoy Bishop's poetry, they might also enjoy the fiction and descriptive pieces offered in this collection.

POSSIBLE CONNECTIONS TO OTHER SELECTIONS

Elizabeth Bishop, "Manners" (text p. 713)
Adrienne Rich, "Living in Sin" (text p. 1115)

FLORENCE CASSEN MAYERS, *All-American Sestina* (p. 888)

In a sense, this poem is an inverted sestina since the first words of each line (rather than the end words) conform to the conventions of a sestina. The poem runs through a series of American clichés involving the numbers one through six and fits them into this difficult poetic form. Mayers departs from her own scheme a few times, though: what should be "six" in the third stanza is "sixty-" (line 14) and it wraps around to the next line, "four-dollar question"; and "hole in one" (27) in stanza five, and "high five" (34) in stanza six break the pattern of having the number begin the line.

Students might debate about whether this poem raises important themes or whether it's just a clever exercise. You may want to gear discussion toward a consideration of what is particularly "All-American" about the clichés in the poem. (Is the fact that they are clichés all-American?) It might help to try to classify the images; the categories may vary, but most seem to have something to do with a kind of consumer hucksterism: "one-day sale" (8), "five-year warranty" (9), "sixty-four-dollar question" (14–15); or with nostalgia: "five-cent cigar" (5), "one-room schoolhouse" (36); or with excess: "six-pack

Bud" (7), "two-pound lobster" (17), "four-wheel drive" (25). Students may come up with entirely different categories. Encourage them to be flexible when creating these categories. Do they see an emerging pattern that might help to define "All-American"? Do any of the phrases not fit neatly into any category? A comparison to Cummings's "next to of course god america i" (text p. 805) may highlight these themes. But does Mayers critique America in the same way that Cummings does? Is it possible to read the poem as a celebration rather than a critique? Or is it simply a neutral portrait? In any case, why does she choose this form to represent it?

POSSIBLE CONNECTIONS TO OTHER SELECTIONS

E. E. Cummings, "next to of course god america i" (question #1, following)
Tato Laviera, "AmeRícan" (text p. 918)

CONNECTION QUESTION IN TEXT (p. 889) WITH ANSWER

1. Describe and compare the strategy used to create meaning in "All-American Sestina" with that used by Cummings in "next to of course god america i" (p. 805). .

    Both poems rely on the distance between relatively meaningless American cultural clichés and real ideas to create meaning, but the speaker of Cummings's poem builds toward a definite point. In Mayers's sestina there is little progress. The poem's meaning wouldn't change much if the stanzas were rearranged; meaning comes primarily from the building panorama of clichés. Cummings's speaker begins with hollow phrases and departs from there to try to convince his audience that the war dead performed their duties cheerfully.

EPIGRAM

SAMUEL TAYLOR COLERIDGE, *What Is an Epigram?* (p. 889)

A. R. AMMONS, *Coward* (p. 890)

DAVID McCORD, *Epitaph on a Waiter* (p. 890)

PAUL LAURENCE DUNBAR, *Theology* (p. 890)

Note how crucial the technique of word selection becomes in poems that use as few words as these. Have students write in prose the ideas conveyed in each of the first three epigrams. These summaries will probably be considerably more verbose and less witty than the poems from which they stem. Which specific words in each epigram are used to condense meanings that might normally be expressed by means of longer words or phrases?

Also consider how important titles become in the epigrams by Ammons, McCord, and Dunbar. Have the students discuss how each epigram would be different if it were presented without its title. Ammons's could be a statement of family pride. McCord's title informs the reader of his subject's occupation and his decease, whereas the poem might refer to anyone who had gone through life exceedingly preoccupied. What does McCord's poem imply about the waiter without saying it specifically? For how much of Dunbar's poem does the title "Theology" seem appropriate? Which words contribute to the serious tone implied by the title? Where does the meaning seem to shift?

Note: For a list of resources for teaching Coleridge, see manual page 387.

LIMERICK

ANONYMOUS, *There was a young lady named Bright* (p. 890)

LAURENCE PERRINE, *The limerick's never averse* (p. 891)

The name "limerick" derives from a form of extemporaneous nonsense verse that always ends with the refrain, "Will you come up to Limerick?" The five-line anapestic verses we now call limericks evolved during the nineteenth century at the hands of humorous versifiers like Edward Lear (1812–1888), as well as numerous anonymous writers.

The extemporaneous nature of limericks is an indication of the ease with which they can be composed. After reviewing the examples in the book, ask the students to compose some limericks, either individually or in small groups.

In addition to overtly bawdy situations, the limerick often relies upon puns and other wordplay for its humor. "There was a young lady named Bright" plays on the term *relative* to draw attention to the possibility, implicit in certain theories of modern physics, that you can arrive in a place before you leave it. The joke of Laurence Perrine's "The limerick's never averse" depends upon a simple pun. You might draw students' attention to Perrine's departures from pure anapestic meter in the poem's first, fourth, and fifth lines. Do these variations in meter contribute anything to the poem?

You may wish to use a discussion of limericks to reinforce the point that anapestic meter — like the dactylic meter of "Hickory, dickory, dock" (text p. 857) — is used almost exclusively in light, humorous, or children's verse.

HAIKU

MATSUO BASHŌ, *Under cherry trees* (p. 891)

Bashō is usually considered the greatest of the haiku poets. He was born near Kyoto, growing up as the companion of a local nobleman's son. He moved to Edo (now called Tokyo) when he was twenty-three and eventually became a recluse, living outside the city in a hut. He made several long journeys, always relying for food and shelter on the generosity of local Buddhist temples and on other poets. *The Narrow Road to the Deep North,* a collection of interlocked prose and haiku chronicling one of these journeys, is perhaps his best-known work in the West.

ETHERIDGE KNIGHT, *Eastern Guard Tower* (p. 892)

Often, as in Knight's "Eastern Guard Tower," a contemporary poet will use the tradition of the haiku form to make a point about the relation of humanity to nature. Note how the convicts are compared to lizards.

Whereas Bashō's "Under cherry trees" images a moment of restfulness, quietude, and delicate sensual pleasure, Knight's "Eastern Guard Tower" depends for its effect on the reader's ability to relate the title to the scene described. It portrays a moment of anguished aloneness.

In contrast to epigrams, which tend to be witty, terse observations made at a distance, often passing judgments on concepts, qualities, or persons, haiku are more likely to evoke landscape, atmosphere, or another person meaningful to the poet. Haiku tend to be more imagistic than intellectual, more suggestive than pointed. Having the class write haiku can teach much concerning image, connotation, and sound.

RESOURCES FOR TEACHING

Haiku. 19 min., color, 1974. Beta, VHS, ¾″ U-matic cassette, 16-mm film. An overview of this poetic form. Distributed by AIMS Media, Inc.

Etheridge Knight I [recording]. 1 cassette (29 min.), 1986. Distributed by New Letters on the Air.

Etheridge Knight II [recording]. 1 cassette (29 min.), 1989. Distributed by New Letters on the Air.

Etheridge Knight: So My Soul Can Sing [recording]. 1 cassette (50 min.). Distributed by Watershed Tapes.

ELEGY

SEAMUS HEANEY, *Mid-term Break* (p. 892)

This elegy commemorates the death of the speaker's brother at the age of four. It is written in poignant, terse flashes of memory. It might be considered a narrative poem as well as an elegy. How does the story unfold? Do the events of the child's death matter more or less than the emotions of the speaker or the reactions of the adults around him?

The starkness of the images in this poem tells us a lot about the speaker. He observes the scenes as if from a distance, trying to control his own reactions to the tragedy. The simple details of the baby cooing and laughing (unaware of the tragedy) and the old men greeting the speaker awkwardly make the young boy's death even more somber and haunting.

The last line tells us more about the boy than we know until this point. He is four years old. Standing apart, the line suggests that the poem is another kind of vessel for the young boy's life. As the coffin holds his body, the poem remembers him long after death.

POSSIBLE CONNECTIONS TO OTHER SELECTIONS

A. E. Housman, "To an Athlete Dying Young" (question #1, following)
John Updike, "Dog's Death" (text p. 673)

CONNECTION QUESTION IN TEXT (p. 893) WITH ANSWER

1. Compare Heaney's elegy with A. E. Housman's "To an Athlete Dying Young" (text p. 1101). Which do you find more moving? Explain why.

   The rhymes and regular meter in "To an Athlete Dying Young" give that poem a more formal, more public tone than the stark, conversational tone of Heaney's elegy. Heaney's little brother is not mythologized the way Housman's hero is. The athlete is an older boy who has presumably accomplished more than the young child. Heaney's poem reads as both elegy and catharsis for the speaker, whereas Housman's speaker is at some distance from the dead boy he commemorates.

ANDREW HUDGINS, *Elegy for My Father, Who Is Not Dead* (p. 893)

The speaker of this poem, unlike his father who is "ready" (line 2) to die, is not convinced "about the world beyond this world" (4). His father seems ready to die, happy "in the sureness of his faith" (3) that his journey into the afterlife will be like a vacation to a place where he will wait for his son to join him. The speaker is skeptical; he "can't / just say good-bye as cheerfully / as if he were embarking on a trip" (14–16). The difference in their attitudes is represented in terms of a ship; the speaker is convinced only that his father's "ship's gone down" (19) while the father is convinced that he will eventually wave and shout "welcome back" (21) to his son when his son's time comes.

The poem raises a crucial question: will the son adopt his father's attitude when he himself is closer to death, or is he simply more skeptical than his father? Both options are raised; the speaker acknowledges, "He's ready. I am not" (14), but he also says "I do not think he is right" (13). Does our attitude toward death change as we get older because we have accepted our mortality, or is belief in the afterlife a defense mechanism? This question is central to the poem's interpretation, as is the speaker's focus: is he more concerned about his father's death or his own? The poem is rather self-involved for an "elegy." Is the poet playing with two senses of the term "elegy" — a poem of mourning and a meditation on death?

POSSIBLE CONNECTIONS TO OTHER SELECTIONS

Donald Hall, "Letter with No Address" (text p. 1153)
Dylan Thomas, "Do not go gentle into that good night" (question #1, following)

CONNECTION QUESTION IN TEXT (p. 894) WITH ANSWER

1. Write an essay comparing attitudes toward death in this poem and in Dylan Thomas's "Do not go gentle into that good night" (p. 885). Both speakers invoke their fathers, nearer death than they are: what impact does this have?

    Thomas's "Do not go gentle into that good night" brings the speaker and his father into direct contact, which is a good starting point for contrasting these two poems. Would the speaker of Hudgins's poem express his sentiments differently if he were speaking to his father? Is there any trace of doubt or cynicism apparent in Thomas's speaker?

O D E

PERCY BYSSHE SHELLEY, *Ode to the West Wind* (p. 894)

Percy Bysshe Shelley was born to wealth in Horsham, Sussex. Educated in conventional privileges, he was taunted by his schoolmates for his unconventionality and lack of physical prowess. His rebellion against this environment helped make him both a nonconformist and a democrat. He was expelled from Oxford in 1811 for coauthoring a pamphlet called *The Necessity of Atheism*. He eventually married Mary Wollstonecraft Godwin and in 1818 settled in Italy, where he wrote his most highly regarded work, including "Prometheus Unbound" and "Ode to the West Wind." Shelley drowned while sailing with a friend, and his ashes were buried in a cemetery in Rome near the graves of his son, William Shelley, and John Keats.

The west wind in England is hailed as the harbinger of spring. As an introduction to this ode, you might have the students read the anonymous "Western Wind" (text p. 688).

The tercets and couplets that form each section of this ode should pose no problems; basically, the tercets interweave (*aba, bcb, cdc, ded, ee*). Since Shelley is describing wind, the ethereal element, it is appropriate that the sounds of the couplet (*ee*), which appear at the end of every twelfth line in the first three sections, should have an airy, wind-rushed quality, as in "hear," "atmosphere," "fear."

The first three sections describe the powers the wind has in nature — on land in autumn, in the clouds in "the dying year" (winter), and on the bay (a mixture of land and sea) in the summer. When Shelley turns to his own problems, including his sense of despair and his need for inspiration (sections IV and V), the rhyme of the couplet (*ee*) is changed and a more mournful, weighted sound ("bowed," "proud") is substituted. The rhyme scheme almost makes the poem generalize in the final section, when "Wind" and the promises of spring are bestowed upon "mankind."

For a close reading of this ode, see S. C. Wilcox's, "Imagery, Ideas, and Design in Shelley's 'Ode to the West Wind,' " *Studies in Philosophy* 47 (October 1950): 634–649.

As a three-page writing assignment, ask students to analyze the symbolic meaning of the west wind.

POSSIBLE CONNECTIONS TO OTHER SELECTIONS

Sophie Cabot Black, "August" (text p. 785)
Henry Wadsworth Longfellow, "Snow-Flakes" (text p. 1106)

RESOURCES FOR TEACHING

The Poetry of Shelley [recording]. 1 cassette. Distributed by Caedmon/Harper-Audio.
Treasury of Percy Bysshe Shelley [recording]. 1 cassette. Distributed by Spoken Arts.
See also "English Literature: Romantic Period," "English Romantic Poetry," "Introduction to English Poetry," and "Palgrave's Golden Treasury of English Poetry" in the appendix of Film, Video, and Audiocassette Resources.

PICTURE POEM

MICHAEL McFEE, *In Medias Res* (p. 897)

Students will probably have fun identifying the puns in this portly poem. A handful for consideration: "His waist / like the plot / thickens" (lines 1–3) — just as in a murder mystery, his increasing girth is out to get him, as the darker tone of the second half of this poem implies. "Wedding / pants" (3–4) — do we read this as the pants from the suit he wore at his wedding, no doubt a smaller size, or as the waist "wedding," or uniting, with the waistband of the pants? "Breathtaking" (4) no longer means spellbinding but rather a kind of choking. The "cinch" (5) can be read either as a girth or belt, or a snap, an easy thing to do.

PARODY

PETER DE VRIES, *To His Importunate Mistress* (p. 898)

Money is at the root of the distress in this work. In contrast, Marvell's main complaint was lack of time (text p. 729). "Picaresque" (line 7) is used in the sense of "our roguish affair." De Vries imitates Marvell's idiom quite closely. He picks up on the middle to high level of diction, the long sentences with verbs separated from their objects, and Marvell's rather Latinate style with the verbs coming at the ends of the sentences.

POSSIBLE CONNECTION TO ANOTHER SELECTION

Anthony Hecht, "The Dover Bitch" (question #1, following)

CONNECTION QUESTION IN TEXT (p. 899) WITH ANSWER

1. Read Anthony Hecht's "The Dover Bitch" (p. 1096), a parody of Arnold's "Dover Beach" (p. 757). Write an essay comparing the effectiveness of Hecht's parody with that of De Vries's "To His Importunate Mistress." Which parody do you prefer? Explain why.

   The parodies have different aims: Hecht's parody goes at Arnold's poem directly, faulting the speaker for his effete lack of attunement to his lover's sexual desires, whereas De Vries's parody satirizes our culture, which seems to demand that we spend our time making money, not making love. De Vries's parody is also closer to the original in terms of its tone. Hecht's parody is more colloquial than the original, countering Arnold's measured lines with phrases like "etc. etc." (line 5) and "Anyway" (20). Students should articulate what makes a parody effective rather than simply stating their preference for one or the other.

X. J. KENNEDY, *A Visit from St. Sigmund* (p. 899)

You might begin a discussion of "A Visit from St. Sigmund" by brainstorming in class about what students already know about Freud. Many students will undoubtedly have some prior knowledge of psychoanalytic theory, and because Freudian psychology has become part of our cultural literacy, even students with minimal knowledge of Freud's theories can enjoy this parody of Moore's "A Visit from St. Nicholas." To introduce students to some of Freud's theories, you might want to have them read Freud's "On the Oedipus Complex" (text p. 1305) or read about the literary applications of Freud's psychoanalytic theories on text page 2029. Kennedy's tone in this poem is humorously satirical; at every opportunity he gives psychoanalysis a jab as he plays with the central tenets of Freud's theories. Mead's opening quotation provides Kennedy with a springboard into the poem. Her comparison between Santa and Freud is appropriate since both have become cultural icons — paternal figures concerned with the behavior (both good and bad) of girls and boys.

You might have students identify specific passages from the poem where the poet uses humor to gently poke fun at psychoanalytic humor. Responses might include the substitution of Freud's "baggage" (hangups, psychoses, a couch, symbols, subliminal meanings, the unconscious, phallic jokes) for the "baggage" of St. Nicholas in the original poem (stockings, reindeer, a sack, a sleigh, a jolly laugh, and so on).

You may want to read the original poem in conjunction with the parody to show how the poet manipulates Moore's famous poem. Students will see that Kennedy merely uses the original poem as the scaffold for "A Visit from St. Sigmund." The real joke here is on Freud, and the Christmas references simply add depth and richness to the humor Kennedy employs.

POSSIBLE CONNECTION TO ANOTHER SELECTION

Blanche Farley, "The Lover Not Taken" (text p. 1005)

PERSPECTIVE

ROBERT MORGAN, *On the Shape of a Poem* (p. 900)

Students might enjoy analyzing Morgan's own "Mountain Graveyard" (text p. 686) in light of his idea that "all language is both mental and sacramental, is not 'real' but is the working of lip and tongue to subvert the 'real.'" How does his anagrammatic, spare prose "subvert the 'real'"?

Elizabeth Bishop's "Sestina" in this chapter (text p. 887) or Dylan Thomas's villanelle "Do not go gentle into that good night" (text p. 885) are good examples to use when discussing Morgan's statement that "poems empearl irritating facts until they become opalescent spheres of moment, not so much résumés of history as of human faculties working with pain."

Ask students to think about form in other aspects of their lives — the formal behavior at a funeral, for example, as a way of dealing with painful emotion.

ELAINE MITCHELL, *Form* (p. 901)

By comparing form to a corset, Mitchell develops the idea that there is a time and a place to use form in poetry and a time and a place not to use it. Ask students to identify in the poem the various moments when the poet suggests that form can be helpful. Responses might include that it can "shape and deceive" (line 5), "It / 's an ace up your sleeve" (7–8), "it / might be a resource" (12–13), or "your grateful slave" (14). Then ask them to identify places where the poet warns that form can prove too confining, such as "Don't try to force it" (3), "Ouch, too tight a corset" (6), "No need to force it" (9), and "sometimes divorce it" (16). Ultimately, Mitchell seems to be suggesting that poets need to recognize when form works to their advantage and when it is forced. When form is forced, poets need to be willing to abandon it rather than continue to impose form where it doesn't work.

By adhering to poetic form herself (three-line stanzas — except the final stanza — constructed with an *aba* rhyme scheme throughout) the poet forces her own poem to conform to the restrictions of form she's set up. Indeed, she creates a very controlled rhythm (dactylic dimeter) and rhyme scheme to provide the poem with structure. Some students may recognize that, ironically, Mitchell forces words together and pulls them apart in totally outrageous ways in order to maintain the form she's established. Ask students to consider whether this effect is intentional.

23

Open Form

Whereas traditional forms depend on the interplay of the poet's current speech and an established form, open form hinges on the poet's (and the reader's) ability to discover a form that works toward the overall effect the poet wishes to produce. Just as in the previous chapter, each of the poems here can form the basis of a rewarding discussion about how form relates to content. With open form, the poet theoretically has absolute control over the form chosen, although some may choose a fairly constraining pattern to guide the poem — witness Peter Meinke's "ABC of Aerobics." As a result of this freedom, the poem must actually withstand closer and more critical reading, as each formal choice takes on greater significance.

Poems like E. E. Cummings's "in Just-" obviously foreground the layout of the poem on the page as a formal technique. In fact, some of Cummings's poems cannot to be read aloud because of their formal experimentation. Cummings's poems, like those of William Carlos Williams, tend toward spareness and intense focus on the medium of language. By contrast, a poet like Whitman uses repetition, catalog, and long rhythmic units to create a sense of plenitude and richness, a spilling over of language onto the page.

For some students, a poem like Galway Kinnell's "After Making Love We Hear Footsteps" may seem to be formless. This results from Kinnell's "plain speech" style and the seeming randomness of the line breaks. You may find it productive to push students to examine the breaks and rhythms in the poem more closely. The breaks serve to create units of meaning and to insert very slight pauses in the reading, which help create rhythms that add to the overall mood of the poem. You might ask students why Kinnell chooses to put a stanza break between lines 18 and 19. Why not run the whole poem together? In both traditional and open forms, stanza breaks create a pause in which ideas can shift, focuses can change, or previous statements can be reassessed. Line breaks can do this on a much smaller scale. In either event, the white space on the page can be as telling as what is said in words.

Similarly, the absence of regular metrics or stanzas does not mean the absence of structure. Tato Laviera's "AmeRícan" demonstrates a use of repetition that is reminiscent of Whitman and serves to create a similar sense of flow and plenitude.

As an exercise, you might have your students experiment with line breaks by taking a poem from the book and redoing the breaks. They might then give that poem to another student and have that student evaluate the new poem, asking themselves "Has the meaning of the poem (or parts of the poem) changed?" This exercise may help to emphasize felicitous or infelicitous choices in poetic structure. A related exercise might have students create found poems by taking a piece of prose and inserting line breaks. Students could again evaluate the results, looking for meanings that have been altered or significances that have been added by the change in form.

E. E. CUMMINGS, *in Just-* (p. 902)

Exactly how poems operate as a graphic medium on our visual sense is not well understood by critics. The open-endedness of the question provides a good occasion for students to make their own guesses. Notice, for example, that the most important thematic word in this poem, *spring,* either is set off from the line (as in line 2) or appears by itself, as in lines 9 and 18. In fact, the placement of *spring* at approximately the beginning, middle, and end of the poem is almost an organizational motif. Another repeated phrase, "whistles far and wee," also is placed first on one line (5) with "whistles" later receiving separational emphasis, over two lines (12 and 13), with "far and wee" receiving space — like long pulses on the whistle — and, at the close of the poem, on separate lines, as though the sound of the whistle were still present but moving away.

The whistle is, of course, united with spring as a modern rendition of Pan's pipes drawing Persephone from the underworld and awakening the calls of birds and the sounds of wildlife. In response to the "goat-footed" (Pan) balloon man's pipes, "bettyandisbel" come running — the elision of their names mimicking the pronunciation, the swift movement, even the perception patterns of children.

Many other word patterns offer themselves for discussion in this poem. These comments are only a beginning, and an enthusiastic class can discover much more.

POSSIBLE CONNECTION TO ANOTHER SELECTION

Robert Frost, "Two Tramps in Mud Time" (text p. 991)

WALT WHITMAN, From *I Sing the Body Electric* (p. 903)

Whitman's outpouring is an homage to the body, the soul, and poetry all at once. In a word, Whitman offers here an anatomy of wonder.

The rhythm of this portion of the poem is striking. Notice how many of the lines begin with a trochee or a spondee. The initial heavy stresses lend a kind of relentless thoroughness to Whitman's catalog of the human body. You might have the class scan a portion of the poem, say from line 25 to line 30. The lines change from heavily accented to a lighter, roughly iambic rhythm that suggests "the continual changes of the flex of the mouth."

The chief difficulty is, of course, discerning the exact relationship between these things. We tend to think of them as separate from each other. Does Whitman's poem help us to unify them in our minds? The poem lists a number of body parts: do any of them tend to stand out or to form any sort of unexpected patterns?

POSSIBLE CONNECTION TO ANOTHER SELECTION

Jane Hirschfield, "The Lives of the Heart" (text p. 1159)

PERSPECTIVE

WALT WHITMAN, *On Rhyme and Meter* (p. 904)

In addition to assigning Consideration 3 as a writing topic, you might ask students to write a few paragraphs about Whitman's use of catalogs or lists as an element of the organic form he espouses. The excerpt from *I Sing the Body Electric* (text p. 903) is especially useful for this exercise. Why is Whitman's tactic of listing appropriate to his subject?

GALWAY KINNELL, *After Making Love We Hear Footsteps* (p. 905)

Kinnell's poetry is known for its directness, precision, and carefully controlled idiom. In his *Book of Nightmares,* from which this poem is taken, he explores the difficult project of explaining human mortality to our children. Love is his answer in many of the poems, but it requires confronting physical as well as emotional issues.

This is a popular poem with students because it vividly presents a scene that is familiar to many of them. Ask them to describe the speaker. What does his language tell us about his character?

In an essay, you might ask students to explore the poem's auditory appeal. How do the various sounds create a mood for the speaker's discussion of his relationship to his child and his wife?

POSSIBLE CONNECTIONS TO OTHER SELECTIONS

Robert Frost, "Home Burial" (question #1, following)
Donald Hall, "My Son, My Executioner" (text p. 1093)
Peter Meinke, "The ABC of Aerobics" (text p. 922)

CONNECTION QUESTION IN TEXT (p. 906) WITH ANSWER

1. Discuss how this poem helps to bring into focus the sense of loss Frost evokes in "Home Burial" (p. 980).

    In concrete images such as the baseball pajamas and the expression "loving and snuggling," Kinnell's speaker establishes a sense of what his child is like. The boy's presence fills the poem as it fills the space between the speaker and his wife. Frost's poem explores what it would be like to have this space suddenly emptied, how he would talk to his wife about their loss, how it would affect their relationship. Frost's speaker's relationship to his wife is painfully awkward, just the opposite of Kinnell's. As Kinnell's poem overflows with affection and love, Frost's echoes in emptiness, silence, grief, and loss.

WILLIAM CARLOS WILLIAMS, *The Red Wheelbarrow* (p. 906)

This poem has a syllabically structured form, like a haiku, of four and two, three and two, three and two, and four and two syllables in each couplet. Also like a haiku, this poem is imagistic and suggestive rather than directly representational. Each couplet contains two stresses in its first line and one in its second.

X. J. Kennedy, in a footnote to the poem that appears in his *Introduction to Poetry,* Sixth Edition, notes that according to a librarian's account, Williams was "gazing from the window of the house where one of his patients, a small girl, lay suspended between life and death" (Boston: Little, 1986, p. 32). This information does enrich the first phrase, "so much depends," which seems to speak of a sympathetic vitality exchanged between ourselves and the objects of our landscape. Without this biographical detail, the poem is usually described as an example of Imagism, in which the image is made to speak for itself.

Does the poem "improve" with the librarian's recollection? This question might be taken up in a writing assignment.

TIP FROM THE FIELD

To help students see the value in pure imagery, try connecting and comparing the importance of images in poetry to those in visual art. Students are often biased by their expectation that poems must have deep meanings. Conversely, they expect art to simply present them with something pleasing to look at and are intimidated if visual art expresses deep meaning. You might discuss the Imagism movement, in which poets embraced the use of imagery alone to convey a poem's emotion and message, and then show slides of modern art in which the image is everything (i.e., Charles Demuth's "I Saw the Figure 5 in Gold" or anything by Andy Warhol). Then have your students write their own version of a poem like William Carlos Williams's "The Red Wheelbarrow" purely for the enjoyment of their own images.

— ROBIN CALITRI, *Merced College*

POSSIBLE CONNECTION TO ANOTHER SELECTION

William Carlos Williams, "Poem" (text p. 753)

DENISE LEVERTOV, *Gathered at the River* (p. 907)

Levertov is a fine example of a poet who has used her energies and gifts to speak her views on human rights and political issues, including the U.S. presence in Vietnam, oppression in Nicaragua and El Salvador, and the manufacture of nuclear weapons and power plants. In this poem she catches the image of a strikingly contemporary gesture, the launching of small candle boats, in a communal act of witness against the atrocities of the past and what might occur in the future.

You might begin by commenting on how the poem opens with a fragment — "As if the trees were not indifferent." Why is this a good opening in terms of the rest of the poem? The reference to trees introduces the central image of the poem, one that will obtain symbolic import by the close. Another obvious question to ask is how the events of Hiroshima and Nagasaki are different from other military events of the past and how the trees illustrate that difference. In lines 12–16 the difference is spelled out with an underscoring of the idea that war is no longer just a "human war" but a war against nature, with the trees as a kind of natural synecdoche. At the close of the poem, the trees become a symbol for what could be lost if people are unsuccessful in arresting the possibility of nuclear war. The trees, in their "slow and innocent wisdom," seem to stand for growth (bole/branch), protection (shade), and continuing life (pollen). Although pollen is the most evanescent of the trees' properties, it ensures the continuance of the life cycle and therefore serves as an appropriate close to the poem.

By all means, teach this poem in conjunction with Levertov's own remarks on it (text p. 909). Writing assignments could be organized around the tone of the poem, the appropriateness of the trees as symbol, or the need to revive the idea of heroes and heroines in the contemporary world.

POSSIBLE CONNECTIONS TO OTHER SELECTIONS

Robert Frost, "Design" (question #1, following)
Gerard Manley Hopkins, "God's Grandeur," "Pied Beauty" (question #2, following)

1. In her comments on "Gathered at the River" (p. 909), Levertov affirms her "underlying belief in a great design, a potential harmony which can be violated or be sustained." How does Frost's "Design" (p. 993) comment on Levertov's beliefs? Explain whether you agree with Levertov or not.

   Levertov's notion of a "great design, a potential harmony" struggles against the selfish intervention of human desires in this poem. Were it not for our "war against earth, / against nature," we might hope for the actualization of the potential she describes. In Frost's poem the malevolent images are natural, indicating that Frost's view of nature's design may be darker than Levertov's. Unlike Levertov's speaker, the speaker in "Design" finds a "darkness to appall" in a natural setting.

2. Levertov also expresses a concern in her essay for the necessity of having "a sense of the sacredness of the earthly creation" and mentions that Gerard Manley Hopkins has always been one of her favorite poets. Write an essay comparing "Gathered at the River" with Hopkins's "God's Grandeur" (p. 837) or "Pied Beauty" (p. 1099). What significant similarities do you find?

   In their comparison of one of the Hopkins poems with Levertov's, ask students to pay particular attention to the poet's relationship to his or her subject. They will notice that Hopkins has much more cause for celebration than does Levertov, perhaps because of their different eras. Levertov has clearly seen more horror than Hopkins has; thus she is less celebratory and more foreboding.

DENISE LEVERTOV, *On "Gathered at the River"* (p. 909)

There are several possible approaches to this perspective. First, instructors might provide copies or excerpts from Edgar Allan Poe's essay "The Philosophy of Composition," in which he describes his process of composing "The Raven." Ask students to compare Poe's and Levertov's discussions of their inspirations and writing processes. Both essays provide students with an intimate view of the poetic process.

Levertov's essay can serve as an excellent model for students. Encourage them to construct a short poem and then to write a similar explanation of the influences, intentions, and accomplishments of the poem. They might enjoy reading each other's work and discussing it before reading the accompanying explanations.

Another topic for discussion would be Levertov's identification, at the end of this piece, of the significant lines from her poem. Following her example, students might create a précis of another poem by isolating its most important elements. They should also compare the complete text of Levertov's poem — included in the "Album of Contemporary Poems" in Chapter 27 (p. 1148) — with the excerpts included in this essay.

MARILYN NELSON WANIEK, *Emily Dickinson's Defunct* (p. 912)

You might begin discussion of this poem by asking what associations students have with Emily Dickinson. For some background information, it might be interesting to read the text's introduction to Dickinson on page 925 and the Perspectives by Dickinson, Higginson, and Todd that follow the collection of Dickinson's poems on pages 952-954. Dickinson is thought to have been somewhat of a recluse, a woman isolated in her home and in her room, writing her life away in solitude and silence.

Waniek's poem presents a Dickinson that is radically different; this Dickinson is a tough woman, earthy, and bold. Ask students to provide specific examples from the poem that redefine Dickinson in this light. Responses might include references to Dickinson being "dressed for action" (6), smelling human (12), and being a "two-fisted woman" (25). In this way, Waniek's poem effectively revises (or at least plays with) the image of Dickinson we've become accustomed to, imagining that underneath her reclusive exterior and "gray old lady / clothes" (5–6) there was a wilder and more adventuresome woman — an idea that is borne out in Dickinson's poetry.

The title of Waniek's poem functions in several ways, and it may be interesting to ask students to discuss or write briefly about the title. *Defunct* means extinct, or no longer living. Having died in 1886, Emily Dickinson is of course literally defunct. But the title may also suggest that the Emily Dickinson we've known in the past is defunct, for a revised image of the New England poet is being suggested by the poem.

After studying the poem, you may wish to ask students to read some Dickinson poems in order to identify connections between Dickinson's poems and the allusions contained in Waniek's poem.

POSSIBLE CONNECTIONS TO OTHER SELECTIONS

E. E. Cummings, "Buffalo Bill 's" (question #1, following)
Emily Dickinson, "I heard a Fly buzz — when I died —" (question #1, following)

CONNECTION QUESTION IN TEXT (p. 913) WITH ANSWER

1. Waniek alludes to at least two other poems in "Emily Dickinson's Defunct." The title refers to E. E. Cummings's "Buffalo Bill 's" (p. 1087) and the final lines (27–30) refer to "I heard a Fly buzz — when I died —" (p. 946). Read those poems and write an essay discussing how they affect your reading of Waniek's poem.

    All three poems take on the topic of death, and on the surface all three seem to equate being dead with being "defunct," as the titles of Waniek's and Cummings's poem indicate and as the final line of Dickinson's poem emphasizes: "I could not see to see —." Yet there is the sense that death is not final, that it does not render us "defunct." Waniek's and Cummings's poems celebrate the vitality of their subjects after their deaths, and Dickinson's poem posits a life after death, even after the speaker loses her sight in the final line. Death is staved off through the lack of decisive end punctuation in Cummings's and Dickinson's poems, and the buzzing of the flies in Waniek's poem suggests an ongoing celebration of the life of this poet.

JIM DANIELS, *Short-order Cook* (p. 913)

Under the pressure of time and the scrutinizing gazes of the counter girls, the speaker of this poem, a short-order cook, rises to the challenge of an unusually large order. He summons all the grace he can and completes the order, celebrating the cycle of "pressure, responsibility, success" (line 27).

The poem's structure contributes to the rhythm of the speaker's situation: the breaks between the first and second stanzas act as pauses before the frenzied activity of the third stanza. The slashes between lines in the third stanza serve to contribute to the frenzied pace of the speaker's activity. Does anything else motivate this speaker besides "responsibility" (27)? The counter girls, not the "average joe," are his audience. How does their interaction alter his behavior?

Students may be quick to find the humor in this poem, because the speaker takes his job so seriously. You might want to begin a discussion by listing as many jobs as your students have had. Were/are there times when they have felt as seriously the "responsibility" associated with work? What other situations (that might evoke diction as elevated) arise at work? Does work, or attitudes toward work, ever have social implications? If so, what?

POSSIBLE CONNECTIONS TO OTHER SELECTIONS

Seamus Heaney, "The Pitchfork" (text p. 760)

Aron Keesbury, "Song to a Waitress" (question #1, following)

CONNECTION QUESTION IN TEXT (p. 914) WITH ANSWER

1. Write a narrative poem or prose poem in which you imagine an encounter between this short-order cook and the speaker of Aron Keesbury's "Song to a Waitress" (p. 872).

    Although both speakers might be found in the same place, this one is far less surly than Keesbury's. He seems intensely aware of his surroundings at all times, whereas the patron in "Song to a Waitress" has been lulled into a kind of hypnotic stupor. We might admire this speaker for his cheerful attention to his work and we might steer clear of Keesbury's speaker. Would the encounter between them necessarily take the form of an outright conflict?

CAROLYN FORCHÉ, *The Colonel* (p. 914)

It may be true ("What you have heard is true"), but is it poetry? Students will probably be surprised to find this paragraph of ostensible prose in the poetry section of the anthology, and you may want to bring in other examples of prose poetry by Charles Baudelaire or W. S. Merwin to illustrate the idea that this form is a continuing tradition.

In "The Colonel" the apocryphal (what you have heard to be true) becomes realized as apocalypse. Reality here knows a variegated texture in which the daily papers and pet dogs are conjoined offhandedly with the omnipresent pistol on the couch. As in poetry (and not prose), the real world and the fictional world, the natural and the fantastic, are placed alongside each other without the pointers of transition, causality, or connection. The effect is to merge the real and the surreal in an amalgam of potent horror that blurs the line between the two. An example of this merging occurs between the introduction of the "cop show" in sentence 7 and the reference to the broken bottles (used to scoop out kneecaps) in sentence 9. The arenas of violence shift back and forth between the TV screen and the living room, with the moon (sentence 6) arcing its ominous pendulum over the house like a swinging hangman's rope or the glare of the inquisitor-torturer's lamp.

This discussion is intended as an illustration of the suggestive power of prose poetry. Words, images, even patterns of speech and silence ricochet off one another to create meanings beyond themselves. The poem comes to an end when the forces of its own energy collide and cannot break apart again. The horrifying evidence of the actual killings (the bags of ears) metamorphoses into a surreal horror show as the ears ("like dried peach halves") become alive in water. Likewise, language as both damnation ("go fuck themselves") and salvation (poetry) meet head on in the colonel's taunt and the fact of the poem itself.

You might explore the close of the poem with students or ask them to describe in a brief essay the import and tone of the final two sentences. Is Forché intimating here that both poetry and a voice beyond the colonel's might someday be heard?

POSSIBLE CONNECTION TO ANOTHER SELECTION

Sharon Olds, "Rite of Passage" (text p. 915)

RESOURCES FOR TEACHING

Carolyn Forché [recording]. 1 cassette (29 min.), 1989. Distributed by New Letters on the Air.
Carolyn Forché: Ourselves or Nothing [recording]. 1 cassette (58 min.), 1983. Distributed by Watershed Tapes.

SHARON OLDS, *Rite of Passage* (p. 915)

Olds's work is often focused on gender distinctions and characteristics. In "Rite of Passage," Olds emphasizes the highly masculine qualities inherent in males of any age. The title refers not only to the birthday party — a ritual by which we celebrate milestones in the maturation process — but also the boys' transition from child to adult behavior. Even six- and seven-year-olds demonstrate adult male characteristics: "Hands in pockets, they stand around / jostling, jockeying for place, small fights / breaking out and calming" (lines 5–7). They also emulate adult male behavior by comparing themselves to each other and by valuing power, force, assertiveness: "They eye each other, seeing themselves / tiny in the other's pupils. They clear their / throats a lot, a room of small bankers, / they fold their arms and frown" (11–12). The final lines, in which "they clear their throats / like Generals, they relax and get down to / playing war" (24–26), provide an overt context for much of the preceding covert activity. Socializing is akin to war: at this party, even the cake — "round and heavy as a / turret" (13–14) — is evocative of combat.

The power in Olds's poem lies in her insistence in the final lines, where the birthday boy assures his guests, *"We could easily kill a two-year-old"* (22), that this transition occurs much earlier than we might commonly expect. The "clear voice" of this child contrasts sharply with the thoughts he expresses, indicating dissonance between the image of a child and the reality of that image. Ultimately, the "rite of passage" refers less to the son's celebrating a birthday than to our own recognition that these children contain and manifest even at this early age the energy and the desire for brutality.

POSSIBLE CONNECTIONS TO OTHER SELECTIONS

Carolyn Forché, "The Colonel" (question #1, following)
Wilfred Owen, "Dulce et Decorum Est" (question #2, following)
Gary Soto, "Behind Grandma's House" (text p. 823)

CONNECTIONS QUESTIONS IN TEXT (p. 916) WITH ANSWERS

1. In an essay discuss the treatment of violence in "Rite of Passage" and Carolyn Forché's "The Colonel" (p. 914). To what extent might the colonel be regarded as an adult version of the generals in Olds's poem?

    The colonel in Forché's poem is a demented individual who brings out a bag of dried human ears at a dinner party. The children/generals in Olds's poem are young boys who, although they say that they could kill a two-year-old, have no real intention of doing so. Both the colonel and the boys exhibit our somewhat disturbing human tendencies toward violence, and the boys are playing war while the colonel is living it. Still, it is likely that most of the boys, if not all of them, will learn how to suppress such tendencies or to find a better outlet for them than the colonel has found.

2. Discuss the use of irony in "Rite of Passage" and Owen's "Dulce et Decorum Est" (p. 763). Which do you think is a more effective antiwar poem? Explain why.

In both cases, young boys participate in warfare, somewhat unwillingly at first. The images of actual warfare and death in Owen's poem are likely to make it the popular choice for a more effective antiwar poem. Students are likely to see Olds's poem as nothing more than a birthday party, which is its central irony. The boys at the birthday party might turn into bankers rather than soldiers, so the critique of war is somewhat dispersed.

RESOURCES FOR TEACHING

Sharon Olds [recording]. 1 cassette (29 min.), 1992. Distributed by New Letters on the Air.

Sharon Olds: Coming Back to Life [recording]. 1 cassette (60 min.). Distributed by Audio-Forum.

Michael O'Brien & Sharon Olds [recording]. 1 cassette (29 min.). Distributed by New Letters on the Air.

See also "Moyers: The Power of the Word" in the appendix of Film, Video, and Audiocassette Resources.

CAROLYNN HOY, *In the Summer Kitchen* (p. 916)

The simple details of this poem offer a vivid impression of a poignant moment that the speaker experiences while doing the wash with her grandmother. Though only the briefest mention is made of the infant Harry's death, the depth of her grandmother's loss is made evident to the granddaughter. This moment provides an intimate emotional context for the spearing, "churning and scooping" that goes on in the first stanza. The speaker takes in the significance of the grandmother's loss as quickly as the grandmother turns away from it to continue with the wash. Apparently the speaker knows enough about her grandmother and her grandmother knows enough about grief so that each refuses to dwell on the loss. Instead, the granddaughter takes her grandmother's cue to snap to the attention required by the immediate moment of doing the laundry — and by life itself. Even so, "as straight and squared" as the grandmother launders the moment, something does pass "from her hand to mine" in addition to the wash. The speaker understands the intense self-control of her grandmother and recognizes "The dignity of it all," a dignity that is passed on in the speaker's tribute to her grandmother in the form of a tightly controlled poem that might serve as the epitaph for her "chiseled headstone." Students who read carefully will find the diction and images in this poem perfectly aligned with its meanings.

POSSIBLE CONNECTION TO ANOTHER SELECTION

Emily Dickinson, "The Bustle in a House" (question #1, following)

CONNECTION QUESTION IN TEXT (p. 917) WITH ANSWER

1. Compare the tone of this poem with that of Emily Dickinson's "The Bustle in a House" (p. 950).

Both poems are characterized by silence and solemnity. The "bustle" in each case takes a back seat to the silence with which it is undertaken. The poets achieve this effect in different ways, though: Hoy builds toward the sharp, spare language of the final two stanzas, whereas Dickinson's form is evenly eerie throughout her short poem.

ALLEN GINSBERG, *First Party at Ken Kesey's with Hell's Angels* (p. 917)

This poem describes a disorderly if not chaotic late-night party scene and concludes with the image of four police cars arriving on the scene, presumably to put an end to the revelry. Students will most likely be familiar with the type of scene Ginsberg describes, and a few will probably be familiar with both Kesey and Ginsberg, counterculture icons of the '50s and '60s. As with many "Beat" poems, this one demands to be read aloud, allowing the lines to create their own rhythm in conjunction with one's breathing, like an improvised riff on a saxophone. Would a poem like this one have a different effect if it were written in a stricter poetic form?

"Hell's Angels" in the title helps to set the scene and tone for this poem. You may want to begin discussion by asking students whether they would find this scene inviting. Though the party is with the notorious motorcycle gang, Ginsberg paints a fairly bucolic scene by using words like "cool" (line 1), "shade" (2), and "stars dim" (3), for example. It isn't until "blast" in line 8 that the speaker introduces any rowdiness. With this setup, what effect do the "red lights" of the police cars have, "revolving in the leaves" (19)? Is the image threatening? Or do the police cars fit in as another part of the scene? Are there "good guys" or "bad guys" in this police intervention?

POSSIBLE CONNECTIONS TO OTHER SELECTIONS

William Hathaway, "Oh, Oh" (question #1, following)
Etheridge Knight, "Eastern Guard Tower" (text p. 892)

CONNECTION QUESTION IN TEXT (p. 917) WITH ANSWER

1. Write an essay that compares the impact of this poem's ending with that of Hathaway's "Oh, Oh" (p. 675).

   A comparison between this poem and Hathaway's "Oh, Oh" is especially interesting because Hell's Angels are the source of anxiety in "Oh, Oh," but the police are that source of anxiety in "First Party . . ." Furthermore, Hell's Angels are good guys, or at least neutral figures, in Ginsberg's poem. Yet students might not interpret the police as altogether negative in Ginsberg's poem. Are they simply part of the tableau he creates?

RESOURCES FOR TEACHING

Allen Ginsberg [video]. Color, Beta, VHS, ¾" U-matic cassette (50 min.). Writers on Writing Series. Distributed by The Roland Collection.
Allen Ginsberg: When the Muse Calls, Answer! [video]. Color, VHS (30 min.). Distributed by Filmic Archives.
Potpourri of Poetry — Summer, Nineteen Seventy-Five [recording]. 1 cassette (60 min.). Distributed by Watershed Tapes.

ANONYMOUS, *The Frog* (p. 918)

Although a number of violations of grammatical rules appear in this poem, such as lack of agreement between subject and verb: "bird . . . are" (line 1), or "he hop" (3), or double negatives: "He ain't go no" (4), there is a certain structure to its content. Following the odd assertion that the frog is "a wonderful bird" (1), the poet catalogs the frog's characteristics and follows them up with a list of what the frog lacks. The final line is a sort of culmination of both approaches: "When he sit, he sit on what he ain't got almost" (6). And although the literal meaning of the poem and its ungrammatical sentences might seem confusing, the poet provides a clear image of the frog, almost in spite of the language. The repetition of words such as *almost* and *hardly* and the reliance on many one-syllable words contribute to the overall rhythmic pattern of the work. You might ask students what the effect of comparing a frog to a bird is in this poem.

POSSIBLE CONNECTION TO ANOTHER SELECTION

William Blake, "Ah Sun-flower" (text p. 1078)

TATO LAVIERA, *AmeRícan* (p. 918)

"AmeRícan" relies on a complex structure and innovative use of language for its power. Encourage students to examine the components and the physical layout of each section of this ever-changing, ever-moving poem. Each of the first three stanzas begins with the phrase "we gave birth to a new generation." The new generation is composed of those AmeRícans who will gather the elements of their culture and move into the mainstream American culture represented by New York. The seventh stanza (lines 21–24) highlights the poem's narrative development and the poet's creative use of language. Marking the transition between native and American culture, the poet embodies the literal movement, the disorientation, and the character of the new environment through the rearrangement and repetition of *across, forth,* and *back.* Appropriately, residence in New York (an island connected by bridges) is indicated by the line "our trips are walking bridges" (24). What other meaning is indicated by this line?

The eighth stanza breaks from the form established by the preceding stanzas. Ask students why it is appropriate to omit the beginning word "AmeRícan" here. In what way is this physical detail a response to the "marginality that gobbled us up abruptly!" (31)? In what other ways do the content and tone of this stanza contrast with the rest of the poem?

The poem is infused with the poet's sense of both Puerto Rican and American cultures. Encourage students to note the comparisons between the first and second halves of this poem, in which the poet touches on the music, spirit, and language of each culture. Also, students might notice instances (particularly toward the end of this poem) in which the cultures seem fused — for example, in words such as *spanglish* (41).

What is the tone of the final two stanzas? Literally, there is a celebration of the myth of America — "home of the brave, the land of the free." The penultimate stanza alludes to the understanding fostered by our Puritan forefathers that America is God's chosen country, "a city on a hill" that should be an example to all nations. The lines in which the poet refers to "our energies / collectively invested to find other civil- / izations" (52–54) also touch on our history of Manifest Destiny. The final stanza conveys the joy experienced by an assimilated AmeRícan, yet there is also considerable loss of identity in the speaker's "dream to take the accent from / the altercation, and be proud to call / myself american" (57–59).

POSSIBLE CONNECTIONS TO OTHER SELECTIONS

Joseph Bruchac, "Ellis Island" (text p. 921)
Chitra Banerjee Divakaruni, "Indian Movie, New Jersey" (question #1, following)

CONNECTION QUESTION IN TEXT (p. 920) WITH ANSWER

1. In an essay consider the themes, styles, and tones of "AmeRícan" and Divakaruni's "Indian Movie, New Jersey" (p. 819).

    Both poems consider the plight of immigrants in America who live a kind of liminal existence between their native culture and mainstream American culture. Laveria's poem is more of a celebration of this liminal state than Divakaruni's is, though; both poets sense a blending of the two cultures, but the Indian immigrants and their families in Divakaruni's poem are alienated and discriminated against. Laveria's poem uses a hybrid language and a new poetic form to celebrate the new, hybrid culture that is the subject of his poem. It is ultimately a more hopeful rendition of the immigrant experience.

THOM WARD, *Vasectomy* (p. 920)

This poem acts as a critique of modern capitalist thought, as its dedication to Adam Smith makes clear. The poet reveals in terse, direct language the gulf that exists between those who own or manage factories and those who work in them. The speaker describes a situation in which factory workers continue to work while the company's hierarchy makes other plans. The final lines make the speaker's intent clear, as he describes the textile mills as "wicked" (line 23) and asks the rhetorical question, "what possible good, / is supply without demand?" (24–25).

Students may not be familiar with the theories of Smith, but they do know something about the morality of the marketplace, and much of our current free-market system is indebted to Smith's thought. You can approach his theories in a general way, by having students extract ideas about free-market economics based on the poem's content, or by providing some background on Smith's theories, most famously advanced in *The Wealth of Nations*. In either case, ask students how the poem serves as a critique. What makes us certain of the speaker's intent? Is his tone consistent throughout the poem? You might want to postpone a discussion of the title until after some of these more fundamental questions are addressed.

POSSIBLE CONNECTION TO ANOTHER SELECTION

Marge Piercy, "The Secretary Chant" (text p. 671)

JOSEPH BRUCHAC, *Ellis Island* (p. 921)

In this poem, Bruchac recounts his own visit to Ellis Island and describes the conflicting emotions that he feels as a descendent of both European immigrants and Native Americans. As the grandson of European immigrants he is "the answerer of [their] dreams" (lines 16–17). However, in the third stanza, he confesses discomfort with this understanding of how he has fulfilled his grandparents' dreams, since those were the dreams of only one set of his forebears. The other part of his blood is Native American: "only one part of my blood loves that memory. / Another voice speaks / of native lands / within this nation" (18–21). Here the speaker implies that the two voices within him are in conflict, for the fulfillment of dreams for the one voice meant a tremendous loss for the dreams of the other voice. Have students find specific lines in the poem where the poet describes this conflict.

In this way, the speaker sees the two parts of his heritage as diametrically opposed. "Success" for one set of grandparents meant the destruction of the dreams of his other ancestors.

In discussing this poem, it may be helpful to ask students about the significance of the word "owned." It appears twice in the poem — at the end of the first stanza about the Slovakian grandparents and again in the third stanza in regard to the loss sustained by the Native American ancestors — and as a concept it may provide a way of concretely understanding the difference between the dreams of the settlers and the dreams of the Native American ancestors.

POSSIBLE CONNECTION TO ANOTHER SELECTION

Tato Laviera, "AmeRícan" (question #1, following)

CONNECTION QUESTION IN TEXT (p. 921) WITH ANSWER

1. Write an essay that discusses the speakers' attitudes toward immigration in "Ellis Island" and in Laviera's "AmeRícan" (p. 918).

   Laviera's poem believes that cultures have blended in America to form a new one: "AmeRícan salutes all folklores, / european, indian, black, spanish" (lines 10–11), and it is optimistic that the new generation will realize their own version of the American dream. Bruchac's poem is less confident that cultures blend in America. His doubts center around the notion that peoples of European descent have driven out the indigenous peoples of America. These cultures do not mix, in Bruchac's poem, which is a tale of invasion rather than a celebration of the American promise of equality.

RESOURCES FOR TEACHING

Joseph Bruchac [recording]. 1 cassette (29 min.), 1983. Distributed by New Letters on the Air.

Joseph Bruchac Two [recording]. 1 cassette (29 min.), 1993. Distributed by New Letters on the Air.

PETER MEINKE, *The ABC of Aerobics* (p. 922)

Born in Brooklyn, Peter Meinke often experiments with form, preferring to let the poem dictate its own form. Works whose titles begin "The ABC of . . ." usually are primers designed to teach the basic elements of a subject. You might start discussion of this poem by asking whether it fulfills the expectations its title sets up. In a kind of playful, semisatiric thumbing of the nose at cholesterol-level and heart-rate calculators, the poem at least acknowledges the obligations of its title. The speaker, apparently, has tried to ward off the effects of aging by jogging, but he expends all this effort with a despairing sense of his past sins and the dark forebodings of his genetic history manifested in the portrait of Uncle George. Small wonder, then, that his thoughts turn to Shirley Clark, and the poem concludes with the speaker "breathing hard" and gasping for his lost flame at his own "maximal heart rate."

At least two aspects of this poem merit some consideration. One is the carefully controlled use of consonance and alliteration, often for humorous effect. Notice, for example, the alternating *l*- and *b*-sounds in line 12 followed by the nasal hiss of "my / medical history noxious marsh." Later, in a spoofing of health and fitness fads, Meinke shows the direction of his true inclinations by exchanging "zen and zucchini" for "drinking and dreaming."

The second aspect of this poem that students should feel comfortable enough to enjoy is the humor, which derives in part from the poem's dip into the vernacular. "Probably I shall keel off the john like / queer Uncle George," Meinke unabashedly tells us in line 16, while he describes the lucky lover who married the fabled Shirley as a "turkey" who lacks all aesthetic appreciation for her wondrous earlobes. We are inclined to like the speaker in this poem, and both his personality and the radiated humor act as rhetorical devices, helping us to feel the way he feels about "The ABC of aerobics," which, by the way, takes us to the end of the alphabet with "zen and zucchini."

Critical studies of Meinke's work include Philip Jason's "Speaking to Us All" in *Poet Lore* (Washington, D.C.: Heldref Publications, 1982), and Eric Nelson's "Trying to Surprise God" in *Mickle Street Review* (Camden: Walt Whitman House Association, 1983).

POSSIBLE CONNECTIONS TO OTHER SELECTIONS

Galway Kinnell, "After Making Love We Hear Footsteps" (question #2, following)
James Merrill, "Casual Wear" (text p. 817)
Sharon Olds, "Sex without Love" (question #1, following)

CONNECTIONS QUESTIONS IN TEXT (p. 922) WITH ANSWERS

1. Write an essay comparing the way Olds connects sex and exercise in "Sex without Love" (p. 740) with Meinke's treatment here.

    Olds's subject is really not exercise and its obsessions, but sex. Her analogy to exercise explores the absence of mutual experience or feeling in sex without love. Meinke's concern *is* exercise. Like Olds, he sees exercise as a desperate attempt to fight off the inevitable process of aging. The difference in the poems' attitudes toward exercise is a matter of diction and theme. Whereas Olds thinks that exercise involves a competition with oneself, Meinke reveals that it is really a struggle against "death and fatty tissue." Meinke's images of exercise are darker and more colloquial.

2. Compare the voices in this poem with those in Kinnell's "After Making Love We Hear Footsteps" (p. 905). Which do you find more appealing? Why?

    Kinnell's poem celebrates a child as a sign of life and love, whereas Meinke's criticizes our culture's inability to accept death. Kinnell's poem will probably appeal to your more optimistic students; the more cynical will be comfortable with Meinke's view.

GARY SOTO, *Mexicans Begin Jogging* (p. 923)

Born in America but mistaken for a Mexican, the speaker of this poem is encouraged by his factory boss to run out the back door and across the Mexican border when the border patrol arrives. Rather than protest, the speaker runs along with a number of Mexicans, yelling *vivas* to the land of "baseball, milkshakes, and those sociologists" (line 18) who are apparently keeping track of demographics.

It is noteworthy that the speaker doesn't protest his boss's orders but joins the throng of jogging Mexicans because he is "on [the boss's] time" (11). Why wouldn't he simply stand his ground and show proof that he is a U.S. citizen? The key may lie in the word "wag" (12), which describes a comic person or wit in addition to its familiar associations with movement: to move from side to side (as in "tail"), or even to depart. The speaker's parting gesture, after all, is "a great silly grin" (21). The joke is on the boss, or the border patrol, or on America in general with its paranoid sociologists. Although the tone is somewhat comic, the subject is serious, whether students take it to be the exploitation of workers from developing nations, or prejudice based on appearance (i.e., the speaker is taken to be Mexican because he looks like he is). What effect does the tone have on a consideration of these subjects? Is there a "point" to his irony?

POSSIBLE CONNECTIONS TO OTHER SELECTIONS

Peter Meinke, "The ABC of Aerobics" (question #1, following)
Thom Ward, "Vasectomy" (text p. 920)

CONNECTION QUESTION IN TEXT (p. 923) WITH ANSWER

1.   Compare the speakers' ironic attitudes toward exercise in this poem and in Meinke's "The ABC of Aerobics" (p. 922).

Whereas each poem uses running as a vehicle for meditation, Gary Soto's speaker runs to avoid the border patrol, and the speaker of "The ABC of Aerobics" exercises for exercise's sake. For each speaker, exercise is somewhat futile: Soto's speaker doesn't really need to be running, as he is an American, and Meinke's speaker comes to realize that if he had love, it would replace the exercise. (Meinke's speaker spends lines 1–16 discussing how, regardless of exercise, the city's air is still filthy, and how it does him little good anyway because of "tobacco, lard and bourbon" [12].)

FOUND POEM

DONALD JUSTICE, *Order in the Streets* (p. 924)

The poem outlines a process, with each step in a separate stanza. As we read the poem, we observe the process with the speaker. The word *jeep,* without an article, is repeated at the beginnings of three stanzas, lending an air of impersonality to its actions, as if there were no driver. The poem is itself impersonal, reducing "Order in the Streets" to a series of mechanized steps, devoid of human presence.

POSSIBLE CONNECTION TO ANOTHER SELECTION

Sharon Olds, "Rite of Passage" (text p. 915)

24

A Study of Three Poets: Emily Dickinson, Robert Frost, and Langston Hughes

EMILY DICKINSON

There are several difficulties in teaching Dickinson. One lies in having students un-learn previous assumptions about her, assumptions dealt with wonderfully in Marilyn Nelson Waniek's "Emily Dickinson's Defunct." Emily Dickinson was, in fact, a real person, and did, from time to time, get out of the house. Dickinson can be read as a poet of passion and exuberance, as well as irony and playfulness. The popular image of her as an agoraphobic introvert has done a disservice to such readings. Emphasizing that she was an actual human being can help students find a juncture between the erotic Dickinson, the death-obsessed Dickinson, the religious Dickinson, the playful Dickinson, and so on.

In addition, students may find many of her poems to be extremely challenging, though some may seem deceptively simple. When you ask students to "get their hands dirty" with these poems, they may find that they can dig much deeper than they initially thought. The challenging poems are often difficult because of Dickinson's use of occasionally unfamiliar vocabulary, wordplay, understatement, and gaps in her poetry. You may find it useful to encourage students to bring to bear all the skills they have developed in previous chapters, including reading the poems aloud and writing about them.

ROBERT FROST

Similarly to Dickinson, Frost may have a somewhat sanitized image in the minds of some students. The introduction addresses this point, and the section from Trilling helps greatly to break down these preconceptions. If students remain unconvinced, "Home Burial" and "Out, Out — " should provide ample evidence of the dark side of Frost.

Many of Frost's poems change on a second or third close reading — the text offers "The Road Not Taken" as an example of this. "Mending Wall" and "Nothing Gold Can Stay" also exhibit this behavior. Frost can provide a good opportunity for students to pay attention to their own reading habits. You might assign short writings that ask students to not only interpret the poems, but also to notice how their interpretations might change between readings.

LANGSTON HUGHES

Of the three poets in this chapter, Hughes perhaps demands most to be read aloud: his use of blues and jazz in the structuring of his poems rewards such reading. Additionally, this section may be enriched by the inclusion of audiovisual material dealing with the Harlem Renaissance and jazz. Hughes self-consciously puts himself at the juncture of popular culture and the intellectual and political questions of his time, and you might find it useful to provide some of this background for students, or to have students do their own research and presentations on it. These presentations might be done singly or as group projects, focusing on such topics as jazz and blues music, the situation of African Americans and the struggle for civil rights during Hughes's lifetime, the history of the Harlem Renaissance, labor and radicalism in the 1930s, and so forth. Such presentations have the advantage of making a great deal of information available to the class with relatively little work on the part of any individual, and encouraging students to be active contributors of knowledge to the classroom environment.

Students' attitudes about race will be inescapable in this section. Nearly every poem in this section could be the focal point of a controversial discussion in class. You might want to foreground these issues early in the discussion, asking students to write about whether or not Hughes has any relevance to current racial issues. This will help students verbalize their own assumptions about race in a space that is not directly confrontational.

EMILY DICKINSON

If I can stop one Heart from breaking and *If I shouldn't be alive* (pp. 928, 929)

You might wish to impress on your class the difference in quality between these two poems by means of a prereading experiment. Before your students have read the introductory text for this section, show them copies of the two poems with key words removed, and have them attempt to fill in the blanks. They will probably have no trouble with phrases like "in vain," "Robin," or "his Nest again" in the first poem, but do any of them anticipate "Granite lip" in the second?

You might begin discussion of "If I can stop" by asking students to consider the comments on sentimentality and the greeting-card tradition in the text (pp. 691-694). Dickinson's relation to such popular occasional verse is, after all, not so far-fetched, since she is reputed to have honored birthdays and other social occasions by composing poems. Ask students to speculate on why this poem was so popularly successful and then to explore its limitations. The poem's simplicity and the extent to which it recounts what we *think* it should are among its popular virtues. If students have trouble seeing the poem's limitations, ask them if it is possible to live life with only one rule of conduct. Would they consider their entire lives successful if they saved one robin? You might also speculate with students on why the least common denominator of a poet's work is so often what the popular mind accepts. Recall as a parallel Walt Whitman's poem on Lincoln, "O Captain! My Captain!" — a rhymed lyric that has found its way into many high-school anthologies and may be even more popular since its use in the film *Dead Poets Society*.

"If I shouldn't be alive" is much more in keeping with Dickinson's usual ironic mode. In what ways does this poem seem to be like the previous one? What emotions are evoked by the use of the Robin in each poem? Where does "If I shouldn't be alive" break away from the world of sentimentality evoked by "If I can stop one Heart . . ."? What does the speaker's concern that she might be thought ungrateful, suggested by the second stanza, say about her? How do the speakers of these two poems differ?

As a way of enabling students to appreciate the master stroke of the "Granite lip" in the last line, you might have them rewrite the line so that it steers the poem back toward a more conventional expression.

POSSIBLE CONNECTION TO ANOTHER SELECTION ("IF I SHOULDN'T BE ALIVE")

Emily Dickinson, "Because I could not stop for Death —" (text p. 948)

The Thought beneath so slight a film — (p. 931)

Just as laces and mists (both light, partial coverings) reveal the wearer or the mountain range, so a veiled expression reveals the inner thought or opinion. Dickinson is here implying that the delicate covering makes the eye work harder to see the form behind the veil; therefore, misted objects appear in sharper outline.

Ask students to suggest other metaphors Dickinson might have used to describe the distinctness of things that are partially hidden. Depending on your class, you might be able to discuss one of the more obvious examples: whether or not seminudity is more erotic than complete nakedness. Why does Dickinson use such totally different metaphors — women's clothing and a mountain range — to make her point here? Is there any connection between the two? Do your students agree with Dickinson's premise? Are things more distinct, or simply more intriguing, when the imagination must become involved? Does one see another person's thoughts more clearly when a "film" necessitates working harder to understand, or is it just as likely that the "understanding" that results is a hybrid of two persons' thoughts?

POSSIBLE CONNECTIONS TO OTHER SELECTIONS

Emily Dickinson, "Portraits are to daily faces" (text p. 934)
——, "Tell all the Truth but tell it slant —" (text p. 951)

To make a prairie it takes a clover and one bee (p. 931)

"To make a prairie" reads like a recipe — add this to that and you will get the desired result. But it could just as well be a call for props in a theater production: take these items and add a little reflective imagination and the result will be a prairie, itself a symbol of open-endedness and freedom of spirit.

To enable students to understand the poem more clearly, you might ask them to explore the idea of essential ingredients by writing their own "recipe" poem: How do you make a family? A term paper? A painting? What happens to each of these entities as various ingredients are removed? What cannot be removed without destroying the entity or changing its character completely?

POSSIBLE CONNECTIONS TO OTHER SELECTIONS

Emily Dickinson, "I felt a Cleaving in my Mind —" (text p. 950)
Robert Frost, "Mending Wall" (text p. 979)

Success is counted sweetest (p. 932)

The power of this poem, to some degree, is its intangibility. We puzzle over how desire enables those who will never succeed to know success better than those who actually achieve it. Ask students to talk about the comparison of success to "a nectar" (line 3). It is odd that the verb *comprehend* should be paired with nectar; what does it mean to comprehend? When they begin to talk about the pairing of understanding and physical images, ask students to think about "need" (4) as both a physical and an intellectual desire for success.

You might also have students discuss the word *burst* in the final line. Are the failures the true achievers? If so, what is it they achieve?

POSSIBLE CONNECTIONS TO OTHER SELECTIONS

Emily Dickinson, "I like a look of Agony," (text p. 938)

——, "Water, is taught by thirst" (text p. 933)

John Keats, "Ode on a Grecian Urn" (question #1, following)

CONNECTION QUESTION IN TEXT (p. 933) WITH ANSWER

1. In an essay, compare the themes of this poem with those of John Keats's "Ode on a Grecian Urn" (p. 741).

   The themes of both "Success is counted sweetest" and "Ode on a Grecian Urn" have to do with wanting. Dickinson holds that success, or as she later calls it, "victory" (line 8), are "counted sweetest / by those who ne'er succeed" (1–2). In other words, the want of success makes success itself seem better. To use a cliché, the grass is always greener.... Similarly, Keats's image of the lovers forever chasing one another recalls the agony of the unsuccessful listener in Dickinson's poem. Yet the agony is not entirely negative. Consider how sweetly the success in Keats's poem is counted.

Water, is taught by thirst (p. 933)

Thematically, this poem reiterates the contention in previous Dickinson poems, such as "Success is counted sweetest" (text p. 932) and "The Thought beneath so slight a film —" (text p. 931), that the inability to grasp something physically brings its essential qualities into sharper focus. It might be interesting to have students suggest what Dickinson's pattern is in this poem. The first four lines appear to work by oppositions: water is defined by its lack, land is defined by the oceans surrounding it, transport (ecstasy) by agony, and peace by war. But how is "Memorial Mold" related to love (line 5), and how can a bird be defined in relation to snow? The images in the poem seem to move from the concrete to the abstract (although the last line seems to subvert this reading). Perhaps the reader is meant to consider the more abstract connotations of the words in the last line. What are some of the ideas or feelings that birds and snow call to mind? Are any of these ideas opposites?

POSSIBLE CONNECTIONS TO OTHER SELECTIONS

Emily Dickinson, " 'Heaven' — is what I cannot reach!" (text p. 936)

——, "I like a look of Agony," (text p. 938)

——, "Success is counted sweetest" (question #1, following)

CONNECTION QUESTION IN TEXT (p. 933) WITH ANSWER

1. What does this poem have in common with the preceding poem, "Success is counted sweetest"? Which poem do you think is more effective? Explain why.

   Both poems argue that we learn through deprivation. We gain not just through necessity, but through experiencing desperate circumstances. Students are likely to argue that this poem is more effective because it emphasizes its theme through repetition and variation. But "Success is counted sweetest" is at once more specific and broader in scope. It might be interesting to revisit this question after you have covered more of Dickinson's poetry or to have students try to isolate what they believe her most effective (or affecting) poem is.

Safe in their Alabaster Chambers — (1859 version) (p. 933) and *Safe in their Alabaster Chambers* — (1861 version) (p. 934)

Probably the most physically obvious change Dickinson made in revising this poem was the combining of the last two lines in the first stanza into one line. The latter poem seems more regular because its line and rhyme schemes are the same in both stanzas. The change also has the effect of de-emphasizing the more pleasant image of the original last two lines — the satin rafters — and emphasizing the colder, harder image of the stone. The emphasis becomes even more pronounced with the addition of the strong punctuation at the end of line 5 in the 1861 version.

The physical changes in the first stanza, coupled with a complete change of imagery for the second stanza, result in a different tone for the two versions of the poem. In the 1859 version, the dead are lamented, but life goes on around their tombs in anticipation of their eventual resurrection at the end of the world (note that in line 4 they only "sleep"). In the 1861 version of the poem, the dead "lie" in their graves and the larger universe continues in its course as though human deaths are of little importance. The second poem's mention of "Diadems" and "Doges" (9) serves to emphasize that even the fall of the earth's most powerful people makes little impact on the universe. The human relationship to nature here is more like that in Stephen Crane's "A Man Said to the Universe" (text p. 805).

You might have students note at this point Dickinson's emphasis on white, translucent things in her imagery. Have students recall such images from earlier poems. They might mention film, lace, mountain mists, or snow. Note the contrast between Dickinson's conviction that we comprehend life more clearly through the mists and Emerson's idea that we should ideally become like a "transparent eyeball" in order to know Nature.

POSSIBLE CONNECTION TO ANOTHER SELECTION (1859 version)

Emily Dickinson, "Apparently with no surprise" (text p. 967)

POSSIBLE CONNECTIONS TO OTHER SELECTIONS (1861 version)

Emily Dickinson, "Apparently with no surprise" (text p. 967)
Robert Frost, "Design" (question #1, following)

CONNECTION QUESTION IN TEXT (p. 934) **WITH ANSWER**

1. Compare the theme in the 1861 version with the theme of Robert Frost's "Design" (p. 993).

   Both poems have to do with perspective and proportion, focusing first on something small and then pulling back to examine how those smaller things fit into a larger scheme. Frost's spider and moth retain their significance despite the ironic final line, "If design govern in a thing so small." Dickinson's "meek members of the Resurrection" (line 4), by contrast, are rendered insignificant by the entire second stanza. They are faceless and unimportant; the poet does not bother to pause and observe them, unlike Frost's speaker who concentrates on the spider, moth, and flower in detail before dismissing them.

Portraits are to daily faces (p. 934)

Before asking students to discuss the analogy presented in "Portraits," you might want to remind them of the analogy sections on their SAT or ACT tests. They probably were at some point taught the strategy of making a connection between one pair of words and trying to apply it to a second pair. What happens when your students try to apply this strategy to Dickinson's poem? One difficulty is that it is hard to determine whether the comparison in the first line is meant to be taken in a positive or a negative manner. Is a portrait a daily face that is perfected and idealized, captured so that it never grows old? Or is it a static, posed rendering of something that was meant to be alive and constantly changing? The word *pedantic* in line 3 suggests a negative connotation for the second term in each analogy. The sunshine is ostentatious in its glory — in its "satin Vest." Do your students object to the characterization of bright sun as "pedantic"? After all, there is nothing inherently inferior about sunshine — or about living human faces, for that matter.

POSSIBLE CONNECTIONS TO OTHER SELECTIONS

Emily Dickinson, " 'Faith' is a fine invention" (text p. 966)
——, "Tell all the Truth but tell it slant —" (text p. 951)
——, "The Thought beneath so slight a film —" (question #3, following)
Robert Francis, "Catch" (question #1, following)
Robert Frost, "Birches" (text p. 986)
——, "Mending Wall" (text p. 979)

CONNECTIONS QUESTIONS IN TEXT (p. 935) WITH ANSWERS

1. Compare Dickinson's view of poetry in this poem with Francis's perspective in "Catch" (p. 676). What important similarities and differences do you find?

   In both poems the reader must work hard to understand the meaning. Dickinson's poem embodies this circumstance, whereas Francis's illustrates it. But we have the impression that Francis believes in authorial intention, that there is a single "point" that the reader can "get," even if that point is obscure. Dickinson's poem (and her poetry in general), presents wide gaps between the reader and poet; we are not sure if we are meant to understand exactly what one of her poems means, nor if that meaning can remain stable over multiple readings.

3. How is the theme of this poem related to the central idea in "The Thought beneath so slight a film —" (p. 931)?

   Portraits are held to be superior to daily faces presumably because they allow the viewer to interpret them and to regard them with a sense of wonder. The thought beneath a slight film also allows for interpretation and awe. In both cases, art is preferred to quotidian existence.

Some keep the Sabbath going to Church — (p. 935)

One way to help students grasp more concretely the ideas Dickinson posits here is to have them draw up a chart comparing the practices of the "I" and the "Some" in this poem. How does the level of comparison shift between the first two stanzas and the third? The most important comparisons come in the last stanza; like the Puritans, the speaker claims that his or her religious practices result in a direct relationship to God, with no middleman. While the earlier lines may suggest a "to each his own" approach to religion, stanza three leaves little room for doubting which experience the speaker considers to be "real" religion. Discuss the distinction made in the last two lines between focusing on the goal one is journeying toward and focusing on the journey itself. Which attitude do your students feel reflects their own outlook?

POSSIBLE CONNECTIONS TO OTHER SELECTIONS

Gerard Manley Hopkins, "Pied Beauty" (text p. 1099)

Walt Whitman, "When I Heard the Learn'd Astronomer" (question #1, following)

CONNECTION QUESTION IN TEXT (p. 936) WITH ANSWER

1. Write an essay that discusses nature in this poem and in Walt Whitman's "When I Heard the Learn'd Astronomer" (p. 1124).

   For both poets, nature is sacred and should be approached through direct experience rather than through the filter of other human perspectives. Although both speakers value their direct experience of nature, they contextualize it differently: for Whitman's speaker it is an alternative to science and for Dickinson's speaker it is an alternative to religion. These contexts give very different meanings to "nature." Science, especially astronomy, is a way of explaining natural phenomena, but religion is a way of providing moral instruction, a human phenomenon. Both speakers demonstrate the same impulse, but their quests differ in specific ways.

I taste a liquor never brewed — (p. 936)

As the speaker in "Some keep the Sabbath" finds true religion in nature, the speaker in this poem finds true intoxication there. While the controlling metaphor is that of drunkenness, successive stanzas of the poem relate specific images of intoxication to increasingly transcendent aspects of nature. The first four lines focus on the physical properties of the "liquor"; what the speaker drinks in from nature surpasses the finest Rhine wine (you might wish to compare this image to that of the "nectar" imbibed in "Success is counted sweetest," text p. 932).

The second stanza picks up on the effects of the "Alcohol," comparing the speaker's state to that of a person who has been drinking and is now clearly intoxicated. Why does Dickinson use the word *reeling* here rather than a more negative word such as *staggering* or *stumbling*?

The third stanza moves away from the human world to lift the speaker above even other "natural" drunks, the butterflies and bees. These creatures can be "cut off" when they've had one too many (a flower, for example, can run out of nectar), but the speaker is able to continue drinking in natural beauty as long as he or she wishes.

The fourth stanza rises to an even higher comparison, to the saints and angels in heaven. The speaker does not suggest that the heavenly creatures experience any kind of intoxication that compares to his or her inebriation. The point seems to be that the speaker will be raised to the level of "Seraphs" and "Saints," who will take notice of him or her. Does the fact that the speaker does not attribute any intoxication to the angels suggest anything about the attitude toward heaven expressed in this poem? Shouldn't celestial beings be so ecstatic about being in the presence of God that they wouldn't notice a mere human interloper?

Possible Connections to Other Selections

Emily Dickinson, "A narrow Fellow in the Grass" (text p. 2)
Galway Kinnell, "Blackberry Eating" (question #2, following)

Connection Question in Text (p. 936) with Answer

2. Discuss the tone created by the images in this poem and in Kinnell's "Blackberry Eating" (p. 832).

Dickinson's speaker is drunk on the tastes, sights, and smells of nature, but we don't have a clear sense of what those specific sensations are. Kinnell's poem appeals to our senses of touch and hearing as well as taste. Blackberries and words are palpable things that have a certain feel in one's mouth. Even the unusual adjective "icy," applied to both "black blackberries" (line 2) and "black language" (13), enhances this sensation. Ultimately, Kinnell's poem is about the specific experience of blackberry eating, which we can experience vicariously, whereas Dickinson's poem is about the effects of drinking in nature, which we must experience in our own way.

"Heaven" — is what I cannot reach! (p. 936)

You might begin discussion of this poem by having students recall other stories they have encountered that deal with the attraction of "forbidden fruit." The first stanza may allude to the story of Adam and Eve and/or to the myth of Tantalus, who was punished for trying to deceive and humiliate the gods by being placed in a pool in Hades, where the water at his feet receded every time he tried to take a drink, and the luscious fruits growing above his head moved away whenever he tried to pluck them to assuage his hunger. Can your students think of other tales that emphasize the same idea? Does this affirm or contradict their own experiences? Why does this speaker consider the unattainable to represent heaven? What does this say about him or her?

Besides the apple that is out of reach, what other images of the unattainable does Dickinson employ in this poem? The last stanza is particularly difficult in its syntax as well as its diction. How, for example, can "afternoons" (line 9) be a "decoy" (10)?

As a further topic for discussion, or as a writing assignment, you might wish to have students consider other Dickinson poems that posit a thesis similar to or different from this one.

Possible Connections to Other Selections

Diane Ackerman, "A Fine, a Private Place" (question #2, following)
Katerina Angheláki-Rooke, "Jealousy" (text p. 1138)
Emily Dickinson, "I like a look of Agony," (text p. 938)
——, "Water, is taught by thirst" (text p. 933)
Linda Hogan, "Hunger" (text p. 1160)

Connection Question in Text (p. 937) with Answer

2. Discuss the speakers' attitudes toward pleasure in this poem and in Ackerman's "A Fine, a Private Place" (p. 734).

For the speaker of this poem, pleasure is always just out of reach. She can presumably *see* the objects of her pleasure, but the experience is frustrating nonetheless, as the allusion to Tantalus makes clear. Whereas Dickinson's speaker cannot reach the apple on the tree, Ackerman's speaker is fully able to grab the peach at the end of her poem and sink her teeth into it; she is, of course, also able to experience her unusual sexual tryst and to relive it through memory. Hers is a much less inhibited attitude toward pleasure; she can and does experience it and enjoy it. Dickinson's speaker can neither experience nor enjoy the things she desires.

Of Bronze — and Blaze — (p. 937)

The speaker here takes her cue from nature, observing the splendor of the northern lights in the nighttime sky, which infect her "simple spirit" (line 8), causing her to "take vaster attitudes — / And strut upon my stem" (9-10). She uses her "Arrogance" (13) to imagine that her works will last for centuries.

The speaker's attitude toward both the northern lights and toward herself is more complex than it might appear. She builds up arrogance, following the lead of the northern sky which is "So preconcerted with itself" (4), and she feels that her "Splendors . . . will entertain the Centuries" (14, 16). Yet she also feels insignificant, strutting on something as fragile as a "stem" and imagining herself, dead, as nothing more than "An Island in dishonored Grass" (18). This conflicting attitude has something to do with her relationship to society: is the speaker trying to make some connection with humanity, or does she truly want to be like the northern lights, distant and unconcerned? She only mentions humanity in abstract or oblique ways: her splendors will entertain the *centuries* — more abstract than, say, future generations; and "Men," the object of the northern lights' disdain, are coupled with "Oxygen" (14). The speaker projects into the future to imagine herself dead: does she also seem to imagine that she is in some senses already dead to the world?

The tone of this poem shifts ever so subtly, from one of awe to one of almost morbid self-analysis. Where does the shift occur? The pattern of dashes in the first five lines slows down the rhythm in a way that alters the tone. You might want to go through a few out-loud readings of the poem until someone manages to highlight the difference between the tones of the two stanzas.

POSSIBLE CONNECTIONS TO OTHER SELECTIONS

Stephen Crane, "A Man Said to the Universe" (question #1, following)
Emily Dickinson, "I heard a Fly buzz — when I died —" (text p. 946)
John Keats, "On First Looking into Chapman's Homer" (question #2, following)
William Shakespeare, "Not marble, nor the gilded monuments" (text p. 1116)

CONNECTIONS QUESTIONS IN TEXT (p. 938) WITH ANSWERS

1. Compare the theme of this poem with that of Crane's "A Man Said to the Universe" (p. 805).

    Crane's poem posits a single man against the rest of the universe. In Dickinson's poem, the speaker acts in concert with the universe, to an extent. Dickinson's universe is, like Crane's, without obligation to the speaker, but her true sense of alienation comes from the rift between her and human society.

2. In an essay compare the sense of wonder expressed in "Of Bronze — and Blaze —" and in Keats's "On First Looking into Chapman's Homer" (p. 879).

The sense of wonder in Keats's poem is expressed in terms of discovery. The vast space he describes at the end of the poem has a different quality than the vastness that Dickinson describes. Her sense of wonder is tied up with her admiration of the "Unconcern" of the northern lights. It is as disconnected as Keats's wonder is connected.

I like a look of Agony, (p. 938)

You might want to ask your class whether the speaker in this poem has an outlook similar to or different from those of the speakers in other Dickinson poems they have read. Whereas many of the previous speakers have professed a love of things half seen, this one seems obsessed with certainty. Ask students to point out words that have to do with truth or falsehood; they will be able to find several in this short verse. Is death the only certainty for human beings? Are there any other times when it is possible to be certain that the image a person projects is an accurate one? Note also the words *I like* in line 1 and the characterization of Anguish as "homely" in the last line. Does this speaker actually find pleasure in people's death throes?

Flannery O'Connor once wrote, in justifying her use of violent encounters in her fiction, that "it is the extreme situation that best reveals what we are essentially." What would the speaker of this poem say to such a statement?

POSSIBLE CONNECTIONS TO OTHER SELECTIONS

Emily Dickinson, "The Bustle in a House" (text p. 950)
——, " 'Heaven' — is what I cannot reach!" (question #1, following)
——, "Success is counted sweetest" (question #1, following)
——, "Water, is taught by thirst" (text p. 933)

CONNECTION QUESTION IN TEXT (p. 938) WITH ANSWER

1. Write an essay on Dickinson's attitudes toward pain and deprivation, using this poem, " 'Heaven' — is what I cannot reach!" (p. 936), and "Success is counted sweetest" (p. 932) as the basis for your discussion.

   According to these poems, it would seem that Dickinson is something of an ascetic, if not a masochist. Each poem describes a blissful state that the speaker cannot achieve. Yet each poem also describes a yearning; that is, in each poem the speaker is not content with her state of deprivation and pain so much as she uses that state to gauge her emotions. In this poem, the desired condition is not necessarily death but rather honest purity. The same could be said for the other two poems as well: on the surface, the speaker inclines toward death, but unadulterated honesty — so rare in our daily lives — is at the heart of her quest.

I'm Nobody! Who are you? (p. 938)

The speaker in this poem employs great diplomacy, using the first stanza of the poem to create a "you and me against the world" camaraderie with the reader before going on to characterize that world, in the second stanza, as "an admiring Bog" (line 8). Why is it important that the reader accept the premise of the first stanza? Is a reader likely to accept it?

In line 6, the speaker compares a public person to a frog. You might have your class discuss what is meant by this, and whether or not it is an accurate simile. What is it that the speaker finds so appalling about being well known? Do your students agree that being famous would be "dreary"? Dickinson wrote in another poem that "Publication — is the Auction / Of the Mind of Man." Consider the use of the word *advertise* in line 4 of "I'm Nobody!" Is the same issue at stake in both poems, or not? Can your students think of ways in which modern celebrities auction their minds? Do they play to "an admiring Bog"?

POSSIBLE CONNECTIONS TO OTHER SELECTIONS

Emily Dickinson, "Wild Nights — Wild Nights!" (text p. 939)
Walt Whitman, "One's-Self I Sing" (question #1, following)

CONNECTION QUESTION IN TEXT (p. 939) WITH ANSWER

1. Contrast the sense of self in this poem and Walt Whitman's "One's-Self I Sing" (p. 1124).

   Dickinson's speaker finds it "dreary" (line 5) to advertise the self to society, which becomes "an admiring Bog" (8). Yet she is not entirely self-effacing. She defines herself against mainstream society, even finding another nonconformist in the addressee with whom to align herself. Whitman's speaker is interested in defining the self in accordance with society rather than against society. His self is at once "a simple separate person" (1) and part of the mass of humanity, the complete form. One variation on this question is to ask students if they believe that Whitman's speaker would celebrate the self that Dickinson's speaker projects or to ask them if they believe that her speaker fits Whitman's definition of the Modern Man in his final stanza of his poem.

Wild Nights — Wild Nights! (p. 939)

A class discussion of this poem could focus on a few well-chosen words. Researching the etymology of *luxury* (line 4) will leave no room for doubt as to the intended eroticism of the poem; it comes from the Latin *luxuria,* which was used to express lust as well as extravagant pleasures of a more general sort, which it has now come to mean. You might also discuss the use of natural imagery in the second and third stanzas. The heart in stanza two has no more need of compass or chart. Ask your students what these images mean to them. They seem to imply attention to order, rules, and laws. These images are set aside in the third stanza in favor of Eden and the sea.

A study of "Wild Nights" provides an excellent opportunity to discuss the possibility of disparity between the author of a work and the created narrator who speaks within the work. Students may wish to dismiss the eroticism of this poem if they have stereotyped Dickinson as a pure spinster in a white dress. However, the speaker of this poem cannot be specifically identified as Dickinson. Indeed, it is debatable whether the speaker is male or female.

POSSIBLE CONNECTIONS TO OTHER SELECTIONS

Margaret Atwood, "you fit into me" (question #1, following)
Emily Dickinson, "I'm Nobody! Who are you?" (text p. 938)

CONNECTION QUESTION IN TEXT (p. 939) **WITH ANSWER**

1. Write an essay that compares the voice, figures of speech, and theme of this poem with those of Atwood's "you fit into me" (p. 777).

    Atwood's poem is characterized by sarcasm and irony, as though the speaker is trying to flatter her addressee only to deflate him with a wry insult. The speaker of Dickinson's poem is much more sincere, desiring sexual union without anticipating the pain that Atwood's speaker focuses on. The imagery of this poem suggests security, whereas Atwood's imagery upends such security and replaces it with a disturbing image of pain: a fish hook in a human eye.

I cannot dance upon my Toes — (p. 940)

The speaker of this poem makes up for her bodily shortcomings with her imagination. She has never learned ballet, or rather "No Man instructed" her (line 2). Her attitude toward the ballet world is haughty; she imagines that, had she "Ballet knowledge" (5), she would "Pirouette to blanch a Troupe — / Or lay a Prima, mad" (7–8).

But the speaker is not fantasizing simply about dancing. Ballet in fact seems to be a metaphor for "the Art / I mention — easy — Here" (17–18). (The speaker admits that the scenario she describes takes place "among my mind" [3].) Is the art she mentions simply the exercise of her imagination, or is it poetry? Is she suggesting a hierarchy of art in the final line, describing the fullness of opera? In creating this hierarchy, what is her attitude toward dance? Consider the imagery in stanzas 3 and 4; does she have any use for this airy, birdlike art? Does the phrasing of the poem's first line contribute to our sense of this attitude? The final stanza may provide the most difficulty, but once students have discerned exactly what "the Art" is in line 16, they will have an easier time with "it" in the final line. Since her art is a private one, what is her attitude toward the "Audiences" (11), the applauding "House" (16), and the "Placard" (19) advertising public arts like ballet and opera?

POSSIBLE CONNECTIONS TO OTHER SELECTIONS

Emily Dickinson, "I dwell in Possibility —" (text p. 943)
——, "This is my letter to the World" (text p. 942)
——, "To make a prairie it takes a clover and one bee" (question #1, following)

CONNECTION QUESTION IN TEXT (p. 940) **WITH ANSWER**

1. Consider the power of "mind" in this poem and in "To make a prairie it takes a clover and one bee" (p. 931).

    The imagination in "To make a prairie" is imbued with vast power, needing only itself, in a pinch, to create something. In this poem, the power of the mind is somewhat more limited, yet just as powerful. The speaker conjures up audiences and transforms herself into a public performer; her art is as "full as Opera." Yet the mind here transforms; in the other poem, it creates.

What Soft — Cherubic Creatures — (p. 940)

A brief discussion of societal expectations for women in the mid–nineteenth century may help students to appreciate Dickinson's satirical intent in this poem. A woman was expected to be "the Angel in the House" who exerted a spiritual influence on those around her and made family life harmonious. In her book *Dimity Convictions: The American Woman in the Nineteenth Century* (Athens: Ohio UP, 1976), which draws its title from this poem, Barbara Welter notes that "religion or piety was the core of woman's virtue, the source of her strength," and that "religion belonged to woman by divine right, a gift of God and nature." Further, woman was to use her "purifying passionless love [to bring] erring man back to Christ." Among other evidence from mid-nineteenth-century women's magazines, Welter cites a poem that appeared in an 1847 *Ladies' Companion*. The title alone — "The Triumph of the Spiritual over the Sensual" (*Dimity Convictions* 21-22) — is enough to convey the sense of disembodied spirituality Dickinson attacks in the poem.

Ask students to notice the particular adjectives the poet uses to describe the "Gentlewomen." They are "Soft," "Cherubic" (line 1), and "refined" (6), but by the end of the poem they are "Brittle" (11). The crucial lines 7–8, which divide the positive from the negative attributes, are especially important. Not only are the women disconnected from both the human and the divine, but their attitudes would seem, by extension, to dissociate them from the central tenet of Christianity, that God became man. The last two lines make it clear that the first stanza is intended to be read satirically. How might the comparisons to "Plush" (3) and to a "Star" (4) be construed negatively? Notice the two uses of the word *ashamed*, in lines 8 and 12. Who is ashamed in each case? What is the effect of the repetition of this word?

POSSIBLE CONNECTIONS TO OTHER SELECTIONS

Emily Dickinson, " 'Faith' is a fine invention" (question #1, following)

Christina Georgina Rossetti, "Some Ladies Dress in Muslin Full and White" (text p. 1116)

CONNECTION QUESTION IN TEXT (p. 941) WITH ANSWER

1. How are the "Gentlewomen" in this poem similar to the "Gentlemen" in " 'Faith' is a fine invention" (p. 966)?

    Dickinson attacks the false faith of "gentlemen" and "gentlewomen" in these poems. Both groups pretend to be pious, but Dickinson characterizes them as hypocritical and superficial, with no clear sense of redemption and no knowledge of their souls.

The Soul selects her own Society — (p. 941)

You might begin a discussion of this poem by asking students to consider whether the image projected here matches the image of a female who spends her life in near solitude. They are likely to notice that one stereotypically assumes that a woman remains alone because she has no other choice (more so when this poem was written than today), whereas the "Soul" described here operates from a position of power. The verbs associated with the soul are all active: she "selects" (line 1), "shuts" (2), chooses (10), and closes off her attention (12), unmoved by chariots (5) or even emperors (7).

How does the meter in lines 10 and 12 reinforce what is happening in the poem at this point? What seems to be the purpose of the soul's restrictions on her society? You might have the students discuss both the limitations and the benefits of such exclusiveness. Do they think the advantages outweigh the disadvantages, or vice versa? What does the speaker of the poem think? How do you know?

Emily Dickinson, "I dwell in Possibility —" (text p. 943)

———, "Much Madness is divinest Sense —" (text p. 942)

This is my letter to the World (p. 942)

The critical gaps in this poem are wide indeed; students could debate at length about the meaning of nature's "News" (line 3) or "Message" (5), and also of "Hands I cannot see" (6). It might be good to isolate all of the descriptive words first: "simple" (3), "tender" (4), "Sweet" (7), and "tenderly" (8). These are words that might appear in an unproblematic love poem. Yet the tone of this poem does not seem to be governed by these words: why not? How would students characterize the tone? And does their impression come from the first two lines of the poem, from their knowledge of Dickinson's life, from their discussion of other poems by her, or from the mysterious (if not eerie) second stanza? Another way into the poem is to characterize its first-person subject. This poem uses the first person as much (per line) as nearly any other Dickinson poem. What is the relationship, really, between the poem's "I" and the addressee, the "Sweet countrymen" of line 7?

POSSIBLE CONNECTIONS TO OTHER SELECTIONS

Emily Dickinson, " 'Heaven' — is what I cannot reach!" (question #2, following)

———, "The Soul selects her own Society —" (question #1, following)

Donald Hall, "Letter with No Address" (text p. 1093)

Linda Pastan, "Marks" (text p. 791)

CONNECTIONS QUESTIONS IN TEXT (p. 942) WITH ANSWERS

1. In an essay compare the tone of this poem with that of "The Soul selects her own Society —" (p. 941).

   The tone of this poem is considerably more personal than that of "The Soul selects her own Society —," which seems detached by comparison. There is also something less final in this poem; there is hope that her countrymen will still judge tenderly of her, whereas "The Soul selects her own Society —" describes something final — a shut door, valves closed like stone.

2. Consider in an essay how "This is my letter to the World" might be explained using the themes in " 'Heaven' — is what I cannot reach!" (p. 936).

   A possible connection between the two poems lies in the frustration that the speaker feels: the message committed to unseen hands or the fruit or the heaven that lie beyond the speaker's grasp. What power does the speaker have over her situation, in either case?

Much Madness is divinest Sense — (p. 942)

This poem could be the epigram of the radical or the artist. For all its endorsement of "madness," however, its structure is extremely controlled — from the mirror-imaged paradoxes that open the poem to the balancing of "Assent" and "Demur" and the consonance of "Demur" and "dangerous." Try to explore with the class some applications of the paradoxes. One might think, for example, of the "divine sense" shown by the Shakespearean fool.

POSSIBLE CONNECTIONS TO OTHER SELECTIONS

Emily Dickinson, "The Soul selects her own Society —" (question #1, following)

Walt Whitman, "One Hour to Madness and Joy" (text p. 1123)

CONNECTION QUESTION IN TEXT (p. 943) WITH ANSWER

1. Discuss the theme of self-reliance in this poem and "The Soul selects her own Society —" (p. 941).

    In this poem Dickinson scorns conformity, specifically in terms of the often wrong-headed attempt to separate sense from insanity. The theme is that we must try to see beyond the notion that consensus necessarily equals what is right. (You might highlight the fact that the poem was written in 1862, at the start of the Civil War; before this period, slavery was accepted in America because it reflected a majority opinion.) Dickinson focuses on the individual in "The Soul selects her own Society —," turning the focus away from the majority and to the individual who decides for oneself what is right, good, or just by aligning oneself only with others who share the same beliefs, even if those others represent a minority.

I dwell in Possibility — (p. 943)

In the first two lines of the poem, the speaker sets up the general premise that poetry is superior to prose. The imagery employed in the next ten lines specifies the reason that the speaker values poetry. One possible strategy for teaching the poem is to explore the metaphor of the house and then return to the original premise and ask students whether they find it convincing.

As in "I taste a liquor never brewed —", the imagery in this poem moves outward from man-made, earthly examples to examples from nature to a final image of the supernatural. In lines 3 and 4, the speaker compares poetry to prose as though they were both houses. Why is it important that the comparison focuses specifically on the windows and doors of the house? The second stanza draws the metaphor outward to compare the rooms and roof of the house of poetry to entities in nature. The chambers in the house are likened to cedar trees (line 5), trees known for the durability of their wood and for their longevity. The cedars of Lebanon are also a familiar biblical allusion. According to the first book of Kings, the house of Solomon was built "of the forest of Lebanon . . . upon four rows of cedar pillars, with cedar beams upon the pillars" (vii.2); the lover in the Song of Solomon sings, "The beams of our house are cedar" (i.17). The roof of the house of poetry is compared to the sky (7–8), but again the speaker adds a qualifier — the word *everlasting* (7) — to raise this roof to an even higher level. The final word of the poem — *paradise* — ends the comparison at the farthest possible reaches of expansiveness.

Returning to the comparison made in the opening lines, students will probably see that the speaker considers poetry to be the "fairer House" on the basis of its capacity to expand, to open up to ever wider capacities. A fruitful discussion might result from the question of whether or not students agree with the speaker of this poem. Can they think of examples of prose that are expansive, or poetry that is narrow? How does the example of Dickinson's own prose — her letter to Higginson (text p. 952) — fit into this argument?

POSSIBLE CONNECTIONS TO OTHER SELECTIONS

Emily Dickinson, "The Soul selects her own Society —" (text p. 941)

T. E. Hulme, "On the Differences between Poetry and Prose" (question #1, following)

1. Compare what this poem says about poetry and prose with Hulme's comments in the perspective "On the Differences between Poetry and Prose" (p. 774).

   Hulme contrasts the symbolic nature of prose with the metaphorical and imagistic properties of poetry. For him, poetry employs a "visual concrete" language. Dickinson argues that poetry is less confined than prose, which is a different point altogether. For her, poetic language is about the endless possibilities for signification in poetry. Her version of poetry is ethereal, taking us through the "Everlasting Roof" of "The Gambrels of the Sky" (lines 7–8), whereas Hulme sees poetry as "a pedestrian taking you over the ground." Of course, for him prose is no more ethereal, but simply more direct, like "a train which delivers you at a destination." Prose for Dickinson is simply more constrained than poetry is, a house with fewer windows, inferior doors, and an actual roof.

This was a Poet — It Is That (p. 943)

In this poem the speaker defines poetry by contrasting it to ordinary experience and perception. The poet distills extraordinary perfumes from ordinary flowers, and discloses a picture that we had not seen before. The speaker endows the poet with "a Fortune — / Exterior — to Time" (lines 15–16) and depicts the rest of the world as living in "ceaseless Poverty" (12).

This poem is complicated by its first line, which sounds like a eulogy: "This was a poet." Why does the speaker use the past tense here? The tense never stays still for long — ironic given that the poem's final gesture is to declare the poet's "Fortune — / Exterior — to Time" (16). Is the speaker's intent to define the role of a poet or to make some philosophical statement about art and time? You can deepen this discussion even further by pointing out that "Attar" (4), in addition to being a perfume derived from flowers, is also the name of a thirteenth-century Persian poet. The timeless fortune of a poet also contrasts nicely with "the familiar species / That perished by the Door" (5–6), which can signify something ordinary that simply lives and dies, unlike the poet, who is extraordinary and who lives on through verse.

POSSIBLE CONNECTIONS TO OTHER SELECTIONS

Emily Dickinson, "A Bird came down the Walk" (question #2, following)

——, "I dwell in Possibility" (question #1, following)

——, "Of Bronze — and Blaze —" (text p. 937)

John Keats, "When I have fears that I may cease to be" (text p. 1103)

William Shakespeare, "Not marble, nor the gilded monuments" (text p. 1116)

CONNECTIONS QUESTIONS IN TEXT (p. 944) WITH ANSWERS

1. Write an essay about a life lived in imagination as depicted in this poem and in "I dwell in Possibility —" (p. 943).

   The first line of this poem again presents difficulty. The poet does not truly seem "exterior to time" if he or she is dead. "I dwell in Possibility —" seems much more eternal, with its final gesture of gathering Paradise.

2. Discuss "A Bird came down the Walk —" (p. 829) as an example of a poem that "Distills amazing sense / From ordinary Meanings —" (lines 2–3).

The contrast between the first and last stanzas of "A Bird came down the Walk —" demonstrates this definition well. The sense of a mundane occurrence is expanded through the poet's transformation. A bird hopping and eating becomes the source of wonderment at the vast mysteries of nature and a metaphor of humanity's humble relationship to the universe.

I read my sentence — steadily — (p. 944)

The speaker of this poem is handed a death sentence, which she reads carefully in order to ensure that she has understood it accurately. She prepares her soul to meet death, only to learn that they are already "acquainted" (line 11), even "friends" (12). In other words, the sentence is inevitable and predestined; the speaker really has no role of which to speak.

The metaphor of death as a "sentence" is also a pun, made evident by the fact that the speaker reads it, inspecting "its extremest clause" (4). Students might begin to interpret the first line to mean "I reviewed my life," or even "I revised my writing." Do either of these readings hold up throughout the poem? As a way of explaining line 7, it might help to point out that it was common for judges in nineteenth- and early twentieth-century America to follow a death sentence with the phrase "May God have mercy on your soul."

The speaker's attitude toward death will probably yield the most fruitful discussion. Her *soul* is nonchalant toward death, but where is the speaker in relation to her soul? If the soul has foreknowledge of death, what is it that causes us to fear death? Is it our bodies, frightened of decay? Is it our rational selves? Perhaps students won't think that the speaker is sincere in the final line, "And there, the Matter ends," in that she is acting blasé about the business of death as a defense mechanism against the horror of it. Point out that "Matter" could also be taken as a pun, in the sense of being both an "encounter" and matter as bodily existence (in contrast to the soul).

POSSIBLE CONNECTIONS TO OTHER SELECTIONS

Emily Dickinson, "Because I could not stop for Death" (question #1, following)
——, "I heard a Fly buzz — when I died —" (text p. 274)
——, "I like a look of Agony" (question #2, following)
Andrew Hudgins, "Elegy for My Father, Who Is Not Dead" (text p. 893)
Dylan Thomas, "Do not go gentle into that good night" (text p. 885)
Miller Williams, "Thinking About Bill, Dead of AIDS" (text p. 1125)

CONNECTIONS QUESTIONS IN TEXT (p. 945) WITH ANSWERS

1. Compare the treatment of death in this poem and in "Because I could not stop for Death —" (p. 948).

    Death is a mannered thing in both poems. There is a formality about it, like a polite but grim gentleman. Death seems to deliver the speaker somewhere in "Because I could not stop for Death —", though not in some eternal place as she had surmised. Here death is not only final, but instant; "the Matter ends" just as abruptly as the poem ends.

2. In an essay discuss the "Agony" in this poem and in "I like a look of Agony," (p. 938).

    Agony in both cases comes with death, and it seems to happen only once. You can't rehearse this agony, in other words. Yet does it really seem like agony in this poem?

The final four lines indicate that what may appear to others as "a look of agony" is actually less painful than it might appear.

The Grass so little has to do — (p. 945)

In this fantasy, the speaker wishes she had a life as simple as grass. The speaker's wish comes at the end of the poem, once the initial subject of the poem, grass, has died and been converted into hay, and after the simple life of grass has proven to be less simple than we might imagine. By metaphorically connecting grass to royalty, the speaker seems to realize that the easy life has its complications — and excitements and beauty. The final line, "I wish I were a Hay," is open to interpretation, but one implication is certainly that the speaker comes to realize that even — or especially — in death, the grass's life is one to envy.

Compared to other poems by Dickinson, this one is less difficult in terms of diction, so students may be tempted to reduce it to a single idea. You can complicate the poem's theme considerably by emphasizing the way in which the speaker personifies grass: how might another poet have conceived of grass differently? It might be interesting to have students try their hands at construing grass in ways other than Dickinson does: as something to be trod upon, mowed down, fertilized, torn up during a football game, and so on. This speaker has the sensibility of someone whose life tends toward the leisurely, it seems. There is no laboring, even during harvest time; hard work equals entertainment. Treatment of the same subject might play very differently in another poet's hands. But is the speaker sentimental? Or is she, like the speakers of so many other poems by Dickinson, preoccupied with death and with avoiding societal obligations?

POSSIBLE CONNECTIONS TO OTHER SELECTIONS

William Blake, "Ah Sun-flower" (text p. 1078)

Emily Dickinson, "Presentiment — is that long Shadow — on the lawn —" (question #1, following)

Robert Frost, "Stopping by Woods on a Snowy Evening" (question #2, folllowing)

William Wordsworth, "I Wandered Lonely as a Cloud" (text p. 467)

CONNECTIONS QUESTIONS IN TEXT (p. 945) WITH ANSWERS

1. Discuss the tone of this poem and "Presentiment — is that long Shadow — on the lawn —" (p. 777).

   Because it begins with a concept (presentiment) rather than with an object (grass), "Presentiment" feels much more philosophical than this poem does. "The Grass so little has to do —" reads like a flight of fancy by comparison, like someone making pictures out of clouds; yet its subject is ultimately serious. This difference in tone affects the way we initially approach the poem, but does it affect our interpretation of it?

2. In an essay compare the speakers' contemplation of death in this poem and in Robert Frost's "Stopping by Woods on a Snowy Evening" (p. 989).

   Since the "I" of Dickinson's poem doesn't make its presence known until the final line, death seems more abstract than it does for Frost's speaker, whom we come to know over the course of the poem. Death in Dickinson's poem seems a relief from the bustle of living, as it does in Frost's poem; but here it is less mysterious than the "lovely, dark and deep" woods of Frost's poem.

After great pain, a formal feeling comes — (p. 946)

In an interesting inversion of her often-used technique of using metaphors from life to explore the territory of death and beyond, Dickinson in this poem uses a metaphor of death — the ceremony of a funeral — to evoke an image of one who has dealt with great pain in life. It is interesting that psychologists consider the funeral ritual to be generally more valuable for the survivors than for the deceased, because this poem is about survivors and how they are able eventually to get past their pain. In addition to the controlling image of a funeral, the poet uses two other strategies to convey the idea of a place that is past pain. Dickinson's choices of words here abound in objects and adjectives that permeate the poem with a sense of numbed feelings. If you ask your students to point out some of these words, they might mention "formal" (line 1), "tombs" (2), "stiff" (3), "mechanical" (5), "wooden" (7), "Quartz" and "stone" (9), "Lead" (10), and "Snow" (12), among others.

The entire poem deals with life after the initial sharp pain of loss has subsided. Lines 12–13 concern the movement from palpable discomfort, to apathetic stupor, to true release. Ask your students if their own experiences with pain confirm or repudiate this scenario. Does the speaker hedge a bit in line 11? Are there other human rituals besides funerals by which we formally let go of pain?

POSSIBLE CONNECTIONS TO OTHER SELECTIONS

Emily Dickinson, "The Bustle in a House" (question #1, following)
Robert Frost, "Home Burial" (text p. 980)
Donald Hall, "Letter with No Address" (text p. 1153)

CONNECTION QUESTION IN TEXT (p. 946) WITH ANSWER

1. How might this poem be read as a kind of sequel to "The Bustle in a House" (p. 950)?

    The poems might be looked at as stages one goes through when coping with loss. "The Bustle in a House" describes an immediate return to daily routine following death, almost a denial about the gravity of the situation even though this bustle is the "solemnest of industries / Enacted upon Earth" (lines 3–4). This poem describes the emotions that might follow the immediate need to return to the relative order of everyday life, the gradual process that allows us to let go of our grief.

I heard a Fly buzz — when I died — (p. 946)

This poem is typical of Dickinson's work as a willed act of imagination fathoming life after death and realizing the dark void and limitation of mortal knowledge. David Porter in *Dickinson: The Modern Idiom* (Cambridge: Harvard UP, 1981) observes:

> At a stroke, Dickinson brilliantly extracted the apt metonymical emblem of the essential modern condition: her intrusive housefly. . . . The fly takes the place of the savior; irreverence and doubt have taken the place of revelation. Her fly, then, "With Blue — uncertain stumbling Buzz" is uncomprehension, derangement itself. It is noise breaking the silence, not the world's true speech but, externalized, the buzz of ceaseless consciousness. (239)

You might introduce this idea and then, either in discussion or in a writing assignment, ask the class to explore the tone of this poem and its accordance with Porter's comment.

POSSIBLE CONNECTIONS TO OTHER SELECTIONS

Emily Dickinson, "There's a certain Slant of light" (text p. 2106)
Marilyn Nelson Waniek, "Emily Dickinson's Defunct" (text p. 912)
Walt Whitman, "A Noiseless Patient Spider" (question #1, following)

CONNECTION QUESTION IN TEXT (p. 947) WITH ANSWER

1. Contrast the symbolic significance of the fly with the spider in Whitman's "A Noiseless Patient Spider" (p. 788).

    The fly in Dickinson's poem is a kind of otherworldly messenger that fills up the space between death and life. Still, there is no connection between the fly and the speaker, nor does the fly seem to belong to the other world, unlike Whitman's spider, whose job is to connect the soul with the world of the living.

One need not be a Chamber — to be Haunted — (p. 947)

This poem, in gothic fashion, describes the psychological terrors of the brain and how it can be haunted by partially repressed, horrifying memories more frightening than real horrors. The first stanza devalues external horrors in comparison to internal ones and explains that "The Brain has Corridors" (line 3) that have the potential to be far scarier than corridors in any haunted house.

You might begin discussion of this poem by asking students to explain Dickinson's comparisons between external and internal "hauntings." What words or lines most effectively characterize the speaker's fear of himself or herself? Ask your class to consider how each stanza is divided into an examination of both external and internal terrors. Each stanza concludes that the inner horrors are much harder to face than the outer ones. For example, the fourth stanza asserts that it is easier to protect oneself from an external "Assassin" (15) than it is to close the door on one's memory. You might ask your class to discuss why one's own personal "hauntings" might be scarier than facing any "External Ghost" (6).

You might also ask your students to consider the tone of this poem. Could it be read as a sort of warning? To whom and from whom? Consider also the poem as an eerie message from an insane mind. Still another vantage point would be to read the poem as a relatively objective discussion of psychological terror. Ask students what words and phrases contribute to their perception of the tone of the poem.

POSSIBLE CONNECTIONS TO OTHER SELECTIONS

Edgar Allan Poe, "The Haunted Palace" (question #1, following)
Jim Stevens, "Schizophrenia" (question #1, following)

CONNECTION QUESTION IN TEXT (p. 948) WITH ANSWER

1. Compare and contrast this poem with Poe's "The Haunted Palace" (p. 800) and Stevens's "Schizophrenia" (p. 788). In an essay explain which poem you find the most frightening.

All three poems advance the idea that minds are more likely to be haunted than structures are. All three poems also use haunted structures as metaphors for some sort of mental disorder, yet they do so in different ways. Dickinson's poem is the most direct in terms of this metaphor since it explicitly links the mind and a haunted chamber in the first stanza. Stevens's poem only intimates the connection between mind and building in the title, and Poe never explicitly makes the connection, although it is apparent to the careful reader.

Because I could not stop for Death — (p. 948)

Here is one Dickinson poem in which the speaker manages to go beyond the moment of death. The tone changes in the exact center of the poem, from the carefree attitude of a person on a day's leisurely ride through town and out into the country, to the chill of the realization that he or she is heading for the grave. However, the final images are not those of horror but of interest in the passage from time to eternity, and its ramifications.

The first line of the poem makes the reader aware of the speaker's lack of control over the situation; Death is clearly in charge. Still, as Death is described as kind (line 2) and civil (8), and as Immortality is along for the ride, the situation is not immediately threatening. In the third stanza, the carriage takes the speaker metaphorically through three stages of life: youth, represented by the school children; maturity, represented by the fields of grain; and old age, pictured as the setting sun.

Lines 13 and 14, which describe the chill felt as the sun goes down, constitute the turning point of the poem. Both the figurative language and the rhythm pattern signal a change. Dickinson abruptly reverses the alternating four-foot, three-foot metrical pattern of the first twelve lines so that line 13 contains the same number of feet as the line that immediately precedes it. The caesura after "Or rather" serves to emphasize the speaker's double take. You might wish to discuss the speaker's tone as the poem concludes.

POSSIBLE CONNECTIONS TO OTHER SELECTIONS

Emily Dickinson, "Apparently with no surprise" (question #1, following)
——, "If I shouldn't be alive" (text p. 929)
——, "I read my sentence — steadily —" (text p. 944)

CONNECTION QUESTION IN TEXT (p. 949) WITH ANSWER

1. Compare the tone of this poem with that of Dickinson's "Apparently with no surprise" (p. 967).

   Both poems cast the process of death as something methodical and mannerly. Yet this poem sounds more philosophical than "Apparently with no surprise," perhaps because its subject is human death as opposed to the cycles of nature. There are also a multitude of dashes in this poem, whereas the other one ends with a period, making it sound more like a clever observation than a deep meditation.

A Light exists in Spring (p. 949)

This poem, like the light it describes, is frustratingly evasive. The first line makes it seem as though a scene is to be described, but in actuality the speaker only sketches the roughest outline. The "Light" (line 1), the "Color" (5), even the "Lawn" (9) and "Horizons" (13) are just suggestions of a landscape. Our attention is on the landscape, but the speaker's attention is elsewhere: on the mood she perceives.

There is something irrational and ineffable about the light, and the speaker admits it by acknowledging that "Science cannot overtake" (7) its color, yet "Human Nature feels" (8) it. The light seems always just beyond our reach; in line 12, "It almost speaks" to us, and by line 16 "It passes and we stay." You might begin discussion by having students color in the picture that the speaker has sketched: what do they see? How would they describe the light? Perhaps those students versed in the visual arts could compare it to the work of an artist (like Edward Hopper, perhaps, or Winslow Homer). They are likely to describe a scene void of people, even though the subject shifts from "you" (12) to "we" (16). The word "Solitary" (6) haunts the scene. Is it possible to feel such melancholy, such "A quality of loss" (17) in public, or is this type of perception limited to those times when we are alone with nature? Such a discussion might lead into an analysis of the final two lines, in which "Trade," something apparently base existing between people, interferes with "a Sacrament," something holy existing between an individual soul and God.

POSSIBLE CONNECTIONS TO OTHER SELECTIONS

Sophie Cabot Black, "August" (text p. 785)

E. E. Cummings, "In Just-" (question #1, following)

Emily Dickinson, " 'Heaven' — is what I cannot reach!" (text p. 936)

——, "I heard a Fly buzz — when I died —" (question #2, following)

——, "There's a certain Slant of light" (question #2, following)

Margaret Holley, "Peepers" (text p. 764)

William Carlos Williams, "Spring and All" (text p. 1126)

CONNECTIONS QUESTIONS IN TEXT (p. 949) WITH ANSWERS

1. Discuss the treatment of spring in this poem and in Cummings's "in Just-" (p. 902).

   The isolation of this poem contrasts nicely with Cummings's "in Just-", which is a celebration of the social rites of spring. The world of "A Light exists in Spring" seems far from "puddle-wonderful."

2. In an essay compare Dickinson's use of "light" in this poem, in "I heard a Fly buzz — when I died —" (p. 946), and in "There's a certain Slant of light" (p. 2082).

   The light in this poem is mysterious, similar to the mystery of life and sight in her "I heard a Fly buzz — when I died —". In "There's a certain Slant of light," light is palpable, a physical object "That oppresses, like the Heft / of Cathedral Tunes" (lines 3–4). This simile is also somewhat evasive since it compares the weight of light to the weight of sound, neither of which has any mass. Is light in Dickinson's poetry meant to illuminate something, or does it serve to create a pictorial effect of some kind?

I felt a Cleaving in my Mind — (p. 950)

This poem describes an experience of mental disintegration or serious psychological strain. The speaker relates the feeling that his or her "Brain had split" (line 2), and that as a result, the speaker's thoughts become increasingly disjointed. Eventually they seem to unravel, like balls of yarn rolling across the floor. You might discuss with your students this likening of the unraveling balls of yarn (7–8) to a mental breakdown. Ask them what is so effective about connecting the homely, domestic image of yarn with the anguish of psychological decay.

Structured in perfect iambic pentameter and incorporating full rhymes, this Dickinson poem is unusual in its regularity. Much of the power of "I felt a Cleaving" lies in its sharp contrast between form and content. Discuss with your students the disparity between its smooth patterns of rhythm and rhyme and its disturbing theme. Point out that the first stanza reads almost like a jingle — how do the soothing musical qualities of the poem increase the horror of the experience? Poetically, the speaker's thoughts are joined together seamlessly, in perfect sequence. Yet this is precisely what the speaker claims is impossible for him or her to do. Ask your students to speculate why Dickinson would write such a smooth poem to describe such a jarring experience.

You might also consider asking your students to investigate the dictionary meanings of several words in this poem. Interestingly, "cleave" is defined as both "to separate" and "to adhere," and "ravel," which is actually a synonym for "unravel," means both "to entangle" and "to disentangle." You might ask your students to consider some of the possible implications of these double meanings.

POSSIBLE CONNECTIONS TO OTHER SELECTIONS

Emily Dickinson, "To make a prairie it takes a clover and one bee" (question #1, following)
John Keats, "Ode to a Nightingale" (text p. 851)

CONNECTION QUESTION IN TEXT (p. 950) WITH ANSWER

1. Compare the power of the speaker's mind described here with the power of imagination described in "To make a prairie it takes a clover and one bee" (p. 931).

    The speaker in this poem is relatively powerless. The cleaving of her mind is beyond her control, and she is not able to mend it, as when one wakes from a dream and tries to fall asleep again to see how it will turn out. In "To make a prairie" the mind has the power to create even without the things of the earth, but it is unclear whether the mind has the power to consciously create in itself a state of reverie.

The Bustle in a House (p. 950)

The images in this poem suggest that getting on with mundane, everyday activities helps us to move beyond the pain of death. In contrast, the use of the funeral metaphor in "After great pain" (text p. 946) promotes the idea that a formal ritual helps us to accomplish this purpose. You might ask students which method strikes them as being more effective. Look closely at the diction in line 7. The phrase "We shall not want" echoes the Twenty-third Psalm, a hymn of comfort and confidence in God's support at the time of death. But does the expression also imply that even though we don't want to deal with any thought other than being reunited with the loved one in eternity, the reality may not be so simple?

In *Literary Women* (Garden City: Doubleday, 1976), Ellen Moers claims that "Emily Dickinson was self-consciously female in poetic voice, and more boldly so than is often recognized" (61). Does the imagery in this poem confirm or repudiate Moers's assertion? Ask your students to consider the many speakers they have encountered in Dickinson's poems. Is her poetic voice generally identifiable as female? If so, how? If not, how would you characterize her poetic voice(s)?

POSSIBLE CONNECTIONS TO OTHER SELECTIONS

Emily Dickinson, "After great pain, a formal feeling comes —" (text p. 946)
——, "I like a look of Agony," (question #2, following)
Donald Hall, "Letter with No Address" (text p. 1153)
Carolynn Hoy, "In the Summer Kitchen" (text p. 916)

CONNECTION QUESTION IN TEXT (p. 951) WITH ANSWER

2. How does this poem qualify "I like a look of Agony," (p. 938)? Does it contradict the latter poem? Explain why or why not.

    The focus of the two poems is slightly different since there is no "I" in this poem. "I like a look of Agony," raises questions about the speaker, whereas this poem states a more objective truth. Yet both poems treat the subject of death and its effects, and in that respect there is a slight contradiction between them since this one ends with the notion of eternity, whereas "I like a look of Agony" concentrates on the physical death of a person without alluding to the state of the soul afterward.

Tell all the Truth but tell it slant — (p. 951)

You might open consideration of "Tell all the Truth" by having students discuss how the speaker characterizes "Truth." The imagery used here centers around the idea of light; in only eight lines, the poet uses "slant" (line 1), "bright" (3), "Lightning" (5), "dazzle" (7), and "blind" (8), besides the punning reference in the word *delight* (3). The speaker considers direct truth to be a light so powerful that it is capable of blinding. Students may suggest other contexts in which they have seen this idea expressed. Biblical stories often recount appearances of God as a light too blinding to be looked at directly. What is it about Truth, which after all only allows us to see things as they really are, that is potentially so destructive?

Don't let your students miss the exquisite word choices in lines 3 and 4 as Dickinson contrasts human fallibility — "our infirm Delight" (De-light?) — with the perfection of "Truth's superb surprise."

How does poetry in general affirm this poem's thesis? Would you expect a writer who believed this premise to prefer writing poetry to writing prose?

POSSIBLE CONNECTIONS TO OTHER SELECTIONS

Emily Dickinson, "I know that He exists" (question #1, following)
——, "Portraits are to daily faces" (text p. 934)
——, "The Thought beneath so slight a film —" (text p. 931)

CONNECTION QUESTION IN TEXT (p. 951) WITH ANSWER

1. How does the first stanza of "I know that He exists" (p. 967) suggest an idea similar to this poem's? Why do you think the last eight lines of the former aren't similar in theme to this poem?

    Both poems argue that the truth is not necessarily obvious or that the deepest truths are cloaked in mystery. The difference in theme between the two poems has to do with the difference of the subjects: the implications of "truth" are not as grave as the implications of God's existence.

From all the Jails the Boys and Girls (p. 951)

Here is a perfect poem for the last day of the semester! Dickinson captures the joy and energy of children released from school by playing trios of images against one another. The "Jails" of the first line and the "Prison" and "keep" — a pun that evokes both a sense of being held and the medieval image of a castle dungeon — in the fourth express the confinement the children endure during the school day. The released prisoners "leap" (line 2), and "storm" and "stun" (5) the world into which they escape. The sense of attacking life to demand everything it has to give is unmistakable, especially when one considers the use of transcendent words such as "ecstatically" (2), "beloved" (3), and "bliss" (6). The triple alliteration of *F*s in the last two lines attempts to bring things back down to earth. You might ask your students whether or not the last two lines have the tempering effect that the bearers of the frowns hope to convey. With which feeling does the end of the poem leave students?

POSSIBLE CONNECTIONS TO OTHER SELECTIONS

William Blake, "The Garden of Love" (text p. 1078)

Cornelius Eady, "The Supremes" (text p. 1150)

Robert Frost, " 'Out, Out —' " (question #2, following)

Judy Page Heitzman, "The Schoolroom on the Second Floor of the Knitting Mill" (text p. 1158)

CONNECTION QUESTION IN TEXT (p. 952) WITH ANSWER

2.   In an essay discuss the treatment of childhood in this poem and in Robert Frost's " 'Out, Out —' " (p. 987).

Both poems — particularly Frost's bleak allusion to *Macbeth* — paint a fairly depressing portrait of childhood. Frost's picture indicates, not only by the more obvious "child at heart," "doing a man's work" (line 24), but also the apron-clad sister, that the children in this poem work, and work hard. Furthermore, the parents, after their extremely brief horror, return to work. Childhood is hard in " 'Out, Out —' ". Similarly, Dickinson's children of "solid bliss" (6) come out of the "Jails" (1) (presumably of their homes), and have fun, only to return in the end to their parents, who are their "foes" (8) and wear predatory "Frowns" (7).

The difference between the two poems, however, is that in Frost's poem, life seems hard for everybody. Perhaps it is so for the "Frowns" in "From all the Jails the Boys and Girls," but it is never stated. One last note: the children in Dickinson's poem actually do have a little fun. Frost doesn't indicate any such thing in " 'Out, Out —' ".

PERSPECTIVES ON DICKINSON

Dickinson's Description of Herself (p. 952)

Probably the most immediately evident characteristic of Dickinson's personal correspondence is that, as in her poetry, the language comes in spurts interspersed with an abundance of dashes. Also, as in her poetry, she uses numerous metaphors. Have your students explore some of these metaphors, such as Dickinson's reference to criticism of her poetry as "surgery" (paragraph 2) and her discussion of "undressed thought" (3). Do such metaphors hide or clarify her meaning?

Dickinson's comment that she had written only "one or two" poems before that winter, when in fact she had written nearly three hundred, could lead to a discussion of the constructed self that appears even in personal correspondence. Have your students consider how they might write about last weekend's party in a letter to their parents as opposed to a letter to their best friend from high school. Without necessarily being dishonest, we generally shape any presentation of self depending on how we wish to appear to a particular audience. How do you suppose Dickinson appeared to Higginson when he first read this letter?

THOMAS WENTWORTH HIGGINSON, *On Meeting Dickinson for the First Time* (p. 953)

The first part of Higginson's letter to his wife reports his encounter with Emily Dickinson at her home in Amherst in a fairly straightforward fashion. If your students have read the poet's letter describing herself to Higginson, you might ask them to consider how closely the poet's description of herself matches his observations. Although Higginson refers to the poet's manner and appearance as childlike three times in a short space, he is also struck by her wisdom when she begins to speak to him.

Dickinson's definition of poetry would be an interesting topic for class discussion. Students might be encouraged to talk about the aptness and/or the limitations of her definition. Should all poetry produce the violent reaction in a reader that she describes? Would Dickinson's own works qualify as poetry according to her definition? The last comments of Dickinson that Higginson records, concerning her relation to the outside world, also merit consideration. Why would she have such an extreme reaction to the thought of mixing in society? Which of her comments might Mrs. Higginson have considered foolish?

MABEL LOOMIS TODD, *The* Character *of Amherst* (p. 954)

While Todd refers to Emily Dickinson both as a character and as a myth, her examples in this letter tend to cast Dickinson more as a ghost; several times she notes that no one ever sees the poet. None of her characterizations of Dickinson is particularly positive. Referring to someone as a "character" usually denotes unusual, even amusing behavior, and portraying that person as a ghost suggests that that person has no substance. Todd does not even use the term *myth* in its powerful, archetypal sense, but more to connote something unreal or not to be believed. The comments in this letter would seem to negate Dickinson's thesis, often stated in her poetry, that things seen half-veiled are more clearly seen than things in plain view. You might ask students what Todd's observations about Dickinson reveal about Todd herself and about the way Dickinson may have been perceived by her Amherst neighbors. As a topic for writing or for class discussion, you may wish to have your students piece together information from this letter and the previous two in order to produce a composite "portrait" of Emily Dickinson. However, what may emerge from these pieces is the enigmatic quality of her character.

RICHARD WILBUR, *On Dickinson's Sense of Privation* (p. 954)

According to Wilbur, Dickinson's fascination with the concept of want, both human and personal, emerges in her poetry in two ways. Her apprehension of God as a distant, unresponsive deity compels her to write satirical poetry protesting this situation on behalf of other human beings. However, the poet who rages against an uncaring creator on behalf of her fellow creatures also tolerates such privations and emulates such aloofness on a personal level. For Dickinson, "less is more" is merely another Christian paradox to be savored, such as the paradoxes of dying to live or freeing oneself by becoming a slave. In fact, depriving herself of everything possible, especially human companionship, seems to have been Dickinson's technique for achieving that appreciation for and knowledge of what she and other humans were missing that inspired her poetry. You may wish to have your students discuss this second premise more thoroughly; it may be a difficult concept for those not accustomed to dealing with paradox. Do they see any parallels in their own lives or in the culture at large to the idea that, as Wilbur says, "privation is more plentiful than plenty"? Can they think of times when deprivation has produced positive results, or do they feel that Dickinson uses this highly contradictory premise as a rationalization for her own eccentricities?

SANDRA M. GILBERT AND SUSAN GUBAR, *On Dickinson's White Dress* (p. 955)

You might wish to preface your discussion of this piece with a freewriting exercise in which your students explore their own associations with whiteness. Do their connotations mostly involve positive qualities, negative qualities, or nothingness? Gilbert and Gubar contrast William Sherwood's assertion that Dickinson's white dress was a sign of her commitment to the Christian mystery of death and resurrection with Melville's suggestion that whiteness may be the "all-color of atheism." They go on to suggest that whiteness may have been, for Dickinson, the perfect expression of a fascination with paradox and irony, that she was drawn to the color precisely because it was capable of representing opposite ends of any spectrum. You might ask your students whether they find any of the above theories convincing before having them propose their own theories as to why Dickinson wore only white (see question #3 in the text, p. 956).

You might caution your students that Gilbert and Gubar's characterization of the dress on display at the Dickinson homestead as "larger than most readers would have expected" is not shared by all who have seen it. Given the feminist perspective of Gilbert and Gubar's work, why might they emphasize the size of Dickinson's dress in this manner?

KARL KELLER, *Robert Frost on Dickinson* (p. 956)

Using Frost's words about Dickinson, Keller suggests that Frost had mixed feelings about his predecessor's deviations from regular rhyme and meter. On the one hand, two of Keller's quotes from Frost specifically mention that Frost feels Dickinson's strength in these situations, as though her urgency to communicate truth clashed with the limitations of form and she was determined that truth emerge the winner. On the other hand, another Frost quote attributes Dickinson's variations to her haste to move along to the next poem, a sign of weakness rather than strength. You might wish to have your students discuss whether or not these comments are necessarily inconsistent. Could Frost have found Dickinson's battles with form appropriate in some poems and careless in others? Could he have found her flouting the principles of rhyme and meter generally inappropriate, but admirable in some respects? What is Keller trying to prove by using these particular quotes? Does he suggest that they are contradictory?

Frost's comments about poetry give us another definition to think about. Do your students agree that "Poetry is play. . . . Poetry is fooling"? Does Frost seem to be talking about writing poetry, reading poetry, or both?

As a writing or a discussion topic, you might have your students respond to Frost's assertion, "I deny in a good poem or a good life that there is compromise."

CYNTHIA GRIFFIN WOLFF, *On the Many Voices in Dickinson's Poetry* (p. 958)

Wolff acknowledges the multiplicity of voices represented by the speakers in Dickinson's poems, from child to housewife to passionate woman to New England Puritan. However, she insists that the presence of these different voices affirms cohesion rather than indicates a fragmentation of the poet's psyche. According to Wolff, what the voices have in common is a concern with specific human problems, particularly those problems that threaten "the coherence of the self." Thus, the many voices become not a difficulty to be overcome but a tool by which the poet seeks to overcome difficulties. Wolff is especially adamant in her assertion that the voice selected for any particular poem does not represent the poet's particular mood of the moment, but is a "calculated tactic," a part of her artistic technique, an aspect of an individual poem that is as carefully chosen as any of the poem's words might be.

In discussing this passage, you might ask your students to consider whether they have different "voices" for different occasions and what determines how they speak at any given time. Do they get a sense of unity in reading Dickinson's poetry? If it is true that Dickinson again and again returns to the idea of encounters that threaten "the coherence of the self," what are some of these encounters, and in what ways are they threatening?

PAULA BENNETT, *On "I heard a Fly buzz — when I died —"* (p. 959)

According to Bennett, the fly in Dickinson's poem represents humankind's ignorance of what awaits us after death. This ignorance is dramatically emphasized in Dickinson's poem by the dying speaker, who, anticipating a divine experience at her death, is shocked when she is assailed by the buzzing of a fly instead. Ask students if they agree with Bennett's assertion that Dickinson's conclusion about death and the afterlife in this poem is that "we don't know much." Are there other ways to interpret Dickinson's depiction of the dying moment? Is Dickinson's poem necessarily, as Bennett puts it, a "grim joke" about the fate of human corpses — to be devoured by flies?

JOAN KIRKBY, *On the Fragility of Language in Dickinson's Poetry* (p. 960)

According to Kirkby, the abyss in Dickinson's poetry appears "in the moment of transition between an old meaning and a new meaning" of a word or words. The power of Dickinson's poetry derives from her ability to span this abyss between meanings and transform language into more potent and "dangerous" forms. You might begin discussing this perspective with your students by asking them to point out moments in Dickinson's poems in which she "challenge[s] familiar and comfortable assumptions" about the meanings of particular words. Discussing how Dickinson uses unusual combinations of words in order to create meaning may lead to a better understanding of this concept of the abyss. You might also ask your students to respond to Kirkby's description of language as potentially "frightening" or "inadequate." In what ways does Dickinson's poetry seem to corroborate this statement?

GALWAY KINNELL, *The Deconstruction of Emily Dickinson* (p. 961)

The speaker of this poem arrives at a public lecture on Dickinson late. He tries to contribute to the conversation about Dickinson and publication by reciting one of her poems, but he is interrupted by the professor. He would like to retort with some snappy witticism when the professor allows him to continue, but he finds himself weakly reciting the poem, "like a schoolboy called upon in class" (line 53). His final gesture is to return to his private dialogue with Dickinson, one which he keeps up in his mind, "But she was silent" (66).

The speaker feels that the professor's approach to Dickinson's poetry and/or her life overlooks the poetry in favor of the critical method, by seeking to unearth meaning by digging into the etymology of words and revealing their ambiguity. The speaker criticizes the professor for failing to listen to Dickinson (30), for wanting to hear himself speak rather than to hear the words of the author (34–35), and for misunderstanding the context of Dickinson's words as he delves into etymology (46). The irony is that the speaker never *says* any of this in public. Like Dickinson, he is trapped by his own shyness, or his reluctance to be a public spectacle, and his one public gesture of reciting the poem fails because he is unable to speak with forcefulness after the professor's spiel. It is also ironic that the speaker arrives after the lecture takes place, indicating that he did not care to hear it, but still feels the need to contribute. Perhaps this line of inquiry might help students respond to the question about the difference between a poet's response and a critic's response to poetry: where do their differing senses of authority come from? (Note that "authority" begins with the word "author," and recall the professor's etymological reading.) Have students witnessed people at lectures, or even in classes, who always feel the need to voice their opinion or to argue with the point that is being presented?

At some point during this discussion, you might want to bring your discussion of the theme of the poem back to Dickinson: why is this type of critique-in-poetry particularly useful when applied to a poet like Dickinson? Is she a poet whose words are meant to be "uprooted" (29), or is it best just to "listen" (30) to her? Which other poets might be equally appropriate for such a discussion, and why? And what of Dickinson's silence at the end of the poem: has she failed the speaker, or has he failed her? Is his connection to her superficial, or is her presence in the poem meant to tell us something deep about the speaker's experience? One final point to consider is the striking difference between Kinnell's poem and Dickinson's poetry in terms of form, language, and rhythm. Can students discern any similarities between Kinnell's poetics and Dickinson's? Would it have been appropriate, or even possible, to write this poem in Dickinson's style, with elliptical dashes, irregular capitalization, and steady rhythm?

POSSIBLE CONNECTIONS TO OTHER SELECTIONS

Marilyn Nelson Waniek, "Emily Dickinson's Defunct" (text p. 912)
Miller Williams, "Excuse Me," (text p. 708)

TWO COMPLEMENTARY CRITICAL READINGS

CHARLES R. ANDERSON, *Eroticism in "Wild Nights — Wild Nights!"* (p. 963)

Anderson finds, in the declaration "Wild Nights should be / Our luxury" (lines 4–5), the image that contains all the other images in Dickinson's poem. According to Anderson, Dickinson's theme is that love is intense but temporal. He discusses the poem's other images, such as those of Eden and storms, in terms of how they emphasize these qualities of love. Each figure the poet uses, from Anderson's perspective, contains a double reference to ecstasy and brevity, and the phrase "Wild Nights" refers to the tumult outside and inside the lovers' paradise. Anderson's argument is consistent and brings all the major figurative language of the poem together in support of a common theme. What he does not deal with in depth is the "frank eroticism" of the poem that he mentions at the beginning of his discussion. You might ask your students how erotic they find the poem to be. Is it truly sensual, or does it just upset our expectations of this particular poet? Another possible topic for discussion is the relationship of this poem to themes found in Dickinson's other work. Is her frequent emphasis on how the narrowness of an experience intensifies our response to it connected with the qualities of love she foregrounds here?

DAVID S. REYNOLDS, *Popular Literature and "Wild Nights — Wild Nights!"* (p. 964)

Reynolds contrasts the rhetoric of Dickinson's poem with that of the sensational literature of her day to support his thesis that the greatness of Dickinson's "Wild Nights" lies in its being erotic and distinct from the lesser literature of the genre. He argues that in the first stanza, the yoking of the sensational adjective "wild" to the natural image of the "Night" serves to "purify" sexual desire (note that Reynolds ignores Dickinson's use of the word *luxury*, which Anderson focused on in the previous piece in order to highlight the poem's eroticism). In the next stanza, the more abstract natural images of sea and harbor further distance the passion expressed in the poem from crude sensationalism. The reference to "Eden," in the last stanza, adds a religious quality to the images that precede it. The cumulative effect, according to Reynolds, is the expression of intense but unconsummated sexual longing without the accompanying connotations of prurience. One question for students to consider, assuming they find Reynolds's argument convincing, is whether or not sexual passion abstracted in this way remains erotic.

ADDITIONAL DICKINSON POEMS ACCOMPANYING QUESTIONS FOR WRITING ABOUT AN AUTHOR IN DEPTH

"Faith" is a fine invention (p. 966)

This poem highlights a witty, even satirical side of Dickinson. Have students note the words that define each of the alternative ways of seeing. "Faith" is an "invention" (line 1), and microscopes are "prudent" (3). When examining Dickinson's diction, it is helpful to note the variety of possible definitions for ordinary words used in an unusual manner. *Invention* not only means a created or fabricated thing; it also carries the more archaic sense of an unusual discovery or a find. Likewise, while *prudence* has a rather stilted, utilitarian ring to it in the twentieth century, it once meant having the capacity to see divine truth. You might want to ask your class whether they feel the speaker favors religion or science. Since both faith and microscopes are meant to help people perceive directly rather than through a mist, is it possible that the poet favors neither side in this argument?

Ask your students what they think of Charles R. Anderson's comment on this poem in *Emily Dickinson's Poetry* (New York: Holt, 1960): "This is a word game, not a poem" (35).

POSSIBLE CONNECTIONS TO OTHER SELECTIONS

Emily Dickinson, "Portraits are to daily faces" (text p. 934)

——, "What Soft — Cherubic Creatures —" (text p. 940)

325

I know that He exists (p. 967)

Dickinson here seems to be at the cutting edge of modern sensibility and its dare-seeking fascination with death. The poem begins as a testimony of faith in the existence of a God who is clearly an Old Testament figure. If you ask students how the poem's speaker characterizes this deity, they may note the attributes of refinement, hiddenness, and removal from the gross affairs of earthly life. With this in mind, the tone of the next stanza, in which God seems to be the orchestrator of a cosmic game of hide-and-seek between Himself and whichever of His creatures will play, and in which the reward is "Bliss" (line 7), may be puzzling to students. The word *fond* in line 6 begins to sow a seed of doubt about the rules of this game. Does it mean "affectionate" or is it being used in its older sense of "foolish"?

In the third stanza, the speaker more fully comprehends the meaning of the game: finding God can mean finding oneself in God at the moment of death. Instead of death being a discovery that begins a condition of everlasting bliss, one may be confronted with an abrupt and everlasting ending. "Death's — stiff — stare" (12) caps three lines of halting verse, further emphasized by the hardness of the alliteration (you may wish to read these lines aloud so that students will appreciate their impact). By the third stanza, the ironic barb pierces through the texture of ordinary language. Instead of saying that the joke has gone too far, the speaker substitutes the verb *crawled,* which summons up the image of the serpent in the Garden of Eden in addition to bringing the lofty language of the first stanza down to earth.

This poem receives a brief but adequate discussion in Karl Keller's *The Only Kangaroo among the Beauty* (Baltimore: Johns Hopkins UP, 1979, p. 63). Keller observes that the "tone of voice moves from mouthed platitude to personal complaint." Ask your students if they agree with this assessment.

POSSIBLE CONNECTIONS TO OTHER SELECTIONS

Emily Dickinson, "Tell all the Truth but tell it slant —" (text p. 951)
Robert Frost, "Design" (text p. 993)

I never saw a Moor — (p. 967)

This straightforward profession of faith follows a pattern of expansion of imagery from the natural to the supernatural. Despite its simplicity, it reflects sound theology; one of the basic theological proofs of the existence of God is the existence of the universe. Ask your students if the poem would be as effective if the first stanza relied on images of man-made things such as the Pyramids. Why or why not? How would it change the impact of the poem if the stanzas were reversed?

POSSIBLE CONNECTION TO ANOTHER SELECTION

Emily Dickinson, " 'Heaven' — is what I cannot reach!" (text p. 936)

Apparently with no surprise (p. 967)

While a first reading of "Apparently with no surprise" seems to present the reader with a picture of death in an uncaring, mechanistic universe overseen by a callous God, a closer look reveals a more ambiguous attitude on the part of the speaker. Most of the poem deals with an ordinary natural process, an early-morning frost that kills a flower.

Framing this event is the viewpoint of the speaker, who acknowledges by means of the word *apparently* that his or her perspective may not be correct. According to the speaker, God is not involved in the event, other than to observe and to approve, as the speaker apparently does not. An examination of the adjectives and adverbs used in the poem reinforces the uncertainty of tone for which we have been prepared by the opening word. "No surprise" (line 1), "accidental power" (4), and the Sun proceeding "unmoved" (6) suggest a vision of nature as devoid of feeling. However, how can anything proceed and at the same time be *un*moved? How can power be used forcefully, as "beheads" (3) and "Assassin" (5) imply, and yet be accidental? The description of the frost as a "blonde Assassin" in line 5 is particularly worth class discussion. Does the noun *Assassin* suggest that the frost is consciously evil? What about the adjective *blonde*? You may wish to have your students recall other images of whiteness in Dickinson's poetry. Can they come to any conclusions as to the connotations this color has for her?

POSSIBLE CONNECTIONS TO OTHER SELECTIONS

Emily Dickinson, "Because I could not stop for Death —" (text p. 948)

——, "Safe in their Alabaster Chambers —" (1859 version) (text p. 933)

ADDITIONAL RESOURCES FOR TEACHING DICKINSON

SELECTED BIBLIOGRAPHY

Anderson, Charles R. *Emily Dickinson's Poetry.* New York: Holt, 1960.

Bennett, Paula. *Emily Dickinson: Woman Poet.* Iowa City: U of Iowa P, 1990.

Bloom, Harold, ed. *Emily Dickinson.* New York: Chelsea, 1985.

Chase, Richard. *Emily Dickinson.* New York: William Sloane Assocs., 1951.

Dickinson, Emily. *The Complete Poems of Emily Dickinson.* Ed. Thomas H. Johnson. Boston: Little, 1955.

——. *The Letters of Emily Dickinson.* Ed. Thomas H. Johnson and Theodora Ward. Cambridge: Belknap Press of Harvard UP, 1958.

——. *The Master Letters of Emily Dickinson.* Ed. Ralph W. Franklin. Amherst: Amherst College P, 1986.

Diehl, Joanne Feit. *Dickinson and the Romantic Imagination.* Princeton: Princeton UP, 1981.

Farr, Judith. *The Passion of Emily Dickinson.* Cambridge: Harvard UP, 1992.

Ferlazzo, Paul J., ed. *Critical Essays on Emily Dickinson.* Boston: Hall, 1984.

Johnson, Thomas H. *Emily Dickinson: An Interpretive Biography.* New York: Atheneum, 1955.

Juhasz, Suzanne, ed. *Feminist Critics Read Emily Dickinson.* Bloomington: Indiana UP, 1983.

Leyda, Jay. *The Years and Hours of Emily Dickinson.* New Haven: Yale UP, 1960.

Orzeck, Martin and Robert Weisbuch, eds. *Dickinson and Audience.* Ann Arbor: University of Michigan Press, 1996.

Patterson, Rebecca. *Emily Dickinson's Imagery.* Amherst: U of Massachusetts P, 1979.

Porter, David. *Dickinson, the Modern Idiom.* Cambridge: Harvard UP, 1981.

Smith, Martha Nell. *Rowing in Eden: Rereading Emily Dickinson.* Austin: U of Texas P, 1992.

Stocks, Kenneth. *Emily Dickinson and the Modern Consciousness: A Poet of Our Time.* New York: St. Martin's, 1988.

Stonum, Gary Lee. *The Dickinson Sublime.* Madison: U of Wisconsin P, 1990.

Wardrop, Daneen. *Emily Dickinson's Gothic: Goblin with a Gauge.* Iowa City: University of Iowa Press, 1996.

AUDIOVISUAL RESOURCES

Emily Dickinson: The Belle of Amherst. 90 min., color, 1980. Beta, VHS, ¾″ U-matic cassette. With Julie Harris. Distributed by Cifex Corporation.

Emily Dickinson: A Brighter Garden [recording]. 1 cassette (15 min.). Distributed by Spoken Arts.

Emily Dickinson: A Certain Slant of Light. 29 min., color, 1978. Beta, VHS, ¾″ U-matic cassette, 16-mm film. Explores Dickinson's life and environment. Narrated by Julie Harris. Distributed by Pyramid Film and Video.

Emily Dickinson. 22 min., color, 1978. Beta, VHS, ¾″ U-matic cassette. A film about the poet and her poems. Part of the "Authors" series. Distributed by Journal Films Inc.

Emily Dickinson [recording]. 1 cassette. Distributed by Recorded Books.

Emily Dickinson: Poems and Letters [recording]. 2 cassettes. Distributed by Recorded Books.

Emily Dickinson Recalled in Song [recording]. 1 cassette (30 min.). Distributed by Audio-Forum.

Emily Dickinson: Magic Prison — A Dialogue Set to Music. 35 min., color, 1969. Beta, VHS, ¾″ U-matic cassette, 16-mm film. Dramatizes the letters between Dickinson and Colonel T. W. Higginson. With an introduction by Archibald MacLeish and music by Ezra Laderman. Distributed by Britannica Films.

Emily Dickinson: An Interpretation with Music. 18 min., color, VHS. A musical presentation of "Because I could not stop for Death —". Distributed by Films for the Humanities and Sciences.

Emily Dickinson: Selected Poems [recording]. 4 cassettes (360 min.), 1993. Read by Mary Woods. Distributed by Blackstone Audio Books.

Emily Dickinson: A Self-Portrait [recording]. 2 cassettes (90 min.). Distributed by Caedmon/HarperAudio, Filmic Archives.

Fifty Poems of Emily Dickinson [recording]. 1 cassette (45 min.). Distributed by Dove Audio.

Poems and Letters of Emily Dickinson [recording]. 1 cassette. Distributed by Caedmon/HarperAudio.

Poems by Emily Dickinson [recording]. 2 cassettes (236 min.), 1986. Distributed by Audio Book Contractors.

Poems of Emily Dickinson [recording]. 1 cassette. Distributed by Spoken Arts.

Poems of Emily Dickinson & Lizette Woodworth Reese [recording]. 1 cassette (60 min.), 1981. Unabridged edition. Part of the "Poetic Heritage Series." Distributed by Summer Stream.

Seventy-Five Poems [recording]. 2 cassettes (2 hrs., 15 min.), 1990. Distributed by Recorded Books.

See also "Inner Ear, Parts 3 and 4," "Introduction to English Poetry," "Voices and Vision," and "With a Feminine Touch" in the Appendix of Film, Video, and Audiocassette Resources.

TIP FROM THE FIELD

I have my students become "experts" on one of the poets treated in depth in the anthology. The students then work in pairs and "team-teach" their poet to two other students who are experts on another poet.

— KARLA WALTERS, *University of New Mexico*

ROBERT FROST

The Road Not Taken (p. 976)

This poem has traditionally been read as the poet's embracing of the "less traveled" road of Emersonian self-reliance, but the middle two stanzas complicate such a reading.

Ask students to read the first and last stanzas alone and then to notice that in the middle two stanzas, the speaker actually seems to equivocate as to whether or not the roads were actually different. After reading those two stanzas, do they trust the assertion that "I took the one less traveled by" (line 19)? In "The Figure a Poem Makes" (text p. 998), Frost states that a poem can provide "a momentary stay against confusion." Against what kind of "confusion" is the poet working? How do the uses of rhyme, meter, and stanza form work against confusion? Is there a "clarification of life" (another of Frost's claims for poetry) in this poem?

At least three times in this poem (2, 4, and 15), the word *I* disrupts the iambic rhythm. Why would the poet do this? What is the effect of the dash at the end of line 18?

Richard Poirier, in *Robert Frost: The Work of Knowing* (New York: Oxford UP, 1977), claims that Frost's poems are often about the making of poetry. Is there any sense in which this poem could refer to writing poetry? For instance, do a poet's choices of rhyme, meter, or metaphor at the beginning of a poem dictate how the rest of the poem will proceed? Do poets try to choose roads not taken by their predecessors in order to be original? Are they sometimes unable to return to standard forms later, once they have launched out on a new poetic path?

As a writing assignment, you might ask your students to discuss or write about decisions they have made that closed off other choices for them.

POSSIBLE CONNECTION TO ANOTHER SELECTION

George Herbert, "The Collar" (text p. 1097)

The Pasture (p. 978)

Ask students to suggest reasons why Frost chose to place "The Pasture" at the beginning of several volumes of his poetry. What might readers of this poem infer about the poems that followed? Could the references to raking the leaves away and watching the water clear in lines 3 and 4 suggest something more than the performance of spring chores?

Notice that the speaker twice informs the reader that "I shan't be gone long" (lines 4 and 8). The need to return to stable ground after going out and making discoveries is a recurring theme in Frost's poetry, as is evident in "Birches" and "Stopping by Woods on a Snowy Evening." Poems wherein the return is not assured — "Acquainted with the Night," for example — tend to be much more negative in tone. They often foreground what Lionel Trilling called the "terrifying" side of Robert Frost. How does Frost's practice of using a fixed form, such as blank verse or sonnet, yet altering the form by varying the meter or rhyme schemes (something he frequently does through the use of dialogue) demonstrate a similar desire to return to stable ground? Does this put the poet's often-quoted comment that writing free verse is like "playing tennis with the net down" in a different light? Is writing free verse, for Frost, more like casting loose from all one's moorings without an anchor?

POSSIBLE CONNECTIONS TO OTHER SELECTIONS

Robert Frost, "After Apple-Picking" (text p. 983)
Walt Whitman, "One's-Self I Sing" (text p. 1124)

Mending Wall (p. 979)

Students may already be familiar with this work from their high-school reading. Although the poem is often considered an indictment of walls and barriers of any sort, Frost probably did not have such a liberal point of view in mind. After all, the speaker initiates the mending, and he repeats the line "Something there is that doesn't love a wall." For him, mending the wall is a spring ritual — a kind of counteraction to spirits or elves or the nameless "Something" that tears down walls over the winter. It is gesture, ritual, and a reestablishment of old lines, this business of mending walls. The speaker teases his neighbor with the idea that the apple trees won't invade the pines, but to some measure he grants his conservative neighbor his due.

POSSIBLE CONNECTIONS TO OTHER SELECTIONS

Emily Dickinson, "Portraits are to daily faces" (text p. 934)
——, "To make a prairie it takes a clover and one bee" (question #1, following)
Ruth Fainlight, "Flower Feet" (text p. 724)
Robert Frost, "Neither Out Far nor In Deep" (question #2, following)

CONNECTIONS QUESTIONS IN TEXT (p. 980) WITH ANSWERS

1. How do you think the neighbor in this poem would respond to Dickinson's idea of imagination in "To make a prairie it takes a clover and one bee" (p. 931)?

    The neighbor in "Mending Wall" might accuse the speaker in Dickinson's poem of being foolish and impractical. Dickinson's speaker does not seem to think that boundaries make people happier, but the neighbor's experience has proved to him that "Good fences make good neighbors." The speaker in Frost's poem, more open to the kind of imagination Dickinson celebrates, wants his neighbor to imagine that elves have brought the wall down — but the neighbor probably won't.

2. What similarities and differences does the neighbor have with the people Robert Frost describes in "Neither Out Far nor In Deep" (p. 993)?

    In both poems Frost presents people who seem to be content with a single point of view, resisting new or even alternative views of the world. The neighbor, "like an old-stone savage armed," appears to be part of some primeval mystery that fascinates the speaker in "Mending Wall." In contrast, the people in "Neither Out Far nor In Deep" are the ones transfixed by a mystery — that of the vast ocean.

Home Burial (p. 980)

"Home Burial" is a dialogue in blank verse between a husband and wife who have recently lost their child and who have different ways of coping with loss. One way to begin discussion is to consider the form of the poem: does it seem more like a poem or a miniature play? How does the rhythm of the poem affect its theme? The haunting repetition of the word "don't" in line 31, for example, is realistic dialogue when we consider the tension behind the situation, but it also serves to mark a turning point in the poem. At what other points in the poem do similar repetitions occur, and do they also mark turning points in the dramatic situation, or do they reveal something about the psychological state of the characters?

Biographical criticism is beginning to come back into fashion, and you might remind the class of some of the introductory notes on Frost in this chapter before discussing the poem. Clearly the speaker is more matter-of-fact than his wife, and there is decidedly a communication problem between them. Note how Frost splits their dialogue in the interrupted iambic lines. But doesn't the husband deserve some special commendation for possessing the courage and integrity to initiate a confrontation with his wife? Discussion of the poem might also consider the value that ancients and moderns alike ascribe to a catharsis of emotions.

You might, if the class seems at all responsive, examine the speaker's claim that "a man must partly give up being a man / With women-folk" (lines 52–53). What does this statement mean? Has feminism done anything to challenge what are uniquely man's and uniquely woman's provinces of concern?

POSSIBLE CONNECTIONS TO OTHER SELECTIONS

Emily Dickinson, "After great pain, a formal feeling comes —" (text p. 946)
Robert Frost, " 'Out, Out —' " (text p. 987)
Jane Kenyon, "The Blue Bowl" (text p. 768)

After Apple-Picking (p. 983)

The sense of things undone and the approach of "winter sleep" seem to betoken a symbolic use of apple picking in this poem. Moreover, the speaker has already had an experience this day — seeing the world through a skim of ice — that predisposes him to view things strangely or aslant. At any rate, he dreams, appropriately enough, of apple harvesting. Apples take on connotations of golden opportunity and inspire fear lest one should fall. As harvest, they represent a rich, fruitful life, but as the speaker admits, "I am overtired / Of the great harvest I myself desired" (lines 28–29).

Apples are symbolically rich, suggesting everything from temptation in the garden of Eden, with overtones of knowledge and desire, to the idea of a prize difficult to attain, as in the golden apples of Hesperides that Hercules had to obtain as his eleventh labor. Here they can be read as representing the fruit of experience.

Refer students to Donald J. Greiner's "On What Comes 'After Apple-Picking' " (text p. 1004) for a critical perspective on this poem.

POSSIBLE CONNECTIONS TO OTHER SELECTIONS

Robert Frost, "Two Tramps in Mud Time" (text p. 991)
John Keats, "To Autumn" (text p. 771)

The Wood-Pile (p. 984)

This poem is a lyric meditation with relatively little narrative content. The speaker, considering a scene in nature, thinks about his personal relationship to the forest, a bird, and an unknown woodcutter who long ago abandoned a pile of firewood. The speaker seems to be spiritually lost and "far from home" (line 9); he seeks some sort of meaning in the unused woodpile, but he finds none. The poem ends with a bleak image of the "slow smokeless burning of decay" (40) and gives no sense that the speaker has found the significance he longs for.

For a segment of the poem, the speaker's attention is captured by "A small bird" (10) that flew by him and alighted nearby. You might ask your students to describe how the speaker is affected by the arrival and departure of this little bird. At first he is delighted by its appearance, but then is saddened to realize that the bird considers him a threat. You might ask your class to consider the speaker's statement when the little bird flies away: "I forgot him." Is the bird really forgotten?

You might also discuss with the class the meaning of the woodpile itself. What does this unused cord of firewood suggest to the speaker? The speaker recognizes that the woodcutter must have been someone who could accept unrewarded effort and "who lived in turning to fresh tasks" (35). How does this description of the woodcutter differ from the character of the speaker?

POSSIBLE CONNECTIONS TO OTHER SELECTIONS

Robert Frost, "Come In" (text p. 994)

———, "Nothing Gold Can Stay" (question #2, following)

———, "Stopping by Woods on a Snowy Evening" (text p. 989)

CONNECTION QUESTION IN TEXT (p. 986) WITH ANSWER

2. Discuss the speaker's sense of time in "The Wood-Pile" and in "Nothing Gold Can Stay" (p. 989).

   The speaker of this poem is disoriented in terms of both time and space as he walks in the woods. The wood pile offers him a chance to orient himself since it is something man-made in a natural setting that appears otherwise untouched by humanity. Yet this structure leaves him with a vision of "slow smokeless burning of decay" (line 40), which is not easily quantifiable or discernible. But the speaker of "Nothing Gold Can Stay" ranges beyond decay — which can happen within a person's lifetime — to contemplate an ongoing cycle. Hours and days are metaphorical in this poem, which takes us all the way back to Eden. Human time in this poem defers entirely to the cycles of nature.

Birches (p. 986)

This poem is a meditative recollection of being a boyhood swinger of birches. In the last third of the poem, the speaker thinks about reliving that experience as a way of escaping from his life, which sometimes seems "weary of considerations." Swinging on birches represents a limber freedom, the elation of conquest, and the physical pleasure of the free-fall swish groundward. Note, in contrast, Frost's description of what ice storms do to birches. Images like "shattering and avalanching on the snow-crust" suggest a harsh brittleness. The speaker in the end opts for Earth over Heaven because he (like Keats, to some extent) has learned that "Earth's the right place for love."

Frost's blank verse lends a conversational ease to this piece, with its digressions for observation or for memory. A more rigid form, such as rhymed couplets, would work against this ease.

In a writing assignment, students might analyze the different forms of knowing in "Birches," contrasting Truth's matter-of-factness (lines 21–22) and the pull of life's "considerations" (43) with boyhood assurance and the continuing powers of dream and imagination.

POSSIBLE CONNECTIONS TO OTHER SELECTIONS

Emily Dickinson, "Portraits are to daily faces" (text p. 934)

Pablo Neruda, "Sweetness, Always" (text p. 1141)

" 'Out, Out —' " (p. 987)

So often when disaster strikes, we tend to notice the timing of events. Frost implies here that "they" might have given the boy an extra half-hour and thereby averted the disaster. This perspective, coupled with the final line, in which the family seems to go on with life and ordinary tasks, can appear callous. But compare the wife's chastisement of her husband in "Home Burial" (text p. 980). Is the attitude callousness, or is it, rather, the impulse of an earth-rooted sensibility that refuses pain its custom of breaking the routine of life-sustaining chores and rituals? Very little in this poem seems to be a criticism of the survivors; rather, like *Macbeth* and the famous speech that proclaims life's shadowy nature (text p. 776), it seems to acknowledge the tenuous hold we have on life.

POSSIBLE CONNECTIONS TO OTHER SELECTIONS

Stephen Crane, "A Man Said to the Universe" (question #3, following)
Emily Dickinson, "From all the Jails the Boys and Girls" (text p. 951)
Robert Frost, "Home Burial" (question #2, following)
——, "Nothing Gold Can Stay" (question #1, following)

CONNECTIONS QUESTIONS IN TEXT (p. 988) WITH ANSWERS

1. What are the similarities and differences in theme between this poem and Frost's "Nothing Gold Can Stay" (p. 989)?

   In this poem the speaker presents a tragic experience involving human beings or property and then sets it in the larger context of the natural world. In "Nothing Gold Can Stay," the focus is on the natural world and the feeling of an Edenic spring.

2. Write an essay comparing how grief is handled by the boy's family in this poem and the couple in "Home Burial" (p. 980).

   Grief separates the couple in "Home Burial," as the wife accuses the husband of being unfeeling when the husband suggests that they must go on living despite their child's death. Miscommunication lingers in the split lines as well as in the situation of the couple, separated by the length of a staircase. In " 'Out, Out —' " the bereaved "turned to their affairs," choosing the response of the man in "Home Burial." Death unites them in that it reaffirms their commitment to the duty of living.

3. Compare the tone and theme of " 'Out, Out —' " and those of Crane's "A Man Said to the Universe" (p. 805).

   " 'Out, Out —' " and Crane's poem share a moral view that there is little ground on which humanity and the universe might meet. Crane's tone is slightly humorous, whereas Frost's approach is more poignant, but both rely heavily on dialogue to make their opinions known. Frost's borrowing from *Macbeth*, as well as the subject of the dead boy, gives his poem a more tragic quality than is present in Crane's sobering message.

Fire and Ice (p. 988)

With a kind of diabolic irony, the theories for the way the world might end grow as our knowledge and technology increase. Students can probably supply a number of earth-ending disaster theories: overheating of the earth because we are moving sunward; the greenhouse effect with the chemical destruction of the ozone layer; war, apocalypse, or "nuclear winter"; a change in the earth's orbit away from the sun; the return of the ice age; and so on. Frost here also speaks of the metaphoric powers of hatred (ice) and desire (fire) as destroyers of the earth. To say that ice would "suffice" to end the world is a prime example of understatement.

POSSIBLE CONNECTION TO ANOTHER SELECTION

William Butler Yeats, "The Second Coming" (text p. 1133)

Stopping by Woods on a Snowy Evening (p. 989)

With very few words, Frost here creates a sense of brooding mystery as the speaker stops his horse in a desolate landscape between wood and frozen lake. The attraction of the woods is their darkness, the intimation they offer of losing oneself in them. The speaker gazes into them with a kind of wishfulness, while his horse shakes his bells, a reminder to get on with the business of living. The repetition in the last lines denotes a literal recognition that the speaker must move on and connotes that there is much to be done before life ends.

You might use the final question in the text as a brief writing assignment to show how rhyme relates and interlocks the stanzas and offers in the final stanza (*dddd*) a strong sense of closure.

POSSIBLE CONNECTIONS TO OTHER SELECTIONS

Robert Frost, "The Wood-Pile" (text p. 984)
Henry Wadsworth Longfellow, "Snow-Flakes" (text p. 1106)

Nothing Gold Can Stay (p. 989)

Students often misread the first image in this poem as the brilliant golds of fall fading into winter. Caution them to read carefully; the poem describes the early days of *spring*, when the leaf buds (in New England, at least) emerge in a brief burst of yellowish-green before turning their deeper summer green. The other images in the poem, dawn losing its colors and becoming the brighter but less colorful day and the ideal of Eden becoming the reality of life after the Fall, reinforce the sense of loss. You might ask your students to consider the ambiguous nature of the images used in this poem. The speaker certainly takes a negative viewpoint: the leaf "subsides," Eden "sank," and the dawn "goes down." But isn't it true that what early spring gives way to is the glory of summer, and dawn to the fullness of the day? Also, the loss of Eden is often referred to as a "fortunate fall." Why do you suppose there is no indication of the other side of these images? Why would Frost use such ambiguous images, when the gold of autumn fading into winter would fit so much better with the tone of the poem? Do your students agree with the speaker's negative appraisal of the passing of time?

POSSIBLE CONNECTIONS TO OTHER SELECTIONS

Robert Frost, " 'Out, Out —' " (text p. 987)
——, "The Wood-Pile" (text p. 984)
Robert Herrick, "To the Virgins, to Make Much of Time" (question #1, following)

CONNECTION QUESTION IN TEXT (p. 990) WITH ANSWER

1. Write an essay comparing the tone and theme of "Nothing Gold Can Stay" with Herrick's "To the Virgins, to Make Much of Time" (p. 728).

Both poems have as their basis the idea that youth is ephemeral and that life passes quickly and inevitably. Herrick's poem offers advice regarding this condition, while Frost's presents it as a universal truth. The tone of Herrick's poem is somewhat lighter (without explicit reference, for instance, to "grief") since it keeps its young audience in mind. His purpose is ultimately rhetorical; Frost's is philosophical.

Once by the Pacific (p. 990)

This sonnet is about the encroaching dangers to civilization that the speaker envisions; it may be interpreted as a general warning to humanity. The forces of nature represent the forces of war and destruction and, like nature, are seen as powerful, potentially devastating, and impossible to thwart.

Much of the power of this poem arises from the poet's remarkably effective use of understatement. You might remind students of this poetic convention and ask them to point out examples in the poem. Lines 12 and 13 both incorporate brilliant understatements; "Someone" (12) really means *everyone*, and "more than ocean-water broken" (13) really suggests that *everything* would be broken.

You might also ask your students to consider the effect of the final line of the poem. How is God portrayed in this dreadful scenario of earthly destruction? Do your students think that "God's last *Put out the Light*" (14) is uttered angrily or regretfully? Why? You might also point out to students that this final line is an interesting reversal of the biblical proclamation "Let there be light," which began the world's existence. How does this biblical allusion add to the effect of this sonnet?

POSSIBLE CONNECTIONS TO OTHER SELECTIONS

Stephen Crane, "A Man Said to the Universe" (text p. 805)
Robert Frost, "Neither Out Far nor In Deep" (question #1, following)

CONNECTION QUESTION IN TEXT (p. 990) WITH ANSWER

1. Write an essay that discusses Frost's use of the ocean in "Once by the Pacific" and in "Neither Out Far nor In Deep" (p. 993).

   The ocean in "Once by the Pacific" is at war with the land in an apocalyptic fantasy. Its fierceness, made ironic by the fact that it is "pacific" (or peaceful), has its counterpart in the stalwart land. In "Neither Out Far nor In Deep," the ocean is not symbolic of God's power but is rather reflective of humanity's inability to comprehend mystery.

Two Tramps in Mud Time (p. 991)

As the speaker chops wood, two tramps emerge from the forest and indicate that they should chop his wood for pay. The speaker reflects on the job he is doing in the precarious season of spring, and inwardly debates whether he should allow them to step in since they have clearly spent more time cutting wood than he has. He concludes that it is noble of him to continue to do this task himself, to fulfill his "object in living," which "is to unite / My avocation and my vocation" (lines 66–67), and the simple task of splitting wood takes on a lofty significance, "done / For Heaven and the future's sakes" (71–72).

The title of the poem seems somewhat misdirected, since the poem is largely about the speaker rather than the tramps. Lines 13–16 begin to characterize the speaker as someone who has led a measured life but who also has a soul that contains some pent-up passion. You may want to begin discussion by having students consider the dual poles of the speaker's personality: his need to foster both his "avocation and [his] vocation" (67), or the dual perspectives that permit his "two eyes" to "make one in sight" (68). The spring setting is thus appropriate because, switching between March, April, and May, it acts as a metaphor for the balance of the speaker's personality; why else is it appropriate? Would autumn, another transitional season, work the same way? Consider also the way the speaker plays with notions of "work" and "play." Is his "task" more work or play, even though he brings the terms together in line 70? What constitutes work?

You may also want to consider the form of the poem. It relies unfailingly on end-rhyme (switching a, b, a, b, c, d, c, d, etc.) and a steady rhythm to unify its stanzas. (If you have worked with scansion in the chapter on "Patterns of Rhythm," this poem is a good candidate). How does the poet's method compare with the speaker's pride in his work? Are the even stanzas meant to mirror the "Good blocks of oak" (9) that the speaker splits so that they fall "splinterless as a cloven rock" (12)? Are there any "splinters" (that is, irregularities or imperfections) in the poem?

POSSIBLE CONNECTIONS TO OTHER SELECTIONS

Julia Alvarez, "Woman's Work" (text p. 886)
William Blake, "The Chimney Sweeper" (text p. 822)
Robert Frost, "After Apple-Picking" (question #1, following)
Seamus Heaney, "The Pitchfork" (text p. 760)

CONNECTION QUESTION IN TEXT (p. 992) WITH ANSWER

1. In an essay discuss attitudes toward work in this poem and in "After Apple-Picking" (p. 983).

    Work in this poem is the opportunity to demonstrate mastery. The speaker, who is affected by the tramps' perception of him as unfit to perform the task of chopping wood, rises to the challenge and proves that he can unite his task and his calling — manual labor and poetry — through his quest for perfection. The speaker of "After Apple-Picking" is overtired of his chore. The setting is fall (as opposed to spring in this poem), and he seems weary, like the passing of the year. This speaker has no perspective when regarding his work; viewing his life through a sheet of ice only magnifies the burden of it. The speaker of "Two Tramps in Mud Time" is blessed with a dual perspective, as he makes clear in the final stanza, and therefore his work does not feel like a burden to him.

Design (p. 993)

The opening octave of this sonnet is highly descriptive and imagistic in its presentation of spider, flower, and moth, all white. The sestet asks the question of design: who assembled all these elements in just such a way as to ensure that the moth would end up where the spider was — inside a "heal-all" (ironic name for this flower), its "dead wings carried like a paper kite"? Frost has in mind the old argument of design to prove the existence of God. There must be a prime mover and creator; otherwise, the world would not be as magnificent as it is. But what of the existence of evil in this design, Frost asks. The final two lines posit choices: either there is a malevolent mover (the "design of darkness to appall") or, on this small scale of moth and spider, evil occurs merely by chance ("If design govern . . ."). The rhyme scheme is *abba, abba, acaa, cc,* and its control provides a tight interlocking of ideas and the strong closure of the couplet.

Randall Jarrell's remarks on the imagery and ideas here are superb; he appreciates this poem with a poet's admiration (see his *Poetry and the Age* [New York: Farrar, 1953, 1972], pp. 45–49). He notes, for example, the babylike qualities of "dimpled . . . fat and white" (not pink) as applied to the spider. Note, too, how appropriate the word *appall* is since it indicates both the terror and the funereal darkness in this malevolently white trinity of images.

A comparison with the original version of this poem, "In White" (text p. 996), should prove that "Design" is much stronger. The title of the revised version, the closing two lines, and several changes in image and diction make for a more effective and thematically focused poem.

As a writing assignment, you might ask students either to compare this poem with its original version or to analyze the use of whiteness in "Design" and show how the associations with the idea of whiteness contrast with the usual suggestions of innocence and purity.

POSSIBLE CONNECTIONS TO OTHER SELECTIONS

Emily Dickinson, "I know that He exists" (question #2, following)
———, "Safe in their Alabaster Chambers —" (1861 version, text p. 934)
Robert Frost, "In White" (text p. 996)
William Hathaway, "Oh, Oh" (question #1, following)
Denise Levertov, "Gathered at the River" (text p. 907)
Edna St. Vincent Millay, "I will put Chaos into fourteen lines" (text p. 882)

CONNECTIONS QUESTIONS IN TEXT (p. 993) WITH ANSWERS

1. Compare the ironic tone of "Design" with the tone of Hathaway's "Oh, Oh" (p. 675). What would you have to change in Hathaway's poem to make it more like Frost's?

    Hathaway's "Oh, Oh" has a far less serious tone than Frost's poem, as the poet plays a joke on his audience, beginning the poem in a slaphappy, conversational tone, only to change it to a note of impending doom. To be more like Frost's poem, "Oh, Oh" would have to make its audience aware of the entire situation from the beginning.

2. In an essay discuss Frost's view of God in this poem and Dickinson's perspective in "I know that He exists" (p. 967).

    In "Design" the speaker questions the existence of God by suggesting that only a malevolent deity could preside over the relentless mechanisms of nature, whereby one species destroys another to survive. In "I know that He exists," Dickinson's speaker speculates not on the nature of God, but just on the hiddenness — the absence against which she must assert her belief. Frost is less comfortable with a God who must be malevolent than with no God at all. God's absence is what troubles Dickinson.

Neither Out Far nor In Deep (p. 993)

This poem, particularly in its last stanza, comments on humanity's limitations in comprehending the infinite, the unknown, the inhuman and vast. Again, Randall Jarrell's comment is useful. He writes, "It would be hard to find anything more unpleasant to say about people than that last stanza; but Frost doesn't say it unpleasantly — he says it with flat ease" (*Poetry and the Age* 42–43). You might organize a writing assignment around the tone of this poem.

POSSIBLE CONNECTIONS TO OTHER SELECTIONS

Robert Frost, "Mending Wall" (text p. 979)
——, "The Most of It" (text p. 995)
——, "Once by the Pacific" (text p. 990)

Come In (p. 994)

The speaker of this poem fancies that a thrush has called to him from the woods, beckoning him to come in and "lament" (line 16). It is dusk, but in the woods it is dark. The speaker decides that perhaps he isn't being asked to come into the woods, and even if he had been, he will not go tonight because he is "out for stars" (17).

Students might find it helpful to discuss some of the metaphorical possibilities for the word "dark" before deciding which ones might apply to this poem: darkness can connote a certain lack of knowledge (as in "the dark ages"), or it might refer to something otherworldly (Milton's "darkness visible"), or simply mysterious (which is reinforced in this poem by the forest setting, often the site of mystery or soul-searching). If you have worked with Dickinson and with a few other poems by Frost, students might be inclined to interpret darkness as death.

No matter how darkness is interpreted, the night setting is crucial to our interpretation of the poem. The very way the speaker thinks changes at night. Is this also true with your students? It is a time of contemplation, perhaps also of melancholy (the thrush's invitation is to "lament"). But this darkness is not absolute; it is dusk, not pitch black. The speaker subtly defines and redefines the quality of light on this night: the dusk of the first stanza is further defined in the second stanza, in which it is too dark for the thrush to "better its perch for the night," (7) but not so dark that the bird has ceased to sing. The speaker is still looking back toward "The last of the light of the sun" (9) in the third stanza, and in the fourth he intimates that there are degrees of darkness within the woods. In the final stanza he tells us that he is looking for stars, a different kind of night-time illumination. While he is going through this restless description of light, he is also recording the thrush's song. You might ask students to consider the relationship between light and sound in this poem. How does the interplay between them reinforce (or even produce) the poem's theme?

POSSIBLE CONNECTIONS TO OTHER SELECTIONS

Robert Frost, "The Pasture" (question #1, following)
——, "Stopping by Woods on a Snowy Evening" (text p. 989)
Henry Wadsworth Longfellow, "Snow-Flakes" (text p. 1106)

CONNECTION QUESTION IN TEXT (p. 995) WITH ANSWER

1. Write an essay comparing the themes of "Come In" with those of "The Pasture" (p. 978). How might each poem be regarded as a kind of invitation?

The invitation in this poem is a beckoning voice from nature, a common trope in the poetry of Ralph Waldo Emerson. The invitation comes in the form of a song, and "The Pasture" too has songlike qualities. Yet this poem reads more like an internal monologue, a speaker debating with himself. In "The Pasture," there is a human solidarity posited by the invitation, an implied trust between the speaker and the addressee.

The Silken Tent (p. 995)

This Shakespearean sonnet uses an extended conceit to compare one woman's equipoise to the silken tent that remains erect on a summer's day. The center-positioned cedar pole, we are told, points "heavenward," and this detail, as well as the silken substance of the tent, suggests the spiritual centeredness of the person. She seems serenely balanced but not aloof from human affairs, since the ties that connect her soul to their groundward stakes are those of "love and thought." Only by slight changes ("the capriciousness of summer air") is she made to feel these ties, which are more connection than bondage. Overall, the tone of the poem, enhanced by the sounds of the words, suggests serenity.

Since the poem is a Shakespearean sonnet, you can begin discussion by considering that form: does the final couplet of the poem change the meaning of the three quatrains before it? Do the quatrains suggest a development of the argument in three distinct points? To what end does Frost use other poetic devices in the poem, such as alliteration? The sonnet was originally titled "In Praise of Your Poise" and was written for Frost's secretary, Kay Morrison.

POSSIBLE CONNECTIONS TO OTHER SELECTIONS

Robert Herrick, "Delight in Disorder" (text p. 865)
William Shakespeare, "Shall I compare thee to a summer's day?" (text p. 881)

The Most of It (p. 995)

In this poem, which is somewhat more cryptic than many of Frost's, a solitary man calls out across a lake and receives only "the mocking echo of his own" (line 4) voice in response. Although "nothing ever came of what he cried" (9), a great buck does appear one morning, swimming toward him and making its way onto his shore.

In contrast to the concrete imagery and voices of some other Frost poems, such as "Two Tramps in Mud Time," this poem almost has the tone of a parable, or a story from mythology. The subject is nondescript, making him seem almost archetypal. Ask students to try to describe him: who is he? What is his goal? What is his life like when he is not calling out across the lake? They will have to fill in considerably; details such as "Instead of proving human when it neared" (14) suggest that he does have expectations. His actions provide a natural contrast to those of the buck, who is characterized by his forcefulness, his power, if not his grace (he stumbles in line 19). If students are content to say that the buck is an emblem of nature, what aspect of nature is the poet emphasizing? What aspect of humanity?

The title is enigmatic. Based on the poem's content and its tone, "it" seems to refer to something broadly philosophical, yet the title sounds like a colloquialism tossed out in conversation. If students have a hard time advancing an interpretation of the title, begin by asking whether they think "it" refers to something within the poem or outside of it. The literal possibilities within the poem are few (the echo, the lake, the buck), so once students have exhausted these they may be more willing to look outside the poem's literal meaning.

POSSIBLE CONNECTIONS TO OTHER SELECTIONS

Emily Dickinson, "The Soul selects her own Society —" (question #2, following)

Robert Frost, "Stopping by Woods on a Snowy Evening" (text p. 989)

——, "Two Tramps in Mud Time" (question #1, following)

N. Scott Momaday, "The Bear" (text p. 1110)

Edgar Allan Poe, "Alone" (text p. 1115)

CONNECTIONS QUESTIONS IN TEXT (p. 996) WITH ANSWERS

1. Write an essay that compares the images of nature in "The Most of It" with those in "Two Tramps in Mud Time" (p. 991). Is nature presented the same way in the two poems? What ideas about nature are expressed by their imagery?

   In "Two Tramps in Mud Time," the poet describes a delicate balance in nature: on one hand we control nature, but for the most part it lies well beyond our control. The speaker of that poem divides wood into neat, split logs, but he also acknowledges how temperamental spring can be. In this poem, the speaker seems to have no control of nature, which is vast and indifferent. Even so, it does seemingly respond to him.

2. Compare and contrast ideas about solitude in this poem and in Dickinson's "The Soul selects her own Society —" (p. 941).

   In Dickinson's poem, solitude is based on the soul's selection; it has considerable power. Yet the speaker in the final stanza has little power over the soul. The speaker of Frost's poem similarly lacks control; it could be said that his soul is selected rather than that his soul has selected something. Even so, he has apparently chosen to live in solitude.

PERSPECTIVES ON FROST

"In White": Frost's Early Version of "Design" (p. 996)

Many of the alterations Frost made in changing "In White" to "Design" have the effect of shifting the poem's focus from an individual occurrence to a more generalized one, from the questioning of a single death to the questioning of the force that caused, or allowed, the death to occur.

Students could begin by noting as many differences as they can find between the two poems. Probably the most obvious is the change in title. Whereas the title of the earlier poem announces a concern with the color white, which seems to represent death, the later title suggests a larger concern: the question of order (or the lack of it) in the universe.

Frost retained the sonnet form when he revised, but the rhyme scheme for the sestet changes from six lines with the same rhyme to the much more complex *abaabb*. This throws a sharper emphasis on the last two lines of "Design," the lines in which the poet suggests that events are shaped either by forces of evil or not at all.

Ask students to discuss how changes in individual word choices affect the poem. Some of the most striking of these are the change from "dented" to "dimpled" in line 1 and from "lifeless" to "rigid" in line 3 (i.e., even more dead, as though rigor mortis has set in). Another interesting change is that whereas the poem once *began* with a general observation and *ended* with the very personal "I," it now *begins* with "I" and moves outward to *end* with a general statement. Also note the use of the word *if* in the last line of the final version of "Design." This is one of Frost's favorite ways of injecting ambivalence and uncertainty into his poems.

POSSIBLE CONNECTION TO ANOTHER SELECTION

Robert Frost, "Design" (text p. 993)

Frost on the Living Part of a Poem (p. 997)

Intonation in musicians' parlance refers to pitch and the idea of playing in tune. Does Frost use the word in that sense here? If not, what does he mean later on by the "accent of sense" and how the word *come* can appear in different passages as a third, fourth, fifth, and sixth note?

In introducing this prose passage, you might point out that poets construct poetry out of fairly near-at-hand vocabularies, words we have already tasted on our tongues. One of the appeals of poetry is the physical way we intone its sounds, even when we read silently, so that we become in a sense a resonating chamber for the poem. It might be well to recall too that poetry originally was a spoken, not a written medium, and those things that were regarded as important enough to be remembered were put in verse.

Frost makes several unqualified statements here. Students, by and large, receive as part of their first-year college training the advice to be chary of the committed word. You might spend some of the class discussion exploring when and where rhetoric must be unequivocating.

AMY LOWELL, *On Frost's Realistic Technique* (p. 998)

Elsewhere in her review, Lowell describes Frost's vision as "grimly ironic." She goes on: "Mr. Frost's book reveals a disease which is eating into the vitals of our New England life, at least in its rural communities." In discussing the characters in Frost's poems she calls them "the leftovers of old stock, morbid, pursued by phantoms, slowly sinking to insanity." You might ask students to find evidence for Lowell's observations in the Frost poems in this chapter. Are there opposite tendencies in these characters that save them from what Lowell describes as a "disease eating into the vitals"?

Frost on the Figure a Poem Makes (p. 998)

In this introduction to his *Collected Poems,* Frost calls the sounds of a poem "the gold in the ore." Perhaps the best way to discuss Frost's assertion is to put it to the test. How do Frost's own poems stand up? How does he use sound? His more conversational poems, such as "Home Burial," provide insight into individual characters through an imitation of their speech patterns. The contemplative poem, exemplified by "Birches" or "After Apple-Picking," can be analyzed both for the speaker's character as it is revealed in his diction and for the way sounds both reaffirm and undermine the speaker's point.

Poems are, according to Frost, spontaneous in that they are derived from the poet's imagination as it interacts with his surroundings. But the imagination is not groundless because poets take many of their ideas from what they've read, often unconsciously: "They stick to nothing deliberately, but let what will stick to them like burrs where they walk in the fields." Frost's belief in the predestination of poetry involves the idea that the poem is an act of belief, of faith: "It must be a revelation, or a series of revelations, as much for the poet as for the reader." Not entirely the product of either spontaneity or predestination, the poem takes on a life of its own: "Like a piece of ice on a hot stove the poem must ride on its own melting."

In giving up claims to democracy and political freedom, Frost resists the process of naming something that supposedly is without limitation. Once defined as "free," whatever we call free ceases to be just that. Frost uses as an example our "free" school system, which forces students to remain in it until a certain age; it is, therefore, not free. Resisting confining labels, Frost as an artist is more able to reach a world audience; once he states a political bias, his art is one of exclusion. You might ask students to examine Frost's statements in the context of the more political poems in the Album of World Literature.

Frost on the Way to Read a Poem (p. 1000)

Experience with one or two poems by an author often eases the way for reading other poems by him or her. But will reading "Birches," for example, prepare the way for understanding "Fire and Ice"? Not necessarily. Beyond our literary experience, some of our "life learning" enters into the reading of poems as well.

The image of reader as "revolving dog" also seems a little discomforting, no matter what one's feelings about dogs. Poetry reading requires a certain point of stability, like the cedar pole in "The Silken Tent." Without it, one might be at a loss to distinguish sentiment from the sentimental, the power of the image from the fascination of the ornament.

You might ask students to try Frost's advice with two or three of his own poems. They can read one in the light of another and then write about the experience.

LIONEL TRILLING, *On Frost as a Terrifying Poet* (p. 1001)

With a take your students may find surprising, Trilling objects to the Frost of readers who use the poet to promote their causes: Frost as simple American, Frost as simple poet, Frost as modernist with a twist. He argues, using D. H. Lawrence's conception of the American writer, that Frost is a truly radical poet, in a tradition of radical American thinkers whose poetic work "is carried out by the representation of the terrible actualities of life in a new way."

To introduce them to Frost's biography (and how it affects his world-view and poetry) you might refer students to Lawrance Thompson's three-volume biography of Frost: *Robert Frost: The Early Years, 1874–1915; Robert Frost: The Years of Triumph, 1915–1938,* and Lawrance Thompson and R. H. Winnick, *Robert Frost: The Later Years, 1938–1963* (New York: Holt, 1966, 1970, 1976). For a more contemporary and controversial biography, consult William H. Pritchard's *Frost: A Literary Life Reconsidered* (New York: Oxford UP, 1984).

HERBERT R. COURSEN JR., *A Parodic Interpretation of "Stopping by Woods on a Snowy Evening"* (p. 1003)

This critical spoof offers a fine opportunity to articulate just what we seek from literary criticism and why we accept one writer's word and reject another's. One important factor in the Frost poem that is not considered here is tone and the speaker's own fascination with the woods, which are "lovely, dark, and deep."

If we were to isolate factors that mark good literary criticism, we might speak of (1) completeness (Are there any significant details omitted?); (2) coherence (Coursen advertises the simplicity of his theory but then talks at length about veiled allusions and obfuscation); and (3) fidelity to experience (No, Virginia, a horse is never a reindeer, not even on Christmas Eve). Good criticism avoids the overly ingenious.

This spoof also lends itself to a review of principles of good writing, which students have probably already acquired in a composition course. You might ask, too, what it was that inspired Coursen to write this essay. What, in other words, is he objecting to in the practice of literary criticism?

DONALD J. GREINER, *On What Comes "After Apple-Picking"* (p. 1004)

Students might be encouraged to use Greiner's analysis as a model for their own analysis of another Frost poem — "Birches" (text p. 986), for example, or "Mending Wall" (text p. 979) — a poem they would nominate as great. You might point out to them the way Greiner moves effortlessly between comments about Frost's technical brilliance (demonstrated in Frost's use of rhyme, varied line lengths, and meter) and speculations about the poem's final implications. Greiner links the technical concerns with the poem's meaning, as when he notes that "the meter invariably returns to the predominant rhythm of iambic pentameter as the meditator struggles to keep his balance in uncertainty as he has kept it on the ladder of his life."

BLANCHE FARLEY, *The Lover Not Taken* (p. 1005)

The fun of parodies derives in part from recognition of their sources — in this instance "The Road Not Taken." In Farley's parody, we see again the distressed speaker who wants to have it both ways. As is usually the case with Frost's deliberators, the woman in this poem seems to have many hours to devote to "mulling." Farley mimics Frost's faint archaisms with the line (present in both poems) "Somewhere ages and ages hence." She also plays with and lightly satirizes the rigors of Frost's blank-verse line. Notice, for example, how she carries over the key word that would round out the sense of the line between lines 8 and 9, only to accommodate the pentameter scansion. At the close of her poem, Farley plays down the need for choosing and asserts that there was no difference between the lovers. Appropriately for this parody, she closes with a heroic couplet.

DEREK WALCOTT, *The Road Taken* (p. 1006)

Pay careful attention to Walcott's definition of an uncle as students respond to Walcott's description of Frost as "avuncular" rather than "paternal." Students may tend to read their impressions of their *own* uncles into Frost's character. This might not be a bad thing, in terms of extending Walcott's analogy — in what *other* ways can Frost be said to be avuncular? — but Walcott qualifies his analogy in specific ways. Also, note that Walcott seems to answer his own rhetorical question in the second paragraph, but the answer may not satisfy. What is it about the American character that craves an uncle? "Because uncles are wiser than fathers" seems ironic in its simplicity, and students may want to offer other responses.

If students select a poem demonstrating that Frost is a "master ironist," they have a number to select from; but what about those students who don't think that Frost is a master ironist? Can they find opposite evidence? Much depends on a careful definition of "mastery" rather than of irony; for instance, if mastery denotes subtlety, " 'Out, Out! —' " could be used to illustrate that Frost is decidedly *not* a master ironist!

If you are working with either of the other two poets which the anthology covers in depth — Dickinson or Hughes — you might want to try to apply Walcott's terms "democratic" and "autocratic" to these other poets as a way of comparing them with Frost. Do these terms mean as much when applied to the other writers, or are the terms only useful insofar as they compare Whitman and Frost? There are also ample examples of Whitman's poetry in the anthology, which students can use to test Walcott's observations.

TWO COMPLEMENTARY CRITICAL READINGS

RICHARD POIRIER, *On Emotional Suffocation in "Home Burial"* (p. 1007)

You could begin class discussion of this perspective by asking students to find particular moments in Frost's poem that suggest that the couple's home has become, as Poirier suggests, a "mental hospital." What is it about this couple that reveals both their profound suffering and their perceived inability to escape their circumstances? You might ask your students to compare and contrast the anguish of the husband and the wife. In what ways are both of them emotionally suffocating in the house and in their relationship?

Poirier argues that "Home Burial" suggests "alienation, secretiveness, [and] male intimidation" (paragraph 3); where in the poem do your students find examples of these qualities? Do they agree with Poirier's interpretation? Does your class wholly identify with one character rather than the other? If not, you might explore the reasons class sympathy is divided between the husband and wife. Why might one elicit more sympathy from the reader than the other?

KATHERINE KEARNS, *On the Symbolic Setting of "Home Burial"* (p. 1008)

Kearns asserts that "the woman can 'see' through the window and into the grave in a way her husband cannot." You might open class discussion by asking students to describe these different ways of "seeing." Why do they see differently, and what does each of them see? Kearns also states that the husband and wife in "Home Burial" are "in profound imbalance." Ask your students to explain how they might be considered imbalanced. Responses might include not only the physical but the emotional reactions of the two to their young son's death and the fact that their marriage is in great danger of being permanently "unbalanced" by the woman's escape. Class discussion might also encompass Kearns's idea that this poem is caught up not only in the issues surrounding the death of a child, but also in those surrounding the institution of marriage itself and the "rights and privileges" that are associated with marriage. You might ask your students which issue they believe to be the primary one, and why.

ADDITIONAL RESOURCES FOR TEACHING FROST

SELECTED BIBLIOGRAPHY

Bagby, George F. *Frost and the Book of Nature.* Knoxville: U of Tennessee P, 1993.
Bloom, Harold, ed. *Robert Frost.* New York: Chelsea, 1986.
Brodsky, Joseph. *Homage to Robert Frost.* New York: Farrar, Straus & Giroux, 1996.

Cox, James Melville, ed. *Robert Frost: A Collection of Critical Essays.* Englewood Cliffs: Prentice, 1962.

Frost, Robert. *Interviews with Robert Frost.* Ed. Edward Connery Lathem. New York: Holt, 1966.

——. *The Poetry of Robert Frost.* Ed. Edward Connery Lathem. New York: Holt, 1979.

——. *Robert Frost: A Time to Talk.* Ed. Robert Francis. Amherst: U of Massachusetts P, 1972.

——. *Robert Frost on Writing.* Ed. Elaine Barry. New Brunswick: Rutgers UP, 1973.

——. *Selected Letters.* Ed. Lawrance Thompson. New York: Holt, 1964.

——. *Selected Prose.* Ed. Hyde Cox and Edward Connery Lathem. New York: Holt, 1966.

Gerber, Philip L. *Critical Essays on Robert Frost.* Boston: Hall, 1982.

Kearns, Katherine. *Robert Frost and a Poetics of Appetite.* Cambridge, Eng.: Cambridge UP, 1994.

Marcus, Mordecai. *The Poems of Robert Frost: An Explication.* Boston: Hall, 1991.

Meyers, Jeffrey, ed. *Early Frost: The First Three Books.* Hopewell: Ecco Press, 1996.

Monteiro, George. *Robert Frost and the New England Renaissance.* Lexington: UP of Kentucky, 1988.

Oster, Judith. *Toward Robert Frost: The Reader and the Poet.* Athens: U of Georgia P, 1992.

Poirier, Richard. *Robert Frost: The Work of Knowing.* New York: Oxford UP, 1977.

Pritchard, William H. *Frost: A Literary Life Reconsidered.* New York: Oxford UP, 1984.

Squires, James Radcliffe. *The Major Themes of Robert Frost.* Ann Arbor: U of Michigan P, 1969.

Thompson, Lawrance. *Fire and Ice: The Art and Thought of Robert Frost.* New York: Russell, 1970.

——. *Robert Frost: The Early Years, 1874–1915.* New York: Holt, 1966.

——. *Robert Frost: The Years of Triumph, 1915–1938.* New York: Holt, 1970.

Thompson, Lawrance, and R. H. Winnick. *Robert Frost: The Later Years, 1938–1963.* New York: Holt, 1982.

AUDIOVISUAL RESOURCES

Afterglow: A Tribute to Robert Frost. 35 min., color, 1989. Beta, VHS, ¾" U-matic cassette. Starring and directed by Burgess Meredith. Distributed by Pyramid Film and Video.

Robert Frost: A First Acquaintance. 16 min., color, 1974. Beta, VHS, ¾" U-matic cassette, 16-mm film. An examination of Frost's life through his poems. Distributed by Films for the Humanities and Sciences.

Frost and Whitman. 30 min., b/w, 1963. Beta, VHS, ½" open reel (EIAJ), ¾" U-matic cassette, 2" quadraplex open reel. Will Geer performs excerpts from the two poets' works. Distributed by New York State Education Department.

An Interview with Robert Frost. 30 min., b/w. Beta, VHS, ¾" U-matic cassette. Bela Kornitzer interviews Frost, who reads from his poetry. Distributed by Social Studies School Service.

Robert Frost: A Lover's Quarrel with the World. 40 min., b/w, 1970. Beta, VHS, ¾" U-matic cassette, 16-mm film. A documentary film on Frost's philosophic and artistic ideas. Distributed by Phoenix/BFA Films.

Robert Frost. 10 min., color, 1972. Beta, VHS, ¾" U-matic cassette, 16-mm film. A biographical sketch of the poet. Distributed by AIMS Media Inc.

Robert Frost in Recital [recording]. 1 cassette. Distributed by Caedmon/Harper-Audio.

Robert Frost Reads [recording]. 1 cassette (60 min.), 1987. From The Poet Anniversary Series. Distributed by Caedmon/HarperAudio.

Robert Frost Reads His Poems [recording]. 1 cassette (55 min.), 1965. Distributed by Audio-Forum.

Robert Frost Reads His Poetry [recording]. 1 cassette (48 min.). Distributed by Recorded Books.

Robert Frost Reads "The Road Not Taken" & Other Poems [recording]. 1 cassette. Distributed by Caedmon/HarperAudio.

Robert Frost's New England. 22 min., color, 1976. Beta, VHS, ¾″ U-matic cassette, 16-mm film, special-order formats. Ancillary materials available. Explores some of Frost's poetry relating to New England and its seasons. Distributed by Churchill Media.

Robert Frost: Twentieth-Century Poetry in English: Recordings of Poets Reading Their Own Poetry, No. 6 [recording]. Distributed by the Library of Congress.

Robert Frost [recording]. 1 cassette, 1981. Includes "The Pasture" and "Stopping by Woods on a Snowy Evening." Distributed by the Library of Congress.

See also "Literature: The Synthesis of Poetry," "Modern American Poetry," "Poetry by Americans," "The Poet's Voice," "Voices and Vision," and "Caedmon Treasury of Modern Poets Reading Their Own Poetry" in the appendix of Film, Video, and Audiocassette Resources.

LANGSTON HUGHES

The Negro Speaks of Rivers (p. 1010)

Since rivers are clearly the central image in this poem, you might begin discussion of "The Negro Speaks of Rivers" by asking students what ideas they commonly associate with rivers. How do associations such as fertility, life, timelessness, and exploration add to the poem's meaning? Also note that the Euphrates River is one of the legendary rivers that bordered the Garden of Eden. How does this association with the Christian myth of creation add to the meaning of the poem? It may be helpful for your students to recognize the geographic locations of these rivers and the fact that they flow in different directions. The Nile and the Congo are African rivers, the Euphrates flows through Turkey and Iraq, and the Mississippi splits the United States. You might ask your students what these diverse locations and directions suggest about the speaker's history.

Another important dimension of this poem is Hughes's use of time. Notice how the speaker stands outside of historical time; the narrative "I" has experienced these times and places over the course of human existence. You might ask students to explore the connection between the timeless narrator and the endurance and timelessness of rivers.

Consider the serious tone of this poem. Ask your students if they think this poem can be interpreted as a celebration. If so, what is the speaker celebrating, and what details contribute to this interpretation? Ask students to consider how the speaker has taken an active role in the history described in the poem ("I bathed . . ." [line 5], "I built my hut near the Congo . . ." [6], "I looked upon the Nile and raised the pyramids . . ." [7], etc.). What do these actions suggest about the history of the "Negro" in the title?

POSSIBLE CONNECTIONS TO OTHER SELECTIONS

Maya Angelou, "Africa" (text p. 1073)
Langston Hughes, "Negro" (text p. 1016)

I, Too (p. 1014)

This poem reveals the speaker's optimism about the future of race relations in America despite the overwhelming discrimination that he must endure daily. The speaker's acknowledgment that "I am the darker brother" (line 2) indicates the brotherhood between blacks and whites that he feels. In the final line the speaker asserts, "I, too, am America" (18), demonstrating his unwavering belief in his rightful national identity and equal standing in society.

In class discussion, consider how this poem incorporates images of racial injustice yet still manages to suggest a hopeful outlook for the future. Ask students to examine the image of the "darker brother" (2) sent to the kitchen to eat. Segregation was still firmly in place when this poem was written; how does the image of eating in the kitchen expose the racial injustices the speaker is forced to endure? You might ask your students to examine the reaction of the speaker to his "banishment" to the kitchen (5–7). What do they think this reaction to discrimination reveals about the speaker?

Ask students to discuss or write about the attitude of the speaker toward his current situation and toward America. Is his optimistic vision of the future clouded by his present predicament? The speaker's pride and confidence in the future are evident in his declaration that "Tomorrow / I'll be at the table / When company comes" (8–10). Discuss how this conviction helps him sustain his vision of a racially unified nation. You might raise the issue of why the speaker longs for acceptance in America, a country that has denied him his freedom for so long. Examine the speaker's prediction that race relations will improve owing to both the strength of black Americans and the shame of white Americans. How has this prophecy of 1925 been realized or not realized?

POSSIBLE CONNECTIONS TO OTHER SELECTIONS

Lucille Clifton, "come home from the movies" (text p. 791)
Countee Cullen, "Yet Do I Marvel" (text p. 1086)
Michael S. Harper, "Grandfather" (text p. 1095)
Langston Hughes, "Dinner Guest: Me" (text p. 1033)

Negro (p. 1016)

This poem chronicles the history of exploitation that black people have endured through the ages. The speaker acknowledges the broad history of the black experience, including slavery, the unappreciated role that blacks have had in the building of civilizations, the positive contributions blacks have made as artists, and the extent to which blacks have been victimized around the world.

Notice that the role of the speaker shifts throughout the poem; the speaker has been a slave, a worker, a singer, and a victim. Yet the self-definition of the speaker does not vary; the poem begins and ends with the line "I am a Negro" (lines 1, 19). Ask students to consider how this change in verb tense (from the present to the past and then back to the present) contributes to the speaker's personal and collective sense of identity. You might ask students to consider why the speaker, presumably an American "Negro," nevertheless identifies so closely with "my Africa" (3, 19).

Ask students to discuss, in terms of space and time, the scope of the racial exploitation this poem addresses. In the second stanza, the speaker offers two examples of his enslavement: to Caesar and to Washington (5–6). Ask your students how this image adds to their historical understanding of Caesar. Ask them also to consider the contrasting images of Washington as a revolutionary freedom fighter and as a colonial slave owner. Students might discuss or write about how this poem forces the reader to reconsider and reevaluate particular details of history.

The repetition of the first and last stanza brings this poem full circle; what words or phrases suggest the speaker's ability to endure hardships and victimization? You may want to ask students if they can see other ways in which the experiences of the speaker may be considered "cyclical." Do your students think that this poetic "cycle" suggests that the speaker recognizes no improvement in the living conditions of blacks in America?

POSSIBLE CONNECTIONS TO OTHER SELECTIONS

William Blake, "The Chimney Sweeper" (question #2, following)
Langston Hughes, "Dream Variations" (text p. 1018)
———, "The Negro Speaks of Rivers" (text p. 1010)

CONNECTION QUESTION IN TEXT (p. 1016) WITH ANSWER

2. Write an essay comparing the treatment of oppression in "Negro" with that in Blake's "The Chimney Sweeper" (p. 822).

Both Blake and Hughes point to specific rather than general oppression. Blake speaks of the experience of the two chimney sweepers (while incidentally mentioning the other "thousands of sweepers"), and indicting, by association, the system that forces them into the job. Hughes's speaker, on the other hand, reaches further, assuming the archetypal personality of Negro "slaves" (line 4), "workers" (7), "singers" (10), and "victims" (14) throughout history. Whereas (ironically, or not) Blake's characters have a chance, through death, of redemption, Hughes seems to indicate, in the first and last stanzas, some redemption in being "black like the depths of [his] Africa."

Danse Africaine (p. 1017)

This poetic rendition of an African dance relies heavily on the sound-value of the repetition of words like "low," "slow," "beat," and "tom-toms." The effect of these sounds is that the music "Stirs your blood" (lines 5, 15). In attempting to link the sounds with meaning students may respond that the poem has no meaning, that it is "simply" designed to create a mood. If they respond this way, you may have to back up a bit and talk about poetic meaning: who creates it, for whom does it exist, and so on. The "meaning" of this poem might lie in the relationship between the speaker and the addressee, if not the poet and the reader. Why the startling command to "Dance!" in line 6? What is the effect of the repeated line "Stirs your blood"? What is the meaning of that phrase? It connotes some kind of passion, or the exercise of vitality; what might be the manifestations of that stirring?

POSSIBLE CONNECTIONS TO OTHER SELECTIONS

Martín Espada, "Latin Night at the Pawnshop" (text p. 726)
Langston Hughes, "Formula" (question #1, following)
Edgar Allan Poe, "The Bells" (text p. 838)
Jean Toomer, "Reapers" (text p. 844)

CONNECTION QUESTION IN TEXT (p. 1017) WITH ANSWER

1.   Try rewriting this poem based on the prescription for poetry in "Formula" (p. 1021).

Students may have different responses to this question; on one hand, "Danse Africaine" does not "treat / Of lofty things" (lines 1–2) in the sense that it is about something human and primal rather than about something ethereal. At the same time, this poem describes a beautiful moment of a girl whirling softly in a circle of light, but it does not account for the "earthly pain [which] / Is everywhere" (12–13). "Formula" describes not only the content of poetry, but also the method that should be used in treating this content. Is it possible to argue that this poem doesn't need to be rewritten in order to conform to the definition of poetry in "Formula"?

Jazzonia (p. 1017)

This poem creates both a visual and an aural effect, something like viewing a modernist painting while listening to jazz. On one level the poem serves as a vivid description of a Harlem nightclub in which "Six long-headed jazzers play" (lines 4, 17), but the sense of the poem extends outward with allusions to Eve and Cleopatra and with glimpses of "rivers of the soul" (2, 8, 15).

The repeated and varied lines about the tree ("silver" in line 1, "singing" in line 7, "shining" in line 14) and the lines about the rivers of the soul that follow them are a good way into the poem. What is the relationship between this tree and the rivers of the soul? How do students interpret the tree? What kind of mind might describe a tree as either silver, singing, or shining? The variations within these and other lines in the poem make sense when we consider the title; if you have access to a jazz recording from the 1920s, especially a live recording in which performers allow themselves a good deal of improvisation and variations on a theme, it would be helpful to play it when discussing Hughes's poetry, and especially appropriate when discussing this poem.

The fourth stanza is likely to provide some difficulties, especially when taken along with the rest of the poem. It stands apart, first because of its odd number of lines, but also because its words seem unconnected to the rest of the poem. Point out that these musings about Eve and Cleopatra are initiated in lines 5 and 6 when the speaker describes a dancing girl. Students may be baffled as to why he would choose such archetypal female figures to describe this dancing girl, but he has, after all, been describing the soul in terms of rivers and trees. If you work with the two complementary readings by Countee Cullen and Onwuchekwa Jemie at the end of this chapter, "Jazzonia" might be a good place to apply them. Does this poem address universal themes, or is it limited by its setting in a Harlem cabaret?

POSSIBLE CONNECTIONS TO OTHER SELECTIONS

Elizabeth Alexander, "Harlem Birthday Party" (text p. 1148)
Allen Ginsberg, "First Party at Ken Kesey's with Hell's Angels" (text p. 917)
Langston Hughes, "Danse Africaine" (question #1, following)
———, "Rent-Party Shout: For a Lady Dancer" (text p. 1023)

CONNECTION QUESTION IN TEXT (p. 1018) WITH ANSWER

1.   Compare in an essay the rhythms of "Jazzonia" and "Danse Africaine" (p. 1017).

The rhythms of "Jazzonia" are more even than those in "Danse Africaine," in which the expected rhythms shift because of lines like "Dance!" (line 6). Despite the repetition of lines and phrases, "Danse Africaine" employs an irregular scheme; "Jazzonia" is smoother. Each is consistent with the types of music it describes.

Dream Variations (p. 1018)

The dreamlike qualities of this poem seem to surface more easily when read aloud; you may wish to ask a student, or several students, to read this poem to the class. Notice how the natural rhythms of the lines speed up or slow down to reflect the natural rhythms of the daytime or the nighttime.

Have your students consider the "dream" in this poem as a description of an idyllic experience without boundaries or inhibitions. How do vibrant, energetic words like "whirl" (line 3), "dance" (3), and "fling" (10) suggest the speaker's desire to transcend conventional restrictions? Ask students to connect this abstract dream of freedom with the social and political climate of the 1920s, in which African Americans could not generally enjoy uninhibited freedom. Overall, how does this dream motif reflect the black experience in America?

Ask your students to consider the way that active images and words (such as "To fling my arms wide" [1] and "To whirl and to dance" [3]) are associated with the "white day" (4), and calmer, more subdued words (such as "cool" [5], "gently" [7], and "tenderly" [16]) are linked to the nighttime. Compare the speaker's vision of day and night. Ask your students how they can be different and yet both be incorporated into the "dream." You might also point out that there are an equal number of lines describing the day and the night. Yet the speaker directly identifies with the nighttime ("Dark like me" [8], "Black like me" [17]). Ask your class how these details influence the reader's understanding of the speaker.

POSSIBLE CONNECTIONS TO OTHER SELECTIONS

Langston Hughes, "Dream Boogie" (question #2, following)
———, "Negro" (text p. 1016)

CONNECTION QUESTION IN TEXT (p. 1019) WITH ANSWER

2. Discuss the significance of the dream in this poem and in "Dream Boogie" (p. 1029).

The dream in this poem connotes an American dream, a hope for a better future; but this dream is also like a literal dream with surreal imagery. As the title indicates, there are slight variations between the two stanzas: the "white day" (line 4) becomes the "quick day" (13) for instance, and "Dark like me" (8) becomes "Black like me" (17). The dream in "Dream Boogie" is the "dream deferred" that is a recognizable hallmark of Hughes's poetry. It is not dreamlike in a literal sense, but rather the dream of a future of equality. The dream is deferred in this poem to the point that it is forgotten.

Johannesburg Mines (p. 1019)

Hughes creates a very stark and political poem out of the statistical fact that 240,000 native Africans work in the Johannesburg mines. The social implications of this poem about exploitation, victimization, and colonization are designed to force some level of consideration on the part of the reader. Ask your students why South Africa, even today, is such a highly suggestive setting. What sort of automatic response does South Africa elicit from readers? You might ask students to discuss what they know about South Africa, including recent political developments. How (if at all) do they believe that conditions there have changed since Hughes wrote this poem in 1925?

Ask students what they feel the tone of this poem is. It may be described, in part, as angry, serious, stunned, outraged, and sober. The fact that there are "240,000 natives / Working in the / Johannesburg mines" (lines 7–9) may lead students to question this exploitative social system. The mines are presumably owned by whites, and black Africans work in the mines because they have few employment opportunities. This subjugation of the natives by nonnative whites becomes at least part of the theme of this poem. Ask students how they see Hughes's radical political ideology evidenced in this brief poem. How would an American worker in 1925 relate to this poem? How would an American worker today react?

POSSIBLE CONNECTIONS TO OTHER SELECTIONS

William Blake, "The Chimney Sweeper" (text p. 822)

T. E. Hulme, "On the Differences between Poetry and Prose" (question #1, following)

CONNECTION QUESTION IN TEXT (p. 1019) WITH ANSWER

1. Read the Perspective by Hulme, "On the Differences between Poetry and Prose" (p. 774), and write an essay on why you think "Johannesburg Mines" is best described as poetry or prose.

    Hulme aside, "Johannesburg Mines" is verse, and it uses the theme-and-improvised-variation on the theme characteristic of much of Hughes's poetry, so the argument for poetry is stronger than that for prose despite the conversational tone of the poem. Hulme argues that the language of poetry is "a visual concrete one," and this poem upholds that definition. Prose, according to Hulme, is given to abstract signs and counters. Little or nothing about Hughes's poem is abstract.

The Weary Blues (p. 1019)

The rhythmical, rhyming lines of "The Weary Blues" suggest that this poem is like the lyrics to a blues song. Singing the blues is depicted as an emotional release — an outlet that is necessary in order to survive one's painful, lonely life. The blues are intensely personal, "Coming from a black man's soul" (line 15). The "drowsy syncopated tune" (1), the "melancholy tone" (16) of the singer's voice, and the "lazy sway" (6) of his body all combine to reveal that the subject of his song may be the weariness of both body and soul. To begin class discussion ask students what the theme of this poem might be and what details in "The Weary Blues" make the theme evident.

The turbulent emotions of the singer are reflected in the lyrics of his song; first he resolves to put aside his troubles and live on (20–21), but then he feels like giving up and wishes that he were dead (27–30). Yet in spite of the admission that "I ain't happy no mo' / And I wish that I had died" (29–30), "The Weary Blues" may be interpreted as a life-affirming experience. Through the melancholy song, the singer is purged of his personal pain long enough to sleep deeply and enjoy at least a temporary respite from his troubles. Thus the blues may be seen as cathartic, changing pain into peace. You might ask your students to discuss which elements of the poem contribute to this catharsis and what the relationship might be between the singer and the speaker. Has the speaker undergone any sort of catharsis as well?

Ask students to think about certain details of this scene, such as the "old gas light" (5) and the "rickety stool" (12). How do these details and others contribute to the overall effect of the poem? This poem employs many sensual images; ask students to consider which details the poet uses to make the reader "see" or "feel" this scene.

POSSIBLE CONNECTION TO ANOTHER SELECTION

Langston Hughes, "Lenox Avenue: Midnight" (question #1, following)

CONNECTION QUESTION IN TEXT (p. 1020) WITH ANSWER

1. Discuss "The Weary Blues" and "Lenox Avenue: Midnight" (p. 1022) as vignettes of urban life in America. Do you think that, although written more than seventy years ago, they are still credible descriptions of city life? Explain why or why not.

   Some details of urban life have changed since Hughes's time. In these poems specifically, urban life is characterized by jazz and blues rhythms, gas lights, and the rumble of streetcars. The new urban rhythms belong to rap and hip-hop; gas lights seem romantic and quaint compared to today's streetlights, and the rumble of streetcars is also obsolete and, most likely, less deafening than the street noises of today. Students might argue that the weariness that weighs on these two poems has been replaced by a frenetic vitality and the danger that goes along with it. Rage has replaced feelings of weariness and pain. It might be interesting to have students write a contemporary update of Hughes's poems with these changes in mind.

Cross (p. 1020)

This brief poem, using stark and simple language, deals with the complicated and often painful issue of biracial identity. There is also the hint of a slave-master relationship between the speaker's father and mother, based on the father's dying in a "fine big house" (line 9) and the mother dying "in a shack" (10). In this poem Hughes suggests some of the implications of miscegenation, including the emotional stress and insecurity of children born of forced interracial relationships. Ask your students to discuss some of the difficulties they may recognize as inherent in trying to forge a biracial identity in America, both when Hughes was writing and today.

Ask your students how the title of the poem, "Cross," may be interpreted on several levels. Possible responses might include the facts that the speaker's identity is a "cross" between races, that the cross is a religious symbol of suffering and persecution, and that "cross" may refer to the anger the speaker feels toward his or her parents for making the speaker "neither white nor black" (12). You might ask your students which interpretation of the title seems to add the most meaning to the poem.

Since the speaker's parents are both dead, the speaker no longer has anyone to curse for his or her racial in-betweenness. The speaker must now begin a personal journey toward some sense of racial identity. Interestingly, the speaker's preoccupation seems to be not where to live, but where to die. Ask your students why this is so and how the speaker's insecurity about where he or she will die adds meaning to the issue of acceptance into a society that devalues biracial people.

POSSIBLE CONNECTIONS TO OTHER SELECTIONS

Robert Francis, "On 'Hard' Poetry" (question #1, following)
Langston Hughes, "Red Silk Stockings" (text p. 1022)

CONNECTION QUESTION IN TEXT (p. 1021) WITH ANSWER

1. Read the Perspective by Francis, "On 'Hard' Poetry" (p. 697), and write an essay explaining why you would characterize "Cross" as "hard" or "soft" poetry.

   This poem is neither soft in form, since it follows a strict scheme of rhyme and meter, nor soft in thought and feeling, since it addresses its tough subject head-on. There is no excess verbiage, nothing to "water down" the ideas, imagery, or direct language. It would be difficult to argue that this poem is anything but "hard," according to Francis's perspective. In the second half of his perspective, he implies that there are degrees of hardness, and students may debate the relative hardness of this poem. As a way of addressing this point even further, it might help to have students compare this poem to another poem by Hughes that they believe is softer than this one, and to yet another poem which is harder.

Formula (p. 1021)

"Formula" parodies romantic misunderstandings about poetry which suggest that good poems have only idyllic, extravagantly elegant subjects. The speaker mocks this attitude, particularly in his repeated suggestion that poetry ought to be about "birds with wings" (lines 4, 16). This poem itself does not adhere to its own "formula." While it ostensibly suggests that poetry should be restricted to "lofty things" (2, 14), "Formula" is clearly not a poem about such idealized images.

By denying that poetry should be "dirty," the speaker actually manages to establish the facts "That roses / In manure grow" (7–8) and "That earthly pain / Is everywhere" (11–12). You may want to ask your students how the poem seems to contradict itself and what effect these apparent contradictions might have on the reader.

You may wish to explain to students that "The Muse of Poetry" (5, 9) is a mythical goddess who was called upon by ancient poets for inspiration. Ask your students how the Muse is treated in this poem. Can certain information be withheld from the Muse of Poetry?

Langston Hughes's poetry, in general, deals with the "earthly pain" (11) of life; clearly he as a poet does not subscribe to the ideas put forth in this poem. You may wish to open class discussion by asking students why they think Hughes wrote such a mocking poem about lofty, idealistic poetry. What could he have been trying to accomplish? Possible responses might include the idea that through satirizing "lofty" poetry, Hughes may be suggesting that one cannot separate the pain of life from one's art, or that poetry that ignores earthly pain cannot be very real or valuable.

POSSIBLE CONNECTIONS TO OTHER SELECTIONS

Helen Farries, "Magic of Love" (question #2, following)
Archibald MacLeish, "Ars Poetica" (text p. 1107)

CONNECTION QUESTION IN TEXT (p. 1022) WITH ANSWER

2. Write an essay that explains how Farries's "Magic of Love" (p. 692) conforms to the ideas about poetry presented in "Formula."

   This question should give students plenty of room to explore the parodic intent of Hughes's poem. There is no trace of earthly pain or of the manure that fertilizes roses in Farries's greeting-card verse. Her poem attempts to emphasize that it is lofty and soaring by ending each stanza with an exclamation point. Moreover, it is formulaic verse, which aligns it with the title of Hughes's poem. It might be fun to have students rewrite "Magic of Love" with an awareness of earthly pain or of the manure in which roses grow. Is it possible to do so while maintaining the poem's tone or theme?

Lenox Avenue: Midnight (p. 1022)

You might begin discussion of this poem by closely examining the first two lines: "The rhythm of life / Is a jazz rhythm." Ask students why jazz and life are so closely connected. Possible responses might include the ideas that jazz, like life, includes solos, improvisations, varied tempos, and melodies that can range from the joyful to the melancholy. Jazz (and life) is unpredictable and often unrehearsed; therein lies much of its beauty and appeal. Ask students to think also about how the word "Honey" (lines 3, 12) in the poem functions in several different ways. For example, "Honey" could be the person the speaker is addressing, or "Honey" could be the sweet heaviness that characterizes both jazz rhythms and life.

You might continue the discussion by asking students why the poet believes that "The gods are laughing at us" (4, 14). The poet seems to be describing the vast distance between human and godly experience; gods are so far away, or perhaps are so cruel, that they laugh instead of weep for the pain they see on Lenox Avenue.

Ask students to consider how the setting of this poem, midnight on Lenox Avenue in Harlem, contributes to its meaning. Lenox Avenue is the backdrop for the speaker's (and Hughes's) life — it is the place where his life is "located." Our own "Lenox Avenues" are the places where we see our own lives, where we see ourselves reflected in our surroundings. You might ask students to explore, in discussion or in a writing assignment, the places that best characterize their own life experiences.

POSSIBLE CONNECTIONS TO OTHER SELECTIONS

Stephen Crane, "A Man Said to the Universe" (text p. 805)
Emily Dickinson, "I know that He exists" (question #1, following)
Thomas Hardy, "Hap" (question #2, following)
Langston Hughes, "Jazzonia" (text p. 1017)
Octavio Paz, "The Street" (text p. 1143)

CONNECTIONS QUESTIONS IN TEXT (p. 1022) WITH ANSWERS

1. In an essay compare the theme of this poem with that of Dickinson's "I know that He exists" (p. 967).

    The supreme being in each poem, whether it be God or gods, is distant from humanity and playful at our expense. Hughes's poem implies that the gods are laughing at the way we live our lives. The poem is vital, beginning with "the rhythm of life." Dickinson's poem meditates on the relationship between death and life. For her, the game that God plays with us has a deadly serious element that has to do with the relationship between life and the afterlife, a relationship that Hughes does not address specifically.

2. Compare and contrast the speaker's tone in this poem with the tone of the speaker in Thomas Hardy's "Hap" (p. 1093).

Hardy's speaker, like Hughes's, imagines gods that are laughing at him, but they are laughing because they take pleasure in his pain and suffering. He realizes that this scenario is not accurate, that the pain we must suffer is a product of chance or fate, the wills only of Time or Casualty. The gods in Hughes's poem do not depress the speaker in the same way that they depress Hardy's speaker. He does not seem to change his behavior as a result of the laughter of the gods, but rather to describe the scene as he sees it. He is in this sense more detached than Hardy's speaker is.

Red Silk Stockings (p. 1022)

The speaker of this poem urges his addressee, a black woman, to wear red silk stockings so that "de white boys" (line 3) will admire her. The speaker implies that the white boys will do more than admire her, though, since he predicts that "tomorrow's chile'll / Be a high yaller" (8–9): that is, a mixed-race child. The speaker is contemptuous toward the addressee, who evidently thinks that she's "too pretty" (7) for him and for the rest of the black boys. His advice to her is motivated by his scorn rather than by his concern for her best interests.

Students might jump to the conclusion that Hughes is the speaker. You can contrast this poem with almost any other by him to point out the difference between the language this speaker uses and Hughes's typical poetic voice. ("Rent-Party Shout . . ." may be the exception.) Do they feel that Hughes is making a broad statement about race relations, or is he just allowing a voice he has heard to speak in his poetry? Like many of Hughes's other poems, this one relies on repetition for emphasis, but the meter of the lines and the length of the three stanzas are irregular. What is the effect of repeating the last two lines from the first stanza as the third stanza? How would the poem read differently if the third stanza were omitted? In general, why is repetition such a prevalent device in Hughes's poetry?

POSSIBLE CONNECTIONS TO OTHER SELECTIONS

Gwendolyn Brooks, "We Real Cool" (text p. 743)
M. Carl Holman, "Mr. Z" (text p. 1098)
Langston Hughes, "Dinner Guest: Me" (question #1, following)
———, "Rent-Party Shout: For a Lady Dancer" (text p. 1023)

CONNECTION QUESTION IN TEXT (p. 1023) WITH ANSWER

1. Write an essay that compares relations between whites and blacks in this poem and in "Dinner Guest: Me" (p. 1033).

   The connection to "Dinner Guest: Me" must take into consideration the publication dates of the poem ("Red Silk Stockings" was published nearly forty years earlier). If students feel that Hughes's depiction of race relations has changed based on these two poems, can they account for that change in terms of history?

Rent-Party Shout: For a Lady Dancer (p. 1023)

This poem sounds as much like a song lyric as it does a poem; the short lines make the tempo fast and sharp, like the words themselves. You may wish to ask students to consider this "shout" as a story; ask them to describe the speaker's situation and her feelings toward her "man." Ask your students if they see any humor in this "shout." Responses might include the speaker's declaration that "I knows I can find him / When he's in de ground —" (15–16) — her jealousy is taken to a bitingly satirical extreme.

Ask students to describe the setting of this poem. Point out that the backdrop to this piece is desperate poverty, where friends and neighbors have to help raise a person's rent money. So the music played at such a party would need to be energetic, entertaining, and cathartic enough to distract the partyers from their own personal troubles. In this way, "Rent-Party Shout" can be interpreted simultaneously as a threat to the wayward man and as a necessary release for the singer herself. Ask students to discuss what might be considered "therapeutic" about this woman's singing about her troubles.

You might also consider asking your students, in discussion or in writing, to draw comparisons between "Rent-Party Shout" and other poems in which Hughes incorporates song lyrics, such as "The Weary Blues" (text p. 1019). Ask them to describe how the lyrics contribute to the meanings of the poems.

POSSIBLE CONNECTION TO ANOTHER SELECTION

Langston Hughes, "Dream Boogie" (text p. 1029)

The English (p. 1024)

This political poem describes the cruel hypocrisy of the English, who, in Hughes's opinion, economically and culturally exploit peoples all over the world while still adhering to their traditional rituals of etiquette and decorum. You might consider opening discussion of this poem by asking students to examine their own social and political stereotypes of the English. Social stereotypes might include the stuffy, aloof, formal attitudes of the English; political stereotypes might include the English history of cultural exploitation and imperialism. Students might note that this poem is the result of juxtaposing these two sets of stereotypes.

Ask students to deduce where these British ships might be doing most of their "business." Details such as "hot rivers" (line 6), "oil" (10), "fruit" (10), "cocoa beans" (11), and "gold" (11) suggest that Africa is at least one victim of England's plundering. Ask your class to examine the suggestiveness of line 9: "Buy, sell, or rob." How do these three verbs suggest the potential ruthlessness of the English?

Hair combing is a deeply symbolic act in this poem and you might ask students what it represents. Responses could include the notion of the hypocrisy of the English, who concern themselves with insignificant and vain details while they exploit the resources of the world, or perhaps the calculating coldness of a people who are undaunted by their own intrusion into foreign lands. You might also ask students to consider whether or not this poem is at all dated. Is England's imperial influence still affecting other nations in the manner that Hughes discusses?

POSSIBLE CONNECTIONS TO OTHER SELECTIONS

Li Ho, "A Beautiful Girl Combs Her Hair" (question #1, following)
D. H. Lawrence, "The English Are So Nice!" (text p. 745)

CONNECTION QUESTION IN TEXT (p. 1024) WITH ANSWER

1. Write an essay that discusses hair combing as symbolic action in this poem and in Ho's "A Beautiful Girl Combs Her Hair" (p. 706).

The gesture of hair combing in Hughes's poem is ironic, in terms of symbolic action, since it implies nobility or civility even as the English who comb their hair commit atrocities through their imperial plundering. It is the hypocritical gesture of one who purports to appear mannered without thinking through his actions. The girl in Li Ho's poem combs her hair as a way of fashioning herself or arranging herself to appear especially beautiful. Through her attention to her appearance, she attempts to enhance her beauty, but her final gesture of breaking a spray of cherry blossoms indicates that she might also be unaware of the import of her actions. Because the relationship between the speaker and the subject of this poem is unclear, it is more difficult to discern the ultimate meaning of her action than it is to understand the speaker's attitude toward his subject in Hughes's poem.

Note on Commercial Theatre (p. 1024)

By 1940 black American arts such as jazz had gone mainstream, but they had also, according to this speaker, begun to be about something other than black experience. The speaker of this poem resents the appropriation and devitalization of black culture in America but looks forward optimistically to a time when these cultural forms will again reflect his (or her?) experience. Students may find a number of parallels to contemporary culture; encourage them to think in terms beyond race to consider what happens whenever any powerful majority culture appropriates aspects of a minority culture. You might need to emphasize that there is a distinct difference between a crossover audience for a particular genre and a weakening of that genre through commercialization. It is crucial in this sense to consider Hughes's speaker, especially since he ends the poem with the line, "Yes, it'll be me." Who is he or she? Is his or her identity generic? Where does his or her identity come from? And what about the relationship between the speaker and his or her audience: is the poem a call to other black people to take up this struggle? Note the visual effect of the poem, the way its lines are whittled down until the speaker arrives at the final realization, "Yes, it'll be me" (line 20), almost as if the poem is pointing us to its true subject: the need to focus on and take control of the self.

POSSIBLE CONNECTIONS TO OTHER SELECTIONS

Amiri Baraka, "SOS" (text p. 1077)
Marilyn Bowering, "Wishing Africa" (text p. 743)
Langston Hughes, "Frederick Douglass: 1817–1895" (question #1, following)
——, "The Weary Blues" (text p. 1019)
Julio Marzán, "Ethnic Poetry" (text p. 816)
Derek Walcott, "The Virgins" (text p. 723)

CONNECTION QUESTION IN TEXT (p. 1025) WITH ANSWER

1. Compare in an essay the tone and theme of this poem and "Frederick Douglass: 1817–1895" (p. 1034).

   The speaker of this poem is essentially optimistic, a characteristic, according to Donald B. Gibson's essay at the end of this chapter, of Hughes in general. Is this speaker's optimism closer to the optimism of the speaker of "Frederick Douglass: 1817–1895" or to the optimism of Douglass himself, as he is depicted in that poem?

Ballad of the Landlord (p. 1025)

In his poetry Hughes was often concerned with incorporating the rhythms and feeling of blues and jazz. It's not difficult to imagine "Ballad of the Landlord" as a slow blues. Whereas the results of the protagonist's rebellion are anything but unfamiliar, his willingness to fight for what little is his — and the verve with which he speaks of that struggle — affords him a certain nobility even though the landlord undeniably "wins." The poem also shows in derisive terms the idiocy of the landlord's and authorities' overreaction to reasonable and modest concerns about safety (even the landlord's) and comfort.

Ask your students how this poem might be interpreted as political and social commentary. You might point out to them that the tenant is not jailed for his legitimate complaints about the condition of his home, but because the landlord unfairly accuses him of being a political radical. As a background for this poem, you might discuss with your students the influence of Senator McCarthy's anticommunist initiatives in 1950s America and how this poem reflects the rampant political paranoia of that era. Students might also consider manifestations today of a social system that tends to victimize the powerless and defend the privileged.

POSSIBLE CONNECTIONS TO OTHER SELECTIONS

Aron Keesbury, "Song to a Waitress" (text p. 872)

Wole Soyinka, "Telephone Conversation" (question #1, following)

CONNECTION QUESTION IN TEXT (p. 1026) WITH ANSWER

1. Write an essay on landlords based on this poem and Soyinka's "Telephone Conversation" (p. 681).

    Landlords are either indifferent toward their tenants, discriminatory, or both based on these two poems. Both landlords seem complicit in a larger pattern of societal discrimination. It could be argued that they are more than complicit in this pattern, that they represent the worst aspects of the societal divisions fostered by modern capitalist society.

Midnight Raffle (p. 1026)

This speaker's night didn't go as he had planned, but he neglects to tell us anything specific about his disappointment. The night is described as a raffle that costs the speaker a "nickel" (lines 1, 5, 9), which seems both metaphorical and literal: it is the price he pays for his failed adventure — that is, his subway fare. Students might spend some time discussing these levels of meaning; we "take a chance" when we play a raffle, after all. What sort of chance do they think the speaker takes when he plays this "raffle of the night" (2)? The speaker also loses his "time" (6); consider all of the economic metaphors that we use when discussing time (we spend it, we invest it, we save it, we waste it, etc.). What type of loss is this speaker describing? Is it different from "the dream deferred" which Hughes describes in "Harlem" (text p. 1030)? How do the final two lines help or hinder our interpretation of the rest of the poem?

POSSIBLE CONNECTIONS TO OTHER SELECTIONS

Regina Barreca, "Nighttime Fires" (text p. 688)

Lucille Clifton, "come home from the movies" (text p. 791)

Langston Hughes, "doorknobs" (question #1, following)

1. Compare in an essay the meaning of home in "Midnight Raffle" and "doorknobs" (p. 1032).

    Home in this poem is a place where nothing happens; the speaker takes a chance by going out into the night and he loses his money and his time. He figures that he might as well have stayed home since he didn't get anything for his troubles. In "doorknobs," home is a place where things happen, but only when they come in from the outside. The final line intimates that we have no control over these invasions of our home. The speaker of "Midnight Raffle" also seems to have no control, but he tries to take control by leaving his home in order to find a way to butter his bread. Home is "safe" in this poem, though; in "doorknobs," it is just the opposite. The difference can be accounted for partially by the two different types of speakers who narrate these poems.

Theme for English B (p. 1027)

This poem reads like a personal narrative, and indeed it does embody certain elements of Hughes's life. For example, "the college on the hill above Harlem" (line 9) is a reference to Columbia University, where Hughes was (briefly) a student. Therefore, asking a student to read this narrative to the class might make the speaker's story appear more poignant than if it were read in silence. You might ask students to pay particular attention to lines 21–26. The speaker defines himself in terms of the things he likes, which are nearly universal in their appeal, and recognizes that "being colored doesn't make [him] *not* like / the same things other folks like who are other races" (25–26). Ask students how this observation complicates the speaker's understanding of his relationship with the white college instructor and with whites in general.

You might also ask students how the double meaning of "theme" adds to the meaning of the poem. The speaker's assignment is to write a one-page "theme," that is, a brief composition. But the subject, or "theme," of that "theme" is far broader and more complicated: race relations and personal experiences. You might ask students if they noticed any other words with more than one interpretation in the context of this poem. One example might be the word *colored,* which means both that the writer is black and that he has been "colored," that is, affected, by the racial conditions into which he was born.

Ask your class to consider, in discussion or in a brief writing assignment, the importance of lines 31–33. How does the speaker understand himself and the white instructor to be part of each other? Why does he consider this to be particularly "American" (33)? You might also ask your students to think about this poem in the context of other poems in which Hughes attempts to define what is "American," such as "I, Too" (text p. 1014). How would your students describe Hughes's vision of America?

POSSIBLE CONNECTIONS TO OTHER SELECTIONS

Chitra Banerjee Divakaruni, "Indian Movie, New Jersey" (question #2, following)
Mark Halliday, "Graded Paper" (text p. 1156)

CONNECTION QUESTION IN TEXT (p. 1028) WITH ANSWER

2. Discuss the attitudes expressed toward the United States in this poem and in Divakaruni's "Indian Movie, New Jersey" (p. 819).

Both poems express the uneasiness of being a minority in white America. There is a grudging relationship between the minority and majority cultures, expressed in Hughes's poem as "You are white — / yet a part of me, as I am part of you. / That's American" (lines 31–33). The Indians in Divakaruni's poem do not even have that much of a connection to white America. They can only dream their version of the American dream while they are in the dim foyer of a movie theater, isolated from the rest of the culture. You might introduce the phrase "melting pot" when students address this question: has that metaphor ever accurately described our nation? How would the speakers of each of these poems respond to it?

Juke Box Love Song (p. 1028)

Transforming the energy of a Harlem night, this speaker makes it into a love song for his lover. He would have to reduce the rumble of the buses and subways, but other than that the heartbeat (line 7) of the night produces a "drumbeat" (7) suitable for dancing. Through the vehicle of a song (traditional in love and in Hughes's Harlem), the speaker connects the Harlem night itself with his lover, the "sweet brown Harlem girl" (12). To the speaker, Harlem is so full of such "natural" music and he of such love for the girl, that the two become intertwined in an imaginary "dance . . . till day" (10, 11).

Ask students if there are places where they feel connected to a person, even if the person isn't there. What about these places reminds them of the person? Are their associations as strong as Hughes's? This poem is rich with imagery; compare students' impressions of Harlem, past or present, with their impression of it based on this poem alone. Hughes's images are purely positive. Are they as positive in the rest of his poetry?

POSSIBLE CONNECTIONS TO OTHER SELECTIONS

Joseph Brodsky, "Love Song" (text p. 845)
Langston Hughes, "Danse Africaine" (text p. 1017)
———, "Red Silk Stockings" (question #1, following)
Timothy Steele, "An Aubade" (text p. 761)

CONNECTION QUESTION IN TEXT (p. 1029) WITH ANSWER

1. Compare the tone of this poem with "Red Silk Stockings" (p. 1022). Which poem do you prefer? Explain why.

   The speaker of "Red Silk Stockings" provides an obvious contrast to this speaker; this speaker dotes on both Harlem and his "sweet brown Harlem girl." The music in "Juke Box Love Song" is dancing music, and the speaker's idea is to "wrap around" (line 2) the girl. Compare the diction and ideas to the sarcastic speaker in "Red Silk Stockings" who entreats the woman to show off her legs to "de white boys" (3). Taken together, do all of the various voices that speak in Hughes's poetry provide a varied portrait of Harlem in the first half of the century? Are some categories of voices more prominent than others?

Dream Boogie (p. 1029)

This poem, like many of Hughes's others, relies heavily on musical influences. You might ask your students what makes this poem so closely resemble a song. Responses might include the fast-paced rhymes of the first stanza and the final four lines, which sound more like lyrics than the conclusion of a poem.

You might also ask your students about the voices in this poem, which seem to interrupt each other. The voice in line 7 is interrupted by a new voice that poses the question: *"You think / It's a happy beat?"* (lines 8–9). This question seems to refer back to "The boogie-woogie rumble / Of a dream deferred" (3–4) in the first stanza. Ask students to examine the meaning of this "rumble" — to what or to whom is the speaker referring? Students might mention that the "rumble" could allude to the lives of those black Americans who cannot achieve their dreams in this country, and that the beat, or rhythm, of their lives is not necessarily a happy one. Students might connect this poem to blues music, which can appear to be uplifting but in fact may be deeply melancholy and troubled.

Ask students to comment on the final four lines of this poem. Have them speculate on why Hughes ended his poem this way. Who might this poem be specifically addressing? You might also ask your students to discuss "The boogie-woogie rumble / of a dream deferred" (3–4) in the context of the next Hughes poem in this collection: "Harlem" (text p. 1030).

POSSIBLE CONNECTIONS TO OTHER SELECTIONS

Langston Hughes, "Dream Variations" (question #2, following)
——, "Harlem" (text p. 1030)

CONNECTION QUESTION IN TEXT (p. 1030) WITH ANSWER

2. How are the "dreams" different in "Dream Boogie" and "Dream Variations" (p. 1018)?

    Both dreams connote hope for the future, but the dream in this poem does not seem to connote a literal dream as well, as it does in "Dream Variations." In other words, this poem's sensibility is wide awake. "Dream Variations" has an impressionistic quality, making its dream both literal and figurative.

Harlem (p. 1030)

Discussion of this poem might be couched in a discussion of how your students define "the American Dream." You might ask your class to discuss or to compile a list of their associations with the American Dream. Their responses might include education, financial security, hopeful prospects for their children, social status, respect, justice, and so on. You might then ask your students how people might be affected if they found their "dreams" to be unattainable for social, political, economic, or racial reasons. This discussion leads into a discussion of the poetic similes that Hughes uses to describe the results of the dreams themselves, when they are "deferred" (line 1).

Ask your students to consider the words that Hughes uses to describe the possible results of "a dream deferred." Words such as "dry up" (2), "fester" (4), "stink" (6), "crust and sugar over" (7), and "sag" (9) offer very diverse images of decay and deterioration. Ask them if they recognize any sort of progression in these images, from the raisin that dries up fairly harmlessly, to a sore that causes pain to an individual, to rotten meat and sweets gone bad, which can poison several, to a heavy load that can burden many. The final alternative that Hughes offers is that a deferred dream might "explode" (11). Ask students how this final possibility is different from the previous ones and how this violent image of explosion might be related to the social and political realities in the United States at the time Hughes wrote this poem. Although this poem predates the civil rights movement, the 1950s were a time of great social upheaval and tense race relations in America. You might ask your students to discuss whether or not this poem may be interpreted as a threat to white Americans who contribute to "deferring" the dreams of minority Americans.

POSSIBLE CONNECTIONS TO OTHER SELECTIONS

Langston Hughes, "Dream Boogie" (text p. 1029)
———, "Frederick Douglass: 1817–1895" (text p. 1034)
James Merrill, "Casual Wear" (question #1, following)

CONNECTION QUESTION IN TEXT (p. 1030) WITH ANSWER

1. Write an essay on the themes of "Harlem" and Merrill's "Casual Wear" (p. 817).

    The theme of "Casual Wear" is that the lives of strangers can meet randomly and result in tragedy. The theme of "Harlem" also ends in tragedy, but it is not so specific or individualized. It is the direct result of a "dream deferred," whereas the terrorist in Merrill's poem is not necessarily a disillusioned dreamer, although he may be disillusioned in general.

Un-American Investigators (p. 1030)

To appreciate this poem, it is important for your students to have some understanding of the political climate of the 1950s and the operations of the congressional Special Committee on Un-American Activities. You might begin class discussion by asking students what they know about McCarthyism and the influence of the Special Committee. This background information may assist students in recognizing that the members of this committee are, according to the tone of the poem and the vision of the speaker, as "un-American" as the activities they are supposedly investigating.

You might ask your students to examine carefully the words the poet uses to describe the investigators on this committee. The "fat" (line 1) and "smug" (2) investigators are sharply contrasted with the "brave" (7) victims of their interrogation. Furthermore, the repeated fact that the "committee shivers / with delight in / Its manure" (21–23) clearly condemns their actions for being arbitrary, intrusive, and corrupt.

Given the radical political background of Langston Hughes and the communist sympathies he held for many years, you might ask students to discuss the risks the poet might have been taking in satirizing this very powerful committee in 1953. In discussion or in a writing assignment, you might ask students to compare and contrast this poem with some of Hughes's earlier, more hopeful poems about America such as "I, Too" (p. 1014). You might also ask your class how the "victim" in this poem differs from the "victims" in other poems by Hughes. In this case, the person summoned before the Committee is named Lipshitz, a Jewish name. Students might recognize that there are no specific racial issues addressed in this poem; the speaker is attacking a committee that scapegoats unfortunate individuals from many different backgrounds.

POSSIBLE CONNECTIONS TO OTHER SELECTIONS

E. E. Cummings, "next to of course god america i" (question #1, following)
N. Scott Momaday, "The Bear" (text p. 1110)

1. Write an essay that connects the committee described in this poem with the speaker in Cummings's "next to of course god america i" (p. 805). What do they have in common?

   The committee in this poem and the speaker in Cummings's are both smug and filled with empty patriotism and a false sense of religion. Both try to manipulate and influence others while preserving their own polished self-image.

Old Walt (p. 1031)

This poem has been interpreted as a celebration of the poetry of Walt Whitman (1819–1892). To begin class discussion, you might ask your students what they already know about Whitman. Important details might include the fact that Whitman considered himself to be a poet of the people and that he tried to include the common man in his poetry by using common language. Given this fact, you might ask your students to make some comparisons between Hughes and Whitman. How might the two poets be considered "poets of the people"? Ask your students to give examples of Hughes's poems that are particularly directed toward the "common man." You might also mention to your students that Whitman's poetry has been noted for its long lists of people or details, intended to include many different kinds of people and situations.

It might also be useful to have students characterize the tone of this poem. The speaker refers to Whitman as "Old Walt" (lines 1, 10); ask your students what this familiarity reveals about the speaker's attitude toward Whitman. What other details do they believe might contribute to the tone of the poem?

POSSIBLE CONNECTIONS TO OTHER SELECTIONS

Langston Hughes, "Frederick Douglass: 1817–1895" (question #1, following)
Walt Whitman, "There Was a Child Went Forth" (text p. 463)

CONNECTION QUESTION IN TEXT (p. 1032) WITH ANSWER

1. How does Hughes's tribute to Whitman compare with his tribute to Frederick Douglass (p. 1034)?

   Hughes's respect for Douglass as a person is more evident than his respect for Whitman. He admires what Whitman did — his endless pleasure in seeking and finding truth through his poetry — but he admires Douglass both for what he did and for who he was. Even the titles of the poems indicate the difference in tone between them: Hughes's respect for "Old Walt" is fondness, as opposed to the unmitigated admiration and formal tribute he shows Douglass.

doorknobs (p. 1032)

You might begin discussion of this poem by offering some historical context to your students. Ask them what they know about the social and political climate of the early 1960s in America. The civil rights movement was gaining momentum when this poem was published, and the nation was facing an important turning point. In this context, ask your students what the "doorknob on a door / that turns to let in life" (lines 2–3) might represent. Ask them to explain what might be so terrifying about a metaphorical doorknob turning and opening the door to "life."

Students might also consider the uncertainty and fear that the speaker feels toward whoever might be behind that door, waiting to enter. Ask them to examine the implications of the description that the "life / on two feet standing" (3–4) may be male or female, drunk or sober, happy or terrified. Ask your students to characterize the speaker in this poem. What details in the poem contribute to the readers' understanding of the speaker's persona?

Stylistically, this poem is very different from the other Hughes poems in this collection. One unusual detail is that "doorknobs" is one long sentence that may be read both literally and symbolically. You might ask students to examine the final three lines. Why might the "yesterday" (24) that is "not of our own doing" (25) be so terrifying to the speaker?

POSSIBLE CONNECTION TO ANOTHER SELECTION

Jim Stevens, "Schizophrenia" (question #1, following)

CONNECTION QUESTION IN TEXT (p. 1033) WITH ANSWER

1. Write an essay comparing the theme of this poem with that of Stevens's "Schizophrenia" (p. 788).

   Both poems play with the psychological tension between physical places and the people who inhabit them. Both imply that the terror associated with doorknobs or other elements of houses symbolizes the terror of the people who are shut up in those houses. Yet the two poems differ subtly in their treatment of the subject: Stevens's poem uses his house as a metaphor for a troubled mind whereas Hughes's doorknob is symbolic.

Dinner Guest: Me (p. 1033)

It is important for students to know that "the Negro Problem" was at one time a common term used by whites to refer to the complicated issues of civil rights and the social treatment of blacks in America. The speaker's immediate announcement that "I know I am / The Negro Problem" (lines 1–2) reveals both the speaker's understanding of this term and his keen sense of the irony of his situation, in which white guests at an elegant dinner party inquire of their single black companion the details of the black American experience. This scenario ridicules the white "quasi-liberalism" of the 1960s.

Ask your students to consider the white diners' statement, "I'm so ashamed of being white" (14), in the context of this luxurious lobster dinner on Park Avenue. Do they see humor in this remark? Empathy? Sarcasm? You might ask your students to discuss the speaker's impression of the white diners. Do they believe the speaker when he says "To be a Problem on / Park Avenue at eight / is not so bad" (18–20)? What does it cost the speaker to partake of this lavish dinner?

You might also ask your students to consider the way Langston Hughes uses setting in his poems, particularly his tendency to name actual streets in New York in order to set the scene for his readers. Ask your class to compare Hughes's mention of Park Avenue (20) in this poem with his reference to Lenox Avenue – in "The Weary Blues" (text p. 1019) and "Lenox Avenue: Midnight" (text p. 1022). You might ask your students how Hughes incorporates these specific streets into his poetry so that even someone who has never been to New York understands these points of reference.

POSSIBLE CONNECTIONS TO OTHER SELECTIONS

M. Carl Holman, "Mr. Z" (text p. 1098)

Maxine Hong Kingston, "Restaurant" (question #1, following)

CONNECTION QUESTION IN TEXT (p. 1033) **WITH ANSWER**

1. Write an essay on each speaker's treatment of the diners in this poem and in Kingston's "Restaurant" (p. 849).

   The diners in both poems are complacent about their country's problems. In Kingston's poem, though, the diners seem oblivious to the problems. There is no connection between the speaker and the diners once the former has prepared dinner for the latter. The speaker in Hughes's poem is aware of the problems; he even describes himself as "the Problem" in lines 19 and 22. His complacency stems not from ignorance but from the fact that he has been wooed by the white diners who seek solace from him, if not solutions.

Frederick Douglass: 1817–1895 (p. 1034)

You might begin class discussion by asking your students to share what they already know about Frederick Douglass. Important points that may arise might include the facts that Douglass was born a slave, escaped from his master, and became a well-known and well-respected abolitionist, writer, orator, and freedom fighter for all oppressed people in America. In this poem, Hughes seems to be celebrating Douglass's personal courage, spirit, and dedication to his beliefs. Douglass overcame seemingly insurmountable odds to become the mouthpiece for all those Americans who were not free and could not speak for themselves.

You might ask your students to consider the second stanza: *"Who would be free / Themselves must strike / The first blow*, he said" (lines 18–20). Hughes attributes these lines to Douglass addressing the slaves. Ask your students how those words might have been interpreted more broadly in 1966 and if this poem can be interpreted as an incitement to violence. You might further this idea by asking your class to debate whether or not using violence to gain freedom is justifiable.

You might ask your students, in discussion or in writing, to examine the seemingly contradictory final two lines of this poem: "He died in 1895. / *He is not dead*" (21–22). Ask your students to explain in what sense Douglass is not dead. If his spirit lives on, in what form does it endure?

POSSIBLE CONNECTION TO ANOTHER SELECTION

Galway Kinnell, "The Deconstruction of Emily Dickinson" (text p. 961)

CONNECTION QUESTION IN TEXT (p. 1034) **WITH ANSWER**

1. How is the speaker's attitude toward violence in this poem similar to that of the speaker in Hughes's "Harlem" (p. 1030)?

   Violence is not construed as negative in either poem. In this poem, it is necessary for Douglass to employ violence in order to realize his life's goal. In "Harlem," violence is an inevitable outcome, or at least a possibility. It is not necessarily positive, but given the choice of other possibilities Hughes presents for a dream deferred, it is the best option.

PERSPECTIVES ON HUGHES

Hughes on Racial Shame and Pride (p. 1034)

Ask your students to discuss the possible reasons why Hughes feels that "it is the duty of the younger Negro artist" to make black people realize "I am a Negro — and beautiful." Ask your students how Hughes performs this "duty," citing specific examples from his poetry that celebrate the black American identity. In this perspective, Hughes describes the black Philadelphia clubwoman who is ashamed of her heritage and denies a "true picture of herself" as "near white in soul." Ask your students how Hughes seems to be characterizing "whiteness" and "blackness." What aspects of this clubwoman's character seem particularly offensive to Hughes? Do your students sense any sympathy that Hughes might feel for her?

Hughes on Harlem Rent Parties (p. 1035)

Hughes describes rent parties in a deeply nostalgic tone; ask your students what details in the Perspective suggest that he longs to reexperience these evenings of "dancing and singing and impromptu entertaining." You might also open discussion about this perspective by asking your students to identify details of these rent parties that Hughes does not include in this description. For instance, Hughes makes no mention of the impoverished, desperate conditions that forced people to throw rent parties in the first place. He eliminates any mention of human suffering in his celebration of the warm, compassionate community spirit that these social gatherings fostered.

You might ask your students to look closely at the invitation card. Have them consider the language used. Nowadays would they consider these cards to be offensive in any way? This might lead into a class discussion about the nature of "labels" to define people in terms of their color; ask them to articulate some of the reasons the term "yellow girls" might not be as acceptable now as it was in the 1930s.

DONALD B. GIBSON, The Essential Optimism of Hughes and Whitman (p. 1036)

One way to open discussion about this Perspective is to ask your students how many agree with Gibson's description of Hughes and how many do not. Using evidence from Hughes's poetry, ask your class to debate whether or not Hughes had any genuine sense of racial injustice as evil. They might pay particular attention to the ways in which Hughes's poetry changed and developed over the years. You could ask them, in discussion or in writing, to compare Hughes's social vision of America in the 1920s with his vision in the 1960s.

Gibson maintains that Hughes could not have written "The Negro Speaks of Rivers" or "I, Too" in the 1960s; ask your students if they agree with this statement. In the 1920s, Hughes was a young man full of hope for his country; in the 1960s, he was an adult who had witnessed the disintegration of the civil rights movement and had perceived little actual improvement in race relations in America. You might ask your students to discuss whether or not they think Hughes might have developed a more threatening, real sense of evil over the years.

JAMES A. EMANUEL, Hughes's Attitudes toward Religion (p. 1037)

In this Perspective, Emanuel cites Hughes's comment that he (Hughes) is against "the misuse of religion." Ask your students to reread some of Hughes's poems, looking for religious images and symbols. If they can identify the influence of religion in one or more poems, have them discuss whether Hughes "misuses" Christianity, as he was accused of doing. If he seems to dismiss or embrace Christianity, is he also dismissing or embracing Christians?

You might also ask your students to comment on Hughes's statement that "we live in a world . . . of solid earth and vegetables and a need for jobs and a need for housing." How and where do they recognize Hughes's practical understanding of worldly needs in his poetry? You might also discuss with your students Hughes's acknowledgment that his formative religious experiences related more to music than to preaching. How does this musical influence surface in his poetry?

RICHARD K. BARKSDALE, *On Censoring "Ballad of the Landlord"* (p. 1038)

You might approach this Perspective by asking students to discuss current social tensions between the "haves" and "have-nots" in our society or between whites and blacks. Would a poem or story written today about social inequality and oppression have the same incendiary potential that it did in the 1960s? Ask them to articulate why they do or do not think so. You might help students to understand the social climate at the time of the poem's censoring by reminding your class about the Rodney King beating and subsequent riots in Los Angeles in 1992. Ask them to consider how a poem about police brutality written in the 1970s might take on "new meanings reflecting the times" in the 1990s. Ask students to think of other examples of texts acquiring new meanings as time passes.

Hughes's "Ballad of the Landlord" was censored ostensibly to avoid exacerbating racial tensions between whites and blacks. This plan obviously backfired, resulting in a great deal of unanticipated attention to this particular poem. This might lead into a class discussion about the nature of censorship and whether or not censoring inflammatory literature can be a useful way of soothing social tensions.

STEVEN C. TRACY, *A Reading of "The Weary Blues"* (p. 1039)

Using this Perspective as a guide, you might ask students to describe the relationship between the speaker and the performer in "The Weary Blues." Can they argue that this relationship is compromised in any way because the two do not actually speak to each other? Can they argue that the relationship is maintained precisely because the two people do not actually connect as individuals? Ask your students to use details from the poem as evidence to support their theories.

The distinction that Tracy makes between the "accepted Western sound" of the piano and the music that the performer plays in the poem seems to be rooted in the piano's long history as a classical European instrument. You might ask students to discuss how the "transformation" of the piano and other instruments in jazz and blues music has added to the effect of these "newer" musical genres.

DAVID CHINITZ, *The Romanticization of Africa in the 1920s* (p. 1040)

Students may find this passage tough going, but it is worthwhile to spend some time reading it closely. Part of the difficulty may come from the discourse (words like "atavism"), part from their potential lack of understanding of the historical context for such a discussion. It is important not only that they understand the tenets of primitivism, but also to understand Chinitz's take on this development (he refers to "clichés" at one point, indicating that he thinks this primitivist strain is a little hokey). Is there any such romanticization of African culture today? If not, do students find post–World War I disillusionment to be a valid explanation of why this romanticization took place in the 1920s?

Many of Hughes's poems from the 1920s can be productively examined through Chinitz's lens. As far as some later poems that show Hughes rejecting this mind-set, "Note on Commercial Theatre," "Harlem," and "Dinner Guest: Me" work well.

TWO COMPLEMENTARY CRITICAL READINGS

COUNTEE CULLEN, *On Racial Poetry* (p. 1041)

It is interesting to note that Countee Cullen, a black poet, quarrels with Hughes's insistence on writing about what Cullen calls "strictly Negro themes." He says that he admires the "jazz poems" that are included in *The Weary Blues*, but regards them merely as "interlopers in the company of the truly beautiful poems in other sections of the book," which do not deal so specifically with the black experience in America.

It is important for your students to take into consideration the era in which Cullen was writing. In 1926, black American artists were only beginning to be recognized by white mainstream audiences, and Cullen might have feared that Hughes would be marginalized or dismissed entirely for becoming a "racial artist" as opposed to an artist "pure and simple." Ask your students to discuss what Cullen may have meant by the term "racial artist." Is that term at all relevant today? Or may all contemporary artists be considered "artists pure and simple"?

ONWUCHEKWA JEMIE, *On Universal Poetry* (p. 1042)

Onwuchekwa Jemie's Perspective, written a half-century later than Countee Cullen's, takes issue with Cullen's conviction that an artist's work will be considered more universally relevant and important if that artist avoids dealing with "racial material." Jemie accuses Cullen of equating "universal" with "white" or "Western," thereby denying the universal qualities of all human experience regardless of racial background. Jemie challenges the notion that black experiences are less appropriate than white experiences when comparing artistic merit and extends Hughes's own argument about the value and universality of the African American experience.

Ask your students to notice how Cullen discounts precisely the qualities in Hughes's writing that Jemie so ardently celebrates. How might your students account for this difference, based on the time periods that produced these two perspectives? One might argue that Jemie's defense of the black experience as universal might extend to other minority experiences, such as those of women, Hispanics, Jews, and homosexuals. Ask your students to discuss this possibility, and then ask them what makes a particular experience "universally" meaningful. You might also discuss with your class the possibility that describing the specific experiences of particular groups as universally relevant might detract from the meaning of that experience in some way. Ask your students whether they agree or disagree with that possibility, and why.

ADDITIONAL RESOURCES FOR TEACHING HUGHES

SELECTED BIBLIOGRAPHY

Bloom, Harold. *Langston Hughes.* New York: Chelsea, 1988.

Bonner, Pat E. *Sassy Jazz and Slo' Draggin' Blues: Music in the Poetry of Langston Hughes.* New York: Lang, 1992.

Emanuel, James A. *Langston Hughes*. New York: Twayne, 1967.

Gates, Henry Louis Jr., ed. *Langston Hughes: Critical Perspectives Past and Present*. New York: Penguin USA, 1993.

Hughes, Langston. *The Collected Poetry of Langston Hughes*. Ed. Arnold Rampersad. New York: Knopf, 1994.

Jemie, Onwuchekwa. *Langston Hughes: An Introduction to the Poetry*. New York: Columbia UP, 1976.

Miller, R. Baxter. *The Art and Imagination of Langston Hughes*. Lexington: UP of Kentucky, 1989.

Mullen, Edward J., ed. *Critical Essays on Langston Hughes*. Boston: Hall, 1986.

O'Daniel, Therman B., ed. *Langston Hughes, Black Genius: A Critical Evaluation*. New York: Morrow, 1971.

Tracy, Steven C. *Langston Hughes and the Blues*. Urbana: U of Illinois P, 1988.

AUDIOVISUAL RESOURCES

Langston Hughes. 24 min., color, 1971. Beta, VHS, ¾" U-matic cassette, 16-mm film. A biographical sketch of the poet. Distributed by Carousel Film and Video.

Langston Hughes: The Dream Keeper [video]. Color, VHS (60 min.), 1988. Distributed by the Annenberg/CPB Collection.

Langston Hughes: Dream Keeper and Other Poems [recording]. 1 cassette, 1955. Distributed by Smithsonian/Folkways Recordings.

Langston Hughes: The Making of a Poet [recording]. 1 cassette (30 min.). Read by the poet. Distributed by National Public Radio.

Langston Hughes: Poetry & Reflections [recording]. 1 cassette. Performed by the author. Distributed by Caedmon/HarperAudio.

Looking for Langston [video]. Color, VHS (45 min.), 1992. Produced by Isaac Julien. Distributed by Water Bearer Films.

Langston Hughes Reads [recording]. 1 cassette (50 min.). Distributed by Caedmon/HarperAudio, Filmic Archives.

Langston Hughes Reads and Talks about His Poems [recording]. 1 cassette. Includes "The Negro Speaks of Rivers" and "Dream Boogie." Distributed by Spoken Arts.

Langston Hughes: Simple Stories [recording]. 1 cassette. Performed by Ossie Davis. Distributed by Caedmon/HarperAudio.

The Poetry of Langston Hughes [recording]. 2 cassettes. Performed by Ruby Dee and Ossie Davis. Distributed by Caedmon/HarperAudio.

The Voice of Langston Hughes: Selected Poetry and Prose [recording]. 1 cassette or CD (38 min.). Selections from the years 1925–1932. The author reads poetry from "The Dream Keeper and Other Poems" and "Simple Speaks His Mind" and narrates his texts from "The Story of Jazz," "Rhythms of the World," and "The Glory of Negro History." Distributed by Smithsonian/Folkways Recordings.

See also "Harlem Renaissance: The Black Poets," "The Harlem Renaissance and Beyond," "Modern American Poetry," "Twentieth-Century Poets Reading Their Work," and "Voices and Vision" in the appendix of Film, Video, and Audiocassette Resources.

25

Critical Case Study: T. S. Eliot's "The Love Song of J. Alfred Prufrock"

One of the problems you may encounter with this chapter is that the presence of material by professional critics may intimidate students into silence about their own readings. You may find it appropriate to have students articulate their own approaches to the poem before they turn to critical sources. On the other hand, critical sources can help in students' understandings of a poem, particularly one as complex as this. If students seem to be having trouble with the poem, you might direct them to one or more of the critical selections.

Another difficulty students may have with this chapter lies in their ability to deal with competing critical attitudes toward the same poem. Students tend to fall into an easy relativism, claiming that each approach highlights a different aspect of the poem and that each is equally valid. While this is true, it would be fair to put a bit of pressure on this attitude. The critical perspectives provided here are incommensurable in many ways. You might recognize this in class, and assign an informal writing or hold a class discussion centered around the question "Which of these readings are better and why?" This discussion should lead into considerations of evidence and argumentation, as well as situation or context: why certain readings are better for certain purposes, or more interesting to certain audiences. This will help students when it comes time for them to write using outside sources, as it will give them valuable experience with thinking critically about other positions.

T. S. ELIOT, *The Love Song of J. Alfred Prufrock* (p. 1045)

This dramatic monologue is difficult but well worth the time spent analyzing the speaker, imagery, tone, and setting. Begin with the title — is the poem actually a love song? Is Eliot undercutting the promise of a love song with the name J. Alfred Prufrock? Names carry connotations and images; what does this name project?

The epigraph from Dante seems to ensure both the culpability and the sincerity of the speaker. After reading the poem, are we, too, to be counted among those who will never reveal what we know?

The organization of this monologue is easy enough to describe. Up until line 83, Prufrock tries to ask the overwhelming question. In lines 84–86, we learn that he has been afraid to ask it. From line 87 to the end, Prufrock tries to explain his failure by citing the likelihood that he would be misunderstood or by making the disclaimer that he is a minor character, certainly no Prince Hamlet. Notice how the idea of "dare" charts Prufrock's growing submissiveness in the poem from "Do I dare / Disturb the universe?" to "Have I the strength to force the moment to its crisis?" (which rhymes lamely with "tea and cakes and ices") and, finally, "Do I dare to eat a peach?"

You might ask students to select images they enjoy. Consider, for example, Prufrock's assertion that he has measured out his life in the shallowness of the ladies Prufrock associates with: "In the room the women come and go / Talking of Michelangelo" (lines 13–14). The poem offers many opportunities to explore the nuances of language and the suggestive power of image as a means of drawing a character portrait and suggesting something about a particular social milieu at a particular time in modern history.

Grover Smith, in his *T. S. Eliot's Poetry and Plays* (Chicago: U of Chicago P, 1960), provides extensive background and critical comment on this poem.

As a writing assignment, you might ask the class to explore a pattern of images in the poem — those of crustaceans near the end, for example — and how that pattern adds to the theme. You might also ask the class to give a close reading of a particular passage — the final three lines come to mind — for explication.

POSSIBLE CONNECTIONS TO OTHER SELECTIONS

John Keats, "La Belle Dame sans Merci" (text p. 1103)
Alberto Ríos, "Seniors" (text p. 702)
Wallace Stevens, "The Emperor of Ice-Cream" (text p. 1120)
Walt Whitman, "One's-Self I Sing" (question #1, following)

CONNECTION QUESTION IN TEXT (p. 1049) WITH ANSWER

1. Write an essay comparing Prufrock's sense of himself as an individual with that of Walt Whitman's speaker in "One's-Self I Sing" (p. 1124).

    These two songs have very different melodies as well as harmonies. Eliot's "love song" is really a dirge for an individual whose isolation from society far outweighs his connection to it. Prufrock never manages to connect himself with any other figure in his poem, except for the "eternal Footman" who snickers at him. His tone is morbid, self-pitying at best, as opposed to Whitman's speaker, who celebrates all aspects of both the individual and of the society he or she belongs to. The "Life immense in passion, pulse, and power" (6) that he celebrates has drained out of Prufrock "like a patient etherized upon a table" (3). Whitman's speaker is eternally awakening to life, Eliot's is eternally dying.

RESOURCE FOR TEACHING

T. S. Eliot Reading "The Love Song of J. Alfred Prufrock" [recording]. 1 cassette. Distributed by HarperAudio.

ELISABETH SCHNEIDER, *Hints of Eliot in Prufrock* (p. 1049)

Schneider acknowledges that literal details of Eliot's life do not match those of Prufrock, yet asserts that "Prufrock was Eliot, though Eliot was much more than Prufrock." Her essay suggests that readers look at the internal workings of the mind of Prufrock, rather than the details of his life, for links to the poet who created him. What kind of "character profile" of Eliot could students create by using Prufrock's personality as a model? What does Schneider mean by her statement that "Eliot was much more than Prufrock?" Does Schneider's comment that "friends who knew the young Eliot almost all describe him, *retrospectively* but convincingly, in Prufrockian terms" (emphasis added) strengthen or weaken her argument? Does the fact that Eliot was in his early twenties when he wrote the poem (around 1910–1911) argue for or against a biographical interpretation?

BARBARA EVERETT, *The Problem of Tone in Prufrock* (p. 1050)

Everett asserts that it is difficult to describe tone in Eliot's poetry because the voice in his poems "seems disinterested in what opinions it may happen to be expressing." That is, the distance that Eliot establishes between the speaker and the scene is so great that the tone of the voice becomes unrecognizable and, to some extent, undefinable. You might ask students to locate particular moments in the poem when this detachment becomes especially noticeable. What might this suggest about Prufrock's character? Everett quotes from the poem: "I have known them all already, known them all." You might ask your class to discuss how this retrospective moment in the poem complements Everett's argument for the speaker's detachment from the action.

MICHAEL L. BAUMANN, *The "Overwhelming Question" for Prufrock* (p. 1051)

Baumann's formalist approach cites specific passages in the text of "Prufrock" to argue that the "overwhelming question" facing Eliot's character is whether or not to commit suicide. In particular, he mentions the allusion to John the Baptist (lines 81–83) and the references to drowning in the closing lines of the poem to substantiate his thesis. You might ask your students why he does not also use the reference to Lazarus. Are there other passages regarding death that Baumann does not choose to discuss? In concentrating on a few examples and developing them thoroughly in order to make his point, does he ignore details that would weaken his theory? Do your students agree with Baumann that the "overwhelming question" concerns suicide? What else might it be?

FREDERIK L. RUSCH, *Society and Character in "The Love Song of J. Alfred Prufrock"* (p. 1053)

Rusch utilizes the socio-psychological theories of Erich Fromm to pose yet another possible interpretation of Prufrock's "overwhelming question." Fromm contends that because human beings are separated by their self-consciousness from nature, they turn to human society for a sense of belonging. Prufrock's dilemma is that he is alienated by the depersonalizing structure of modern life. Rusch argues that Prufrock understands his alienation but does not know what to do about it. He concludes that Prufrock's solution is an imaginary return to the animal state, suggested by the image of the "ragged claws" in the sea at the end of the poem. The significance of water as an archetypal symbol of the unconscious or of rebirth lends further credence to Rusch's conclusion. The essay ties in nicely with Baumann's argument by supporting the depiction of Prufrock as a hopelessly depressed man, although its conclusion differs.

It might be interesting to discuss with your students whether Fromm's work and Rusch's analysis of Prufrock's dilemma are gender-based. That is, do women, who historically have grown up knowing they are separate from the power structures of society, suffer the same shock of alienation Fromm describes? Do women feel the same disconnectedness from other human beings that men do?

ROBERT SWARD, *A Personal Analysis of "The Love Song of J. Alfred Prufrock"* (p. 1055)

If students do not think that this dialogue approach to criticism is serious, point out that it has been used since Plato, if not before, and revived by modern critics such as Oscar Wilde. This dialogue between a sailor and a ranking officer is highly stylized, although it seems to rely on earthy sailor-talk (like how the T. S. of Eliot's name stands for "Tough Shit"), it seems like a fictionalized portrait, if not a fictional one. You might ask students to select passages of the essay that indicate that Sward's narrative couldn't really have happened that way; is the essay truly "personal"? Why is this setting, on a ship en route to Korea with sailors drinking rum out of coffee cups, crucial to this particular reading of the poem? Although it seems radically different from the other critical selections in terms of tone, point out that this reading has many elements in common with the other readings, such as the need to sort through Eliot's biography, the analysis both of Prufrock's character and Eliot's method in conjunction with one another, and the will to construct Prufrock as a kind of "everyman" at the end of the essay. If students attempt to analyze another poem using Sward's method, do they embellish their account at all by relying on some device like a dialogue? If not, will the reading suffer, or will it be that much fresher for its honesty?

ADDITIONAL RESOURCES FOR TEACHING

Four Quartets [recording]. 1 cassette. Distributed by Caedmon/HarperAudio.

The Mysteries of Mr. Eliot. 62 min., color, 1973. Beta, VHS, ¾″ U-matic cassette, 16-mm film. A biographical film about the poet. Distributed by Insight Media and CRM Films.

T. S. Eliot: Selected Poems [recording]. 49 min., 1971. The author reads his poetry, including "The Waste Land." Distributed by Caedmon/HarperAudio.

T. S. Eliot and George Orwell [recording]. 1 cassette (41 min.), 1953. Read by Stephen Spender. Distributed by Audio-Forum.

T. S. Eliot: Twentieth-Century Poetry in English: Recordings of Poets Reading Their Own Poetry, No. 3 [recording]. Distributed by the Library of Congress.

See also "Modern American Poetry," "The Poet's Voice," "Voices and Vision," and "Caedmon Treasury of Modern Poets Reading Their Own Poetry" in the appendix of Film, Video, and Audiocassette Resources.

26

Cultural Case Study:
Julia Alvarez's "Queens, 1963"

This chapter presents a poem along with various materials that will aid students in understanding the historical and cultural context of the poem. This may seem a great departure to students if the class has previously taken a more formalist approach, or even to students who have dealt with the poems more thematically, as it grounds discussion in a consideration of a specific historical moment. The poem could stand on its own, even based on the limited knowledge that most students have of recent history. However, the other materials can show students what can be added to the understanding of a poem by a careful investigation of its cultural context.

The poem "Queens, 1963" deals with issues of neighborliness, immigration, and racism. It is followed by an excerpt from an interview with Alvarez (the full text of which is available online — see Additional Resources for Teaching). The interview presents in a concise form many of the pressures that Alvarez felt as an immigrant and that have informed her poetry. It puts a human face on some of the events listed in the chronology, and can be useful to students in that capacity.

The other resources deal more with the wider cultural context of New York and America at the time. The ad for Gibson's Homes may initially be puzzling to the students. However, the picture in the ad can give them a sense of the physical environment in which the events of the poem took place. Students' experiences with "neighborhoods" can vary widely, from rural to suburban to urban, and this may help them more clearly understand the setting. The newspaper article provides a complementary picture of life in Queens. Students may or may not be cynical about such obvious public relations rhetoric; considering this article in relation to the poem may provide for an interesting discussion.

In stark contrast to these sanitized views of life in Queens, the photograph of the demonstrator and police reveals a hidden underside that is not all light and air. You might find it appropriate to point out that the picture was taken the same year as the events in the poem and the newspaper article; dissent was contemporaneous with images of the "good life," a fact that the poem also acknowledges, in its portrayal of the darker side of the "good neighborhood."

As an interesting exercise for this unit, you might have students do a similar cultural case study for one of the other poems in the text, or a cultural portfolio of a place familiar to them: either their hometown or where they are going to school. You may find that it is easier on students if you make this an assignment for small groups, which will enable them to cover more ground with less work.

Queens, 1963 (p. 1063)

This poem deals with the childhood experience of an immigrant girl in Queens who discovers open racism for the first time. It contains an interesting meditation on immigration, assimilation into a culture, and racism.

When a black family moves into the neighborhood that the immigrants have only recently joined, the speaker sees racism covered over by a variety of guises: the Haralambides's desire to avoid trouble, Mr. Scott's separatism, Mrs. Bernstein's seemingly enlightened position undercut by her worry over property values. These are counterpointed by the presence of the police, which shows even official involvement in trying to maintain barriers between the races. The speaker tries for a connection, a welcoming wave, but fails to bridge the gap, one that she can bridge only through sympathy and imagination. The final image of the poem retreats to an idyllic moment before any immigration. This final affirmation of a land before immigrants of any sort serves to undercut the self-righteousness of the immigrants in the poem, and points out that all the property owners were, at one point, immigrants themselves.

The connections between immigrants wanting to assimilate themselves into America and the racism perpetrated against African Americans makes this a particularly fascinating poem. You might ask your students if they believe that the black family will be integrated into the neighborhood in a year, just the Alvarez family, or if they believe the dynamic will be fundamentally different this time. Lorraine Hansberry's play *A Raisin in the Sun* would be a particularly interesting parallel text to consider in this case.

Students may misunderstand the presence of the police car in line 68, and believe that the family is being arrested for some reason. A close reading provides no evidence of this however: merely that the police are performing a subtle kind of intimidation on the family, making them feel like criminals despite the fact that they have committed no crime. This may be a touchy point for students who have accepted the current police-heavy answers being offered for social problems.

This poem can be read as indicting American culture on many levels, from personal reactions to civil servants to supposedly impersonal property values. Students, however, may be uncomfortable with this kind of reading. You might want to take this into account in the class discussion, and use the analyses of the later cultural materials to present this idea in a less threatening manner, one that will enable productive discussion and disagreement.

If you have been following the previous chapters and dealing with formal issues in the course, you may find it interesting to have students apply their skills in these areas to this poem, particularly noting the use of significant detail and irony.

MARNY REQUA, *From an Interview with Julia Alvarez* (p. 1066)

The interview raises several themes that are important to a consideration of the poem: immigration, cultural identity, and belonging. Alvarez speaks of the old "model for the immigrant," which meant buying into the American melting-pot ideology, an ideology that has since come under fire from a variety of sources. She also speaks of being caught between two worlds, American and Caribbean. It is precisely this sense of not-quite-belonging that enables the sympathetic identification between Alvarez and the black girl across the street.

An Advertisement for Tudor Row Houses (p. 1067)

As mentioned above, this ad can be puzzling to students, who may be unsure why it was included. In addition to giving them a better sense of the scene of the poem, it can give insight into the rhetoric of American identity in the first part of the century. You might encourage students to examine the selling points: driveways, low pricing, ideal for children, sewers, and so on. What do these selling points say about the promise of "the good life" in America? It is no coincidence that the development is billed as "The Perfect Low Priced American Home," particularly given the immigrant populations that came to occupy it. It is also interesting that the establishments mentioned are schools, churches, stores, and amusements. You might ask students how these institutions relate to ideas about "the American Dream" and the idealized versions of America popular throughout the century.

Additionally, you might encourage students to make connections between this ad and the interview, to articulate how it might appeal to the kinds of immigrants Alvarez describes, people all too eager to become American. You might also draw some connections in terms of style and rhetoric to the newspaper article that follows: in forty-three years, the perceptions of "the good life" in Queens appear to have remained largely unchanged. Another approach would be to ask students to evaluate this ad for irony, particularly in light of the poem and the photograph of the demonstrator.

Queens: "The 'Fair' Borough" (p. 1068)

The questions given in the text can help anchor a discussion of this article, focusing on the ironies revealed by its juxtaposition with the poem and photograph. You might find it helpful to ask students why the brochure was produced in the first place. Why is there a need to " 'reacquaint our residents' with the borough's history and present stature?" What sort of function is this brochure actually performing? Another interesting detail worth comment is the historical note at the end of the article: how does this fact about religious freedom mesh with the story America tells about itself, and how does the poem call this story into question?

NORMAN LEAR, "Talkin' about Prejudice" in Queens (From Meet the Bunkers) (p. 1069)

Though presumably taking place in Queens in 1971, eight years after Julia Alvarez's "Queens, 1963," this episode of the popular *All in the Family* sitcom highlights similar racial tensions that existed for Alvarez's speaker. For one thing, even before Lionel's entrance, the conversation focuses largely on race. In the scene presented here, the issue remains in the forefront of the characters' consciousness — and as the centerpiece of conversation. You may want to have students look for specific lingual clues that present each character's view on race. When the class has characterized the overall racial climate of Queens in 1971 that Lear shows us, have them do the same thing with "Queens, 1963." What climate changes seem to have taken place in the eight years between these selections? How would your students characterize these changes? Is one view more hopeful? More cynical?

A Civil Rights Demonstration (photograph) (p. 1072)

This photograph stands in stark contrast to the happy pictures of Queens life offered in the previous two entries. You might have students note the visual composition of the photograph: the dark wall of police cutting off the protestors, and the one protestor's face clearly visible in the center of the photo, staring at the camera. You might want to talk as a class about the power of such images, and similar images of demonstrations in civil rights protests and at Kent State. You might also have the class draw connections between the presence and function of police in this photograph and in the poem.

ADDITIONAL RESOURCES FOR TEACHING

SELECTED BIBLIOGRAPHY

Alvarez, Julia. *The Other Side/El Otro Lado: Poems.* New York: Dutton, 1995. The collection from which this poem is taken.

——. *Something to Declare: Essays.* Chapel Hill: Algonquin, 1998.

Requa, Marny. "The Politics of Fiction." *Frontera* 5 (29 Jan. 1997). <http://www.fronteramag.com/issue5/Alvarez>. The magazine itself might be an interesting resource for students to explore.

AUDIOVISUAL SOURCES

Julia Alvarez. 60 min., 1997, videocassette. Alvarez reads new poems and prose. Available through interlibrary loan from Appalachian State University.

Julia Alvarez Reads from *How the Garcia Girls Lost Their Accents* and Talks about the Dominican American Immigrant Experience. [recording]. 1 cassette. Newport Beach: Moveable Feast, 1990.

27

A Collection of Poems

MAYA ANGELOU, *Africa* (p. 1073)

This poem describes the continent of Africa as a woman, emphasizing her history of oppression and predicting her triumph in the future. You might begin a conversation about this poem by pointing out the contrasts between the anthropomorphized female Africa in each of the three stanzas. In each stanza, the meaning of the entire section is reflected in the poet's repeated use of the word *lain*. For instance, in the first stanza, "lain" refers to a sensual, even sexual Africa in years of rich repose, while in the second stanza, "lain" refers to an Africa that is violated and beaten. In the final stanza, Africa is no longer lying; rather, she is now rising and striding with images of strength and determination.

Like the poem "Wishing Africa" by Marilyn Bowering (text p. 743), this poem uses color to contrast geographic or emotional states of being — an observation that may make a good writing assignment. For instance, in Angelou's poem, the first stanza ends its vision of a rich, ripe Africa with the lines "Thus has she lain / Black through the years" (lines 7–8). This dark richness is contrasted in the second stanza with images of whiteness, coldness, and bloodlessness — "rime white and cold" (10) — which convey the violence brought to the sons, daughters, and continent of Africa herself.

You may wish to ask students who Angelou believes brought this violence to Africa and her children. Which lines of the poem can they cite as evidence? What is the predominant tone of the poem? Ask students also to consider whether it is significant that the repeated line "Thus she has lain" (1, 6) is changed in the final stanza to "although she *had* lain" (25).

POSSIBLE CONNECTIONS TO OTHER SELECTIONS

Langston Hughes, "The Negro Speaks of Rivers" (text p. 1010)

Wole Soyinka, "Future Plans" (text p. 1145)

RESOURCES FOR TEACHING

Maya Angelou. 30 min., color, 1982. Beta, VHS, ½" open reel (EIAJ), ¾" U-matic cassette. Robert Cromie talks with the poet. A two-part series. Distributed by Nebraska Educational Television Network.

Maya Angelou [recording]. 1 cassette (60 min.). Angelou reads from "And Still I Rise." With Heywood Hale Broun. Distributed by Audio-Forum.

Maya Angelou [recording]. 1 cassette (30 min.). The poet reads from her poetry, talks about her memoirs, and discusses her refusal to speak for three years as a child. Distributed by Tapes for Readers.

Maya Angelou [recording]. 2 cassettes (150 min.), 1993. Angelou's biography. Distributed by Chelsea House Publishers.

Maya Angelou: I Know Why the Caged Bird Sings [recording]. 2 cassettes (179 min.). Angelou's autobiography. Distributed by Random Audiobooks.

Maya Angelou: Making Magic in the World [recording]. 1 cassette (60 min.), 1988. Presents a trip from the Deep South to the heart of Africa and back again. Presented by New Dimensions Radio.

See also "Literature: The Synthesis of Poetry" in the appendix of Film, Video, and Audiocassette Resources.

ANONYMOUS, *Bonny Barbara Allan* (p. 1074), *Lord Randal* (p. 1075)

Ballads can provide a good introduction to poetry, for they demonstrate many devices of other poetic forms — such as rhyme, meter, and image — within a narrative framework. Ballads, however, often begin abruptly, and the reader must infer the details that preceded their action. They employ simple language, tell their story through narrated events and dialogue, and often use refrains. The folk ballad was at its height in England and Scotland in the sixteenth and seventeenth centuries. These ballads were not written down but were passed along through an oral tradition, with the original author remaining anonymous. Literary ballads are derivatives of the folk ballad tradition. John Keats's "La Belle Dame sans Merci" (text p. 1103) is an example.

Notice how often these ballads refer to broken love relationships. What can you infer about the relationships of the people in these ballads? Is it always one sex or the other who suffers? Is there a relationship between these ballads and modern-day popular songs? "Scarborough Fair" (text p. 827) might provide the basis for a discussion of the romantic situations presented in these ballads and the durability of such old "songs." Despite the list of impossible tasks that the speaker presents to his former lover as the price of reconciliation, the refrain names garden herbs associated with female power. Thyme traditionally is thought to enhance courage, sage wisdom, and rosemary memory, and parsley was used to decorate tombs — but both sage and rosemary had the additional connotations of growing in gardens where women ruled the households. You might wish to have your students speculate on how such "mixed messages" might have been incorporated into this ballad. Also, "Scarborough Fair" was the basis for an antiwar song by the folk-rock duo Simon and Garfunkel in the 1960s. Your students might be interested in hearing how this old folk song was adapted for twentieth-century purposes.

Despite their ostensible narrative directness, ballads can be highly suggestive (rather than straightforward) in their presentation. Psychological motivation is often implied rather than spelled out. To explore this point, you might request, for example, that students in a two-to-three-page essay examine and compare the reasons for and effects of the vengeful acts of Barbara Allan and Frankie.

All these ballads contain central characters whose awareness (and, hence, voice) comes into full power near the moment of their death. Again, this observation seems to support the psychological realism and suggestive truth that ballads can convey.

TIP FROM THE FIELD

When teaching "Lord Randal" and other ballads, I begin by reading the selection aloud or playing a recording of it, followed by a recording of early blues music from Mississippi (i.e., songs by Robert Johnson or Howlin' Wolf). In conjunction, I distribute the lyrics from the blues songs to the class. I then ask my students to compare these two oral-based forms.

— TIMOTHY PETERS, *Boston University*

ANONYMOUS, *Scottsboro* (p. 1076)

Ballads often speak the concerns of a culture, giving voice and hope to an oppressed people by encouraging them to keep their spirit alive in harsh circumstances. The black American folk tradition contains many examples of this kind of ballad. Written long after the Civil War, "Scottsboro" addresses a particular political situation, the Scottsboro case. The poet draws on the tradition of black folk ballads, finding a way to speak in a context where his words are not welcome.

POSSIBLE CONNECTION TO ANOTHER SELECTION

Langston Hughes, "Ballad of the Landlord" (text p. 1025)

W. H. AUDEN, *The Unknown Citizen* (p. 1076)

Clearly, the speaker of this poem is not Auden himself; and the distance between what the speaker says and what we assume Auden feels makes for a sharply satiric poem about this "unknown" yet statistically well-documented citizen. The important question for the class is, at what point and in what way do they realize they are reading satire? Focus first on the epitaph, its impersonal numbers and its precise rhymes. In the opening lines, consider how to reconcile "sainthood" with "One against whom there was no official complaint." Students familiar with George Orwell's fiction will probably enjoy this caricature of bureaucracy. You may want to explore the fine line that separates duty and regard for civic law from blind obedience.

POSSIBLE CONNECTION TO ANOTHER SELECTION

James Merrill, "Casual Wear" (text p. 817)

MARGARET AVISON, *Tennis* (p. 1077)

Avison's poem focuses and reflects on the sensory aspects of a seemingly rigid, methodical sport. Rather than allow the framework of the sonnet form to restrict her description of playing tennis, she explores the possibilities that lie in metric deviation. Avison writes about the physical exhilaration of the game, as well as its visual appeal, lending the whole sonnet a sweeping, lyrical quality that is uncommon in most traditional sonnets: "Dancing white galliardes at tape or net / Till point, on the wire's tip, or the long bum- / ing arc to nethercourt marks game and set." (lines 7, 8). Avison sees unrestricted possibility within the basic rules of tennis, and also relishes that same sense of possibility in the writing of her sonnet. The game of tennis is transformed into an insular, fantastical world where the opponents can become poets themselves and "Score liquid Euclids in foolscaps of air" (line 14).

There are many visual and metrical "surprises" in this poem, such as the breakup of the word *buming* at the end of the line 7. Also surprising is the appearance of the words *The albinos* in line 12. What are some other "surprises," metrical or otherwise, in this sonnet? Have your students explain how these devices contribute to the overall liberation of the form. At what point does the poem transform from a mere description of the action of a game to something more imaginative?

POSSIBLE CONNECTIONS TO OTHER SELECTIONS

Peter Meinke, "The ABC of Aerobics" (text p. 922)
David Solway, "Windsurfing" (text p. 755)

AMIRI BARAKA, *SOS* (p. 1077)

Baraka, who changed his name from LeRoi Jones in the 1960s, was the major poetic voice of the civil rights movement during that decade. His poetry is always social commentary, the subject often race relations, and his style is sometimes likened to that of Beat Generation writers such as Allen Ginsberg.

This spare poem borrows the language of two-way radio to send a message, but the meaning of that message depends on the reader's interpretation of "come in" (lines 3, 6), which is changed to "come / on in" (6–7) at the end of the poem. In terms of two-way radio, "come in" means simply "respond." That meaning is certainly inherent in Baraka's poem, but what are some of the other connotations of the phrase? You also might want to ask students to write a continuation of this poem: once the addressees ("all black people" [2]) have responded, what will the speaker say next? Does the title help them to speculate about what the message will be?

POSSIBLE CONNECTIONS TO OTHER SELECTIONS

Lucille Clifton, "come home from the movies" (text p. 791)
M. Carl Holman, "Mr. Z" (text p. 1098)
Langston Hughes, "Red Silk Stockings" (text p. 1022)

RESOURCES FOR TEACHING

Amiri Baraka [recording]. 1 cassette (29 min.), 1988. Distributed by New Letters on the Air.
LeRoi Jones/Imamu Amiri Baraka [recording]. 1 cassette, 1976. Distributed by Everett/Edwards.

WILLIAM BLAKE, *The Garden of Love* (p. 1078)

This brief lyric poses in customary Blakean fashion the natural, free-flowing, and childlike expression of love against the restrictive and repressive adult structures of organized religion. The dialogue between the two is effectively demonstrated in the closing two lines, with their internal rhyme patterns, in particular the rhyming of "briars" (of the priests) and "desires" (of the young boy). The process of growing into adulthood is costly, according to Blake; it requires the exchange of simple pleasures for conventional morality.

POSSIBLE CONNECTION TO ANOTHER SELECTION

Emily Dickinson, "From all the Jails the Boys and Girls" (text p. 951)

WILLIAM BLAKE, *Ah Sun-flower* (p. 1078)

Addressing the sunflower, Blake also addresses issues of time, life, and rejuvenation. The sunflower, "weary of time" seeks to go where, both literally and metaphorically, it cannot go. At first, the poem seems fairly simple. The symbol of the sunflower, rooted in place, but looking toward the sun, seems to indicate a sad irony about the flower's position in the world. But as the poem moves on, it seems more hopeful: the sunflower wants to go to a place of apparent redemption where "the Youth pined away with desire, / And the pale Virgin shrouded in snow" (lines 5–6) "Arise" (7). Yet when the two arise, they, in turn, want to go where the sunflower also wants to go. It is a circular bit of reasoning, and it reinforces the original picture of a sunflower (itself circular), circling around forever, wanting.

A good way into the poem is to ask students what the Youth and the Virgin have in common. True, they are both dead, and they both "arise" (if only in the imagination of the poem), but is there anything else? That the Youth pined and the Virgin is a virgin indicate that they missed something in life. How do they relate to the sunflower?

POSSIBLE CONNECTION TO ANOTHER SELECTION

Robert Frost, "Stopping by Woods on a Snowy Evening" (text p. 989)

ROBERT BLY, *Snowfall in the Afternoon* (p. 1078)

In these four three-line stanzas, the speaker of this poem describes an almost hallucinatory winter scene. By the end of the poem the distant barn has fully transformed into a ship, emphasizing the speaker's transforming perception, influenced by the hypnotic falling snow. You might begin discussion by talking about the structure of this poem. Bly very deliberately separates the stanzas by giving them numbers, and you might ask students to consider how the poem might read differently if the stanzas were merely separated by space. Do the numbers provide a sense of progression or differentiation between the various stanzas? Ask students to consider also whether the structure of the poem reflects the poem's content.

Examine in class the contrasts that Bly sets up in the poem — between the images of snow and darkness in the first two stanzas and the images of moving away and moving toward in the third and fourth stanzas. Ask students to consider these images and describe how they affect the mood of the poem.

Have students examine the final line of the poem: "All the sailors on deck have been blind for many years" (line 12). Who are the sailors on deck, and why might they be blind?

POSSIBLE CONNECTIONS TO OTHER SELECTIONS

Robert Bly, "Snowbanks North of the House" (text p. 809)
Henry Wadsworth Longfellow, "Snow-Flakes" (text p. 1106)

ROBERT BLY, *Waking from Sleep* (p. 1079)

Bly suggests that the awakening body is like a harbor at dawn (stanzas 1, 3, and 4) and that the body asleep is like the country in winter (2). Ask students to discuss whether these metaphors seem appropriate. The ordering of the stanzas might indicate that the speaker's usual process of waking involves an initial move toward consciousness, followed by one last pull toward sleep before he wakes up entirely. Ask students to consider how they typically wake up in the morning and to suggest a metaphor that matches their own process. Who is the "master" (line 12) who has left for the day?

POSSIBLE CONNECTION TO ANOTHER SELECTION

Timothy Steele, "An Aubade" (text p. 761)

ROO BORSON, *Talk* (p. 1079)

This poem is a minute discussion of character and conversation as it is engendered in both men and women of different generations. The poet's point of view is the view of the casual street observer who focuses in on the use of "talk" and offers the reader very revealing thumbnail sketches of gender relationships.

Some of the most interesting perspectives that the poet offers are the glimpses of the characters' thoughts as they are revealed through their mannerisms. "Sometimes, looking at a girl, it / almost occurs to them, but they can't make it out, / they go pawing toward it through the fog" (lines 3–4). You may want to discuss with your students how the placement of the line breaks in the poem reflect the distracted, disjointed nature of the elderly men.

Another item for discussion would be to carefully scrutinize the ways in which the poet has used her words sparingly but effectively, to create a concise and thought-provoking analysis of men and women of different generations. What, does it seem, have the old men lost as a result of time and age? How do the young women, characterized as confused, compare with the young men? The old men? Ask your students if they think that the young women are bound to turn out like the old women in the poem. Why is it important to "know the value of oranges" (11)?

Finally, is the poet somehow linking herself with the young men in the last two lines of the poem by finally admitting her artistic tinkering with the people she observes?

POSSIBLE CONNECTION TO ANOTHER SELECTION

A. E. Housman, "When I was one-and-twenty" (text p. 864)

ANNE BRADSTREET, *Before the Birth of One of Her Children* (p. 1080)

Until Anne Bradstreet's brother-in-law took a collection of her poems to London and had it published in 1650, no resident of the New World had published a book of poetry. Bradstreet's work enjoyed popularity in England and America. She was born and grew up on the estate of the earl of Lincoln, whose affairs her father managed. Bradstreet's father was eager to provide his daughter with the best possible education. When she was seventeen she and her new husband, Simon Bradstreet, sailed for Massachusetts, where she lived the rest of her life.

As a child Bradstreet contracted rheumatic fever, and its lifelong effects compounded the dangers attending seventeenth-century childbirth. What may seem at first an overdramatized farewell to a loved one can be viewed in this context as a sober reflection on life's capriciousness and an understandable wish to maintain some influence on the living. Perhaps the most striking moment in the poem occurs in line 16, when the only inexact end rhyme ("grave") coincides with a crucial change in tone and purpose. What had been a summary of Puritan attitudes (deeply felt, to be sure) toward life and death and a gently serious offering of "best wishes" to the speaker's husband becomes, with that crack in the voice, a plea to be remembered well.

You might discuss the appropriateness of the poet's choosing heroic couplets for this subject: how does the symmetry of the lines affect our understanding of the subject? You might also consider the way the speaker constructs her audience, like someone writing a diary. Is this truly private verse? Or does the speaker sense that people other than her children will read the poem?

POSSIBLE CONNECTIONS TO OTHER SELECTIONS

Anne Bradstreet, "The Author to Her Book" (text p. 778)
John Donne, "A Valediction: Forbidding Mourning" (text p. 790)

ANNE BRADSTREET, *To My Dear and Loving Husband* (p. 1080)

Anne Bradstreet, Anglo-America's first female poet, is noted for her Puritan devotion, her belief that all worldly delights are meaningless when placed in the context of the afterlife. Yet there is an ambiguous strain within her poetry that complicates this position; she is human, and thus drawn to worldly things. Note how she describes not only love but heaven in terms of material wealth. With this ambiguity in mind, ask students to assess whether Bradstreet's devotion is directed more toward her husband here on earth or toward the eternal rewards of heaven. The final two lines are themselves ambiguous; she does indicate that she believes in eternal life, but she also declares that at some point she and her husband will "live no more" (line 12). You might also point out that the final two lines comprise the only part of the poem not written in heroic couplets (they are 11 syllables each), a fact that adds to their ambiguity. Students might also enjoy discussing the tone of the poem as a dedication to one's husband: does the speaker seem warm? Rational? Self-absorbed or self-effacing?

POSSIBLE CONNECTIONS TO OTHER SELECTIONS

John Donne, "A Valediction: Forbidding Mourning" (text p. 790)

William Shakespeare, "When, in disgrace with Fortune and men's eyes" (text p. 1118)

GWENDOLYN BROOKS, *The Mother* (p. 1081)

This poem discusses a controversial issue in very contradictory images. The difference between the title and the first word points out this contradiction immediately. Isn't an abortion about *not* being a mother? Students may tend to simplify this poem because abortion is a heated moral and ethical issue. Urge them to consider the way the poem talks about the experience. They might begin by noting the matter-of-factness of the first stanza: the perfect rhymed couplets, the direct statements. This directness breaks down in the second stanza, as "You" shifts to "I."

Ask students to compare the first and second stanzas. How, for example, does *sweet,* a word that appears in both stanzas, mean something different each time? The rhyme scheme changes in the second stanza. How does this change affect the speaker's attitude toward her experience? She speaks of "I" and "you" in the second stanza. Is this poem directed to her unborn children, or to herself? Why does she list the events of her children's lost lives in lines 15–20? How does this listing affect the reader? Does the speaker effectively separate herself from her lost children, or is she somewhat confused about their loss? She returns to the direct statement at the end of the stanza, perhaps trying to regain control over herself. In the third stanza, the speaker admits that she is unsure of how to describe her experience in order to say "the truth" (line 28). Ask students to identify possible meanings for this truth. Is it definable? Finally, you might consider why the last stanza is separated from the rest.

A writing assignment might ask students to discuss at length the form of the poem. How does the structure illustrate the speaker's feelings or change of feeling?

POSSIBLE CONNECTION TO ANOTHER SELECTION

Anne Bradstreet, "Before the Birth of One of Her Children" (text p. 1080)

ROBERT BROWNING, *Meeting at Night* and *Parting at Morning* (p. 1082)

The titles of these two lyrics ask that they be taught together. Have students summarize in a writing assignment the poems' themes and suggest their complementarity. Here are portrayed the coexisting desires in human beings for the bonds of love and the freedom of adventure. Discuss with the class the use of natural imagery in each poem and the relative displacement of the sense of a speaker.

You might also ask students if we can still read these poems with the unhesitating acceptance of the divisions that Browning seems to take for granted, namely, that Eros and the night world are linked in the acceptance of the feminine, but that the day world of action and adventure is the exclusive realm of man.

GEORGE GORDON, LORD BYRON, *She Walks in Beauty* (p. 1082)

In the nineteenth century, George Gordon, Lord Byron, was commonly considered the greatest of the Romantic poets. He spent his childhood with his mother in Aberdeen, Scotland, in deprived circumstances despite an aristocratic heritage. In *Childe Harold, Don Juan,* and much of his other work, Byron chronicled the adventures of one or another example of what came to be known as the "Byronic hero," a gloomy, lusty, guilt-ridden individualist. The poet died of fever while participating in the Greek fight for independence from Turkey.

The title and first line of "She Walks in Beauty" can be an excellent entrance to the poem's explication. Students might puzzle over what it means to walk *in* beauty: is the beauty like a wrap or a cloud? The simile "like the night" hinges on that image. You might ask students if the speaker makes nature subservient to the woman, or the reverse. You might point out "gaudy" (line 6), a strange adjective for describing the day, to draw attention to the speaker's attitude toward nature.

Note the mood of timeless adoration in the second stanza. There is really no movement, only an exclamation of wonder. The exclamation is even more direct in the final stanza, where the woman's visage becomes a reflection of her spotless character. Students might explore the images in all three stanzas, looking for shifts from natural to social. How does the speaker move from "like the night" (1) to "a mind" (17) and "a heart" (18)? Why would he want to describe a woman in these terms? What effect does this description have on our idea of her? Do we really know her by the end of the poem?

For discussion of Byron's poetry, consult *Byron: Wrath and Rhyme*, edited by Alan Bold (London: Vision, 1983); Frederick Garber's *Self, Text, and Romantic Irony: The Example of Byron* (Princeton: Princeton UP, 1988); and Peter Mannings's *Byron and His Fictions* (Detroit: Wayne State U, 1978).

POSSIBLE CONNECTION TO ANOTHER SELECTION

William Wordsworth, "The Solitary Reaper" (text p. 1128)

RESOURCES FOR TEACHING

Lord Byron: Selected Poems [recording]. 2 cassettes (180 min.). Read by Frederick Davidson. Distributed by Blackstone Audio Books.

The Essential Byron [recording]. 1 cassette. Unabridged edition. Distributed by Listening Library.

The Poetry of Byron [recording]. 1 cassette. Distributed by Caedmon/HarperAudio.

Treasury of George Gordon, Lord Byron [recording]. 1 cassette. Distributed by Spoken Arts.

See also "English Literature: Romantic Period," "English Romantic Poetry," "Palgrave's Treasury of English Poetry," and "The Young Romantics" in the appendix of Film, Video, and Audiocassette Resources.

LUCILLE CLIFTON, *for deLawd* (p. 1083)

This poem provides an opportunity to explore delicacies of tone. Ask students to describe the speaker's attitude toward those people who "say they have a hard time / understanding." Does she defend her world against their definitions in order to incriminate them?

The violence that kills the sons remains unnamed in the poem. Given the year that the poem was written, 1969, you might ask students to discuss the speaker's attitude toward violence in the black community in general and families in particular. Have students consider the possible sources of violence that could have influenced Clifton's writings in the late 1960s, including the assassinations of Martin Luther King Jr. and Malcolm X, the civil rights movement, the Watts riot, and the Vietnam War. Ask students to discuss why the poet chose not to state the specific source(s) of violence that led to murdered sons (line 11). What kind of reader response is produced by leaving out the source of violence?

You might also draw students' attention to the grammatical ambiguity of the word *grief* in line 16; this word seems to be both subject and object, painting the mothers as both victims and survivors.

POSSIBLE CONNECTION TO ANOTHER SELECTION

Etheridge Knight, "A Watts Mother Mourns While Boiling Beans" (text p. 1104)

SAMUEL TAYLOR COLERIDGE, *Kubla Khan: or, a Vision in a Dream* (p. 1083)

Samuel Taylor Coleridge was born in Ottery St. Mary, Devonshire, but was sent to school in London, where he impressed his teachers and classmates (among whom was Charles Lamb) as an extremely precocious child. He attended Cambridge without taking a degree, enlisted for a short tour of duty in the Light Dragoons (a cavalry unit), planned a utopian community in America with Robert Southey, and married Southey's sister-in-law. He met William Wordsworth in 1795 and published *Lyrical Ballads* with him three years later. Coleridge became an opium addict in 1800–1801 because of the heavy doses of laudanum he'd taken to relieve the pain of several ailments, principally rheumatism. For the last eighteen years of his life, he was under the care (and under the roof) of Dr. James Gillman, writing steadily but never able to sustain the concentration needed to complete the large projects he kept planning.

Reputedly, "Kubla Khan" came to Coleridge "as in a vision" after he took a prescribed anodyne and fell into a deep sleep. What Coleridge was able to write down upon waking is only a fragment of what he dreamed. Figures such as the "pleasure-dome" and "the sacred river" take on an allegorical cast and suggest the power that inspires the writing of poetry. Although phrases such as "sunless sea" and "lifeless ocean" appear gloomy, they could also suggest mystery and the atmosphere conducive to bringing forth poems.

For a reading of this poem, consult Humphrey House's "Kubla Khan, Christabel, and Dejection," in *Coleridge* (London: Hart-Davis, 1953), reprinted in *Romanticism and Consciousness,* edited by Harold Bloom (New York: Norton, 1970). Another good essay to turn to is "The Daemonic in 'Kubla Khan': Toward Interpretation" by Charles I. Patterson Jr., in *PMLA* 89 (October 1974): 1033–1042. Patterson points out, for example, that the river in the poem is "sacred" because it seems to be possessed by a god who infuses in the poet a vision of beauty. Likewise, he identifies the "deep delight" mentioned in line 44 as "a daemonic inspiration." In a writing assignment you might ask students to explore imagery and sound patterns in order to demonstrate how Coleridge uses words to embody and suggest the idea that poetry is truly a "pleasure-dome," visionary and demonically inspired.

You could initiate discussion by asking students to locate and discuss the way Coleridge employs unusual language to describe the scene and to shape our perceptions of it. What is the effect, for instance, of alliteration in line 25 ("Five miles meandering with a mazy motion")?

POSSIBLE CONNECTIONS TO OTHER SELECTIONS

John Keats, "Ode to a Nightingale" (text p. 851)
William Butler Yeats, "Sailing to Byzantium" (text p. 1132)

RESOURCES FOR TEACHING

The Poetry of Coleridge [recording]. 1 cassette. Distributed by Caedmon/Harper-Audio.
Samuel Taylor Coleridge: The Fountain and the Cave. 57 min., color, 1974. Beta, VHS, ¾″ U-matic cassette. A biography of the poet, filmed on location. Narrated by Paul Scofield. Distributed by Pyramid Film and Video.
Samuel Taylor Coleridge: "The Rime of the Ancient Mariner" & Other Great Poems [recording]. 2 cassettes. From the Cassette Bookshelf Series. Distributed by Listening Library.
Samuel Taylor Coleridge: "The Rime of the Ancient Mariner" & Other Poems [recording]. 1 cassette. Distributed by Spoken Arts.
See also "English Romantic Poetry," "Palgrave's Golden Treasury of English Poetry," and "Romantic Pioneers" in the appendix of Film, Video, and Audiocassette Resources.

WILLIAM COWPER, *Epitaph on a Hare* (p. 1085)

The relationship between the speaker and the deceased rabbit is worth discussing since the animal is not quite fully domesticated (as is the speaker's cat), nor is it fully wild. Although the rabbit is the "surliest of his kind" (line 5), he also causes the speaker to smile (36), which may explain why the speaker takes care of the animal in the first place. The selections below all deal with the death of an animal as well. By comparing this poem to any of these others, you can open a discussion of the type of speakers who people these poems. Is Cowper's speaker sensitive or pragmatic? To what degree does the form of this poem affect its tone?

POSSIBLE CONNECTIONS TO OTHER SELECTIONS

Andrew Hudgins, "Seventeen" (text p. 813)
Jane Kenyon, "The Blue Bowl" (text p. 768)

William Stafford, "Traveling through the Dark" (text p. 813)
John Updike, "Dog's Death" (text p. 673)
Ronald Wallace, "Dogs" (text p. 1164)

VICTOR HERNÁNDEZ CRUZ, *Anonymous* (p. 1086)

Beginning *in medias res*, the speaker tells us how things would have been different if he had "lived in those olden times" (line 1), presumably in fifteenth- or sixteenth-century England rather than in contemporary Manhattan. He is playing with the conventions of being a poet, which, based on the title and on lines 2 and 3, has much to do with one's name. According to the speaker, the life of a poet of yore consisted of the constant search for rhyme and of the ability to use the words "*alas* and *hath*" (7). The poet uses these words, but their use is heavily ironic since the poet lives on the Lower East Side of Manhattan rather than in the English court during the Renaissance. The poet's exact intent is not immediately obvious. His poem is somewhat experimental, eschewing punctuation (for the most part) and including words whose meaning isn't immediately obvious from the context (such as "measurement termination surprise" in line 5 or "Within thou *mambo* of much more haste" in line 19).

Before students begin to dig into some of these more obscure lines, you might begin a discussion by considering the implication of the title. "Anonymous" is occasionally the way we designate the author of a poem, but it is rarely the title. What do the names of poets sometimes connote? Do we read a poem differently if we know it is by a famous poet such as Shakespeare, or Eliot, or Wordsworth? If you have time, you might even begin such a discussion by having students read and discuss two poems without knowing the names of the authors, perhaps one by a "famous" author and one by a lesser-known author. When you reveal the authors' names, does it make a difference?

POSSIBLE CONNECTIONS TO OTHER SELECTIONS

Julio Marzán, "Ethnic Poetry" (text p. 816)
Miller Williams, "Excuse Me" (text p. 708)

COUNTEE CULLEN, *Yet Do I Marvel* (p. 1086)

This speaker addresses some age-old questions about the mystery of God's works, but concludes the poem by adding his own situation as a black poet to this list of mysteries. The allusions to Tantalus and Sisyphus aren't accidental; Tantalus represents a dream just out of reach and Sisyphus represents eternal struggle. Both of these situations are relevant to the black poet of 1925, and relevant to larger questions of God's goodness. It is interesting to note that, whereas the speaker addresses God, the examples by which he questions God's benevolence stem from the "pagan" classical mythology, mirroring, perhaps, the alienation the speaker feels.

Students have to fill in quite a bit here, though; the situation of the black poet might be difficult, but why is his situation mysterious, or as the title and the penultimate line suggest, marvelous? What is the relationship between God and the speaker? Is this God indifferent, capricious, omniscient, cruel, or all of the above?

POSSIBLE CONNECTIONS TO OTHER SELECTIONS

Gerard Manley Hopkins, "God's Grandeur" (text p. 837)
Langston Hughes, "Negro" (text p. 1016)

E. E. CUMMINGS, *Buffalo Bill 's* (p. 1087)

An interesting few moments of class discussion could address whether Cummings is singing the praises of Buffalo Bill in this poem. How does the word *defunct* strike our ears, especially in the second line of the poem? What is the speaker's tone as he asks the concluding question? Is he sincere or contemptuous?

POSSIBLE CONNECTION TO ANOTHER SELECTION

Marilyn Nelson Waniek, "Emily Dickinson's Defunct" (text p. 912)

E. E. CUMMINGS, *since feeling is first* (p. 1087)

Once again in the head-heart debate, the heart comes out the winner in this poem. The eliding of the syntax supports the value of feeling over rational thought. Students will probably enjoy the syntactical turn of line 3, which can either complete line 2 or be the subject of line 4. Considering the mention of death and its prominent position in the poem, you might explore with the class — or use as a writing assignment — a defense of this as a *carpe diem* poem.

POSSIBLE CONNECTION TO ANOTHER SELECTION

John Donne, "The Flea" (text p. 1090)

MARY DI MICHELE, *As in the Beginning* (p. 1087)

In this poem, the author focuses on her father's hands, and how their appearance reflects the hardships he has had to endure in life. She begins the poem by asserting the basic knowledge that "A man has two hands" (line 1), acknowledging this fact as if it were an inalienable right that all men have, and that has been denied her father because of his work. "$250 for each digit &/or $100 for a joint" (8) hardly seeming compensation enough for her father's loss.

Throughout this poem, there is a distinct sense of an even greater loss than the loss of her father's fingers — there is also the poet's loss of the person her father was when he was young, and still unmarked by hardships: "give me my father's hands still brown and uncallused, / beautiful hands that broke bread for us at table" (20–21). The poet presents the reader with an image of her father as he once was, almost as if she were trying to go back in time and physically reconstruct him. This is evident in the last four lines in the poem, with the appearance of the words "whole," open," and "warm" "as they were in the beginning" (25).

To begin a discussion of this poem with students, you might want to focus on the title. How does this biblical reference reflect the circumstances of the poem? You also might want to discuss the poet's role as writer in the poem (see 12–13). How does the act of writing help the poet come to terms with her father's condition? What is the intended effect of the poet directly addressing her readers in lines 14–15? Ask your students to determine whom the poet is speaking to when she repeats the phrase "give me" in the second section of the poem.

POSSIBLE CONNECTIONS TO OTHER SELECTIONS

Julia Alvarez, "Woman's Work" (text p. 886)
Andrew Hudgins, "Elegy for My Father, Who Is Not Dead" (text p. 893)

GREGORY DJANIKIAN, *When I First Saw Snow* (p. 1088)

This is a poem of transformation — a moment that is much larger and more significant in the poet's life than the simple event it describes. Ask students to point to specific lines in the poem that describe in detail the feel of this moment. Students are likely to point out the red bows (line 13), the dusting of snow on the gray planks of the porch (17), the smell of the pine tree (6), the feel of the sticky sap on his fingers (5), and, most particularly, the sounds (the music, the sound of the Monopoly game in progress, his boot buckles, and the imagined whistling of the train).

These images are woven together to effectively re-create the speaker's first experience of snow, but they take on larger relevance within the context of the beginning and ending of the poem. After reading the poem in class, you may wish to ask students about the beginning and the end — what do they make of the "papers" the family is waiting for (3)? How does an understanding of that phrase affect an understanding of the final two lines of the poem?

POSSIBLE CONNECTIONS TO OTHER SELECTIONS

Elizabeth Alexander, "Harlem Birthday Party" (text p. 1148)

John Keats, "On First Looking into Chapman's Homer" (text p. 879)

JOHN DONNE, *The Apparition* (p. 1089)

Donne's poem carries the Renaissance conceit of the lover, pining away at the mercy of a cruel and scornful mistress, one step further; after the lover has died from his mistress's neglect, he takes his revenge by coming back to haunt her. Ask students to notice the various means by which the speaker seeks to characterize his former love. He calls her a "murderess" in the very first line. How else does he attempt to cast her in a bad light? Students may need to be informed that quicksilver (line 12) — mercury — was a common treatment for venereal disease in Donne's day. Do your students trust the speaker's description of his former love? What are the implications of the fact that there are actually *two* ghosts, the speaker (4) and the woman (13), in this poem? Notice that Donne uses three different metrical lengths in the first four lines. What is the effect of this constant change of rhythm and of the rhyme between "dead" and "bed" in these lines?

POSSIBLE CONNECTIONS TO OTHER SELECTIONS

Robin Becker, "Shopping" (text p. 794)

John Donne, "The Flea" (text p. 1090)

JOHN DONNE, *Batter My Heart* (p. 1089)

Christian and Romantic traditions come together in this sonnet. Employing Christian tradition, Donne here portrays the soul as a maiden with Christ as her bridegroom. Borrowing from Petrarchan materials, Donne images the reluctant woman as a castle and her lover as the invading army. Without alluding to any particular tradition, we can also observe in this poem two modes of male aggression, namely, the waging of war and the pursuit of romantic conquest, again blended into a strong and brilliantly rendered metaphysical conceit. Donne is imploring his "three-personed" God to take strong measures against the enemy, Satan. In a typical metaphysical paradox, Donne moreover asks God to save him from Satan by imprisoning him within God's grace.

Rhythm and sound work remarkably in this sonnet to enforce its meaning. Review the heavy-stressed opening line — which sounds like the pounding of a relentless fist and is followed by the strong reiterated plosives of "break, blow, burn."

Mark Jarman, "Unholy Sonnet" (text p. 884)

JOHN DONNE, *Death Be Not Proud* (p. 1090)

Many students will have read this sonnet in high school. It should serve as a reminder that the logic of a poem can be as tightly constructed as that of any other form of rhetorical argument. In the frame of Donne's religious belief, which promises life after death, death is a very brief moment and is, furthermore, slave to the darker dealings of fate. As usual Donne has a sense of the rhythmic force of words. Notice the quartet of heavy-stressed beats in his opening injunction; the sonnet concludes with another group of four stressed syllables.

Ask students to compare in a brief essay the attitude toward death taken by Donne in this poem and by Dickinson in "Because I could not stop for Death —" (text p. 948).

POSSIBLE CONNECTION TO ANOTHER SELECTION

Mark Jarman, "Unholy Sonnet" (text p. 884)

JOHN DONNE, *The Flea* (p. 1090)

An interesting discussion or writing topic could be organized around the tradition of the *carpe diem* poem and how this poem both accommodates and alters that tradition.

The wit here is ingenious, and after the individual sections of the poem are explained, more time might be needed to review the parts and give the class a sense of the total effect of the poem's operations.

The reason the speaker even bothers to comment on the flea stems from his belief that a commingling of blood during intercourse (here, admittedly, by the agency of the flea) may result in conception. Hence his belief that the lovers must be "yea more than" united and that the flea's body has become a kind of "marriage temple." For the woman to crush the flea (which she does) is a multiple crime because in so doing she commits murder, suicide, and sacrilege (of the temple) and figuratively destroys the possible progeny. The flea in its death, though, also stands as logical emblem for why this courtship should be consummated. The reasoning is that little if any innocence or honor is spent in killing the flea, then, likewise, neither of those commodities would be spent "when thou yield'st to me."

One way to begin discussion is to consider the poem as an exercise in the making of meaning: what does the flea represent to the speaker, and how does its meaning change as the poem progresses? What, in effect, is the relation between the flea and the poem?

POSSIBLE CONNECTIONS TO OTHER SELECTIONS

Sally Croft, "Home-Baked Bread" (text p. 768)
John Donne, "Song" (text p. 844)

DAVID DONNELL, *The Canadian Prairies View of Literature* (p. 1091)

Donnell has flipped the perspective of this poem around in order to shed some light on the ways in which subject matter can influence the very creation of a poem or piece of literature. Donnell takes us on a tour of the rural landscape of Canada, and allows each environment to speak for itself as to the ways in which it should be and has been represented in art.

It is important to note the sudden, ironic gestures that the poet lends to his subject matter. For example, you might want to discuss with your students the sometimes conversational tone that the poem adopts. For example, "towns are alright; Ontario towns are urban; French towns are European; / the action should take place on a farm between April and October; / nature is quiet during winter; when it snows, there's a lot of it" (lines 6–8). Each item in this list is representational, rather than concrete. Discuss with your students what these images point to, and where they can be found elsewhere in literature. Would it be justifiable to say that the author is indicating some probable, stereotypical locales in which Canadian literature generally takes place, such as in "beverage rooms and cheap hotels" (13–14)? What does the author intend by the sudden appearance of Indians and Metis (15)?

It will also be important to discuss how the poet uses the semicolon in this poem to create a pastiche of images that can be put together to create a whole picture. How does this type of punctuation contribute to the overall effect of the poem?

POSSIBLE CONNECTION TO ANOTHER SELECTION

Robert Morgan, "On the Shape of a Poem" (text p. 900)

GEORGE ELIOT [MARY ANN EVANS], *In a London Drawingroom* (p. 1092)

This poem could more accurately be titled "*From* a London Drawingroom" since the speaker's gaze seems to be directed entirely outward, through a window that makes London (or even the world) seem like a prison. The colors are drab, the people are lifeless, the architecture monotonous. Despite the monotony of the landscape, everyone is in constant motion, which is part of the problem; "No figure lingering / Pauses to feed the hunger of the eye / Or rest a little on the lap of life" (lines 9–11). Ask students to unpack these lines; what do they imply about these people and their surroundings, or about the relationship between this speaker and the rest of the world? What is meant by the phrase "multiplied identity" (16)? And in the last two lines, what do students suppose "men" are being punished for? By whom? The relationship between humankind and nature is also worth pursuing; we have presumably created the "smoke" of the first line, and the "solid fog" of the fourth line; yet the punishment seems to come from elsewhere. This poem is a good example of how an outward-looking description really reflects inward psychology.

POSSIBLE CONNECTIONS TO OTHER SELECTIONS

Matthew Arnold, "Dover Beach" (text p. 757)
Emily Dickinson, "I cannot dance upon my Toes —" (text p. 940)
T. S. Eliot, "The Love Song of J. Alfred Prufrock" (text p. 1045)
Robert Hass, "Happiness" (text p. 707)

LOUISE GLÜCK, *The School Children* (p. 1092)

You might begin a discussion of this poem by pointing out the richness of color contained in the poem — the red and gold of apples (line 3), the blue and yellow of the wool overcoats (10), and the gray limbs of the fruit trees at the end of the poem (13). Ask students to consider the significance of these colors in the poem. Why is there such a contrast between the bright colors at the beginning of the poem and the gray at the end of the poem?

In the poem, the mothers of the children who are going forward are working very hard, laboring to gather apples. Ask students to interpret the "forward" movement of the children. Possible responses might include literally going forward to school and figuratively going forward into the future.

The apples are described as words of "another language" (4), suggesting that the women may be migrant or immigrant workers and speak a language other than English. Ask students to consider what the apples represent to the women laborers.

Ask students who the people are "who wait behind great desks" (6) and what "offerings" they are receiving (7). Keeping in mind the apple imagery, some students will likely interpret this passage literally and understand the people behind the desks to be teachers who are receiving the children and, in the tradition of education, apples as well. Another possible interpretation is that they are the rich and powerful owners of the orchards for whom the women are working.

Ask students to consider the meaning of the final stanza. Discuss how the red and gold apples represent "a way out" (12). Consider also the scarcity of the apples among "the gray limbs of the fruit trees" (13) — trees that are not full of fruit and of hope, but that are sterile, colorless, and hopeless. Why does the poet use the word *ammunition* to describe the apples in the final line? What, in the end, is the poet saying about the lives and the future of these school children?

POSSIBLE CONNECTIONS TO OTHER SELECTIONS

Emily Dickinson, "From all the Jails the Boys and Girls" (text p. 951)

Cornelius Eady, "The Supremes" (text p. 1150)

Judy Page Heitzman, "The Schoolroom on the Second Floor of the Knitting Mill" (text p. 1158)

DONALD HALL, *My Son, My Executioner* (p. 1093)

You might discuss the title of this short rhymed lyric. Is *executioner* too strong and somehow too long a word to be applied to an infant? Hall explores a paradox that comes through with metaphysical clarity in this tightly controlled verse. The son is a way of sustaining the family name, hence conferring "immortality," and a sign of his parents' aging.

POSSIBLE CONNECTION TO ANOTHER SELECTION

Anne Bradstreet, "Before the Birth of One of Her Children" (text p. 1080)

THOMAS HARDY, *Hap* (p. 1093)

Bad luck, pain, and sorrow seem so happenstance, Hardy says in this sonnet. Does the attitude of the speaker ring true? He claims that it would be easier to bear ill chance if some vengeful god would openly proclaim his malevolent designs. Discuss with the class why even the machinations of some divinity appear preferable to the silent, indeterminate (and inhuman) operations of caprice.

POSSIBLE CONNECTION TO ANOTHER SELECTION

Langston Hughes, "Lenox Avenue: Midnight" (text p. 1022)

THOMAS HARDY, *The Ruined Maid* (p. 1093)

This humorous dialogue between two country girls raises questions about class, language, and morality. One maid has been "ruined" — that is, she has fallen sexually — yet the result is not public shame but rather the realization of her dream, which is to break out of her socioeconomic class. Much of the humor depends upon the word "ruined," which connotes a state of spiritual and material impoverishment and which is presumably used by the country girls' elders to instruct their behavior. The "ruined" maid is rewarded with earthly riches, with the trappings of the privileged classes, while the chaste maid is yoked to her mundane existence. The rest of the humor comes in the final line, in which the ruined maid's speech reverts to its original unpolished state when she declares to the other girl, "You ain't ruined."

The poem seems, however, more than simply humorous. Hardy seems to be making a broader point about the constraints of moral instruction. Is the final line meant to imply that one can never really lose one's past? How does the poem's form, particularly the repeated phrase "said she," in conjunction with the tripping anapests, contribute to its tone?

POSSIBLE CONNECTIONS TO OTHER SELECTIONS

Katharyn Howd Machan, "Hazel Tells LaVerne" (text p. 725)
Adrienne Rich, "Living in Sin" (text p. 1115)

JOY HARJO, *Fishing* (p. 1094)

This is a very rich prose poem by Native American poet Joy Harjo. You may want to open a discussion of this poem by pointing out the difference between what students usually consider "poetry" and the prose form of this poem. (The prose poem is introduced in the text on page 905.) Ask students what makes this piece a poem. One possible exercise is to have students rewrite the first few lines in more conventional poetic lines. What is the effect of these changes? Why might Harjo have chosen to use the prose poem format?

In the poem, the speaker describes a fishing trip she has promised to make with her friend, Louis. Later she admits that "This / is the only place I can keep that promise, inside a poem as familiar to him / as the banks of his favorite fishing place" (12–14). Ask students to interpret these lines. Possible responses include that the poet never really does go to Louis's favorite spot along the river, or that the poem is the only way she can fish *with Louis* anymore.

The speaker makes several connections between fishing and dying throughout the poem. In class examine lines 18–27. Although it is never stated directly, she hints that Louis is dead. Additional references to death include the fossils and ashes in line 15; the fish asking "When is that old Creek coming back?" (16), then going on to refer to Louis in the past tense; and the poet stating that "Last night I dreamed I tried to die, I was going to / look for

Louis" (18–19). Near the end of the poem, the speaker says, "I know most fishers to be liars most of the time. Even Louis when it / came to fishing, or even dying" (26–27).

The content of this poem could be divided into several sections, and it may be interesting to ask students to identify where they see these sections occurring. The first section might be the opening lines that present fish as heroic survivors; the second section could include the lines that introduce Louis as a friend and a fisher; the third section could be the dream sequence; and the final section could be the ending, in which the speaker explores the connection between fishing, dying, and the mystery of life.

After discussing the poem, you may wish to have students write about the characters that appear. What do we know about Louis — both literally and figuratively — from the poem? What do we know about the narrator? What do we know about their relationship?

POSSIBLE CONNECTIONS TO OTHER SELECTIONS

Elizabeth Bishop, "The Fish" (text p. 682)
N. Scott Momaday, "The Bear" (text p. 1110)

RESOURCES FOR TEACHING

Joy Harjo [recording]. 1 cassette (29 min.), 1991. The author plays her saxophone and reads from her work. Distributed by New Letters on the Air.
Joy Harjo & Barney Bush [recording]. 1 cassette (29 min.), 1983. Native American poets Harjo and Bush read from their work. Distributed by New Letters on the Air.
Joy Harjo: Furious Light [recording]. 1 cassette (56 min.), 1986. Selected poems with musical accompaniment. Distributed by Watershed Tapes.

MICHAEL S. HARPER, *Grandfather* (p. 1095)

This open form poem pays homage to the speaker's grandfather, who was subject to racial prejudice in the early part of the twentieth century. The speaker plays his memories for us like a movie. His earliest memory of his grandfather is of his resistance to racist neighbors who tried to burn his house down after seeing the movie *Birth of a Nation*. These neighbors act as though they are "in a movie they'd just seen" (line 8) rather than acting as a result of seeing the movie. The final stanza is a montage of the grandfather's life, "the film / played backwards on his grandson's eyes" (47–48). What is the effect of using film as a metaphor for his nostalgia? In each stanza, the term "nation" is used, but to different effects. What is the speaker's point about nationhood, and how does his grandfather help him to arrive at his definition of nationhood? Is the poem personal or public in nature? That is, is the speaker's grandfather just that, or is he meant to be somehow representative of his race?

POSSIBLE CONNECTIONS TO OTHER SELECTIONS

Elizabeth Alexander, "Harlem Birthday Party" (text p. 1148)
Jimmy Santiago Baca, "Green Chile" (text p. 758)
Langston Hughes, "The Weary Blues" (text p. 1019)

RESOURCE FOR TEACHING

Hear Where Coltrane Is [recording]. 1 cassette (60 min.), 1971, 1984. Poems accompanied by music. Distributed by Watershed Tapes.

ANTHONY HECHT, *The Dover Bitch* (p. 1096)

The subtitle of this poem is "A Criticism of Life," and Hecht indirectly makes his criticism by having as a backdrop Arnold's "Dover Beach" (text p. 757). That poem too was a criticism of society, of declining religious values and the disappearance of a moral center. The tone of this poem is initially amusing; the young woman is not going to be treated "as a sort of mournful cosmic last resort." She desires a relationship more carnal than platonic. The speaker obliges her, and now, in what seems to be a continuing casual relationship, he occasionally brings her perfume, called *Nuit d'Amour*. At the edges of this poem we still hear the sound of Arnold's armies of the night, a reminiscence that doesn't make the current times seem so much worse but does make our moral comprehension of them so much more slight and haphazard.

POSSIBLE CONNECTIONS TO OTHER SELECTIONS

Matthew Arnold, "Dover Beach" (text p. 757)
Peter De Vries, "To His Importunate Mistress" (text p. 898)

GEORGE HERBERT, *The Collar* (p. 1097)

Herbert's poems were published after his death. Many of them deal with the hesitancy of commitment he felt before becoming an Anglican priest.

The title "The Collar" echoes *choler* (anger) and suggests the work collar that binds horses in their traces as well as the clerical collar. Explore with the class how the speaker's situation, the stress he feels, and his particular argument gradually emerge. In his meditation, he tries to argue himself out of his position of submission. His life is free; he deserves more than thorns. He would like to have some of the world's secular awards. The speaker then admonishes himself to forget the feeble restrictions — his "rope of sands." But when all is said and done, he capitulates. You might observe how this poem demonstrates a strong measure of psychological insight.

As a writing assignment, you might ask the class to explore in a two- to three-page paper how rhythm reinforces the meaning in this poem.

POSSIBLE CONNECTION TO ANOTHER SELECTION

Sir Philip Sidney, "Loving in Truth, and Fain in Verse My Love to Show" (text p. 1119)

LINDA HOGAN, *Song for My Name* (p. 1098)

You might want to begin a discussion of this poem by reminding students that in Native American tradition, names carry great significance, often reflecting or defining some important characteristic about a person. In fact, some Native Americans are given two names — a public name, which is used, and a private name that is kept secret in order to preserve its power.

In this poem, the speaker explores the significance of her own name — a name that she sees as a point of connection to her Native American heritage. You might ask students to identify the contrast that Hogan sets up in the poem between the darkness of the old woman's hair (lines 2–3), the grandfather's dark hands (7), and the "women / with black hair / and men with eyes like night" (11–13) and the mother, who is described as a "white dove" (19). In the mother's "own land," images of whiteness abound (20–22).

Ask students to consider why the speaker's father is not mentioned in the poem. It is this contrast between her mother and what we can assume to be her father's family that is the focus of the poem. The name the speaker is given reflects her Native American heritage, but she feels caught between cultures — she is "a woman living / between the white moon / and the red sun" (30–32). On a number of occasions, the speaker refers to her name as an indication of hardship. She writes, "It means no money / tomorrow" (13–14); "If you have a name like this, / there's never enough water" (26); and "There is too much heat" (26). Ask students why the speaker never actually tells us her name. Explore the implications of the speaker's Native American ancestry. Which world is she "waiting to leave" (32)?

As a writing assignment, you may wish to compare this speaker's sense of being caught between two cultures with the similar sense in "Ellis Island" by Joseph Bruchac (text p. 921).

POSSIBLE CONNECTIONS TO OTHER SELECTIONS

Jimmy Santiago Baca, "Green Chile" (text p. 758)

Ben Jonson, "On My First Son" (text p. 1102)

RESOURCE FOR TEACHING

Linda Hogan [recording]. 1 cassette (29 min.), 1990. Distributed by New Letters on the Air.

M. CARL HOLMAN, *Mr. Z* (p. 1098)

Students will readily perceive the irony of this poem: the man who lived so that his racial identity was all but obliterated earned as his summary obituary the reductive, faint, and defaming praise "One of the most distinguished members of his race." His loss is a double loss, to be sure; not only did he fail finally to be judged according to white standards (those he aspired to) but in the process of living up to those standards he "flourish[ed] without [the] roots" of his own racial identity. Review the poem for its ironic phrases. You may have to explain that racial, religious, and ethnic differences were often suppressed in favor of assimilation and that the celebration of and return to these differences is a relatively recent tendency.

POSSIBLE CONNECTIONS TO OTHER SELECTIONS

Elizabeth Alexander, "Harlem Birthday Party" (text p. 1148)

Paul Laurence Dunbar, "We Wear the Mask" (text p. 808)

GERARD MANLEY HOPKINS, *Pied Beauty* (p. 1099)

It seems appropriate for Hopkins to have used so many innovations in style, structure, and diction in a poem that glorifies God — the only entity "whose beauty is past change" (line 10) — by observing the great variety present in the earth and sky. Ask students to point out examples of poetic innovation in this poem and to suggest their effects on the poem.

In form, "Pied Beauty" is what Hopkins termed a "curtal [that is, shortened] sonnet." Not only is it shortened, but it is shortened to exactly three-fourths of a traditional sonnet: the "octet" is six lines, the "sestet" four and a half. Having compressed the sonnet structure to ten and a half lines, Hopkins must make careful word choices to convey meaning in fewer words. Note the hyphenated words, which are his own creations; is it possible to understand the meanings of these made-up compounds? Compare Hopkins's practice of creating new words to that of Lewis Carroll in "Jabberwocky" (text p. 841).

Students will need to know what *pied* means (patchy in color; splotched). How do the many synonyms for *pied* in the first few lines emphasize the theme of the poem? How does the repetition of the *le* sound (dappled, couple, stipple, tackle, fickle, freckled, adazzle) add a sense of rhythm and unity to this poem's untraditional metrics?

POSSIBLE CONNECTION TO ANOTHER SELECTION

E. E. Cummings, "in Just-" (text p. 902)

GERARD MANLEY HOPKINS, *The Windhover* (p. 1100)

At the midpoint of his poetic career, Hopkins considered this poem "the best thing I ever wrote" (*The Letters of Gerard Manley Hopkins to Robert Bridges,* edited by C. C. Abbott, rev. 1955 [New York: Oxford UP], 85). Regardless of the poem's quality, students should be forewarned that this is a difficult work by a difficult poet. It may help them to know that even literary specialists have had a difficult time agreeing on the poem's exact meaning. In fact, Tom Dunne's Hopkins bibliography (1976) lists nearly one hundred different readings of the poem before 1970. With this in mind, you might ask students to discuss the overall feeling conveyed by this lyric, rather than expecting them to be able to explicate it line by line. In general, the poem begins with the speaker's observation of a kestrel hawk in flight. The speaker is drawn from passive observation into passionate feeling for the "ecstasy" (line 5) of the bird's soaring freedom: "My heart in hiding / Stirred for a bird, — the achieve of, the mastery of the thing!" (7–8). It then occurs to the speaker that the bird's creator is "a billion / Times told lovelier, more dangerous" (9–10) than the creature, and his awe expands to consider an even greater power.

Have students note that the poem is addressed "To Christ our Lord." The speaker directly speaks to Christ as "my chevalier" in line 11. Realizing that the poem is addressed to Christ leads to an interpretation of the final lines as references to Christ's suffering and death. Despite Christ's earthly humility (the "blue-bleak embers" of line 13), his true glory — "gold-vermilion" (14) — is revealed when he falls, galls, and gashes himself (14).

One might approach "The Windhover" structurally by comparing it to the less complex poem that precedes it in the text. In "The Windhover," as in "Pied Beauty," Hopkins alters the sonnet form to suit his purposes. Discuss how "The Windhover" conforms to and deviates from traditional sonnet form. In particular, note its division into thirteen lines and the indication of the "turn" not at the beginning of the sestet but with the poet's emphasis on the word *and* in line 9. How do these deviations from the traditional sonnet form affect the poem's meaning?

Also worth discussing are the striking use of alliteration in the first long line and the poet's choices of unusual words, as seen in previous poems. Note that to the poet, a Jesuit priest, the "billion" in line 10 is not hyperbole; if anything, it is an understatement.

Fortunately, a number of glosses and extended critical interpretations of the works of this difficult poet are available. Among these are Graham Storey's *A Preface to Hopkins* (London and New York: Longman, 1981); Paul Mariani's *A Commentary on the Complete Poems of Gerard Manley Hopkins* (Ithaca: Cornell UP, 1969); *Hopkins: A Collection of Critical*

Essays, edited by Geoffrey Hartman (Englewood Cliffs: Twentieth-Century Views/
Prentice-Hall, 1966); and J. Hillis Miller's *The Disappearance of God* (Cambridge: Harvard
UP, 1963).

POSSIBLE CONNECTION TO ANOTHER SELECTION

Gerard Manley Hopkins, "God's Grandeur" (text p. 837)

A. E. HOUSMAN, *Is my team ploughing* (p. 1100)

This poem is in ballad form, with a typical question-response exchange between the
Shropshire lad who has died and a supposedly impersonal voice that answers his queries.
The surprise comes, of course, with the introduction of the second "I," who has a decid-
edly vested interest in the earthly life of the deceased.

You might ask students to trace the development of the worldly objects the speaker
is interested in: what is the effect of his beginning with his team of horses and ending
with questions about his girl and his friend? Does the development say anything about
his sense of priority, or is the effect meant only to heighten the poem's final irony?

POSSIBLE CONNECTION TO ANOTHER SELECTION

Emily Dickinson, "Because I could not stop for Death —" (text p. 948)

A. E. HOUSMAN, *To an Athlete Dying Young* (p. 1101)

You might discuss this poem in relation to the *carpe diem* tradition. Is it perverse to
imagine such a connection in a poem that treats youth and death? Many students will
have read this poem in high school. They might enjoy picking out recurrent words and
themes — such as "shoulder-high" in stanzas I and II, "shady" in stanza IV, and "shade" in
stanza VI; the various thresholds and sills or doorways in the poem; and the image of
both the laurel and the rose as evanescent tokens of glory and youth — and exploring
their function in the poem.

POSSIBLE CONNECTION TO ANOTHER SELECTION

Seamus Heaney, "Mid-term Break" (text p. 892)

BEN JONSON, *On My First Son* (p. 1102)

A father's deep grief for his lost child as expressed in this beautiful epitaph needs
little explication. However, the poem contains several ideas worthy of class discussion.
Why does the poet think that we should envy those who die at an early age? Do your students agree? Do they think the poet believes it himself? How can a child be considered a
"best piece of poetry" (line 10)? Have students suggest paraphrases for the last two lines,
which are confusing because of the convoluted grammatical construction. Do these lines
mean that the poet has learned a lesson about not caring too much for earthly joys, a
reading that the use of the word *lent* in line 3 supports? Is he proposing that his great at-
tachment to the child had something to do with his death?

POSSIBLE CONNECTION TO ANOTHER SELECTION

Anne Bradstreet, "Before the Birth of One of Her Children" (text p. 1080)

BEN JONSON, *To Celia* (p. 1102)

This poem is a laudatory devotion to a lover in which the speaker moves through conceits of drinking in the first stanza and conceits of the tribute of a rose in the second. This poem is in fact a good opportunity to examine a Petrarchan conceit, or rather, two conceits. After students have worked through each stanza, you might ask them if there is a definite relationship between them. Does the poem read like two poems, or do the two stanzas depend upon each other in a fundamental way?

You may also want to discuss whether the poem seems to be a bit *too* devotional; students may find the speaker's praise for his lover to be a bit too much, a bit unbelievable. You may want to discuss how poetic conventions change over time. Jonson's Celia is an exaggerated lover (her name connotes heaven), but that type of love or devotion was the subject of poetry in seventeenth-century England. An interesting writing assignment might be to have students trace the way in which such devotion changes over time by selecting representative love poems from the seventeenth century through the present.

POSSIBLE CONNECTIONS TO OTHER SELECTIONS

Joseph Brodsky, "Love Song" (text p. 845)
Robert Herrick, "Upon Julia's Clothes" (text p. 878)
Christopher Marlowe, "The Passionate Shepherd to His Love" (text p. 1108)
William Shakespeare, "Not marble, nor the gilded monuments" (text p. 1116)

JOHN KEATS, *When I have fears that I may cease to be* (p. 1103)

The fears described in this sonnet are increasingly human, mortal, and intimate. Keats fears first that death may cut short the writing of his imagined "high-piled books"; then that he may never trace the "shadows" of "huge cloudy symbols of a high romance"; and, finally, that he might not see his beloved again. In the couplet, love and fame sink to nothingness, but Keats confronts his fear and is deepened by the experience.

There is a subtle order to the presentation of Keats's objects of regret. In a writing assignment, you might ask the class to comment on how one item seems to lead to the next and how their arrangement lends form and substance to this sonnet.

POSSIBLE CONNECTIONS TO OTHER SELECTIONS

Emily Dickinson, "This was a Poet — It Is That" (text p. 943)
William Shakespeare, "Not marble, nor the gilded monuments" (text p. 1116)

JOHN KEATS, *La Belle Dame sans Merci* (p. 1103)

You might read this ballad in connection with other ballads in this book. How is it that ballads have stood the test of time and continued to appeal to many generations of listeners and readers? Is this ballad any different from medieval ballads? Is it more suggestive, perhaps, of a state of mind?

The opening three stanzas hold a descriptive value for the reader, for they present the knight as pale, ill, possibly aging and dying. The stanzas possess a rhetorical value as well, for they whet our curiosity. Just why is the knight trapped in this withered landscape?

The femme fatale figure goes back at least to Homeric legend and the wiles of Circe. Note how the "belle dame" appeals here to several senses — with her appearance, her voice, the foods she offers, the physical comforts of sleep. Above all else, though, she seems otherworldly, and Keats here seems to insist on her elfin qualities, her wild eyes, and her strange language.

Words change meaning and grow in and out of popularity over generations (even decades). Contrast the way we might use *enthrall* today (with what subjects) and what Keats intends by "La Belle Dame sans Merci / Hath thee in Thrall!" (lines 39–40). Note how the shortened line of each quatrain gives both a sense of closure and the chill of an inescapable doom.

In his well-known essay on the poem, Earl R. Wasserman begins by remarking, "It would be difficult in any reading of Keats's ballad not to be enthralled by the haunting power of its rhythm, by its delicate intermingling of the fragile and the grotesque, the tender and the weird, and by the perfect economy with which these effects are achieved" (from "La Belle Dame sans Merci," in his *The Finer Tone: Keats's Major Poems* [Baltimore: Johns Hopkins UP, 1953, 1967], 65–83, and reprinted in *English Romantic Poets: Modern Essays in Criticism,* edited by M. H. Abrams [New York: Oxford UP, 1960], 365–380). In a writing assignment you might ask students to select any one of these elements and discuss it with several examples to show how it shapes the tone and mood of the poem.

Other studies of this poem include Jane Cohen's "Keats's Humor in 'La Belle Dame sans Merci,' " *Keats-Shelley Journal* 17 (1968): 10–13, and Bernice Slote's "The Climate of Keats's 'La Belle Dame sans Merci,' " *Modern Language Quarterly* 21 (1960): 195–207.

POSSIBLE CONNECTIONS TO OTHER SELECTIONS

Anonymous, "Bonny Barbara Allan" (text p. 1074)

Emily Dickinson, "Because I could not stop for Death —" (text p. 948)

ETHERIDGE KNIGHT, *A Watts Mother Mourns While Boiling Beans* (p. 1104)

One of the most striking aspects of this poem is its sound patterns. Alliteration ("blooming," "born," "bold," "blood") and assonance ("blooming," "blood") project the mother's (speaker's) anxiety and apprehension. She cannot just grieve, for she must worry about her husband's dinner. Ask students to think about how the sound patterns influence their reading of this poem, both literally and figuratively. Does the poem *demand* to be read a certain way? How does this reading affect its meaning?

POSSIBLE CONNECTION TO ANOTHER SELECTION

Lucille Clifton, "for deLawd" (text p. 1083)

PHILIP LARKIN, *This Be the Verse* (p. 1105)

At once indicting and absolving parenthood for the faults and woes of the world, this poem's depth goes beyond the humor and unexpectedness of its blunt first line. Students are likely to find some humor here because, or in spite of, Larkin's particularly "non-poetic" diction. But this poem is more than a simple cynical witticism.

Larkin builds a funny tone by inverting the syntax of the first line (which places the shocking "fuck" as the poem's second word), by lightening the tone with mocking language such as "just for you" in line 4, and by using childish words like "mum and dad" (line 1). Furthermore, readers may not expect this kind of "talk" from a poet — especially one who is espousing as serious a point as "man hands misery to man" (9). The contrast in the speaker's two levels of diction is, itself, funny, but at the same time, calls greater attention to the more serious, if not beautiful lines: "It deepens like a coastal shelf" (10). The glib ending, in particular, both humorously undermines the more serious message and enhances it by contrast.

You may want to begin a discussion by trying to characterize the speaker. Apart from the techniques of the poet, why would this speaker be funny when there is such a sad message sitting there in the middle of his diatribe? Is the speaker sad?

POSSIBLE CONNECTIONS TO OTHER SELECTIONS

Robert Bly, "Sitting Down to Dinner" (text p. 824)
Queen Latifah, "The Evil That Men Do" (text p. 695)

LI-YOUNG LEE, *Eating Together* (p. 1105)

This poem describes in meticulous detail a family eating dinner and then shifts to a metaphorical consideration of the speaker's father. The description of the father suggests that he has died. Encourage students to notice the sensual images that Lee uses to describe the meal in the first 8 lines of this poem. Every detail of the meal is given in great detail — from the exact food eaten to the precise way the mother will hold the fish between her fingers. Consider what the effect is of sharing the intricate details of the meal. Why might the poet wish to re-create the scene so carefully?

Point out the shift in the poem that occurs in line 9, where the poet moves from language that is literal to language that is figurative and metaphoric. Ask students what actual event do they suppose the poet is describing in this section. Are the images the poet chooses effective? What do students make of the poem's final line, "without any travelers, and lonely for no one" (12)?

Lee titles this poem "Eating Together" and describes his family gathered around the table for lunch. Ask students whether it is symbolic that his mother "will / taste the sweetest meat of the head" (6) the way his father did "weeks ago" (9). Consider whether this is a possible foreshadowing, representing a shift in the family hierarchy. Or is it simply a point of familial connection?

POSSIBLE CONNECTIONS TO OTHER SELECTIONS

Indira Sant, "Household Fires" (text p. 1144)
Dylan Thomas, "Do not go gentle into that good night" (text p. 885)

RESOURCES FOR TEACHING

Li-Young Lee: The City in Which I Love You [recording]. 1 cassette (29 min.), 1990. Reads from his book, which was the year's Lamont Poetry Selection. Distributed by New Letters on the Air.

See also "A Movable Feast" in the appendix of Film, Video, and Audiocassette Resources.

PHILIP LEVINE, *The Simple Truth* (p. 1105)

"The Simple Truth" is partially a definition of the poet's poetics, and partially a meditation on friendship, simplicity, and truth. He argues for simplicity, for truth, for the obvious that "must be said without elegance, meter and rhyme" (line 20), but he also tells a story using figurative language, and describes scenes rich with meaning. It might be best to begin by discussing what the speaker means by "simple" and "true"; do students believe that poetry seeks to convey truth, or rather that it tries to obscure the truth by cloaking it in poetic conventions? Is it possible that certain events or bits of knowledge of poetry "must stand for themselves" (24)? If they agree with the speaker's assertion, you might want to test it against some of the elements of this poem: how is it possible, for instance, to "taste what [he's] saying" (27–28)? When he uses onions, potatoes, salt, and butter as metaphors for the truth, is he stating the truth simply? And what do students make of his final gesture of renaming salt as a "metal" (33) or of referring to "a form we have no words for" (34)? This poem is a complex definition of truth within poetry, and it might be appropriate to consider it either toward the beginning or toward the end of the course.

POSSIBLE CONNECTIONS TO OTHER SELECTIONS

Langston Hughes, "Formula" (text p. 1021)

Marianne Moore, "Poetry" (text p. 1111)

HENRY WADSWORTH LONGFELLOW, *Snow-Flakes* (p. 1106)

The snow, generally described in terms of emotions and falterings of the human spirit, is taken in this poem to reveal something about "the troubled sky" (line 11) and "our cloudy fancies" (7) at the same time. The air is personified; the speaker insists that the snow is this poem which reveals "the secret of despair, / Long in its cloudy bosom hoarded" (15–16).

A good place to begin discussion is with the question of the speaker, who removes himself from the scene as much as possible. The only time he alludes to himself at all is with the plural pronoun "our" in line 7. What type of person must he be? Do we assume that he is feeling troubled, that he is full of grief and despair? What is his relationship to the scene that he is witnessing?

POSSIBLE CONNECTIONS TO OTHER SELECTIONS

Robert Frost, "Stopping by Woods on a Snowy Evening" (text p. 989)

Percy Bysshe Shelley, "Ode to the West Wind" (text p. 894)

RESOURCES FOR TEACHING

The Best-Loved Poems of Longfellow [recording]. 1 cassette (55 min.), 1966. Read by Hal Holbrook. Distributed by Caedmon/HarperAudio.

Songs of Hiawatha and More Poems [recording]. 3 cassettes (3 hours, 9 minutes). Distributed by Audio Book Contractors.

Treasury of Henry Wadsworth Longfellow [recording]. 1 cassette (54 min.), 1986. Distributed by Spoken Arts.

AUDRE LORDE, *Hanging Fire* (p. 1107)

This poem should be accessible enough to your students, who probably remember all too clearly what life felt like at age fourteen. You might either as a writing assignment or in class discussion ask students to supply and talk about lines from this poem that seem to ring especially true to their own memories of adolescence. Consider, for example, the opening five lines, expressing bewilderment over a physical body that seems no longer one's own, accompanied by the awakenings and trials of first love directed toward someone whose own maturing processes seem at a standstill. Students might also want to comment on the range of emotional pitches the speaker feels, including the adolescent anxiety and imaginative investment in death.

The three stanzas share a refrain — made up of the most rhythmic lines in the poem: "and momma's in the bedroom / with the door closed." You may want to touch lightly on the similarities this poem shares with the ballad tradition and comment on how this refrain effects a sense of closure in a poem that composes itself primarily according to the cadences of speech rhythms and fairly spontaneous thought patterns. The repetition of this line also lends a certain poignance to the speaker's voice. By the end of the poem, we have a clear sense that she will not receive much help from the person who could be expected to help her while she is "hanging fire." You might ask how long one goes through life "hanging fire."

POSSIBLE CONNECTION TO ANOTHER SELECTION

Indira Sant, "Household Fires" (text p. 1144)

RESOURCES FOR TEACHING

Audre Lorde [recording]. 1 cassette (29 min.), 1979. The author reads her poetry and discusses her ideas about poetry and her experiences in West Africa. Distributed by New Letters on the Air.

Audre Lorde: Shorelines [recording]. 1 cassette (53 min.), 1985. Distributed by Watershed Tapes.

ARCHIBALD MACLEISH, *Ars Poetica* (p. 1107)

In the first eight lines of his poem, MacLeish poses what seems to be a paradox: he states that a poem, which is an arrangement of words on a page, should be "mute," "Dumb," "Silent," and "wordless." Note, however, that the word *as* follows each of these adjectives; this suggests that poetry accomplishes its purpose not through the words, but by means of the metaphorical images created by the words. Poetry addresses itself not to the intellect, but to deeper, more abstract, more emotional levels. You might have students examine some of the metaphors employed in this poem. To what senses are they directed? What emotions do the images evoke? In lines 19–22, MacLeish gives examples of emotions that can be conveyed by specific images. How well do these images evoke the specified emotions? Can your students suggest other images that evoke grief or love? What image might convey hate? Fear?

The final two lines of the poem create another paradox: the poet/speaker who has argued against prosaic forms in favor of metaphorical images suddenly states this thesis directly. Do your students think the speaker mistrusts the reader's ability to comprehend the poem without a prosaic thesis statement? Note that the speaker's previous reiterations that "A poem should," are consistently followed by metaphors, whereas the statement "A poem should not" is followed by a direct assertion. Is the speaker, having demonstrated what a poem should be, now showing us what a poem should not be? Can your students suggest another explanation for the unpoetic format of these last two lines?

CHRISTOPHER MARLOWE, *The Passionate Shepherd to His Love* (p. 1108)

Marlowe was the first English dramatist to use blank verse in his plays. He completed a master of arts at Cambridge in 1587 and was stabbed to death six years later, having lived an eventful, though somewhat mysterious, life.

Anyone with an ounce of romance will respond favorably to this pastoral lyric, whose speaker pledges to do the impossible (yet how inviting to entertain the vision of "a thousand fragrant posies" on demand!) if only his beloved will be his love. What lovers have not believed, for a time at least, that they could "all the pleasures prove," that all the pleasure the world offered was there for the taking?

It's significant, of course, that his song is sung in May, the month when spring takes firm hold (in England, at least) and when the end of winter was (and still is) celebrated with great exuberance.

POSSIBLE CONNECTIONS TO OTHER SELECTIONS

John Donne, "The Sun Rising" (text p. 705)
William Shakespeare, "When, in disgrace with Fortune and men's eyes" (text p. 1118)
Richard Wilbur, "A Late Aubade" (text p. 732)

RESOURCES FOR TEACHING

Christopher Marlowe: Elizabethan Love Poems [recording]. 1 cassette (50 min.). Unabridged edition. Distributed by Spoken Arts.
See also "Medieval and Elizabethan Poetry" and "Palgrave's Golden Treasury of English Poetry" in the appendix of Film, Video, and Audiocassette Resources.

HERMAN MELVILLE, *The Maldive Shark* (p. 1109)

The title of this poem leads us away from the pilot-fish, who could be considered the true subject of the poem. The poem begins by reinforcing the title, "About the Shark," and it also ends with a description of "the dotard lethargic and dull" (line 15). Yet the rest of the poem is about the "sleek little pilot-fish" (3) who serve as the shark's "Eyes and brains" (15). You might want to spend a few minutes discussing the effect of naming the poem after the shark rather than after the pilot-fish before moving into a broader interpretation of the poem. Are students likely to try to extract some human "truth" out of Melville's description of nature? Does the poem encourage us to do so at all? By using the distinctly human words "friends" and "friendly" (13), Melville personifies the relationship between the fish, and hints at an allegorical meaning. The pilot-fish "guide [the shark] to prey," giving the shark his food, but "never partake" (13–14). In return, the little fish are given safety, and clemency from his wrath. You may want to discuss Melville's take on the nature of friendships and how human relations mirror the fish in this poem.

Students who have read *Moby-Dick* are likely to notice that the shark is described as "Pale" twice and that his teeth are emphatically white; those same students might be encouraged to try to emphasize the philosophical nature of Melville's writing.

POSSIBLE CONNECTIONS TO OTHER SELECTIONS

Robert Frost, "Design" (text p. 993)
N. Scott Momaday, "The Bear" (text p. 1110)

JOHN MILTON, *On the Late Massacre in Piedmont* (p. 1109)

Born in London, Milton began writing poetry at the age of fifteen. He had a remarkable aptitude for languages, mastering Latin, Greek, Hebrew, and most modern European languages before he completed his education in 1637. After earning his master's degree from Christ's College, Cambridge University, in 1632, he disappointed expectations that he would become a minister and embarked instead on a six-year period of carefully self-designed study in which he read everything he could. (The eyestrain caused by his voracious study eventually led to his blindness in 1651.)

Milton dedicated his literary talent to the causes of religious and civil freedom during the years 1640 to 1660, writing Puritan propaganda and numerous political and social tracts. Milton argued vociferously on many issues: "Of Reformation Touching Church Discipline in England" (1641) denounced the episcopacy; his troubled relationship with seventeen-year-old Mary Powell, who left him after one month of marriage, inspired him to support the legalization of divorce in "Doctrine and Discipline of Divorce" (1643); "Areopagitica," (1644), one of his most famous polemics, argued the necessity of a free press; and his defense of the murder of King Charles I in "The Tenure of Kings and Magistrates" (1649), although contributing to his appointment as the secretary for foreign languages in Cromwell's government, nearly got him executed when the monarchy was restored in 1660.

He was arrested, but friends and colleagues intervened on his behalf, and he was eventually released. Blind and unemployed, he returned to his poetry and a quiet life with his third wife, Elizabeth Minshull. It was during these last years of his life that Milton produced (by dictating to relatives, friends, and paid assistants) his most famous and substantial works: the epic poems *Paradise Lost* (1667) and *Paradise Regained* (1671) and the verse drama *Samson Agonistes* (1671).

"On the Late Massacre in Piedmont" is a sonnet of accountability — in an almost bookkeeper sense of the term. The basic premise is contractual. The Waldenses have preserved piety and faith in God over four centuries; now God should avenge their massacre. *Even*, as the first word of line 3, is an imperative verb form, as in *Even the score*. Scorekeeping, in fact, matters in this sonnet, and students might find it a good exercise in reading to identify and analyze the numerical images. Nature, moreover, is shown as sympathetic to the Waldenses, for it redoubles the sound of their lamentations. The passage ends with the elliptical phrase "and they / To heaven." Syntax again provides the verb *redoubled* and says, in effect, that the hills echoed the moans to heaven. Milton expresses the wish that future generations of Waldenses will augment their number "a hundredfold" to offset the Pope's power.

You might ask students to write an analytical and persuasive essay proving that this is either a plea for vengeance or the expression of a hope that the Waldenses will receive God's protection and strength throughout history.

POSSIBLE CONNECTIONS TO OTHER SELECTIONS

Wilfred Owen, "Dulce et Decorum Est" (text p. 763)
Alfred, Lord Tennyson, "The Charge of the Light Brigade" (text p. 870)

RESOURCES FOR TEACHING

Milton. 28 min., color, 1989. Beta, VHS, ¾" U-matic cassette. Looks at Milton's sonnets to his wife Katherine and *Paradise Lost*. Distributed by Films for the Humanities and Sciences.

Milton and 17th Century Poetry. 35 min., color, 1989. Beta, VHS, ¾″ U-matic cassette. A study of Milton and other metaphysical poets. Distributed by Films for the Humanities and Sciences.

Milton by Himself. 27 min., color, 1989. Beta, VHS, ¾″ U-matic cassette. A biography constructed from Milton's autobiographical writings. Distributed by Films for the Humanities and Sciences.

Milton the Puritan: Portrait of a Mind [recording]. 10 cassettes (1 hr., 30 min. each). Distributed by Books on Tape.

The Poetry of John Milton [recording]. 1 cassette. Distributed by Caedmon/HarperAudio.

Treasury of John Milton [recording]. 1 cassette. Distributed by Spoken Arts.

See also "Introduction to English Poetry" and "Palgrave's Golden Treasury of English Poetry" in the appendix of Film, Video, and Audiocassette Resources.

JOHN MILTON, *When I consider how my light is spent* (p. 1110)

This sonnet is sometimes mistakenly titled "On His Blindness." You might begin by asking just what the topic of Milton's meditation is. He seems to be at midlife, neither old nor young. If Milton's blindness comes to mind as the subject, does that idea accommodate itself to the description "And that one talent which is death to hide / Lodged with me useless"? It would take some ingenuity to make blindness the equivalent of "talent" here. Far better to let "talent" stand in its old (biblical) and new senses and refer to Milton's poetic capability. At any rate, a discussion of this sonnet should prove useful in developing students' ability to select or discard extraliterary details in connection with a poem.

POSSIBLE CONNECTIONS TO OTHER SELECTIONS

Anne Bradstreet, "To My Dear and Loving Husband" (text p. 1080)

Ben Jonson, "On My First Son" (text p. 1102)

John Keats, "When I have fears that I may cease to be" (text p. 1103)

N. SCOTT MOMADAY, *The Bear* (p. 1110)

This poem investigates not only the character of the bear (who is only named as such in the title), but also the speaker's perception of him. The poem is largely about how we perceive nature, and how this perception changes according to rules that we do not expect or even understand. The poet leads us through a series of revelations about his subject, who is endowed with "old age" (line 6), "valor" (7), and "courage" (8), and then, as the speaker looks more closely, we see the effect of human hunting on the bear. It is as though we are there with the speaker, seeing the bear as he sees him, and losing sight of him as the speaker does. The bear is evasive, but the speaker is too; he does not paint himself into the picture. Sight is described in passive terms, first as a vague "ruse of vision" (1), and later the bear is "Seen" (9), then finally, "is gone . . . from sight" (17–18). What is the relationship between the speaker and the bear? And what is the speaker's relationship with us? Are we complicit in the bear's decline? If it's possible to establish these relationships, what is our relationship with the bear?

POSSIBLE CONNECTIONS TO OTHER SELECTIONS

James Dickey, "Deer Among Cattle" (text p. 766)

Robert Frost, "The Most of It" (text p. 995)

House Made of Dawn [recording]. 7 cassettes (7 hours). Distributed by Books on Tape.

N. Scott Momaday. 50 min., color. The author discusses the creative sources for his work. Distributed by Films for the Humanities and Sciences.

N. Scott Momaday: House Made of Dawn [recording]. 1 cassette (39 min.). Momaday reads excerpts from his stories. Distributed by the American Audio Prose Library.

N. Scott Momaday Reading [recording]. 2 cassettes (109 min.), 1983. Distributed by American Audio Prose Library.

MARIANNE MOORE, *Poetry* (p. 1111)

Moore was editor of *The Dial,* a literary magazine, from 1925 until its demise in 1929, so if this poem at times sounds like a manifesto, it is probably because it shares in the self-consciousness of an American literary scene that was trying to establish its own identity and formulate a modernist aesthetic.

You might pair this poem with MacLeish's "Ars Poetica" (text p. 1107). Would MacLeish have liked "Poetry," or would he have found it too discursive, too much like prose? What precisely does Moore find objectionable about some poetry — possibly its stilted expressions, its overworked compulsion toward ornamentation, its "prettiness"? What do you suppose she means by "the genuine," and what images does she use to suggest it? The material after a colon usually explains the material preceding it. Is this the case at the beginning of stanza IV? Would Moore endorse the idea that anything can be material for a poem? What, if any, provisos or exceptions would she make?

These questions should help students begin to see not only what Moore is saying but also how similar the process of analysis can be in extracting ideas from either prose or poetry.

POSSIBLE CONNECTIONS TO OTHER SELECTIONS

Langston Hughes, "Formula" (text p. 1021)
Archibald MacLeish, "Ars Poetica" (text p. 1107)
Miller Williams, "Excuse Me" (text p. 708)

RESOURCES FOR TEACHING

Marianne Moore Reading Her Poems & Fables from La Fontaine [recording]. 1 cassette. Distributed by Caedmon/HarperAudio.

Marianne Moore Reads Her Poetry [recording]. 1 cassette (22 min.), 1965. Distributed by Audio-Forum.

See also "Inner Ear, Parts 3 and 4," "Modern American Poetry," "The Poet's Voice," "Voices and Vision," and "Caedmon Treasury of Modern Poets Reading Their Own Poetry" in the appendix of Film, Video, and Audiocassette Resources.

WILFRED OWEN, *Arms and the Boy* (p. 1112)

This poem emphasizes the tragic loss of innocence that results from sending boys to war — or, more specifically, from introducing them to violence. That which transforms a boy into a killer seems to reside outside of the boy and within the implements, the arms, of war. There is an implicit pun in "arms"; the poet proposes that a boy is first introduced to military arms through touching them — that is, through the tactile use of his own arms. The final stanza intimates that God (or nature) has no role in warfare, that our teeth are for eating and that our bodies are generally not created (or have not evolved) for war. Does the poem seem entirely a product of World War I, or is its sentiment still relevant? How has warfare changed since Owen's time? Could his argument be productively applied to the problem of gun control in contemporary America?

On another tack: how does the poet's use of conventions such as alliteration, personification, and slant rhyme enhance the way he presents his argument? Consider the rhyming pairs together: "blade" and "blood" (lines 1, 2); "flash" and "flesh" (3, 4); "bulletleads" and "lads" (5, 6); "teeth" and "death" (7, 8); and the concluding stanza, "apple" and "supple" (9, 10); and "heels" and "curls." The pairs together form a much bleaker narrative, mirroring that of the whole poem. Being imperfect rhymes, they create a disturbing sense, and enhance the message.

POSSIBLE CONNECTIONS TO OTHER SELECTIONS

Wilfred Owen, "Dulce et Decorum Est" (text p. 763)

Alfred, Lord Tennyson, "The Charge of the Light Brigade" (text p. 870)

MARGE PIERCY, *Barbie Doll* (p. 1112)

This poem uses our culture's icon of perfection, the Barbie Doll, to describe how society's expectations can damage or even destroy a child. Instructors might focus on the "girlchild" (line 1) as a kind of property belonging to her society: the only things that seem to matter in her world are how she is perceived, what people say to her, and what they say about her. Significantly, she remains nameless, and although Piercy tells us that "She was healthy, tested intelligent, / possessed strong arms and back" (7–8), because of a classmate's expressed perception of her appearance, "She went to and fro apologizing" (10). Ironically, only after the young woman has killed herself — and benefited from "the undertaker's cosmetics" (20) — does she finally achieve society's approval.

Ask students to explain the significance of the title. How does the concept of a "Barbie doll" connect with the description of the toys in the first stanza or the final description of the young woman in the casket? Note how this young woman is encouraged to behave: "to play coy, / . . . to come on hearty, / exercise, diet, smile and wheedle" (12–14). None of these instructions is concerned with developing her individual talents; instead, they are singularly focused on socializing her into conforming to patriarchal expectations. She is a commodity not unlike a car: as Piercy writes, "Her good nature wore out / like a fan belt" (15–16).

Do students find the situation described in "Barbie Doll" completely ludicrous? What aspects of modern culture might suggest that Piercy's depiction is surprisingly accurate? Instructors might touch on the high rate of eating disorders among young women, for instance, or point out the longevity of Barbie-making. Or, students might construct a parable featuring a "boychild" as a companion piece to "Barbie Doll." Either of these approaches should provoke a spirited discussion.

POSSIBLE CONNECTIONS TO OTHER SELECTIONS

Robert Bly, "Sitting Down to Dinner" (text p. 824)

Indira Sant, "Household Fires" (text p. 1144)

SYLVIA PLATH, *Daddy* (p. 1113)

Read this poem aloud before you begin teaching it. That way the class will hear some of the insistent and bizarre nursery-rhyme repetitions of sound that hammer their way through it. The critic A. Alvarez describes "Daddy" as a love poem. That idea, given the tone and imagery, might surprise some students, but it can be related to Plath's own comment on her father's early death and her attempt to cut through the entanglements of a relationship that never had a chance to mature.

The person we need most to love but are unable to is the one most likely to be projected in an effigy of hatred. One wants to exorcise what one cannot embrace. The most memorable feature of this poem is the string of transformations Plath projects on the father. From the inorganic statue to the mythical vampire (killed by a stake "in" the heart), the transforming range could not be wider. In this imaginative process Plath begins to think that she is a Jew and that her father is with the German Luftwaffe and then with the armored tank division ("panzer-man"). She eventually connects him with Fascism and the sadomasochism of male aggression against women. The real picture of Otto Plath as teacher is suddenly rendered in Plath's mind as surreal — father as devil. The crescendo of memories and images reaches its peak when Plath recalls an earlier suicide attempt (one she described, in fact, in her novel *The Bell Jar*). She also seems to implicate her husband, the British poet Ted Hughes, in this memory, as she portrays him in the roles of torturer and vampire.

Plath is often described as a "confessional poet." Despite the highly idiosyncratic nature of this poem, what in it allows for a sharing of this personal experience with a wide and impersonal audience? What, if any, are the universal themes touched on here? You might develop one of these questions into a writing assignment.

POSSIBLE CONNECTIONS TO OTHER SELECTIONS

Philip Larkin, "This Be the Verse" (text p. 1105)
Linda Pastan, "Marks" (text p. 791)
Dylan Thomas, "Do not go gentle into that good night" (text p. 885)

SYLVIA PLATH, *Metaphors* (p. 1115)

Miraculously, this poem is a self-reflective text with nine lines of nine beats each and a nine-letter title all addressing a nine-month phenomenon.

Riddles that focus on the idea of birth in all likelihood antedate King Oedipus; for birth itself, particularly to the woman carrying the child, is always a riddle — of that which is not me, yet of me; apart from me, and yet within. You might for a moment pause to consider the literary characteristics of riddles, with their paradoxes and the surprise and delight they engender when their answers are discovered.

This poem is useful too in discussing tone. The speaker here is self-jesting in her description and seems to accept with good grace the pregnancy's inexorable progress.

POSSIBLE CONNECTIONS TO OTHER SELECTIONS

Sylvia Plath, "Mirror" (text p. 786)
———, "Mushrooms" (text p. 842)

EDGAR ALLAN POE, *Alone* (p. 1115)

With elliptical dashes reminiscent of Dickinson, this speaker describes his isolation from society, building up toward a vision, in the final line, of a "demon" that haunts his mind. The poem is deeply psychological; the speaker never tells us what "The mystery which binds me still" (line 12) is, other than to describe its form as a cloud in the shape of a demon. Students will undoubtedly speculate about the speaker in contemporary psychological terms, possibly casting him as antisocial ("I have not seen / As others saw" [2–3]), depressed ("I could not awaken / My heart to joy" [6–7]), or alienated ("all I lov'd — I lov'd alone" [8]). Why does the speaker choose to explain his condition in terms of things outside himself, specifically in terms of nature? What is the effect of projecting one's psychological state onto a landscape? Consider, also, how the speaker describes himself largely in terms of what he is not.

If you have worked with Dickinson, it will be interesting to compare the style of this poem to any one by her; do the dashes function in the same way in Poe's poem as they do in Dickinson's poetry? Do they seem as effective, or even as necessary, as they are to Dickinson's poetics? The final dash in "Alone" leaves open a number of possibilities; if the poem were to continue, what is the speaker likely to tell us next?

POSSIBLE CONNECTIONS TO OTHER SELECTIONS

Emily Dickinson, "I'm Nobody! Who are you?" (text p. 938)
——, "The Soul selects her own Society —" (text p. 941)

ADRIENNE RICH, *Living in Sin* (p. 1115)

This poem describes the experience of a woman whose love affair is anything but romantic. She focuses on the details of the room in which she and her lover meet, and they reveal her profound discontentment with her situation. Students will enjoy the title and its ironic reversal in context with the poem. Rich was married at the time she wrote this, but her "sin" was to see through the myth of romantic bliss in a one-room flat to the harsh particulars of daytime reality. Compare the roles of the man and the woman here. What might be some of the "minor demons"?

The images in this poem are worth examining. In lines 4–6, for example, the romantic point of view becomes an artful still life, a painting by Renoir perhaps.

POSSIBLE CONNECTIONS TO OTHER SELECTIONS

Thomas Hardy, "The Ruined Maid" (text p. 1093)
Sharon Olds, "Sex without Love" (text p. 740)

RESOURCES FOR TEACHING

Adrienne Rich: Planetarium: A Retrospective, 1950 to 1980 [recording]. 1 cassette (63 min.), 1986. Part of the YM-YWHA Poetry Center Series. Distributed by Watershed Tapes.

The Poetry of Adrienne Rich [recording]. 1 cassette (36 min.), 1968. Part of the YM-YWHA Poetry Center Series. Distributed by Audio-Forum.

Adrienne Rich: Tracking the Contradictions: Poems 1981–1985 [recording]. 1 cassette (53 min.), 1986. Distributed by Watershed Tapes.

See also "Poets in Person, No. 4" [recording] in the appendix of Film, Video, and Audiocassette Resources.

CHRISTINA GEORGINA ROSSETTI, *Some Ladies Dress in Muslin Full and White* (p. 1116)

The speaker of this poem transforms from a rather benign observer of fashion into a misanthrope who would selectively eliminate men and women based on what they are wearing. You might ask students to locate the precise moments where her attitude seems to shift: does anything cause it? You might first ask them what they think the poet's tone or intention is. Which words indicate that light humor is the intended tone, and which words make the poem seem a biting satire? The poem may allow you to discuss the aggressive nature of humor, the very fine line between comedy and tragedy. Do students know anyone, or can they think of examples of professional comedians, whose brand of humor reveals antisocial tendencies? What motivates these humorists? Would they put Rossetti's speaker in the same camp?

POSSIBLE CONNECTIONS TO OTHER SELECTIONS

Emily Dickinson, "I'm Nobody! Who are you?" (text p. 938)

Charles Martin, "Victoria's Secret" (text p. 867)

WILLIAM SHAKESPEARE (pp. 1116–1118)

Shakespeare's sonnets have been widely discussed. Some books that may offer useful observations on them include *A Casebook of Shakespeare's Sonnets,* edited by Gerald Willen and Victor B. Reed; Edward Hubler's *The Sense of Shakespeare's Sonnets* (Westport: Greenwood, 1976); and *Shakespeare's Sonnets,* edited with commentary by Stephen Booth (New Haven: Yale UP, 1977). The two songs given in this section, "Spring" and "Winter," are discussed by Bertrand Bronson in *Modern Language Notes* 63 (1948) and by C. L. Barber in *Shakespeare's Festive Comedy* (Princeton: Princeton UP, 1972).

WILLIAM SHAKESPEARE, *Not marble, nor the gilded monuments* (p. 1116)

The central point of this poem, that poetry, more than any monument, possesses the power to immortalize its subject, was a common one in the Petrarchan love sonnets of Shakespeare's day. This same conceit appears in Shakespeare's "Shall I compare thee to a summer's day?" (text p. 881). Have students find conventional images of permanence in the poem. With what destructive forces are these images juxtaposed? Even marble, the most durable of building materials, becomes "unswept stone" when it is "besmeared with sluttish time" (line 4), the most destructive force of all. Yet according to the poet, his lover will live until judgment day in "this powerful rhyme" (2). How do your students respond to this conceit? Can a poem immortalize a person? Do poems last forever? Can students suggest other things that might last longer, other ways of achieving immortality?

POSSIBLE CONNECTIONS TO OTHER SELECTIONS

Emily Dickinson, "This was a Poet — It Is That" (text p. 943)

John Keats, "Ode on a Grecian Urn" (text p. 741)

WILLIAM SHAKESPEARE, *That time of year thou mayst in me behold*
(p. 1117)

Images of death and decay predominate in this sonnet. Ask students to identify the different metaphors for death that are presented in the poem's three quatrains. The first quatrain evokes the approach of winter as dying leaves drift to the ground; the image of "bare ruined choirs" in line 4 would probably have reminded Shakespeare's contemporaries of the many monastery churches that had gone to ruin in the wake of Henry VIII's dissolution of the English monasteries in the 1530s. The second quatrain evokes images of falling night; the third, of a dying fire whose embers are being extinguished by its own ashes.

The tone of the poem's concluding couplet could be a topic for class debate. Do students find the grimness of the first three quatrains to be mitigated by the poem's last two lines? The speaker seems to be suggesting to his friend or lover that the inevitability of death should sharpen his or her appreciation of the speaker's affections. Ask students to compare the portrayal of love as an anodyne against the inevitability of death in this poem with that idea as expressed in Matthew Arnold's "Dover Beach" (text p. 757).

POSSIBLE CONNECTIONS TO OTHER SELECTIONS

Matthew Arnold, "Dover Beach" (text p. 757)

Anne Bradstreet, "To My Dear and Loving Husband" (text p. 1080)

Robert Hass, "Happiness" (text p. 707)

Richard Wilbur, "A Late Aubade" (text p. 732)

WILLIAM SHAKESPEARE, *When forty winters shall besiege thy brow*
(p. 1117)

"When forty winters shall besiege thy brow" provides another excellent example of the form of an English, or Shakespearean, sonnet. The central concept of the poem is expressed through three complementary quatrains, and the rhyme scheme — *abab cdcd efef gg* — adheres to the traditional Shakespearean sonnet form. Students unfamiliar with sonnet form should be referred to Chapter 22, "Poetic Forms," for a fuller explanation of the genre. They should then be encouraged to consider how form and content complement each other in this sonnet.

It may be useful to suggest that the sonnet is a well-organized argument. Generally, Shakespeare marshals his rhetoric to convince his audience — both the person addressed in the sonnet and the poem's readers — of a specific truth. Here, the poet warns the youthful subject of the poem that age, like winter, offers no true sustenance, and that the best antidote to old age is children. The poet's powers of persuasion rest primarily on threats: in the first quatrain, he depicts the physical effects of "forty winters" (line 1) and predicts that "Thy youth's proud livery, so gazed on now / Will be a tattered weed" (3–4). The second quatrain extends this rhetorical approach: the beauty of youth and "the treasure of thy lusty days" (6) are reduced merely to "deep-sunken eyes" (7) and "all-eating shame and thriftless praise" (8). In the final quatrain, Shakespeare offers an alternative to what he has depicted as a wasteful life: instead of having nothing to show for youth, the addressee might instead say, "This fair child of mine / Shall sum my count and make my old excuse" (10–11). In addition, the beauty of the parent's youth will live on in the next generation. The couplet emphasizes the advantages of the alternative described by the third quatrain: "This were to be new made when thou art old, / And see thy blood warm

413

when thou feel'st it cold" (13–14). The final line smoothly blends with the opening line, touching on the harsher aspects of "forty winters" and yet contrasting the potential emptiness with the warmth offered by the poet's suggested alternative.

POSSIBLE CONNECTIONS TO OTHER SELECTIONS

Anne Bradstreet, "Before the Birth of One of Her Children" (text p. 1080)

Ben Jonson, "On My First Son" (text p. 1102)

WILLIAM SHAKESPEARE, *When, in disgrace with Fortune and men's eyes* (p. 1118)

This sonnet posits a future scenario in which the speaker will be outcast because of his fortune. He claims that he will be comforted by remembering his idyllic time with his lover, which presumably occurs in the present. A good starting point for analysis of this poem is its diction, since it contains several words — *bootless, featured, scope* — whose meanings have changed. Another interesting point for discussion is the religious allusion in line 12. Students might be invited to entertain the possibility that the "thee" in line 10 and "thy" in line 13 refer not to the conventional Petrarchan lover, but to God.

The sonnet's structure also merits attention. Ask students to compare the arrangement of the quatrains and concluding couplet in this poem with that of the other Shakespearean sonnets in the text. In which of the poems is there a sharp logical break between the quatrains and the couplet, and in which does this break occur after the octave? Is there any obvious relation between structure and content?

POSSIBLE CONNECTIONS TO OTHER SELECTIONS

John Donne, "A Valediction: Forbidding Mourning" (text p. 790)

William Shakespeare, "That time of year thou mayst in me behold" (text p. 1117)

PERCY BYSSHE SHELLEY, *Ozymandias* (p. 1118)

Many students will have read this Petrarchan sonnet in high school. You might begin by asking whether in an unintentionally ironic way Ozymandias may have been right; although he is far from outdistancing the rest of humanity in possessions and power, his statue is a reminder that all things are subject to decay and is thus a source of despair. The sonnet, despite its familiarity, still surprises by the quality of its versification. Observe in line 6 the delayed placement of "well," which underscores the closing cautionary note. The final lines, moreover, with the alliterated "boundless and bare" and "lone and level," do suggest the infinite reaches of both the desert and time.

POSSIBLE CONNECTIONS TO OTHER SELECTIONS

John Keats, "Ode on a Grecian Urn" (text p. 741)

William Butler Yeats, "Sailing to Byzantium" (text p. 1132)

SIR PHILIP SIDNEY, *Loving in Truth, and Fain in Verse My Love to Show* (p. 1119)

This sonnet's irregular meter matches its speaker's labored attempt to write it. Ask students to scan its lines, looking for irregularities. For example, the trochees at the beginnings of lines 1, 3, 4, 13, and so on illustrate the forced style that the speaker is trying to avert, while the irregular meter in line 9 aptly illustrates "words . . . halting forth."

Ask students to think about the images the speaker uses to describe his struggle to find the perfect writing style. His "sunburnt brain" (8) and the pregnancy metaphor ("great with child to speak" [12]) evoke an overfull, overcooked speaker who has worked too hard and gained little. How does the final line affirm our suspicions that there may be an easier way to write? Of course, Sidney has constructed his poem to make us feel this affirmation in the end.

Studies of this sonnet are included in the following discussions of *Astrophel and Stella* ("Loving in Truth" is the first sonnet in that sequence): David Kalsone's *Sidney's Poetry* (New York: Norton, 1970); Richard Lanham's "Pure and Impure Persuasion," and Collin Williamson's "Structure and Syntax in *Astrophel and Stella*" (both in *Essential Articles for the Study of Sir Philip Sidney*, edited by Arthur Kinney [Hamden: Archon, 1986]).

POSSIBLE CONNECTION TO ANOTHER SELECTION

George Herbert, "The Collar" (text p. 1097)

GARY SOTO, *Black Hair* (p. 1119)

The speaker of this poem, reflecting on his youth, recalls baseball games, specifically games involving his hero, Hector Moreno. Hector becomes a mythical figure in the speaker's mind, "Quick and hard with turned muscles" (line 8), but the speaker is also "brilliant with [*his*] body" (1, 21) as he sits in the bleachers. There is a connection between them, the player and the fan, which is not easily defined but which is crucial to an understanding of the poem. You might ask students to locate all references to the way the body is used in the poem. What does the speaker mean when he declares "I was brilliant with my body"? Does that meaning change as the poem progresses? You might have to pause to consider the tension between metaphor and descriptive language in the poem, which begins with the title. The speaker's identity is tied up not only with the way he uses his body but with physical aspects of his ethnicity: black hair and brown skin. If those aspects connect him with Hector Moreno, what inhibits his identity? What can we assume about his home life based on the cryptic description of his parents at the end of the first stanza?

POSSIBLE CONNECTIONS TO OTHER SELECTIONS

Martín Espada, "Coca-Cola and Coco Frío" (text p. 1151)
Gary Soto, "Mexicans Begin Jogging" (text p. 923)
Robert Wallace, "The Double-Play" (text p. 1122)

WALLACE STEVENS, *The Emperor of Ice-Cream* (p. 1120)

Even more than a parting word to the old woman about to be buried, this poem is a celebration of her mourners, who could still touch imagination's fire despite their impoverished surroundings. By covering the woman in her own embroidered winding sheet ("fantails" here are fantail pigeons), transforming the cigar roller into ice-cream creator, and gathering together like extras in a film extravaganza, they celebrate and affirm the gaudy, bawdy vitality of their lives, together with their creative power to "Let be be finale of seem." As a note, "deal" is furniture made of cheap wood, lacquered over to look more expensive.

You may want to ask students why the emperor of ice-cream is an emperor. Is this an indication that he knows how to move people through the pleasure principle, perhaps?

A Collection of Poems

POSSIBLE CONNECTIONS TO OTHER SELECTIONS

E. E. Cummings, "Buffalo Bill 's" (text p. 1087)
T. S. Eliot, "The Love Song of J. Alfred Prufrock" (text p. 1045)

RESOURCES FOR TEACHING

Wallace Stevens Reads [recording]. 1 cassette (60 min.), 1987. Part of The Poet Anniversary Series. Distributed by Caedmon/HarperAudio.
Wallace Stevens Reading His Poems [recording]. 1 cassette. Distributed by Caedmon/HarperAudio.
See also "Inner Ear, Parts 3 and 4," "Modern American Poetry," "The Poet's Voice," "Voices and Vision," and "Caedmon Treasury of Modern Poets Reading Their Own Poetry" in the appendix of Film, Video, and Audiocassette Resources.

ALFRED, LORD TENNYSON, *Ulysses* (p. 1120)

Tennyson was only twenty-four when he wrote this monologue, magnificently creating the thoughts that must have plagued this hero who had striven with the gods. The poem is written in blank verse and preserves a certain conversational eloquence through its use of parallelism. Consider the infinitives in "How dull it is to pause, to make an end, / To rust unburnished, not to shine in use!" (lines 22–23). Ulysses seems to be passing on his power and authority to his son Telemachus, who will, apparently, have a gentler, less warlike (though no less important) kind of work to do. You might ask the class what they suppose Ulysses has in mind when he says in the final stanza, "Some work of noble note, may yet be done." Could this poem bear some autobiographical reflection on the life of a poet? This question could prompt a brief research paper.

POSSIBLE CONNECTIONS TO OTHER SELECTIONS

Emily Dickinson, "This was a Poet — It Is That" (text p. 943)
William Butler Yeats, "Sailing to Byzantium" (text p. 1132)

ROBERT WALLACE, *The Double-Play* (p. 1122)

You might in teaching this poem ask the class the following questions: In the terms of the game, what literally happened? (Outs were made at second, then first base.) For what other reason is this poem called "The Double-Play"? (Words are object, then subject of the sentence or phrase; from their syntactic position, they demonstrate a double play.) For a clear example, examine how "the ball" is used in the second tercet. Does this syntactic double play serve any purpose? (It does, for it suggests the split-second fluidity of motion and the quick redirection of the ball necessary to make the double play.) Overall, the poem suggests analogically the relation of baseball to poetry — another sort of double play.

POSSIBLE CONNECTION TO ANOTHER SELECTION

Robert Francis, "The Pitcher" (text p. 850)

EDMUND WALLER, *Go, Lovely Rose* (p. 1123)

Metaphor can be the subject of a class discussion of this poem. The personified rose is ordered to perform the speaker's duty of convincing his beloved to "come forth" and

416

accept praise. The praise, though, is enclosed in the metaphoric association of her with the rose. You might ask students to consider this poem as a lesson in how metaphor works. How does the speaker direct the rose to act?

In stanza II, the rose and the beloved become interchangeable. Ask students why they think the speaker makes the shift to the desert. What does this tell us about his beloved? Why might she shun praise? Line 15, "And not blush so to be admired," presents a paradox. Students will enjoy figuring out that the woman blushes, looking like a rose, but she is supposed to take her flattery (a comparison of her to a rose!) more easily, which would make her pale, and unlike the rose. The final stanza concludes this persuasion to love, with a warning to the woman. What is the speaker trying to urge her to do? How does the rose figure in the persuasion?

In an essay you might ask students to characterize the tone and diction in the poem. What vocabulary or vocabularies does the speaker draw from to persuade his love to rush into his arms?

POSSIBLE CONNECTIONS TO OTHER SELECTIONS

Robert Herrick, "To the Virgins, to Make Much of Time" (text p. 728)
Richard Wilbur, "A Late Aubade" (text p. 732)

RESOURCE FOR TEACHING

See "Palgrave's Golden Treasury of English Poetry" in the appendix of Film, Video, and Audiocassette Resources.

WALT WHITMAN, *One Hour to Madness and Joy* (p. 1123)

Students may be taken aback by Whitman's explosive liberation, both in the unconstrained form of his poem and in its theme. This poem unleashes the poet's feelings in a rush of ecstasy; he has given in to passion, or to "madness and joy," and it has liberated in him a host of emotions to which he gives voice. The cause for this release seems to be a storm; the speaker muses, "What do my shouts amid lightnings and raging winds mean?" (line 3). His feeling is thus tied to "the best of Nature" (13); yet the speaker is not simply shouting to and communing with nature. His message exists for the benefit of his "children" (5), for a "bridegroom and bride" (6), and for an unspecified "you" (12). Is the poem meant to be instructive, or do students feel that it is purely an outpouring of the individual soul? The speaker seems to argue for a radical individualism in the final stanza, but as in all of Whitman, the spirit of the individual exists in confluence with the soul of society. The poem is written in terms that are not defined or illustrated as such; how do students interpret the various constraints, or "anchors and holds" (17), that Whitman refers to? What is "the puzzle, the thrice-tied knot" of line 10? In what ways does the form of the poem reinforce its theme?

POSSIBLE CONNECTIONS TO OTHER SELECTIONS

John Keats, "Ode to a Nightingale" (text p. 851)
Percy Bysshe Shelley, "Ode to the West Wind" (text p. 894)
Walt Whitman, "One's-Self I Sing" (text p. 1124)
——, "The Soul, reaching, throwing out for love" (text p. 789)

WALT WHITMAN, *One's-Self I Sing* (p. 1124)

This poem opens *Leaves of Grass* and is a kind of bugle announcement of several of Whitman's fondly held themes: the individual as both separate and a member of the democratic community; the equality of the sexes; the importance of both body and soul; and the "divinity" of modern humanity, which is not subject to kingly law. Some students will probably hear echoes of the opening lines of a traditional epic poem. Whitman is inverting epic convention somewhat by not singing of arms and men with the requisite bowings to the gods, but hailing the individual self.

As a writing assignment, you might ask the class to describe how and why this brief poem is a good opening for a book of poems. You might also ask students to say what seems particularly American about the poem.

POSSIBLE CONNECTION TO ANOTHER SELECTION

Emily Dickinson, "I'm Nobody! Who are you?" (text p. 938)

WALT WHITMAN, *When I Heard the Learn'd Astronomer* (p. 1124)

Whitman's poem sets forth in verse the often-debated argument over the relative values of art and science; true to the traditions of American romanticism, art is the winner in Whitman's view. You might ask your students to recall other instances in which they have seen this issue debated. Which side seemed to have the stronger argument in each case? Is this necessarily an either/or debate? That is, are art and science ever interconnected? What about stanzaic and metrical patterns, in which art depends on numbers? (You might ask students why a poet like Whitman might not be impressed with this particular example.) Can your students think of any poet whose use of imagery or structures depends on scientific principles? Does science owe anything to the power of the artist's imagination?

POSSIBLE CONNECTION TO ANOTHER SELECTION

Emily Dickinson, "Some keep the Sabbath going to Church —" (text p. 935)

RICHARD WILBUR, *Love Calls Us to the Things of This World* (p. 1124)

You might begin a discussion of this poem by talking about how a poet controls and convinces us of the truth of metaphors. Wilbur spends some time describing the motions of the wind-tossed laundry in order for us to see the laundry as "angels," and thus offer his prayer (lines 21–23) for a heaven on Earth.

To live as soul in a mock heaven would be incomplete, to say the least. The soul, like someone trying to sleep a while longer, resists the "punctual rape" of the day, which calls the soul back into the world of business and reality. Only when the sun rises does the soul out of "bitter love" join with the waking body and take down the laundry, an image for heaven. As it dismantles heaven, it clothes this daily world, without moral consideration for who wears the laundry — itself an act of graciousness and love. The nuns "keeping their difficult balance" suggest both the literal act of walking and the spiritual act of mediating between things of this world and things of the next.

You might review in class discussion phrases such as "punctual rape" (19), "every blessed day" (19), and "bitter love" (26).

POSSIBLE CONNECTION TO ANOTHER SELECTION

Walt Whitman, "The Soul, reaching, throwing out for love" (text p. 789)

MILLER WILLIAMS, *Thinking About Bill, Dead of AIDS* (p. 1125)

Williams's poem is about the experience of watching a friend with AIDS deal with the world around him as he succumbs to the disease. In the first stanza, the speaker admits ignorance of the processes by which the body turns on itself. Ask students to point out the metaphors of battle or war that the speaker uses to describe the onslaught of AIDS: "blood surrenders" (line 2), "rescinding all its normal orders" (4), "defenders of flesh" (5), "betraying the head" (5), and "pulling its guards back from all its borders" (6).

The second stanza moves from describing what is happening in Bill's body to describing the responses of others to his disease. Students may find line 9 particularly evocative — "your eyes drained of any reprimand." In the last three stanzas, the speaker explains the response of the "we" of the poem. Ask students to consider who the "we" represents. You may wish to pay special attention to lines like "partly to persuade / both you and us . . . that we were loving and were not afraid" (10-12), "stopping, though, to set our smiles at the door" (15), and "we didn't know what look would hurt you least" (18). What emotion is the speaker intending to convey? Ask students to identify the conflict that occurs in this part of the poem. Who experiences this tension? Discuss whether this underlying conflict is ever resolved.

POSSIBLE CONNECTIONS TO OTHER SELECTIONS

Donald Hall, "Letter with No Address" (text p. 1153)
Robert Hayden, "Those Winter Sundays" (text p. 672)
Andrew Hudgins, "Elegy for My Father, Who Is Not Dead" (text p. 893)

RESOURCES FOR TEACHING

Miller Williams [recording]. 1 cassette (29 min.), 1985. Distributed by New Letters on the Air.
Poems of Miller Williams [recording]. 1 cassette. Read by the author. Distributed by Spoken Arts.
The Poetry of Miller Williams [recording]. 1 cassette (26 min.), 1969. Part of the YM-YWHA Poetry Center Series. Distributed by Audio-Forum.

WILLIAM CARLOS WILLIAMS, *Spring and All* (p. 1126)

All sounds a good deal like *fall,* and indeed there is something autumnal about Williams's chill spring, with its "reddish/purplish" bushes and "dead, brown leaves." But these tokens of death actually bespeak a quickening life of the season that connotes rebirth. The images of human birth are not far from Williams's mind in this poem, as he talks about the nameless "They" who come into the world naked. Syntactically "They" (line 16) stands for the vegetation of grass, wild carrot leaf, and the rest (all), but we do not know this until after the pronoun appears. Williams can thus have it both ways and point to both a human and a nonhuman world.

Williams's spring, like so many of his subjects, is earth-rooted, literally. No surface change here; this profound "change" is " rooted" far down, so that life springs forth from its depths.

You might ask the class whether there is any significance in the setting of the poem — by the road to the contagious hospital.

POSSIBLE CONNECTIONS TO OTHER SELECTIONS

Margaret Atwood, "February" (text p. 784)

Wislawa Szymborska, "End and Beginning" (text p. 1146)

WILLIAM CARLOS WILLIAMS, *This Is Just to Say* (p. 1127)

Three possible writing assignments can be organized around this poem: (1) an essay talking about line breaks, necessary brevity, and careful word choice that validates this seemingly conversational statement as poetry; (2) a found poem, using a scrap of conversation or some lines from a short story, to make a poem about the length of this one; (3) a parody of this poem.

POSSIBLE CONNECTIONS TO OTHER SELECTIONS

Helen Chasin, "The Word *Plum*" (text p. 851)

Donald Justice, "Order in the Streets" (text p. 924)

Ezra Pound, "In a Station of the Metro" (text p. 772)

WILLIAM WORDSWORTH, *I Wandered Lonely as a Cloud* (p. 1127)

The speaker of this poem finds comfort for his loneliness in nature. His connection to daffodils comforts him even in memory. In his preface to *Lyrical Ballads*, Wordsworth describes poetry as "the spontaneous overflow of powerful feelings: it takes its origin from emotion recollected in tranquillity." To some extent, this quotation explains the "wealth" that Wordsworth alludes to in line 18, for while reclining on his couch he can recall the heightened sense of pleasure the daffodils first brought him. From his mood of loneliness, he moves to a state of gladness. What else characterizes how the daffodils appear to him? Seemingly, they are a token of cosmic splendor in their extensiveness and golden sparkle.

POSSIBLE CONNECTIONS TO OTHER SELECTIONS

Emily Dickinson, "A Bird came down the Walk —" (text p. 829)

Robert Frost, "Come In" (text p. 994)

Robert Hass, "Happiness" (text p. 707)

WILLIAM WORDSWORTH, *A Slumber Did My Spirit Seal* (p. 1128)

This is one of Wordsworth's "Lucy poems," and the "she" in line 3 alludes to Lucy. Apparently, this poem marks a loss for which the poet was unprepared. He was asleep to the possibilities of aging and death, and Lucy now seems well beyond the province of earthly years and more the spirit of eternal time. Is there a paradox in this poem? Probably so. The speaker's dream, which he had had in a more pleasant period, when he felt that they were both beyond the effects of time, turns out to be for Lucy ironically accurate, for like the rocks and stones and trees, she is now unaffected by the passage of time.

POSSIBLE CONNECTIONS TO OTHER SELECTIONS

John Keats, "When I have fears that I may cease to be" (text p. 1103)

Percy Bysshe Shelley, "Ozymandias" (text p. 1118)

WILLIAM WORDSWORTH, *The Solitary Reaper* (p. 1128)

This poem seems to spill over its limits as fit lyric to become a spontaneous overflow of powerful feeling. Ask the class to note how many boundaries are exceeded here. In stanza I, for example, the song overflows the vales. In the final stanza the song seems without end, and the hearer hears it long after he leaves the singer behind. Implied too in the second and third stanzas is the song's ability to transcend place and history. As with other poetic figures of Wordsworth, this solitary reaper and her song provide a way into perceiving an order of existence beneath the surface. You might ask the class if it matters at all that the singer is female.

POSSIBLE CONNECTIONS TO OTHER SELECTIONS

William Blake, "The Chimney Sweeper" (text p. 822)
Langston Hughes, "The Weary Blues" (text p. 1019)

JAMES WRIGHT, *A Blessing* (p. 1129)

This poem stands apart from many other late modern poems in its unabashed happiness. In a century of cynicism, the communion between humanity and nature in this poem almost makes us suspicious. Nothing should pose difficulty in this poetic narrative of a man who approaches "two Indian ponies" (line 3) except for the final two lines, which posit a bizarre transformation of the speaker into a flowering plant. He makes it sound as if he is *able* to step out of his body: "if I stepped out of my body I would break / into blossom" (22–23). The slight rest at the line break after the word "break" gives us pause; there is something not right about this scene. On the surface the poem seems almost naïve; but is there something else going on? What else seems "off" about the poem? Does the fantastic tone of the majority of the poem clash with the concrete, localized setting described in the first line? Is there something disturbing about the way the speaker and the ponies interact?

POSSIBLE CONNECTIONS TO OTHER SELECTIONS

James Dickey, "Deer Among Cattle" (text p. 766)
Robert Frost, "Design" (text p. 993)
Robert Hass, "Happiness" (text p. 707)

MITSUYE YAMADA, *A Bedtime Story* (p. 1129)

Irony is this poem's most striking feature. A father tells his child an ancient story from his culture (we presume), and his daughter, the speaker, is unable to understand the story's message. To figure out the speaker's inability to grasp this message, we must look into the way the story is framed. At the beginning of the poem, the time is nonspecific; the father begins his story as many stories begin: "Once upon a time" (line 1). At the end of the story, the speaker describes where the story is told, "In the comfort of our / hilltop home in Seattle / overlooking the valley" (40–42). This tension between the timeless and the present indicate a gap between father and daughter that goes beyond a typical generation gap. The daughter cannot grasp the moral of her father's story because she is safe and comfortable, and, presumably, privileged. The irony is that she cannot identify with the woman in the story who is turned away from houses in town, identifying instead with the townspeople who turn the old woman away. The speaker can no more see the message of the story than the people in that town can see the beauty of the moon. As readers of the poem, we are put in a similar position: what are we to take away from the story, frame-tale and all? Do students identify with the daughter (who wants a fuller story with a more exciting plot), with the father (who wants to pass on a piece of his culture), with both, with neither, or with the woman in the story? One way to enter such a discussion is to ask students how they read the poem's tone; is it meant to be humorous or instructive? Compare the poem's tone with that of the legend recounted.

POSSIBLE CONNECTIONS TO OTHER SELECTIONS

Julia Alvarez, "Woman's Work" (text p. 886)

Margaret Atwood, "Bored" (text p. 737)

Jimmy Santiago Baca, "Green Chile" (text p. 758)

WILLIAM BUTLER YEATS, *Adam's Curse* (p. 1130)

The poet is addressing his beloved, Maud Gonne. "That beautiful mild woman" is Gonne's sister, Kathleen. The idea at the poem's center is that, with Adam's curse, nothing can be achieved except by hard labor. Indeed, all is work, including the making of poems and the nurturing of beauty in women. Natural images reflect the failing of the love between the speaker and his beloved. We hear then the final bitter victory of Adam's curse: the demise of the tradition of the courtier and "the old high way of love." The study of books, the craft of letters, and the demeanor of high courtesy — all have been made to seem trivial, and as a result the grace of this continuing courtship can find no validation for its style. You might initiate discussion by asking students to connect the themes of the poem with the themes they extrapolate from the story of Eden, particularly in terms of gender roles.

Maud Gonne married Major MacBride a year after this poem was written.

POSSIBLE CONNECTION TO ANOTHER SELECTION

Timothy Steele, "An Aubade" (text p. 761)

WILLIAM BUTLER YEATS, *Crazy Jane Talks with the Bishop* (p. 1131)

Tradition has it that the fool is the purveyor of truth, and Crazy Jane, whose retort to the bishop is that "fair needs foul," is no exception. The paradoxical mutualities that Crazy Jane endorses find other correspondences in the last stanza, where the romantic ideal of love, we are told, pitches its mansion in "the place of excrement." Puns on *sole* and *whole* also invite a commingling of the platonic with the blatantly physical. According to John Unterecker, the bishop in the poem was a divinity student turned down by Jane for Jack the Journeyman. The bishop banished Jack, but Jane remained true to him *(A Reader's Guide to William Butler Yeats* [New York: Noonday, 1959]).

POSSIBLE CONNECTION TO ANOTHER SELECTION

Thomas Hardy, "The Ruined Maid" (text p. 1093)

WILLIAM BUTLER YEATS, *Leda and the Swan* (p. 1132)

Some references in this poem might require clarification: the offspring of Leda and Zeus (as swan) was Helen, the most beautiful of women, who married Menelaus but was later awarded to Paris. Paris took her to Troy with him, thus occasioning the Trojan War and the death of Agamemnon, the leader of the Greeks. Agamemnon was married to Clytemnestra, Helen's sister.

According to Yeats's view, this rape marks a turning point in history and the downward spiraling of the gyres. The moment is dark and fraught with the onset of much tragedy that Leda cannot possibly know, yet she does seem to take on a measure of Zeus's power and come closer to assuming a consciousness of the divine than is ordinarily possible. One point to consider in class discussion is Yeats's use of the rhetorical question in this poem. Does the poem suggest any answers to these questions? What do they do to the tone of the poem?

POSSIBLE CONNECTION TO ANOTHER SELECTION

William Butler Yeats, "The Second Coming" (text p. 1133)

WILLIAM BUTLER YEATS, *Sailing to Byzantium* (p. 1132)

Byzantium, in historical terms, was the capital of the Eastern Roman Empire and was the holy city of Greek Orthodoxy. Explore with the class what Byzantium symbolically represents, especially in terms of Yeats's career as a poet. In a note to the poem, Yeats commented, "I have read somewhere that in the Emperor's Palace at Byzantium was a tree made of gold and silver and artificial birds that sang" (*The Collected Poems of William Butler Yeats* [New York: Macmillan, 1972], 453). Increasingly in his later poems, Yeats turned to art rather than nature as a means of transcending time.

POSSIBLE CONNECTIONS TO OTHER SELECTIONS

John Keats, "Ode on a Grecian Urn" (text p. 741)
William Shakespeare, "Not marble, nor the gilded monuments" (text p. 1116)

WILLIAM BUTLER YEATS, *The Second Coming* (p. 1133)

The pattern here of the falcon circling around the falconer indicates the pattern of the gyre, now tracing its widest circle and thus least subject to the control of the falconer. "Mere anarchy" is loosed on a world troubled by recent wars (World War I and the Russian Revolution). Yeats later claimed he was describing the rise of Fascism in Europe. What kind of order will assume its place over the next two thousand years, if the nature of that world is imaged by a description of the annunciating beast as blank, pitiless, and rough?

POSSIBLE CONNECTIONS TO OTHER SELECTIONS

Robert Frost, "Fire and Ice" (text p. 988)
William Butler Yeats, "Leda and the Swan" (text p. 1132)

DALE ZIEROTH, *Time over Earth* (p. 1134)

The speaker in this poem tries to come to terms with the sensation of flight and travel. He is led to contemplate the differences in time spent over earth and time spent on earth. The speaker is intent on comparing the actions of what is occurring in the plane with the other passengers and his own fears of being suspended above earth. While the plane glides over "bank after bank of cloud / and the sudden open hole for rock or snow" (lines 1, 2) the other passengers wrestle with newspapers and "offer comments" (10) and "fight ennui" (6). Items such as "foam seats" (20) seem trite in comparison with the detrimental nature of being in flight. Meanwhile, the speaker cannot help but dwell on the immensity of the darkness and the uncertainty of making it back down to earth.

In the second part of the poem, the speaker realizes that he is unchanged by his experiences in the air. That "beam" (22) he relied upon to get the plane safely to the ground is forgotten in the prospect of discovering a new place on earth, along with all the others who are just as much in a rush to discover it as he is. He is soon to discover that in sleep, his subconscious has recorded all he has seen and feared in the plane, and he is changed with the realization that his state of suspension and fear have left an impression on him and can just as easily be experienced in those last moments before sleep.

You might enter into a discussion of this poem by asking students to compare the speaker's state of mind when he is in the air with what he experiences before he goes to sleep. What information has he gleaned from being in the plane, and how has that affected his everyday perspective? What is the poet's intention when he focuses on the actions of the other passengers on the plane?

POSSIBLE CONNECTIONS TO OTHER SELECTIONS

Emily Dickinson, "Because I could not stop for Death —" (text p. 948)
Robert Frost, "Acquainted with the Night" (text p. 798)

AN ALBUM OF WORLD LITERATURE

The poems in this section give students an opportunity to experience over fifty years of world literature written from often contradictory perspectives. The poems range from general comments on modern sensibility to more specific pleas for relief from the political upheaval that has torn apart many of the countries represented. Although it is hardly necessary to teach them chronologically, the poems do present some of the major historic events of the twentieth century, including World War II and the revolutions that have racked Central and South American countries in the latter part of the century.

In different ways, each poet acknowledges that history is not outside us but within us, shaping our sense of reality. Pablo Neruda reminds us that we can enhance life by appreciating one of the simplest and most pleasurable aspects of physical experience: taste. In contrast, Wislawa Szymborska confronts the devastation of hatred. Keeping the memory of this incident alive challenges readers of the poem to act to prevent such devastation in the future, but, perhaps more poignant, to confront our complicity in the violence as participants in what can be an oppressive Western culture.

Students will read these poems not only for historical and geographical information but for new perspectives on their own lives as well. Your class will have to reassess the reading they have done in English courses throughout their scholastic careers. How many readings from cultures other than their own have they encountered? What might be the effect of this very limited education?

Questioning their own biases will lead students to open up the poems to the extent that they realize that world literature is not simply about some "Other"; it is about all of us, living in an ever-contracting world where we must think as much about our labels and notions of "the Other" as we do about ourselves.

ANNA AKHMATOVA, *Dedication* (p. 1135)

The speaker's situation in this poem is not exactly clear from a superficial reading, and students will have to read it carefully and repeatedly to discern it. The speaker spent "two years . . . in hell" (line 24) — that is, in a Russian prison camp — and is now reflecting upon those days, wondering what happened to her fellow prisoners, her "partners in . . . dread" (8). The poem begins and ends with a meditation about these partners, but the actual circumstances of their imprisonment are described, somewhat vaguely, in the body of the poem. What do students see as the most memorable image of the poem? Do the images clarify a theme? Does the tone or theme of the poem shift when someone moans, "Whose sentence is decreed?" in line 17?

POSSIBLE CONNECTIONS TO OTHER SELECTIONS

Emily Dickinson, "I read my sentence — steadily —" (question #2, following)
Faiz Ahmed Faiz, "If You Look at the City from Here" (question #1, following)
John Milton, "On the Late Massacre in Piedmont" (text p. 1109)
Wilfred Owen, "Dulce et Decorum Est" (text p. 763)

CONNECTIONS QUESTIONS IN TEXT (p. 1136) WITH ANSWERS

1. Compare the metaphors of imprisonment in "Dedication" and Faiz Ahmed Faiz's "If You Look at the City from Here" (p. 1139).

    One obvious difference is that Faiz is describing a city as a prison whereas Akhmatova is describing a prison. In "Dedication," prison is constructed as an eerie daylong ritual, beginning "As if for early mass," and ending with hope singing, but "from afar." Faiz's poem contains little hope; by the end of the poem, when he offers a choice between blood and roses, we are fairly certain to choose blood, so negative has been the imagery up until that point. Faiz offers no hope, "no way out," whereas in Akhmatova's poem, the speaker seems to have gotten beyond the horror of imprisonment; her final gesture is to cry "Hail and Farewell!"

2. Write an essay on the "sentence" decreed in this poem and in Emily Dickinson's "I read my sentence — steadily —" (p. 944).

    The sentence in this poem is pretty clearly unjust, although the poet does not come right out and say so. (Censorship may have been a factor.) The sentence in Dickinson's poem is death, but it doesn't necessarily seem unjust, but rather surprising, or inevitable. In both cases, the speaker is powerless to change her circumstances, but that fact seems more painful in "Dedication" since the circumstances are artificial.

RESOURCES FOR TEACHING

Anna Akhmatova: Selected Poems [recording]. 1 cassette (60 min.). Akhmatova reads her poems in Russian. Includes transcript. Distributed by Interlingua VA.

The Anna Akhmatova File. 65 min., color, 1989. Beta, VHS. Documentary of the Russian poet. Russian with English subtitles. Distributed by Facets Multimedia, Inc.

Fear and the Muse: The Story of Anna Akhmatova [video]. Color, VHS (60 min.), 1995. With voices of Claire Bloom and Christopher Reeve. Distributed by Mystic Fire Video.

CLARIBEL ALEGRÍA, *I Am Mirror* (p. 1136)

Born in Estelí, Nicaragua, Alegría moved to El Salvador six months later; she therefore considers herself more Salvadoran than Nicaraguan. She attended George Washington University, graduating in 1948, and is married to the American writer Darwin J. Flakoll. She received the Casa de las Americas prize of Cuba in 1978 for her book *Sobrevivo*. Alegría and her husband have lived in many foreign countries; they now divide their time between Majorca, Spain, and Managua, Nicaragua.

The speaker in this poem describes her attempts to feel again after she has been numbed by violence. She looks for her identity in the mirror, only to see herself as another person; note her use of third-person pronouns to refer to herself: "she also pricks herself" (line 11). In an ironic twist of Descartes's *Cogito ergo sum,* the speaker feels her arm, saying, "I hurt / therefore I exist" (32–33). Her attention continually turns to the horror around her as she alternates between scenes of violence and an attempt to keep her identity amid the turmoil. In a series of negations that begins in line 44, the speaker denies the violence, losing her self in the process. She cannot sustain an identity and survive, so she becomes an object: "I am a blank mirror" (48).

In a writing assignment, you might ask students to trace the two strands of images in this poem: the images the speaker uses to describe herself and the images of violence. They might construct an argument explaining the relationship between the two, discussing the effect of the images on the poem's tone and theme.

POSSIBLE CONNECTIONS TO OTHER SELECTIONS

William Blake, "London" (text p. 762)

Sylvia Plath, "Mirror" (question #1, following)

CONNECTION QUESTION IN TEXT (p. 1138) WITH ANSWER

1. Compare the ways Alegría uses mirror images to reflect life in El Salvador with Plath's concerns in "Mirror" (p. 786).

   Plath's speaker is first mirror, then lake. In a reversal of Alegría's technique, in which the speaker becomes the mirror, Plath shows how the mirror absorbs the woman looking into it. Both poets play with the notion of women as objects, but Alegría does so to reflect the turmoil in war-torn El Salvador, whereas Plath considers the woman's aging process and approaching death.

RESOURCES FOR TEACHING

Claribel Alegría: Who Raised Up This Prison's Bars? [recording]. 1 cassette (58 min.), 1988. Alegría reads her poems in Spanish, with translations by Carolyn Forché. Distributed by Watershed Tapes.

Claribel Alegría [recording]. 1 cassette (29 min.), 1991. The Nicaraguan poet and writer talks about her autobiographical novel, *Luisa in RealityLand.* Distributed by New Letters on the Air.

KATERINA ANGHELÁKI-ROOKE, *Jealousy* (p. 1138)

Ask students to consider what the speaker knows about the couple in the poem and how she knows it. Is this simply a poem of speculation? Does the speaker admit anything that she *doesn't* know about the couple's relationship?

Discuss the role of landscape in this poem. Throughout the poem, the poet moves between describing the surroundings and describing the couple. Ask your students how the landscape connects to the individuals described in the poem. Note the transformation of images that occurs as the poem progresses. Early on, "the rural / landscapes [are] in ruins" (line 3) and the earth "is still mute / and alone before it becomes a butterfly" (9-10); later, "the dry branches retreat / in memory" (25-26); and at the end of the poem "the landscape starts anew within them / in full spring" (27-28). What might such a transformation indicate? At what point in the poem does the transformation begin to occur? In a writing assignment, you might ask students to discuss who or what is symbolically changing in this poem.

Ask students to consider what the speaker's attitude toward love is. Explore how the details the speaker includes make her at times seem to be a vicarious participant in the romantic encounter.

POSSIBLE CONNECTION TO ANOTHER SELECTION

Emily Dickinson, " 'Heaven' — is what I cannot reach!" (question #1, following)

CONNECTION QUESTION IN TEXT (p. 1139) WITH ANSWER

1. Compare the speaker's attitude toward desire in "Jealousy" with that of the speaker in Emily Dickinson's " 'Heaven' — is what I cannot reach!" (p. 936).

   Both Angheláki-Rooke and Dickinson present desire as something observed but not participated in, a sort of paradise that is unattainable. In Dickinson's poem, heaven is the unreachable beauty of an afternoon of which she is enamored but by which she has been spurned; in "Jealousy," the speaker remains on the outside looking in on a love affair, unable to intervene despite her knowledge of and interest in what is going on.

FAIZ AHMED FAIZ, *If You Look at the City from Here* (p. 1139)

The poem, an extended analogy comparing a city to a prison, does not answer for us a crucial question: where is "here" (lines 1, 11)? The "concentric circles" of line 2 and the "distant lamps" of line 18 indicate that the speaker is probably at a distance from the city. The question then becomes, why does distance from the city cause the speaker to alter his perspective? How would the city be seen differently if the speaker were on the streets of the city? Why is everyone placed on the same level, without "dignity" (12), when one is not close to them? And who imprisons them: is it some unnamed governmental force, or the physical city, or is it the people themselves? The impression that Faiz creates is vivid, but quite open to interpretation.

POSSIBLE CONNECTIONS TO OTHER SELECTIONS

William Blake, "London" (question #1, following)
George Eliot, "In a London Drawingroom" (text p. 1092)
Langston Hughes, "Midnight Raffle" (text p. 1026)
Rainer Maria Rilke, "The Panther" (question #2, following)

CONNECTIONS QUESTIONS IN TEXT (p. 1140) WITH ANSWERS

1. Compare the treatment of the city in this poem and in Blake's "London" (p. 762).

In Blake's "London," the manacles of imprisonment are clearly "mind-forged." That is to say, we have created them through limitations in our thinking. The source of the manacles in Faiz's poem is less defined. There are striking similarities in the two descriptions, such as blood running down walls; but in Blake, we sense the origin of social ills based on the professions of people in the city (Chimney-sweeper, Soldier, Harlot). In Faiz, we are given no such clues.

2. Write an essay on the meaning of confinement in Faiz's poem and in Rilke's "The Panther" (p. 767).

A main difference between these two poems is that the perspective is radically different. In Rilke's poem, it is as if we are in the cage with the panther, and there does not seem to be any world outside. In Faiz's poem, we know that there is a world beyond the city because we are outside of it along with the speaker. Although it looks as though there is no way out of the city, there must be. In the case of the panther, there truly is no way out.

XU GANG, *Red Azalea on the Cliff* (p. 1140)

"Red Azalea on the Cliff" is a poem of paradoxes. The smiling azalea of the first line makes the speaker's heart "shudder with fear" (line 3). Hidden within beauty is the threat of disaster (5) — an idea that is central to the poem. Likewise, the sweetness of the flower encloses slyness, and its intimacy embraces distance (21–22).

In light of these paradoxes, encourage students to discuss what the red azalea might represent. What seems to be the relationship between humans and nature in the poem? Discuss what the red flower has to do with love.

Ask students to consider the last two lines of the poem, in particular, their meaning in light of Xu Gang's role in the Cultural Revolution and his later disillusionment.

POSSIBLE CONNECTIONS TO OTHER SELECTIONS

William Blake, "The Sick Rose" (question #1, following)
John Keats, "La Belle Dame sans Merci" (text p. 1103)

CONNECTION QUESTION IN TEXT (p. 1141) WITH ANSWER

1. Compare the significance of the flower in "Red Azalea on the Cliff" with that of the flower in Blake's "The Sick Rose" (p. 807).

In these poems, the flowers may be read as symbols of love, beauty, passion, innocence, and so on. In each poem, those symbolic elements are undermined by a hidden presence that works oppositionally — a force that threatens to destroy what is lovely and good. In "Red Azalea," the beauty of the flower conceals the danger in trying to reach it on the cliffside; in "The Sick Rose," the bed of crimson joy in which the rose is growing hides the invisible sick worm. In each case, love and beauty, passion and innocence are undermined by the danger and destruction that paradoxically lie within the flowers. The difference is, of course, that in "Red Azalea" the destructive force is part of the beauty of the plant — the environment in which it needs to grow, on the cliff where there is no road. In "The Sick Rose," the worm is not a part of the beauty of the flower; its only function is to destroy, and it is killing the rose with its "dark secret love."

PABLO NERUDA, *Sweetness, Always* (p. 1141)

In an essay on "impure poetry," Chilean-born Pablo Neruda defended the importance to the poet's craft of not-so-nice images and words. Neruda criticized American poets for ignoring politics to pursue their own, "loftier" pleasures. Art was life for Neruda; he believed that poetry must be kept near the bone, where it originates, and not elevated to irrelevancy. "Sweetness, Always" illustrates this point in delicious, sense-appealing imagery, which contrasts with the dullness of more abstract poetry. The speaker defends the poor, the politically oppressed, the mundane, and the earthy as the truly valuable subjects for poetry.

The poem appeals to the sense of taste, pointing out that even the builders of great monuments have to eat. Talking about the body makes Neruda's appeal appropriate for every man and woman. Poems do indeed feed the world, although clearly the poets Neruda distrusts claim that feeding is not their job: "We are not feeding the world." Working from the extremes of underground and sky, Neruda focuses on the earth — at the level of the people: "and the poor adults' also." He derides the typical monuments of human power in favor of the food that creates living monuments of joy and misery — human beings.

Neruda's poetry has been discussed in Manuel Duran and Margery Safir's *Earth Tones* (Bloomington: Indiana UP, 1980); Rene de Costa's *The Poetry of Pablo Neruda* (Cambridge: Harvard UP, 1979); and "Pablo Neruda, 1904–1973," *Modern Poetry Studies* 5.1 (1974).

POSSIBLE CONNECTIONS TO OTHER SELECTIONS

Helen Chasin, "The Word *Plum*" (question #2, following)
Robert Frost, "Birches" (question #1, following)
Galway Kinnell, "Blackberry Eating" (question #2, following)

CONNECTIONS QUESTIONS IN TEXT (p. 1143) WITH ANSWERS

1. Compare the view of life offered in this poem with that in Frost's "Birches" (p. 986).

   The speaker's call for "sweetness, always" in Neruda's poem asks us to avoid vanity and seek "Verses of pastry which melt / into milk and sugar in the mouth" (lines 12–13). The speaker in Frost's "Birches" wishes to "get away from the earth awhile" (48) and then return and start over again. Although both speakers ask us to return to earthly things, Neruda's speaker asks us to return to the sweetness of existence, whereas Frost's urges first an escape from a life "like a pathless wood" (44) in order to return to earth.

2. Write an essay that discusses Kinnell's "Blackberry Eating" (p. 832) and Chasin's "The Word *Plum*" (p. 851) as the sort of "eatable" poetry the speaker calls for in this poem.

   In Kinnell's "Blackberry Eating" and Chasin's "The Word *Plum*," the fruits could easily represent the "sweetness" the speaker asks for in Neruda's poem. The plum and the blackberries invite listeners to experience the world through a single, sensuous image, without much concern for "deep, philosophical" issues.

RESOURCES FOR TEACHING

Pablo Neruda: Poet. 30 min., b/w, 1972. Beta, VHS, ¾" U-matic cassette. A profile of the poet. Distributed by Cinema Guild.

Pablo Neruda: Selected Poems [recording]. 1 cassette. In Spanish. Distributed by Applause Productions.

Yo Soy Pablo Neruda. 29 min., b/w, 1967. Beta, VHS, ¾″ U-matic cassette, 16-mm film. A profile of the poet. Narrated by Sir Anthony Quayle. Distributed by Films for the Humanities and Sciences.

OCTAVIO PAZ, *The Street* (p. 1143)

A Mexican poet of metamorphic surrealism, Octavio Paz has influenced many writers, including William Carlos Williams, Denise Levertov, and Muriel Rukeyser, each of whom has translated him. He has served the Mexican diplomatic service in Paris, New Delhi, and New York.

Students may let this poem too easily defeat them or too easily collapse into platitudes: "OK, a guy becomes his own shadow or he can't tell whether he's real or not." The poem's simple diction, pleasing (and very frequent) rhymes, and skillful alliteration work in opposition to its mournful tone and shadowy imagery, a tension that mirrors the speaker's situation: the everyday world of streets, leaves, stones, and people is not at all everyday. Nothing has definition on "The Street" (note the references to night, blindness, and awkwardness and to the unstated reasons for the pursuit), yet the urgent certainty of the "narrative" is almost palpable.

You might ask students to change all the verbs in the poem to the past tense and comment on the resulting differences in tone. Other questions that would yield productive discussion or writing include: How would the poem's effect be altered if it ended with line 11? How does the speaker know the street is "long" if he walks "in blackness"? How can stones be anything but "silent"? To what extent could the poem's logic be considered dream logic?

POSSIBLE CONNECTIONS TO OTHER SELECTIONS

Robert Frost, "Acquainted with the Night" (question #1, following)
Langston Hughes, "Lenox Avenue: Midnight" (question #2, following)

CONNECTIONS QUESTIONS IN TEXT (p. 1143) WITH ANSWERS

1. How does the speaker's anxiety in this poem compare with that in Frost's "Acquainted with the Night" (p. 798)?

   Frost's speaker in "Acquainted with the Night" vacillates between himself and the outside world, alternating between images of light and darkness, good and evil. Paz's speaker begins and ends in darkness, in the solipsistic prison of his own mind. Whereas Frost's speaker seems indecisive and brooding, Paz's is forever fixed in darkness, without hope. Frost's speaker feels alone in a realistic night setting where he sees "one luminary clock against the sky." His poem conveys loneliness rather than anxiety. Paz's scene, in contrast, is the landscape of persecution and nightmare.

2. Write an essay comparing the tone of this poem and that of Hughes's "Lenox Avenue: Midnight" (p. 1022).

   Both Paz and Hughes set their poems on particular streets, and the setting affects the tone of the poems. The tone of Hughes's poem is one of melancholy, shaped by the jazz "rhythm of life" (line 1). The image of the gods laughing at the "weary heat of pain" (6) is oppressive and hopeless. Likewise, Paz's speaker does not leave any room for hope or escape from his own consciousness; thus, the tone of both poems is dismal.

RESOURCES FOR TEACHING

Octavio Paz: An Uncommon Poet. 28 min., color, 198?. Beta, VHS, ¾″ U-matic cassette, 16-mm film. The poet talks about the distinctions between his two careers: poet and political activist. Distributed by Films for the Humanities and Sciences.

See also "Moyers: The Power of the Word" in the appendix of Film, Video, and Audiocassette Resources.

INDIRA SANT, *Household Fires* (p. 1144)

This poem delineates the roles (or "jobs") of four children in an Indian household. The father's role is only suggested, but the poem's final focus is on the mother, who seems to be caving in as a result of the demands placed on her. You might explore in discussion the effect of the way this poem is arranged: where are our sympathies? And would they be different if the poem were ordered differently? The poem categorizes the roles of the children in terms of gender, but also in terms of age. Is there a clear-cut hierarchy based on these criteria? If there were a sixth stanza about the father's "job," what would it be like and where would it most effectively be placed?

POSSIBLE CONNECTIONS TO OTHER SELECTIONS

Julia Alvarez, "Woman's Work" (text p. 886)
Chitra Banerjee Divakuruni, "Indian Movie, New Jersey" (question #2, following)
Elaine Magarrell, "The Joy of Cooking" (text p. 792)
Linda Pastan, "Marks" (text p. 791)
Sylvia Plath, "Daddy" (question #1, following)

CONNECTIONS QUESTIONS IN TEXT (p. 1144) WITH ANSWERS

1. Implicit in this poem is the father's presence. Compare the treatment of the father in "Household Fires" and Plath's "Daddy" (p. 1113).

   The key word in this question is "implicit." The father is cleverly hidden in "Household Fires," whereas the father in "Daddy," whether or not he is taken as the speaker's actual father, is attacked directly. "Household Fires" also seems to be representative of a broader cultural pattern, whereas the father in "Daddy" is more individualized. Finally, the speaker's problem with "daddy" in Plath's poem is personal, between the two of them; in Sant's poem, the conflict does not exist between two people but amidst an entire family.

2. Write an essay that compares the life described in this poem with Divakuruni's "Indian Movie, New Jersey" (p. 819).

   The focus of Divakuruni's poem is a cultural divide that brings families closer together. Indian culture is held up for praise, and no one's "mind . . . gets burned" as the mother's mind does in Sant's poem (lines 33–34). Their excursion to the movies at least enables them to forget about the troubles within their families while bonding with other Indians. In Sant's poem, the outside world doesn't factor into the family strife. Yet both poems seem stifling, as though there is no real way out of this pattern.

A Collection of Poems

WOLE SOYINKA, *Future Plans* (p. 1145)

Students may be intimidated by the demands placed on the reader in this poem — a complete understanding of "Future Plans" requires a rather extensive familiarity with world history. Soyinka is highly specific in naming the leaders from around the world who have become notorious for their dishonesty, their ruthless annihilation of those who objected to their policies, and their disregard for basic human rights. He ruthlessly satirizes their behavior and suggests that the information the people are allowed access to is not always accurate. For instance, those leaders whom we might consider to be "enemies" may in fact be in league (or, as Soyinka suggests in his pairing of Meir and Arafat, in bed).

One means of opening up class discussion of the poem is to encourage students to research one or more of the names listed here and to briefly report in class on their findings. However, even without a specific understanding of the variety of atrocities practiced by the leaders referred to in "Future Plans," students might easily perceive the intensity of the poem's irony. The first stanza, with its reference to "Forgers, framers, / Fabricators Inter- / national" (lines 2–3), conveys Soyinka's attitude toward the leaders whose names follow. In line 20, he epitomizes the corruption that is the subject of his poem when he writes of "Contraceptives stacked beneath the papal bunk" — an image that contrasts sharply with the Catholic mandate that church leaders take vows of celibacy and chastity. The final line of the poem provides a means of better understanding the title: here, Soyinka ominously notes that there are "more to come" (21) in the line of oppressive, dishonest leaders. Soyinka's sharp criticisms are not limited to any particular region of the world; in "Future Plans," he asserts that corruption is common to all human societies.

POSSIBLE CONNECTIONS TO OTHER SELECTIONS

Kenneth Fearing, "AD" (question #1, following)
Dylan Thomas, "The Hand That Signed the Paper" (text p. 781)

CONNECTION QUESTION IN TEXT (p. 1146) WITH ANSWER

1. Discuss the political satire in "Future Plans" and in Fearing's "AD" (p. 803).

    Soyinka and Fearing rely on an almost comic tone in establishing their satirical views; they also adapt familiar patterns as they organize their arguments. Soyinka rates his subjects according to the Mach scheme; he also arranges his observations according to the agenda of a business meeting, including a calling to order and an agenda for unfinished business — "Projects in view" (11). Fearing also converts an ordinary form — a want ad — into the ideal method of conveying his satire on the mentality of a warmonger. The structure of these poems parallels their content: both poets build their satires on an outrage that such unacceptable beliefs and behaviors are evident on a regular basis.

WISLAWA SZYMBORSKA, *End and Beginning* (p. 1146)

In teaching this poem, it may be useful to begin by examining the context, pointing out that it was written by a Polish poet who was born in 1923, between World War I and World War II. Thus, the poet grew up in the years immediately following World War I, and it is possible that some of the material for this poem comes from sources from his early childhood. The poem uses powerful images to depict the chaos and the enormous rebuilding efforts that follow a war — any war, it seems, since in line 1 the poet uses the phrase "each war" rather than identifying a particular war. The repetition of the word "somebody" throughout the poem intensifies the reader's sense of the endless tasks involved in putting things in order and speaks to the universal and anonymous nature of individual and communal recovery.

The images of war throughout the poem create powerful pictures and are set against the final image of someone reclining in the grass with a stalk of rye in their teeth. This image contrasts with the preceding exhausting, pain-filled images, and it may be useful to have students speculate on just how this image functions and what the word "ogling" (line 47) implies. Is this final image a picture of tranquillity or withdrawal; diffidence or transcendence; resignation or peace? Is the "somebody" who reclines the poet who continues to observe, the rebuilder who is finally at rest, or the blissfully ignorant individual who is satisfied with "knowing nothing" (37–42)?

There is room for a great deal of discussion here, for students' interpretations of the final image will color their interpretation of the poem as a whole. The poem is surely an indictment of those who fail or are unable to remember the effects of war; at the same time, the final image remains ambiguous. Have students consider the meaning of the title. "End and Beginning" may signify the end of war and the beginning of peace, or it may signify the end of war and the beginning of an ignorance that will eventually lead to war once more.

An effective short writing assignment would be to have students write an essay comparing the treatment of war in "End and Beginning" to the treatment of war in one of the following poems: Matthew Arnold's "Dover Beach" (text p. 757); Wilfred Owen's "Dulce et Decorum Est" (text p. 763); or Walt Whitman's "Calvary Crossing a Ford" (text p. 754).

TOMAS TRANSTROMER, *April and Silence* (p. 1148)

Students may find their traditional romantic notions about the connotations of spring challenged by Transtromer's poem, in which "Spring lies desolate" (line 1). However, "April and Silence" is part of a tradition in which poets have expounded on the negative qualities of spring. For example, Transtromer's opening line recalls that of Eliot's "The Wasteland": the cruelest month. The speaker's depression manifests itself throughout the poem. He focuses almost solely on what he lacks, on what he cannot achieve, and on his own inability to gain control. As he notes, "I am carried in my shadow / like a violin / in its black box" (7–9). Perhaps because of the limitations of translation, the poem may seem flat to some readers — some students may argue that the speaker is merely suffering from light deprivation. You might ask students whether they are inspired to empathize with the speaker of the poem. Why or why not?

POSSIBLE CONNECTION TO ANOTHER SELECTION

William Carlos Williams, "Spring and All" (question #1, following)

CONNECTION QUESTION IN TEXT (p. 1148) WITH ANSWER

1. Discuss the description of spring in this poem and in William Carlos Williams's "Spring and All" (p. 1126).

   By the time April rolls around, we are so desperate for warmth and new growth that if the weather remains wintery, our souls contract and we become pessimists. If spring comes early, we are somehow more optimistic. Transtromer's "April and Silence" is reminiscent of our thoughts while enduring a late spring, when all we can recognize is what we are unable to achieve. Williams's "Spring and All," in contrast, reminds us of the moment when winter turns to spring and the dormant plants awaken.

RESOURCE FOR TEACHING

Tomas Transtromer: The Blue House [recording]. 1 cassette (58 min.), 1986. Distributed by Watershed Tapes.

AN ALBUM OF CONTEMPORARY POEMS

Both the difficulties and the rewards of contemporary poetry derive from the same characteristics; namely, there are no set principles for the construction of contemporary poetry or the range of its style. It can be structured in stanzas, or in open free-verse paragraphs, or even as an uninterrupted block of prose. Contemporary poetry is as likely to be rhymed as unrhymed. The level of diction can be lofty and elegant or it can be spiced with slang, as in Peter Meinke's "The ABC of Aerobics" (text p. 922). In short, the idea of decorum, if it exists at all in contemporary poetry, is open ended.

Thematically, the field for discovering material for poems is also more extensive than ever before. Some of the poems here take as their motive an area of public concern relevant not only to the country of the poet but to an area other than or far more inclusive than a specific nation. We are living in an age that has given new meaning to the word *global,* and North American poetry especially seems to reflect this broadened interest. Other poems, such as Donald Hall's "Letter with No Address," embody a more private concern and voice the particular anxieties and observations of the individual. One point, though, that students should grasp is that our age does not dictate either an introspective poetry bound to extol and explore nature and the human mind or a public poetry pitched for a celebration of reason, country, and the famous. We can, and do, address both public and private issues, and certain poems, such as Elizabeth Alexander's "Harlem Birthday Party" and Yusef Komunyakaa's "Facing It," manage to merge the dialectic of *polis* and *poesis.*

Without question, contemporary poets write about the age-old issues of love and death and the pain of growing up, but these themes, seemingly so essential and enduring, are changed by recent history, technology, and our systems of belief and values. Knowledge of the casualness of death and one's consequent vulnerability, as well as the prospect of mass extinction, also influences the way poets today think and write about death. The world of the contemporary poet is violent and nonsensical, but it is also diverse and exotic.

The poetry included here exhibits a wide range of techniques and levels of diction. The tools for reading poetry learned in earlier chapters will find their fullest application here. On the whole, though, the poems are highly accessible and offer a fine occasion for you and your students to observe the events, vocabulary, and concerns of the day worked into a poetic context. Perhaps that context will enable all of us to articulate more clearly what we desire, value, and wish to protect in this world.

ELIZABETH ALEXANDER, *Harlem Birthday Party* (p. 1148)

This poem reads like a prose narrative that serves both as a description of the speaker's grandfather's life and of his ninetieth birthday party. Students may wonder why this poem is written in verse as opposed to prose. It is a valid question. A good place to start discussion might be with the question of selection: what are some of the details that the speaker includes that do not seem to "fit in" with a simple prose narrative? A good example is the detail about the speaker and her boyfriend Gustavo buying pillows before they return from New York to Philadelphia. Why is that detail included? How does it compare to the description of Harlem in the first two stanzas? Do the characters in the poem besides the speaker and her grandfather fit into some pattern? Perhaps not; perhaps that is what makes this poem unique. Our attempts to analyze it as we would analyze another poem are frustrated. Yet there is something resonant about the dichotomy the poem sets up between special events and everyday details. The poem contains famous people on one side and ordinary people on the other; it describes the details of a menu and the way someone's life was changed as a result of talking to the speaker's grandfather. Does the poem attempt to reconcile the ordinary and the extraordinary?

POSSIBLE CONNECTIONS TO OTHER SELECTIONS

Michael S. Harper, "Grandfather" (text p. 1095)
M. Carl Holman, "Mr. Z" (question #2, following)
Langston Hughes, "Lenox Avenue: Midnight" (text p. 1022)

CONNECTION QUESTION IN TEXT (p. 1150) WITH ANSWER

2. Write an essay that compares the grandfather's identity in "Harlem Birthday Party" with the man described in Holman's "Mr. Z." (p. 1098).

   Mr. Z and the speaker's grandfather in "Harlem Birthday Party" are direct opposites in terms of their racial identity. The former eschews his blackness entirely since he was "Taught early that his mother's skin was the sign of error" (line 1). The latter wants "to stay / in the neighborhood" (5-6) for his birthday party, and this gesture is symbolic of his general attitude toward his cultural heritage. He was born in Jamaica and lived in Harlem; those are the facts of his life, and they speak volumes about his identity. He never pretended to nor was attracted by anything else, in stark contrast to Mr. Z, whose "palate shrank from cornbread, yams and collards" (12).

CORNELIUS EADY, *The Supremes* (p. 1150)

This savagely cynical poem describes the fatalism of schoolchildren, who are "born to be gray" (line 1) — to conform. The poem, which continues to rely on dull-toned colors to paint its picture, is all about a soul-killing conformity that causes children to point out and ridicule any differences that exist between themselves and others. A good place to begin discussion is with the "long scream" (5, 18) that exists in the back of the schoolchildren's minds. Is this a scream of protest? Of ängst? Of outrage? Students are likely to have experienced or witnessed the type of divisiveness that exists between the students in this poem. Where does it come from? Where does Eady think it comes from? There are a few possible answers to this question: the parents who "shook their heads and waited" (13) for their children to conform, the sometimes mind-numbing institution of primary education, the children themselves, the undefined "they" of line 25, or something like fate. In what sense can the wigs, lipstick, and sequins of the final lines be considered "self-defense"? How do the last three lines change our understanding of the speaker, or his classmates?

POSSIBLE CONNECTIONS TO OTHER SELECTIONS

Robert Bly, "Sitting Down to Dinner" (text p. 824)

Emily Dickinson, "From all the Jails the Boys and Girls" (question #2, following)

Judy Page Heitzman, "The Schoolroom on the Second Floor of the Knitting Mill" (question #1, following)

Louis Simpson, "In the Suburbs" (text p. 746)

CONNECTIONS QUESTIONS IN TEXT (p. 1151) WITH ANSWERS

1. Discuss the speakers' memories of school in "The Supremes" and in Judy Page Heitzman's "The Schoolroom on the Second Floor of the Knitting Mill" (p. 1158).

    In Heitzman's poem, the schoolteacher, Mrs. Lawrence, is singled out for her cruelty to children. Her desire to keep children "in line" is institutionally sanctioned, but her criticism of the speaker's leadership skills is unthoughtful. There is no "Mrs. Lawrence" to blame in "The Supremes." The children are victimized as much by their own human nature as they are by any one teacher, or by elementary school more generally.

2. In an essay compare the themes of "The Supremes" and Dickinson's "From all the Jails the Boys and Girls" (p. 951).

    The "long scream" of Eady's poem is released and transformed into "Bliss" in Dickinson's poem, but only temporarily. In both cases, school seems to represent a kind of imprisonment; yet in Dickinson's poem, the imprisonment is literal, whereas the prisons in Eady's poem are at least partially psychological or sociological.

MARTÍN ESPADA, *Coca-Cola and Coco Frío* (p. 1151)

The cultural dichotomy set up by this poem is implicit in the title; a child of Puerto Rican descent is surprised to find that Puerto Ricans are more likely to drink Coca-Cola than to drink coconut milk. The boy is ultimately confused as to why his culture has been overshadowed by one that seems to him shallow by comparison. The implication in the final line is that Puerto Rican culture — as shown through the metaphor of coconut milk — is ultimately more nourishing than the version of American culture that has overshadowed the island. Besides the obvious analogy between coconut milk and mother's milk in the final lines, what other evidence is there in the poem that the two beverages are not to be taken at face value but rather as symbolic of broader issues?

POSSIBLE CONNECTIONS TO OTHER SELECTIONS

Martín Espada, "Latin Night at the Pawnshop" (text p. 726)

Langston Hughes, "Theme for English B" (question #1, following)

Tato Laviera, "AmeRícan" (question #2, following)

Gary Soto, "Mexicans Begin Jogging" (text p. 923)

Mitsuye Yamada, "A Bedtime Story" (text p. 1129)

CONNECTIONS QUESTIONS IN TEXT (p. 1152) WITH ANSWERS

1. Compare what the boy in this poem discovers about Puerto Rico with what the speaker learns in Hughes's "Theme for English B" (p. 1027).

In both poems, two cultures mingle, but not altogether comfortably. The boy in Espada's poem marvels at Puerto Rico's inattention to itself in favor of America. There is a judgment implicit in his marveling, though; something has certainly been lost (or wasted) in this process. The speaker of Hughes's poem acknowledges that, though differences and animosity might exist between himself and his white professor, that's the way things are. Their relationship is more symbiotic, as he sees it, than the relationship between the United States and Puerto Rico in Espada's poem, in which Puerto Rican identity is almost completely overshadowed by American consumer culture.

2. Write an essay discussing the images used to describe Puerto Rico and the United States in this poem and in Laviera's "AmeRícan" (p. 918).

Although the tone of "AmeRícan" shifts throughout the poem, it can be said in general that it is a more positive poem than "Coca-Cola and Coco Frío" in terms of the way U.S. and Puerto Rican cultures mix. One particularly interesting point to contrast in the two poems is the use of music: Pedro Flores, plena-rhythms, and jíbaro in Laviera's poem as opposed to Coca-Cola jingles from World War II in Espada's. Furthermore, the new generation in "AmeRícan" seems much more vital than the "fat boy" of Espada's poem. Language is another way to compare the two poems as a way of examining their treatment of their subject; in Laviera's poem, rules of standard English are ignored and a new hybrid language ensues, whereas in Espada's poem women sing songs "in a language they did not speak" (25).

DEBORAH GARRISON, *She Was Waiting to Be Told* (p. 1152)

In "She Was Waiting to Be Told," Garrison describes a Pygmalion-like relationship in which a man has, essentially, trained a woman to behave exactly as he wishes: "to wear a short black slip / and red lipstick, / how to order a glass of red wine / and finish it" (lines 1–4). According to the description of her talents in the first fifteen lines of this poem, she is the perfect social accessory. Yet Garrison provides us with a "turn" in line 16 when she suggests that the man only thinks he has trained the woman well. The remainder of the poem proposes an alternate reading of the "text" of the woman's behavior. Although the man may think that she is becoming more intimate with him by adhering to his wishes and fulfilling his needs, in reality, as the last stanza suggests, she may have been slipping away from him. "She Was Waiting to Be Told" is an excellent example of a poem that juxtaposes conflicting perspectives. Students might enjoy writing about the relationship described in this poem from the woman's point of view, or possibly from the perspective of one of the friends mentioned in the second stanza.

POSSIBLE CONNECTIONS TO OTHER SELECTIONS

John Keats, "La Belle Dame sans Merci" (text p. 1103)
Richard Wilbur, "A Late Aubade" (question #2, following)

CONNECTION QUESTION IN TEXT (p. 1153) WITH ANSWER

2. Discuss the relationship between the man and the woman in Garrison's poem and the lovers in Wilbur's "A Late Aubade" (p. 732).

Both poems depict a male character's paternalistic reading of a woman's behavior and choices. In Garrison's poem, the man approves of his lover because she seems able to intuit his every need and because his society looks upon her as quite a prize:

"So your confidence grows. / She doesn't ask what you want / because she knows" (13–15). In Wilbur's poem, the narrator enumerates the many choices his lover could have made to be elsewhere: "You could be sitting now in a carrel / Turning some liver-spotted page, / Or rising in an elevator-cage / Toward Ladies' Apparel" (1–4). All of the male speaker's judgments of his lover's other possible activities are tainted by derogatory or demeaning adjectives such as "raucous" (5), "unhappy" (9), or "bleak" (10). Clearly, her highest priority is to be with him: "Think of all the time you are not / wasting, and would not care to waste" (13–14). The second half of Garrison's poem serves as a retort to both men and an alternative to the assumptions they have made about their lovers.

DONALD HALL, *Letter with No Address* (p. 1153)

The speaker of this poem, grief-stricken over the death of his wife, writes her a letter in which he describes both the events of his day-to-day life and his lingering emotions over her death. It is a devastatingly honest poem, hiding nothing from the reader. Much of the real heartbreak comes from the speaker's need to share even the most mundane details of his life with his wife. This is not a highflown "poetic" love, but a very deep, real, everyday love. The truly heart-rending irony is that the speaker especially needs his wife now, after, and because of, her death. You might begin by asking how students feel when they read something so personal. It is, after all, a "letter with no address"; do they feel as though they have stumbled upon someone's mail or diary? Is the speaker's purpose in writing the poem part of the way he deals with grief, or does the poem also serve another purpose, perhaps to connect his soul with that of his wife? In either case, where does the reader fit in?

The poem is also noteworthy for its vivid imagery. Much of this imagery serves to connect the world of the living and the world of the dead, or to show how these two worlds overlap. One way of opening up discussion is to have students locate two images in the poem, one that defines the poem's overall tone and another that seems to clash with this tone, then to work through the poet's reasoning for including both images. (For example, how do students reconcile the opening image of dying daffodils with the final image of automobiles as a symbol of lewd sexuality?)

POSSIBLE CONNECTIONS TO OTHER SELECTIONS

Emily Dickinson, "The Bustle in a House" (question #1, following)
Robert Frost, "Home Burial" (question #2, following)
Andrew Hudgins, "Elegy for My Father, Who Is Not Dead" (text p. 893)

CONNECTIONS QUESTIONS IN TEXT (p. 1155) WITH ANSWERS

1. Compare how the speaker copes with grief in "Letter with No Address" with the speaker in Dickinson's "The Bustle in a House" (p. 950).

    It might be said that the speaker in Hall's poem is "Sweeping up the heart / And putting Love away" (Dickinson lines 5–6), but it seems as if this process will continue indefinitely, whereas in Dickinson it seems to be a way to return to routine. The speaker in "Letter with No Address" also describes his routine, but this routine doesn't allow him to forget the past. It doesn't seem as though he will ever be able to, yet that fact doesn't seem to be the source of misery in his life. The ongoing presence of his wife is just as inevitable as her death was. Yet there is something "solemn" about his bustling through life just as the bustle in Dickinson's poem "Is solemnest of industries" (3). Is his writing of this poem akin to "The Sweeping up the Heart" in Dickinson's poem?

2. Write an essay on the tone of this poem and Frost's "Home Burial" (p. 980).

    There is nothing of the animosity between Frost's couple in Hall's poem. The tone of "Letter with No Address" is solemn, touching, the world seen clearly through watery eyes. The speakers of Frost's poem are in a different phase of grief. They lash out at one another in bitterness and anger. Two common ways of dealing with loss are to focus on it intensely and to return to routine as though it didn't happen. In Frost's poem, the man and woman cannot understand the way the other has reacted. In Hall's poem, the two ways are reconciled in one person, who relies on both in turn.

MARK HALLIDAY, *Graded Paper* (p. 1156)

Students may enjoy analyzing Halliday's characterization of this professor who soliloquizes about the merits and faults of his student's paper. Ask students to identify the professor's biggest objection to the paper. What pleases him about it? What displeases him? How much does the professor seem to have in common with the student, as far as we can tell from the comments included in "Graded Paper"?

The professor begins by noting those aspects of the student's paper that please him: "your main argument about the poet's ambivalence — / how he loves the very things he attacks — / is mostly persuasive and always engaging" (lines 2–4). The remainder of the poem incorporates the professor's criticisms of the work, and those criticisms are made in a highly organized fashion. First, the professor comments on the paper's thesis. He then moves on to the supporting ideas, the language, and the punctuation, winding up with some quasi-encouraging comments. The grade, an "A–", is a symbol of the grader's own ambivalence toward the student. What prompts the "minus"? A partial answer lies in the professor's acknowledgment that "You are not / me, finally" (35–36) as well as his comments on age — his own and his student's — throughout the poem.

POSSIBLE CONNECTIONS TO OTHER SELECTIONS

Robert Browning, "My Last Duchess" (question #1, following)
Marilyn Hacker, "Groves of Academe" (text p. 848)

CONNECTION QUESTION IN TEXT (p. 1157) WITH ANSWER

1. Compare the ways in which Halliday reveals the speaker's character in this poem with the strategies used by Robert Browning in "My Last Duchess" (p. 821).

    Like Browning, Halliday establishes the characterization of the speaker of his poem through the speaker's expression of his likes and dislikes. When the professor in "Graded Paper" scoffs at a line from his student's paper, which makes an assumption about a previous era, he notes that the year was "only forty years ago, after all!" (21) — indicating that he is much older than his student and remembers the year in question through personal experience. Likewise, in "My Last Duchess," the duke notes that his wife "had / A heart — how shall I say? — too soon made glad, / Too easily impressed; she liked whate'er / She looked on" (21–24). From this comment, we can infer that the duke was jealous of the duchess's attention to anything other than himself. As readers of these poems, we are able to construct our own portraits of the professor and the duke through the evidence contained in their own words.

ROBERT HASS, *A Story About the Body* (p. 1157)

As the title indicates, this poem is indeed a story about the body. You might want to begin by discussing in what ways bodies appear in the poem: What is it that the young composer loves about the Japanese woman? How does he respond when she tells him about her double mastectomy?

It's obvious that the body of the Japanese woman is central to this poem. However, you might ask students to explore in writing how this piece is about the young man's body as well: What is the symbolism of the gift of rose petals that cover dead bees (lines 13–17)? What is the woman trying to tell the young man through this gift? You may also want to ask your students to consider what they think the poet is saying about beauty, desire, and love.

POSSIBLE CONNECTIONS TO OTHER SELECTIONS

Joan Murray, "Play-by-Play" (text p. 1163)

John Frederick Nims, "Love Poem" (question #1, following)

CONNECTION QUESTION IN TEXT (p. 1158) WITH ANSWER

1. Discuss the treatments of love in "A Story About the Body" and John Frederick Nims's "Love Poem" (p. 693).

   Recalling Shakespeare's "My mistress' eyes are nothing like the sun" (text p. 882), Nims's speaker expresses admiration for his beloved despite her physical setbacks — in this case, clumsiness. In fact, like Shakespeare's, Nims's speaker seems to *revel* in his love's awkwardness — and treats love as transcendent of body. In contrast, the "radiance" that Hass's speaker "had carried around in his belly and chest cavity — like music — withered very quickly" (lines 9–10) when he found out that the woman he was courting had had a double mastectomy and lost her breasts. That lost "love" is lost *because* the woman's body is not what the speaker expected. Hass reveals that this love is not at all the same kind of love that Shakespeare and Nims appreciate. Instead, it is a love based on the body's regularities rather than a love that flourishes despite a body's "irregularities."

JUDY PAGE HEITZMAN, *The Schoolroom on the Second Floor of the Knitting Mill* (p. 1158)

The narrator comments in the opening lines of Heitzman's poem that she misses her teacher, Mrs. Lawrence. This establishes an impression of the teacher — that she has made an unforgettable, positive impact on the narrator — that the last stanza chillingly contradicts. Ask students to assess the initial description of Mrs. Lawrence, in which the narrator explains that "While most of us copied letters out of books, / Mrs. Lawrence carved and cleaned her nails" (lines 1–2). Clearly, the narrator is not in an interactive classroom — the task of copying letters seems less an effective pedagogical approach than drudgery. In addition, the teacher obviously withholds her attention from her students. Why, then, does Mrs. Lawrence's comment have such a dramatic impact on the narrator, not only in her memory of that day, but throughout her life?

Students may find themselves inspired by this poem to write about their own childhood memories, as well as the effect of the past on the present.

POSSIBLE CONNECTIONS TO OTHER SELECTIONS

Emily Dickinson, "From all the Jails the Boys and Girls" (question #1, following)
Cornelius Eady, "The Supremes" (text p. 1150)

CONNECTION QUESTION IN TEXT (p. 1159) WITH ANSWER

1. Compare the representations and meanings of being a schoolchild in this poem and in Dickinson's "From all the Jails the Boys and Girls" (p. 951).

    Dickinson's poem overtly emphasizes the stifling nature of the schoolroom and equates the schoolchildren with inmates. As Heitzman's narrator remembers it, the atmosphere of the schoolroom is stuffy, and the classroom is overwhelmed by its urban nature — the chimney looming overhead and the fire escape. In addition, there are limitations on the children's behavior and freedom of thought. The students are only approved of when they follow the teacher's instructions to the letter. The crime committed by the speaker of Heitzman's poem is that she allows the children to crowd over the threshold of the door to the playground (line 19). This supports Dickinson's assessment of school as a "Prison" (4) and her suggestion that "From all the Jails the Boys and Girls / Ecstatically leap" (1-2).

JANE HIRSHFIELD, *The Lives of the Heart* (p. 1159)

Students may be overwhelmed by the riot of metaphors that make up this poem. It is virtually impossible to comprehend the poem as a whole or to paraphrase its "meaning"; discussion is best undertaken by examining the metaphors individually. Depending on the number of students in your class, you might choose to assign one or two lines to each student and to have the students explore them. As the discussion evolves, try to place these metaphors into categories: In what clusters do the images fall? Does a pattern form before the poem shifts in line 29? One recurrent motif has to do with the formation of the earth, but that motif doesn't necessarily present itself as dominant because it is just as fragmented as the rest of the motifs. Do any metaphors seem particularly incomprehensible? Do we have a clearer understanding of "the lives of the heart" by the end of the poem, or is part of its purpose to show us the difficulty in defining them?

POSSIBLE CONNECTIONS TO OTHER SELECTIONS

Alice Jones, "The Foot" (question #2, following)
Jim Stevens, "Schizophrenia" (question #1, following)
Walt Whitman, "The Soul, reaching, throwing out for love" (text p. 789)

CONNECTIONS QUESTIONS IN TEXT (p. 1160) WITH ANSWERS

1. Discuss the use of personification in this poem and Jim Stevens's "Schizophrenia" (p. 788).

    "Schizophrenia" uses personification in a much more systematic way than does "The Lives of the Heart." In Stevens's poem, the house is the subject; it acts as a person throughout the poem. In Hirshfield's poem, personification is one of many ways with which the poet describes the lives of the heart. Its personified aspects don't necessarily stand out any more than its animal or mineral aspects. The lives of the heart seem passive as well as active; personification isn't necessarily more helpful than any other form of metaphor.

2. Write an essay that compares the diction and images of "The Lives of the Heart" and Alice Jones's "The Foot" (p. 863).

    "The Foot" is described largely in scientific terms, gradually moving away from scientific language and toward the final image that reduces the foot to a kind of claw. "The Lives of the Heart" are described partially in scientific terms ("ligneous" in line 1, "calcified" in line 4), but that is only part of the spectrum of imagery associated with them. Perhaps it is a function of the subject; feet seem more easily defined than hearts do because of the endless metaphorical possibilities of the latter. As a result, "The Foot" seems to consider all of the possibilities of feet whereas "The Lives of the Heart" seems to expand the sense of its subject to the point that we are likely to feel distant from the subject at the end of the poem.

LINDA HOGAN, *Hunger* (p. 1160)

To begin a discussion of this poem, you may wish to introduce students to the concept of a series poem — that is, a poem that provides readers with some sort of list, including some variations in the list for the sake of interest. Ask students to recreate the list that provides the structure of this poem. Notice how several of the stanzas begin with the word "Hunger" followed by a verb in which hunger is personified, for example, "Hunger crosses" (line 1), "Hunger was" (10), "Hunger knows" (15), and "Hunger lives" (30).

As you talk further about these images of hunger, students may discover some common threads between the descriptions of hunger and the descriptions of men in this poem. Both are said to sit on the ship and cry (lines 3, 9, and 35), and the way both hunger and the men are sated is through female images, particularly images of dolphins who are "like women" taken from the sea so that the men can "have their way with them" (13–14, 44–45).

Although at times it seems that Hunger represents a hunger for food, there are moments in the poem where it becomes clear that Hunger is more than a physical need for nourishment or sustenance. Ask students what they think Hunger represents.

Finally, you may wish to spend some time talking about the final stanza. Consider the line, "the body that wants to live beyond itself" (39). Ask students to interpret this line. Does their understanding of this line help explain the kinds of hunger the poet has in mind? Examine also the imagery at the end of the poem: "wanting to be inside, / to drink / and be held in / the thin, clear milk of the gods" (46–49). What significance is assigned based on gender in this poem, and what ultimately satisfies Hunger and the men in the poem?

POSSIBLE CONNECTIONS TO OTHER SELECTIONS

Sally Croft, "Home-Baked Bread" (question #2, following)
Emily Dickinson, " 'Heaven' — is what I cannot reach!" (text p. 936)

CONNECTION QUESTION IN TEXT (p. 1161) WITH ANSWER

2. Discuss the relationship between love and hunger in this poem and in Croft's "Home-Baked Bread" (p. 768).

    In both "Hunger" and "Home-Baked Bread," food is viewed as more than food. Both poems see food as a source of comfort, and more important, as something sexual. In "Home-Baked Bread," the imagery is unabashedly sexual as the poet suggests that there is a "cunning triumph" involved in baking bread that metamorphoses into other more overtly sexual triumphs. In "Hunger," Hogan suggests that Hunger is in reality an unattainable longing and desire that can never be satisfied.

YUSEF KOMUNYAKAA, *Facing It* (p. 1162)

The speaker of "Facing It" perceives the glossy granite of the Vietnam Memorial as a sort of mirror through which the faces and responses of other visitors are reflected. Appropriately, he reflects on his present experience of facing the memorial and his past involvement in Vietnam. The poem suggests that in a sense the memorial contains the casualties and veterans of Vietnam — an eerie reminder that for those who never returned from combat, or whose remains were never returned to their families, the memorial is the sole physical reminder of their existence. In the final lines of the poem, the speaker imagines that a woman is trying to erase the names engraved on the memorial (line 30). Revising his interpretation of her action, he asserts that she is touching the person whose name is engraved there, that she is "brushing a boy's hair" (31). An alternate interpretation of these lines would suggest that the memorial is reflecting the woman's brushing of an actual, living boy's hair, and that the gesture is suggestive of American lack of interest in either the experiences of those who served in Vietnam or their needs as a result of the conflict. You might ask students which of these interpretations they find more convincing.

POSSIBLE CONNECTIONS TO OTHER SELECTIONS

E. E. Cummings, "next to of course god america i" (question #1, following)
Mary Jo Salter, "Welcome to Hiroshima" (text p. 703)

CONNECTION QUESTION IN TEXT (p. 1162) WITH ANSWER

1. Discuss the speakers' attitudes toward war in "Facing It" and Cummings's "next to of course god america i" (p. 805).

    Readers who compare these poems must recognize the great difference between the American response to previous wars and reactions to the Vietnam War. Previously, American soldiers had generally been hailed as heroes and the wars they fought in had been perceived as necessary for the affirmation of truth, justice, and democracy. Cummings's satire on the rallies, parades, and spirit of righteousness displayed by those who upheld the cause of war reflects his perception of the "patriotic spirit" as empty rhetoric.

    The Vietnam War, in contrast, never received the whole-hearted support of the American public, and its veterans are still fighting for the benefits enjoyed by those who fought in previous wars. Komunyakaa's speaker, someone who experienced the horror of combat in Vietnam, is genuinely moved when he confronts the "58,022 names" (line 14) etched in the granite of the memorial; he is "half-expecting to find / my own in letters like smoke" (15–16). Unlike Cummings, his focus is not on patriotism as a subject, but on his personal, emotional, spiritual reaction to the specifics and the aftermath of the Vietnam War.

JOAN MURRAY, *Play-By-Play* (p. 1163)

This series of hypothetical questions makes us consider the effect of older women gazing at and admiring the bodies of young men. One way to begin discussion is to try to answer each of the questions, read exactly as it is written, as a way to try to determine the speaker's intent in raising the questions. That is, are there implicit answers to the questions? It is a very different thing to ask "I wonder how men would react if they knew that women occasionally scrutinized their bodies" than it is to phrase the questions as the speaker of this poem does, in careful detail with a definite setting. Consider the word "caress" (line 16). If discussion strays too far into general questions of the effect of the female gaze, you might need to bring students back to the specific nature of this poem. It is all about perception, as the final lines make clear. One possible assignment is to have students write a poem from the perspective of these young men, either how they see themselves or how they see the women who are gazing at them. Try to encourage students to recognize the fine line between appreciation of beauty and sexual desire in this poem; how might the poem be different if the poem did not take place at an artist's colony with "marble Naiads" (21) as part of the background?

POSSIBLE CONNECTIONS TO OTHER SELECTIONS

Diane Ackerman, "A Fine, a Private Place" (question #1, following)
Robert Herrick, "To the Virgins, to Make Much of Time" (text p. 728)
Timothy Steele, "An Aubade" (question #2, following)

CONNECTIONS QUESTIONS IN TEXT (p. 1164) WITH ANSWERS

1. Compare the voice of the speaker in "Play-By-Play" with that of Ackerman's in "A Fine, a Private Place" (p. 734).

   The speaker of "A Fine, a Private Place" never enters the poem as a first-person subject, unlike the speaker of "Play-By-Play." On the other hand, the speaker of Murray's poem remains distant through her use of hypothetical questions, whereas the speaker of Ackerman's poem narrates not only a series of events but the emotions that attended them. In this sense, Ackerman's poem is more of a "play-by-play," whereas Murray's asks, "what if we were to play?"

2. Write an essay on the speaker's gaze in this poem and in Steele's "An Aubade" (p. 761).

   A primary difference is that the speaker of Steele's poem obviously knows the object of his gaze intimately. There is no sense of invasiveness since she is obviously aware of his gaze and doesn't seem to mind it. The objects of the gaze in Murray's poem, though, do not necessarily know that they are being watched. Of course, the question remains as to whether the women in this poem are watching the men for a kind of sexual gratification or if they are appreciating and discussing them aesthetically. In both cases, the objects of the gaze are rendered in terms of their inherent beauty, but in Murray's poem there is the nagging sense that the men on the softball field might feel violated since they haven't in any way consented to being watched.

RONALD WALLACE, *Dogs* (p. 1164)

Discussing dogs, this speaker investigates his long-lasting guilt over accidentally hitting and subsequently killing a dog. He begins with the childhood memory of "hit[ting] one with / a baseball bat. An accident" (lines 1–2). The dog is put to sleep. From there he moves to a series of the most ignoble acts that dogs have inflicted on him, to the one act that gives him the most pain: those dogs "whose slow eyes gazed at me, in love" (14).

The basic form of the Petrarchan sonnet calls attention to the way in which emotion is presented in the poem. At what points does the poem's tone shift, and what is our emotional response when it does? For a speaker who's "been barked at, bitten, nipped, knocked flat, slobbered over, humped, sprayed, beshat" (9–10), it might seem unusual for the most painful act to have been being the recipient of love. But the speaker (presumably an adult looking back) has endured years of "the lasting wrath / of memory's flagellation" (5–6), which the couplet recalls from the octave. He feels guilty.

POSSIBLE CONNECTIONS TO OTHER SELECTIONS

Andrew Hudgins, "Seventeen" (text p. 813)

Jane Kenyon, "The Blue Bowl" (text p. 768)

William Shakespeare, "My mistress' eyes are nothing like the sun" (question #2, following)

John Updike, "Dog's Death" (question #1, following)

CONNECTIONS QUESTIONS IN TEXT (p. 1165) WITH ANSWERS

1. Compare this poem's theme with that in John Updike's "Dog's Death" (p. 673).

   Both speakers try to act as if the death of a dog is simply accidental, but their lives (or deaths) resonate anyway, causing pain in the lives of the speakers. Dogs seem helpless in both poems, as though waiting expectantly for humans to do something that will end their lives. But the speaker of Updike's poem doesn't seem to suffer the same "flagellation" of memory that Wallace's speaker suffers. The speaker of "Dogs" suffers guilt; the speaker of "Dog's Death" suffers pity. What do we suffer as we read each poem?

2. In an essay discuss the strategies used in this sonnet and William Shakespeare's "My mistress' eyes are nothing like the sun" (p. 882) to create emotion in the reader.

   In both poems, the speaker relies on humor before expressing tenderness in the final two lines, but the effect is different. Shakespeare's sonnet is humorous throughout; there is no disturbing undercurrent like the one that taints the beginning of Wallace's poem. "Dogs," in a sense, manipulates our emotions more than Shakespeare's sonnet does because it drags us back and forth throughout the poem between deep, affecting pain and a light treatment of its subject.

D R A M A

28

Reading Drama

Before beginning a class unit on drama, you may want to find out if many of your students have seen a play performed. Most of them will probably have had some exposure to drama on stage, but for many that exposure may have been limited to a school or church play during childhood. If possible, arrange for your students to view a live play while they study drama. Many colleges have theater departments that produce a show every semester. If live drama is not available, try showing a video of a play to your class. (This manual suggests several.) Seeing a show as a class will give you the opportunity to discuss certain theatrical conventions, staging challenges, casting, and other elements of drama which cannot be represented in a written script.

This unit's opening section, "Reading Drama Responsively" (p. 1169) highlights the benefits of reading drama instead of (or in addition to) viewing it. Ask your students about their experiences reading drama. Do they agree that there are some advantages to reading a play over watching one? Discuss the role of imagination. How does their imagination affect the way they read a play they haven't seen?

Comparing Susan Glaspell's *Trifles* (p. 1172) to her short story version entitled, "A Jury of Her Peers" (p. 1182) should generate a good discussion about drama as a *genre*. Have students note the changes from the play to the story, including more detailed descriptions in the story and the story's addition of a third-person narrator who provides background material. Why were these changes made? Is one genre more effective than the other in presenting this plot? By examining ways in which the play differs from the story, you can achieve a good sense of how the elements of drama work and how drama differs from other literary mediums even when it is not being performed.

Students will probably enjoy reading David Ives's *Sure Thing* (p. 1189) and Larry David's episode of *Seinfeld* (p. 1199). Both short readings are good illustrations of the importance of timing in drama. You may even want to have students read scenes from these plays out loud to get a sense of how the humor plays to an audience. Starting the unit off with a *Seinfeld* episode will remind your students that theater has almost always been, and continues to be, entertainment for the masses.

SUSAN GLASPELL, *Trifles* (p. 1172)

A discussion of the elements of drama in *Trifles* appears on pages 1185–1188 in the text; this discussion alludes to most of the questions that follow the play.

The stark, gloomy setting (discussed on pp. 1185–1186) evokes the hard life Mr. Wright imposed on his wife. Within this cold environment, the relationship between the Wrights is immediately and subtly recapitulated in the opening scene by Glaspell's having the men dominate the room as they stand by the stove, while the two women remain timidly near the door. The sympathy that we increasingly feel for Mrs. Peters and Mrs. Hale will eventually be extended to Mrs. Wright, despite the fact that she murdered her husband.

Exposition (discussed on p. 1186) is used throughout to characterize Mr. and Mrs. Wright; Glaspell makes us feel as if we know the essential qualities of this couple even though we never actually see them. Just as the dialogue reveals their characters, it displays the insensitivity of the men, whose self-importance blinds them to the clues woven into the domestic setting, which they dismiss as mere "trifles." The women understand what these details reveal, for example, that the bird cage and dead bird offer evidence concerning Mrs. Wright's motive for murdering her husband. The cage (now broken) symbolizes the lifeless, joyless, confining marriage Mrs. Wright had to endure, and the bird (strangled) suggests both the husband and the wife, Minnie Foster, who used to sing in the choir. Although the women recognize the significance of these objects as well as of the identical knots Mrs. Wright used on her husband and on her sewing, they will not give this evidence to the men because, as women, they empathize with Mrs. Wright's circumstances.

Trifles is packed with irony. On a second reading, the dialogue takes on a strong ironic flavor, for example when the sheriff says there's "nothing here but kitchen things" (p. 1174) or when the county attorney sarcastically asks, "What would we do without the ladies?" (p. 1174) and expresses mild surprise to Mrs. Hale about her being "loyal to her sex" (p. 1175).

The play's title comments on the kind of evidence that *could* be used to convict Mrs. Wright if the men were not so smugly certain of their powers of observation. What appears to be unimportant in the play — the domestic details and the two women — turns out to be powerfully significant. In the final line, Mrs. Hale answers the county attorney's condescending question about Mrs. Wright's sewing. She is standing center stage, he by the door so that their positions are the reverse of what they were in the opening scene. She has the dead canary in her pocket and Mrs. Wright's fate on her lips, but she chooses to exonerate her.

Mrs. Wright is tried by "A Jury of Her Peers" (the short story title); Mrs. Hale and Mrs. Peters penetrate the meaning of what appears only trifling to the men and go beyond conventional, shallow perceptions to discover and empathize with Mrs. Wright's reasons for killing her husband. *Trifles*, although written in 1916, has a distinctly contemporary quality because its feminist perspectives make a convincing case for women stepping outside general attitudes and oppressive values to be true to their own experience. This play is well worth comparing with Henrik Ibsen's *A Doll House* (p. 1564), especially in terms of characterization and theme.

TIP FROM THE FIELD

When teaching the play *Trifles*, I divide my class in half and have one half write a final act determining the fate of Mrs. Wright in accordance with the time period of the play. The other half writes a final act in accordance with today's social and legal mores.

— OLGA LYLES, *University of Nevada*

POSSIBLE CONNECTIONS TO OTHER SELECTIONS

Kate Chopin, "The Story of an Hour" (text p. 10)

Andre Dubus, "Killings" (text p. 81)

Henrik Ibsen, *A Doll House* (text p. 1564)

David Ives, *Sure Thing* (text p. 1189)

Sophocles, *Oedipus the King* (text p. 1224)

RESOURCES FOR TEACHING

Trifles. 21 min., color, 1979. Beta, VHS. Distributed by Phoenix/BFA Films.

Trifles. 22 min., b/w, 1981. Beta, VHS, ¾" U-matic cassette. Distributed by Centre Communications.

PERSPECTIVE

SUSAN GLASPELL, *From the Short Story Version of* Trifles (p. 1182)

The play's opening description immediately gives us information about the Wrights' "gloomy" kitchen; the story, however, can take us beyond the kitchen so that we get a larger view of the house from a little hill. We are told that to Mrs. Hale, the house looked "lonesome." The story, of course, can provide more details through the narrator.

The story begins with characterizations of Mr. and Mrs. Peters ("she didn't seem like a sheriff's wife") as well as Mrs. Hale. The women take more central roles earlier on in the story than in the play. The story also permits us to get inside Mrs. Hale's mind to learn her feelings of guilt for not having visited Mrs. Wright earlier. This intimacy emphasizes Mrs. Hale's perspective and suggests why Glaspell uses the title "A Jury of Her Peers." The story seems to focus more on justice than on the "trifles" overlooked by the men. Perhaps this slight shift in emphasis occurs because the trifles — the sewing, bird cage, and dead canary — make for good stage business.

DAVID IVES, *Sure Thing* (p. 1189)

CONSIDERATIONS FOR CRITICAL THINKING AND WRITING (p. 1195)

1. Even though Ives provides us with very little information about the setting of the play, we understand that the action takes place in a relatively busy place (indicated both by one of Bill's early pick-up lines and the fact that he cannot seem to get a waiter's attention). Yet the anonymity of the place also suggests that the setting is not really important; Ives is satirizing any sort of "pick-up scene" between two strangers.

2. The ringing bell, which relentlessly interrupts the dialogue throughout the play, indicates moments where the characters can go back in time and have the opportunity to revise their words. Students may note that the ringing bell in a sense divides the play into dozens of miniscenes, as the conversation between Bill and Betty is continually reworked and the characters, in a sense, "start over."

3. Students might consider Betty to be the antagonist and Bill to be the protagonist of the play, insofar as Betty is the character with most of the power to terminate their conversation and Bill is the character who is constantly struggling to say the right thing. Conflicts arise throughout the conversation, as one or the other says some-

thing offensive, ridiculous, or merely bizarre. Yet the overall conflict is an internal one, resulting from the struggle of individuals to create public identities that others will find acceptable, attractive, and interesting.

4. The characters' struggles to create acceptable identities complicate the formulaic "boy-meets-girl" plotline, since we are inclined to think that when two people are attracted to each other it is because they are "destined" to be together, and not because they invent clever and highly idealized versions of themselves in order to get past their first impressions. The climax of the play seems to occur at the ringing of the final bell; after this point, Bill and Betty get along so well that there is no further need for them to "back up" and start over. They reach a more comfortable level of conversation and discover that they have some similar likes and dislikes, which leads to their decision to stay together.

5. The play is farcical; nevertheless its theme may be described as the difficulties of really knowing other people and of knowing oneself. Bill and Betty try to mold themselves to fit what they think are the expectations of others. For example, Bill disregards his true sense of identity and invents colleges, grade-point averages, political leanings, anything at all in order to keep Betty interested. One might say that they succeed in their endeavors; they are together at the end of the conversation. But students should consider what Ives suggests are the implications of beginning a relationship based on the false impressions that preceded that final ringing bell.

6. The title of the play is ironic because at no particular point during Bill and Betty's conversation is their future together a "sure thing" — only through backpedaling and revising their conversation are they able to connect. Their relationship can be considered a "sure thing" only in the sense that in the world that Ives created they can redo their conversation as many times as they want, until they get it right.

7. Just as Bill explains that it is important to "hit these things at the right moment or it's no good" (p. 1191), Ives inserts the ringing bell at precisely the moments when the conversation goes out of control and one person is ready to dismiss the other. Ives's sense of timing also extends to the length and shape of the conversation; in spite of the humor, Bill and Betty's first encounter couldn't go on forever. Ives brings his audience just to the point when it seems doubtful that the two characters will *ever* "connect," and then he lets them connect with a comic intensity that pokes fun at all romantic "pick-ups."

POSSIBLE CONNECTION TO ANOTHER SELECTION

Susan Glaspell, *Trifles* (text p. 1172)

LARRY DAVID, *From "The Pitch," a* Seinfeld *Episode* (p. 1199)

CONSIDERATIONS FOR CRITICAL THINKING AND WRITING (p. 1205)

1. George's idea that the proposed show should be about "nothing" is brilliant, because it perfectly describes the much-ado-about-nothing quality of most *Seinfeld* plots. Many *Seinfeld* episodes deal with the fragments that make up our daily lives, such as finding an apartment, standing in bank lines, coping with needy neighbors, picking up clothes at the dry cleaner's, getting short-changed, or visiting parents. These seemingly mundane incidents become dramatic vignettes of the characters' personal

lives. For example, one Emmy-winning episode, titled "The Contest," focused on the characters' attempts to avoid masturbating. As prurient as this episode may sound, it was, in fact, a good-natured, humorous treatment of a sensitive subject. Although these plots about "nothing" are comic, they provide astute observations about human nature and social interactions.

2. Whether students are asked to discuss or write about how they think the "Suits" look, they are likely to have some fun with this question. Television executives come in all sizes and shapes, of course, but the stage direction calling for "Suits" emphasizes the conservative, uniform, bottom-line sensibility that characterizes the people in this highly competitive business. In "The Pitch," the suits and ties worn by Stu and Jay make clear that they are more engaged in business than in entertainment.

3. George spells Crespi's name correctly, but his childish enthusiasm for getting it right suggests that there is something oddly wrong with George: here's a man who doesn't have much else to claim as an achievement in his life. Later, his misspelling of Dalrymple's name indicates that this particular talent, like George's others, is hit-or-miss. In addition to provoking laughter and making the audience wince, George's spelling sheds some light on his idea that the pilot should be about "nothing," because nothing is really going on in his life.

4. As the discussion about *Seinfeld* in the text indicates, the major characters in the show are an odd lot. Kramer's assertion that "people want to watch freaks" is true of the show, but with an important qualification: although the characters find themselves in bizarre comic situations, audiences do not perceive them as abnormal in a freakish way. Instead, the characters seem more familiar than foreign, more hilarious than monstrous. We tend to identify with these characters' foibles and mild eccentricities, so we regard them less as "freaks" than as versions of relatives, friends, colleagues, and even ourselves.

5. The humorous nature of most of the script's scenes is alluded to in the discussion that appears in the text. Students should have no difficulty analyzing how the humor is used to complicate Jerry's and George's efforts to come up with a pilot that the television executives will approve. The humor in *Seinfeld* is a version of a comedy of manners concerned with the intrigues of (supposedly) sophisticated New York City characters whose witty conversations and verbal duels are matched by their absurd and ridiculous violations of social conventions and decorum — not to mention common sense.

6. It is difficult to imagine that any student will prefer reading the script to viewing the show, but their reasons for their preference should prove revealing. The trick here is to get students to explain how the script is brought to life by the quality of the show's ensemble acting and to explain how the script serves as an effective vehicle for the actors' considerable skills and talent. If there is time to view an episode as a class and then to discuss the quality of the writing that goes into the script, students will understand how important the script's language and plotting are to the show's success.

POSSIBLE CONNECTION TO ANOTHER SELECTION

David Ives, *Sure Thing* (text p. 1189)

PERSPECTIVE

GEOFFREY O'BRIEN, *On* Seinfeld *as Sitcom Moneymaker* (p. 1207)

The final episode of *Seinfeld* aired on May 14, 1998; your students may be fans of the sitcom, but they may not know the extent to which media pundits and devoted viewers mourned the passing of this "show about nothing." Nick at Nite's *TV Land* paid homage by showing nothing during the hour that the final episode was on, explaining that "nothing is more important than the last episode of *Seinfeld*. . . . *TV Land* is honored to pre-empt an hour of programming for this historic and monumental occasion."

Your students also may not know the enormous sums of money generated around the show, which pulled in 200 million dollars a year in advertising sales. For the final episode, 30-second advertising spots sold for a record-setting average of 1.7 million dollars.

You may want to start by asking your students whether they like the show and find it funny — and whether they do or not, what they think the qualities are about it that made it so popular. Is it truly a show about nothing? Does it matter that these are all single, white professionals living in nice apartments in New York City? If, as O'Brien writes, *Seinfeld* is the "defining sitcom of our age," what exactly does that say about our age? You might ask students to think about entertainment other than *Seinfeld*. Why are actors and athletes paid so much? What role does advertising play? What observations can they make about American culture based on the cost of entertainment, whether it be a popular TV show, a blockbuster movie, or a playoff game?

29

Writing about Drama

QUESTIONS FOR RESPONSIVE READING AND WRITING

Considering the Questions for Responsive Reading and Writing about drama in this chapter might prove especially useful to your students, many of whom may be relatively new to the study of drama. Remind them, of course, that not every question will speak to the issues raised in every play, but that these questions may be treated as a starting point for a closer investigation into the meaning and significance of a particular play or plays. These questions cannot be answered in a single word; many of them require a paragraph or more of explanation. Thus, you might encourage your students to be as specific as possible when attempting to answer any of these questions; the more details that they can provide, the more interesting and relevant their answers will be.

One way to incorporate these questions into your class might be to break your students up into small groups, and ask each group to respond to three or four questions using a play the class has read. By coming up with specific examples from the play to support their answers, students will become more familiar with both the technique of analyzing dramatic literature and the terms commonly used to discuss it. These in-class responses could be turned into short writing assignments and may provide the foundations for more detailed written analyses in the future.

Another way to use these questions effectively might be to assign one question to each of your students and ask them to write a brief, one- or two-page essay answering the given question using a specific play. This is also an important opportunity for students to practice documenting quoted material from the play itself and to become more familiar with the conventions of dramatic literature in general.

A SAMPLE PAPER

The sample student paper titled "The Feminist Evidence in *Trifles*" (p. 1213) offers a strong feminist interpretation of the play by Susan Glaspell. Ask your students to examine what makes this interpretation so convincing. You might ask your class to pay particular attention to the way that this student writer incorporates material directly from the play in order to support the main thesis of the paper. And, as no paper is ever perfect, you might ask your class to suggest specific ways that this essay might have been improved in another revision. Using sample essays in this way can offer your class not only a useful model of a well-argued analytical interpretation of a play, but also provide them with some helpful experience critiquing the work of another student writer. This critiquing may prove useful to your students when they revise drafts of their own papers or in any sort of peer-editing situation.

30

A Study of Sophocles

Students (and their teachers) may be surprised at how much they enjoy studying classical Greek drama. Despite the significant barriers of time and place that separate contemporary audiences from Sophocles, these plays continue to hold our fascination. Robert Fagles's accessible translations of *Oedipus the King* and *Antigone* should pose no language difficulties for students, and the complex characterizations will draw readers in. Nonetheless, there are important conventions of classical Greek drama that may be puzzling. Have your students read and discuss the chapter's section on "Theatrical Conventions of Greek Drama" (p. 1218) before beginning the plays. Many of them may be familiar with Aristotle's definition of "tragedy," but it bears going over in detail. As this section notes, it is important not to reduce tragic characters to a single "fatal flaw," but to see the "hamartia" of Oedipus and Antigone in a larger context.

In order to emphasize the difference between the conventional and the literary use of the term "tragedy," you might ask students to bring in newspaper articles and discuss them in light of the classic definition. Using concrete and familiar examples, students can then determine, for example, that a car accident is less classically "tragic" than the downfall of a successful politician whose political greatness is overshadowed by a personal flaw or a bad decision.

Many of your students will have read *Oedipus the King* (p. 1224) in the past and those who have not will certainly be familiar with the story through Freud's "Oedipus Complex." No doubt there will be vigorous debate about Freud's interpretation of the play (p. 1305). Do students really see Oedipus's actions as "the fulfillment of our childhood wishes," as Freud claims? In today's talk-show culture, we are all armchair psychologists to some degree, and students should be encouraged to "analyze" the play in light of Freud's assessment. Reading J. T. Sheppard's translation of lines 1433–1550 of the play (p. 1306) will enable them to view the work in another way. How does the elevated language affect their reading? Would students have been as likely to analyze the work in modern terms had this been the translation they read? Comparing the language of the two translations can promote some fruitful discussion about the role of translation in the way we approach a work of literature. Muriel Rukeyser's "Myth" (p. 1309) provides a different angle on the same theme, as we read her take on the translation of the word "man."

R. G. A. Buxton's (p. 1314) and Cynthia P. Gardiner's (p. 1315) critical essays about *Antigone* (p. 1267) will be useful sources for framing classroom discussion or essays. Antigone is classically heroic and undeniably sympathetic, but some students may agree with Buxton that there are "problematic aspects of her behavior." Through a careful reading of the play and the critical responses to the play, students can assess the degree to which these two critical readings complement one another and the degree to which they diverge. They will quickly become critics themselves as they try to negotiate their own positions among those of the critics excerpted here.

One way to conclude this unit is to discuss *Oedipus the King* and *Antigone* as companion pieces. Ask students what similarities they see in terms of the plays' themes, characterizations, or structures. Using these plays as examples, what generalizations can students make about classical drama in general and Sophocles in particular? As the term progresses, it will be useful to return to this discussion and ask students to what degree they see the influence of classical Greek drama on later works.

SOPHOCLES, *Oedipus the King* (p. 1224)

Student discussions of this play are likely to center on Oedipus's powerful character and the fate that has been prophesied for him. The two compete for our attention, and the ironies associated with each raise intriguing questions about human freedom and fate. For a broad range of critical responses to the play see *Oedipus Tyrannus*, edited by Luci Berkowitz and Theodore F. Brunner (New York: Norton, 1970).

CONSIDERATIONS FOR CRITICAL THINKING AND WRITING (p. 1265)

2. The opening scene presents Oedipus as a powerful king who has defeated the Sphinx and ruled successfully for many years. The priest's speech (lines 16–69) offers this exposition and characterizes Oedipus as the "first of men" (41) and the "best of men" (57). The city turns to heroic Oedipus to save it once again.

3–5. Oedipus's fury at Tiresias for initially refusing to tell his "dreadful secrets" (374) establishes Oedipus's fierce determination to discover the truth. His quick temper and unreasonableness are also revealed when he accuses Tiresias of conspiring with Creon to usurp the throne (431–459). Oedipus's rage renders him, in a sense, blind (the ironies abound) to the information Tiresias directly tells him: "I say you are the murderer you hunt" (413).

When Oedipus also accuses Creon of treason, Creon correctly assesses a significant element — an error or frailty — of Oedipus's personality as a "crude, mindless stubbornness" that has caused Oedipus to lose his "sense of balance" (615–616). Oedipus's absolute insistence on learning who murdered Laius shows him to be a decisive leader while simultaneously exposing him to the consequences of making public the message from Delphi and his cursing of the murderer of Laius.

Oedipus's self-confidence, determination, and disregard for consequences propel him toward his goal and his destruction. His downfall is not brought about solely by the gods or fate but by the nature of his own remarkable character. The gods may know what will inevitably happen, but it is Oedipus's personality — especially his proud temper — that causes it to happen. As much as he is responsible for the suffering in the play, he is the victim of it. His virtues as well as his vices contribute to his horror and shame.

6. Irony is pervasive in the play, but the greatest irony is that the murderer Oedipus seeks is himself. He sets out to save the city, to appease the gods, and to see that justice is done, but all his altruistic efforts bring ruin on himself. Ignorant of the truth, Oedipus is consistently used as a vehicle for dramatic irony because we know more than he does; this strategy allows Sophocles to charge Oedipus's speeches with additional meanings that the protagonist only gradually comes to perceive. A review of Oedipus's early speeches will yield numerous instances of dramatic irony, as when he declares that if anyone knows about the murder of Laius that person must report to

Oedipus "even if he must denounce himself" (257). His curse on the murderer (280–314) is especially rich in ironic foreshadowings.

7.   The Chorus voices community values of reason, order, and moderation. It knows better than to defy the gods, and it firmly condemns human pride (for instance, in lines 963–980). It reacts to and comments on the action and also links scenes. In contrast to Jocasta's rejection of the oracles, the Chorus worries about the irreverence it observes. Its final words confirm the unpredictable ironies that we must endure: "Count no man happy till he dies, free of pain at last."

8.   Tiresias's blindness does not prevent him from seeing the truth of Oedipus's past. His insight is in ironic contrast to Oedipus, who sees physically but is blind to the pattern of events that defines his life. Once Oedipus does see the truth, he blinds himself, a fitting punishment that will not allow him to escape his suffering. Oedipus does not choose suicide because to live is even more painful; he takes complete responsibility for what has happened and accepts his suffering as his destiny.

1, 9. Students should be encouraged to examine both Oedipus's irrational willfulness — which his behavior demonstrates and the Chorus comments on — and prophecies, coincidences, and actions that transform a powerful, bold man into a tragic figure whose only remaining dignity is in complete suffering. What happens to Oedipus raises questions concerning human guilt and innocence and cosmic justice. Students are likely to recognize that though Oedipus's circumstances are specific to himself, the larger issues he encounters are relevant to them too.

10. In *The Interpretation of Dreams*, Sigmund Freud reads the play as a manifestation of men's unconscious desire to replace their fathers and have sexual relations with their mothers. In healthy personalities this jealousy and sexual impulse are overcome and suppressed. Jocasta urges Oedipus not to worry that this has happened to him (1074–1078). Certainly Oedipus had no conscious design to marry his mother; he is appalled by the possibility. But Freud would argue that a significant part of our fascination with this play is our identification with Oedipus's fears. Students with some background in psychology will probably be eager to pursue the question; others are likely to be wary and skeptical.

POSSIBLE CONNECTIONS TO OTHER SELECTIONS

Susan Glaspell, *Trifles* (text p. 1172)

David Henry Hwang, *M. Butterfly* (text p. 1675)

Henrik Ibsen, *A Doll House* (text p. 1564)

William Shakespeare, *Hamlet, Prince of Denmark* (text p. 1383)

———, *The Tempest* (text p. 1483)

Sophocles, *Antigone* (text p. 1267)

Wole Soyinka, *The Strong Breed* (text p. 1919)

Tennessee Williams, *The Glass Menagerie* (text p. 1864)

RESOURCES FOR TEACHING

SELECTED BIBLIOGRAPHY

Bloom, Harold. *Sophocles' Oedipus Rex*. New York: Chelsea, 1988.

Edmonds, Lowell. *Oedipus: The Ancient Legend and Its Later Analogues*. Baltimore: Johns Hopkins UP, 1985.

Fergusson, Francis. *The Idea of a Theater.* Princeton: Princeton UP, 1949. 14–53.

Knox, Bernard M. *Oedipus at Thebes: Sophocles' Tragic Hero and His Time.* New York: Norton, 1971.

AUDIOVISUAL RESOURCES

Oedipus Rex. 20 min., color, 1957. Beta, VHS, ¾″ U-matic cassette. A performance by deaf actors. Distributed by Gallaudet University Library.

Oedipus Rex. 87 min., color, 1957. VHS, 16-mm film. With Douglas Campbell, Douglas Rain, Eric House, and Eleanor Stuart. Based on William Yeats's translation. Directed by Tyrone Guthrie. Contained and highly structured rendering by the Stratford (Ontario) Festival Players. Distributed by Water Bearer Films. Available for rental from member institutions of the Consortium of College and University Media Centers.

Oedipus the King. 97 min., color, 1967. VHS. With Donald Sutherland, Christopher Plummer, Lilli Palmer, Orson Welles, Cyril Cusack, Richard Johnson, and Roger Livesey. Directed by Philip Saville. Simplified film version of the play, filmed in Greece using an old amphitheater to serve as the background for much of the action. Distributed by Crossroads Video.

Oedipus the King. 45 min., color, 1975. Beta, VHS, ¾″ U-matic cassette, 16-mm film. With Anthony Quayle, James Mason, Claire Bloom, and Ian Richardson. A production by the Athens Classical Theatre Company, with an English soundtrack. Distributed by Films for the Humanities and Sciences. Available for rental from member institutions of the Consortium of College and University Media Centers.

Oedipus Tyrannus. 60 min., color, 1978. Beta, VHS, ¾″ U-matic cassette. Hosted by Jose Ferrer. Shown from the point where Oedipus is informed of the death of his father. Expository portion shows scenes of Greek theaters and recounts Aristotle's definition of tragedy. Distributed by Films, Inc.

Oedipus the King. 120 min., color, 1987. VHS. With John Gielgud, Michael Pennington, and Claire Bloom. Distributed by Films for the Humanities and Sciences.

Oedipus Rex [recording]. 2 cassettes. Translated by William Butler Yeats. Performed by Douglas Campbell and Eric House. Dramatization. Distributed by Caedmon/HarperAudio.

Oedipus Rex: Age of Sophocles, I. 31 min., color and b/w, 1959. Beta, VHS, ¾″ U-matic cassette, 16-mm film. Discusses Greek civilization, the classic Greek theater, and the theme of man's fundamental nature. Distributed by Britannica Films. Available for rental from member institutions of the Consortium of College and University Media Centers.

Oedipus Rex: The Character of Oedipus, II. 31 min., color and b/w, 1959. Beta, VHS, 3/4″ U-matic cassette, 16-mm film. Debates whether Oedipus's trouble is a result of character flaws or of fate. Distributed by Britannica Films. Available for rental from member institutions of the Consortium of College and University Media Centers.

Oedipus Rex: Man and God, III. 30 min., color and b/w, 1959. Beta, VHS, ¾″ U-matic cassette, 16-mm film. Deals with the idea that Oedipus, although a worldly ruler, cannot overcome the gods and his destiny. Distributed by Britannica Films. Available for rental from member institutions of the Consortium of College and University Media Centers.

Oedipus Rex: Recovery of Oedipus, IV. 30 min., color and b/w, 1959. Beta, VHS, ¾″ U-matic cassette, 16-mm film. Deals with man's existence between God and beast. Distributed by Britannica Films. Available for rental from member institutions of the Consortium of College and University Media Centers.

The Rise of Greek Tragedy, Sophocles: Oedipus the King. 45 min., color, 198?. Beta, VHS, ¾" U-matic cassette, 16-mm film. With James Mason, Claire Bloom, and Ian Richardson, and narrated by Anthony Quayle. The play is photographed in the ancient Greek theater of Amphiaraion and uses tragic masks. Distributed by Films for the Humanities and Sciences. Available for rental from member institutions of the Consortium of College and University Media Centers.

SOPHOCLES, *Antigone* (p. 1267)

The conflict in this play derives from two powerful characters — Antigone and Creon — and the two principles they represent. Antigone's loyalty is to her family, individual conscience, and religious law. Creon, however, defines his duty as the enforcement of civil law to maintain order. This produces tensions between human laws and religious law and between the individual and the state. Sophocles complicates the moral choices each character makes by revealing their personalities so that their choices are not merely abstract sets of principles. Therein lies the drama.

CONSIDERATIONS FOR CRITICAL THINKING AND WRITING (p. 1302)

1. Creon forbids Polynices' burial to punish Antigone's rebellious brother. Antigone, however, refuses to abide by this decree because she pledges her allegiance to religious law rather than civil law. The central conflict of the play revolves around whether one should obey the law of the land or follow one's conscience. Students will probably be divided in their loyalties to Creon's (lines 210–214) or Antigone's (510–524) position. Sophocles does not make the choice easy.

2. The Chorus, rejecting extremes, makes a plea for moderation and reasonableness; "the laws of the land" must be combined with "the justice of the gods" if the city is to prosper (410–412). "Reckless daring" (415) of any kind jeopardizes both individuals and the state. Although the Chorus celebrates the power and genius of humankind, it also emphasizes the importance of subordinating human will to that of the gods (377–416).

3. Ismene serves as a foil to Antigone because she urges her sister to be "sensible," to remember that women cannot resist the strength of men and that they must "submit" to "the ones who stand in power" (60–81). Ismene recognizes her sister's passions and sees her as a quixotic romantic "in love with impossibility" (104) and "off on a hopeless quest" (107). Students may find Ismene's position weak and overly cautious, but they are also likely to find Antigone's rejection of Ismene's attempts to martyr herself along with her sister coldly extreme. Perhaps the fairest assessment of each sister's values and sensibilities is voiced by Antigone when she tells Ismene that "your wisdom appealed to one world — mine, another" (629). Both sisters can lay claim to truth, but neither's position is wholly adequate to live in both worlds.

4. With great self-control Haemon calmly pleads for Antigone's life by informing his father that public opinion is against her execution. Haemon is deferential and loving when he urges Creon not to "be quite so single-minded, self-involved / or assume the world is wrong and you are right." He pleads with Creon "not to be too rigid" (789–797). Haemon's demeanor changes abruptly and radically when he realizes that his father will not pardon Antigone. Haemon's despair and suicide are plausible because he has lost his father and his lover. Indeed, his rashness identifies him as his father's son and as a sympathetic mate for Antigone.

5. Creon's angry reaction to Antigone's disobedience is informed, in part, by what he perceives to be a threat not only to his authority but also to his manhood: "I'm not the man, not now: she is the man / if this victory goes to her and she goes free" (542–543). He insists that "no woman is going to lord it over me" (594). He tells Haemon to "never lose your sense of judgment over a woman" (724) and "never be rated / inferior to a woman, never" (761–762). For additional moments when Creon expresses contempt for women, see lines 837–838 and 849.

6. Both Creon and Antigone must share responsibility for what happens. If neither had acted so rigidly and precipitously, the outcome might have been different. However, Creon must assume more responsibility for the tragedy because he has the power and authority to change his orders. Both appear to be guilty of the "stubbornness" that Tiresias says "brands you for stupidity — pride is a crime" (1137–1138). Antigone loses her life, but Creon's suffering is finally greater because he must accept the guilt for his son's and wife's deaths.

POSSIBLE CONNECTIONS TO OTHER SELECTIONS

Henrik Ibsen, *A Doll House* (text p. 1564)
William Shakespeare, *Hamlet, Prince of Denmark* (text p. 1383)
Sophocles, *Oedipus the King* (text p. 1224)
Tennessee Williams, *The Glass Menagerie* (text p. 1864)

RESOURCES FOR TEACHING

SELECTED BIBLIOGRAPHY

Brown, Andrew. *A New Companion to Greek Tragedy*. Totowa: Barnes, 1983.
Linforth, I. M. *Antigone and Creon*. Berkeley: U of California P, 1961.

AUDIOVISUAL RESOURCES

Antigone. 88 min., b/w, 1962. 16-mm film. With Irene Papas. Directed by George Tzavellas. In Greek, with subtitles. Distributed by Films, Inc.

Antigone. 120 min., 1987. Beta, VHS, ¾" U-matic cassette. With Juliet Stevenson, John Shrapnel, and John Gielgud. Staged version. Distributed by Films for the Humanities and Sciences. Available for rental from member institutions of the Consortium of College and University Media Centers.

Antigone [recording]. 2 cassettes. Dramatization of the Fitts and Fitzgerald translation. Performed by Dorothy Tutin and Max Adrian. Distributed by Caedmon/Harper-Audio.

PERSPECTIVES ON SOPHOCLES

ARISTOTLE, *On Tragic Character* (p. 1303)

The tragic figure, according to Aristotle, "does not fall into misfortune through vice or depravity" but through "some mistake" (paragraph 1). Neither extreme virtue nor vice is appropriate because these characteristics do not produce in the audience the emotional intensity of "pity and fear."

Aristotle's objection to a woman being "manly or formidable in the way I mean" should produce considerable class debate. Perhaps a discussion of Creon's attitude toward women in *Antigone* can be related to Aristotle's comments.

Aristotle argues that characters should be made "handsomer . . . than they are in reality" because a character's qualities on the stage have to be perceived by an audience at a distance.

SIGMUND FREUD, *On the Oedipus Complex* (p. 1305)

Students may agree or disagree with the notion that the Oedipus complex is the "key to the tragedy," but it is certainly an important critical aspect of the play and should not be dismissed too quickly. It is important for students to understand the substantial influence of Freud's ideas about dream interpretation on both psychology and literature; you might ask them to think of other instances in which the Oedipus complex is played out in literature or in some other area.

However, Freud's vision of tragic character differs from Aristotle's in that Freud believes that tragic characters do not necessarily have to make mistakes; they are subject to the mysterious workings of their subconscious minds and act according to their very human reactions to the subconscious.

SOPHOCLES, *Another Translation of a Scene from* Oedipus the King (p. 1306)

Fagles's more modern diction and tone (lines 1433–1549) are less poetically embellished than Sheppard's. Consider, for example, these lines spoken by the Chorus:

Unhappy in thy fortune and the wit
That shows it thee. Would thou hadst never known. (Sheppard)

Pitiful, you suffer so, you understand so much . . .
I wish you'd never known. (Fagles)

Fagles's version is considerably more direct and less mannered than Sheppard's translation, with its many *O*s and *Alas*es. Although there are no differences significant enough to affect our interpretation of the scene, it is fair to say that in Fagle's translation Oedipus sounds to the modern ear like a man who is truly suffering rather than declaiming.

MURIEL RUKEYSER, *On* Oedipus the King (p. 1309)

The "myth" of the title does not merely indicate a mythical allusion; it also refers to the mistaken notion that "when you say man . . . you include women." Although Sophocles' play does not address the issue of equality of the sexes, Rukeyser indicates — with good humor — that the unresolved issue is the cause of great unhappiness and even catastrophe. Her colloquial rendering of Oedipus's second encounter with the Sphinx gives the episode just the right updated tone to establish its relevance to the reader.

JEAN ANOUILH, *A Scene from* Antigone (p. 1310)

Creon refuses to bury Polynices because he believes that refusal will help preserve "peace and order" in Thebes. Unlike Sophocles' Creon, who refuses to be bested by a woman, Anouilh's acts out of a firmer sense of duty and responsibility. He is not a tyrant (being too "fastidious"); instead, he is trapped by circumstances that, he thinks, make his actions necessary to save the ship of state. Anouilh seems more sympathetic to Creon than Sophocles does. Antigone's position is surely morally purer, but she makes her choice in an abstract, absolute context, while Creon is finally anchored in historic circumstances, conditions that Anouilh found parallel to the German occupation of France.

MAURICE SAGOFF, *A Humorous Distillation of Antigone* (p. 1312)

Sagoff actually manages to tuck a significant portion of the play into his poem, particularly in lines 7–8, where he alludes to the theme. Creon and Antigone are given short shrift, but that, of course, is the nature of a shrinklit and part of its breezy fun.

BERNARD KNOX, *On Oedipus and Human Freedom* (p. 1313)

Knox argues that Oedipus's freedom to find out the truth about himself is both heroic and admirable — and that in choosing to search to find out who he is, Oedipus is exercising what is perhaps the only *real* human freedom. Invite students to seriously consider Knox's positive reading of what is traditionally considered a fairly bleak play about lack of agency. What is gained if you consider Oedipus free rather than trapped by circumstances outside of his control? Is it better to think of Oedipus as a hero or as a victim?

TWO COMPLEMENTARY CRITICAL READINGS

R. G. A. BUXTON, *The Major Critical Issue in Antigone* (p. 1314)

Buxton evaluates the moral positions of Creon and Antigone almost as though they were mirror images of one another. According to Buxton, while Creon plainly goes too far, the noble sentiments that he expresses in his opening speech, as well as the magnitude of the tragedy that befalls him, prevent us from perceiving him as a total blackguard. On the other hand, while Antigone is clearly admirable, Sophocles endows her with defects that prevent us from seeing her as a saint. You might ask your students to point to examples of positive or sympathetic aspects of Creon's character and negative aspects of Antigone's. Do any of these traits change our ultimate judgment of either character? If not, what do they add to the play? What do your students think of the contention at the close of this passage that the downfalls of Antigone and Creon are "separate in nature"? Might their respective downfalls be seen as interconnected?

CYNTHIA P. GARDINER, *The Function of the Chorus in Antigone* (p. 1315)

Gardiner asserts that "nearly everyone agrees" that Antigone is right and Creon wrong in Sophocles' play. She then suggests that the Chorus can be considered an independent persona whose judgment of the two characters throughout the play determines for the audience how "right" or "wrong" they are. One approach to testing Gardiner's thesis would be to choose specific speeches by the chorus and have students suggest whether any aspects of the speeches imply support of Creon or of Antigone. In particular, you might look at the Chorus's first and last speeches (lines 117–179 and 1238–1273, or the closing lines, 1466–1470) and ask students whether there seems to be any change in attitude on the part of the chorus as to where its loyalties lie. Is the judgment of the Chorus the only way, or the best way, for the reader or viewer of the play to assess the two characters?

ADDITIONAL RESOURCES FOR TEACHING SOPHOCLES

SELECTED BIBLIOGRAPHY

Bloom, Harold, ed. *Sophocles*. New York: Chelsea, 1990.

Bowra, Sir Maurice. *Sophoclean Tragedy*. Oxford: Clarendon, 1944.

Gardiner, Cynthia P. *The Sophoclean Chorus: A Study of Character and Function*. Iowa City: U of Iowa P, 1987.

Hogan, James C. *A Commentary on the Plays of Sophocles*. Carbondale: Southern Illinois UP, 1991.

Woodard, T. M., ed. *Sophocles: A Collection of Critical Essays*. Englewood Cliffs: Prentice, 1966.

AUDIOVISUAL RESOURCES

Drama: How It Began. 30 min., b/w, 1957. 16-mm film. Discusses the early beginnings of the theater. Explains the techniques of the Greek theater and how playwriting developed. Illustrates the chorus technique with a scene from *Oedipus the King*. Distributed by the Indiana University Instructional Support Services.

The Greek Theater: Greece 478–336 B.C. 26 min., color, 1979. 16-mm film. Professor Eric Handley of University College and the Institute for Classical Studies, London, discusses the classical Greek theater, focusing on the theaters at Epidauros and Athens. Contrasts the ancient and modern theatrical experiences and discusses such aspects of drama as costume, acting, and the function of the chorus. Distributed by Media Guild.

Greek Tragedy [recording]. 1 cassette. Works of Euripides and Sophocles. Performed by Katina Paxinou and Alexis Minotis. Distributed by Caedmon/HarperAudio.

The Theatre in Ancient Greece. 26 min., color, 1989. Beta, VHS, ¾″ U-matic cassette. Program explores ancient theater design, the origins of tragedy, the audience, the comparative roles of the writer/director and actors, and the use of landscape in many plays. Examines the theaters of Herodus, Atticus, Epidauros, Corinth, and numerous others. Distributed by Films for the Humanities and Sciences.

31

A Study of William Shakespeare

Most college students have read at least one William Shakespeare play in high school, usually *Romeo and Juliet* or *Julius Caesar*. Recent mainstream movie versions of *Hamlet, Much Ado about Nothing, Richard III*, and *Romeo and Juliet* may have exposed more people to his works, so few students will approach this chapter as true Shakespeare novices. You may want to begin your introduction to this chapter by asking your students to write about or discuss what they already know about Shakespeare and his writings. Many of them will be familiar with his life as a London actor and playwright, his association with the Globe Theatre, and the three basic categories of history plays, comedies, and tragedies into which his works fall. Invite students to contribute their own knowledge to your initial discussion about Shakespeare, then fill in the gaps by reading and discussing the chapter's introduction, which provides important background. Students may be surprised at how much they already know.

Nonetheless, many of them are likely to be intimidated by the prospect of studying three of Shakespeare's major plays in depth. Much of this intimidation stems from Shakespeare's reputation as the "greatest" writer in English as well as the daunting language of his plays. Believing that they need years of schooling and expertise to truly understand Shakespeare's greatness, students may shy away from reading his works. These apprehensions should be discussed openly in tandem with reading "A Note on Reading Shakespeare" (p. 1325) from this chapter. You may even want to lead a discussion "translating" some passages into "hip," contemporary English to highlight the universal themes that the plays included here encompass. Once students feel they have permission to "read Shakespeare's work as best [as they] can" (p. 1326), they will be more open to the pleasure that a study of William Shakespeare has to offer.

The perspectives at the end of this chapter reflect different approaches to Shakespeare's theater from the sixteenth-century to the present. You need not limit your use of the perspectives to their specific subjects. Louis Adrian Montrose's "On Amazonian Mythology in *A Midsummer Night's Dream*" (p. 1552) will help to frame important discussions about gender and power in *A Midsummer Night's Dream* (p. 1327), but this article can also be applied to *Hamlet* (p. 1383) and *The Tempest* (p. 1483), two other plays in which characters are caught between the opposing forces of masculinity and femininity. Similarly, James Kincaid's claim that "comedy is the whole story — the narrative which refuses to leave things out" in "On the Value of Comedy in the Face of Tragedy" (p. 1553) might be applied to *Hamlet* for further evaluation. One could certainly argue that *Hamlet's* length and scope, though undeniably tragic, share with comedy the refusal to leave things out. Such discussions in which the three plays are analyzed together will reveal the complexity of Shakespeare's vision and the difficulty of easily categorizing his works.

Students who enjoyed applying Freudian psychology to *Oedipus the King* in Chapter 30 may find it interesting to continue their analysis on Hamlet. In addition to his own reading of Hamlet's motives, Freud suggests some other possible explanations for Hamlet's refusal to act against Claudius (p. 1546). Some students may not dismiss these other explanations as quickly as Freud did. Other readings about *Hamlet* by Jan Kott (p. 1547) and Coppélia Kahn (p. 1548) survey a few of the numerous ways the play has been read and produced. You may wish to divide your class into small groups, assigning one reading for each group to discuss in detail. The class can later reconvene, argue the merits of each reading, and offer some interpretations of their own.

The perspectives following *The Tempest* offer a good introduction to postcolonial theory and criticism, using Caliban as an important symbol of England's imperialism. After discussing other approaches to this play, ask students why they think the role and significance of Caliban has been central to criticism of *The Tempest*. What is their response to G. Wilson Knight's praise for England's "will to raise savage people from superstition and blood sacrifice . . . to a more enlightened existence" in "Prospero's Civilizing Influence" (p. 1555)? No doubt most students will find some of Knight's ideas offensive and even racist, and many will sympathize with Caliban. Still, many will also be uneasy with Caliban's character and admit that they find him a frightening savage in need of a little civilizing. These opposite responses may well coexist for some students: another example of the way Shakespeare's plays defy easy interpretation.

As you conclude this chapter, you might ask students to account for Shakespeare's continued popularity and even his recent return to popular culture (via movies). Do they see his works and characters, as Samuel Johnson did, as universal (p. 1545)? Or do they agree more with Alden T. Vaughn in "Caliban as a Sociopolitical Symbol" (p. 1556)? Referring specifically to *The Tempest*, Vaughn writes, "New situations give the play's characters new meanings" (p. 1557). What "new situations" in contemporary America give Shakespeare "new meaning" for your students?

WILLIAM SHAKESPEARE, *A Midsummer Night's Dream* (p. 1327)

For a comprehensive annotated bibliography of criticism on the play, see *A Midsummer Night's Dream: An Annotated Bibliography*, edited by D. Allen Carroll (New York: Garland, 1986). There have been several attempts to associate the play with a specific wedding, among them E. K. Chamber's essay, cited in the selected bibliography (manual p. 469). Chambers argues that the play was written to be performed at the wedding of William Stanley, Earl of Derby, to Lady Elizabeth Vere on January 26, 1595. The reading of the play by G. Wilson Knight in *The Shakespearean Tempest* (1932; rpt. Methuen, 1953) discusses the interplay of imagery and thus emphasizes the play's formal properties over its historical context. C. L. Barber's highly influential *Shakespeare's Festive Comedy* (1959; rpt. Princeton UP, 1972) takes a sociological approach by considering many of Shakespeare's romantic comedies, including *A Midsummer Night's Dream*, in light of their relation to English holiday traditions.

CONSIDERATIONS FOR CRITICAL THINKING AND WRITING (p. 1381)

1. The title of *A Midsummer Night's Dream* creates at least two immediate expectations. First, the relationship between dreams and reality is a prominent theme in the play. Shakespeare recognized that dreams are expressions of our profoundest longings and desires; he also understood that we often dismiss them as trifles that are not to be taken too seriously. In *Midsummer*, he explores deep human longings, the desire to fall in love and marry, and encourages us to see the play as trivial entertainment, "No more yielding but a dream," as Puck says in the epilogue. Dreams and references to dreams occur throughout the play: for example, Hermia awakens from a nightmare

(one with interesting Freudian implications) in Act II, Scene ii, to discover Lysander is missing, while Bottom believes his transformation into an ass was a dream. Theseus's opening speech in Act V is worth examining as an exploration of the relation between illusion and reality.

The play's title also draws our attention to the time of year when the action occurs; it is a *midsummer* night's dream. In Shakespeare's England, the summer solstice, the longest day of the year, was commonly associated with madness and with fertility rituals whose origins were rooted in pre-Christian antiquity. Shakespeare's title would thus have connoted an atmosphere of celebration and sexual license for an Elizabethan audience.

2. Shakespeare's removal of the action in *A Midsummer Night's Dream* from the city of Athens to the forest signals a loosening of the restraints that threaten to prevent the young lovers from freely selecting their own mates. In Shakespeare's day, ancient Athens was associated with the highest level of civilization humankind had ever achieved, and the playwright strengthens this connotation by making Theseus, who is traditionally portrayed as the strongest and wisest of rulers, the chief human authority figure in the play. For Shakespeare's audiences, Athens would have represented civilization, order, and social stability.

The forest represents Athens's opposite, a world in which disorder and confusion reign. While the strong patriarchal ruler Theseus has a nominal counterpart in Oberon, the true spirit of the forest is represented by the mischievous Puck. Puck represents *misrule*, the inversion of normal social restrictions. When the four young lovers cross the boundary that separates urban, civilized Athens from the wild world of the forest, they enter a topsy-turvy world in which lovers switch allegiance at a moment's notice, the girls chase the boys rather than the other way around, and Titania, the queen of the fairies, falls in love with an ass.

In the end, however, the social rules represented by Theseus and Athens have not only been reasserted, they have clearly been strengthened by their temporary suspension. When the four lovers waken from their "dream" at the end of Act IV, they are reintegrated into society by Theseus, an assimilation symbolized by the group marriage of Act V. Similarly, the dissension in the fairy world is healed by the play's end when the marital spat between Oberon and Titania is amicably resolved.

3. In Shakespearean comedy, marriage commonly functions as a symbol of order restored. The marriage of Theseus and Hippolyta brackets the main action of *A Midsummer Night's Dream*. The play opens with Theseus announcing his impending wedding to Hippolyta, the queen of the Amazons, whom he has conquered in battle. The marriage thus connotes not only the natural harmony of male-female bonding but also a political alliance designed to prevent further warfare between two peoples.

The harmony represented by Theseus and Hippolyta's wedding is disrupted, however, by Egeus's desire to force Hermia to marry Demetrius against her will. While Hippolyta is Theseus's prisoner, there is no suggestion that she is averse to the marriage. Egeus's extreme patriarchalism contrasts unfavorably with the more benign rule of Theseus.

Egeus's unreasonably domineering attitude results in the flight of the young lovers into the forest, where, with the aid of the fairies, they work out their relationships. Tellingly, it is precisely when the lovers waken from their "dream" that Theseus and Hippolyta reappear in the play near the end of Act IV. In keeping with the general symbolism of marriage in comedy, the reintegration of Hermia, Lysander, Helena, and Demetrius into society as adults is symbolized by their inclusion in Theseus and Hippolyta's nuptials.

4. *A Midsummer Night's Dream* is one of Shakespeare's earlier comedies, and the play's four young lovers lack the brilliant delineation of individual character that the play-wright would achieve in subsequent comedies. Indeed, Lysander and Demetrius are virtually interchangeable; they possess the virtues and defects of male youth. Both are spirited and courageous; they are also stubborn and hot-headed. Both also seem somewhat opportunistic: Demetrius, we learn early on, "Made love to Nedar's daughter, Helena, / And won her soul" (I.i.107–108) before switching his affections to Hermia. Similarly, Lysander shows no squeamishness about running away with Hermia after Theseus rules against him in Act I.

. The two young women in the play, while scarcely displaying the brilliantly captivat-ing personalities of a Rosalind or a Viola, are considerably more individuated than their boyfriends. Their differing temperaments are related to the differing physical characteristics we may deduce from the insults Lysander and Demetrius hurl at Her-mia and that Hermia flings at Helena in Act III, Scene ii. Hermia is described, and has traditionally been cast, as small and dark, with a sharp tongue and a hot temper. By contrast, Helena is fair, tall, and timid; she is "a right maid for [her] cowardice" (III.ii.303). Interestingly, it is Helena who displays perhaps the most growth of any of the four young lovers. When she pursues Demetrius into the woods, her lack of self-esteem is appalling even for a farce: she literally is willing to be treated like a dog. When she imagines that her friends have united to make her the butt of their jokes, however, she responds with some spirit, and her tone is one of genuine hurt. Hermia, too, may experience some emotional growth in Act III, Scene ii, as she realizes that she has gone from being avidly pursued by two young men to having been rejected by them both. For a headstrong girl accustomed to having her way, suddenly to find herself spurned by both her lovers is sobering.

5. The essence of Bottom's comic appeal is his complete absence of self-awareness. The oafish, ignorant weaver sees himself as a splendid actor; not only does he see no rea-son he should not be cast as Pyramus in the artisans' play, he wishes to play all the other parts as well. He also displays no surprise whatever when the beautiful fairy queen, Titania, falls passionately in love with him. To the audience, however, Bot-tom's shortcomings as both an actor and a lover are patently obvious. He is, literally and figuratively, an ass.

Yet Bottom is not the only character in the play who suffers from a lack of self-awareness. A lack of reflectiveness is evident in the four young lovers, who are as dog-gedly bent on having their own ways as Nick Bottom is on playing all the parts in the artisan's play. We must wonder why Hermia and Helena feel they will die if they can-not have the men of their choice, for Demetrius and Lysander seem interchangeable. Oberon's desire for the changeling boy is rooted in a similar lack of self-awareness; it is clearly as much a consequence of his personal vanity and need for ascendancy over Titania as it is a product of concern for the boy's welfare. Thus, other characters be-sides Bottom suffer from self-delusion; the difference is that they do not have the ex-cuse of stupidity.

6. The opening scene of *A Midsummer Night's Dream* makes it clear from the outset that we are in a male-dominated world. Theseus begins the play by anticipating his mar-riage to Hippolyta, the Amazon warrior queen whom he has captured by force of

arms. Almost immediately, Egeus enters and demands the death penalty for the disobedient Hermia. Lysander's revelation that Demetrius had previously wooed Helena is reproved by Theseus but is clearly not regarded as any impediment to Demetrius's marriage to Hermia, since that is what her father desires. Although he mitigates the Athenian death penalty for Hermia to a lifetime in a nunnery, Theseus does not question Egeus's fundamental right to dictate Hermia's choice of a mate, as his speech to her in lines 46–52 makes clear.

This tone of patriarchal domination also extends to the world of the fairies. Oberon's ire results from Titania's disobedience, and in the end he gets his way. While a modern audience might look askance on the ease with which the fairy king reestablishes his authority, most members of Shakespeare's audience would have regarded the patriarchalism of the play's "real" and fairy worlds as normative.

The play's four female characters are drawn with varying degrees of distinctiveness. Hippolyta has little depth; she says almost nothing until the last act, and even then her lines seem chiefly designed to give Theseus an opportunity to display his wisdom (in his famous speech of lines 2–22) and sense of *noblesse oblige* toward the artisans' wretched play. Titania possesses more substance; her speech to Oberon in II.i.121–137 shows genuine concern about the changeling's welfare, and most of us probably feel she has gotten a bit of a raw deal by the play's end. Hermia and Helena, unlike Lysander and Demetrius, are different from each other both in appearance and temperament. They also relate to their men differently. Hermia is more assertive — some might say domineering. She is accustomed to having her own way, and when she realizes that Lysander and Demetrius are pursuing Helena, she is first incredulous and then aggressive. Helena's behavior, on the other hand, when she invites Demetrius to treat her as he would his dog, constitutes a parody of female passiveness. Both young women undergo changes during the course of the play. By Scene iv Hermia seems somewhat chastened, Helena a little more self-confident. Shakespeare seems to suggest that such moderation is a necessary prelude to each woman's making a mature commitment to marriage.

7.   Puck's remark to Oberon (III.ii.115) ostensibly refers to the foolish conduct of Lysander and Demetrius under the spell of Oberon's potion. In a larger thematic sense, however, *A Midsummer Night's Dream* is filled with foolishness on the part of many of the characters, mortal and fairy. Egeus is foolish in his unreasoning paternalism; Lysander and Hermia in their precipitate flight from Athens; Demetrius in his fickle rejection of Helena and his unmanly abuse of her continued affection. Oberon's insistence on having his way is almost childish, and Titania's refusal to negotiate on the subject of custody of the changeling violates the spirit of compromise that characterizes most healthy marriages.

8.   Puck directs the barely controlled chaos of the lovers' "fond pageant," and at times we must wonder if even Oberon has control over this mischievous sprite. Indeed, Oberon seems to wonder about this himself: "This is thy negligence. Still thou mistak'st," he tells Puck, "Or else thou committ'st thy knaveries willfully" (III.ii.346–347). Puck's explanation for his error is plausible; nevertheless, he makes no bones about the fact that he is delighted with the consequences of his mistake. This is the pattern throughout the play; while Oberon represents a nominal authority figure in the fairy kingdom, it is Puck who controls the action. It is fitting that the actor who plays Puck speaks the play's epilogue, which reminds the audience that what they have just seen should be given no more importance than a dream.

Throughout the play we have seen Puck as a director of sorts. In the epilogue, when he promises to "mend" those parts of the play that do not please, he is identified with the role of author. We are reminded by Puck's speech that at the original production of this play he spoke on behalf of a living author who could conceivably "mend" those parts of the production that the audience found unsatisfactory.

9. In Act V, the four groups of characters are brought together by means of the symbolic harmony of the marriage ritual. Theseus and Hippolyta, who represent rational authority and stability, are married along with Hermia, Lysander, Demetrius, and Helena. This triple wedding signals the reacceptance of the young people into Athenian society, and the royal wedding is blessed by the royalty of the fairy world, Oberon and Titania. Even the artisans' silly play has symbolic significance. It represents a gift offered, as Theseus observes to Hippolyta, in "simpleness and duty" (V.i.83).

A Midsummer Night's Dream resembles modern television situation comedies in that all its complex conflicts are satisfactorily resolved in the end — at least on the surface. In the conventional television situation comedy, an initially stable situation is complicated by some sort of conflict so that order has to be restored. As in Shakespeare's play, this complication often stems from thwarted desire. In a typical I Love Lucy episode, for example, the stable domesticity of the Ricardo's middle-class life is disrupted when Lucy embarks on some crazy scheme. Chaos invariably ensues, but by the end of the show order has been restored. Students should be encouraged to apply this basic comic movement from order, to disruption, and back to order to an episode of their own favorite sitcom.

10. A Midsummer Night's Dream provides a wealth of comic scenes for analysis, ranging from the verbal comedy of Helena's exchange with Demetrius in II.i to the outrageous slapstick of the Pyramus and Thisbe play. Many scenes combine both verbal and physical humor. For example, the encounter between the four young lovers in III.ii depends for its comic effect partly on the verbal barbs the lovers toss at each other. Equally important, however, is the scene's physical comedy as Lysander tries to shake off Hermia as he would a burr, and he and Demetrius try to prevent her from attacking Helena.

11. The Pyramus and Thisbe play in A Midsummer Night's Dream is Shakespeare's parody of the early Elizabethan interludes he knew from his youth and may, perhaps, have performed in as a young actor in London. It is a comic exaggeration of such crude works as Thomas Preston's Cambises, King of Persia — although, as anyone who has read the latter play can attest, it is not much of an exaggeration. The artisans' incompetence as actors, of course, further intensifies the humor already inherent in the play's clumsy verse.

Thematically, however, the play-within-the-play constitutes a sophisticated comment on the relationship of illusion to reality. Theseus opens the fifth act of the play with a lengthy speech on the power of the imagination, and when Hippolyta complains of the silliness of the play after hearing its first few lines, her husband comments, "The best of this kind are but shadows; and the worst are no worse, if imagination amend them," adding, "If we imagine no worse of [the actors] than they of themselves, they may pass for excellent men" (V.i.205–206, 208–209). In other words, if the three newly married couples are willing to utilize their imaginations to compensate for the deficiencies of the play's script and acting, it will be the equal of a well-written, skillfully presented production. Since Bottom and his companions present the play "with good will" (V.i.110), the aristocrats ought to receive it in the same spirit and use their superior imaginations to "amend" its deficiencies. By appealing to the sense of *noblesse oblige* on the part of his original aristocratic audience, Shakespeare invites them to accept his play, *A Midsummer Night's Dream,* in the same charitable spirit as that with which Theseus and his court accept the artisans' inept interlude.

The plot of *Pyramus and Thisbe* is also significant. It is a tragedy of star-crossed lovers — the sort of play *A Midsummer Night's Dream* might have become had it not been for the benign intervention of Oberon and Puck in the young lovers' affairs.

Finally, the plot of the play may be something of an inside joke for Shakespeare and his audience, since many scholars believe that the play he had written directly before *A Midsummer Night's Dream* was *Romeo and Juliet,* another tale of star-crossed lovers who "kill [themselves] most gallant for love."

12. There are several points in the play at which we are aware that the action might take a tragic turn. First, Hermia faces a possible death penalty for resisting her father's will, although Theseus does commute this penalty to life imprisonment in a nunnery. The fighting match between Hermia and Helena in the woods has decidedly nasty and even violent overtones, and when Lysander and Demetrius withdraw to fight, they might actually hurt each other if Puck does not intervene.

On the whole, however, the edge of danger in *A Midsummer Night's Dream* is not so pronounced as in some of Shakespeare's later comedies, especially the so-called problem comedies, such as *All's Well That Ends Well* and *Measure for Measure.* The Athenian marriage law with which Egeus threatens his daughter is so draconian that we are probably not meant to take it very seriously, and the conflict between the young couples is obviously adolescent in tone. It is conceivable that the play could be transformed into a tragedy, but it would be more like the artisans' *Pyramus and Thisbe* play than like *Romeo and Juliet.*

POSSIBLE CONNECTIONS TO OTHER SELECTIONS

Anton Chekhov, *The Proposal: A Jest in One Act* (text p. 1615)

Henrik Ibsen, *A Doll House* (text p. 1564)

Jane Martin, *Rodeo* (text p. 1657)

Tim O'Brien, "How to Tell a True War Story" (text p. 555)

William Shakespeare, *Hamlet, Prince of Denmark* (text p. 1383)

———, *The Tempest* (text p. 1483)

RESOURCES FOR TEACHING

SELECTED BIBLIOGRAPHY

Chambers, E. K. "The Occasion of *A Midsummer Night's Dream.*" *A Book of Homage to Shakespeare.* Ed. Israel Gollancz. London: Oxford UP, 1916. 154–160.

Dent, R. W. "Imagination in *A Midsummer Night's Dream.*" *Studies in English Literature* 35 (1964): 115–129.

Leggatt, Alexander. *Shakespeare's Comedy of Love.* London: Methuen, 1974.

Price, Anthony, ed. *Shakespeare's* A Midsummer Night's Dream: *A Casebook.* London: Macmillan, 1983.

Warren, Roger. A Midsummer Night's Dream: *Text and Performance.* London: Macmillan, 1983.

AUDIOVISUAL RESOURCES

A Midsummer Night's Dream. 117 min., b/w, 1935. VHS. With James Cagney, Mickey Rooney, Olivia de Havilland, Dick Powell, and Joe E. Brown. Directed by William Dieterle and Max Reinhardt. See local retailer.

A Midsummer Night's Dream. 111 min., b/w, 1963. Beta, VHS. With Patrick Allen, Eira Heath, Cyril Luckham, Tony Bateman, Jill Bennett. A Live BBC-TV performance, with Mendelssohn's incidental music. Distributed by Video Yesteryear.

A Midsummer Night's Dream. 120 min., 1968. Beta, VHS, 16-mm film. With Diana Rigg and David Warner. Directed by Peter Hall. A Royal Shakespeare Company performance. Distributed by Drama Classics Video. Available for rental from member institutions of the Consortium of College and University Media Centers.

A Midsummer Night's Dream. 120 min., color, 1982. Beta, VHS. With Helen Mirren, Peter McEnry, and Brian Clover. See local retailer. Available for rental from member institutions of the Consortium of College and University Media Centers.

A Midsummer Night's Dream. 165 min., color, 1983. Beta, VHS, ¾″ U-matic cassette. With William Hurt and Michelle Shay. A lively interpretation by Joseph Papp. Distributed by Films for the Humanities and Sciences. Available for rental from member institutions of the Consortium of College and University Media Centers.

A Midsummer Night's Dream. 194 min., color, 1987. Beta, VHS. With Ileana Cotrubas, James Bowman, and Curt Appelgren. Directed by Peter Hall. A performance of the Benjamin Britten opera, taped at the Glyndebourne Festival Opera. Distributed by Films, Inc.

A Midsummer Night's Dream [recording]. 1 cassette. Dramatization performed by the Folio Theatre Players. Distributed by Spoken Arts.

A Midsummer Night's Dream [recording]. 3 cassettes (text included). Dramatization performed by Paul Scofield and Joy Parker. Distributed by Caedmon/HarperAudio.

A Midsummer Night's Dream [recording]. 1 cassette (60 min.), 1985. Dramatization performed by Stanley Holloway and Sarah Churchill. Living in Shakespeare Series. Distributed by Crown Publishers.

A Midsummer Night's Dream [recording]. 2 cassettes (120 min.). Performed by Robert Helpmann and Moira Shearer. An Old Vic production. Distributed by Durkin Hayes Publishing.

A Midsummer Night's Dream: Introduction to the Play. 26 min., color, 1970. Introduction to famous scenes and characters. Distributed by Phoenix/BFA Films and Video.

WILLIAM SHAKESPEARE, *Hamlet, Prince of Denmark* (p. 1383)

Two standard sources for the study of *Hamlet* are A. C. Bradley's *Shakespearean Tragedy* (1904; rpt. New York: St. Martin's, 1965) and Harley Granville-Barker's "Preface to *Hamlet*," in his *Prefaces to Shakespeare*, vol. I (Princeton: Princeton UP, 1946). Both discuss character and motivation in detail. A useful study of the relation of imagery to character is Maynard Mack's "The World of *Hamlet*," *Yale Review* 41 (1952): 502–523, reprinted in *Shakespeare: Modern Essays in Criticism*, rev. ed., edited by Leonard F. Dean (New York: Oxford UP, 1967), 242–262. Useful too is Harold Jenkins's introduction in the 1982 Arden edition. He sorts through the criticism and offers a sensible, adaptable reading.

TIP FROM THE FIELD

I have students see videotapes of the famous "To be, or not to be" soliloquy from three different productions of *Hamlet*. I then ask them to write an essay comparing the version they like best to the text and explain why they prefer it over the other two.

— RICHARD STONER, *Broome Community College*

CONSIDERATIONS FOR CRITICAL THINKING AND WRITING (p. 1480)

1. (See also question 5.) Hamlet's attempts to define his own character in a corrupt world, his fear of death (apparently resulting from his new view of the world's corruption), the fact that death is an inevitable consequence of revenge, the fact that his image of the world is so wrapped up in his now-horrible image of his mother, even his legitimate desire (at least in a revenge-play world) to send Claudius to hell — all cause delay.

2. Insofar as Claudius's advice generalizes from the traditional Boethian consolation, it is sensible. But if we look back at this advice after we hear of Claudius's crime, his speech's sensibility is undercut by his lurking suspicion of Hamlet. Hamlet cannot heed the advice because it does not address his particular grief, deeply felt because he remembers his father as "Hyperion" (see his first soliloquy, I.ii.129–159). Nor can the advice smooth over other complications in Hamlet's mood arising from his hatred of the "satyr" Claudius and his revulsion at his mother's incestuous "frailty."

3. Polonius's advice to Laertes is sound, albeit in its political content rather than its moral or ethical content. It thus reflects Polonius's political role in court as well as the delicate, sometimes finicky care with which a courtier must conduct himself. Polonius's political view of life is asserted more clearly when he sends Reynaldo to spy on Laertes (II.i.3–72).

4. When Horatio first tells him of the ghost's appearance, Hamlet immediately offers an interpretation that hints at prophecy: "I doubt some foul play" (I.ii.255), and later, when the ghost beckons him, he says, "My fate cries out" (I.iv.81). So there is evidence of Hamlet's foreboding early on. And the fact that the ghost's revelation of the crime (I.v.60–76) nearly repeats Hamlet's first soliloquy makes the suggestion of prophetic insight more plausible. The ghost's principal demand is that Hamlet "revenge his foul and most unnatural murder" (I.v.25); three secondary demands are

> Let not the royal bed of Denmark be
> A couch for . . . damned incest. . . .
> Taint not thy mind, nor let thy soul contrive
> Against thy mother aught. (I.v.82–86)

Hamlet has difficulty fulfilling all of these.

5. What we know of Hamlet before his father's death comes in snippets from other characters. Claudius identifies him as a student (I.ii.113). Laertes and Ophelia (and Hamlet himself) speak of his love for Ophelia (I.iii.14–16, III.i.113–141, V.i.237–239). Laertes and Ophelia remark on his greatness as a prince (I.iii.17, III.i.142–146). Claudius too recognizes and fears his popularity (IV.iii.1–5) and power (III.i.158–159). And Fortinbras says, in the end, that Hamlet would have "proved most royal" (V.ii.368). We also see him actively fearless in pursuing the ghost (I.v.1–32); we hear him speak knowledgeably on the theater (II.ii.393–485, III.ii.1–36); and he proves himself an expert swordsman. In addition we are given subtler indications of his former character. Hamlet's friendship with Horatio is evidence of his gentle nature. His language is richly imaginative. Even the stability he shows after his return from sea and his "readiness" to face his task and his death bespeak a personality that was the "rose of the fair state" (III.i.144).

The initial change in Hamlet occurs before the play begins: with his father's death and his mother's hasty remarriage, the ideas upon which he based his life and his view of the world have been severely shaken. His references to his father as Hyperion and to his mother's doting love for his father, coupled with his pained speech to Rosencrantz and Guildenstern about the earth, the heavens, and humanity all gone to corruption (II.ii.277-290), suggest that his former image of the world was somewhat idealistic. That Hamlet has been robbed of the crown, that the world is now rank, humanity a "quintessence of dust," the king a satyr, and the queen an incestuous beast point to the utter destruction of Hamlet's ideological basis for living. With this sudden demolition comes near madness. Upon receiving news of the murder, Hamlet barely avoids total distraction (I.v.92-112), but he never, apparently, falls into true madness. His verbal antics are usually contrived, such as those with which he fends off Polonius. When his verbal violence is aimed at Ophelia, particularly in III.i, or at Gertrude in the closet scene (III.iv), he seems closer to madness. But uncontrolled passion is probably a better way to describe these expressions of Hamlet's mental condition. In general we might say that in exchanges with the women in the play, Hamlet tends toward passionate distraction.

But intermingled with these shifts between feigned madness and violent passion are the soliloquies. While each contains the conflict between reason and passion, between action and inaction, and each ends with a determination to act that remains unfulfilled, there is also from the first soliloquy to the last a traceable development toward logical and rhetorical control. The first (I.ii.129-159) shifts topics frantically, apparently by rapid associations. The second major soliloquy (II.ii.499-557) progresses emotionally, but each topic is more clearly separated, as if Hamlet were becoming aware of and beginning to control his distraction. The third (III.i.56-90), following hard upon the second, flows smoothly but maintains a delicate tension, only seemingly resolved, between the personal fear of death and the general fear. Its conclusive "Thus conscience does make cowards of us all" is a statement both individual and communal. The last major soliloquy (IV.iv.32-66) is clearly logical, moving from controlled personal reflection, to the contrary example, to the particular application of the contrary to Hamlet himself.

This various, sometimes contradictory mental activity creates for us a character unlike any other. Our sense of Hamlet as a tragic hero depends largely on his (and our) endurance through this chaotic progress toward the courageous stability we see in Acts IV and V.

6. The dramatic purpose of the play within the play is to verify the ghost's story and to trap Claudius into revealing his guilt. Its themes refer to Gertrude's inconstancy in love. (She, however, as the closet scene will show, is deaf to all this.) One other interesting feature is the player king's speech (III.ii.165-194) on the changeability of human affection; its tone suggests acceptance of human frailty.

7. Ophelia is only indirectly connected with the crime. Because Hamlet feels that the world, including himself, has become sinfully corrupt (see his soliloquy and the nunnery scene, III.i.56-141) and because he sees women as being a source of corruption in two senses — as lusting beasts and as bearers of children — he feels that Ophelia must necessarily be corrupt. In III.i, Hamlet's vehemence comes from this view of the world and Ophelia's place in it. (In III.ii, however, Hamlet's crudities are aimed through Ophelia at Gertrude and Claudius.) Ophelia's fall into madness mirrors Hamlet's. Having lived, it seems, solely according to the guidance of Polonius, Laertes, and perhaps Hamlet, she has no strength to bear up when her supports collapse. With Polonius dead, Hamlet, whom she loved, a murderer and madman, and Laertes absent, she crumbles.

8. Hamlet's words to Gertrude after she calls the killing of Polonius "a rash and bloody deed" — "almost as bad, good mother / As kill a king and marry with his brother" (III.iv.28–30) — are a slip that reveals Hamlet's belief that she is deeply, conspiratorially guilty. Her crime, however, seems to be one of omission as well as commission. In setting up a "glass" wherein she will see her soul, Hamlet hits on an image appropriate to his mother's failure to perceive what has occurred. In presenting the pictures of his father and Claudius and returning to an analogy to the gods in describing his father, Hamlet indicates that he feels compelled to reveal to his mother what he has seen and learned. His words must call up the same torment in her that he has felt.

9. The two questions will probably give rise to opposing responses. The likelihood of sympathy for Claudius depends to a great extent on the reader because Claudius expresses remorse for his crime and unwillingness to make reparation. One particular source of sympathy will be the speech's closeness logically, rhetorically, and thematically to Hamlet's soliloquies. But sympathy in whatever degree survives only as long as Claudius is on his knees. The safest answer to why Hamlet does not kill Claudius is Hamlet's own: perfect revenge requires that Claudius suffer as much as or more than Hamlet's father did. Perhaps, too, Hamlet wishes Claudius to feel torment equal to his own — the idea of infernal or purgatorial punishment has been strong in Hamlet since the ghost's revelation.

10. This question addresses one of the central complexities of the play — Hamlet finds himself bound by external command to act on a situation that is, in one sense, outside himself and, in another, deeply personal. Because of his complex emotional involvements, he is slow to act. His various perceptions of corruption combine to retard the fulfillment of a seemingly simple command. From the closet scene on, we watch Hamlet come to terms with these ideas of corruption. Cathartic images occupy his mind — the dead Polonius (Hamlet is now an active agent in dealing death), the stricken mother, the ghost again, the planned destruction of Rosencrantz and Guildenstern, Fortinbras's army marching to death for an "eggshell," the graveyard, Yorick's skull, foul-smelling, and Ophelia's corpse.

    Through this process of images and actions, Hamlet also comes to terms with corruption and death, including his own, and reaches a spiritual stability, a conception of humanity and the universe, that frees him to act and die. Because we share with him this movement and conclude with him, however unconsciously, that there has been some "special providence" at work, we can have little or no sense of his moral culpability.

11. Fortinbras is the foil toward which Hamlet seems to move. In structural terms, he is Hamlet's most important foil. His situation as described by Horatio (I.i.80–107) parallels Hamlet's before we meet Hamlet, and Fortinbras's action serves twice as a contrast to Hamlet's inaction (I.ii.17–33, IV.iv.32–66). His appearance in the final scene concludes the play on a note of order and stability. His armor (he is the only living character to be seen prepared for battle) finally opens the play to a world of action beyond the confines of Denmark.

12. The humor of the play is remarkable for its poignant commentary on the central themes. Hamlet's joke about the "funeral baked meats" (I.ii.180), his satiric assaults on Polonius (II.ii.173–214), his initial quips with Rosencrantz and Guildenstern (II.ii.215–256), his bitter sexual jibes at Ophelia's expense (III.ii.97–118), his dark humor regarding Polonius's body and death (III.iv.214–216, IV.iii.18–35), the gravedig-

ger's callous joking, and Hamlet's thoughts on the deaths of ladies and great men (V.i.65–184) — all reflect on the many forms of corruption that Hamlet contemplates. Often the humor reveals the pain inherent in his thoughts and a desire to be released from them. In the gravedigger scene, there is a nice shift toward a more pathetic although resolved opinion of death and corruption. Such humor, one of the many mirrors of Hamlet's evolution, differs from the humor in the comedies because of its dark tones and its tragic import.

POSSIBLE CONNECTIONS TO OTHER SELECTIONS

T. S. Eliot, "The Love Song of J. Alfred Prufrock" (text p. 1045)

David Henry Hwang, *M. Butterfly* (text p. 1675)

Henrik Ibsen, *A Doll House* (text p. 1564)

Jane Martin, *Rodeo* (text p. 1657)

Arthur Miller, *Death of a Salesman* (text p. 1795)

William Shakespeare, *A Midsummer Night's Dream* (text p. 1327)

——, *The Tempest* (text p. 1483)

Sophocles, *Antigone* (text p. 1267)

——, *Oedipus the King* (text p. 1224)

RESOURCES FOR TEACHING

SELECTED BIBLIOGRAPHY

Bloom, Harold, ed. *William Shakespeare's* Hamlet. New York: Chelsea, 1986.
Mack, Maynard. "The World of Hamlet." *Yale Review* 41 (1952): 502–523.
Prosser, Eleanor. *Hamlet and Revenge.* Stanford: Stanford UP, 1967.
Wilson, John Dover. *What Happens in* Hamlet. Cambridge: Cambridge UP, 1967.

AUDIOVISUAL RESOURCES

Approaches to Hamlet. 45 min., color, 1979. Beta, VHS, ¾" U-matic cassette, 16-mm film. Includes footage of the four greatest Hamlets of this century: John Barrymore, Laurence Olivier, John Gielgud, and Nicol Williamson. Shows a young actor learning the role. Narrated by Gielgud. Distributed by Films for the Humanities and Sciences. Available for rental from member institutions of the Consortium of College and University Media Centers.

Discovering Hamlet. 53 min., color, 1990. VHS, ¾" U-matic cassette. An exposition of the play, hosted by Patrick Stewart, including a behind-the-scenes look at a production by the Birmingham Repertory Theatre. Distributed by PBS Video.

Hamlet. 242 min., color, 1996. VHS. Directed by Kenneth Branagh. Starring Kenneth Branagh, Kate Winslet, John Gielgud, Jack Lemmon, Julie Christie, Gerard Depardieu, Judy Dench, and others. Distributed by Columbia Tristar Home Video.

Hamlet. 153 min., b/w, 1948. VHS and 16-mm film. With Laurence Olivier, Basil Sydney, Felix Aylmer, Jean Simmons, Stanley Holloway, Peter Cushing, and Christopher Lee. Voice of John Gielgud. Directed by Olivier. Photographed in Denmark. Cut scenes include all of Rosencrantz and Guildenstern. Emphasizes Oedipal implications in the play. Video: see local retailer. Film: Learning Corporation of America. Available for rental from member institutions of the Consortium of College and University Media Centers.

Hamlet. 115 min., color, 1969. Beta, VHS, 16-mm film. With Nicol Williamson. Directed by Tony Richardson. Distributed by Learning Corporation of America. Available for rental from member institutions of the Consortium of College and University Media Centers.

Hamlet. 150 min., color, 1979. Beta, VHS, ¾" U-matic cassette, other formats by special arrangement. Directed by Derek Jacobi. Distributed by Time-Life Video.

Hamlet. 135 min., color, 1990. VHS. With Mel Gibson, Glenn Close, Alan Bates, Paul Scofield, Ian Holm, and Helena Bonham Carter. Directed by Franco Zeffirelli. See local retailer.

Hamlet [recording]. 3 cassettes (210 min.), 1993. Performed by Kenneth Branagh. Distributed by Bantam Audio Publishers.

Hamlet [recording]. 4 cassettes. Dramatization performed by Paul Scofield and Diana Wynyard. Distributed by Caedmon/HarperAudio.

Hamlet [recording]. 1 cassette (60 min.), 1985. Dramatization performed by Michael Redgrave. Living Shakespeare Series. Distributed by Crown Publishers.

Hamlet [recording]. 2 cassettes (120 min.). With John Gielgud and Old Vic Company. Distributed by Durkin Hayes Publishing.

Hamlet [recording]. 1 cassette (51 min.). Performed by Dublin Gate Theatre. Using key scenes and bridges, a complete telling of *Hamlet*. Distributed by Spoken Arts.

Hamlet: The Age of Elizabeth, I. 30 min., color, 1959. Beta, VHS, ¾" U-matic cassette, 16-mm film. An introduction to Elizabethan theater. Distributed by Britannica Films. Available for rental from member institutions of the Consortium of College and University Media Centers.

Hamlet: What Happens in Hamlet, II. 30 min., color and b/w, 1959. Beta, VHS, 3/4" U-matic cassette, 16-mm film. Analyzes the play as a ghost story, a detective story, and a revenge story. Uses scenes from Acts I, III, and V to introduce the principal characters and present the structure of each substory. Distributed by Britannica Films. Available for rental from member institutions of the Consortium of College and University Media Centers.

Hamlet: The Poisoned Kingdom, III. 30 min., color, 1959. Beta, VHS, ¾" U-matic cassette, 16-mm film. Observes that poisoning in the play, both literal and figurative, affects all the characters. Distributed by Britannica Films. Available for rental from member institutions of the Consortium of College and University Media Centers.

Hamlet: The Readiness Is All, IV. 30 min., color, 1959. Beta, VHS, ¾" U-matic cassette, 16-mm film. *Hamlet* is presented as a coming-of-age story. Distributed by Britannica Films. Available for rental from member institutions of the Consortium of College and University Media Centers.

Hamlet: The Trouble with Hamlet. 23 min., color, 1969. 16-mm film. Emphasizes Hamlet's existentialist dilemma. Distributed by the National Broadcasting Company. Available for rental from member institutions of the Consortium of College and University Media Centers.

The Tragedy of Hamlet: Prince of Denmark. 22 min., color, 1988. VHS. Actors depict Shakespeare and his contemporary, Richard Burbage, rehearsing the play. "Shakespeare" gives a line-by-line analysis of scenes from the play along with insight into plot and character. Part of the Shakespeare in Rehearsal Series. Distributed by Coronet/MTI Film & Video. Available for rental from member institutions of the Consortium of College and University Media Centers.

WILLIAM SHAKESPEARE, *The Tempest* (p. 1483)

In *Shakespeare's Last Plays* (Chatto and Windus, 1938), the noted historicist critic E. M. W. Tillyard argues that the later plays pursue the same basic pattern of "prosperity, destruction, and regeneration" that the great tragedies do but bring them to comic endings. Another influential reading is that of the great archetypal critic Northrop Frye, whose views are set forth in an introduction to *The Tempest* published by Penguin Books (1959). More recently, the feminist critic Marilyn French has argued in *Shakespeare's Division of Experience* (New York: Summit, 1981) that it is Prospero's feminine qualities that enable him to forgive his enemies and administer justice.

CONSIDERATIONS FOR CRITICAL THINKING AND WRITING (p. 1542)

1. Whatever sympathy we have for Caliban stems from our knowledge that prior to Prospero and Miranda's arrival on the island he was lord of all he surveyed. From our present historical perspective, it is tempting to compare Prospero's harsh treatment of Caliban with the domination and exploitation of aboriginal peoples in the Americas by sixteenth- and seventeenth-century European explorers. Unlike Ariel, Caliban is unable to accept servitude as a condition of freedom. The question as to whether Caliban is primarily a victim or a villain might lead to a classroom discussion on the differences between how Shakespeare's contemporaries viewed the kind of patriarchal dominance Prospero exercises and how we see such dominance now.

2. Ariel, as his name implies, is a light, airy spirit, while Caliban is gross, earthy, and malformed. The two differ markedly in their attitudes toward their servitude to Prospero. Ariel, who was imprisoned in a tree by Caliban's mother, Sycorax, when he refused to follow her "abhorred commands," was freed by Prospero to be the wizard's assistant. Although the spirit sometimes chafes at his subordinate status, he recognizes that obedience to Prospero is the quickest route to freedom. In return for the prompt execution of his instructions, Prospero promises Ariel his freedom, a promise he makes good at the play's end. Their master-servant relationship is one that is mutually beneficial.

    Caliban, on the other hand, has broken faith with Prospero before the action of the play begins. Prospero claims that he attempted to treat Caliban as an equal and educate him along with Miranda, but that Caliban repaid this trust by attempting to molest her. The spawn of a witch and a devil, Caliban is congenitally incapable of normal, loving relationships based on equality — he must either be completely dominant, as he was before Prospero's arrival on the island, or a slave who is driven by threats and punishments. Even when Caliban tries to break free of Prospero's control, he does so by pledging his allegiance to the drunken servants Stephano and Trinculo, whom he worships as gods. Thus, we see that Caliban can never truly be free, since he is as much a prisoner of his base nature as Ariel was a prisoner of the "cloven pine" in which Sycorax placed him.

3. Miranda is the perfect product of a humanistic education. She is kind, compassionate, and intelligent, but thanks partly to the negative example provided by Caliban, she is not naive. Brought to the island as a small child, she has been educated by her father in laboratory-perfect conditions; prior to the shipwreck of the king and his courtiers, she is unsullied by any contact with the "real" world of imperfect human beings that she and Prospero left behind. This is a world, as we quickly see, of greed and passion — a world in which brother betrays brother for power and wealth. The plot of Sebastian against Alonso, as well as the antics of Stephano and Trinculo, make it clear that human nature has not improved during Prospero and Miranda's absence.

At the same time, Prospero recognizes that while the conditions of Miranda's education might be perfect, they are also sterile. One of the play's principal themes is the reintegration of Miranda into human society, for only by means of such reintegration can she escape the oblivion of a loveless (and sexless) future. Miranda and Ferdinand symbolize the future in the play, a future that holds the promise of renewal of human life, through marriage, without necessarily renewing the foibles and crimes of the preceding generation.

4. Prospero immediately recognizes the mutual attraction between his daughter and Ferdinand, but he pretends hostility toward the young prince and forces him to perform manual labor. His reason for deliberately putting obstacles between the young lovers is that "too light winning / [will] Make the prize light" (I.ii.454–455). He fears that if Ferdinand gets Miranda too easily, he may undervalue her as a wife. Prospero's deliberate obstructionism gives the two young people, especially in Act III, Scene i, a chance to further develop as rounded characters. In this scene, we see further evidence of Miranda's compassionate nature and of Ferdinand's gentleness and virtue.

5. Caliban's attitude toward Miranda is essentially that of a rapist. When Prospero reminds Caliban of how he attempted to "violate / The honor of my child" when Prospero lodged him in his cell, Caliban responds with laughter: "Oho, oho! Would't had been done! / Thou dids't prevent me; I had peopled else / This isle with Calibans" (I.ii.353–355). He sees her as an object to be used for breeding. Later, when he persuades the drunken Stephano to murder Prospero, Caliban uses similar imagery, describing Miranda as one who will "bring thee forth brave brood" (III.ii.98) — "brood" being a term normally associated with sows.

Ferdinand sees Miranda quite differently; in his speech at the beginning of Act III he draws our attention once again to her gentleness and compassion. His desire for her is far loftier than the debased lust of Caliban. Furthermore, he willingly suffers the degrading labor Prospero has put him to because that labor also serves Miranda. In this, he contrasts notably with Caliban, whom we see early in the play performing the same sorts of labor but with great resentment. Ferdinand, however, recognizes that sometimes "poor matters / Point to rich ends" (III.i.3–4).

6. The parallel murder plots underscore the level of corruption in the so-called civilized world that Prospero left behind when he came to the island. Stephano and Trinculo, led by Caliban, plan to kill Prospero and make themselves lords of the island. Their drunken bluster is hard to take seriously; however, their actions act as an antimasque that intensifies the seriousness of Antonio and Sebastian's plans. Antonio, we are aware, has already betrayed a brother, although he stopped short of murder. Sebastian, egged on by Antonio, is prepared to commit even that crime to gain Alonso's kingdom. We doubt that Stephano and Trinculo's plan could ever succeed, since they are so thoroughly inebriated, but the very ineffectualness of their efforts makes us view the courtiers' murder plot more seriously.

7. Different students will undoubtedly have varying perspectives on Prospero's personality. There can be little doubt that historically Shakespeare saw Prospero as a figure who transcends the normal human impulse for revenge in favor of a quasi-Christian philosophy of enlightened forgiveness. Furthermore, most members of Shakespeare's audience would have been of the opinion that while patriarchalism could be taken to unhealthy extremes, patriarchy itself was normative as a social system.

Nevertheless, part of Shakespeare's greatness as an artist lies in his ability to create characters who resist easy categorization. Prospero is a loving father to Miranda and a benevolent dictator of his island kingdom. Still, he is a dictator, and he expects to be obeyed. When Ariel sulks at his servitude, Prospero becomes peremptory and then threatening toward him. He treats Caliban with a harshness that at times seems to cross over into cruelty. Encourage students to debate the justice of Prospero's conduct in each case and his overall effectiveness as the ruler of his island.

Be sure to see also the critical readings by G. Wilson Knight (p. 1555) and Alden T. Vaughn (p. 1556), as well as the comments on these readings in this manual.

8. Gonzalo's ideal commonwealth bears a notable similarity to the commonwealth of Sir Thomas More's *Utopia*: it is a perfect communist society from which all injustice, greed, and violence have been eliminated. Shakespeare undoubtedly had More's work in mind when he wrote this scene. More's Utopia is situated on an island similar to the one on which Alonso and his court are stranded, and there is even a direct allusion to More's work when the dejected Alonso tells Gonzalo, "Thou dost talk nothing to me" (II.i.159), since *utopia* means "nowhere." (In case any of Shakespeare's audience missed the joke, he repeats it several times in the next few lines.)

Sebastian and Antonio's response to Gonzalo's description of his ideal commonwealth is crudely cynical. Sebastian sarcastically observes that while Gonzalo maintains that his commonwealth would have no sovereignty, "Yet he would be king on't" (II.i.146). Much as we dislike these two and admire Gonzalo, we may feel that they have a point. You might ask students whether they feel a utopian society such as the one Gonzalo describes could actually exist.

9. Stephano's remark has several layers of meaning. His first thought on encountering Caliban, who appears to have four legs because Trinculo is hiding under his cloak, is to capture him for personal profit. His giving Caliban wine to drink is therefore a self-interested rather than an altruistic act. In addition, because the drunken Stephano does not realize that Trinculo is hiding under Caliban's cloak, he literally cannot tell who his own friend is. Finally, and most important, Stephano's statement represents a truth about the world of the play, especially the world the king and his courtiers have brought to the island. In the preceding scene, we have seen Sebastian and Antonio plotting to murder Alonso. This is indeed a world in which one cannot tell who one's friends are.

10. Prospero's comparison of life to a play follows the masque that he and Ariel have staged for the newly betrothed Miranda and Ferdinand. Before the masque can conclude, however, Prospero "starts suddenly" (IV.i.138 sd.) because he knows through his magic that Stephano, Trinculo, and Caliban are nearing to carry through their plot to murder him.

The interrupted masque in this scene draws our attention to the many masque-like qualities of *The Tempest*. Masques in Shakespeare's day were highly ornate (and expensive) entertainments usually staged at court. Often, members of the nobility, including King James, played parts. The ostensible purpose of the masque was edification and instruction as well as entertainment. The plots often revolved around a retelling of some popular story from classical mythology, frequently chosen to illustrate the particular virtues of the member of the aristocracy sponsoring the masque. In the interrupted masque of *The Tempest*, Prospero seems bent on presenting a play that will bless the newly engaged young couple's fertility and, perhaps, instruct them in the proper values of married love. In a larger sense, *The Tempest* is a masque, that is, a highly mythic play populated by larger-than-life figures and concerned with inculcating a moral lesson as well as offering entertainment.

The typical masque also often included an "antimasque," a comic scene or scenes that involved grotesque or absurd characters in a parody of the main action. The antimasque interrupted the main action of the court masque; similarly, the clowns' ridiculous murder plot, which parodies the far more serious plot of Sebastian and Antonio against Alonso, interrupts Prospero's masque. Prospero's philosophical comments about the relation between life and illusion suggest that just as the antimasque of Caliban's plot impinges upon the play-within-the-play, death, the great interrupter, will one day "dissolve" all reality. Prospero is aware that while he may foil Caliban's clumsy murder scheme, he cannot escape his own mortality.

11. Shakespeare is somewhat vague about the source of Prospero's magical powers, but we quickly see that he exercises his art for good and derives his knowledge from books rather than through commerce with the devil. Sycorax, on the other hand, was clearly a witch, banished from "Argier" for practicing "mischiefs manifold and sorceries terrible" (I.ii.266–267). Caliban, her son, was "got by the devil himself" (I.ii.323), according to Prospero.

There is also a clear difference between Prospero and Sycorax in the use they make of their magical powers. For Sycorax, the power she gained through sorcery was an end in itself; when Ariel refused to obey her commands, she imprisoned him in a tree, where he remained until Prospero freed him. For Prospero, magic is a means to an end. Specifically, he seeks his reentry and, more important, his daughter's, into society along with a restoration of her hereditary rights. When Prospero's magic has fulfilled its purpose, he willingly "drown[s his] book" (V.i.57) and rejoins normal human society.

12. Caliban's speech in I.ii.334–338 alludes to the difficulties Prospero and Miranda must have encountered when they first arrived on the island and leads us to speculate as to whether they might have perished had Caliban not been there to help them find food and water. In most other parts of the play, however, nature is represented as essentially neutral, neither intrinsically benevolent nor malevolent. The storm symbolizes nature at its most destructive, but we soon learn that Prospero conjured up the tempest for his own purposes. Caliban, who has had no other tutor but nature, is wicked and vicious, but he is the progeny of a witch and a devil. These examples of the "evil" of nature are therefore equivocal.

In most respects, the natural world is presented as morally superior to so-called civilization in *The Tempest*. Caliban grumbles and threatens, but he is too cowardly to try to kill Prospero until he meets up with Stephano and Trinculo and has his courage fortified with the "civilized" invention of wine. Antonio, another representative of civilization, has betrayed his brother Prospero with the acquiescence of Alonso, who is, in turn, about to be betrayed by his brother Sebastian. However, the play does not suggest that civilization is unequivocally corrupt, since the civilized world has also produced the virtuous Gonzalo and Ferdinand.

POSSIBLE CONNECTIONS TO OTHER SELECTIONS

William Shakespeare, *Hamlet, Prince of Denmark* (text p. 1383)

———, *A Midsummer Night's Dream* (text p. 1327)

Sophocles, *Oedipus the King* (text p. 1224)

Tennessee Williams, *The Glass Menagerie* (text p. 1864)

RESOURCES FOR TEACHING

SELECTED BIBLIOGRAPHY

Bamber, Linda. *Comic Women, Tragic Men.* Stanford: Stanford UP, 1982.

Cantor, Paul A. "Prospero's Republic: The Politics of Shakespeare's *The Tempest.*" *Shakespeare as Political Thinker.* Ed. John Alvis and Thomas West. Durham: Carolina Academic Press, 1981. 239–255.

Champion, Larry S. *The Evolution of Shakespeare's Comedy.* Cambridge: Harvard UP, 1970.

Kernan, Alvin B. *The Playwright as Magician.* New Haven: Yale UP, 1979.

AUDIOVISUAL RESOURCES

Prospero's Books. 1992. Directed by Peter Greenaway. With John Gielgud, Erland Josephson, Michael Clark, Tom Bell, and Kenneth Cranham. See local retailer.

The Tempest. 76 min., color, 1963. Beta, VHS, ¾" U-matic cassette. With Maurice Evans, Richard Burton, Roddy McDowall, Lee Remick, and Tom Poston. Directed by George Schaefer. Distributed by Films for the Humanities and Sciences. Available for rental from member institutions of the Consortium of College and University Media Centers.

The Tempest. 150 min., color, 1980. Beta, VHS, ¾" U-matic cassette, other formats by special arrangement. Distributed by Time-Life Video. Available for rental from member institutions of the Consortium of College and University Media Centers.

Tempest. 140 min., color, 1982. Beta, VHS (stereo). With John Cassavetes, Gena Rowlands, Susan Sarandon, Vittorio Gassman, and Raul Julia. Directed by Paul Mazursky. A New York architect abandons city life to live on a barren Greek island with his daughter. See local retailer.

The Tempest. 2 cassettes (126 min.), color, 1983. Beta, VHS, ¾" U-matic cassette. With Efrem Zimbalist, William H. Basset, Ted Sorrel, Kay E. Kuter, Edward Edwards, Nicholas Hammond, and Ron Palillo. Directed by William Woodman. Puts American actors on an artist's re-creation of the Globe Theatre stage. Distributed by Kultur and Britannica Films. Available for rental from member institutions of the Consortium of College and University Media Centers.

The Tempest [recording]. 1 cassette. Dramatization performed by the Folio Theatre Players. Distributed by Spoken Arts.

The Tempest [recording]. 3 cassettes (text included). Dramatization performed by Michael Redgrave and Vanessa Redgrave. Distributed by Caedmon/HarperAudio.

The Tempest: O Brave New World. 23 min., color, 1969. 16-mm film. Explores the problem of evil in the play. Distributed by the National Broadcasting Company. Available for rental from member institutions of the Consortium of College and University Media Centers.

PERSPECTIVES ON SHAKESPEARE

Objections to the Elizabethan Theater by the Mayor of London (p. 1543)

Plays, says the mayor, are a bad influence on idle people and the young, who may be inclined to a variety of "lewd & ungodly practises." They are the cause of diseases of the body, mind, and soul. Examples of similar or related late-twentieth-century opinions are readily discoverable. Complaints about violence or sexual immorality in books, movies and, to a lesser extent, plays are heard with regularity from religious organizations, some feminist groups, and the government. Those in favor of restrictions might argue that art affects our perceptions of the world and, therefore, our actions. Those in favor of unrestricted expression might argue that art forms such as Shakespeare's plays do not incite action because they resolve the emotional tensions they create through a cathartic process.

LISA JARDINE, *On Boy Actors in Female Roles* (p. 1544)

Jardine shakes up the conventional view that though Renaissance plays featured female characters played by young boys, the audiences "saw" a woman if the garb were right. She suggests that, in fact, they saw young boys, and that many polemics of the period railed against the sexual depravity and perversion stirred up by such transvestites. You might want to start discussion by asking students to imagine how they would see one of Shakespeare's heroines differently if *she* were played by a *he* — if Juliet, Miranda, or Ophelia were played by Leonardo di Caprio, for example (in a wig and a dress, of course). Many of Shakespeare's heroines cross-dress within the context of the play itself, and mistaken identity is further confused if the girl dressed up as a boy (and winning female attention as a result) is *actually* a boy.

It's difficult for us to imagine Shakespeare — our canonical Bard — being as controversial as heavy metal and horror movies are today, but Jardine offers ample evidence in *Still Harping on Daughters* that such, in fact, was the case. (Students should also read "Objections to the Elizabethan Theater by the Mayor of London," p. 1543, for another voice of alarm about the evils of the stage.) Have students spend some time brainstorming about potentially threatening or dangerous aspects of *A Midsummer Night's Dream* when it was first performed in what we would call today right-wing England. They will probably take Jardine's cue and start by observing that each of the young lovers would have been played by men or boys, but encourage them to think carefully about the setting, plot, and fantasy characters and try to imagine what warnings the Mayor of London or Dr. John Rainoldes might have offered.

SAMUEL JOHNSON, *On Shakespeare's Characters* (p. 1545)

As an additional writing assignment, you might ask students to consider Claudius in light of Johnson's assessment that in the writing of Shakespeare a character is "commonly a species." Ask students to discuss the attributes of the "species" of Claudius. What in the world of the play suggests that Claudius's treachery is not simply idiosyncratic or confined to one uniquely malevolent figure?

SIGMUND FREUD, *On Repression in* Hamlet (p. 1546)

Ask students to write an essay supporting or refuting Freud's analysis of Hamlet by citing additional evidence from the play.

JAN KOTT, *On Producing* Hamlet (p. 1547)

Because of its variety of themes — military, Christian, sexual, psychological, and so on — the play opens itself to interpretation from all sides, as this perspective indicates. Research into productions will show a wide diversity of treatments.

A reasonable argument for truth to Elizabethan theatrical practices can be found in Harley Granville-Barker's "Preface to *Hamlet*" (see entry on *Hamlet*). The problem with interpretations based too closely on current ideas or events is that they tend to disguise the play behind an apparently "really meaningful" significance.

Discussions should lead to a better understanding of situation, character psychology as expressed in dress, interpretation of character, and a better reading of the play as a whole. Showing a film or videotape production will help get such discussions started.

COPPÉLIA KAHN, *On Cuckoldry in* Hamlet (p. 1548)

Kahn suggests that by examining the frequently ignored issue of cuckoldry in *Hamlet*, readers may be afforded a more insightful glimpse into the complicated relationship between Hamlet and his dead father. You might ask your students to discuss what they believe to be the "conventions of cuckoldry" that Kahn mentions, which she maintains free the wronged husband from any blame whatsoever. Do these conventions still exist in any form today?

Your class might also discuss evidence in the play that supports or contradicts Kahn's idea that cuckoldry influences Hamlet's feelings toward his father. How might Hamlet's feelings toward his mother and father have been different had adultery not played such a crucial role in their situation? Does his status as a cuckold undermine King Hamlet's role in the play? You might ask your students to examine, in class discussion or in a writing assignment, whether the cuckolding of a king makes him a more or a less sympathetic character to the audience. Would this level of sympathy differ between an Elizabethan audience and a modern audience?

RUSSELL JACKSON, *A Film Diary of the Shooting of Kenneth Branagh's* Hamlet (p. 1550)

Jackson's diary records the beginning of rehearsals for Branagh's *Hamlet*, during which the actors and director are working out character motivations and nuances of plot in their interpretation of the play. You might want to watch the play together as a class and then talk about other ways that the plot and characters could be read (Gertrude, for example, has not traditionally been read as the good mother). You may also want to discuss how the text of any play, and this one in particular, changes between reading and performance.

LOUIS ADRIAN MONTROSE, *On Amazonian Mythology in* A Midsummer Night's Dream (p. 1552)

You might begin discussion of Montrose's account of Amazonian mythology in *A Midsummer Night's Dream* by asking students to recount what they already know about the Amazons. In what previous contexts have they encountered this myth, and in what respects does the word *Amazon* have positive or negative connotations? A discussion of these connotations might lead into a class analysis of the relation between the Amazonian myth and Shakespeare's play, considering as well the ways in which an Elizabethan audience might react to the Amazons versus the way a modern audience might.

Montrose maintains that *A Midsummer Night's Dream* explores "different crucial transitions in the male and female life cycles." You might ask your students to examine this notion of "crucial transitions" more closely and discuss if and why these transitional periods are critical to the play.

Montrose also addresses the issue of the possession of women in the play. You might ask your class to consider the implications of this masculine desire to dominate and indeed "own" the feminine. How might reactions today differ from those of Shakespeare's original audiences?

JAMES KINCAID, *On the Value of Comedy in the Face of Tragedy* (p. 1553)

The irreverent tone of Kincaid's remarks mirrors his thesis, which asserts that comedy is superior to tragedy because of its greater expansiveness. Kincaid calls tragedy "unified and coherent, formally balanced and elegantly tight" (paragraph 2). He argues that tragedy is constrained by its rigid structure from presenting the human experience in all its complexity and richness.

When we consider a comedy like *A Midsummer Night's Dream*, Kincaid's assertion that comedy "gives" rather than takes seems accurate. The overall spirit of the play is effectively summed up by Puck's concluding speech, which is governed by a clear eagerness to please. When it comes to tragedy, however, it can be argued that Kincaid's assertions rest on an overly simplistic definition of the genre. His definition of tragedy is fundamentally Aristotelian in its emphasis on a tight, formal structure and absence of distracting subplots. You might ask your students to consider whether Kincaid's argument is equally applicable to Shakespearean tragedy, with its looser observance of the classical unities and wider range of characters and situations. In *Hamlet*, for example, the graveyard scene, while it is usually termed "comic relief," also contributes to one of the play's major themes: how human beings come to terms with their mortality. The humor of the scene is not an intrusion; it forms an integral part of the artistic fabric of the play. It may therefore be claimed that Shakespearean tragedy is inclusive in much the same way that Shakespearean comedy is.

TWO COMPLEMENTARY CRITICAL READINGS

G. WILSON KNIGHT, *Prospero's Civilizing Influence* (p. 1555)

Knight describes Prospero as "Plato's philosopher-king betrayed by Machiavellian policy" (paragraph 2) and asserts that he represents much of what is best in the British character, especially its "blend of unbending integrity and wide catholicity" (3). Knight's assessment will appear more than a little jingoistic to most contemporary readers, as will his claim that one of the overriding accomplishments of British imperialism was "to raise savage peoples . . . to a more enlightened existence" (5). In discussing this passage, students might be invited to consider whether, in light of our current attitudes toward imperialism and colonialism, there is anything defensible in Knight's statements. Is it, for example, possible to separate Knight's clear belief in the moral superiority of British culture from his claim that Prospero resembles those English explorers who, like the Puritans, "follow[ed] their soul-cravings across the sea and there work[ed] out the controlled magic of personal integration" (4)?

ALDEN T. VAUGHAN, *Caliban as a Sociopolitical Symbol* (p. 1556)

In this passage, Vaughan first comments on the tendency of many Shakespeare critics "to signify a social or political position by invoking a familiar Shakespearean phrase or character" (paragraph 1) and then describes how Caliban has been used during the twentieth century as both an "exemplar of imperialist oppressors" and an "emblem of oppressed natives" (3). Vaughan observes that while traditional Shakespeare criticism and scholarship have focused on trying to reconstruct Shakespeare's intentions in creating a character like Caliban, some more recent critics regard Shakespeare's intentions as irrelevant and interpret Caliban in light of present-day cultural and political concerns. The view of Caliban as a victim of imperialist aggression, which has been advanced by some critics, may be contrasted with G. Wilson Knight's view of Prospero as a bearer of "enlightened" values.

ADDITIONAL RESOURCES FOR TEACHING SHAKESPEARE

SELECTED BIBLIOGRAPHY

Barber, C. L. *Shakespeare's Festive Comedy*. Princeton: Princeton UP, 1968.

Bradley, A. C. *Shakespearean Tragedy*. New York: Meridian, 1955.

Dusinberre, Juliet. *Shakespeare and the Nature of Women*. London: Macmillan, 1975.

Frye, Northrup. *On Shakespeare*. New Haven: Yale UP, 1986.

Goddard, Harold C. *The Meaning of Shakespeare*. Chicago: U of Chicago P, 1951.

Kermode, Frank, ed. *Four Centuries of Shakespearean Criticism*. New York: Avon, 1974.

Righter, Anne. *Shakespeare and the Idea of the Play*. Harmondsworth, England: Penguin Ltd. in association with Chatto and Windus, 1967.

Schoenbaum, Samuel. *William Shakespeare: A Documentary Life*. New York: Oxford UP, 1975.

Spivak, Bernard. *Shakespeare and the Allegory of Evil: The History of a Metaphor in Relation to His Major Villains*. New York: Columbia UP, 1958.

AUDIOVISUAL RESOURCES

Behind-the-Scenes Views of Shakespeare: Shakespeare and His Theatre [recording]. 1 cassette (60 min.). Read by Daniel Seltzer. Explores Shakespeare and the characteristics of his works, suggesting how to watch a play. Distributed by National Public Radio.

Behind-the-Scenes Views of Shakespeare: Shakespeare in Our Time [recording]. 1 cassette (60 min.). Read by Maynard Mack, Jr. Discusses Shakespeare from a modern perspective and addresses the issue of to what extent he is and is not our contemporary. Distributed by National Public Radio.

Behind-the-Scenes Views of Shakespeare: Shakespeare the Man [recording]. 1 cassette (60 min.). Portrays Shakespeare as reflected in his work and in the surviving facts and myths about his life. Distributed by National Public Radio.

The Life and Times of William Shakespeare: 1, The Historical Setting. 25 min., color, 1978. VHS. An overview of Elizabethan England. Distributed by the University of Wyoming Audio-Visual Services. Available for rental from member institutions of the Consortium of College and University Media Centers.

The Life and Times of William Shakespeare: 2, English Drama. 20 min., color, 1978. VHS. A history of drama from that of the Greeks to that of Shakespeare's time. Distributed by the University of Wyoming Audio-Visual Services.

The Life and Times of William Shakespeare: 3, Stratford Years. 18 min., color, 1978. VHS. Deals with Shakespeare's early life. Distributed by the University of Wyoming Audio-Visual Services. Available for rental from member institutions of the Consortium of College and University Media Centers.

The Life and Times of William Shakespeare: 4, London Years. 33 min., color, 1978. VHS. A history of the center of the English-speaking world. Distributed by the University of Wyoming Audio-Visual Services. Available for rental from member institutions of the Consortium of College and University Media Centers.

The Life and Times of William Shakespeare: 5, Globe Theatre. 27 min., color, 1978. VHS. A study of the Globe and English theatres. Distributed by the University of

Wyoming Audio-Visual Services. Available for rental from member institutions of the Consortium of College and University Media Centers.

Shakespearean Tragedy. 40 min., color, 1984. Beta, VHS, ¾" U-matic cassette. Focuses on *Hamlet* and *Macbeth*. Distributed by Films for the Humanities and Sciences.

Shakespeare and His Stage. 47 min., color, 1975. VHS, 16-mm film. Provides a montage of Shakespearean background, including scenes from Hamlet and the preparation of various actors for the role. Distributed by Films for the Humanities and Sciences. Available for rental from member institutions of the Consortium of College and University Media Centers.

Shakespeare and His Theatre: The Gentle Shakespeare. 28 min., color. VHS. A history of Shakespeare's life in the theatre and an examination of his work. Distributed by Films for the Humanities and Sciences.

Shakespeare and the Globe. 31 min., color, 1985. VHS. A survey of Shakespeare's life, work, and cultural milieu. Distributed by Films for the Humanities and Sciences. Available for rental from member institutions of the Consortium of College and University Media Centers.

Shakespeare's Heritage. 29 min., color, 1988. 16-mm film. Narrated by Anthony Quayle. Explores the life of the playwright and his hometown of Stratford. Distributed by Britannica Films. Available for rental from member institutions of the Consortium of College and University Media Centers.

Shakespeare's Theater. 13 min., color, 1946. 16-mm film. Re-creates the experience of going to a play at the Globe Theatre in Shakespeare's time. Distributed by Indiana University Instructional Support Services.

Shakespeare's Theater. 28 min., b/w, 1952. 16-mm film. Hosted by Frank Baxter. A discussion of the evolution of Elizabethan theater and the original staging of Shakespeare's plays. Available for rental from member institutions of the Consortium of College and University Media Centers.

Shakespeare's Theater: The Globe Playhouse. 18 min., b/w, 1953. VHS. Provides a model of the Globe Theatre and a discussion of the original staging of some of Shakespeare's plays. Distributed by the University of California Extension Media Center. Available for rental from member institutions of the Consortium of College and University Media Centers.

Shakespeare's World and Shakespeare's London. 29 min., b/w, 1952. 16-mm film. Hosted by Frank Baxter. Re-creates the climate of Renaissance England that allowed Shakespeare's genius to flourish. Distributed by Films, Inc. Available for rental from member institutions of the Consortium of College and University Media Centers.

The Two Traditions. 50 min., color, 1983. VHS. Deals with the problem of overcoming barriers of time and culture to make Shakespeare relevant today. Examples from *Hamlet, Coriolanus, The Merchant of Venice*, and *Othello*. Part of the Playing Shakespeare Series. Distributed by Films for the Humanities and Sciences.

Understanding Shakespeare: His Sources. 20 min., color, 1972. Beta, VHS, ¾" U-matic cassette, 16-mm film, other formats by special arrangement. Examines how Shakespeare's plays grew out of sources available to him, and how he enhanced the material with his own imagination. Distributed by Coronet/MTI Film & Video. Available for rental from member institutions of the Consortium of College and University Media Centers.

32

Modern Drama

The characters and situations in Henrik Ibsen's *A Doll House* (p. 1564) and Anton Chekhov's *The Proposal* (p. 1615) will be accessible to most of your students. The everyday concerns of the characters, the natural dialogue, and the familiar domestic settings that characterize dramatic realism should ensure that students have no trouble following the plots of these plays.

These plays may even seem so accessible that it is easy to forget that the conventions of realism, like those of Greek or Shakespearean drama, are still literary conventions. While we may be more familiar with a picture-frame stage than a Greek amphitheater, we must keep in mind that such settings are used to create the *illusion* of reality and are not actual reflections of reality itself. We are still suspending our disbelief when we pretend we can see through a wall that is really not there, or that the painted background through a window represents an actual outdoor scene. Engage your students in a discussion of the realistic conventions used in *A Doll House* and *The Proposal*. Is there anything in these plays (such as setting, character, or dialogue) that gives the appearance of reality, but that, upon further analysis, proves to be a carefully selected artistic technique — and maybe even *un*real?

A Doll House will undoubtedly give rise to some debate among your students as to Nora's morality in committing forgery and her wisdom in choosing to leave her family in order to discover herself. While most students fault Torvald for his hypocrisy in caring more about the way his wife's actions appear to the public than about her reasons for committing them, some students will nonetheless be uncomfortable with any mother who chooses to leave her children. A close examination of Nora's rationale will help students move beyond their initial "gut" response to her decision and analyze it more objectively. Read Ibsen's own "Notes for *A Doll House*" (p. 1613) as a class to help you frame the inevitable discussion about the role of gender in this play. He writes that "there are two kinds of spiritual law, two kinds of conscience, one in man and another, altogether different, in woman" (p. 1613). Students may intellectually reject this claim, yet intuitively feel its truth with regard to *A Doll House*. What are the moral and legal implications of Ibsen's ideas? It might be useful to introduce your students to the work of feminist sociologist Carol Gilligan, whose book *In a Different Voice* addresses the difference between male and female morality. For more perspectives and suggestions on teaching this play, see Chapter 33, "Critical Case Study: Henrik Ibsen's *A Doll House*" (p. 1627).

The types of misunderstandings that lead up to the crisis in *A Doll House* contribute to the light comedy of Anton Chekhov's *The Proposal*. Although the result of these misunderstandings is far more serious in Ibsen's play than in Chekhov's, the same atmosphere of confusion and missed opportunities pervades in both plays. After reading both works, you might ask students to write about or discuss the effectiveness of misunderstandings as a stage technique. Why has this method of advancing plot been used from Sophocles to Shakespeare to Chekhov?

Both of these plays feature women who are essentially the property of their fathers or husbands. Although *The Proposal* ends in a marriage rather than a marital separation, it is clear that this marriage will be filled with conflict. Ask your students to compare the endings of the two plays in this chapter. Which do they consider more positive? You might apply Chekhov's "On What Artists Do Best" (p. 1625) to the endings of both plays: Do either of them attempt to solve problems or merely to pose them? Encourage a discussion in which students explore the role of drama in identifying and solving society's problems. This discussion can of course be expanded to include almost any other play in the anthology, but will be especially relevant to other modern works such as Lorraine Hansberry's *A Raisin in the Sun* (p. 1730) or Arthur Miller's *Death of a Salesman* (p. 1795).

HENRIK IBSEN, *A Doll House* (p. 1564)

In the final scene of this play, just before Nora walks out on Helmer, he instructs her that she is "before all else . . . a wife and mother." Ever since the play was first performed in 1879, Nora's reply has inspired feminists: "I don't believe in that any more. I believe that, before all else, I'm a human being, no less than you — or anyway, that I ought to try to become one." As a social problem play, *A Doll House* dramatizes Nora's growth from Helmer's little pet and doll to an autonomous adult who refuses to obey rules imposed on her by a male-dominated society (see Ibsen's notes on *A Doll House* [p. 1613] for his comments on "masculine society").

Ibsen, however, preferred to see Nora's decision in a larger context. In a speech before a Norwegian women's rights group that honored him in 1898, he insisted that

> I have been more of a poet and less of a social philosopher than most people have been inclined to think. I am grateful for your toast, but I can't claim the honor of ever having worked consciously for women's rights. I'm not even sure what women's rights are. To me it has seemed a matter of human rights.

Ibsen is being more than simply coy here. He conceives of Nora's problems in broad human terms, not in polemical reformist ones. The play invites both readings, and students should be encouraged to keep each in focus.

TIPS FROM THE FIELD

When I teach *A Doll House*, I have students choose a character from the play. You may find it best to assign a group of three or four students to each of the main characters and have the remaining students assume the roles of the children and the nanny. You might also want one or two students to assume the role of Ibsen. At the following class, I group the students together by role and have them discuss their character. I also have them prepare at least one question directed toward another character about any aspect of the play. The class then comes together in a circle with everyone wearing a name tag of their character. Discussion follows with all students "in character" for the rest of the class meeting.

— CATHERINE RUSCO, *Muskegon Community College*

After they read Ibsen's *A Doll House*, I have my students write an entry in Nora's diary. They may choose to date the entry before, during, or after the action of the play takes place. My students especially enjoy tracing Nora's thought process as she decides whether or not she should abandon her children.

— ELIZABETH KLEINFELD, *Red Rocks Community College*

CONSIDERATIONS FOR CRITICAL THINKING AND WRITING (p. 1612)

1. The title points to the Helmers' unreal domestic arrangement. Nora chooses to stop this game when she realizes that she can no longer play her assigned role.

2. Nora lies about trivial matters, such as the macaroons, and she deceives her husband about the source of the money that helped restore him to health, but these lies are not to be seen as moral lapses because the trivial lies are inconsequential and her deception about the money is selfless. What is significant is that Nora's *life* is a lie because Helmer has no real idea who she is as a human being.

3. Helmer expects Nora to be a submissive helpmate who leaves all the important matters to the man of the house. He treats her more like a child than a wife. His affectionate terms for her are condescending, perhaps even dehumanizing.

4. The confident expectations of security and happiness that Nora has expressed to Mrs. Linde have been miserably deflated by the end of Act I. Nora worries that Helmer will regard her with the same contempt he heaps on Krogstad, and worse, she fears that her husband will judge her to be a destructive influence on their children. The Christmas tree — a symbol of domestic well-being and happiness in Act I — is stripped and ragged at the beginning of Act II, when Nora's world is threatened by both Krogstad's possible betrayal and Helmer's possible harsh judgment. Other symbols include Nora's desperately wild dance, Dr. Rank's fatal illness (the sins of the fathers), and Nora's removal of her masquerade costume as she moves closer to the truth of her circumstances.

5. Although Dr. Rank's characterization has been referred to as unimportant because he is not directly related to advancing the plot, his interest in talking with Nora and understanding her character provides a contrast with Helmer's behavior. Moreover, like Nora, Dr. Rank has been adversely affected by his father's corruption.

6. Krogstad and Mrs. Linde are reunited in what appears to be an honest, lasting relationship just as the Helmers are splitting up.

7. Krogstad's decision not to expose Nora's secret is motivated by his love for Mrs. Linde. Many readers find this abrupt romantic reconstruction of his character unconvincing.

8. Nora rejects Helmer's attempts to start over because she realizes that she's never been truly happy as his "doll-wife." Helmer's character is to some degree sympathetic if only because he is thoroughly bewildered and incapable of understanding the transformation his little "squirrel" has undergone.

9. We don't know what will become of Nora after she leaves her husband. Although she arrives at a mature understanding of herself as an adult woman, that recognition shatters the pattern of her life and forces her to confront her new freedom on her own. Even if we imagine her as fulfilled and happy in the future, her life at the close of the play takes on tragic proportions because she is thrown completely back on herself. A discussion of this topic will help bring students to the heart of the play.

10. This alternate ending is a "barbaric outrage" because it undercuts the seriousness of Nora's plight and the significance of her discovery about her life. Moreover, it represents a calculated sentimentalization of the issues raised in the play.

11. Ibsen proposes no solutions to the problems he depicts concerning Nora's individualism and the repressive social conventions and responsibilities she rejects. If we

imagine the inclusion of solutions, we can also imagine the play turning oppressively didactic. Ibsen knew what he was doing in leaving the solutions to his audience.

12. The play certainly reflects the kinds of problems we might encounter in our everyday lives. The characters look and sound real. Less true to life are Krogstad's transformation from villain to generous lover, the two forgeries, and the fairly obvious use of symbols such as the Christmas tree and Nora's dance.

POSSIBLE CONNECTIONS TO OTHER SELECTIONS

Anton Chekhov, *The Proposal: A Jest in One Act* (text p. 1615)
Susan Glaspell, *Trifles* (text p. 1172)
Gail Godwin, "A Sorrowful Woman" (text p. 33)
William Shakespeare, *Hamlet, Prince of Denmark* (text p. 1383)
——, *A Midsummer Night's Dream* (text p. 1327)
Sophocles, *Antigone* (text p. 1267)
——, *Oedipus the King* (text p. 1224)

RESOURCES FOR TEACHING

A Doll's House. 89 min., b/w, 1959. Beta, VHS, ¾″ U-matic cassette. With Julie Harris, Christopher Plummer, Jason Robards, Hume Cronyn, Eileen Heckart, and Richard Thomas. An original television production. See local retailer.

A Doll's House. 98 min., color, 1973. VHS, 16-mm film. With Jane Fonda, Edward Fox, Trevor Howard, and David Warner. Screenplay by Christopher Hampton. Video: see local retailer. Distributed by Prism Entertainment. Available for rental from member institutions of the Consortium of College and University Media Centers.

A Doll's House. 39 min., color, 1977. Beta, VHS, ¾″ U-matic cassette. With Claire Bloom. Distributed by AIMS Multimedia.

A Doll's House. 96 min., color, 1989. Beta, VHS. With Claire Bloom, Anthony Hopkins, Ralph Richardson, Denholm Elliott, Anna Massey, and Edith Evans. Directed by Patrick Garland. Distributed by Hemdale Home Video.

A Doll's House [recording]. 3 cassettes (180 min.), 1993. Read by Flo Gibson. Distributed by Audio Book Contractors.

A Doll's House [recording]. 3 cassettes. Translated by Christopher Hampton. Dramatization performed by Claire Bloom and Donald Madden. Distributed by Caedmon/HarperAudio.

A Doll's House, Part I. 34 min., color, 1968. Beta, VHS, ¾″ U-matic cassette, 16-mm film. "The Destruction of Illusion." Norris Houghton discusses the subsurface tensions that make up the play. Distributed by Britannica Films. Available for rental from member institutions of the Consortium of College and University Media Centers.

A Doll's House, Part II. 29 min., color, 1968. Beta, VHS, ¾″ U-matic cassette, 16-mm film. "Ibsen's Themes." Norris Houghton examines the cast of characters and the themes in the play. Distributed by Britannica Films. Available for rental from member institutions of the Consortium of College and University Media Centers.

Ibsen's Life and Times, Part I: Youth and Self-Imposed Exile. 28 min., color. VHS. The conflict between individual and society is illustrated in scenes from *Ghosts*, featuring Beatrice Straight as Mrs. Alving. Includes a biographical segment on the playwright. Distributed by Insight Media.

Ibsen's Life and Times, Part II: The Later Years. 24 min., color. VHS. Includes scenes from *The Master Builder* and *Lady from the Sea,* emphasizing the realism in Ibsen's plays. A biographical segment includes on-location footage. Distributed by Insight Media.

PERSPECTIVE

HENRIK IBSEN, *Notes for* A Doll House (p. 1613)

Ibsen seems to suggest here that "masculine society" lives by the letter of the law and will not take into account extenuating circumstances, such as Nora's altruistic reasons for forging her father's signature on the loan. This is a correct assessment of Helmer, but whether it is also an accurate observation of today's society is a subject for debate.

When Nora heads for the door, getting past Helmer is perhaps easy compared with facing the disapproval she will encounter on the other side. The social pressures she will have to endure as a wife and mother who has abandoned her family will be formidable.

ANTON CHEKHOV, *The Proposal: A Jest in One Act* (p. 1615)

Although *The Proposal* is light rather than profound, hilarious rather than probing, it does offer a perspective on human relationships that goes beyond comic observations. As broadly funny as the characters reveal themselves to be, they are also outraged and angry at the possibility of anything — whether property or status — being denied to them. We can agree to laugh at their instinctive covetousness and silliness because the consequences are easily and humorously resolved, but we are also aware that these "landowners" feel more vulnerable than self-possessed about themselves.

CONSIDERATIONS FOR CRITICAL THINKING AND WRITING (p. 1624)

1. The three hundred years of history informing this property dispute cannot be sorted out and resolved based upon the conflicting assertions made by each family. What is important is that each family, with its ancient grievances and competing status, demands recognition from the other, but neither is flexible enough to yield any ground. Hence these arguments escalate to mutual charges of landgrabbing, embezzlement, madness, alcoholism, gambling, sexual immorality, and even physical deformity.

2. Choobukov assumes that Lomov has come to him to ask for money, and he immediately determines that "He's not getting any." This instantaneous response establishes the defensive nature of Choobukov's character and begins the repeated patterns of misunderstanding throughout the play.

3. Lomov's shiverings, palpitations, sharp pains, and insomnia render him a comic figure whose strength is apparent only when he's challenged by Choobukov and Natalyia. The fact that Lomov is presented in so unattractive a light only makes Natalyia's desire to marry him that much more desperate a wish. In the final scene, he does not so much propose marriage as succumb to it.

4. In a sense Lomov's request for Choobukov's daughter's hand in marriage is a means of collecting "the goods" for these landowners. Natalyia represents a form of currency that can be exchanged between them to ensure peace and stability between

their families, and she willingly (if not urgently) allows herself to be offered as a kind of commodity in order to secure marital status.

5. Lomov and Natalyia are both outraged by the possibility of suffering an injustice and are quick to go on the defensive. They engage in a shouting match that devolves to a clipped exchange of "ours" and "mine." When they feel threatened they both respond in a self-protective (and almost self-destructive) manner. Neither character seems capable of understanding and acting in his or her own best interests for very long.

6. Once again Lomov and Natalyia instinctively disagree — because of their pride — over an unimportant matter. Choobukov is drawn into the dispute only to make things worse. The fact that the characters are sidetracked from the real issue of marriage to arguing over bits of property and the reputation of hunting dogs suggests their farcical nature. Indeed, versions of this kind of behavior can be found in contemporary television situation comedies.

7. Choobukov's description can be read both literally and ironically. Given their characters, conflict and argument come naturally to Natalyia and Lomov. That's who they are and so that must be part of their relationship. Moreover, there is the suggestion that all marriages, to one degree or another, are joined in mutual combat. In addition, Choobukov's description is filled with irony, because although conflict may be the central fact of their lives together, there can be little hope that their family will be happy in any conventional sense that includes peace and harmony.

8. The present translator, Elisaveta Fen, chooses *The Proposal* as her title over previous translations as *The Marriage Proposal*. By dropping "marriage" from the title, Fen suggests that the proposal is not only about marriage but also about the economic status and security that marriage meant in nineteenth-century Russia.

POSSIBLE CONNECTIONS TO OTHER SELECTIONS

Henrik Ibsen, *A Doll House* (text p. 1564)
William Shakespeare, *A Midsummer Night's Dream* (text p. 1327)

RESOURCES FOR TEACHING

Anton Chekhov: A Writer's Life. 37 min., b/w, 1974. Beta, VHS, ¾″ U-matic cassette. A biographical portrait of the playwright. Distributed by Films for the Humanities and Sciences. Available for rental from member institutions of the Consortium of College and University Media Centers.

Chekhov [recording]. 12 cassettes (90 min. each), 1989. By Henri Troyat, read by Wolfram Kandinsky. A biography of the writer. Distributed by Books on Tape.

Chekhov: Humanity's Advocate [recording]. 1 cassette (46 min.), 1968. By Ernest J. Simmons. Explores various facets of Chekhov's works and his artistic principals. Classics of Russian Literature Series. Distributed by Audio-Forum.

Chekhov and the Moscow Art Theatre. 13 min., color. Beta, VHS, 16-mm film. Yuri Zavadsky uses the Stanislavsky method in directing scenes from *The Cherry Orchard*. The program is set in the context of the Moscow Art Theatre and the Russian countryside. Distributed by IASTA. Available for rental from member institutions of the Consortium of College and University Media Centers.

PERSPECTIVE

ANTON CHEKHOV, *On What Artists Do Best* (p. 1625)

As a development of Consideration 2, ask students to define the problem Chekhov sets himself in *The Proposal*. What are "the right questions" that he asks — through the characters and the action — in order to achieve his purpose?

33

A Critical Case Study:
Henrik Ibsen's *A Doll House*

This chapter could be ideally taught in conjunction with Chapter 37, "Critical Strategies for Reading." The critical perspectives provided on Ibsen's play offer a sampling of several ways to directly apply the various critical approaches discussed in that chapter. As students respond to these readings, they may be surprised at how varied the critical issues are and how open the possibilities for interpretation.

After reading "A Nineteenth-Century Husband's Letter to His Wife" (p. 1628), you might want to go over Kathy Atner's student essay, "On the Other Side of the Slammed Door in *A Doll House*" (p. 1639). If your class has a writing component, you can use this paper to demonstrate certain aspects of writing that you stress in your class. The paper contains examples of a solid thesis statement, well-chosen and well-handled quotations, logical organization, and other characteristics of good writing. This paper can also be a useful tool for modeling peer revision. Have the students critique this paper as they would one of their classmates', with a specific evaluation of the paper's strengths and weaknesses. This activity will give them an idea of what to look for when they help one another revise their work.

This chapter provides a number of options for paper assignments. You could ask students to respond to the ideas in any of the critical articles. Students can write about the importance of economics or the notion of absences discussed in Barry Witham and John Lutterbie's "A Marxist Approach to *A Doll House*" (p. 1630) and Joan Templeton's "Is *A Doll House* a Feminist Text?" (p. 1635), which cites those who dismiss Ibsen's feminism. Your students may wish to develop their own feminist reading of the play in response to these critics. In addition to these possible paper topics, you might invite your students to write a paper on a different play using one of the critical approaches demonstrated in this chapter and discussed in Chapter 37. Or ask students to research *A Doll House* (or another play), and bring in and write about a critical article that uses one or more of the critical approaches they have studied. Regardless of what students write about, the Questions for Writing (p. 1636) will help them focus their ideas and get started.

Even if you are not using this chapter as a topic for student papers, the readings provide interesting additional perspectives on the play. In addition to reading them as examples of separate critical approaches, these essays can also be read in conjunction with one another to provide even more interpretations. What happens, for example, when students bring together Carol Strongin Tufts's ideas about Nora's narcissism in "A Psychoanalytical Reading of Nora" (p. 1632) and Joan Templeton's thoughts about Ibsen's feminism? Students will probably find that analyzing these and the chapter's other essays together both complicates and complements their theories.

A Nineteenth-Century Husband's Letter to His Wife (p. 1628)

Marcus's attitude toward his wife Ulrike as expressed in this letter may remind your students of Helmer's attitude toward Nora, especially at the point in the play when he first learns from Krogstad's letter how she has deceived him. Both men place the blame entirely on their wives. Marcus writes, "you, alone, carry the guilt of all the misfortune" (paragraph 1). He also refers to his wife's "false ambitions" and her "stubbornness." However, Helmer at least displays some affection for Nora in the play. Although Marcus describes himself in his signature as "unhappy," there is little other evidence of affection in his letter. He is possibly being sensitive to her feelings by letting her know that their children are healthy, but in most respects the letter contains only his personal concerns and his list of ultimatums. Do your students see any differences in the ways the two men treat their wives? What does the reader learn about Marcus from his letter? What does his desire to control all the details of the household say about him? Is it possible to infer anything positive about him, such as a talent for organization and efficiency, from his lists of regulations? Encourage your students to try to read Marcus's letter from a nineteenth-century perspective: why would "many in the world" envy Ulrike if she chose to return to her husband?

BARRY WITHAM AND JOHN LUTTERBIE, *A Marxist Approach to* A Doll House (p. 1630)

Witham and Lutterbie's discussion of economics as a subversive force in human relationships could offer important insights into Nora and Torvald's relationship. You might ask your students to consider, possibly in writing, ways in which their marriage has been shaped by financial concerns. Is economics the prevalent shaping force, or are there other powers that must be considered? You might also ask your class to examine closely the idea that "financial enslavement is symptomatic of other forms of enslavement" (p. 1630). Do your students believe that Witham and Lutterbie exaggerate the importance of the play's economics, or are they correct in diagnosing the source of Nora's difficulties?

Consider also the authors' assertion that "the function of women in this society was . . . artificial" (p. 1631). Can your students find evidence of this in the play? Do they see this subservient female role as a characteristic of past societies, or does it still exist today? In what forms? You might discuss with your class whether Nora's desertion of her family might be considered a victory or a defeat. For whom? In economic terms, what might Nora be facing as an estranged wife?

CAROL STRONGIN TUFTS, *A Psychoanalytic Reading of Nora* (p. 1632)

Tufts uses the American Psychiatric Association's definition of *narcissism* as a framework for presenting her argument about Nora's character. She claims that the application of this definition to Nora will enable readers to see her as multidimensional and complex, rather than as a "totally sympathetic victim turned romantic heroine" (paragraph 2). One could argue that Tufts's reading of Nora and her discussion of the reactions of modern audiences to the play are reductive rather than complex. Do your students see Nora as "totally sympathetic"? Would the play have remained popular for over one hundred years if audiences considered the characters to be as one-dimensional as Tufts claims? Despite her measured phrases, Tufts clearly wants the reader to "diagnose" Nora in terms of her narcissism and to downplay her heroism. Could any other characters in the play be accused of narcissism?

You might also have students consider Tufts's assessment of Ibsen's words at the beginning of this excerpt. Is he really being "sarcastic" about audience response, as she claims, or is he simply recognizing that authors do not have complete control over how their work is interpreted?

JOAN TEMPLETON, *Is* A Doll House *a Feminist Text?* (p. 1635)

Templeton's piece incorporates the tirades of several respected critics who do not feel that *A Doll House* should be referred to as a feminist text. However, Templeton's choice of such strident quotations, as well as her presentation of them and her use of the term *backlash* in the title of the essay from which this piece is excerpted, imply that she thinks the various critics are protesting too much. The first line of the perspective, in which Templeton writes that Ibsen has been "saved from feminism," may well be sarcastic in tone. The quote from R. M. Adams with which the excerpt closes — "Nora has no sex" — is patently absurd. While the critics Templeton cites may have been responding with extreme criticism to extreme feminist claims, is any purpose served by their vehemence? Does it have the effect of encouraging a reader to take a more balanced look at the play?

R. M. Adams's assertion that Nora has no sex is worth further consideration. Certainly Nora must have universal qualities in order for audiences to empathize with her, but how much difference does it make to the play that she is female? How could Ibsen have written a play with this theme about a man? What kind of man would such a character have had to have been? Who might have been controlling him?

34

Experimental Trends in Drama

This chapter contains three short plays or excerpts of plays that demonstrate twentieth-century examples of nonrealistic theater. Have students read the chapter's introduction to get a sense of the different movements in experimental drama. Although much of this theater may seem strange to them, today's college students are essentially modernists: the concepts of the "antihero" and "tragicomedy" will likely be familiar.

If students have read Samuel Beckett's well-known play *Waiting for Godot* (and many of them may have), they know not to expect much in the way of realism from his writings. Still, even *Godot* features social interactions between a number of characters. *Krapp's Last Tape* (p. 1649) features only one individual interacting with voices of his former self recorded on tape over a number of years. Martin Esslin's "On the Theater of the Absurd" (p. 1656) should provide some perspective on this play, as well as some ideas for discussion. Esslin compares theater of the absurd with Greek tragedy and other religious drama, a connection many of your students may find a stretch. In a class discussion, invite them to see how far they can take this comparison.

Krapp's Last Tape is a series of monologues interrupted by commentary by Krapp himself. The two excerpts in this chapter, from Jane Martin's *Rodeo* (p. 1657) and Anna Deavere Smith's *Twilight: Los Angeles, 1992* (p. 1661) also present monologues in unusual ways. The characters differ significantly in all three works, but each author uses monologues to reveal characters and explore an issue or situation. It might be useful to divide your students into three groups and have each group discuss the use of monologues in one work. Ask them what makes this type of drama experimental. Can it be viewed as a reaction against realism? What does the monologue enable a playwright to reveal that a more conventional exposition of the drama does not?

While these plays are not likely to be "difficult" for college readers to understand, they may be perplexing on other levels. Help your students to see that Beckett finds meaning in meaninglessness, that behind Big Eight's rodeo jargon and slang lie some profound insight into corporate culture, and that the fragmentary glimpses of Los Angeles provided by Smith can give us a more complete vision of America's racial battleground.

SAMUEL BECKETT, *Krapp's Last Tape* (p. 1649)

A single character on a stage with a tape recorder does not sound like a very promising dramatic situation, but Beckett manages to evoke the essence of Krapp's life in a brief, concentrated period of time, an essence that Krapp barely articulates or understands. Krapp's surprised, bewildered, and even contemptuous response to his earlier selves on the tapes serves as a dramatic reminder of how we are changed by time and experience. Beckett's Krapp is a comic figure whose serious purpose is to remind us that we are often strangers to ourselves. For a discussion of how this type of theater makes us "aware of man's precarious and mysterious position in the universe" see Martin Esslin, *On the Theater of the Absurd* (p. 1656).

TIP FROM THE FIELD

To help the class appreciate the comedy in *Krapp's Last Tape*, I have students perform the opening pantomime while one student reads the stage directions.

— SR. ANNE DENISE BRENNAN, *College of Mt. St. Vincent*

CONSIDERATIONS FOR CRITICAL THINKING AND WRITING (p. 1655)

1. If the play were set in the present, we might dismiss Krapp as an odd old man too unlike us to reveal anything to us about ourselves. By setting the play on "a late evening in the future," Beckett emphasizes Krapp's role as a representative figure. He is, after all, the only person in the landscape of the play. As Krapp (on tape) muses, "The earth might be uninhabited" (p. 1653). He might be the last person alive. The future setting lends an ominous weight to that speculation.

2. Krapp's present physical condition — his purple nose (ravaged by alcohol), short trousers, baggy pockets, white face — makes him look like a clown or a music-hall tramp. He can hardly hear, see, or walk. Although he is a shabby, ridiculous figure, the tape recordings and his reactions to them provide us with a serious look at his inner life that is both intriguing and puzzling.

3. The recordings serve as Krapp's journal. Each year he records his impressions of important events; these are then reviewed on subsequent birthdays. The tapes give him access to a memory that he appears to have lost and, because of that loss, he frequently seems surprised by his own words, which come from an earlier self he no longer knows or understands.

4. The many pauses show Krapp responding to himself. They range from simple reflections, meditations, regret, and nostalgia to incredulity at his own naiveté.

5–6. The sixty-nine-year-old Krapp regards his thirty-nine-year-old self as a "young whelp" full of "resolutions" and "aspirations" (p. 1651), while the thirty-nine-year-old finds his twenty-eight-year-old self to be callow (p. 1654). The older Krapp is revolted by the pretentiousness of his thirty-nine-year-old revelations about himself; he refuses to listen to them and fast-forwards the tape to a lyrical moment when he had made love in a boat and then renounced love in favor of a "fire" in him. Writing, he believed, would become his life's work. Sadly, he had rejected love and life for the sale of "seventeen copies" (p. 1654) of his work.

7. Krapp sees his life as blank. He was wrong about rejecting love, and he is now paying the price as he faces the rest of his life. Instead of discovering meaning in his recordings, he is confronted with a record of painful errors that have led him to isolation, alienation, and a sense of futility.

8. Krapp is not heroic in any conventional sense, but he does fit the general definition of an antihero who is "bewildered, ineffectual, deluded, and lost" (p. 1646).

9. "Farewell to love" would be an appropriate subtitle for the play because while at thirty-nine Krapp thought he was recording a moment of insight when he rejected love to explore his inner "dark," at sixty-nine, he sees that he recorded the moment when he turned from the possibilities of love and life, which he has now permanently lost.

10. At the end of the play, Krapp is more conscious of his loneliness. This recognition does appear to have changed his present life because instead of behaving clownishly he now sits motionless, staring into space and listening to silence. He has nothing more to say.

POSSIBLE CONNECTIONS TO OTHER SELECTIONS

Robert Frost, *"The Road Not Taken"* (text p. 976)
David Henry Hwang, *M. Butterfly* (text p. 1675)
Arthur Miller, *Death of a Salesman* (text p. 1795)

RESOURCES FOR TEACHING

Krapp's Last Tape [recording]. 1 cassette, 1986. Part of the Sound of Modern Drama series, in which modern playwrights read and discuss their work. Distributed by Spoken Arts.
Samuel Beckett [recording]. 1 cassette. Performed by Cyril Cusack. Distributed by Caedmon/HarperAudio.
Samuel Beckett. 80 min., color, 1989. Beta, VHS, ¾" U-matic cassette. An autobiographical portrait of Beckett's artistic life, presented through his work. Distributed by Films for the Humanities and Sciences.

PERSPECTIVE

MARTIN ESSLIN, *On the Theater of the Absurd* (p. 1656)

The essential difference between the absurdists' assumptions about "ultimate realities" and earlier perspectives is, according to Esslin, that the absurdists posit a world devoid of absolute values, in which there is no common agreement on what is true or false. No doctrines, no myths, no system of values provides ready answers to the disturbing questions the absurdists raise concerning human existence. Because individuals in absurdist dramas can take no comfort in shared values and identities, they are, like Beckett's Krapp, thrown upon their own experiences. Whatever meaning there is in their lives is derived from their own situations. Unlike a Sophocles, Shakespeare, or Ibsen play, in which community expectations represent powerful forces and values, absurdist drama presents "one man's descent into the depths of his personality, his dreams, fantasies, and nightmares" (paragraph 2).

JANE MARTIN, *Rodeo* (p. 1657)

Martin's brief monologue in the voice of Big Eight/Lurlene, a woman whose whole life has been involved in rodeo, hardly seems to be the stuff of engaging drama. However, the author's talent for drawing the audience into the lives of her characters soon makes her a sympathetic, then an empathetic character. By the time she utters her challenge — "[L]ook out, honey! They want to make them a dollar out of what you love. Dress *you* up like Minnie Mouse. Sell your rodeo" (p. 1659) — the audience is more than ready to accept Big Eight as an individual and her plight as something that is a danger to us all.

CONSIDERATIONS FOR CRITICAL THINKING AND WRITING (p. 1659)

1. Martin presents Big Eight to the audience in such a way as to play into audience preconceptions about rodeo people. Consider the stage directions, which place her

among horse equipment, dressed in jeans and a workshirt, drinking beer and listening to "Tanya Tucker . . . or some other female country-western vocalist" (p. 1657). Big Eight's later comments indicate that she probably chews tobacco, and her dialect stamps her as uneducated and crude. Martin allows, even encourages, the audience to prejudge her character, and the character of rodeo, then works to force us to see the other aspects of both the woman and the rodeo that exist beneath the stereotypical trappings. Big Eight turns out to be funny, touching, and wise, though uneducated. Audiences may be surprised to learn of the importance rodeo places on family life, as exemplified by the Tilsons and their five children on the circuit. By the time the audience learns that Big Eight has a real name — Lurlene — it is ready to accept her as a human being and lament the very human problem she exemplifies: that decent and caring people are pushed out of the way in the name of progress and the name of profit.

2. Rodeo is probably the most genuinely American of sports, having had its origin in the American West of the 1880s. Its events — saddle-bronc riding, bareback horse riding, bull riding, calf roping, steer dogging, and barrel racing — developed from skills necessary for cowboys on cattle drives. Rodeo probably began as an end-of-the-roundup celebration and competition. Rodeo has not historically been a "money" sport. Although six-time world champion Larry Mahan earned about $50,000 at the peak of his career, most rodeo participants only earn $15,000 to $20,000 per year, out of which they must pay all their living and traveling expenses. There is a certain lyricism in Big Eight's repeated lament of how the rodeo "used to be." According to Big Eight, the participants were cowboys and, more important, families of cowboys. The audiences were knowledgeable about and appreciative of rodeo skills — they "knew what they were lookin' at" because they "had a horse of their own back home" (p. 1658). As she sums it up at the end of the dialogue, "Rodeo used to be people ridin' horses for the pleasure of people who rode horses" (p. 1659). According to Big Eight, rodeo changed when business people realized they could make money from it: "they figure if ya love it, they can sell it" (p. 1659). But the investors who brought money into rodeo also brought a new set of rules, all meant to make the event marketable. They brought in clowns, costumes, and Astro-Turf. Largely through their efforts, Big Eight says, rodeo has become a group of hired performers playing to a crowd of "disco babies and dee-vorce lawyers."

3. Big Eight's language is full of slang and often crude. It helps to characterize her as tough and close to the earth. The colorful vocabulary she often employs enables the audience to feel the excitement and vitality of her character and her life. To emphasize this point, you might have students rewrite a few of her lines in standard English and compare their rewrites to the liveliness of the original. It is also interesting to note that Big Eight stereotypes businessmen and actors in cigarette commercials in much the same way as the new rodeo owners — and the audience — attempt to stereotype her.

4. Big Eight's sense of humor relies on crudity and exaggeration. Much of her humor is either sexual or scatological, but not mean. Audiences of the play are likely to accept her as funny and likable. She probably expresses a lot of things members of the audience would love to say but wouldn't dare to.

5. As noted in the answer to Question 1, Martin initially presents Big Eight as a stereotype. However, the audience quickly gets to know her as a daughter, a hard worker, a funny woman, and an idealist whose dreams are being shattered. By the time she re-

lates her story of being fired from the rodeo, the audience is ready to at least sympathize with her plight. Her final warning to her audience that the merchandisers will one day try to sell what *they* love serves to underscore the broader implications of her story.

Two further considerations might develop in a discussion of this question. Do any of your students dislike Big Eight by the end of the play? Is it possible, once we realize that she has been fired from the rodeo, to consider this monologue as "sour grapes" on the part of a poor loser? Also, you might encourage your students to discuss other instances in modern life where business interests have entered into areas that are supposedly "off-limits." College basketball is one possible example. Another example is the Whittle Corporation's offer to equip American schools with high-tech video equipment on the condition that they be allowed to broadcast a daily newscast, including commercials, to the classrooms. Is any aspect of modern life "safe" from advertising? Should certain areas be kept free of such influences? Is business's entry into new areas always negative?

6.   The aspect of rodeo that Big Eight mentions the most is the importance of family and community. The play opens with the story she tells about how she received her nickname from her father for staying on a bucking horse. The rodeo is "us" to Big Eight: "We'd jest git us to a bar and tell each other lies about how good we were" (p. 1658). The outsiders who come in and change the rodeo are "they." Significantly, one of the things the businessmen have done is to change the character of the people who participate in the rodeo. At the end of the monologue, we find out that neither Big Eight nor the Tilson family is involved any longer. The rodeo has been transformed from a closely-knit community to a business.

POSSIBLE CONNECTIONS TO OTHER SELECTIONS

Stephen Crane, "The Bride Comes to Yellow Sky" (text p. 249)
Arthur Miller, *Death of a Salesman* (text p. 1795)
William Shakespeare, *Hamlet, Prince of Denmark* (text p. 1383)
———, *A Midsummer Night's Dream* (text p. 1327)
Anna Deavere Smith, From *Twilight: Los Angeles, 1992* (text p. 1661)

ANNA DEAVERE SMITH, *From* Twilight: Los Angeles, 1992 (p. 1661)

Anna Deavere Smith's *Twilight: Los Angeles, 1992*, based on the savage 1991 beating of Rodney King by Los Angeles police officers and the ensuing violence that erupted in the city, has been commended in part because the author manages to provide a sense of unity to the play in spite of its fragmentary nature. You might ask your students to discuss the many themes present in the text, including the central themes of retributive violence, skewed justice, and the search for order in an anarchic world. Smith incorporates a variety of viewpoints in her monologues and clearly does not envision the problems in Los Angeles and elsewhere as simply a black-white issue. Students may benefit from a discussion of why *Twilight* takes on such a multicultural dimension. You might also ask your class if Smith seems to come to any particular conclusions, based on the excerpt found in the text. Can your students find value in this piece even if no concrete conclusions are suggested?

CONSIDERATIONS FOR CRITICAL THINKING AND WRITING (p. 1671)

1.   Smith's arrangement of her interviewees' words on the page transforms what were at one time conversational monologues into poetry. As poetry, these monologues be-

come subject to critical interpretation that could involve the analysis of poetic terminology and conventions. For example, Jason Sanford's story makes use of poetic
devices such as repetition and rhyme, which enhance the effect of his story on the
reader.

2. Michael Zinzun's story may be regarded as a kind of play in miniature, because his
    narrative relates a series of actions that parallel the conventional dramatic form. The
    narrator (the protagonist) first describes the setting (1:00 A.M. in the street during an
    incident of police brutality) and then establishes the conflict between himself and
    the Los Angeles police officers (the antagonist). The climactic moment occurs when
    the police smash Zinzun's face with a flashlight and it "explode[s] the optic nerve to
    the brain, / ya see, / and boom (*he snaps his fingers*) / that [is] it" (p. 1663). At this
    point the narrative of the fight ends and Zinzun explains the resolution (the hospi-
    tal trip, the trial) and the conclusion (he spends the money he was awarded in the
    lawsuit fighting police abuse) of this miniature drama.

3. Jason Sanford's description of his encounters with the Los Angeles police reveals
    that he, described by the author as a "handsome white man" (p. 1663), recognizes
    that he is not treated as brutally by the police as he would have been were he black. In
    spite of the fact that he has had only limited personal experience with African Ameri-
    cans, Sanford understands that because he looks like "an all-American white boy,"
    he is "seen by the police totally different / than a black man" (p. 1665).

4. Michael Zinzun and Julio Menjivar were both innocent members of minority groups
    who became victims of police brutality. Zinzun was beaten, however, because he
    tried to intervene on the part of another black man who was being abused by the po-
    lice; Menjivar was an onlooker who was "only standing there / watching what was /
    happening" (p. 1665) when he was dragged into the fray. At the end of the mono-
    logues, we learn that Zinzun, who was permanently disabled by the police, continues
    to look beyond his personal plight to the unfortunate circumstances of others who
    suffer at the hands of the police. Conversely, Menjivar considers the irony of his own
    personal tragedy: "Now I have a record. / Aha, and a two-hundred-fifty-dollar / fine /
    and probation for / three years" (p. 1667).

5. Mrs. Young-Soon Han's bitterness may derive from her loss of the liquor store as
    well as her frustration with an America that alienates those of Korean ancestry and
    does not recognize their social difficulties. Her mood shifts from deep disillusion-
    ment and despair to anger to a deep sadness and sympathy for other minorities who
    are also suffering. The pauses in the monologue add to the reader's understanding
    of Mrs. Young-Soon Han as a real person; her pauses indicate varying degrees of em-
    phasis or uncertainty that increase her effectiveness as an authentic voice describing
    the Korean American experience.

6. Students might take this question in any number of directions; fruitful topics for
    these dialogues might include the ramifications of recent congressional efforts to re-
    duce spending on programs for the poor, the O. J. Simpson murder trial, and Ameri-
    ca's treatment of illegal immigrants.

POSSIBLE CONNECTIONS TO OTHER SELECTIONS

Lorraine Hansberry, *A Raisin in the Sun* (question #2, following)

Jane Martin, *Rodeo* (question #1, following)

CONNECTIONS QUESTIONS IN TEXT (p. 1671) **WITH ANSWERS**

1. Compare and contrast one of Smith's monologues with the style and content of Jane Martin's *Rodeo* (p. 1657).

    Smith's monologue called "Swallowing the Bitterness," by Mrs. Young-Soon Han, contains some of the same wistful, unpretentious social commentary that character-izes Jane Martin's *Rodeo*. Young-Soon Han is a Korean woman whose liquor store was destroyed in the Los Angeles riots, and this event has clearly altered forever her idealistic vision of America. She begins her monologue by saying "Until last year / I believed America is the best" (p. 1668); the rest of her monologue describes her anger at the injustice that runs unchecked in this country and her longing to be able to be-lieve in the mythical America where everyone is truly equal and protected under the law.

    Martin's monologue begins on a regretful note that is somewhat similar to Mrs. Han's; Big Eight opens the play by saying "Shoot — Rodeo's just goin' to hell in a handbasket" (p. 1657). While there are obvious differences between the violence of the Los Angeles riots and the transformation of the American rodeo, both women are mourning the passing of something very important to them — something that served as a symbol of the country they want so badly to love. These "passings" sug-gest the loss of a time in which they could trust in certain truths, believe in certain standards, depend on the existence of certain things. Now, these women seem to say, the values and the priorities of the modern world no longer match their values and priorities. Racism, commercialization, and greed have led to a world full of sadness, injustice, and malevolence.

2. In an essay discuss the attitudes toward race expressed in Smith's monologues with those expressed in Lorraine Hansberry's *A Raisin in the Sun* (p. 1730).

    Your students may note, in their essays, that Smith's monologues incorporate sev-eral different racial perspectives, while Hansberry's play tackles white/black racism exclusively. Yet this does not make Hansberry's approach to race any simpler; indeed, the attitudes toward race expressed in both pieces are complicated and, in many cases, extremely painful. Smith's monologues address the diverse and divisive nature of racial relations; the voices of the piece belong to a black man, a white man, a His-panic man, and a Korean woman. All of them, to some degree, describe the ways in which they feel distanced from those who do not look like them. The white man, for example, admits his understanding that police treat him in a particular way because he looks like an "all-American white boy" (p. 1664). And the Korean woman asks "Why do we [Koreans] have to be left out [of society]?" (p. 1668). The voices of the black man, the El Salvadoran man, and the Korean woman identify strongly with the victimization of their respective racial groups, while the white man indirectly ac-knowledges their victimization by admitting the preferential treatment, based on race, that he receives. These voices represent, on a microcosmic level, the inability of larger groups of people to communicate with each other and to reach beyond the prejudices, misunderstandings, fears, and stereotypes that racism fosters.

    The attitudes toward race that become evident in Lorraine Hansberry's *A Raisin in the Sun* are equally wrenching, but are somewhat more limited in focus. Hansberry tack-les the issue of race by demonstrating, through the circumstances surrounding the Younger family, both racial pride and racial tensions. Racial pride is bound up most obviously in the character of Asagai, whose influence leads Beneatha to embrace her

African heritage and denounce what Asagai sees as "assimilationist." Under his tute-lage, Beneatha changes her hair, her dress, and even her name to reflect what she en-visions as her true ethnicity. But Asagai, who is significantly an African and not an African American, is not responsible for every moment of racial pride that appears in the play; ultimately the Youngers themselves pull together and rise above the shame that Mr. Lindner, a white resident of Clybourne Park, tries to instill in them. Hans-berry's play also plunges into turbulent racial issues by tackling the problems of seg-regated housing, economic barriers (the wealthy George versus the struggling Youngers), and the dilemma of assimilating into a racist society. Hansberry, like Smith, makes abstract racial problems personal, by allowing the usually silent voices of the victimized and the underprivileged to be heard.

35

Cultural Case Study: David Henry Hwang's *M. Butterfly*

Like the Critical Case Study of Henrik Ibsen's *A Doll House*, the Cultural Case Study for David Henry Hwang's *M. Butterfly* (p. 1675) is an opportunity to study a play in depth. In addition to the play itself, the chapter provides a number of materials that will enable students to understand the play in its cultural and historical context. Even if your class has been focusing primarily on formalist approaches to literature, they have likely practiced some cultural criticism in reading some of the perspectives following other works in this anthology. Introduce your class to the concept of cultural criticism by having them read the chapter introduction, which defines cultural criticism and compares a formalist approach to Susan Glaspell's *Trifles* to a cultural one. Once students have a sense of what cultural criticism is, you could do a brainstorming exercise as a class, generating a list of questions that cultural critics might ask about a work. To get started you might suggest some questions yourself: What major historical events are relevant to the writing and setting of this work? Does the work make reference to any other literary or artistic sources? What kinds of documents (laws, letters, conduct books) define the relationships between the sexes, classes, and races? What does the author's biography tell us about this work? Once you get them started, your students will likely come up with a number of relevant questions of their own. The documents in this chapter will provide answers to many of their questions, as well as help to generate some new ones.

M. Butterfly lends itself well to a cultural critique because it is based on an actual news story, it makes use of another artistic genre, and it is essentially *about* culture, or the clash of cultures — East and West, female and male. Before introducing students to some of the cultural documents, it is important that they have a good understanding of the play itself; the shifts in time and place, and the use of the opera are important elements of the work that might pose some initial difficulty for students. The best way to address any problems students might have with an initial reading is to study the play's formal elements as you have done with other works in this anthology.

"A Plot Synopsis of *Madame Butterfly*" (p. 1722) might be an exception to the above suggestion. Depending on what you want to emphasize, you might wish to have your students read this summary of the opera *before* having them read the play. This knowledge will enable them to follow Gallimard's "description" of the opera and to help them trace the reversals that come at the play's end.

Consider reading "The News Source for *M. Butterfly*" (p. 1723) in conjunction with your analysis of the photograph of Shi Pei Pu (p. 1725). Students will probably know that Hwang's play is based on a true story, but the details of the news story combined with the visual image of Shi will no doubt fascinate them. As you compare the play to the newspaper account, you can generate a discussion about the choices artists make based on the details Hwang selects for emphasis. You might connect this discussion back to the discussion of the opera, asking why Hwang might add this artistic layer to the story.

"A Theater Review of *M. Butterfly*" (p. 1726) and "An Interview with David Henry Hwang" (p. 1727) will give students a sense of the author's intentions regarding his own play and the way that play is received by an audience. Your students probably will not be surprised to note the gaps between the intended effect and the received effect; they may, however, be surprised at the number of common ideas. In general, the play Hwang intended to write is the one Rich experienced. Ask students to find ideas in the review and in the interview with which they agree and disagree. A discussion question following the review asks them to write a review of their own (p. 1727); you might also ask them to write an interview. What questions would *they* ask David Henry Hwang? Based on the play and the other documents, how do they think he would answer their questions?

As a research project, you might have students locate some other documents that would be relevant to a study of *M. Butterfly*. These might include examples of cultural stereotyping between East and West (photos, articles, movies), information about homosexuality in communist China, or additional reviews of the play. As this chapter demonstrates, studying a work from additional cultural perspectives exposes additional layers of understanding.

DAVID HENRY HWANG, *M. Butterfly* (p. 1675)

M. Butterfly opened on Broadway in March 1988 with John Lithgow in the role of Gallimard and B. D. Wong (an actor whose name does not give away his gender) portraying Song Liling. Students may find themselves carried far into the play by the absurdity of the premise, a man in love with a man whom he believes to be a woman, before realizing the seriousness of Hwang's larger themes.

CONSIDERATIONS FOR CRITICAL THINKING AND WRITING (p. 1721)

1. Certainly we are meant to despise Gallimard's arrogance in cultural, sexual, and diplomatic matters; we cheer Song's assessment of his superficiality in Act I, Scene vi. Throughout the play, the audience has reasons to dislike him. Nevertheless, the self-deprecating sense of humor he displays in his speeches to the audience ("I've become a patron saint of the socially inept" [p. 1678]) and the vulnerability so obvious in his dealings with his old friend Marc make us sympathize and perhaps identify with him. Furthermore, he does eventually fall in love with Song and loses everything because of the relationship.

2. Nearly all the characters display at least one kind of prejudice. There is sexism on both sides of the bamboo curtain, as Marc and Song ("only a man knows how a woman is supposed to act" [p. 1707]) demonstrate. Helga is biased against Chinese culture, Chin against homosexuals, to name but a few examples.

3. Gallimard's reactions to Song's letters reveal his motivations at the beginning of their relationship. He will not respond to dignified begging, to the asexual (and therefore more equal) term *friend*, or to anger. Only complete submission and humiliation make him feel powerful enough to return. Gallimard does not want to exercise his power over Song (i.e., by tearing her clothes off); he does, however, want to be sure that he *can*.

4. Both are essentially foils who help to further define Gallimard. There is a point at which Marc and his friend have similar sexual attitudes, but Gallimard shows a greater capacity for growth. For instance, Marc considers Gallimard "crazy" when he feels ashamed of his behavior regarding Song's letters. Marc makes Gallimard seem

much less despicable by comparison; it is Marc, not Gallimard, who finally fits the Pinkerton role.

Helga is slightly more sympathetic. Gallimard admits he married her for ambition, not love; this and his cold announcement that he wants a divorce display a side of him that counterbalances some of his positive qualities. On the other hand, the complete lack of feeling with which Hwang presents Helga helps the audience to comprehend what was missing in Gallimard's life when he became involved with Song.

5. The real "Gallimard" claimed that his meetings with the actor always took place hastily and in the dark, a claim Hwang at least partially reinforces by the way he presents their first meetings and by the fact that Gallimard never sees Song naked. Chin suggests homosexuality as the explanation; the scene between the two toward the end of the play (Act III, Scene ii) gives credence to this interpretation. Song claims Gallimard believed because he wanted so much to believe and because his Western attitude toward the East dictated that "being an Oriental, I [Song] could never be completely a man" (p. 1716). Since this is the last explanation offered, and Gallimard essentially agrees with at least the first part of it, it is possibly the most convincing. However, the question is intended to provoke discussion rather than a definitive answer.

6. Early in the play, Gallimard equates Asian women with centerfold models because both are "women who put their total worth at less than sixty-six cents" (p. 1681). Further, both appeal to his sense of power: the centerfold is a fantasy figure and will perform whatever Gallimard's imagination dictates. This provocative submissiveness is also an important part of Gallimard's fantasy about Asian women.

Later, Gallimard's centerfold reappears as Renee, with whom he has an "extra-extramarital" affair. At this point, he discovers that Renee's total lack of inhibition renders her almost "masculine" to him; nevertheless, he continues to see her to force Song into further submissiveness.

7. By overlapping scenes from present and past, reality and fantasy, and even from two separate plays, Hwang reinforces the interconnectedness of his themes. The play is not merely an attempt to address separate problems — sexism, racism, and imperialism — within the confines of a single work. Hwang's contention is that these attitudes are all part of the same problem: the need to dominate another in order to feel complete — a need that has disastrous consequences.

Hwang has the characters move in and out of the various plays being enacted, with many of them taking on two or three roles and even stepping out of character to relate directly to the audience. This shifting of roles and direct address of the audience constantly remind the audience that it is watching a play; *M. Butterfly* thus becomes a metadrama, a drama about drama, about role-playing, about the illusions we are capable of creating — and believing in.

8. The role reversal begins taking place gradually, before the final scene, once Gallimard falls in love with Song and wants to marry him/her. Prior to that time, Gallimard controls the relationship; afterward, Song assumes more and more power, so the final reversal is a culmination rather than a sudden reversal. Both Gallimard and the audience come to realize the depth of Madame Butterfly's love, a love that has little to do with a stereotypical vision of Oriental submissiveness. This love raises

the play beyond all of its "isms" to a story of love and loss, which finally touches even Song.

9.   The absurd situation upon which the play is based is enough to elicit embarrassed laughter from the outset. Hwang's quotations from the song lyrics of David Bowie and Iggy Pop further augment the light mood. Gallimard portrays himself as a clown in his first speech. Throughout the play, there are hilarious moments — Renee's discussion of Gallimard's "weenie," the revolutionary rhetoric of Chin's meetings with Song, Song's repartee with the trial judge. Nevertheless, the drama's themes and ultimate outcome are tragic. True to tragic form, Gallimard becomes enlightened only when it is too late for him to do anything about it except die. Perhaps the play should be considered a tragicomedy.

10. Despite the many awards *M. Butterfly* has garnered, the play has not received universal acclaim. Some critics have faulted it for the heavy-handed way in which Hwang links Western sexism to the events in Vietnam rather than letting the audience draw its own conclusions. Others claim that Hwang reinforces racial stereotypes: that his use of a Japanese character for a story based in China says that "all Orientals are alike" and that the play as a whole reinforces a "Mata Hari" image of Asian women — beautiful but dangerous. In a writing assignment, you might ask students to respond to these criticisms.

POSSIBLE CONNECTIONS TO OTHER SELECTIONS

Alison Baker, "Better Be Ready 'Bout Half Past Eight" (text p. 617)
Samuel Beckett, *Krapp's Last Tape* (text p. 1649)
Yukio Mishima, "Patriotism" (question #3, following)
William Shakespeare, *Hamlet, Prince of Denmark* (question #2, following)
Sophocles, *Oedipus the King* (question #1, following)
Tennessee Williams, *The Glass Menagerie* (text p. 1864)

CONNECTIONS QUESTIONS IN TEXT (p. 1721) WITH ANSWERS

1.   At first glance Rene Gallimard and Sophocles' Oedipus in *Oedipus the King* (p. 1224) are very different kinds of characters, but how might their situations — particularly their discoveries about themselves — be compared? What significant similarities do you find in these two characters? Explain whether you think Gallimard can be seen as a tragic character.

Both Gallimard and Oedipus fail to perceive crucial information about the world around them, the lack of which results in their entering into love relationships that have disastrous results in both a personal and a political sense. Oedipus kills his father and marries his mother, and the gods punish his society with a plague for his sins. Gallimard's long-term extramarital relationship with Song — who turns out to be a man — includes passing classified intelligence information to a hostile government. Both characters eventually come to disgrace.

Students may find both similarities and differences between the two characters. On the surface, the differences are most obvious: Oedipus is a great man, a hero to his people, a confident and courageous leader, a man wise enough to solve the riddle of the Sphinx. Gallimard, on the other hand, falls into Song's trap largely because he is insecure and only marginally competent in any aspect of his life — "the patron saint of the socially inept," as he puts it. However, the falls of both men stem from their inability to accept the truth about their lives. Blindness is an apt metaphor in both plays. Again, Gallimard seems the more culpable — how could anyone carry on a twenty-year love affair without knowing the gender of his lover? — but is this as blameworthy as Oedipus's stubborn refusal to accept the words of both the oracle and the seer Tiresias?

Your students may disagree as to whether Gallimard should be considered a tragic hero. Perhaps it would help to compare him to a more modern figure of tragedy such as Arthur Miller's Willy Loman, who is flawed but displays a certain kind of greatness, rather than to a classical figure such as Oedipus. Gallimard is despicable in some respects but sympathetic in others. Does anything about him suggest greatness or nobility? After reviewing the characteristics of tragedy discussed on pages 1221–1223 with your students, you might ask them whether or not Gallimard's situation arouses the cathartic feelings of pity and fear. Do we feel somehow connected to Gallimard, despite some of his more despicable qualities? Does his situation suggest that there are things in all our lives that we refuse to face and warn us of the consequences of such blindness?

2. Compare the function of Puccini's *Madame Butterfly* in *M. Butterfly* with that of the play within the play in Shakespeare's *Hamlet* (p. 1383). How are these internal dramatic actions used to comment on the events of each larger play? How is role playing relevant to the theme of each play?

Hwang uses Gallimard's summary of the plot of *Madame Butterfly* to enhance the audience's understanding of the characters of Gallimard and Song; further, the placement of the summary close to the beginning of *M. Butterfly*, and Gallimard's re-creation of Butterfly's end as his own, enables the audience to grasp the connections between sexual, racial, and cultural imperialism, which are central to Hwang's play. In contrast, the play in *Hamlet* is directed primarily at the characters, and although Claudius's reaction is of interest to the audience, it provides them with no new information, since Claudius's treachery has already been exposed.

However, the use of embedded drama in each play serves to call attention to the theme of role playing. The play within a play in *Hamlet* calls attention to Claudius, who has assumed the role of the concerned uncle/father figure when he actually is the murderer. In addition, Hamlet's life comes to depend on his ability to play the role of the madman until he has the opportunity to avenge his father's death. Hwang's use of *Madame Butterfly* serves to emphasize that Song is an actor. By having Gallimard and Marc act out important scenes from the Puccini opera, Hwang draws our attention to the variety of roles that people play in their private lives. With several characters playing more than one role in Hwang's play, the audience is forced to consider the many illusions we create for ourselves — the roles we accept and are forced to play out.

3. Compare and contrast the way women are represented in *M. Butterfly* and in Yukio Mishima's short story "Patriotism" (p. 593).

The chief "female" characters in "Patriotism" and *M. Butterfly*, Reiko and Song Liling, are represented as submissive to the males in all respects. Their actions are controlled by the male characters. Reiko's lieutenant becomes the "sun" in her life; even her suicide is dictated by his actions. The narrator of "Patriotism" tells us that ever since Reiko's marriage, "her husband's existence had been her own existence" (p.

606). In *M. Butterfly*, Song Liling observes, "Only a man knows how a woman is supposed to act" (p. 1707).

However, both the narrator and the lieutenant in "Patriotism" respond to the "woman's" submissiveness with the utmost respect. The lieutenant is filled with admiration by his wife's request to follow his suicide with her own — even though he attributes it to the excellent way in which he has "educated" her. The story projects a deep respect for all those in society — men and women — who understand their respective roles and fulfill them well. In *M. Butterfly*, on the other hand, the submissive role is an act on the part of Song, and both Gallimard and Song regard "Butterfly's" submissiveness disdainfully. Song looks at Gallimard's attitude toward "her" demeanor as merely another example of the West's refusal to consider Asians as equals. Gallimard recognizes the thrill of power he gets from dominating his lover. At one point, he refers to Song as "a vessel to contain my humiliation" (p. 1704).

RESOURCES FOR TEACHING

M. Butterfly [recording]. 2 cassettes (118 min.). Starring John Lithgow and B. D. Wong. Distributed by L.A. Theatre Works.

M. Butterfly. 101 min., color, 1993. Beta, VHS. A film adaptation starring Jeremy Irons. Distributed by Warner Home Video.

HAROLD ROSENTHAL AND JOHN WARRACK, *A Plot Synopsis of* Madame Butterfly (p. 1722)

CONSIDERATIONS FOR CRITICAL THINKING AND WRITING (p. 1723)

1. By comparing his situation to the opera, Gallimard elevates what would otherwise be a rather sordid and bizarre story of sexual and political betrayal to the level of a tragic romance. The opera reinforces and romanticizes the stereotype of the docile, submissive Asian woman, a stereotype in which Gallimard wants desperately to believe in order to reinforce his own masculinity. Ironically, his relationship with Song ends up having the opposite effect, making Gallimard the object of cocktail-party jokes. His suicide ultimately places him in the role of the tragic Butterfly rather than the brash American naval officer with whom he had originally identified.

2. Gallimard's account emphasizes the casual and transient nature of Pinkerton's feelings for Butterfly and the trusting and lasting adoration of his bride. Gallimard stays fairly close to the original plot, but he leaves out the sacrifices Butterfly has made to marry Pinkerton, the renouncement of her religion and family.

3. Certainly Gallimard originally chooses to identify with Pinkerton, comparing himself to men "who are not handsome, nor brave . . . but somehow believe, like Pinkerton, that we deserve a Butterfly" (p. 1681). He fantasizes about having the same kind of power over Song that Pinkerton has over Butterfly. By the end of the play, we realize that it has been Song all along controlling Gallimard for her own purposes. Unwittingly, Gallimard is more like the blindly devoted bride who has lost everything for love than the husband who controls the relationship.

4. As a class, you might listen to parts of the opera that correspond to Gallimard's retelling. How does his version differ in effect from the experience of actually listening to the music? Students who are moved by music or have some musical background

will be especially likely to have a new understanding of why Gallimard was so swept up by the opera and by Song's performance.

RICHARD BERNSTEIN, *The News Source for* M. Butterfly (p. 1723)

CONSIDERATIONS FOR CRITICAL THINKING AND WRITING (p. 1724)

1. Many of the details from the news source appear in Hwang's play. The affair between the two men, the birth of the child, the espionage, and, of course, the Frenchman's ignorance regarding his lover's gender have been retained. Hwang even stays faithful to some smaller details. For example, from reading Bernstein's article, we learn that the case "has been the talk of Paris" (p. 1723), something Gallimard tells us in the play's opening. Despite these connections, Hwang adapts the facts of the case to suit his artistic and political ends. The news article makes no mention of Boursicot's wife, and some of the details and timing of the affair are altered.

2. Without an understanding of the actual event that inspired *M. Butterfly,* students might find the premise so unbelievable that they might have a hard time engaging with the play on its cultural, artistic, or political levels.

3. Students with any knowledge of basic anatomy will undoubtedly find it hard to believe that a person involved in a twenty-year sexual relationship would have no knowledge of his lover's gender. Taken alone, the explanation that Mr. Shi "was shy" is inadequate, but in the context of the Eastern and Western stereotypes and the relations highlighted in *M. Butterfly,* the explanation might make more sense. Clearly Boursicot/Gallimard believed in the "Chinese custom" because it suited his preconceived notions of female Asian sexuality.

Shi Pei Pu in The Story of the Butterfly (p. 1725)

CONSIDERATIONS FOR CRITICAL THINKING AND WRITING (p. 1725)

1. The photograph of a delicate looking Shi elaborately dressed and made up is decidedly androgynous. If students have doubts as to Boursicot/Gallimard's honesty, this picture can help explain how powerful costume and presentation can be when creating an overall effect.

2. The white face, the elaborate Oriental robe and headpiece, and the ambivalent facial expression combine to reinforce Western stereotypes of the exotic and mysterious East. Ironically, while Song manipulates this image of the East successfully, she never hides her disdain for it and for those who accept it. After Song vows never to play Madame Butterfly again, even Gallimard wryly admits that his fantasies about the East are misguided: "So much for protecting her in my big Western arms" (p. 1685), he says.

FRANK RICH, *A Theater Review of* M. Butterfly (p. 1726)

CONSIDERATIONS FOR CRITICAL THINKING AND WRITING (p. 1727)

1. Rich refers to "the clashing and blending" (p. 1726) of culture and gender, major themes of the play that are reflected in the "clashing and blending" of *M. Butterfly*'s structure. The play makes frequent shifts — from the present in Gallimard's jail cell to the early days of Gallimard and Song's relationship, from a retelling of Galli-

mard's own story to a retelling of *Madame Butterfly*. These shifts parallel the many shifts from male to female, from West to East, that the play's characters are trying to negotiate.

2. Hwang compares Gallimard's personal sexism and racism to the larger political conflict between the United States and Vietnam. Yet according to Rich, he does not force this "ideological leap"; instead, Hwang creates a situation in which these culture and gender roles are more universal. Gallimard's attitude toward Asian women, for example, is similar to his attitude toward pornographic photos.

3. In arguing that the play "is overly explicit," students might point to Song's lecturing Gallimard on the political implications of *Madame Butterfly* (I.vi), or his analysis on the witness stand as to why Gallimard was fooled ("You expect Oriental countries to submit to your guns and you expect Oriental women to be submissive to your men" [p. 1716]). Some students will find this didacticism more of a flaw than others will. Ask students to define to what degree an explicit thesis detracts from or adds to their enjoyment of a play.

4. Like Frank Rich's review, students' reviews should address issues of casting, plot, and staging. They might also want to consider the script adaptations necessary to bring this play to the screen.

DAVID SAVRAN, *An Interview with David Henry Hwang* (p. 1727)

CONSIDERATIONS FOR CRITICAL THINKING AND WRITING (p. 1728)

1. Hwang thinks Song should be played by a man because he wants the audience to be as seduced by the character as Gallimard is. To use a female actor, he suggests, would be a deliberate deception on the audience and would also be unfair to the actress in the role. While some students may agree with this perspective, others might argue that Song's appeal to Gallimard would be more convincing if she were played by a woman.

2. As Hwang points out in his interview, it would be ideal if students could read this play for the first time without knowing Song's real gender, but many will already know the story's outcome. This knowledge may make them dismiss Gallimard as a pathetic buffoon, but it may also make him more sympathetic. They will also react differently to Song, seeing ulterior motives behind her protestations of modesty and servility.

3. You might encourage students without much background in the subject to research the Vietnam War and America's attitudes toward it, comparing the language used to justify involvement in the war with statements by Gallimard and Song. Students might also consider the way our culturally constructed mythologies, like the opera *Madame Butterfly*, contribute to our attitudes toward nation, race, and gender. Hwang states that systems of domination are essentially based on economic factors. Remind students to consider the role of economics as they link imperialism, racism, and sexism in their essays.

36

A Collection of Plays

There are a number of ways to make use of this chapter. The Perspectives and the Connections Questions that follow the plays will give you the flexibility to study a few of the works in depth or to move more quickly through the chapter in order to cover more ground.

This chapter groups plays into several categories: The first few plays represent a range of dramatic styles and techniques from the classic modern tragedy, *Death of a Salesman* (p. 1795), to Hansberry's charged *A Raisin in the Sun* (p. 1730). Then, "An Album of World Literature" links plays from two very different countries — Ireland and Nigeria — to demonstrate the types of drama being written worldwide. The final section, "An Album of Contemporary Plays," reveals the scope of current theater from the humorous, to the political, to the absurd, to the realistic. These categories suggest obvious ways of grouping the plays for teaching, but you need not feel bound by them.

You could also organize these works by theme. A unit on the American family in drama, for example, would come together well by selecting from Lorraine Hansberry's *A Raisin in the Sun,* Arthur Miller's *Death of a Salesman,* Tennessee Williams's *The Glass Menagerie* (p. 1864), Wendy Wasserstein's *Tender Offer* (p. 1956), and August Wilson's *The Piano Lesson* (p. 1962). Use the Connections Questions, Possible Connections to Other Selections, and the appendix in this manual, "Suggested Thematic Units for Discussion and Writing," to suggest other ways of grouping these plays.

LORRAINE HANSBERRY, *A Raisin in the Sun* (p. 1730)

Like the characters in Williams's and Miller's plays, the members of the Younger family in Hansberry's play are caught up in their dreams of a better future. However, their situation is complicated by the fact that they are an African American family living in a racist society. At first, a life insurance check seems to promise the answer to their dreams, but as they come to understand that they have conflicting ambitions, they must struggle to find a way to move into the future as a family without sacrificing their individual goals.

POSSIBLE CONNECTIONS TO OTHER SELECTIONS

Langston Hughes, "Harlem" (text p. 1030)

Arthur Miller, *Death of a Salesman* (text p. 1795)

Anna Deavere Smith, From *Twilight: Los Angeles, 1992* (text p. 1661)

Tennessee Williams, *The Glass Menagerie* (text p. 1864)

August Wilson, *The Piano Lesson* (text p. 1962)

RESOURCES FOR TEACHING

A Raisin in the Sun. 128 min., b/w, 1961. Beta, VHS. With Sidney Poitier, Claudia McNeil, and Ruby Dee. Directed by Daniel Petrie. See local retailer. Available for rental from member institutions of the Consortium of College and University Media Centers.

A Raisin in the Sun. 171 min., color, 1989. Beta, VHS. With Danny Glover, Esther Rolle, and Starletta DuPois. Directed by Bill Duke. An "American Playhouse," made-for-television production. See local retailer.

A Raisin in the Sun [recording]. 2 cassettes, 2 hr., 21 min. Dramatization performed by Ossie Davis and Ruby Dee. Distributed by Caedmon/HarperAudio.

Black Theatre Movement from *A Raisin in the Sun* to the Present. 130 min., color, 1979, 16-mm film. Traces the Black Theatre Movement from its roots in Hansberry's play to the current black plays and musicals on Broadway. Includes interviews with performers, writers, and directors, as well as footage from plays and theatre pieces from around the country. Available for rental from member institutions of the Consortium of College and University Media Centers.

Lorraine Hansberry: The Black Experience in the Creation of Drama. 35 min., color, 1975. Beta, VHS, ¾″ U-matic cassette. With Sidney Poitier, Ruby Dee, and Al Freeman, Jr. Narrated by Claudia McNeil. A profile of the playwright's life and work. Distributed by Films for the Humanities and Sciences.

Lorraine Hansberry Speaks Out: Art and the Black Revolution [recording]. 1 cassette. By Lorraine Hansberry, edited by Robert Nemiroff. Distributed by Caedmon/HarperAudio.

To Be Young, Gifted, and Black. 90 min., color, 1981. Beta, VHS, ½″ open reel (EIAJ), ¾″ U-matic cassette, 16-mm film. With Ruby Dee, Al Freeman, Jr., Claudia McNeil, Barbara Barrie, Lauren Jones, Roy Scheider, and Blythe Danner. A play about the life of Lorraine Hansberry. Distributed by Monterey Home Video. Available for rental from member institutions of the Consortium of College and University Media Centers.

ARTHUR MILLER, *Death of a Salesman* (p. 1795)

Willy Loman's intentions are the best; he wants what the "American Dream" of success promises: in addition to security, comfort, and possessions, he longs for love and respect. Unfortunately, he is all too willing to sacrifice the highest human values to achieve his dreams. He is a salesman who, ironically, sells himself; he fails to realize that he loses much more than he can possibly gain by lying, cheating, or stealing. His aspirations reflect everyone's longings, but his dream falls far short of the kind of idealism associated with his father's hard work and perseverance. He mistakes brand names for true values and in doing so earns the name of "Lo[w] man."

POSSIBLE CONNECTIONS TO OTHER SELECTIONS

Samuel Beckett, *Krapp's Last Tape* (text p. 1649)

Lorraine Hansberry, *A Raisin in the Sun* (text p. 1730)

Tato Laviera, "AmeRícan" (text p. 918)

Jane Martin, *Rodeo* (text p. 1657)

William Shakespeare, *Hamlet, Prince of Denmark* (text p. 1383)

Wole Soyinka, *The Strong Breed* (text p. 1919)

Tennessee Williams, *The Glass Menagerie* (text p. 1864)

August Wilson, *The Piano Lesson* (text p. 1962)

RESOURCES FOR TEACHING

Arthur Miller. 25 min., color, 1982. Beta, VHS, ¾″ U-matic cassette. Explores themes in the works of Arthur Miller. Distributed by Films, Inc., Video.

Death of a Salesman [recording]. 2 cassettes, 2 hr., 16 min. Dramatization performed by Lee J. Cobb and Mildred Dunnock. Distributed by Caedmon/HarperAudio.

Death of a Salesman. 135 min., color, 1985. Beta, VHS. With Dustin Hoffman, John Malkovich, Charles Durning, and Stephen Lang. Directed by Volker Schlondorff. A made-for-TV adaptation of the play. Distributed by Orion Home Video, Facets Multimedia, Warner Home Video.

Private Conversations on the Set of *Death of a Salesman*. 82 min., color, 1985. Beta, VHS. With Arthur Miller, Dustin Hoffman, Volker Schlondorff, and John Malkovich. This PBS documentary presents heated discussions between actor, director, and playwright. Various interpretations of the play emerge and viewers gain insight into how each part contributed to the final production. See local retailer.

ARTHUR MILLER, *Tragedy and the Common Man* (p. 1860)

Miller argues here that our modern scientific understanding of human behavior makes tragedy less accessible to us because we tend to approach behavior from a clinical or sociological perspective rather than as an individual's "total compulsion to evaluate himself justly" (paragraph 5). This, coupled with the apparent "paucity of heroes among us," (1) seems to limit the possibilities for tragedy.

Unlike Aristotle, who argued that the tragic hero must be an extraordinary person, Miller makes a case for the "common man." Such a person knows "the underlying fear of being displaced, the disaster inherent in being torn away from our chosen image of what and who we are in this world" (10).

The final paragraphs of the excerpt make a distinction between pathos and tragedy. Unlike a tragic character, a pathetic one is to be pitied because he could not possibly have won against superior forces. A tragic figure is someone who might have succeeded but did not.

ARTHUR MILLER, *On Biff and Willy Loman* (p. 1863)

As a development of Miller's remarks, ask students to comment on why the self-realization of Biff is not a weightier counterbalance to Willy's disaster. Does this "flaw" compromise the play as tragedy? If not, why not?

TENNESSEE WILLIAMS, *The Glass Menagerie* (p. 1864)

Williams depicts a fragile world founded on illusions. Amanda, Laura, Tom, and Jim indulge their own illusions, but so does the world at large as it rushes toward the devastation of total war. Instead of sensing danger, society steeps itself in drink, dance, music, movies, sex, and anything else that pushes reality aside. This tendency characterizes the general tenor of things both inside and outside the family. The play dramatizes a family and a culture that are trapped in its dreams of self-fulfillment.

TIPS FROM THE FIELD

With any selection, I find it useful to elicit discussion by posing a specific interpretive problem. For example, when teaching *The Glass Menagerie* I ask students why Tennessee Williams ends the play with Laura blowing out the candles. Once directed to something so specific, students tend to examine the text carefully as they try to answer the question. Because it is also interpretive, an answer that "works" leads them to a deeper understanding of the selection.

— ROBERT M. ST. JOHN, *DePaul University*

After my students read *The Glass Menagerie,* I have them read E. E. Cummings's poem "somewhere I have never traveled, gladly beyond." In class, we analyze the images of power and frailty in the poem. This serves as an excellent prelude to a discussion of the themes of the play. I then ask students to consider why Williams chose to precede his play with the line from Cummings's poem.

— THOMAS S. EDWARDS, *Westbrook College*

POSSIBLE CONNECTIONS TO OTHER SELECTIONS

Lorraine Hansberry, *A Raisin in the Sun* (text p. 1730)

David Henry Hwang, *M. Butterfly* (text p. 1675)

Arthur Miller, *Death of a Salesman* (text p. 1795)

William Shakespeare, *The Tempest* (text p. 1483)

Sophocles, *Antigone* (text p. 1267)

——, *Oedipus the King* (text p. 1224)

August Wilson, *The Piano Lesson* (text p. 1962)

RESOURCES FOR TEACHING

The Glass Menagerie. 134 min., color, 1987. Beta, VHS. With Joanne Woodward, Karen Allen, John Malkovich, and James Naughton. Directed by Paul Newman. See local retailer.

The Glass Menagerie [recording]. 2 cassettes. 1 hour, 49 min., unabridged. Dramatization performed by Montgomery Clift and Julie Harris. Distributed by Caedmon/HarperAudio.

The Glass Menagerie [recording]. Read by Tennessee Williams. Includes "The Yellow Bird" (short story) and poems. Distributed by the American Audio Prose Library.

In the Country of Tennessee Williams. 30 min., color, 1977. Beta, VHS, ½" reel, ¾" U-matic cassette, 2" Quad. A one-act play about how Williams developed as a writer. Distributed by the New York State Education Department.

Tennessee Williams Reads *The Glass Menagerie* and Others [recording]. 1 cassette. 45 min. Complete selections. Read by Tennessee Williams. Includes *The Glass Menagerie* (opening monologue and closing scene), "Cried the Fox," "The Eyes," "The Summer Belvedere," "Some Poems Meant for Music: Little Horse," "Which Is My Little Boy," "Little One," "Gold-Tooth Blues," "Kitchen-Door Blues," "Heavenly Grass," and "The Yellow Bird." Distributed by Caedmon/HarperAudio.

TENNESSEE WILLIAMS, *Production Notes to* The Glass Menagerie (p. 1908)

Williams's assertion that the "theater of realistic conventions" is "exhausted" is overstated, at least insofar as audiences are concerned. The perennial popularity of realistic plays indicates that although many gifted playwrights are impatient with realistic conventions, audiences find them entertaining and rewarding. Indeed, the decision to drop the screen owing to the "extraordinary power of Miss Taylor's performance" (paragraph 3) suggests that an effective actress speaking Williams's dialogue does not require such a device. The nostalgia, fragility, and radiance that Williams seeks to evoke with the music and lighting are a useful summary of the play's tone.

TENNESSEE WILLIAMS, *On Theme* (p. 1910)

Williams makes a distinction between "the story I was trying to tell" and the themes that critics try to pinpoint in his work. The multitude of questions his work elicits, even though he claims he is never intentionally obscure, argues for the complexity of his art as well as for the complexity of life as he depicts it. His comments also indicate that the story, rather than the "lesson" about life the story is meant to convey, comes first with him. You might ask your students to consider other writers they have encountered in this anthology. Do any writers state their themes in a more clear-cut way than Williams does? Do any of them seem especially vague or difficult to pin down?

AN ALBUM OF WORLD LITERATURE

The plays in this album exhibit many of the characteristics discussed in the prefaces to the world albums of fiction and poetry. Like Yukio Mishima's short story "Patriotism" (p. 593), *The Strong Breed* depicts the customs of a culture that will be foreign to most students. The universality of the scapegoat theme in Soyinka's play may offer students a way of connecting their own concerns to those of the playwright.

Soyinka's exploration of a tribal society in need of coming to terms with the modern world echoes the concerns of several of the world poets whose countries are saddled with poor leaders and face instability and revolution. Soyinka's own poem "Future Plans" (p. 1145) bitterly satirizes those government figures for whom lies and corruption are a way of life.

BRIAN FRIEL, *From* Molly Sweeney (p. 1911)

Students may have a hard time thinking of *Molly Sweeney* as a play. Through a series of monologues by the three characters — Molly, her husband Frank, and her doctor, Mr. Rice — Brian Friel unfolds his drama about a blind Irish woman who opts for surgery to regain her sight. There are few stage directions and there is no interaction between the characters. We learn the story by hearing it retold from three different perspectives, not by witnessing the actual events ourselves. A discussion of this play can lead to some interesting conclusions about point of view. Consider, for example, the way that Molly's troubled response to being able to see is depicted in this excerpt from Act Two. Frank suggests a shadow on the joyous moment when Molly can first identify colors by telling us that "her expression was open and joyous. But as I said good night I had a feeling she wasn't as joyous as she looked." Later, Molly struggles to describe her reaction: "I tried to explain to Frank once how — I suppose how *terrifying* it all was." And Mr. Rice clinically observes, after the operation on her second eye, that "she could now see from a medical point of view. From a psychological point of view she was still blind. In other words she now had to learn to see." It is clear from this excerpt that part of Molly does not want to see, despite the fact that everyone around her is celebrating her restored sight. By juxtaposing these different accounts through monologue, Friel manages to present a complex, tangled story about Molly, Frank, and Mr. Rice. There is no single "truth," but only differing perspectives on what the truth might be.

Though the physical setting on the stage is spare, the larger setting of Ireland plays an indirect but important role. You may wish to discuss how Irish identity, a depressed economy, and political turmoil might shape the characters of marginal people like the Sweeneys and Dr. Rice.

POSSIBLE CONNECTIONS TO OTHER SELECTIONS

Samuel Beckett, *Krapp's Last Tape* (question #1, following)
Susan Glaspell, *Trifles* (text p. 1172)

David Henry Hwang, *M. Butterfly* (text p. 1675)
Jane Martin, *Rodeo* (question #3, following)
Anna Deavere Smith, From *Twilight: Los Angeles, 1992* (text p. 1661)
Sophocles, *Oedipus the King* (question #2, following)

Connections Questions in Text (p. 1918) with Answers

1. Discuss the themes of *Molly Sweeney* and Samuel Beckett's *Krapp's Last Tape* (p. 1649). What kind of recognition or understanding do the protagonists have at the end of each play?

    In both plays, the title characters learn an important lesson about themselves too late. Neither Krapp nor Molly realize it at the time, but each rejects happiness and peace of mind in favor of the vague promise of future betterment. It takes thirty years, but listening to tapes of his old self leads Krapp to conclude that he was a fool to reject love for writing. Similarly, in agreeing to have her sight restored, Molly discards her comfortable life for a confusing one in which none of her senses can be relied upon. Molly's blindness had never been a handicap for her. Her other senses, combined with her sharp intelligence, had enabled her to enjoy a full life surrounded by friends, work, and recreation.

    By the end of both plays, Krapp and Molly are resigned to their situations; Krapp's claim that he "wouldn't want [his best years] back" (p. 1655) contains a note of regret that is absent from Molly's final lines: "[I]t seems to be all right. And why should I question any of it anymore?" (p. 1911). Still, any consolation we might take from her assurance is undercut by the fact that Molly will probably spend the rest of her life alone in a rest home, unable to distinguish fantasy from reality.

2. Discuss the significance of blindness in *Molly Sweeney* and in Sophocles' *Oedipus the King* (p. 1224). How is blindness used for symbolic purposes in each play?

    In both of these plays, as well as numerous other works of literature, sight and blindness are powerful symbols for the human capacity to understand and to fail (sometimes willfully) to understand. In the case of Oedipus and Molly Sweeney, their experiences with blindness and sight leave them both between vision and blindness, both metaphorical and literal.

    "What good were eyes to me? / Nothing I could see could bring me joy" (p. 1260), laments Oedipus after he destroys his eyes. These words could apply to Molly Sweeney's experience with vision as well. Although Oedipus was literally sighted, he was metaphorically blind, unable to "see" the truth about his own past and his own life. Once he sees this truth, the idea of literal sight is unbearable to him and he blinds himself. Molly Sweeney's case is the reverse. As the play opens, she is literally blind, but metaphorically she sees clearly. Once Dr. Rice restores her literal vision to her, she loses her ability to attach meaning to what she sees. By the end of the play, she is unsure whether she sees anything at all.

3. In an essay, compare Brian Friel's techniques for revealing characters in *Molly Sweeney* with Jane Martin's in *Rodeo* (p. 1657). What important similarities do you find in the playwrights' use of monologues?

    Before asking them to write a direct comparison between *Molly Sweeney* and *Rodeo*, you might invite your students to freewrite about the monologue as a dramatic convention. Unlike a soliloquy, which usually represents the inner thoughts of a character, a monologue is a speech intended for listeners. A close study of the speech patterns in a monologue can reveal the speaker's character in surprising ways. In *Rodeo*, Big Eight may reveal her lack of formal education by her ungrammatical sentences and frequent use of slang, but she also reveals her enthusiasm and sincerity in the frequent exclamations that punctuate her stories — "Shoot . . . Heck! . . . Ha! . . . I ain't lyin' " (p. 1658). In contrast, Mr. Rice's elevated language in *Molly Sweeney* reveals him to be a highly educated, if slightly pretentious, character. You could expand this assignment by asking them to examine monologues from other plays. Anna Deavere Smith's *Twilight: Los Angeles, 1992* and David Henry Hwang's *M. Butterfly* contain thought-provoking examples.

WOLE SOYINKA, *The Strong Breed* (p. 1919)

Soyinka learned his stagecraft firsthand. After attending University College in Ibadan, Nigeria, for two years, he graduated with honors in 1957 from Leeds University in England. He taught school and became a script reader for Royal Court Theatre in London, learning the mechanics of play direction and stage production. During this period, he also participated in a writers' group and acted in dramatic improvisations. Success came quickly: Soyinka's first three plays — *The Swamp Dwellers* (1958), *The Invention* (1959), and *The Lion and the Jewel* (1959) — were all produced in London, and *The Swamp Dwellers* and *The Lion and the Jewel* were both staged in Ibadan to enthusiastic response.

After studying African traditional drama on a Rockefeller Foundation grant, Soyinka became a lecturer in English at the University of Ife in 1962, only to resign the next year in protest against the imprisonment of Chief Awolowo, a western Nigerian tribal leader. For the next two years, Soyinka devoted himself to various forms of social protest and to the development of a Nigerian theater. His writing during this time reflected even more deeply the influence of the traditional dramatic form of Yoruba tribal ritual, especially harvest festivals.

Soyinka returned to academic life as senior lecturer at the University of Lagos in 1965. In August 1967, just before becoming chair of the Drama Department at the University of Ibadan, he was arrested on suspicion of supporting Biafran rebels. He spent the next twenty-six months in prison, fifteen of them in solitary confinement. His autobiographical *The Man Died* (1972) records much of this experience.

Soyinka's most important Western influences include Samuel Beckett and Bertolt Brecht (he based his comedy *Opera Wonyosi* [1977] on Brecht's *Three Penny Opera*), but even his most satiric or absurdist work expresses some affirmation of traditional values, albeit sometimes in terms of the bitter cost of their disintegration.

Soyinka's plays include *A Dance of the Forests* (1960), *The Trials of Brother Jero* (1961), *Kongi's Harvest* (1965), *Madmen and Specialists* (1970), and *Death and the King's Horseman* (1976).

When *The Strong Breed* opened in New York, Wole Soyinka was in prison in Nigeria for aiding Biafran leaders in the civil war against the Nigerian government. Soyinka said at the time that he was trying to arrange a cease-fire between the warring factions. In Eman, Soyinka creates a central character whose life is sacrificed in the attempt to negotiate a balance between tribal customs and the larger world.

POSSIBLE CONNECTIONS TO OTHER SELECTIONS

Arthur Miller, *Death of a Salesman* (question #2, following)

Sophocles, *Oedipus the King* (question #1, following)
August Wilson, *The Piano Lesson* (text p. 1962)

CONNECTIONS QUESTIONS IN TEXT (p. 1942) WITH ANSWERS

1. Compare and contrast Eman's role as a scapegoat with that of Oedipus in Sophocles' *Oedipus the King* (p. 1224).

    Both Eman and Oedipus serve as scapegoat figures for their respective communities. Eman dies in a ritual that is meant to purge the village of all its sins but in this case probably purges the village of the need to continue the barbaric custom in the future. Oedipus offers himself as a scapegoat in order to rescue Thebes from the plague that has descended upon it. Nevertheless, there are many differences in the two scapegoat figures and in the way they carry out the rituals of atonement. Eman is a stranger in the village, while Oedipus is the king of Thebes; even though Oedipus at first believes he is a stranger from another land, it turns out he is not only a native, but the rightful heir to the throne. The village rite in which Eman becomes involved is a yearly custom of a primitive society; the village "sins" being atoned for have very little to do with the scapegoat figure. On the other hand, the situation in Thebes is a specific disaster for which Oedipus is responsible. Without knowing it, he has killed the king his father and married his mother. When he realizes this, he blinds himself and has himself led into exile. Eman is also a willing sacrificial victim, although he offers himself in the place of the idiot Ifada, whom the village leaders have chosen as the victim. He is hunted through the village and killed by a trap set in the forest, whereas Oedipus does not actually die in the play. Both sacrifices, though in different and complex ways, have the effect of revitalizing the communities for which the scapegoat figures sacrifice themselves.

2. How does the use of flashbacks provide essential information about the two protagonists in *The Strong Breed* and in Miller's *Death of a Salesman* (p. 1795)?

    In both cases, the playwrights use flashbacks to provide the audience with details about the characters' pasts that are essential to a full understanding of how they have come to their present situations. In the case of Eman, we see his most recent memory first — his last encounter with his father before his father's final scapegoat rite and Eman's departure from his village. The next two flashbacks take us back farther, to his encounter with Omae in the midst of his puberty rite, and to her funeral after she has died bearing his son. Each scene makes the audience more aware of Eman's nobility, his compassion, his courage, and the pain he bears.

    Willy's flashbacks begin with the most distant and move forward in time. The audience becomes progressively more aware of how he has put his hopes on Biff's becoming a famous athlete, how he has encouraged Biff to believe he can be successful merely by being and not by doing, and how he has never looked at himself or his family realistically. The final episode from the past reveals the crucial encounter between Willy and Biff and "The Woman" in Willy's Boston hotel room, an encounter that destroys Biff's image of his father and, for years, destroys Biff himself. While the flashback episodes in both plays enable us to perceive the main characters more clearly, we tend to see Eman more positively and Willy more negatively because of them.

3. Read the discussion of mythological criticism (p. 2037) in Chapter 37, "Critical Strategies for Reading." Explain what you think a mythological critic would have to say about *The Strong Breed*.

The most important mythological aspect of the play involves Eman as the "dying god" who is sacrificed for the good of the community. The discussions of the scapegoat in Connections Question 1, and in James Gibb's Perspective (p. 1942), constitute mythic interpretations of the play. In the largest sense, *The Strong Breed* enacts a death/resurrection myth; the tribe's killing of Eman is the low point of the play, occurring close to midnight on the last night of the old year. Yet sacrificing a victim who is not a stranger to them leads the villagers to break with custom and refuse to lay their curses on him. This ensures a new life for the villagers, a movement onto a higher plane where, perhaps, the sacrificial purging of guilt can be accomplished by remembering rather than dismembering.

One mythic pattern not discussed directly in any of these interpretations is that of reconciliation with the father, an event that usually takes place at some point during a heroic quest. Eman's heritage as a member of the "strong breed" is to be a scapegoat figure for his own tribe. His final departure from his village ends with estrangement from his father, because he will not be there to take his place in the annual ritual. By becoming a scapegoat, Eman is reunited with his father, a point that is made clear by means of his final vision, when he follows his father into the forest and to his death.

RESOURCE FOR TEACHING

Wole Soyinka. 50 min., color, 1985. VHS. ¾" U-matic cassette. An interview with the playwright, who discusses political and cultural life in Africa and the United States and what it means to be an artist. Distributed by The Roland Collection.

PERSPECTIVE

JAMES GIBB, *Ritual Sacrifice in* The Strong Breed (p. 1942)

You might discuss with your students the ways in which *The Strong Breed* is and is not "a passion play"; that is, how is Eman's situation similar to and different from Christ's? One interesting fact about Eman is that, unlike Christ, he is *not* put to death by his own people. He has also had a deeply affecting love relationship with a woman. Do these considerations affect our understanding of him as a sacrificial victim in any way?

Christ and Obatala are not the only scapegoat figures you might mention. In *The Golden Bough,* Sir James George Frazer asserts that scapegoat rituals were very common in primitive societies. Frazer, however, distinguishes between animal scapegoats, human but "expendable" persons used as scapegoats, and godlike scapegoats. What kind of scapegoat is Eman? Can your students suggest other literary or historical figures who might be considered scapegoats — Oedipus, King Lear, or Gandhi, for instance? Are there "scapegoats" in contemporary society (i.e., people who sacrifice themselves for the good of the community)?

AN ALBUM OF CONTEMPORARY PLAYS

WILLIAM SEEBRING, *The Original Last Wish Baby* (p. 1944)

Satirizing "a nation known for its thirst of spectacle" (p. 1948), William Seebring's *The Original Last Wish Baby* should resonate with students on a number of levels. Like many other contemporary dramas, this play eschews any semblance of realism by creating a series of ludicrous characters and situations. Yet the issues invoked by Seebring are ones that most students will recognize. Using irony and humor, Seebring creates an implausible situation, a live baby born without a heart, to demonstrate the opportunism prevalent in American culture. The hospital executive and his assistant focus exclusively on the liability and profit that the "miracle" baby represents. Even the baby's mother is complicitous in manipulating sentiment for commercial reward. The play contains a number of comical scenes, as when the baby's "heart was delivered separately by a surprised New Jersey woman on her way home" (p. 1945). Yet Seebring also addresses serious issues such as abortion and euthanasia with the play's "Right to Extended Life" movement.

POSSIBLE CONNECTIONS TO OTHER SELECTIONS

Samuel Beckett, *Krapp's Last Tape* (text p. 1649)
T. Coraghessan Boyle, "Carnal Knowledge" (question #3, following)
Anna Deavere Smith, *Twilight: Los Angeles, 1992* (question #2, following)

CONNECTIONS QUESTIONS IN TEXT (p. 1955) WITH ANSWERS

2. Discuss the implicit social commentary in *The Original Last Wish Baby* and in Anna Deavere Smith's *Twilight: Los Angeles, 1992* (p. 1661).

    Both plays portray a divided, culturally bankrupt America. By juxtaposing voices from different races and social classes, Smith reveals a pattern of police brutality and societal racism. In a more satiric mode, Seebring's vast cast of characters reveals a pattern of individuals using their economic power and shrill ideologies to further their own interests. Although neither Smith nor Seebring provide any solutions or draw any conclusions, both expose tears in America's social fabric through carefully chosen episodes.

3. Write an essay comparing the satire in *The Original Last Wish Baby* with the satire in T. Coraghessan Boyle's "Carnal Knowledge" (p. 276). Which satire do you find more effective? Explain why.

    Both writers aim their satire at radical special-interest groups. Boyle spots the inconsistencies and absurdities of animal rights activists through the earnest but self-righteous Alena, while Seebring points out the fanatical lengths to which the abortion and euthanasia debates have been driven. As they begin to write this essay, students should focus on the difference between the genres of fiction and drama and on the effect that that difference has on point of view. In *The Original Last Wish Baby,* we are equally attached to (or detached from) the play's characters, all of whom represent stock "types" drawn from today's culture. The satire works because the audience can stand outside the play's action and judge the characters and situations objectively. In "Carnal Knowledge," the first-person narrator, someone who "never really thought much about meat" (p. 276), is more like most of us. As a result, we share his wry perspective on the story's events. Your students' conclusion that one is "more effective" than the other may be dependent on whether they prefer a detached perspective or a more involved one.

WENDY WASSERSTEIN, *Tender Offer* (p. 1956)

In a brief, one-act play, Wendy Wasserstein reveals the complex emotions of love, anger, and confusion in the relationship between a busy father and his nine-year-old daughter. Ask students to note Wasserstein's careful use of language, specifically the language of business and finance, as they read this play. Paul tells Lisa she doesn't "want to go about [her] business," which is exactly the point; she's not interested in business and wishes her father were less interested as well. Though his business isolates him from his daughter, it is ultimately the language of business that enables him to communicate with her honestly for the first time. By asking Lisa to "put a bid on the table" (p. 1959) and by offering to "make a tender offer" (p. 1960), Paul breaks down the barrier between them. In this context, the cold language of business has another, more "tender" side. Students will probably have strong opinions about this short piece. Are they sympathetic to the father? Do they feel that Lisa is being unfair? You might also ask them to consider the play's absent mother. What are her roles and responsibilities in the family?

POSSIBLE CONNECTIONS TO OTHER SELECTIONS

Jane Martin, *Rodeo* (question #2, following)
Arthur Miller, *Death of a Salesman* (text p. 1795)

CONNECTION QUESTION IN TEXT (p. 1961) WITH ANSWER

2. *Tender Offer* and Jane Martin's *Rodeo* (p. 1657) are extremely brief dramatic works that present conflicts in which business serves as an antagonist. Write an essay on the nature of the conflicts in each play and how business is the source of those conflicts.

   In both plays "business" is an abstract antagonist without a human face, in sharp contrast to the very real characters who are confronting its forces. Suggest that students list the similarities and differences regarding the two plays' attitudes toward business in order to generate ideas for their papers. In both cases business interferes with spontaneity and family. Even though Big Eight's monologue does not directly address her relationship with her own family, she tells us that before the rodeo was run by big business it "used to be a family thing" (p. 1658).

AUGUST WILSON, *The Piano Lesson* (p. 1962)

In spite of its setting in the 1930s, August Wilson's *The Piano Lesson* offers important insights into the struggle of black Americans, even today, in terms of financial gain and social acceptance. The pivotal conflict between Berniece and her brother Boy Willie essentially involves a choice between loyalty to the past and faith in the future; the characters are divided on this issue, and your students may be as well. You might use this play to discuss elements of superstition and magical realism with your class; Boy Willie's climactic battle with Sutter's ghost brings together aspects of the physical and the spiritual selves that fuel this intricate story.

POSSIBLE CONNECTIONS TO OTHER SELECTIONS

Ralph Ellison, "Battle Royal" (question #3, following)
Lorraine Hansberry, *A Raisin in the Sun* (question #2, following)
Arthur Miller, *Death of a Salesman* (text p. 1795)
Wole Soyinka, *The Strong Breed* (question #1, following)
Tennessee Williams, *The Glass Menagerie* (text p. 1864)

CONNECTIONS QUESTIONS IN TEXT (p. 2017) WITH ANSWERS

1. Discuss the significance of custom and the past in *The Piano Lesson* and Wole Soyinka's *The Strong Breed* (p. 1919).

In both *The Piano Lesson* and *The Strong Breed*, past and custom are virtually inseparable from present daily life. In Wilson's play, the characters' actions in the present are often directly dictated by their relationships with the past. For example, Berniece's fierce determination to keep the piano out of her brother's hands reveals the extent to which her past experiences influence her present decisions. On another level, the pervasive presence of the blues in *The Piano Lesson* signifies the entire history of black oppression in America. The characters sing the blues as both a mourning and a celebration of the past; the melancholy lyrics reveal both suffering and the ability to endure. On still another level, the significance of the past is revealed through the regular appearance of ghosts. At one point Avery, the preacher, is called upon to exorcise the house of the spirits of the dead. Yet chants and prayers do not replace the need for the characters to face their collective past, and it is only when Berniece finally plays the piano that the ghosts of their past are quieted.

In Soyinka's *The Strong Breed*, the past and custom also play a critical role. The fact that much of the story is told in the form of flashbacks reveals the importance of facing the past in order to understand the present. Furthermore, Soyinka's story of a tribal society coming to terms with the modern world suggests the many difficulties inherent in trying to reconcile the past with the present. For example, the villagers still sacrifice Eman as a scapegoat, but they break their custom of cursing the sacrificial victim because Eman is not a stranger to them. This implies an important change in the perspective of the tribal community; while they remained true to their ritual, they altered their customs to suit their particular present-day circumstances. Thus, Soyinka may be suggesting that while customs and rituals provide certain cultural foundations, these customs may be transformed in order to meet the needs of life in the present.

2.   In an essay, discuss the importance of African heritage in *The Piano Lesson* and Lorraine Hansberry's *A Raisin in the Sun* (p. 1730).

Your students' essays might explore more thoroughly some of the following points. The world of Wilson's *The Piano Lesson* is strongly connected to issues of heritage. The piano itself is perhaps the primary symbol of this connection between the present and the past, but it is not the only aspect of the characters' battle to understand their history. Part of the friction between Berniece and Boy Willie can be attributed to their conflicting beliefs about what their ancestors would have wanted them to do. Berniece believes in treating the piano as a sacred memorial to the past; Boy Willie believes that using the piano to acquire his own land and secure his future is a more appropriate way to honor the dead. Doaker and Wining Boy also represent, to some extent, the different ways that one's heritage (in this case, one's slave heritage) can be recognized. And the powerful presence of Sutter's ghost in the play reminds all the characters of the need to reckon with the past and to respect the dead before embracing one's own future.

In Hansberry's *A Raisin in the Sun,* the character of Asagai, Beneatha's African boyfriend, becomes a symbol of the African heritage that the Youngers share but that only Beneatha, an impressionable college student, openly embraces. Asagai teaches Beneatha to respect her African background and to distrust the "assimilationist" tendencies of African Americans. Beneatha's family, especially Walter, find Asagai's foreignness alienating and strange. But even Walter, at the beginning of Act II, gets "into the act" and adopts, for a drunken moment, the persona of an African warrior. The recognition and celebration of African heritage in *A Raisin in the Sun* represents both racial pride and a return to almost a state of grace, in which there is no segregation, no racism, and no black pain caused by white privilege. Hansberry presents the celebration of African heritage not as a solution to the racial problems that exist in America, but as a means to instill a certain measure of racial pride that is integral for African Americans if solutions to racism in America are to be found.

3. How might the narrator's experience in Ralph Ellison's "Battle Royal" (p. 223) be used to shed light on the conflicts in *The Piano Lesson*?

One important way that the narrator's experience in "Battle Royal" can be used to illuminate *The Piano Lesson* is by examining the conflicting loyalties that the narrator experiences, and the ways that one's loyalties influence one's identity. His grandfather's dying words haunt the boy like a ghost, yet he does not fully understand their implications. In spite of this lack of complete understanding, however, the narrator's identity as a successful student who is recognized by the white community does make him somewhat uneasy. During the "battle royal," this sense of unease becomes genuinely painful as the narrator attempts to reconcile his loyalty to his education and his promising future with his loyalty to his race and his own sense of personal dignity. During the course of the evening, the narrator passes between two sets of radically different social expectations. He transforms, in an instant, from "nigger" fighter entertaining the drunk white audience to boy scholar, recipient of a scholarship that will help him to serve "his people" in appropriate ways in the future. His discomfort in adapting to both of these roles to please the white people becomes evident in his dream, in which he realizes that his accommodation of both roles only adds to his overall sense of powerlessness.

The Piano Lesson also examines issues of loyalty and the reasons behind people's decisions to adhere to certain sets of social expectations. Wining Boy, for example, regrets that he sacrificed his own identity to adapt to the persona of the "piano player." And both Boy Willie and Berniece struggle to justify their conflicting loyalties to the past. These loyalties help to define their present identities, their relationships with others, and their visions of their futures. Berniece demonstrates one level of these conflicting loyalties in her reluctance to marry Avery because she does not want to betray Crawley, Maretha's dead father. Boy Willie, on the other hand, thinks that marrying Avery would not be a betrayal of the past, any more than selling the piano would be. Thus Wilson's characters demonstrate that reckoning with one's past and defining one's loyalties (symbolized at the end of the play by the struggle with Sutter's ghost) are a critical part of defining one's identity.

RESOURCE FOR TEACHING

August Wilson: Writing the Blues. 30 min., color, 1988. VHS, ¾" U-matic cassette. In an interview with Bill Moyers, Wilson discusses the importance of the blues in his life and writing. Focuses on his 1984 play *Ma Rainey's Black Bottom*. Distributed by Films for the Humanities and Sciences.

37

Critical Strategies for Reading

Although there is an emphasis on critical strategies for reading throughout the fifth edition of *The Bedford Introduction to Literature*, this chapter brings into focus an increasing tendency in introductory literature classes to make students aware of critical approaches to literature used by contemporary theorists. The treatment of the eleven major approaches discussed in this chapter — formalist, biographical, psychological, historical (including Marxist, new historicist, and cultural criticism), gender (including feminist and gay and lesbian criticism), mythological, reader-response, and deconstructionist — is designed to supplement the more general Questions for Responsive Reading and Writing that are provided in each genre section (for fiction, see p. 41; poetry, p. 711; drama, p. 1211). These critical strategies range from long-standing traditional approaches, such as those practiced by biographical and historical critics, to more recent and controversial perspectives represented, for example, by feminist and deconstructionist critics.

By introducing students to competing critical strategies, you can help them to understand that there are varying strategies for talking about literary works. A familiarity with some of the basic assumptions of these strategies and with the types of questions raised by particular ways of reading will aid students in keeping their bearing during class discussions as well as in the deep water of the secondary readings they're likely to encounter for their writing assignments. After studying this chapter, students should have a firmer sense that there can be many valid and interesting readings of the same work. Their recognition should open up some of the interpretive possibilities offered by any given text while simultaneously encouraging students to feel more confident about how their own reading raises particular kinds of questions and leads them into the text. In short, this chapter can empower students to think through their own critical interpretations in relation to a number of critical contexts.

This chapter can be assigned at any point during the course. Some instructors may find it useful to assign the chapter at the start of the course so that students are aware of the range of critical approaches from the beginning. Many students are likely to raise more informed and sophisticated questions about texts as a result of having been exposed to these critical strategies. Instructors who wish to introduce this chapter early in the course may want to take a look at the appendix in this manual entitled "Perspectives by Critical Strategies for Reading," which organizes the perspectives throughout the book by the critical strategy they most exemplify. Other instructors may prefer to lead up to the critical perspectives and assign the chapter later in the course as a means of pulling together the elements of literature taken up during the preceding weeks. When you do assign the chapter, however, remind students to first read Kate Chopin's "The Story of an Hour" (p. 10), since each of the critical approaches is applied to that particular work as well as to other texts.

The purpose of this chapter is not to transform students into Annette Kolodnys or Northrup Fryes (although the chapter's Selected Bibliography might serve to introduce those critics to students); instead, the purpose is to suggest how texts can be variously interpreted by looking through different critical lenses. Despite the intimidating fact that literary criticism is an enormous and complex field, it can be usefully introduced as part of the intellectual landscape to even beginning students.

The Perspectives provide a small sampling of some of the issues that can be raised about the critical strategies discussed in the chapter. Sontag's objections to interpreting texts (p. 2048) should strike a familiar chord (if for different reasons) among students who are more comfortable leaving works of art "alone" rather than interpreting them. But Sontag's claim that interpretation makes art "manageable" and "comfortable" can be challenged by having students read Fetterley's feminist treatment of "A Rose for Emily" (p. 2048), a reading that's worth connecting to the ideological commitments articulated by Kolodny, who demands that criticism reject "intellectual neutrality" (p. 2050).

The Perspective by Thomas (p. 2053) offers a politically sensitive reading of "Ode on a Grecian Urn" as a "social text" that suggests how a new historicist approach to a work enriches our understanding of both the past and the present. The final four perspectives, by Rabinowitz (p. 2055), Hawkins (p. 2058), Dickstein (p. 2060), and Steiner (p. 2061) invite students to join in the current debates over the canon and the purpose of literary studies.

PERSPECTIVES ON CRITICAL READING

SUSAN SONTAG, *Against Interpretation* (p. 2048)

Sontag argues against interpretation on the grounds that any interpretation reduces the multiple facets of a work of art to a single meaning. Like Wordsworth — who wrote, "Sweet is the lore which Nature brings; / Our meddling intellect / Misshapes the beauteous forms of things: We murder to dissect" — Sontag uses a Romantic argument. The most important dimensions of art are grasped best by feeling, not thinking — through "energy and sensual capability," as she puts it. Further, she claims that the attraction of an intellectual approach to art is the feeling of control such an approach provides. You might divide your class according to whether or not they agree with Sontag and have them debate the question of whether interpretation opens up or closes off a piece of literature, using one of the critical essays in this book as a basis for the debate.

JUDITH FETTERLEY, *A Feminist Reading of "A Rose for Emily"* (p. 2048)

Fetterley effectively compares two tableaus to convince her readers that "A Rose for Emily" is "the story of how to murder your gentleman caller and get away with it" (paragraph 1) and "a story of the patriarchy" (1). The first tableau, depicting Emily and her father, reveals his oppression of her; the second tableau, in which the men of the town break into Emily's upstairs bedroom, indicates her response to the oppression, her counteroppression. Relying on such concrete examples, and supporting them with articulate, specific defense of her feminist theories, Fetterley makes it difficult for an audience to discount her reading. Encourage students to discover other examples that support Fetterley's reading, or encourage them to rely on the specifics of the text in discounting her argument. Are Fetterley's assertions about oppression and Emily's response to it solely gender-based? Could this argument prevail even if stripped of its specifically feminist ideology?

ANNETTE KOLODNY, *On the Commitments of Feminist Criticism* (p. 2050)

Kolodny argues that the implication of sociological approaches to literature is that critics who take such consciously ideological approaches should extend their concerns beyond literature into society. She opposes an "ivory-tower" approach to literature — one that restricts the exploration of ideas to the classroom. Certain critics have argued that the outlook on literature and life that Kolodny and other feminist critics propose is an ideology specifically constructed to push political aims into the classroom. Feminist critics have responded to such attacks by noting that all approaches to literature are informed by a particular critic's ideology. For example, the critic who chooses to ignore the sexual stereotyping of women in literature is making a political choice. You might encourage your students to discuss situations in which they have been aware of an instructor's ideological approach. How did such an awareness affect their response to the course?

ANDREW P. DEBICKI, *New Criticism and Deconstructionism: Two Attitudes in Teaching Poetry* (p. 2050)

Encourage students to define in their own language each of the strategies discussed by Debicki in this perspective. A somewhat simplistic interpretation of the New Critical strategy would be that it involves a search for meaning through unity of content and form, a recognition of the whole as a collection of complementary parts. A deconstructionist reading, however, arises from a recognition of the disunity of a work: a dissonance between content and form, for example, or the confusion caused by an apparently inappropriate metaphor or tone. Once students have achieved some understanding of each of these approaches, ask them to apply the approaches to another poem from the anthology. For instance, Roethke's "My Papa's Waltz" (p. 871) might provide an appropriate example for such an exercise. Students might benefit from writing both a New Critical and a deconstructionist interpretation of a work; they might also acquire more confidence in their abilities to exercise such approaches by doing group work. For instance, a class might reasonably divide into New Critics and deconstructionists to discuss a poem.

BROOK THOMAS, *A New Historical Approach to Keats's "Ode on a Grecian Urn"* (p. 2053)

Thomas's essay describes three historical approaches to "Ode on a Grecian Urn." In each case, he suggests that contemplating the poem, and the urn, has particular implications for present-day readers that either differ from or completely contradict attitudes of the time when Keats wrote the poem. His first consideration is the attitude the poem projects about the relation between art and the past. Keats, he says, suggests that art "both keeps alive a sense of beauty in a world of change and gives us a sense of the felt life of the past" (paragraph 3). However, this conflicts with our modern sense of history, which is that time is irrevocable and that history is a record of specific people and events, not a generic "felt life." In looking at the poem in a second way, students might consider the political conditions in Keats's time that encouraged the British to consider themselves heirs to the great civilization of Greece and to experience nostalgia for a simpler, more pastoral past. Thomas expects that this consideration will spur students on to contemplate how contemporary attitudes toward history are shaped by present events. Finally, Thomas suggests that looking at the urn as an historical object leads to a consideration of the rise of art museums in Europe and the manner in which ancient countries were plundered for their art in order to stock these museums. This raises issues concerning the "political consequences of our cultural heritage" (6). In each case, he contends that the ultimate value of a historical look at the "Grecian Urn" is to encourage students to consider their own views of history and how these views were formed. As he puts it, art itself is a "social text."

You might ask students to compare Thomas's approach with Annette Kolodny's (p. 2050). Both critics seek to place art in a social context. How do your students respond to such a project? What is lost, and what is gained, by looking at a piece of literature as a "social text"?

PETER RABINOWITZ, *On Close Readings* (p. 2055)

You might begin discussion of this passage by asking your students to describe what they believe to be "canonical" literature, and why. Rabinowitz argues that artificial distortions of texts by readers contribute to the definition of the literary canon. Your students might discuss whether they believe Rabinowitz's claims to be an important threat to literary studies. You might encourage students to consider possible examples of texts that have become highly popular or highly controversial as a result of mirroring the *reader's* expectations or desires and not the external world. Examples might include incidents of book-banning for perceived racist or sexist material or best-sellers that reflect idealized fantasies. You might also ask your students to articulate the differences they perceive in "real reading" and "reading for class." What differentiates these two kinds of reading? Why do some people consider reading for class less "real" than "real reading"? Invite your students to debate Rabinowitz's ideas about a more "pluralistic" approach to literature. Do they believe that close reading should be eclipsed by reading techniques that encompass more "personal and cultural situations"?

HARRIET HAWKINS, *Should We Study* King Kong *or* King Lear? (p. 2058)

Students may enjoy debating the merits of the "classics" versus the value of "popular" cultural artifacts (you can direct them to Chapter 1, which includes an excerpt from a Harlequin romance and a short story by Gail Godwin, in order to provide them with a focus for such a debate). Students might compare books they feel have been "beaten into the ground" by their teachers with such "popular" texts as comic books, television programs, and rock lyrics. In addition, encourage students to compare the contents of college literature anthologies as a means of ascertaining where the editors of such books "stand" on the subject of the canon. What works are anthologized most frequently? What "new" works seem to be creeping into college texts? What conclusions can be drawn from the way in which bookstores and student unions display and categorize their books? What cultural and economic assumptions seem evident from such displays? Finally, students might construct their own syllabus for a college English class.

MORRIS DICKSTEIN, *On the Social Responsibility of the Critic* (p. 2060)

Students may be quick to cite examples of the ways in which electronic media such as television, film, video games, and computer software (especially the Internet and other computerized information sources) have eclipsed the printed word. Indeed, it can be argued that these forms of electronic media have substantially weakened the potential influence of written texts. You might ask your class to discuss how Dickstein attempts to reinvest "ordinary reading" with the power that he believes is being stolen not only by new technology, but also, and more important, by literary critics themselves. Encourage your students to consider carefully what Dickstein envisions as the moral responsibility of the critic. Does his description of critics as possessors of "a public trust" ignore any aspects of the literary critic's role? Interesting perspectives might arise from an in-class debate, a writing assignment, or a class discussion focused on your students' understanding of the role of literary criticism and literary critics.

WENDY STEINER, *On the Critics' Readership* (p. 2061)

In this passage, Wendy Steiner raises several academic issues of audience, style, and atmosphere that have doubtless occurred — in one form or another — to your students. You may want to begin a discussion about Steiner's essay by asking students which aspects of the argument they find most salient: That academic writing is losing or has lost its audience? That past academics have alienated their audience? What does Steiner's take seem to be? What should be done? In any case, it may be productive to relate Steiner's experience to that of your students writing papers for their classes — a relatively small leap of thought. To whom do they write when assigned a paper in, say, a literature class? A general audience? The teacher who assigned the paper? Do they feel torn? If so, how is their writing affected?

RESOURCES FOR TEACHING

SELECTED BIBLIOGRAPHY ON THE TEACHING OF LITERATURE

Adler, Mortimer J., and Charles Van Doren. *How to Read a Book.* New York: Simon, 1972.

Bunge, Nancy L. *Finding the Words: Conversations with Writers Who Teach.* Athens: Ohio UP, 1985.

Guerin, Wilfred L., et al. *A Handbook of Critical Approaches to Literature.* New York: Harper, 1979.

Koch, Kenneth. *Rose, Where Did You Get That Red?* New York: Vintage, 1974.

Lipschultz, Geri. "Fishing in the Holy Waters." *College English* 48.1 (1986): 34–39.

Ponsot, Marie, and Rosemary Deen. *Beat Not the Poor Desk.* Upper Montclair: Boynton, 1982. 154–180.

Pound, Ezra. *ABC of Reading.* New York: New Directions, 1960.

Young, Gloria L. "Teaching Poetry: Another Method." *Teaching English in the Two-Year College* (Feb. 1987): 52–56.

Supplementing *The Bedford Introduction to Literature* with Volumes in Bedford's Case Studies in Contemporary Criticism Series

Instructors who wish to supplement *The Bedford Introduction to Literature* with a longer work may be interested in the volumes in Bedford's Case Studies in Contemporary Criticism series, which are now available with the fifth edition at a special price.

Titles available in the Case Studies series include *The Awakening, The Dead, Death in Venice, Frankenstein, Great Expectations, Gulliver's Travels, Hamlet, Heart of Darkness, The House of Mirth, Howards End, Jane Eyre, A Portrait of the Artist as a Young Man, The Scarlet Letter, The Secret Sharer, Tess of the D'Urbervilles, The Turn of the Screw, The Wife of Bath's Prologue and Tale,* and *Wuthering Heights.* Volumes from the Bedford Cultural Editions, the Bedford Shakespeare Series, and Case Studies in Critical Controversy include *The Adventures of Huckleberry Finn, The Blithedale Romance, The Commerce of Everyday Life: Selections from* THE SPECTATOR *and* THE TATLER, *Evelina, The First Part of King Henry the Fourth, Life in the Iron-Mills, The Rape of the Lock, Reading the West: An Anthology of Dime Westerns, The Taming of the Shrew,* and *The Yellow Wallpaper.*

Each volume reprints an authoritative complete text of a classic literary work together with five essays that examine the work from five contemporary critical perspectives, such as new historicism, cultural criticism, feminist and gender criticism, reader-response criticism, psychoanalytic criticism, Marxist criticism, and deconstruction. Each volume also includes a succinct introduction to the history, principles, and practices of the critical perspectives it covers. These volumes provide a useful supplement for instructors who want to cover the different schools of literary theory in more depth than is provided in Chapter 37 of *The Bedford Introduction to Literature*, Fifth Edition.

The critical essays in each volume of the Case Studies series can serve as models for helping students to understand how to apply a particular approach to works anthologized in *The Bedford Introduction to Literature*. In addition, the literary works in the Case Studies series can be compared in style and content to any number of the selections in the anthology. The following suggestions for using *The Awakening, The Dead,* or *Heart of Darkness* should serve to indicate how the Case Studies titles might be taught along with *The Bedford Introduction to Literature*.

The Awakening can be conveniently paired with Kate Chopin's "The Story of an Hour" (p. 10), because many of the feminist, psychological, economic, deconstructionist, and reader-response issues that can be addressed in the novel are also present in the short story. For example, in Elaine Showalter's discussion of "Tradition and the Female Talent: *The Awakening* as a Solitary Book" students will find a feminist analysis of the novel that offers important literary contexts which comment on "female plots and feminine endings" in nineteenth-century fiction. This discussion sheds light on both the novel and the short story. The information Showalter provides about literary traditions and the feminist perspective she uses could also be usefully connected to Henrik Ibsen's *A Doll House* (p. 1564) and the Perspective titled "A Nineteenth-Century Husband's Letter to His Wife"

(p. 1628). Taken together these resonant works could provide a fascinating unit on feminist perspectives about women and literature. In addition, the remaining critical essays in the volume offer other provocative approaches from differing perspectives: Margit Stange, "Personal Property: Exchange Value and the Female Self in *The Awakening*" (new historicism); Cynthia Griffin Wolff, "Thanatos and Eros: Kate Chopin's *The Awakening*" (psychoanalytic); Patricia S. Yaeger, " 'A Language Which Nobody Understood': Emancipatory Strategies in *The Awakening*" (deconstruction); and Paula A. Treichler, "The Construction of Ambiguity in *The Awakening*: A Linguistic Analysis" (reader–response).

The Dead offers especially rich possibilities for comparison with the new Cultural Case Study of James Joyce's "Eveline" (p. 507). John Paul Riquelme's deconstructionist reading of Gabriel Conroy in "For Whom the Snow Taps: Style and Repetition in 'The Dead' " presents the protagonist as "an example of a self-deluded person who is startled into a process of reconsidering what he has thought about himself and about those around him," but Riquelme notes that "there are difficulties in establishing precisely what the effect on Gabriel at the story's end is and what it will be in the future." This observation offers a potential model for discussing Eveline as well as any number of characters whose insights are rendered ambiguous. Other essays in the volume are Daniel R. Schwarz, "Gabriel Conroy's Psyche: Character as Concept in Joyce's 'The Dead' " (psychoanalytic); Peter J. Rabinowitz, " 'A Symbol of Something': Interpretive Vertigo in 'The Dead' " (reader-response); Michael Levenson, "Living History in 'The Dead' " (new historicism); and Margaret Norris, "Not the Girl She Was at All: Women in 'The Dead' " (feminist).

The second edition of the Case Study on *Heart of Darkness* includes Peter J. Rabinowitz, "Reader Response, Reader Responsibilty: *Heart of Darkness* and the Politics of Displacement" (reader-response); Johanna Smith, " 'Too Beautiful Altogether': Ideologies of Gender and Empire in *Heart of Darkness*" (feminist); J. Hillis Miller, "*Heart of Darkness* Revisited" (deconstruction); Brook Thomas, "Preserving and Keeping Order by Killing Time in *Heart of Darkness*" (new historicism); and Patrick Brantlinger, "*Heart of Darkness*: Anti-imperialism, Racism, or Impressionism" (cultural). Each of these essays opens up the text so that students will be primed to make connections to other works in the anthology, particularly those in which violence, race, and cultural imperialism are central. Among the works that might be fruitfully compared with *Heart of Darkness* are:

Ruth Prawer Jhabvala, "The Englishwoman" (p. 160)

Ralph Ellison, "Battle Royal" (p. 223)

Yukio Mishima, "Patriotism" (p. 593)

Gish Jen, "In the American Society" (p. 643)

Wole Soyinka, "Telephone Conversation" (p. 681)

Marilyn Bowering, "Wishing Africa" (p. 743)

James Merrill, "Casual Wear" (p. 817)

Carolyn Forché, "The Colonel" (p. 914)

Langston Hughes, "Johannesburg Mines" (p. 1019) and "The English" (p. 1024)

William Shakespeare, *The Tempest* (p. 1483)

David Henry Hwang, *M. Butterfly* (p. 1675)

Anna Deavere Smith, from *Twilight: Los Angeles, 1992* (p. 1661)

Each of the titles in the Bedford Case Studies series provides instructors with an opportunity to supplement the anthology with a longer work and to deepen the introduction to critical theory provided in Chapter 37, "Critical Strategies for Reading." To obtain complimentary copies of any of these titles, please call the Bedford/St. Martin's College Desk at 1-800-446-8923 or contact your local Bedford/St. Martin's sales representative.

Perspectives by Critical Strategies for Reading

The following list organizes the Perspectives throughout *The Bedford Introduction to Literature* by the Critical Strategies for Reading discussed in Chapter 37. The Perspectives are listed below the critical strategy they best exemplify (though not all Perspectives appear here.) The strategies are in the order in which they appear in *The Bedford Introduction to Literature*. By no means comprehensive, this list is meant to serve as a quick reference for instructors interested in teaching the critical strategies by showing them in action, most often applied to specific works that students have read.

FORMALIST STRATEGIES (text p. 2025)

Michael L. Baumann, *The "Overwhelming Question" for Prufrock* (text p. 1051, manual p. 372)
Andrew P. Debicki, *New Criticism and Deconstructionism: Two Attitudes in Teaching Poetry* (text p. 2050, manual p. 527)
James Ferguson, *Narrative Strategy in "Barn Burning"* (text p. 500, manual p. 95)
Richard Poirier, *On Emotional Suffocation in "Home Burial"* (text p. 1007, manual p. 344)
Steven C. Tracy, *A Reading of "The Weary Blues"* (text p. 1039, manual p. 367)

BIOGRAPHICAL STRATEGIES (text p. 2027)

James A. Emanuel, *Hughes's Attitudes toward Religion* (text p. 1037, manual p. 366)
Sigmund Freud, *On Repression in* Hamlet (text p. 1546, manual p. 481)
Sandra M. Gilbert and Susan Gubar, *On Dickinson's White Dress* (text p. 955, manual p. 322)
Nathaniel Hawthorne, *On Herman Melville's Philosophic Stance* (text p. 138, manual p. 27)
Josephine Hendin, *On O'Connor's Refusal to "Do Pretty"* (text p. 425, manual p. 82)
Jane Hiles, *Blood Ties in "Barn Burning"* (text p. 494, manual p. 94)
Karl Keller, *Robert Frost on Dickinson* (text p. 956, manual p. 322)
Edward Kessler, *On O'Connor's Use of History* (text p. 426, manual p. 82)
Amy Lowell, *On Frost's Realistic Technique* (text p. 998, manual p. 341)
Herman Melville, *On Nathaniel Hawthorne's Tragic Vision* (text p. 364, manual p. 73)
O'Connor on Faith (text p. 421, manual p. 81)
Elisabeth Schneider, *Hints of Eliot in Prufrock* (text p. 1049, manual p. 371)
Joan Templeton, *Is* A Doll House *a Feminist Text?* (text p. 1635, manual p. 495)
Richard Wilbur, *On Dickinson's Sense of Privation* (text p. 954, manual p. 321)

PSYCHOLOGICAL STRATEGIES (text p. 2029)

Sigmund Freud, *On Repression in* Hamlet (text p. 1546, manual p. 481)
Sigmund Freud, *On the Oedipus Complex* (text p. 1305, manual p. 460)
Coppélia Kahn, *On Cuckoldry in* Hamlet (text p. 1548, manual p. 482)
Katherine Kearns, *On the Symbolic Setting of "Home Burial"* (text p. 1008, manual p. 344)
James Quinn and Ross Baldessarini, *A Psychological Reading of "The Birthmark"* (text p. 366, manual p. 73)
Frederik L. Rusch, *Society and Character in "The Love Song of J. Alfred Prufrock"* (text p. 1053, manual p. 372)
Carol Strongin Tufts, *A Psychoanalytic Reading of Nora* (text p. 1632, manual p. 494)
Gayle Edward Wilson, *Conflict in "Barn Burning"* (text p. 497, manual p. 95)

HISTORICAL STRATEGIES (text p. 2031)

A. Marxist Criticism (text p. 2033)
Thomas P. Adler, *The Political Basis of Lorraine Hansberry's Art* (text p. 1793)
Benjamin DeMott, *Abner Snopes as a Victim of Class* (text p. 496, manual p. 95)
Barry Witham and John Lutterbie, *A Marxist Approach to* A Doll House (text p. 1630, manual p. 494)

B. New Historicist Criticism (text p. 2033)
Richard K. Barksdale, *On Censoring "Ballad of the Landlord"* (text p. 1038, manual p. 367)
Louis Adrian Montrose, *On Amazonian Mythology in* A Midsummer Night's Dream (text p. 1152, manual p. 482)
David S. Reynolds, *Popular Literature and "Wild Nights — Wild Nights!"* (text p. 964, manual p. 325)
Brook Thomas, *A New Historical Approach to Keats's "Ode on a Grecian Urn"* (text p. 277, manual p. 527)
Alden T. Vaughan, *Caliban as a Sociopolitical Symbol* (text p. 1556, manual p. 483)

C. Cultural Criticism (text p. 2034)
David Chinitz, *The Romanticization of Africa in the 1920s* (text p. 1040, manual p. 367)
James Kincaid, *On the Value of Comedy in the Face of Tragedy* (text p. 1553, manual p. 483)
Tania Modleski, *The Popularity of Romance Novels* (text p. 38, manual p. 6)

GENDER STRATEGIES (text p. 2035)

Bernard Duyfhuizen, *"To His Coy Mistress": On How a Female Might Respond* (text p. 731, manual p. 168)
Judith Fetterly, *A Feminist Reading of "The Birthmark"* (text p. 365, manual p. 73)
Judith Fetterly, *A Feminist Reading of "A Rose for Emily"* (text p. 2072, manual p. 526)
Annette Kolodny, *On the Commitments of Feminist Criticism* (text p. 2050, manual p. 527)
Tania Modleski, *The Popularity of Romance Novels* (text p. 38, manual p. 6)
Louis Adrian Montrose, *On Amazonian Mythology in* A Midsummer Night's Dream (text p. 1152, manual p. 482)
Joan Templeton, *Is* A Doll House *a Feminist Text?* (text p. 1635, manual p. 495)

MYTHOLOGICAL STRATEGIES (text p. 2037)

READER-RESPONSE STRATEGIES (text p. 2039)

DECONSTRUCTIONIST STRATEGIES (text p. 2041)

The following thematic units offer a selected list of titles from *The Bedford Introduction to Literature*. These selections of fiction, poetry, and drama are organized around a particular subject or theme and can be used to generate topics for discussion and writing. The lists are intended to be representative rather than exhaustive, suggestive rather than definitive. One or more of the thematic groupings might be useful for encouraging students to create additional thematic categories based on their readings. Students' own perceptions of how the works are linked may prove to be particularly revealing.

HOME AND FAMILY

FICTION

Raymond Carver, *Popular Mechanics*, 272
Andre Dubus, *Killings*, 81
William Faulkner, *Barn Burning*, 481
Gail Godwin, *A Sorrowful Woman*, 33
James Joyce, *Eveline*, 512
Alice Munro, *Miles City, Montana*, 458
Alice Munro, *An Ounce of Cure*, 434

POETRY

Margaret Atwood, *Bored*, 737
Margaret Atwood, *February*, 784
Gwendolyn Brooks, *The Mother*, 1081
Emily Dickinson, *The Bustle in a House*, 950
Robert Frost, *Home Burial*, 980
Rachel Hadas, *The Red Hat*, 864
Donald Hall, *Letter with No Address*, 1153
Donald Hall, *My Son, My Executioner*, 1093
Robert Hayden, *Those Winter Sundays*, 672
Andrew Hudgins, *Elegy for My Father, Who Is Not Dead*, 893
Galway Kinnell, *After Making Love We Hear Footsteps*, 905
Philip Larkin, *This Be the Verse*, 1105
Faye Myenne Ng, *A Red Sweater*, 235
Sharon Olds, *Rite of Passage*, 915
Sylvia Plath, *Daddy*, 1113
Theodore Roethke, *My Papa's Waltz*, 871

DRAMA

Anton Chekhov, *The Proposal: A Jest in One Act,* 1615
Lorraine Hansberry, *A Raisin in the Sun,* 1730
Sophocles, *Oedipus the King,* 1224
Tennessee Williams, *The Glass Menagerie,* 1864
August Wilson, *The Piano Lesson,* 1962

QUESTIONS FOR DISCUSSION AND WRITING

1. Discuss the attitudes toward fathers presented in Carver's "Popular Mechanics," Dubus's "Killings," Atwood's "Bored," Hudgins's "Elegy for My Father, Who Is Not Dead," Plath's "Daddy," Roethke's "My Papa's Waltz," and Wilson's *The Piano Lesson.* How successful are these men as fathers? How do these various works, taken together, offer a complex view of fathers?

2. Discuss the attitudes toward mothers presented in Godwin's "A Sorrowful Woman," Joyce's "Eveline," Brooks's "The Mother," Frost's "Home Burial," Hansberry's *A Raisin in the Sun,* Sophocles' *Oedipus the King,* and Williams's *The Glass Menagerie.* Explain how these women respond to the challenges they face as mothers.

3. Describe how the families in *A Raisin in the Sun, The Glass Menagerie,* and *The Piano Lesson* respond to the changes that inform their lives. What similarities do you find in their responses?

4. Choose any five works and discuss the treatment of children in them. To what extent are children at the center of the conflicts in the works?

5. Consider the endings of each of the short stories on the list. What do these endings have in common? Are they neatly tied up or left unresolved? What do they suggest about the nature of home and family?

6. What is the nature of the conflict in "Popular Mechanics"? Choose one other work in which the conflict is similar and develop a detailed comparison.

7. Discuss the importance of family grief in "Killings," "The Bustle in a House," "Home Burial," and *Oedipus the King.* How does grief reveal character in these works?

8. Compare the views of the young boys in "Rite of Passage" to any five fathers included in the list. How does Olds's assessment of the boys' futures square with their adult counterparts?

9. Compare the themes of "After Making Love We Hear Footsteps" and "My Son, My Executioner." What accounts for the warm tone of these poems? Explain whether or not you think either one can be charged with being sentimental.

LOVE AND ITS COMPLICATIONS

FICTION

Alison Baker, *Better Be Ready 'Bout Half Past Eight,* 617
Anton Chekhov, *The Lady with the Pet Dog,* 185
William Faulkner, *A Rose for Emily,* 72
Dagoberto Gilb, *Love in L.A.,* 265
Nathaniel Hawthorne, *Rappaccini's Daughter,* 341
Alice Munro, *How I Met My Husband,* 442

Alice Munro, *Prue*, 454
Joyce Carol Oates, *The Lady with the Pet Dog*, 200
Flannery O'Connor, *Good Country People*, 392
Karen Van Der Zee, from *A Secret Sorrow*, 25
Fay Weldon, *IND AFF, or Out of Love in Sarajevo*, 153

POETRY

Diane Ackerman, *A Fine, a Private Place*, 734
Margaret Atwood, *you fit into me*, 777
Sally Croft, *Home-Baked Bread*, 768
E. E. Cummings, *since feeling is first*, 1087
Emily Dickinson, *Wild Nights — Wild Nights!* 939
T. S. Eliot, *The Love Song of J. Alfred Prufrock*, 1045
Robert Herrick, *To the Virgins, to Make Much of Time*, 728
John Keats, *La Belle Dame sans Merci*, 1103
Andrew Marvell, *To His Coy Mistress*, 729
Sharon Olds, *Sex without Love*, 740
William Shakespeare, *My mistress' eyes are nothing like the sun*, 882
Cathy Song, *The White Porch*, 772
Richard Wilbur, *A Late Aubade*, 732

DRAMA

Susan Glaspell, *Trifles*, 1172
David Henry Hwang, *M. Butterfly*, 1675
Henrik Ibsen, *A Doll House*, 1564
David Ives, *Sure Thing*, 1189
William Shakespeare, *A Midsummer Night's Dream*, 1327

QUESTIONS FOR DISCUSSION AND WRITING

1. Using the following pairs of works, explore how men and women agree and differ in their expectations about love: Chekhov's and Oates's "The Lady with the Pet Dog"; Marvell's "To His Coy Mistress" and Ackerman's "A Fine, a Private Place"; and Hwang's *M. Butterfly* and Ives's *Sure Thing*.

2. Discuss Cummings's "since feeling is first," Herrick's "To the Virgins, to Make Much of Time," and Wilbur's "A Late Aubade" as *carpe diem* poems. (This type of poem is defined on p. 728 of the text.) Pay particular attention to the speakers' tones in the poems. What do they have in common?

3. How might Keats's "La Belle Dame sans Merci" be used as a commentary on Hwang's *M. Butterfly*?

4. Despite their bizarre plots, how can Faulkner's "A Rose for Emily" and O'Connor's "Good Country People" nevertheless be regarded as love stories?

5. Explain why love fails in Eliot's "The Love Song of J. Alfred Prufrock" and in Ibsen's *A Doll House*.

6. Compare the humorous tone of Shakespeare's "My mistress' eyes are nothing like the sun" with that of Atwood's "you fit into me."

7. Compare the sensuousness and sensuality in Croft's "Home-Baked Bread" and Song's "The White Porch." What is the effect of the implicit — rather than the explicit — nature of the sexuality in each poem?

8. Discuss the significance of marriage in the plots of Shakespeare's *A Midsummer Night's Dream* and Van Der Zee's excerpt from *A Secret Sorrow*.

9. Consider Dickinson's "Wild Nights — Wild Nights!," Olds's "Sex without Love," and Weldon's "IND AFF, or Out of Love in Sarajevo" as commenting upon one another. What do these works suggest to you about sexuality and love?

THE NATURAL WORLD

FICTION

T. Coraghessan Boyle, *Carnal Knowledge,* 276
Edgar Rice Burroughs, from *Tarzan of the Apes,* 62
Kate Chopin, *The Story of an Hour,* 10
Nathaniel Hawthorne, *Young Goodman Brown,* 310
Tim O'Brien, *How to Tell a True War Story,* 555
Tobias Wolff, *Powder,* 665

POETRY

Elizabeth Bishop, *The Fish,* 682
William Blake, *The Tyger,* 868
James Dickey, *Deer Among Cattle,* 766
Emily Dickinson, *A narrow Fellow in the Grass,* 2
Robert Frost, *Design,* 993
Margaret Holley, *Peepers,* 764
Gerard Manley Hopkins, *Pied Beauty,* 1099
John Keats, *To Autumn,* 771
Galway Kinnell, *Blackberry Eating,* 832
N. Scott Momaday, *The Bear,* 1110
Alden Nowlan, *The Bull Moose,* 815
William Stafford, *Traveling through the Dark,* 813
William Carlos Williams, *Spring and All,* 1126

DRAMA

Brian Friel, From *Molly Sweeney,* 1911
William Shakespeare, *A Midsummer Night's Dream,* 1327
William Shakespeare, *The Tempest,* 1483

QUESTIONS FOR DISCUSSION AND WRITING

1. Describe how nature serves as an antagonist in the excerpt from Burroughs's *Tarzan of the Apes* and Shakespeare's *The Tempest* or *A Midsummer Night's Dream*. How are conflicts in the plot reflected in nature?

2. How does nature function as a protagonist in Wolff's "Powder" and Chopin's "The Story of an Hour"?

3. Consider imagery in Bishop's "The Fish," Blake's "The Tyger," Dickey's "Deer Among Cattle," and Holley's "Peepers." To what extent do the poems go beyond the subjects they describe?

4. Consider the role that sense of sight plays in knowing the world for the protagonist of Friel's *Molly Sweeney*. Choose any work from the list and describe the scene as Molly might have seen it, both before and after her sight is restored.

5. Compare the imagery and themes of Keats's "To Autumn" and Williams's "Spring and All." Which poem appeals to you more? Explain why.

6. Discuss Hopkins's attitude toward nature in "Pied Beauty" and Frost's in "Design." What connections does each poem make between nature and God?

7. Compare the attitudes toward nature in Hawthorne's "Young Goodman Brown" and O'Brien's "How to Tell a True War Story." How is nature used to develop the themes of each story?

8. How is nature used to critique societal values in Nowlan's "Bull Moose" and Boyle's "Carnal Knowledge"?

OTHER CULTURES

FICTION

POETRY

DRAMA

QUESTIONS FOR DISCUSSION AND WRITING

1. Choose a work from the list and explain how it causes you to adjust or reassess your own cultural assumptions in order to understand and appreciate the perspective offered in the work.

2. Explain the significance of ritual in Mishima's "Patriotism" and Soyinka's *The Strong Breed*. Consider whether there are any comparable rituals in your own culture.

3. How do the protagonists of "The Tenant" and "Broken Transformers" feel about American products and American culture? Do American values clash with the values of other cultures in these stories? To what purpose?

4. Compare Alegría's treatment of violence in "I Am Mirror" with that of Allende in "The Judge's Wife." How does the violence in these works compare with your sense of violence in American culture?

5. Discuss Baca's and Divakaruni's respective attitudes toward their own cultures in "Green Chile" and "Indian Movie, New Jersey."

6. How is Indian culture compared with Western culture in Jhabvala's "The Englishwoman" and Divakaruni's "Indian Movie, New Jersey"?

7. How are the simplest experiences in Neruda's "Sweetness, Always" and Djanikian's "When I First Saw Snow" rendered significant? Why are they significant?

8. Discuss the tone of Paz's "The Street" and Transtromer's "April and Silence." Despite their brevity each evokes a depth of feeling. What feelings are evoked by the tone of each poem?

9. How do generational differences account for the speakers' attitudes toward their cultures in Yamada's "A Bedtime Story" and Salter's "Welcome to Hiroshima"?

WORK AND BUSINESS

FICTION

POETRY

Katharyn Howd Machan, *Hazel Tells LaVerne*, 725
Marge Piercy, *The Secretary Chant*, 671
Edwin Arlington Robinson, *Richard Cory*, 802
Jean Toomer, *Reapers*, 844

DRAMA

Jane Martin, *Rodeo*, 1657
Arthur Miller, *Death of a Salesman*, 1795
Anna Deavere Smith, "Swallowing the Bitterness" from *Twilight: Los Angeles, 1992*, 1668

QUESTIONS FOR DISCUSSION AND WRITING

1. Consider attitudes toward success in Ellison's "Battle Royal," Dickinson's "Success is counted sweetest," and Robinson's "Richard Cory." How is true success defined and measured in these works?

2. How is humor used to characterize the world of work in Melville's "Bartleby, the Scrivener," Machan's "Hazel Tells LaVerne," Piercy's "The Secretary Chant," and Martin's *Rodeo*? What serious points about work are made through the use of humor in these selections?

3. Choose a single work for each of the three genres that, in your opinion, presents the most severe judgment upon business as a dehumanizing process.

4. What is the function of Lengel in Updike's "A & P" and the lawyer in Melville's "Bartleby, the Scrivener"? How does each character serve to represent business attitudes? Do you think their characterizations are essentially similar or different?

5. Compare Mr. Chang's ties to his cultural past in Jen's "In the American Society" with Mr. Z's ties to his past in Holman's poem. How do such ties affect each character's aspirations?

6. Discuss the significance of the images used in Hughes's "Johannesburg Mines" and Blake's "The Chimney Sweeper." What attitudes toward work emerge from these images?

7. How are advertisements and commercialism used as a means to comment upon societal values in Fearing's "AD"?

8. Compare the use of symbolism in Toomer's "Reapers" and Frost's "After Apple-Picking." How and for what purpose is work symbolized in each poem?

9. Discuss the speakers' attitudes toward work expressed in Kingston's "Restaurant" and Smith's "Swallowing the Bitterness" from *Twilight: Los Angeles, 1992*.

Connections Between Selections Suggested in Text and Manual

The following list of works linked by connections is organized by genre (Fiction, Poetry, and Drama). Within each genre section the listings are arranged alphabetically by author. When a Connection question posed in the text is answered in the instructor's manual, the page reference is to the manual itself.

FICTION: LIST OF CONNECTIONS BETWEEN SELECTIONS BY AUTHOR

AUTHOR, STORY	CONNECTED TO:
Isabel Allende, *The Judge's Wife*	Andre Dubus, *Killings* (manual p. 118) Bessie Head, *The Prisoner Who Wore Glasses* (text p. 587) Flannery O'Connor *A Good Man Is Hard to Find* (text p. 381)
Margaret Atwood, *There Was Once*	Toni Cade Bambara, *The Lesson* (text p. 179) T. Coraghessan Boyle, *Carnal Knowledge* (manual p. 52)
Alison Baker, *Better Be Ready 'Bout Half Past Eight*	T. Coraghessan Boyle, *Carnal Knowledge* (text p. 276) Andre Dubus, *Killings* (manual p. 130) David Henry Hwang, *M. Butterfly* (text p. 1675)
Toni Cade Bambara, *The Lesson*	Sandra Cisneros, *Barbie-Q* (text p. 218) Ralph Ellison, *Battle Royal* (text p. 223) Katherine Mansfield, *Miss Brill* (text p. 258) Flannery O'Connor, *A Good Man Is Hard to Find* (text p. 381)
George Bowering, *A Short Story*	Andre Dubus, *Killings* (manual p. 64) Stephen King, *Suffer the Little Children* (text p. 535)
T. Coraghessan Boyle, *Carnal Knowledge*	Alison Baker, *Better Be Ready 'Bout Half Past Eight* (text p. 617) Nathaniel Hawthorne, *Young Goodman Brown* (text p. 310) Edgar Allan Poe, *The Purloined Letter* (text p. 564)
Edgar Rice Burroughs, from *Tarzan of the Apes*	Tim O'Brien, *How to Tell a True War Story* (text p. 555) Karen Van Der Zee, from *A Secret Sorrow* (text p. 25)

AUTHOR, STORY	CONNECTED TO:
Raymond Carver, *Popular Mechanics*	Sandra Cisneros, *Barbie-Q* (text p. 218)
Anton Chekhov, *The Lady with the Pet Dog*	Joyce Carol Oates, *The Lady with the Pet Dog* (text p. 200)
Kate Chopin, *The Story of an Hour*	Dagoberto Gilb, *Love in L.A.* (text p. 265)
	Susan Glaspell, *Trifles* (text p. 1172)
	Yukio Mishima, *Patriotism* (text p. 593)
Sandra Cisneros, *Barbie-Q*	Toni Cade Bambara, *The Lesson* (text p. 179)
	Raymond Carver, *Popular Mechanics* (text p. 272)
	Colette, *The Hand* (text p. 220)
	Ralph Ellison, *Battle Royal* (text p. 223)
	Dagoberto Gilb, *Love in L.A.* (text p. 265)
Colette [Sidonie-Gabrielle Colette], *The Hand*	Sandra Cisneros, *Barbie-Q* (text p. 218)
	Gail Godwin, *A Sorrowful Woman* (text p. 33)
	Nathaniel Hawthorne, *The Birthmark* (text p. 329)
	John Updike, *A & P* (text p. 576)
Stephen Crane, *The Bride Comes to Yellow Sky*	William Faulkner, *A Rose for Emily* (text p. 72)
	Katherine Mansfield, *Miss Brill* (text p. 258)
	Jane Martin, *Rodeo* (text p. 1657)
Charles Dickens, from *Hard Times*	Toni Cade Bambara, *The Lesson* (text p. 179)
	Nathaniel Hawthorne, *Young Goodman Brown* (text p. 310)
Andre Dubus, *Killings*	Isabel Allende, *The Judge's Wife* (text p. 581)
	Alison Baker, *Better Be Ready 'Bout Half Past Eight* (text p. 617)
	William Faulkner, *Barn Burning* (text p. 481)
	William Faulkner, *A Rose for Emily* (text p. 72)
	Susan Glaspell, *Trifles* (text p. 1172)
	Gish Jen, *In the American Society* (text p. 643)
Ralph Ellison, *Battle Royal*	Toni Cade Bambara, *The Lesson* (text p. 179)
	Paul Laurence Dunbar, *We Wear the Mask* (text p. 808)
	William Faulkner, *A Rose for Emily* (text p. 72)
	Bessie Head, *The Prisoner Who Wore Glasses* (text p. 587)
	M. Carl Holman, *Mr. Z* (text p. 1098)
	Flannery O'Connor, *Revelation* (text p. 407)
	August Wilson, *The Piano Lesson* (text p. 1962)

Suggested Connections Between Selections

AUTHOR, STORY	CONNECTED TO:
William Faulkner, *Barn Burning*	Andre Dubus, *Killings* (text p. 81)
	William Faulkner, *A Rose for Emily* (text p. 72)
	Bessie Head, *The Prisoner Who Wore Glasses* (text p. 587)
	Flannery O'Connor, *A Good Man Is Hard to Find* (text p. 381)
William Faulkner, *A Rose for Emily*	Stephen Crane, *The Bride Comes to Yellow Sky* (text p. 250)
	Emily Dickinson, *The Soul selects her own Society —* (text p. 941)
	Ralph Ellison, *Battle Royal* (text p. 223)
	William Faulkner, *Barn Burning* (text p. 481)
	Yukio Mishima, *Patriotism* (manual p. 15)
Richard Ford, *Bascombe, in Realty*	Mark Halliday, *Young Man on Sixth Avenue* (manual p. 132)
	Susan Minot, *Lust* (text p. 290)
	Alice Munro, *An Ounce of Cure* (manual p. 132)
Dagoberto Gilb, *Love in L.A.*	Sandra Cisneros, *Barbie-Q* (text p. 218)
Gail Godwin, *A Sorrowful Woman*	Colette, *The Hand* (text p. 220)
	Emily Dickinson, *Much Madness is divinest Sense —* (text p. 942)
	Henrik Ibsen, *A Doll House* (text p. 1564)
	Herman Melville, *Bartleby, the Scrivener* (text p. 113)
	Linda Pastan, *Marks* (text p. 791)
Mark Halliday, *Young Man on Sixth Avenue*	T. S. Eliot, *The Love Song of J. Alfred Prufrock* (text p. 1045)
	Herman Melville, *Bartleby, the Scrivener* (manual p. 14)
Nathaniel Hawthorne, *The Birthmark*	Colette, *The Hand* (text p. 220)
	Emily Dickinson, *Success is counted sweetest* (text p. 932)
	Nathaniel Hawthorne, *The Minister's Black Veil* (text p. 320)
	Nathaniel Hawthorne, *Young Goodman Brown* (text p. 310)
	Yukio Mishima, *Patriotism* (text p. 593)
	Flannery O'Connor, *A Good Man Is Hard to Find* (text p. 381)
	Fay Weldon, *IND AFF, or Out of Love in Sarajevo* (text p. 153)
Nathaniel Hawthorne, *The Minister's Black Veil*	Nathaniel Hawthorne, *The Birthmark* (text p. 329)
	Nathaniel Hawthorne, *Young Goodman Brown* (text p. 310)

AUTHOR, STORY	CONNECTED TO:
Nathaniel Hawthorne, *Rappaccini's Daughter*	Gail Godwin, *A Sorrowful Woman* (text p. 33) Nathaniel Hawthorne, *The Birthmark* (manual p. 72)
Nathaniel Hawthorne, *Young Goodman Brown*	T. Coraghessan Boyle, *Carnal Knowledge* (text p. 276) Nathaniel Hawthorne, *The Birthmark* (text p. 329) Nathaniel Hawthorne, *The Minister's Black Veil* (text p. 320) Herman Melville, *Bartleby, the Scrivener* (text p. 113)
Bessie Head, *The Prisoner Who Wore Glasses*	Isabel Allende, *The Judge's Wife* (text p. 581) Ralph Ellison, *Battle Royal* (manual p. 120) William Faulkner, *Barn Burning* (manual p. 121)
Ernest Hemingway, *Soldier's Home*	Gish Jen, *In the American Society* (text p. 643) James Joyce, *Eveline* (text p. 512) Yukio Mishima, *Patriotism* (text p. 593) Tim O'Brien, *How to Tell a True War Story* (text p. 555)
Gish Jen, *In the American Society*	Ernest Hemingway, *Soldier's Home* (text p. 145) Yukio Mishima, *Patriotism* (manual p. 134) Flannery O'Connor, *A Good Man Is Hard to Find* (manual p. 134)
Ruth Prawer Jhabvala, *The Englishwoman*	Gail Godwin, *A Sorrowful Woman* (text p. 33) Ernest Hemingway, *Soldier's Home* (text p. 145) James Joyce, *Eveline* (text p. 512)
Charles Johnson, *Exchange Value*	Toni Cade Bambara, *The Lesson* (text p. 179) Flannery O'Connor, *The Turkey* (text p. 373)
James Joyce, *Eveline*	Ernest Hemingway, *Soldier's Home* (text p. 145) Naguib Mahfouz, *The Answer Is No* (text p. 591)
Franz Kafka, *A Hunger Artist*	Herman Melville, *Bartleby, the Scrivener* (text p. 113)
Jamaica Kincaid, *Girl*	Susan Minot, *Lust* (text p. 290) Alice Munro, *Miles City, Montana* (text p. 458)
Stephen King, *Suffer the Little Children*	Charles Dickens, from *Hard Times* (text p. 98) Flannery O'Connor, *A Good Man Is Hard to Find* (text p. 381)

AUTHOR, STORY	CONNECTED TO:
D. H. Lawrence, *The Horse Dealer's Daughter*	Yukio Mishima, *Patriotism* (text p. 593) Fay Weldon, *IND AFF, or Out of Love in Sarajevo* (text p. 153)
Naguib Mahfouz, *The Answer Is No*	James Joyce, *Eveline* (text p. 512) Fay Weldon, *IND AFF, or Out of Love in Sarajevo* (manual p. 122)
Katherine Mansfield, *Miss Brill*	Stephen Crane, *The Bride Comes to Yellow Sky* (text p. 250) James Joyce, *Eveline* (text p. 512) Fay Weldon, *IND AFF, or Out of Love in Sarajevo* (text p. 153)
Herman Melville, *Bartleby, the Scrivener*	Emily Dickinson, *There's a certain Slant of Light* (text p. 2082) Robert Frost, *Mending Wall* (text p. 979) Gail Godwin, *A Sorrowful Woman* (text p. 33) Nathaniel Hawthorne, *Young Goodman Brown* (text p. 310) Franz Kafka, *A Hunger Artist* (text p. 528)
Susan Minot, *Lust*	Jamaica Kincaid, *Girl* (text p. 534) Alice Munro, *An Ounce of Cure* (manual p. 62) David Updike, *Summer* (manual p. 62)
Yukio Mishima, *Patriotism*	Kate Chopin, *The Story of an Hour* (manual p. 124) William Faulkner, *A Rose for Emily* (text p. 72) Nathaniel Hawthorne, *The Birthmark* (text p. 329) Ernest Hemingway, *Soldier's Home* (text p. 145) David Henry Hwang, *M. Butterfly* (text p. 1675) Gish Jen, *In the American Society* (text p. 643) D. H. Lawrence, *The Horse Dealer's Daughter* (manual p. 125) Tim O'Brien, *How to Tell a True War Story* (manual p. 124)
Bharati Mukherjee, *The Tenant*	Raymond Carver, *Popular Mechanics* (manual p. 23) William Faulkner, *Barn Burning* (text p. 481) Alice Munro, *Prue* (manual p. 24)
Alice Munro, *Miles City, Montana*	T. S. Eliot, *The Love Song of J. Alfred Prufrock* (text p. 1045) Alice Munro, *An Ounce of Cure* (manual p. 89) Flannery O'Connor, *The Turkey* (manual p. 89)

AUTHOR, STORY	CONNECTED TO:
Alice Munro, *An Ounce of Cure*	George Bowering, *A Short Story* (text p. 298) Susan Minot, *Lust* (text p. 290) David Updike, *Summer* (text p. 169)
Alice Munro, *Prue*	Colette, *The Hand* (text p. 454) Katherine Mansfield, *Miss Brill* (text p. 258)
Fae Myenne Ng, *A Red Sweater*	Toni Cade Bambara, *The Lesson* (text p. 179) Gish Jen, *In the American Society* (manual p. 50) Bharati Mukherjee, *The Tenant* (manual p. 50)
Joyce Carol Oates, *The Lady with the Pet Dog*	Anton Chekhov, *The Lady with the Pet Dog* (text p. 185) Fay Weldon, *IND AFF, or Out of Love in Sarajevo* (text p. 153)
Joyce Carol Oates, *The Night Nurse*	Nathaniel Hawthorne, *Young Goodman Brown* (manual p. 137) Stephen King, *Suffer the Little Children* (manual p. 136) Alice Munro, *Miles City, Montana* (text p. 458)
Tim O'Brien, *How to Tell a True War Story*	Edgar Rice Burroughs, from *Tarzan of the Apes* (text p. 62) Ernest Hemingway, *Soldier's Home* (text p. 145) Yusef Komunyakaa, *Facing It* (text p. 1162) Yukio Mishima, *Patriotism* (text p. 593) William Shakespeare, *A Midsummer Night's Dream* (text p. 1327)
Flannery O'Connor, *Good Country People*	Ernest Hemingway, *Soldier's Home* (text p. 145) Flannery O'Connor, *Revelation* (text p. 407)
Flannery O'Connor, *A Good Man Is Hard to Find*	Isabel Allende, *The Judge's Wife* (text p. 581) Toni Cade Bambara, *The Lesson* (text p. 179) William Faulkner, *Barn Burning* (text p. 481) Nathaniel Hawthorne, *The Birthmark* (text p. 329) Gish Jen, *In the American Society* (text p. 643) Flannery O'Connor, *Revelation* (text p. 407)
Flannery O'Connor, *Revelation*	Emily Dickinson, *What Soft — Cherubic Creatures —* (text p. 940) Ralph Ellison, *Battle Royal* (text p. 223) Flannery O'Connor, *Good Country People* (text p. 392) Flannery O'Connor, *A Good Man Is Hard to Find* (text p. 381) John Updike, *A & P* (text p. 576)

Suggested Connections Between Selections

AUTHOR, STORY	**CONNECTED TO:**
Flannery O'Connor, *The Turkey*	Nathaniel Hawthorne, *The Minister's Black Veil* (text p. 320) Flannery O'Connor, *Good Country People* (manual p. 77) Flannery O'Connor, *Revelation* (manual p. 76)
Edgar Allan Poe, *The Purloined Letter*	T. Coraghessan Boyle, *Carnal Knowledge* (text p. 276)
Leon Rooke, *Sweethearts*	Margaret Atwood, *There Was Once* (text p. 247) A. L. Bader, *Nothing Happens in Modern Short Stories* (manual p. 29) John Updike, *A & P* (text p. 576)
Bi Shumin, *Broken Transformers*	Sandra Cisneros, *Barbie-Q* (manual p. 127) Charles Johnson, *Exchange Value* (manual p. 127) Alice Munro, *Miles City, Montana* (text p. 458)
David Updike, *Summer*	Dagoberto Gilb, *Love in L.A.* (manual p. 38) Leon Rooke, *Sweethearts* (text p. 141) John Updike, *A & P* (manual p. 38)
John Updike, *A & P*	Colette, *The Hand* (text p. 220) Ernest Hemingway, *Soldier's Home* (text p. 145) Flannery O'Connor, *Revelation* (text p. 407)
Karen Van Der Zee, from *A Secret Sorrow*	Edgar Rice Burroughs, from *Tarzan of the Apes* (text p. 62) Gail Godwin, *A Sorrowful Woman* (text p. 33)
Fay Weldon, *IND AFF, or Out of Love in Sarajevo*	Mark Halliday, *Graded Paper* (text p. 1156) Nathaniel Hawthorne, *The Birthmark* (manual p. 34) D. H. Lawrence, *The Horse Dealer's Daughter* (manual p. 34) Naguib Mahfouz, *The Answer Is No* (text p. 591) Katherine Mansfield, *Miss Brill* (text p. 258) Joyce Carol Oates, *The Lady with the Pet Dog* (manual p. 34)
Tobias Wolff, *Powder*	Margaret Atwood, *Bored* (text p. 737) William Faulkner, *Barn Burning* (manual p. 139) David Updike, *Summer* (manual p. 139)

POETRY: LIST OF CONNECTIONS BETWEEN POEMS BY AUTHOR

AUTHOR, POEM	CONNECTED TO:
Diane Ackerman, *A Fine, a Private Place*	Marilyn Bowering, *Wishing Africa* (text p. 743) Emily Dickinson, *"Heaven"— is what I cannot reach!* (text p. 936) Langston Hughes, *Jazzonia* (text p. 342) Andrew Marvell, *To His Coy Mistress* (manual p. 171)
Anna Akhmatova, *Dedication*	Emily Dickinson, *I read my sentence — steadily —* (manual p. 425) Faiz Ahmed Faiz, *If You Look at the City from Here* (manual p. 425) John Milton, *On the Late Massacre in Piedmont* (text p. 1109) Wilfred Owen, *Dulce et Decorum Est* (text p. 763)
Claribel Alegría, *I Am Mirror*	William Blake, *London* (text p. 762) Sylvia Plath, *Mirror* (manual p. 426)
Elizabeth Alexander, *Harlem Birthday Party*	Michael S. Harper, *Grandfather* (text p. 1095) M. Carl Holman, *Mr. Z* (manual p. 435) Langston Hughes, *Lenox Avenue: Midnight* (text p. 1022)
Julia Alvarez, *Woman's Work*	Jim Daniels, *Short-order Cook* (text p. 913) Dylan Thomas, *Do not go gentle into that good night* (manual p. 272)
Maya Angelou, *Africa*	Langston Hughes, *The Negro Speaks of Rivers* (text p. 1010) Wole Soyinka, *Future Plans* (text p. 1145)
Katerina Angheláki-Rooke, *Jealousy*	Emily Dickinson, *"Heaven"— is what I cannot reach!* (manual p. 427)
Anonymous, *Scarborough Fair*	Anonymous, *Bonny Barbara Allan* (text p. 1074) John Donne, *A Valediction: Forbidding Mourning* (text p. 790)
Anonymous, *Scottsboro*	Langston Hughes, *Ballad of the Landlord* (text p. 1025)
Anonymous, *Western Wind*	Timothy Steele, *An Aubade* (text p. 761)
Richard Armour, *Going to Extremes*	Margaret Atwood, *you fit into me* (text p. 777)
Matthew Arnold, *Dover Beach*	Anthony Hecht, *The Dover Bitch* (manual p. 187) Wilfred Owen, *Dulce et Decorum Est* (manual p. 187)

AUTHOR, POEM	CONNECTED TO:
John Ashbery, *Paradoxes and Oxymorons*	Robert Francis, *Catch* (text p. 676) Miller Williams, *Excuse Me* (text p. 708)
Margaret Atwood, *Bored*	Robert Hayden, *Those Winter Sundays* (manual p. 172)
Margaret Atwood, *February*	Stephen Crane, *A Man Said to the Universe* (text p. 805) Richard Wilbur, *A Late Aubade* (text p. 732)
Margaret Atwood, *you fit into me*	Emily Dickinson, *Wild Nights — Wild Nights!* (text p. 939)
W. H. Auden, *The Unknown Citizen*	James Merrill, *Casual Wear* (text p. 817)
Jimmy Santiago Baca, *Green Chile*	Seamus Heaney, *The Pitchfork* (text p. 760) Bonnie Jacobson, *On Being Served Apples* (text p. 753)
Amiri Baraka, *SOS*	Lucille Clifton, *come home from the movies* (text p. 791) M. Carl Holman, *Mr. Z* (text p. 1098) Langston Hughes, *Red Silk Stockings* (text p. 1022)
Regina Barreca, *Nighttime Fires*	Michael Harper, *Grandfather* (text p. 1095) Robert Hayden, *Those Winter Sundays* (text p. 672)
Matsuo Bashō, *Under cherry trees*	William Carlos Williams, *Poem* (text p. 753)
Robin Becker, *Shopping*	Emily Dickinson, *The Bustle in a House* (manual p. 217) Sylvia Plath, *Mirror* (text p. 786)
Elizabeth Bishop, *The Fish*	Joy Harjo, *Fishing* (text p. 1094) Seamus Heaney, *The Pitchfork* (text p. 760) N. Scott Momaday, *The Bear* (text p. 1110) David Solway, *Windsurfing,* (text p. 755)
Elizabeth Bishop, *Manners*	D. H. Lawrence, *The English Are So Nice!* (text p. 745)
Elizabeth Bishop, *Sestina*	Elizabeth Bishop, *Manners* (text p. 713) Adrienne Rich, *Living in Sin* (text p. 1115)
Sophie Cabot Black, *August*	Margaret Atwood, *February* (manual p. 209) James Dickey, *Deer Among Cattle* (text p. 766) Jane Kenyon, *Surprise* (text p. 806)
William Blake, *Ah Sun-flower*	Robert Frost, *Stopping by Woods on a Snowy Evening* (text p. 989)
William Blake, *The Chimney Sweeper*	Paul Laurence Dunbar, *We Wear the Mask* (text p. 808) Langston Hughes, *Negro* (text p. 1016)
William Blake, *The Garden of Love*	Emily Dickinson, *From all the Jails the Boys and Girls* (text p. 951)

AUTHOR, POEM	CONNECTED TO:
William Blake, *The Lamb*	William Wordsworth, *I Wandered Lonely as a Cloud* (text p. 1127)
William Blake, *The Little Black Boy*	William Blake, *The Lamb* (text p. 868)
William Blake, *London*	Claribel Alegría, *I Am Mirror* (text p. 1136)
	George Eliot, *In a London Drawingroom* (text p. 1092)
	Faiz Ahmed Faiz, *If You Look at the City from Here* (text p. 1139)
William Blake, *The Sick Rose*	William Blake, *Ah Sun-flower* (text p. 1078)
	Robert Frost, *Design* (text p. 993)
William Blake, *The Tyger*	William Wordsworth, *I Wandered Lonely as a Cloud* (text p. 1127)
Robert Bly, *Sitting Down to Dinner*	Robert Frost, *Birches* (text p. 986)
	Judy Page Heitzman, *The Schoolroom on the Second Floor of the Knitting Mill* (manual p. 236)
Robert Bly, *Snowbanks North of the House*	William Blake, *London* (text p. 762)
	Robert Bly, *Snowfall in the Afternoon* (text p. 1078)
	William Butler Yeats, *The Second Coming* (text p. 1133)
Robert Bly, *Snowfall in the Afternoon*	Robert Bly, *Snowbanks North of the House* (text p. 809)
	Henry Wadsworth Longfellow, *Snow-Flakes* (text p. 1106)
Marilyn Bowering, *Wishing Africa*	Diane Ackerman, *A Fine, a Private Place* (text p. 734)
	Rainer Maria Rilke, *The Panther* (text p. 767)
Anne Bradstreet, *The Author to Her Book*	William Shakespeare, *Not marble, nor the gilded monuments* (text p. 1116)
Anne Bradstreet, *Before the Birth of One of Her Children*	Anne Bradstreet, *The Author to Her Book* (text p. 778)
	John Donne, *A Valediction: Forbidding Mourning* (text p. 790)
Anne Bradstreet, *To My Dear and Loving Husband*	John Donne, *A Valediction: Forbidding Mourning* (text p. 790)
	William Shakespeare, *When, in disgrace with Fortune and men's eyes* (text p. 1118)
Joseph Brodsky, *Love Song*	Aron Keesbury, *Song to a Waitress* (text p. 872)
	William Shakespeare, *My mistress' eyes are nothing like the sun* (text p. 882)
Gwendolyn Brooks, *The Bean Eaters*	Li-Young Lee, *Eating Together* (text p. 1105)
Gwendolyn Brooks, *The Mother*	Anne Bradstreet, *Before the Birth of One of Her Children* (text p. 1080)

AUTHOR, POEM	CONNECTED TO:
Gwendolyn Brooks, *We Real Cool*	Langston Hughes, *Jazzonia* (text p. 1017)
Elizabeth Barrett Browning, *Grief*	E. E. Cummings, *since feeling is first* (text p. 1087) Emily Dickinson, *I like a look of Agony* (text p. 938)
Robert Browning, *My Last Duchess*	Mark Halliday, *Graded Paper* (manual p. 439) Katharyn Howd Machan, *Hazel Tells LaVerne* (manual p. 233)
Joseph Bruchac, *Ellis Island*	Tato Laviera, *AmeRícan* (manual p. 293)
George Gordon, Lord Byron, *She Walks in Beauty*	William Wordsworth, *The Solitary Reaper* (text p. 1128)
Lewis Carroll [Charles Lutwidge Dodgson], *Jabberwocky*	May Swenson, *A Nosty Fright* (manual p. 243)
Rosario Castellanos, *Chess*	Robin Becker, *Shopping* (text p. 794) Sylvia Plath, *Daddy* (text p. 1113)
Helen Chasin, *The Word* Plum	Galway Kinnell, *Blackberry Eating* (manual p. 251) Robert Morgan, *Mountain Graveyard* (text p. 686) Pablo Neruda, *Sweetness, Always* (manual p. 429)
John Ciardi, *Suburban*	Louis Simpson, *In the Suburbs* (manual p. 179) Wole Soyinka, *Telephone Conversation* (text p. 681)
Amy Clampitt, *Dancers Exercising*	John Donne, *The Sun Rising* (text p. 705) Robert Hass, *Happiness* (text p. 707)
Lucille Clifton, *come home from the movies*	Amiri Baraka, *SOS* (text p. 1077) Langston Hughes, *Red Silk Stockings* (text p. 1022)
Lucille Clifton, *for deLawd*	Etheridge Knight, *A Watts Mother Mourns While Boiling Beans* (text p. 1104)
Samuel Taylor Coleridge, *Kubla Khan: or, a Vision in a Dream*	John Keats, *Ode to a Nightingale* (text p. 851) William Butler Yeats, *Sailing to Byzantium* (text p. 1132)
Edmund Conti, *Pragmatist*	Samuel Taylor Coleridge, *What Is an Epigram?* (text p. 889) William Hathaway, *Oh, Oh* (text p. 675)
Wendy Cope, *Lonely Hearts*	Robin Becker, *Shopping* (text p. 794) Joseph Brodsky, *Love Song* (text p. 845)
William Cowper, *Epitaph on a Hare*	Andrew Hudgins, *Seventeen* (text p. 813) Jane Kenyon, *The Blue Bowl* (text p. 768) William Stafford, *Traveling through the Dark* (text p. 813) John Updike, *Dog's Death* (text p. 673) Ronald Wallace, *Dogs* (text p. 1164)

AUTHOR, POEM	CONNECTED TO:
Stephen Crane, *A Man Said to the Universe*	Robert Frost, "*Out, Out —*" (manual p. 333)
	Thomas Hardy, *The Convergence of the Twain* (text p. 738)
	Langston Hughes, *Lenox Avenue: Midnight* (text p. 1022)
Sally Croft, *Home-Baked Bread*	Carolyn Kizer, *Food for Love* (text p. 769)
	Elaine Magarrell, *The Joy of Cooking* (manual p. 215)
	Cathy Song, *The White Porch* (manual p. 201)
Victor Hernandez Cruz, *Anonymous*	Julio Marzán, *Ethnic Poetry* (text p. 816)
	Miller Williams, *Excuse Me* (text p. 708)
Countee Cullen, *Saturday's Child*	Lucille Clifton, *for deLawd* (text p. 1083)
	Edgar Allan Poe, *Alone* (text p. 1115)
Countee Cullen, *Yet Do I Marvel*	Gerard Manley Hopkins, *God's Grandeur* (text p. 837)
	Langston Hughes, *Negro* (text p. 1016)
E. E. Cummings, *anyone lived in a pretty how town*	Emily Dickinson, *I'm Nobody! Who are you?* (text p. 938)
E. E. Cummings, *Buffalo Bill 's*	Marilyn Nelson Waniek, *Emily Dickinson's Defunct* (text p. 912)
E. E. Cummings, *in Just-*	Robert Frost, *Two Tramps in Mud Time* (text p. 991)
E. E. Cummings, *l(a*	Robert Morgan, *Mountain Graveyard* (text p. 686)
E. E. Cummings, *next to of course god america i*	Langston Hughes, *Un-American Investigators* (text p. 1030)
	Yusef Komunyakaa, *Facing It* (manual p. 443)
	Florence Cassen Mayers, *All-American Sestina* (text p. 888)
E. E. Cummings, *she being Brand*	Sharon Olds, *Sex without Love* (manual p. 174)
	Marge Piercy, *The Secretary Chant* (text p. 671)
Jim Daniels, *Short-order Cook*	Seamus Heaney, *The Pitchfork* (text p. 760)
	Aron Keesbury, *Song to a Waitress* (manual p. 287)
Peter De Vries, *To His Importunate Mistress*	Anthony Hecht, *The Dover Bitch* (manual p. 279)
James Dickey, *Deer Among Cattle*	William Blake, *The Tyger* (text p. 868)
	Rainer Maria Rilke, *The Panther* (manual p. 195)
Emily Dickinson, *After great pain, a formal feeling comes —*	Emily Dickinson, *The Bustle in a House* (manual p. 314)
	Robert Frost, *Home Burial* (text p. 980)
	Donald Hall, *Letter with No Address* (text p. 1153)

AUTHOR, POEM	**CONNECTED TO:**
Emily Dickinson, *Apparently with no surprise*	Emily Dickinson, *Because I could not stop for Death* — (text p. 948)
	Emily Dickinson, *Safe in their Alabaster Chambers* — (1859 version) (text p. 933)
Emily Dickinson, *Because I could not stop for Death* —	Emily Dickinson, *Apparently with no surprise* (manual p. 316)
	Emily Dickinson, *If I shouldn't be alive* (text p. 929)
	Emily Dickinson, *I read my sentence — steadily* — (text p. 944)
Emily Dickinson, *A Bird came down the Walk* —	Rainer Maria Rilke, *The Panther* (text p. 767)
Emily Dickinson, *The Bustle in a House*	Emily Dickinson, *After great pain, a formal feeling comes* — (text p. 946)
	Emily Dickinson, *I like a look of Agony* (manual p. 319)
	Donald Hall, *Letter with No Address* (text p. 1153)
	Carolynn Hoy, *In the Summer Kitchen* (text p. 916)
Emily Dickinson, *"Faith" is a fine invention*	Emily Dickinson, *Portraits are to daily faces* (text p. 934)
	Emily Dickinson, *What Soft — Cherubic Creatures* — (text p. 940)
Emily Dickinson, *From all the Jails the Boys and Girls*	William Blake, *The Garden of Love* (text p. 1078)
	Cornelius Eady, *The Supremes* (text p. 1150)
	Robert Frost, *"Out, Out —"* (manual p. 320)
	Judy Page Heitzman, *The Schoolroom on the Second Floor of the Knitting Mill* (text p. 1158)
Emily Dickinson, *"Heaven"— is what I cannot reach!*	Diane Ackerman, *A Fine, a Private Place* (text p. 734)
	Katerina Angheláki-Rooke, *Jealousy* (manual p. 427)
	Emily Dickinson, *I like a look of Agony* (text p. 938)
	Emily Dickinson, *Water, is taught by thirst* (text p. 933)
	Linda Hogan, *Hunger* (text p. 1160)
Emily Dickinson, *I cannot dance upon my Toes* —	Emily Dickinson, *I dwell in Possibility* — (text p. 943)
	Emily Dickinson, *This is my letter to the World* (text p. 942)
	Emily Dickinson, *To make a prairie it takes a clover and one bee* (manual p. 307)
Emily Dickinson, *I dwell in Possibility* —	Emily Dickinson, *The Soul selects her own Society* — (text p. 941)

AUTHOR, POEM	CONNECTED TO:
Emily Dickinson, *I dwell in Possibility —* (cont.)	T. E. Hulme, *On the Differences between Poetry and Prose* (manual p. 311)
Emily Dickinson, *I felt a Cleaving in my Mind —*	Emily Dickinson, *To make a prairie it takes a clover and one bee* (manual p. 318)
	John Keats, *Ode to a Nightingale* (text p. 851)
Emily Dickinson, *If I can stop one Heart from breaking*	Emily Dickinson, *Because I could not stop for Death —* (text p. 948)
Emily Dickinson, *If I shouldn't be alive*	Emily Dickinson, *Because I could not stop for Death —* (text p. 948)
Emily Dickinson, *I heard a Fly buzz — when I died —*	Emily Dickinson, *There's a certain Slant of light* (text p. 2082)
	Marilyn Nelson Waniek, *Emily Dickinson's Defunct* (text p. 912)
	Walt Whitman, *A Noiseless Patient Spider* (manual p. 315)
Emily Dickinson, *I know that He exists*	Emily Dickinson, *Tell all the Truth but tell it slant —* (text p. 951)
	Robert Frost, *Design* (manual p. 337)
Emily Dickinson, *I like a look of Agony*	Emily Dickinson, *The Bustle in a House* (text p. 950)
	Emily Dickinson, *"Heaven" — is what I cannot reach!* (manual p. 305)
	Emily Dickinson, *Success is counted sweetest* (manual p. 305)
	Emily Dickinson, *Water, is taught by thirst* (text p. 933)
	Robert Hass, *Happiness* (manual p. 158)
Emily Dickinson, *I'm Nobody! Who are you?*	Emily Dickinson, *Wild Nights — Wild Nights!* (text p. 939)
	Walt Whitman, *One's-Self I Sing* (manual p. 306)
Emily Dickinson, *I never saw a Moor —*	Emily Dickinson, *"Heaven"— is what I cannot reach!* (text p. 936)
Emily Dickinson, *I read my sentence — steadily —*	Emily Dickinson, *Because I could not stop for Death —* (manual p. 312)
	Emily Dickinson, *I heard a Fly buzz — when I died —* (text p. 946)
	Emily Dickinson, *I like a look of Agony* (manual p. 312)
	Andrew Hudgins, *Elegy for My Father, Who Is Not Dead* (text p. 893)
	Dylan Thomas, *Do not go gentle into that good night* (text p. 885)
	Miller Williams, *Thinking About Bill, Dead of AIDS* (text p. 1125)
Emily Dickinson, *I taste a liquor never brewed —*	Emily Dickinson, *A narrow Fellow in the Grass* (text p. 2)
	Galway Kinnell, *Blackberry Eating* (manual p. 303)

AUTHOR, POEM	**CONNECTED TO:**
Emily Dickinson, *A Light exists in Spring*	Sophie Cabot Black, *August* (text p. 785)
	E. E. Cummings, *in Just-* (manual p. 317)
	Emily Dickinson, *"Heaven"— is what I cannot reach!* (text p. 936)
	Emily Dickinson, *I heard a Fly buzz — when I died* (manual p. 317)
	Emily Dickinson, *There's a certain Slant of light* (text p. 2082)
	Margaret Holley, *Peepers* (text p. 764)
	William Carlos Williams, *Spring and All* (text p. 1126)
Emily Dickinson, *Much Madness is divinest Sense —*	Emily Dickinson, *The Soul selects her own Society —* (manual p. 310)
	Walt Whitman, *One Hour to Madness and Joy* (text p. 1123)
Emily Dickinson, *Of Bronze — and Blaze —*	Stephen Crane, *A Man Said to the Universe* (manual p. 304)
	Emily Dickinson, *I heard a Fly buzz — when I died —* (text p. 946)
	John Keats, *On First Looking into Chapman's Homer* (manual p. 304)
	William Shakespeare, *Not marble, nor the gilded monuments* (text p. 1116)
Emily Dickinson, *One need not be a Chamber — to be Haunted —*	Edgar Allan Poe, *The Haunted Palace* (manual p. 315)
	Jim Stevens, *Schizophrenia* (manual p. 315)
Emily Dickinson, *Portraits are to daily faces*	Emily Dickinson, *"Faith" is a fine invention* (text p. 966)
	Emily Dickinson, *Tell all the Truth but tell it slant —* (text p. 951)
	Emily Dickinson, *The Thought beneath so slight a film —* (manual p. 301)
	Robert Francis, *Catch* (text p. 676)
	Robert Frost, *Birches* (text p. 986)
	Robert Frost, *Mending Wall* (text p. 979)
Emily Dickinson, *Presentiment — is that long Shadow — on the lawn —*	Robert Frost, *"Out, Out —"* (text p. 987)
Emily Dickinson, *Safe in their Alabaster Chambers —* (1859 version)	Emily Dickinson, *Apparently with no surprise* (text p. 967)
Emily Dickinson, *Safe in their Alabaster Chambers —* (1861 version)	Emily Dickinson, *Apparently with no surprise* (text p. 967)
	Robert Frost, *Design* (manual p. 300)
Emily Dickinson, *Some keep the Sabbath going to Church —*	Gerard Manley Hopkins, *Pied Beauty* (text p. 1099)
	Walt Whitman, *When I Heard the Learn'd Astronomer* (manual p. 302)
Emily Dickinson, *The Soul selects her own Society —*	Emily Dickinson, *I dwell in Possibility —* (text p. 943)

Author, Poem	**Connected to:**
Emily Dickinson, *The Soul selects her own Society —* (cont.)	Emily Dickinson, *Much Madness is divinest Sense —* (text p. 942)
Emily Dickinson, *Success is counted sweetest*	Emily Dickinson, *I like a look of Agony* (text p. 938)
	Emily Dickinson, *Water, is taught by thirst* (text p. 933)
	John Keats, *Ode on a Grecian Urn* (manual p. 299)
Emily Dickinson, *Tell all the Truth but tell it slant —*	Emily Dickinson, *I know that He exists* (manual p. 319)
	Emily Dickinson, *Portraits are to daily faces* (text p. 934)
	Emily Dickinson, *The Thought beneath so slight a film —* (text p. 931)
Emily Dickinson, *This is my letter to the World*	Emily Dickinson, *"Heaven"— is what I cannot reach!* (manual p. 309)
	Emily Dickinson, *The Soul selects her own Society —* (manual p. 309)
	Donald Hall, *Letter with No Address* (text p. 1153)
	Linda Pastan, *Marks* (text p. 791)
Emily Dickinson, *This was a Poet — It Is That*	Emily Dickinson, *A Bird came down the Walk —* (manual p. 311)
	Emily Dickinson, *I dwell in Possibility —* (manual p. 311)
	Emily Dickinson, *Of Bronze — and Blaze —* (text p. 937)
	John Keats, *When I have fears that I may cease to be* (text p. 1103)
	William Shakespeare, *Not marble, nor the gilded monuments* (text p. 1116)
Emily Dickinson, *The Thought beneath so slight a film —*	Emily Dickinson, *Portraits are to daily faces* (text p. 934)
	Emily Dickinson, *Tell all the Truth but tell it slant —* (text p. 951)
Emily Dickinson, *To make a prairie it takes a clover and one bee*	Emily Dickinson, *I felt a Cleaving in my Mind —* (text p. 950)
	Robert Frost, *Mending Wall* (manual p. 330)
Emily Dickinson, *Water, is taught by thirst*	Emily Dickinson, *"Heaven"— is what I cannot reach!* (text p. 936)
	Emily Dickinson, *I like a look of Agony* (text p. 938)
	Emily Dickinson, *Success is counted sweetest* (manual p. 299)
Emily Dickinson, *What Soft — Cherubic Creatures —*	Emily Dickinson, *"Faith" is a fine invention* (manual p. 308)

AUTHOR, POEM	CONNECTED TO:
Emily Dickinson, *What Soft — Cherubic Creatures —* (cont.)	Christina Georgina Rossetti, *Some Ladies Dress in Muslin Full and White* (text p. 1116)
Emily Dickinson, *Wild Nights — Wild Nights!*	Margaret Atwood, *you fit into me* (manual p. 307)
	Emily Dickinson, *I'm Nobody! Who are you?* (text p. 938)
Chitra Banerjee Divakaruni, *Indian Movie, New Jersey*	Langston Hughes, *Theme for English B* (text p. 1027)
	Tato Laviera, *AmeRícan* (text p. 918)
Gregory Djanikian, *When I First Saw Snow*	Elizabeth Alexander, *Harlem Birthday Party* (text p. 1148)
	John Keats, *On First Looking into Chapman's Homer* (text p. 879)
John Donne, *The Apparition*	Robin Becker, *Shopping* (text p. 794)
	John Donne, *The Flea* (text p. 1090)
John Donne, *Batter My Heart*	Mark Jarman, *Unholy Sonnet* (text p. 884)
John Donne, *Death Be Not Proud*	Mark Jarman, *Unholy Sonnet* (text p. 884)
John Donne, *The Flea*	Sally Croft, *Home-Baked Bread* (text p. 768)
	John Donne, *Song* (text p. 844)
	John Donne, *The Sun Rising* (text p. 705)
John Donne, *Hymn to God, My God, in My Sickness*	John Donne, *Batter My Heart* (text p. 1089)
	George Herbert, *The Collar* (text p. 1097)
John Donne, *Song*	Anonymous, *Scarborough Fair* (text p. 827)
John Donne, *The Sun Rising*	John Donne, *The Flea* (text p. 1090)
	Andrew Marvell, *To His Coy Mistress* (text p. 729)
	Richard Wilbur, *A Late Aubade* (manual p. 156)
John Donne, *A Valediction: Forbidding Mourning*	Anne Bradstreet, *To My Dear and Loving Husband* (text p. 1080)
	John Donne, *The Flea* (text p. 1090)
	William Shakespeare, *Shall I compare thee to a summer's day?* (text p. 881)
Paul Laurence Dunbar, *We Wear the Mask*	William Blake, *The Chimney Sweeper* (text p. 822)
Cornelius Eady, *The Supremes*	Robert Bly, *Sitting Down to Dinner* (text p. 824)
	Emily Dickinson, *From all the Jails the Boys and Girls* (manual p. 436)
	Judy Page Heitzman, *The Schoolroom on the Second Floor of the Knitting Mill* (manual p. 436)
	Louis Simpson, *In the Suburbs* (text p. 746)
George Eliot, *In a London Drawingroom*	Matthew Arnold, *Dover Beach* (text p. 757)
	Emily Dickinson, *I cannot dance upon my Toes —* (text p. 940)
	T. S. Eliot, *The Love Song of J. Alfred Prufrock* (text p. 1045)
	Robert Hass, *Happiness* (text p. 707)
T. S. Eliot, *The Love Song of J. Alfred Prufrock*	John Keats, *La Belle Dame sans Merci* (text p. 1103)
	Alberto Ríos, *Seniors* (manual p. 154)

558

AUTHOR, POEM	CONNECTED TO:
T. S. Eliot, *The Love Song of J. Alfred Prufrock* (cont.)	Wallace Stevens, *The Emperor of Ice-Cream* (text p. 1120) Walt Whitman, *One's-Self I Sing* (manual p. 371)
Louise Erdrich, *Windigo*	Margaret Holley, *Peepers* (text p. 764) William Butler Yeats, *Leda and the Swan* (text p. 1132)
Martín Espada, *Coca-Cola and Coco Frío*	Martín Espada, *Latin Night at the Pawnshop* (text p. 726) Langston Hughes, *Theme for English B* (manual p. 436) Tato Laviera, *AmeRícan* (manual p. 437) Gary Soto, *Mexicans Begin Jogging* (text p. 923) Mitsuye Yamada, *A Bedtime Story* (text p. 1129)
Martín Espada, *Latin Night at the Pawnshop*	Thom Ward, *Vasectomy* (text p. 920)
Ruth Fainlight, *Flower Feet*	Robert Frost, *Mending Wall* (manual p. 164) James Merrill, *Casual Wear* (manual p. 164) Janice Mirikitani, *Recipe* (text p. 803)
Faiz Ahmed Faiz, *If You Look at the City from Here*	William Blake, *London* (manual p. 427) George Eliot, *In a London Drawingroom* (text p. 1092) Langston Hughes, *Midnight Raffle* (text p. 1026) Rainer Maria Rilke, *The Panther* (manual p. 428)
Blanche Farley, *The Lover Not Taken*	Robert Frost, *The Road Not Taken* (text p. 976)
Helen Farries, *Magic of Love*	Langston Hughes, *Formula* (text p. 1021)
Kenneth Fearing, *AD*	Janice Mirikitani, *Recipe* (text p. 803) Wole Soyinka, *Future Plans* (manual p. 432)
Carolyn Forché, *The Colonel*	Sharon Olds, *Rite of Passage* (text p. 915)
Robert Francis, *Catch*	Emily Dickinson, *Portraits are to daily faces* (text p. 934) Robert Francis, *The Pitcher* (text p. 850) Robert Wallace, *The Double-Play* (text p. 1122)
Robert Francis, *The Pitcher*	Robert Francis, *Catch* (text p. 676) Robert Wallace, *The Double-Play* (manual p. 250)
Robert Frost, *Acquainted with the Night*	T. S. Eliot, *The Love Song of J. Alfred Prufrock* (text p. 1045) Robert Frost, *Stopping by Woods on a Snowy Evening* (text p. 989) Octavio Paz, *The Street* (manual p. 430)

AUTHOR, POEM	CONNECTED TO:
Robert Frost, *After Apple-Picking*	Robert Frost, *Two Tramps in Mud Time* (text p. 991) John Keats, *To Autumn* (manual p. 200)
Robert Frost, *Birches*	Emily Dickinson, *Portraits are to daily faces* (text p. 934) Pablo Neruda, *Sweetness, Always* (manual p. 429)
Robert Frost, *Come In*	Robert Frost, *Stopping by Woods on a Snowy Evening* (text p. 989) Henry Wadsworth Longfellow, *Snow-Flakes* (text p. 1106)
Robert Frost, *Design*	Emily Dickinson, *I know that He exists* (manual p. 337) Emily Dickinson, *Safe in their Alabaster Chambers* — (1861 version) (text p. 934) Robert Frost, *In White* (text p. 996) William Hathaway, *Oh, Oh* (manual p. 337) Denise Levertov, *Gathered at the River* (manual p. 285) Edna St. Vincent Millay, *I will put Chaos into fourteen lines* (manual p. 269)
Robert Frost, *Fire and Ice*	William Butler Yeats, *The Second Coming* (text p. 1133)
Robert Frost, *Home Burial*	Emily Dickinson, *After great pain, a formal feeling comes* — (text p. 946) Robert Frost, *"Out, Out —"* (manual p. 333) Jane Kenyon, *The Blue Bowl* (text p. 768)
Robert Frost, *Mending Wall*	Emily Dickinson, *Portraits are to daily faces* (text p. 934) Emily Dickinson, *To make a prairie it takes a clover and one bee* (manual p. 330) Ruth Fainlight, *Flower Feet* (manual p. 164) Robert Frost, *Neither Out Far nor In Deep* (manual p. 330)
Robert Frost, *The Most of It*	Emily Dickinson, *The Soul Selects her own Society* — (manual p. 340) Robert Frost, *Stopping by Woods on a Snowy Evening* (text p. 989) Robert Frost, *Two Tramps in Mud Time* (manual p. 340) N. Scott Momaday, *The Bear* (text p. 1110) Edgar Allan Poe, *Alone* (text p. 1115)
Robert Frost, *Neither Out Far nor In Deep*	Robert Frost, *Mending Wall* (text p. 979) Robert Frost, *The Most of It* (text p. 995) Robert Frost, *Once by the Pacific* (text p. 990)

AUTHOR, POEM	CONNECTED TO:
Robert Frost, *Nothing Gold Can Stay*	Robert Frost, *"Out, Out —"* (text p. 987) Robert Frost, *The Wood-Pile* (text p. 984) Robert Herrick, *To the Virgins, to Make Much of Time* (text p. 728)
Robert Frost, *Once by the Pacific*	Stephen Crane, *A Man Said to the Universe* (text p. 805) Robert Frost, *Neither Out Far nor In Deep* (manual p. 335)
Robert Frost, *"Out, Out —"*	Stephen Crane, *A Man Said to the Universe* (manual p. 333) Emily Dickinson, *From all the Jails the Boys and Girls* (text p. 951) Robert Frost, *Home Burial* (manual p. 333) Robert Frost, *Nothing Gold Can Stay* (manual p. 333)
Robert Frost, *The Pasture*	Robert Frost, *After Apple-Picking* (text p. 983) Walt Whitman, *One's-Self I Sing* (text p. 1124)
Robert Frost, *The Road Not Taken*	George Herbert, *The Collar* (text p. 1097)
Robert Frost, *The Silken Tent*	Robert Herrick, *Delight in Disorder* (text p. 865) William Shakespeare, *Shall I compare thee to a summer's day?* (text p. 881)
Robert Frost, *Stopping by Woods on a Snowy Evening*	Robert Frost, *The Wood-Pile* (text p. 984) Henry Wadsworth Longfellow, *Snow-Flakes* (text p. 1106)
Robert Frost, *Two Tramps in Mud Time*	Julia Alvarez, *Woman's Work* (text p. 886) William Blake, *The Chimney Sweeper* (text p. 822) Robert Frost, *After Apple-Picking* (manual p. 336) Seamus Heaney, *The Pitchfork* (text p. 760)
Robert Frost, *The Wood-Pile*	Robert Frost, *Come In* (text p. 994) Robert Frost, *Nothing Gold Can Stay* (manual p. 332) Robert Frost, *Stopping by Woods on a Snowy Evening* (text p. 989)
Deborah Garrison, *She Was Waiting to Be Told*	John Keats, *La Belle Dame sans Merci* (text p. 1103) Richard Wilbur, *A Late Aubade* (manual p. 437)
Allen Ginsberg, *First Party at Ken Kesey's with Hell's Angels*	William Hathaway, *Oh, Oh* (manual p. 290) Etheridge Knight, *Eastern Guard Tower* (text p. 892)
Louise Glück, *The School Children*	Emily Dickinson, *From all the Jails the Boys and Girls* (text p. 951) Cornelius Eady, *The Supremes* (text p. 1150) Judy Page Heitzman, *The Schoolroom on the Second Floor of the Knitting Mill* (text p. 1158)

AUTHOR, POEM	CONNECTED TO:
H. D. [Hilda Doolittle], *Heat*	Ezra Pound, *In a Station of the Metro* (text p. 772) William Carlos Williams, *Poem* (text p. 753)
Marilyn Hacker, *Groves of Academe*	Robert Browning, *My Last Duchess* (text p. 821) Mark Halliday, *Graded Paper* (manual p. 248)
Rachel Hadas, *The Red Hat*	Robert Bly, *Sitting Down to Dinner* (manual p. 257) Sharon Olds, *Rite of Passage* (text p. 915)
Donald Hall, *Letter with No Address*	Emily Dickinson, *The Bustle in a House* (manual p. 438) Robert Frost, *Home Burial* (manual p. 439) Andrew Hudgins, *Elegy for My Father, Who Is Not Dead* (text p. 893)
Donald Hall, *My Son, My Executioner*	Anne Bradstreet, *Before the Birth of One of Her Children* (text p. 1080)
Donald Hall, *Scenic View*	Robert Frost, *The Most of It* (text p. 995) James Wright, *A Blessing* (text p. 1129)
Mark Halliday, *Graded Paper*	Robert Browning, *My Last Duchess* (manual p. 439) Marilyn Hacker, *Groves of Academe* (text p. 848)
Thomas Hardy, *The Convergence of the Twain*	Stephen Crane, *A Man Said to the Universe* (text p. 805) David R. Slavitt, *Titanic* (text p. 739) Wallace Stevens, *The Emperor of Ice-Cream* (text p. 1120)
Thomas Hardy, *Hap*	Langston Hughes, *Lenox Avenue: Midnight* (text p. 1022)
Thomas Hardy, *The Ruined Maid*	Philip Larkin, *A Study of Reading Habits* (text p. 684) Katharyn Howd Machan, *Hazel Tells LaVerne* (text p. 725) Adrienne Rich, *Living in Sin* (text p. 1115)
Joy Harjo, *Fishing*	Elizabeth Bishop, *The Fish* (text p. 682) N. Scott Momaday, *The Bear* (text p. 1110)
Michael S. Harper, *Grandfather*	Elizabeth Alexander, *Harlem Birthday Party* (text p. 1148) Jimmy Santiago Baca, *Green Chile* (text p. 758) Regina Barreca, *Nighttime Fires* (text p. 688) Langston Hughes, *The Weary Blues* (text p. 1019)
Robert Hass, *Happiness*	James Dickey, *Deer Among Cattle* (text p. 766) Emily Dickinson, *I like a look of Agony* (manual p. 158)

AUTHOR, POEM	CONNECTED TO:
Robert Hass, *A Story About the Body*	Joan Murray, *Play-By-Play* (text p. 1163)
William Hathaway, *Oh, Oh*	Robert Frost, *Design* (manual p. 337)
	Wyatt Prunty, *Elderly Lady Crossing on Green* (manual p. 153)
Robert Hayden, *Those Winter Sundays*	Margaret Atwood, *Bored* (text p. 737)
	Regina Barreca, *Nighttime Fires* (text p. 688)
	Andrew Hudgins, *Elegy for My Father, Who Is Not Dead* (text p. 893)
	Theodore Roethke, *My Papa's Waltz* (text p. 871)
Seamus Heaney, *Mid-term Break*	A. E. Housman, *To an Athlete Dying Young* (manual p. 276)
	John Updike, *Dog's Death* (text p. 673)
Seamus Heaney, *The Pitchfork*	Jimmy Santiago Baca, *Green Chile* (text p. 758)
	Elizabeth Bishop, *The Fish* (text p. 682)
Anthony Hecht, *The Dover Bitch*	Matthew Arnold, *Dover Beach* (manual p. 187)
	Peter De Vries, *To His Importunate Mistress* (text p. 898)
Judy Page Heitzman, *The Schoolroom on the Second Floor of the Knitting Mill*	Emily Dickinson, *From all the Jails the Boys and Girls* (manual p. 441)
	Cornelius Eady, *The Supremes* (text p. 1150)
George Herbert, *The Collar*	Sir Philip Sidney, *Loving in Truth, and Fain in Verse My Love to Show* (text p. 1119)
Robert Herrick, *Delight in Disorder*	Ben Jonson, *Still to Be Neat* (manual p. 258)
Robert Herrick, *To the Virgins, to Make Much of Time*	Robert Frost, *Nothing Gold Can Stay* (text p. 989)
	Edmund Waller, *Go, Lovely Rose* (text p. 1123)
	Richard Wilbur, *A Late Aubade* (text p. 732)
Robert Herrick, *Upon Julia's Clothes*	Paul Humphrey, *Blow* (manual p. 266)
William Heyen, *The Trains*	Mary Jo Salter, *Welcome to Hiroshima* (text p. 703)
Conrad Hilberry, *The Frying Pan*	Julia Alvarez, *Woman's Work* (text p. 886)
	Bonnie Jacobson, *On Being Served Apples* (text p. 753)
Jane Hirshfield, *The Lives of the Heart*	Alice Jones, *The Foot* (manual p. 442)
	Jim Stevens, *Schizophrenia* (manual p. 441)
	Walt Whitman, *The Soul, reaching, throwing out for love* (text p. 789)
Li Ho, *A Beautiful Girl Combs Her Hair*	Langston Hughes, *The English* (text p. 1024)
	Sylvia Plath, *Mirror* (text p. 786)

AUTHOR, POEM	CONNECTED TO:
Li Ho, *A Beautiful Girl Combs Her Hair* (cont.)	David Solway, *Windsurfing* (text p. 755) Cathy Song, *The White Porch* (manual p. 157)
Linda Hogan, *Hunger*	Sally Croft, *Home-Baked Bread* (manual p. 442) Emily Dickinson, *"Heaven" — is what I cannot reach!* (text p. 936)
Linda Hogan, *Song for My Name*	Jimmy Santiago Baca, *Green Chile* (text p. 758) Ben Jonson, *On My First Son* (text p. 1102)
Margaret Holley, *Peepers*	Sylvia Plath, *Mushrooms* (text p. 172)
M. Carl Holman, *Mr. Z*	Elizabeth Alexander, *Harlem Birthday Party* (text p. 1148) Paul Laurence Dunbar, *We Wear the Mask* (text p. 808)
Gerard Manley Hopkins, *God's Grandeur*	Denise Levertov, *Gathered at the River* (manual p. 283) William Wordsworth, *The World Is Too Much with Us* (manual p. 267)
Gerard Manley Hopkins, *Pied Beauty*	E. E. Cummings, *in Just-* (text p. 902)
Gerard Manley Hopkins, *Spring and Fall*	Gerard Manley Hopkins, *The Windhover* (text p. 1100)
Gerard Manley Hopkins, *The Windhover*	Gerard Manley Hopkins, *God's Grandeur* (text p. 837)
A. E. Housman, *Is my team ploughing*	Emily Dickinson, *Because I could not stop for Death —* (text p. 948)
A. E. Housman, *Loveliest of trees, the cherry now*	Robert Frost, *The Road Not Taken* (text p. 976) Robert Herrick, *To the Virgins, to Make Much of Time* (text p. 728)
A. E. Housman, *When I was one-and-twenty*	Margaret Atwood, *Bored* (text p. 737) Robert Frost, *Birches* (text p. 986)
Carolynn Hoy, *In the Summer Kitchen*	Emily Dickinson, *The Bustle in a House* (text p. 950)
Andrew Hudgins, *Elegy for My Father, Who Is Not Dead*	Donald Hall, *Letter with No Address* (text p. 1153) Robert Hayden, *Those Winter Sundays* (text p. 672) Dylan Thomas, *Do not go gentle into that good night* (manual p. 277)
Andrew Hudgins, *Seventeen*	Jane Kenyon, *The Blue Bowl* (text p. 99) William Stafford, *Traveling through the Dark* (manual p. 228)
Langston Hughes, *Ballad of the Landlord*	Aron Keesbury, *Song to a Waitress* (text p. 872) Wole Soyinka, *Telephone Conversation* (text p. 681)

AUTHOR, POEM	CONNECTED TO:
Langston Hughes, *Cross*	Robert Francis, *On "Hard" Poetry* (manual p. 353)
	Langston Hughes, *Red Silk Stockings* (text p. 1022)
Langston Hughes, *Danse Africaine*	Martín Espada, *Latin Night at the Pawnshop* (text p. 726)
	Langston Hughes, *Formula* (manual p. 349)
	Edgar Allan Poe, *The Bells* (text p. 838)
	Jean Toomer, *Reapers* (text p. 844)
Langston Hughes, *Dinner Guest: Me*	M. Carl Holman, *Mr. Z* (text p. 1098)
	Maxine Hong Kingston, *Restaurant* (manual p. 365)
Langston Hughes, *doorknobs*	Jim Stevens, *Schizophrenia* (manual p. 364)
Langston Hughes, *Dream Boogie*	Langston Hughes, *Dream Variations* (manual p. 361)
	Langston Hughes, *Harlem* (text p. 1030)
Langston Hughes, *Dream Variations*	Langston Hughes, *Dream Boogie* (manual p. 350)
	Langston Hughes, *Negro* (text p. 1016)
Langston Hughes, *The English*	Li Ho, *A Beautiful Girl Combs Her Hair* (manual p. 356)
	D. H. Lawrence, *The English Are So Nice!* (manual p. 178)
Langston Hughes, *Formula*	Helen Farries, *Magic of Love* (text p. 692)
	Archibald MacLeish, *Ars Poetica* (text p. 1107)
Langston Hughes, *Frederick Douglass: 1817–1895*	Langston Hughes, *Harlem* (manual p. 365)
	Galway Kinnell, *The Deconstruction of Emily Dickinson* (text p. 961)
Langston Hughes, *Harlem*	Langston Hughes, *Dream Boogie* (text p. 1029)
	Langston Hughes, *Frederick Douglass: 1817–1895* (text p. 1034)
	James Merrill, *Casual Wear* (manual p. 362)
Langston Hughes, *Jazzonia*	Diane Ackerman, *A Fine, a Private Place* (text p. 734)
	Elizabeth Alexander, *Harlem Birthday Party* (text p. 1148)
	Allen Ginsberg, *First Party at Ken Kesey's with Hell's Angels* (text p. 917)
	Langston Hughes, *Danse Africaine* (manual p. 349)
	Langston Hughes, *Rent-Party Shout: For a Lady Dancer* (text p. 1023)

AUTHOR, POEM	CONNECTED TO:
Langston Hughes, *Johannesburg Mines*	William Blake, *The Chimney Sweeper* (text p. 822) T. E. Hulme, *On the Differences between Poetry and Prose* (manual p. 351)
Langston Hughes, *Juke Box Love Song*	Joseph Brodsky, *Love Song* (text p. 845) Langston Hughes, *Danse Africaine* (text p. 1017) Langston Hughes, *Red Silk Stockings* (manual p. 360) Timothy Steele, *An Aubade* (text p. 761)
Langston Hughes, *Lenox Avenue: Midnight*	Stephen Crane, *A Man Said to the Universe* (text p. 805) Emily Dickinson, *I know that He exists* (manual p. 354) Thomas Hardy, *Hap* (manual p. 354) Langston Hughes, *Jazzonia* (text p. 1017) Octavio Paz, *The Street* (manual p. 430)
Langston Hughes, *Midnight Raffle*	Regina Barreca, *Nighttime Fires* (text p. 688) Lucille Clifton, *come home from the movies* (text p. 791) Langston Hughes, *doorknobs* (manual p. 359)
Langston Hughes, *Negro*	William Blake, *The Chimney Sweeper* (manual p. 348) Langston Hughes, *Dream Variations* (text p. 1018) Langston Hughes, *The Negro Speaks of Rivers* (text p. 1010)
Langston Hughes, *Note on Commercial Theatre*	Amiri Baraka, *SOS* (text p. 1077) Marilyn Bowering, *Wishing Africa* (text p. 743) Langston Hughes, *Frederick Douglass: 1817–1895* (manual p. 357) Langston Hughes, *The Weary Blues* (text p. 1019) Julio Marzán, *Ethnic Poetry* (text p. 816) Derek Walcott, *The Virgins* (text p. 723)
Langston Hughes, *Old Walt*	Langston Hughes, *Frederick Douglass: 1817–1895* (manual p. 363)
Langston Hughes, *Red Silk Stockings*	Gwendolyn Brooks, *We Real Cool* (text p. 743) M. Carl Holman, *Mr. Z* (text p. 1098) Langston Hughes, *Dinner Guest: Me* (manual p. 355) Langston Hughes, *Rent-Party Shout: For a Lady Dancer* (text p. 1023)

AUTHOR, POEM	**CONNECTED TO:**
Langston Hughes, *Rent-Party Shout: For a Lady Dancer*	Langston Hughes, *Dream Boogie* (text p. 1029)
Langston Hughes, *Theme for English B*	Chitra Banerjee Divakaruni, *Indian Movie, New Jersey* (manual p. 359)
	Mark Halliday, *Graded Paper* (text p. 1156)
Langston Hughes, *Un-American Investigators*	E. E. Cummings, *next to of course god america i* (manual p. 363)
	N. Scott Momaday, *The Bear* (text p. 1110)
Langston Hughes, *The Weary Blues*	Langston Hughes, *Lenox Avenue: Midnight* (manual p. 352)
Ted Hughes, *Thistles*	Sylvia Plath, *Mushrooms* (text p. 842)
Paul Humphrey, *Blow*	Robert Herrick, *Upon Julia's Clothes* (text p. 878)
Bonnie Jacobson, *On Being Served Apples*	Jimmy Santiago Baca, *Green Chile* (text p. 758)
	Conrad Hilberry, *The Frying Pan* (text p. 807)
	Alice Walker, *a woman is not a potted plant* (text p. 700)
Mark Jarman, *Unholy Sonnet*	John Donne, *Batter My Heart* (text p. 1089)
	John Donne, *Death Be Not Proud* (text p. 1090)
Randall Jarrell, *The Death of the Ball Turret Gunner*	Wilfred Owen, *Dulce et Decorum Est* (text p. 763)
	Alfred, Lord Tennyson, *The Charge of the Light Brigade* (text p. 870)
Alice Jones, *The Foot*	Wilfred Owen, *Arms and the Boy* (text p. 1112)
Ben Jonson, *On My First Son*	Anne Bradstreet, *Before the Birth of One of Her Children* (text p. 1080)
Ben Jonson, *Still to Be Neat*	Robert Herrick, *Delight in Disorder* (manual p. 258)
Ben Jonson, *To Celia*	Joseph Brodsky, *Love Song* (text p. 845)
	Robert Herrick, *Upon Julia's Clothes* (text p. 878)
	Christopher Marlowe, *The Passionate Shepherd to His Love* (text p. 1108)
	William Shakespeare, *Not marble, nor the gilded monuments* (text p. 1116)
John Keats, *La Belle Dame sans Merci*	Anonymous, *Bonny Barbara Allan* (text p. 1074)
	Emily Dickinson, *Because I could not stop for Death* — (text p. 948)

AUTHOR, POEM	CONNECTED TO:
John Keats, *Bright star! would I were steadfast as thou art —*	Emily Dickinson, *Of Bronze — and Blaze —* (text p. 937)
John Keats, *Ode on a Grecian Urn*	Andrew Marvell, *To His Coy Mistress* (manual p. 175)
John Keats, *Ode to a Nightingale*	Robert Frost, *Come In* (text p. 994)
	Percy Bysshe Shelley, *Ode to the West Wind* (text p. 894)
John Keats, *On First Looking into Chapman's Homer*	Robert Hass, *Happiness* (text p. 707)
	Walt Whitman, *One Hour to Madness and Joy* (text p. 1123)
John Keats, *To Autumn*	Robert Frost, *After Apple-Picking* (manual p. 200)
	John Keats, *Ode on a Grecian Urn* (manual p. 176)
	Theodore Roethke, *Root Cellar* (text p. 756)
John Keats, *When I have fears that I may cease to be*	Emily Dickinson, *This was a Poet — It Is That* (text p. 943)
	William Shakespeare, *Not marble, nor the gilded monuments* (text p. 1116)
Aron Keesbury, *Song to a Waitress*	Jim Daniels, *Short-order Cook* (text p. 913)
	Katharyn Howd Machan, *Hazel Tells LaVerne* (text p. 725)
	Wyatt Prunty, *Elderly Lady Crossing on Green* (text p. 701)
Jane Kenyon, *The Blue Bowl*	Rachel Hadas, *The Red Hat* (text p. 864)
	John Updike, *Dog's Death* (text p. 673)
Jane Kenyon, *Surprise*	William Hathaway, *Oh, Oh* (manual p. 222)
	Sharon Olds, *Rite of Passage* (manual p. 222)
Maxine Hong Kingston, *Restaurant*	Langston Hughes, *Dinner Guest: Me* (text p. 1033)
	Carolyn Kizer, *Food for Love* (text p. 769)
	Elaine Magarrell, *The Joy of Cooking* (text p. 792)
Galway Kinnell, *After Making Love We Hear Footsteps*	Robert Frost, *Home Burial* (manual p. 283)
	Donald Hall, *My Son, My Executioner* (text p. 1093)
	Peter Meinke, *The ABC of Aerobics* (manual p. 294)
Galway Kinnell, *Blackberry Eating*	Helen Chasin, *The Word Plum* (text p. 851)
	Emily Dickinson, *I taste a liquor never brewed —* (text p. 936)
	Pablo Neruda, *Sweetness, Always* (manual p. 429)
Carolyn Kizer, *Food for Love*	Sally Croft, *Home-Baked Bread* (text p. 768)
	Maxine Hong Kingston, *Restaurant* (text p. 849)

AUTHOR, POEM	CONNECTED TO:
Carolyn Kizer, *Food for Love* (cont.)	Elaine Magarrell, *The Joy of Cooking* (text p. 792)
	Andrew Marvell, *To His Coy Mistress* (text p. 729)
Etheridge Knight, *A Watts Mother Mourns While Boiling Beans*	Lucille Clifton, *for deLawd* (text p. 1083)
Yusef Komunyakaa, *Facing It*	E. E. Cummings, *next to of course god america i* (manual p. 443)
	Mary Jo Salter, *Welcome to Hiroshima* (text p. 703)
Maxine Kumin, *Woodchucks*	William Stafford, *Traveling through the Dark* (text p. 813)
Philip Larkin, *A Study of Reading Habits*	Thomas Hardy, *The Ruined Maid* (text p. 1093)
	Marianne Moore, *Poetry* (text p. 1111)
Philip Larkin, *This Be the Verse*	Robert Bly, *Sitting Down to Dinner* (text p. 824)
	Queen Latifah, *The Evil That Men Do* (text p. 695)
Tato Laviera, *AmeRícan*	Joseph Bruchac, *Ellis Island* (text p. 921)
	Chitra Banerjee Divakaruni, *Indian Movie, New Jersey* (text p. 819)
D. H. Lawrence, *The English Are So Nice!*	Langston Hughes, *The English* (manual p. 178)
Li-Young Lee, *Eating Together*	Indira Sant, *Household Fires* (text p. 1144)
	Dylan Thomas, *Do not go gentle into that good night* (text p. 885)
Denise Levertov, *Gathered at the River*	Robert Frost, *Design* (manual p. 285)
	Gerard Manley Hopkins, *God's Grandeur, Pied Beauty* (manual p. 285)
	Mary Jo Salter, *Welcome to Hiroshima* (manual p. 155)
Denise Levertov, *News Items*	Langston Hughes, *Johannesburg Mines* (text p. 1019)
	Queen Latifah, *The Evil That Men Do* (text p. 695)
	Thom Ward, *Vasectomy* (text p. 920)
Philip Levine, *The Simple Truth*	Langston Hughes, *Formula* (text p. 1021)
	Marianne Moore, *Poetry* (text p. 1111)
J. Patrick Lewis, *The Unkindest Cut*	Queen Latifah, *The Evil That Men Do* (text p. 695)
	Dorothy Parker, *One Perfect Rose* (text p. 869)
Henry Wadsworth Longfellow, *Snow-Flakes*	Robert Frost, *Stopping by Woods on a Snowy Evening* (text p. 989)
	Percy Bysshe Shelley, *Ode to the West Wind* (text p. 894)
Audre Lorde, *Hanging Fire*	Indira Sant, *Household Fires* (text p. 1144)

AUTHOR, POEM	CONNECTED TO:
Katharyn Howd Machan, *Hazel Tells LaVerne*	Robert Browning, *My Last Duchess* (manual p. 165) Thomas Hardy, *The Ruined Maid* (text p. 1093) Marge Piercy, *The Secretary Chant* (text p. 671)
Elaine Magarrell, *The Joy of Cooking*	Sally Croft, *Home-Baked Bread* (manual p. 215) Maxine Hong Kingston, *Restaurant* (text p. 849) Carolyn Kizer, *Food for Love* (text p. 769)
Christopher Marlowe, *The Passionate Shepherd to His Love*	John Donne, *The Sun Rising* (text p. 705) William Shakespeare, *When, in disgrace with Fortune and men's eyes* (text p. 1118) Richard Wilbur, *A Late Aubade* (text p. 732)
Charles Martin, *Victoria's Secret*	Robin Becker, *Shopping* (text p. 794) Kenneth Fearing, *AD* (manual p. 259)
Andrew Marvell, *To His Coy Mistress*	Diane Ackerman, *A Fine, a Private Place* (text p. 734) John Donne, *The Sun Rising* (text p. 705) John Keats, *Ode on a Grecian Urn* (manual p. 175) Carolyn Kizer, *Food for Love* (text p. 769) Richard Wilbur, *A Late Aubade* (text p. 732)
Julio Marzán, *Ethnic Poetry*	Robert Frost, *Mending Wall* (text p. 979) Langston Hughes, *Formula* (manual p. 229) D. H. Lawrence, *The English Are So Nice!* (text p. 745)
Florence Cassen Mayers, *All-American Sestina*	E. E. Cummings, *next to of course god america i* (manual p. 274) Tato Laviera, *AmeRícan* (text p. 918) Louis Simpson, *In the Suburbs* (text p. 746)
Peter Meinke, *The ABC of Aerobics*	Galway Kinnell, *After Making Love We Hear Footsteps* (manual p. 294) James Merrill, *Casual Wear* (manual p. 230) Sharon Olds, *Sex without Love* (manual p. 294)
Herman Melville, *The Maldive Shark*	Robert Frost, *Design* (text p. 993) N. Scott Momaday, *The Bear* (text p. 1110)
James Merrill, *Casual Wear*	W. H. Auden, *The Unknown Citizen* (text p. 1076) Ruth Fainlight, *Flower Feet* (manual p. 164) Peter Meinke, *The ABC of Aerobics* (manual p. 230)
Edna St. Vincent Millay, *I will put Chaos into fourteen lines*	Robert Frost, *Design* (manual p. 269)

AUTHOR, POEM	CONNECTED TO:
Edna St. Vincent Millay, *What Lips My Lips Have Kissed*	Robert Herrick, *To the Virgins, to Make Much of Time* (text p. 728) William Butler Yeats, *Sailing to Byzantium* (text p. 1132)
John Milton, *On the Late Massacre in Piedmont*	Wilfred Owen, *Dulce et Decorum Est* (text p. 763) Alfred, Lord Tennyson, *The Charge of the Light Brigade* (text p. 870)
John Milton, *When I consider how my light is spent*	Anne Bradstreet, *To My Dear and Loving Husband* (text p. 1080) Ben Jonson, *On My First Son* (text p. 1102) John Keats, *When I have fears that I may cease to be* (text p. 1103)
Janice Mirikitani, *Recipe*	Ruth Fainlight, *Flower Feet* (text p. 724) Kenneth Fearing, *AD* (text p. 803)
N. Scott Momaday, *The Bear*	James Dickey, *Deer Among Cattle* (text p. 766) Robert Frost, *The Most of It* (text p. 995)
Janice Townley Moore, *To a Wasp*	John Donne, *The Flea* (text p. 1090) David McCord, *Epitaph on a Waiter* (text p. 890)
Marianne Moore, *Poetry*	Langston Hughes, *Formula* (text p. 1021) Archibald MacLeish, *Ars Poetica* (text p. 1107) Miller Williams, *Excuse Me* (text p. 708)
Robert Morgan, *Mountain Graveyard*	Helen Chasin, *The Word Plum* (text p. 851) E. E. Cummings, *l(a* (text p. 687)
Joan Murray, *Play-By-Play*	Diane Ackerman, *A Fine, a Private Place* (manual p. 444) Robert Herrick, *To the Virgins, to Make Much of Time* (text p. 728) Timothy Steele, *An Aubade* (manual p. 444)
Pablo Neruda, *Sweetness, Always*	Helen Chasin, *The Word Plum* (manual p. 429) Robert Frost, *Birches* (manual p. 429) Galway Kinnell, *Blackberry Eating* (manual p. 429)
John Frederick Nims, *Love Poem*	William Shakespeare, *My mistress' eyes are nothing like the sun* (text p. 882)
Alden Nowlan, *The Bull Moose*	William Stafford, *Traveling through the Dark* (text p. 813)
Sharon Olds, *Rite of Passage*	Carolyn Forché, *The Colonel* (text p. 914) Wilfred Owen, *Dulce et Decorum Est* (text p. 763) Gary Soto, *Behind Grandma's House* (text p. 823)

AUTHOR, POEM	CONNECTED TO:
Sharon Olds, *Sex without Love*	E. E. Cummings, *she being Brand* (manual p. 174) Peter Meinke, *The ABC of Aerobics* (manual p. 294) Alberto Ríos, *Seniors* (manual p. 154) Richard Wilbur, *A Late Aubade* (manual p. 174)
Mary Oliver, *The Black Snake*	Elizabeth Bishop, *The Fish* (text p. 682) Andrew Hudgins, *Seventeen* (text p. 813) William Stafford, *Traveling through the Dark* (text p. 813)
Wilfred Owen, *Arms and the Boy*	Wilfred Owen, *Dulce et Decorum Est* (text p. 763) Alfred, Lord Tennyson, *The Charge of the Light Brigade* (text p. 870)
Wilfred Owen, *Dulce et Decorum Est*	Matthew Arnold, *Dover Beach* (manual p. 187) Randall Jarrell, *The Death of the Ball Turret Gunner* (text p. 720) Sharon Olds, *Rite of Passage* (text p. 915)
Linda Pastan, *Marks*	Julia Alvarez, *Woman's Work* (text p. 886) Indira Sant, *Household Fires* (text p. 1144)
Octavio Paz, *The Street*	Robert Frost, *Acquainted with the Night* (manual p. 430) Langston Hughes, *Lenox Avenue: Midnight* (manual p. 430)
Molly Peacock, *Desire*	Diane Ackerman, *A Fine, a Private Place* (manual p. 270) Walt Whitman, from *I Sing the Body Electric* (text p. 903)
Stephen Perry, *Blue Spruce*	Regina Barreca, *Nighttime Fires* (text p. 688) Theodore Roethke, *My Papa's Waltz* (text p. 871)
Marge Piercy, *Barbie Doll*	Robert Bly, *Sitting Down to Dinner* (text p. 824) Indira Sant, *Household Fires* (text p. 1144)
Marge Piercy, *The Secretary Chant*	E. E. Cummings, *she being Brand* (text p. 721) Katharyn Howd Machan, *Hazel Tells LaVerne* (text p. 725) Alice Walker, *a woman is not a potted plant* (manual p. 152)
Sylvia Plath, *Daddy*	Philip Larkin, *This Be the Verse* (text p. 1105) Linda Pastan, *Marks* (text p. 791)
Sylvia Plath, *Metaphors*	Sylvia Plath, *Mirror* (text p. 786) Sylvia Plath, *Mushrooms* (text p. 842)

AUTHOR, POEM	CONNECTED TO:
Sylvia Plath, *Mirror*	Claribel Alegría, *I Am Mirror* (text p. 1136) Li Ho, *A Beautiful Girl Combs Her Hair* (text p. 706)
Edgar Allan Poe, *Alone*	Emily Dickinson, *I'm Nobody! Who are you?* (text p. 938) Emily Dickinson, *The Soul selects her own Society —* (text p. 941)
Edgar Allan Poe, *The Bells*	Anonymous, *Bonny Barbara Allan* (text p. 1074) Robert Southey, *The Cataract of Lodore* (manual p. 242)
Edgar Allan Poe, *The Haunted Palace*	Emily Dickinson, *One need not be a Chamber — to be Haunted —* (text p. 947) Jim Stevens, *Schizophrenia* (text p. 788)
Alexander Pope, from *An Essay on Criticism*	Langston Hughes, *Formula* (text p. 1021)
Ezra Pound, *In a Station of the Metro*	Emily Dickinson, *I dwell in Possibility —* (text p. 943) Langston Hughes, *Johannesburg Mines* (text p. 1019) William Carlos Williams, *Poem* (text p. 753)
Wyatt Prunty, *Elderly Lady Crossing on Green*	William Hathaway, *Oh, Oh* (manual p. 153) Aron Keesbury, *Song to a Waitress* (text p. 872)
Queen Latifah, *The Evil That Men Do*	Bruce Springsteen, *Streets of Philadelphia* (manual p. 150)
Henry Reed, *Naming of Parts*	E. E. Cummings, *she being Brand* (text p. 721) Linda Pastan, *Marks* (text p. 791)
Adrienne Rich, *Living in Sin*	Thomas Hardy, *The Ruined Maid* (text p. 1093) Sharon Olds, *Sex without Love* (text p. 740)
Rainer Maria Rilke, *The Panther*	Marilyn Bowering, *Wishing Africa* (text p. 743) Emily Dickinson, *A Bird came down the Walk —* (manual p. 196)
Alberto Ríos, *Seniors*	T. S. Eliot, *The Love Song of J. Alfred Prufrock* (manual p. 154) Sharon Olds, *Sex without Love* (manual p. 154)
Edwin Arlington Robinson, *Richard Cory*	M. Carl Holman, *Mr. Z* (text p. 1098) Percy Bysshe Shelley, *Ozymandias* (text p. 1118)
Theodore Roethke, *My Papa's Waltz*	Regina Barreca, *Nighttime Fires* (text p. 688) Robert Hayden,*Those Winter Sundays* (text p. 672) Dylan Thomas, *Do not go gentle into that good night* (text p. 885)

AUTHOR, POEM	CONNECTED TO:
Theodore Roethke, *Root Cellar*	John Keats, *To Autumn* (text p. 771)
Christina Georgina Rossetti, *Some Ladies Dress in Muslin Full and White*	Emily Dickinson, *I'm Nobody! Who are you?* (text p. 938)
	Charles Martin, *Victoria's Secret* (text p. 867)
Mary Jo Salter, *Welcome to Hiroshima*	Denise Levertov, *Gathered at the River* (manual p. 155)
Indira Sant, *Household Fires*	Julia Alvarez, *Woman's Work* (text p. 886)
	Chitra Banerjee Divakaruni, *Indian Movie, New Jersey* (manual p. 431)
	Elaine Magarrell, *The Joy of Cooking* (text p. 792)
	Linda Pastan, *Marks* (text p. 791)
	Sylvia Plath, *Daddy* (manual p. 431)
Anne Sexton, *Lobster*	Herman Melville, *The Maldive Shark* (text p. 1109)
	N. Scott Momaday, *The Bear* (text p. 1110)
William Shakespeare, *My mistress' eyes are nothing like the sun*	William Shakespeare, *Shall I compare thee to a summer's day?* (text p. 881)
	Alice Walker, *a woman is not a potted plant* (text p. 700)
William Shakespeare, *Not marble, nor the gilded monuments*	Emily Dickinson, *This is a Poet — It Is That* (text p. 943)
	John Keats, *Ode on a Grecian Urn* (text p. 741)
William Shakespeare, *Shall I compare thee to a summer's day?*	John Frederick Nims, *Love Poem* (text p. 693)
	William Shakespeare, *My mistress' eyes are nothing like the sun* (text p. 882)
William Shakespeare, *That time of year thou mayst in me behold*	Matthew Arnold, *Dover Beach* (text p. 757)
	Anne Bradstreet, *To My Dear and Loving Husband* (text p. 1080)
	Robert Hass, *Happiness* (text p. 707)
	Richard Wilbur, *A Late Aubade* (text p. 732)
William Shakespeare, *When forty winters shall besiege thy brow*	Anne Bradstreet, *Before the Birth of One of Her Children* (text p. 1080)
	Ben Jonson, *On My First Son* (text p. 1102)
William Shakespeare, *When, in disgrace with Fortune and men's eyes*	John Donne, *A Valediction: Forbidding Mourning* (text p. 790)
	William Shakespeare, *That time of year thou mayst in me behold* (text p. 1117)
Percy Bysshe Shelley, *Ode to the West Wind*	Sophie Cabot Black, *August* (text p. 785)
	Henry Wadsworth Longfellow, *Snow-Flakes* (text p. 1106)
Percy Bysshe Shelley, *Ozymandias*	John Keats, *Ode on a Grecian Urn* (text p. 741)
	William Butler Yeats, *Sailing to Byzantium* (text p. 1132)

AUTHOR, POEM	CONNECTED TO:
Sir Philip Sidney, *Loving in Truth, and Fain in Verse My Love to Show*	George Herbert, *The Collar* (text p. 1097)
Louis Simpson, *In the Suburbs*	John Ciardi, *Suburban* (manual p. 179) Florence Cassen Mayers, *All-American Sestina* (text p. 888)
David R. Slavitt, *Titanic*	Thomas Hardy, *The Convergence of the Twain* (manual p. 173)
Ernest Slyman, *Lightning Bugs*	Ezra Pound, *In a Station of the Metro* (text p. 772)
David Solway, *Windsurfing*	Elizabeth Bishop, *The Fish* (text p. 682) Li Ho, *A Beautiful Girl Combs Her Hair* (text p. 706)
Cathy Song, *The White Porch*	Sally Croft, *Home-Baked Bread* (manual p. 201) Li Ho, *A Beautiful Girl Combs Her Hair* (manual p. 157)
Gary Soto, *Behind Grandma's House*	Sharon Olds, *Rite of Passage* (text p. 915)
Gary Soto, *Black Hair*	Martín Espada, *Coca-Cola and Coco Frío* (text p. 1150) Gary Soto, *Mexicans Begin Jogging* (text p. 923) Robert Wallace, *The Double-Play* (text p. 1122)
Gary Soto, *Mexicans Begin Jogging*	Peter Meinke, *The ABC of Aerobics* (manual p. 295) Wole Soyinka, *Telephone Conversation* (text p. 681) Thom Ward, *Vasectomy* (text p. 920)
Robert Southey, from *The Cataract of Lodore*	Greg Williamson, *Waterfall* (text p. 874)
Wole Soyinka, *Future Plans*	Kenneth Fearing, *AD* (manual p. 432) Dylan Thomas, *The Hand That Signed the Paper* (text p. 781)
Wole Soyinka, *Telephone Conversation*	Chitra Banerjee Divakaruni, *Indian Movie, New Jersey* (text p. 819) Langston Hughes, *Ballad of the Landlord* (text p. 1025) Gary Soto, *Mexicans Begin Jogging* (text p. 923)
Bruce Springsteen, *Streets of Philadelphia*	Robert Francis, *On "Hard" Poetry* (text p. 697) Queen Latifah, *The Evil That Men Do* (manual p. 150)
William Stafford, *Traveling through the Dark*	Andrew Hudgins, *Seventeen* (text p. 813) Langston Hughes, *Dream Variations* (text p. 1018)

Suggested Connections Between Selections

AUTHOR, POEM	CONNECTED TO:
William Stafford, *Traveling through the Dark* (cont.)	Alden Nowlan, *The Bull Moose* (text p. 815) John Updike, *Dog's Death* (text p. 673)
Timothy Steele, *An Aubade*	Anonymous, *Western Wind* (text p. 688) Robert Herrick, *To the Virgins, to Make Much of Time* (text p. 728) Richard Wilbur, *A Late Aubade* (manual p. 191)
Jim Stevens, *Schizophrenia*	Emily Dickinson, *One need not be a Chamber — to be Haunted* — (text p. 947) Langston Hughes, *doorknobs* (text p. 1032) Edgar Allan Poe, *The Haunted Palace* (text p. 800)
Wallace Stevens, *The Emperor of Ice-Cream*	E. E. Cummings, *Buffalo Bill 's* (text p. 1087) T. S. Eliot, *The Love Song of J. Alfred Prufrock* (text p. 1045)
May Swenson, *A Nosty Fright*	Lewis Carroll [Charles Lutwidge Dodgson], *Jabberwocky* (manual p. 243)
Alfred, Lord Tennyson, *The Charge of the Light Brigade*	Randall Jarrell, *The Death of the Ball Turret Gunner* (text p. 720) Wilfred Owen, *Dulce et Decorum Est* (manual p. 261) Walt Whitman, *Cavalry Crossing a Ford* (text p. 754)
Alfred, Lord Tennyson, *Ulysses*	Emily Dickinson, *This was a Poet — It Is That* (text p. 943) William Butler Yeats, *Sailing to Byzantium* (text p. 1132)
Dylan Thomas, *Do not go gentle into that good night*	Sylvia Plath, *Daddy* (text p. 1113)
Dylan Thomas, *The Hand That Signed the Paper*	Alice Jones, *The Foot* (text p. 863) Wilfred Owen, *Arms and the Boy* (text p. 1112) Wole Soyinka, *Future Plans* (text p. 1145)
Jean Toomer, *Reapers*	William Blake, *The Chimney Sweeper* (text p. 822) Countee Cullen, *Yet Do I Marvel* (text p. 1086) Derek Walcott, *The Virgins* (text p. 723)
Tomas Transtromer, *April and Silence*	William Carlos Williams, *Spring and All* (manual p. 433)
John Updike, *Dog's Death*	Seamus Heaney, *Mid-term Break* (text p. 892) Jane Kenyon, *The Blue Bowl* (text p. 768) Ronald Wallace, *Dogs* (text p. 1164)
Derek Walcott, *The Virgins*	Jean Toomer, *Reapers* (text p. 844) Thom Ward, *Vasectomy* (text p. 920)

AUTHOR, POEM	CONNECTED TO:
Alice Walker, *a woman is not a potted plant*	Bonnie Jacobson, *On Being Served Apples* (text p. 753) Marge Piercy, *The Secretary Chant* (manual p. 152) William Shakespeare, *My mistress' eyes are nothing like the sun* (text p. 882)
Robert Wallace, *The Double-Play*	Robert Francis, *Catch* (text p. 676)
Ronald Wallace, *Dogs*	Andrew Hudgins, *Seventeen* (text p. 813) Jane Kenyon, *The Blue Bowl* (text p. 768) William Shakespeare, *My mistress' eyes are nothing like the sun* (manual p. 445) John Updike, *Dog's Death* (manual p. 445)
Edmund Waller, *Go, Lovely Rose*	Robert Herrick, *To the Virgins, to Make Much of Time* (text p. 728) Richard Wilbur, *A Late Aubade* (text p. 732)
Marilyn Nelson Waniek, *Emily Dickinson's Defunct*	E. E. Cummings, *Buffalo Bill 's* (manual p. 286) Emily Dickinson, *I heard a Fly buzz — when I died —* (manual p. 286)
Thom Ward, *Vasectomy*	Martín Espada, *Latin Night at the Pawnshop* (text p. 726) Marge Piercy, *The Secretary Chant* (text p. 671) Derek Walcott, *The Virgins* (text p. 723)
Walt Whitman, *Cavalry Crossing a Ford*	Faiz Ahmed Faiz, *If You Look at the City from Here* (text p. 1139) William Carlos Williams, *Poem* (text p. 753)
Walt Whitman, from *I Sing the Body Electric*	Jane Hirschfield, *The Lives of the Heart* (text p. 1159)
Walt Whitman, *A Noiseless Patient Spider*	Emily Dickinson, *I heard a Fly buzz — when I died —* (text p. 946) Walt Whitman, *The Soul, reaching, throwing out for love* (text p. 789)
Walt Whitman, *One Hour to Madness and Joy*	John Keats, *Ode to a Nightingale* (text p. 851) Percy Bysshe Shelley, *Ode to the West Wind* (text p. 894) Walt Whitman, *One's-Self I Sing* (text p. 1124) Walt Whitman, *The Soul, reaching, throwing out for love* (text p. 789)
Walt Whitman, *One's-Self I Sing*	Emily Dickinson, *I'm Nobody! Who are you?* (text p. 938)

Suggested Connections Between Selections

AUTHOR, POEM	CONNECTED TO:
Walt Whitman, *When I Heard the Learn'd Astronomer*	Emily Dickinson, *Some keep the Sabbath going to Church —* (text p. 935)
Richard Wilbur, *A Late Aubade*	John Donne, *The Sun Rising* (manual p. 156)
	Deborah Garrison, *She Was Waiting to Be Told* (manual p. 437)
	Robert Herrick, *To the Virgins, to Make Much of Time* (text p. 728)
	Andrew Marvell, *To His Coy Mistress* (text p. 729)
	Sharon Olds, *Sex without Love* (manual p. 174)
	Edmund Waller, *Go, Lovely Rose* (text p. 1123)
Richard Wilbur, *Love Calls Us to the Things of This World*	Walt Whitman, *The Soul, reaching, throwing out for love* (text p. 789)
Miller Williams, *Excuse Me*	Archibald MacLeish, *Ars Poetica* (text p. 1107)
Miller Williams, *Thinking About Bill, Dead of AIDS*	Donald Hall, *Letter with No Address* (text p. 1153)
	Robert Hayden, *Those Winter Sundays* (text p. 672)
	Andrew Hudgins, *Elegy for My Father, Who Is Not Dead* (text p. 893)
William Carlos Williams, *Poem*	Matsuo Bashō, *Under cherry trees* (text p. 891)
	Ezra Pound, *In a Station of the Metro* (text p. 772)
	Walt Whitman, *Cavalry Crossing a Ford* (text p. 754)
William Carlos Williams, *The Red Wheelbarrow*	William Carlos Williams, *Poem* (text p. 753)
William Carlos Williams, *Spring and All*	Margaret Atwood, *February* (text p. 784)
	Wislawa Szymborska, *End and Beginning* (text p. 1146)
William Carlos Williams, *This Is Just to Say*	Helen Chasin, *The Word Plum* (text p. 851)
	Donald Justice, *Order in the Streets* (text p. 924)
	Ezra Pound, *In a Station of the Metro* (text p. 772)
Greg Williamson, *Waterfall*	Edgar Allan Poe, *The Bells* (text p. 838)
William Wordsworth, *I Wandered Lonely as a Cloud*	Emily Dickinson, *A Bird came down the Walk —* (text p. 829)
	Robert Frost, *Come In* (text p. 994)
	Robert Hass, *Happiness* (text p. 707)

AUTHOR, POEM	CONNECTED TO:
William Wordsworth, *London, 1802*	William Blake, *London* (text p. 762) George Eliot, *In a London Drawingroom* (text p. 1092)
William Wordsworth, *My Heart Leaps Up*	William Blake, *The Lamb* (text p. 868)
William Wordsworth, *A Slumber Did My Spirit Seal*	John Keats, *When I have fears that I may cease to be* (text p. 1103) Percy Bysshe Shelley, *Ozymandias* (text p. 1118)
William Wordsworth, *The Solitary Reaper*	William Blake, *The Chimney Sweeper* (text p. 822) Langston Hughes, *The Weary Blues* (text p. 1019)
William Wordsworth, *The World Is Too Much with Us*	Gerard Manley Hopkins, *God's Grandeur* (manual p. 267)
James Wright, *A Blessing*	James Dickey, *Deer Among Cattle* (text p. 766) Robert Frost, *Design* (text p. 993) Robert Hass, *Happiness* (text p. 707)
Xu Gang, *Red Azalea on the Cliff*	William Blake, *The Sick Rose* (manual p. 428) John Keats, *La Belle Dame sans Merci* (text p. 1103)
Mitsuye Yamada, *A Bedtime Story*	Julia Alvarez, *Woman's Work* (text p. 886) Margaret Atwood, *Bored* (text p. 737) Jimmy Santiago Baca, *Green Chile* (text p. 758)
William Butler Yeats, *Adam's Curse*	Timothy Steele, *An Aubade* (text p. 761)
William Butler Yeats, *Crazy Jane Talks with the Bishop*	Thomas Hardy, *The Ruined Maid* (text p. 1093)
William Butler Yeats, *Leda and the Swan*	William Butler Yeats, *The Second Coming* (text p. 1133)
William Butler Yeats, *Sailing to Byzantium*	John Keats, *Ode on a Grecian Urn* (text p. 741) William Shakespeare, *Not marble, nor the gilded monuments* (text p. 1116)
William Butler Yeats, *The Second Coming*	Robert Frost, *Fire and Ice* (text p. 988) William Butler Yeats, *Leda and the Swan* (text p. 1132)
William Butler Yeats, *That the Night Come*	Emily Dickinson, *I read my sentence — steadily —* (text p. 944)

DRAMA: LIST OF CONNECTIONS BETWEEN SELECTIONS BY AUTHOR

AUTHOR, PLAY	CONNECTED TO:
Samuel Beckett, *Krapp's Last Tape*	Robert Frost, *The Road Not Taken* (text p. 976)
	David Henry Hwang, *M. Butterfly* (text p. 1675)
	Arthur Miller, *Death of a Salesman* (text p. 1795)
Anton Chekhov, *The Proposal: A Jest in One Act*	Henrik Ibsen, *A Doll House* (text p. 1615)
	William Shakespeare, *A Midsummer Night's Dream* (text p. 1327)
Larry David, from "The Pitch," a *Seinfeld* Episode	David Ives, *Sure Thing* (text p. 1189)
Brian Friel, from *Molly Sweeney*	Samuel Beckett, *Krapp's Last Tape* (manual p. 517)
	Susan Glaspell, *Trifles* (text p. 1172)
	David Henry Hwang, *M. Butterfly* (text p. 1675)
	Jane Martin, *Rodeo* (manual p. 517)
	Anna Deavere Smith, from *Twilight: Los Angeles, 1992* (text p. 1661)
	Sophocles, *Oedipus the King* (manual p. 517)
Susan Glaspell, *Trifles*	Kate Chopin, *The Story of an Hour* (text p. 10)
	Andre Dubus, *Killings* (text p. 81)
	Henrik Ibsen, *A Doll House* (text p. 1564)
	David Ives, *Sure Thing* (text p. 1189)
	Sophocles, *Oedipus the King* (text p. 1124)
Lorraine Hansberry, *A Raisin in the Sun*	Arthur Miller, *Death of a Salesman* (text p. 1795)
	Anna Deavere Smith, from *Twilight: Los Angeles, 1992* (text p. 1661)
	Tennessee Williams, *The Glass Menagerie* (text p. 1864)
	August Wilson, *The Piano Lesson* (text p. 1962)
David Henry Hwang, *M. Butterfly*	Alison Baker, *Better Be Ready 'Bout Half Past Eight* (text p. 617)
	Samuel Beckett, *Krapp's Last Tape* (text p. 1649)
	Yukio Mishima, *Patriotism* (manual p. 508)
	William Shakespeare, *Hamlet, Prince of Denmark* (manual p. 508)
	Sophocles, *Oedipus the King* (manual p. 507)
	Tennessee Williams, *The Glass Menagerie* (text p. 1864)

AUTHOR, PLAY	CONNECTED TO:
Henrik Ibsen, *A Doll House*	Anton Chekhov, *The Proposal: A Jest in One Act* (text p. 1615) Susan Glaspell, *Trifles* (text p. 1172) Gail Godwin, *A Sorrowful Woman* (text p. 33) William Shakespeare, *Hamlet, Prince of Denmark* (text p. 1383) William Shakespeare, *A Midsummer Night's Dream* (text p. 1327) Sophocles, *Antigone* (text p. 1267) Sophocles, *Oedipus the King* (text p. 1224)
David Ives, *Sure Thing*	Susan Glaspell, *Trifles* (text p. 1172)
Jane Martin, *Rodeo*	Stephen Crane, *The Bride Comes to Yellow Sky* (text p. 250) Arthur Miller, *Death of a Salesman* (text p. 1795) William Shakespeare, *Hamlet, Prince of Denmark* (text p. 1383) William Shakespeare, *A Midsummer Night's Dream* (text p. 1327) Anna Deavere Smith, from *Twilight: Los Angeles, 1992* (text p. 1661)
Arthur Miller, *Death of a Salesman*	Samuel Beckett, *Krapp's Last Tape* (text p. 1649) Lorraine Hansberry, *A Raisin in the Sun* (text p. 1730) Tato Laviera, *AmeRícan* (text p. 918) Jane Martin, *Rodeo* (text p. 1657) William Shakespeare, *Hamlet, Prince of Denmark* (text p. 1383) Wole Soyinka, *The Strong Breed* (text p. 1919) Tennessee Williams, *The Glass Menagerie* (text p. 1864) August Wilson, *The Piano Lesson* (text p. 1962)
William Seebring, *The Original Last Wish Baby*	Samuel Beckett, *Krapp's Last Tape* (text p. 1649) T. Coraghessan Boyle, *Carnal Knowledge* (manual p. 521) Larry David, *Seinfeld* (text p. 1199) Anna Deavere Smith, from *Twilight: Los Angeles, 1992* (manual p. 521)
William Shakespeare, *Hamlet, Prince of Denmark*	T. S. Eliot, *The Love Song of J. Alfred Prufrock* (text p. 1045) David Henry Hwang, *M. Butterfly* (text p. 1675)

AUTHOR, PLAY	CONNECTED TO:
William Shakespeare, *Hamlet, Prince of Denmark* (cont.)	Henrik Ibsen, *A Doll House* (text p. 1564)
	Jane Martin, *Rodeo* (text p. 1657)
	Arthur Miller, *Death of a Salesman* (text p. 1795)
	William Shakespeare, *A Midsummer Night's Dream* (text p. 1327)
	William Shakespeare, *The Tempest* (text p. 1483)
	Sophocles, *Antigone* (text p. 1267)
	Sophocles, *Oedipus the King* (text p. 1224)
William Shakespeare, *A Midsummer Night's Dream*	Anton Chekhov, *The Proposal: A Jest in One Act* (text p. 1615)
	Henrik Ibsen, *A Doll House* (text p. 1564)
	Jane Martin, *Rodeo* (text p. 1657)
	Tim O'Brien, *How to Tell a True War Story* (text p. 555)
	William Shakespeare, *Hamlet, Prince of Denmark* (text p. 1383)
	William Shakespeare, *The Tempest* (text p. 1483)
William Shakespeare, *The Tempest*	William Shakespeare, *Hamlet, Prince of Denmark* (text p. 1383)
	William Shakespeare, *A Midsummer Night's Dream* (text p. 1327)
	Sophocles, *Oedipus the King* (text p. 1224)
	Tennessee Williams, *The Glass Menagerie* (text p. 1864)
Anna Deavere Smith, from *Twilight: Los Angeles, 1992*	Lorraine Hansberry, *A Raisin in the Sun* (manual p. 502)
	Jane Martin, *Rodeo* (manual p. 502)
Sophocles, *Antigone*	Henrik Ibsen, *A Doll House* (text p. 1564)
	William Shakespeare, *Hamlet, Prince of Denmark* (text p. 1383)
	Sophocles, *Oedipus the King* (text p. 1224)
	Tennessee Williams, *The Glass Menagerie* (text p. 1864)
Sophocles, *Oedipus the King*	Susan Glaspell, *Trifles* (text p. 1172)
	David Henry Hwang, *M. Butterfly* (text p. 1675)
	Henrik Ibsen, *A Doll House* (text p. 1564)
	William Shakespeare, *Hamlet, Prince of Denmark* (text p. 1383)
	William Shakespeare, *The Tempest* (text p. 1483)
	Sophocles, *Antigone* (text p. 1267)
	Wole Soyinka, *The Strong Breed* (text p. 1919)

AUTHOR, PLAY	CONNECTED TO:
Sophocles, *Oedipus the King* (cont.)	Tennessee Williams, *The Glass Menagerie* (text p. 1864)
Wole Soyinka, *The Strong Breed*	Arthur Miller, *Death of a Salesman* (manual p. 519)
	Sophocles, *Oedipus the King* (manual p. 519)
	August Wilson, *The Piano Lesson* (text p. 1962)
Wendy Wasserstein, *Tender Offer*	Jane Martin, *Rodeo* (manual p. 522)
	Arthur Miller, *Death of a Salesman* (text p. 1795)
Tennessee Williams, *The Glass Menagerie*	Lorraine Hansberry, *A Raisin in the Sun* (text p. 1730)
	David Henry Hwang, *M. Butterfly* (text p. 1675)
	Arthur Miller, *Death of a Salesman* (text p. 1795)
	William Shakespeare, *The Tempest* (text p. 1483)
	Sophocles, *Antigone* (text p. 1267)
	Sophocles, *Oedipus the King* (text p. 1224)
	August Wilson, *The Piano Lesson* (text p. 1962)
August Wilson, *The Piano Lesson*	Ralph Ellison, *Battle Royal* (manual p. 524)
	Lorraine Hansberry, *A Raisin in the Sun* (manual p. 523)
	Arthur Miller, *Death of a Salesman* (text p. 1795)
	Wole Soyinka, *The Strong Breed* (manual p. 522)
	Tennessee Williams, *The Glass Menagerie* (text p. 1864)

The following list of resources is organized by genre (Fiction, Poetry, and Drama), and within each genre section the listings are alphabetically arranged by author. Resources include films and videos of theatrical performances, tapes of poets reading their own work, videos of short stories adapted for film and for the stage, interviews with authors, and films and videos that provide biographical information on an author or general information on a particular period or genre. This list is not intended to be exhaustive; rather, it is meant to provide a number of exciting possibilities for supplementing and provoking class discussion.

Many of the films and videos in this list will be most readily available from a local retailer. If not, you may contact the distributor by using the addresses and phone numbers provided at the end of the list. The films and videos marked with an asterisk (*) are available for rental from member institutions of the Consortium of College and University Media Centers. For further information, consult *The Educational Film & Video Locater*, published by R. R. Bowker.

FICTION

Isabel Allende

Giving Birth, Finding Form [recording].
1 cassette (90 min.), 1993.
Authors Isabel Allende, Alice Walker, and Jean Shinoda Bolen discuss their lives and work.
Distributed by Sounds True.

Isabel Allende: The Woman's Voice in Latin American Literature.
56 min., color, 1991.
VHS.
The author discusses the emotions that inform her fiction and the events that set them in motion.
Distributed by Films for the Humanities and Sciences.

Margaret Atwood

*Atwood and Family.
30 min., color, 1989.
Beta, VHS, ¾" U-matic cassette, 16-mm film.

Atwood talks about her life and work.
Distributed by the National Film Board of Canada.

Interview with Margaret Atwood [recording].
1 cassette (56 min.).
Covers Atwood's feminism, nationalism, themes, and craft.
Distributed by American Audio Prose Library.

Toni Cade Bambara

Interview with Toni Cade Bambara [recording].
1 cassette (58 min.).
Discussion of Bambara's origins, work habits, publishing, and writing.
Distributed by American Audio Prose Library.

Edgar Rice Burroughs

Tarzan of the Apes [recording].
6 cassettes (90 min. each).

Read by Walter Costello.
Distributed by Books on Tape.

Raymond Carver

Interview with Raymond Carver
[recording].
1 cassette (51 min.).
Stimulating introduction to Carver's life
and work.
Distributed by American Audio Prose Library.

Raymond Carver.
50 min., color, 1996.
VHS.
Fellow writers, Carver's wife, and others
discuss his lower-middle-class roots in
the Northwest as the source of inspiration for his characters and stories. A
BBC Production. From the "Great
Writers of the 20th Century" Series.
Distributed by Films for the Humanities
and Sciences.

Readings [recording].
1 cassette (51 min.).
Distributed by American Audio Prose Library.

Short Cuts.
189 min., color, 1993.
Cast: Jennifer Jason Leigh, Tim Robbins,
Madeleine Stowe, Frances McDor-
mand, Peter Gallagher, Lily Tomlin,
Andie MacDowell, Jack Lemmon, Lyle
Lovett, Huey Lewis, Matthew Modine,
Lili Taylor, Christopher Penn, Robert
Downey Jr. Directed by Robert Altman.
Distributed by Columbia Tristar Home
Video.

Anton Chekhov

*Anton Chekhov: A Writer's Life.
37 min., color and b/w, 1983.
Beta, VHS, ¾" U-matic cassette.
A biographical portrait of the writer.
Distributed by Films for the Humanities
and Sciences.

The Lady with the Dog.
86 min., b/w, 1960.
Beta, VHS.

In Russian, with English subtitles.
Distributed by White Star, Facets Multimedia, Inc., Tapeworm Video Distributors.

Kate Chopin

Kate Chopin's "The Story of an Hour."
24 min., color, 1982.
½" open reel (EIAJ), 16-mm film.
A dramatization of the story, with an examination of Chopin's life.
Distributed by Ishtar.

Colette [Sidonie-Gabrielle Colette]

*Colette.
30 min., b/w, 1950.
16-mm film.
Still photos and live footage provide the
background for Colette's own narration. In French with English subtitles.
Out of print.

Stephen Crane

The Bride Comes to Yellow Sky
[recording].
1 cassette (50 min.), 1983.
Read by Walter Zimmerman and Jim Killavey. Illustrates the contrasting sides
of Crane's art — the humorous and
the gruesome.
Distributed by Jimcin Recordings.

The Red Badge of Courage and Other Stories
[recording].
6 cassettes (6 hrs., 39 min.), 1976.
Includes title story, "The Mystery of Heroism," "The Open Boat," and "The
Bride Comes to Yellow Sky."
Distributed by Listening Library.

The Red Badge of Courage and Other Stories
[recording].
9 cassettes (60 min. each).
Read by Michael Pritchard. Includes "The
Bride Comes to Yellow Sky," "The
Blue Hotel," and "The Open Boat."
Distributed by Books on Tape.

Charles Dickens

Charles Dickens: An Introduction to His Life
and Work.

27 min., color, 1979.
Beta, VHS, ¾″ U-matic cassette, special-order formats.
An introduction to Dickens's life and work.
Distributed by the International Film Bureau.

The Charles Dickens Show.
52 min., color, 1973.
Beta, VHS, ¾″ U-matic cassette, 16-mm film.
Deals with the writer and his times. Includes dramatization from his life and works.
Distributed by the International Film Bureau.

Hard Times.
240 min., color, 1977.
Beta, VHS, ¾″ U-matic cassette.
A TV adaptation of the novel.
Distributed by WNET/Thirteen Non-Broadcast.

Hard Times *[recording].*
16 hrs., 8 cassettes.
Read by Frederick Davison.
Distributed by Blackstone Audio.

Andre Dubus

Andre Dubus: Reading *[recording].*
1 cassette (51 min.).
The writer reads his work and discusses the writing process.
Distributed by American Audio Prose Library.

Andre Dubus: Interview *[recording].*
1 cassette (50 min.).
The writer reads his works and discusses the writing process.
Distributed by American Audio Prose Library.

William Faulkner

Barn Burning.
41 min., color, 1980.
Beta, VHS, 16-mm film.
With Tommy Lee Jones.
Same program available in **"The American Short Story Series II"** on manual p. 591. See local retailer.

Collected Short Stories of William Faulkner, Volumes 1 and 2
[recording].
Volume 1, 11 90-min. cassettes; Volume 2, 11 90-min. cassettes.
Read by Wolfram Kandinsky and Michael Kramer. (Volume 2 includes "A Rose for Emily.")
Distributed by Books on Tape.

The Long Hot Summer.
118 min., color, 1958.
Beta, VHS.
A film adaptation of "Barn Burning." Directed by Martin Ritt. With Paul Newman, Orson Welles, Joanne Woodward, Lee Remick, Anthony Franciosa, Angela Lansbury, and Richard Anderson.
See local retailer.

The Long Hot Summer.
172 min., color, 1986.
Beta, VHS.
A made-for-TV version of "Barn Burning." Directed by Stuart Cooper. With Don Johnson, Cybill Shepherd, Judith Ivey, Jason Robards, and Ava Gardner.
See local retailer.

*A Rose for Emily.
27 min., color, 1983.
Beta, VHS, ¾″ U-matic cassette, 16-mm film.
Distributed by Pyramid Film and Video.

A Rose for Emily (William Faulkner).
27 min., color, 1983.
VHS.
Cast: Anjelica Huston. Narrated by John Houseman.
Distributed by Pyramid Film & Video.

William Faulkner: A Life on Paper.
120 min., color, 1980.
Beta, VHS, ¾″ U-matic cassette.
A documentary biography. With Lauren Bacall, Howard Hawks, Anita Loos, George Plimpton, Tennessee Williams, and Jill Faulkner Summers (the author's daughter).
Distributed by Films, Inc.

*William Faulkner's Mississippi.
49 min., color and b/w, 1965.
Beta, VHS, ¾" U-matic cassette.
Deals with Faulkner's life and works.
Distributed by Benchmark Films.

Richard Ford

Richard Ford: The Sportswriter (First chapter) and Rock Springs (short story) [recording].
1 cassette (89 min.).
Distributed by American Audio Prose Library.

Interview [recording].
1 cassette (55 min.).
Pulitzer Prize–winning Ford discusses his writing and personal life.
Distributed by American Audio Prose Library.

Gail Godwin

Interview [recording].
1 cassette (56 min.).
Godwin discusses the recurring themes and concerns in her fiction.
Distributed by American Audio Prose Library.

Nathaniel Hawthorne

The Birthmark [recording].
1 cassette (63 min.). Read by Walter Zimmerman.
Distributed by Jimcin Recordings.

Favorite Stories by Nathaniel Hawthorne, Vol. 1 [recording].
2 cassettes (2 hrs., 30 min.).
Read by Walter Zimmerman and John Chatty. Includes "Dr. Heidegger's Experiment" and "The Minister's Black Veil."
Distributed by Jimcin Recordings.

The Minister's Black Veil [recording].
1 cassette (82 min.).
Read by Walter Zimmerman and John Chatty. Includes "Young Goodman Brown."
Distributed by Jimcin Recordings.

The Minister's Black Veil [recording].
1 cassette.
Distributed by Spoken Arts.

*Nathaniel Hawthorne: Light in the Shadows.
23 min., color, 1982.
Beta, VHS, ¾" U-matic cassette, 16-mm film, special-order formats.
A background of the author's life and works, especially *The Scarlet Letter* and *The House of the Seven Gables*.
Distributed by the International Film Bureau.

*Young Goodman Brown.
30 min., color, 1972.
Beta, VHS, ¾" U-matic cassette, 16-mm film.
Distributed by Pyramid Film and Video.

Ernest Hemingway

Ernest Hemingway.
53 min., color, 1983.
VHS.
This program explores Hemingway's life and literary psyche through the eyes of those who knew him. A BBC Production. Part of the "Great Writers of the 20th Century" series.
Distributed by Films for the Humanities and Sciences.

Ernest Hemingway: A Life Story [recording].
Part 1, 11 cassettes, Part 2, 10 cassettes (1 hr., 30 min. per cassette).
Read by Christopher Hunt. Draws from Hemingway's diaries, letters, and unpublished writing as well as personal testimony from the people who played a part in the author's life.
Distributed by Blackstone·Audio Books

*Hemingway.
18 min., b/w, 1993.
Beta, VHS, ¾" U-matic cassette, 16-mm film.
A biography using rare stills and motion-picture footage. Narrated by Chet Huntley.
Distributed by Thomas Klise Company.

Hemingway: Up in Michigan, the Early Years
28 min., color, 1986.
Beta, VHS, ¾″ U-matic cassette.
A literary biography of the writer.
Distributed by Centre Communications.

Soldier's Home. See "The American Short Story Series I" on manual
p. 591.

Charles Johnson

Charles Johnson.
29 min., color, 1993.
VHS.
This program shows how Charles Johnson blends black folk tales, Zen parables, eighteenth-century picaresque novels, and twentieth-century philosophy into his storytelling.
Distributed by Films for the Humanities and Sciences.

In Black and White: Charles Johnson.
27 min., color, 1992.
VHS.
Johnson describes his literary objective: to explore classic metaphysical questions from East and West against the backdrop of American life and history.
Distributed by California Newsreel.

See "In Black and White: Conversations with African American Writers" on manual p. 591.

James Joyce

"The Dead" and Other Stories from Dubliners [recording].
2 cassettes (2 hrs., 15 min.).
Distributed by Audio Partners.

James Joyce.
50 min., color, 1996.
VHS.
Critics and those who knew Joyce trace events in his life through passages in *Ulysses* and other works, including *Dubliners*, the collection of short stories, and the semiautobiographical novel *A Portrait of the Artist as a Young Man*. A BBC Production. Part of the "Great Writers of the 20th Century" series.
Distributed by Films for the Humanities and Sciences.

James Joyce's Women.
91 min., color, 1983.
Beta, VHS.
Actors portray Joyce's wife plus Molly Bloom and two of his female characters. Adapted and produced by Fionnula Flanagan. With Flanagan, Timothy E. O'Grady, Chris O'Neill.
See local retailer.

Dubliners by James Joyce [recording].
6 cassettes (90 min. each).
Read by Jim Killavey. "The Dead" and fourteen other short stories of Irish life.
Distributed by Jimcin Recordings.

Dubliners [recording].
8 cassettes (60 min. each).
Read by David Case.
Distributed by Books on Tape.

Franz Kafka

Franz Kafka.
22 min., color, 1994.
VHS.
A literary portrait of the author.
Distributed by Klise Company.

The Trials of Franz Kafka.
15 min., b/w, 198?.
Beta, VHS, ¾″ U-matic cassette.
Kafka's life and times, told in his own words. Narrated by Kurt Vonnegut.
Distributed by Films for the Humanities and Sciences.

Jamaica Kincaid

Readings [recording].
1 cassette (60 min.).
Jamaica Kincaid reads excerpts from *Annie John*, *At the Bottom of the River* (including "Girl") and *Lucy*.
Distributed by American Audio Prose Library.

Interview with Jamaica Kincaid
    [recording].
1 cassette (59 min.).
Kincaid describes her move from Antigua to the United States and her British colonial education.
Distributed by American Audio Prose Library.

D. H. Lawrence

England, My England [recording].
8 cassettes (60 min. each).
Read by Richard Brown. Includes readings of "The Horse Dealer's Daughter," "The Primrose Path," and others.
Distributed by Books on Tape.

*D. H. Lawrence.
30 min., color, 1984.
VHS, 16-mm film.
A biographical portrait of the writer. Includes his views on war and censorship. Part of the "Famous Author" series.
Distributed by Britannica Films.

The Horse Dealer's Daughter.
30 min., color, 1984.
VHS. Close-captioned.
Distributed by Monterey Home Video.

D. H. Lawrence.
53 min., color, 1984.
VHS.
Lawrence biographer John Worthen and others who knew the writer discuss the author's life, his many love affairs, and his turbulent marriage to his wife, Frieda. The program contains some profanity and should be previewed before being shown to students. A BBC Production. Part of the "Great Writers of the 20th Century" series.
Distributed by Films for the Humanities and Sciences.

Herman Melville

*Herman Melville.
22 min., color, 1978.
Beta, VHS, ¾" U-matic cassette, 16-mm film.

Ancillary materials available. Part of the "Authors" series of biographies.
Distributed by Journal Films, Inc.

*Herman Melville: Consider the Sea.
28 min., color, 1982.
Beta, VHS, ¾" U-matic cassette, 16-mm film, special-order formats.
Deals with the author and his relationship with the sea. Major works discussed include *Moby-Dick, Billy Budd,* and "Bartleby, the Scrivener."
Distributed by the International Film Bureau.

Melville: Six Short Novels [recording].
8 cassettes (60 min. each).
Read by Dan Lazar. Includes "Bartleby, the Scrivener," "The Apple Tree Table," "My Chimney," and "The Happy Failure."
Distributed by Books on Tape.

*Herman Melville: Damned in Paradise.
90 min., color, 1986.
Beta, VHS, ¾" U-matic cassette.
Documents Melville's personal and intellectual history.
Distributed by Pyramid Film and Video.

Bartleby.
79 min., color, 1970.
VHS.
Cast: Paul Scofield, John McEnery. Directed by Anthony Friedman.
Distributed by White Star.

Bartleby.
60 min., color, 197?.
VHS.
Distributed by Maryland Public Television.

Bartleby.
28 min., color, 1969.
VHS.
Distributed by Britannica Films.

Bartleby.
29 min., b&w, 1965.
VHS.
Videotape from the "American Story Classics" series.
Distributed by Film Video Library.

Bartleby, the Scrivener *[recording].*
1 cassette (90 min.).
Read by Walter Zimmerman.
Distributed by Jimcin Recordings.

Bharati Mukherjee

Bharati Mukherjee: Conquering America.
30 min., color, 1994.
VHS.
In this interview with Bill Moyers, Mukherjee discusses America's newest immigrants and the building resentment and tensions between our country's various cultures.
Distributed by Films for the Humanities and Sciences.

Alice Munro

Interview with Alice Munro *[recording].*
1 cassette (72 min.).
Munro discusses influences, feminism, and Canadian literature.
Distributed by American Audio Prose Library.

Joyce Carol Oates

Joyce Carol Oates *[recording].*
1 cassette (29 min.), 1989.
The author talks about her writing habits.
Distributed by Letters on the Air.

Joyce Carol Oates.
28 min., color, 1994.
VHS.
Oates discusses her work as both a writer and teacher, her craft and methods, and the major themes of her novels, short stories, and poems.
Distributed by Films for the Humanities and Sciences.

Edgar Allan Poe

Edgar Allan Poe: Terror of the Soul.
60 min., color, 1995.
Beta, VHS.
A biography revealing Poe's creative genius and personal experiences through dramatic re-creations of important scenes from his work and life. Includes dramatizations of Poe classics such as "The Tell-Tale Heart" performed by Treat Williams, John Heard, and Rene Auberjonois.
Distributed by PBS Video.

Edgar Allan Poe Stories *[recording].*
2 cassettes (2 hrs., 5 min.).
Six stories performed by Basil Rathbone.
Distributed by Caedmon/HarperAudio.

"The Fall of the House of Usher": And Other Poems and Tales *[recording].*
1 cassette (44 min.).
Abridged. Performed by Basil Rathbone. Includes "The Fall of the House of Usher," "The Tell-Tale Heart," "The Haunted Palace," and "The Bells."
Distributed by Caedmon/Harper.

The Purloined Letter and Poems *[recording].*
1 cassette (60 min.).
Abridged. Performed by Anthony Quayle. Includes "The Purloined Letter," "The Valley of Unrest," and "A Dream within a Dream."
Distributed by Books on Tape.

John Updike

John Updike.
30 min., b/w, 1966.
16-mm film.
Discusses Updike's beliefs and attitudes. The author reads selections from his works.
Distributed by Indiana University Instructional Support Services.

Selected Stories by John Updike *[recording]*
2 cassettes (2 hrs., 49 min.), 1985.
Updike reads six unabridged stories: "A & P," "Pigeon Feathers," "The Family Meadow," "The Witnesses," "The Alligators," and "Separating."
Distributed by Random Audiobooks.

What Makes Rabbit Run?
29 min., color, 1986.
VHS, 16-mm film.

Updike reads from his works and discusses his life.
Distributed by Barr Entertainment.

Writers: John Updike.
30 min., b/w, 1966.
¾" U-matic cassette, 16-mm film, special order formats.
An interview with the writer.
Distributed by Indiana University Instructional Support Services.

Tobias Wolff

Interview [recording].
1 cassette (56 min.).
Discussion of stories and storytelling.
Distributed by American Audio Prose Library.

GENERAL

The American Short Story Series I.
45 min./program, color, 1978.
Beta, VHS, ¾" U-matic cassette, 16-mm film.
Ancillary materials available. Includes nine film adaptations of short stories that appeared on PBS: "Parker Adderson, Philosopher," "The Jolly Corner," "The Blue Hotel," "I'm a Fool," "Soldier's Home," "Bernice Bobs Her Hair," "Almos' a Man," "The Displaced Person," and "The Music School."
Distributed by Coronet/MTI Film & Video.

The American Short Story Series II.
50 min./program, color, 1980.
Beta, VHS, ¾" U-matic cassette, 16-mm film.
Eight programs: "The Golden Honeymoon," "Paul's Case," "The Greatest Man in the World," "Rappaccini's Daughter," "The Jilting of Granny Weatherall," "The Sky Is Grey," "The Man That Corrupted Hadleyburg," and "Barn Burning." With Geraldine Fitzgerald, Brad Davis, and Tommy Lee Jones.
Distributed by Coronet/MTI Film & Video.

The Authors Series.
22 min./program, color, 1978.
Beta, VHS, ¾" U-matic cassette, 16-mm film.
Programs deal with biographical information as related to the creative process. Five programs: James Fenimore Cooper, Stephen Crane, Emily Dickinson, Henry James, and Herman Melville.
Distributed by Journal Films.

Dialogue.
20 min., b/w, 1974.
Beta, VHS, ¾" U-matic cassette.
Mr. and Mrs. Alfred A. Knopf remember the authors they worked with, including John Updike and Albert Camus.
Distributed by Phoenix/BFA Films.

Exploring the Short Story: For Entertainment and Comprehension.
37 min., color, 1976.
Beta, VHS, ¾" U-matic cassette.
Ancillary materials available. Deals with character, plot, setting, style, theme, and point of view.
Distributed by the Center for Humanities, Inc.

Great American Short Stories, Vol. I [recording].
7 cassettes (90 min. each), 1981.
Includes "Bartleby, the Scrivener," "The Minister's Black Veil," and fourteen others.
Distributed by Jimcin Recordings and Books on Tape.

Great American Short Stories, Vol. II [recording].
7 cassettes (90 min. each), 1984.
Includes "The Bride Comes to Yellow Sky," "The Birthmark," and fifteen others.
Distributed by Jimcin Recordings and Books on Tape.

In Black and White: Conversations with African American Writers.
Approx. 30 min./program, color, 1992.
VHS.
Interviews with African American writers Alice Walker, August Wilson, Charles

Johnson, Gloria Naylor, John Wideman, and Toni Morrison.
Distributed by California Newsreel.

A Movable Feast.
30 min./program, color, 1991.
VHS.
Hosted by Tom Vitale. Profiles eight contemporary writers: (1) Allen Ginsberg; (2) Joyce Carol Oates; (3) Li-Young Lee; (4) Sonia Sanchez; (5) T. Coraghessan Boyle; (6) T. R. Pearson; (7) Trey Ellis; (8) W. S. Merwin.
Distributed by Acorn Media.

*The Short Story.
20 min., color, 1962.
16-mm film.
A history of the American short story.

Women in Literature, The Short Story:
  A Collection [recording].
5 cassettes (7 hrs., 30 min.), 1984.

Various readers. Includes "The Story of an Hour" by Kate Chopin and other works by Edith Wharton, Willa Cather, Mary E. Wilkins Freeman, Sarah Orne Jewett, George Sand, Frances Gilchrist Wood, and Selma Laerloff.
Distributed by Jimcin Recordings and Books on Tape.

*The Writer in America.
29 min./program, color, 1979.
Beta, VHS, ¾" U-matic cassette, 16-mm film.
Interviews with eight contemporary writers: (1) Eudora Welty; (2) Ross MacDonald; (3) Janet Flanner; (4) John Gardner; (5) Toni Morrison; (6) Wright Morris; (7) Robert Duncan; (8) Muriel Rukeyser.
Distributed by Coronet/MTI Film & Video.

POETRY

AI

AI [recording].
1 cassette (29 min.), 1988.
AI reads from her book *Sin* and discusses her writing and mixed ethnicity.
Distributed by New Letters on the Air.

Anna Akhmatova

Anna Akhmatova: Selected Poems
  [recording].
1 cassette (60 min.).
Akhmatova reads her poems in Russian. Includes transcript.
Distributed by Interlingua VA.

The Anna Akhmatova File.
65 min., color, 1989.
Beta, VHS.
Documentary of the Russian poet. Russian with English subtitles.
Distributed by Facets Multimedia, Inc.

Fear and the Muse: The Story of Anna
  Akhmatova.
Color, VHS (60 min.), 1995.

With voices of Claire Bloom and Christopher Reeve.
Distributed by Mystic Fire Video.

Claribel Alegría

Claribel Alegría: Who Raised Up This
  Prison's Bars? [recording].
1 cassette (58 min.), 1988.
Alegría reads her poems in Spanish, with translations by Carolyn Forché.
Distributed by Watershed Tapes.

Claribel Alegría [recording].
1 cassette (29 min.), 1991.
The Nicaraguan poet and writer talks about her autobiographical novel *Luisa in Reality Land*.
Distributed by New Letters on the Air.

A. R. Ammons

A. R. Ammons [recording].
1 cassette (29 min.), 1984.
Distributed by New Letters on the Air.

Maya Angelou

Maya Angelou.
30 min., color, 1982.
Beta, VHS, ½" open reel (EIAJ), ¾" U-matic cassette.
Robert Cromie talks with the poet. A two-part series.
Distributed by Nebraska Educational Television Network.

Maya Angelou [recording].
1 cassette (60 min.).
Angelou reads from "And Still I Rise." With Heywood Hale Broun.
Distributed by Audio-Forum.

Maya Angelou [recording].
1 cassette (30 min.).
The poet reads from her poetry, talks about her memoirs, and discusses her refusal to speak for three years as a child.
Distributed by Tapes for Readers.

Maya Angelou [recording].
2 cassettes (150 min.), 1993.
Angelou's biography.
Distributed by Chelsea House Publishers.

Maya Angelou: I Know Why the Caged Bird Sings [recording].
2 cassettes (179 min.).
Angelou's autobiography.
Distributed by Random Audiobooks.

Maya Angelou: Making Magic in the World [recording].
1 cassette (60 min.), 1988.
Presents a trip from the Deep South to the heart of Africa and back again.
Distributed by New Dimensions Radio.

See also *"Literature: The Synthesis of Poetry"* on manual p. 619.

Matthew Arnold

Treasury of Matthew Arnold [recording].
1 cassette.
Distributed by Spoken Arts.

See also *"Literature: The Synthesis of Poetry," "Palgrave's Golden Treasury of English Poetry,"* and *"Victo-*

rian Poetry" (film and recording) on manual pp. 619–622.

John Ashbery

John Ashbery [recording].
1 cassette (29 min.), 1986.
Distributed by New Letters on the Air.

The Poetry of John Ashbery [recording].
1 cassette (39 min.), 1967.
Part of the YM-YWHA Poetry Center Series.
Distributed by Audio-Forum.

John Ashbery: Songs We Know Best [recording].
1 cassette (60 min.), 1989.
Distributed by Watershed Tapes.

See also *"The Poet's Voice," "Poets in Person, No. 5"* (recording), and *"Potpourri of Poetry"* on manual pp. 620–621.

Magaret Atwood

The Poetry and Voice of Margaret Atwood [recording].
1 cassette (59 min.), 1977.
Distributed by Caedmon/HarperAudio.

Margaret Atwood Reads [recording].
1 cassette (36 min.).
Distributed by Caedmon/HarperAudio

W. H. Auden

The Poetry of W. H. Auden, Part I [recording].
1 cassette (50 min.), 1953.
Part of the YM-YWHA Poetry Center Series.
Distributed by Audio-Forum.

The Poetry of W. H. Auden, Part II [recording].
1 cassette (59 min.), 1966.
Part of the YM-YWHA Poetry Center Series.
Distributed by Audio-Forum.

W. H. Auden [recording].
1 cassette (48 min.).
Read by the poet.
Distributed by Spoken Arts.

W. H. Auden and the Writers of the 1930s [recording].
1 cassette (59 min.), 1953.
Read by Stephen Spender.
Distributed by Audio-Forum.

W. H. Auden Reading [recording].
1 cassette.
The poet reads his work.
Distributed by Caedmon/HarperAudio.

W. H. Auden Remembered [recording].
1 cassette (56 min.).
Read by Heywood H. Broun and Stephen Spender. From the Broun Radio Series.
Distributed by Audio-Forum.

See also *"Caedmon Treasury of Modern Poets Reading Their Own Poetry," "The Poet's Voice,"* and *"Twentieth-Century Poets Reading Their Work"* on manual pp. 618–621.

Jimmy Santiago Baca

Jimmy Santiago Baca [recording].
1 cassette (29 min.), 1991.
Distributed by New Letters on the Air.

Amiri Baraka

Amiri Baraka [recording].
1 cassette (29 min.), 1988.
Distributed by New Letters on the Air.

Le Roi Jones/Imamu Amiri Baraka [recording].
1 cassette, 1976.
Distributed by Everett/Edwards.

John Berryman

John Berryman.
See *"The Poet's Voice"* on manual p. 620.

Elizabeth Bishop

Delmore Schwartz, Richard Blackmur, Stephen Spender, and Elizabeth Bishop.
1 cassette.
Distributed by the Library of Congress.

See also *"Voices and Vision"* on manual p. 622.

William Blake

*Essay on William Blake.
52 min., color, 1969.
¾″ U-matic cassette, 16-mm film, special-order formats.
A profile of the poet.
Distributed by Indiana University Instructional Support Services.

The Poetry of William Blake [recording].
1 cassette.
Distributed by Caedmon/HarperAudio.

Poetry of William Blake [recording].
1 cassette.
Distributed by Spoken Arts.

*William Blake.
26 min., color, 1973.
16-mm film.
Hosted by Kenneth Clark. Focuses on Blake's drawings and engravings.
Distributed by Pyramid Film and Video.

William Blake.
30 min.
VHS.
A dramatization of Blake's inner world.
Distributed by Insight Media.

William Blake.
57 min., color, 1976.
Beta, VHS, ¾″ U-matic cassette, special-order formats.
A biographical portrait.
Distributed by Time-Life Video.

William Blake: The Book of Thel [recording].
1 cassette.
Distributed by Audio-Forum.

William Blake: Selected Poems [recording].
2 cassettes (180 min.), 1992.
Includes "Tyger! Tyger!" and "A Poison Tree."
Distributed by Blackstone Audio Books.

William Blake: The Marriage of Heaven and Hell.
30 min., color, 1984.
¾″ U-matic cassette.
Dramatizes the life of Blake and his wife

Catherine. With Anne Baxter and George Rose.
Distributed by Modern Talking Picture Service.

William Blake: Something About Poetry *[recording].*
1 cassette (22 min.), 1969.
Distributed by Audio-Forum.

See also *"Introduction to English Poetry"* and *"Romantic Pioneers"* on manual pp. 619–621.

***William Blake: Poems** [recording].*
1 cassette (80 min.).
Distributed by HighBridge.

Robert Bly

The Poetry of Robert Bly *[recording].*
1 cassette (38 min.), 1966.
Part of the YM-YWHA Poetry Series.
Distributed by Audio-Forum.

Robert Bly I & II *[recording].*
1 cassette (60 min.), 1979, 1991.
Distributed by New Letters on the Air.

Robert Bly: Booth and Bly, Poets.
30 min., color, 1978.
½" open reel (EIAJ), ¾" U-matic cassette.
A four-part series of workshops and readings by the poets.
Distributed by Nebraska Educational Television Network.

Robert Bly: An Evening of Poetry *[recording].*
2 cassettes.
Distributed by Sound Horizons.

Robert Bly: Fairy Tales for Men and Women *[recording].*
90 min., 1987.
Bly applies psychoanalytical analysis to poetry.
Distributed by Ally Press.

Robert Bly: For the Stomach — Selected Poems, 1974 *[recording].*
64 min.
Bly reads his poetry.
Distributed by Watershed Tapes.

Robert Bly: The Human Shadow *[recording].*

2 cassettes.
Distributed by Mystic Fire.

Robert Bly: A Man Writes to a Part of Himself.
57 min., color, 1978.
¾" U-matic cassette, special-order formats.
Poetry and conversation with the writer.
Distributed by Intermedia Arts of Minnesota.

Robert Bly: Poetry East and West *[recording].*
140 min., 1983.
Bly gives a poetry lecture, accompanied by the dulcimer.
Distributed by Dolphin Tapes.

Robert Bly: Poetry in Motion.
30 min., color, 1981.
Beta, VHS, ¾" U-matic cassette.
Video biographies of three poets: Robert Bly, Frederick Marfred, and Thomas McGrath.
Distributed by Intermedia Arts of Minnesota.

Robert Bly: Poetry Reading — An Ancient Tradition *[recording].*
2 cassettes (150 min.), 1983.
Bly talks about the oral tradition in poetry.
Distributed by Dolphin Tapes.

Robert Bly — A Home in the Dark Grass: Poems & Meditations on Solitudes, Families, Disciplines *[recording].*
2 cassettes (131 min.), 1991.
Distributed by Ally Press Audio.

Robert Bly: Poems of Kabir *[recording].*
2 cassettes (1 hr., 59 min.), 1977, 1995.
Distributed by Audio Literature.

Robert Bly: Poems of Kabir *[recording].*
1 cassette.
Distributed by Ally Press.

Robert Bly: Selected Poems *[recording].*
2 cassettes (131 min.), 1987.
Distributed by Ally Press.

Robert Bly: The Six Powers of Poetry *[recording].*

1 cassette (90 min.), 1983.
A lecture from the San Jose Poetry Center.
Distributed by Dolphin Tapes.

See also *"Moyers: The Power of the Word"* on manual p. 620.

Anne Bradstreet

Anne Bradstreet [recording].
1 cassette, 1976.
Distributed by Everett/Edwards.

Joseph Brodsky

Joseph Brodsky: A Maddening Space.
Color, VHS (60 min.), 1989.
Center for Visual History in association with Channel 4. Produced by Sasha Alpert, directed/written by Lawrence Pitkethly, narrated by Jason Robards. Distributed by Mystic Fire Video.

Joseph Brodsky Reads His Poetry [recording].
1 cassette (30 min.), 1988.
Distributed by Caedmon/HarperAudio.

Joseph Brodsky: Winter [recording].
1 cassette (64 min.).
In Russian and English.
Distributed by Watershed Tapes.

Gwendolyn Brooks

*Gwendolyn Brooks.
30 min., b/w, 1966.
¾" U-matic cassette, 16-mm film, special-order formats.
Brooks talks about her life and poetry.
Distributed by Indiana University Instructional Support Services.

Gwendolyn Brooks I & II [recording].
1 cassette (60 min.), 1988, 1989.
Distributed by New Letters on the Air.

Gwendolyn Brooks Reading Her Poetry [recording].
1 cassette.
Distributed by Caedmon/HarperAudio.

See also *"The Harlem Renaissance and Beyond"* on manual p. 619.

Elizabeth Barrett Browning

Elizabeth Barrett Browning: Sonnets from the Portuguese [recording].
1 cassette.
Performed by Katherine Cornell and Anthony Quayle.
Distributed by Caedmon/HarperAudio.

Elizabeth Barrett Browning: Sonnets from the Portuguese [recording].
1 cassette.
Read by Penelope Lee.
Distributed by Spoken Arts.

See also *"Victorian Poetry"* (film and recording) on manual p. 622.

Robert Browning

Robert Browning: "My Last Duchess" & Other Poems [recording].
1 cassette.
Distributed by Caedmon/HarperAudio.

Robert Browning: Selected Poems [recording].
4 cassettes (360 min.).
Read by Frederick Davidson.
Distributed by Blackstone Audio Books.

The Poetry of Browning [recording].
1 cassette.
Distributed by Caedmon/HarperAudio.

*Robert Browning — His Life and Poetry.
21 min., color, 1972.
Beta, VHS, ¾" U-matic cassette, 16-mm film, special-order format.
A dramatization of Browning's life and several of his poems, including "My Last Duchess."
Distributed by International Film Bureau.

Treasury of Robert Browning [recording].
1 cassette.
Distributed by Spoken Arts.

See also *"Victorian Poetry"* (recording) on manual p. 622.

Joseph Bruchac

Joseph Bruchac [recording].
1 cassette (29 min.), 1983.
Distributed by New Letters on the Air.

Joseph Bruchac Two *[recording].*
1 cassette (29 min.), 1993.
Distributed by New Letters on the Air.

Robert Burns

Robert Burns: Love and Liberty.
38 min., color, 1985.
Beta, VHS, ¾″ U-matic cassette.
Burns's lyrics are sung and read aloud.
Distributed by Films for the Humanities
    and Sciences.

Robert Burns: Love Songs *[recording].*
1 cassette.
Distributed by Spoken Arts.

*Robert Burns: The Poetry of Robert
    Burns & Border Ballads*
    [recording].
1 cassette.
Distributed by Caedmon/HarperAudio.

See also *"Palgrave's Golden Treasury of
    English Poetry"* on manual p. 620.

George Gordon, Lord Byron

Lord Byron: Selected Poems *[recording].*
2 cassettes (180 min.).
Read by Frederick Davidson.
Distributed by Blackstone Audio Books.

The Essential Byron *[recording].*
1 cassette.
Unabridged edition.
Distributed by Listening Library.

The Poetry of Byron *[recording].*
1 cassette.
Distributed by Caedmon/HarperAudio.

Treasury of George Gordon, Lord Byron
    [recording].
1 cassette.
Distributed by Spoken Arts.

See also *"English Literature: Romantic Peri-
    od," "English Romantic Poetry," "Pal-
    grave's Golden Treasury of English
    Poetry,"* and *"The Young Romantics"*
    on manual pp. 618–622.

Lewis Carroll

Treasury of Lewis Carroll *[recording].*

1 cassette.
Distributed by Spoken Arts.

See also *"Victorian Poetry"* (recording) on
    manual p. 622.

John Ciardi

As If: Poems Selected and Read by John Ciardi
    [recording].
1 cassette, 1955.
Distributed by Smithsonian/Folkways Re-
    cordings.

*Hans Juergensen & John Ciardi: World War
    II* *[recording].*
1 cassette (29 min.).
Distributed by New Letters on the Air.

The Poetry of John Ciardi
    [recording].
1 cassette (56 min.), 1964.
Distributed by Audio-Forum.

John Ciardi *[recording].*
1 cassette, 1991.
Distributed by Audio-Forum.

John Ciardi, I & II *[recording].*
1 cassette (60 min.), 1983, 1984.
The author reads poems about war, Italy,
    and aging.
Distributed by New Letters on the Air.

*John Ciardi: Twentieth-Century Poets
    in English: Recordings of Poets
    Reading Their Own Poetry, No. 27*
    [recording].
Distributed by the Library of Congress.

*John Ciardi: You Read to Me, I'll Read
    to You* *[recording].*
1 cassette, 1992.
Distributed by Spoken Arts.

Lucille Clifton

Lucille Clifton *[recording].*
1 cassette (29 min.), 1989.
Distributed by New Letters on the Air.

Lucille Clifton: The Place for Keeping
    [recording].
1 cassette (45 min.).
Distributed by Watershed Tapes.

Samuel Taylor Coleridge

Samuel Taylor Coleridge: The Fountain and the Cave.
57 min., color, 1974.
Beta, VHS, ¾″ U-matic cassette.
A biography of the poet, filmed on location. Narrated by Paul Scofield.
Distributed by Pyramid Film and Video.

The Poetry of Coleridge [recording].
1 cassette.
Distributed by Caedmon/HarperAudio.

Samuel Taylor Coleridge: The Rime of the Ancient Mariner & Other Poems [recording].
1 cassette.
Distributed by Spoken Arts.

Samuel Taylor Coleridge: The Rime of the Ancient Mariner & Other Great Poems [recording].
2 cassettes.
From the Cassette Bookshelf Series.
Distributed by Listening Library.

See also *"English Romantic Poetry," "Palgrave's Golden Treasury of English Poetry,"* and *"Romantic Pioneers"* on manual pp. 618–621.

Countee Cullen

The Poetry of Countee Cullen [recording].
1 cassette.
Distributed by Caedmon/HarperAudio.

Countee Cullen: The Lost Zoo [recording].
1 cassette.
Distributed by Caedmon/HarperAudio.

See also *"The Harlem Renaissance and Beyond"* and *"Modern American Poetry"* on manual p. 619.

E. E. Cummings

E. E. Cummings Reading His Poetry [recording].
1 cassette.
Distributed by Caedmon/HarperAudio.

E. E. Cummings Reads [recording].
1 cassette (60 min.), 1987.
From The Poet Anniversary Series.
Distributed by Caedmon/HarperAudio.

E. E. Cummings Reads His Collected Poetry, 1920–1940, & Prose [recording].
2 cassettes (79 min.).
Distributed by Caedmon/HarperAudio.

E. E. Cummings Reads His Collected Poetry, 1943–1958 [recording]
2 cassettes.
Distributed by Caedmon/HarperAudio.

*E. E. Cummings: The Making of a Poet.
24 min., 1978.
Beta, VHS, ¾″ U-matic cassette.
A profile of Cummings told in his own words.
Distributed by Films for the Humanities and Sciences.

E. E. Cummings: Nonlectures [recordings].
6 cassettes.
(1) I & My Parents; (2) I & Their Son; (3) I & Self-discovery; (4) I & You & Is; (5) I & Now & Him; (6) I & Am & Santa Claus.
Distributed by Caedmon/HarperAudio.

Poems of E. E. Cummings [recording].
1 cassette (60 min.), 1981.
Part of the Poetic Heritage Series.
Distributed by Summer Stream.

E. E. Cummings: Twentieth-Century Poetry in English: Recordings of Poets Reading Their Own Poetry, No. 5 [recording].
Distributed by the Library of Congress.

See also *"Caedmon Treasury of Modern Poets Reading Their Own Poetry," "Inner Ear, Parts 5 and 6,"* and *"Poetry for People Who Hate Poetry"* on manual pp. 618–620.

James Dickey

James Dickey.
Color, VHS (30 min.), 1989.
A production of the University of South Carolina and the South Carolina ETV Network.
Distributed by PBS Video.

James Dickey [recording].
1 cassette (29 min.), 1987.
Distributed by New Letters on the Air.

James Dickey [recording].
1 cassette, 1976.
Distributed by Tapes for Readers.

James Dickey Reads His Poetry &
Prose [recording].
1 cassette, 1972.
Distributed by Caedmon/HarperAudio.

The Poems of James Dickey [recording].
1 cassette (52 min.), 1967.
Distributed by Spoken Arts.

Emily Dickinson

Emily Dickinson: A Brighter Garden
[recording].
1 cassette (15 min.).
Distributed by Spoken Arts.

Emily Dickinson: A Self-Portrait
[recording].
2 cassettes (90 min.).
Distributed by Caedmon/HarperAudio,
Filmic Archives.

Fifty Poems of Emily Dickinson
[recording].
1 cassette (45 min.).
Distributed by Dove Audio.

Emily Dickinson: Seventy-Five Poems
[recording].
2 cassettes (2 hours, 15 min.), 1990.
Distributed by Recorded Books.

*Emily Dickinson: The Belle of Amherst.
90 min., color, 1980.
Beta, VHS, ¾" U-matic cassette.
With Julie Harris.
Distributed by Cifex Corporation.

*Emily Dickinson: A Certain Slant of
Light.
29 min., color, 1978.
Beta, VHS, ¾" U-matic cassette, 16-mm film.
Explores Dickinson's life and environment. Narrated by Julie Harris.
Distributed by Pyramid Film and Video.

Emily Dickinson: Magic Prison —
A Dialogue Set to Music.
35 min., color, 1969.
Beta, VHS, ¾" U-matic cassette, 16-mm film.

Dramatizes the letters between Dickinson and Colonel T. W. Higginson. With an introduction by Archibald MacLeish and music by Ezra Laderman.
Distributed by Britannica Films.

Emily Dickinson: Poems and Letters
[recording].
2 cassettes.
Distributed by Recorded Books.

Emily Dickinson: Selected Poems
[recording].
4 cassettes (360 min.), 1993.
Read by Mary Woods.
Distributed by Blackstone Audio Books.

Poems and Letters of Emily Dickinson
[recording].
1 cassette.
Distributed by Caedmon/HarperAudio.

*Emily Dickinson.
22 min., color, 1978.
Beta, VHS, ¾" U-matic cassette.
A film about the poet and her poems. Part of the "Authors" series.
Distributed by Journal Films Inc.

Emily Dickinson [recording].
1 cassette.
Distributed by Recorded Books.

Emily Dickinson Recalled in Song
[recording].
1 cassette (30 min.).
Distributed by Audio-Forum.

Poems by Emily Dickinson [recording].
2 cassettes (236 min.), 1986.
Distributed by Audio Book Contractors.

Poems of Emily Dickinson [recording].
1 cassette.
Distributed by Spoken Arts.

Poems of Emily Dickinson & Lizette
Woodworth Reese [recording].
1 cassette (60 min.), 1981.
Unabridged edition. Part of the "Poetic Heritage Series."
Distributed by Summer Stream.

See also *"Inner Ear, Parts 3 and 4," "Introduction to English Poetry," "Voices and Vision,"* and *"With a*

Feminine Touch" on manual pp. 619–622.

John Donne

Essential Donne [recording].
From the Essential Poets Series.
Distributed by Listening Library.

John Donne.
40 min., color.
VHS.
Discusses the poet's life and works.
Distributed by Insight Media.

John Donne: Love Poems [recording].
1 cassette.
Distributed by Recorded Books.

John Donne: Selected Poems [recording].
2 cassettes (180 min.), 1992.
Read by Frederick Davidson.
Distributed by Blackstone Audio Books.

*The Love Poems of John Donne
    [recording].*
1 cassette.
Distributed by Caedmon/HarperAudio.

Treasury of John Donne [recording].
1 cassette.
Distributed by Spoken Arts.

See also *"Metaphysical and Devotional Po-
    etry"* and *"Palgrave's Golden Treasury
    of English Poetry"* on manual pp.
    619–620.

Paul Laurence Dunbar

**Paul Laurence Dunbar: American
    Poet.*
14 min., color, 1966.
Beta, VHS, ¾" U-matic cassette, 16-mm
film, open-captioned.
A biographical sketch of the poet.
Distributed by Phoenix/BFA Films.

*Paul Laurence Dunbar.
22 min., color, 1973.
Beta, VHS, ¾" U-matic cassette.
A biographical tribute to the poet. Di-
rected by Carlton Moss.
Distributed by Pyramid Film and Video.

T. S. Eliot

*The Mysterious Mr. Eliot.
62 min., color, 1973.
Beta, VHS, ¾" U-matic cassette, 16-mm film.
A biographical film about the poet.
Distributed by Insight Media and CRM
    Films.

T. S. Eliot: Selected Poems [recording].
1 cassette (49 min.), 1971.
The author reads his poetry, including
    "The Waste Land."
Distributed by Caedmon/HarperAudio.

T. S. Eliot: Four Quartets [recording].
1 cassette.
Distributed by Caedmon/HarperAudio.

*T. S. Eliot: Twentieth-Century Poetry in
    English: Recordings of Poets Reading
    Their Own Poetry, No. 3 [recording].*
Distributed by the Library of Congress.

T. S. Eliot and George Orwell [recording].
1 cassette (41 min.), 1953.
Read by Stephen Spender.
Distributed by Caedmon/HarperAudio.

*T. S. Eliot Reading "The Love Song of
    J. Alfred Prufrock" [recording].*
1 cassette.
Distributed by Caedmon/HarperAudio.

*T. S. Eliot Reading "The Waste Land" &
    Other Poems [recording].*
1 cassette.
Distributed by Caedmon/HarperAudio.

See also *"Caedmon Treasury of Modern Po-
    ets Reading Their Own Poetry," "Mod-
    ern American Poetry," "The Poet's
    Voice,"* and *"Voices and Vision"* on
    manual pp. 618–622.

Carolyn Forché

Carolyn Forché [recording].
1 cassette (29 min.), 1989.
Distributed by New Letters on the Air.

*Carolyn Forché: Ourselves or Nothing
    [recording].*
1 cassette (58 min.), 1983.
Distributed by Watershed Tapes.

Robert Frost

Afterglow: A Tribute to Robert Frost.
35 min., color, 1989.
Beta, VHS, ¾" U-matic cassette.
Starring and directed by Burgess Meredith.
Distributed by Pyramid Film and Video.

Robert Frost [recording].
1 cassette, 1981.
Includes "The Pasture" and "Stopping by Woods on a Snowy Evening."
Distributed by the Library of Congress

*Robert Frost: A First Acquaintance.
16 min., color, 1974.
Beta, VHS, ¾" U-matic cassette, 16-mm film.
An examination of Frost's life through his poems.
Distributed by Films for the Humanities and Sciences.

Frost and Whitman.
30 min., b/w, 1963.
Beta, VHS, ½" open reel (EIAJ), ¾" U-matic cassette, 2" quadraplex open reel.
Will Geer performs excerpts from the two poets' works.
Distributed by New York State Education Department.

An Interview with Robert Frost.
30 min., b/w, 1952.
Beta, VHS, ¾" U-matic cassette.
Bela Kornitzer interviews Frost, who reads from his poetry.
Distributed by Social Studies School Service.

*Robert Frost: A Lover's Quarrel with the World.
40 min., b/w, 1970.
Beta, VHS, ¾" U-matic cassette, 16-mm film.
A documentary film on Frost's philosophic and artistic ideas.
Distributed by Phoenix/BFA Films.

*Robert Frost.
10 min., color, 1972.
Beta, VHS, ¾" U-matic cassette, 16-mm film.

A biographical sketch of the poet.
Distributed by AIMS Media Inc.

Robert Frost in Recital [recording].
1 cassette.
Distributed by Caedmon/HarperAudio.

Robert Frost Reads [recording].
1 cassette (60 min.), 1987.
From The Poet Anniversary Series.
Distributed by Caedmon/HarperAudio.

Robert Frost Reads His Poems [recording].
1 cassette (55 min.), 1965.
Distributed by Audio-Forum.

Robert Frost Reads His Poetry [recording].
1 cassette (48 min.).
Distributed by Recorded Books.

Robert Frost Reads "The Road Not Taken" & Other Poems [recording].
1 cassette.
Distributed by Caedmon/HarperAudio.

*Robert Frost's New England.
22 min., color, 1976.
Beta, VHS, ¾" U-matic cassette, 16-mm film, special-order formats. Ancillary materials available.
Explores some of Frost's poetry relating to New England and its seasons.
Distributed by Churchill Media.

Robert Frost: Twentieth-Century Poetry in English: Recordings of Poets Reading Their Own Poetry, No. 6 [recording].
Distributed by the Library of Congress.

See also *"Caedmon Treasury of Modern Poets Reading Their Own Poetry," "Literature: The Synthesis of Poetry," "Modern American Poetry," "Poetry by Americans," "The Poet's Voice,"* and *"Voices and Vision"* on manual pp. 618–622.

Allen Ginsberg

Allen Ginsberg [recording].
1 cassette (29 min.), 1988.
The author talks about the Beat move-

ment and his ongoing battle against censorship.
Distributed by New Letters on the Air.

Allen Ginsberg: First Blues [recording].
Recorded in the 1970s, these songs represent Ginsberg's earliest experiments combining improvised text with music.
Distributed by Poet's Audio Center.

Allen Ginsberg.
Color, Beta, VHS, ¾" U-matic cassette (50 min.).
Part of the Writers on Writing Series.
Distributed by The Roland Collection.

Allen Ginsberg: When the Muse Calls, Answer!
Color, VHS (30 min.).
Distributed by Filmic Archives.

Allen Ginsberg: Potpourri of Poetry — Summer, Nineteen Seventy-Five [recording].
1 cassette.
Distributed by Caedmon/HarperAudio.

The Life and Times of Allen Ginsberg.
83 min., color, 1993.
VHS.
Chronicles the life of the poet, with commentary from Abbie Hoffman, Ken Kesey, Jack Kerouac, Joan Baez, and others.
Distributed by First Run/Icarus Films.

See also *"Fried Shoes, Cooked Diamonds," "A Movable Feast," "Poets in Person," "The Poet's Voice," "Potpourri of Poetry,"* and *"Spoken Arts Treasury of American Jewish Poets Reading Their Poems, Vol. VI,"* on manual pp. 618–621.

H. D. [Hilda Doolittle]

H. D. [Hilda Doolittle]: Helen in Egypt [recording].
1 cassette (39 min.).
Part of the Archive Series.
Distributed by Watershed Tapes.

Marilyn Hacker

Marilyn Hacker: The Poetry and Voice of Marilyn Hacker [recording].
1 cassette.
Distributed by Caedmon/HarperAudio.

Donald Hall

Donald Hall: Prose and Poetry [recording].
2 cassettes (93 min.), 1997.
Distributed by Audio Bookshelf.

Donald Hall [recording].
1 cassette (29 min.), 1987.
Distributed by New Letters on the Air.

Donald Hall [recording].
1 cassette (29 min.), 1987.
Distributed by Spoken Arts.

Donald Hall and Jane Kenyon: A Life Together.
60 min., color.
VHS.
Bill Moyers interviews these husband-and-wife poets at their home in New Hampshire.
Distributed by Films for the Humanities and Sciences.

Donald Hall: Names of Horses [recording].
1 cassette (53 min.), 1986.
Distributed by Watershed Tapes.

The Poetry of Donald Hall [recording].
1 cassette (26 min.), 1964.
Part of the YM-YWHA Poetry Center Series.
Distributed by Audio-Forum.

Thomas Hardy

The Poetry of Thomas Hardy [recording].
1 cassette.
Distributed by Caedmon/HarperAudio.

See also *"Introduction to English Poetry," "Romantics and Realists,"* and *"Victorian Poetry"* (recording) on manual pp. 619–622.

Joy Harjo

Joy Harjo [recording].
1 cassette (29 min.), 1991.
The author plays the saxophone and reads from her work.
Distributed by New Letters on the Air.

Joy Harjo & Barney Bush [recording].
1 cassette (29 min.), 1983.
Native American poets Harjo and Bush read from their work.
Distributed by New Letters on the Air.

Joy Harjo: Furious Light [recording].
1 cassette (56 min.), 1986.
Selected poems with musical accompaniment.
Distributed by Watershed Tapes.

Michael S. Harper

Michael S. Harper: Hear Where Coltrane Is [recording].
1 cassette (60 min.), 1971, 1984. Poems accompanied by music.
Distributed by Watershed Tapes.

Robert Hass

Robert Hass: A Story About the Body [recording].
1 cassette, 1988.
Distributed by Watershed Tapes.

William Hathaway

William Hathaway [recording].
1 cassette (29 min.), 1984.
Distributed by New Letters on the Air.

Seamus Heaney

Seamus Heaney [recording].
2 cassettes, 1990.
Heaney reads his own work and a personal selection of classic poems by Shakespeare, Marvell, Hardy, Yeats, Blake, and others.
Distributed by Poet's Audio Center.

Seamus Heaney: Stepping Stones [recording].
1 cassette (72 min.), 1996.
Distributed by Penguin Audiobooks.

*Seamus Heaney: Poet in Limboland.
29 min., color, 1972.
Beta, VHS, ¾″ U-matic cassette, 16-mm film.
Heaney discusses his poetry and political problems in Ireland.
Distributed by Films for the Humanities and Sciences.

Anthony Hecht

Anthony Hecht I & II [recording].
1 cassette (60 min.), 1985, 1988.
Distributed by New Letters on the Air.

George Herbert

See *"Introduction to English Poetry"* and *"Metaphysical and Devotional Poetry"* on manual p. 619.

Robert Herrick

See *"Palgrave's Golden Treasury of English Poetry"* on manual p. 620.

Linda Hogan

Linda Hogan [recording].
1 cassette (29 min.), 1990.
Distributed by New Letters on the Air.

Gerard Manley Hopkins

The Poetry of Gerard Manley Hopkins [recording].
1 cassette.
Distributed by Caedmon/HarperAudio.

Gerard Manley Hopkins: The Wreck of the Deutschland [recording].
1 cassette.
Distributed by Audio-Forum.

See also *"Romantics and Realists"* and *"Victorian Poetry"* (recording) on manual pp. 621–622.

A. E. Housman

A. E. Housman: "A Shropshire Lad" & Other Poetry [recording].
1 cassette.
Distributed by Caedmon/HarperAudio.

See also *"Romantics and Realists"* and *"Victorian Poetry"* (recording) on manual pp. 621–622.

Langston Hughes

*Langston Hughes.
24 min., color, 1971.
Beta, VHS, ¾″ U-matic cassette, 16-mm film.
A biographical sketch of the poet.
Distributed by Carousel Film & Video.

Langston Hughes: The Dream Keeper.
Color, VHS (60 min.), 1988.
Distributed by the Annenberg/CPB Collection.

Langston Hughes: Looking for Langston.
Color, VHS (45 min.), 1992. Produced by Isaac Julien.
Distributed by Water Bearer Films.

Langston Hughes Reads [recording].
1 cassette (50 min.).
Distributed by Caedmon/HarperAudio, Filmic Archives.

Langston Hughes Reads and Talks about His Poems [recording].
1 cassette. (42 min.).
Distributed by Dove Audio.

Langston Hughes: Dream Keeper and Other Poems [recording].
1 cassette, 1955.
Distributed by Smithsonian/Folkways Recordings.

Langston Hughes: The Making of a Poet [recording].
1 cassette (30 min.).
Read by the poet.
Distributed by National Public Radio.

Langston Hughes: Poetry & Reflections [recording].
1 cassette.
Performed by the author.
Distributed by Caedmon/HarperAudio.

Langston Hughes Reads and Talks about His Poems [recording].
1 cassette.

Includes "The Negro Speaks of Rivers" and "Dream Boogie."
Distributed by Spoken Arts.

The Poetry of Langston Hughes [recording].
2 cassettes.
Performed by Ruby Dee and Ossie Davis.
Distributed by Caedmon/HarperAudio.

The Voice of Langston Hughes: Selected Poetry and Prose [recording].
1 cassette or CD (38 min.).
Selections from the years 1925–1932. The author reads poetry from *"The Dream Keeper" and Other Poems* and *Simple Speaks His Mind,* and he narrates his text from *The Story of Jazz, Rhythms of the World,* and *The Glory of Negro History.*
Distributed by Smithsonian/Folkways Recordings.

Langston Hughes: Simple Stories [recording].
1 cassette.
Performed by Ossie Davis.
Distributed by Caedmon/HarperAudio.

See also *"Harlem Renaissance: The Black Poets," "The Harlem Renaissance and Beyond," "Modern American Poetry," "Twentieth-Century Poets Reading Their Work,"* and *"Voices and Vision"* on manual pp. 619–622.

Randall Jarrell

Randall Jarrell: The Bat Poet [recording].
1 cassette.
Distributed by Caedmon/HarperAudio.

The Poetry of Randall Jarrell [recording].
1 cassette (67 min.), 1963.
Part of the YM-YWHA Poetry Center Series.
Distributed by Audio-Forum.

Randall Jarrell Reads and Discusses His Poems against War [recording].
1 cassette.
Distributed by Caedmon/HarperAudio.

See also *"The Poet's Voice"* on manual p. 621.

Ben Jonson

Ben Jonson: Poetry of the Early Seventeenth Century [recording].
1 cassette.
Distributed by Spoken Arts.

Donald Justice

Donald Justice: "Childhood" & Other Poems [recording].
1 cassette (55 min.), 1985.
Distributed by Watershed Tapes.

Donald Justice I & II [recording].
1 cassette (60 min.), 1984, 1989.
Distributed by New Letters on the Air.

John Keats

*John Keats — His Life and Death.
55 min., color, 1973.
Beta, VHS, ¾″ U-matic cassette, 16-mm film.
Extended version of *"John Keats — Poet"* (see below). Explores the poet's affair with Fanny Browne and the events surrounding his death. Written by Archibald MacLeish.
Distributed by Britannica Films.

*John Keats — Poet.
31 min., color, 1973.
Beta, VHS, ¾″ U-matic cassette, 16-mm film.
A biography of the poet, with excerpts from his letters and poems. Written by Archibald MacLeish.
Distributed by Britannica Films.

John Keats: Selected Poems [recording].
2 cassettes (180 min.), 1993.
Read by Frederick Davidson.
Distributed by Blackstone Audio Books.

John Keats: Odes [recording].
1 cassette.
Distributed by Audio-Forum.

The Poetry of Keats [recording].
1 cassette.
Distributed by Caedmon/HarperAudio.

Treasury of John Keats [recording].
1 cassette.
Distributed by Spoken Arts.

See also *"English Literature: Romantic Period," "Palgrave's Golden Treasury of English Poetry,"* and *"The Young Romantics"* on manual pp. 618–622.

X. J. Kennedy

X. J. Kennedy: Is Seeing Believing? [recording].
1 cassette (60 min.), 1985.
Distributed by Watershed Tapes.

Jane Kenyon

Jane Kenyon [recording].
1 cassette, 1987.
Distributed by New Letters on the Air.

Maxine Hong Kingston

Maxine Hong Kingston [recording].
1 cassette, 1986.
Interview.
Distributed by American Audio Prose Library.

The Stories of Maxine Hong Kingston.
54 min., color, 1990.
VHS.
Kingston discusses her perspective of the "Great American Melting Pot."
Distributed by University of Washington Educational Media Collection.

Galway Kinnell

Galway Kinnell I & II [recording].
1 cassette (60 min.), 1982, 1991.
Distributed by New Letters on the Air.

The Poetry of Galway Kinnell [recording].
1 cassette (33 min.), 1965.
Part of the YM-YWHA Poetry Center Series.
Distributed by Audio-Forum.

The Poetry & Voice of Galway Kinnell [recording].
1 cassette.
Distributed by Caedmon/HarperAudio.

See also *"Moyers: The Power of the Word"* on manual p. 620.

Carolyn Kizer

Carolyn Kizer: An Ear to the Earth [recording].
1 cassette (63 min.), 1977.
Distributed by Watershed Tapes.

Carolyn Kizer [recording].
1 cassette (29 min.), 1985.
Distributed by New Letters on the Air.

Carolyn Kizer: Reading Her Poetry [recording].
1 cassette.
Distributed by Sound Photosynthesis.

Carolyn Kizer: Selected Poems [recording].
1 cassette (63 min.), 1977.
Distributed by Watershed Tapes.

Etheridge Knight

Etheridge Knight I [recording].
1 cassette (29 min.), 1986.
Distributed by New Letters on the Air.

Etheridge Knight II [recording].
1 cassette (29 min.), 1989.
Distributed by New Letters on the Air.

Etheridge Knight: So My Soul Can Sing [recording].
1 cassette (50 min.).
Distributed by Watershed Tapes.

Maxine Kumin

Maxine Kumin: Progress Report [recording].
1 cassette (42 min.), 1976.
Distributed by Watershed Tapes.

Maxine Kumin I & II [recording].
1 cassette (60 min.), 1980, 1987.
Distributed by New Letters on the Air.

See also *"Poets in Person, No. 2"* (recording) on manual p. 621.

D. H. Lawrence

Poems of D. H. Lawrence [recording].

1 cassette (36 min.).
Distributed by Spoken Arts.

Li-Young Lee

Li-Young Lee: The City in Which I Love You [recording].
1 cassette (29 min.), 1990.
Reads from his book, which was the year's Lamont Poetry Selection.
Distributed by New Letters on the Air.

See also *"A Movable Feast,"* which features a discussion of "Always a Rose," on manual p. 620.

Denise Levertov

Denise Levertov [recording].
1 cassette (29 min.), 1983.
The author reads her poems and discusses political activism and the responsibility of a writer.
Distributed by New Letters on the Air.

Denise Levertov: The Acolyte [recording].
1 cassette (63 min.), 1985.
Distributed by Watershed Tapes.

*Poetry: Denise Levertov and Charles Olson.
30 min., b/w, 1966.
¾″ U-matic cassette, 16-mm film, special-order formats.
An introduction to the two poets' work.
Distributed by Indiana University Instructional Support Services.

The Poetry of Denise Levertov [recording].
1 cassette (37 min.), 1965.
Part of the YM-YWHA Poetry Center Series.
Distributed by Audio-Forum.

See also *"Spoken Arts Treasury of American Jewish Poets Reading Their Poems, Vol. V"* on manual p. 621.

Philip Levine

Philip Levine [recording].
1 cassette (29 min.), 1986.
Distributed by New Letters on the Air.

Philip Levine: Hear Me [recording].
1 cassette (62 min.), 1977.
Features selected poems.
Distributed by Watershed Tapes, Audio-Forum.

The Poetry and Voice of Philip Levine
[recording].
1 cassette.
Distributed by Caedmon/HarperAudio.

See also *"Spoken Arts Treasury of American Poets Reading Their Poems, Vol. II"* on manual p. 621.

Henry Wadsworth Longfellow

Henry Wadsworth Longfellow:
The Best-Loved Poems of Longfellow
[recording].
1 cassette (55 min.), 1996. Read by Hal Holbrook.
Distributed by Caedmon/HarperAudio.

Henry Wadsworth Longfellow: Songs of Hiawatha and More Poems
[recording].
3 cassettes (3 hours, 9 minutes.).
Distributed by Audio Book Contractors.

Treasury of Henry Wadsworth Longfellow
[recording].
1 cassette (54 min.), 1986.
Distributed by Spoken Arts.

Audre Lorde

Audre Lorde [recording].
1 cassette (29 min.), 1979.
The author reads her poetry and discusses her ideas about poetry and her experiences in West Africa.
Distributed by New Letters on the Air.

Audre Lorde: Shorelines [recording].
1 cassette (53 min.), 1985.
Distributed by Watershed Tapes.

Archibald MacLeish

Archibald MacLeish Reads His Poetry
[recording].
1 cassette.
Distributed by Caedmon/HarperAudio.

Archibald MacLeish: Twentieth-Century Poetry in English: Recordings of Poets Reading Their Own Poetry: Nine Pulitzer Prize Poets, No. 29 [recording].
Distributed by the Library of Congress.

See also *"Caedmon Treasury of Modern Poets Reading Their Own Poetry"* on manual p. 618.

Christopher Marlowe

Christopher Marlowe: Elizabethan Love Poems [recording].
1 cassette (50 min.).
Unabridged edition.
Distributed by Spoken Arts.

See also *"Medieval and Elizabethan Poetry"* and *"Palgrave's Golden Treasury of English Poetry"* on manual pp. 619–620.

Andrew Marvell

Andrew Marvell: Ralph Richardson Reads Andrew Marvell [recording].
1 cassette.
Distributed by Audio-Forum.

See also *"Metaphysical and Devotional Poetry"* on manual p. 619.

James Merrill

James Merrill: Reflected Houses [recording].
1 cassette (60 min.), 1988.
Distributed by Watershed Tapes.

James Merrill: Voices from Sandover.
116 min., color.
A dramatic adaptation of Merrill's "The Changing Light at Sandover" and a summation of the poetic thought of this influential American poet. The cassette concludes with an interview of Merrill by Helen Vendler.
Distributed by Films for the Humanities and Sciences.

See also *"Poets in Person, No. 4"* on manual p. 620.

Edna St. Vincent Millay

Edna St. Vincent Millay: Renascence.
60 min., color.
A biography of the poet.
Distributed by Films for the Humanities and Sciences.

Poems of Edna St. Vincent Millay [recording].
1 cassette (60 min.), 1981.
Part of the Poetic Heritage Series.
Distributed by Summer Stream.

Poetry of Edna St. Vincent Millay [recording].
1 cassette.
Distributed by Caedmon/HarperAudio.

See also *"With a Feminine Touch"* on manual p. 622.

John Milton

*Milton.
28 min., color, 1989.
Beta, VHS, ¾" U-matic cassette.
Looks at Milton's sonnets to his wife Katherine and "Paradise Lost."
Distributed by Films for the Humanities and Sciences.

*Milton and 17th Century Poetry.
35 min., color, 1989.
Beta, VHS, ¾" U-matic cassette.
A study of Milton and other metaphysical poets.
Distributed by Films for the Humanities and Sciences.

Milton by Himself.
27 min., color, 1989.
Beta, VHS, ¾" U-matic cassette.
A biography constructed from Milton's autobiographical writings.
Distributed by Films for the Humanities and Sciences.

Milton the Puritan: Portrait of a Mind [recording].
10 cassettes (15 hours).
Distributed by Books on Tape.

The Poetry of John Milton [recording].
1 cassette.
Distributed by Caedmon/HarperAudio.

Treasury of John Milton [recording].
1 cassette.
Distributed by Spoken Arts.

See also *"Introduction to English Poetry"* and *"Palgrave's Golden Treasury of English Poetry"* on manual pp. 619 and 620.

N. Scott Momaday

N. Scott Momaday.
50 min., color.
The author discusses the creative sources of his work.
Distributed by Films for the Humanities and Sciences.

N. Scott Momaday: House Made of Dawn [recording].
1 cassette (39 min.).
Momaday reads excerpts from his stories.
Distributed by the American Audio Prose Library.

N. Scott Momaday: House Made of Dawn [recording].
7 cassettes (7 hours).
Distributed by Books on Tape.

N. Scott Momaday Reading [recording].
2 cassettes (109 min.), 1983.
Distributed by American Audio Prose Library.

Marianne Moore

Marianne Moore Reading Her Poems & Fables from La Fontaine [recording].
1 cassette.
Distributed by Caedmon/HarperAudio.

Marianne Moore Reads Her Poetry [recording].
1 cassette (22 min.), 1965.
Distributed by Audio-Forum.

See also *"Caedmon Treasury of Modern Poets Reading Their Own Poetry," "Inner Ear, Parts 3 and 4," "Modern American Poetry," "The Poet's Voice,"* and *"Voices and Vision,"* on manual pp. 618–622.

Pablo Neruda

Pablo Neruda: Poet.
30 min., b/w, 1972.
Beta, VHS, ¾″ U-matic cassette.
A profile of the poet.
Distributed by Cinema Guild.

Pablo Neruda: Selected Poems
    [recording].
1 cassette.
In Spanish.
Distributed by Applause Productions.

*Yo Soy Pablo Neruda.
29 min., b/w, 1967.
Beta, VHS, ¾″ U-matic, 16-mm film.
A profile of the poet. Narrated by Sir An-
    thony Quayle.
Distributed by Films for the Humanities
    and Sciences.

John Frederick Nims

John Frederick Nims [recording].
1 cassette (29 min.), 1986.
A reading by the Chicago poet.
Distributed by New Letters on the Air.

Sharon Olds

Sharon Olds [recording].
1 cassette (29 min.), 1992.
Distributed by New Letters on the Air.

Sharon Olds: Coming Back to Life
    [recording].
1 cassette (60 min.).
Distributed by Audio-Forum.

Michael O'Brien & Sharon Olds
    [recording].
1 cassette (29 min.).
Distributed by New Letters on the Air.

See also *"Moyers: The Power of the Word"*
    on manual p. 620.

Wilfred Owen

Wilfred Owen: War Requiem.
Color & b/w, VHS (92 min.), 1988.
Written and directed by Derek Jarman,
    music by Benjamin Britten.
Distributed by Mystic Fire Video.

Wilfred Owen: War Requiem [recording].
2 compact discs, 1993.
Distributed by Deutsche Grammophone.

*The Pity of War: From the Works of Wilfred
    Owen.*
58 min., color, 1987.
Beta, VHS, ¾″ U-matic cassette.
A documentary drawn from Owen's po-
    ems, diaries, and letters.
Distributed by Films for the Humanities
    and Sciences.

Dorothy Parker

Dorothy Parker [recording].
2 cassettes.
Read by Mary M. Lewis.
Distributed by Cassette Works.

*An Informal Hour with Dorothy
    Parker [recording].*
1 cassette.
The author reads her short story "Horsie"
    as well as twenty-six poems.
Distributed by Spoken Arts.

See also *"Spoken Arts Treasury of American
    Jewish Poets Reading Their Poems, Vol.
    1"* on manual p. 621.

Linda Pastan

Linda Pastan [recording].
1 cassette (29 min.).
Distributed by New Letters on the Air.

Linda Pastan: Mosaic [recording]
1 cassette (51 min.), 1988.
Distributed by Watershed Tapes.

Octavio Paz

*Octavio Paz: An Uncommon Poet.
28 min., color, 198?.
Beta, VHS, ¾″ U-matic cassette, 16-mm
    film.
The poet talks about the distinctions be-
    tween his two careers: poet and politi-
    cal activist.
Distributed by Films for the Humanities
    and Sciences.

See also *"Moyers: The Power of the Word"*
    on manual p. 620.

Marge Piercy

Marge Piercy: At the Core [recording].
1 cassette (58 min.), 1977.
Distributed by Watershed Tapes.

Sylvia Plath

Sylvia Plath: The Bell Jar.
113 min., color, 1979.
Beta, VHS.
Based on Plath's semiautobiographical novel.
See local retailer.

Sylvia Plath.
Color, VHS (1988).
Distributed by Annenberg/CPB Collection and Mystic Fire.

Sylvia Plath.
4 programs (30 min. each), color, 1974.
VHS, ½" open reel (EIAJ), ¾" U-matic cassette, 2" quadraplex open reel.
A biographical examination of the poet and her work.
Distributed by New York State Education Department.

Sylvia Plath [recording].
1 cassette (48 min.), 1962.
A historic reading of fifteen poems recorded the month before the poet's suicide.
Distributed by Poet's Audio Center.

Sylvia Plath: Letters Home.
90 min., color, 1985.
Beta, VHS, ¾" U-matic cassette.
Staged version of Plath's letters to her mother.
Distributed by Films for the Humanities and Sciences.

Sylvia Plath, Part I: The Struggle.
30 min., color, 1974.
Beta, VHS, ½" open reel (EIAJ), ¾" U-matic cassette, 2" quadraplex open reel.
A dramatization of Plath's poetry by The Royal Shakespeare Company.
Distributed by New York State Education Department.

Sylvia Plath, Part II: Getting There.
30 min., color, 1974.
Beta, VHS, ½" open reel (EIAJ), ¾" U-matic cassette, 2" quadraplex open reel.
Plath's poems are set to music by Elizabeth Swados and performed by Michele Collison.
Distributed by New York State Education Department.

Sylvia Plath Reading Her Poetry [recording].
1 cassette.
Distributed by Caedmon/HarperAudio.

Sylvia Plath Reads [recording].
1 cassette (60 min.), 1987.
From The Poet Anniversary Series.
Distributed by Caedmon/HarperAudio.

See also *"The Poet's Voice," "Voices and Vision,"* and *"With a Feminine Touch"* on manual pp. 621–622.

Edgar Allan Poe

Edgar Allan Poe: "The Raven," "The Bells," and Other Poems [recording].
1 cassette.
Distributed by Spoken Arts.

Edgar Allan Poe [recording].
2 cassettes (2 hours).
Distributed by Dove Audio.

See also *"Poetry by Americans"* on manual p. 620.

Alexander Pope

Treasury of Alexander Pope [recording].
1 cassette.
Distributed by Spoken Arts.

See also *"English Literature: Eighteenth Century"* and *"Restoration and Augustan Poetry"* on manual pp. 618 and 621.

Ezra Pound

Ezra Pound Reading "Cantico Del Sole," "Canto Ninety-Nine" & Other Poems [recording].
2 cassettes.
Distributed by Caedmon/HarperAudio.

*Ezra Pound: Poet's Poet.
29 min., b/w, 1970.
Beta, VHS, ¾″ U-matic cassette, 16-mm film.
A profile of Pound and his influence on later poets.
Distributed by Films for the Humanities and Sciences.

See also *"Caedmon Treasury of Modern Poets Reading Their Own Poetry," "Modern American Poetry," "The Poet's Voice,"* and *"Voices and Vision,"* on manual pp. 618–622.

Adrienne Rich

*Adrienne Rich: Planetarium:
A Retrospective 1950 to 1980
[recording].*
1 cassette (63 min.), 1986.
Part of the YM-YWHA Poetry Center Series.
Distributed by Watershed Tapes.

*The Poetry of Adrienne Rich
[recording].*
1 cassette (36 min.), 1968.
Part of the YM-YWHA Poetry Center Series.
Distributed by Audio-Forum.

*Adrienne Rich: Tracking the Contradictions:
Poems 1981–1985
[recording].*
1 cassette (53 min.), 1986.
Distributed by Watershed Tapes.

See also *"Poets in Person, No. 4"* on manual p. 621.

Rainer Maria Rilke

*The Poetry of Rainer Maria Rilke
[recording].*
1 cassette.
In German.
Distributed by Caedmon/HarperAudio.

*Rainer Maria Rilke: Selected Poems
[recording].*
2 cassettes (118 min.), 1988.
From the Spiritual Classics on Cassette Series.

Distributed by Audio Literature.
Alberto A. Ríos

Alberto A. Ríos

*Alberto A. Ríos: Reading His Poetry
[recording].*
1 cassette.
Distributed by Sound Photosynthesis.

See also *"Birthright: Growing Up Hispanic"* on manual p. 618.

Theodore Roethke

The Poetry of Theodore Roethke [recording].
1 cassette (36 min.).
Part of the YM-YWHA Poetry Center Series.
Distributed by Audio-Forum.

Theodore Roethke [recording].
1 cassette (48 min.), 1972.
A posthumous collection of Roethke reading his poetry.
Distributed by Caedmon/HarperAudio.

*Theodore Roethke: Twentieth-Century
Poetry in English: Recordings of
Poets Reading Their Own Poetry,
No. 10 [recording].*
Distributed by the Library of Congress.

*Words for the Wind: Read by Theodore
Roethke [recording].*
1 cassette, 1962.
Distributed by Smithsonian/Folkways Recordings.

See *"The Poet's Voice"* on manual p. 621.

William Shakespeare

***William Shakespeare: Poetry and Hidden
Poetry.**
53 min., color, 1984.
A microexamination of Shakespeare's poetry and its hidden meanings. Produced by the Royal Shakespeare Company.
Distributed by Films for the Humanities and Sciences.

Selected Sonnets by Shakespeare.
40 min., color, 1984.
Beta, VHS, ¾″ U-matic cassette.

Features readings by Ben Kingsley and Jane Lapotaire.
Distributed by Films for the Humanities and Sciences.

Selected Sonnets of Shakespeare *[recording]*.
1 cassette.
Distributed by Spoken Arts.

William Shakespeare: The Sonnets *[recording]*.
1 cassette.
Distributed by Recorded Books.

William Shakespeare Sonnets *[recording]*.
2 cassettes (120 min.).
Distributed by Caedmon/HarperAudio.

William Shakespeare's Sonnets.
150 min., color, 1984.
Beta, VHS, ¾″ U-matic cassette.
An in-depth look at fifteen of Shakespeare's sonnets. With Ben Kingsley, Roger Reese, Claire Bloom, Jane Lapotaire, A. L. Rowse, and Stephen Spender.
Distributed by Films for the Humanities and Sciences.

See also ***"England: Background of Literature," "Introduction to English Poetry," "Medieval and Elizabethan Poetry," "Palgrave's Golden Treasury of English Poetry,"*** and ***"Poetry for People Who Hate Poetry"*** on manual pp. 619–620.

Percy Bysshe Shelley

The Poetry of Shelley *[recording]*.
1 cassette.
Distributed by Caedmon/HarperAudio.

Treasury of Percy Bysshe Shelley *[recording]*.
1 cassette.
Distributed by Spoken Arts.
See also ***"English Literature: Romantic Period," "English Romantic Poetry," "Introduction to English Poetry,"*** and ***"Palgrave's Golden Treasury of English Poetry"*** on manual pp. 618–620.

Louis Simpson

Louis Simpson *[recording]*.
1 cassette (29 min.), 1983.
Distributed by New Letters on the Air.

Louis Simpson: Physical Universe *[recording]*.
1 cassette (57 min.), 1985.
Distributed by Watershed Tapes.

Gary Soto

Gary Soto I & II *[recording]*.
1 cassette (60 min.), 1982, 1992.
The author reads his work and talks about the recent rise of Chicano literature.
Distributed by New Letters on the Air.

See also ***"Poets in Person, No. 7"*** on manual p. 620.

Bruce Springsteen

Bruce Springsteen's Greatest Hits *[recording]*.
1 CD.
Contains Springsteen's hit single "Streets of Philadelphia."
Distributed by Columbia Records.

Philadelphia.
125 min., color, 1994.
VHS.
Film starring Tom Hanks and Denzel Washington and featuring Bruce Springsteen's hit single "Streets of Philadelphia."
See local retailer.

William Stafford

William Stafford I & II *[recording]*.
1 cassette (60 min.), 1983, 1984.
The author reads his poetry and discusses politics, poetry, and the writing process.
Distributed by New Letters on the Air.

William Stafford: Troubleshooting *[recording]*.
1 cassette (50 min.), 1984.
Distributed by Watershed Tapes.

See also ***"Moyers: The Power of the Word"*** on manual p. 620.

Wallace Stevens

Wallace Stevens Reads [recording].
1 cassette (60 min.), 1987.
Part of The Poet Anniversary Series.
Distributed by Caedmon/HarperAudio.

Wallace Stevens Reading His Poems
[recording].
1 cassette.
Distributed by Caedmon/HarperAudio.

See also *"Caedmon Treasury of Modern Poets Reading Their Own Poetry," "Inner Ear, Parts 3 and 4," "Modern American Poetry," "The Poet's Voice,"* and *"Voices and Vision,"* on manual pp. 618–622.

May Swenson

The Poetry of May Swenson [recording].
1 cassette (32 min.), 1963.
Part of the YM-YWHA Poetry Center Series.
Distributed by Audio-Forum.

The Poetry and Voice of May Swenson
[recording].
1 cassette.
Distributed by Caedmon/HarperAudio.

Alfred, Lord Tennyson

Treasury of Alfred, Lord Tennyson
[recording].
1 cassette.
Read by Robert Speaight.
Includes "Ulysses," "The Lotus Eaters," and "The Charge of the Light Brigade."
Distributed by Spoken Arts.

The Poetry of Tennyson [recording].
1 cassette.
Distributed by Caedmon/HarperAudio.

Alfred, Lord Tennyson: Portrait of a Poet [recording].
1 cassette (53 min.).
Distributed by Watershed Tapes.

See also *"England: Background of Literature," "Palgrave's Golden Treasury of English Poetry,"* and *"Victorian*

Poetry" (film and recording) on manual pp. 618–622.

Dylan Thomas

*The Days of Dylan Thomas.
21 min., b/w, 1965.
Beta, VHS, ¾" U-matic cassette, 16-mm film.
A biography of the poet.
Distributed by CRM Films.

Dylan Thomas [recording].
4 cassettes.
Distributed by Caedmon/HarperAudio.

Dylan Thomas.
25 min., color, 1982.
Beta, VHS, ¾" U-matic cassette.
A portrait of the poet.
Distributed by Films, Inc.

*A Dylan Thomas Memoir.
28 min., color, 1972.
Beta, VHS, ¾" U-matic cassette, 16-mm film.
A character study of the poet.
Distributed by Pyramid Film and Video.

Dylan Thomas Soundbook [recording].
4 cassettes.
Read by the author.
Distributed by Caedmon/HarperAudio.

Dylan Thomas Reading "And Death Shall Have No Dominion" & Other Poems [recording].
1 cassette.
Distributed by Caedmon/HarperAudio.

Dylan Thomas Reading His Poetry
[recording].
2 cassettes.
Distributed by Caedmon/HarperAudio.

Dylan Thomas Reading "Quite Early One Morning" & Other Poems
[recording].
1 cassette.
Distributed by Caedmon/HarperAudio.

Dylan Thomas Reading "Over Sir John's Hill" & Other Poems [recording].
1 cassette.
Distributed by Caedmon/HarperAudio.

Dylan Thomas Reads a Personal Anthology [recording].
1 cassette.
Distributed by Caedmon/HarperAudio.

An Evening with Dylan Thomas [recording].
1 cassette.
Distributed by Caedmon/HarperAudio.

Dylan Thomas: In Country Heaven — The Evolution of a Poem [recording].
1 cassette.
Distributed by Caedmon/HarperAudio.

Dylan Thomas: A Portrait.
26 min., color, 1989.
Beta, VHS, ¾″ U-matic cassette.
A biographical film.
Distributed by Films for the Humanities and Sciences.

Dylan Thomas: An Appreciation [recording].
1 cassette.
Distributed by Audio-Forum.

Dylan Thomas: Under Milkwood [recording].
2 cassettes (90 min.).
Distributed by S & S Audio.

The Wales of Dylan Thomas.
Color, 1989.
Images of Wales in Thomas's poetry, prose, and drama.
Distributed by Films for the Humanities and Sciences.

See also *"Caedmon Treasury of Modern Poets Reading Their Own Poetry"* on manual p. 618.

Tomas Transtromer

Tomas Transtromer: The Blue House [recording].
1 cassette (58 min.), 1986.
Distributed by Watershed Tapes.

John Updike

John Updike, I and II [recording].
2 cassettes (58 min.), 1987.
Distributed by New Letters on the Air.

The Poetry of John Updike [recording].
1 cassette (47 min.), 1967.
Part of the YM-YWHA Poetry Center Series.
Distributed by Audio-Forum.

Derek Walcott

Bill Moyer's A World of Ideas: Derek Walcott.
Color, VHS (29 min.), 1989.
Distributed by PBS Video.

Derek Walcott Reads [recording].
1 cassette (90 min.).
Distributed by Caedmon/HarperAudio.

Omeros [recording].
1 cassette (29 min.), 1990.
Distributed by New Letters on the Air.

**Walcott on Poetry* [recording].*
1 cassette.
Distributed by the Center for National Humanities.

Alice Walker

Alice Walker: Interview with Kay Bonetti [recording].
2 cassettes (82 min.), 1988.
Distributed by American Audio Prose Library.

Edmund Waller

See *"Palgrave's Golden Treasury of English Poetry"* on manual p. 620.

Walt Whitman

Walt Whitman: "Crossing Brooklyn Ferry" & Other Poems [recording].
1 cassette.
Distributed by Caedmon/HarperAudio.

Walt Whitman: American Poet, 1819–1892 [recording].
Color, VHS (30 min.), 1994
Distributed by Kultur.

The Democratic Vistas of Walt Whitman [recording].
1 cassette (22 min.), 1968.
By Louis Untermeyer. Part of the Makers of the Modern World Series.
Distributed by Audio-Forum.

Walt Whitman: Endlessly Rocking.
21 min., color, 1986.
Beta, VHS, ¾" U-matic cassette.
Shows a teacher's unsuccessful attempts to interest her students in Whitman.
Distributed by Centre Communications.

Walt Whitman: Frost and Whitman.
30 min., b/w, 1963.
Beta, VHS, ½" open reel (EIAJ), ¾" U-matic cassette, 2" quadraplex open reel.
Will Geer performs excerpts from the two poets' works.
Distributed by New York State Education Department.

Walt Whitman: Galway Kinnell Reads Walt Whitman [recording].
1 cassette (59 min.).
Kinnell reads excerpts from "Song of Myself," "I Sing the Body Electric," and several shorter poems.
Distributed by Sound Rx.

Walt Whitman: The Living Tradition.
20 min., color, 1983.
Beta, VHS, ¾" U-matic cassette.
Allen Ginsberg reads Whitman's poetry.
Distributed by Centre Communications.

Walt Whitman: Memoranda during the War: From Specimen Days [recording].
240 min.
Distributed by Recorded Books.

Walt Whitman: Orson Welles Reads "Song of Myself" [recording].
1 cassette.
Distributed by Audio-Forum.

Walt Whitman: Poet for a New Age.
29 min., color, 1972.
Beta, VHS, ¾" U-matic cassette, 16-mm film.
A study of the poet.
Distributed by Britannica Films.

Readings of Walt Whitman [recording].
1 cassette, 1957.
Distributed by Smithsonian/Folkways Recordings.

Treasury of Walt Whitman: Leaves of Grass, I & II [recording].
2 cassettes (92 min.).
Unabridged edition.
Distributed by Spoken Arts.

Walt Whitman: Twentieth-Century Poetry in English, Nos. 13–17 [recording].
From the Leaves of Grass Centennial Series.
Distributed by the Library of Congress.

Walt Whitman.
10 min., color, 1972.
Beta, VHS, ¾" U-matic cassette, 16-mm film, open captioned.
Readings and a discussion of Whitman's life. Hosted by Efrem Zimbalist Jr.
Distributed by AIMS Media Inc.

Walt Whitman.
12 min., color, 1989.
Beta, VHS, ¾" U-matic cassette.
Examines Whitman's poetic language.
Distributed by Films for the Humanities and Sciences.

Walt Whitman's Civil War.
15 min., color, 1988.
Beta, VHS, ¾" U-matic cassette.
Discusses Whitman's perspective on the war.
Distributed by Churchill Media.

See also *"Poetry by Americans"* and *"Voices and Vision"* on manual pp. 620 and 622.

Richard Wilbur

Richard Wilbur [recording].
1 cassette (29 min.), 1990.
The author reads his poems and talks about early influences and censorship.
Distributed by New Letters on the Air.

Poems of Richard Wilbur [recording].
1 cassette.
Distributed by Spoken Arts.

Poetry — Richard Wilbur and Robert Lowell.
30 min., b/w, 1966.
¾" U-matic cassette, 16-mm film, special-order formats.

Interviews with the two poets.
Distributed by Indiana University Instructional Support Services.

Richard Wilbur Reading His Poetry
[recording].
1 cassette.
Distributed by Caedmon/HarperAudio.

See also *"Caedmon Treasury of Modern Poets Reading Their Own Poetry"* and *"Twentieth-Century Poets Reading Their Work"* on manual pp. 618 and 621.

Miller Williams

Miller Williams *[recording].*
1 cassette (29 min.), 1985.
Distributed by New Letters on the Air.

Poems of Miller Williams *[recording].*
1 cassette.
Read by the author.
Distributed by Spoken Arts.

The Poetry of Miller Williams
[recording].
1 cassette (26 min.), 1969.
Part of the YM-YWHA Poetry Center Series.
Distributed by Audio-Forum.

William Carlos Williams

William Carlos Williams Reads His Poetry
[recording].
1 cassette.
Distributed by Caedmon/HarperAudio.

William Carlos Williams: People and the Stones: Selected Poems
[recording].
1 cassette (60 min.).
Distributed by Watershed Tapes.

See also *"Caedmon Treasury of Modern Poets Reading Their Own Poetry," "Inner Ear, Part 1," "The Poet's Voice,"* and *"Voices and Vision"* on manual pp. 618–622.

William Wordsworth

William Wordsworth: Selected Poems
[recording].

2 cassettes (180 min.).
Read by Frederick Davidson.
Distributed by Blackstone Audio Books.

The Poetry of Wordsworth *[recording].*
1 cassette.
Distributed by Caedmon/HarperAudio.

Treasury of William Wordsworth
[recording].
1 cassette.
Distributed by Spoken Arts.

William Wordsworth: William and Dorothy.
52 min., color, 1989.
Beta, VHS, ¾" U-matic cassette.
Explores Wordsworth's poetry and his troubled relationship with his sister. Directed by Ken Russell.
Distributed by Films for the Humanities and Sciences.

*William Wordsworth.
28 min., color, 1989.
Beta, VHS, ¾" U-matic cassette.
An examination of the poet's work set against the Lake District, subject for many of the poems.
Distributed by Films for the Humanities and Sciences.

William Wordsworth and the English Lakes.
15 min., color, 1989.
Beta, VHS, ¾" U-matic cassette.
Looks at Wordsworth's use of language.
Distributed by Films for the Humanities and Sciences.

See also *"English Literature: Romantic Period," "English Romantic Poetry," "Introduction to English Poetry," "Palgrave's Golden Treasury of English Poetry," "Romantic Pioneers,"* and *"The Young Romantics"* on manual pp. 618–622.

James Wright

The Poetry & Voice of James Wright
[recording].
1 cassette.
Distributed by Caedmon/HarperAudio.

William Butler Yeats

Dylan Thomas Reads the Poetry of W. B. Yeats & Others [recording].
1 cassette.
Includes readings of Yeats, Louis MacNeice, George Barker, Walter de la Mare, W. H. Davies, D. H. Lawrence, and W. H. Auden.
Distributed by Caedmon/HarperAudio.

The Love Poems of William Butler Yeats.
30 min., b/w, 1967.
Beta, VHS, ½" open reel (EIAJ), ¾" U-matic cassette, 2" quadraplex open reel.
Selections from the poet's works.
Distributed by New York State Education Department.

Poems by W. B. Yeats and Poems for Several Voices.
1 cassette, 1973.
Includes "Sailing to Byzantium" and features poems by Thomas Hardy, Robert Graves, and Gerard Manley Hopkins. Read by V. C. Clinton-Baddeley, Jill Balcon, and M. Westbury.
Distributed by Smithsonian/Folkways Recordings.

Poems of William Butler Yeats [recording].
1 cassette.
Distributed by Spoken Arts.

The Poetry of William Butler Yeats [recording].
1 cassette.
Distributed by Caedmon/HarperAudio.

William Butler Yeats, et al.: Treasury of Irish Verse, Folk Tales, & Ballads [recording].
6 cassettes (294 min.), 1986.
Distributed by Spoken Arts.

William Butler Yeats: Twentieth-Century Poets Read Their Works [recording].
6 cassettes (270 min.), 1986.
Distributed by Spoken Arts.

W. B. Yeats [recording].
1 cassette (49 min.), 1953.
Read by Stephen Spender.
Distributed by Audio-Forum.

*Yeats Country.
19 min., color, 1965.
VHS, ¾" U-matic cassette, 16-mm film.
Juxtaposes Yeats's poetry with scenes of the Ireland he wrote about.
Distributed by International Film Bureau.

Yeats Remembered.
30 min.
VHS.
Biographical film using period photographs and interviews with the poet and his family.
Distributed by Insight Media.

See also *"Caedmon Treasury of Modern Poets Reading Their Own Poetry," "Introduction to English Poetry,"* and *"Twentieth-Century Poets Reading Their Own Work"* on manual pp. 618–621.

GENERAL

Anthology of Nineteenth Century American Poets [recording].
1 cassette.
Includes Longfellow, Holmes, Whittier, Lowell, Emerson, Poe, and Whitman.
Distributed by Spoken Arts.

Anthology of Contemporary American Poetry [recording].
1 cassette, 1961.
Includes poems by John Ciardi, Richard Ebhardt, Theodore Roethke, Howard Nemerov, Galway Kinnell, Donald Justice, May Swenson, Richard Wilbur, Karl Shapiro, and others.
Distributed by Smithsonian/Folkways Recordings.

Anthology of Negro Poets [recording].
1 cassette, 1954.
Includes the poetry of Langston Hughes, Sterling Brown, Claude McKay, Countee Cullen, Margaret Walter, and Gwendolyn Brooks.

Distributed by Smithsonian/Folkways Recordings.

Archive of Recorded Poetry and Literature.
Library of Congress

Birthright: Growing Up Hispanic.
59 min., color, 1989.
VHS, Beta, ¾" U-matic cassette.
Focuses on the achievements of Hispanic American writers. Includes the work of Alberto Ríos and Judith Ortiz Cofer.
Distributed by Cinema Guild.

Caedmon Treasury of Modern Poets Reading Their Own Poetry [recording].
2 cassettes (95 min.).
Includes T. S. Eliot, W. B. Yeats, W. H. Auden, Edith Sitwell, Dylan Thomas, Robert Graves, Gertrude Stein, Archibald MacLeish, E. E. Cummings, Marianne Moore, Stephen Spender, Conrad Aiken, Robert Frost, William Carlos Williams, Wallace Stevens, Ezra Pound, Richard Wilbur, and others.
Distributed by Caedmon/HarperCollins.

Conversation Pieces: Short Poems by Thomas, Hardy, Housman, Auden, Keats, and Others [recording].
1 cassette, 1964.
Distributed by Smithsonian/Folkways Recordings.

*England: Background of Literature.
11 min., color, 1962.
Beta, VHS, ¾" U-matic cassette, 16-mm film, special-order formats.
Presents the works of English writers Shakespeare, Dickens, and Tennyson against the backgrounds that inspired them.
Distributed by Coronet/MTI Film & Video.

*English Literature: Eighteenth Century.
14 min., color, 1958.
Beta, VHS, ¾" U-matic cassette, 16-mm film, special-order formats.
Treats the work of Addison and Steele, Pope, Swift, and others.
Distributed by Coronet/MTI Film & Video.

*English Literature: Romantic Period.
13 min., color, 1957.
Beta, VHS, ¾" U-matic cassette, 16-mm film, special-order formats.
Includes selections from Wordsworth, Byron, Shelley, Keats, and others.
Distributed by Coronet/MTI Film & Video.

*English Literature: Seventeenth Century.
13 min., color, 1958.
Beta, VHS, ¾" U-matic cassette, 16-mm film, special-order formats.
Examines works by Jonson, Pepys, and others.
Distributed by Coronet/MTI Film & Video.

English Romantic Poetry: Coleridge, Shelley, Byron, Wordsworth [recording].
3 cassettes.
Distributed by Recorded Books.

*Fried Shoes, Cooked Diamonds.
55 min., color, 1982.
Beta, VHS, ¾" U-matic cassette.
Documents a summer at the Jack Kerouac School of Poetics at the Naropa Institute in Boulder, Colorado. Features such poets from the Beat generation as Allen Ginsberg, Gregory Corso, William S. Burroughs, Peter Orlovsky, and Timothy Leary.
Distributed by Centre Communications, Inc. and Mystic Fire.

Great Poets of the Romantic Age [recording].
6 cassettes (270 min.), 1986.
Distributed by Spoken Arts.

*Haiku.
19 min., color, 1974.
Beta, VHS, ¾" U-matic cassette, 16-mm film.

An overview of this poetic form.
Distributed by AIMS Media Inc.

*Harlem Renaissance: The Black Poets.
20 min., color, 198?.
Beta, VHS, ¾″ U-matic cassette, 16-mm film.
Discusses this era, including an examination of Georgia Douglas Johnson, Fenton Johnson, W. E. B. Du Bois, and Langston Hughes.
Distributed by Carousel Film & Video.

The Harlem Renaissance and Beyond.
31 min., 1989.
VHS.
A still-image program with excerpts from Countee Cullen, Langston Hughes, Claude McKay, Gwendolyn Brooks, Alice Walker, and Richard Wright.
Distributed by Insight Media.

Inner Ear, Part 1 [recording].
1 cassette (60 min.).
Includes the poetry of Carl Sandburg and William Carlos Williams.
Distributed by National Public Radio.

Inner Ear, Parts 3 and 4 [recording].
1 cassette (60 min.).
Emily Dickinson, Marianne Moore, and Wallace Stevens.
Distributed by National Public Radio.

Inner Ear, Parts 5 and 6 [recording].
1 cassette (60 min.).
E. E. Cummings and Gary Snyder.
Distributed by National Public Radio.

In Their Own Voices: A Century of Recorded Poetry [recording].
4 compact discs.
Distributed by Rhino Records.

*Introduction to English Poetry.
28 min., color, 1989.
Beta, VHS, ¾″ U-matic cassette.
Introduces students to English verse, with readings from Chaucer, Shakespeare, Herbert, Milton, Swift, Blake, Wordsworth, Shelley, Emily Brontë, Dickinson, Hardy, Yeats, and Ted Hughes.
Distributed by Films for the Humanities and Sciences.

*Lannan Literary Series.
26 cassettes (60 min. each), color, VHS, 1989-1991.
Carolyn Forché, Allen Ginsberg, Louise Glück, Galway Kinnell, W. S. Merwin, Lucille Clifton, Czeslaw Milosz, Octavio Paz, Yehuda Amichai, Joy Harjo, Victor Hernandez Cruz, Kay Boyle, Alice Walker, Ishmael Reed, Richard Wilbur, Carlos Fuentes, Robert Creeley, Larry Heinemann, Sonya Sanchez, Andrei Voznesensky, Ernesto Cardenal, Anne Waldman, Sharon Olds, Amiri Baraka, Gary Snyder.
Distributed by The Lannan Foundation/Metropolitan Pictures/EZTV.

Literature: The Synthesis of Poetry.
30 min.
VHS.
Hosted by Maya Angelou, who reads some of her own work, as well as the poetry of Frost, Sandburg, and Arnold.
Distributed by Insight Media.

Medieval and Elizabethan Poetry.
28 min., color, 1989.
Beta, VHS, ¾″ U-matic cassette.
Examines trends of the period, focusing on John Skelton, Thomas Wyatt, Tichborne, Nashe, Walter Raleigh, Marlowe, Drayton, and Shakespeare.
Distributed by Films for the Humanities and Sciences.

*Metaphysical and Devotional Poetry.
28 min., color, 1989.
Beta, VHS, ¾″ U-matic cassette.
Looks at the works of John Donne, George Herbert, and Andrew Marvell.
Distributed by Films for the Humanities and Sciences.

Modern American Poetry.
45 min., 1989.
VHS.
Hosted by Helen Vendler. Deals with poets from between the World Wars: Eliot, Pound, Stevens, Cullen, Hughes, Frost, Moore, and Crane. Focuses on development of an American, as distinct from European, voice.
Distributed by Insight Media.

A Movable Feast.
8 programs (30 min. each), color, 1991. VHS.

Hosted by Tom Vitale. Profiles eight contemporary writers: (1) Allen Ginsberg; (2) Joyce Carol Oates; (3) Li-Young Lee; (4) Sonia Sanchez; (5) T. Coraghessan Boyle; (6) T. R. Pearson; (7) Trey Ellis; (8) W. S. Merwin. Distributed by Acorn Media.

Moyers: The Power of the Word.
6 programs (60 min. each), color, 1989. Beta, VHS, ¾" U-matic cassette.

Bill Moyers talks with modern poets: James Autry, Quincy Troupe, Joy Harjo, Mary Tallmountain, Gerald Stern, Li-Young Lee, Stanley Kunitz, Sharon Olds, William Stafford, W. S. Merwin, Galway Kinnell, Robert Bly, and Octavio Paz. Distributed by PBS Video.

Palgrave's Golden Treasury of English Poetry [recording].
2 cassettes.

Includes Marlowe, Shakespeare, Barnefield, Wyatt, Lyly, Donne, Herrick, Dryden, Waller, Lovelace, Milton, Gray, Rogers, Burns, Goldsmith, Keats, Wordsworth, Byron, Shelley, Coleridge, Tennyson, Arnold, and Crashaw. Distributed by Caedmon/HarperAudio.

Poems from Black Africa [recording].
1 cassette.

Many poets and poems from Africa, including oral traditions from various parts of the continent (Nigeria, South Africa, Ghana, and others). Distributed by Caedmon/HarperAudio.

Poetic Forms [recording].
5 cassettes (5 hours), 1988.

Includes the list poem, the ode, the prose poem, the sonnet, the haiku, the blues poem, the villanelle, the ballad, the acrostic, and free verse. Distributed by Teachers & Writers Collaborative.

*Poetry: A Beginner's Guide.
26 min., color, 1986.

Beta, VHS, ¾" U-matic cassette.

Interviews contemporary poets and examines the tools they use. Distributed by Coronet/MTI Film & Video.

*Poetry by Americans.
4 programs (10 min. each), color, 1988. Beta, VHS, ¾" U-matic cassette, 16-mm film.

Robert Frost, Edgar Allan Poe, James Weldon Johnson, and Walt Whitman. Narrated by Leonard Nimoy, Lorne Greene, Raymond St. Jacques, and Efrem Zimbalist Jr. Distributed by AIMS Media Inc.

*Poetry for People Who Hate Poetry.
3 programs (15 min. each), color, 1980. Beta, VHS, ¾" U-matic cassette, special-order formats.

Roger Steffens makes poetry accessible to students. Three programs: (1) About words; (2) E. E. Cummings; (3) Shakespeare. Distributed by Churchill Media.

Poetry in Motion.
90 min., color, 1982. Laser optical videodisc.

A performance anthology of twenty-four North American poets, including Ntozake Shange, Amiri Baraka, Anne Waldman, William Burroughs, Ted Berrigan, John Cage, and Tom Waits. Performed by Ntozake Shange, Amiri Baraka, and Anne Waldman. Distributed by Voyager Company.

The Poet's Voice [recording].
6 cassettes.

From the tape archive of the Poetry Room, Harvard University. Includes John Ashbery, W. H. Auden, John Berryman, T. S. Eliot, Robert Frost, Allen Ginsberg, Randall Jarrell, Robinson Jeffers, Marianne Moore, Sylvia Plath, Ezra Pound, Theodore Roethke, Wallace Stevens, and William Carlos Williams. Distributed by Watershed Tapes.

***Poets in Person: A Series on American Poets & Their Art** [recording].*

7 programs (30 min. each), 1991.

Thirteen poets in conversation, reading their poems, discussing their lives, their work, and the changing styles in contemporary American poetry: (1) Allen Ginsberg; (2) Karl Shapiro, Maxine Kumin; (3) W. S. Merwin, Gwendolyn Brooks; (4) James Merrill, Adrienne Rich; (5) John Ashbery, Sharon Olds; (6) Charles Wright, Rita Dove; (7) Gary Soto, A. R. Ammons.

Distributed by Modern Poetry.

***Potpourri of Poetry — from the Jack Kerouac School of Disembodied Poetics, Summer 1975** [recording].*

1 cassette (60 min.), 1975.

Allen Ginsberg, Dianne DiPrima, John Ashbery, Ted Berrigan, Philip Whalen, and others.

Distributed by Watershed Tapes.

*Restoration and Augustan Poetry.

28 min., color, 1989.

Beta, VHS, ¾" U-matic cassette.

Discusses the age of satire in England, including the Earl of Rochester, John Dryden, Jonathan Swift, and Alexander Pope.

Distributed by Films for the Humanities and Sciences.

*Romantic Pioneers.

28 min., color, 1989.

Beta, VHS, ¾" U-matic cassette.

Readings of poems by Christopher Smart, William Blake, William Wordsworth, and Samuel Taylor Coleridge.

Distributed by Films for the Humanities and Sciences.

*Romantics and Realists.

28 min., color, 1989.

Beta, VHS, ¾" U-matic cassette.

Discusses Thomas Hardy, Gerard Manley Hopkins, A. E. Housman, and Rudyard Kipling.

Distributed by Films for the Humanities and Sciences.

***Serenade: Poets of New York** [recording].*

1 cassette, 1957.

Read by Aaron Kramer, Maxwell Maxwell, and Bodenheim.

Distributed by Smithsonian/Folkways Recordings.

***Spoken Arts Treasury of American Jewish Poets Reading Their Poems** [recording].*

7 cassettes.

Includes the work of Dorothy Parker, Phillip Levine, Anthony Hecht, Denise Levertov, Allen Ginsberg, and John Hollander.

Distributed by Spoken Arts.

***The Spoken Arts Treasury of 100 Modern American Poets Reading Their Poems** [recording].*

1985.

Distributed by Spoken Arts.

A Survey of English and American Poetry.

16 programs (28 min. each), color, 1987.

Beta, VHS, ¾" U-matic cassette.

A history and anthology of English-language poetry. Programs include: (1) Introduction to English Poetry; (2) Old English Poetry; (3) Chaucer; (4) Medieval to Elizabethan Poetry; (5) The Maturing Shakespeare; (6) Metaphysical and Devotional Poetry; (7) Milton; (8) Restoration and Augustan Poetry; (9) Romantic Pioneers; (10) William Wordsworth; (11) The Younger Romantics; (12) Victorian Poetry; (13) American Pioneers; (14) Romantics and Realists; (15) The Earlier Twentieth Century; (16) The Later Twentieth Century.

Distributed by Films for the Humanities and Sciences.

Teaching Poetry.

30 min., color, 1990.

VHS.

A new approach to teaching poetry. Includes discussion questions and homework assignments.

Distributed by Video Aided Instruction.

***Twentieth-Century Poets in English: Recordings of Poets Reading Their Own Poetry** [recording].*

33 volumes.
Distributed by the Library of Congress.

Twentieth-Century Poets Reading Their Work *[recording]*.
6 cassettes.
Includes William Butler Yeats, Stephen Spender, Langston Hughes, W. H. Auden, Richard Wilbur, and James Dickey.
Distributed by Spoken Arts.

****Victorian Poetry*.**
28 min., color, 1989.
Beta, VHS, ¾″ U-matic cassette.
An examination of works by Alfred, Lord Tennyson, Emily Brontë, Christina Rossetti, Elizabeth Barrett Browning, Matthew Arnold, and Algernon Swinburne.
Distributed by Films for the Humanities and Sciences.

Victorian Poetry *[recording]*.
3 cassettes.
Includes John Henry; E. B. Browning; Edward Fitzgerald; Alfred, Lord Tennyson; W. M. Thackeray; Robert Browning; Edward Lear; Charlotte Brontë; Emily Brontë; A. H. Clough; Charles Kingsley; George Eliot; Matthew Arnold; George Meredith; Dante Gabriel Rossetti; Christina Rossetti; Lewis Carroll; James Thomson; Algernon Charles Swinburne; Thomas Hardy; Gerard Manley Hopkins; Coventry Patmore; Robert Bridges; William Ernest Henley; R. L. Stevenson; Oscar Wilde; A. E. Housman; Francis

Thompson; George Santayana; Arthur Symons; and Rudyard Kipling.
Distributed by Caedmon/HarperAudio.

****Voices and Vision*.**
13 programs (60 min. each), color, 1988.
Beta, VHS, ¾″ U-matic cassette.
A series exploring the lives of some of America's best poets. Hosted by Joseph Brodsky, Mary McCarthy, James Baldwin, and Adrienne Rich. Programs include: (1) Elizabeth Bishop; (2) Hart Crane; (3) Emily Dickinson; (4) T. S. Eliot; (5) Robert Frost; (6) Langston Hughes; (7) Robert Lowell; (8) Marianne Moore; (9) Sylvia Plath; (10) Ezra Pound; (11) Wallace Stevens; (12) Walt Whitman; (13) William Carlos Williams.
Distributed by the Annenberg/CPB Collection.

***With a Feminine Touch*.**
45 min., color, 1990.
VHS.
Readings from Emily Dickinson, Anne Brontë, Charlotte Brontë, Emily Brontë, Sylvia Plath, and Edna St. Vincent Millay. Read by Valerie Harper and Claire Bloom.
Distributed by Monterey Home Video.

***The Young Romantics*.**
28 min., color, 1989.
Beta, VHS, ¾″ U-matic cassette.
Features the work of John Keats, William Wordsworth, and Lord Byron.
Distributed by Films for the Humanities and Sciences.

DRAMA

Samuel Beckett

Krapp's Last Tape *[recording]*.
1 cassette, 1986.
Part of the "Sound of Modern Drama" series, in which modern playwrights read and discuss their work.
Distributed by Spoken Arts.

Samuel Beckett *[recording]*.
1 cassette.

Performed by Cyril Cusack.
Distributed by Caedmon/HarperAudio.

***Samuel Beckett*.**
80 min., color, 1989.
Beta, VHS, ¾″ U-matic cassette.
An autobiographical portrait of Beckett's artistic life, presented through his work.
Distributed by Films for the Humanities and Sciences.

Anton Chekhov

Anton Chekhov: A Writer's Life.
37 min., b/w, 1974.
Beta, VHS, ¾" U-matic cassette.
A biographical portrait of the playwright.
Distributed by Films for the Humanities
and Sciences.

Chekhov [recording].
12 cassettes (90 min. each), 1989.
By Henri Troyat, read by Wolfram Kandinsky. A biography of the writer.
Distributed by Books on Tape.

Chekhov: Humanity's Advocate [recording].
1 cassette (46 min.), 1968.
By Ernest J. Simmons. Explores various
facets of Chekhov's works and his artistic principles. Classics of Russian
Literature Series.
Distributed by Audio-Forum.

Chekhov and the Moscow Art Theatre.
13 min., color.
Beta, VHS, 16-mm film. Yuri Zavadsky
uses the Stanislavsky method in directing scenes from *The Cherry Orchard*. Program is set in the context of
the Moscow Art Theatre and the Russian countryside.
Distributed by IASTA.

Susan Glaspell

Trifles.
21 min., color, 1979.
Beta, VHS.
Distributed by Phoenix/BFA Films.

Trifles.
22 min., b/w, 1981.
Beta, VHS, ¾" U-matic cassette.
Distributed by Centre Communications.

Lorraine Hansberry

A Raisin in the Sun.
128 min., b/w, 1961.
Beta, VHS.
With Sidney Poitier, Claudia McNeil, and
Ruby Dee. Directed by Daniel Petrie.
See local retailer.

A Raisin in the Sun.
171 min., color, 1989.
Beta, VHS.
With Danny Glover, Esther Rolle, and
Starletta DuPois. Directed by Bill
Duke. An "American Playhouse"
made-for-television production.
See local retailer.

A Raisin in the Sun [recording].
2 cassettes, (2 hours, 21 min.)
Dramatization performed by Ossie Davis
and Ruby Dee.
Distributed by Caedmon/HarperAudio.

Black Theatre Movement from A Raisin in the Sun to the Present.
130 min., color, 1979.
16-mm film.
Traces the Black Theatre Movement from
its roots in Hansberry's play to the
current black plays and musicals on
Broadway. Includes interviews with
performers, writers, and directors, as
well as footage from plays and theatre
pieces from around the country.

Lorraine Hansberry: The Black Experience in the Creation of Drama.
35 min., color, 1975.
Beta, VHS, ¾" U-matic cassette.
With Sidney Poitier, Ruby Dee, and Al
Freeman Jr. Narrated by Claudia
McNeil. A profile of the playwright's
life and work.
Distributed by Films for the Humanities
and Sciences.

Lorraine Hansberry Speaks Out: Art and the Black Revolution [recording].
1 cassette.
By Lorraine Hansberry, edited by Robert
Nemiroff.
Distributed by Caedmon/HarperAudio.

To Be Young, Gifted, and Black.
90 min., color, 1981.
Beta, VHS, ½" open reel (EIAJ), ¾" U-matic
cassette, 16-mm film.
With Ruby Dee, Al Freeman Jr., Claudia
McNeil, Barbara Barrie, Lauren Jones,
Roy Scheider, and Blythe Danner. A

play about the life of Lorraine Hansberry.
Distributed by Monterey Home Video.

David Henry Hwang

M. Butterfly [recording].
2 cassettes (118 min.).
Starring John Lithgow and B. D. Wong.
Distributed by L.A. Theatre Works.

M. Butterfly.
101 min., color, 1993.
Beta, VHS.
A film adaptation of Hwang's acclaimed play starring Jeremy Irons.
Distributed by Warner Home Video.

Henrik Ibsen

A Doll's House.
89 min., b/w, 1959.
Beta, VHS, ¾" U-matic cassette.
With Julie Harris, Christopher Plummer, Jason Robards, Hume Cronyn, Eileen Heckart, and Richard Thomas. An original television production.
See local retailer.

*A Doll's House.
98 min., color, 1973.
VHS, 16-mm film.
With Jane Fonda, Edward Fox, Trevor Howard, and David Warner. Screenplay by Christopher Hampton.
Video: See local retailer.
Distributed by Prism Entertainment.

A Doll's House.
39 min., color, 1977.
Beta, VHS, ¾" U-matic cassette.
With Claire Bloom.
Distributed by AIMS Multimedia.

A Doll's House.
96 min., color, 1989.
Beta, VHS.
With Claire Bloom, Anthony Hopkins, Ralph Richardson, Denholm Elliott, Anna Massey, and Edith Evans. Directed by Patrick Garland.
Distributed by Hemdale Home Video.

A Doll's House [recording].

3 cassettes (180 min.), 1993.
Read by Flo Gibson.
Distributed by Audio Book Contractors.

A Doll's House [recording].
3 cassettes.
Translated by Christopher Hampton.
Dramatization performed by Claire Bloom and Donald Madden.
Distributed by Caedmon/HarperAudio.

*A Doll's House, Part I.
34 min., color, 1968.
Beta, VHS, ¾" U-matic cassette, 16-mm film.
"The Destruction of Illusion." Norris Houghton discusses the subsurface tensions that make up the play.
Distributed by Britannica Films.

*A Doll's House, Part II.
29 min., color, 1968.
Beta, VHS, ¾" U-matic cassette, 16-mm film.
"Ibsen's Themes." Norris Houghton examines the cast of characters and the themes in the play.
Distributed by Britannica Films.

Ibsen's Life and Times, Part I: Youth and Self-Imposed Exile.
28 min., color. VHS.
The conflict between individual and society is illustrated in scenes from *Ghosts*, featuring Beatrice Straight as Mrs. Alving. Includes a biographical segment on the playwright.
Distributed by Insight Media.

Ibsen's Life and Times, Part II: The Later Years.
24 min., color. VHS.
Includes scenes from *The Master Builder* and *Lady from the Sea*, emphasizing the realism in Ibsen's plays. A biographical segment includes on-location footage.
Distributed by Insight Media.

Arthur Miller

Arthur Miller.
25 min., color, 1982.
Beta, VHS, ¾" U-matic cassette.

Explores themes in the works of Arthur Miller.
Distributed by Films, Inc., Video.

Death of a Salesman [recording].
2 cassettes (2 hrs., 16 min.), unabridged.
Dramatization performed by Lee J. Cobb and Mildred Dunnock.
Distributed by Caedmon/HarperAudio.

Death of a Salesman.
135 min., color, 1985.
Beta, VHS.
With Dustin Hoffman, John Malkovich, Charles Durning, and Stephen Lang. Directed by Volker Schlondorff. A made-for-television adaptation of the play.
Distributed by Orion Home Video, Facets Multimedia, Warner Home Video.

Private Conversations on the Set of Death of a Salesman.
82 min., color, 1985.
Beta, VHS.
With Arthur Miller, Dustin Hoffman, Volker Schlondorff, and John Malkovich. This PBS documentary presents heated discussion between actor, director, and playwright. Various interpretations of the play emerge and viewers gain insight into how each part contributed to the final production.
See local retailer.

William Shakespeare

Hamlet

Hamlet.
242 min., color, 1996.
VHS.
Directed by Kenneth Branagh. Starring Kenneth Branagh, Kate Winslet, John Gielgud, Jack Lemmon, Julie Christie, Gerard Depardieu, Judy Dench, and others.
Distributed by Columbia Tristar Home Video.

*Hamlet.
153 min., b/w, 1948.
VHS and 16-mm film.
With Laurence Olivier, Basil Sydney, Felix Aylmer, Jean Simmons, Stanley Holloway, Peter Cushing, and Christopher Lee. Voice of John Gielgud. Directed by Olivier. Photographed in Denmark. Cut scenes include all of Rosencrantz and Guildenstern. Emphasizes Oedipal implications in the play.
Video: see local retailer.
Film: Learning Corporation of America.

*Hamlet.
115 min., color, 1969.
Beta, VHS, 16-mm film.
With Nicol Williamson. Directed by Tony Richardson.
Distributed by Learning Corporation of America.

Hamlet.
150 min., color, 1979.
Beta, VHS, ¾" U-matic cassette, other formats by special arrangement.
Directed by Derek Jacobi.
Distributed by Time-Life Video.

Hamlet.
135 min., color, 1990.
VHS.
With Mel Gibson, Glenn Close, Alan Bates, Paul Scofield, Ian Holm, and Helena Bonham Carter. Directed by Franco Zeffirelli.
See local retailer.

Hamlet [recording].
3 cassettes (210 min.), 1993.
Performed by Kenneth Branagh.
Distributed by Bantam Audio Publishers.

Hamlet [recording].
4 cassettes.
Dramatization performed by Paul Scofield and Diana Wynyard.
Distributed by Caedmon/HarperAudio.

Hamlet [recording].
1 cassette (60 min.), 1985.
Dramatization performed by Michael Redgrave. Part of the Living Shakespeare Series.
Distributed by Crown Publishers.

Hamlet [recording].
2 cassettes (120 min.).

With John Gielgud and Old Vic Company. Distributed by Durkin Hayes Publishing.

Hamlet [recording].
1 cassette (51 min.).
Performed by Dublin Gate Theatre. Using key scenes and bridges, a complete telling of Hamlet.
Distributed by Spoken Arts.

*Approaches to Hamlet.
45 min., color, 1979.
Beta, VHS, ¾″ U-matic cassette, 16-mm film.
Includes footage of the four greatest Hamlets of this century: John Barrymore, Laurence Olivier, John Gielgud, and Nicol Williamson. Shows a young actor learning the role. Narrated by Gielgud.
Distributed by Films for the Humanities and Sciences.

Discovering Hamlet.
53 min., color, 1990.
VHS, ¾″ U-matic cassette.
An exposition of the play, hosted by Patrick Stewart, including a behind-the-scenes look at a production by the Birmingham Repertory Theatre.
Distributed by PBS Video.

*Hamlet: The Age of Elizabeth, I.
30 min., color, 1959.
Beta, VHS, ¾″ U-matic cassette, 16-mm film.
An introduction to Elizabethan theater.
Distributed by Britannica Films.

*Hamlet: What Happens in Hamlet, II.
30 min., color and b/w, 1959.
Beta, VHS, ¾″ U-matic cassette, 16-mm film.
Analyzes the play as a ghost story, a detective story, and a revenge story. Uses scenes from Acts I, III, and V to introduce the principal characters and present the structure of each substory.
Distributed by Britannica Films.

*Hamlet: The Poisoned Kingdom, III.
30 min., color, 1959.
Beta, VHS, ¾″ U-matic cassette, 16-mm film.
Observes that poisoning in the play, both literal and figurative, affects all the characters.
Distributed by Britannica Films.

*Hamlet: The Readiness is All, IV.
30 min., color, 1959.
Beta, VHS, ¾″ U-matic cassette, 16-mm film.
Hamlet is presented as a coming-of-age story.
Distributed by Britannica Films.

*Hamlet: The Trouble with Hamlet.
23 min., color, 1969.
16-mm film.
Emphasizes Hamlet's existentialist dilemma.
Distributed by the National Broadcasting Company.

*The Tragedy of Hamlet: Prince of Denmark.
22 min., color, 1988.
VHS.
Actors depict Shakespeare and his contemporary, Richard Burbage, rehearsing the play. "Shakespeare" gives a line-by-line analysis of scenes from the play, along with insight into plot and character. Part of the Shakespeare in Rehearsal Series.
Distributed by Coronet/MTI Film & Video.

A Midsummer Night's Dream

A Midsummer Night's Dream.
117 min., b/w, 1935.
VHS.
With James Cagney, Mickey Rooney, Olivia de Havilland, Dick Powell, and Joe E. Brown. Directed by William Dieterle and Max Reinhardt.
See local retailer.

A Midsummer Night's Dream.
111 min., b/w, 1963.
Beta, VHS.
With Patrick Allen, Eira Heath, Cyril Luckham, Tony Bateman, Jill Bennett. A live BBC-TV performance, with Mendelssohn's incidental music.
Distributed by Video Yesteryear.

*A Midsummer Night's Dream.
120 min., 1968.

Beta, VHS, 16-mm film.
With Diana Rigg and David Warner. Directed by Peter Hall. A Royal Shakespeare Company performance.
Distributed by Drama Classics Video.

*A Midsummer Night's Dream.
120 min., color, 1982.
Beta, VHS.
With Helen Mirren, Peter McEnry, and Brian Clover.
See local retailer.

*A Midsummer Night's Dream.
165 min., color, 1983.
Beta, VHS, ¾″ U-matic cassette.
With William Hurt and Michelle Shay. A lively interpretation by Joseph Papp.
Distributed by Films for the Humanities and Sciences.

A Midsummer Night's Dream.
194 min., color, 1987.
Beta, VHS.
With Ileana Cotrubas, James Bowman, and Curt Appelgren. Directed by Peter Hall. A performance of the Benjamin Britten opera, taped at the Glyndebourne Festival Opera.
Distributed by Films, Inc.

A Midsummer Night's Dream [recording].
1 cassette.
Dramatization performed by the Folio Theatre Players.
Distributed by Spoken Arts.

A Midsummer Night's Dream
[recording].
3 cassettes (text included).
Dramatization performed by Paul Scofield and Joy Parker.
Distributed by Caedmon/HarperAudio.

A Midsummer Night's Dream
[recording].
1 cassette (60 min.), 1985.
Dramatization performed by Stanley Holloway and Sarah Churchill. Part of the Living in Shakespeare Series.
Distributed by Crown Publishers.

A Midsummer Night's Dream
[recording].

2 cassettes (120 min.).
Performed by Robert Helpmann and Moira Shearer. An Old Vic production.
Distributed by Durkin Hayes Publishing.

A Midsummer Night's Dream: Introduction to the Play.
26 min., color, 1970.
Introduction to famous scenes and characters.
Distributed by Phoenix/BFA Films and Video.

The Tempest
*The Tempest.
76 min., color, 1963.
Beta, VHS, ¾″ U-matic cassette.
With Maurice Evans, Richard Burton, Roddy McDowall, Lee Remick, and Tom Poston. Directed by George Schaefer.
Distributed by Films for the Humanities and Sciences.

*The Tempest.
150 min., color, 1980.
Beta, VHS, ¾″ U-matic cassette, other formats by special arrangement.
Distributed by Time-Life Video.

Tempest.
140 min., color, 1982.
Beta, VHS (stereo).
With John Cassavetes, Gena Rowlands, Susan Sarandon, Vittorio Gassman, and Raul Julia. Directed by Paul Mazursky. A York architect abandons city life to live on a barren Greek island with his daughter.
See local retailer.

*The Tempest.
2 cassettes (126 min.), color, 1983.
Beta, VHS, ¾″ U-matic cassette.
With Efrem Zimbalist, William H. Basset, Ted Sorrel, Kay E. Kuter, Edward Edwards, Nicholas Hammond, and Ron Palillo. Directed by William Woodman. Puts American actors on an artist's re-creation of the Globe Theatre stage.
Distributed by Kultur and Britannica Films.

The Tempest [recording].
1 cassette.
Dramatization performed by the Folio Theatre Players.
Distributed by Spoken Arts.

The Tempest [recording].
3 cassettes (text included).
Dramatization performed by Michael Redgrave and Vanessa Redgrave.
Distributed by Caedmon/HarperAudio.

Prospero's Books.
1992.
Directed by Peter Greenaway. With John Gielgud, Erland Josephson, Michael Clark, Tom Bell, and Kenneth Cranham.
See local retailer.

*The Tempest: O Brave World.
23 min., color, 1969.
16-mm film.
Explores the problem of evil in the play.
Distributed by the National Broadcasting Company.

GENERAL

Behind-the-Scenes Views of Shakespeare: Shakespeare and His Theatre [recording].
1 cassette (60 min.).
Read by Daniel Seltzer. Explores Shakespeare and the characteristics of his works suggesting how to watch a play.
Distributed by National Public Radio.

Behind-the-Scenes Views of Shakespeare: Shakespeare in Our Time [recording].
1 cassette (60 min.).
Read by Maynard Mack Jr. Discusses Shakespeare from a modern perspective, and addresses the issue of to what extent he is and is not our contemporary.
Distributed by National Public Radio.

Behind-the-Scenes Views of Shakespeare: Shakespeare the Man [recording].
1 cassette (60 min.).

Portrays Shakespeare as reflected in his work and in the facts and myths about his life that have survived.
Distributed by National Public Radio.

*The Life and Times of William Shakespeare 1: The Historical Setting.
25 min., color, 1978.
VHS.
An overview of Elizabethan England.
Distributed by the University of Wyoming Audio-Visual Services.

*The Life and Times of William Shakespeare 2: English Drama.
20 min., color, 1978.
VHS.
History of drama from that of the Greeks to that of Shakespeare's time.
Distributed by the University of Wyoming Audio-Visual Services.

*The Life and Times of William Shakespeare 3: Stratford Years.
18 min., color, 1978.
VHS.
Deals with Shakespeare's early life.
Distributed by the University of Wyoming Audio-Visual Services.

*The Life and Times of William Shakespeare 4: London Years.
33 min., color, 1978.
VHS.
A history of the center of the English-speaking world.
Distributed by the University of Wyoming Audio-Visual Services.

*The Life and Times of William Shakespeare 5: Globe Theatre.
27 min., color, 1978.
VHS.
A study of the Globe and English theatre.
Distributed by the University of Wyoming Audio-Visual Services.

*Shakespeare and His Stage.
47 min., color, 1975.
VHS.
16-mm film.
Provides a montage of Shakespearean background, including scenes from

Hamlet and the preparation of various actors for the role.
Distributed by Films for the Humanities and Sciences.

Shakespeare and His Theatre: The Gentle Shakespeare.
28 min., color.
VHS.
A history of Shakespeare's life in the theatre and an examination of his work.
Distributed by Films for the Humanities and Sciences.

*Shakespeare and the Globe.
31 min., color, 1985.
VHS.
A survey of Shakespeare's life, work, and cultural milieu.
Distributed by Films for the Humanities and Sciences.

Shakespearean Tragedy.
40 min., color, 1984.
Beta, VHS, ¾" U-matic cassette.
Focuses on *Hamlet* and *Macbeth*.
Distributed by Films for the Humanities and Sciences.

*Shakespeare's Heritage.
29 min., color, 1988.
16-mm film.
Narrated by Anthony Quayle. Explores the life of the playwright and his hometown of Stratford.
Distributed by Britannica Films.

*Shakespeare's Theater.
13 min., color, 1946.
16-mm film.
Re-creates the experience of going to a play at the Globe Theatre in Shakespeare's time.
Distributed by the Indiana University Instructional Support Services.

*Shakespeare's Theater.
28 min., b/w, 1952.
16-mm film.
Hosted by Frank Baxter. A discussion of the evolution of Elizabethan theater and the original staging of Shakespeare's plays.

*Shakespeare's Theater: The Globe Playhouse.
18 min., b/w, 1953.
VHS.
Provides a model of the Globe Theater and a discussion of the original staging of some of Shakespeare's plays.
Distributed by the University of California Extension Media Center.

*Shakespeare's World and Shakespeare's London.
29 min., b/w, 1952.
16-mm film.
Hosted by Frank Baxter. Re-creates the climate of Renaissance England that allowed Shakespeare's genius to flourish.
Distributed by Films, Inc.

The Two Traditions.
50 min., color, 1983.
VHS.
Deals with the problem of overcoming barriers of time and culture to make Shakespeare relevant today. Examples from *Hamlet, Coriolanus, The Merchant of Venice*, and *Othello*. Part of the Playing Shakespeare Series.
Distributed by Films for the Humanities and Sciences.

*Understanding Shakespeare: His Sources.
20 min., color, 1972.
Beta, VHS, ¾" U-matic cassette, 16-mm film, other formats by special arrangement. Examines how Shakespeare's plays grew out of sources available to him, and how he enhanced the material with his own imagination.
Distributed by Coronet/MTI Film & Video.

Sophocles

Antigone

Antigone.
88 min., b/w, 1962.
16-mm film.
With Irene Papas. Directed by George Tzavellas. In Greek, with subtitles.
Distributed by Films, Inc.

*Antigone.
120 min., 1987.
Beta, VHS, ¾″ U-matic cassette. With Juliet Stevenson, John Shrapnel, and John Gielgud. Staged version.
Distributed by Films for the Humanities and Sciences.

Antigone [recording].
2 cassettes.
Dramatization of the Fitts and Fitzerald translation. Performed by Dorothy Tutin and Max Adrian.
Distributed by Caedmon/HarperAudio.

Oedipus Rex

Oedipus Rex.
20 min., color, 1957.
Beta, VHS, ¾″ U-matic cassette.
A performance by deaf actors.
Distributed by Gallaudet University Library.

*Oedipus Rex.
87 min., color, 1957.
VHS, 16-mm film.
With Douglas Campbell, Douglas Rain, Eric House, and Eleanor Stuart. Based on William Yeats's translation. Directed by Tyrone Guthrie. Contained and highly structured rendering by the Stratford (Ontario) Festival Players.
Distributed by Water Bearer Films.

Oedipus the King.
97 min., color, 1967.
VHS.
With Donald Sutherland, Christopher Plummer, Lilli Palmer, Orson Welles, Cyril Cusack, Richard Johnson, and Roger Livesey. Directed by Philip Saville. Simplified film version of the play, filmed in Greece using an old amphitheater to serve as the background for much of the action.
Distributed by Crossroads Video.

*Oedipus the King.
45 min., color, 1975.
Beta, VHS, ¾″ U-matic cassette, 16-mm film.

With Anthony Quayle, James Mason, Claire Bloom, and Ian Richardson. A production by the Athens Classical Theatre Company, with an English soundtrack.
Distributed by Films for the Humanities and Sciences.

Oedipus Tyrannus.
60 min., color, 1978.
Beta, VHS, ¾″ U-matic cassette.
Hosted by Jose Ferrer. Shown from the point where Oedipus is informed of the death of his father. Expository portion shows scenes of Greek theaters and recounts Aristotle's definition of tragedy.
Distributed by Films, Inc.

Oedipus the King.
120 min., color, 1987.
VHS.
With John Gielgud, Michael Pennington, and Claire Bloom.
Distributed by Films for the Humanities and Sciences.

Oedipus Rex [recording].
2 cassettes.
Translated by William Butler Yeats. Performed by Douglas Campbell and Eric House. Dramatization.
Distributed by Caedmon/HarperAudio.

*Oedipus Rex: Age of Sophocles, I.
31 min., color and b/w, 1959.
Beta, VHS, ¾″ U-matic cassette, 16-mm film.
Discusses Greek civilization, the classic Greek theater, and the theme of man's fundamental nature.
Distributed by Britannica Films.

*Oedipus Rex: The Character of Oedipus, II.
31 min., color and b/w, 1959.
Beta, VHS, ¾″ U-matic cassette, 16-mm film.
Debates whether Oedipus's trouble is a result of character flaws or of fate.
Distributed by Britannica Films.

*Oedipus Rex: Man and God, III.
30 min., color and b/w, 1959.

Beta, VHS, ¾" U-matic cassette, 16-mm film.

Deals with the idea that Oedipus, although a worldly ruler, cannot overcome the gods and his destiny.

Distributed by Britannica Films.

Oedipus Rex: Recovery of Oedipus, IV.
30 min., color and b/w, 1959.
Beta, VHS, ¾" U-matic cassette, 16-mm film.

Deals with man's existence in between God and beast.

Distributed by Britannica Films

The Rise of Greek Tragedy, Sophocles: Oedipus the King.
45 min., color, 198?.
Beta, VHS, ¾" U-matic cassette, 16-mm film.

With James Mason, Claire Bloom, and Ian Richardson. Narrated by Anthony Quayle. The play is photographed in the ancient Greek theater of Amphiaraion and uses tragic masks.

Distributed by Films for the Humanities and Sciences.

Wole Soyinka

Wole Soyinka.
50 min., color, 1985.
VHS, ¾" U-matic cassette.

An interview with the playwright, who discusses political and cultural life in Africa and the United States and what it means to be an artist.

Distributed by The Roland Collection.

Tennessee Williams

The Glass Menagerie.
134 min., color, 1987.
Beta, VHS.

With Joanne Woodward, Karen Allen, John Malkovich, and James Naughton. Directed by Paul Newman.

See local retailer.

The Glass Menagerie [recording].
2 cassettes.
1 hr., 49 min., unabridged.
Dramatization performed by Montgomery

Clift and Julie Harris.

Distributed by Caedmon/HarperAudio.

The Glass Menagerie [recording].
Read by Tennessee Williams.
Includes "The Yellow Bird" (short story) and poems.

Distributed by the American Audio Prose Library.

Tennessee Williams Reads The Glass Menagerie and Others [recording].
1 cassette. (45 min.).

Complete selections. Read by Tennessee Williams. Includes *The Glass Menagerie* (opening monologue and closing scene), "Cried the Fox," "The Eyes," "The Summer Belvedere," "Some Poems Meant for Music: Little Horse," "Which Is My Little Boy," "Little One," "Gold-Tooth Blues," "Kitchen-Door Blues," "Heavenly Grass," and "The Yellow Bird."

Distributed by Caedmon/HarperAudio.

In the Country of Tennessee Williams.
30 min., color, 1977.
Beta, VHS, ½" reel, ¾" U-matic cassette, 2" Quad.

A one-act play about how Williams developed as a writer.

Distributed by the York State Education Department.

GENERAL

Black Theatre: The Making of a Movement.
113 min., color, 1978.
VHS.

A look at black theatre born from the civil rights movement of the fifties, sixties, and seventies. Recollections from Ossie Davis, James Earl Jones, Amiri Baraka, and Ntozake Shange.

Distributed by California Newsreel.

A Day at the Globe.
30 min., color.
VHS.

Starts with a brief overview of early drama and of seventeenth-century England, then discusses the Globe Theatre, using still images. Explains how actors, artisans, and other company members prepared for performances, and presents dramatic readings, period costumes, music, and sound effects in order to help students envision how Shakespearean drama actually looked.

Distributed by Insight Media.

Drama Comes of Age.
30 min., b/w, 1957.
16-mm film.

Discusses the Shakespearean theater and neoclassic drama. Demonstrates early realism with a scene from *Hedda Gabler.*

Distributed by the Indiana University Instructional Support Services.

Drama: How It Began.
30 min., b/w, 1957.
16-mm film.

Discusses the beginnings of the theater. Explains the techniques of the Greek theater and how playwriting developed. Illustrates the chorus technique with a scene from *Oedipus the King.*

Distributed by the Indiana University Instructional Support Services.

Echoes of Jacobean England.
45 min., color.
VHS.

Re-creates the liberal arts in seventeenth-century England. Features authentically performed music, contemporary literature, scenes of daily life, and period setting to provide a background for the works of Shakespeare, Dryden, John Donne, and John Dowland.

Distributed by Films for the Humanities and Sciences.

The Elizabethan Age.
30 min., color.
VHS.

A discussion of the resurgence of enthusiasm for the arts and letters that swept seventeenth-century England. Uses original sources.

Distributed by Insight Media.

Greek Tragedy *[recording].*
1 cassette.

Works of Euripides and Sophocles, performed by Katina Paxinou and Alexis Minotis.

Distributed by Caedmon/HarperAudio.

The Theatre in Ancient Greece.
26 min., color, 1989.
Beta, VHS, ¾" U-matic cassette.

Program explores ancient theatre design, the origins of tragedy, the audience, the comparative roles of the writer/director and actors, and the use of landscape in many plays. Examines the theaters of Herodus, Atticus, Epidauros, Corinth, and numerous others.

Distributed by Films for the Humanities and Sciences.

DIRECTORY OF DISTRIBUTORS

Acorn Media
7910 Woodmont Avenue
Suite 350
Bethesda, MD 20814
(301) 907-0030
(800) 999-0212

AIMS Media Inc.
9710 DeSoto Ave.
Chatsworth, CA 91311-9409
(818) 773-4300
(800) 367-2467

Ally Press
524 Orleans St.
St. Paul, MN 55107
(612) 291-2652

American Audio Prose Library
P.O. Box 842
Columbia, MO 65205
(573) 443-0361
(800) 447-2275

Annenberg/CPB Collection
P.O. Box 2345
South Burlington, VT 05407-2345

Applause Productions
85-A Fernwood Lane
Roslyn, NY 11576
(516) 365-1259
(800) 253-5351

Audio Alternatives
P.O. Box 405
Chappaqua, NY 10514
(914) 238-5943

Audio Book Contractors
P.O. Box 40115
Washington, DC 20016
(202) 363-3429

Audio Bookshelf
174 Prescott Hill Road
Northport, ME 04849
(800) 234-1713

Audio Brandon Films
See **Films, Inc.**

Audio-Forum
Jeffrey Norton Publishers
96 Broad St.
Guilford, CT 06437
(203) 453-9794
(800) 243-1234

Audio Literature
P.O. Box 7123
Berkeley, CA 94707
(800) 841-2665

Audio Partners
1700 4th Street
Berkeley, CA 94710
(510) 528-1444
(800) 788-3123

Bantam Audio Publishers
A division of Bantam Doubleday
    Dell
2451 South Wolf Road
Des Plaines, IL 60018
(800) 323-9872

Barr Entertainment
12801 Schabarum Ave.
P.O. Box 7878
Irwindale, CA 91706
(818) 338-7878

Benchmark Films
569 North State Road
Briarcliff Manor, NY 10510
(914) 762-3838

Blackstone Audio Books
P.O. Box 969
Ashland, OR 97520
(541) 482-9239
(800) 729-2665

Books in Motion
E. 9212 Montgomery
Suite 501
Spokane, WA 99206
(509) 922-1646
(800) 752-3199

Books on Tape
P.O. Box 7900
Newport Beach, CA 92658
(714) 548-5525
(800) 626-3333

Britannica Films
310 South Michigan Ave.
Chicago, IL 60604
(800) 747-8503

Caedmon/HarperAudio
P.O. Box 588
Dunmore, PA 18512
(717) 343-4761
(800) 242-7737
(800) 982-4377 (in Pennsylvania)

California Newsreel
149 Ninth Street
Suite 420
San Francisco, CA 94103
(415) 621-6196
(800) 621-6196

Carousel Film & Video
260 Fifth Ave.
Suite 405
New York, NY 10001
(212) 683-1660
(800) 683-1660

Cassette Works
125 North Aspen
Azusa, CA 91702
(818) 969-6699
(800) 423-8273

Center for Humanities, Inc.
Box 1000
Mount Kisco, NY 10549
(914) 666-4100
(800) 431-1242

Centre Communications
1800 30th St.
Suite 207
Boulder, CO 80301
(800) 886-1166

Chelsea House Publishers
Division of Main Line Book Co.
P.O. Box 914
Brommall, PA 19008
(610) 353-5166
(800) 848-2665

Churchill Media
6901 Woodley Ave.
Van Nuys, CA 91406-4844
(818) 778-1978
(800) 334-7830

Cifex Corporation
1 Teconic Hills Center
Southampton, NY 11968
(516) 283-4795

Cinema Guild
1697 Broadway
Suite 506
New York, NY 10019
(212) 246-5522
(800) 723-5522

Columbia Records
550 Madison Avenue
New York, NY 10022-3211
(212) 833-8000

Columbia Tristar Home Video
Sony Pictures Plaza
10202 West Washington Boulevard
Culver City, CA 90232
(310) 244-4000

Coronet/MTI Film & Video
P.O. Box 2649
Columbus, OH 43216
(800) 221-1274

CRM Films
2215 Faraday Ave.
Carlsbad, CA 92008-7295
(619) 431-9800
(800) 421-0833

Crossroads Video
15 Buckminster Lane
Manhasset, NY 11030
(516) 741-2155

Crown Publishers
See **Random Audiobooks**

Direct Cinema Limited, Inc.
P.O. Box 10003
Santa Monica, CA 90410
(310) 396-4774
(800) 345-6748

Dolphin Tapes
P.O. Box 71
Esalen Hot Springs
Big Sur, CA 93920
(408) 667-2252

Dove Audio
301 North Canon Drive
Beverly Hills, CA 90210

Drama Classics Video
P.O. Box 2128
Manorhaven, NY 11050
(516) 767-7576
(800) 892-0860

Durkin Hayes Publishing
1 Colomba Drive
Niagara Falls, NY 14305
(716) 298-5150
(800) 962-5200
Canadian address:
3375 North Service Road
Unit B7
Burlington, ON
CANADA L79 3G2
(905) 335-0393
(800) 263-5224

Facets Multimedia, Inc.
1517 W. Fullerton Ave.
Chicago, IL 60614
(800) 331-6197

**Films for the Humanities
and Sciences**
P.O. Box 2053
Princeton, NJ 08543-2053
(609) 275-1400
(800) 257-5126

Films, Inc.
5547 North Ravenswood Ave.
Chicago, IL 60640-1199
(800) 323-4312

First Run/Icarus Films
153 Waverly Place
New York, NY 10014
(212) 727-1711
(800) 876-1710

Gallaudet University Library
Gallaudet Media Distribution
800 Florida Avenue, NE
Washington, DC 20002
(202) 651-5579
(202) 651-5440

Home Vision Cinema
5547 North Ravenswood Avenue
Chicago, IL 60640-1199
(773) 878-2600
(800) 826-3456

IASTA
310 West 56th Street, #1B
New York, NY 10019
(212) 581-3133

**Indiana University Instructional
Support Services**
Franklin Hall, Room 0001
Bloomington, IN 47405-5901
(812) 855-2853

Insight Media
2162 Broadway
New York, NY 10024
(212) 721-6316
(800) 233-9910

Interlingua VA
2615 Columbia Pike
P.O. Box 4132
Arlington, VA 22204
(703) 920-6644

Intermedia Arts of Minnesota
425 Ontario St. SE
Minneapolis, MN 55414
(612) 627-4444

International Film Bureau
332 S. Michigan Ave.
Suite 450
Chicago, IL 60604-4382
(312) 427-4545
(800) 432-2241

Ishtar
15030 Ventura Blvd.
Suite 766
Sherman Oaks, CA 91403
(800) 428-7136

Jimcin Recordings
P.O. Box 536
Portsmouth, RI 02871
(401) 847-5148
(800) 538-3034

Journal Films, Inc.
1560 Sherman Avenue, Suite 100
Evanston, IL 60201
(312) 328-6700
(800) 323-5448

Thomas S. Klise Company
P.O. Box 317
Waterford, CT 06385
(860) 442-4449
(800) 937-0092

Kultur
195 Highway #36
West Long Branch, NJ 07764
(908) 229-2343
(800) 458-5887

L.A. Theatre Works
681 Venice Boulevard
Venice, CA 90291
(800) 708-8863

Learning Corporation of America
See **Coronet/MTI Film & Video**

Library of Congress
orders to:
Superintendent of Documents
P.O. Box 371954
Pittsburgh, PA 15250-7954
(202) 783-3238

Listening Library
1 Park Ave.
Old Greenwich, CT 06870
(203) 637-3616
(800) 243-4504

Maryland Public Television
11767 Owings Mills Blvd.
Owings Mills, MD 21117
(410) 356-5600

Media Concepts Press
331 North Broad St.
Philadelphia, PA 19107
(215) 923-2545

Media Guild
11722 Sorrento Valley Rd., Suite E
San Diego, CA 92121
(619) 755-9191
(800) 886-9191

Modern Poetry
60 W. Walton Street
Chicago, IL 60610
(312) 255-3703

Modern Talking Picture Service
4707 140th Avenue North
Suite 105
Clearwater, FL 34622
(813) 541-7571
(800) 243-6877

Monterey Home Video
28038 Dorothy Drive
Suite 1
Agoura Hills, CA 91301
(818) 597-0047
(800) 424-2593

Mystic Fire
P.O. Box 9323
South Burlington, VT 05407
(800) 292-9001

National Broadcasting Company
30 Rockefeller Plaza
New York, NY 10112
(212) 664-4444

National Film Board of Canada
16th Floor
1251 Avenue of the Americas
New York, NY 10020-1173
(212) 586-5131

National Public Radio
Audience Services
635 Massachusetts Avenue NW
Washington, DC 20001
(202) 414-3232

**Nebraska Educational
    Television Network**
Public Affairs Unit
1800 N. 33 St.
Lincoln, NE 68583
(402) 472-3611

New Dimensions Radio
P.O. Box 569
Ukiah, CA 95482
(707) 468-5215
(800) 935-8273

New Letters on the Air
University of Missouri at Kansas City
5100 Rockhill Rd.
Kansas City, MO 64110
(816) 235-1168

New York State Education Department
Media Distribution Network
Room C-7, Concourse Level
Cultural Education Center
Albany, NY 12230
(518) 474-1265

PBS Video
1320 Braddock Place
Alexandria, VA 22314-1698
(703) 739-5380

Phoenix/BFA Films
2349 Chaffee Drive
St. Louis, MO 63146
(314) 569-0211
(800) 421-2304

Poet's Audio Center
P.O. Box 50145
Washington, DC 20091-0145
(202) 722-9105

Pyramid Film & Video
P.O. Box 1048
Santa Monica, CA 90406-1048
(310) 828-7577
(800) 221-1274

Random Audiobooks
400 Hahn Rd.
Westminster, MD 21157
(800) 733-3000

Recorded Books
270 Skipjack Rd.
Prince Frederick, MD 20678
(301) 535-5590
(800) 638-1304

Rhino Records
10635 Santa Monica Boulevard
Los Angeles, CA 90025-4900

The Roland Collection
22D Hollywood Avenue
Hohokus, NJ 07423
(201) 251-8200

S & S Audio
795 Abbot Blvd.
Fort Lee, NJ 07024
(201) 224-3100
(800) 734-4758

Smithsonian/Folkways Recordings
Office of Folklife Programs
955 L'Enfant Plaza, Suite 2600
Smithsonian Institution
Washington, DC 20560
(202) 287-3262

Sound Horizons
250 W. 57th St.
Suite 1517
New York, NY 10107
(212) 956-6235
(800) 524-8355

Sound Photosynthesis
P.O. Box 2111
Mill Valley, CA 94942-2111
(415) 383-6712

Sound Rx
See **Audio Alternatives**

Sounds True
P.O. Box 8010
Boulder, CO 80306-8010
(303) 663-3151
(800) 333-9185

Spoken Arts
P.O. Box 100
New Rochelle, NY 10801
(800) 326-4090

Summer Stream
P.O. Box 6056
Santa Barbara, CA 93160
(805) 962-6540

Tapes for Readers
4410 Lingan Road
Washington, DC 20007
(202) 338-1215

Tapeworm Video Distributors
27833 Avenue Hopkins
Unit 6
Valencia, CA 91355
(805) 257-4904

Teachers & Writers Collaborative
5 Union Square W.
New York, NY 10003
(212) 691-6590

Time-Life Video
Customer Service
1450 East Parham Rd.
Richmond, VA 23280
(703) 838-7000
(800) 621-7026

**University of California
Extension Media Center**
2000 Center Street
Suite 400
Berkeley, CA 94704
(510) 642-0460

**University of Washington Educational
Media Collection**
Kane Hall, DG-10
Seattle, WA 98195
(206) 543-9909

University of Wyoming Audiovisual Services
Box 3273
Laramie, WY 82071
(307) 766-3184

Video Aided Instruction
P.O. Box 332
Roslyn Heights, NY 11577
(800) 238-1512

The Video Catalog
1000 Westgate Drive
Saint Paul, MN 55114
(612) 659-3700
(212) 334-0340

Video Yesteryear
Box C
Sandy Hook, CT 06482
(203) 426-2574
(800) 243-0987

Voyager Company
1 Bridge Street
Irvington, NY 10533
(914) 591-5500
(800) 446-2001

Water Bearer Films
205 West End Ave.
Suite 24H
New York, NY 10023
(212) 580-8185
(800) 551-8304

Watershed Tapes
Dist. by Inland Book Co.
P.O. Box 120261
East Haven, CT 06512
(203) 467-4257
(800) 243-0138

White Star
195 Highway 36
West Long Branch, NJ 07764
(732) 229-2343

WNET/Thirteen Non-Broadcast
356 West 58th St.
New York, NY 10019
(212) 560-2000
(800) 367-2467

Available on both compact disc and audiotape, *Literature Aloud* offers a range of classic and contemporary short stories, poems, and excerpted plays from *The Bedford Introduction to Literature,* Fifth Edition. All selections are read either by the authors themselves or by other celebrated writers or actors. With its selections from all three genres and its focus on the voice of the writer, *Literature Aloud* provides students with the unique opportunity to hear the literature that they study.

FICTION

James Joyce, *Eveline* (read by Gabriel Byrne) (Chapter 12, p. 512)
Jamaica Kincaid, *Girl* (read by Jamaica Kincaid) (Chapter 13, p. 534)
John Updike, *A & P* (read by John Updike) (Chapter 13, p. 576)

POETRY

Regina Barreca, *Nighttime Fires* (read by Regina Barreca) (Chapter 14, p. 688)
Elizabeth Bishop, *The Fish* (read by Randall Jarrell) (Chapter 14, p. 682)
Robert Bly, *Snowbanks North of the House* (read by Robert Bly) (Chapter 19, p. 809)
Gwendolyn Brooks, *The Mother* (read by Gwendolyn Brooks) (Chapter 27, p. 1081)
Gwendolyn Brooks, *We Real Cool* (read by Gwendolyn Brooks) (Chapter 16, p. 743)
E. E. Cummings, *next to of course god america i* (read by E. E. Cummings) (Chapter 19, p. 805)
Emily Dickinson, *I heard a Fly buzz — when I died —* (read by Glenda Jackson) (Chapter 24, p. 946)
Emily Dickinson, *I heard a Fly buzz — when I died —* (read by Robert Pinsky) (Chapter 24, p. 946)
Emily Dickinson, *Presentiment — is that long Shadow — on the lawn* (read by Meryl Streep) (Chapter 18, p. 777)
Emily Dickinson, *The Soul selects her own Society* (read by Julie Harris) (Chapter 24, p. 941)
Emily Dickinson, *There's a certain Slant of light* (read by Sharon Stone) (Chapter 38, p. 2082)
Emily Dickinson, *There's a certain Slant of light* (read by Julie Harris) (Chapter 38, p. 2082)
Emily Dickinson, *What Soft — Cherubic Creatures —* (read by Robert Pinsky) (Chapter 24, p. 940)
Emily Dickinson, *What Soft — Cherubic Creatures —* (read by Julie Harris) (Chapter 24, p. 940)
Emily Dickinson, *Wild Nights — Wild Nights!* (read by Robert Pinsky) (Chapter 24, p. 939)

John Donne, *The Flea* (read by Richard Burton) (Chapter 27, p. 1090)

John Donne, *Song: Sweetest love, I do not go* (read by Richard Burton) (Chapter 20, p. 844)

John Donne, *The Sun Rising* (read by Richard Burton) (Chapter 14, p. 705)

T. S. Eliot, *The Love Song of J. Alfred Prufrock* (read by T. S. Eliot) (Chapter 25, p. 1045)

Carolyn Forché, *The Colonel* (read by Carolyn Forché) (Chapter 23, p. 914)

Robert Frost, *Acquainted with the Night* (read by Robert Frost) (Chapter 19, p. 798)

Robert Frost, *After Apple-Picking* (read by Robert Frost) (Chapter 24, p. 983)

Robert Frost, *Birches* (read by Robert Frost) (Chapter 24, p. 986)

Robert Frost, *Mending Wall* (read by Robert Frost) (Chapter 24, p. 979)

Donald Hall, *Letter with No Address* (read by Donald Hall) (Chapter 27, p. 1153)

Anthony Hecht, *The Dover Bitch* (read by Anthony Hecht) (Chapter 27, p. 1096)

Judy Page Heitzman, *The Schoolroom on the Second Floor of the Knitting Mill* (read by Judy Page Heitzman) (Chapter 27, p. 1158)

Langston Hughes, *Dream Boogie* (read by Langston Hughes) (Chapter 24, p. 1029)

Langston Hughes, *Dream Variations* (read by Langston Hughes) (Chapter 24, p. 1018)

Langston Hughes, *Harlem* (read by Langston Hughes) (Chapter 24, p. 1030)

Langston Hughes, *Negro* (read by Langston Hughes) (Chapter 24, p. 1016)

Langston Hughes, *The Negro Speaks of Rivers* (read by Langston Hughes) (Chapter 24, p. 1010)

Langston Hughes, *The Weary Blues* (read by Langston Hughes) (Chapter 24, p. 1019)

John Keats, *La Belle Dame sans Merci* (read by Sir Ralph Richardson) (Chapter 27, p. 1103)

John Keats, *Ode on a Grecian Urn* (read by Sir Ralph Richardson) (Chapter 16, p. 741)

John Keats, *When I have fears that I may cease to be* (read by Sir Ralph Richardson) (Chapter 27, p. 1103)

Aron Keesbury, *Song to a Waitress* (read by Aron Keesbury) (Chapter 21, p. 872)

X. J. Kennedy, *A Visit from St. Sigmund* (read by X. J. Kennedy) (Chapter 22, p. 899)

Jane Kenyon, *The Blue Bowl* (read by Donald Hall) (Chapter 17, p. 768)

Galway Kinnell, *After Making Love We Hear Footsteps* (read by Galway Kinnell) (Chapter 23, p. 905)

Galway Kinnell, *Blackberry Eating* (read by Galway Kinnell) (Chapter 20, p. 832)

Etheridge Knight, *A Watts Mother Mourns While Boiling Beans* (read by Etheridge Knight) (Chapter 27, p. 1104)

Maxine Kumin, *Woodchucks* (read by Maxine Kumin) (Chapter 16, p. 727)

Denise Levertov, *Gathered at the River* (read by Denise Levertov) (Chapter 23, p. 907)

Kathryn Howd Machan, *Hazel Tells LaVerne* (read by Kathryn Howd Machan) (Chapter 16, p. 725)

Sharon Olds, *Rite of Passage* (read by Sharon Olds) (Chapter 23, p. 915)

Dorothy Parker, *One Perfect Rose* (read by Dorothy Parker) (Chapter 21, p. 869)

Linda Pastan, *Marks* (read by Linda Pastan) (Chapter 18, p. 791)

Sylvia Plath, *Daddy* (read by Sylvia Plath) (Chapter 27, p. 1113)

Theodore Roethke, *My Papa's Waltz* (read by Theodore Roethke) (Chapter 21, p. 871)

William Shakespeare, *My mistress' eyes are nothing like the sun* (read by Sir John Gielgud) (Chapter 22, p. 882)

William Shakespeare, *Not marble, nor the gilded monuments* (read by Sir John Gielgud) (Chapter 27, p. 1116)

William Shakespeare, *Shall I compare thee to a summer's day?* (read by Sir John Gielgud) (Chapter 22, p. 881)

William Shakespeare, *When forty winters shall besiege thy brow* (read by Sir John Gielgud) (Chapter 27, p. 1117)

Gary Soto, *Black Hair* (read by Gary Soto) (Chapter 27, p. 1119)

Dylan Thomas, *Do not go gentle into that good night* (read by Dylan Thomas) (Chapter 22, p. 885)

Richard Wilbur, *Love Calls Us to the Things of This World* (read by Richard Wilbur) (Chapter 27, p. 1124)

William Carlos Williams, *The Red Wheelbarrow* (read by William Carlos Williams) (Chapter 23, p. 906)

James Wright, *A Blessing* (read by James Wright) (Chapter 27, p. 1129)

William Butler Yeats, *That the Night Come* (read by Samantha Eggar) (Chapter 21, p. 862)

William Butler Yeats, *Adam's Curse* (read by Julie Sands) (Chapter 27, p. 1130)

DRAMA

Ingmar Bergman, Scene from *Nora,* a stage adaptation of Henrik Ibsen's *A Doll House* (performed by Linda Purl, David Dukes, Robert Foxworth, Natalija Nogulich, and John Vickery) From Act III (Chapter 32, p. 1598)

David Henry Hwang, A Scene from *M. Butterfly* (performed by John Lithgow and B. D. Wong) Act III, Scene 1 (Chapter 35, p. 1715)

William Shakespeare, A Scene from *Hamlet* (performed by Sir John Gielgud) From Act III, Scene 1 ("To be or not to be . . .") (Chapter 31, p. 1424)

William Shakespeare, Two Scenes from *Hamlet* (performed by Kenneth Branagh) From Act III, Scene 1 ("To be or not to be . . .") (Chapter 31, p. 1424); Act III, Scene 4 ("The Queen's Closet") (Chapter 31, p. 1441)

ORDERING INFORMATION

Literature Aloud is available to adopters of *The Bedford Introduction to Literature,* Fifth Edition. To obtain a compact disc or cassette, please contact your local Bedford/St. Martin's sales representative, or call Bedford/St. Martin's at 1-800-446-8923.

Index

642

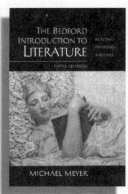